Generalized Theory of Electrical Machines

OTHER BOOKS BY THE SAME AUTHOR

- Electric Machines (ISBN: 978-93-86173-29-4)
- Electrical Machinery (ISBN: 978-93-89139-10-5)
- Electrical Machines - I (ISBN: 978-93-86173-44-7)
- Electrical Machines - II (ISBN: 978-93-86173-60-7)
- Power Electronics (ISBN: 978-81-95123-12-4)

Generalized Theory of Electrical Machines

DR. P. S. BIMBHRA
Ph.D., M.E.(Hons.), F.I.E. (India), M.I.S.T.E.
Ex-Dean. Ex-Professor and Head,
Electrical and Electronics Engineering Department
Thapar Institute of Engineering and Technology
Patiala-147004

KHANNA BOOK PUBLISHING CO. (P) LTD.
Publisher of Engineering and Computer Books
4C/4344, Ansari Road, Darya Ganj, New Delhi-110002
Phone : 011-23244447-48 **Mobile:** +91-9910909320
E-mail : contact@khannabooks.com
Website : www.khannabooks.com

Dear Readers,

To prevent the piracy, this book is secured with HIGH SECURITY HOLOGRAM on the front title cover. In case you don't find the hologram on the front cover title, please write us to at *contact@khannabooks.com* or whatsapp us at +91-99109 09320 and avail special gift voucher for yourself.

Specimen of Hologram on front Cover title:

Moreover, there is a SPECIAL DISCOUNT COUPON for you with EVERY HOLOGRAM.

How to avail this SPECIAL DISCOUNT:

Step 1: Scratch the hologram
Step 2: Under the scratch area, your "coupon code" is available
Step 3: Logon to *www.khannabooks.com*
Step 4: Use your "coupon code" in the shopping cart and get your copy at a special discount
Step 5: Enjoy your reading!

Thanks,
Khanna Publishing House

Price: ₹ 495.00

GENERALIZED THEORY OF ELECTRICAL MACHINES

Dr. P.S. Bimbhra

ISBN: 978-93-91505-08-0

Seventh Revised Edition: 2021

Published by:

Khanna Book Publishing Co. (P) Ltd.
4C/4344, Ansari Road, Darya Ganj, New Delhi-110 002
Phone: 011-23244447-48 **Mobile:** +91-9910909320
E-mail: contact@khannabooks.com

Printed in India by: Sanjeev Offset Printers

To

My Wife

For her Continuous Encouragement

Preface

It has been a matter of great controversy about whether the electrical machines theory be taught by generalized approach or by conventional approach. Some people argue that generalized approach provides little understanding of a real machine and they emphasize their line of reasoning by quoting some jokes. The author feels that first physical concepts of electrical machines be taught to the students along with an extensive laboratory course. Then the generalized theory of electrical machines can be taught with advantage, in conjunction with a set of appropriate laboratory experiments. An untoward behaviour of the machine should be explored by the students themselves and in case they fail, the instructor incharge should help them. For example, if the direction of motor rotation turns out to be wrong in any experiment, then students should be made to think so as to correct the direction of rotation. This type of laboratory course work would definitely obviate absurd answers from the students and would go a long way in imparting a real physical understanding of the various types of electrical machines.

In the earlier stages, the machine worked in isolation and its steady-state analysis was sufficient to be known. Now the electrical machine forms an integral part of a large system comprising of other components as well. In feedback control systems, a motor operates mainly under transient and dynamic conditions. In view of these facts, the transient and dynamic analysis of electrical machines and systems have gained importance and therefore the students must be taught the art of reducing a practical problem to an accurate mathematical model. The generalized theory of electrical machines, emphasizing the basic similarities of all the machines, now forms the basis of mathematical-machine modelling. The magnetic field view-point leads to steady-state analysis, whereas the generalized approach leads to steady-state, transient and dynamic analysis. The ability of a teacher to corelate the two independent treatments in the class leads to a better understanding of the subject.

The coupled circuit theory of synchronous machines makes use of the Park's transformation. First of all, the voltage equation $v = ri + p\psi$ is written for each phase and then the flux linkages ψ are expressed in terms of self and mutual inductances. These voltage and flux-linkage equations are then transformed to d–q variables by using Park's transformations. This process of transformation from phase variables to d–q variables is so tedius and cumbersome that students lose sight of what is going on in the machine. In this regard, G. Kron wrote as follows: "The author has seen hundreds of student engineers in company courses start the study of Park's equations with zest, then after several weeks of relentless manipulations of the $\cos(\theta - 120)$ and $\sin(\theta - 240)$ terms, give up in disgust. By the time they thought they understood the dc machine type equations, the students were all ready and willing to become executives and vice-presidents rather than synchronous machine experts." With generalized approach, the synchronous machine equations in d–q variables can be obtained by a simple graphical method of writing the machine equations, from merely observing the primitive machine. It may be concluded from above that generalized approach for polyphase synchronous and in-duction machines is simpler than the coupled-circuit approach.

It is sometimes argued that generalized approach can't take saturation into consideration. Actually, this approach is more useful for studying the transient and dynamic behaviour of electrical machines and of interconnected electrical machine systems. This does not mean that this approach fails to do the steady-state analysis. In order to highlight the various factors effecting the transient performance and to study the dynamic system problems, it is relatively of much less importance to take magnetic saturation into consideration. Saturation can, however, be taken into account but with the use of computers.

The physical understanding of single-phase induction motors and asymmetrical operation of 3-phase induction motors can be better appreciated by counter-rotating field theory associated with symmetrical component concepts. It is because of this reason that single-phase induction motor is dealt with in detail by double revolving field theory, in addition to the generalized concepts. The physical approach is presented in this book where the generalized approach becomes too involved for the undergraduate students.

In the present edition, some material of the book has been reworded and rewritten so as to make the presentation easily comprehensible. More illustrative examples mainly from IAS, IES and GATE and other Competitive Examinations have been added and problem material with answers, at the end of each chapter, has been considerably enlarged.

With recent advances in power electronics and microelectronics, new electric machine types like brushless dc motors, variable reluctance motors etc. are found in modern electric drive systems. Keeping these advances into consideration, also devoted to the discussion of brushless dc, variable reluctance and stepping motors, is included in the book. An appendix, containing objective-type questions pertaining to the topics covered in this book, is given in the end.

A great deal of time has gone into the updating of the fourth edition, and I must acknowledge the patience exhibited by my wife and children, though at a great inconvenience to them.

The author would welcome the advice and suggestions leading to the improvement of the book.

Dr. P. S. BIMBHRA

Contents

Chapter			*Pages*

1 Elements of Generalized Theory

Rotating electrical machines work on the same basic principles. The various types differ from each other in their winding arrangements and in the method of exciting these windings. The attempts to unify the piecemeal treatment of rotating electrical machines has led to the concept of generalized theory, or two-axis theory, of electrical machines. The idea behind the generalised theory stemmed from the efforts of A. Blondel whose work is now known as Blondel's two-reaction theory of salient-pole synchronous machines. The work of Blondel was then investigated in detail by Doherty and Nickle leading to the publication of a series of papers.

Subsequently, R.H. Park, in his classic paper [1], developed general two-axis equations of the synchronous machines by making use of appropriate transformations. Park's ideas were then developed by Gabriel Kron to deal with all rotating electrical machines in a systematic manner by tensor analysis. However, W.J. Gibbs [2] simplified the work of Kron by applying matrices to the analysis of electrical machines. This unified treatment of rotating electrical machines, developed by Kron, is now called *generalized theory of electrical machines or two-axis theory of electrical machines*, for which either tensors or matrices may be employed. In this book, elementary matrix algebra is used as a mathematical tool for studying this generalized approach.

The object of this chapter is to develop the basic elements of generalized theory and to derive the general equations for both voltages and torques. These general equations, applicable to almost all types of rotating electrical machines, can deal comprehensively with their steady-state, dynamic and transient analysis.

1.1 ESSENTIALS OF ROTATING ELECTRICAL MACHINES

From the construction and operation point of view, rotating electrical machines have many common essential features. The purpose of this article is to describe these essential features which are illustrated in Fig. 1.1.

(*i*) There is an outer stationary member called *stator* and an inner rotating member, called *rotor*. The latter is mounted in bearings which are fixed to the stationary member.

(*ii*) Both the stator and rotor carry concentric cylindrical cores. These are made up of ferromagnetic material and are usually fabricated from laminated steel sheets to provide optimum electric and magnetic characteristics.

(*iii*) The clearance between the two cylindrical ferromagnetic cores is called the *air-gap*. The coupling between electrical and mechanical systems is through the electromagnetic field present in the air-gap.

(*iv*) A common magnetic flux ϕ crosses the air gap from one core to the other in a combined magnetic circuit. This magnetic flux ϕ, in crossing the air-gap, causes the production of alternate N and S poles on both stator and rotor. Such a magnetic system with alternate N and S poles along its air-gap periphery is called *hetropolar system.*

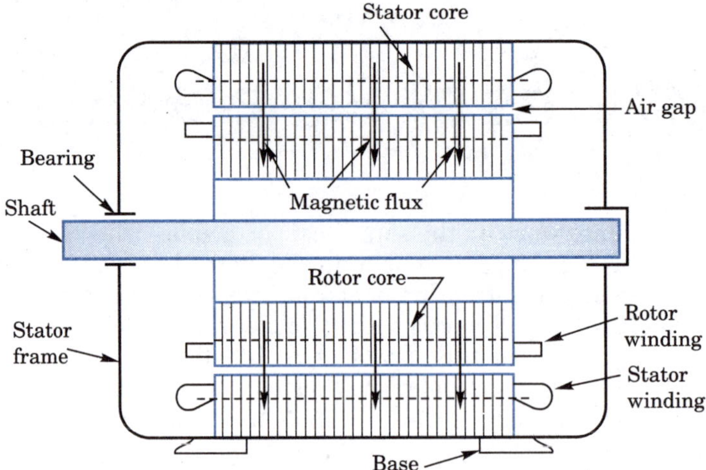

Fig. 1.1: Common geometrical configuration of all rotating electrical machines.

(*v*) The important feature of all machines is that the two cylindrical ferromagnetic surfaces, a short distance apart, move relative to one another for electro-mechanical energy conversion.

The cylindrical surface on either element may be continuous (neglecting slot openings) or may have salient poles. Near the air-gap surface of each or either element, conductors run parallel to the axis of cylinders. These conductors are suitably connected to form the machine windings.

Thus the general arrangement is the same for all types of rotating electrical machines. The various types differ basically, in the distribution of the conductors forming the windings and in whether the two members have continuous cylindrical surfaces or salient poles. The operation of any given machine depends on the nature of the excitations applied to its windings.

1.2 CONVENTIONS

In the development of the generalized machine theory, certain conventions have been adopted and they are consistently maintained throughout, for an intelligent appreciation of the theory. A brief outline of them is given below:

(*i*) The distribution of current and flux under one pair of poles, repeats itself under all other pairs of poles as shown in Fig. 1.2 (*a*), whatever the actual number of pole-pairs may be. Hence any machine can be replaced by an equivalent two-pole machine and the generalized machine theory is developed in terms of two-pole machines. This is done in order to avoid ambiguity with different electrical and mechanical angles. The number of poles must, of course, be introduced in determining the torque (increased) and speed (reduced) of the machine.

(*ii*) Each winding of the actual machine or each part of the winding forming a single circuit is represented in the idealised or basic two-pole machine by a single coil. For rotor, these single coils, occupy only a part of the radius and for stator, the coils are shown on one side of the machine only. This is essential to indicate the positive direction of currents and m.m.fs. For instance, a three phase synchronous machine without damper bars, necessitates one coil *F* for field winding and three coils *A, B, C* for three phase windings as illustrated in Fig. 1.2 (*b*).

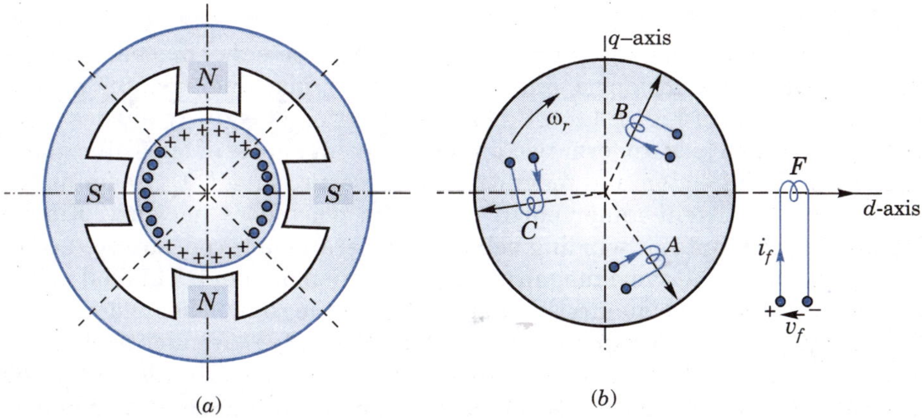

Fig. 1.2: (*a*) Four-pole electrical machine, (*b*) Synchronous machine.

(*iii*) The axis of the poles around which the field winding is wound, is called the *direct axis* of the machine, while the axis 90° away from it is called the *quadrature* axis as shown in Fig. 1.2 (*b*). It is customary to take *d*-axis as horizontal and *q*-axis as vertical.

(*iv*) The positive direction of the current in any coil is towards the coil in the lead nearer to the centre of the diagram. The positive direction of flux linking a coil is radially outwards along the axis of the coil, as indicated by arrow-heads along the axes of the coils in Fig. 1.2 (*b*).

(*v*) Lower case v represents the voltage impressed on the coil from an external source and i, the current measured in the same direction as v. This is also indicated in Fig. 1.2 (*b*). This means that the instantaneous power vi flows into the circuit from outside and this corresponds to motor operation. Reversal of either v or i means generator action, though it is customary to reverse i.

(*vi*) The positive direction of rotation of rotor is taken as clockwise and torque is also taken positive when acting in the sense of positive rotation.

(*vii*) Capital L and X are used for total (*i.e.* self) inductance and the corresponding reactance respectively. The leakage inductance and reactance are represented by the lower case letters l and x respectively.

(*viii*) Capital letters are used to indicate the coils and the corresponding lower case letters serve as subscripts for the voltages, currents, impedances etc. For example, in Fig. 1.2 (*b*), voltage v_f and current i_f pertain to the coil *F;* similarly v_a, i_a would pertain to coil *A*.

(*ix*) The dot convention, if used anywhere, is the same as adopted for circuit analysis.

(*x*) The torque conventions in detail, are discussed in Art. 3.2.

1.3 THE BASIC TWO-POLE MACHINE

The theory is developed for a basic or an idealised two-pole machine, which is closely related to the actual machine. As stated earlier, each part of the winding forming a single circuit, is represented by a single coil in the basic two-pole machine. Thus, a basic two-pole machine is one in which each coil represents each part of the winding forming a single circuit of actual machine.

1.3.1 Commutator Machines

Some of the a.c. machines employ commutator winding, while d.c. machines are invariably fitted with commutators. Consider a simple two-pole d.c. machine, running as a separately excited motor, as shown in Fig. 1.3 (*a*). Commutator action effectively divides the armature winding, along the brush axis, to form two uniform current sheets of opposite polarity. As the armature rotates, the direction and magnitude of armature m.m.f. F_{qr} remains unchanged, since the direction of current under north and south poles does not vary. From magnetic considerations, the commutator winding behaves as a stationary concentrated coil as shown in Fig. 1.3 (*b*), producing the same magnitude and direction of m.m.f. This coil is indicated by letters *QR*, the letter *Q* for the quadrature axis and *R* for the rotor. The field produced by *N*, *S* poles in Fig. 1.3 (*a*), and that produced by coil *DS* in Fig. 1.3 (*b*) are identical in all respects. For total equivalence, the stationary concentrated coil generates the same rotational voltage as that generated by the commutator winding, when acting as a generator. When acting as a motor, the same torque is developed for the same currents in the coil *QR* and in the commutator winding. Such a coil is fictitious one and as it is to be used to represent commutator windings, it is given the identifying name of *pseudo-stationary coil or quasi-stationary coil.* Thus the properties of the pseudo-stationary coil located on the moving element are similar to those possessed by a commutator winding and can be summarised as follows:

(*i*) A current in a coil produces a field which is stationary in space.

(*ii*) A rotational voltage can however be induced in the coil by virtue of its being on the moving element, though the coil does not move.

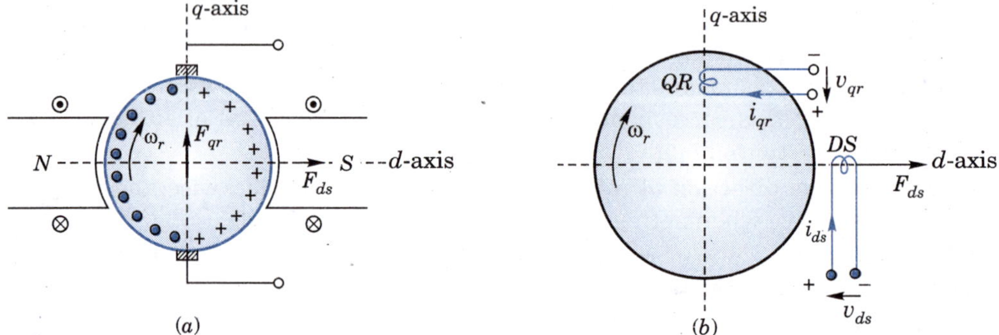

Fig. 1.3: (*a*) Separately excited d.c. motor and (*b*) its basic two-pole machine representation.

Note that the pseudo-stationary coil on the moving element here is along the *q*-axis. For convinience, the *d*-axis is taken horizontal and *q*-axis vertical, as stated before.

In general, it may be stated that a pseudo-stationary coil is always taken along the *d*- or *q*-axis and is indicated in the diagram *inside a circle*, which represents the rotating element of the machine.

1.3.2 D.C. Compound Machine

In Fig. 1.3 (*b*) is drawn the idealised two-pole machine diagram for a d.c. shunt machine, the shunt field winding being separately excited. The d.c. compound machine, in addition to the shunt winding, carries a series field winding on the main poles. Thus the basic machine diagram for a d.c. compound machine can be drawn by having one more coil *DSE* on the *d*-axis stationary element, as shown in Fig. 1.4 (*a*). Some readers may draw the coil *DSE* as shown in Fig. 1.4 (*b*). Though it is correct, yet it is convenient to show the coil *DSE* on the right of the centre of the circle as shown in Fig. 1.4 (*a*). Here coil *DSE* represents series field winding on main poles. At present no mention is made of differential or cumulative compounding and the coils representing the various windings are shown with no interconnections amongst them.

Henceforth, if there are one or two coils on stator (or rotor) *d*-axis, these will be shown on the right of centre of the circle. For one, two or more coils on the stator (or rotor) *q*-axis, these will accordingly be shown above the centre of the circle.

1.3.3 D.C. Shunt Machine with Interpoles

Since the interpoles are 90° away from the main poles and are on the stationary element, the basic machine diagram is shown in Fig. 1.4 (*c*), with coil *QS* representing the interpoles. Note that the direction of currents etc. is not indicated in the coils yet as the whole attention is focussed for the proper representation of the basic machine.

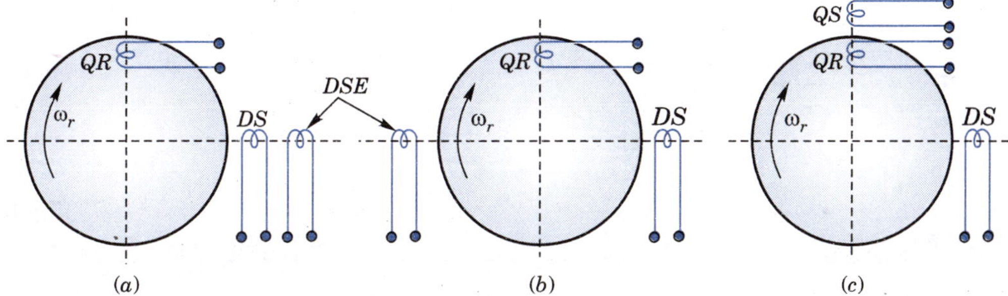

Fig. 1.4: Basic machine representation of (*a*) and (*b*) D.C. compound machine and (*c*) D.C. shunt machine with interpoles.

1.3.4 Amplidyne

A schematic diagram of the amplidyne is given in Fig. 1.5 (*a*). The field winding *F* and compensating winding are along the same axis and are on the stationary member. These can be shown as *DS* (*D* for the *d*-axis and *S* for stator) and *DC* (compensating winding) respectively on the stationary element.

Two brushes *A, B* on the armature are along the axis of the main field winding *F* and the armature reaction m.m.f. due to this pair of brushes shall also be along the same axis, *i.e.* *d*-axis. Thus a coil *DR* on the rotating element and producing the same m.m.f., will represent these two brushes *A* and *B*. The other two brushes *C* and *D*, 90° away from the axis of the winding *F*, can be replaced by coil *QR*, along the *q*-axis on the moving element. If coil *DC* is omitted in Fig. 1.5 (*b*), the resulting basic machine diagram is for the metadyne.

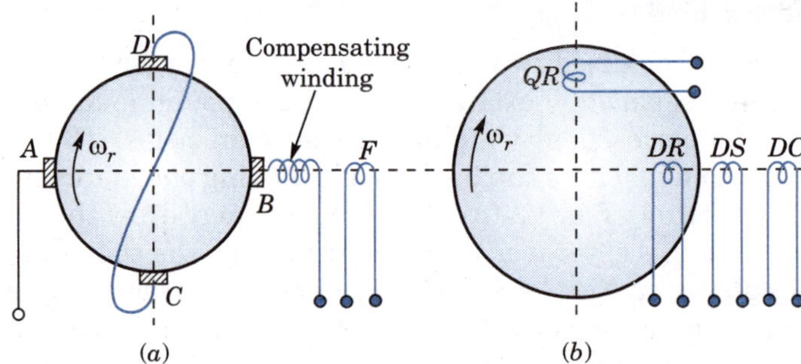

Fig. 1.5: Amplidyne. (*a*) Its schematic representation and (*b*) Its basic machine representation.

1.3.5 Single Phase A.C. Series Machine

The stator carries a single phase winding, which is excited by a.c. and a single coil *DS* is enough to represent it. The rotor carries a winding whose magnetic axis is 90° away from the stator winding axis. Hence a coil *QR* represents it, as shown in Fig. 1.6 (*b*). The same basic machine diagram also represents d.c. series machine, dc shunt machine or dc separately excited machine.

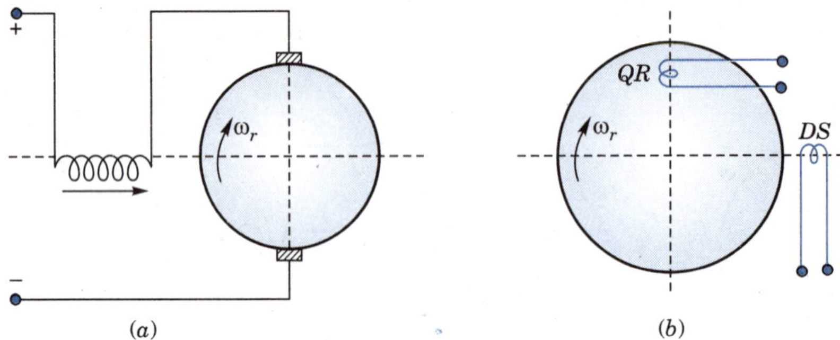

Fig. 1.6: Single phase a.c. series machine, (*a*) Schematic, and (*b*) Basic machine representations.

1.3.6 Repulsion Motor

It consists of a single phase stator winding which is shown by a single coil *D* in Fig. 1.7 (*a*), along the *d*-axis. Its rotor consists of a commutator winding with a pair of short-circuited brushes displaced from stator field axis or *d*-axis by an angle α as shown in Fig. 1.7 (*a*). The field due

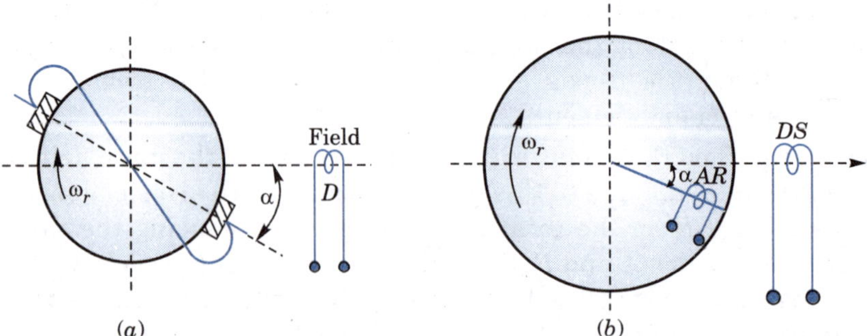

Fig. 1.7: (*a*) Schematic diagram, and (*b*) Basic machine representation of a repulsion motor.

to the rotor currents is aligned along the brush axis and this has a component at right angle to the d-axis. Their interaction results in the production of a torque. The basic two pole machine diagram of Fig. 1.7 (a) can easily be drawn, as illustrated in Fig. 1.7 (b). In this figure, coil AR, displaced by an angle α from d-axis, represents the commutator winding. Coil DS represents single-phase stator winding.

1.3.7 (a) Synchronous Machine without Dampers

For the purpose of analysis, it is immaterial which of the two elements (armature winding and field winding) of the machine rotates and which is stationary, since machine operation depends only on the relative motion between them. Salient pole synchronous machines have usually its three-phase armature winding on the stator and the field winding on the rotor, though the machines with the reverse arrangement are also built. The theory applies to either arrangement. However, it is convenient to take the salient pole element to be stationary and to indicate it on the diagram as the outer member.

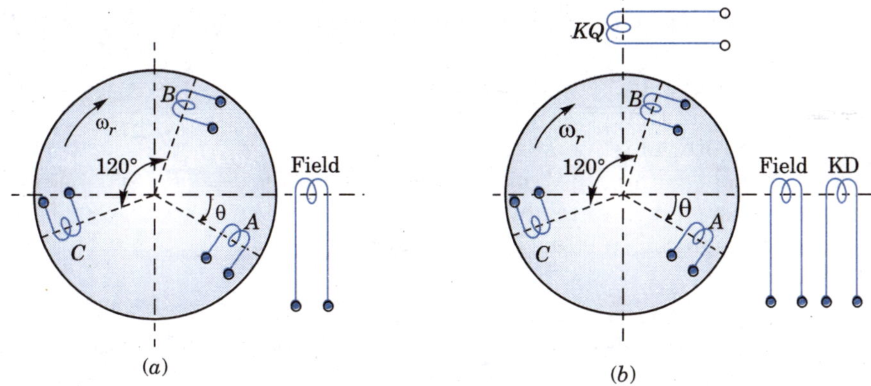

Fig. 1.8: Basic two pole machine representation of a three-phase synchronous machine, (a) Without damper bars, (b) With damper bars.

In general, it may be stated that if any machine has salient poles, they are taken on the stator. The generalized machine theory fails to embrace the treatment of machines, which have salient poles both on the stator and rotor, as in the case of an inductor alternator.

An idealised three-phase salient pole synchronous machine without damper bars is shown in Fig. 1.8 (a). Here the phase A forming a part of the three-phase winding, constitutes a single circuit and thus it is represented in the basic machine diagram by a single coil A. The coil representing armature phase A makes an angle θ in a clockwise direction with the d-axis and the choice of phase A is arbitrary *i.e.*, phase B or C could have been at an angle θ from the field axis.

For Fig. 1.8 (a), the armature phase B is represented by a single coil with its axis 120° away from that of the coil A. Phase C is also shown in a like manner. The field winding is indicated by a coil marked, 'field', on the d-axis.

Note here that A, B, C are not pseudo-stationary coils, likewise these are not shown along d- or q-axis.

1.3.7 (b) Synchronous Machine with Dampers

The commonest form of damper winding consists of squirrel cage bars in the pole-faces connected together at the ends by rings or segments. In addition to the damper bars, there are also eddy current paths in the iron, whether solid or laminated, of the magnetic system. All these circuits react to changes in the flux of the machine and for a complete representation in the basic machine, a large number of circuits is necessary. Therefore, exact analysis is difficult to achieve. In order to obtain a workable theory, all the synchronous machines are studied with one amortisseur *KD* in the *d*-axis and another *KQ* in the quadrature axis as shown in Fig. 1.8 (*b*). The amortisseurs in the *d*- and *q*-axes may be thought of as equivalent to all the amortisseur circuits in a synchronous machine.

1.3.8 Three-Phase Induction Machines

The three-phase winding on the stator can be represented by three coils *A, B* and *C* but with a space angle of 120° amongst them. Phase *A* winding is taken along *d*-axis for convenience. The rotor carries a slip ring winding or a short circuited cage. In the former case, it is easier to represent the slip ring winding on the basic machine diagram, just as for the armature of the synchronous machine. A cage rotor is rather more complex, but in so far as it can, and does produce an armature reaction m.m.f. substantially identical with that of a slip ring winding, the representation of cage rotor must be identical with that of a slip-ring rotor. Thus, both the types of rotors of a three-phase induction motor are represented by three coils *a, b, c* on the rotor, though displaced from each other by a space angle of 120°, Fig. 1.9.

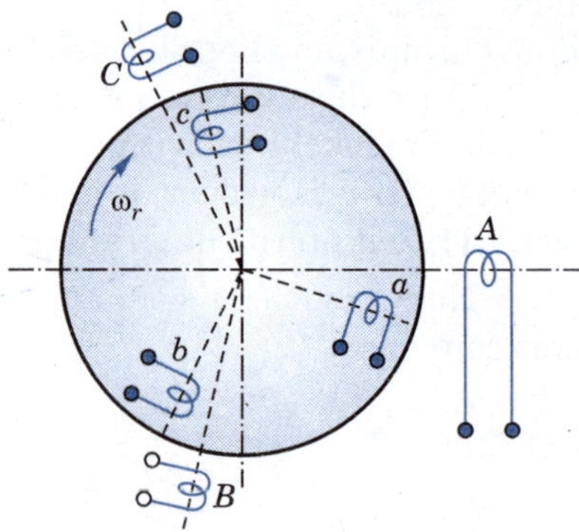

Fig. 1.9: Basic two-pole machine diagram for a three-phase induction machine.

In general, the basic two pole machine diagrams for any type of rotating electrical machine, can be drawn by knowing (*i*) the stator and rotor configuration, salient pole member being taken as stationary (*ii*) the winding arrangements on both stator and rotor, and (*iii*) the position of the brushes on the rotor, if present.

1.4 THE PER UNIT SYSTEM

In the generalized machine theory, as in the power systems, per unit system has been used, since it possesses many advantages.

Consider the coil *A*, Fig. 1.10 (*a*), of N_a turns in which current i_a sets up flux ϕ_a along its axis.

For a linear system, the self-inductance is defined as the flux linkage with a winding per ampere in the same winding.

$$\therefore \quad \text{Self-inductance of coil } A = L_a = \frac{N_a \phi_a}{i_a} = \frac{\psi_a}{i_a}$$

The voltage equation for coil *A* is

$$v_a = r_a i_a + \frac{d}{dt}(L_a i_a) \quad \text{or} \quad v_a = r_a i_a + \frac{d}{dt}(\psi_a)$$

$$= r_a i_a + p\psi_a \qquad \text{...(1.1)}$$

Here *p* is the derivative operator *d*/*dt*.

Now consider another coil *B* of Fig. 1.10 (*b*) with N_b turns.

$\therefore$ Self inductance of coil $B = \dfrac{N_b \phi_b}{i_b} = \dfrac{\psi_b}{i_b}$

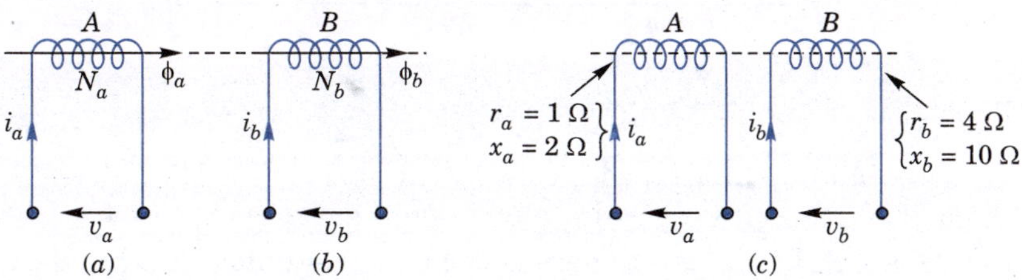

Fig. 1.10: (*a*) Coil *A* with N_a turns, (*b*) Coil *B* with N_b turns, (*c*) Coils *A* and *B* together with magnetic flux in the same direction.

The voltage equation for coil *B* is, $v_b = r_b i_b + p\psi_b$ ...(1.2)

Now let coil *A* be placed near coil *B* as shown in Fig. 1.10 (*c*) such that their magnetic axes coincide and the flux set up by both of them is in the same direction.

Assume the parameters of coil *A* as $r_a = 1\ \Omega$, $x_a = 2\ \Omega$ and of coil *B* as $r_b = 4\ \Omega$, $x_b = 10\ \Omega$ with 400 volts across *A* and 2000 volts across *B*. The resulting currents are taken to be 10 Amps and 2 Amps respectively.

For coil *A*:

Base impedance $Z_{base} = \dfrac{400}{10} = 40\ \Omega$

$\therefore$ $r_{a(p.u.)} = \dfrac{1}{40} = 0.025,$ $x_a(p.u.) = \dfrac{2}{40} = 0.050$

For coil *B*:

Base impedance $Z_{base} = \dfrac{2000}{2} = 1000\ \Omega$

$\therefore$ $r_{b(p.u.)} = \dfrac{4}{1000} = 0.004,$ $x_{b(p.u.)} = \dfrac{10}{1000} = 0.010.$

Referring the parameters to 400 volt side

$$r_a' = r_a + \left(\frac{N_a}{N_b}\right)^2 r_b = 1 + \frac{4}{25} = \frac{29}{25}\ \Omega$$

$\therefore$ $r_a'{}_{(p.u.)} = \dfrac{29}{25} \times \dfrac{1}{40} = 0.029$ p.u.

Similarly $x_a'{}_{(p.u.)} = \dfrac{60}{25} \times \dfrac{1}{40} = 0.060$ p.u.

Also from $r_{a(p.u.)}$ and $r_{b(p.u.)}$,

$$r_a'{}_{(p.u.)} = r_{a(p.u.)} + r_{b(p.u.)} = 0.029 \text{ p.u.}$$

$\therefore$ With per unit system, $\dfrac{N_a}{N_b} = 1.$

Thus when the per unit system is used, the turns ratio is equivalent to unity. Or in other words, it can be presumed that each winding (or coil) has one turn or the same number of effective turns when per unit system is used.

Now $$L_a = \frac{\text{Total flux linkages with coil } A}{i_a \text{ (current in coil } A)}$$
$$= \frac{\text{(Mutual + Leakage) flux linkage with coil } A}{i_a}$$
$$= \frac{\Phi_{ma}N_a + \Phi_{la}N_a}{i_a}$$

where Φ_{ma} is the mutual flux linking both coils by the current in coil A alone (*i.e.* with $i_b = 0$)
and ϕ_{la} is the leakage flux linking coil A alone, see Fig. 1.11 (*a*).

Now leakage flux linkages per ampere is the leakage inductance represented by l.

Thus, leakage inductance of coil A, $l_a = \dfrac{\phi_{ia}N_a}{i_a}$.

From above, self-inductance of coil A is,

$$L_a = \frac{\phi_{ma}N_a}{i_a} + l_a \quad \text{or} \quad L_a = \frac{\phi_{ma}N_b}{i_a} \cdot \frac{N_a}{N_b} + l_a \qquad ...(1.3)$$

Mutual inductance is defined as the flux linkages with a coil per ampere in another coil. Here $\phi_{ma} N_b$ is the flux linkages with coil B, set up by the current i_a in coil A alone.

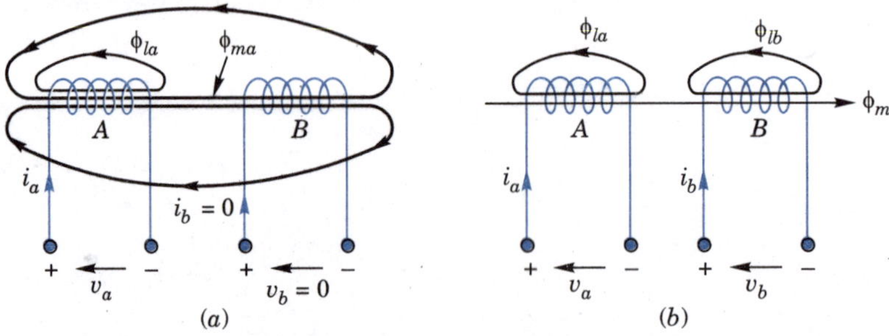

Fig. 1.11: (*a*) Coil *A* alone carrying i_a and producing mutual flux ϕ_{ma} (*b*) Both coils carrying currents and the resultant mutual flux is ϕ_m.

$$\therefore \quad L_a = M_{ab} \cdot \frac{N_a}{N_b} + l_a.$$

If per unit system is used ; $\dfrac{N_a}{N_b} = 1$

$$\therefore \quad L_a = M_{ab} + l_a \qquad ...(1.4)$$

$$\text{Similarly} \quad L_a = M_{ba} + l_b \qquad ...(1.5)$$

$$\text{Now} \quad M_{ab} = \frac{\phi_{ma}N_b}{i_a} = \frac{N_a i_a}{\text{Reluctance}} \cdot \frac{N_b}{i_a} = N_a N_b \text{ Permeance.}$$

$$\text{Also} \quad M_{ba} = \frac{\phi_{mb}N_a}{i_b} = \frac{N_b i_b}{\text{Reluctance}} \cdot \frac{N_a}{i_b} = N_a N_b \text{ Permeance}$$

$$\therefore \quad M_{ab} = M_{ba} = M \text{ (say)}$$

$$\therefore \quad L_a = M + l_a \quad \text{and} \quad L_b = M + l_b.$$

Thus in per unit system

Self-inductance = Mutual inductance + Leakage inductance

Also $\phi_{ma} = Mi_a$ and $\phi_{mb} = Mi_b$

When both coils A and B carry currents, the resultant mutual flux (by superposition) see Fig. 1.11 (*b*), is

$$\phi_m = \phi_{ma} + \phi_{mb} = M(i_a + i_b) \qquad \text{...[1.6 (a)]}$$

$\therefore$ Mutual flux linkages with either coil = $M(i_a + i_b)$

since in p.u. system each coil or winding has one turn only.

Similarly, for three mutually-coupled coils A, B and C, the mutual flux linkages with any one coil would be given by,

$$\psi = M(i_a + i_b + i_c) \qquad \text{...[1.6 (b)]}$$

Thus the advantages of p.u. system are

(*i*) number of turns do not enter into the equations and

(*ii*) self-inductance of a coil is obtained by merely adding its mutual and leakage inductances.

1.5 TRANSFORMER WITH A MOVABLE SECONDARY

Consider an ideal transformer with 100 turns in the primary and 250 turns in the secondary. Primary P is supplied with 400 volts and if the magnetic axes of P and S coincide, Fig. 1.12 (*a*), the voltage induced in the secondary will be 1000 volts.

The secondary is now moved so that the magnetic axes of P and S are at an angle θ as shown in Fig. 1.12 (*b*). The voltage induced in the secondary will now be given by 1000 cos θ volts. So if

$\theta = 30°$, voltage induced in S = 1000 cos 30° = 866 volts

$\theta = 45°$, voltage induced in S = 1000 cos 45° = 707 volts

$\theta = 60°$, voltage induced in S = 1000 cos 60° = 500 volts

$\theta = 90°$, voltage induced in S = 1000 cos 90° = 0 volts

Thus if the magnetic axes of P and S are 90° away from each other, the voltage induced in S due to transformer action is zero.

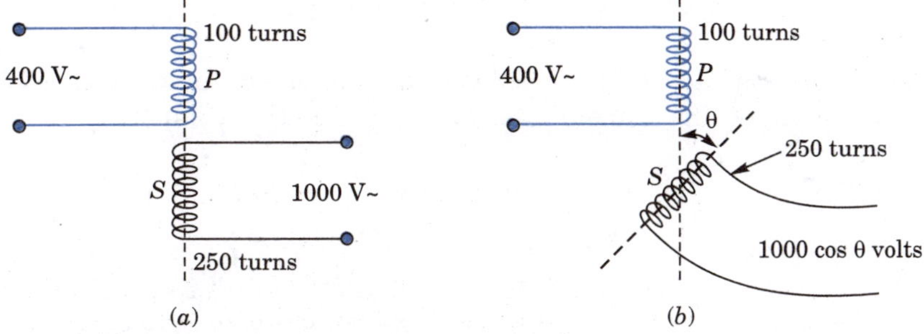

Fig. 1.12: Transformer with primary and secondary winding magnetic axes (*a*) coincident (*b*) at an angle θ.

1.6 TRANSFORMER AND SPEED VOLTAGES IN THE ARMATURE

Consider a field coil DS along the d-axis, and on the stationary element as shown in Fig. 1.13 (*a*). Though it has only one turn, the magnetic flux produced by it is assumed to be distributed sinusoidally in space and is time varying in nature. Another similar coil *DR* along the *d*-axis, is on the moving element. The alternating magnetic flux produced by i_{ds} in coil *DS* links *DR* and let its magnitude at the instant shown in Fig. 1.13 (*a*) be

$$\psi_{md} = M_d i_{ds}$$

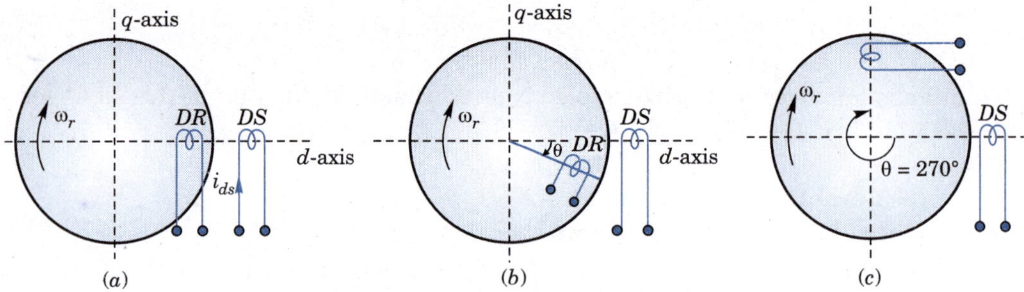

Fig. 1.13: Coils *DS*, *DR* with different positions.

Here M_d is the mutual inductance between coils *DS* and *DR* and i_{ds} is the exciting current at this particular instant in coil *DS*.

Let the coil *DR,* on the moving element, traverse an angle θ in time, say *t* seconds, such that $\theta = \omega_r t$ radians, see Fig. 1.13 (*b*).

∴ The flux linkages with *DR,* after time *t* seconds, are

$$= \psi_{md} \cos\theta = (M_d i_{ds}) \cos\theta.$$

According to Faraday's Law, the e.m.f. induced in coil *DR,* at this instant, is given by

$$e = -\frac{d}{dt}(\psi_{md}\cos\theta) \quad \text{...(1.7)}$$

$$= +\psi_{md}\sin\theta\frac{d\theta}{dt} - \cos\theta\frac{d}{dt}(\psi_{md})$$

$$= +\psi_{md}\,\omega_r \sin\theta - \cos\theta\, p\psi_{md}$$

$$= +\psi_{md}\,\omega_r \sin\theta - \cos\theta\, M_d\,(pi_{ds}) \quad \text{...(1.8)}$$

where $\dfrac{d\theta}{dt} = p\theta = \omega_r$.

The first term in Eq. (1.8) is the speed voltage component, because speed ω_r appears in it. The other term is called the transformer voltage, since this component involves the time derivative of current i_{ds}.

When θ = 270°, in the direction of rotation, as shown in Fig. 1.13 (*c*)

$$e_q = \omega_r\,\psi_{md}\,\sin 270° - 0$$

$$= +\,\omega_r\,\psi_{md}\,\sin(180° + 90°) = -\,\omega_r\psi_{md} \quad \text{...(1.9)}$$

With the e.m.f. *e,* the subscript *q* has been added, because with a rotation of θ = 270°, the axis of coil *DR* coincides with the *q*-axis.

When $\theta = 0,\ e_d = -M_d\,(pi_{ds}) = -p\psi_{md}$ ...(1.10)

Now consider another field coil *QS* and an armature coil *QR* as shown in Fig. 1.14 (*a*), and let ψ_{mq} be the mutual flux linkages at the instant shown.

After time *t* seconds, the flux linkages with coil *QR* are, $= \psi_{mq}\cos\theta$

where $\theta = \omega_r t$.

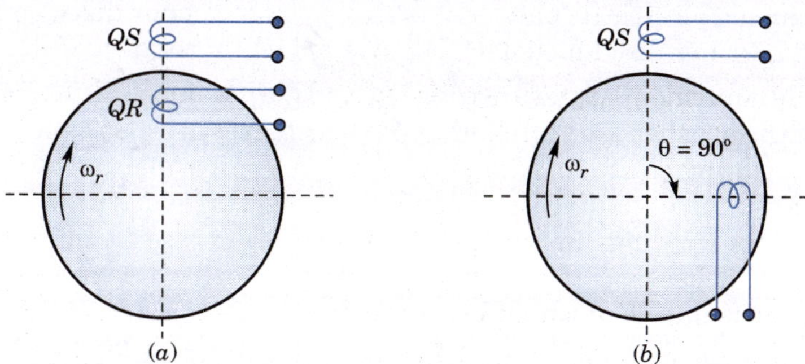

Fig. 1.14: Coils *QS* and *QR*. (*a*) Along the same axis, (*b*) 90° away from each other.

As earlier, the e.m.f. induced in coil *QR* is given by

$$e = -\frac{d}{dt}(\psi_{mq} \cos\theta)$$

$$= +\omega_r\, \psi_{mq} \sin\theta - \cos\theta\, p\psi_{mq} \qquad \text{...(1.11)}$$

When $\theta = 90°$ as shown in Fig. 1.14 (*b*),

$$e_d = +\omega_r \psi_{mq} \qquad \text{...(1.12)}$$

When $\theta = 0°$; $\quad e_q = -p\psi_{mq} \qquad \text{...(1.13)}$

It is seen from above that (*i*) the magnitude of the speed voltages is maximum, when the moving coil is magnetically at right angles to the other coil, Eqs. (1.9) and (1.12) and (*ii*) the magnitude of the transformer voltages is maximum when the two coils are aligned magnetically along the same axis, Eqs. (1.10) and (1.13).

1.7 KRON'S PRIMITIVE MACHINE

The Kron's primitive machine with stationary axes is shown in Fig. 1.15 (*a*). This machine consists of a stationary field winding *DS* in the direct axis, an independent stationary field winding *QS* at right angles to *d*-axis, *i.e.* in the quadrature axis. The machine has one rotating armature winding brought out to a commutator. Two sets of brushes are provided which are magnetically perpendicular to each other, with one brush set in the *d*-axis and the other in the *q*-axis. The idealised or basic two-pole machine diagram for this machine can easily be drawn and it is as shown in Fig. 1.15 (*b*).

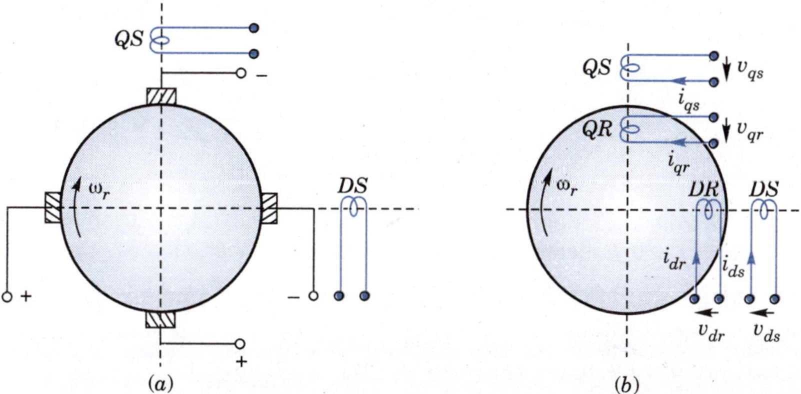

Fig. 1.15: (*a*) Kron's primitive machine. (*b*) Its basic two-pole representation.

This equivalent electrical network is called the "generalized machine", "Kron's primitive machine", "generalised model or two-axis model" of rotating electrical machines.

Note that the equivalent armature coils *DR* and *QR* produce stationary fluxes along the brush axes, only if the brushes are stationary. The brush axes are also called commutator axes or Park's axes. If the brushes are rotating, the corresponding armature coil fluxes will also be rotating. Single armature winding is made to act as two electrically and magnetically independent armature windings in quadrature, due to the presence of two brush sets. This representation is valid because the system is assumed to be linear both electrically and magnetically and the principle of superposition is applicable.

This generalized primitive machine can be shown to be equivalent to any of the rotating electrical machines with an appropriate number of coils on each fixed axis. Some machines may require fewer than four coils to represent them, while others may require more. For the ordinary d.c. machine, the generalized or two-axis machine diagram requires only two coils, *DS* for the field winding and *QR* for the armature. Thus the coils *DR* and *QS* will have to be omitted from Fig. 1.15 (*b*), to obtain a generalized, or two-axis, machine diagram for this machine, as shown in Fig. 1.3 (*b*). For an amplidyne coil *QS* should be omitted, while an additional coil *DC* on the direct axis, to represent the compensating winding, would have to be added to the stationary member, as shown in Fig. 1.5 (*b*).

Some of the basic two-pole machines are similar to the generalized or primitive machine, as discussed above, but if they are not, it is necessary to make a conversion. The process of conversion from the actual coils of the machine itself (*i.e.* the basic two-pole machine) to the equivalent *d*- and *q*-axes of the generalized machine or *vice-versa* is known as a *transformation*. For instance, in the case of a three phase winding on the stator, a transformation must be made to the equivalent coils *DS* and *QS*, in such a manner that the magnitude and direction of m.m.f. set up by the three-phase currents i_a, i_b, i_c and the two coil currents i_{ds}, i_{qs} is identical. The rotor of this machine should not know whether the rotating m.m.f. wave is produced by three phase currents i_a, i_b, i_c or by two coil (or phase) currents i_{ds}, i_{qs}. Thus the generalized machine diagram, or two-axis model, for a 3-phase induction machine is as shown in Fig. 1.16 (*a*).

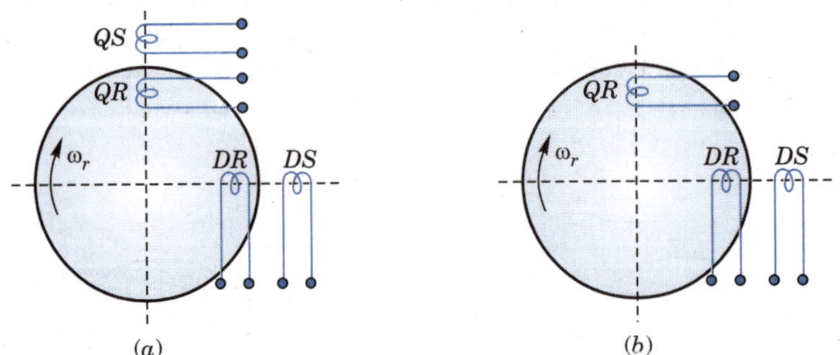

Fig. 1.16: Primitive (or generalized) machine diagrams, (*a*) Induction machine, (*b*) Synchronous machine (without damper bars).

Similarly the primitive machine diagram for a synchronous machine (without damper bars) is as shown in Fig. 1.16 (*b*).

Note that there are no electrical connections between windings of the Kron's primitive machine, generalized machine, or two-axis model.

Some fundamental assumptions are required to use the primitive machine:

(*i*) The m.m.f. distribution along the air-gap periphery is sinusoidal. This effectively neglects space harmonics and their effect on torque and on induced voltages.

(*ii*) Saturation and hysteresis are neglected, *i.e.*, linear coupled circuit theory is assumed valid.

(*iii*) Slots do not cause appreciable variation of inductances with the relative movement between stator and rotor. This along with (*i*) means that self and mutual inductances vary sinusoidally as the rotor moves.

In addition to these assumptions, it should be noted that the two coils *DR* and *QR* on the moving element of Fig. 1.15 (*b*), are pseudo-stationary coils. Since the coils are mechanically identical, the electrical resistance will be same for both coils. The inductances can differ, since the magnetic reluctance in the two axes, need not be the same. These will be the same in a machine with a uniform air gap.

1.7.1 Leakage Flux in Machines with more than Two Windings

In case of two mutually coupled coils, the leakage flux is defined as the flux which links one coil only, but not the other. For more than two coils, any one of them has a different leakage flux with respect to each of the others. To illustrate this, consider three coils *A, B, C* as shown in Fig. 1.17 (*a*) where each coil has ϕ_{la}, ϕ_{lb}, ϕ_{lc} as its leakage flux respectively. ϕ_{lbc} is also the leakage flux, since it does not link coil *A*. Similarly ϕ_{lab} and ϕ_{lca} (not shown in the figure) can also be the leakage fluxes. Thus the exact analysis of three coils requires six leakage fluxes and hence six leakage inductances, making the analysis more involved.

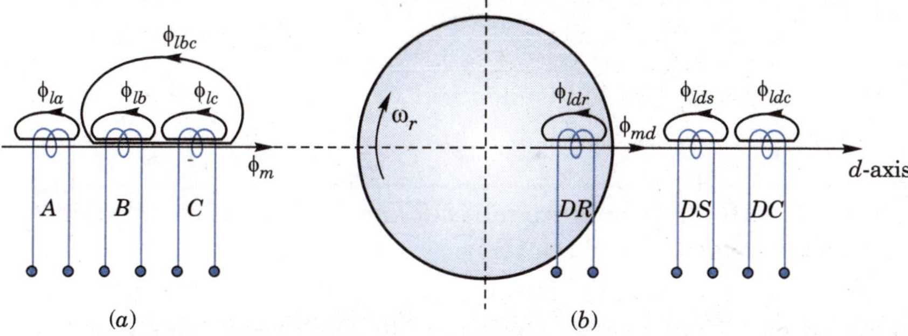

Fig. 1.17: (*a*) Leakage fluxes shown for three coils A, *B*, C. (*b*) Coils *DR, DS* and *DC* along the *d*-axis.

For practical purposes, it is sufficiently accurate to assume that a common mutual magnetic flux links all the windings and each winding has its own leakage flux. It amounts to using one common mutual inductance and a single leakage inductance for each winding.

Now let the three coils along the direct axis be designated as *DR, DS* and *DC,* as shown in Fig. 1.17 (*b*).

Self-inductance of each coil will be the sum of the mutual inductance and leakage inductance of that coil.

∴ Self-inductance of coil $DR = L_{dr} = M_d + l_{dr}$

Self-inductance of coil $DS = L_{ds} = M_d + l_{ds}$

and Self-inductance of coil $DC = L_{dc} = M_d + l_{dc}$

Here M_d is the mutual inductance between the three coils *DR, DS* and *DC*. The resultant mutual flux linkages due to the three *d*-axis coils-currents, Fig. 1.17 (*b*) as per Eq. (1.6), are

$$\psi_{md} = M_d\,(i_{dr} + i_{ds} + i_{dc}) \qquad \text{...(1.14)}$$

As stated before, Eq. (1.14) is valid on the assumption that (*i*) all parameters are referred to per unit system or (*ii*) all parameters are referred to any one coil or (*iii*) coils *DS*, *DR, DC* are single-turn coils. However, the flux produced by these coils is distributed sinusoidally in space.

If coils *DS* and *DC* are on the stationary element and *DR* on the rotor as illustrated in Fig. 1.17 (*b*), then total direct axis flux linkages with the armature coil *DR* on the rotor are:

$$\psi_d = \psi_{md} + l_{dr}\,i_{dr}$$
$$= M_d\,(i_{ds} + i_{dc} + i_{dr}) + l_{dr}\,i_{dr} = L_{dr} i_{dr} + M_d\,(i_{ds} + i_{dc}) \qquad \text{...(1.15)}$$

In obtaining the armature voltage equations, the armature leakage flux and sinusoidal air-gap flux must be assumed to act identically.

1.7.2 Voltage Equations

At this stage, the voltage equations for the primitive machine of Fig. 1.15 (*b*), can be written as follows:

Stator field coil DS. Its resistance is r_{ds} and total inductance is $L_{ds} = (M_d + l_{ds})$. It is mutually coupled with any other *d*-axis coil, *i.e.*, when the voltage equation for the *DS* circuit is to be written, the mutual (*i.e.*, transformer) effect of other *d*-axis coils must be considered. *Q*-axis coils *QS*, *QR* can have no effect on *DS* and no rotational voltages appear in it, since the coil *DS* is on the stationary element. Thus the applied voltage v_{ds} must account for the components given by

$$v_{ds} = r_{ds}\,i_{ds} + L_{ds} p i_{ds} + M_d p i_{dr} \qquad \text{...(1.16)}$$

Stator field coil QS. This coil is identical with coil *DS,* so that applied voltage v_{qs} is given by

$$v_{qs} = r_{qs}\,i_{qs} + L_{qs}\,p i_{qs} + M_q\,p i_{qr} \qquad \text{...(1.17)}$$

Armature coil DR. The armature coils *DR* and *QR* are the pseudo-stationary coils and they have rotational voltages induced in them.

$$v_{dr} = r_{dr}\,i_{dr} + L_{dr} p i_{dr} + M_d p i_{ds} - e_{dr} \qquad \text{(induced rotational voltage)}$$

The negative sign before the induced rotational voltage in the above equation is due to the fact that, if other voltage drops are neglected, the induced voltage is equal and opposite to the applied voltage. Referring to Eq. (1.12) and noting that rotational e.m.f. in coil *DR* appears due to *q*-axis flux, we get,

$$e_{dr} = +\,\omega_r \psi_q$$

In the rotational e.m.f. relation e_{dr} as given above, note that total armature flux linkage ψ_q (and not ψ_{mq}) are taken into consideration as assumed before.

Substitution of the value of e_{dr} in the expression for v_{dr} gives

$$v_{dr} = r_{dr}\,i_{dr} + L_{dr} p i_{dr} + M_d p i_{ds} - \omega_r\,\psi_q$$

Here ψ_q, the total flux linkages with the armature in *q*-axis, is given by,

$$\psi_q = M_q (i_{qs} + i_{qr}) + l_{qr}\,i_{qr}$$

Thus

$$v_{dr} = r_{dr}\,i_{dr} + L_{dr}\,p i_{dr} + M_d p i_{ds} - \omega_r M_q (i_{qs} + i_{qr}) - \omega_r l_{qr}\,i_{qr}$$
$$= r_{dr} i_{dr} + L_{dr}\,p i_{dr} + M_d\,p i_{ds} - \omega_r L_{qr} i_{qr} - \omega_r M_q i_{qs} \qquad \text{...(1.18)}$$

Armature coil QR. This coil is similar to coil *DR* and, therefore adopting the above procedure, the applied voltage v_{qr} must have the components:

$$v_{qr} = r_{qr}\, i_{qr} + L_{qr} p i_{qr} + M_q p i_{qs} + \omega_r L_{dr} i_{dr} + \omega_r M_d i_{ds} \quad \text{...(1.19)}$$

Equations in matrix form. The above four equations from (1.16) to (1.19) can be written down rapidly in matrix form as illustrated below:

			ds	qs	dr	qr		
v_{ds}		ds	$r_{ds} + L_{ds}p$		$M_d p$		i_{ds}	
v_{qs}	=	qs		$r_{qs} + L_{qs}p$		$M_q p$	i_{qs}	
v_{dr}		dr	$M_d p$	$-M_q\omega_r$	$r_{dr} + L_{dr}p$	$-\omega_r L_{qr}$	i_{dr}	...(1.20)
v_{qr}		qr	$\omega_r M_d$	$M_q p$	$\omega_r L_{dr}$	$r_{qr} + L_{qr}p$	i_{qr}	

The matrices should be written in pigeon-box form as above, instead of using the brackets as done in mathematics. This will facilitate in identifying an element as belonging to a particular part of the system. The identifying index is written outside the pigeon-box for both rows and columns in Eq. (1.20).

In the matrix Eq. (1.20), the left hand side matrix is called the *voltage matrix* and on the right hand side, the four-column matrix, is referred to as the *impedance matrix* or operational impedance matrix, whereas one-column matrix, a *current matrix*. It will be observed from the impedance matrix that the main diagonal boxes or compartments contain only the self-impedances, while the remaining ones contain mutual impedances or rotational emf's where any exist. The voltage v_{ds} equals the sum of the product of *ds* row impedances with the column of currents. The rotational e.m.f. terms appear only in last two rows. It should be noted that every co-efficient of p in row *dr* appears again in row *qr* in the same column but with p replaced by ω_r. Similarly every coefficient of p in row *qr* appears in row *dr* in the same column but with p replaced by $(-\omega_r)$.

Note that all the terms of the impedance matrix in Eq. (1.20) are positive except some of the terms involving speed ω_r. The thought process for ascertaining the correct sign for the rotational voltage terms can be described as below:

The armature coil under consideration say *QR* will have rotational voltage in it due to a flux 90° away from it, *i.e.* the *d*-axis flux. So move the coil *QR* by $\pi/2$ so that it is aligned along *d*-axis. Since the motion is in the reference positive direction of rotation, the sign for the rotational voltage term is positive. Coil *QR* is then conceived to be mutually coupled with *DS*, thus $+ M_d\omega_r$ term now appears due to coil *DS*, but coil *QR* is completely embraced by coil *DR*, therefore the rotational voltage term is $+ L_{dr}\omega_r$. Likewise for coil *DR* to align along *q*-axis, motion is opposite to the reference positive direction of rotation and thus $- M_q\omega_r$ and $- L_{qr}\omega_r$ appear as rotational voltage terms due to coils *QS* and *QR* respectively.

If there are more *d*- or *q*-axis coils, they can be considered by incorporating one row and one column for each. If certain coils are absent, then columns and rows pertaining to these coils are deleted.

One thing must be noted about the terms $M_d p$ and $M_d\omega_r$ appearing in Eq. (1.20). M_d in the term $M_d p$, is the mutual inductance between coils *DS* and *DR* (on the same magnetic axis) due to the transformer action and may be called *transformer mutual inductance.* M_d, in the term $M_d\omega_r$, is the mutual inductance between coils DS and QR (magnetic axis in quadrature, *i.e.*, 90° apart) due to rotation and may be called *rotational mutual inductance* or *motional inductance.* The transformer mutual inductance is different from the rotational mutual inductance but they are taken as same for all practical purposes and to simplify the analysis.

In abbreviated form, the matrix Eq. (1.20) can be written as

[Voltage column matrix] = [Impedance matrix] [Current-column matrix]

$$[v] = [Z]\,[i] \qquad \text{or} \qquad [v] = \{[R] + [L]p + [G]\omega_r\}\,[i]$$

where $[R]$ = 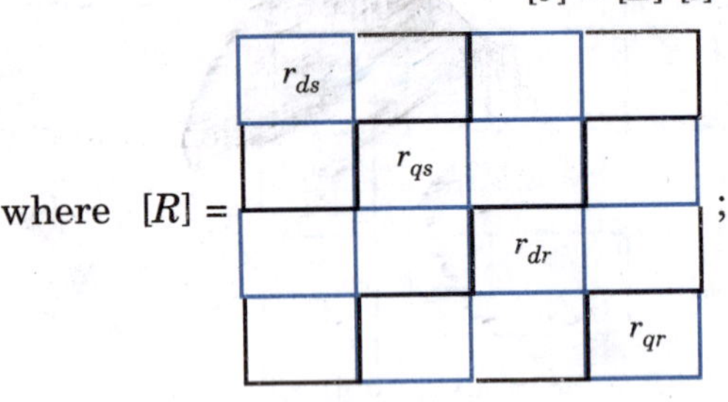

; $[L]$ = 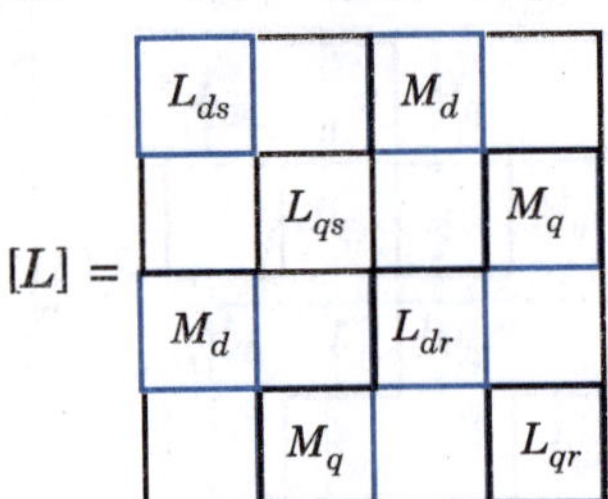

and $[G]$ = 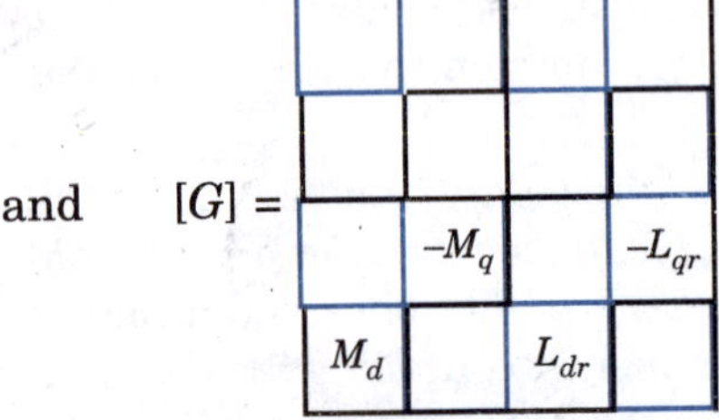

$[R]$ is the resistance matrix and possesses elements in the main diagonal only. $[L]$ is the inductance matrix and $[G]$ is the *motional inductance matrix* or *torque matrix.*

Now total electrical power input P_i into the four electrical ports of the machine is given by,

$$P_i = v_{ds}i_{ds} + v_{qs}i_{qs} + v_{dr}i_{dr} + v_{qr}i_{qr}$$

which in matrix form is

$$P_i = \begin{bmatrix} i_{ds} & i_{qs} & i_{dr} & i_{qr} \end{bmatrix} \begin{bmatrix} v_{ds} \\ v_{qs} \\ v_{dr} \\ v_{qr} \end{bmatrix} = [i_t]\,[v] \qquad \text{...(1.21)}$$

Here $[i_t]$ is the transpose of the current column matrix $[i]$.

Substitution of the value of $[v]$ in Eq. (1.21) gives

$$P_i = [i_t]\,\{[R] + [L]p + [G]\omega_r\}\,[i]$$

$$= [i_t][R][i] + [i_t][L]p[i] + \omega_r[i_t][G][i] \qquad \text{...(1.22)}$$

The terms on the right hand side of Eq. (1.22), are now examined in detail.

First term on the right hand side is given by,

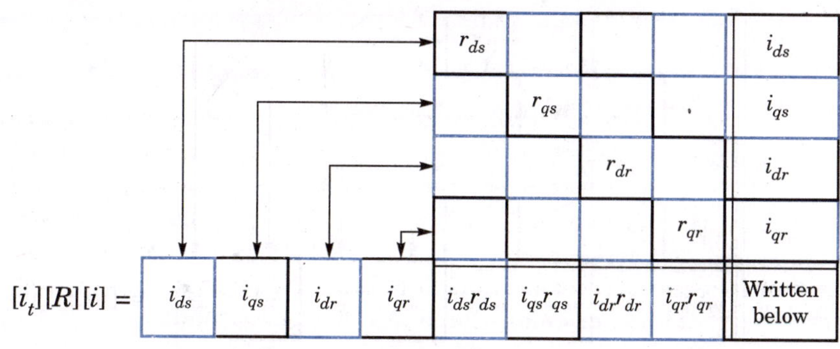

$$= i_{ds}^2 r_{ds} + i_{qs}^2 r_{qs} + i_{dr}^2 r_{dr} + i_{qr}^2 r_{qr}$$

= Resistance or ohmic loss in the four windings.

Thus the first term in Eq. (1.22) is the sum of ohmic losses in all the four windings.

Second term on the right hand side of Eq. (1.22) is

$$\begin{array}{c|cccc|c} & L_{ds}p & & M_dp & & i_{ds} \\ & & L_{qs}p & & M_qp & i_{qs} \\ & M_dp & & L_{dr}p & & i_{dr} \\ & & M_qp & & L_{qr}p & i_{qr} \\ \hline [i_t][L]p[i] = \begin{bmatrix} i_{ds} & i_{qs} & i_{dr} & i_{qr} \end{bmatrix} & \begin{matrix} i_{ds}L_{ds}p \\ + \\ i_{dr}M_dp \end{matrix} & \begin{matrix} i_{qs}L_{qs}p \\ + \\ i_{qr}M_qp \end{matrix} & \begin{matrix} i_{ds}M_dp \\ + \\ i_{dr}L_{dr}p \end{matrix} & \begin{matrix} i_{qs}M_qp \\ + \\ i_{qr}L_{qr}p \end{matrix} & \text{Written below} \end{array}$$

$$= i_{ds}L_{ds}pi_{ds} + i_{dr}M_dpi_{ds} + i_{qs}L_{qs}pi_{qs} + i_{qr}M_qpi_{qs} + i_{ds}M_dpi_{dr}$$
$$+ i_{dr}L_{dr}pi_{dr} + i_{qs}M_qpi_{qr} + i_{qr}L_{qr}pi_{qr}$$

Writing first the terms containing self-inductances and then the terms having mutual inductances, the above equation can be written as

$$[i_t][L]p[i] = [i_{ds}L_{ds}pi_{ds} + i_{qs}L_{qs}pi_{qs} + i_{dr}L_{dr}pi_{dr} + i_{qr}L_{qr}pi_{qr}]$$
$$+ [i_{ds}M_dpi_{dr} + i_{qs}M_qpi_{qr} + i_{dr}M_dpi_{ds} + i_{qr}M_qpi_{qs}] \qquad ...(1.23)$$

The energy W_1 stored in a magnetic field due to self-inductance L and current i is given by,

$$W_1 = \frac{1}{2}L \cdot i^2$$

$$\therefore \qquad \frac{dW_1}{dt} = \frac{1}{2} L2i \cdot \frac{di}{dt} = (iLpi)$$

= Rate at which energy stored in the self field changes.

Also the energy stored in a magnetic field, due to mutual inductance is,

$$W_2 = Mi_1i_2$$

$$\therefore \qquad \frac{dW_2}{dt} = i_1Mpi_2 + i_2Mpi_1$$

= Rate at which stored energy in the mutual field changes.

Thus the second term in Eq. (1.22), *i.e.*, Eq. (1.23) comprises of two components: (*i*) The first component represents the rate at which the stored magnetic energy in the self-fields changes or it represents the power being stored in self-fields, (*ii*) The second component is the rate at which the stored magnetic energy in the mutual fields changes or it represents the power being stored in the mutual fields. It may be stated, in general, that the second term in Eq. (1.22) corresponds to the power being stored in the magnetic fields.

According to the principle of conservation of energy, the energy must be conserved and the energy balance must be maintained, *i.e.*,

Power input = Power lost + Power stored + Power output.

Since the system under consideration is a rotating one, third term in Eq. (1.22) must represent the electrical power being converted to mechanical form. Thus

P = Power being converted from electrical to mechanical form.

$$= \omega_r[i_t]\ [G]\ [i] \qquad \text{...(1.24)}$$

But T_e = Electrical torque

$$= \frac{P}{\omega_r} = [i_t]\ [G]\ [i] \qquad \text{...(1.25)}$$

Substitution of the values of $[i_t]$, $[G]$ and $[i]$ in Eq. (1.25), gives

$$\begin{array}{c|cccc|c} & & & & & i_{ds} \\ & & & & & i_{qs} \\ & & -M_q & & -L_{qr} & i_{dr} \\ & M_d & & L_{dr} & & i_{qr} \\ \hline T_e = \begin{bmatrix} i_{ds} & i_{qs} & i_{dr} & i_{qr} \end{bmatrix} & i_{qr} \cdot M_d & -i_{dr}M_q & i_{qr} \cdot L_{dr} & -i_{dr}L_{qr} & \text{Written below} \end{array}$$

$$= i_{qr} \cdot M_d \cdot i_{ds} - i_{dr}M_qi_{qs} + i_{qr}L_{dr}i_{dr} - i_{dr}L_{qr}i_{qr}$$

$$= M_d \cdot i_{ds}i_{qr} - M_q \cdot i_{qs}i_{dr} + (L_{dr} - L_{qr})\, i_{dr}i_{qr} \qquad \text{...(1.26)}$$

A careful examination of Eq. (1.26) reveals that the development of electrical torque T_e, requires the interaction between two currents which must be in quadrature. Currents on the same axis don't contribute to the production of electrical torque.

In Eq. (1.26), the torque component $(L_{dr} - L_{qr})\, i_{dr}i_{qr}$ is known as the reluctance torque and is present only in salient-pole machines in which $L_{dr} > L_{qr}$. With uniform air-gap machines, $L_{dr} = L_{qr}$ and the reluctance torque vanishes. The first two terms in Eq. (1.26) define the electromagnetic torque. Note that in a generalized machine (or two-axis machine), the reluctance torque requires the existance of two currents on the rotor (or stator), but space displaced from each other by 90° ; the electromagnetic torque requires the existence of one current on the stator and the other current on the rotor and these must also be in space quadrature (*i.e.*, 90° away from each other).

In Eq. (1.26), d- and q-axes armature flux linkages ψ_d and ψ_q can be included as follows:

$$\begin{aligned} T_e &= M_d \cdot i_{qr} \cdot l_{ds} + (M_d + l_{dr})\, i_{dr} i_{qr} - M_q i_{qs} i_{dr} - (M_q + l_{qr}) i_{dr} i_{qr} \\ &= i_{qr}\, [M_d(i_{ds} + i_{dr}) + l_{dr} i_{dr}] - i_{dr}\, [M_q(i_{qs} + i_{qr}) + l_{qr} i_{qr}] \\ &= i_{qr}\psi_d - i_{dr}\psi_q \end{aligned} \quad ...(1.27a)$$

The first term is due to the interaction between the q-axis armature current and the d-axis flux and has positive sign showing it to be a motoring term. The second component is due to the interaction between the d-axis armature current and q-axis flux and has a negative sign indicating it to be a generating term. No torque is produced by interaction between the flux and current on the same axis.

The torque given by Eq. (1.27a) is for a two-pole machine. For any number of poles,

$$\begin{bmatrix}\text{Speed in electrical} \\ \text{radians/sec, } \omega_r\end{bmatrix} = \left(\frac{\text{Poles}}{2}\right)\begin{bmatrix}\text{Speed in mechanical} \\ \text{radians/sec, } \omega_m\end{bmatrix}$$

$$\therefore \qquad T_e = \frac{\text{Power}}{\text{Speed in mechanical radians/sec, } \omega_m}$$

$$= \frac{\omega_r\, [i_t]\, [G]\, [i]}{[\omega_r/(\text{poles}/2)]} = \left[\frac{\text{Poles}}{2}\right] [i_t]\, [G]\, [i]$$

$$= \left(\frac{\text{Poles}}{2}\right) [i_{qr}\psi_d - i_{dr}\psi_q] \quad ...(1.27b)$$

1.8 ANALYSIS OF ELECTRICAL MACHINES

Some additional information, essential for the analysis of electrical machines is given here.

1.8.1 Concept of Phasors

A phasor or complexor (also called a sinor) is a time independent quantity which is used to describe a sinusoid completely. In order to illustrate it, let an alternating current, as a function of time, be expressed as

$$i = I_m \cos(\omega t + \sigma) \quad ...(1.28)$$

where I_m = maximum value of current, $\omega = (2\pi)$ (frequency in Hz)

and σ = phase angle of the current i with respect to the time origin, see Fig. 1.18 (a).

Now $\qquad e^{j(\omega t + \sigma)} = \cos(\omega t + \sigma) \pm j \sin(\omega t + \sigma)$

Taking the real parts of both sides, we get

$$Re\, [e^{j(\omega t + \sigma)}] = \cos(\omega t + \sigma)$$

In the above relation, Re stands for 'real part of'. Introducing the above relation in Eq. (1.28),

$$\begin{aligned} i &= Re\, [I_m e^{j(\omega t + \sigma)}] \\ &= Re\left[\sqrt{2}\left(\frac{I_m}{\sqrt{2}} e^{j\sigma}\right) e^{j\omega t}\right] \end{aligned} \quad ...(1.29)$$

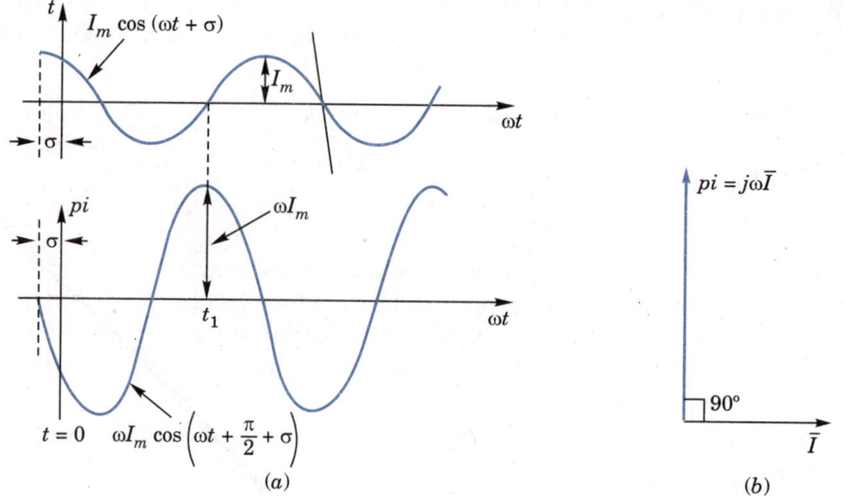

Fig. 1.18: Effect of p operating on i (a) waveforms of i and pi (b) phasor diagram at instant t_1.

Now the two characteristics which distinguish $I_m \cos(\omega t + \sigma)$, from all other sinusoidal currents of the same frequency are, (i) the amplitude I_m and (ii) the phase angle σ. Thus the time-invariant complex quantity $\left(\frac{I_m}{\sqrt{2}}\right) e^{j\sigma}$, carries all the essential information required to describe a sinusoid completely, assuming that the frequency is known. This term $\frac{I_m}{\sqrt{2}} e^{j\sigma}$, a time-invariant complex quantity is called a phasor $\bar{I}$ (bar over I) and is defined as

$$\bar{I} = \frac{I_m}{\sqrt{2}} . e^{j\sigma} = \frac{I_m}{\sqrt{2}} \angle\sigma \qquad ...(1.30)$$

Magnitude of phasor $= \frac{I_m}{\sqrt{2}} = \text{r.m.s. } I$

∴ Eq. (1.30) becomes $\bar{I} = Ie^{j\sigma} = I\angle\sigma$ ...(1.31)

Eq. (1.29) can also be written as

$$i = Re\,[\sqrt{2}\;\bar{I}\,e^{j\omega t}] \qquad ...(1.32)$$

The advantage of using phasor notation is that the sinusoids can be handled as complex quantities and the manipulations of the equations become simpler to get the required solution. The application of complex numbers for solving the steady-state a.c. circuit problems may already be known to the reader.

A differential equation for an a.c. circuit or machine carrying sinusoidal currents or voltages, can be converted to a phasor equation as follows:

Differentiation with respect to time, of the current given by Eq. (1.28) gives

$$pi = \frac{di}{dt} = -\omega I_m \sin(\omega t + \sigma)$$

$$= \omega I_m \cos\left(\overline{\omega t + \sigma} + \frac{\pi}{2}\right) \qquad ...(1.33)$$

In Fig. 1.18 (*a*), $i = I_m \cos(\omega t + \sigma)$, and di/dt as given by Eq. (1.33) are plotted as a functions of time. The amplitude of current i is I_m and Fig. 1.18 (*a*) shows that amplitude of pi is ωI_m. In Fig. 1.18 (*b*), a phasor diagram is drawn at time t_1 where i is represented by a phasor of length $\bar{I} = I_m/\sqrt{2}$ and di/dt by a phasor of length $\omega\bar{I}$. Note that at time t_1, current i is passing through zero, whereas derivative of current pi is maximum and equal to ωI_m. It is seen from this figure that phasor $\omega\bar{I}$ representing pi leads by 90° the phasor $\bar{I}$ that represents current i. Mathematically, this can be written as

$$pi = \frac{di}{dt} = j\omega\bar{I} \qquad \text{...(1.34)}$$

Thus a differential equation can be converted to phasor equation

(*i*) by replacing p by $j\omega$ and

(*ii*) at the same time, replacing instantaneous values by their corresponding phasors.

For example, an instantaneous voltage equation for an R-L circuit is

$$v = (R + Lp)\, i \qquad \text{...(1.35)}$$

If applied voltage is sinusoidal, then r.m.s. phasor equation is obtained by putting $p = j\omega$ and replacing v and i by their respective phasors $\bar{V}$ and $\bar{I}$. So, Eq. (1.35) in phasor form is

$$\bar{V} = (R + j\omega L)\bar{I} \qquad \text{...(1.36)}$$

Power in A.C. circuits. Let the voltage V applied to a circuit result in a current I and assume the current I to lag behind the voltage V by an angle θ as shown in Fig. 1.19. Phasors $\bar{V}$ and $\bar{I}$ make angle α and β respectively, with the reference axis. Thus, in view of Eq. (1.31), the phasors $\bar{V}$ and $\bar{I}$ can be written as

$$\bar{V} = Ve^{j\alpha} \qquad \text{and} \qquad \bar{I} = Ie^{j\beta}$$

Now power in a.c. circuit

$$\begin{aligned} P &= VI\cos\theta \\ &= VI\cos(\alpha - \beta) \\ &= Re\,[VIe^{j(\alpha-\beta)}] \\ &= Re\,[Ve^{j\alpha} . Ie^{-j\beta}] \end{aligned}$$

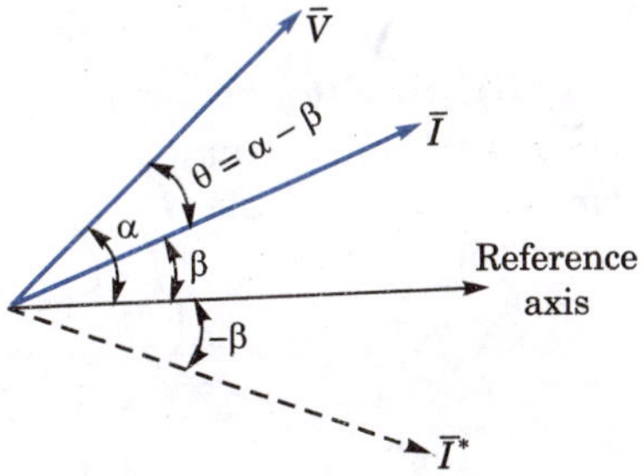

Fig. 1.19: Phasor diagram for an inductive circuit.

But conjugate of phasor $\bar{I}$ is given by $\bar{I}^* = Ie^{-j\beta}$

Thus the power in an a.c. circuit can be written as

$$P = Re[\bar{V}\,\bar{I}^*] \qquad \text{...(1.37)}$$

Also $\qquad \bar{V}\,\bar{I}^* = VIe^{j(\alpha-\beta)} = VI\cos\theta + jVI\sin\theta = P + jQ.$

Taking the real parts of both sides

$$P = Re[\bar{V}\,\bar{I}^*] = VI\cos\theta$$

If imaginary parts [*Img*] are taken, then

$$Q = Img\,[\bar{V}\,\bar{I}^*] = VI\sin\theta \qquad \text{...(1.38)}$$

Also, $\qquad Q = VI\sin\theta = \dfrac{P}{\cos\theta}\sin\theta = P\tan\theta \qquad \text{...(1.38}a\text{)}$

With I lagging V as in an inductive circuit, both θ (= $\alpha - \beta$) and Q are positive.

In other words, it can be stated that a lagging power factor load absorbs both P and Q from the source. For example, a 3-phase induction motor operates invariably at a lagging p.f.;

it, therefore, absorbs both power P (in watts) and reactive power Q (in VAr) from the supply system.

A leading p.f. load will absorb P from the source and give out Q to the source. For example, a 3-phase synchronous motor working at a leading p.f. absorbs power from the source but returns reactive power to the source.

1.8.2 Operational Method

This method involves the replacement of d/dt by p, d^2/dt^2 by p^2 etc. in the differential equations. The operator p is then treated as an algebraic quantity in the manipulations of the equations.

An operator is a symbol which states that a particular operation is to be performed on the quantity to which it applies and which is called the operand. Thus in the expression $y = \cos x$; the cos is a symbol for certain familiar operation and x is the operand.

It is common practice to represent the inverse operation by a unit negative exponent. Thus in $x = \cos^{-1} y$, the $\cos^{-1}$ is the inverse operator to cos, meaning that when they are applied together their effects get cancelled. For example

$$\cos^{-1} \cos x = \cos \cos^{-1} x = x.$$

So far as p is concerned, the inverse operator will be written p^{-1} which is then defined as that operator which annuls the effect of p, so that

$$p^{-1}pf(t) = pp^{-1} f(t) = f(t).$$

The operator p^{-1} is thus an integration, since it cancels the effect of differentiation.

Also $$pp\, f(t) = p^2 f(t)$$

and $$p^m p^n f(t) = p^{m+n} f(t)$$

Unit Step function. It is defined as that discontinuous function of the time which is zero until time t equals zero and unity thereafter as shown in Fig. 1.20 (a). Mathematically it can be expressed as:

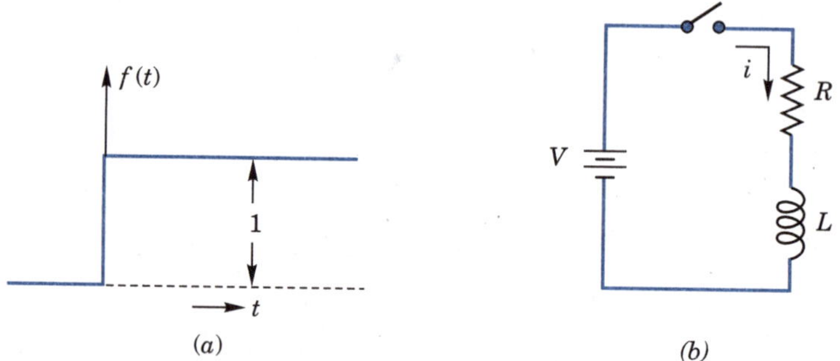

Fig. 1.20: (a) Unit step function; (b) a voltage V suddenly applied to R-L circuit.

$$f(t) = 0 \qquad t \le 0-$$
$$= 1 \qquad t \ge 0+$$

If a source of one volt d.c. is suddenly impressed on a circuit, say R and L in series, the network equation is

$$Ri + L\frac{di}{dt} = 1$$

In operational form, $$(R + Lp)i = \mathbf{1}$$

If the applied voltage is zero for $t \leq 0-$ and has the constant value V for $t \geq 0+$, the applied voltage is called a step-function voltage and equals $V\mathbf{1}$ where $\mathbf{1}$ is the Heaviside's unit step function. The circuit equation can now be written as,

$$(R + Lp)i = V\mathbf{1} \qquad \text{or} \quad i = \frac{V\mathbf{1}}{R + Lp} \qquad ...(1.39)$$

Eq. (1.39) is normally known as operational expression for the current i. The right hand side of the above equation means to get a function of t, no longer involving p.

Eq. (1.39) can be transformed to complex variables by replacing the

(*i*) derivative operator p by complex frequency s,

(*ii*) unit-step function $\mathbf{1}$ by $1/s$.

In view of the above, Eq. (1.39) in s domain is,

$$I(s) = \frac{V(s)}{(R + sL)s} \qquad ...(1.40)$$

Here variables $I(s)$ and $V(s)$ are the complex amplitudes of the corresponding time variables and Eq. (1.40) is an algebraic equation in complex frequency s. The time-domain solution of Eq. (1.40) can be obtained by taking its Laplace inverse by usual methods.

PROBLEMS

1.1. (*a*) With the help of a suitable diagram, describe the common essential features of rotating electrical machines.

(*b*) Explain how a rotating commutator winding can be represented by a pseudo-stationary coil on the moving element. Enumerate the properties possessed by this coil.

(*c*) A coil moves in a time varying magnetic field whose spatial distribution along the air-gap periphery is sinusoidal. Find an expression for voltage induced in the coil identifying the terms therein.

1.2. (*a*) What is Kron's primitive machine (or generalized model of rotating electrical machines) ? How are the various windings of a machine represented by the primitive machine ?

(*b*) Develop volt-ampere equations for the two-axis model of rotating electrical machines. Express these in matrix form. What observations are made from the impedance matrix so obtained.

1.3. Obtain an expression for the electrical torque of the Kron's primitive machine. Show that no torque is produced by interaction between the flux and current on the same axis.

1.4. Draw the (*i*) basic two-pole machine diagrams and (*ii*) primitive machine diagrams for the following machines:

D.C. compound machine, amplidyne, repulsion motor, polyphase induction machine, Schrage motor, single phase induction motor, synchronous machine with amortisseurs.

Describe briefly how these are obtained.

1.5. (*a*) Is phasor a time variant quantity ? Explain.

(*b*) How can a differential equation for an a.c. circuit or machine be converted to a phasor equation ? Illustrate your answer by assuming current $i = I_m \sin(\omega t + \sigma)$.

(*c*) Prove that the active and reactive powers in an inductive circuit are given by,

$$P = Re\,[\overline{V}\,\overline{I}^*] \text{ and } Q = Img\,[\overline{V}\,\overline{I}^*]$$

respectively. Here $\overline{V}$ is the voltage phasor and $\overline{I}^*$ is the conjugate of current phasor. Does a leading power factor load absorbs Q from the source or give out Q to the source? Discuss.

2
Linear Transformations in Machines

It has been stated earlier that the primitive machine can be shown equivalent to any of the rotating electrical machines. The rotor winding of the primitive machine is fitted with commutator and brushes and the rotor magnetic field is space and time invariant. The electrical machines, most closely resembling the primitive machine are d.c. machines, since these are also constructed with commutator plus brushes and the field produced in them is space and time invariant. Thus the d.c. machines are equivalent to the primitive machine with appropriate number of coils on each fixed axis and no transformation is necessary.

A wide variety of rotating machines are polyphase a.c. machines constructed in a different manner than the primitive machine. In such cases, the primitive machine can also be employed in the analysis, provided the rotating polyphase winding on the rotor and the stationary polyphase winding on the stator can be represented by the *d-q* axes coils of the primitive machine. The process of replacing one set of variables by another related set of variables is called *winding transformation* or merely, transformation.

The term "linear transformation" means that the transformation from old to new set of variables or *vice-versa*, is governed by linear equations*. The idea of using linear transformations, for simplifying the solution, is not new to the reader. He must have used logarithms for doing the multiplication or division of two or more numbers. For example, for multiplying two numbers, we take the $\log_{10}$ of both the numbers, add them and then take the inverse by the use of logarithm tables to get the required multiplication. This is done primarily for simplifying the process of multiplication; logarithm is thus an example of linear transformation. Similarly, the Laplace transform is also a linear transformation. It transforms the time-domain (old variables) equation to *s*-domain (new variables) equation and after manipulations, we again get the required time-domain solution. The equations relating the symmetrical components of currents with 3-phase currents are equivalent to a linear transformation. The process of referring secondary quantities to primary or primary quantities to secondary in a transformer is also equivalent to a linear transformation. Note that the transformation from old to new set of variables is carried out merely for making the calculations simpler and less laborious.

The equations expressing old variables in terms of new variables *or vice versa* are called *transformation equations*. These equations, when written in matrix, have the following general form:

---

*An equation each of whose term is a first degree term in the variables is called a linear algebraic equation. A linear equation does not involve squares, higher powers of the variables or their products.

[New variables] = [Transformation matrix] [Old variables]

or [Old variables] = [Transformation matrix] [New variables]

The *transformation matrix* may, therefore, be defined as a matrix, containing the coefficients relating the old and new variables.

Linear transformations in electrical machines are usually carried out for the purpose of obtaining new equations which are fewer in number or are more easily solved. For example, a 3-phase machine requires three voltage equations whereas its generalized model requires only two voltage equations which can be solved more easily as compared to three voltage equations. Further, the circuit equations for a 3-phase machine are more complicated because of the magnetic coupling amongst the three-phase windings, but this is not the case in the generalized (or two-axis) model, in which m.m.f. acting along one axis has no mutual coupling with the m.m.f. acting along the other axis.

A transformation can be arbitrary, selected purely on mathematical grounds to get a suitable matrix, which results in simplifying the process of obtaining the solution of a problem. However, most of the transformations used here have physical meaning, though it is not necessary for a transformation to correspond to any physical equivalent.

2.1 INVARIANCE OF POWER

As already stated, the transformations are made from old variables to new variables, so as to yield an easier solution of the problem. Generally two transformations, one for the voltage and the other for the current, have to be considered. The voltage transformations may be different from the current transformations since the rules of matrix algebra, do not put any restriction on the choice of the two transformations. But the two transformations should be so related that the power in one set of variables, is the same as the power in new set of variables, taking the system as a whole in both cases. This principle of maintaining the power same under transformation from old to new set of variables is known as *invariance of power* or *power invariance.*

If power is variant (not invariant) under transformation, power and torques can be determined only from currents expressed in original system of reference axes. In other words, if the currents in the new set of variables are obtained, it will be essential to transform them, back to the original set of variables before power or torques are calculated. However, if the transformations correspond to the power invariance, power and torques, calculated either from the new set of variables or from the original system of variables will yield identical results.

In machine analysis, generally rotor currents are transformed and the necessary condition for doing this is that the transformed system of currents must produce an m.m.f. identical with that of the original system of currents, so far as magnitude and direction are concerned. In other words, the m.m.fs produced in the two cases, must be time and space invariant. The equivalence of m.m.fs is obtained by resolving the instantaneous rotor m.m.f. along any convenient axes, say α, β or d, q axes and the necessary transformation thereby obtained. The stator m.m.fs can be treated in a similar manner. Some of the transformations are discussed in what follows.

2.2 TRANSFORMATION FROM A DISPLACED BRUSH-AXIS

If a commutator machine has brushes displaced from *d-* or *q-axes,* a transformation is necessary from the displaced brush axis to *d-q* axes.

Suppose one set of brushes, denoted by *AA*, makes an angle α with the *d*-axis as shown in Fig. 2.1(*a*). The armature establishes an m.m.f. F_a along its brush axis, Fig. 2.1. This m.m.f. F_a can be resolved along *d*-axis as F_d and along *q*-axis as F_q, where

$$F_d = F_a \sin \alpha \quad \text{and} \quad F_q = F_a \cos \alpha$$

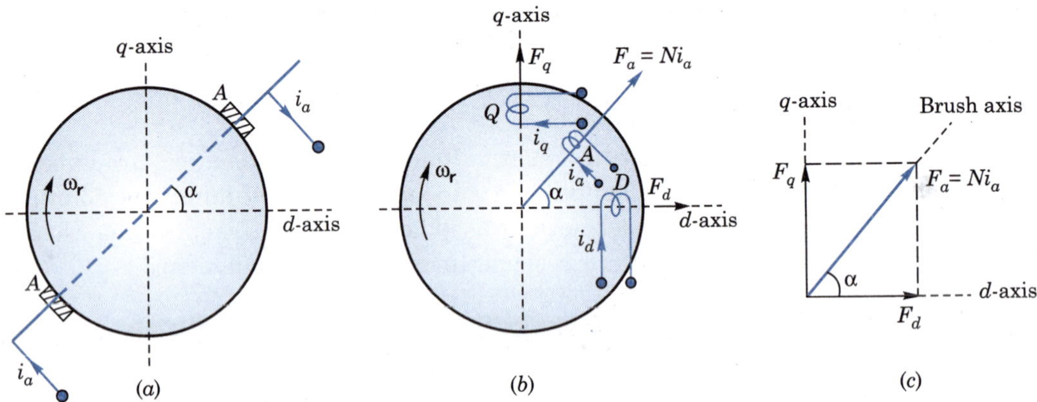

Fig. 2.1: (*a*) One set of displaced brushes (*b*) its *d-q* equivalent (*c*) brush-shifting transformation.

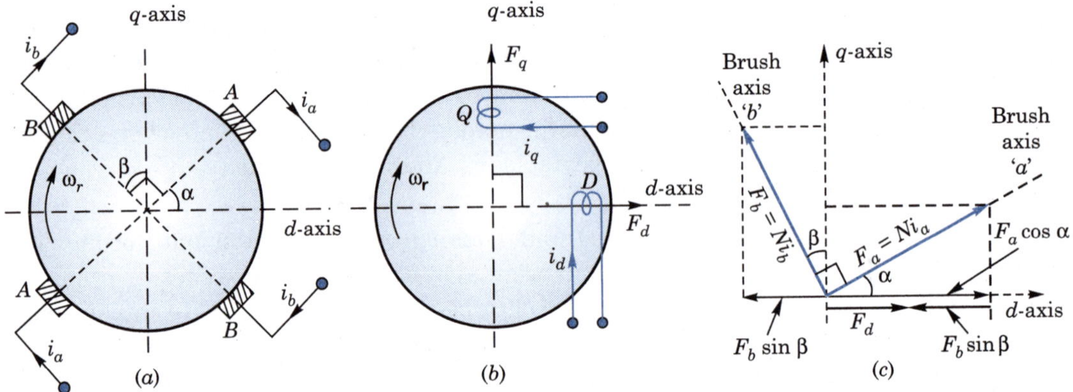

Fig. 2.2: (*a*) Two sets of displaced brushes (*b*) its *d-q* equivalent (*c*) brush-shifting transformation.

Assuming equal number of turns in both armature and *d-q* coils, we get

$$Ni_d = Ni_a \sin \alpha$$

or and

$$\left.\begin{aligned} i_d &= i_a \sin \alpha \\ i_q &= i_a \cos \alpha \end{aligned}\right\} \qquad \ldots(2.1)$$

Thus two coils *D* and *Q* in Fig. 2.1 (*b*), with the currents given above, are required to establish the equivalence of m.m.fs.

In addition to brush pair *AA*, consider another set of brushes *BB* making an angle β with *q*-axis as shown in Fig. 2.2 (*a*). The m.m.fs set up by the brush-pairs *AA* and *BB* are F_a

and F_b respectively, Fig. 2.2 (*c*). The *d-q* axes coils, *D* and *Q*, set up m.m.fs F_d and F_q along their respective axis, Fig. 2.2 (*b*). The resolution of m.m.fs F_a and F_b, along *d-q* axes gives

$$F_d = F_a \cos \alpha - F_b \sin \beta$$

and

$$F_q = F_a \sin \alpha + F_b \cos \beta$$

Assuming equal number of turns as above, we get

$$\left.\begin{aligned} i_d &= i_a \cos \alpha - i_b \sin \beta \\ i_q &= i_a \sin \alpha + i_b \cos \beta \end{aligned}\right\} \quad \text{...(2.2)}$$

2.3 TRANSFORMATIONS IN ELECTRICAL MACHINES

The dynamic modelling of three-phase synchronous machines or three-phase induction machines can be obtained from the generalised machine, or two-axis model of Fig. 1.15(*b*). This model can, however, be used only if three-phase variables *a*, *b*, *c* are related to two-axis variables *d*, *q*, *O*. A simple way to derive the transformations relating the three-phase and two-axis variables is to (*i*) first relate the 3-phase variables to 2-phase variables and (*ii*) then related 2-phase variables to two-axis variables and (*iii*) finally relate the 3-phase variables to *dqo* variables. This is what is done in the following pages.

2.3.1 Three-phase to two-phase transformation (*a*, *b*, *c* to α, β, *o*)

A symmetrical 2-pole, 3-phase winding on the rotor is represented by three coils *A*, *B*, *C*; each of *N* effective turns and mutually displaced by 120° as shown in Fig. 2.3 (*a*). Maximum values of mmfs F_a, F_b and F_c are shown along their respective phase-axes. The combined effect of these three mmfs, results in a constant amplitude rotating mmf, which revolves at a constant angular velocity depending on the poles and frequency.

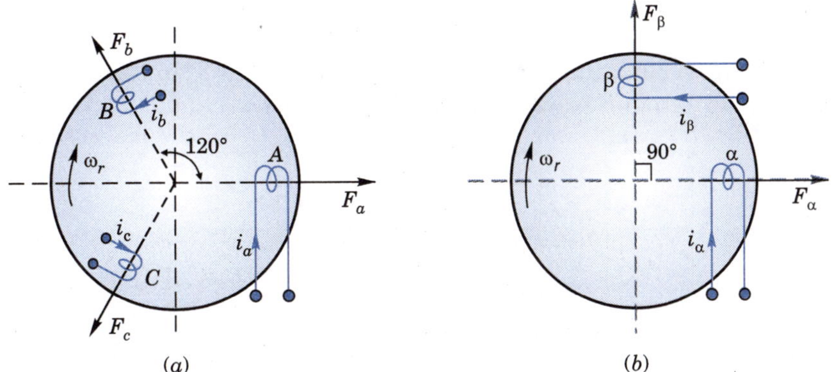

Fig. 2.3: Balanced windings on the rotor (*a*) three-phase winding and (*b*) two-phase winding.

If the three-phase currents are

$$i_a = I_m \cos \omega t$$

$$i_b = I_m \cos (\omega t - 120°) \quad \text{and} \quad i_c = I_m \cos (\omega t - 240°)$$

then, these three currents would produce an mmf of constant magnitude $\frac{3 I_m N}{2}$ rotating with respect to the three-phase winding at the time frequency. The space-phase angle (120°) between the windings must comply with the time-phase angle (120°) between the currents.

In Fig. 2.3 (*b*), a balanced two-phase winding is represented by two orthogonal coils α, β on the rotor. For convinience in transformation, the axis of phase '*A*' and '*a*' are taken to be coincident.

If two-phase currents

$$i_\alpha = I_m \cos \omega t \quad \text{and} \quad i_\beta = I_m \cos(\omega t - 90°) = I_m \sin \omega t$$

flow in the two-phase winding, the result will be an mmf of constant magnitude $I_m N$, revolving with respect to two-phase winding at the time frequency of phase currents.

The three-phase variables can be replaced by two-phase variables if the parity between three-and two-phases is established. This parity, or equivalence, is usually based on making equal the mmfs produced by three-phase and two-phase windings.

Assume N to be the effective number of turns per phase in a three-phase winding and $\frac{3}{2}N$ as the effective number of turns per phase in a two-phase winding. As stated before, axes of phase-*A* and phase-α are taken to coincide as shown in Fig. 2.3 (*a*) and (*b*). The mmfs in 3-phase and 2-phase windings can be rendered equal in magnitude by resolving the instantaneous three-phase mmfs along the α-β axis. Resolving first along α-axis, reference to Fig. 2.3 gives

$$\frac{3}{2}N \,.\, i_\alpha = N\,[i_a \cos 0° + i_b \cos 120° + i_c \cos 240°]$$

or

$$i_\alpha = \frac{2}{3}\left[i_a - \frac{1}{2}(i_b + i_c)\right] \qquad ...(2.3)$$

Similarly,

$$\frac{3}{2}N \,.\, i_\beta = N\,[i_a \sin 0° + i_b \sin 120° + i_c \sin 240°]$$

or

$$i_\beta = \frac{2}{3}\left[0 + \frac{\sqrt{3}}{2}(i_b - i_c)\right] \qquad ...(2.4)$$

The transformation equations giving the new currents i_α, i_β in terms of i_a, i_b, i_c can be expressed in matrix form from Eqs. (2.3) and (2.4) as under.

$$\begin{bmatrix} i_\alpha \\ i_\beta \end{bmatrix} = \frac{2}{3}\begin{bmatrix} 1 & -\frac{1}{2} & -\frac{1}{2} \\ & \frac{\sqrt{3}}{2} & -\frac{\sqrt{3}}{2} \end{bmatrix}\begin{bmatrix} i_a \\ i_b \\ i_c \end{bmatrix} \qquad ...(2.5)$$

The transformation matrix, containing the constant coefficients, is a singular one and thus i_a, i_b, i_c cannot be obtained from i_α, i_β; since inverse of a singular matrix does not exist. The matrix can be made square matrix if there is a third equation of constraint amongst i_a, i_b and i_c. Since the magnitude and direction of the mmf produced by two or three phase systems are identical, the third current in terms of i_a, i_b, i_c should not produce any resultant air-gap mmf. The only abvious choice is, therefore, the *zero-sequence current* i_0 which is defined as

$$i_o = \frac{1}{3}(i_a + i_b + i_c)$$

Note that zero-sequence current does not produce any rotating mmf and here the factor (1/3) is chosen just to suit the transformation. The three-phase currents i_a, i_b, i_c are thus related to two-phase current i_a, i_b, i_0 as under

$$\begin{bmatrix} i_\alpha \\ i_\beta \\ i_0 \end{bmatrix} = \frac{2}{3} \begin{array}{c} \\ \alpha \\ \beta \\ 0 \end{array} \begin{array}{c} \begin{array}{ccc} a & b & c \end{array} \\ \begin{bmatrix} 1 & -\frac{1}{2} & -\frac{1}{2} \\ & \frac{\sqrt{3}}{2} & -\frac{\sqrt{3}}{2} \\ \frac{1}{2} & \frac{1}{2} & \frac{1}{2} \end{bmatrix} \end{array} \begin{bmatrix} i_a \\ i_b \\ i_c \end{bmatrix} \quad \text{...(2.6)}$$

The transformation matrix in Eq. (2.6) is now non-singular and its inverse can be easily obtained.

Let $[A] = \frac{2}{3} \begin{bmatrix} 1 & -\frac{1}{2} & -\frac{1}{2} \\ & \frac{\sqrt{3}}{2} & -\frac{\sqrt{3}}{2} \\ \frac{1}{2} & \frac{1}{2} & \frac{1}{2} \end{bmatrix} = \begin{bmatrix} \frac{2}{3} & -\frac{1}{3} & -\frac{1}{3} \\ & \frac{1}{\sqrt{3}} & -\frac{1}{\sqrt{3}} \\ \frac{1}{3} & \frac{1}{3} & \frac{1}{3} \end{bmatrix}$

Now $\quad |A| = \frac{2}{3}\left[\frac{1}{3\sqrt{3}} + \frac{1}{3\sqrt{3}}\right] + \frac{1}{3}\left[\frac{1}{3\sqrt{3}} + \frac{1}{3\sqrt{3}}\right] = \frac{2}{3\sqrt{3}}$

Co-factor of $[A] = \begin{bmatrix} \frac{2}{3\sqrt{3}} & -\frac{1}{3\sqrt{3}} & -\frac{1}{3\sqrt{3}} \\ & \frac{1}{3} & -\frac{1}{3} \\ \frac{2}{3\sqrt{3}} & \frac{2}{3\sqrt{3}} & \frac{2}{3\sqrt{3}} \end{bmatrix}$

Inverse of matrix $\quad [A] = [A]^{-1} = \frac{1}{|A|}$ [transpose of co-factor matrix A]

$$\therefore \quad [A]^{-1} = \frac{3\sqrt{3}}{2} \begin{bmatrix} \frac{2}{3\sqrt{3}} & & \frac{2}{3\sqrt{3}} \\ -\frac{1}{3\sqrt{3}} & \frac{1}{3} & \frac{2}{3\sqrt{3}} \\ -\frac{1}{3\sqrt{3}} & -\frac{1}{3} & \frac{2}{3\sqrt{3}} \end{bmatrix} = \begin{array}{c} \\ a \\ b \\ c \end{array} \begin{array}{c} \begin{array}{ccc} \alpha & \beta & 0 \end{array} \\ \begin{bmatrix} 1 & & 1 \\ -\frac{1}{2} & \frac{\sqrt{3}}{2} & 1 \\ -\frac{1}{2} & -\frac{\sqrt{3}}{2} & 1 \end{bmatrix} \end{array}$$

$$\therefore \quad \begin{bmatrix} i_a \\ i_b \\ i_c \end{bmatrix} = \begin{array}{c} \\ a \\ b \\ c \end{array} \begin{array}{c} \alpha \quad\quad \beta \quad\quad 0 \\ \begin{bmatrix} 1 & & 1 \\ -\frac{1}{2} & \frac{\sqrt{3}}{2} & 1 \\ -\frac{1}{2} & -\frac{\sqrt{3}}{2} & 1 \end{bmatrix} \end{array} \begin{bmatrix} i_\alpha \\ i_\beta \\ i_0 \end{bmatrix} \quad ...(2.7a)$$

or

$$\begin{bmatrix} i_a \\ i_b \\ i_c \end{bmatrix} = \begin{bmatrix} \cos 0^\circ & \sin 0^\circ & 1 \\ \cos \frac{2\pi}{3} & \sin \frac{2\pi}{3} & 1 \\ \cos \frac{4\pi}{3} & \sin \frac{4\pi}{3} & 1 \end{bmatrix} \begin{bmatrix} i_\alpha \\ i_\beta \\ i_0 \end{bmatrix}. \quad ...(2.7b)$$

If zero-sequence current is not present, then i_a, i_b, i_c may be obtained by omitting the last column (marked 0) of the transformation matrix of Eq. (2.7).

In Fig. 2.3, three-phase and two-phase windings are shown on the rotor and for convinience, the axis of phase 'α' is taken to coincide with the axis of phase 'A'. Since the two rotors rotate at the same angular velocity and in the same direction, axis of phase α continues coinciding the axis of phase A. In other words, the rotating 2-phase axes α, β and the rotating 3-phase axes a, b, c; moving in one direction at the same angular speed, are at rest with respect to each other. Consequently, the transformation matrix relating the 3-phase and 2-phase variables, has constant coefficients, as in Eqs. (2.6) and (2.7). It can be stated here that the transformation from 3-phase rotating axes to 2-phase rotating axes is the transformation from rotating reference frame a, b, c to rotating reference frame α, β, 0.

2.3.2 Two-phase to two-axis transformation (α-β to d-q)

The transformation from three-phase (or two-phase) variables to d-q variables possess the advantage that volt-ampere equations in d-q variables have constant coefficients. Such equations in d-q variables can, therefore, be solved easily. The object of this part of article is to derive the transformation from two-phase to d-q variables, *i.e.* from α-β to d-q variables.

In Fig. 2.4 (a), two-phase winding α-β is shown on the rotor making an angle θ with stationary d-q axes. At time $t = 0$, $\theta = 0$ and at any time t, $\theta = \omega_r t$ where ω_r = rotor angular velocity in rad/sec in clockwise direction. Fig. 2.4 (b) shows two stationary rotor coils D, Q aligned respectively along the direct and quadrature axes. At the instant the coils α, β and D, Q are shown in Fig. 2.4 (a) and (b), the mmf space phasors F_α, F_β for α, β windings and F_d, F_q for D, Q windings are shown below in Fig. 2.4 (a) and (b) respectively. Assuming that the effective number of turns in α, β and D, Q windings is the same, mmfs F_α and F_β can be resolved along the d- and q-axes, giving the relationship.

$$F_d = F_\alpha \cos\theta + F_\beta \sin\theta \qquad \text{or} \quad Ni_d = Ni_\alpha \cos\theta + N\,.\,i_\beta \sin\theta$$

or

$$i_d = i_\alpha \cos\theta + i_\beta \sin\theta$$

Similarly,

$$i_q = -\,i_\alpha \sin\theta + i_\beta \cos\theta$$

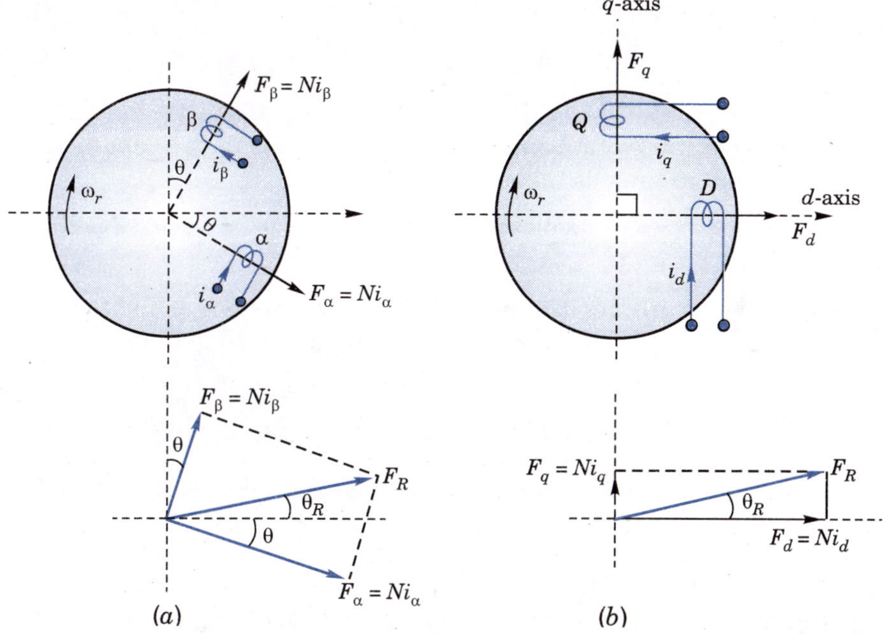

Fig. 2.4: (*a*) Rotating axes α, β with rotating space phasors F_α, F_β
(*b*) Stationary axes *d*, *q* with stationary space phasors F_d, F_q.

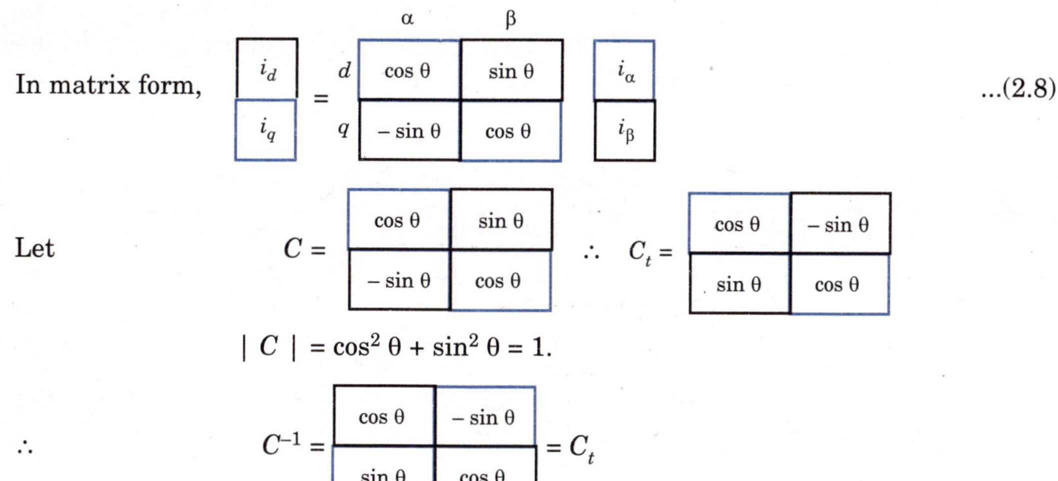

In matrix form,

$$\begin{bmatrix} i_d \\ i_q \end{bmatrix} = \begin{array}{c} \\ d \\ q \end{array} \begin{array}{cc} \alpha & \beta \\ \hline \cos\theta & \sin\theta \\ -\sin\theta & \cos\theta \end{array} \begin{bmatrix} i_\alpha \\ i_\beta \end{bmatrix} \qquad ...(2.8)$$

Let

$$C = \begin{bmatrix} \cos\theta & \sin\theta \\ -\sin\theta & \cos\theta \end{bmatrix} \quad \therefore \quad C_t = \begin{bmatrix} \cos\theta & -\sin\theta \\ \sin\theta & \cos\theta \end{bmatrix}$$

$$|\,C\,| = \cos^2\theta + \sin^2\theta = 1.$$

$$\therefore \qquad C^{-1} = \begin{bmatrix} \cos\theta & -\sin\theta \\ \sin\theta & \cos\theta \end{bmatrix} = C_t$$

As $C^{-1} = C_t$, the matrix is orthogonal and the voltage and current have identical transformations.

$$\therefore \qquad \begin{bmatrix} i_\alpha \\ i_\beta \end{bmatrix} = \begin{array}{c} \\ \alpha \\ \beta \end{array} \begin{array}{cc} d & q \\ \hline \cos\theta & -\sin\theta \\ \sin\theta & \cos\theta \end{array} \begin{bmatrix} i_d \\ i_q \end{bmatrix} \qquad ...(2.9)$$

Let the currents in d-q axes windings be functions of time and be given by

$$i_d = I_m \sin(\omega t + \phi)$$

and

$$i_q = I_m \cos(\omega t + \phi)$$

where ϕ is a constant arbitrary phase angle. The equivalent currents i_α and i_β can be obtained with the help of Eq. (2.9) where θ is taken equal to ωt.

$$\therefore \quad i_\alpha = I_m [\sin(\omega t + \phi) \cos \omega t - \cos(\omega t + \phi) \sin \omega t] = I_m \sin \phi$$

Similarly,

$$i_\beta = I_m \cos \phi$$

Thus, time-varying currents in stationary D-Q coils produce an mmf which is identical with the mmf produced by constant (or dc) currents in rotating α, β coils.

If coils α, β are stationary, dc currents in them would set up stationary mmf. Now if these coils are made to rotate at a certain constant speed, their mmf would also rotate at the same speed and in the same direction. It has been shown above that identical rotating mmf is also produced by two-phase currents $i_d = I_m \sin(\omega t + \phi)$ and $i_q = I_m \cos(\omega t + \phi)$ flowing in two stationary D, Q coils. Note that the space angle of 90° in between D, Q coils agrees with the time-angle of 90° between the two currents i_d and i_q.

2.3.3 Three-phase to Two-axis Transformation (*a*, *b*, *c* to *d*, *q*, *o*)

Transformations from 3-phase to 2-phase variables and from two-phase to d, q variables have already been obtained. These transformations lend themselves easily to obtain abc to dqO transformations.

In the transformation from dq to $\alpha\beta$, Eq. (2.9), zero-sequence current is not transformed. But if it exists, it can be taken into account in matrix C, by an additional row and an additional column, containing a unity as their common element. Thus

$$\begin{bmatrix} i_\alpha \\ i_\beta \\ i_0 \end{bmatrix} = \begin{array}{c} \\ \alpha \\ \beta \\ 0 \end{array} \begin{array}{c} \begin{array}{ccc} d & q & O \end{array} \\ \begin{bmatrix} \cos\theta & -\sin\theta & \\ \sin\theta & \cos\theta & \\ & & 1 \end{bmatrix} \end{array} \begin{bmatrix} i_d \\ i_q \\ i_O \end{bmatrix} \quad \ldots(2.10)$$

The transformation from 2-phase to 3-phase, *i.e.*, from $\alpha\beta O$ to abc is given by Eq. (2.7*b*). Substituting the values of i_α, i_β, i_0 from Eq. (2.10) in Eq. (2.7*b*), we get

$$\begin{bmatrix} i_a \\ i_b \\ i_c \end{bmatrix} = \begin{array}{c} \\ a \\ b \\ c \end{array} \begin{array}{c} \begin{array}{ccc} \alpha & \beta & O \end{array} \\ \begin{bmatrix} \cos 0^\circ & \sin 0^\circ & 1 \\ \cos\frac{2\pi}{3} & \sin\frac{2\pi}{3} & 1 \\ \cos\frac{4\pi}{3} & \sin\frac{4\pi}{3} & 1 \end{bmatrix} \end{array} \begin{array}{c} \\ \alpha \\ \beta \\ O \end{array} \begin{array}{c} \begin{array}{ccc} d & q & O \end{array} \\ \begin{bmatrix} \cos\theta & -\sin\theta & \\ \sin\theta & \cos\theta & \\ & & 1 \end{bmatrix} \end{array} \begin{bmatrix} i_d \\ i_q \\ i_O \end{bmatrix}$$

$$\therefore \quad \begin{bmatrix} i_a \\ i_b \\ i_c \end{bmatrix} = \begin{array}{c} a \\ b \\ c \end{array} \overset{\begin{array}{ccc} d & q & O \end{array}}{\begin{bmatrix} \cos\theta & -\sin\theta & 1 \\ \cos\left(\theta - \frac{2\pi}{3}\right) & -\sin\left(\theta - \frac{2\pi}{3}\right) & 1 \\ \cos\left(\theta - \frac{4\pi}{3}\right) & -\sin\left(\theta - \frac{4\pi}{3}\right) & 1 \end{bmatrix}} \begin{bmatrix} i_d \\ i_q \\ i_O \end{bmatrix} \qquad \text{...(2.11)}$$

Zero-sequence current can be inducted into Eq. (2.8) as under,

$$\begin{bmatrix} i_d \\ i_q \\ i_O \end{bmatrix} = \begin{array}{c} d \\ q \\ O \end{array} \overset{\begin{array}{ccc} \alpha & \beta & O \end{array}}{\begin{bmatrix} \cos\theta & \sin\theta & \\ -\sin\theta & \cos\theta & \\ & & 1 \end{bmatrix}} \begin{bmatrix} i_\alpha \\ i_\beta \\ i_O \end{bmatrix}$$

Substituting the values of i_α, i_β, i_0 from Eq. (2.6) into the above relation, we get

$$\begin{bmatrix} i_d \\ i_q \\ i_O \end{bmatrix} = \begin{array}{c} d \\ q \\ O \end{array} \overset{\begin{array}{ccc} \alpha & \beta & O \end{array}}{\begin{bmatrix} \cos\theta & \sin\theta & \\ -\sin\theta & \cos\theta & \\ & & 1 \end{bmatrix}} \times \frac{2}{3} \begin{array}{c} \alpha \\ \beta \\ O \end{array} \overset{\begin{array}{ccc} a & b & c \end{array}}{\begin{bmatrix} \cos\theta & \cos\frac{2\pi}{3} & \cos\frac{4\pi}{3} \\ \sin\theta & \sin\frac{2\pi}{3} & \sin\frac{4\pi}{3} \\ \frac{1}{2} & \frac{1}{2} & \frac{1}{2} \end{bmatrix}} \begin{bmatrix} i_a \\ i_b \\ i_c \end{bmatrix}$$

$$\therefore \quad \begin{bmatrix} i_d \\ i_q \\ i_O \end{bmatrix} = \frac{2}{3} \begin{bmatrix} \cos\theta & \cos\left(\theta - \frac{2\pi}{3}\right) & \cos\left(\theta - \frac{4\pi}{3}\right) \\ -\sin\theta & -\sin\left(\theta - \frac{2\pi}{3}\right) & -\sin\left(\theta - \frac{4\pi}{3}\right) \\ \frac{1}{2} & \frac{1}{2} & \frac{1}{2} \end{bmatrix} \begin{bmatrix} i_a \\ i_b \\ i_c \end{bmatrix} \qquad \text{...(2.12)}$$

Axes voltages v_d, v_q, v_0 are related to armature-phase voltages v_a, v_b, v_c by identical expressions as given by Eqs. (2.11) and (2.12). Note that factor $\frac{2}{3}$ appears when transformation from *abc* to *dqO* is required but it does not exist in *dqO* to *abc* transformation.

The transformation Eqns. (2.11) and (2.12), relating three-phase and *dq* variables are called **Park's transformations**.

The D, Q coils may be on the rotor as in Fig. 2.4 (*b*) or on the stator along d-q axes. In practice, the stator may have single-phase, two-phase or three-phase windings. The stator axes a, b, c or α, β will be stationary relative to the stator and its windings. The stator two-phase axes α, β may coincide with d, q axes and thus there is no disparity between α, β and d, q axes in case of stator. So if the stator carries

(*i*) single-phase winding, it is taken along d-axis,

(*ii*) two-phase winding, these are taken along d-q axes,

(*iii*) three-phase winding, transformation has to be made from three-phase axes to α, β or d, q axes, though the coefficient of the transformation matrix would be constant.

2.4 POWER INVARIANCE

During the transformation from 3-phase to 2-phase variables, or from 3-phase to dqO variables, it is imperative that total power in any electrical machine, in any reference frame, should remain the same. Only then, the modelling in any reference frame would be valid. Here the power in three-phase and dqO variable is examined.

The instantaneous power input to a three-phase stator is

$$p_i = v_a i_a + v_b i_b + v_c i_c = [v_a \quad v_b \quad v_c] \begin{bmatrix} i_a \\ i_b \\ i_c \end{bmatrix}$$

But
$$\begin{bmatrix} v_a \\ v_b \\ v_c \end{bmatrix} = [v_{abc}] \quad \therefore \quad [v_a \quad v_b \quad v_c] = [v_{abc}]_t$$

$\therefore$
$$p_i = [v_{abc}]_t \, [i_{abc}] \qquad \text{...(2.13)}$$

The equivalent *abc* voltages in terms of dqO voltages, from Eq. (2.11), are

$$[v_{abc}] = [A] \, [v_{dqo}] \qquad \text{...(2.14)}$$

Similarly,
$$[i_{abc}] = [A] \, [i_{dqo}] \qquad \text{...(2.15)}$$

Taking the transpose of Eq. (2.14), we get

$$[v_{abc}]_t = [v_{dqO}]_t \, [A]_t \qquad \text{...(2.16)}$$

The transpose of Eq. (2.14) will interchange rows and columns on both sides and for the matrix product to be confirmable, the relation of Eq. (2.16) must hold good.

Making the substitution from Eqs. (2.15) and (2.16) in Eq. (2.13), we get

$$p_i = [v_{dqO}]_t \, [A]_t \, [A] \, [i_{dqO}] \qquad \text{...(2.17)}$$

From Eq. (2.11),

$$[A] = \begin{bmatrix} \cos\theta & -\sin\theta & 1 \\ \cos\left(\theta - \frac{2\pi}{3}\right) & -\sin\left(\theta - \frac{2\pi}{3}\right) & 1 \\ \cos\left(\theta - \frac{4\pi}{3}\right) & -\sin\left(\theta - \frac{4\pi}{3}\right) & 1 \end{bmatrix}$$

Substituting $[A]_t$ and $[A]$ in Eq. (2.17) gives

$$p_i = [v_{dqO}]_t \begin{bmatrix} \cos\theta & \cos\left(\theta - \frac{2\pi}{3}\right) & \cos\left(\theta - \frac{4\pi}{3}\right) \\ -\sin\theta & -\sin\left(\theta - \frac{2\pi}{3}\right) & -\sin\left(\theta - \frac{4\pi}{3}\right) \\ 1 & 1 & 1 \end{bmatrix} \begin{bmatrix} \cos\theta & -\sin\theta & 1 \\ \cos\left(\theta - \frac{2\pi}{3}\right) & -\sin\left(\theta - \frac{2\pi}{3}\right) & 1 \\ \cos\left(\theta - \frac{4\pi}{3}\right) & -\sin\left(\theta - \frac{4\pi}{3}\right) & 1 \end{bmatrix} [i_{dqO}]$$

For manipulating the above multiplication, use of trigonometric relations listed in appendix *B* gives

$$p_i = [v_d \quad v_q \quad v_O] \begin{bmatrix} \frac{3}{2} & 0 & 0 \\ 0 & \frac{3}{2} & 0 \\ 0 & 0 & 3 \end{bmatrix} \begin{bmatrix} i_d \\ i_q \\ i_O \end{bmatrix}$$

$$= \frac{3}{2}\,[v_d i_d + v_q i_q + 2v_O i_O]$$

For balanced 3-phase machines, zero-sequence currents cannot exist.

$$\therefore \qquad p_i = \frac{3}{2}\,[v_d i_d + v_q i_q] \qquad \text{...(2.18)}$$

Example 2.1. *A 3-phase induction motor has the following data: 5 kW, 400 V, 50 Hz, 4-pole, 0.8 pf, delta-connected.*

Find the dqO voltages and currents when working under rated voltage and rated load conditions. Also calculate the total powr from dqO variables. Assume d-axis coinciding the rotor phase-a axis at t = 0.

Solution. Per phase applied voltage = 400 V

For phase a, $\qquad v_a = \sqrt{2}\,.\,400 \sin \omega t$

$$v_b = \sqrt{2}\,.\,400 \sin(\omega t - 120°) \quad \text{and} \quad v_c = \sqrt{2}\,.\,400 \sin(\omega t - 240°)$$

As rotor phase-a axis is assumed to coincide stator d-axis, $\theta = 0$ in Eq. (2.12).

$$\therefore \qquad v_d = \frac{2}{3}\,[v_a \cos 0° + v_b \cos(-120°) + v_c \cos(-240°)]$$

$$= \frac{2}{3}\left[v_a - \frac{1}{2}(v_b + v_c)\right]$$

For a 3-phase balanced system, $v_a + v_b + v_c = 0$

$\therefore \qquad (v_b + v_c) = -v_a$. This gives

$$v_d = \frac{2}{3}\left[v_a + \frac{1}{2}v_a\right] = v_a = \sqrt{2} \times 400 \sin \omega t$$

$$v_q = \frac{2}{3}\left[0 - \frac{\sqrt{3}}{2}v_b + \frac{\sqrt{3}}{2}v_c\right] = \frac{1}{\sqrt{3}}[v_c - v_b]$$

Substituting the value of v_b, v_c, we get

$$v_q = \frac{1}{\sqrt{3}}[V_m \sin(\omega t - 240°) - V_m \sin(\omega t - 120°)]$$

$$= \frac{V_m}{\sqrt{3}}\left[-\frac{1}{2}\sin\omega t + \frac{\sqrt{3}}{2}\cos\omega t + \frac{1}{2}\sin\omega t + \frac{\sqrt{3}}{2}\cos\omega t\right]$$

$$= V_m \cos\omega t = \sqrt{2} \times 400 \cos\omega t = \sqrt{2} \times 400 \angle 90° = j\sqrt{2} \times 400 \text{ V}$$

Rms value of $V_d = 400$ V and $V_q = j\,400$ V

As expected, the two-phase voltages are in quadrature with V_d as reference, V_q leads V_d by 90°.

$$\text{Per-phase current in 3-phase motor} = \frac{5000}{3 \times 400 \times 0.8} = 5.2083 = 5.21 \text{ A}$$

Instantaneous phase-a current, $i_a = \sqrt{2} \times 5.21 \sin(\omega t - \phi)$

where $\phi = \cos^{-1}(0.8)$

$$i_b = \sqrt{2} \times 5.21 \sin(\omega t - \phi - 120°)$$

and $i_c = \sqrt{2} \times 5.21 \sin(\omega t - \phi - 240°)$

From Eq. (2.12), with $\theta = 0$, we have

$$i_d = \frac{2}{3}\left[i_b - \frac{1}{2}(i_b + i_c)\right] = i_a = \sqrt{2} \times 5.21 \sin(\omega t - \phi)$$

and

$$i_q = \frac{2}{3}\left[\frac{\sqrt{3}}{2}(i_C - i_B)\right] = \frac{1}{\sqrt{3}}[i_c - i_b]$$

$$= \frac{1}{\sqrt{3}}[I_m \sin(\omega t - \phi - 240°) - I_m \sin(\omega t - \phi - 120°]$$

$$= I_m \cos(\omega t - \phi) = \sqrt{2} \times 5.21 \cos(\omega t - \phi)$$

Rms value of $I_d = 5.21$ A and $I_q = j\,5.21$ A

The dq currents are also displaced from each other by 90° with i_q leading i_d by 90° (just like v_q leading v_d by 90°).

The power can be calculated from d-q variables from Eq. (2.18).

$$\therefore \quad p_i = \frac{3}{2}[400 \times 5.21 \times 0.8 + 400 \times 5.21 \times 0.8] = 5001.6 \simeq 5000 \text{ W}$$

2.5 PHYSICAL CONCEPTS OF PARK'S TRANSFORMATIONS

Equations governing the transformation of three-phase variables to dqO variables, or vice-versa, are called Park's transformations. Therefore, Eqs. (2.11) and (2.12) constitute Park's transformations. For understanding the physical concepts of these transformations, let the three-phase currents i_a, i_b, i_c be given by

$$i_a = I_m \cos(\omega t + \alpha)$$

$$i_b = I_m \cos\left(\omega t + \alpha - \frac{2\pi}{3}\right) \quad \text{and} \quad i_c = I_m \cos\left(\omega t + \alpha - \frac{4\pi}{3}\right)$$

where I_m = maximum value of armature phase currents and α = phase-angle of i_a with respect to time origin.

From Eq. (2.12), $$i_d = \frac{2}{3}\left[i_a \cos\theta + i_b \cos(\theta - 120°) + i_c \cos(\theta - 240°)\right] \quad ...(2.12)$$

Here θ is the angle which d-axis makes with phase a-axis at any time t. Assuming $\theta = 0°$ at time $t = 0$, then at any time t, $\theta = \omega t$; where ω is the synchronous speed at which rotor is running. Substitution of i_a, i_b, i_c in Eq. (2.12) with $\theta = \omega t$ gives d-axis current i_d as under.

$$i_d = \frac{2}{3} I_m \left[\cos\omega t \cos(\omega t + \alpha) + \cos\left(\omega t - \frac{2\pi}{3}\right)\cos\left(\omega t + \alpha - \frac{2\pi}{3}\right) + \cos\left(\omega t - \frac{4\pi}{3}\right)\cos\left(\omega t + \alpha - \frac{4\pi}{3}\right)\right]$$

Using the trigonometric identity, $\cos A \cos B = \frac{1}{2}[\cos(A+B) + \cos(A-B)]$, we get

$$i_d = \frac{2}{3} \cdot I_m \cdot \frac{1}{2}\left[\cos(2\omega t + \alpha) + \cos\alpha + \cos\left(2\omega t + \alpha - \frac{4\pi}{3}\right) + \cos\alpha + \cos\left(2\omega t + \alpha - \frac{2\pi}{3}\right) + \cos\alpha\right]$$

$$= \frac{2}{3} I_m \cdot \frac{1}{2}\,[3\cos\alpha] = I_m \cos\alpha \quad ...(2.19a)$$

Similarly, $$i_q = I_m \sin\alpha \quad ...(2.19b)$$

It is seen from above that i_d, i_q are constant dc currents. These two currents flowing in direct and quadrature axes winding produce the same type of field as produced by three-phase currents i_a, i_b, i_c. The above may be interpretted by saying that balanced alternating currents in *abc* reference frame get converted to direct currents *dqO* reference frame.

Now the physical picture of Park's transformations, as applicable to 3-phase synchronous and 3-phase induction machines is presented.

2.5.1 Three-phase Synchronous Machines

A synchronous machine may have field winding on the rotor and armature winding on the stator, Fig. 2.5 (*a*); or field winding on the stator and armature winding on the rotor, Fig. 2.6 (*a*). Here, the application of Park's transformations to synchronous machines is presented with field winding on the rotor and then with field winding on the stator.

(*i*) Field-winding on the rotor: Stator currents i_a, i_b, i_c in three-phase armature winding produce constant amplitude rotating mmf wave. This stator mmf is resolved along *d-q* axes which are stationary with respect to field-winding axis. Since field-winding on rotor rotates at synchronous speed, the *d-q* axes must also rotate at synchronous speed so that magnetic field produced by constant *d-q* currents is at rest with respect to rotating rotor field. This can happen only if currents i_d and i_q enter and leave a two-axis fictitious commutator winding on the stator. Current i_d is, therefore, equivalent to a brush current entering and leaving the two-axis commutator winding on stator, through a pair of brushes aligned along the field-winding axis. Similarly, current i_q is equivalent to a brush current entering and leaving the two-axis commutator winding on the stator, through a second pair of brushes aligned along q-axis of the field. The two-axis commutator winding on stator is fictitious and is assumed sinusoidally distributed along the air-gap periphery. Since field winding on rotor is revolving at synchronous speed and the brushes are attached to the d-q axes of the field winding, the brushes must also rotate at synchronous speed in the direction of rotor rotation as shown in Fig. 2.5 (*b*). Only then, the field winding axis would remain in line with direct axis. Here, the Park's transformations are basically with respect to rotating d-q reference frame, fixed on the rotor. Since the d-q axes rotate at synchronous speed, in synchronism with rotating magnetic field, the Park's transformation is also referred to as **synchronously-rotating reference frame**.

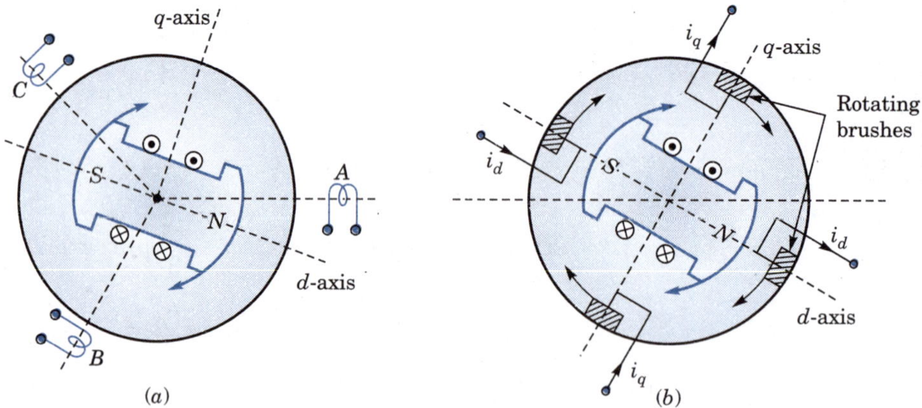

Fig. 2.5: (*a*) Three-phase synchronous machine with field winding on the rotor and (*b*) representation of Park's transformations.

In Fig. 2.5 (*a*) and (*b*), the stator mmf wave, with respect to an observer sitting on the rotor, is stationary and constant in magnitude. In Fig. 2.5 (*b*), the stator mmf is rotating clockwise at synchronous speed, because the field winding is also rotating clockwise at the same speed. Thus, the stator mmf wave and field piles are stationary with respect to each other (a condition necessary for the successful steady-state operation of a synchronous machine).

***(ii)* Field winding on the stator:** With field winding on stator, the three-phase armature winding would naturally be on the rotor as shown in Fig. 2.6 (*a*). If armature mmf rotates anticlockwise with respect to rotor, then the rotor must rotate clockwise at synchronous speed, so that armature mmf wave in the air gap is stationary with respect to field poles (an essential condition for synchronous machine operation). Since the field winding is on the stator, the resultant air-gap field must be stationary in space. The d-q axes, being fixed with respect to standstill field winding, are now stationary. The armature is now equivalent to dc type armature winding with two pairs of stationary brushes as shown in Fig. 2.6 (*b*).

Now the currents i_d, i_q as given by Eq. (2.19) are equivalent to two brush currents entering and leaving the two-axis sine distributed commutator winding on the rotor, through two pairs of brushes aligned along d- and q-axes respectively. The field winding is stationary, therefore, d-q axes are also stationary. Since the brushes are always attached to the d-q axes, the brushes must now be stationary as shown in Fig. 2.6 (*b*).

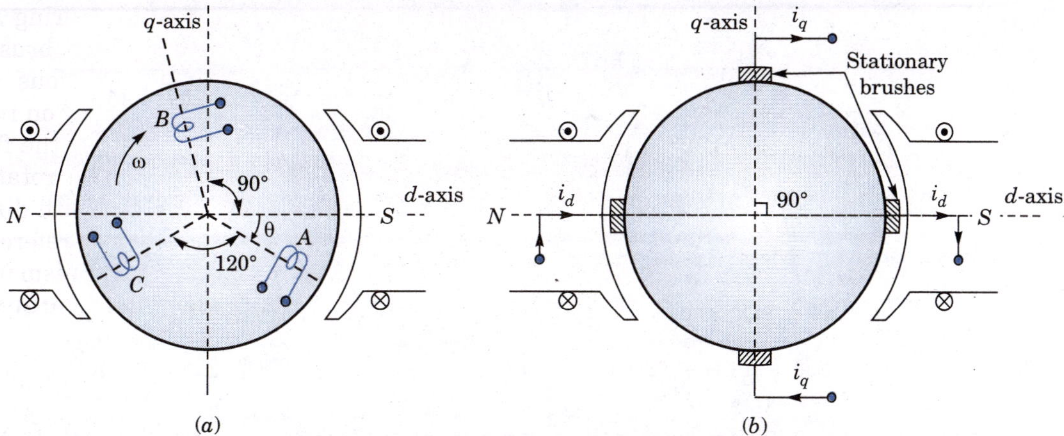

Fig. 2.6: Three-phase synchronous machine (*a*) with field winding on stator and (*b*) its two-axis model.

Here the transformations are basically with respect to stationary *d-q* reference frame, because *d-q* axes are fixed relative to field on stator. As the reference frame is attached to stator, the *dqO* transformation in Fig. 2.6 (*b*) is usually called *stator reference frame.*

From the foregoing, it can be stated that Fig. 2.6 (*b*) represents the two-axis model of a polyphase synchronous machine with field on stator. This model is used in this book, because it leads to simpler analysis of synchronous machines by the use of generalized theory. Reference to Art. 1.7 shows that the generalized model, or two-axis model, of Fig. 2.6 (*b*) is as shown in Fig. 1.16 (*b*), where coils *DR*, *QR* represent brush pairs along *d*, *q* axes respectively and coil *DS* represents the field winding on the stator of a synchronous machine. Note that Fig. 2.6 (*b*) also represents a metadyne, with no compensating winding, see Fig. 1.5 (*b*).

Actually, Park's transformation as depicted in Fig. 2.5 (*b*) formed the starting point for Gabriel Kron to develop two-axis theory of electrical machines [3] which has now come to be known as *generalized theory of electrical machines.*

Example 2.2. *A 2-pole, 3-phase synchronous machine is carrying the following three balanced currents:*

$$i_a = I_m \cos \omega t,\ i_b = I_m \cos (\omega t - 120°) \text{ and } i_c = I_m \cos (\omega t - 240°).$$

Calculate the dqO components of armature currents in case rotor-phase a axis coincides with the stator field winding axis at t = 0. Rotor is running at synchronous speed ω.

Solution. Here, at $t = 0$, $i_a = I_m \cos 0° = I_m$. This shows that rotor rotating mmf is aligned along the rotor-phase a axis* at $t = 0$.

From Eq. (2.12),
$$i_d = \frac{2}{3}\,[i_a \cos \theta + i_b \cos (\theta - 120°) + i_c \cos (\theta - 240°)] \quad ...(i)$$

It is given that angle between rotor-phase a axis and stator field axis at $t = 0$ is zero, *i.e.*, $\theta = 0$ at $t = 0$. As rotor speed is ω rad/sec, angle θ at any time *t* is ω*t*, *i.e.*, $\theta = \omega t$. Substituting the values of i_a, i_b, i_c and $\theta = \omega t$ in Eq. (*i*), we get

$$i_d = \frac{2}{3} I_m\,[\cos \omega t \cos \omega t + \cos (\omega t - 120°)\,.\,\cos (\omega t - 120°)$$
$$+ \cos (\omega t - 240°)\,.\,\cos (\omega t - 240°)]$$

It is known that $\cos^2 \omega t = \frac{1}{2}(1 + \cos 2\omega t)$

$$\therefore \quad i_d = \frac{2}{3} \cdot I_m \cdot \frac{1}{2} [1 + \cos 2\,\omega t + 1 + \cos(2\omega t - 120°) + 1 + \cos(2\omega t - 240°)]$$

But $\cos 2\omega t + \cos(2\omega t - 120°) + \cos(2\omega t - 240°) = 0$

$$\therefore \quad i_d = \frac{2}{3} \cdot I_m \cdot \frac{1}{2}(3) = I_m$$

Similarly,

$$i_q = -\frac{2}{3} I_m [\cos \omega t \sin \omega t + \cos(\omega t - 120°) \sin(\omega t - 120°) + \cos(\omega t - 240°) \sin(\omega t - 240°)]$$

But $[\sin \omega t \cos \omega t + \sin(\omega t - 120°) \cos(\omega t - 120°) + \sin(\omega t - 240°) \cos(\omega t - 240°)] = 0$

$$\therefore \quad i_q = 0$$

Since three-phase currents produce synchronously rotating mmf wave and the armature winding on rotor is also running at the same speed but opposite to the rotating mmf, peak of rotor rotating mmf wave remains stationary along the stator-field-winding axis, *i.e.*, direct axis, under the conditions stated above. This shows that rotor phase currents create only direct-axis flux which can be produced by d-axis current $i_d = I_m$ alone. Thus, dqO components of rotor-phase currents consists of direct-axis component only and $i_q = i_0 = 0$.

2.5.2 Three-phase induction machines

For applying generalized theory to polyphase induction machines, it is essential to have d-q axes fixed in the stator structure. Since the stator three-phase winding ABC and dq axes are stationary with respect to each other, the transformation matrix for ABC to dqO variables, or vice-versa, must have constant coefficients. The transformation equations relating the 3-phase ABC and dqO currents on the stator can be obtained from Eq. (2.12) by replacing θ by zero, on the assumption that phase A-axis coincides with d-axis. Therefore,

$$\begin{bmatrix} i_d \\ i_q \\ i_O \end{bmatrix} = \frac{2}{3} \begin{bmatrix} \cos\theta & \cos\left(\theta - \frac{2\pi}{3}\right) & \cos\left(\theta - \frac{4\pi}{3}\right) \\ \sin\theta & \sin\left(\theta - \frac{2\pi}{3}\right) & \sin\left(\theta - \frac{4\pi}{3}\right) \\ \frac{1}{2} & \frac{1}{2} & \frac{1}{2} \end{bmatrix} \begin{bmatrix} i_A \\ i_B \\ i_C \end{bmatrix} \quad \text{...(2.20)}$$

In Eq. (2.20), subscripts stands for stator and has been added to indicate that dqO currents are on the stator. Let the three-phase currents be given by

$$i_A = I_m \cos(\omega t + \alpha), \; i_B = I_m \cos\left(\omega t + \alpha - \frac{2\pi}{3}\right)$$

and

$$i_C = I_m \cos\left(\omega t + \alpha - \frac{4\pi}{3}\right)$$

where $I_m = \sqrt{2}$ (rms value of current, I) and α = phase angle of i_A with time origin.

*The armature mmf produced by 3-phase currents in 3-phase balanced winding results in a rotating mmf wave, directed along the axis of that phase which carries the maximum current at that instant.

The value of i_{ds}, from Eq. (2.20) with $\theta = 0$, is given by

$$i_{ds} = \frac{2}{3} I_m \left[\cos 0 \cos(\omega t + \alpha) + \cos\frac{2\pi}{3}\cos\left(\omega t + \alpha - \frac{2\pi}{3}\right) + \cos\frac{4\pi}{3}\cos\left(\omega t + \alpha - \frac{4\pi}{3}\right)\right]$$

$$= \frac{2}{3} . I_m . \frac{1}{2}[3\cos(\omega t + \alpha)] = I_m \cos(\omega t + \alpha) \qquad ...(2.21)$$

Similarly, $$i_{qs} = I_m \sin(\omega t + \alpha) \qquad ...(2.22)$$

Eqs. (2.21) and (2.22) reveal that d-q axes components of currents are also functions of time and are displaced from each other by a time-phase angle of 90°. This shows that i_{ds}, i_{qs} constitute a 2-phase system of currents having a frequency equal to the three-phase supply frequency. The m.m.fs produced by 2-phase currents i_{ds}, i_{qs} and 3-phase currents i_A, i_B, i_C are identical in all respects.

For rotor, three-phase to d-q axes transformation is given by Eq. (2.12). The d-q axes rotor currents i_{dr}, i_{qr} must be at line frequency, because coils *DR*, *QR* representing the rotor are stationary with respect to the stator. More about these transformations is discussed in Art. 5.1.

2.6 TRANSFORMED IMPEDANCE MATRIX

Let [*C*] be the matrix which transforms old variables i_1, i_2, i_3 to new variables i_1', i_2'

such that $$[i_{123}] = [C]\,[i_{12}']$$

or $$[i] = [C]\,[i'] \qquad ...(2.23)$$

where [*i*] represents old variables and [*i*′] the new variables. Taking the transpose of Eq. (2.23),

$$[i_t] = [i_t']\,[C_t] \qquad ...(2.24)$$

Power in old variables $P = [i_t][v]$ and power in new variables

$$P' = [i_t'][v']$$

For total power invariance,

$$[i_t']\,[v'] = [i_t][v].$$

From Eq. (2.24), $$[i_t'][v'] = [i_t'][C_t][v]$$

or $$[v'] = [C_t][v] \qquad ...(2.25)$$

Thus the new voltage matrix is obtained by premultiplying the old voltage matrix by $[C_t]$.

But $$[v] = [Z][i]$$

∴ From Eq. (2.25); $$[v'] = [C_t]\,[Z]\,[i]$$

and from Eq. (2.23) $$[v'] = [C_t][Z][C][i']$$

Also $$[v'] = [Z'][i'] = [C_t][Z][C][i']$$

∴ New impedance matrix

$$[Z'] = [C_t][Z][C] \qquad ...(2.26)$$

Eq. (2.26) shows that the new impedance matrix *Z'* can be obtained from the old impedance matrix *Z* by premultiplying it by $[C_t]$ and postmultiplying it by [*C*].

If voltages and currents are expressed in complex notation, then

Power = *Re* [Product of conjugate of current and voltage phasor]

$$= Re\{\bar{I}^*\bar{V}\} \qquad ...(1.37)$$

It should be noted that $\bar{I}^*$ and $\bar{V}$, required to obtain power, are not in matrix form.

From Eqs. (1.21) and (1.37), the expression of power in terms of complex notation is

$$\text{Power} = Re\{[\bar{I}_t^*][\bar{V}]\} \quad ...(2.27)$$

where $[\bar{I}_t^*]$ and $[\bar{V}]$ are in matrix form.

Let $[\bar{I}']$ and $[\bar{V}']$ be the new (transformed) currents and voltages so that the power in new variables is $Re\ [\bar{I}_t'^*][\bar{V}']$.

Suppose the new currents are related to old currents by the following equations:

$$\left.\begin{aligned} \bar{I}_1 &= C_{11}\bar{I}_1' + C_{12}\bar{I}_2' + C_{13}\bar{I}_3' \\ \bar{I}_2 &= C_{21}\bar{I}_1' + C_{22}\bar{I}_2' + C_{23}\bar{I}_3'. \end{aligned}\right\} \quad ...(2.28)$$

In matrix form

$$\begin{bmatrix} \bar{I}_1 \\ \bar{I}_2 \end{bmatrix} = \begin{bmatrix} C_{11} & C_{12} & C_{13} \\ C_{21} & C_{22} & C_{23} \end{bmatrix} \begin{bmatrix} \bar{I}'_1 \\ \bar{I}'_2 \\ \bar{I}'_3 \end{bmatrix}$$

or

$$[\bar{I}] = [C][\bar{I}'] \quad ...(2.29)$$

Hence $[C]$ is the connection matrix which relates the old and new variables.

If volt-amperes in the two systems of variables are to be invariant, then with complex notation,

$$[\bar{I}_t'^*][\bar{V}'] = [\bar{I}_t^*]\,[\bar{V}] \quad ...(2.30)$$

Conjugate of Eq. (2.29) is $[\bar{I}^*] = [C^*][\bar{I}'^*]$

and its transpose is $[\bar{I}_t^*] = [\bar{I}_t'^*]\,[C_t^*]$

Substitution of $[\bar{I}_t^*]$ in Eq. (2.30) gives,

$$[\bar{I}_t'^*][\bar{V}'] = [\bar{I}_t'^*]\,[C_t^*]\,[\bar{V}] \quad ...(2.31)$$

Since $[\bar{I}_t'^*]$ exists on both sides of Eq. (2.31), every element of the matrix obtained after the product of $[C_t^*]\,[\bar{V}]$ must be equal to the corresponding element of matrix $[\bar{V}']$

i.e., $[\bar{V}'] = [C_t^*]\,[\bar{V}]$

But $[\bar{V}] = [Z]\,[\bar{I}]$

$\therefore$ $[\bar{V}'] = [C_t^*]\,[Z]\,[\bar{I}] = [C_t^*]\,[Z]\,[C]\,[\bar{I}']$

Also $[\bar{V}'] = [Z']\,[\bar{I}'] = [C_t^*]\,[Z]\,[C]\,[\bar{I}']$

$$\therefore \quad [Z'] = [C_t^*]\,[Z]\,[C] \quad ...(2.32)$$

In obtaining the new impedance matrix $[Z']$ the current transformation matrix $[C]$ and $[C_t]$ or $[C_t^*]$ have been used, since it is convenient to find $[C]$, when there are interconnections between the coils of the primitive machine or between machine and other circuit elements.

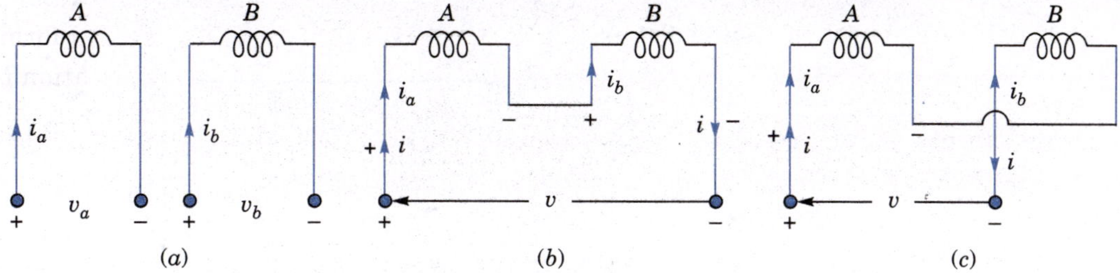

Fig. 2.7: Pertaining to the use of connection matrix.

Note that the transformation matrix obtained from a knowledge of the connections between the coils or the circuit elements, is called a *connection matrix* and it is usually represented by $[C]$. The method of writing connection matrix $[C]$ and its use is now demonstrated by taking a simple system consisting of two mutually coupled coils as shown in Fig. 2.7.

For coil A, the voltage equation is

$$v_a = r_a i_a + L_a p i_a + M p i_b \qquad ...(2.33)$$

For coil B, the voltage equation is

$$v_b = r_b i_b + L_b p i_b + M p i_a \qquad ...(2.34)$$

Here M is the mutual inductance between coils A and B. Eqs. (2.33) and (2.34) can be written in matrix form as

$$\begin{bmatrix} v_a \\ v_b \end{bmatrix} = \begin{bmatrix} r_a + L_a p & Mp \\ Mp & r_b + L_a p \end{bmatrix} \begin{bmatrix} i_a \\ i_b \end{bmatrix}$$

When coils A and B are interconnected as shown in Fig. 2.7 (b), then it is seen that new current i is in the same direction as old currents i_a and i_b. In view of this,

$$i_a = i \text{ and } i_b = i.$$

This can be expressed in matrix form as

$$\begin{bmatrix} i_a \\ i_b \end{bmatrix} = \begin{bmatrix} 1 \\ 1 \end{bmatrix} \begin{bmatrix} i \end{bmatrix} = [C][i].$$

Here the connection matrix $[C]$ transforms the old variables i_a, i_b to new variable i.

$$\therefore \quad \text{Connection matrix, } [C] = \begin{bmatrix} 1 \\ 1 \end{bmatrix}$$

The new voltage matrix, as per Eq. (2.25), is

$$[v'] = [C_t]\ [v] = \begin{bmatrix} 1 & 1 \end{bmatrix} \begin{bmatrix} v_a \\ v_b \end{bmatrix} = \begin{bmatrix} v_a + v_b \end{bmatrix}$$

The new impedence matrix, as per Eq. (2.26), is

$$[Z'] = [C_t]\,[Z]\,[C] = \begin{array}{cc|ccc} & & r_a + L_a p & Mp & 1 \\ & & Mp & r_b + L_b p & 1 \\ \hline 1 & 1 & \begin{matrix} r_a + L_a p \\ + Mp \end{matrix} & \begin{matrix} r_b + L_b p \\ + Mp \end{matrix} & \begin{matrix} \text{Written} \\ \text{below} \end{matrix} \end{array}$$

$$= [(r_a + r_b) + (.L_a + L_b + 2M)p].$$

Thus the voltage equation, for Fig. 2.7 (*b*), in new set of variables is

$$[v'] = [Z'][i]$$

$$[v_a + v_b] = [(r_a + r_b) + (L_a + L_b + 2M)p]\ [i]$$

or $$[v] = [(r_a + r_b) + (L_a + L_b + 2M)p][i]$$

or $$v = (r_a + r_b)\, i + (L_a + L_b + 2M)pi \qquad \text{...(2.35)}$$

Though Eq. (2.35) may be obtained by some other method also, yet the method of using connection matrix [*C*] is simple and more systematic.

If the coils *A* and *B* are interconnected as shown in Fig. 2.7 (*c*), then it is seen that the new current *i* is in the direction of i_a, but is opposite to i_b. In view of this,

$$i_a = i \quad \text{and} \quad i_b = -\,i.$$

In matrix form,

$$\begin{bmatrix} i_a \\ i_b \end{bmatrix} = \begin{bmatrix} 1 \\ -1 \end{bmatrix} \begin{bmatrix} i \end{bmatrix}$$

Thus the connection matrix for Fig. 2.7 (*c*), is $[C] = \begin{bmatrix} 1 \\ -1 \end{bmatrix}$

New voltage matrix and new impedance matrix can be obtained respectively from Eqs. (2.25) and (2.26). The result is

$$[v_a - v_b] = [(r_a + r_b) + (L_a + L_b - 2M)p]\ [i] \qquad \text{...(2.36)}$$

The method of using connection matrix is widely applicable to any number of interconnected coils (or circuits). The example illustrated in Fig. 2.7 demonstrates how conveniently the network equations for Fig. 2.7 (*b*) and (*c*) can be derived with the help of connection matrix [*C*].

2.7 HOW TO APPLY GENERALIZED THEORY

It is appropriate here to outline the general method of applying generalized theory to any of the rotating electrical machines.

(*a*) First of all, the basic two-pole machine model is drawn, using the smallest number of coils to represent the machine under consideration. Saliency is kept on the stator.

(*b*) The primitive (or generalized) machine diagram is drawn with suitable number of coils on direct and quadrature axes. This model is now related to the basic two-pole machine representation, either directly or by suitable transformation. Note that there are no inter-connections between the coils of the primitive machine.

(*c*) Write the generalized voltage equations for the primitive machine, in matrix form. One must be able to write these equations, simply by giving the thought process to the primitive machine representation as outlined in Art. 1.7.

(*d*) The generalized equations, *i.e.*, voltage matrix, transient impedance matrix and current matrix, may be transformed to new variables if there are interconnections between windings. The new variables may be the actual values or other fictitious values.

(*e*) Other suitable constraints can be specified by knowing the construction of the rotating machine under survey. A few are listed below:

(*i*) If all the windings of the machine are identical and uniformly distributed, then the resistances of *d*-*q* axes of this winding, are equal.

(*ii*) The self-inductances of the *d*-*q* axes of a symmetrical winding are equal if the air gap is uniform, in other words if the reluctance offered to *d* and *q*-axes fluxes is same.

The matrix obtained with suitable transformations and constraints is the transient impedance matrix for the machine, in terms of stationary reference axes. From these, the solutions for (*i*) steady state a.c. or d.c. and (*ii*) transient electrical conditions or in terms of instantaneous a.c. conditions can be obtained.

A due consideration to the air-gap m.m.f. or flux must be given to obtain steady state conditions. If the resultant air-gap flux is

(*i*) stationary (or space and time invariant) with respect to the stator, replace p by zero as in d.c. machines, synchronous machines with field winding on the stator;

(*ii*) rotating at synchronous speed with respect to the stator, replace p by $j\omega$ ($\omega = 2\pi f$) as in polyphase induction machines;

(*iii*) rotating at a speed other than synchronous speed, say $k\omega$ with respect to the stator, replace p by $jk\omega$, as in Schrage motor etc;

(*iv*) pulsating in nature at an angular frequency ω, replace p by $j\omega$, as in a.c. single phase machines.

The replacing of p by $j\omega$ or $jk\omega$ in (*ii*), (*iii*) or (*iv*) results in r.m.s. phasor equations as illustrated in Art. 1.8.

2.8 ELECTRICAL TORQUE

The torque can be calculated by writing down first the motional inductance matrix or torque matrix $[G]$, consisting of the co-efficient of ω_r terms from the transient impedance matrix of the machine. Then, as per Eq. (1.25), electrical torque is

$$T_e = [i_t][G][i] \qquad \text{...(1.25)}$$

The torque obtained by Eq. (1.25) is the transient torque at any instant of time. The instantaneous power converted to electrical torque is

$$\begin{aligned} P &= \omega_r T_e = \omega_r \,.\, [i_t][G][i] \\ &= [i_t]\,\omega_r\,[G][i] = [i_t][v_r] \end{aligned} \qquad \text{...(2.37)}$$

The subscript r with voltage matrix $[v]$ in Eq. (2.37), is used to indicate that $[v_r]$ is the rotational voltage matrix and it is given by the product $\omega_r[G][i]$.

For steady state a.c. conditions, the power in terms of complex numbers, from Eq. (1.37) is,

$$P = Re\ [\bar{I}^* \ \bar{V}].$$

Thus, corresponding to the electrical torque T_e, the electrical power P in terms of complex numbers, from Eq. 2.27), is given by

$$P = Re\ \{[\bar{I}_t^*][\bar{V}_r]\} \qquad ...(2.38)$$

Now $\qquad v_r] = \omega_r\ [G][i]$

In phasor form, $\qquad [\bar{V}_r] = \omega_r\ [G][\bar{I}]$

Substitution of $[\bar{V}_r]$ in Eq. (2.38) gives

$$P = Re\ \{[\bar{I}_t^*]\omega_r\ [G][\bar{I}]\} \qquad ...(2.39)$$

Here $\bar{I}_t^*$ denotes the transpose of the conjugate of phasor current $\bar{I}$.

∴ Mean electrical torque,

$$T_e = \frac{P}{\omega_r} = R_e\{[\bar{I}_t^*]\ [G][\bar{I}\,]\} \qquad ...(2.40)$$

It should be noted that the torque matrix [G] must be taken from the transient impedance matrix of the machine. Eq. (2.40) gives steady state torque for a 2-pole machine. For the number of poles greater than two,

$$T_e = \frac{P}{\text{Speed in mechanical radians per sec, } \omega_m}$$

But speed in electrical radians per sec.

$$\omega_r = (\text{Pole pairs})\ \omega_m, \qquad T_e = \frac{P}{\omega_r/\text{pole pairs}}$$

Substitution of the value of P from Eq. (2.39) gives electrical torque as

$$T_e = Re\left\{\left(\frac{\omega_r}{\omega_r/\text{pole pairs}}\right)[\bar{I}_t^*]\ [G]\ [\bar{I}]\right\}$$

$$= (\text{pole pairs})\ R_e\ \{[\bar{I}_t^*]\ [G]\ [\bar{I}]\} \qquad ...(2.41)$$

2.9 RESTRICTIONS OF THE GENERALIZED THEORY OF MACHINES

There are some restrictions in representing a rotating electrical machine by its d-q axes equivalent, *i.e.* primitive machine model. It will be worthwhile to review them here.

(*i*) The generalized machine theory can't be applied to machines in which both stator and rotor are salient as in an inductor alternator. This is due to the fact that the d-q axes of the primitive machine can't be fixed with respect to the stator or rotor of the inductor alternator.

(*ii*) The non-salient element of the machine must have balanced windings. A single phase alternator, possesses unbalanced windings on the cylindrical element of the machine and this, therefore, can't be studied with this theory.

(iii) Brush contact phenomena, commutation effects and surge phenomena can't be represented in the primitive machine and, therefore, need separate considerations. Similarly, the effect of slotting and skew, stray load loss, eddy-current phenomenon, mechanical features such as vibration, noise, critical speed etc. have to be studied separately.

PROBLEMS

2.1. *(a)* What do you understand by the term 'linear transformation' as used in electrical machines? Illustrate your answer with suitable examples.

(b) Explain the basic reasons of using transformations in electrical machines.

(c) Explain the term 'invariance of power' as applied to electrical machines.

What is the advantage of having power invariance during the transformations?

(d) On what basis are the transformations carried out in electrical machines? Explain.

2.2. Obtain identical transformations for currents and voltages from a rotating balanced three-phase (*a, b, c*) winding to a rotating balanced two-phase (α, β) winding. The transformation matrix so obtained is singular. How is it made square and why? Express *abc* variables in terms of αβ variables by taking inverse of the square matrix.

2.3. *(a)* Derive the transformations for currents between a rotating balanced 2-phase (α, β) winding and a pseudo-stationary two-phase (*d, q*) winding. Assume equal turns on all coils. Show that the transpose of current transformation matrix is equal to its inverse.

(b) For steady state balanced operation with

$$i_\alpha = I_m \cos(\omega t + \phi)$$

and
$$i_\beta = I_m \sin(\omega t + \phi),$$

determine *d-q* axes currents and show that these are steady dc values. Take α-axis coinciding *d*-axis at $t = 0$ and rotor sped = ω rad/sec. **[Ans.** $i_d = I_m \cos\phi$, $i_q = I_m \sin\phi$]

2.4. Deduce Park's transformations relating the three-phase currents of a synchronous machine to its corresponding *dqO* currents through the use of two-phase to three-phase transformations.

Express three-phase currents in terms of *d-q* axes currents and its inverse.

2.5. Power input to three-phase stator is given by $v_a i_a + v_b i_b + v_c i_c$. Express this power input in terms of *dqO* variables by using Park's transformations.

2.6. What is meant by 'power invariance'? If current connection matrix [*C*] is given, find the new voltage matrix and the transformed impedance matrix in case the currents are:

(a) instantaneous, and

(b) expressed in complex notation.

2.7. What is a connection matrix? Explain, with a suitable example, its use for obtaining the transformed (or new) impedance matrix and new voltage matrix.

Give the advantages of using a connection matrix [*C*].

2.8. A three-phase alternator has the following rating:

80 MVA, 11 kV, 50 Hz, 10 poles, 0.9 pf, star-connection.

Find *dqO* voltages and currents under rated conditions. Calculate also the total power from *dqO* variables. Assume *d*-axis coinciding the rotor phase-*a* axis at $t = 0$.

[Ans. $v_d = \sqrt{2} \times 6351 \sin\omega t$, $v_q = \sqrt{2} \times 6351 \cos\omega t$; 72 MW]

2.9. Much of the literature in electrical machinery also uses Park's transformations in the following form:

$$\begin{bmatrix} i_d \\ i_q \\ i_O \end{bmatrix} = \sqrt{\frac{2}{3}} \begin{bmatrix} \cos\theta & \cos\left(\theta - \frac{2\pi}{3}\right) & \cos\left(\theta - \frac{4\pi}{3}\right) \\ -\sin\theta & -\sin\left(\theta - \frac{2\pi}{3}\right) & -\sin\left(\theta - \frac{4\pi}{3}\right) \\ \frac{1}{\sqrt{2}} & \frac{1}{\sqrt{2}} & \frac{1}{\sqrt{2}} \end{bmatrix} \begin{bmatrix} i_a \\ i_b \\ i_c \end{bmatrix}$$

Obtain the inverse of the above transformation matrix by assuming $\theta = 0$. Then induct the angle θ in the inverse matrix and show that the transpose of transformation matrix is equal to its inverse.

2.10. Power input to a 3-phase stator is given by $v_a i_a + v_b i_b + v_c i_c$. Express this power in dqO variables by using the following transformation:

$$\begin{bmatrix} v_a \\ v_b \\ v_c \end{bmatrix} = \sqrt{\frac{2}{3}} \begin{bmatrix} \cos\theta & -\sin\theta & \frac{1}{\sqrt{2}} \\ \cos\left(\theta - \frac{2\pi}{3}\right) & -\sin\left(\theta - \frac{2\pi}{3}\right) & \frac{1}{\sqrt{2}} \\ \cos\left(\theta - \frac{4\pi}{3}\right) & -\sin\left(\theta - \frac{4\pi}{3}\right) & \frac{1}{\sqrt{2}} \end{bmatrix} \begin{bmatrix} v_d \\ v_q \\ v_O \end{bmatrix}$$

[**Ans.** $v_d i_d + v_q i_q + v_0 i_0$]

2.11. In a 2-pole, 3-phase synchronous machine, the armature currents are as under:

$i_a = I_m \sin \omega t$, $i_b = I_m \sin (\omega t - 120°)$

$i_c = I_m \sin (\omega t - 240°)$

In case stator field-winding axis coincides with the rotor phase-*a* axis at $t = 0$, find dqO components of armature currents. Rotor is running at synchronous speed.

[**Ans.** $i_d = 0$, $i_q = -I_m$. **Hint.** Negative sign for current i_q means the resultant q-axis flux is directed towards the centre along the q-axis.]

2.12. (*a*) Outline the various steps of applying the generalized theory to various rotating electrical machines.

(*b*) Explain clearly, how the operator p is replaced by

(*i*) zero in case of a synchronous machine with its field winding on the stator and

(*ii*) $js\omega$ in case of Schrage motor.

2.13. (*a*) If the currents are given in complex notation, derive an expression for the electrical torque T_e, for any number of poles.

(*b*) List the various limitations of the generalized theory of electrical machines.

2.14. A 3-phase, 4-pole, 60-Hz, squirrel-cage induction motor develops a torque of 300 Nm at rated phase voltage of 240 V. The three-phase stator winding is now replaced by 2-phase stator winding for which the number of poles, effective number of turns per phase and conductor size are not changed. Will this induction motor be able to operate? If so, compute:

(*a*) the rated phase voltage of the two-phase induction motor.

(*b*) the torque, if the two-phase induction motor is energized at rated phase voltage obtained in part (*a*), from a 2-phase 50 Hz supply system; ignore the losses.

(*c*) the rating in kW for both 3-phase and 2-phase induction motors.

[**Hint.** (*a*) Subscripts 1 and 2 are used for three and two phase induction motors respectively.

Since the conductor size remains unchanged, $I_2 = I_1$. The magnitude of rotating mmf for 3-phase induction motor is $\frac{3}{2} I_m N_1$ and that for 2-phase induction motor is $I_m N_1$.

$\therefore$ Rated phase voltage of 2-phase induction motor $= \frac{2}{3} \times 240 = 160$ V

(*b*) Torque, $T_1 = \frac{3E_1I_1}{\omega_1}$ and $T_2 = \frac{2E_2I_2}{\omega_2}$

$$\therefore \quad \frac{T_1}{T_2} = \frac{3E_1I_1}{2E_2I_2} \cdot \frac{\omega_2}{\omega_1} \quad \text{or} \quad \frac{300}{T_2} = \frac{3(240)\,I_1}{2(160)\,I_1} \cdot \frac{50}{60}$$

$$\therefore \quad T_2 = 300 \times \frac{6}{5} \times \frac{32}{72} = 160 \text{ Nm}$$

(*c*) $P_1 = T_1\omega_1 = T_1 \cdot \frac{4\pi f_1}{P} = 300 \times \frac{4\pi \times 60}{4} = 18\pi$ kW

$P_2 = T_2\omega_2 = 8\pi$ kW]

2.15. A 3-phase, 8-pole, 50 Hz, squirrel-cage induction motor develops a torque of 200 Nm at rated phase voltage of 240 V. The 3-phase stator winding is now replaced by two-phase stator winding for which the number of poles and conductor size remain unchanged. If total number of stator turns in both 3-phase and 2-phase induction motors are the same, find:

(*a*) the rated phase voltage of the 2-phase induction motor.

(*b*) the torque, in case the two-phase induction motor is energized at rated phase voltage obtained in part (*a*), from a 2-phase 50 Hz supply system; ignore the losses.

(*c*) the rating in kW for both the motors. [**Ans.** (*a*) 360 V (*b*) 200 Nm (*c*) 5π kW for both]

3
D.C. Machines

Direct current machines are the most versatile energy-conversion devices. Their outstanding advantage is that the volt-ampere or speed-torque characteristics of these machines are very much flexible and easily adaptable for both steady-state and dynamic operations. Their inherent characteristics can be modified further by making use of the feedback control circuits. The reader of this chapter is assumed to be fully familiar with the physical concepts of d.c. machines and their steady-state behaviour. The object of this chapter is to study both the transient and dynamic analysis of d.c. machines, however, their steady-state behaviour is also presented with much less emphasis.

The direct current machine is a non-uniform air-gap machine. The concentrated field winding is wound on the salient poles which are fitted to the yoke. The armature winding, on rotor, is distributed in slots and connected to the commutator segments. The d-axis of the primitive machine is along the field poles and its q-axis is along the brush-axis. This means that for any d.c. machine, the basic two-pole machine and Kron's primitive machine are identical and, therefore, no transformation is required. But for a particular d.c. machine under consideration, the number of coils along d- and q-axes may be fewer or more than that of Kron's primitive machine. Some fundamental assumptions for the use of primitive machine are already given in Art. 1.7. In addition to them, the following assumptions pertaining to the use of generalized mathematical model of d.c. machines are also useful.

(*i*) The armature m.m.f. along the q-axis is assumed to have no effect on the total direct axis flux. The reader, familiar with the effect of armature mmf, should come to think that this assumption means the neglect of demagnetising effect of armature m.m.f. on the main-pole flux.

(*ii*) The brushes are assumed to be narrow so that the coil-sides undergoing commutation are midway between the field poles. This assumption means that the stationary armature m.m.f. wave is always directed along the quadrature axis.

(*iii*) Effects of magnetic saturation are neglected. This means that linear coupled circuit theory is assumed valid, magnetic super-position is permissible and inductances are constant.

With these idealizing assumptions, it is possible to concentrate more on the factors effecting the transient and dynamic performance of d.c. machine systems, which otherwise would be difficult without the use of a computer.

3.1 SEPARATELY EXCITED D.C. GENERATORS

In this article, steady-state and transient analysis of separately excited d.c. generators are dealt with. Their sudden short-circuit analysis is also presented here.

When a machine is working as a generator, the output quantities of interest are the armature voltage, current or the power.

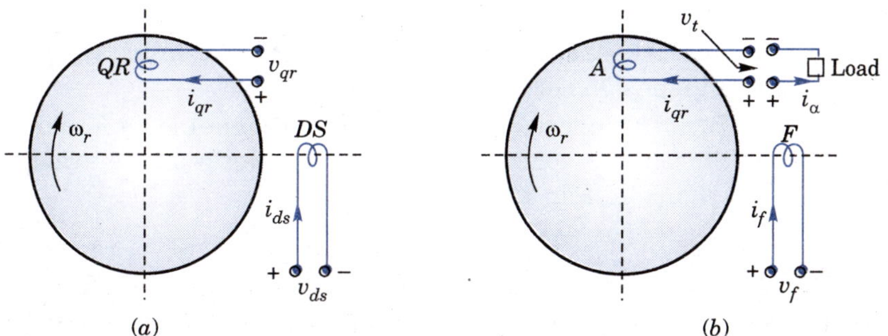

Fig. 3.1: Separately-excited d.c. generator. (*a*) Its mathematical model. (*b*) Load connected to armature *A*.

For the separately excited d.c. machine, the generalized mathematical model is as shown in Fig. 3.1 (*a*). The voltage equations for this model can be written in a manner described in Art. 1.7.2 or else the voltage equations can be written from Eq. (1.20) by omitting rows and columns pertaining to coils *qs* and *dr*. These voltage equations in matrix form are,

$$\begin{bmatrix} v_{ds} \\ v_{qr} \end{bmatrix} = \begin{matrix} & ds & qr \\ ds & r_{ds} + L_{ds}p & \\ qr & M_d\omega_r & r_{qr} + L_{qr}p \end{matrix} \begin{bmatrix} i_{ds} \\ i_{qr} \end{bmatrix} \qquad \text{...(3.1)}$$

One should, however, endeavour to write the above voltage equations without referring to Eq. (1.20).

The reader may ask here as to how the mutual inductance term M_d is appearing in Eq. (3.1), when the two coils *DS* and *QR* are in quadrature. It may be recalled that any coil along *d*- or *q*-axis on the armature will have rotational e.m.f. induced in it by a flux in quadrature with it. Here $M_d \cdot \omega_r \cdot i_{ds}$ is the rotational e.m.f. in armature, due to field current i_{ds} and as described earlier, M_d may be thought of as the mutual inductance between coils *DS* and *QR*, owing to rotation only. In view of this, M_d is also called the *rotational mutual inductance* or *motional inductance*. That M_d has the dimensions of inductance can be proved as under:

In a d.c. machine, the generated e.m.f. is given by

$$E_a = \frac{\Phi ZnP}{a} \text{ volts.}$$

where Φ is the flux in Wb per pole, Z is the total number of armature conductors, n is the speed in r.p.s., P is the number of poles and a is the number of parallel paths.

Now $$\omega_m = \text{speed in mech. rad./sec.} = 2\pi n.$$

$$\therefore \qquad E_a = \frac{\Phi Z\omega_m}{2\pi} \cdot \frac{P}{a}.$$

Also $\omega_m = \frac{2}{P}$ (Speed in electrical rad./sec.) $= \frac{2}{P} \cdot \omega_r$

Thus $E_a = \frac{\Phi Z}{2\pi} \cdot \frac{2}{P} \cdot \omega_r \cdot \frac{P}{a} = \frac{\Phi Z}{\pi a} \cdot \omega_r \cdot$

From Eq. (3.1), the steady state generated e.m.f. at no load is $M_d \cdot \omega_r \cdot I_{ds}$.

$$\therefore \quad M_d\, \omega_r\, I_{ds} = \frac{\Phi Z}{\pi a} \cdot \omega_r \quad \text{or} \quad M_d = \frac{\Phi Z}{\pi a} \cdot \frac{1}{I_{ds}}$$

The right hand side is seen to be the equivalent flux linkages per ampere and consequently M_d has the dimensions of inductance.

For simplicity, in Fig. 3.1 (*b*), coils *DS* and *QR* are designated by *F* and *A* for field and armature, respectively. Since the machine is acting as a generator, the armature current i_a will be opposite to i_{qr}, as shown in Fig. 3.1 (*b*).

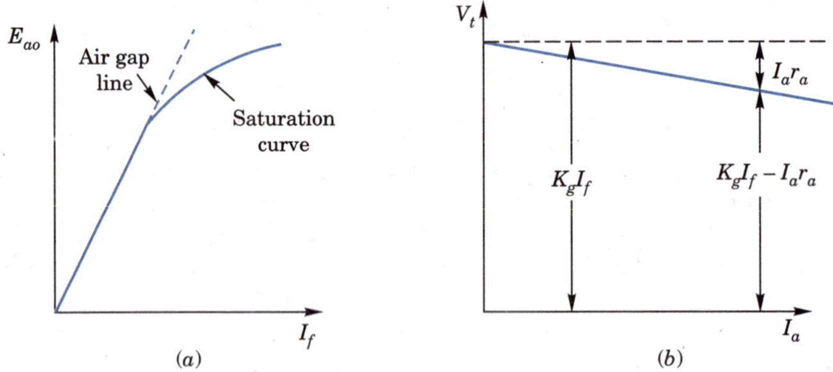

Fig. 3.2: Separately-excited d.c. generator. (*a*) Its saturation curve and (*b*) Its volt-ampere characteristics.

Thus $i_{qr} = -i_a$ and $i_{ds} = i_f$

$$\left.\begin{aligned} v_f &= (r_f + L_f p)\, i_f \\ v_t &= M_d \omega_r i_f - (r_a + L_a p)\, i_a \end{aligned}\right\} \quad \text{...[3.1 (a)]}$$

Here v_t is the armature terminal voltage.

Eq. [3.1 (*a*)] is applicable both to steady state and transient analysis of a separately excited d.c. generator.

(*a*) **Steady state analysis.** In d.c. machines, the steady-state analysis can be obtained from the transient equation by putting $p = 0$.

So the steady state equations, from Eq. [3.1 (*a*)], are

$$\left.\begin{aligned} V_f &= r_f\, I_f \\ V_t &= M_d \omega_r I_f - r_a\, I_a \end{aligned}\right\} \quad \text{...(3.2)}$$

At no load, $I_a = 0$, therefore, no-load armature terminal voltage is

$$M_d\, \omega_{ro} I_f = E_{ao} \quad \text{...(3.3)}$$

Note that here E_{ao} is the armature generated e.m.f. at no load and at a constant speed of ω_{ro}. The plot of E_{ao} versus I_f gives the saturation, or magnetization, curve as shown in Fig. 3.2 (*a*). The armature generated e.m.f. E_a at any other speed ω_r is,

$$E_a = \frac{E_{ao}}{\omega_{ro}} \cdot \omega_r = M_d \omega_r I_f = K_g I_f.$$

Thus the armature terminal voltage at any load current I_a is

$$V_t = \frac{M_d \omega_r V_f}{r_f} - r_a I_a \quad \text{...(3.4)}$$

$$= K_g I_f - r_a I_a$$

where $K_g = M_d \omega_r$ = generated e.m.f. constant/field ampere at speed ω_r.

Eq. (3.3), which gives the open-circuit, saturation, or magnetization, curve of the machine, shows that the armature voltage E_{ao} increases with field current linearly. However, when field current saturates the magnetic path, M_d begins to decrease and the plot of E_{ao} versus I_f is as shown in Fig. 3.2 (*a*). Eq. (3.4) gives the volt-ampere, external, or load, characteristics of a separately excited d.c. generator, which is illustrated in Fig. 3.2 (*b*).

(*b*) Transient analysis. Here the transient analysis of a separately excited d.c. generator is investigated under different operating conditions.

(*i*) With sudden application of step-field excitation to the field, the variation of armature terminal voltage is studied with load current $i_a = 0$ and for constant no-load speed ω_{ro}.

Since V_f is the step excitation, the field circuit equation becomes

$$V_f \mathbf{1} = (r_f + L_f p)\, i_f$$

For zero armature current, $i_a = 0$, the no-load armature terminal voltage corresponding to a no-load speed ω_{ro} is,

$$e_{ao} = M_d \omega_{ro} i_f - 0.$$

$$\therefore \qquad e_{ao} = \frac{M_d \omega_{ro} V_f}{r_f (1 + \tau_f p)} \mathbf{1}$$

where $\tau_f = L_f / r_f$ = field time constant.

This gives,

$$e_{ao} = \frac{M_d\, \omega_{ro} \,.\, V_f}{r_f (1 + \tau_f p)} \mathbf{1} = \frac{E_{ao}}{(1 + \tau_f p)} \mathbf{1} \quad \text{...(3.5)}$$

The above equation in s-domain becomes

$$E_{ao}(s) = \frac{E_{ao}}{s(1 + \tau_f s)} = \frac{E_{ao}}{s \,.\, \tau_f \left(s + \dfrac{1}{\tau_f}\right)}$$

Its Laplace-inverse is

$$e_{ao}(t) = E_{ao}\left(1 - e^{-t/\tau_f}\right) \quad \text{...(3.6)}$$

This equation gives the characteristics illustrated in Fig. 3.3.

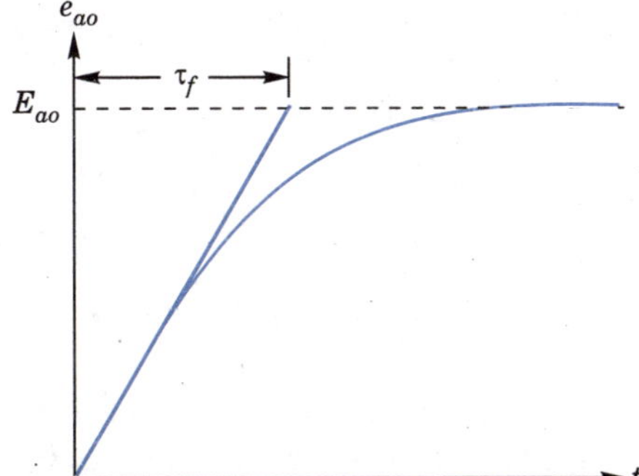

Fig. 3.3: Variation of armature terminal voltage of a separately excited d.c. generator, to a step-field input.

(*ii*) Same as in (*i*), but here armature current i_a is not zero and speed is ω_r. Now the performance equations, from Eq. 3.1 (*a*) are,

$$V_f \mathbf{1} = (r_f + L_f p)\, i_f$$

$$v_t = M_d \omega_r i_f - (r_a + L_a p)\, i_a$$

or

$$v_t = \frac{M_d\, \omega_r V_f}{r_f (1 + \tau_f p)} \mathbf{1} - (r_a + L_a p)\, i_a$$

The voltage v_a exists across the load also and if the load is inductive (R_L in series with L_L), the load current is then given by,

$$i_a = \frac{v_t}{R_L + L_L p}$$

$$\therefore \qquad i_a (R_L + L_L p) = \frac{E_a}{(1+\tau_f p)} \mathbf{1} - (r_a + L_a p)\, i_a$$

The above equation in s-domain is

$$I_a(s)\,[R_L + sL_L] = \frac{E_a}{s(1+\tau_f s)} - I_a(s)\,(r_a + sL_a)$$

or

$$I_a(s) = \frac{E_a}{s(r_a + R_L)(1+s\tau_f)(1+s\tau)} \qquad \text{...(3.7)}$$

where $\tau = \dfrac{L_a + L_L}{r_a + R_L}$ = effective armature time constant.

If the difference between τ_f and τ is large enough, then the smaller of the two time constants may be neglected for simplifying the computation of i_a. Thus the major delay in build up of i_a will be that due to the larger time constant only.

However, if the time constants τ_f and τ are comparable, none of them can be neglected and the value of i_a must be obtained accordingly.

Since $V_t(s) = (R_L + sL_L)\, I_a(s)$, the load voltage $V_L(s) = V_t(s)$ in s-domain is given by

$$V_L(s) = V_t(s) = \frac{E_a\,.(R_L + sL_L)}{s(r_a + R_L)(1+s\tau_f)(1+s\tau)} \qquad \text{...(3.8)}$$

Example 3.1. *A separately excited d.c. generator running at* $\dfrac{4500}{\pi}$ *r.p.m. has the following parameters:*

$r_f = 80\ \Omega$; $L_f = 40$ H; $r_a = 0.1\ \Omega$; $L_a = 0.3$ mH. Motional inductance $M_d = 0.8$ H.

(or generated e.m.f. constant $K_g = M_d \omega_r = 120$ volts/field amp.)

(a) The field is unexcited and the armature is open.

Find the armature voltage as a function of time and sketch it, if a constant voltage of 160 volts is suddenly impressed across the field terminals.

(b) Sketch the rise of armature current in part (a), if the armature terminals are initially short-circuited.

(c) Armature voltage has attained steady value in part (a). Now the armature is suddenly connected to a load of resistance 1.1 ohm in series with an inductance of 1.7 mH. Determine (i) armature current and (ii) the armature terminal voltage as functions of time.

(d) In part (c), find the electrical torque as a function of time. Obtain the mean value of torque also.

(e) In part (c), after the armature current has become steady state, an additional resistance of 0.4 Ω is inserted in the load circuit. Find the armature current, after this change.

Solution. (*a*) From Eq. (3.6), the no-load armature terminal voltage as a function of time is given by

$$e_a = \frac{M_d \omega_r V_f}{r_f}(1 - e^{-t/\tau_f})$$

where $\tau_f = \frac{L_f}{r_f} = \frac{1}{2}$ sec

$$\therefore \qquad e_a = \frac{0.8 \times 2\pi \times (4500)(160)}{80 \times 60 \times \pi}(1 - e^{-2t}) = 240\,(1 - e^{-2t}) \text{ volts.}$$

Sketch is drawn in Fig. 3.4 (*a*).

(*b*) The rise of armature current is given by Eq. (3.7).

Here $r_a = 0.1\ \Omega;$ $\qquad R_L = 0$

$L_a = 0.3$ mH; $\qquad L_L = 0$

$$\tau = \frac{L_a + L_L}{r_a + R_L} = \frac{0.3}{0.1 \times 1000} = 0.003 \text{ sec}$$

$$E_a = 240 \text{ volts.}$$

$$\therefore \quad \text{From Eq. (3.7), } I_a(s) = \frac{240}{0.1s(1+\frac{1}{2}s)(1+0.003s)}$$

Since $\tau = 0.003$ sec. is much less than $\tau_f = 0.5$ sec, τ can be easily neglected, without any appreciable error.

$$\therefore \qquad i_a(t) = 2400\,(1 - e^{-2t}).$$

This is sketched in Fig. 3.4 (*b*).

(*c*) (*i*) Armature voltage has become constant, *i.e.* $E_a = M_d\,\omega_r\,I_f = 240$ volts. Now E_a is suddenly applied across the load. The resulting equations become:

$$V_f = r_f I_f$$

$$V_a(s) = E_a \cdot \frac{1}{s} - (r_a + sL_a)\,I_a(s)$$

But $\qquad v_a(t) = R_L \cdot i_a + L_L \cdot pi_a$

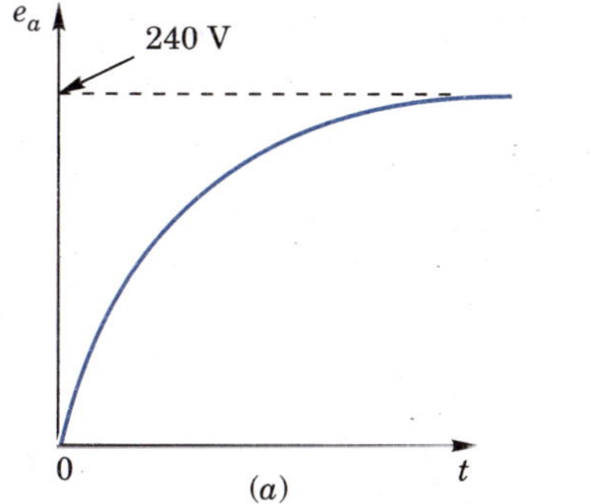

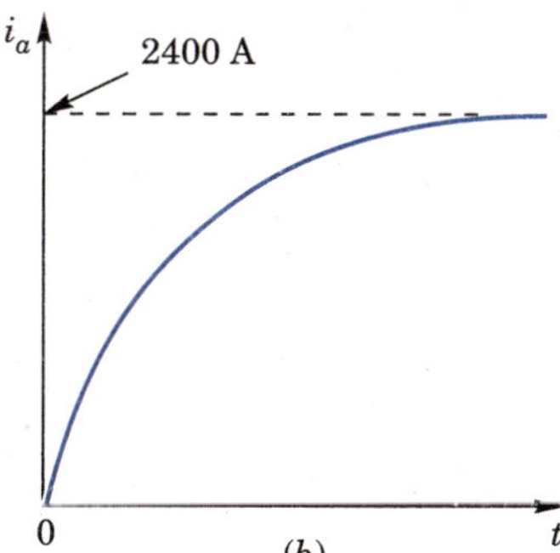

Fig. 3.4: Variation of (*a*) armature voltage with time and (*b*) armature current with time. Example 3.1.

Its Laplace transform is,

$$V_a(s) = (R_L + sL_L)\,I_a(s)$$

$$\therefore \qquad (R_L + sL_L)\,I_a(s) = \frac{E_a}{s} - (r_a + sL_a)\,I_a(s)$$

or $$I_a(s) = \frac{E_a}{s[(r_a + R_L) + s(L_a + L_L)]} = \frac{E_a}{s(r_a + R_L)(1 + s\tau)}$$

Its Laplace inverse is, $i_a(t) = \dfrac{E_a}{r_a + R_L} \cdot (1 - e^{-t/\tau})$

Now $$\tau = \frac{L_a + L_L}{r_a + R_L} = \frac{2}{1.2 \times 1000} = \frac{1}{600} \text{ sec}$$

$\therefore$ $$i_a(t) = \frac{240}{1.2}(1 - e^{-600t}) = 200(1 - e^{-600t})$$

Now v_t = armature terminal voltage or voltage across load

$$= (R_L + L_L \cdot p)\, i_a(t) = (R_L + L_L \cdot p) \frac{E_a}{r_a + R_L}(1 - e^{-t/\tau})$$

$\therefore$ $$v_t(t) = \frac{E_a R_L}{r_a + R_L}(1 - e^{-t/\tau}) + \frac{E_a L_L}{r_a + R_L} e^{-t/\tau} \cdot \frac{1}{\tau}$$

or $$v_t(t) = \frac{E_a R_L}{r_a + R_L}(1 - e^{-t/\tau}) + \frac{E_a L_L}{L_a + L_L} e^{-t/\tau}$$

$$= \frac{240 \times 1.1}{1.2}(1 - e^{-600t}) + \frac{240 \times 1.70}{2.00} e^{-600t}$$

$$v_t(t) = 220 - 16e^{-600t}.$$

This equation shows that just after the load is switched on, the armature terminal voltage at once drops from its no load value of 240 V to (220 – 16) = 204 V. This voltage then rises finally to its steady value of 220 V.

(*d*) $$T_e = -M_d I_f i_a$$

$$= -[0.8 \times 2 \times 200(1 - e^{-600t})] = -320(1 - e^{600t})$$

Average $T_e = -320$ N metres

Negative sign shows that the machine is working as a generator.

(*e*) The steady state current in part (*c*) is 200 amps. At this stage, a resistance change of 0.4 Ω in the armature circuit is equivalent to a step change of voltage equal to (0.4 × 200 **1**), *i.e.*, 80 **1** volts in the load circuit. Thus the value of the changing current i_{ct} is given by,

$$i_{ct} = \frac{80\,\mathbf{1}}{1.6 + 2 \times 10^{-3} p}$$

In *s*-domain, $$I_{ct}(s) = \frac{80}{s(1.6 + 0.002s)}$$

Its Laplace inverse is $i_{ct}(t) = 50(1 - e^{-800t})$

Since the final resultant armature current would be less due to more resistance in the armature circuit, we get

$$i_{final} = I_a - i_{ct} = 200 - 50(1 - e^{-800t}) = (150 + 50e^{-800t}) \text{ Amps.}$$

Note that final resultant armature current is 200 A at $t = 0+$ and 150 A after the transients are over.

Example 3.2. *A separately-excited d.c. generator is connected to R_L. The generator is driven at constant speed, but the voltage source connected to field is such that the expression for field current can be written as,*

$$i_f = I_{fo} + I_f \sin \omega t.$$

Obtain expressions for (i) load current (ii) torque and (iii) power converted from mechanical to electrical. Neglect armature inductance.

Solution. (*i*) From Eq. [3.1 (*a*)], with $L_a = 0$, we get

$$v_t = M_d \omega_r i_f - i_a r_a = i_a R_L$$

$$\therefore \quad i_a = \frac{M_d \omega_r}{r_a + R_L} i_f = \frac{M_d \omega_r}{r_a + R_L} (I_{fo} + I_f \sin \omega_t).$$

(*ii*)

$$T_e = -M_d i_f i_a = -\frac{M_d^2 \omega_r}{(r_a + R_L)} [I_{fo} + I_f \sin \omega t]^2$$

This is the electromagnetic torque converted from mechanical to electrical. So the torque given by the primemover, *i.e.* the magnitude of torque converted from mechanical to electrical is given by,

$$T_{mech} = \frac{M_d^2 \omega_r}{(r_a + R_L)} [I_{fo} + I_f \sin \omega t]^2.$$

(*iii*) Power converted from mechanical to electrical,

$$= T_{mech} \omega_r = \frac{M_d^2 \omega_r^2}{(r_a + R_L)} [I_{fo}^2 + I_f^2 \sin^2 \omega t + 2I_{fo} . I_f \sin \omega t]$$

$$= \frac{M_d^2 \omega_r^2}{(r_a + R_L)} \left[I_{fo}^2 + I_f^2 \frac{1}{2} (1 - \cos 2\omega t) + 2I_{fo} . I_f \sin \omega t \right]$$

$$\therefore \quad \text{Average } P_{mech} = \frac{M_d^2 \omega_r^2}{r_a + R_L} \left(I_{fo}^2 + \frac{1}{2} I_f^2 \right) \qquad \text{...(3.9)}$$

3.1.1 Sudden Short-Circuit for a Separately Excited d.c. Generator

Separately-excited d.c. generators permit the control of the output voltage over a wide range and are used in steel mills in conjunction with Ward-Leonard sets, and to supply d.c. on ships and aircrafts. It is, therefore, of considerable importance to calculate the transient currents, when these generators are suddenly short-circuited. In order to obtain an approximate solution of their short-circuit analysis, the following assumptions are made:

(*i*) Short circuit is instantaneous.

(*ii*) Speed remains unchanged before and after the short-circuit.

(*iii*) Though heavy currents are involved after short-circuit, effects of armature reaction m.m.f. are neglected.

The voltage equations for this machine are

$$\therefore \quad \left. \begin{aligned} v_f &= (r_f + L_f p)\, i_f \\ v_t &= M_d \omega_r i_f - (r_a + L_a p)\, i_a \end{aligned} \right\} \qquad \text{...[3.1 (a)]}$$

Before the short-circuit, the generator is running at constant speed ω_r and developing a voltage of E_a at no load. The effect of short-circuit is to reduce the armature voltage $E_a = M_d\omega_r I_f = K_g I_f$ suddenly to zero, while leaving the field voltage unchanged.

Such a problem can be conveniently handled by means of the principle of superposition. According to this principle, the voltages and currents after the short-circuit are each equal to the sum of (*i*) the original value before the short-circuit and (*ii*) the change resulting from the short-circuit. Thus

$$\begin{bmatrix}\text{Voltage or current} \\ \text{after short circuit}\end{bmatrix} = \begin{bmatrix}\text{Their original values} \\ \text{before short circuit}\end{bmatrix} + \begin{bmatrix}\text{Their superimposed} \\ \text{values resulting from} \\ \text{short circuit}\end{bmatrix}$$

$$\therefore \qquad i_f = i_{fo} + i_{ft}$$

and
$$i_a = i_{ao} + i_{at} \qquad \text{...(3.10)}$$

Here i_f, i_a are the field and armature currents after the short circuit. Further; i_{fo}, i_{ao} are the initial values of field and armature currents before the short circuit (note that here $i_{ao} = 0$); i_{ft}, i_{at} are the superimposed field and armature currents to be obtained from the equations written in terms of superimposed quantities.

For the sudden short-circuit of the separately-excited d.c. generator as stated above, the armature voltage before short circuit is $v_{to} = E_a$ and it changes abruptly to zero after short circuit, *i.e*,. $v_t = 0$. Thus, the superimposed voltage is $v_{tt} = v_t - v_{to} = 0 - E_a = -E_a$. As the superimposed voltage must be suddenly applied, $v_{tt} = -E_a \mathbf{1}$.

For the field circuit, $\quad v_f = v_{fo} + v_{ft}$

Here $\quad v_{fo} = V_f$ (before short circuit)

$v_f = V_f$ (after short circuit)

$\therefore$ Superimposed field voltage,

$$v_{ft} = V_f - V_f = 0$$

Eq. [(3.1 (*a*)] in terms of superimposed quantities is

$$v_{ft} = 0 = (r_f + L_f p)\, i_{ft}$$

$$v_{tt} = -E_a \mathbf{1} = M_d\omega_r i_{ft} - (r_a + L_a p)\, i_{at}$$

$$\therefore \qquad i_{at} = \frac{E_a \mathbf{1}}{r_a + L_a p}$$

In *s*-domain,
$$I_{at}(s) = \frac{E_a}{s(r_a + sL_a)}$$

Its Laplace inverse is

$$i_{at}(t) = \frac{M_d \,.\, \omega_r \,.\, I_f}{r_a}(1 - e^{-t/\tau_a})$$

or
$$i_{at}(t) = \frac{K_g \,.\, I_f}{r_a}(1 - e^{-t/\tau_a})$$

The resultant armature current after the short-circuit is

$$i_a = i_{ao} + i_{at} = 0 + i_{at}$$

$$= \frac{K_g I_f}{r_a}(1 - e^{-t/\tau_a}) \qquad \text{...(3.11)}$$

If the short-circuit occurs some distance away from the generator terminals, the line parameters must be added to the generator.

Then $$i_a = \frac{K_g \cdot I_f}{r_a + R_{line}}(1 - e^{-t/\tau'_a}) \quad ...(3.12)$$

where $\tau_a' = \dfrac{L_a + L_{line}}{r_a + R_{line}}$

Here $K_g = M_d \omega_r$ = generated e.m.f. constant/field Amp.

3.2 SEPARATELY-EXCITED D.C. MOTORS

When a wide range of speed control and torque output are required, d.c. motor is an obvious choice. A separately excited d.c. motor fed from solid-state controlled rectifiers, or from a separately-excited d.c. generator as in Ward-Leonard system, is used extensively for applications requiring wide range of speed control and torque outputs. The object of this article is to study the separately-excited d.c. motors, with emphasis on their dynamic analysis.

When a rotating machine is working as a motor, the output quantities of interest are speed, torque or power. It is desired initially to establish the general torque conventions to be followed in generalized machine theory. Fig. 3.5 illustrates that the application of a mechanical torque T_m to the shaft of the machine results in the rotation of shaft in the reference positive direction for ω_r. It is expressed, in other words, that the torque T_m is also passing into the machine. Likewise, if the electromagnetic torque T_e results in the rotation of the shaft in the reference positive direction for ω_r, it is said that the torque T_e is also passing into the machine. These torques T_e and T_m, have to overcome inertia and damping torques as shown in Fig. 3.5. Thus

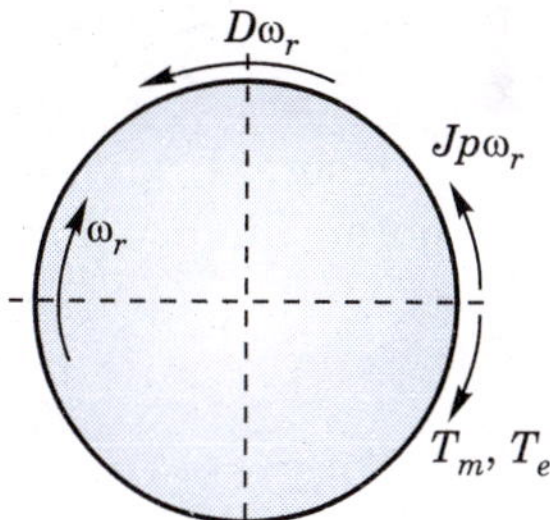

Fig. 3.5: General torque conventions.

$$T_e + T_m = Jp\omega_r + D\omega_r \quad ...(3.13)$$

In the case of a motor, the applied torque T_L (*i.e.* the load torque) causes the torque to flow out of the machine at positive speed.

$\therefore$ $$T_L = -T_m.$$

Thus the dynamic equation for any motor-load combination is

$$T_e = Jp\omega_r + D\omega_r + T_L$$

where J = Polar moment of inertia of motor and load in kgm^2

D = Viscous co-efficient of friction (or viscous damping constant) for moving parts in Nm/radian/sec.

The equations specifying the performance of separately-excited d.c. motor are:

(*i*) Two voltage equations — for two electrical ports.

(*ii*) One torque equation — for one mechanical port.

The voltage equations for the separately-excited d.c. motor, in matrix form are:

$$\begin{bmatrix} v_{ds} \\ v_{qr} \end{bmatrix} = \begin{bmatrix} r_{ds} + L_{ds}p & \\ M_d\omega_r & r_{qr} + L_{qr}P \end{bmatrix} \begin{bmatrix} i_{ds} \\ i_{qr} \end{bmatrix} \qquad ...(3.1)$$

The torque equation can be obtained from the rotational inductance (or torque) matrix G, given by,

$$[G] = \begin{bmatrix} & \\ M_d & \end{bmatrix}$$

$$\begin{array}{lcccc} & & & & i_{ds} \\ & & & M_d & i_{qr} \\ \text{But} \quad T_e = [i_t]\,[G]\,[i] = & i_{dr} & i_{qr} & M_d\, i_{qr} & M_d i_{ds} i_{qr} \end{array}$$

Designating the coil DS, QR by F and A, the equations which control the performance of this motor, under all conditions of operation are:

$$\left.\begin{aligned} v_f &= (r_f + L_f p)\, i_f \\ v_t &= M_d\omega_r i_f + (r_a + L_a p)\, i_a \\ M_d\, i_f i_a &= Jp\omega_r + D\omega_r + T_L \end{aligned}\right] \qquad ...(3.14)$$

Separately-excited d.c. motors are used for an accurate control of speed or torque. For large machines, armature voltage control with constant field excitation is generally used and as such, it will be considered here in detail.

Since the field current is constant, i_f is replaced by I_f and the equations are re-written as under:

$$\left.\begin{aligned} v_t &= M_d\omega_r I_f + (r_a + L_a p) i_a \\ M_d I_f i_a &= Jp\omega_r + D\omega_r + T_L \end{aligned}\right] \qquad ...(3.15)$$

Thus
$$i_a = \frac{v_t - M_d\omega_r I_f}{r_a(1 + \tau_a p)}$$

From the second equation of Eq. (3.15),

$$\frac{M_d I_f (v_t - M_d\omega_r I_f)}{r_a(1 + \tau_a p)} = [Jp\omega_r + D\omega_r + T_L]$$

or
$$\omega_r \left[Jp + D + \frac{M_d^2\, I_f^2}{r_a(1 + \tau_a p)} \right] = \frac{M_d I_f v_t}{r_a(1 + \tau_a p)} - T_L$$

or
$$\omega_r = \frac{M_d I_f v_t}{\left[Jp + D + \dfrac{M_d^2\, I_f^2}{r_a(1 + \tau_a p)} \right] r_a(1 + \tau_a p)} - \frac{T_L}{\left[Jp + D + \dfrac{M_d^2\, I_f^2}{r_a(1 + \tau_a p)} \right]} \qquad ...(3.16)$$

This expression can be simplified further, since τ_a, in general, is small as compared with the motor effective mechanical time constant τ'_m defined below:

$$\therefore \qquad \omega_r = \frac{M_d I_f v_t}{r_a[Jp + D + D_e]} - \frac{T_L}{[Jp + D + D_e]}$$

where $\quad D_e = \frac{M_d^2 I_f^2}{r_a} = \frac{K_m^2}{r_a}$ = Electrical damping constant. ...(3.17 (a))

$$\therefore \qquad \omega_r = \frac{K_m v_t}{r_a(D + D_e)(1 + \tau'_m p)} - \frac{T_L}{(D + D_e)(1 + \tau'_m p)} \qquad \text{...(3.17)}$$

where $\tau'_m = \frac{J}{D + D_e}$ = Effective mechanical time constant of motor and K_m is the motor torque constant in Nm/A or K_m is the generated e.m.f. constant in V-sec/rad.

Note that the motor introduces an electrical viscous damping coefficient $\frac{M_d^2 I_f^2}{r_a} = \frac{K_m^2}{r_a}$ that adds to the mechanical damping constant D of the motor. This has the effect of reducing the effective mechanical time constant of motor, with a corresponding rapid response to load variations.

(*a*) **Steady state analysis.** From Eq. (3.17), the steady-state speed ω_{ro} is,

$$\omega_{ro} = \frac{K_m V_t}{r_a(D + D_e)} - \frac{T_{Lo}}{(D + D_e)} \qquad \text{...(3.18)}$$

The characteristics showing the variation of speed ω_{ro} with load torque T_{Lo}, with V_t as parameter (*i.e.* V_t kept constant at different values) are given in Fig. 3.6 (*a*). With V_t at a particular value, ω_{ro} decreases with increase in load torque. These characteristics of Fig. 3.6 (*a*) are termed as shunt characteristics. Fig. 3.6 (*b*) gives the speed *versus* armature voltage curves with T_{Lo} as parameter. Note that if V_t is increased, ω_{ro} increases linearly. When load torque is present at the time of starting, note that motor does not start until $\frac{M_d I_f V_t}{r_a} = T_{Lo}'$.

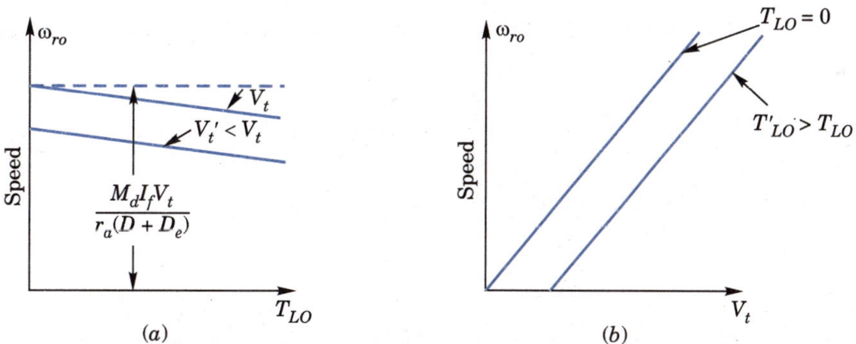

Fig. 3.6: Separately-excited d.c. motor, (*a*) Speed torque characteristics with V_t as parameter, (*b*) Speed-armature voltage characteristics with torque as parameter.

(*b*) **Transient analysis.** The transient expression (3.17) for speed ω_r can be analysed further, for various modes of motor operation, as follows:

(*i*) Load torque $T_L = 0$ and the motor is at rest. With constant field current, the armature voltage is suddenly applied to the armature. Find $\omega_r(t)$.

For the conditions stated here, $v_t = V_t \mathbf{1}$ and $T_L = 0$, therefore, from Eq. (3.17), we get

$$\omega_r = \frac{K_m V_t \mathbf{1}}{r_a (D + D_e)(1 + \tau'_m p)}$$

$$\therefore \qquad \omega_r(t) = \frac{K_m V_t}{r_a (D + D_e)} (1 - e^{-t/\tau'_m}) \qquad ...(3.19)$$

(*ii*) With the motor running at constant no load speed, load torque T_L is suddenly applied. Find $\omega_r(t)$.

The change in speed $\Delta\omega_r$ due to sudden application of T_L is given by the second term of Eq. (3.17).

The first term of Eq. (3.17) does not effect ω_r since V_t is constant.

$$\therefore \qquad \Delta\omega_r = \frac{-T_L \mathbf{1}}{(D + D_e)(1 + \tau'_m p)}$$

$$\therefore \qquad \Delta\omega_r(t) = \frac{-T_L}{D + D_e} (1 - e^{-t/\tau'_m}) \qquad ...[3.19\ (a)]$$

Thus $\omega_r(t)$ = No load speed + Change in speed

$$= \frac{K_m V_t}{r_a (D + D_e)} - \frac{T_L}{D + D_e} (1 - e^{-t/\tau'_m}) \qquad ...(3.20)$$

(*iii*) With load torque T_L, the motor is running under steady conditions, with constant V_t. Now the armature terminal voltage is suddenly increased by an amount ΔV_t. Find $\omega_r(t)$.

Here $$\Delta\omega_r(t) = \frac{K_m \Delta V_t}{r_a (D + D_e)} (1 - e^{-t/\tau'_m})$$

$\therefore$ $\omega_r(t)$ = Initial steady speed + Change in speed

$$= \frac{K_m V_t}{r_a (D + D_e)} - \frac{T_L}{D + D_e} + \frac{K_m \Delta V_t}{r_a (D + D_e)} (1 - e^{-t/\tau'_m})$$

$$= \frac{K_m}{r_a (D + D_e)} (V_t + \Delta V_t) - \frac{T_L}{D + D_e} - \frac{K_m \Delta V_t}{r_a (D + D_e)} \cdot e^{-t/\tau'_m} \qquad ...(3.21)$$

It is seen from Eq. (3.21) that when the transients are over, the new motor speed would attain a value $\frac{K_m \cdot \Delta V_t}{r_a (D + D_e)}$ higher than its initial speed, and this is as expected.

(*iv*) The motor is running at steady state speed, with load torque T_L and constant V_t. The load torque is suddenly changed from T_L to T_{L_1}. Find $\omega_r(t)$.

Here $$\Delta\omega_r(t) = -\frac{T_{L_1} - T_L}{D + D_e} (1 - e^{-t/\tau'_m})$$

$$\therefore \qquad \omega_r(t) = \frac{K_m V_t}{r_a (D + D_e)} - \frac{T_L}{D + D_e} - \frac{T_{L_1} - T_L}{D + D_e} (1 - e^{-t/\tau'_m})$$

$$= \frac{K_m V_t}{r_a (D + D_e)} - \frac{T_{L_1}}{D + D_e} + \frac{T_{L_1} - T_L}{D + D_e} e^{-t/\tau'_m} \qquad ...(3.22)$$

Example 3.3. *A 230 V, separately-excited d.c. motor is driving a constant load torque, with the following data:*

$$r_a = 0.4\ \Omega\ ;\ L_a = 0.01\ H\ ;\ r_f = 115\ \Omega.$$

Motor torque constant

$$K_m = M_d I_f = 2\ Nm/armature\ amp.$$

Friction and windage constant, i.e., D = 0.

The armature current is 50 amperes, with rated voltage across the armature and field. Determine the magnitude of constant load torque. If the armature voltage is suddenly reduced by 20 volts, find the speed as a function of time. Total J = 12 kgm².

Solution.
$$I_f = \frac{V_f}{r_f} = \frac{230}{115} = 2 \text{ Amps.}$$

Now
$$T_e = Jp\omega_r + D\omega_r + T_L$$

Under steady state conditions

$$T_e = M_d I_f I_a = T_L$$

$\therefore$
$$T_L = \text{Constant load torque} = K_m I_a$$
$$= 2 \times 50 = 100 \text{ Nm.}$$

Note that in M.K.S. system of units,

(*i*) K_m (= $M_d I_f$) is the motor torque constant and has the units of Newton-metre/armature ampere.

(*ii*) K_m is also the generated e.m.f. constant and has the units of volt-sec/radian.

The speed under transient condition, from Eq. (3.17), is

$$\omega_r = \frac{K_m v_t}{r_a (D + D_e)(1 + \tau_m' p)} - \frac{T_L}{(D + D_e)(1 + \tau_m' p)} \qquad ...(3.17)$$

where $\tau_m' = \dfrac{J}{D + D_e}$

Here
$$D = 0, \qquad D_e = \frac{M_d^2 I_f^2}{r_a} = \frac{K_m^2}{r_a}$$

and
$$\tau_m = \frac{J r_a}{K_m^2} = \frac{12 \times 0.4}{2 \times 2} = 1.2 \text{ sec}$$

Introducing these changes, Eq. (3.17) becomes,

$\therefore$
$$\omega_r = \frac{v_t}{K_m (1 + \tau_m p)} - \frac{T_L\, r_a}{K_m^2 (1 + \tau_m\, p)}$$

Under steady state conditions, the initial speed is

$$\omega_{ro} = \frac{V_t}{K_m} - \frac{T_L \,.\, r_a}{K_m^2} = \frac{230}{2} - \frac{100 \times 0.4}{2 \times 2} = 105 \text{ rad/sec.}$$

The change in speed, with a sudden decrease of armature voltage (T_L remaining constant) is,

$$\Delta\omega_r = \frac{\Delta V_t \mathbf{1}}{K_m (1 + \tau_m p)} = \frac{20\,.\mathbf{1}}{2(1 + 1.2p)}$$

$$\therefore \qquad \Delta\omega_r(t) = 10\,(1 - e^{-0.833t})$$

Thus speed as a function of time is given by

$$\omega_r(t) = \omega_{ro} - \Delta\omega_r(t) = 95 + 10e^{-0.866t}$$

Example 3.4. *A separately-excited d.c. motor is at rest, with its field winding carrying a steady state current I_f. The motor and load have a total inertia of J kg m^2. Load torque, damping and armature inductance are negligible. If voltage V_t is suddenly impressed across the armature, find the total heat energy dissipated in the armature resistance as the motor accelerates from rest to final steady speed ω_{ro}.*

Solution. The equation (3.15), re-written here under the constraints of this problem, is

$$\left.\begin{aligned} v_t &= K_m\omega_r + r_a i_a \\ K_m i_a &= Jp\omega_r \end{aligned}\right\} \qquad \text{...(3.23)}$$

Since armature voltage V_t is suddenly applied, we get

$$V_t\,\mathbf{1} = K_m\,.\,\omega_r + \frac{Jr_a}{K_m}\,.\,p\omega_r$$

$$\omega_r = \frac{V_t\,\mathbf{1}}{K_m\left(1 + \dfrac{Jr_a}{K_m^2}p\right)} = \frac{V_t\,\mathbf{1}}{K_m(1 + \tau_m p)}$$

where $\tau_m = \dfrac{Jr_a}{K_m^2}$ is the inertial time constant.

The above equation in s-domain is

$$\omega_r(s) = \frac{V_t}{K_m\,.\,s(1 + s\tau_m)}$$

Its time domain solution is

$$\therefore \qquad \omega_r(t) = \frac{V_t}{K_m}(1 - e^{-t/\tau_m})$$

At $t = \infty$, $\quad (\omega_r)_{t=\infty} = \omega_{ro} = \text{final steady speed} = \dfrac{V_t}{K_m}$

Armature current, from Eq. (3.23), is given by

$$i_a = \frac{J}{K_m}p\omega_r = \frac{J}{K_m}\cdot\frac{V_t}{K_m}e^{-t/\tau_m}\cdot\frac{1}{\tau_m}$$

$$= \frac{V_t}{r_a}e^{-t/\tau_m}$$

Total heat energy dissipated in armature resistance r_a, as the motor accelerates from rest to final steady speed ω_{ro}, is

$$= \int_0^\infty i_a^2 r_a\,dt = \int_0^\infty \frac{V_t^2}{r_a}\,.\,e^{-2t/\tau_m}dt = \frac{V_t^2}{r_a}\cdot\frac{\tau_m}{2}$$

$$= \frac{1}{2}J\left(\frac{V_t}{K_m}\right)^2 = \frac{1}{2}J\omega_{ro}^2 \qquad \text{...(3.24)}$$

= Total K.E. stored in the rotating mass.

This example shows that during acceleration from standstill to steady no-load speed ω_{ro}, the total energy loss appearing as heat in the armature circuit of a d.c. motor (shunt excited or separately-excited) is $\frac{1}{2}J\omega_{ro}^2$. This energy loss does not depend upon th acceleration time but depends only on the final no-load speed ω_{ro}. Note that $\frac{1}{2}J\omega_{ro}^2$ is also the kinetic energy stored in the rotating mass. Thus total energy taken from d.c. source is $J\omega_{ro}^2$ and this gives an energy efficiency of 50% during acceleration time.

3.2.1 Sudden Application of Inertia Load

Suppose the separately-excited d.c. motor is running at steady speed ω_1 with its moment of inertia J_1 and damping co-efficient D. The object of this part of the article is to investigate the effect of sudden application of additional inertia load J_2 on to the motor shaft by means of a clutch.

For this problem, the principle of conservation of momentum must be invoked. According to this principle,

Angular momentum just before the load application, *i.e.*, at $t = 0-$ } = Angular moment just after the load application, *i.e.*, at $t = 0+$

or
$$J_1\omega_1 = (J_1 + J_2)\,\omega_2$$

$$\therefore \quad \omega_2 = \frac{J_1\omega_1}{J_1 + J_2}$$

Here ω_2 is the angular speed at $t = 0+$ and ω_1 is the initial steady speed equal to $\frac{T_e}{D}$

The dynamic equation of the motor at $t = 0+$ is

$$T_e = (J_1 + J_2)\,p\omega_r + D\,.\,\omega_r.$$

Its solution consists of (*i*) complementary function, and (*ii*) particular integral, *i.e.*

$$\omega_r = \text{C.F.} + \text{P.I.}, \qquad \text{or} \quad \omega_r(t) = Ae^{-\frac{D}{J_1+J_2}t} + \frac{T_e}{D}$$

At $t = 0+$,
$$\omega_r = \omega_2 = \frac{J_1\omega_1}{J_1 + J_2} = A + \frac{T_e}{D}$$

$$\therefore \quad A = \frac{J_1\omega_1}{J_1 + J_2} - \frac{T_e}{D} = \frac{T_e}{D}\left(\frac{J_1}{J_1 + J_2} - 1\right) \qquad \left[\because \frac{T_e}{D} = \omega_1\right]$$

$$= -\frac{T_e}{D}\cdot\frac{J_2}{J_1 + J_2}$$

Substituting the value of A, we get

$$\omega_r(t) = \frac{T_e}{D}\left[1 - \frac{J_2}{J_1 + J_2}e^{-\frac{D}{J_1+J_2}t}\right]$$

or $$\omega_r(t) = \omega_1 \left[1 - \frac{J_2}{J_1 + J_2} e^{-\frac{D}{J_1+J_2}t}\right] \quad ...(3.25)$$

The motor speed, just after the application of inertia load, *i.e.* at $t = 0+$, from Eq. (3.25), is

$$\omega_r = \frac{J_1\omega_1}{J_1 + J_2} = \omega_2.$$

Final steady speed, after the application of inertia load, *i.e.* at $t = \infty$, from Eq. (3.25), is $\omega_r = \omega_1$. This shows that at the instant of application of inertia load J_2, the speed at once drops to its minimum value of

$$\omega_2 = \frac{J_1\omega_1}{J_1 + J_2}$$

and it finally recovers to its original speed ω_1 with a recovery time constant of $\frac{J_1 + J_2}{D}$ seconds.

Here armature terminal voltage V_t and field current I_f are constant. With a change in speed ω_r, the counter e.m.f. $M_d\,\omega_r I_f$ or $K_g I_f$ changes and as a result of it, the armature current i_a also changes. In view of this the voltage equation for the armature circuit is given by

$$V_t = K_m\,\omega_r - (r_a + L_a p)\,i_a$$

If armature inductance L_a is neglected, then

$$i_a = \frac{V_t}{r_a} - \frac{K_m}{r_a}\omega_r = \frac{V_t}{r_a} - \frac{K_m}{r_a}.\omega_1\left[1 - \frac{J_2}{J_1 + J_2} e^{-\frac{D}{J_1+J_2}t}\right]$$

Just after the load application, *i.e.* at $t = 0\,+$, the armature current becomes

$$i_a = \frac{V_t}{r_a} - \frac{K_m}{r_a}.\omega_1\frac{J_1}{J_1 + J_2} = \frac{V_t}{r_a} - \frac{E_a}{r_a}\frac{J_1}{J_1 + J_2}$$

Final value, *i.e.* at $t = \infty$, the armature current is given by

$$I_a = \frac{V_t}{r_a} - \frac{K_m}{r_a}\omega_1 = \frac{V_t - E_a}{r_a}.$$

This value of armature current is the same as it was before the load application. This shows that at the instant of application of inertia load, the armature current at once increases to its maximum value of

$$\frac{V_t}{r_a} - \frac{E_a}{r_a}.\frac{J_1}{J_1 + J_2}$$

and it finally recovers to its original value of $\frac{V_t - E_a}{r_a}$ with a time constant of $\frac{J_1 + J_2}{D}$ seconds.

Energy Loss. Before the load application, the kinetic energy stored in the rotating mass is

$$W_1 = \frac{1}{2}J_1\omega_1^2 = \frac{1}{2}J_1\left(\frac{T_e}{D}\right)^2$$

Just after the load application, *i.e.* at $t = 0\,+$, the kinetic energy stored in the rotating mass becomes

$$W_2 = \frac{1}{2}(J_1 + J_2)\ (\text{speed at } t = 0\,+)$$

$$= \frac{1}{2}(J_1 + J_2) \cdot \frac{J_1^2 \omega_1^2}{(J_1 + J_2)^2} = \frac{1}{2} \frac{J_1^2}{J_1 + J_2} \omega_1^2.$$

$\therefore$ Kinetic energy loss between the time interval $t = 0-$ and $t = 0+$ is given by

$$W_1 - W_2 = \frac{1}{2} J_1 \omega_1^2 \left(1 - \frac{J_1}{J_1 + J_2}\right)$$

$$= \frac{1}{2} J_1 \omega_1^2 \frac{J_2}{J_1 + J_2} = \begin{pmatrix}\text{Kinetic energy before the} \\ \text{load application}\end{pmatrix} \frac{J_2}{J_1 + J_2}$$

This energy loss appears at the clutch in the form of frictional heat.

3.3 INTERCONNECTION OF MACHINES

The analysis of the individual machine has been considered so far. In practice, however, two or more machines may be connected together, for say, speed control, phase conversion, frequency conversion, energy conversion, etc. For such combinations, the system must be considered as a whole and to do this, the following procedure is adopted.

(*i*) Obtain the transient impedance matrix of each machine and other circuit elements.

(*ii*) Write these as sub-matrices on the principal diagonal of a compound matrix.

(*iii*) From a knowledge of the interconnections, write down the connection matrix and apply it to the above compound matrix.

It must be remembered that inter-connections can be made only between actual winding axes of the machines and not between the fictitious axes obtained by transformation. In d.c. machines, the currents in the equations are the actual currents in external circuits and thus the process is much simpler. But in a.c. machines, the axis currents in the equations, may not be the actual currents in the external circuits and the process is, therefore, much more difficult.

The procedure for the analysis of inter-connected machines is illustrated, by taking a simple d.c. machine system.

3.3.1 Ward-Leonard System of Speed Control

It provides armature voltage control, the field current to the motor being maintained constant through separate connections (not shown). In this scheme, the motor armature current is supplied by a d.c. generator, which is driven at constant speed by a prime-mover (or any motor) as shown in Fig. 3.7.

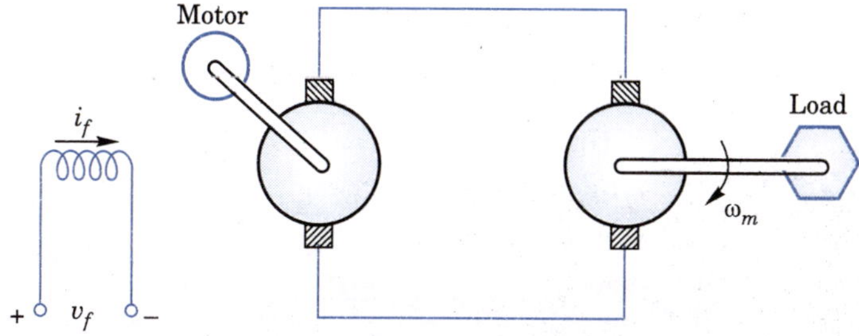

Fig. 3.7: Ward-Leonard system of speed control.

The general voltage equations for the individual machines are given as under :

$$\begin{array}{c} \\ \end{array}\begin{bmatrix} v_{dsg} \\ v_{qrg} \\ v_{dsm} \\ v_{qrm} \end{bmatrix} = \begin{array}{c} \\ dsg \\ qrg \\ dsm \\ qrm \end{array}\begin{array}{cccc} dsg & qrg & dsm & qrm \\ \hline r_{dsg}+L_{dsg}p & & & \\ M_{dg}\omega_g & r_{qrg}+L_{qrg}p & & \\ & & r_{dsm}+L_{dsm}p & \\ & & M_{dm}\omega_m & r_{qrm}+L_{qrm}p \end{array}\begin{bmatrix} i_{dsg} \\ i_{qrg} \\ i_{dsm} \\ i_{qrm} \end{bmatrix}$$

The subscript g refers to generator and subscript m to motor.

From the inter-connections of Fig. 3.8, it is seen that

$$-i_{qrg} = i_{qrm} = i_a \text{ (say)}, \qquad i_{dsg} = i_{fg}\ ;\ i_{dsm} = i_{fm}.$$

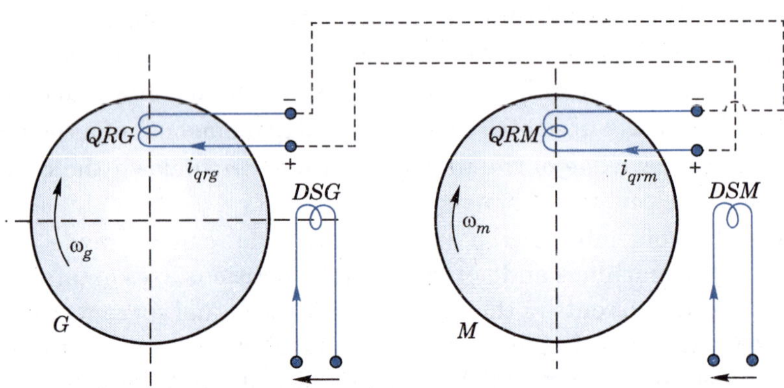

Fig. 3.8: Inter-connection between a d.c. generator and d.c. motor.

Thus the connection matrix relating the old currents with new currents is

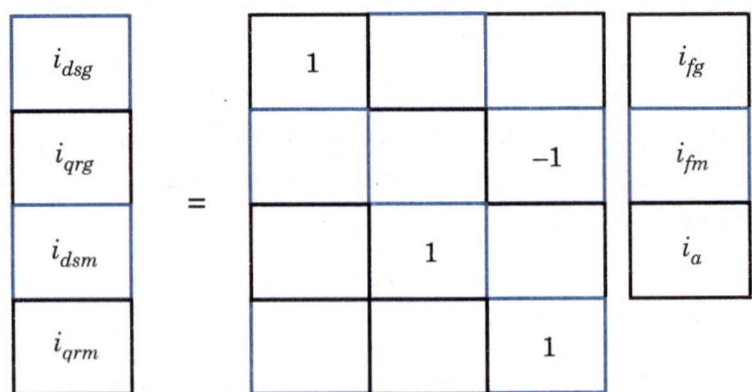

$$\begin{bmatrix} i_{dsg} \\ i_{qrg} \\ i_{dsm} \\ i_{qrm} \end{bmatrix} = \begin{bmatrix} 1 & & \\ & & -1 \\ & 1 & \\ & & 1 \end{bmatrix}\begin{bmatrix} i_{fg} \\ i_{fm} \\ i_a \end{bmatrix}$$

or $$[I] = [C]\ [I']$$

For convinience, here *DSG*, *QRG*, *DSM* and *QRM* are replaced by *FG*, *AG*, *FM* and *AM* respectively. With these subscripts, the new impedance matrix is given by:

$$[Z'] = [C_t]\,[Z]\,[C] = \begin{bmatrix} r_{fg} + L_{fg}p & & \\ & r_{fm} + L_{fm}p & \\ -M_{dg}\omega_g & M_{dm}\omega_m & r_{ag} + r_{am} + p(L_{ag} + L_{am}) \end{bmatrix} \quad \text{...(3.26)}$$

This is the transient impedance matrix for the system as a whole.

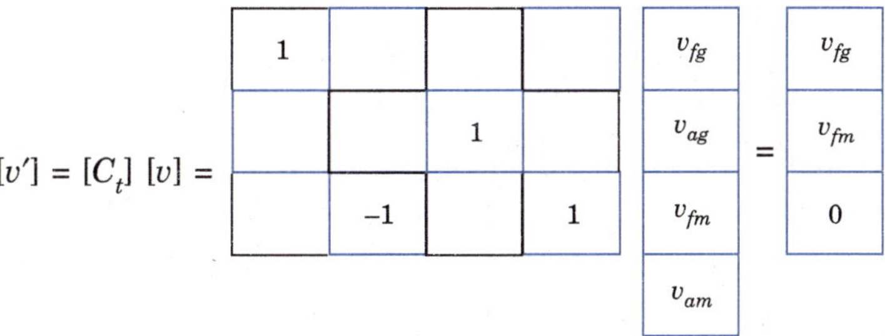

$$[v'] = [C_t]\,[v] = \begin{bmatrix} 1 & & & \\ & & 1 & \\ & -1 & & 1 \end{bmatrix} \begin{bmatrix} v_{fg} \\ v_{ag} \\ v_{fm} \\ v_{am} \end{bmatrix} = \begin{bmatrix} v_{fg} \\ v_{fm} \\ 0 \end{bmatrix}$$

Here $\qquad v_{ag} = v_{am} = v_a$

So, the electrical performance equations for the two machines are :

$$\begin{bmatrix} v_{fg} \\ v_{fm} \\ 0 \end{bmatrix} = \begin{bmatrix} r_{fg} + L_{fg}p & & \\ & r_{fm} + L_{fm}p & \\ -M_{dg}\omega_g & M_{dm}\omega_m & r_{ag} + r_{am} + p\,(L_{ag} + L_{am}) \end{bmatrix} \begin{bmatrix} i_{fg} \\ i_{fm} \\ i_a \end{bmatrix}$$

$$v_{fg} = (r_{fg} + L_{fg}\,p)\,i_{fg}$$

or
$$v_{fm} = (r_{fm} + L_{fm}\,p)\,i_{fm} \quad \text{...(3.27)}$$

$$0 = -M_{dg}\omega_g\,i_{fg} + M_{dm}\,\omega_m\,i_{fm} + (R + Lp)\,i_a$$

where $\qquad R = r_{ag} + r_{am} \quad$ and $\quad L = L_{ag} + L_{am}$

Since motor field current i_{fm} is considered constant, second expression of Eq. (3.27) is not of much importance, it may, therefore, be neglected. At the same time i_{fm} becomes I_{fm} in the third equation.

$\therefore$
$$v_{fg} = (r_{fg} + L_{fg}\,p)\,i_{fg} \quad \text{...(3.28)}$$

$$0 = -M_{dg}\,\omega_g\,i_{fg} + M_{dm}\omega_m\,I_{fm} + (R + Lp)\,i_a \quad \text{...(3.29)}$$

In Eq. (3.29), $M_{dg}\,\omega_g = K_g$ is the generated voltage per unit field current.

It should be noted that for obtaining electro-magnetic torque T_e, only ω_m components from the transient impedance matrix (3.26), are to be taken. Electric torque T_e is found to be $M_{dm}L_{fm}i_a$.

The torque balance equation is

$$M_{dm}\,I_{fm}\,i_a = K_m\,i_a = Jp\omega_m + D\omega_m + T_L \quad \text{...(3.30)}$$

In Eq. (3.30), $M_{dm} I_{fm} = K_m$ is the motor torque constant in Nm per armature current in motor.

Eqs. (3.28), (3.29) and (3.30) describe the behaviour of the Ward-Leonard system, under all operating conditions (with I_{fm} constant).

Eliminating i_a from Eqs. (3.29) and (3.30), we get

$$\left[\frac{M_{dg}\,\omega_g\, i_{fg} - M_{dm}\, I_{fm}\,\omega_m}{R + Lp}\right] M_{dm}\, I_{fm} = Jp\omega_m + D\omega_m + T_L$$

or
$$\left(\frac{K_g\, i_{fg} - K_m\,\omega_m}{R + L\,.\,p}\right) K_m = Jp\,\omega_m + D\omega_m + T_L$$

or
$$\frac{K_g\, K_m}{R + L\,.\,p}\, i_{fg} = \left[Jp + D + \frac{K_m^2}{R + L\,.\,p}\right]\omega_m + T_L$$

Neglecting the armature inductances $(L_{ag} + L_{am})$, *i.e.*, L

$$\omega_m = \frac{K_g\, K_m\, v_{fg}}{r_{fg}\,.\,R(1 + \tau_{fg}\, p)\left[\left(D + \frac{K_m^2}{R}\right) + Jp\right]} - \frac{T_L}{\left[\left(D + \frac{K_m^2}{R}\right) + Jp\right]}$$

Here $\dfrac{K_m^2}{R} = \dfrac{M_{dm}^2\, I_{fm}^2}{R} = D_e$ = electrical damping constant as in Eq. (3.17 (*a*)).

$$\therefore \qquad \omega_m = \frac{K_g\, K_m\, v_{fg}}{r_{fg}\,.\,R\,(1 + \tau_{fg}\, p)(D + D_e)(1 + \tau'_m\, p)} - \frac{T_L}{(D + D_e)(1 + \tau'_m\, p)} \qquad ...(3.31)$$

where $\tau'_m = \dfrac{J}{D + D_e}$ = Effective mechanical time constant.

Eq. (3.31) can be utilised to study any type of disturbance, as done in Art. 3.2.

Steady state speed, from Eq. (3.31) is

$$\omega_{ms} = \frac{K_g K_m v_{fg}}{Rr_{fg}\,(D + D_e)} - \frac{T_L}{D + D_e}.$$

If mechanical damping (friction, windage etc.) $D = 0$, then from Eq. (3.31), we get

$$\omega_m = \frac{K_g K_m v_{fg}}{Rr_{fg}\,(1 + \tau_{fg}\, p)\,.\,\frac{K_m^2}{R}\,(1 + \tau_m\, p)} - \frac{RT_L}{K_m^2\,(1 + \tau_m\, p)}$$

$$= \frac{K_g\,.\,v_{fg}}{K_m\,.\,r_{fg}\,(1 + \tau_{fg}\, p)\,(1 + \tau_m\, p)} - \frac{RT_L}{K_m^2\,(1 + \tau_m\, p)} \qquad ...(3.32)$$

Here $\tau_m = \dfrac{J}{D_e} = \dfrac{JR}{K_m^2}$.

Steady-state motor speed, from Eq. (3.32) is

$$\omega_{ms} = \frac{K_g\,.\,v_{fg}}{K_m\,.\,r_{fg}} - \frac{RT_L}{K_m^2}$$

$$= \frac{K_g}{K_m}\,.\,I_{fg} - \frac{RT_L}{K_m^2} \qquad ...(3.33)$$

Example 3.5. *Two d.c. machines, connected electrically to form a Ward-Leonard system, have the following characteristics:*

Generator : $r_{ag} = 0.4\ \Omega$; $L_{ag} = 0.00$

$r_{fg} = 100\ \Omega$; $L_{fg} = 40\ H$

and $K_g = 600$ *volts/field ampere*

Motor : $r_{am} = 0.6\ \Omega$; $L_{am} = 0.00$

$K_m = 2$ *Nm/armature current.*

Total inertia of motor and load = 10 kg-m²

Mechanical damping coefficient = 1 Nm-sec/rad.

The generator, running at a constant speed, is unexcited but the motor at rest is excited.

(a) A constant voltage of 40 volts is suddenly applied to the generator field. Find how the motor speed rises with time.

(b) After the steady speed is reached in part (a), a load torque of 20 Nm is suddenly applied to the motor shaft. Find the speed variation as a function of time.

Solution.

(a)
$$D_e = \frac{K_m^2}{R} = \frac{(2)^2}{(0.4)+(0.6)} = 4$$

$\therefore$
$$D + D_e = 1 + 4 = 5 \text{ Nm/rad/sec.}$$

$$\tau_m' = \frac{J}{D+D_e} = \frac{10}{5} = 2 \text{ sec.}$$

and
$$\tau_{fg} = L_{fg}/r_{fg} = 0.4 \text{ sec.}$$

From Eq. (3.31), with $T_L = 0$ and with field voltage of 40 V suddenly applied,

$$\omega_m = \frac{(600)(2)(40)\,\mathbf{1}}{1(100)(5)(1+0.4p)(1+2p)} = \frac{96\,\mathbf{1}}{(1+0.4p)(1+2p)}$$

The above equation in s-domain is

$$\omega_m(s) = \frac{96}{s(1+0.4s)(1+2s)} = \frac{120}{s(s+2.5)(s+0.5)}$$

In partial fractions, this can be expressed as

$$\omega_m(s) = \frac{96}{s} + \frac{24}{s+2.5} - \frac{120}{s+0.5}$$

Its time-domain solution is

$$\omega_m(t) = [96 + 24e^{-2.5t} - 120e^{-0.5t}] \text{ rad/sec.}$$

(b) Steady State Speed = 96 rad/sec.

From Eq. (3.31), with V_{fg} constant, a sudden application of load torque gives the change in speed as:

$$\Delta\omega_m = \frac{-20\,\mathbf{1}}{5(1+2p)}$$

The above equation in s-domain is

$$\Delta\omega_m(s) = \frac{-20}{5s(1+2s)} = \frac{-2}{s(s+0.5)}$$

or $\quad \Delta\omega_m(s) = \dfrac{-4}{s} + \dfrac{4}{s+0.5} \quad$ or $\quad \Delta\omega_m(t) = -4(1 - e^{-0.5t})$

$\therefore$ Speed $\quad \omega_m(t) = 96 - 4 + 4e^{-0.5t}$

$= 92 + 4e^{-0.5t}$

3.4 D.C. SERIES MOTOR

The arrangement of this machine is shown in Fig. 3.19 (*a*) and its two-axis model in Fig. 3.19 (*b*).

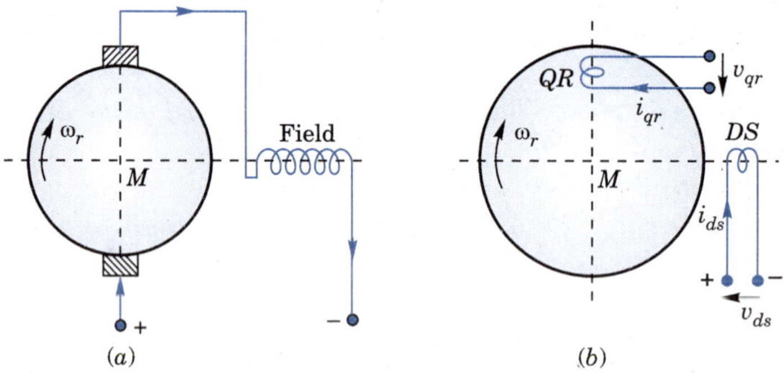

Fig. 3.9: D.C. Series motor. (*a*) Schematic representation and (*b*) Its two-axis model.

The voltage equations are

			ds	qr	
v_{ds}	=	ds	$r_{ds} + L_{ds}p$		i_{ds}
v_{qr}		qr	$M_d\omega_r$	$r_{qr} + L_{qr}p$	i_{qr}

...(3.1)

But in case of series commutator machines, the field and armature are connected in series as shown in Fig. 3.10.

$\therefore \quad i_{ds} = i_{qr} = i_f$

$= i_a = i$ (say)

With this change, voltage equations become

$$v_f = (r_f + L_f p)\, i$$

$$v_a = M_d\,\omega_r\, i + (r_a + L_a p) i$$

But $\quad v = v_a + v_f$

$$\therefore \quad v = [(r_a + r_f) + (L_a + L_f)\, p + M_d\,\omega_r]\, i \qquad ...(3.34)$$

or $\quad v = (R + Lp + M_d\,\omega_r)\, i \qquad ...[3.34\ (a)]$

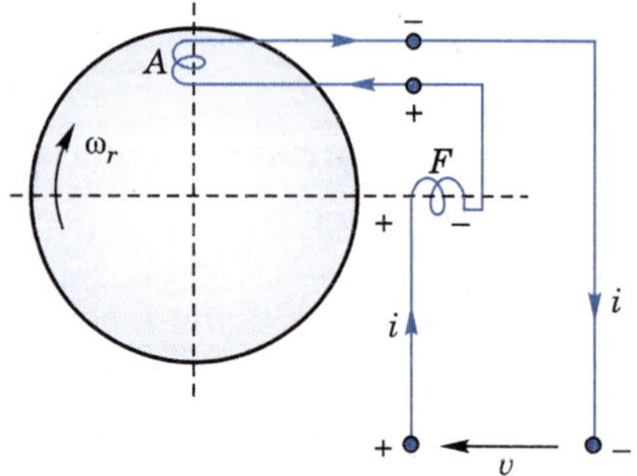

Fig. 3.10: Interconnection of field and armature coils for series motor.

Torque matrix [G] =

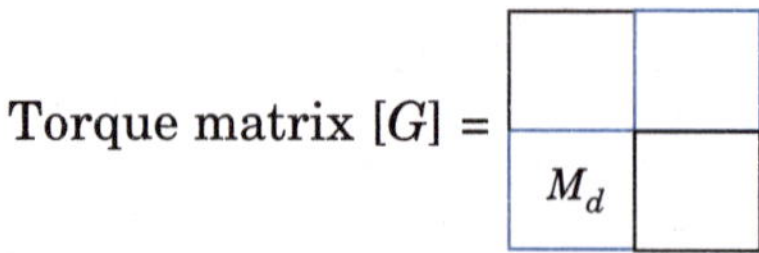

∴ Electro-magnetic torque,

$$T_e = M_d\, i^2 = Jp\omega_r + D\omega_r + T_L \quad \text{...(3.35)}$$

Equations (3.34) and (3.35) are equally valid for d.c. and a.c. single phase series machines.

Steady state analysis. For d.c. machines, p is replaced by zero for steady state conditions.

$$\therefore \quad V = (R + M_d\, \omega_r)\, I$$

or

$$\omega_r = \frac{V - IR}{M_d I} \cong \frac{V}{M_d I} \quad \text{...(3.36)}$$

Steady state torque,

$$T_e = M_d\, I^2 = \frac{V^2}{M_d\, \omega_r^2} \quad \text{...(3.37)}$$

Eq. (3.36) gives speed-current curve of Fig. 3.11 (*a*) and Eq. (3.37) gives torque-current curve of Fig. 3.11 (*b*).

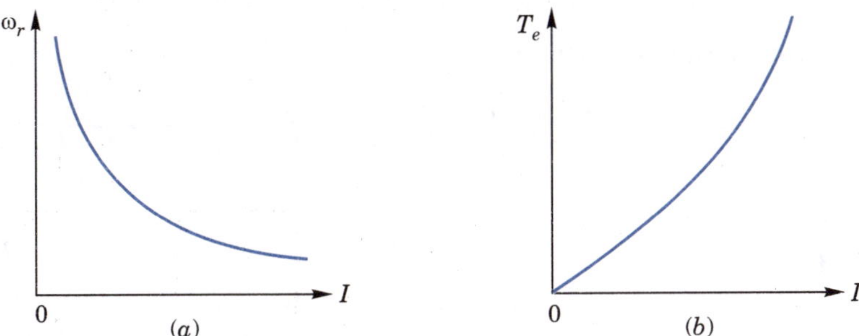

Fig. 3.11: D.C. series motor. (*a*) Speed/current and (*b*) Torque/current characteristics.

3.5 D.C. SHUNT MACHINES

The generalized machine diagram for dc shunt motor is similar to Fig. 3.1 (*a*) and the voltage equations are as given in Eq. (3.1).

3.5.1 Motor Operation

Fig. 3.12 (*a*) gives the schematic diagram for a d.c. shunt motor and the inter-connection between the armature and field winding is shown in Fig. 3.12 (*b*). The voltage equations are

$$\left.\begin{aligned} v_f &= (r_f + L_f p)\, i_f \\ \text{and} \quad v_a &= M_d \omega_r i_f + (r_a + L_a p)\, i_a \end{aligned}\right\} \quad \text{...(3.38)}$$

Steady State analysis. The voltage equations, under steady state are

$$\left.\begin{aligned} V_f &= r_f\, I_f \\ V_a &= M_d \omega_r I_f + r_a\, I_a \end{aligned}\right\}$$

In the d.c. shunt motor, $V_f = V_a = V_t$ (say),

then

$$V_t = r_f I_f \quad \text{and} \quad V_t = M_d \omega_r I_f + r_a I_a$$

$\therefore \qquad I_f = V_t/r_f$

and $$I_a = \frac{V_t}{r_a}\left(1 - \frac{M_d\,\omega_r}{r_f}\right) \qquad \text{...(3.39)}$$

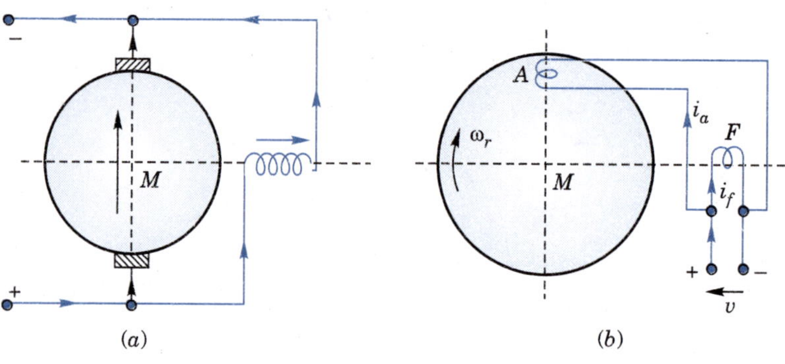

Fig. 3.12: D.C. shunt motor (*a*) Schematic diagram and (*b*) Interconnection between armature and field.

Steady state torque is given as

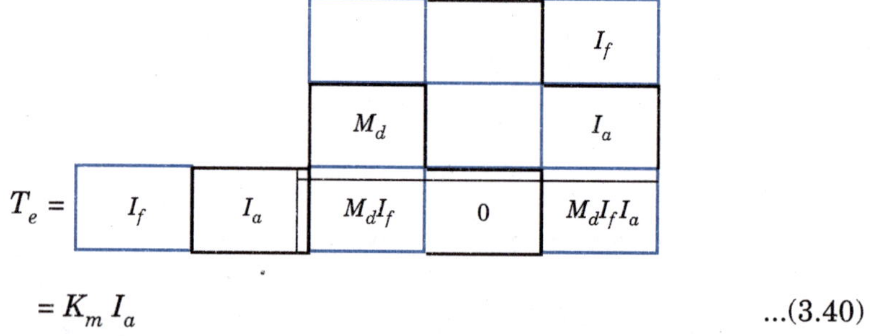

$$= K_m\,I_a \qquad \text{...(3.40)}$$

where $K_m = M_d\,I_f$ = motor torque constant in newton-metre/armature ampere.

Substituting the value of I_a from Eq. (3.39)

$$T_e = \frac{K_m}{r_a}\,[V_t - K_m\omega_r] \qquad \text{...(3.41)}$$

Torque versus armature current characteristics can be obtained from Eq. (3.40) as shown in Fig. 3.13 (*a*). It is a straight line, since the field current remains relatively constant as I_a is increased.

Torque *versus* speed characteristics are obtained with the help of Eq. (3.41), *i.e.*,

$$T_e = \frac{K_m}{r_a}\,[V_t - K_m\omega_r] \qquad \text{...[3.41 (a)]}$$

When $\omega_r = 0$, $$T_e = \frac{K_m V_t}{r_a}$$

The slope of torque/speed characteristic is

$$\frac{dT_e}{d\omega_r} = -\frac{K_m^2}{r_a}$$

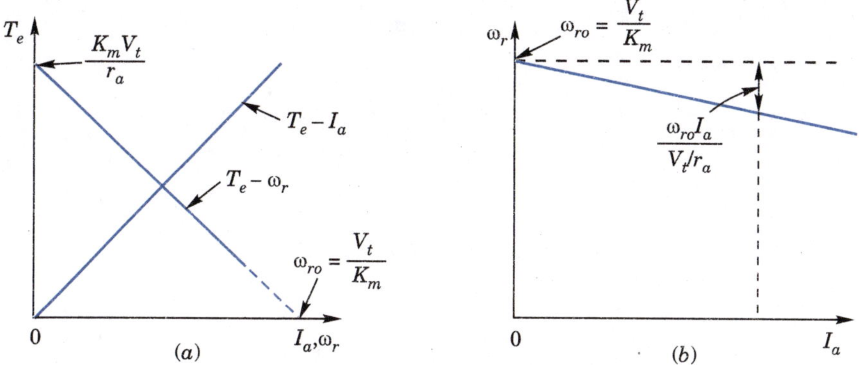

Fig. 3.13: D.C. shunt motor (*a*) torque-speed and torque-armature current characteristics (*b*) speed-current characteristics.

From Eq. (3.39) ; $$I_a = \frac{V_t}{r_a} - \frac{M_a I_f \omega_r}{r_a} = \frac{1}{r_a}(V_t - K_m\omega_r)$$

$\therefore$ $$\omega_r = \frac{V_t}{K_m} - \frac{I_a r_a}{K_m}$$

No-load speed is $$\omega_{ro} = \frac{V_t}{K_m} \qquad [\because I_a = 0 \text{ at no-load}]$$

Thus $$\omega_r = \omega_{ro}\left(1 - \frac{I_a}{V_t/r_a}\right) \qquad ...(3.42)$$

In general $\frac{V_t}{r_a} >> I_a$ and second term in Eq. (3.42) is small. Thus the speed drop with load, is small and the shunt machine can be considered as substantially a constant speed motor.

Also $$T_e = Jp\omega_r + D\omega_r + T_L.$$

Under steady-state conditions, if damping constant D is neglected, from Eq. (3.41),

$$T_e = T_L = \frac{K_m}{r_a}(V_t - K_m\omega_r)$$

or $$\frac{T_L \cdot r_a}{K_m^2} = \frac{V_t}{K_m} - \omega_r = \omega_{ro} - \omega_r$$

or $$\omega_r = \omega_{ro} - \frac{T_L \cdot r_a}{K_m \cdot V_t} \cdot \frac{V_t}{K_m}$$

$\therefore$ $$\omega_r = \omega_{ro}\left[1 - \frac{T_L r_a}{K_m V_t}\right] \qquad ...(3.43)$$

Thus, load torque *versus* speed characteristics can also be obtained from Eq. (3.43).

Example 3.6. *A d.c. shunt motor is running under steady state conditions. Find the condition for maximum torque and obtain its value.*

Solution. $$T_e = \frac{K_m}{r_a}(V_t - K_m\omega_r) \qquad (3.41)$$

$$\therefore \quad \frac{dT_e}{dK_m} = \frac{V_t}{r_a} - \frac{2K_m\omega_r}{r_a}.$$

For obtaining the condition for maximum torque

$$\frac{dT_e}{dK_m} = 0, \text{ i.e.,}$$

$$V_t = 2K_m\omega_r = 2M_d I_f \omega_r = 2E_a.$$

Thus maximum torque is obtained when the counter (or back) e.m.f. E_a is equal to half the terminal voltage.

$$\therefore \quad K_m = \frac{V_t}{2\omega_r}$$

$$\therefore \quad T_{e(\max)} = \frac{K_m}{r_a}\left[V_t - \frac{V_t}{2}\right] = \frac{V_t K_m}{2r_a}.$$

Example 3.7. *A d.c. shunt motor is to be brought to rest by dynamic braking method, which involves disconnecting the armature terminals from the supply and connecting it to a resistor R, the field current remaining uneffected.*

(i) Obtain an expression for motor speed. Solve it for negligible armature inductance.

(ii) Find the value of R so that the speed reduces to zero in minimum possible time.

Solution. The field current remains under steady state and transients appear only in the armature circuit. When the armature terminals are switched across the braking resistance R, *i.e.* at $t = 0\,+$, the armature current is opposite to what it was at $t = 0\,-$. Thus the equations describing the behaviour of this machine are :

$$V_f = r_f I_f$$

$$v_t = i_a R = M_d\omega_r I_f - (r_a + L_a p)\, i_a$$

$$\therefore \quad i_a = \frac{M_d I_f \omega_r}{(r_a + R)(1 + \tau'_a p)} = \frac{K_m\omega_r}{R'(1 + \tau'_a p)}$$

where τ'_a = Effective armature time constant.

$$= \frac{L_a}{r_a + R} = \frac{L_a}{R'}.$$

Generally, torque components due to J and D oppose the electromagnetic torque T_e. But here i_a is reversed and, therefore, T_e is also reversed. Thus, in this problem, T_e is also tending to stop the motor.

$$\therefore \quad -T_e = -M_d I_f I_a = -K_m i_a = Jp\omega_r + D\omega_r$$

Substitution of the value of i_a gives

$$\omega_r\left[Jp + \frac{K_m^2}{R'(1 + \tau'_a p)} + D\right] = 0$$

or $$\omega_r[p^2 JR'\tau'_a + p\,(JR' + D\tau'_a R') + DR' + K^2_m] = 0 \qquad \text{...(3.44)}$$

The solution of the above equation is of the type

$$\omega_r(t) = Ae^{p_1 t} + Be^{p_2 t}$$

where p_1 and p_2 are the roots of the equation,

$$p^2 JR' \tau'_a + p\,(JR' + D\tau'_a R') + (DR' + K^2_m) = 0$$

which are $p = \dfrac{-(JR' + D\tau'_a R') \pm \sqrt{JR' + D\tau'_a R')^2 - 4JR'\,\tau'_a (DR' + K_m^2)}}{2JR'\,\tau'_a}$

If L_a is neglected, τ'_a is zero and the Eq. (3.44) takes the form $\omega_r\,(DR' + K_m{}^2 + p\,.\,JR') = 0$.

Here $$p = -\frac{DR' + K_m^2}{JR'}$$

$\therefore$ $$\omega_r(t) = Ae^{-\frac{DR' + K_m^2}{JR'}t}$$

At $t = 0+\,;\ \omega_r = \omega_{ro} = \text{A}\,.\,1$

$\therefore$ $A = \omega_{ro}$

This gives the motor speed as,

$$\omega_r\,(t) = \omega_{ro}\,.\,\exp\left[-\frac{DR' + K_m^2}{JR'}\right]t \qquad \text{...(3.45)}$$

Thus the speed of the machine falls exponentially as given above.

(*b*) For the speed to come down to zero in minimum possible time, the system must be critically damped, *i.e.*

$$(JR' + D\tau'_a R')^2 = 4JR'\tau'_a DR' + 4JR'\tau'_a K_m{}^2 \qquad \text{or} \qquad R' = \frac{4J\tau'_a K_m^2}{(J - D\tau'_a)^2}$$

$\therefore$ $$R = \frac{4J\tau'_a K_m^2}{(J - D\tau'_a)^2} - r_a\,.$$

If damping D is neglected,

$$R' = \frac{4J\,\tau'_a K_m^2}{J^2} = \frac{4JL_a K_m^2}{J^2\,.\,R'} \qquad \text{or} \qquad R' = 2K_m\,.\,\sqrt{\frac{L_a}{J}}$$

$\therefore$ $$R = 2K_m\,.\,\sqrt{\frac{L_a}{J}} - r_a\,.$$

Example 3.8. *A d.c. shunt motor can be quickly brought to rest by means of plugging, which involves reversing the polarity of the armature supply, the field circuit maintaining the constant field current as before. Obtain an expression for the speed as a function of time.*

Solution. It is easier to use the principle of superposition for this problem. Before plugging, *i.e.*, at $t = 0-$, the armature supply voltage is V_t and at $t = 0+$, it is $-V_t$. Thus

$$v_t = v_{t0} + v_{tt}$$
$$-V_t = V_t + v_{tt}$$

The superimposed voltage is thus

$$v_{tt} = -2V_t\mathbf{1}$$

For the speed $\omega_r = \omega_{ro} + \omega_{rt}$

The performance equations, with negligible L_a and T_L are $V_f = I_f r_f$

$$M_d I_f i_{at} = Jp\omega_{rt} + D\omega_{rt} \qquad \text{and} \qquad -2V_t\,\mathbf{1} = M_d\, I_f\, \omega_{rt} + r_a i_{at}$$

Eliminating i_{at}, $-2V_t\,\mathbf{1} = \omega_{rt}\left[K_m + \frac{Dr_a}{K_m} + \frac{Jr_a}{K_m}\,.\,p\right]$

or

$$\omega_{rt} = \frac{-2V_t\,\mathbf{1}}{\left(K_m + \frac{Dr_a}{K_m}\right)\left[1 + \frac{Jr_a}{K_m^2 + Dr_a}\,p\right]}$$

The above equation in s-domain is

$$\omega_{rt}(s) = \frac{-2V_t}{\left(K_m + \frac{Dr_a}{K_m}\right)s\left[1 + \frac{Jr_a}{K_m^2 + Dr_a}\,s\right]}$$

Its Laplace inverse is $\qquad \omega_{rt}(t) = \dfrac{-2V_t}{K_m + \frac{Dr_a}{K_m}}\left[1 \quad \cdot\left\{-\frac{K_m^2 + Dr_a}{Jr_a}\,.\,t\right\}\right]$

The speed before plugging is

$$\omega_{ro} = \frac{V_t}{K_m + \frac{Dr_a}{K}}$$

$$\therefore \qquad \omega_r(t) = \omega_{ro} + \omega_{rt}(t) = \frac{V_t}{K_m + \frac{Dr_a}{K_m}}\left[2e^{-\frac{(K_m^2 + Dr_a)}{Jr_a}t} - 1\right]. \qquad \text{...(3.46)}$$

Example 3.9. *An ideal d.c. motor with negligible internal power loss operates at no-load with fixed field excitation supplied from a separate source. Write down an expression for the current drawn when the armature is subjected to a varying voltage v_t.*

Determine the constant in this expression if the moment of inertia of the armature is 0.5 kgm² and the armature develops 100 V at a speed of 1000 rpm. [I.A.S., 1989]

Solution. With V_t as the applied voltage to the armature circuit, the voltage equation for the armature circuit is

$$v_t = (r_a + L_a p)\, i_a + E_a$$

With $\qquad r_a = 0$ and $E_a = K_m\omega_r$,

$$v_t = L_a\, pi_a + K_m\omega_r \qquad \text{or} \qquad \omega_r = \frac{v_t - L_a pi_a}{K_m}$$

The torque balance equation for the d.c. motor is

$$T_e = K_m\, i_a = Jp\omega_r$$

or

$$i_a = \frac{J}{K_m}\,p\omega_r = \frac{J}{K_m}\,p\left[\frac{v_t - L_a pi_a}{K_m}\right]$$

or

$$i_a = \frac{(J/K_m^2)\,pv_t}{1 + (J/K_m^2)\,p^2 L_a}$$

Constant in the above expression is $J/K_m^{\ 2}$

Now, at no load, $V_t = 100 \text{ Volts} = K_m \omega_r$

or
$$K_m = \frac{100 \times 60}{2\pi \times 1000} = \frac{3}{\pi}$$

$\therefore$
$$\frac{J}{K_m^2} = 0.5 \times \left(\frac{\pi}{3}\right)^2 = 0.5483.$$

3.6 D.C. COMPOUND MACHINE

The d.c. shunt machine charateristics can be modified by having an additional winding, known as the series field winding, on its main poles. This winding, as the name implies, is connected in series with the armature. The schematic representation of a d.c. compound machine, with its shunt field separately excited is shown in Fig. 3.14 (*a*) and its generalized model in Fig. 3.14 (*b*).

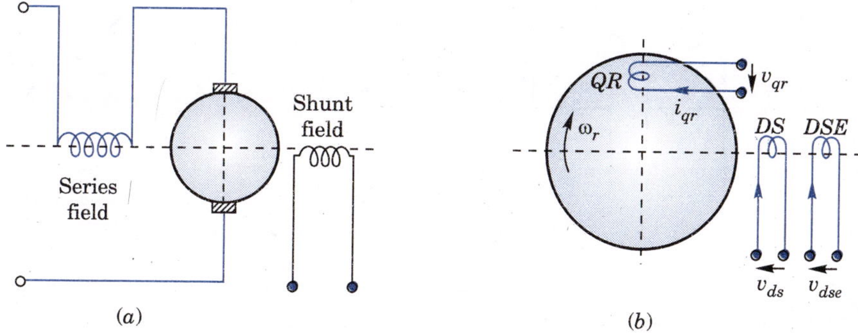

Fig. 3.14: D.C. compound machine. (*a*) Schematic diagram with separately excited shunt field. (*b*) Its generalized model.

The voltage equations in matrix form, written with the help of Fig. 3.14 (*b*), are given below:

$$\begin{bmatrix} v_{ds} \\ v_{dse} \\ v_{qr} \end{bmatrix} = \begin{matrix} ds \\ dse \\ qr \end{matrix} \overset{\begin{matrix} ds & \quad dse & \quad qr \end{matrix}}{\begin{bmatrix} r_{ds} + L_{ds}p & M_d p & \\ M_d p & r_{dse} + L_{dse}p & \\ M_d\omega_r & M_d'\omega_r & r_{qr} + L_{qr}p \end{bmatrix}} \begin{bmatrix} i_{ds} \\ i_{dse} \\ i_{qr} \end{bmatrix} \quad ...(3.47)$$

The motional inductance between coils QR and DSE has been written as M_d', just to avoid confusion between K_g or $M_d \cdot \omega_r$ and K_s or $M_d' \cdot \omega_r$ at a later stage.

Considering the operation of the machine as a separately excited compound generator, see Fig. 3.15 (*a*), we get

$$i_{qr} = -i_a = -i_L, \; i_{ds} = i_f$$

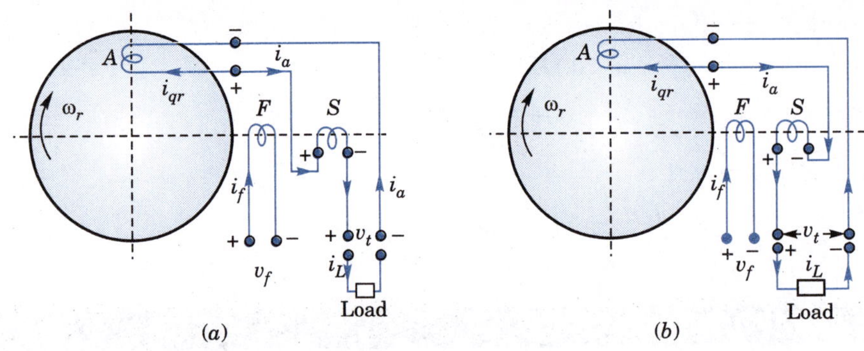

Fig. 3.15: (*a*) Cumulatively compounded separately excited d.c. generator.
(*b*) Differentially compounded separately excited d.c. generator.

In a cumulatively compounded generator, series field aids the shunt field, therefore,

$$i_{dse} = i_a = i_L.$$

In a differentially compounded generator, the two fields oppose each other as shown in Fig. 3.15 (*b*) and therefore

$$i_{dse} = -\,i_a = -\,i_L.$$

$$\therefore \quad \begin{bmatrix} i_{ds} \\ i_{dse} \\ i_{qr} \end{bmatrix} = \begin{bmatrix} 1 & \\ & \pm 1 \\ & -1 \end{bmatrix} \begin{bmatrix} i_f \\ i_a \end{bmatrix}$$

Thus the connection matrix is $[C] = \begin{bmatrix} 1 & \\ & \pm 1 \\ & -1 \end{bmatrix}$

Wherever ± appears, the positive one is for cumulatively and the negative one for the differentially compounded generators. The new impedance matrix after replacing the subscripts *ds*, *dse*, *qr* by *f*, *s* and *a* respectively is

$$[Z'] = [C_t]\,[Z]\,[C] = \begin{bmatrix} r_f + L_f p & \pm M_d p \\ \pm M_d p - M_d \omega_r & \begin{matrix} r_s + L_s p \mp M_d' \omega_r \\ + r_a + L_a p \end{matrix} \end{bmatrix}$$

The new voltage matrix is $[v'] = [C_t]\,[v] = \begin{bmatrix} v_f \\ \pm v_s \\ -v_a \end{bmatrix}$

From Fig. 3.15 (*a*), $v_t = v_L = v_a - v_s$ and from Fig. 3.15 (*b*)

$v_t = v_L = v_a + v_s.$ *i.e.*, $v_t = v_a \pm v_s.$

Thus the new voltage equations in matrix form are

$$\begin{array}{c} \\ f \\ a \end{array}\begin{bmatrix} v_f \\ -v_L \end{bmatrix} = \begin{array}{c|c|c} & f & a \\ \hline f & r_f + L_f p & \pm M_d p \\ a & -M_d\omega_r \pm M_d p & r_s + r_a + (L_s + L_a)p \mp M_d'\omega_r \end{array} \begin{bmatrix} i_f \\ i_a \end{bmatrix} \qquad ...(3.48)$$

or

$$v_f = (r_f + L_f p)\, i_f \pm M_d p i_a$$

$$v_t = v_L = (M_d\, \omega_r \pm M_d\, p)\, i_f - [(r_a + r_s) + (L_a + L_s)\, p \mp M_d'\, \omega_r]\, i_a \qquad ...[3.48\ (a)]$$

Under steady state, the voltage equations become

$$\left.\begin{aligned} V_f &= r_f I_f \\ \text{and} \quad V_t = V_L &= M_d \omega_r I_f \pm M_d' \omega_r I_a - (r_a + r_s) I \end{aligned}\right\} \qquad ...(3.49)$$

Here $M_d\, \omega_r I_f = K_g I_f$ is the generated e.m.f. due to shunt field and $M_d'\, \omega_r I_a = K_s I_a$, that due to series field,

where $K_g = M_d\, \omega_r$ = generated e.m.f. constant/shunt field ampere at ω_r.

and $K_s = M_d' \omega_r$ = generated e.m.f. constant/series field ampere at ω_r.

Equation (3.49) can now be written as

$$\left.\begin{aligned} V_f &= r_f I_f \\ V_c &= K_g I_f \pm K_s I_a - (r_a + r_s) I_a \end{aligned}\right\} \qquad ...[3.49\ (a)]$$

For obtaining flat-compounded generator, the voltage drop due to I_a must be zero. From Eq. (3.49 (*a*)),

$$-(r_a + r_s) \pm K_s = 0.$$

Flat-compounded characteristic can be obtained only for cumulatively compounded generator and the necessary condition is

$$(r_a + r_s) = K_s = M_d'\, \omega_r.$$

For obtaining overcompounded characteristics $K_s > (r_a + r_s)$ and for undercompounded characteristics $K_s < (r_a + r_s)$.

3.6.1 Cumulatively Compounded (Long Shunt) D.C. Motor

Its generalized mathematical model is given in Fig. 3.14 (*b*) and its schematic diagram in Fig. 3.16 (*a*).

Interconnections between the primitive machine coils are illustrated in Fig. 3.16 (*b*).

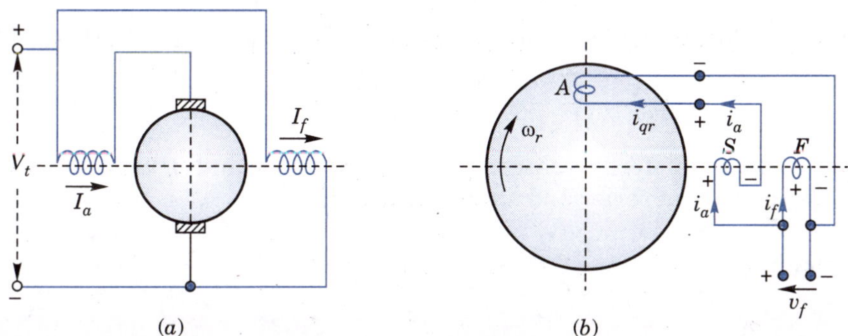

Fig. 3.16: Cumulatively compounded (long shunt) d.c. motor. (*a*) The schematic diagram and (*b*) The interconnections between primitive machine coils.

The voltage equations are the same as in Eq. (3.47).

Here $i_{qr} = i_{dse} = i_a$ and $i_{ds} = i_f$

$$\therefore \quad \begin{bmatrix} i_{ds} \\ i_{dse} \\ i_{qr} \end{bmatrix} = \begin{bmatrix} 1 & \\ & 1 \\ & 1 \end{bmatrix} \begin{bmatrix} i_f \\ i_a \end{bmatrix}$$

The new impedance matrix is

$$[Z'] = [C_t]\,[Z]\,[C] = \begin{bmatrix} r_f + L_f p & M_d p \\ M_d \omega_r + M_d p & r_a + r_s + (L_a + L_s)p + M_d' \omega_r \end{bmatrix}$$

The new voltage matrix is $[v'] = [C_t]\,[v] = \begin{bmatrix} v_f \\ v_s + v_a \end{bmatrix}$ But $v_t = v_s + v_a$

Thus the new voltage equations in matrix form are :

$$\begin{bmatrix} v_f \\ v_t \end{bmatrix} = \begin{array}{c} f \\ a \end{array} \overset{\begin{array}{cc} f & a \end{array}}{\begin{bmatrix} r_f + L_f p & M_d p \\ M_d \omega_r + M_d p & r_a + r_s + (L_a + L_s)p + M_d' \omega_r \end{bmatrix}} \begin{bmatrix} i_f \\ i_a \end{bmatrix} \quad \text{...(3.50)}$$

Under steady-state conditions, the voltage equations become:

$$\left.\begin{aligned} V_f &= r_f I_f \\ V_t &= M_d \,\omega_r I_f + (r_a + r_s)\, I_a + M_d' \,\omega_r I_a \\ \text{or} \quad V_t &= K_g I_f + K_s I_a + (r_a + r_s)\, I_a \end{aligned}\right\} \quad \text{...(3.51)}$$

where K_g and K_s have already been defined.

From Eq. (3.51), $\omega_r\,[M_d I_f + M_d' I_a] = V_t - I_a\,(r_a + r_s)$

$$\therefore \quad \omega_r = \frac{V_t - I_a\,(r_a + r_s)}{M_d I_f + M_d' I_a} \quad \text{...(3.52)}$$

When the armature current (or approximately load current) is zero, the no-load speed is

$$\omega_{ro} = \frac{V_t}{M_d I_f} = \frac{I_f r_f}{M_d I_f} = \frac{r_f}{M_d}.$$

As the load on the motor increases, I_a will also increase and ω_r versus I_a characteristics will be somewhere between series and shunt characteristics.

Also from Eq. (3.51), $V_t = \dfrac{K_g V_t}{r_f} + (r_a + r_s + K_s)\, I_a$

$$\text{or} \quad I_a = \frac{V_t}{r_a + r_s + K_s}\left(1 - \frac{K_g}{r_f}\right)$$

Torque can be found out from the torque matrix [G] obtained from Eq. (3.50).

				i_f
		M_d	M'_d	i_a
$T_e =$ i_f	i_a	$M_d i_a$	$M'_d i_a$	Written ahead

$$T_e = M_d i_f i_a + M_d' i_a^2$$

3.7 LINEARIZATION TECHNIQUES FOR SMALL PERTURBATIONS

For some applications, d.c. machines operate invariably under steady-state conditions, *i.e.*, the various variables remain substantially constant. However, perturbations in applied voltage, load torque etc. do occur and these can be regarded as small-signal inputs. These perturbations cause the appearance of transients before the d.c. machine settles down to new steady-state operating conditions. The behaviour of d.c. machines to such disturbances can be investigated by means of linearization techniques, according to which (*i*) the perturbations are considered to be superimposed on steady-operating points and (*ii*) the squares or products of small variables are neglected. The linear equations so obtained, may be used for examining the steady-state stability of the system.

The use of linearization techniques for small perturbations is illustrated by two examples given below.

Example 3.10. *A 230 V d.c. series motor, running at 150 radians per second, takes 20 amperes from the supply mains. The armature and field resistance are $r_a + r_f = 1.0\ \Omega$. Total $J = 5.4$ kg. m² and $D = 0.02$ Nm-sec / rad.*

(a) Calculate the rotational mutual inductance M_d and the load torque.

(b) If the supply voltage is suddenly reduced to 220 volts with the load torque remaining constant, find the speed as a function of time.

Solution. Neglecting the armature and field inductances, the equations specifying the operation of d.c. series motor, from Eqs. (3.34 *a*) and (3.35), are

$$\left.\begin{aligned} v &= ri + M_d\,\omega_r i \\ M_d\, i^2 &= Jp\omega_r + D\omega_r + T_L \end{aligned}\right\} \qquad \text{...(3.53)}$$

The d.c. series motor is working initially under steady-state conditions. A small change in the supply voltage would cause small changes in i and ω_r, thus making Eq. (3.53) non-linear, because then this equation contains $\omega_r\, i$ (product of two variables ω_r and i) and i^2 (square of the current variable i.) This equation can however be linearized provided the changes in the variables are small.

Here the supply voltage changes from steady value V_o to a slightly different value $V_0 + v_t$, where v_t is time-varying voltage. The corresponding new values of the speed and current are $\omega_{ro} + \omega_{rt}$ and $I_o + i_t$, where ω_{ro} and I_0 are initial steady-state values ; ω_{rt} and i_t are time-varying quantities.

Introduction of these changes in Eq. (3.53) gives

$$\left.\begin{aligned} V_0 + v_t &= r(I_0 + i_t) + M_d(\omega_{r0} + \omega_{rt})(I_0 + i_t) \\ M_d(I_0 + i_t)^2 &= Jp(\omega_{r0} + \omega_{rt}) + D(\omega_{r0} + \omega_{rt}) + T_L + \Delta T_L \end{aligned}\right\} \quad ...(3.54)$$

Under steady-state condition (before the small change in voltage), Eq. (3.53) becomes

$$\left.\begin{aligned} V_0 &= rI_0 + M_d\omega_{r0}I_0 \\ M_d I_0^2 &= D\omega_{r0} + T_L \end{aligned}\right\} \quad ...(3.55)$$

Subtracting Eq. (3.55) from Eq. (3.54), we get the equations containing the time-varying quantities. These equations are,

$$v_t = ri_t + M_d\,\omega_{rt}I_o + M_d\,\omega_{ro}\,i_t \quad ...(3.56)$$

$$2M_dI_oi_t = Jp\omega_{rt} + D\omega_{rt} + \Delta T_L \quad ...(3.57)$$

While obtaining Eqs. (3.56) and (3.57), the terms $\omega_{rt}\,i_t$ (product of two small variables) and i_t^2 (square of small variable i_t) have been neglected and the operator p operating on steady values gives zero.

From Eq. (3.56), $\quad i_t = \dfrac{v_t - M_d I_o\omega_{rt}}{r + M_d\,\omega_{ro}}.$

Substitution of this value of i_t in Eq. (3.57) gives

$$\frac{2M_d\,.\,I_ov_t}{r + M_d\,\omega_{ro}} - \frac{2(M_d\,I_o)^2\,\omega_{rt}}{r + M_d\,\omega_{ro}} = Jp\omega_{rt} + D\omega_{rt} + \Delta T_L$$

or

$$\omega_{rt}\left[Jp + D + \frac{2M_d^2\,I_o^2}{r + M_d\,\omega_{ro}}\right] = \frac{2M_d\,I_ov_t}{r + M_d\,\omega_{ro}} - \Delta T_L$$

$\therefore$

$$\omega_{rt} = \frac{2M_d\,I_ov_t}{(r + M_d\,\omega_{ro})(Jp + D + D_e)} - \frac{\Delta T_L}{(Jp + D + D_e)} \quad ...(3.58)$$

In this problem, load torque is held constant and in view of this $\Delta T_L = 0$. The armature voltage changes by a small amount v_t.

$\therefore$

$$\omega_{rt}(t) = \frac{2M_d\,I_ov_t}{(r + M_d\,\omega_{ro})(D + D_e)}(1 - e^{-t/\tau'_m}) \quad ...(3.59)$$

where $\tau'_m = \dfrac{J}{D + D_e}$ and $D_e = \dfrac{2M_d^2\,I_o^2}{r + M_d\,\omega_{ro}}$

(*a*) Under steady-state conditions, from Eq. (3.55)

$V_o = rI_o + M_d\omega_{ro}I_o, \qquad 230 = (1 + M_d \times 150)\,20$

$\therefore \quad M_d = 0.07$ H.

Also, from Eq. (3.55),

$M_dI_o^2 = D\omega_{ro} + T_L.$

$(0.07)(20)^2 = 0.02 \times 150 + T_L \qquad \therefore \quad T_L = 25$ Nm.

(*b*) $\quad D_e = \dfrac{2[(0.07)(20)]^2}{1 + 0.07 \times 150} = 0.34, \quad \tau'_m = \dfrac{5.4}{0.02 + 0.34} = 15.$

$\therefore$ Change in speed as a function of time, from Eq. (3.59), is

$$\omega_{rt}(t) = \frac{2 \times 0.07 \times 20 \times 10}{(1 + 0.07 \times 150)(0.02 + 0.34)}(1 - e^{-t/15}) = 6.76\,(1 - e^{-0.067t})$$

Since the supply voltage decreases from 230 V to 220 V, the motor speed after this change would be less than the previous value.

Therefore, the motor speed as a function of time is

$$\omega_r(t) = \omega_{ro} - \omega_{rt}(t)$$
$$= 150 - 6.76\,(1 - e^{-0.067t}) = 143.24 + 6.76e^{-0.067t}$$

Example 3.11. *A rheostat is connected in series with the field winding of a d.c. shunt motor, driving a constant load torque under steady-state conditions. Friction and windage torques (i.e. D) are negligible. When the field rheostat is short-circuited, the voltage across the field winding increases only by a small amount. Find the variation of speed after this small perturbation. Neglect the effect of armature inductance.*

Solution. With negligible armature inductance, Eq. (3.38) becomes,

$$\left.\begin{aligned} V_f &= (r_f + L_f p)\, i_f \\ V_a &= M_d\, \omega_r I_f + r_a i_a \end{aligned}\right\} \qquad ...(3.60)$$

Its torque balance equation is

$$T_e = M_d\, i_f\, i_a = Jp\omega_r + T_L \qquad ...(3.61)$$

With rheostat in the field circuit, the steady field current is

$$I_{fo} = \frac{V_f}{r_f + r_{fr}}$$

where r_{fr} = resistance of the shunt field rheostat.

The sudden short circuit of r_{fr} is equivalent to a step change of voltage in the field circuit, which is given by $I_{fo}\, r_{fr}\, \mathbf{1}$.

Thus the field voltage equation involving the small change in resistance r_{fr} is,

$$I_{fo}\, r_{fr}\, \mathbf{1} = (r_f + L_f p)\, i_{ft} \qquad ...(3.62)$$

Introducing the small changes in armature voltage equation of Eq. (3.60) and torque equation (3.61) and then subtracting the steady-state voltage and torque equations, as has been done in Example 3.10, we get the following equations:

$$\left.\begin{aligned} O &= M_d\, \omega_{ro}\, i_{ft} + M_d\, \omega_{rt} I_{fo} + r_a i_{at} \\ M_d I_{fo} i_{at} &+ M_d\, i_{ft} I_{ao} = Jp\omega_{rt} \end{aligned}\right\} \qquad ...(3.63)$$

Elimination of i_{at} from Eq. (3.63) gives

$$\omega_{rt}\left[Jp + \frac{M_d^2\, I_{fo}^2}{r_a}\right] = \left[M_d I_{ao} - \frac{M_d^2\, I_{fo}\omega_{ro}}{r_a}\right] i_{ft}.$$

Substitution of the value of i_{ft} from Eq. (3.62), in the above equation gives

$$\omega_{rt} = \left[\frac{M_d\, I_{ao} r_a}{K_m^2\,(1+\tau_m p)} - \frac{M_d^2\, I_{fo}\,.\,\omega_{ro}}{K_m^2\,(1+\tau_m p)}\right] \frac{I_{fo}\,.\,r_{fr}\,.\,\mathbf{1}}{r_f\,(1+\tau_f p)}$$

Here $\qquad K_m = M_d I_{fo}$ and $\tau_m = \dfrac{J r_a}{K_m^2}$

Also

$$\omega_{rt} = \frac{M_d}{r_f K_m}\left[\frac{I_{ao}\, r_a}{K_m} - \omega_{ro}\right] \frac{I_{fo}\, r_{fr}\, \mathbf{1}}{(1+\tau_f p)(1+\tau_m p)}$$

or
$$\omega_{rt} = \frac{r_{fr}}{r_f}\left[\frac{I_{ao}\,.\,r_a}{K_m} - \omega_{ro}\right]\frac{1}{(1+\tau_f p)(1+\tau_m p)}$$

The above equation in s-domain is

$$\omega_{rt}\,(s) = \frac{r_{fr}}{r_f}\left[\frac{I_{ao}\,.\,r_a}{K_m} - \omega_{ro}\right]\frac{1}{s(1+s\tau_f)(1+s\tau_m)}$$

$$= \frac{r_{fr}}{r_f}\left[\frac{I_{ao}\,.\,r_a}{K_m} - \omega_{ro}\right]\frac{1}{s\,.\,\tau_f\,.\,\tau_m\left(s+\dfrac{1}{\tau_f}\right)\left(s+\dfrac{1}{\tau_m}\right)}$$

After partial fractions, the above can be written as

$$\omega_{rt}\,(s) = \frac{r_{fr}}{r_f}\left[\frac{I_{ao}r_a}{K_m} - \omega_{ro}\right]\left[\frac{1}{s} + \frac{\tau_m}{\tau_f - \tau_m}\cdot\frac{1}{s+\dfrac{1}{\tau_m}} - \frac{\tau_f}{\tau_f - \tau_m}\cdot\frac{1}{s+\dfrac{1}{\tau_f}}\right]$$

Therefore, the change in speed as a function of time is

$$\omega_{rt}\,(t) = \frac{r_{fr}}{r_f}\left[\frac{I_{ao}r_a}{K_m} - \omega_{ro}\right]\left[1 + \frac{\tau_m}{\tau_f - \tau_m}e^{-t/\tau_m} - \frac{\tau_f}{\tau_f - \tau_m}e^{-t/\tau_f}\right] \quad ...(3.64)$$

The resultant speed is

$$\omega_r\,(t) = \text{Initial speed} + \text{Change in speed}$$

$$= \omega_{ro} + \frac{r_{fr}}{r_f}\left[\frac{I_{ao}\,.\,r_a}{K_m} - \omega_{ro}\right]\left[1+\frac{\tau_m}{\tau_f - \tau_m}e^{-t/\tau_m} - \frac{\tau_f}{\tau_f - \tau_m}e^{-t/\tau_f}\right] \quad ...(3.65)$$

After the transients are over, the new steady-state operating speed, from Eq. (3.65), is

$$\omega_r = \omega_{ro} + \frac{r_{fr}}{r_f}\left(\frac{I_{ao}r_a}{K_m} - \omega_{ro}\right)$$

But $\quad \omega_{ro}K_m = V_t$

$$\therefore \quad \omega_r = \omega_{ro} - \frac{r_{fr}}{r_f}\left[\frac{V_t - I_{ao}r_a}{K_m}\right].$$

This shows that new steady-operating speed is less than its value before the perturbation.

3.8 CROSS FIELD MACHINES

Ordinary d.c. machines considered so far, possess only one pair of brushes along q-axes. Cross field machines have brush pairs both along d- and q-axes. Such a d.c. machine, which has two brush sets per pole pair, is called a *metadyne*. The control or field winding on the stator is excited from a separate voltage source. A compensating winding is provided on the stator d-axis to improve performance of the metadyne. This winding is connected in series with d-axis load (or armature) current. The cross-field machines with zero or partial compensation are called metadyne generators. A fully compensated cross-field machine, which is more commonly used as a rotating amplifier, is called an *amplidyne*.

The stator construction of cross-field machines is such that the reluctance offered to the armature d- and q-axes fluxes is same as illustrated in Fig. 3.17 (a). This means that L_d may be taken as equal to L_q.

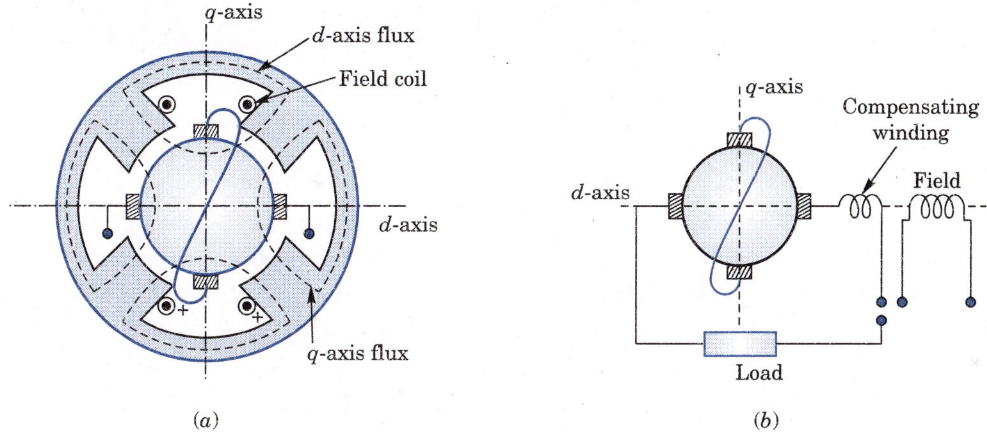

Fig. 3.17: (a) Magnetic flux in a cross-field machine
(b) Basic features of a compensated metadyne generator.

3.8.1 Amplidyne

The basic features of a compensated metadyne generator are depicted in Fig. 3.17 (b). A partially compensated metadyne is not so useful in practice. But, a fully-compensated metadyne generator, called an *amplidyne*, is used extensively to provide power amplification in several applications. In view of this, here the analysis of amplidyne would only be presented.

From Fig. 3.17 (b), a generalized mathematical model of amplidyne can be drawn as shown in Fig. 3.18 (a). The voltage equations from this model of Fig. 3.18 (a) can be written as under.

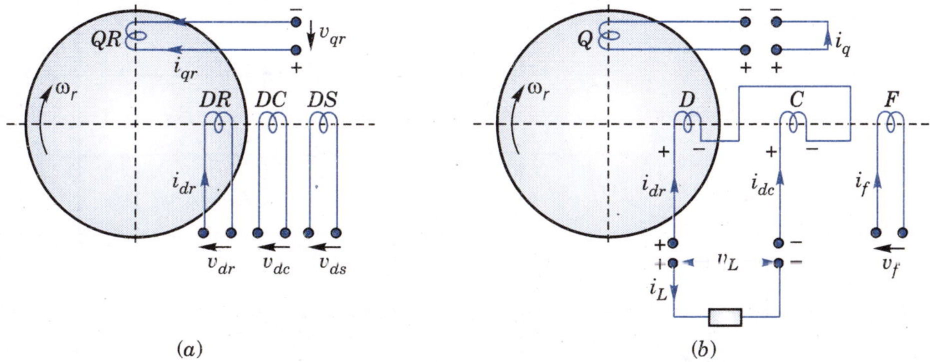

Fig. 3.18: (a) Generalized model of amplidyne and
(b) the interconnection between the various coils of an amplidyne.

$$\begin{bmatrix} v_{ds} \\ v_{dc} \\ v_{dr} \\ v_{qr} \end{bmatrix} = \begin{array}{c} \\ ds \\ dc \\ dr \\ qr \end{array} \begin{array}{c} \begin{array}{cccc} ds & dc & dr & qr \end{array} \\ \begin{bmatrix} r_{ds} + L_{ds}p & M_d p & M_d p & \\ M_d p & r_{dc} + L_{dc}p & M_d p & \\ M_d p & M_d p & r_{dr} + L_{dr}p & -L_{qr}.\omega_r \\ M_d\omega_r & M_d\omega_r & L_{dr}.\omega_r & r_{qr} + L_{qr}.p \end{bmatrix} \end{array} \begin{bmatrix} i_{ds} \\ i_{dc} \\ i_{dr} \\ i_{qr} \end{bmatrix} \quad ...(3.66)$$

For simplicity, *DS*, *DC*, *DR* and *QR* are replaced by *F*, *C*, *D* and *Q*.

Also $r_{dr} = r_{qr} = r_a$

and $L_{dr} = L_{qr} = L_a$ (say), as explained from Fig. 3.17 (*a*).

The machine coils are connected as shown in Fig. 3.18 (*b*) from which it is seen that

$$i_L = -i_{dr} = i_{dc}, \qquad i_{ds} = i_f;\ i_{qr} = -i_q.$$

Load voltage, $v_L = v_d - v_c$

and $v_q = 0$, since *q*-axis brush-pair is short-circuited.

The current relations obtained from Fig. 3.18 (*b*) can be written in matrix form as under.

$$\begin{bmatrix} i_{ds} \\ i_{dc} \\ i_{dr} \\ i_{qr} \end{bmatrix} = \begin{array}{c} \\ ds \\ dc \\ dr \\ qr \end{array} \begin{array}{c} \begin{array}{ccc} f & l & q \end{array} \\ \begin{bmatrix} 1 & & \\ & 1 & \\ & -1 & \\ & & -1 \end{bmatrix} \end{array} \begin{bmatrix} i_f \\ i_L \\ i_q \end{bmatrix}$$

The 4 × 3 matrix given above is the connection matrix [*C*] and now the new impedance matrix $[Z'] = [C_t]\ [Z]\ [C]$ can be obtained.

					$r_f + L_f.p$	$M_d p$	$M_d p$		1		
					$M_d.p$	$r_c + L_c p$	$M_d p$			1	
					$M_d p$	$M_d p$	$r_a + L_a p$	$-L_a.\omega_r$		-1	
					$M_d.\omega_r$	$M_d.\omega_r$	$L_a.\omega_r$	$r_a + L_a.p$			-1
	1				$r_f + L_f.p$	$M_d\,p$	$M_d p$	0	Written below		
$[Z'] =$		1	-1		0	$r_c + L_c.p - M_d\,p$	$M_d.p - r_a - L_a.p$	$L_a.\omega_r$			
				-1	$-M_d\omega_r$	$-M_d\omega_r$	$-L_a\omega_r$	$-r_a - L_a p$			

$$[Z'] = \begin{bmatrix} r_f + L_f \cdot p & & \\ & (r_a + r_c) + (L_a - L_c)p - 2M_d \cdot p & -L_a \cdot \omega_r \\ -M_d\omega_r & \omega_r(L_a - M_d) & r_a + L_a p \end{bmatrix}$$

Now $\quad [v'] = [C_t]\,[v] = \begin{bmatrix} 1 & & & \\ & 1 & -1 & \\ & & & -1 \end{bmatrix} \begin{bmatrix} v_f \\ v_c \\ v_d \\ v_q \end{bmatrix} = \begin{bmatrix} v_f \\ v_c - v_d \\ 0 \end{bmatrix}$

Since $\quad [v'] = [Z']\,[i'] =$

$$\begin{bmatrix} v_f \\ -v_L \\ 0 \end{bmatrix} = \begin{bmatrix} r_f + L_f \cdot p & & \\ & (r_a + r_c) + (L_a + L_c)p - 2M_d \cdot p & -L_a \cdot \omega_r \\ -M_d \cdot \omega_r & \omega_r (L_a - M_d) & r_a + L_a \cdot p \end{bmatrix} \begin{bmatrix} i_f \\ i_L \\ i_q \end{bmatrix} \qquad ...(3.67)$$

or

$$v_f = (r_f + L_f p)\, i_f$$
$$-v_L = [(r_a + r_c) + (L_a + L_c - 2M_d)\,p]\, i_L - L_a \cdot \omega_r \cdot i_q$$
$$0 = -M_d \cdot \omega_r \cdot i_f + \omega_r (L_a - M_d)\, i_L + (r_a + L_a p)\, i_q$$

Third equation from above gives,

$$i_q = \frac{M_d \cdot \omega_r\, i_f - \omega_r (L_a - M_d)\, i_L}{r_a + L_a\, p}$$

Substitution of i_q in second equation gives,

$$\left.\begin{aligned} v_L &= \frac{L_a \cdot M_d \cdot \omega_r^2\, i_f}{r_a + L_a p} - \frac{L_a\, \omega_r^2 (L_a - M_d)\, i_L}{r_a + L_a p} - [(r_a + r_c) + (L_a + L_c - 2M_d)p]\, i_L \\ \text{and} \quad v_f &= (r_f + L_f p)\, i_f \end{aligned}\right\} \qquad ...(3.68)$$

If the leakage impedance between d-axis armature and compensating winding is neglected, then

$$L_a + L_c - 2M_d = (L_a - M_d) + (L_c - M_d) = 0$$

With this, Eq. (3.68) gets simplified as under.

$$\left.\begin{aligned} v_f &= (r_f + L_f p) i_f \\ v_L &= \frac{L_a \cdot M_d \cdot \omega_r^2}{r_a + L_a p}\, i_f - (r_a + r_c)\, i_L \end{aligned}\right\} \qquad ...(3.69)$$

For load $(R_L + L_L p)$, Eq. (3.69) gives

$$i_L = \frac{L_a \,.\, M_d \,.\, \omega_r^2 \,.\, v_f}{r_f \,.\, R \,.\, r_a\,(1+\tau_f\, p)\,(1+\tau_a\, p)\,(1+\tau\, p)} \qquad \text{...(3.69 (a))}$$

where $R = r_a + r_c + R_L$, $\tau = \dfrac{L_L}{R}$ $\quad \tau_a = \dfrac{L_a}{r_a}$ and $\tau_f = \dfrac{L_f}{r_f}$

Under steady-state conditions, if load current is zero, then Eq. (3.69) gives

$$E_d = \text{no-load output voltage} = \frac{L_a \,.\, M_d \,.\, \omega_r^2}{r_a \,.\, r_f} V_f$$

$$\therefore \quad \text{Voltage amplification} = \frac{E_d}{V_f} = \frac{L_a \,.\, M_d \,.\, \omega_r^2}{r_a \,.\, r_f} = A \qquad \text{...(3.70)}$$

Under transient conditions, if $i_L = 0$, then from Eq. (3.69), we get

$$e_d = \text{generated voltage at no load}$$

$$\therefore \quad = \frac{L_a \,.\, M_d \,.\, \omega_r^2 \,.\, v_f}{r_a(1+\tau_a p) \,.\, r_f\,(1+\tau_f p)}$$

$$= \frac{A}{(1+\tau_a p)\,(1+\tau_f p)} \,.\, V_f \qquad \text{...(3.71)}$$

Example 3.12. *A 4 kW, 200 V, 200 rad/sec amplidyne has the following parameters:*

$r_f = 100\ \Omega$; $\quad L_f = 20\ H$; $\quad r_a = 1\ \Omega$;

$L_a = 0.1\ H$; $\quad r_c = 0.5\ \Omega$; $\quad M_d = 1.00\ H.$

(a) Calculate the field current and power gain at rated output.

(b) With the machine running at no-load, 5 V is suddenly applied to the field winding. Find rise of output terminal voltage.

(c) Unexcited amplidyne is running at rated speed with load 8.5 Ω and 5 H connected across its output terminals. Find the rise of output current, when 5 V is suddenly applied to field winding. The leakage flux between armature and compensating windings may be neglected.

(d) After steady state has reached in part (b) ; a load of zero resistance (short-circuit) is switched across the output terminals. Find the output current.

(e) Repeat part (d) ; if the load is 8.5 Ω and 5 H.

Solution. (*a*) Full load current, $I_L = \dfrac{4000}{200} = 20$ A

From Eq. (3.69), $\quad V_L = \dfrac{L_a M_d \omega_r^2}{r_a} \,.\, I_f - (r_c + r_a) I_L$

$$200 = \frac{(0.1)(1.0)(200)^2}{1} I_f - (1.5)(20)$$

$$\therefore \quad I_f = 57.5 \text{ mA}$$

$$\text{Power gain} = \frac{V_L I_L}{V_f I_f} = \frac{(200)(20)}{(0.0575)^2(100)} = 12100.$$

(*b*) From Eq. (3.69); with $i_L = 0$

$$e_{do} = \frac{L_a M_d \omega_r^2 V_f \mathbf{1}}{(r_a + L_a p)(r_f + L_f p)} = \frac{200\,\mathbf{1}}{(1+0.1p)(1+0.2p)}$$

This equation in s-domain is, $E_{d0}(s) = \dfrac{200 \times 50}{s(s+10)(s+5)} = \dfrac{10^4}{s(s+10)(s+5)}$

Its partial fractions are, $E_{d0}(s) = \dfrac{200}{s} + \dfrac{200}{s+10} - \dfrac{400}{s+5}$

Its time-domain solution is, $e_{d0}(t) = 200\,(1 + e^{-10t}) - 400e^{-5t}$.

(*c*) From Eq. (3.69), $V_f \mathbf{1} = (r_f + L_f p)\, i_f$

and $$i_L(R_L + r_a + r_c + L_L p) = \frac{L_a M_d \omega_r^2 i_f}{(r_a + L_a p)}$$

$\therefore$ $$i_L = \frac{L_a M_d \omega_r^2 V_f \mathbf{1}}{r_f . R . r_a (1 + \tau_f p)(1 + \tau_a p)(1 + \tau p)}$$

where $$R = R_L + r_a + r_c$$

and $$\tau = \frac{L_L}{R} = \frac{5}{10} = 0.5$$

Substitution of the various values in the expression for i_L gives

$$i_L = \frac{(0.1)(1)(40{,}000)(5)}{(100)(10)(1+0.2p)(1+0.1p)(1+0.5p)}\mathbf{1}$$

or $$i_L = \frac{20\,\mathbf{1}}{(1+0.2p)(1+0.1p)(1+0.5p)}$$

The current i_L in s-domain is,

$$I_L(s) = \frac{20 \times 5 \times 10 \times 2}{s(s+5)(s+10)(s+2)}$$

or $$I_L(s) = \frac{20}{s} + \frac{26.67}{s+5} - \frac{5}{s+10} - \frac{41.67}{s+2}$$

Its Laplace inverse is, $i_L(t) = 20 + 26.67e^{-5t} - 5e^{-10t} - 41.67e^{-2t}$.

(*d*) The equations specifying the short circuit are

$$0 = (r_f + L_f p)\, i_{ft}$$

$$-V_L \mathbf{1} = \frac{L_a M_d \omega_r^2}{r_a + L_a p} i_{ft} - (r_a + r_c) i_{Lt}$$

$\therefore$ $$i_{Lt} = i_L = \frac{200}{1.5} = 133.33 \text{ Amps.}$$

It is thus seen here that no transients appear in the short circuit current of an amplidyne.

(*e*) The equations giving this load application are

$$0 = (r_f + L_f p)i_{ft}' \qquad -V_L\, \mathbf{1} = \frac{L_a M_d \omega_r^2}{r_a + L_a p}.i_{ft} - [r_c + r_a + R_L + L_L p]\, i_{Lt}$$

$$\therefore \qquad i_{Lt} = i_L = \frac{200}{10 + 5p}\mathbf{1}$$

This equation in *s*-domain is, $I_L(s) = \dfrac{200}{s5(s+2)} = \dfrac{40}{s(s+2)} = \dfrac{20}{s} - \dfrac{20}{s+2}$

Its time-domain solution is,

$$i_{Lt}(t) = i_L(t) = 20\,(1 - e^{-2t}) \text{ Amp.}$$

Example 3.13. *In an idealized amplidyne, one control winding is being used. The internal generated voltage in the quadrature or short-circuited armature axis is K_{qf} volts per ampere in the control winding. The generated voltage in the direct axis armature circuit is K_{dq} volts per ampere in the short-circuited brushes. The effects of any other amplidyne auxiliaries are neglected.*

(a) With the amplidyne unloaded and initially unexcited, show how the d-axis output voltage builds up following the sudden appearance of a voltage V_f at the control winding terminals.

(b) Repeat part (a), when amplidyne is loaded by an impedance of $(R_L + L_L p)$.

Solution. (*a*) A careful examination of Fig. 3.18 (*b*) reveals that for a current i_f in the field winding *F*(*DS*), the speed voltage e_q generated across *q*-axis brushes is given by

$$e_q = M_d \omega_r i_f = K_{qf} i_f = \frac{K_{qf}}{r_f}\cdot\frac{v_f}{1 + \tau_f p} \qquad ...(3.72)$$

$$\therefore \quad Q\text{-axis armature current, } i_q = \frac{e_q}{r_q + L_q p} = \frac{e_q}{r_a + L_a p}$$

Here $\qquad r_d = r_q = r_a \quad \text{and} \quad L_d = L_q = L_a$

The magnitude of speed voltage e_d generated across *d*-axis brushes due to *q*-axis armature current i_q is,

$$e_d = L_a \omega_r i_q = K_{dq} i_q.$$

Substituting the value of i_q in the above expression, we get,

$$e_d = \frac{L_a M_d \omega_r^2}{r_a + L_a p} i_f = \frac{K_{dq} K_{qf}}{r_a + L_a p} i_f.$$

For a fully compensated metadyne, $\qquad e_f = (r_f + L_f p)\, i_f$

$$\therefore \quad \text{No-load } d\text{-axis output voltage is,} \quad e_d = \frac{K_{dq} K_{qf} . v_f}{r_f r_a (1 + \tau_a p)(1 + \tau_f p)} \qquad ...(3.73)$$

For a sudden application of voltage V_f across field winding, $v_f = V_f\, \mathbf{1}$.

$$\therefore \quad D\text{-axis output voltage is,} \quad e_d = \frac{K_{dq} K_{qf} V_f \mathbf{1}}{r_a r_f (1 + \tau_a p)(1 + \tau_f p)} \qquad ...(3.74)$$

Steady-state output voltage, from Eq. (3.73), is,

$$E_d = \frac{K_{dq}K_{qf}}{r_a r_f} V_f = AV_f$$

$\therefore$ No-load d-axis output voltage e_d, from Eq. (3.74), is,

$$e_d = \frac{AV_f \mathbf{1}}{(1+\tau_a p)(1+\tau_f p)} \qquad \text{...(3.75)}$$

Note that Eqs. (3.71) and (3.75) are identical.

Time solution of Eq. (3.75) is given by,

$$e_d(t) = AV_f \left[1 - \frac{\tau_a}{\tau_a - \tau_m} e^{-t/\tau_a} - \frac{\tau_f}{\tau_f - \tau_a} e^{-t/\tau_f}\right] \qquad \text{...(3.76)}$$

(*b*) Now voltage across load is,

$$v_d = v_L = i_L(R_L + L_L p)$$

Also $$v_d = v_L = e_d - i_L(r_c + r_a).$$

Note that for a fully compensated machine, inductance along d-axis is zero.

Substitution of the value of e_d, from Eq. (3.73), gives,

$$v_d = i_L(R_L + L_L p) = \frac{K_{dq}K_{qf}v_f}{r_a r_f(1+\tau_a p)(1+\tau_f p)} - (r_a + r_c)i_L$$

or $$i_L[R_L + r_a + r_c + L_L p] = \frac{K_{dq}K_{qf}v_f}{r_a r_f(1+\tau_a p)(1+\tau_f p)} \qquad \text{...(3.77)}$$

$$i_L = \frac{K_{dq}K_{qf}V_f \mathbf{1}}{r_a r_f R(1+\tau_a p)(1+\tau_f p)(1+\tau p)} \qquad \text{...(3.78)}$$

where $R = R_L + r_a + r_c$ and $\tau = \dfrac{L_L}{R}$.

From Eq. (3.78), i_L as a function of time can be obtained. Direct axis output terminal voltage is

$$v_d = v_L = (R_L + L_L p)\, i_L \qquad \text{...(3.79)}$$

Substituting the value of i_L from Eq. (3.78) in Eq. (3.79), v_L as a function of time can be obtained.

3.9 PARALLEL OPERATION OF D.C. GENERATORS

For a given installed capacity in a power station, either a single large unit or several small units may be installed. Though a single large unit involves less investment, yet it is preferable to have several small units in parallel. The advantages of using several small generators over the use of a single large unit are as follows:

(*a*) **Operating efficiency.** The load on a power station does not remain constant during the whole day. With several units in parallel, the number of generators operating at a time can be changed depending upon the power demand. In this manner, it is possible to operate the generators near their rated capacity. Since a generator operates most efficiently near its rated capacity, the use of several units in parallel has higher operating efficiency and, therefore, reduced operating cost. A single large unit will have to operate at a reduced level for certain periods of the day, consequently it has lower operating efficiency and, therefore, higher operating cost.

(*b*) **Maintenance.** Routine inspection of generators is essential to reduce the possibility of a sudden breakdown. For this purpose, a unit must be shut down and brought to rest, in the mean time the other machines can take care of the load. In case a generator does breakdown, it can be repaired carefully without any rush. This all is not possible with a single large unit. In addition to it, the cost of a standby unit, normally installed in power stations, is much less when several units are installed.

(*c*) **Continuity of service.** With several units at a station, a breakdown of one unit does not matter, because the continuity of service to the consumers can still be maintained though at a reduced level. The continuity of service and reliability of power supply has become so important these days that it is almost universal to install several units in parallel at a power station.

(*d*) **Future extensions.** At the time of designing a power station, provisions are usually made for installing the additional units for future extensions. In case the load demand exceeds the rated plant capacity, more machines can be installed.

In view of the above, it may be stated that as a rule, it is preferable to use several units in parallel than a single large unit at a power station.

In practice, d.c. generators are installed to work in parallel only when the load demands essentially a constant d.c. voltage. For example, for building up the worn-out parts to their original shape in case of expensive equipment, an uninterrupted and constant d.c. voltage is essential. This supply is usually taken from several d.c. generators running in-parallel. If power for electroplating is taken from an a.c. supply undertaking through rectifiers, then an inadvertent dip in the a.c. supply voltage would result in defective electroplating and the expensive equipment under treatment would have to be discarded, thus incurring a huge loss. Therefore, for the building up of worn-out parts to their original shape in case of expensive equipment, an uninterrupted and constant d.c. supply is always taken by operating several d.c. generators in parallel. In addition, d.c. motors are made to operate as d.c. generators in parallel in railway traction system for regenerative braking. This shows that study of parallel operation of d.c. generators is quite important.

The object of this article is to describe the process of connecting two d.c. machines in parallel and then to examine the problems of their load-sharing.

3.9.1 Parallel Operation of Shunt Generators

When several d.c. generators are working in parallel, then positive and negative terminals of all the generators are appropriately connected to two thick copper bars called *bus-bars*. In this part of the article, the method of connecting an incoming d.c. shunt generator with an already loaded generator is described first and then their load sharing is considered. Their operational behaviour, after they are put in parallel, is also examined.

(*a*) **Connections for parallel operation.** The conditions which must be observed at the time of connecting one d.c. generator with another already loaded generator (or generators) are as follows. For convenience, the already loaded generator is numbered 1, whereas the incoming machine is numbered 2.

(*i*) The terminal-polarity of incoming generator 2 must be the same as that of generator 1.

(*ii*) The e.m.f. generated by incoming generator 2 should be almost equal to the terminal voltage of already loaded generator 1.

Fig. 3.19 illustrates the circuit diagram for connecting the two shunt generators in parallel and for fulfilling the above two conditions. Generator 1 is assumed connected to the load and now generator 2 is to be put in parallel with the former. For this purpose, generator 2, with its switches S_2 and S_3 open, is brought upto its rated speed by the prime-mover. The field current of generator 2 is now adjusted so that its generated e.m.f. becomes equal to the terminal voltage of generator 1 – this equality in voltages can be checked by voltmeter V_1 through *DPDT* switch. Now close switch S_3 with S_2 remaining open ; if voltmeter V_2 across switch S_2 reads zero or a very low voltage, then the polarities are correct. In case voltmeter V_2 reads sum of the voltages of generators 1 and 2, the polarities are wrong–these can however be corrected by reversing the terminals of either generator 1 or generator 2. After ascertaining the proper polarities, switch S_3 is opened and S_2 is closed. Now when the generated e.m.f. of machine 2 is equal to the terminal voltage of generator 1, switch S_3 is closed and this connects the two generators in parallel. Since e.m.f. of generator 2 is equal to the terminal voltage of generator 1, generator 2 supplies no current to the load, under these conditions generator 2 is said to be *floating* on the d.c. busbars.

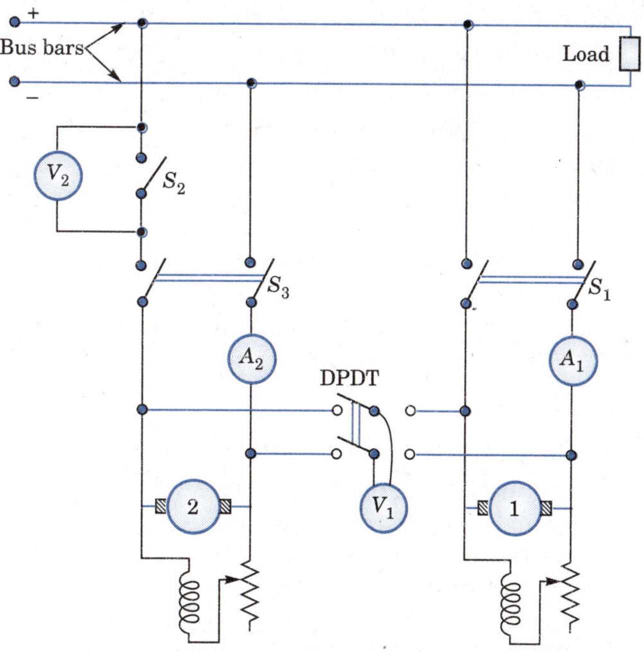

Fig. 3.19: Circuit diagram for connecting two shunt generators in parallel.

It is, however, preferable to have the e.m.f. of incoming generator 2, a few volts (2 to 3 volts) higher than the terminal voltage of generator 1. When this is done, generator 2 begins to supply some load-power as soon as it is switched on in parallel with generator 1. After this, the terminal voltage of machine 2 drops on account of armature reaction, $I_a r_a$ drop and reduction in its field current, so that terminal voltage of both the machines in parallel become equal.

In case generator 2 is floating as indicated by zero reading of ammeter 2, then it can be loaded by increasing either its field current or the driving torque of its prime-mover. Division of the load between the generators can be controlled more easily with the adjustment of field currents, this is, therefore, described here.

(*b*) **Load sharing.** Suppose generator 2 is floating on the line and that generator 1 is carrying the entire load current I_L. An increase in the excitation of generator 2 increases its generated e.m.f. E_a and its load current $\left(= \dfrac{E_a - V_t}{r_a}\right)$ is increased from zero to say I_{L_2} (field current ignored). As a result of it, the speed of prime-mover of generator 2 drops depending upon its speed-load characteristics. The load current of generator 1 becomes $I_{L_1} = I_L - I_{L_2}$. The effect of increasing excitation of generator 2 may also increase the d.c. bus voltage. This voltage can however brought down to its original value merely by decreasing the field current of generator 1–this has the effect of increasing the load on generator 2 to I_{L2}' and of decreasing the load on generator 1 to I_{L_1}' so that $I_{L_1}' + I_{L_2}' = I_L$. The physical concepts pertaining to the load division between two d.c. shunt generators can be understood better by referring to Fig. 3.20.

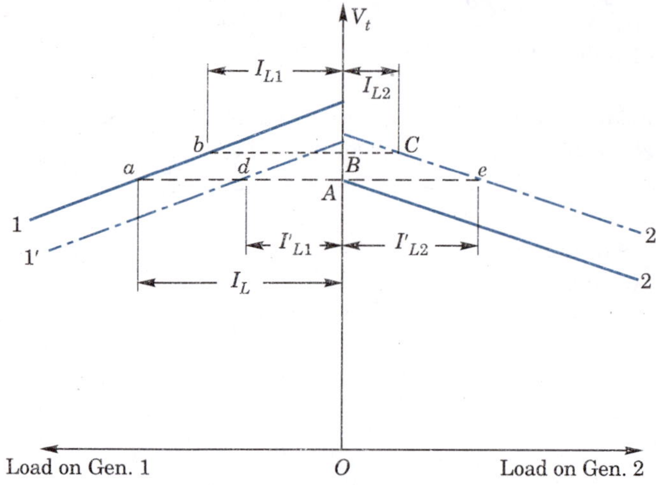

Fig. 3.20: Pertaining to the load division between two d.c. shunt generators.

In Fig. 3.20, *OA* is their common terminal voltage, generator 2 is floating and generator 1 is sharing a total of $Aa = I_L$ so that its operating point is *a*. Now field current of machine 2 is increased so that its $V_t - I_L$ characteristic* is shifted upward to 2′. The load carried by machine 1 is now $Bb = I_{L_1}$ and that carried by machine 2 is $Bc = I_{L_2}$ so that $I_{L_1} + I_{L_2} = I_L$, but now terminal voltage is seen to increase from *OA* to *OB*. In order to keep the d.c. bus-bar voltage constant, decrease the field current of generator 1 suitably so that its $V_t - I_L$ characteristic shifts to 1′. Now the load shared by machine 1 is $Ad = I_{L_1}'$ and that by machine 2 is $Ae = I_{L_2}'$ so that $I_{L_1}' + I_{L_2}' = I_L$ and terminal voltage is *OA* as before.

It may be concluded from above that if load is to be increased on a generator, its field current should be increased ; if load is to be reduced, its field current should be decreased.

(*c*) **Operation.** After the two d.c. shunt generators are put in parallel, the effect of their $V_t - I_L$ characteristics on their operational behaviour is now examined.

Suppose that the two d.c. shunt generators have their same no-load terminal voltage as shown in Fig. 3.21 (*a*). The generator 1 is assumed to have more drooping $V_t - I_L$ characteristic as compared to generator 2.

When the two generators are loaded, their terminal voltages must be equal. For a terminal voltage V_{t_1}, the load on generator 1 is I_{L_1} and that on generator 2 is $I_{L_2} > I_{L_1}$. Their total output current is $I_{L_1} + I_{L_2}$. It is seen from Fig. 3.21 (*a*) that a generator, with more drooping $V_t - I_L$ characteristic, shares less load. Thus two generators of equal ratings can share the load current equally only when their $V_t - I_L$ characteristics are identical.

Sometimes, the two d.c. shunt generators running in parallel may have their open-circuit voltages unequal. For understanding their working, refer to Fig. 3.21 (*b*) where $V_t - I_L$

*The effect of increasing field current of a generator is to increase its E_a and, therefore, the terminal voltage V_t for the same load current I_L. In short, $V_t - I_L$ characteristic of a d.c. generator is shifted upward if its field current is increased.

characteristics of generators 1 and 2 are shown. The total $V_t - I_L$ characteristic is obtained by adding their corresponding abscissa of the two characteristics. When the total load current is zero, their common terminal voltage is OA. The machine 1 works as a generator with power output of $OA \times AC$; whereas machine 2 works as a motor and receives power input of $OA \times AB = OA \times AC$. The machine 2 will continue to work as a motor till the total load current is OD and the common terminal voltage is OF. For the load current OD, generator 1 shares the entire load current OD, whereas machine 2 just floats. As the total load is increased, machine 2 shares less load than machine 1 till the load OE is reached. Beyond load OE, machine 2 shares load greater than that shared by machine 1. If there is any decrease or increase in the load, each generator must take its own share proportionally.

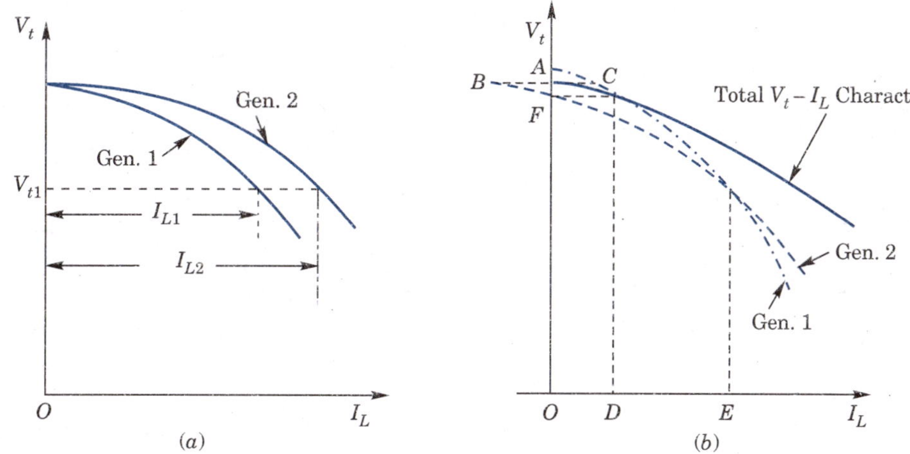

Fig. 3.21: Two dc shunt generators in parallel with (a) drooping $V_t - I_L$ characteristics and (b) open-circuit voltages unequal.

If a generator is to be taken out of service, it should not be switched off while it is sharing a load. It is because a sudden disconnection of the load would cause a heavy sparking at the switching contacts and a sudden transfer of the entire load on to the other machine and this all is objectionable.

Suppose generator 1 is to be taken out of service. For doing so, its excitation is decreased while that of generator 2 is increased till the entire load is transferred to generator 2 as indicated by zero reading of ammeter A_1 in Fig. 3.19. Now the main switch S_1 of generator 1 is opened and the set is brought to rest.

3.9.2 Parallel Operation of Compound Generators

For parallel operation, the compound generators are usually cumulatively compounded so that their terminal voltage remains fairly constant with the variation in load. These generators may be over-compounded which possess rising $V_t - I_L$ characteristics. But the parallel operation of over-compounded generators is not possible without the use of a special connection, called *equalizer*.

In order to illustrate the importance of using an equalizer, suppose that two compound generators are connected in parallel without an equalizer in Fig. 3.22. Now let us assume that e.m.f. of generator 1 goes up due to an increase in its speed or due to an increase in shunt field current. The effect of increase in its e.m.f. causes an increase in the armature current of generator 1. Since most of the armature current passes through the series field winding, this increase in armature current causes the production of more series field flux which aids the shunt field flux. As a result of it, total flux is increased and e.m.f. generated in machine 1 goes up further. This, in turn, increases armature current and, therefore, the series field flux and generated e.m.f. of machine increases still further. This cummulative process causes machine 1 to take more and more share of the load, whereas generator 2 is getting relieved of the load accordingly. Finally the generator 1 carries not only the entire load, but may attempt to drive the machine 2 as a motor.

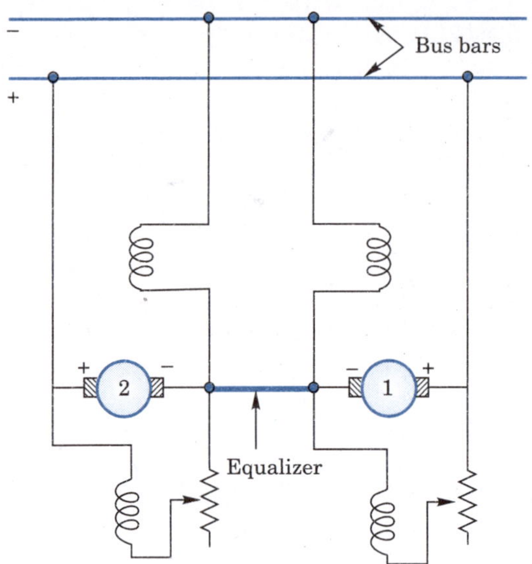

Fig. 3.22: Parallel operation of two compound generators.

Such unstable operation can be avoided by the use of an equalizer. An equalizer is a very low-resistance copper wire, which connects identical terminals having the same polarity as illustrated in Fig. 3.22. This figure reveals that the series field windings of both (or all) the machines get connected in parallel, at one end through the equalizer and at the other end through the main bus. If armature current of one machine increases due to some reason or the other, then this current divides in the parallel-connected series-field windings in a ratio inversely proportional to their resistances. In view of this, the series field excitations of both (or all) the machines increase accordingly. Thus, a change in the load current of one generator effects the series field excitations of all the parallel-connected generators and the cummulative effect leading to instability as described above, is avoided. Note that if the compound generators have drooping $V_t - I_L$ (or external) characteristics, as in differentially compounded generators, no equalizer is required. It is only in over-compounded generators, having rising $V_t - I_L$, or external, characteristics that an equalizer is essential.

If compound generator 1 is already loaded, then machine 2 can be connected in parallel with machine 1 by adopting the method as used for d.c. shunt generators. Load shared by the machines can be controlled by adjusting their shunt-field excitations as done for d.c. shunt machines. Before the two compound generators are connected in parallel, it should be ensured that both the machines are connected properly for over-compounded operation. This can be checked by loading each generator separately. As soon as the incoming compound generator 2 is switched on in parallel with already loaded compound generator 1, then armature current of machine 1 also starts flowing through the series field of machine 2 *via* the equalizer. This has the effect of increasing total flux of machine 2, its generated e.m.f. and, therefore, its armature current does not remain zero, *i.e.* incoming generator 2 can't float. This shows that though the e.m.f. of incoming generator 2 is made equal to the voltage of generator 1 or bus bar ; even then, the machine 2 starts sharing the load as soon as it is put in parallel with machine 1.

If compound generators are fitted with compoles, then the equalizer is connected to the junctions of series field and compole windings as shown in Fig. 3.23 (*a*), so that compole winding carries the entire armature current.

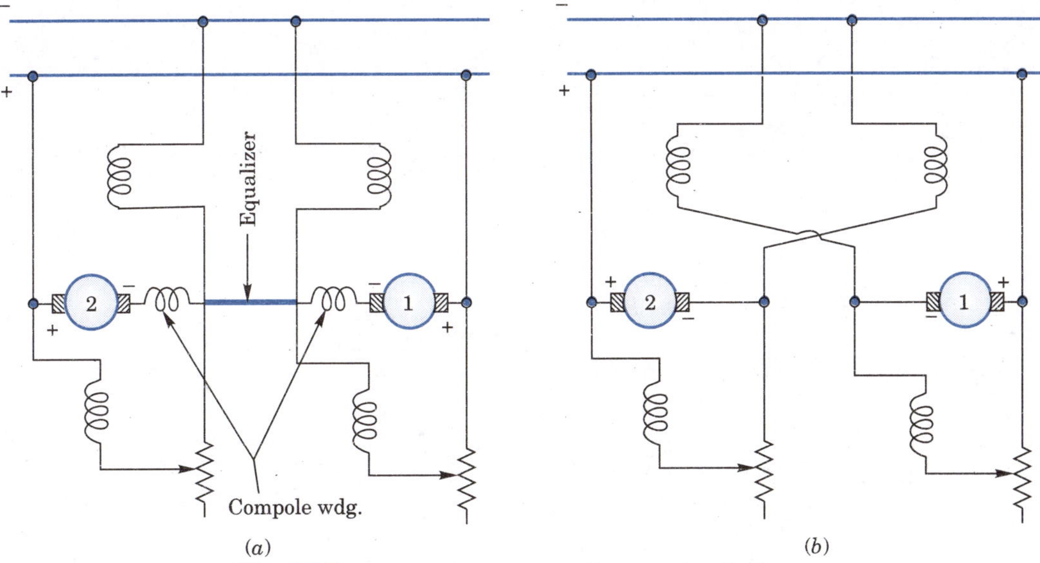

Fig. 3.23: (*a*) Use of equalizer with compole windings.
(*b*) Cross-connection of series windings to avoid the use of equalizer.

If the two compound generators are identical, then cross-connection of the series windings, as shown in Fig. 3.23 (*b*), avoids automatically the unstable operation and equalizer is, therefore, not required. For example, if machine 1 gives excessive output current, then series field ATs strengthen the field of machine 2, whereas field of machine 1 is weakened due to more armature reaction, thus avoiding the conditions which lead to instability.

For satisfactory operation of two compound generators,

(*i*) the resistance of the equalizer should be very small as compared to that of the series-field windings ; and

(*ii*) the series field resistance should be inversely proportional to their ratings.

In case the two compound generators are not identical, these can be successfully operated in parallel by fulfilling the above two conditions. The first condition requires an appropriate low-resistance in series with the series field windings. The second condition, however, requires a diverter across the series field winding. The use of low-resistance and diverter is illustrated in Example 3.19.

Example 3.14. *Two d.c. shunt generators, operating in parallel, share a load current of 200 A. Each generator has an armature resistance of 0.10 Ω and a field resistance of 100 Ω. Their no-load generated e.m.fs. are 250 and 245 volts. Calculate the bus-bar voltage and the power output of each machine.*

Solution. Let the generators 1 and 2 supply load currents of I_{L_1} and I_{L_2} respectively at a common bus voltage V_b.

$$\therefore \qquad I_{L_1} + I_{L_2} = 200 \text{ A}.$$

Subscripts 1 and 2 are used for generators 1 and 2 respectively.

$$\text{Shunt field current for both generators} = \frac{V_b}{100}$$

For generator 1, armature current, $I_{a_1} = I_{L_1} + \dfrac{V_b}{100}$

For generator 2, armature current, $I_{a_2} = I_{L_2} + \dfrac{V_b}{100}$

For generator 1, $E_{a_1} = V_b + I_{a_1} r_a$

or $$250 = V_b + \left(I_{L_1} + \frac{V_b}{100}\right) \times 0.10 \qquad ...(i)$$

Similarly for generator 2, $245 = V_b + \left(I_{L_2} + \dfrac{V_b}{100}\right) \times 0.10$ ...(ii)

Subtraction of Eq. (*ii*) from Eq. (*i*) gives $5 = 0.10\,(I_{L_1} - I_{L_2})$

$\therefore$ $I_{L_1} - I_{L_2} = 50$ But $I_{L_1} + I_{L_2} = 200$

Solution of these two equations give $I_{L_1} = 125$ A and $I_{L_2} = 75$ A

But voltage $V_b = E_{a_1} - I_{a_1} r_a = 250 - \left(125 + \dfrac{V_b}{100}\right)(0.10)$.

Its solution gives $V_b = 237.263$ volts.

Power output of machine 1 $= V_b I_{L_1} = 237.263 \times 125 \times \dfrac{1}{1000} = 29.66$ kW.

Power output of machine 2 $= 237.263 \times 75 \times \dfrac{1}{1000} = 17.795$ kW.

Example 3.15. *Two d.c. shunt generators, connected in parallel, supply a total load of 800 A. The machines have armature resistances of 0.06 Ω and 0.04 Ω, field resistances of 30 Ω and 25 Ω and give no-load e.m.fs. of 440 V and 420 V respectively. Determine the current and power output of each machine.*

Solution. Subscripts 1 and 2 are used for generators 1 and 2 respectively. Let V_b be their common bus voltage.

Total output current, $I_{L_1} + I_{L_2} = 800$ A

For generator 1, $E_{a_1} = V_b + (I_{a_1})\, r_{a_1}$

$$\therefore \quad 440 = V_b + \left(I_{L_1} + \frac{V_b}{30}\right) \times 0.06$$

or $$440 = \frac{501}{500} V_b + 0.06 I_{L_1} \qquad ...(i)$$

For generator 2, $420 = V_b + \left(I_{L_2} + \dfrac{V_b}{25}\right) \times 0.04 = \dfrac{626}{625} V_b + 0.04 I_{L_2}$

But $I_{L_2} = 800 - I_{L_1}$

$$\therefore \quad 420 = \frac{626}{625} V_b + 0.04\,(800 - I_{L_1}) = \frac{626}{625} V_b + 32 - 0.04 I_{L_1}$$

or $$388 = \frac{626}{625} V_b - 0.04 I_{L_1} \qquad ...(ii)$$

Multiplying Eq. (*i*) by 2 and Eq. (*ii*) by 3, we get

$$880 = \frac{501}{250} V_b + 0.12 I_{L_1} = 2.004 V_b + 0.12 I_{L_1}$$

and

$$1164 = 3 \times \frac{626}{625} V_b - 0.12 I_{L_1} = 3.005 V_b - 0.12 I_{L_1}$$

Addition of above two equations gives

$$V_b = \frac{2044}{5.009} = 408.07 \text{ V}$$

Substituting the value of $V_b = 408.07$ V in Eq. (*i*) gives I_{L_1}

$$\therefore \quad 440 = 408.07 \times \frac{501}{500} + 0.06 I_{L_1}$$

or $\quad I_{L_1} = 518.5$ A $\quad$ and $\quad I_{L_2} = 800 - 518.5 = 281.5$ A

$\therefore$ Output of machine 1 $= V_b I_{L_1} = 408.07 \times 518.5$ watts = 211.5843 kW.

Output of machine 2 $= 408.07 \times 281.5$ watts = 114.8717 kW.

Example 3.16. *Two d.c. generators, operating in parallel, supply a total output current of 120 A. The terminal voltage of one machine falls from 250 V at no-load to 230 V at an output current of 70 A. The terminal voltage of second machine is 260 V at no load and 220 V at an output current of 90 A. Their external characteristics are linear.*

(a) Find the current output of each machine.

(b) Find the line voltage and total load in kW when one generator is floating.

Solution. (*a*) For an output current of 70 A, the voltage drop is 250 – 230 = 20 V. Therefore the voltage drop per output ampere is $\frac{20}{70}$ V/amp. If this generator shares a load current I_{L_1}, then its voltage drop is $\frac{2}{7} \times I_{L_1}$ volts.

$$\therefore \quad E_{a_1} = \text{common line votage, } V_t + \frac{2}{7} I_{L_1}$$

or

$$250 = V_t + \frac{2}{7} I_{L_1} \quad \text{...(i)}$$

Similarly, for generator 2,

$$E_{a_2} = V_t + \frac{260 - 220}{90} I_{L_2}$$

or

$$260 = V_t + \frac{4}{9} I_{L_2} \quad \text{...(ii)}$$

Substraction of Eq. (*i*) from Eq. (*ii*) gives

$$10 = \frac{4}{9} I_{L_2} - \frac{2}{7} I_{L_1} \qquad \text{But} \qquad I_{L_1} + I_{L_2} = 120 \text{ A}$$

$$\therefore \quad 10 = \frac{4}{9}(120 - I_{L_1}) - \frac{2}{7} I_{L_1}$$

Its solution gives, $I_{L_1} = 59.35$ A.

$$\therefore \quad I_{L_2} = 120 - 59.35 = 60.65 \text{ A.}$$

From Eq. (*i*), their common line voltage is, $V_t = 250 - \frac{2}{7} \times 59.35 = 233.04$ V.

(*b*) When generator 1 is floating, the line voltage is 250 V. Note that the generator with lower no-load e.m.f. can only float.

Since the no-load e.m.f. of generator 2 is 260 V, a line voltage of 250 V corresponds to voltage drop of 10 volts in its armature.

But the voltage drop for this generator is $\frac{4}{9}$ V/amp.

$$\therefore \text{ Load carried by generator 2 } = \frac{9}{4} \times 10 = 22.5 \text{ A.}$$

$$\text{Power delivered to load } = 22.5 \times 250 \times \frac{1}{1000} = 5.625 \text{ kW.}$$

Example 3.17. *Two d.c. shunt generators, each with an armature resistance of 0.05 Ω, have no-load e.m.fs. of 250 and 245 V, field resistances of 50 and 40 Ω respectively. They are in parallel and supply a total load of 60 kW. How do they share the total load ?*

Solution. Subscipts 1 and 2 are used for generators 1 and 2 respectively.

For generator 1, $$E_{a_1} = V_t + \left(I_{L_1} + \frac{V_t}{50}\right)(0.05)$$

or $$250 = V_t + (I_{L_1} + 0.02V_t)(0.05) \quad ...(i)$$

For generator 2, $$E_{a_2} = V_t + \left(I_{L_2} + \frac{V_t}{40}\right)(0.05)$$

or $$245 = V_t + (I_{L_2} + 0.025V_t)(0.05) \quad ...(ii)$$

Addition of Eqs. (*i*) and (*ii*) gives,

$$495 = 2.00225V_t + 0.05\,(I_{L_1} + I_{L_2})$$

But $$(I_{L_1} + I_{L_2}) = \frac{60{,}000}{V_t}$$

$$\therefore \quad 495 = 2.00225V_t + 0.05\left(\frac{60{,}000}{V_t}\right)$$

or $$2.00225V_t^2 - 495V_t + 3000 = 0$$

Its solution gives $V_t = 241.0$ volts

From Eq. (*i*), $$250 = 241.0 + (I_{L_1} + 0.02 \times 241.0) \times 0.05$$

$$\therefore \quad I_{L_1} = \frac{8.759}{0.05} = 175.18 \text{ A}$$

and $$I_{L_2} = \frac{60{,}000}{241.0} - 175.18 = 73.78 \text{ A}$$

$$\text{Output of machine 1} = V_t I_{L_1} = 241.0 \times 175.18 \times \frac{1}{1000}$$
$$= 42.22 \text{ kW.}$$

$$\text{Output of machine 2} = 241.0 \times 73.78 \times 10^{-3} = 17.78 \text{ kW.}$$

Example 3.18. *Two d.c. generators have the following external characteristics :*

Output current, in A		*0*	*20*	*40*	*50*	*60*	*70*	*80*
Terminal voltage, in V	*M/C 1*	*226*	*224.3*	*221.7*	*220.1*	*218.1*	*215.1*	
	M/C 2	*222*	*221.1*	*219.7*	*218.7*	*217.6*	*216.1*	*214.1*

Find the current shared by each machine and their common terminal voltage, when, in parallel, they supply

(a) a total load of 150 A *(b) a load of resistance 2 Ω.*

Solution. First of all, the external characteristics of machines 1 and 2 are plotted. Then their total characteristic, obtained by adding output currents of both the machines for the same terminal voltage, is also plotted on the same graph paper as shown in Fig. 3.24.

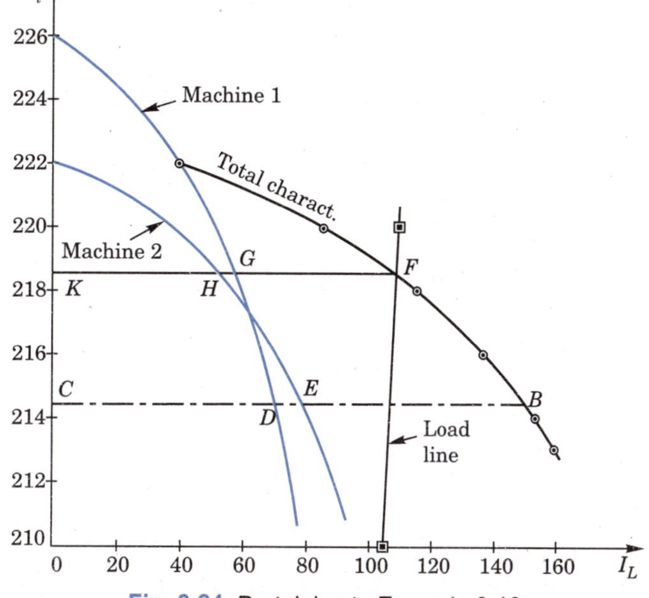

Fig. 3.24: Pertaining to Example 3.18.

(*a*) At 150 A along *x*-axis, a vertical line is drawn meeting the total characteristic at *B*. Now a horizontal line *BC* is drawn as shown in the figure. Then *CD* = 72 A is the current shared by machine 1 and *CE* = 78.5 A is that shared by machine 2. The intercept of *C* gives the common terminal voltage as 214.4 V.

(*b*) The load line pertaining to 2 Ω is drawn as follows :

Load current – 105 A, 110 A

Load voltage – 210 V, 220 V.

These two points are plotted and a line joining them gives the required load line, which intersects the total characteristic at *F*. A horizontal line through *F* meets machine characteristics at points *G*, *H* and the vertical axis at *K*. Then, *KG* = 58.5 A is the current shared by machine 1 and *KH* = 52.5 A is that shared by machine 2. Total output current is *KF* = 109.2 A. Their common terminal voltage, given by the point *K*, is 218.45 V.

Example 3.19. *Two over-compounded short-shunt generators have the following data:*

	Series	*Shunt*	*Rated current*
	(Ω)	(Ω)	(A)
Machine 1	*0.20*	*100*	*120*
Machine 2	*0.10*	*70*	*180*

For machine 1, the output terminal voltage is 230 V for a load current of 120 A.

For machine 2, the output terminal voltages are 230 V and 235 V for load currents of 140 A and 180 A respectively.

It is required that two compound generators, though not identical, should deliver their rated currents to a 230 V bus. This can be achieved by putting resistances r_1 and r_2 as shown in Fig. 3.25.

Determine (a) shunt field currents of both the machines and (b) the values of r_1 and r_2.

Solution. (*a*) For machine 1, the voltage E_1 across the armature terminals at full load is

$$E_1 = 230 + (\text{full load drop in series field resistance})$$

$$= 230 + 120 \times 0.20 = 254 \text{ volts.}$$

∴ Shunt field current of machine 1,

$$I_{f_1} = \frac{E_1}{100} = \frac{254}{100} = 2.54 \text{ A}$$

Since the equalizer connects the two armature in parallel, E_1 must be equal to the voltage E_2 across the armature terminals of machine 2.

$$\therefore \quad E_1 = E_2 = 254 \text{ V}$$

∴ Shunt field current of machine 2 is given by,

$$I_{f_2} = \frac{E_2}{70} = \frac{254}{70} = 3.6286 \text{ A.}$$

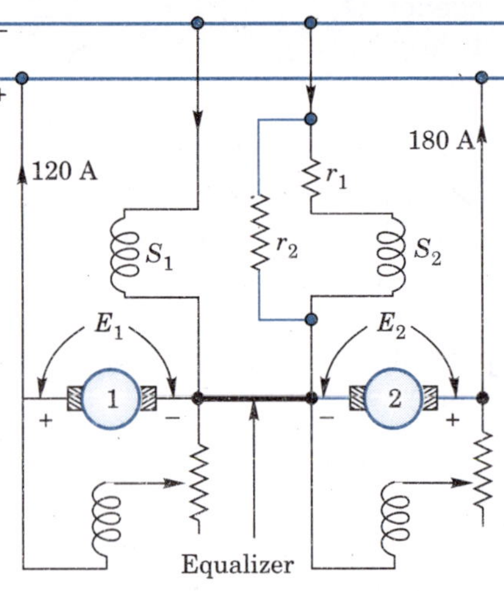

Fig. 3.25: Pertaining to Example 3.19.

(*b*) When machine 1 delivers its rated current of 120 A to the 230 V bus, its voltage across the armature terminals is $E_1 = 254$ V.

Load characteristic of machine 2 reveals that for a bus voltage of 230 V, its output current is 140 A only. For this load current, the voltage E_2 across the armature terminals of machine 2 is

$$E_2 = 230 + 0.10 \times 140 = 244 \text{ V.}$$

But with the use of an equalizer, E_2 must be equal to $E_1 = 254$ volts. In view of this, a voltage drop of 254 – 244 = 10 volts must be allowed to occur across resistance r_1 for a current of 140 A.

$$\therefore \quad r_1 = \frac{10.0}{140} = 0.07143 \ \Omega.$$

Now in the parallel combination of r_2 with r_1 and s_2, the resistance values of r_1 and s_2 are fixed. The value of resistances r_2 should be so chosen that 180 – 140 = 40 A should flow through r_2 when machine 2 is delivering its full-load current of 180 A to the 230 V bus.

Now voltage across r_2 = voltage across $(r_1 + s_2)$

$$= (0.07143 + 0.10) \times 140$$

$$\therefore \quad r_2 = \frac{0.17143 \times 140}{40} = 0.60 \ \Omega.$$

3.10 ELECTRIC BRAKING OF D.C. MOTORS

Electric braking of motors in modern electric drives is becoming increasingly important. With electric braking, the motors can be rapidly brought to rest, or their deceleration can be controlled most effectively as when lowering a load by means of a crane or a hoist. In a planning machine, soon after its stroke is over, the motor should be quickly stopped (by electic braking) so as to get a high rate of production.

There are three important methods for electric braking of d.c. motors ; namely, regenerative braking, counter-current braking (or plugging) and dynamic braking. The object of this article is to describe these three methods of braking and to examine the speed-torque characteristics of d.c. motors as affected by the method of braking employed.

3.10.1 Regenerative Braking

Regenerative braking takes place when the load forces the motor to run at a speed higher than its no-load speed with a constant excitation. Under this condition, the motor counter e.m.f. E_a ($\propto \omega_r \phi$) exceeds the supply voltage, which reverses the direction of motor armature current and electric braking takes place. During regenerative braking, the motor operates as a generator in parallel with the d.c. supply. As the armature current is reversed, the electric energy is returned to the supply circuit.

(*a*) Shunt motors. In d.c. shunt motors, regenerative braking takes place in the simplest manner.

Under normal conditions of motor operation as shown in Fig. 3.26 (*a*), the armature current is given by $I_a = \dfrac{V_t - E_a}{r_a}$

When the load (such as lowering of load by a crane or a hoist) causes the motor speed to be greater than its no-load speed, then counter e.m.f. E_a exceeds V_t. As a result of it, armature current I_a becomes negative and the torque developed by the machine changes sign, *i.e.*, the machine now begins to operate as a generator as shown in Fig. 3.26 (*b*). Under these conditions, the energy is returned to the supply and electric braking results.

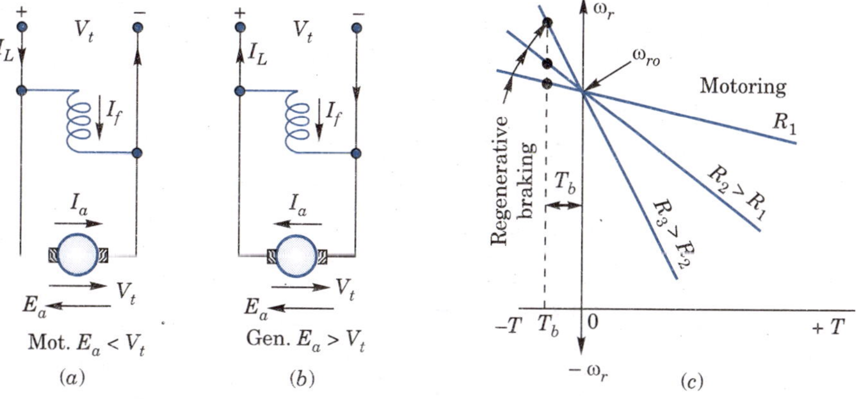

Fig. 3.26: (*a*) and (*b*) Pertaining to the regenerative braking of a d.c. shunt motor, (*c*) Speed-torque characteristics of a d.c. shunt motor during regenerative braking.

Under motor-mode operation, the speed is given by,

$$\omega_r = \frac{V_t - I_a R}{k\phi} = \frac{V_t - I_a R}{K_m}$$

where R is the total armature circuit resistance.

But electromagnetic torque,

$$T_e = k\,\phi\, I_a = K_m\, I_a$$

$$\therefore \qquad \omega_r = \frac{V_t}{K_m} - \frac{T_e R}{K_m^2}$$

$$= \omega_{ro} - \frac{T_e R}{K_m^2} \qquad \text{...(3.80)}$$

Under regenerative braking, I_a is reversed, therefore, braking torque T_b is given by

$$T_b = -\,k\phi I_a = -\,K_m I_a.$$

The speed during regenerative braking is

$$\omega_r = \frac{V_t}{K_m} - \frac{R}{K_m}\left(-\frac{T_b}{K_m}\right) = \omega_{ro} + \frac{T_b R}{K_m^2} \qquad \text{...(3.81)}$$

When braking torque $T_b = 0$, $\omega_r = \omega_{ro}$ and therefore the speed-torque characteristic passes through the point corresponding to the no-load speed $\omega_{ro} = V_t/K_m$ as shown in Fig. 3.26 (*c*). Second term of Eqs. (3.80) and (3.81), *i.e.*, $\frac{R}{K_m^2}$ determines the slope of speed-torque curve. This shows that slope of the speed-torque characteristic during motoring and braking conditions is the same as determined by the total armature circuit resistance R. Thus, the speed-torque characteristic during regenerative braking is merely an extension of the motor characteristic into the second quadrant as shown in Fig. 3.26 (*c*). An examination of this figure reveals that for given braking torque T_b, greater the armature circuit resistance, greater must be the speed for getting the regenerative braking action.

This method of braking can't be used for stopping the motor. As electric energy is returned to the supply, regenerative braking is quite economical. It is employed only for controlling the motor speeds above no-load speed ω_{ro}, when the loads are lowered as in cranes, hoists, lifts etc.

(*b*) Series motors. For d.c. series motors, regenerative braking with a single motor can't be accomplished, because its counter e.m.f. can't exceed the supply voltage. However, if required, the braking can be obtained by connecting the series field in parallel with its armature to get shunt connection. In traction motors, regenerative braking of a group of series motors is quite common, though with suitable modifications.

3.10.2 Counter-current Braking (or Plugging)

There are two methods for braking of d.c. motors by plugging. One method pertains to the lowering of loads as in cranes, hoists etc. and by this method, speeds can't be brought down to zero but can be controlled during their downward journey. This method will not be descussed here.

In the second method, braking of d.c. motors by plugging is achieved by reversing polarity of the voltage applied to the motor armature, but the direction of field current is not reversed. This method is described here in detail.

(a) Shunt motors. Fig. 3.27 (*a*) illustrates the d.c. shunt motor operation. When polarity of the voltage applied to motor armature is reversed as shown in Fig. 3.27 (*b*), braking action by counter-current braking comes into play. It may be seen from Fig. 3.27 (*b*), that with sudden reversal of armature terminal voltage V_t, the total voltage in the armature circuit at once increases to $V_t + E_a$ and there is, therefore, a sudden inrush of armature current. This inrush can, however, be limited by placing an external resistance R_e (usually the starting resistance) in series with armature circuit as shown. The voltage equation for armature circuit, just after plugging, is

$$-V_t = E_a + I_a (r_a + R_e)$$

$$\therefore \qquad I_a = -\frac{V_t + E_a}{r_a + R_e}$$

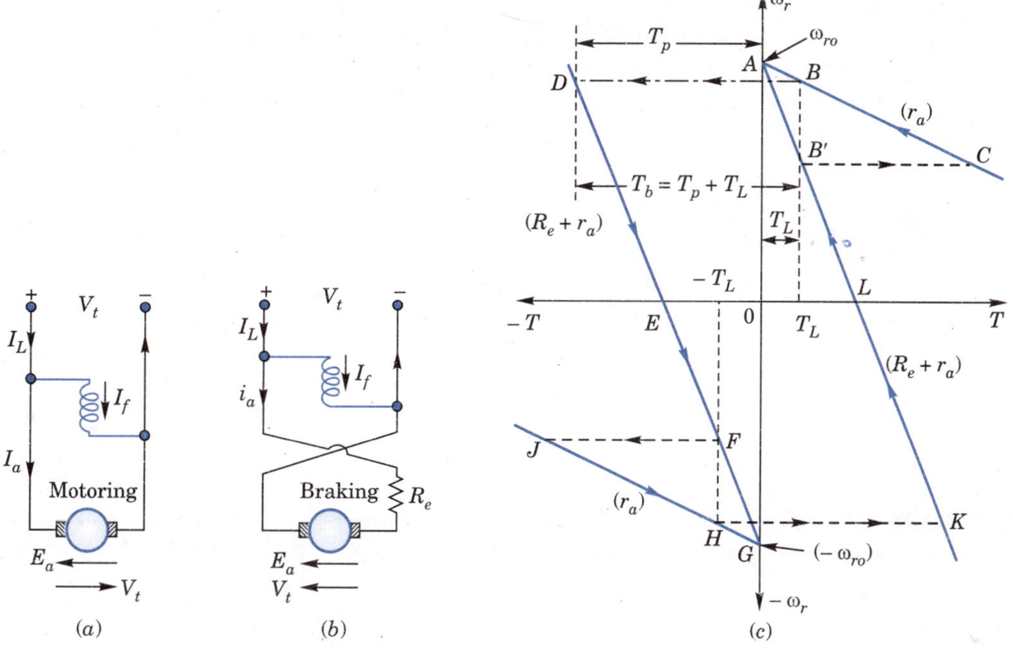

Fig. 3.27: (*a*) and (*b*) Plugging with d.c. shunt motor, (*c*) Speed-torque characteristics of d.c. shunt motor during plugging.

Since the sign of armature current is reversed, with the direction of field current remaining unchanged, the torque developed by the motor is reversed and braking action takes place.

The plugging torque T_p, just after the reversal of armature current, is

$$T_p = k\,\phi\,I_a = K_m\,I_a = -K_m \frac{V_t + E_a}{r_a + R_e} \qquad \text{...(3.82)}$$

Total braking torque T_b, at the instant of plugging, is given by $T_b = T_p + T_L$; this is shown as $DB = T_b$ in Fig. 3.27 (*c*). Here T_L is the load torque at the time of plugging.

For motor operation, the natural speed-torque characteristic is *AC* with no external resistance in the armature circuit. With external resistance R_e in series with armature circuit, the speed-torque characteristic for motor is *ALK*. Line *DEG* is drawn parallel to *ALK* and *GJ* is parallel to AC. Here $OA = \omega_{ro}$ and $OG = -\omega_{ro}$. This means that G would be the operating point if this machine were operated as a motor at no-load in the reversed direction.

For a load torque T_L, B is the operating point in the first quadrant. With the reversal of voltage applied to the armature terminals, the operating point shifts from point B to point D in second quadrant, with the speed remaining the same due to inertia of the rotating parts. Note that external resistance R_e is inserted in series with armature circuit, as soon as polarity of voltage across armature terminals is reversed. The braking torque now slows down the motor according to the speed-torque characteristic DE (parallel to AL) until the motor stops.

As soon as the motor stops as indicated by point E, the supply should be switched off. In case the supply is not disconnected, the motor would begin to rotate in the reversed direction corresponding to point F in third quadrant. It should be noted that as the speed gets reversed in the third quadrant, generated e.m.f. E_a in the armature is also reversed in polarity. Thus E_a in third quadrant acts against the applied voltage V_t and the machine therefore operates as a d.c. motor. This motoring mode in the third quadrant is usually referred to as the *reverse motoring*. If R_e is now cut out from the armature circuit, operating point shifts from F to J and finally to H as shown. Note that GJ in Fig. 3.27 (c) is parallel to the natural speed-torque characteristic AC.

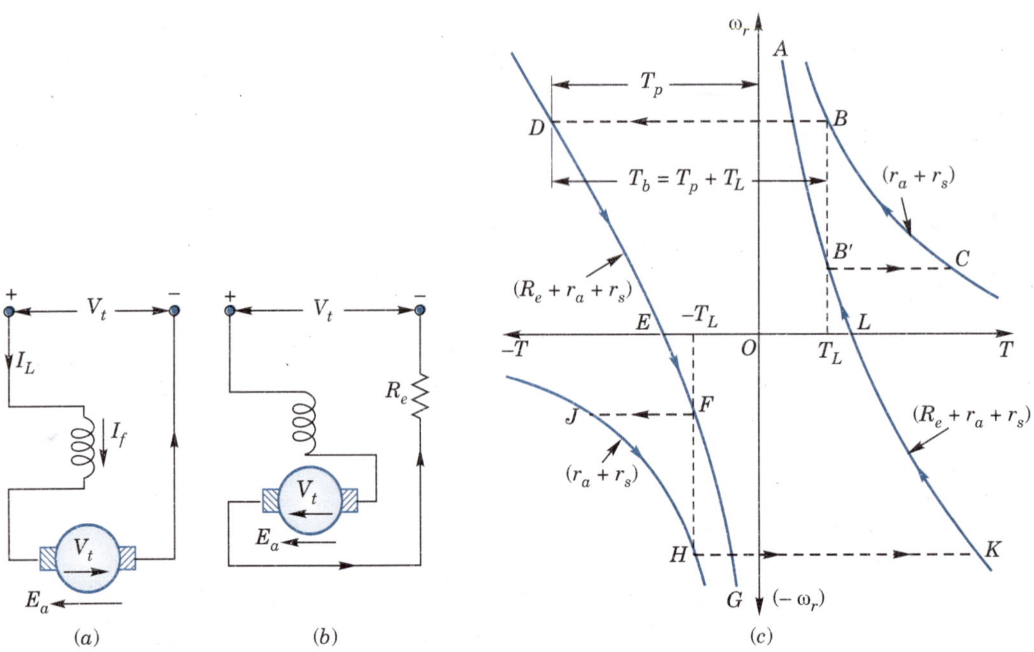

Fig. 3.28: (*a*) and (*b*) Plugging of d.c. series motor, (*c*) Speed torque characteristics of a d.c. series motor during plugging.

With the operating point in the third quadrant, if the voltage applied to the armature terminals is again reversed and R_e is inserted at the same time, the operating point H shifts to point K in fourth quadrant. Braking action by plugging now takes place along KL and B' is final operating point in first quadrant, in case d.c. supply is not switched off for stopping the motor at L. If R_e is now cut out from the armature circuit, the operating point shifts from B' to C and then to B as shown in Fig. 3.27 (c).

(*b*) Series motors. For d.c. series motors, electric braking by plugging is carried out by reversing polarity of the voltage applied to the armature, but with the series-field current-direction remaining unchanged as shown in Fig. 3.28 (*b*). In Fig. 3.28 (*c*), *BC* is the natural speed-torque characteristic, whereas *AB′L* is the speed-torque curve with external resistance R_e in series with armature circuit. For load torque T_L, *B* is the operating point. When polarity of the voltage across armature is reversed with field circuit remaining unchanged, braking torque is developed and the operating point shifts from *B* to *D* in the second quadrant. Note that external resistance R_e is inserted in series with armature circuit, as soon as polarity of voltage across armature terminals is reversed. The motor speed now begins to drop along the speed-torque curve *DE* till the motor stops at *E*. Further explanation is similar to that given for Fig. 3.27 (*c*).

3.10.3 Dynamic Braking

With this method of electric braking, motor armature is first disconnected from the supply circuit and then, it is switched across a resistor with field circuit left unchanged. This method is also called *rheostatic braking* method because of connecting an external resistance across the armature for electric braking.

(*a*) Shunt motors. Fig. 3.29 (*a*) shows the normal operation of a d.c. shunt motor. In order to obtain its dynamic braking, the armature is disconnected from the supply circuit and is then connected across external resistance R_e. The field winding remains connected to the supply as before, this is illustrated in Fig. 3.29 (*b*). As field flux and direction of rotation are the same as before, the counter e.m.f. in Fig. 3.29 (*b*) retains the same polarity as it is during the motor-mode operation. Since V_t reduces to zero, the armature current during dynamic braking is

$$I_a = -\frac{E_a}{R_e + r_a} = -\frac{E_a}{R}.$$

Since field flux ϕ is in the same direction as before and armature current I_a has reversed, the torque gets reversed–the motor begins to operate as a generator and the electric braking takes place. The kinetic energy stored in the rotating parts of the motor

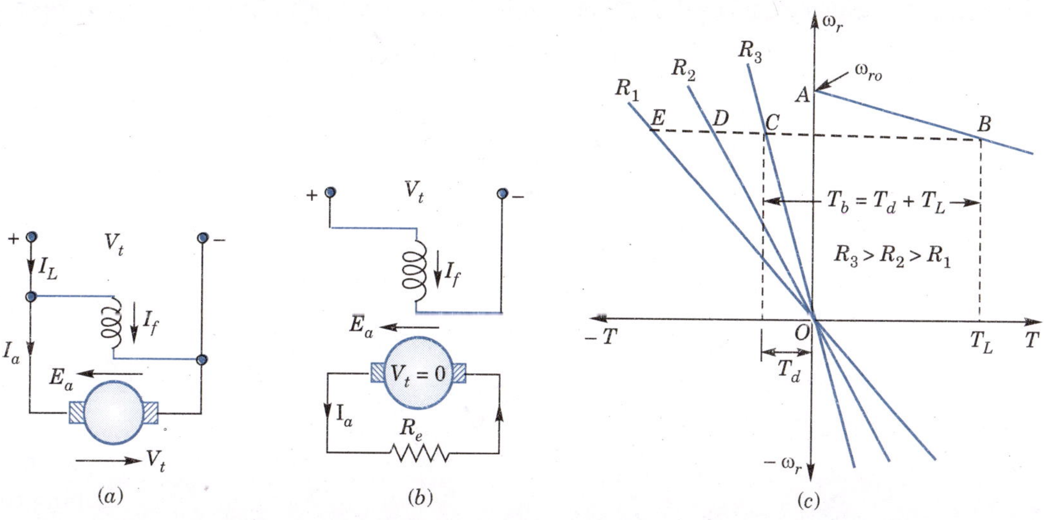

Fig. 3.29: (*a*) and (*b*) Pertaining to the dynamic braking of a d.c. shunt motor (*c*) Speed-torque characteristics of d.c. shunt motor during dynamic braking.

system is now converted to electric energy and dissipated as heat in the braking resistor R_e and armature circuit resistance r_a.

The dynamic braking torque T_d is given by

$$T_d = K_m I_a = -\frac{K_m E_a}{R} = -\frac{K_m^2}{R}\omega_r \qquad \text{...(3.83 (a))}$$

Since the field current remains constant,

$$K_m = k\phi = M_d I_f = \text{constant.}$$

$$\therefore \qquad T_d = -\frac{C}{R}\,\omega_r$$

or

$$\frac{\omega_r}{T_d} = -\frac{R}{C} \qquad \text{...(3.83)}$$

where $C = K_m^2$.

Eq. (3.83) shows that speed-torque characteristic during dynamic braking is a straight line and it passes through the origin, because when $T_d = 0$, $\omega_r = 0$. Greater the value of R, greater is the slope of $\omega_r - T_d$ characteristics and, therefore, less is the dynamic braking torque T_d. This shows that the magnitude of dynamic braking torque can be controlled by a suitable choice of the braking resistor R_e or $R = R_e + r_a$.

Total braking torque T_b at the instant of dynamic braking is given by

$$T_b = T_d + T_L$$

where T_L is the load torque at the instant of dynamic braking.

In Fig. 3.29 (*c*), *B* is the operating point during normal motor-mode operation for load torque T_L. As soon as the machine is connected for dynamic braking, the speed remains practically unchanged and, therefore, the operating point *B* shifts to second quadrant point *C*, *D* or *E* depending upon the armature circuit resistance R_3, R_2 or R_1 respectively. Now the speed drops along speed-torque characteristic *CO* (for R_3) till finally the motor stops at *O*.

(*b*) Series motors. There are two methods of obtaining the dynamic braking of d.c. series motors. In one method, called self-excitation method, both the armature and field windings are disconnected from the supply and connected across resistor R_e. In order that field shall not get demagnetized, the terminals of the field, or the armature, must be interchanged for obtaining the dynamic braking, this is shown in Fig. 3.30 (*b*). After the

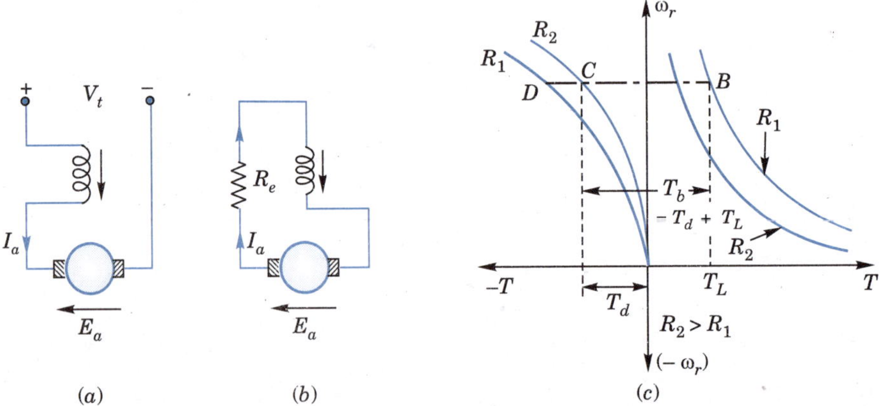

Fig. 3.30: (*a*) and (*b*) Pertaining to dynamic braking of d.c. series motor by self-excitation method. (*c*) Speed-torque curves of d.c. series motor during dynamic braking.

connections are changed from Fig. 3.30 (*a*) to Fig. 3.30 (*b*), self-excited series field builds up and the machine begins to develop braking torque, as the direction of armature current has reversed. The speed-torque characteristics during this type of dynamic braking are shown in the second quadrant of Fig. 3.30 (*c*). Note that braking torque near zero speed is very low.

In the second method, called separate-excitation method, a resistance is inserted in series with the field winding to limit the field current drawn from the supply. The armature is disconnected from the field circuit and is switched across the braking resistor R_e as shown in Fig. 3.31. The speed-torque characteristics during this method of braking are the same as shown in second quadrant of Fig. 3.29 (*c*), because now the series machine is working as a separately-excited d.c. generator during the dynamic braking.

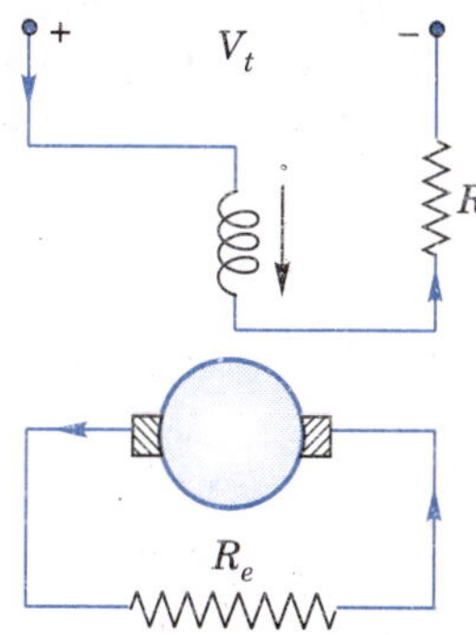

Fig. 3.31: Separate-excitation method of dynamic braking of d.c. series motor.

In industrial applications, dynamic braking is preferred for stopping the drive unit. But for reversing the drives, electric braking by plugging is used.

Example 3.20. *A 15 kW, 240 V, 1500 r.p.m., 72 A d.c. shunt motor has an armature resistance of 0.3 Ω. Neglect the effect of shunt field current.*

(*a*) *This motor is to be operated under regenerative braking conditions. If the armature current returned to the supply is 50 A, calculate the motor speed.*

(*b*) *The motor is braked by plugging when working under rated conditions.*

For limiting the armature current to 1.2 times the rated current, find:

(*i*) *resistance that must be inserted in the armature circuit,*

(*iii*) *braking torque developed by motor,*

(*iii*) *power input from the supply.*

(*c*) *The motor is braked by dynamic braking when working under rated conditions. If the armature current is to be limited to 1.2 times the rated armature current, find the resistance that must be inserted in the armature circuit and the braking torque developed at the motor shaft.*

(*d*) *Repeat part (c), if the motor is initially running at 750 r.p.m. with rated armature current. Neglect saturation.*

Solution. (*a*) Under rated conditions, the counter e.m.f. is,

$$E_{a_1} = V_t - I_a r_a = 240 - 72 \times 0.3 = 218.4 \text{ V}$$

For regenerative braking, generated voltage is,

$$E_{a_2} = V_t + I_a r_a = 240 + 50 \times 0.3 = 255 \text{ V}$$

But

$$\frac{E_{a_1}}{E_{a_2}} = \frac{1500 \times \phi}{N_2 \times \phi},$$

∴

$$N_2 = 1500 \times \frac{255}{218.4} = 1751.37 \text{ r.p.m.}$$

(*b*) Rated shaft torque of motor,

$$T_{e.s} = T_L = \frac{15{,}000 \times 60}{2\pi \times 1500} = 95.493 \text{ Nm}$$

But $T_{e.s} = K_m I_a$,

$\therefore$ $K_m = \frac{95.493}{72} = 1.3263$ Nm/A.

Note that here K_m pertains to shaft torque per unit of armature current.

(*i*) Counter e.m.f. under rated conditions, $E_{a_1} = 218.4$ V

$\therefore$ Resistance that must be inserted in the armature circuit at the time of plugging

$$= \frac{V_t + E_{a_1}}{I_a} - r_a = \frac{240 + 218.4}{1.2 \times 72} - 0.3 = 5.00\ \Omega$$

(*ii*) Initial plugging torque, $T_p = K_m I_a = 1.3263 \times 1.2 \times 72 = 114.592$ Nm

$\therefore$ Total braking torque, $T_b = T_p + T_L = 114.592 + 95.493 = 210.085$ Nm

(*iii*) Power taken from the supply $= \frac{V_t \cdot I_a}{1000} = \frac{240 \times 1.2 \times 72}{1000} = 20.74$ kW

(*c*) Motor counter e.m.f., $E_{a_1} = 218.4$ V

$\therefore$ Inserted resistance $= \frac{218.4}{1.2 \times 72} - 0.3 = 2.228\ \Omega$

Initial dynamic braking torque, $T_d = K_m I_a = 1.3263 \times 1.2 \times 72 = 114.59$ Nm

$\therefore$ Total initial braking torque, $T_b = T_d + T_L = 210.085$ Nm

(*d*) At 750 r.p.m., the counter e.m.f. E_{a_3} is given by

$$\frac{E_{a_3}}{E_{a_1}} = \frac{750 \times \phi}{1500 \times \phi} \quad \text{or} \quad E_{a_3} = \frac{218.4}{2} = 109.2 \text{ V}$$

$\therefore$ Inserted resistance $= \frac{109.2}{1.2 \times 72} - 0.3 = 0.964\ \Omega$

Total braking torque = 210.085 Nm, the same as in part (*c*).

Example 3.21. *A d.c. shunt motor is running at speed ω_1 rad/sec. The moment of inertia of motor armature is J kgm². Damping torque is zero. If the speed of this motor is to be reduced from ω_1 to ω_2 rad/sec by dynamic braking, find the time taken for this speed reduction under the condition of (a) zero load torque and (b) constant load torque T_L.*

Solution. Dynamic braking torque is given by, $T_d = -K_m^2/R \cdot \omega_r$ as per Eq. (3.83 (*a*)). Under dynamic braking conditions, the torque-balance equation for the motor-load combination is

$$-K_m^2/R\ \omega_r = Jp\omega_r + D\omega_r + T_L$$

(*a*) As D is zero and T_L has zero value for this part, the above torque-balance equation becomes

$$-\frac{K_m^2}{R}\omega_r = J\frac{d\omega_r}{dt} \quad \text{or} \quad dt = -\frac{JR}{K_m^2}\frac{d\omega_r}{\omega_r}$$

For the speed to fall from ω_1 to ω_2, the time required is

$$\int_{t_1}^{t_2} dt = -\frac{JR}{K_m^2}\int_{\omega_1}^{\omega_2}\frac{d\omega_r}{\omega_r} = \frac{JR}{K_m^2}\int_{\omega_2}^{\omega_1}\frac{d\omega_r}{\omega_r}$$

or $$(t_2 - t_1) = \Delta t = JR/K_m^2 \ln \omega_1/\omega_2$$

(*b*) When constant load torque is present, the torque-balance equation from above is

$$-\frac{K_m^2}{R}\omega_r = J\frac{d\omega_r}{dt} + T_L \quad \text{or} \quad dt = -\frac{J}{\dfrac{K_m^2}{R}\omega_r + T_L}.\,d\omega_r$$

For the speed to fall from ω_1 to ω_2, the time required is

$$\int_{t_1}^{t_2} dt = \int_{\omega_2}^{\omega_1} \frac{J}{\dfrac{K_m^2}{R}\omega_r + T_L}\,d\omega_r = \frac{J}{K_m^2/R}\left[\ln\left\{\frac{K_m^2}{R}\omega_r + T_L\right\}\right]_{\omega_2}^{\omega_1}$$

or
$$(t_2 - t_1) = \Delta t = \frac{JR}{K_m^2}\ln\left[\frac{\dfrac{K_m^2}{R}\omega_1 + T_L}{\dfrac{K_m^2}{R}\omega_2 + T_L}\right]$$

Example 3.22. *A d.c. series motor has a magnetization curve given by a straight line $E_a = 4.8\,I_a + 200$ at a speed of 800 r.p.m. and for I_a between 20 and 50 A. The series motor shaft is fitted with a pulley of diameter 40 cms and a load of 100 kgs is to be lowered. In order to limit the descending speed of load to a safe value, rheostatic braking is employed. Find the braking resistance to be connected in series with the motor armature circuit for limiting the downward speed to 600 r.p.m. Total motor resistance is 1 Ω. Neglect rotational losses.*

Solution. At 800 r.p.m., $E_a = (4.8I_a + 200)$ volts.

At 600 r.p.m., $E_{a_1} = (4.8\,I_{a_1} + 200) \times 600/800 = 3.6\,I_{a_1} + 150$

Power developed in armature,

$$= E_{a_1}\,.\,I_{a_1} = (3.6\,I_{a_1} + 150)\,I_{a_1} \text{ watts}$$

Armature terminal power $= E_{a_1}I_{a_1} - I_{a_1}^2\,.\,r_a$

Descending load torque $= 100 \times 0.40/2 \times 9.81$ Nm = Rheostatic braking torque, T_d

∴ $T_d = 20 \times 9.81 = 196.2$ Nm

For torque balance, dynamic braking torque = Descending load torque

$$\therefore \quad \frac{(3.6I_{a_1} + 150)\,I_{a_1} - I_{a_1}^2 \times 1}{2\pi \times 600/60} = 196.2 \text{ Nm}$$

or
$$2.6\,I_{a_1}^2 + 150\,I_{a_1} = 12327.61 \quad \text{or} \quad I_{a_1}^2 + 57.692\,I_{a_1} - 4741.39 = 0$$

Its solution gives, $I_{a_1} = 45.81$ A.

Generated voltage at 600 r.p.m. is $E_{a_1} = 3.6 \times 45.81 + 150 = 314.92$ V. If R_b is the braking resistance to be connected in series with armature, then

$$I_{a_1} = \frac{E_{a_1}}{R_b + r_a} = \frac{314.92}{R_b + 1} = 45.81 \qquad \text{or} \quad R_b = 5.874\ \Omega.$$

Example 3.23. *A 150 h.p. 750 r.p.m. d.c. shunt motor has stored energy per h.p. of 5000 Nm. Determine the time taken to start the motor if the load torque is equal to full load torque during the starting period and the current is limited to 1.5 times the full-load current.* *[I.A.S., 1991]*

Solution. Here energy stored = $1/2J\omega^2 = 5000 \times 150$ Nm or Joules

$$\omega = \frac{2\pi \times 750}{60} = 25\pi \text{ rad/sec.}$$

$$\therefore \quad J = \frac{5000 \times 150 \times 2}{(25\pi)^2} = 243.17 \text{ kgm}^2$$

For d.c. motor, the dynamic equation is,

$$T_e = J\frac{d\omega}{dt} + T_L \quad \text{or} \quad d_t = \frac{J}{T_e - T_L}\,d\omega \quad \text{or} \quad t = \frac{J}{T_e - T_L}\,.\,\omega$$

It is given that load torque, T_L = motor full-load torque, $T_{e:fl}$

where $T_{e:fl} = \dfrac{150 \times 746}{25\pi}$ Nm

As current during starting is limited to 1.5 times the full-load current, the starting torque, $T_{e.st} = 1.5\,T_{e.fl}$

$$\therefore \quad t = \frac{J}{T_{e.st} - T_{e.fl}}\,.\,\omega = \frac{243.17 \times 25\pi}{0.5 \times 150 \times 746} \times 25\pi = \mathbf{26.8096 \text{ sec.}}$$

3.11 SOME WORKED EXAMPLES

The object of this article is to solve some typical problems on d.c. machines. Most of these problems have appeared in one or the other competitive examinations.

Example 3.24. *Two series motors are connected to the same supply system and coupled to the same load. The one when running at 500 r.p.m. normally takes a current of 50 amperes ; the other when taking 50 amperes, runs at 1000 r.p.m. ; in each case the supply voltage being 500 V. Neglecting the effects of saturation, at what speed will the motors run when the load current is 100 amperes ? Each motor has a resistance of 0.8 Ω. Calculate also the value of current in each motor under these conditions.*

Solution. As saturation effects are neglected, flux $\phi = CI_a$

For motor one, counter e.m.f. $= V_t - I_a(r_a + r_s) = K_{a_1}C_1I_an_1$

or $$500 - 50 \times 0.8 = K_{a_1}C_1 \times 50 \times 500$$

or $$K_{a_1}C_1 = \frac{460}{25000}$$

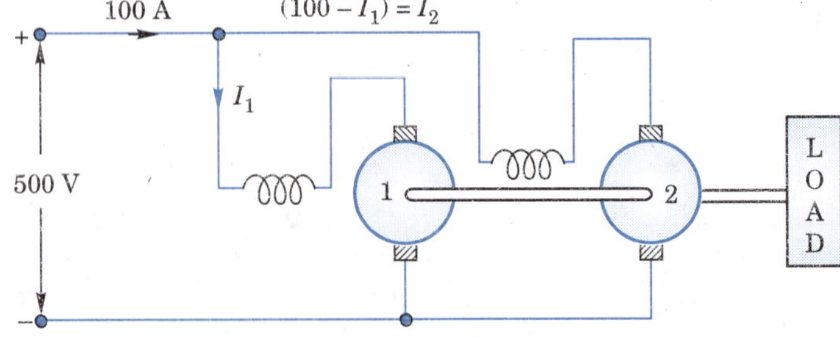

Fig. 3.32: Pertaining to Example 3.24.

For the second motor,

$$500 - 50 \times 0.8 = K_{a_2} C_2 \times 50 \times 1000 \quad \text{or} \quad K_{a_2} C_2 = \frac{460}{50{,}000}$$

$$\frac{K_{a_1} C_1}{K_{a_2} C_2} = \frac{460}{25{,}000} \times \frac{50{,}000}{460} = 2$$

When motors are connected in parallel as shown in Fig. 3.32 and coupled to the same load, then let the current in one motor be I_1. Its counter e.m.f. is, therefore, given by

$$500 - 0.8 I_1 = K_{a_1} C_1 I_1 n \qquad ...(i)$$

For second motor, armature current = $I_2 = 100 - I_1$ and its counter e.m.f. is

$$500 - 0.8\,(100 - I_1) = K_{a_2} C_2 I_2 n \qquad ...(ii)$$

From Eqs. (*i*) and (*ii*), $\dfrac{500 - 0.8 I_1}{500 - (100 - I_1)\,0.8} = \dfrac{K_{a_1} C_1}{K_{a_2} C_2} . \dfrac{I_1}{I_2} = \dfrac{2 I_1}{100 - I_1}$

or $\quad 0.8 I_1^2 + 1420 I_1 - 50{,}000 = 0.00$

Its solution gives, $\quad I_1 = 34.54$ A

$\therefore \quad I_2 = 100 - 34.54 = 65.46$ A

From Eq. (*i*), the speed of the set is given by

$$n = \frac{(500 - 0.8 \times 34.54) \times 25{,}000}{34.54 \times 460} = 743.26 \text{ r.p.m.}$$

Example 3.25. *Two indentical d.c. series motors, each having ratings of 20 kW, 250 V, 1200 r.p.m., are connected in series across a 250 V d.c. supply. They drive a common shaft through reduction gears of 2 :1 and 3 : 1 ratios respectively. Given that the load torque on the common shaft is 500 Nm, calculate the mechanical power delivered to the load, the current taken from the mains, and the voltage across each machine. Assume negligible internal power losses in the machines and negligible saturation effects.*

Solution. Motor counter e.m.f., $E_a = K_a \phi\, \omega$

For no saturation, $\quad \phi = C I_a$ and $E_a = K_a C I_a \omega$

Rated armature current, $\quad I_a = \dfrac{20{,}000}{250} = 80$ A

and $\quad$ rated speed $= \dfrac{2\pi \times 1200}{60} = 40\pi$ rad/sec

$$\therefore \quad E_a = K_a C \,.\, 80 \,.\, 40\pi = V_t - I_a r_a = 250 \qquad [\text{As } r_a = 0]$$

$$\therefore \quad K_a C = \frac{250}{80 \times 40 \times \pi} = \frac{1}{12.8\pi}$$

Motor torque, $\quad T_e = K_a \phi I_a = K_a C I_a^2$

Now power developed by (motor 1 + motor 2) = $T_L \,.\, \omega$

or $\quad K_a C I_a^2\,(2\omega + 3\omega) = 500 \,.\, \omega \quad$ or $\quad K_a C I_a^2 5 = 500$

or $$I_a = \sqrt{\frac{100}{K_a C}} = \sqrt{100 \times 12.8\pi} = 63.413 \text{ A}$$

∴ Current taken from the mains = 63.413 A

For the motors connected in series,

$$K_a C I_a 2\omega + K_a C I_a 3\omega = 250 \text{ volts}$$

or
$$\omega = \frac{2\pi N}{60} = \frac{250}{5 \,.\, K_a C I_a} = \frac{250 \times 12.8\pi}{5 \times 63.413}$$

or
$$N = \frac{50 \times 12.8\pi}{63.413} \times \frac{60}{2\pi} = 302.78 \text{ r.p.m.}$$

Mechanical power delivered to load $= T_L \,.\, \omega = 500 \times \frac{2\pi \times 302.78}{60}$ W = 15.8535 kW

Voltage across motor 1, $V_1 = K_a C I_a \,(2\omega)$

$$= \frac{1}{12.8\pi} \times 63.413 \times 2 \times \frac{2\pi \times 302.78}{60} = 100 \text{ V}$$

Voltage across motor 2, $V_2 = 250 - 100 = 150$ V.

Example 3.26. *One d.c. series motor runs at 600 r.p.m. taking 50 A; another identical series motor runs at 800 r.p.m. taking 50 A ; in each case the supply voltage being 500 V. Each motor has a total resistance of 0.4 Ω . If these motors are coupled mechanically but connected in series across 500 V source taking 50 A, calculate the speed of the machines and the voltage across each machine. Neglect magnetic saturation.*

Solution. For one motor, counter e.m.f.

$$E_{a_1} = 500 - 50 \times 0.4 = K_{a_1} C_1 I_{a_1} n_1 \quad \text{or} \quad K_{a_1} C_1 = \frac{480}{50 \times 600}$$

For second motor,

$$E_{a_2} = 500 - 50 \times 0.4 = K_{a_2} C_2 I_{a_2} n_2 \quad \text{or} \quad K_{a_2} C_2 = \frac{480}{50 \times 800}$$

When the motors are connected in series across 500 V but mechanically coupled, then

$500 - 50\,(0.4 + 0.4)$ = sum of counter e.m.fs. of both the motors.

or
$$460 = \frac{480}{50 \times 600} \times 50 \times n + \frac{480}{50 \times 800} \times 50 \times n$$

or
$$n = \frac{460 \times 600 \times 800}{1400 \times 480} = 328.6 \text{ r.p.m.}$$

∴ Speed of the coupled motors, $n = 328.6$ r.p.m.

Voltage across motor 1 $= \frac{480}{600} \times 328.6 + 50 \times 0.4 = 282.88$ V

Voltage across motor 2 $= \frac{480}{800} \times 328.6 + 50 \times 0.4 = 217.12$ V.

Example 3.27. *A d.c. series motor of total resistance 0.5 Ω runs at a speed of 800 r.p.m. when taking 60 A from 500 V d.c. mains. Now another indentical series motor is mechanically coupled, but connected in series with the first motor. If the set runs at 400 r.p.m. with load torque equal to 2.5 times the original torque, find the current drawn from 500 V d.c. source.*

Solution. Motor counter e.m.f., $E_a = 500 - 60 \times 0.5 = 470$ V

Electromagnetic torque, $T_e = \dfrac{470 \times 60 \times 60}{2\pi \times 800} = 336.6127$ Nm

New load torque $= 2.5 \times 336.6127 = 841.532$ Nm

Torque developed by the set $= \dfrac{(250 - I_a \times 0.5) \times 2 \times I_a \times 60}{2\pi \times 400} = 841.532$

$$I_a^2 - 500I_a + 35250 = 0$$

Its solution gives $I_a = 84.924$ A.

Example 3.28. *For constant power input to two series motors, show that:*

(a) the electric torque developed by them in parallel is one-fourth of that when these are in series,

(b) their operating speed when in parallel is four times that when motors are in series. Neglect magnetic saturation.

Solution. For no magnetic saturation in series motor, $\phi = CI_a$ and electric torque $T_e = K_a\phi I_a = K_a C I_a^2$.

The subscript '*s*' and '*p*' are used to denote quantities for motors in series and parallel respectively.

For constant power input, input line current I_L must be constant as supply voltage V_t is constant.

For series connection of motors, $I_s = I_L$

For parallel connection of motors, $I_p = \dfrac{1}{2} I_L = \dfrac{1}{2} I_s$ or $I_s = 2I_p$

(*a*) Now $T_e = K_a C I_a^2$

$$\therefore \quad T_{e.s} = K_a C I_a^2 = K_a C I_L^2$$

Also $$T_{e.p} = K_a C I_p^2 = K_a C \left(\frac{1}{2} I_L\right)^2 = \frac{1}{4} K_a C I_L^2$$

$$\therefore \quad \frac{T_{e.p}}{T_{e.s}} = \frac{\frac{1}{4} K_a C I_L^2}{K_a C I_L^2} = \frac{1}{4} \text{ or } T_{e.p} = \frac{1}{4} T_{e.s}$$

This shows that electric torque for the motors in parallel is one-fourth of that when these are in series.

(*b*) Motor counter e.m.f.,

$$E_a = V_t - I_a(r_a + r_s) = K_a\phi\omega_r$$

Neglecting voltage drop in $(r_a + r_s)$,

$$E_a = K_a C I_a \omega_r = V_t$$

When in series, $E_{as} = K_a C I_s \cdot \omega_s = K_a C I_L \cdot \omega_s = \dfrac{1}{2} V_t$

When in parallel, $E_{ap} = K_a C I_p \cdot \omega_p = K_a C \cdot \dfrac{1}{2} I_L \cdot \omega_p = V_t$

$$\therefore \quad \frac{E_{ap}}{E_{as}} = \frac{V_t}{\frac{1}{4}V_t} = \frac{\frac{1}{2}K_a CI_L \cdot \omega_p}{K_a CI_L \cdot \omega_s} = \frac{\omega_p}{2\omega_s}$$

or $$\frac{\omega_p}{\omega_s} = 2 \times 2 = 4 \text{ or } \omega_p = 4\omega_s.$$

This shows that speed of motor when in parallel is four-times that when they are in series.

Example 3.29. *A 500 V d.c. separately excited motor with an efficiency of 90% operates an hoist having an efficiency of 70%. Calculate the current taken from the supply mains in order to raise a load of 1000 kgs at a speed of 3 m/sec.*

If rheostatic braking is employed, what resistance must be inserted in the armature circuit in order to lower the load at the same speed.

Solution. Here 1000 kgs is the weight to be lifted up, therefore the resisting force due to gravitational pull = 1000 × 9.81 kg.m/sec^2 = 9810 Newtons.

Power required for lifting this load

$$= 9810 \times 3 \text{ Nm/sec or watts}$$

$$\text{Input to hoist or d.c. motor output} = \frac{9810 \times 3}{\text{hoist efficiency}}$$

$$\text{D.C. motor input required} = \frac{9810 \times 3}{\text{(hoist efficiency) (motor efficiency)}}$$

$$\therefore \quad \text{Current taken by motor from supply mains} = \frac{9810 \times 3}{0.7 \times 0.9 \times 500} = \mathbf{93.428\ A}$$

When the load is being lifted up, the motor is doing the work. During rheostatic braking, the load is doing the work in driving the motor, *i.e.* the power flow is now opposite to that when the load is being lifted up.

Power developed by falling load = 9810 × 3 W = Input to hoist

Output of hoist or input to d.c. motor = 9810 × 3 × hoist η

Armature power developed or output of d.c. motor = 9810 × 3 × hoist η × motor η

$$\therefore \text{Current required in the armature circuit} = \frac{9810 \times 3 \times 0.7 \times 0.9}{500} = 37.082 \text{ A}$$

$$\text{Resistance that must be inserted in the armature circuit} = \frac{500}{37.082} = 13.484\ \Omega.$$

PROBLEMS

3.1. (*a*) For doing the analysis of d.c. machines with the help of Kron's primitive machine, no transformation is required. Why ?

(*b*) Enumerate the assumptions pertaining to the use of generalized mathematical model of d.c. machines.

(*c*) For d.c. machines, show that the motion 1 inductance M_d is given by

$$M_d = \frac{\phi Z}{\pi a} \cdot \frac{1}{I_f}.$$

The symbols used have their usual meaning.

3.2. (*a*) A separately-excited d.c. generator gave no-load output voltage of 240 V at a speed ω_r and for a field current of 3 A. Find $M_d\omega_r$ (= K_g, generated e.m.f. per field ampere).

(*b*) The other constants of the generator of part (*a*) are

$r_f = 60\ \Omega$ $\quad L_f = 60$ H

$r_a = 0.02\ \Omega$ $\quad L_a = 0.01$ H

$R_L = 0.38\ \Omega$ $\quad L_L = 0.$

Find the voltage v_L as a function of time, after 240 V is suddenly applied to the field winding with the armature running at constant speed ω_r.

[**Ans.** (*a*) 80 V/amp (*b*) 304 $(1 - e^{-t})$ V]

3.3. The following constants pertain to a 250 V d.c. separately-excited generator:

Field	:	60 Ω,	30 H
Armature	:	0.03 Ω,	0.02 H
Load	:	1.37 Ω,	1.78 H

Slope of air-gap line – 36 V/field ampere at rated speed.

The generator is initially unexcited but running at rated speed and connected to the load. A 240 V d.c. supply is suddenly switched on to the field coils. Neglecting magnetic non-linearity and any speed changes, find out the variation of armature current as a function of time.

Derive the expression used above. [**Ans.** 102.86 $[1 + 0.636e^{-2t} - 1.636e^{-0.7776t}]$]

3.4. A d.c. series motor drives a load requiring constant torque T_L. The total moment of inertia of the motor and load is J kg-m². The armature circuit resistance, including field winding, is $R\Omega$. Show that the total energy dissipated in the armature circuit, as the speed changes from ω_1 to ω_2, is given by the expression

$$\int_{t_1}^{t_2} i_a^2 R\, dt = \frac{JR}{M_d}(\omega_2 - \omega_1) + \frac{T_L R}{M_d}(t_2 - t_1).$$

3.5. A separately-excited d.c. motor is at rest with its field winding excited. Inertia of rotating parts is J kg-m². Neglect damping and armature inductance.

If voltage V_t is suddenly impressed across the armature terminals, find:

(*a*) the time taken by the motor to come up to 50% of its no-load speed ω_{ro} and the energy lost in the armature during this time.

(*b*) the time taken by the motor to come up to 98.1685% of its no-load speed ω_{ro} and the energy lost in the armature during this time.

Express the time in terms of motor time constant τ_m and the energy in terms of J and ω_{ro}.

[**Hint.** See Example 3.4.]

$$\left[\textbf{Ans.}\ (a)\ 0.693\tau_m,\ 0.25\left(\frac{1}{2}J\omega_{ro}^2\right);\ (b)\ 4\tau_m,\ 0.9637\left(\frac{1}{2}J\omega_{ro}^2\right)\right]$$

3.6. A separately-excited d.c. motor, fed from silicon-controlled rectifiers has the following data:

Total resistance of motor armature and SCR circuit = 0.04 Ω

Total inductance of motor armature and SCR circuit = zero

Source voltage at no-load = 250 V

Inertia of rotating parts, J = 50 kg-m².

Electromechanical conversion constant for motor,

$K_m = 2$ Nm/armature amp.

Friction and windage is negligible.

(*a*) If the d.c. motor takes a no-load current of 10 A, find the motor no-load speed.

(*b*) With the motor running at no-load, a load torque of 600 Nm is suddenly applied to the motor shaft. Find

(*i*) the speed as a function of time and

(*ii*) the ultimate speed drop. [**Ans.** (*a*) 1191.8 r.p.m. (*b*) $(1134.5 + 57.3e^{-2t})$; 57.3 r.p.m.]

3.7. A 230 V d.c. shunt motor has the following constants :

Electromagnetic torque constant, $K_m = 6$

Armature resistance, $r_a = 0.8\ \Omega$

Total moment of inertia, $J = 9$ kg-m²

Fixed losses and armature inductance are negligible.

The motor is operating at rated voltage and on no-load. If it is brought to rest by plugging, find the speed as a function of time. Also find the time taken by the motor to stop.

Derive the expression used above. [**Ans.** $38.33\ (2e^{-5t} - 1)$; 0. 1386 sec]

3.8. Repeat Prob. 3.7, in case the load torque is proportional to speed and its value is 50 Nm at a speed of 100 rad/sec. [**Ans.** $37.91\ (2e^{-5.056t} - 1)$; 0.1371 sec]

3.9. A 200 V d.c. shunt motor has the following data :

$r_a = 0.04\ \Omega, \quad L_a = 0.04$ H, $\quad J = 30$ kg m²

Torque constant, $K_m = 4$ Nm/ampere.

The load torque, proportional to speed, is 80 Nm at a speed of 1000 r.p.m. This motor is dynamically braked with a braking resistor of 0.4 Ω.

(*a*) Find the time taken by the motor speed to become 2% of its initial value. Assume negligible armature inductance for this part only.

(*b*) If it is required that speed should come down to zero in minimum possible time, find the value of external braking resistance required.

(*c*) Repeat part (*b*), if load torque is assumed to be zero.

Derive the various expressions used for parts (*a*), (*b*) and (*c*).

[**Hint.** See Example 3.7.] [**Ans.** 3.161 sec : 0.155 Ω ; 0.252 Ω]

3.10. Write the general voltage equations for a fully-compensated metadyne generator. For a load impedance of $(R_L + L_L p)$ connected across the output terminals, derive the transient and steady-state expressions for the load voltage.

3.11. (*a*) For an amplidyne, derive expressions for voltage gain, current gain and power gain under steady-state conditions.

(*b*) Show that the transfer function for an amplidyne is given by the expression,

$$\frac{I_L(s)}{V_f(s)} = \frac{L_a M_d \omega_r^2}{r_a \cdot r_f \cdot R(1+\tau_a s)(1+\tau_f s)(1+\tau s)}$$

where $R = r_a + r_c + R_L$

and $\tau = \dfrac{L_L}{R}$. [**Hint.** See Eq. (3.69 (*a*))]

3.12. (*a*) Describe the advantages of using several small d.c. generators in parallel over the use of a single large generator.

(*b*) What are the two conditions for connecting two d.c. shunt generators in parallel ?

(c) Explain the procedure of commissioning a d.c. shunt generator in parallel with the other already working in a power station.

3.13. (a) Two d.c. shunt generators are operating in parallel. Explain how the load sharing between them can be controlled by adjusting their field currents.

(b) Two shunt generators, operating in parallel, supply a total load current of 100 A. First generator gives 250 V on no-load and 230 V at a load current of 600 A. The second generator gives 260 V on no-load and 230 V at a load current of 500 A. Assuming linear load characteristics for both the generators, find the current supplied by each generator and the common bus-bar voltage.

[**Ans.** (b) – 42.86 A, 142.86 A, 251.43 V. The machine with – 42.86 A is working as a d.c. shunt motor]

3.14. (a) Show that a d.c. generator with more drooping characteristic shares less load as compared with the other operating in parallel with it.

(b) Two d.c. shunt generators, each with an armature resistance of 0.04 Ω, have no-load e.m.fs. of 253 V and 252 V, field resistances of 50 and 40 Ω respectively. They are operating in parallel and supply a total load of 50 kW. How do they share the total load.

[**Ans.** (b) 28.24 kW, 21.76 kW]

3.15. Two d.c. shunt generators, operating in parallel, share a load current of 300 A. Each generator has an armature resistance of 0.20 Ω and a field resistance of 120 Ω. The no-load generated e.m.fs. of these two machines are 245 and 240 V. Calculate the common line voltage and the power output of each machine. [**Ans.** (b) 212.146 V, 34.474 kW, 29.17 kW]

3.16. The external characteristics of two shunt generators in parallel are as follows :

Load current,	A	: 0,	10,	20,	30,	35,	40,	45,
Terminal voltage, V	M/c 1	: 230,	228.7,	226.4,	223.1,	220.4,	215,	–
	M/c 2	: 227,	226.1,	224.6,	223,	221.2,	219,	216

Find the load current and terminal voltage of each machine, when in parallel they supply, (a) a total load of 75 A and (b) a load of resistance 4 Ω.

[**Ans.** (a) 36.5 A, 39.0 A, 219.5 V (b) 29.5 A, 27.0 A, 223.3 V]

3.17. (a) Why are the compound generators, to be operated in parallel, usually over-compounded ?

(b) Explain clearly the importance of an equalizer for the satisfactory parallel operation of compound generators.

(c) A compound generator is delivering power to a load. As soon as the second compound generator is put in parallel, it starts sharing the load though its no-load e.m.f. is made equal to the line voltage. Explain.

3.18. (a) Explain the procedure of connecting one compound generator in parallel with another already loaded compound generator.

(b) Explain how an equalizer can be avoided in the parallel operation of two identical compound generators.

(c) Explain how the two conditions, for the satisfactory operation of two compound genrators in parallel, can be achieved.

(d) If the compound generators are fitted with interpoles, show where the equalizer should be connected.

3.19. (a) Explain the principle of regenerative braking of d.c. motors. Show that for a given braking torque, greater the armature circuit resistance greater must be the speed for obtaining the regenerative braking action.

(b) Explain how four-quadrant operation of a d.c. series motor is obtained by counter-current braking method.

3.20. (*a*) Explain the principle of counter-current braking of d.c. motors. Describe, with a suitable diagram, how four-quadrant operation of a d.c. shunt motor can be obtained.

(*b*) A 400 V, 750 r.p.m., 70 A d.c. shunt motor has an armature resistance of 0.3 Ω.

When running under rated conditions, the motor is to be braked by plugging with armature current limited to 90 A. What external resistance should be inserted in series with the armature ? Calculate the plugging and total braking torques (*i*) at the time of plugging and (*ii*) when the speed has fallen to 300 r.p.m.

Neglect rotational losses and saturation.

[**Ans.** 8.356 Ω, (*i*) 434.30 Nm, 772.09 Nm (*ii*) 307.51 Nm, 645.3 Nm]

3.21. (*a*) Explain the principle of dynamic braking of d.c. motors.

Show that greater the value of total braking resistance *R*, greater is the slope of speed-torque characteristics during dynamic braking.

(*b*) Compare the three methods of electric braking of d.c. motors.

3.22. A 40 kW, 500 V, 700 r.p.m., d.c. shunt motor has armature circuit resistance of 0.1 Ω and rated current of 100 A. This motor is to be braked by plugging from rated working conditions.

(*a*) Calculate the resistance to be connected in series with armature to limit the initial current to 150 A. Find also the initial plugging and total braking torques.

(*b*) Compute the plugging and total braking torques when the speed has fallen by 25%.

[**Ans.** (*a*) 6.5 Ω, 818.5 Nm, 1366.17 Nm (*b*) 717.23 Nm, 1264.9 Nm.]

3.23. (*a*) A 400 V, 80 A, 1200 r.p.m. d.c. shunt motor has armature circuit resistance of 0.2 Ω. For obtaining regenerative braking torque of 200 Nm, find the speed at which the d.c. machine must run.

(*b*) Repeat part (*a*) in case an external resistance of 0.8 Ω is inserted in the armature circuit.

[**Hint.** Find K_m = 3.056 V-sec/rad and use Eq. (3.81)]

[**Ans.** (*a*) 1290.81 rpm (*b*) 1454.41 rpm.]

3.24. A d.c. shunt motor has counter e.m.f. of 220 V at 1000 r.p.m. Its moment of inertia is 20 kgm^2. Find the time taken to reduce the motor speed from 1000 to 400 r.p.m. by means of dynamic braking when resistance connected across its armature is 5 Ω. Assume that damping torque is absent and (*a*) load torque is zero and (*b*) load torque is 15 Nm.

Derive the expressions used. [**Ans.** (*a*) 20.762 sec (*b*) 16.453 sec]

3.25. Two identical 15 kW, 250 V, 1000 r.p.m. d.c. series motors *A* and *B* are connected in series across a 250 V supply. They drive the same shaft through reduction gearing 3 : 1 and 4 : 1 respectively. If the total load torque on the shaft is 630 Nm, calculate the speed of the shaft, the voltage across each motor and the current from the supply. Neglect losses and assume the magnetic circuits to be unsaturated. [*GATE, 1988*]

[**Ans.** 180.22 r.p.m. ; 107.14 V, 142.86 V ; 47.56 A]

3.26. Repeat Example 3.29 in case motor drives the hoist through reduction gears of ratio 10 : 1. Gears are assumed to have an efficiency of 100%.

[**Hint.** Power on both sides of gears remains unchanged.] [**Ans.** 93.428 A, 13.484 Ω]

4

Polyphase Synchronous Machines

A synchronous machine is an a.c. machine which is provided with a distributed armature winding and a concentrated d.c. field winding. When working as a generator, the armature winding delivers or exports a.c. power and as a motor, it absorbs or imports a.c. power. The field winding, however, always imports d.c. power from a suitable d.c. source for both synchronous-generator and synchronous-motor operations.

The synchronous machines are usually built with field winding on the rotor and armature winding on the stator. This is on account of the fact that large amounts of power from, or to, the stationary armature and small portion of power to the field, can be conducted easily. However, synchronous machines with armature winding on the rotor and field winding on the stator are also being built even at present, for ratings up to about 100 kVA, 400 V or so. Synchronous generators are also called alternators. The generators driven by steam turbines are called *turbo-generators* and those driven by water turbines are called *hydro-generators*. Turbo-generators run at high speeds, these have, therefore, cylindrical-rotor construction; hydro-generators run at low speeds, these have, therefore, salient-pole construction. Synchronous generators driven by internal combustion engines (diesel, petrol or gas engines) are also of the salient-pole construction. Slow-speed synchronous motors are usually of the salient-pole type, though high speed synchronous motors with cylindrical rotor design are also built. A salient-pole synchronous machine is characterised by a non-uniform air gap, whereas a cylindrical-rotor machine has a uniform air-gap.

For applying the generalized theory to the analysis of a polyphase synchronous machine, its field winding is assumed on the stator and armature winding on the rotor. With this change, the operation of the synchronous machine and, therefore, its analysis are unaffected; since for its steady-state working, the relative speed between stator and rotor fields must be zero.

In this chapter, emphasis is given to the transient and dynamic analysis of polyphase (3-phase or 2-phase) synchronous machines, though their steady-state analysis is also presented.

4.1 BASIC SYNCHRONOUS-MACHINE PARAMETERS

A 3-phase synchronous machine has four basic windings (neglecting damper winding); namely three identical and symmetrical armature windings and one field winding. Fig. 4.1 illustrates an elementary two-pole synchronous machine with salient-pole construction. In this figure, the three armature windings are designated by A, B, C and d.c. field winding by F. As stated before, the distributed armature winding is shown on the rotor and concentrated field winding on the salient-pole stator.

The field winding axis is taken as *direct axis* and the inter-polar axis as *quadrature axis*. Phase A axis is displaced from d-axis by an angle θ measured in the direction of rotor rotation. At time $t = 0$, axis of phase A is assumed to coincide with d-axis so that at any time t, $\theta = \omega t$. Here ω is the constant rotor angular velocity in radians per second. At the instant shown in Fig. 4.1, the phase B axis is displaced from d-axis by $120° - \theta$ or $\theta - 120°$ and phase C axis by an angle $\theta - 240°$ $(= \theta + 120°)$. The d- and q- axes remain fixed with the field winding on stator, but the three magnetic axes of three-phase armature phases rotate as the rotor revolves.

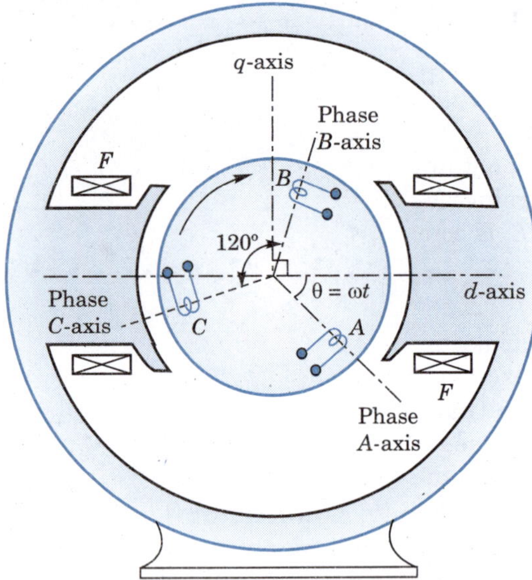

Fig. 4.1: Basic two-pole synchronous machine.

In order to concentrate more on the synchronous machine basic features and to expedite its analysis, the following assumptions are made.

1. Influence of damper bars is neglected, though their effect is considered qualitatively at a later stage.

2. Hysteresis and magnetic saturation are neglected. This means that synchronous machine is magnetically linear and therefore a linear relation exists between flux and current. Consequently, concept of synchronous-machine inductances can be introduced.

3. Space distribution of armature m.m.f. wave and field flux wave are assumed sinusoidal. In fact, in a salient-pole machine, the pole shoes are so shaped as to obtain a sinusoidal reluctance variation along the air-gap periphery.

4. The armature slots do not have any effect on the synchronous-machine inductances.

Both the field and armature windings have their own resistances and self-inductances. In addition, mutual inductances are present between armature and field windings and also amongst the armature-phase windings. All the synchronous-machine inductances, except the field-winding inductance L_f, depend upon the armature orientation with respect to field winding. Consequently, synchronous machine inductances (except L_f) are functions of the time-varying space angle θ. The object of this article is to examine the nature of these inductances and the machine resistances.

4.1.1 Synchronous-machine Resistances

The armature circuit resistances for A, B, C phases are designated by r_a, r_b, r_c respectively. Since the phase windings are identical, the magnitudes of all the three resistances are equal, *i.e.* $r_a = r_b = r_c$. For convenience, we use the symbol r_a for the resistance of phase A and for any of the three phases as well. So here r_a is the armature circuit resistance for any of the three phases and for phase A also. The symbol r_f is used to represent the field-circuit resistance.

4.1.2 Synchronous-machine Inductances

The nature of synchronous-machine inductances can be obtained from an examination of the machine geometry shown in Fig. 4.1.

(*a*) **Field self-inductance.** The air-gap length seen by the field m.m.f. remains constant, whatever the rotor position with respect to field poles may be. As a result of it, the reluctance seen by the field m.m.f. is always constant and consequently field self-inductance L_f is constant.

$$\therefore \qquad L_f = \text{constant} \qquad ...(4.1)$$

(*b*) **Armature to field mutual inductances.** The mutual inductances between armature and field windings vary periodically with space angle θ. When only phase *A* is excited, then for θ = 0 the phase *A* axis and field winding axis coincide and therefore, the mutual inductance M_{af} between phase *A* and field winding *F* is maximum, say M_{afm}. When phase *A* axis is 90° away from field axis (*i.e.* when θ = 90°), then $M_{af} = 0$. For θ = 180°, M_{af} is again maximum but negative, *i.e.* for θ = 180°, $M_{af} = -M_{afm}$.

For θ = 270°, M_{af} is again zero. Thus, in general, the mutual inductance between phase *A* and field winding *F* can be expressed mathematically as

$$M_{af} = M_{afm} \cos \theta \qquad ...(4.2)$$

The variation of mutual inductance M_{af} with space angle θ is shown in Fig. 4.2.

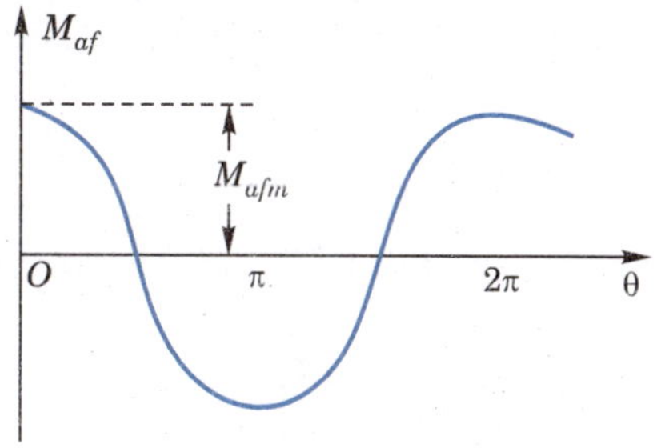

Fig. 4.2: Variation of M_{af} between phase *A* and field winding *F* with space angle θ.

The expressions for mutual inductances M_{bf} and M_{cf} between phases *B*, *C* and the field winding *F* can be obtained by replacing θ in Eq. (4.2) by (θ – 120°) and (θ – 240°) respectively.

$$\therefore \qquad \left.\begin{aligned} M_{bf} &= M_{afm} \cos (\theta - 120°) \\ \text{and} \qquad M_{cf} &= M_{afm} \cos (\theta - 240°) \end{aligned}\right\} \qquad ...(4.3)$$

Note that maximum value of mutual inductance between any one phase and the field winding is M_{afm}, because all the three armature phase windings are identical in all respects.

(*c*) **Armature self-inductances.** The self-inductance of any armature phase is always positive, but it varies peroidically from its maximum to minimum values as the rotor moves. For example, self-inductance L_a of phase *A* is maximum positive when θ = 0°, a minimum when θ = 90°, a maximum positive when θ = 180° and so on. Armature self-inductance for any phase can be obtained by assuming that phase to be excited alone.

Assume that only phase *A* is excited. For current i_a, m.m.f. F_a for phase *A* is given by

$$F_a = N_a i_a \qquad ...(4.4)$$

Here $\quad N_a$ = effective number of per-phase turns

= (winding factor) × (actual per-phase turns)

The armature phase m.m.f. F_a is sinusoidally distributed along the air-gap periphery, it can therefore be represented by phasor $\overline{F_a}$ along the phase *A* axis as shown in Fig. 4.3 (*a*). The armature m.m.f. F_a can be resolved along two components, F_{da} along *d*-axis and F_{qa} along *q*-axis as shown and their values are

$$F_{da} = F_a \cos \theta$$

and

$$F_{qa} = F_a \cos (\theta + 90°) = -F_a \sin \theta.$$

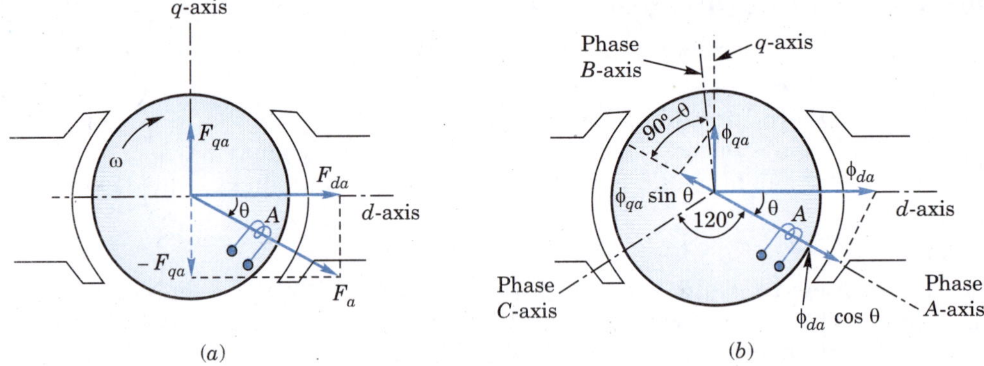

Fig. 4.3: Resolution of (*a*) F_a along *d*- and *q*-axes (*b*) ϕ_{da} and ϕ_{qa} along phase *A*-axis.

The idea of resolving F_a along its *d-q* axes components follows from *two-reaction theory*. The reluctance seen by F_{da} is that due to small air gap under the pole along the *d*-axis and the reluctance offered to F_{qa} is that due to long interpolar air gap along *q*-axis. Component m.m.fs F_{da} and F_{qa} give rise to their corresponding per pole fluxes ϕ_{da} and ϕ_{qa}.

$$\therefore \quad \phi_{da} = \Lambda_d . F_{da}$$

$$\text{and} \quad \phi_{qa} = \Lambda_q . F_{qa} \qquad \text{...(4.5)}$$

Here Λ_d and Λ_q are the effective permeance co-efficients in direct and quadrature axes respectively.

The air-gap flux ϕ_{ga} linking phase *A* winding is obtained by taking the components of ϕ_{da} and ϕ_{qa} along phase *A* axis as shown in Fig. 4.3 (*b*).

$$\therefore \quad \phi_{ga} = \phi_{da} \cos\theta + \phi_{qa} \cos(\theta + 90°)$$

$$= \phi_{da} \cos\theta - \phi_{qa} \sin\theta$$

In Fig. 4.3 (*b*), $\phi_{da} \cos\theta$ and $\phi_{qa} \sin\theta$ are shown opposing each other.

Substitution of the values of ϕ_{da} and ϕ_{qa} in the above equation gives

$$\phi_{ga} = F_{da} \Lambda_d \cos\theta - F_{qa} \Lambda_q \sin\theta$$

$$= F_a (\Lambda_d \cos^2\theta + \Lambda_q \sin^2\theta) \qquad \text{...(4.5a)}$$

With the help of trigonometric relations,

$$\cos^2\theta = \frac{1}{2}(1 + \cos 2\theta)$$

and $\sin^2\theta = \frac{1}{2}(1 - \cos 2\theta)$, Eq. [4.5 (*a*)] can be written as

$$\phi_{ga} = N_a i_a \left[\frac{\Lambda_d + \Lambda_q}{2} + \frac{\Lambda_d - \Lambda_q}{2} \cos 2\theta\right]$$

Now self-inductance is defined as the flux linkages per ampere in the same winding. In view of this, the self-inductance L_{ga} of phase *A* due to air-gap flux ϕ_{ga} is given by

$$L_{ga} = \frac{\phi_{ga} . N_a}{i_a}$$

$$= N_a^2 \left[\frac{\Lambda_d + \Lambda_q}{2} + \frac{\Lambda_d - \Lambda_q}{2} \cos 2\theta\right] \qquad \text{...(4.6)}$$

$$= L_{go} + L_{g2} \cos 2\theta \qquad \text{...(4.7)}$$

In Eq. (4.7), L_{go} is a constant term, whereas L_{g2} is the amplitude of second-harmonic component. There is some flux, produced by phase A, which does not cross the air gap to link the stator. This flux is called leakage flux and can be accounted for by phase leakage inductance l_a. Therefore, total self-inductance L_a of phase A is given by

$$L_a = L_{go} + l_a + L_{g2} \cos 2\theta$$
$$= L_{ao} + L_{g2} \cos 2\theta \qquad ...(4.8)$$

The variation of L_a with space angle θ is depicted in Fig. 4.4. The self-inductance of phases B and C can be obtained by replacing θ in Eq. (4.8) by (θ – 120°) and (θ – 240°) respectively.

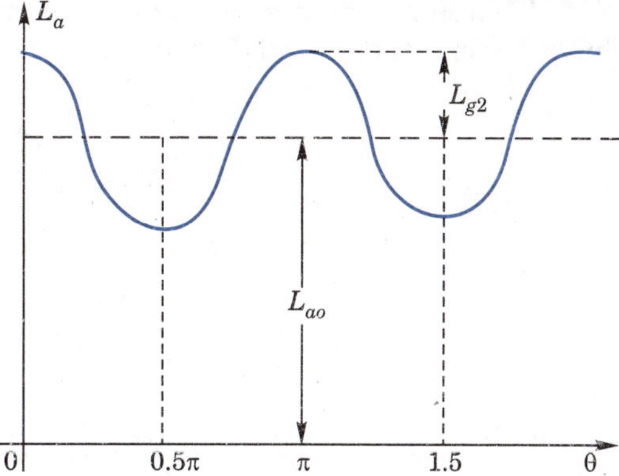

Fig. 4.4: Variation of self-inductance of phase A with space angle θ.

Note that for cylindrical-rotor machines, $L_{g_2} = 0$.

(*d*) **Armature mutual inductances.** The mutual inductance between phases A, B is $M_{ab} = M_{ba}$; between phases B, C is $M_{bc} = M_{cb}$ and between phases C, A is $M_{ca} = M_{ac}$. The mutual inductance $M_{ab} = M_{ba}$ can be found by determining the flux linkages with phase B when only phase A is excited or by determining the flux linkages with phase A when only phase B is excited.

Here assume that phase A alone is excited so that $i_b = i_c = 0$. The armature m.m.f. of phase A produces two *d*-*q* flux-components ϕ_{da} and ϕ_{qa} as given by Eq. (4.5). Fig. 4.3. (*b*) reveals that angle between ϕ_{da} and phase B axis is (120° – θ) or (θ – 120°). Therefore component of ϕ_{da} linking phase B (*i.e.* along the axis of phase B) is $\phi_{da} \cos(\theta - 120°)$.

Similarly, component of ϕ_{qa} linking phase B is

$$\phi_{qa} \cdot \cos(\overline{\theta + 90} - 120°) = \phi_{qa} [\cos(\theta + 90) \cos 120° + \sin(\theta + 90°) \sin 120°]$$
$$= -\phi_{qa} \cdot \sin(\theta - 120°)$$

Therefore, with only phase A excited, the flux linking phase B is given by

$$\phi_{ba} = \text{component of } \phi_{da} \text{ linking phase } B$$
$$+ \text{ component of } \phi_{qa} \text{ linking phase } B$$
$$= \phi_{da} \cos(\theta - 120°) - \phi_{qa} \sin(\theta - 120°)$$
$$= F_a [\Lambda_d \cos\theta \cos(\theta - 120°) + \Lambda_q \sin\theta \sin(\theta - 120°)]$$

Now $$\cos A \cos B = \frac{1}{2} [\cos(A + B) + \cos(A - B)]$$

and $$\sin A \sin B = \frac{1}{2} [\cos(A - B) - \cos(A + B)]$$

∴ $$\phi_{ba} = F_a [\Lambda_d \cdot \frac{1}{2} \cos(2\theta - 120°) + \Lambda_d \cdot \frac{1}{2} \cos 120°]$$
$$+ F_a [\Lambda_q \cdot \frac{1}{2} \cos 120° - \Lambda_q \cdot \frac{1}{2} \cos(2\theta - 120°)]$$

$$= N_a i_a \left[-\frac{\Lambda_d + \Lambda_q}{4} + \frac{\Lambda_d - \Lambda_q}{2} \cos(2\theta - 120°) \right]$$

Therefore, the mutual inductance between phases A and B, due to air-gap flux, when phase A alone is excited is given by

$$M_{ba} = M_{ab} = \frac{(\text{Phase } B \text{ turns})\begin{bmatrix}\text{air-gap flux linking phase} \\ B \text{ due to } i_a \text{ alone}\end{bmatrix}}{i_a} = \frac{N_b \cdot \phi_{ba}}{i_a}$$

The per-phase turns in each of the three phases are equal,

i.e., $N_a = N_b = N_c$

$$\therefore \quad M_{ab} = M_{ba} = \frac{N_a . N_a . i_a}{i_a}\left[-\frac{\Lambda_d + \Lambda_q}{4} + \frac{\Lambda_d - \Lambda_q}{2}\cos(2\theta - 120°)\right]$$

$$= N_a^2\left[-\frac{\Lambda_d + \Lambda_q}{4} + \frac{\Lambda_d - \Lambda_q}{2}\cos(2\theta - 120°)\right] \quad ...(4.9)$$

$$= -\tfrac{1}{2}L_{go} + L_{g2}\cos(2\theta - 120°) \quad ...(4.10)$$

It is seen from Eqs. (4.6) and (4.9) that amplitudes of second-harmonic components (L_{g2}) of self and mutual inductances are equal to $N_a^2 \dfrac{\Lambda_d - \Lambda_q}{2}$. It is also seen that constant component L_{ao}, of self-inductance L_a, in Eq. (4.8) is equal to about twice the constant component $\frac{1}{2}$ L_{go} of mutual inductance M_{ab} or M_{ba} in Eq. (4.10).

The variation of M_{ab} or M_{ba} with space angle θ is as shown in Fig. 4.5, where

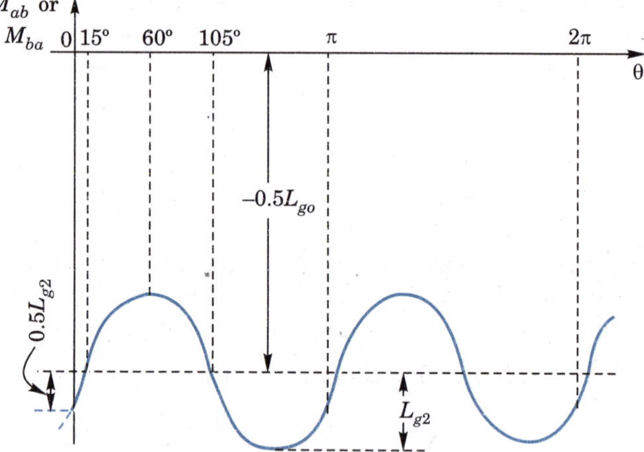

Fig. 4.5: Variation of armature mutual inductance with space angle θ.

for $\theta = 0$, $\quad M_{ab} = -\frac{1}{2}L_{go} - \frac{1}{2}L_{g2}$

for $\theta = 15°$, $\quad M_{ab} = -\frac{1}{2}L_{go}$

for $\theta = 60°$, $\quad M_{ab} = -\frac{1}{2}L_{go} + L_{g2}$

for $\theta = 150°$, $\quad M_{ab} = -\frac{1}{2}L_{go} - L_{g2}$ and so on.

The mutual inductance M_{bc} (between phases B, C) and M_{ca} (between phases C, A) can be obtained by replacing θ in Eq. (4.10) by $(\theta - 120°)$ and $(\theta - 240°)$ respectively.

$$\therefore \quad M_{bc} = -\tfrac{1}{2}L_{go} + L_{g2}\cos(2\theta - 240° - 120°) = -\tfrac{1}{2}L_{go} + L_{g2}\cos 2\theta$$

$$M_{ca} = -\tfrac{1}{2}L_{go} + L_{g2}\cos(2\theta - 480 - 120°) = -\tfrac{1}{2}L_{go} + L_{g2}\cos(2\theta - 240°)$$

For round-rotor machine, $L_{g2} = 0$

The question may arise in the mind of the reader that why the armature mutual inductances are negative. When phase A alone is excited, the component of flux linking with both phases B and C is negative, because phases B, C are dispaced by a space angle of 120° (more than 90°) from phase A. Consequently, the armature mutual-inductances are negative. An examination of the expression ϕ_{ba} shows that negative term $(\Lambda_d + \Lambda_q)/4$ is greater than the positive term $(\Lambda_d - \Lambda_q)/2$ and therefore ϕ_{ba} and M_{ba} (or M_{ab}) are negative.

Summary of Synchronous-machine parameters. All the synchronous machine inductances are defined in terms of five positive inductance parameters L_f, M_{afm}, L_{ao}, L_{g2}, L_{go} and space angle θ expressed in electrical degrees. These five inductance parameters and field and armature circuit resistances are assumed known either by test or from manufacturer's data. The various resistances and inductances for a salient-pole synchronous machine are summarised below.

(*a*) Field-circuit resistance and per phase armature-circuit resistance are given the symbols r_f and r_a respectively.

(*b*) Field self-inductance, L_f = constant.

(*c*) Armature to field mutual inductances,

$$\left.\begin{aligned} M_{af} &= M_{fa} = M_{afm} \cos\theta \\ M_{bf} &= M_{fb} = M_{afm} \cos(\theta - 120°) \\ M_{cf} &= M_{fc} = M_{afm} \cos(\theta - 240°) \end{aligned}\right] \quad ...(4.11)$$

(*d*) Armature self-inductances,

$$\left.\begin{aligned} L_a &= L_{ao} + L_{g2} \cos 2\theta \\ L_b &= L_{ao} + L_{g2} \cos(2\theta - 240°) \\ L_c &= L_{ao} + L_{g2} \cos(2\theta - 120°) \end{aligned}\right] \quad ...(4.12)$$

(*e*) Armature mutual inductances,

$$\left.\begin{aligned} M_{ab} &= M_{ba} = -0.5\, L_{go} + L_{g2} \cos(2\theta - 120°) \\ M_{bc} &= M_{cb} = -0.5\, L_{go} + L_{g2} \cos 2\theta \\ M_{ca} &= M_{ac} = -0.5\, L_{go} + L_{g2} \cos(2\theta - 240°) \end{aligned}\right] \quad ...(4.13)$$

For a round-rotor synchronous machine, $L_{g2} = 0$ because its air gap is uniform.

Thus, for a cylindrical-rotor synchronous machine, the self-inductance of phase A, or any other phases from Eq. (4.12), is

$$L_a = L_b = L_c = L_{ao} = L_{go} + l_a \quad ...(4.12a)$$

As stated before, L_{go} is a constant component of self-inductance and is present due to the space-fundamental component of air-gap flux.

With $L_{g2} = 0$, the mutual inductances between armature phases, from Eq. (4.13), are

$$M_{ab} = M_{bc} = M_{ca} = -0.5\, L_{go} \quad ...(4.13a)$$

It is seen from Eqs. (4.12) and (4.13) that as expected, effects of saliency appear in salient-pole machines in the form of a component inductance that varies with 2θ. This double frequency variation term is associated with armature self-inductances as well as armature mutual-inductances but not with armature-to-field mutual inductances. It is observed from Eq. (4.12) that self-inductance of any armature phase is maximum when that phase axis coincides with the field winding or direct axis. For example, when θ = 0°, phase – a axis coincides with direct axis, phase – a self-inductance L_a (= $L_{ao} + L_{g2}$) is, therefore, maximum.

Eq. (4.13) reveals that armature mutual inductance is maximum (*i.e.* minimum negative), when mid-point of any two phases is aligned with the direct axis. For example, when $\theta = 0°$, the mid-point of phases b and c is along the d-axis, mutual inductance M_{bc} $(= -0.5L_{go} + L_{g2})$ between armature phases b and c is, therefore, maximum.

4.2 GENERAL MACHINE EQUATIONS

The object of this article is to obtain synchronous machine voltage equations in *dqo* variables by the use of coupled-circuit theory and Park's transformations.

The voltage equations for each of the three-phase windings and the field winding have the general form,

$$v = ri + p\psi \qquad ...(4.14)$$

Here v is the applied voltage, r the winding resistance, i the input current and ψ the flux linkages with the winding. For convenience, the differential operator p is used to replace d/dt.

Phase windings A, B, C and field winding F have their own self-inductance and mutual inductances with respect to every other circuit. From an examination of Fig. 4.1, the flux linkages ψ of the 3-phase winding and that of the field winding, in terms of the self and mutual inductances, are

$$\begin{aligned} \psi_a &= L_a i_a + M_{ab} i_b + M_{ac} i_c + M_{af} i_f \\ \psi_b &= M_{ba} i_a + L_b i_b + M_{bc} i_c + M_{bf} i_f \\ \psi_c &= M_{ca} i_a + M_{cb} i_b + L_c i_c + M_{cf} i_f \\ \psi_f &= M_{fa} i_a + M_{fb} i_b + M_{fc} i_c + L_f i_f \end{aligned} \qquad ...(4.15)$$

Here the subscripts a, b, c and f are used to denote respectively the terms pertaining to phases A, B, C and field winding F.

The nature of the various inductances involved in Eq. (4.15) has already been discussed in Art. 4.1 in Eqs. (4.11) to (4.13).

The voltage equation for phase A is

$$\begin{aligned} v_a &= r_a i_a + p\psi_a \\ &= r_a i_a + p[L_a i_a + M_{ab} i_b + M_{ac} i_c + M_{af} i_f] \end{aligned} \qquad ...(4.16)$$

Substitution of the values of L_a, M_{ab} etc. from Eqs. (4.11) to (4.13) in Eq. (4.16) gives

$$\begin{aligned} v_a = r_a i_a + p\,[&(L_{ao} + L_{g2}\cos 2\theta)\, i_a + (-0.5L_{go} + L_{g2}\cos(2\theta - 120°))\, i_b \\ &+ (-0.5L_{go} + L_{g2}\cos(2\theta - 240°))\, i_c + (M_{afm}\cos\theta)\, i_f] \end{aligned} \qquad ...(4.17)$$

The voltage equations for v_b, v_c and v_f can be written similarly as done for obtaining Eq. (4.17). The solution of these four simultaneous equations is quite prohibitive. However, the solution of these equations, describing the synchronous machine operation, can be simplified if these four equations are expressed in terms of *dqo* variables. The procedure of expressing v_a, v_b, v_c in *dqo* variables is given below.

With the help of Park's Eq. (2.12), write down the voltages v_d, v_q, v_o in terms of v_a, v_b, v_c, as follows:

$$\begin{bmatrix} v_d \\ v_q \\ v_o \end{bmatrix} = \frac{2}{3} \begin{bmatrix} \cos\theta & \cos\left(\theta - \frac{2\pi}{3}\right) & \cos\left(\theta - \frac{4\pi}{3}\right) \\ -\sin\theta & -\sin\left(\theta - \frac{2\pi}{3}\right) & -\sin\left(\theta - \frac{4\pi}{3}\right) \\ \frac{1}{\sqrt{2}} & \frac{1}{\sqrt{2}} & \frac{1}{\sqrt{2}} \end{bmatrix} \begin{bmatrix} v_a \\ v_b \\ v_c \end{bmatrix} \quad ...(4.18)$$

Now in Eq. (4.18), substitute the value of v_a as given by Eq. (4.17) and the values of v_b, v_c which are similar to Eq. (4.17). Simplify these resulting equations by recognizig that ψ_d, ψ_q, ψ_o in terms of ψ_a, ψ_b, ψ_c are given by an expression similar to Eq. (4.18). The simpification of these equations give

$$\left.\begin{aligned} v_d &= r_a i_d + p\psi_d - \omega\psi_q \\ v_q &= r_a i_q + p\psi_q + \omega\psi_d \\ v_o &= r_a i_o + p\psi_o \end{aligned}\right\} \quad ...(4.19)$$

In armature voltage equations given by Eq. (4.19), the terms $p\psi_d$ and $p\psi_q$ are transformer voltages. The terms $\omega\psi_q$ and $\omega\psi_d$ are speed, or rotational, voltages. Under balanced operation, v_o is absent.

The voltage equation for the field circuit is given by

$$v_f = r_f i_f + p\psi_f$$

Substitution of the value of ψ_f from Eq. (4.15) gives,

$$v_f = r_f i_f + p\,[M_{fa} i_a + M_{fb} i_b + M_{fc} i_c + L_f i_f]$$

Now substitute the values of M_{fa}, M_{fb}, M_{fc} from Eq. (4.11).

Therefore,

$$\begin{aligned} v_f &= r_f i_f + p\,[M_{afm} \cos\theta \,.\, i_a + M_{afm} \cos(\theta - 120°).\, i_b + M_{afm} \cos(\theta - 240°).\, i_c] + L_f p_{if}] \\ &= r_f i_f + p.\, M_{afm}\,[i_a \cos\theta + i_b \cos(\theta - 120°) + i_c \cos(\theta - 240°)] + L_f p_{if} \end{aligned}$$

From Eq. (4.18),

$$i_d = \frac{2}{3}\,[i_a \cos\theta + i_b \cos(\theta - 120°) + i_c \cos(\theta - 240°)]$$

$$\therefore \qquad v_f = r_f i_f + \frac{3}{2} pM_{afm}\, i_d + L_f p i_f \quad ...(4.20)$$

It can also be proved that

$$\psi_f = L_f i_f + \frac{3}{2} M_{afm} i_d \quad ...(4.21)$$

In Eq. (4.21), M_{afm} is the maximum value of mutual inductance between armature phase '*a*' of three-phase machine and field winding when their magnetic axis coincide. Therefore, M_{afm} may be expressed as

$$M_{afm} = N_a \,.\, N_f \,.\, \Lambda_d$$

where N_a = effective per-phase armature turns in three-phase machine,

N_f = field winding turns

and Λ_d = *d*-axis (or field-winding axis) permeance

For the two-axis model, *d*-axis coil has 3/2 N_a effective turns as per Eq. (2.3). Therefore, the mutual inductance M_d between *d*-axis, or *q*-axis, coil of two-axis (or generalized) machine and the field winding can be expressed as

$$M_d = \frac{3}{2} N_a N_f \Lambda_d = \frac{3}{2} M_{afm} \qquad ...(4.22)$$

In view of this, Eqs. (4.20) and (4.21) can be expressed as

$$v_f = r_f i_f + L_f\, pi_f + M_d\, pi_d$$

and

$$\psi_f = L_f i_f + M_d i_d \qquad ...(4.23)$$

Note that M_d, the mutual inductance between field-winding coil and q-axis, or d-axis, coil, is usually called the **motional inductance**.

The flux linkages ψ_d, ψ_q, ψ_o in terms of i_d, i_q, i_o can be obtained by following the procedure adopted for obtaining Eq. (4.19). Therefore,

$$\left.\begin{aligned} \psi_d &= L_d i_d + M_d i_f \\ \psi_q &= L_q i_q \\ \psi_o &= L_o i_o \end{aligned}\right\} \qquad ...(4.23a)$$

The derivation of Eqs. (4.19) and (4.22) is very unwieldy and laborious. In fact, the manipulations are so tedius and lengthy that the students may loose track of what is going on in the machine. In view of this, these manipulations are not done here.

With this, Eqs. (4.21) and (4.23) become

$$\left.\begin{aligned} \psi_d &= L_d i_d + M_d i_f \\ \psi_d &= L_q i_q \\ \psi_f &= M_d i_d + L_f i_f \\ \psi_o &= L_o i_o \end{aligned}\right\} \qquad ...(4.24)$$

Substitution, from above, the values of ψ_d, ψ_q, ψ_o, in Eq, (4.19) gives,

$$v_d = r_a i_d + L_d pi_d + M_d pi_f - \omega_r L_q i_q \qquad ...(4.25)$$

$$v_q = r_a i_q + L_q pi_q + \omega_r L_d i_d + M_d \omega_r i_f \qquad ...(4.26)$$

$$v_o = r_a i_o + L_o pi_o \qquad ...(4.27)$$

Eq. (4.20) is already re-written as

$$v_f = r_f i_f + L_f pi_f + M_d pi_d \qquad ...(4.28)$$

In Eqs. (4.25) and (4.26), $\omega_r = p\theta$.

In Eq. (4.24), the following new parameters have been introduced.

$$\left.\begin{aligned} L_d &= l_a + \frac{3}{2}(L_{go} + L_{g_2}) \\ L_q &= l_a + \frac{3}{2}(L_{go} - L_{g_2}) \\ L_o &= l_a \end{aligned}\right\} \qquad ...(4.29)$$

From the above equations, $L_d - L_q = 3L_{g_2}$

This shows that difference between L_d and L_q depends upon the amplitude of second harmonic component L_{g_2}.

The new inductance parameters L_d, L_q and L_o, as given by Eq. (4.29), are called, respectively, the *direct-axis synchronous inductance,* the *quadrature-axis synchronous inductance,* and the *zero-sequence inductance.*

The expressions for L_d and L_q are usually written as $L_d = l_a + L_{md}$ and $L_q = l_a + L_{mq}$

Here L_{md} = 3/2 ($L_{go} + L_{g2}$) is called d-axis magnetizing inductance or d-axis armature reaction inductance. Similarly, L_{mq} = 3/2 ($L_{go} - L_{g2}$) is called q-axis magnetizing inductance or q-axis armature-reaction inductance of a salient-pole machine.

For a round-rotor synchronous machine, $L_{g_2} = 0$ and its synchronous inductance L_s, from Eq. (4.29), is

$$L_s = l_a + \frac{3}{2} L_{go} \qquad \text{...[4.29 (a)]}$$

In Eq. (4.29 a), 3/2 L_{go} is usually called magnetizing inductance or armature reaction inductance of a cylindrical-rotor synchronous machine.

Let us now summarise what Park's transformations have done in transforming equations in a, b, c variables to equations in d, q, o variables.

(a) Eq. (4.17) for v_a and similar other three equations for v_b, v_c and v_f have time-varying co-efficients. But Park's transformations have transformed these equations to Eqs. (4.25) to (4.28) which have constant parameters. With constant speed ω_r, Eqs. (4.25) and (4.26) are now linear equations.

(b) In Eq. (4.17), p ($L \cdot i$) gives two terms and there are, therefore, total nine terms. But there are only two to four terms in Eqs. (4.25) to (4.28). This shows that it is much simpler to handle Eqs. (4.25) to (4.28) for steady state, transient and dynamic analysis of synchronous machines.

A study of this article reveals how cumbersome it is to obtain synchronous machine voltage equations (4.25) and (4.26) in dqo variables by using coupled-circuit theory and Park's transformations. This lengthy and laborious procedure can, however, be avoided if the generalized approach is adopted. By this approach, the voltage equations in dqo variables can be written graphically just by observing the generalized (or two-axis) model of a synchronous machine and this is the object of the next Art. 4.3.

Example 4.1. *A basic 3-phase, 2-pole synchronous machine of the salient-pole type has the following inductances, where θ is the angle measured from d-axis to the axis of phase A.*

Phase A self-inductance, $L_a = 0.9 + 0.2 \cos 2\theta$

Mutual inductance between phase A and field winding F, $M_{af} = 8 \cos \theta$.

Mutual inductance between phases B and C, $M_{bc} = -0.4 + 0.2 \cos 2\theta$

(a) *Write expressions for all the self and mutual inductances in terms of* θ.

(b) *Determine* L_d, L_q *and* L_o.

(c) *Repeat parts* (a) *and* (b) *if this machine were a cylindrical-rotor synchronous machine.*

Solution. (a) Self-inductance of phase A,

$$L_a = L_{ao} + L_{g_2} \cos 2\theta = 0.9 + 0.2 \cos 2\theta$$

$$\therefore \qquad L_{ao} = 0.9 \text{ H and } L_{g_2} = 0.2 \text{ H.}$$

Self-inductance of phase B,

$$L_b = L_{ao} + L_{g_2} \cos (2\theta - 240°) = 0.9 + 0.2 \cos (2\theta - 240°)$$

Similarly, $L_c = 0.9 + 0.2 \cos(2\theta - 120°)$

Mutual inductance between A and F,

$$M_{af} = M_{afm} \cos\theta = 8 \cos\theta$$

$\therefore$ $M_{afm} = 8$ H

$\therefore$ $M_{bf} = M_{afm} \cos(\theta - 120°) = 8 \cos(\theta - 120°)$

and $M_{cf} = 8 \cos(\theta - 240°)$

Mutual inductance between B and C,

$$M_{bc} = -0.5L_{go} + L_{g_2} \cos 2\theta = -0.4 + 0.2 \cos 2\theta \text{ (given)}$$

$\therefore$ $L_{go} = 0.8$ H and $L_{g_2} = 0.2$ H

$\therefore$ $M_{ab} = -0.5L_{go} + L_{g_2} \cos(2\theta - 120°) = -0.4 + 0.2 \cos(2\theta - 120°)$

and $M_{ca} = -0.4 + 0.2 \cos(2\theta - 240°)$

(*b*) From Eq. (4.8), $L_{ao} = L_{go} + l_a$ or $0.9 = 0.8 + l_a$

$\therefore$ $l_a = 0.1$ H

From Eq. (4.29),

$$L_d = l_a + 3/2(L_{go} + L_{g_2})$$
$$= 0.1 + 3/2(0.8 + 0.2) = 1.6 \text{ H}$$
$$L_q = l_a + 3/2(L_{go} - L_{g_2})$$
$$= 0.1 + 3/2(0.8 - 0.2) = 1.0 \text{ H}$$
$$L_o = l_a = 0.1 \text{ H}$$

(*c*) For a cylindrical-rotor synchronous machine,

$$L_{g_2} = 0.$$

$\therefore$ $L_a = L_b = L_c = L_{ao} = 0.9$ H

$$M_{af} = 8 \cos\theta,$$
$$M_{bf} = 8 (\cos\theta - 120°),$$
$$M_{cf} = 8 \cos(\theta - 240°)$$
$$M_{ab} = M_{bc} = M_{ca} = -0.5L_{go} = -0.4 \text{ H};$$
$$l_a = 0.1 \text{ H}.$$
$$L_d = l_a + 3/2\, L_{go} = 0.1 + 3/2 \times 0.8 = 1.3 \text{ H}$$
$$L_q = l_a + 3/2\, L_{go} = 1.3 \text{ H}$$

and $L_o = l_a = 0.1$ H

Example 4.2. *A 11 kV, 100 MVA, 50 Hz, 3-phase synchronous generator has the following data:*

Synchronous reactance = 1.2 pu, leakage reactance = 0.1 pu.

Calculate:

(*a*) *synchronous inductance in H*

(*b*) *leakage inductance in H*

(*c*) *self-inductance of phase 'a' in H and in pu and*

(*d*) *armature mutual inductance in H.*

Solution. Base impedances, $Z_b = \dfrac{(kV)_B^2}{MVA} = \dfrac{11^2}{100} = 1.21\ \Omega$

(*a*) Synchronous reactance, $1.2 \text{ pu} = \dfrac{X_s \text{ in } \Omega}{\text{Base impedance}}$

$$\therefore \qquad X_s = 1.21 \times 1.2 = 1.452\ \Omega$$

Synchronous inductance, $\quad L_s = \dfrac{1.452}{2\pi \times 50} = 4.622 \text{ mH}$

(*b*) Leakage reactance in ohms, $x_a = 1.21 \times 0.1 = 0.121\ \Omega$

$\therefore$ Armature leakage inductance, $l_a = \dfrac{0.121}{2\pi \times 50} = 0.3852 \text{ mH}$

(*c*) But $\quad L_s = l_a + \dfrac{3}{2} L_g.$

$$\therefore \qquad L_{go} = \frac{2}{3}[4.622 - 0.3852] = 2.8245 \text{ mH}$$

$\therefore$ Self-inductance of phase a, $L_a = l_a + L_{go} = 0.3852 + 2.8245 = 3.21 \text{ mH}$

Armature-phase reactance $= 2\pi \times 50 \times 3.21 \times 10^{-3}\ \Omega$

$\therefore$ Armature-phase reactance in pu

$$= \frac{2\pi \times 50 \times 3.21 \times 10^{-3}}{1.21} = 0.8334 \text{ pu}$$

(*d*) Armature mutual inductance $= -1/2\, L_{go} = -1/2 \times 2.8245 = -1.4123 \text{ mH}$

4.3 THREE-PHASE SYNCHRONOUS MACHINE (WITH NO AMORTISSEURS)

The synchronous machine voltage Eqs. (4.25) to (4.28) in *dqo* variables can be obtained from phase variable equations though the manipulations involved are quite tedius and lengthy. However, the synchronous machine voltage equations in *d-q* variables can be obtained by a simple graphical method developed in Art. 1.7 and same is adopted in this article.

The primitive machine model or generalized model of a polyphase machine without amortisseurs is illustrated in Fig. 4.6. The stator coil *DS* represents the field winding and the rotor coils *DR*, *QR* represent the polyphase armature winding. In the analysis to follow, the effect of amortisseur circuits (or damper bars) is neglected, so that basic important results are obtained more conviniently.

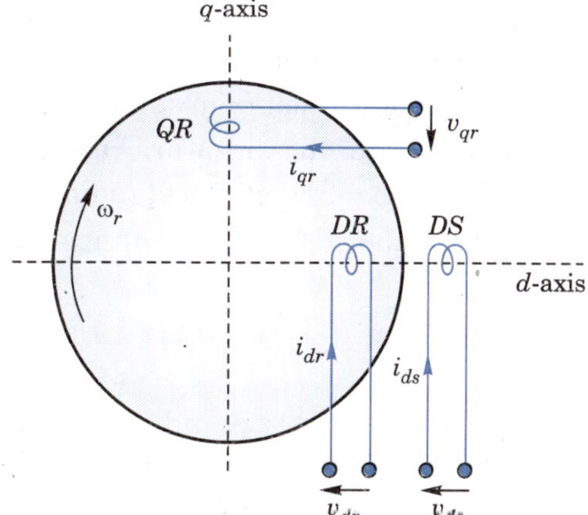

Fig. 4.6: Generalized model of a polyphase synchronous machine.

In Fig. 4.6, the voltages are applied and currents are input currents. In accordance with Art. 1.7.2, the voltage equations in matrix form for the model of Fig. 4.6 are written as follows :

$$\begin{bmatrix} v_{ds} \\ v_{dr} \\ v_{qr} \end{bmatrix} = \begin{matrix} ds \\ dr \\ qr \end{matrix} \overset{\begin{matrix} ds & \quad dr & \quad qr \end{matrix}}{\begin{bmatrix} r_{ds} + L_{ds}p & M_d p & \\ M_d p & r_{dr} + L_{dr}p & -L_{qr}\omega_r \\ M_d \omega_r & M_{dr}\omega_r & r_{qr} + L_{qr}p \end{bmatrix}} \begin{bmatrix} i_{ds} \\ i_{dr} \\ i_{qr} \end{bmatrix} \quad ...(4.30)$$

Now the field winding is designated by F in place of more general DS. Similarly the armature winding DR and QR are designated by D and Q respectively.

Since the armature winding is uniformly distributed and balanced,

$$r_{dr} = r_{qr} = r_a \text{ (say).}$$

With these constraints, the voltage Eq. (4.30) becomes,

$$\left.\begin{aligned} v_f &= (r_f + L_{fp})\, i_f + M_d p i_d \\ v_d &= M_d p i_f + (r_a + L_d p)\, i_d - L_q \omega_r i_q \\ v_q &= M_d \omega_r i_f + L_d \omega_r i_d + (r_a + L_q p) i_q \end{aligned}\right] \quad ...(4.31)$$

The voltage-current relations given by Eq. (4.31) are applicable both for steady-state and transient analysis of synchronous machines.

4.4 BALANCED STEADY-STATE ANALYSIS

With d.c. field winding on the outer fixed member, the stator field does not revolve and is, therefore, stationary in space. Polyphase currents in the armature winding produce synchronously revolving field and for the relative speed between the two fields to be zero, the armature must revolve at synchronous speed opposite to the direction of rotating field. Thus the speed of resultant air-gap flux with respect to stator is zero. In other words, the resultant air-gap flux is stationary in space and in view of this, the operator p must be replaced by zero. On steady state, the armature can run at synchronous speed only, therefore, rotor angular velocity $\omega_r = \omega = 2\pi f$ electrical radians per second.

Thus the steady-state voltage equations, from Eq. (4.31) are ;

$$\left.\begin{aligned} V_f &= r_f I_f \\ v_{do} &= r_a i_{do} - L_q \omega i_{qo} \\ v_{qo} &= M_d \omega I_f + L_d \omega i_{do} + r_a i_{qo} \end{aligned}\right] \quad ...(4.32)$$

The subscript zero indicates constant or d.c. values. In place of v_{do}, v_{qo} etc.; V_d, V_q etc. should have been written, but it is not done here merely to use them at a later stage.

Note that the term $L_q\omega$ is associated with v_{do} and $L_d\omega$ with v_{qo}. These quantities $L_d\omega$ and $L_q\omega$ are known as

$$L_d\omega = X_d, \text{ direct axis synchronous reactance and}$$

$$L_q\omega = X_q, \text{ quadrature axis synchronous reactance.}$$

In order to include these terms, Eq. (4.32) is re-written as,

$$\left.\begin{aligned} v_{do} &= r_a i_{do} - X_q i_{qo} \\ v_{qo} &= M_d \omega I_f + X_d i_{do} + r_a i_{qo} \end{aligned}\right] \quad ...(4.33)$$

4.4.1 Phasor Equations and Phasor Diagrams

In order to determine the performance characteristics of the machine in actual machine axes, *i.e.* *a–b–c* co-ordinates, the transformation from *d*, *q*, *o* to *abc* variables as given by Eq. (2.11) can be used.

Considering phase *a* only, $v_a = [v_{do} \cos \theta - v_{qo} \sin \theta]$

Note that, under balanced 3-phase operation, zero sequence current i_o is zero.

If the axis of phase *a* is coinciding with the *d*-axis at time $t = 0$, then the angle between phase *a* and *d*-axes at any time *t* is $\theta = \omega t$, as illustrated in Fig. 4.7 (*a*).

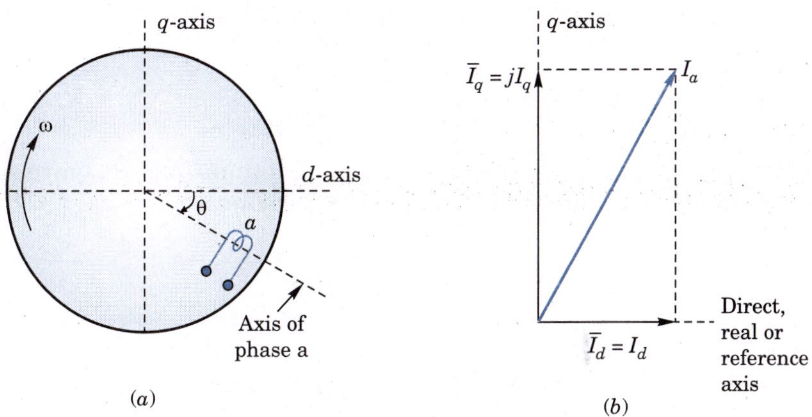

Fig. 4.7: (*a*) Phase – *a* axis at an angle $\theta = \omega t$ from *d*-axis and (*b*) Phasor components of I_a.

$$\therefore \quad v_a = [v_{do} \cos \omega t - v_{qo} \sin \omega t]$$

Now
$$Re\,[v_{do}\, e^{j\omega t}] = v_{do} \cos \omega t$$

and
$$Re\,[jv_{qo}\, e^{j\omega t}] = Re\,[jv_{qo} \cos \omega t - v_{qo} \sin \omega t]$$
$$= -\,v_{qo} \sin \omega t.$$

$$\therefore \quad v_a = Re\,[v_{do}\, e^{j\omega t} + jv_{qo}\, e^{j\omega t}]$$
$$= Re\,[(v_{do} + jv_{qo})\, e^{j\omega t}] \qquad ...(4.34)$$

For phase *a*, let the voltage be given by, $v_a = V_m \cos (\omega t + \sigma)$

where σ is the angle that v_a makes at $t = 0$.

Also
$$v_a = Re\left[\sqrt{2}\,.\frac{V_m}{\sqrt{2}}\,.\,e^{j\sigma}\,.\,e^{j\omega t}\right]$$
$$= Re\,[\sqrt{2}\,.\,\bar{V}_a\,.\,e^{j\omega t}] \qquad ...(4.35)$$

where
$$\bar{V}_a = \frac{V_m}{\sqrt{2}}\,.\,e^{j\sigma} = V_e^{\,j\sigma}$$

In Eqs. (4.34) and (4.35), the term $R_e\,[e^{j\omega t}]$ appears on both sides, this can therefore be cancelled. As a result of it,

$$\bar{V}_a = \frac{v_{do} + jv_{qo}}{\sqrt{2}} = V_d + jV_q \qquad ...(4.36)$$

where
$$V_d = \frac{v_{do}}{\sqrt{2}} \text{ and } V_q = \frac{v_{qo}}{\sqrt{2}}$$

Similarly $$\bar{I}_a = I_d + jI_q \quad ...(4.37)$$

where $$I_d = \frac{i_{do}}{\sqrt{2}} \quad \text{and} \quad I_q = \frac{i_{do}}{\sqrt{2}}$$

Open-circuit conditions. On no-load, $i_a = i_b = i_c = 0$, *i.e.*, the actual armature currents are zero. These zero values when transformed to d-q axes currents are $i_{do} = i_{qo} = 0$. In view of this, Eq. (4.33) becomes

$$v_{do} = 0 \quad \text{and} \quad v_{qo} = M_d \omega I_f.$$

The no-load r.m.s. voltage of phase a, from Eq. (4.36), is

$$\bar{V}_a = \frac{v_{do} + jv_{qo}}{\sqrt{2}} = j\frac{M_d \omega I_f}{\sqrt{2}} = jE_f \quad ...(4.38)$$

where $$E_f = \frac{M_d \omega I_f}{\sqrt{2}} \quad ...(4.39)$$

is called the **excitation emf**, **excitation voltage**, **open-circuit voltage** or **voltage generated at no load.** This voltage can also be expressed in terms of M_{afm}. From Eqs. (4.39) and (4.22),

$$E_f = \frac{M_d \cdot \omega \cdot I_f}{\sqrt{2}} = \frac{3}{2} \cdot \frac{M_{afm} \cdot \omega \cdot I_f}{\sqrt{2}} \quad ...(4.40)$$

Note that M_d in Eq. (4.39) is the motional inductance whereas M_{afm} in Eq. (4.40) is the maximum mutual inductance between field and any one phase of armature winding.

Load conditions. In this case, the voltage of phase a is obtained by the substitution of v_{do}, v_{qo} from Eq. (4.33) in Eq. (4.36) for $\bar{V}_a$.

$$\therefore \quad \bar{V}_a = \frac{v_{do} + jv_{qo}}{\sqrt{2}} = \frac{1}{\sqrt{2}} [r_a i_{do} - X_q i_{qo} + j(M_d \omega I_f + X_d i_{do} + r_a i_{qo})]$$

$$= r_a \bar{I}_a - X_q I_q + jX_d I_d + jE_f \quad ...(4.41)$$

In Eq. (4.41); I_d, I_q and E_f are only magnitudes and not in complex notation. In order to express them as phasors, refer to Fig. 4.7 (*b*), where d-axis is taken as the reference or real-axis. The phasor notation for armature current I_a, in terms of phasors $\bar{I}_d$ and $\bar{I}_q$ can be written as

$$\bar{I}_a = \bar{I}_d + \bar{I}_q$$

From Eq. (4.37), $$\bar{I}_a = \bar{I}_d + \bar{I}_q = I_d + jI_q$$

$$\therefore \quad \bar{I}_d = I_d \text{ and } \bar{I}_q = jI_q \quad \text{or} \quad I_q = -j\bar{I}_q.$$

With these changes, Eq. (4.41) becomes

$$\bar{V}_a = r_a \bar{I}_a + jX_d \bar{I}_d + jX_q \bar{I}_q + jE_f \quad ...(4.42)$$

Eq. (4.42) gives r.m.s. terminal voltage of phase a in phasor notation. By a proper choice, terminal voltage $\bar{V}_b$ for phase b or V_c for phase c may have been obtained. Using V_t to represent the terminal voltage of any one phase, Eq. (4.42) may be written as

$$\bar{V}_t = r_a \bar{I}_a + jX_d \bar{I}_d + jX_q \bar{I}_q + jE_f \quad ...(4.43)$$

Note that Eq. (4.43) is obtained with applied voltages and input armature currents. Therefore, Eq. (4.43) pertains to a synchronous motor and it yields the phasor diagram of Fig. 4.8 (*a*) for a salient-pole type motor.

For a generator, the voltages are generated and the currents are output currents. In view of this, the generator voltage equation can be obtained from motor voltage equation by writing $(-\bar{I}_a)$ in place of $\bar{I}_a$. Therefore, from Eq. (4.43), the generator voltage equation is

$$\bar{V}_t = -r_a\bar{I}_a - j\bar{I}_dX_d - j\bar{I}_qX_q + jE_f$$

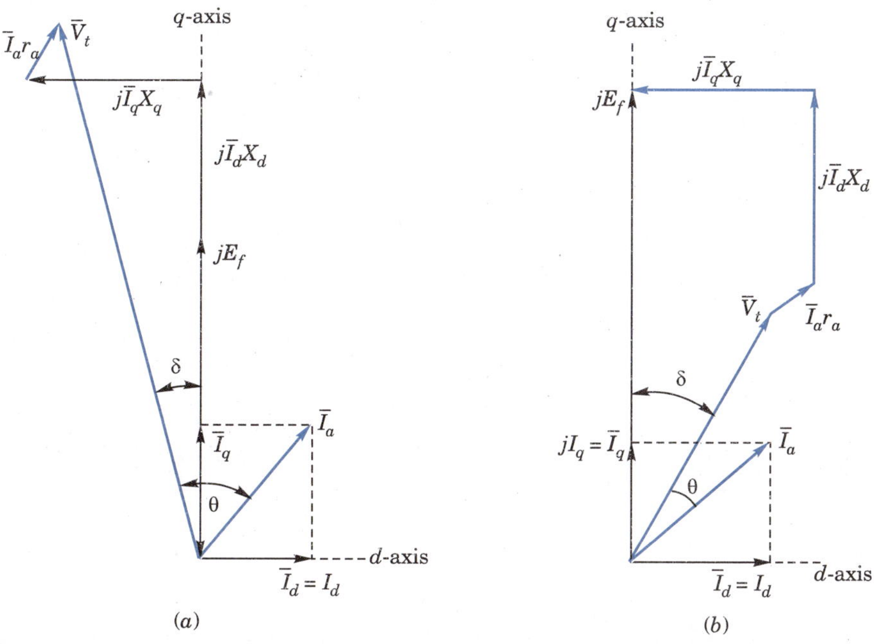

Fig. 4.8: Phasor diagrams for (*a*) synchronous motor and (*b*) synchronous generator.

or $$jE_f = \bar{V}_t + \bar{I}_a r_a + j\bar{I}_dX_d + j\bar{I}_qX_q \quad ...(4.44)$$

Eq. (4.44) gives phasor diagram for a salient-pole synchronous generator as shown in Fig. 4.8 (*b*).

For using the phasor diagrams of Fig. 4.8, the armature current I_a must be resolved into its *d*- and *q*-axis components. Usually V_t, I_a, power-factor angle θ, X_d and X_q are known in a problem. But for calculating I_d and I_q, the internal power-factor angle (δ + θ) for a generator and (θ – δ) for a motor must be known. For this purpose, draw *ab* normal to I_a as shown in Fig. 4.9 ; where for simplicity *j* with E_f is dropped. Since *ab* is 90° away from I_a, it must be a reactance drop, say I_aX. Draw *ac* perpendicular to *ob* (= E_f') as shown in Fig. 4.9.

From generator phasor diagram of Fig. 4.9 (*a*) it is seen that *oab* and *acb* are right angled triangles and, therefore, ∠*bac* = ∠δ +θ.

Thus, $$ac = ab\cos(\delta + \theta) = XI_a\cos(\delta + \theta) = XI_q = de = X_qI_q$$

or $$XI_q = X_qI_q \text{ or } X = X_q.$$

This shows that in Fig. 4.9 (*a*), $ab = I_aX_q$. If *ob* is designated as E_f', then it is seen that

$$\bar{E}_f' = \bar{V}_t + \bar{I}_a r_a + j\bar{I}_aX_q \quad ...(4.45)$$

Note that phasors $\bar{E}_f'$ and $\bar{E}_f$ are directed along the same line.

Thus the phasor sum $\overline{V}_t + \overline{I}_a r_a + j\overline{I}_a X_q$ gives $\overline{E}_f'$ and, therefore, the angular position of the excitation voltage E_f with respect to V_t, *i.e.* the power angle δ is known. From this, angle $(\delta + \theta)$ and, therefore, I_d and I_q can be computed – this is illustrated in Example 4.3. Fig. 4.9 (*a*) also reveals that

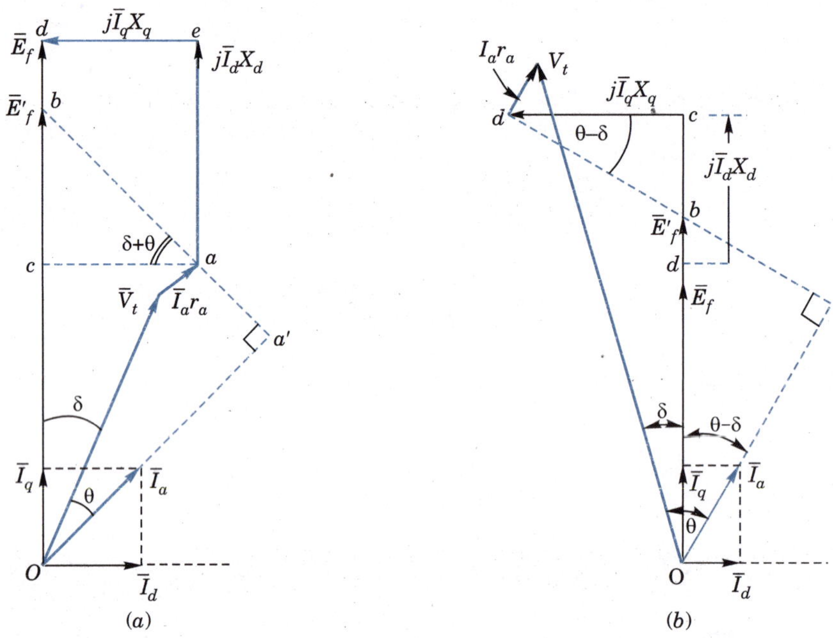

Fig. 4.9: Resolving of I_a into its *d*- and *q*-axes components I_d and I_q for (*a*) generator and (*b*) motor.

$$bd = cd - cb = X_d I_d - X_q I_a \sin(\delta + \theta)$$
$$= X_d I_d - X_q I_d = (X_d - X_q) I_d.$$

Eq. (4.44) may now be written as

$$\overline{E}_f = \overline{V}_t + \overline{I}_a r_a + j\overline{I}_a X_q + j\overline{I}_d (X_d - X_q) \quad ...(4.46)$$

Synchronous-motor phasor diagram of Fig. 4.9 (*b*) reveals that

$$\angle abc = 90 - (\theta - \delta) \quad \text{and} \quad \angle bac = \theta - \delta.$$

$$\therefore \quad ac = ab \cos(\theta - \delta)$$
$$= XI_a \cos(\theta - \delta) = XI_q \quad \text{or} \quad XI_q = X_q I_q$$
$$\therefore \quad X = X_q.$$

Thus the angular position of E_f can be obtained by computing

$$ob = \overline{E}_f' = \overline{V}_t - \overline{I}_a r_a - j\overline{I}_a X_q.$$

This permits the calculation of angle $(\theta - \delta)$, I_d and I_q. Here again $bd = I_d (X_d - X_q)$. Eq. (4.43) may now be re-written as

$$\overline{V}_t = \overline{E}_f + j(X_d - X_q)\overline{I}_d + j\overline{I}_a X_q + \overline{I}_a r_a \quad ...(4.47)$$

It should be noted that E_f *is ahead of* V_t *for a synchronous generator, whereas* E_f *is behind* V_t *for a synchronous motor.*

Eqs. (4.46) and (4.47) include a term $I_d (X_d - X_q)$ which is due to saliency, *i.e.* non-uniform air gap. This quantity reduces to zero for a cylindrical-rotor synchronous machine in which $X_d = X_q$. This saliency factor in salient-pole synchronous machines is quite appreciable, since X_d is approximately 60 to 70% larger than X_q. Even in turbo-alternators, small salient-pole effect is present due to the effect of field-winding slots on q-axis reluctance – consequently X_d differs slightly (about 10%) from X_q in cylindrical-rotor synchronous machines.

Armature current I_a can also be resolved into its d-q components as follows :

From the generator phasor diagram of Fig. 4.9 (*a*), it is seen that

$$\tan(\delta + \theta) = \frac{V_t \sin\theta + I_a X_q}{V_t \cos\theta + I_a r_a} \qquad ...(4.48)$$

From the motor phasor diagram of Fig. 4.9 (*b*), it is seen that

$$\tan(\theta - \delta) = \frac{V_t \sin\theta - I_a X_q}{V_t \cos\theta - I_a r_a} \qquad ...(4.49)$$

A knowledge of $(\theta + \delta)$ in Fig. 4.9 (*a*) and $(\theta - \delta)$ in Fig. 4.9 (*b*) helps in determining I_d and I_q – this is illustrated in Example 4.3.

Cylindrical-rotor synchronous machines. These machines are characterised by uniform air gap so that reluctances along d and q axes are equal. In view of this,

$$X_d = X_q = X_s$$

where X_s is called the *synchronous reactance*.

Thus the voltage equation for a cylindrical-rotor synchronous generator, from Eq. (4.46), is

$$\bar{E}_f = \bar{V}_t + \bar{I}_a (r_a + jX_s) = \bar{V}_t + \bar{I}_a \bar{Z}_s \qquad ...(4.50)$$

Here $(r_a + jX_s) = Z_s$ is called the synchronous impedance. With the help of Eq. (4.50) or from Fig. 4.9 (*a*), the voltage phasor diagram of a cylindrical-rotor alternator is as shown in Fig. 4.10 (*a*). Eq. (4.50) also helps in representing this type of machine by the equivalent circuit of Fig. 4.10 (*b*).

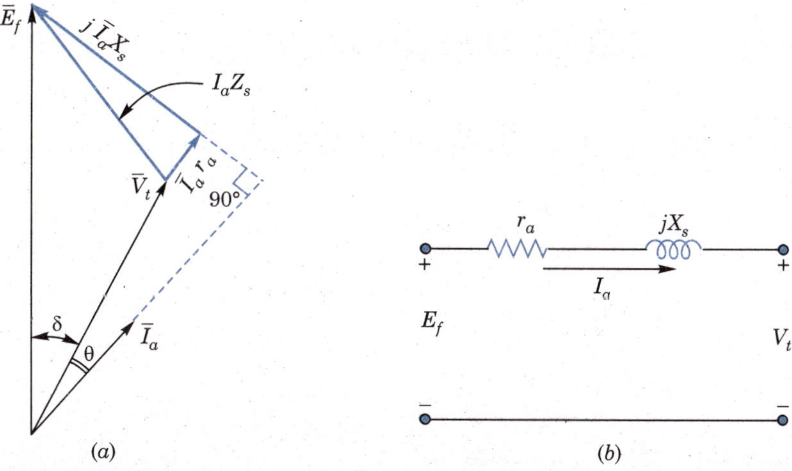

Fig. 4.10: Cylindrical-rotor alternator. (*a*) phasor diagram and (*b*) its equivalent circuit.

For a cylindrical-rotor synchronous motor, the voltage equation from Eq. (4.47) is

$$\overline{V}_t = \overline{E}_f + \overline{I}_a (r_a + jX_s) = \overline{E}_f + \overline{I}_a \overline{Z}_s \qquad ...(4.51)$$

The equivalent circuit of Fig. 4.10 (*b*) is also applicable to motor but with armature current I_a reversed. For cylindrical-rotor synchronous motor, the voltage phasor diagram can be drawn easily.

Example 4.3. *A 3-phase star-connected 50 Hz synchronous generator has direct-axis synchronous reactance of 0.65 p.u. and quadrature axis synchronous reactance of 0.5 p.u. The generator delivers rated kVA at rated voltage. Draw the phasor diagram at full load 0.8 lagging power factor and hence calculate the open-circuit voltage and voltage regulation. Resistance drop at full load is 0.02 p.u.*

Solution. Refer to Fig. 4.9 (*a*). With V_t as a reference phasor,

$$\overline{V}_t = 1 + j0.00$$

$$\therefore \quad \overline{I}_a = 0.8 - j0.60 = 1.00 \angle -36.87^\circ$$

$$j\overline{I}_a X_q = j\,(0.8 - j0.6)\,(0.5) = 0.30 + j0.40$$

$$r_a \overline{I}_a = 0.02\,(0.8 - j0.6) = 0.016 - j0.012$$

Thus
$$\overline{E}_f{}' = \overline{V}_t + r_a \overline{I}_a + j\overline{I}_a X_q$$
$$= (1 + j0.00) + (0.016 - j0.012) + (0.3 + j0.4)$$
$$= 1.316 + j\,0.388 = 1.372 \angle 16.43^\circ.$$

$\therefore$ Load angle $\quad \delta = 16.43^\circ$ and $\angle \delta + \theta = 16.43 + 36.87 = 53.3^\circ$.

Resolving the armature current I_a into its *d-q* components, we get

$$I_d = 1.00 \sin(\delta + \theta) = 1.00 \sin 53.3^\circ = 0.802$$

$$I_q = 1.00 \cos(\delta + \theta) = 1.00 \cos 53.3^\circ = 0.598.$$

An examination of Fig. 4.9 (*a*) reveals that E_f' and E_f are along the same line *od*. In view of this, algebraic sum of E_f' and $I_d (X_d - X_q)$ gives open-circuit voltage or excitation voltage E_f.

$$\therefore \quad E_f = E_f' + I_d (X_d - X_q) = 1.372 + (0.802)(0.15) = 1.4923 \text{ p.u.}$$

$$\therefore \quad \text{Voltage regulation} = \frac{E_f - V_t}{V_t} \times 100 = \frac{1.4923 - 1.00}{1.00} \times 100 = 49.23\%.$$

Another Method

From Eq. (4.48) or from Fig. 4.9 (*a*),

$$\tan(\delta + \theta) = \frac{V_t \sin\theta + I_a X_q}{V_t \cos\theta + I_a r_a} = \frac{0.6 + 0.5}{0.8 + 0.02} = 1.3415$$

$$\therefore \quad (\delta + \theta) = 53.30^\circ$$

Load angle, $\quad \delta = 53.30^\circ - 36.87^\circ = 16.43^\circ.$

D-axis component of armature current is

$$I_d = I_a \sin(\delta + \theta) = 1.00 \sin 53.3^\circ = 0.802.$$

An examination of Fig. 4.9 (*a*) show that

$$E_f = od = V_t \cos\delta + I_a r_a \cos(\delta + \theta) + I_d X_q$$

$$= 1.00 \cos 16.43° + 0.02 \cos 53.3° + 0.802 \times 0.65$$
$$= 0.959 + 0.01196 + 0.5213 = 1.4923.$$

$$\therefore \quad \text{Voltage regulation} = \frac{1.4923 - 1.00}{1.00} \times 100 = 49.23\%$$

Example 4.4. *For a salient-pole synchronous machine with negligible armature resistance, show that the d-axis synchronous reactance X_d can be obtained from its occ and scc.*

Solution. Phasor diagram of Fig. 4.9 (*a*) reveals that with $r_a = 0$

$$V_t \sin \delta = I_q X_q.$$

Under steady state short-circuit conditions, terminal voltage, $V_t = 0$.

$$\therefore \quad I_q X_q = V_t \sin \delta = 0 \text{ or } I_q = 0$$

Now the short-circuit current

$$\bar{I}_{sc} = \bar{I}_d + \bar{I}_q = \bar{I}_d.$$

Thus the phasor diagram of Fig. 4.9 (*a*) under short-circuit conditions and with $r_a = 0$, gets modified to that illustrated in Fig. 4.11. The short-circuit armature current I_{sc} becomes equal to I_d, because $I_q = 0$.

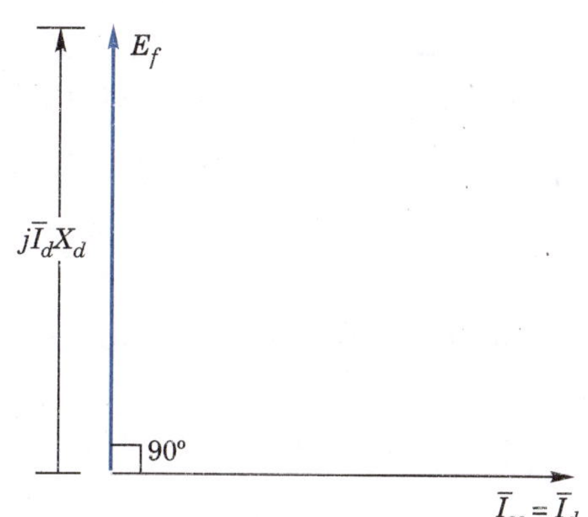

Fig. 4.11: Salient-pole alternator phasor diagram under short-circuit condition and with $r_a = 0$.

From the phasor diagram of Fig. 4.11, it is seen that

$$E_f = I_d X_d \quad \text{or} \quad X_d = \frac{E_f}{I_d} = \frac{E_f}{I_{sc}}$$

The excitation voltage E_f is obtained from *occ* and short-circuit current I_{sc} from *scc*, for the same value of field current. Therefore,

$$X_d = \frac{\text{Open-circuit (or excitation) voltage for a given field current}}{\text{Short-circuit current for the same field current}}$$

The excitation voltage of the synchronous machine, as given by Eq. (4.39), is

$$E_f = \frac{1}{\sqrt{2}} . M_d \omega I_f.$$

Also $\quad X_d = \omega L_d.$

$$I_{sc} = \frac{E_f}{X_d} = \frac{1}{\sqrt{2}} . \frac{M_d . \omega I_f}{\omega L_d} . = \frac{1}{\sqrt{2}} . \frac{M_d I_f}{L_d} \qquad ...(4.52)$$

Here M_d and L_d are synchronous machine constants. Eq. (4.52) shows that for a given field current I_f, the armature short-circuit current remains substantially constant over a wide range of frequency or alternator speed. In view of this, it is not necessary for the alternator speed to be equal to synchronous speed during the short-circuit test. However, at considerably lower speeds, the resistance becomes comparable with reactance and the change in armature short-circuit current is manifested.

4.5 STEADY-STATE POWER-ANGLE CHARACTERISTICS

In this article, power expressions are derived for salient-pole and cylindrical-rotor synchronous machines.

Power input to a 3-phase synchronous machine, from Eq. (2.18), is

$$P = \frac{3}{2}\,[v_d i_d + v_q i_q] \qquad ...(2.18)$$

From above expression, electrical torque can be obtained by substituting speed voltages for v_d, v_q and then dividing it by the shaft-speed in radians per second. The speed voltages, from Eq. (4.31), are $(-L_q\omega_r i_q)$ in v_d and $(M_d\omega_r i_f + L_d\omega_r i_d)$ in v_q. Substituting these in Eq. (2.18) and dividing by speed ω_r, we get total electrical torque as under.

$$T_e = \frac{3}{2}\cdot\frac{1}{\omega_r}\,[-L_q\omega_r i_q i_d + M_d\omega_r i_f i_q + L_d\omega_r i_d i_q]$$

$$= \frac{3}{2}\,[M_d i_q i_f + (L_d - L_q)\,i_d i_q] \qquad ...(4.53a)$$

Under steady state and at synchronous speed, three-phase sychronous power P_e is

$$P_e = \omega T_e = \frac{3}{2}\,[M_q\omega i_{qo}\,I_f + \omega(L_d - L_q)\,i_{do}\cdot i_{qo}]$$

$$\text{Power per phase} = \frac{P_e}{3} = \left[\frac{M_q\,.\,\omega\,.\,I_f}{\sqrt{2}}\right]\frac{i_{qo}}{\sqrt{2}} + (X_d - X_q)\,\frac{i_{do}}{\sqrt{2}}\cdot\frac{i_{qo}}{\sqrt{2}}$$

$$= E_f I_q + (X_d - X_q)\,I_d I_q \qquad ...(4.53)$$

Eq. (4.53) can also be obtained from the relation $P = Re\,\{\overline{V}_t\overline{I}_a^*\}$. Here use that expression for $\overline{V}_t$ that contains $\overline{I}_a$ as many times as is possible, *i.e.* here Eq. (4.47) should be used. In this equation, if resistance drop is neglected, then

$$\overline{V}_t = j(X_d - X_q)\,\overline{I}_d + jX_q\overline{I}_a + \overline{E}_f$$

or $$\overline{V}_t = j\,(X_d - X_q)\,\overline{I}_d + jX_q\overline{I}_a + jE_f \qquad ...(4.54)$$

Here $$\overline{I}_a = I_d + jI_q;$$

∴ $$\overline{I}_a^* = I_d - jI_q$$

∴ $$P = Re\,\{[j\,(X_d - X_q)\,\overline{I}_d + jX_q\overline{I}_a + jE_f][I_d - jI_q]\}$$

$$= E_f I_q + (X_d - X_q)\,\overline{I}_d\,I_q$$

or $$P = E_f I_q + (X_d - X_q)\,I_d I_q \qquad ...(4.53)$$

Note that $(jX_q\overline{I}_a)\,(I_d - jI_q) = jX_q\,(I_d + jI_q)\,(I_d - jI_q) = jX_q\,(I_d^2 + I_q^2)$ is an imaginary term.

If d.c. excitation is reduced to zero, $E_f = 0$ and Eq. (4.53) becomes,

$$P = (X_d - X_q)\,I_d I_q \qquad ...(4.55)$$

This power given by Eq. (4.55) is called the reluctance power and is the basis of operation of a wide variety of reluctance motors.

Many times, it is convenient to include load angle δ in the synchronous power expression of Eq. (4.53). This can easily be done with the help of phasor diagram. The armature resistance r_a is usually quite small in well-designed synchronous machines and if r_a

is neglected, the phasor diagram of Fig. 4.9 (*b*) gets modified to that shown in Fig. 4.12 (*a*). From this figure,

$$V_t \cos \delta = E_f + X_d I_q \quad \text{and} \quad V_t \sin \delta = X_q I_q$$

$$I_d = \frac{V_t \cos \delta - E_f}{X_d} \qquad \text{...(4.56)}$$

and

$$I_q = \frac{V_t \sin \delta}{X_q} \qquad \text{...(4.57)}$$

Substitution of Eqs. (4.56) and (4.57) in Eq. (4.53) gives,

$$P = \frac{V_t E_f}{X_d} \sin \delta + \frac{V_t^2}{2} \left(\frac{1}{X_q} - \frac{1}{X_d} \right) \sin 2\delta \qquad \text{...(4.58)}$$

Eq. (4.58) can also be obtained in an alternative method as follows :

In Fig. 4.12 (*a*), $V_t \cos \delta$ is in phase with I_q and $V_t \sin \delta$ is in phase opposition to I_d. Therefore, synchronous power P is given by

$$P = (V_t \cos \delta)\, I_q - (V_t \sin \delta)\, I_d \qquad \text{...(4.59)}$$

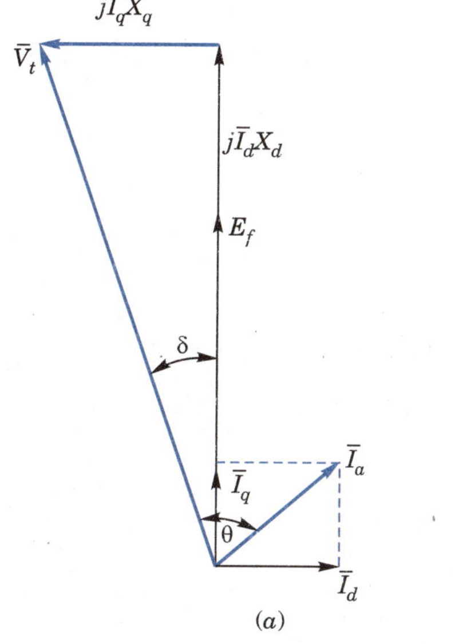

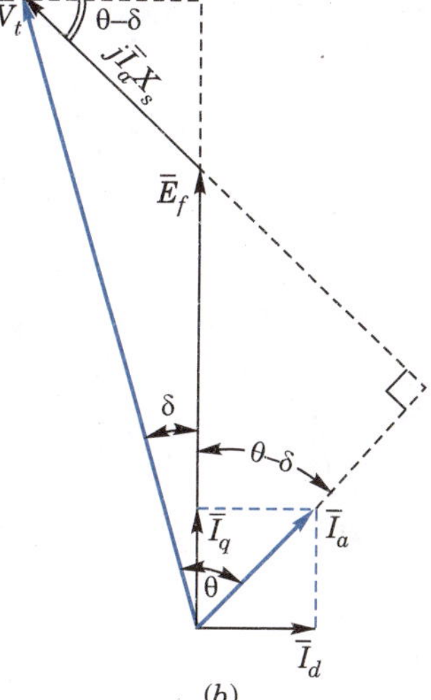

Fig. 4.12: Synchronous motor phasor diagrams with armature resistance ignored (*a*) salient-pole and (*b*) cylindrical-rotor.

Now substitution of Eqs. (4.56) and (4.57) in Eq. (4.59) gives

$$P = \frac{V_t E_f}{X_d} \sin \delta + \frac{V_t^2}{2} \left(\frac{1}{X_q} - \frac{1}{X_d} \right) \sin 2\delta \qquad \text{...(4.58)}$$

The phasor diagram of a cylindrical-rotor synchronous motor, with negligible r_a, is as shown in Fig. 4.12 (*b*). From this figure,

$$V_t \sin \delta = X_s I_a \cos (\theta - \delta) = X_s I_q$$

or

$$I_q = \frac{V_t \sin \delta}{X_s} \qquad \text{...(4.60)}$$

For a round-rotor machine, $X_d = X_q = X_s$, therefore, synchronous power, from Eq. (4.53), is

$$P = E_f I_q \qquad ...(4.61)$$

Substitution of I_q from Eq. (4.60) in Eq. (4.61) gives

$$P = \frac{V_t E_f}{X_s} \sin \delta \qquad ...(4.62)$$

With the help of Eq. (4.62), the variation of power P with δ is plotted in Fig. 4.13 (*a*) to give the power-load angle characteristics of a cylindrical-rotor synchronous machine. Eq. (4.58) gives the power-angle characteristics of a salient-pole sychronous machine, which is illustrated in Fig. 4.13 (*b*). Note that power P for a salient-pole machine consists of a fundamental component $\frac{E_f V_t}{X_d} \sin \delta$ and a second-harmonic component $\frac{V_t^2}{2}\left(\frac{1}{X_q} - \frac{1}{X_d}\right) \sin 2\delta$.

If there is an external reactance X between synchronous machine terminals and the infinite-bus terminals of voltage V_t, then power for a cylindrical-rotor machine, from Eq. (4.62), is

$$P = \frac{E_f V_t}{X_s + X} \sin \delta_1 \qquad ...(4.63)$$

For a salient-pole machine, the power from Eq. (4.58) is

$$P = \frac{E_f V_t}{X_d + X} \sin \delta_1 + \frac{V_t^2}{2}\left(\frac{1}{X_q + X} - \frac{1}{X_d + X}\right) \sin 2\delta_1 \qquad ...(4.64)$$

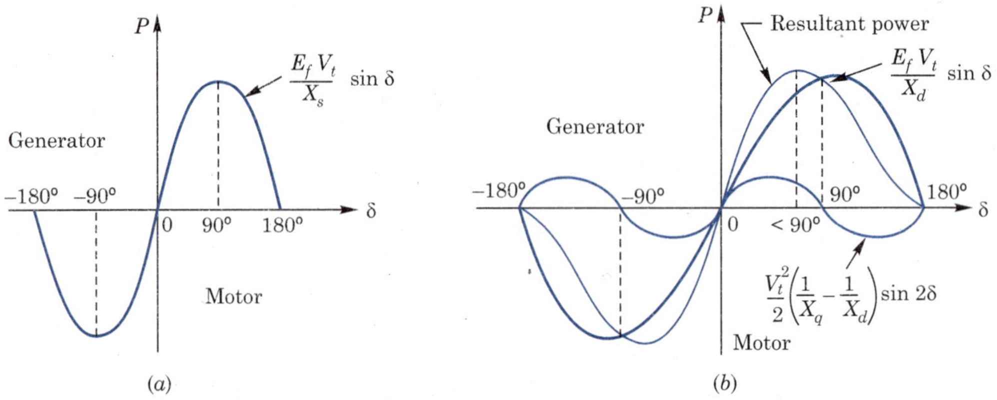

Fig. 4.13: Power-angle characteristics for (*a*) cylindrical-rotor machine and (*b*) salient-pole machine.

In Eqs. (4.63) and (4.64), load angle δ_1 is the time phase angle between infinite bus voltage and the excitation voltage E_f.

Fig. 4.13 (*a*) reveals that maximum power in a cylindrical-rotor machine occurs when $\delta = 90°$. For a salient-pole machine, the maximum power as seen from Fig. 4.13 (*b*) is at a load angle less than 90°. This value of load angle can be obtained from Eq. (4.58) as follows:

$$\frac{dP}{d\delta} = \frac{V_t E_f}{X_d} \cos \delta + V_t^2 \left(\frac{1}{X_q} - \frac{1}{X_d}\right) \cos 2\delta = 0$$

Its solution, with $\cos 2\delta = 2\cos^2\delta - 1$, gives

$$\cos\delta = -\frac{E_f X_q}{4V_t(X_d - X_q)} \pm \sqrt{\frac{1}{2} + \left[\frac{E_f X_q}{4V_t(X_d - X_q)}\right]^2} \quad ...(4.65)$$

In Eq. (4.65), out of ± signs, only positive sign should be used, because negative sign gives ambiguous results. Substitution of angle δ, calculated from Eq. (4.65), in Eq. (4.58) gives the maximum power which is sometimes called the pull-out power.

4.5.1 Reactive Power

The reactive power Q is determined by taking the imaginary part or $\bar{V}_t\bar{I}_a^*$, *i.e.*

$$Q = Img\,\{\bar{V}_t\bar{I}_a^*\}. \quad \text{From Eqs. (4.54) and (4.37),}$$

$$Q = Img\,[\{j(X_d - X_q)\bar{I}_d + jX_q\bar{I}_a + jE_f\}(I_d - jI_q)]$$

$$= (X_d - X_q)I_d^2 + X_q(I_d^2 + I_q^2) + E_f I_d$$

or

$$Q = X_d I_d^2 + X_q I_q^2 + E_f I_d \quad ...(4.66)$$

Eq. (4.66) can also be obtained from the phasor diagram of Fig. 4.12 (*a*) by noting that reactive power is equal to the product of voltage and quadrature lagging component of armature current.

$$\therefore \quad Q = (E_f + X_d I_d)I_d + (X_q I_q)I_q = X_d I_d^2 + X_q I_q^2 + E_f I_d \quad ...(4.66)$$

In Eq. (4.66), substitution of I_d and I_q, from Eq. (4.56) and (4.57) respectively, gives

$$Q = X_d\frac{(V_t\cos\delta - E_f)^2}{X_d^2} + X_d\frac{(V_t^2\sin^2\delta)}{X_q^2} + \frac{E_f(V_t\cos\delta - E_f)}{X_d}$$

or

$$Q = \frac{V_t^2}{X_d} + V_t^2\left(\frac{1}{X_q} - \frac{1}{X_d}\right)\sin^2\delta - \frac{E_f V_t}{X_d}\cos\delta \quad ...(4.67)$$

For a cylindrical-rotor machine, $X_d = X_q = X_s$ and reactive power for this machine, from Eq. (4.67), is given by

$$Q = \frac{V_t}{X_s}(V_t - E_f\cos\delta) \quad ...(4.68)$$

Eq. (4.68) shows that when $E_f \cos\delta = V_t$, *i.e*, under normal excitation, $Q = 0$ and the motor operates at *upf*. In case $E_f\cos\delta < V_t$ *i.e.*, the motor is underexcited, Q is positive which means that motor draws reactive power from the supply lines.

If $E_f\cos\delta > V_t$, *i.e.*, the motor is over-excited, Q is negative and, therefore, the motor delivers reactive power to the supply lines.

For a salient-pole alternator, it can be shown that

$$Q = \frac{E_f V_t}{X_d}\cos\delta - V_t^2\left(\frac{1}{X_q} - \frac{1}{X_d}\right)\sin^2\delta - \frac{V_t^2}{X_d} \quad ...(4.69)$$

and for a cylindrical-rotor alternator

$$Q = \frac{V_t}{X_s}(E_f\cos\delta - V_t) \quad ...(4.70)$$

For both the generator and motor operations, it can be stated in general that an overexcited ($E_f\cos\delta > V_t$) machine delivers or exports reactive power to the supply system; an under-excited ($E_f\cos\delta < V_t$) machine absords, imports or draws reactive power from the supply system.

Example 4.5. *Power input to a 3-phase synchronous machine, in terms of dqo variables, is given by*

$$P = 3/2\ [v_d i_d + v_q i_q]$$

From this, derive an expression for electrical torque in terms of motional-inductance matrix.

Solution. From the given P expression, first obtain Eq. (4.53a), which for convinience, is repeated here.

$$T_e = \frac{3}{2} \cdot [M_d i_q i_f + L_d i_d i_q - L_q i_d i_q] \qquad \text{...(4.53}a\text{)}$$

$$= \frac{3}{2} \cdot \begin{bmatrix} M_d i_q & L_d i_q & -L_q i_d \end{bmatrix} \begin{bmatrix} i_f \\ i_d \\ i_q \end{bmatrix}$$

$$= \frac{3}{2} \cdot \begin{bmatrix} i_f & i_d & i_q \end{bmatrix} \begin{bmatrix} & & \\ & & -L_q \\ M_d & L_d & \end{bmatrix} \begin{bmatrix} i_f \\ i_d \\ i_q \end{bmatrix}$$

with the product of the row and the matrix being $\begin{bmatrix} M_d i_q & L_d i_q & -L_q i_d \end{bmatrix}$.

$$= \frac{3}{2} \cdot [i_t]\ [G]\ [i]$$

Here $[G]$ is the motional-inductance, or torque, matrix. It can be obtained from Eq. (4.30).

Example 4.6. *A salient-pole synchronous motor is fed from an infinite bus. Show how its power varies with load angle δ, as its excitation voltage is reduced from 1.5 per unit to zero. Indicate the points pertaining to the steady-state stability limits.*

Solution. The power-angle curve of the salient-pole synchronous motor with $E_f = 1.50$ *pu* is illustrated in Fig. 4.14. As E_f is reduced, the resultant power P developed by a synchronous motor decreases-this has the effect of shifting the maximum power points towards lower values of load angle. For $E_f = 0$, motor operates as a reluctance motor and the steady-state stability limit is at a load angle of 45°. If all the points pertaining to the steady-state stability limits are joined; a curve, shown

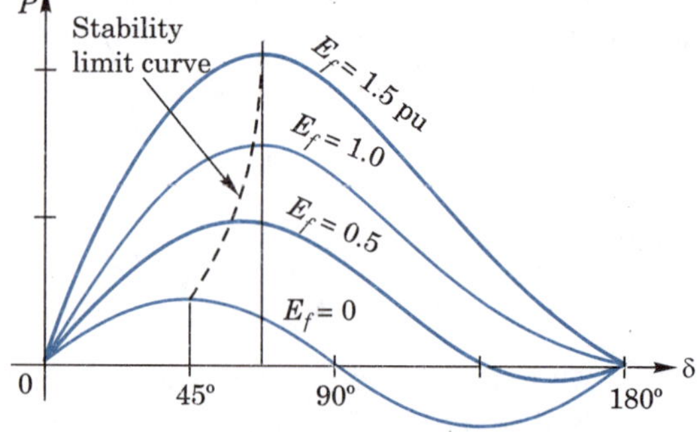

Fig. 4.14: Pertaining to Example 4.6.

dotted in Fig. 4.14, is obtained. It is seen from this figure that resultant power is maximum for load angles of $45° < \delta < 90°$.

Example 4.7. *(a) A cylindrical-rotor synchronous motor, with E_f = 1.5 pu, is connected to an infinite bus. The machine has a synchronous reactance of 1.2 pu and output power delivered to the load is 0.5 pu. With all losses ignored, find the magnitude of reactive power delivered or absorbed, by the synchronous motor.*

(b) If load on the motor is increased to its rated load without any change in its field current, repeat part (a).

(c) With the load as given in part (a), if the excitation voltage is reduced to 0.75, repeat part (a).

Solution. (*a*) For a cylindrical-rotor synchronous motor, the real power, or synchronous power, is given by

$$P = \frac{E_f V_t}{X_s} \sin \delta$$

or

$$0.5 = \frac{1.5 \times 1}{1.20} \sin \delta \quad \text{or} \quad \sin \delta = \frac{1.2 \times 0.5}{1.5} = 0.4\ ; \quad \therefore \quad \cos \delta = 0.9165$$

Reactive power, from Eq. (4.68), is

$$Q = \frac{V_t}{X_s} (V_t - E_f \cos \delta) = \frac{1}{1.2} (1 - 1.5 \times 0.9165) = -0.3125\ pu$$

Since Q is negative, the synchronous motor is delivering reactive power to the infinite bus.

(*b*) Under rated-load conditions,

$$1 = \frac{1.5 \times 1}{1.2} \sin \delta \qquad \text{or} \quad \sin \delta = 0.8 \text{ and } \cos \delta = 0.6.$$

Reactive power, $$Q = \frac{1}{1.2} (1 - 1.5 \times 0.6) = 0.0833\ pu.$$

Here Q is positive, the synchronous motor is, therefore, drawing reactive power from the infinite bus.

(*c*) Here $$0.5 = \frac{0.75 \times 1}{1.2} \sin \delta$$

$\therefore$ $$\sin \delta = 0.8 \quad \text{and} \quad \cos \delta = 0.6$$

$$Q = \frac{1}{1.2} (1 - 0.75 \times 0.6) = 0.4583\ pu.$$

Here also Q is positive, the motor is, therefore, absorbing reactive power from the infinite bus.

Example 4.8. *(a) From the phasor diagram of a cylindrical rotor alternator, show that its power output is given by* $P = \frac{E_f \cdot V_t}{Z_s} \sin(\delta + \alpha_z) - \frac{V_t^2}{Z_s^2} r_a$,

where $\alpha_z = \tan^{-1}\left(\frac{r_a}{X_s}\right)$ *and* $Z_s = (r_a + jX_s)$ *is its synchronous impedance.*

(b) From part (a), find an expression for the maximum power output of the alternator.

Solution. (*a*) For a cylindrical-rotor alternator working at a lagging power factor, the phasor diagram is as shown in Fig. 4.15. Its voltage equation is

$$\bar{E}_f = \bar{V}_t + \bar{I}_a Z_s$$

or

$$\bar{I}_a = \frac{\bar{E}_f}{\bar{Z}_s} - \frac{\bar{V}_t}{\bar{Z}_s} \qquad \text{...(4.71)}$$

The current phasor $\frac{\bar{E}_f}{\bar{Z}_s}$ lags $\bar{E}_f$ by $\theta_z = \tan^{-1}\left(\frac{X_s}{r_a}\right)$ as shown in Fig. 4.15. Similarly current phasor $\bar{V}_t / \bar{Z}_s$ lags $\bar{V}_t$ by θ_z. The difference of $\frac{\bar{E}_f}{\bar{Z}_s}$ and $\frac{\bar{V}_t}{\bar{Z}_s}$, as per Eq. (4.71), gives the armature current I_a.

Now, per phase power output of generator is given by

$$P = V_t I_a \cos\theta.$$

In Fig. 4.15, $I_a \cos\theta = OA = OB - AB$. But $OB = \frac{E_f}{Z_s}\cos(\theta_z - \delta)$ and $AB = OC = \frac{V_t}{Z_s}\cos\theta_z$. In view of this,

$$I_a \cos\theta = \frac{E_f}{Z_s}\cos(\theta_z - \delta) - \frac{V_t}{Z_s}\cos\theta_z$$

$$\therefore \quad P = V_t I_a \cos\theta$$

$$= \frac{E_f V_t}{Z_s}\cos(\theta_z - \delta) - \frac{V_t^2}{Z_s}\cos\theta_z$$

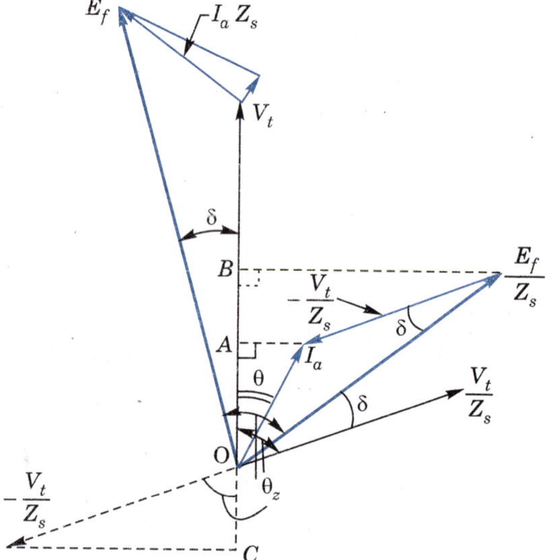

Fig. 4.15: Pertaining to Example 4.8.

But $\cos\theta_z = r_a / Z_s$

and $\theta_z = 90 - \alpha_z$

$$\therefore \quad P = \frac{E_f V_t}{Z_s}\cos[90 - (\delta + \alpha_z)] - \frac{V_t^2}{Z_s^2} r_a$$

$$= \frac{E_f V_t}{Z_s}\sin(\delta + \alpha_z) - \frac{V_t^2}{Z_s^2} r_a \qquad \text{...(4.72)}$$

(*b*) For given values of E_f, V_t and Z_s, maximum alternator output is obtained by differentiating Eq. (4.72) with respect to δ.

$$\therefore \quad \frac{dP}{d\delta} = \frac{E_f V_t}{Z_s}\cos(\delta + \alpha_z) = 0 \quad \text{or} \quad \delta + \alpha_z = 90° \;;\; \therefore \delta = 90 - \alpha_z = \theta_z.$$

Thus, for maximum power output of an alternator, load angle δ = impedance angle θ_z.

$$\therefore \quad P_{max} = \frac{E_f . V_t}{Z_s} - \frac{V_t^2}{Z_s^2} r_a$$

$$= \frac{V_t}{Z_s}\left(E_f - \frac{V_t}{Z_s} r_a\right) \qquad \text{...(4.73)}$$

Example 4.9. *A salient-pole synchronous generator is synchronized with an infinite bus. For zero excitation voltage, draw its phasor diagram and hence obtain an expression for its power factor under maximum power conditions. Neglect armature resistance.*

Solution. The phasor diagram of a salient-pole synchronous generator with $E_f = 0$ and $r_a = 0$ is illustrated in Fig. 4.16 which is drawn by referring to Fig. 4.8 (*b*). With $E_f = 0$, the reluctance power from Eq. (4.58) is given by

$$P = \frac{V_t^2}{2}\left(\frac{1}{X_q} - \frac{1}{X_d}\right) \sin 2\delta$$

Maximum reluctance power P_{max}, is obtained for $\delta = 45°$.

$$\therefore \quad P_{max} = \frac{V_t^2}{2}\left(\frac{1}{X_q} - \frac{1}{X_d}\right) = \frac{V_t^2}{2} \frac{X_d - X_q}{X_d X_q}$$

From Fig. 4.16, it is seen that

$$V_t \sin \delta = I_q X_d \text{ and } V_t \cos \delta = I_d X_d$$

$$\therefore \quad I_q = \frac{V_t \sin \delta}{X_q} \text{ and } I_d = \frac{V_t \cos \delta}{X_d}$$

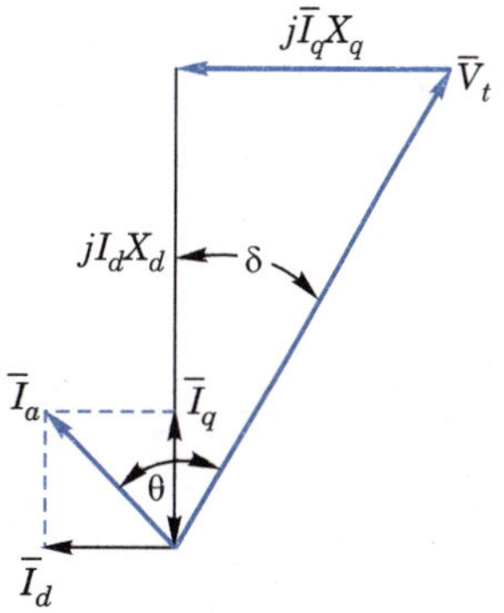

Fig. 4.16: Salient-pole alternator phasor diagram with $E_f = 0$ and $r_a = 0$.

Under maximum power conditions,

$$I_d = \frac{V_t}{X_d} \cos 45° = \frac{1}{\sqrt{2}} \frac{V_t}{X_d} \quad \text{and} \quad I_q = \frac{1}{\sqrt{2}} \frac{V_t}{X_q}$$

$$\therefore \quad I_a = \sqrt{I_d^2 + I_q^2} = \frac{V_t}{\sqrt{2}} \sqrt{\frac{1}{X_d^2} + \frac{1}{X_q^2}} = \frac{V_t}{\sqrt{2}} \cdot \frac{\sqrt{X_d^2 + X_q^2}}{X_d X_q}$$

Now $$V_t I_a \cos \theta = P_{max}$$

$$V_t \frac{V_t}{\sqrt{2}} \cdot \frac{\sqrt{X_d^2 + X_q^2}}{X_d X_q} \cdot \cos \theta = \frac{V_t^2}{2} \cdot \frac{X_d - X_q}{X_d X_q}$$

$$\therefore \quad \cos \theta = \frac{1}{\sqrt{2}} \frac{X_d - X_q}{\sqrt{X_d^2 + X_q^2}}.$$

Example 4.10. *A salient-pole synchronous motor, connected with an infinite bus, is working at no-load. Its field current is gradually reduced to zero and is then reversed.*

(a) Find the magnitude of maximum negative excitation possible.

(b) Find the magnitude of reactive power under the conditions of part (a).

Solution. (*a*) From Eq. (4.58), the power is given by

$$P = \frac{E_f V_t}{X_d} \sin \delta + \frac{V_t^2}{2}\left(\frac{1}{X_q} - \frac{1}{X_d}\right) \sin 2\delta$$

When excitation is made negative, the power is given by

$$P = -\frac{E_f V_t}{X_d} \sin \delta + \frac{V_t^2}{2}\left(\frac{1}{X_q} - \frac{1}{X_d}\right) \sin 2\delta \quad ...(4.74)$$

The magnitude of negative excitation is increased till steady-state limit is reached. With E_f reversed, electromagnetic power and reluctance power are opposing each other, therefore steady-power limit is reached when the motor is just on the verge of losing synchronism. Thus, maximum negative excitation is obtained by equating P to zero in Fig. 4.74.

$$\therefore \quad \frac{E_f V_t}{X_d}\sin\delta = \frac{V_t^2}{2}\left(\frac{1}{X_q}-\frac{1}{X_d}\right)2\sin\delta\cos\delta \quad \text{or} \quad E_f = V_t\left(\frac{X_d}{X_q}-1\right)\cos\delta$$

Since $P = 0$, load angle δ must be zero. Therefore, the magnitude of maximum negative excitation is

$$E_{f\cdot\min} = V_t\left(\frac{X_d}{X_q}-1\right)$$

(*b*) For negative excitation, the reactive power from Eq. (4.67) is

$$Q = \frac{V_t^2}{X_d} + V_t^2\left(\frac{1}{X_q}-\frac{1}{X_d}\right)\sin^2\delta + \frac{E_f V_t}{X_d}\cos\delta$$

Under the condition of maximum negative excitation $E_{f\,.\,\min}$, δ is zero and therefore the reactive power is given by

$$Q = \frac{V_t^2}{X_d} + \frac{E_{f\,\cdot\,\min}V_t}{X_d} = \frac{V_t^2}{X_d} + V_t\left(\frac{X_d}{X_q}-1\right)\cdot\frac{V_t}{X_d}$$

$$= \frac{V_t^2}{X_q} \qquad \text{...(4.75)}$$

Since Q is positive, synchronous motor draws reactive power from the infinite bus.

For the motor at no-load, $V_t I_a \cos\theta = 0$ or $I_a \cos\theta = 0$. Since I_a can't be zero, $\cos\theta$ is zero and therefore $\theta = 90°$. In view of this,

$$Q = V_t I_a \sin 90° = V_t I_a = \frac{V_t^2}{X_q}$$

or

$$X_q = \frac{V_t}{I_a} \qquad \text{...(4.76)}$$

Eq. (4.76) forms the basis of obtaining X_q from the maximum-lagging current test.

4.6 SHORT-CIRCUIT RATIO

Short-cicuit ratio, or *SCR*, of a synchronous machine helps in obtaining an estimate of its operating characteristics. Also, for a given rating and type of the synchronous machine, *SCR* is a measure of its physical size.

SCR is defined as the ratio of field current required to generate rated open-circuit voltage, to the field current required to circulate rated armature current on three-phase short circuit. From *OCC* (at rated speed) and *SCC* of a three-phase synchronous machine as shown in Fig. 4.17, *SCR* is given as

$$SCR = \frac{I_f \text{ for rated } OC \text{ voltage}}{I_f \text{ for rated } SC\ I_a} = \frac{oa}{od}$$

Triangles oab and ode are similar, therefore

$$SCR = \frac{oa}{od} = \frac{ab}{de} \quad ...(4.77)$$

The direct-axis synchronous reactance X_d is defined as the ratio of open-circuit voltage for a given field current, to the armature short-circuit current for the same field current. From Fig. 4.17, for a field current oa, X_d in ohms is given by

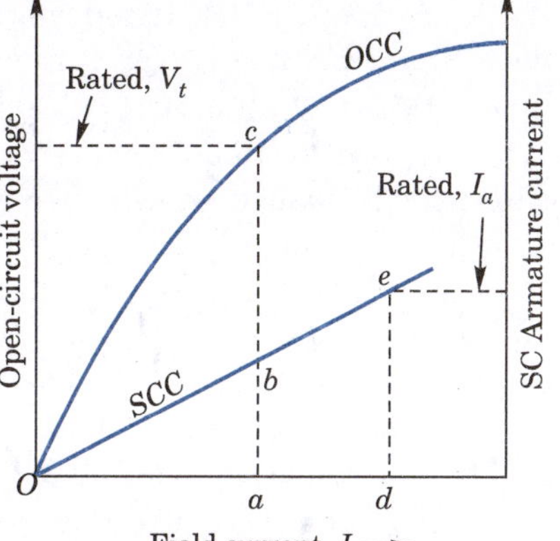

Fig. 4.17: Pertaining to the definition of short-circuit ratio.

$$X_d = \frac{ac}{ab} \Omega$$

$$X_d \text{ in per unit} = \frac{ac}{ab} \cdot \frac{1}{\text{base impedance}}$$

Now,

$$\text{base impedance} = \frac{\text{Per-phase rated voltage}}{\text{Per-phase rated armature current}} = \frac{V_{\text{rated}}}{I_{\text{rated}}} = \frac{ac}{de} \Omega$$

$$\therefore \quad X_d \text{ in per unit} = \frac{ac}{ab} \cdot \frac{1}{\frac{ac}{de}} = \frac{de}{ab}$$

From Eq. (4.77),

$$SCR = \frac{ab}{de} = \frac{1}{\frac{de}{ab}} = \frac{1}{X_d \text{ in per unit}} \quad ...(4.78)$$

It is thus seen that SCR is equal to the reciprocal of per unit value of direct-axis synchronous reactance X_d. In a saturated magnetic circuit, the value of X_d depends upon the degree of saturation. But note that ***SCR is single-valued*** because it pertains to the rated voltage on OCC and rated armature current on SCC.

SCR effects both the physical size and operating characteristics of the synchronous machine. A significance of SCR can be gained from the following considerations:

(*a*) **Low SCR.** Low value of SCR means greater value of X_d. An examination of Fig. 4.8 (*b*), or Fig. 4.10 (*a*) with $X_s = X_d$, shows that low SCR results in large voltage variation with load and thus a poor voltage regulation. Therefore, in order to maintain constant terminal voltage, the field current will have to be varied over a wide range.

Eq. (4.58) or Eq. (4.62) shows that low value of SCR means less synchronous power P and consequently a lower stability limit.

A low value of SCR means more X_d (or X_s) and therefore a low value of synchronizing power $P_s = \left(\frac{E_f \cdot V_t}{X_s} \cos \delta \cdot \Delta\delta \text{ for a round rotor synchronous machine} \right)$. The synchronizing power is transient in nature and comes into play only when there is a disturbance in the system. In other words, the function of P_s is to keep the machine in synchronism. Therefore, a machine with low value of SCR has low synchronizing power and therefore a low tendency for keeping the machine in synchronism with the infinite bus.

A low value of SCR results in low value of armature short-circuit current.

(*b*) **High SCR.** It follows from the foregoing discussion that a synchronous machine with high *SCR* has better voltage regulation and improved steady-state stability limit. The disadvantage of high *SCR* is the high value of armature short-circuit current.

A synchronous generator, feeding a long transmission, or cable, line, may be capacitively loaded in which case the armature current may begin to lead the terminal voltage. The m.m.f. set up by a leading armature current, aids the field m.m.f. and consequently the generated voltage increases. In order to reduce the effect of armature m.m.f. on the field m.m.f. and to retain the voltage under control, air-gap length should be increased, which means a synchronous machine with high *SCR* should be used.

Typical values of *SCR* are : 0.5 to 0.8 for turbo-generators, 1 to 1.4 for hydro-generators and 0.4 for synchronous condensors.

Physical size and cost of the machine. In order to investigate the influence of *SCR* on the physical size and cost of the machine, assume that its air-gap length is doubled. Now the mutual inductance M_d, in terms of *d*-axis reluctance may be written as,

$$M_d \propto \frac{1}{d\text{-axis reluctance}}$$

For negligible saturation, doubling the air-gap length decreases M_d to half of its previous value. For the same open-circuit voltage, therefore, the field current must be doubled as per Eq. (4.39). From Eq. (4.52), the short-circuit current I_{sc} is

$$I_{sc} = \frac{E_f}{X_d} = \frac{M_d \cdot \omega I_f}{\sqrt{2} \cdot \omega L_d} = \frac{M_d I_f}{\sqrt{2} L_d}$$

When the air-gap length is doubled, M_d and L_d are affected equally and therefore field current required for circulating the rated armature short-circuit current remains ths same. It is thus seen from above that when air-gap length is doubled, the field current for generating the same rated excitation voltage is doubled but field current for the rated armature short-circuit current remains unchanged. As per the basic definition of *SCR*, Eq. (4.77), doubling the air-gap length increases *SCR* to double of its previous value. With double the air-gap length, the field current is almost doubled to generate the same open-circuit voltage. A large field current requires greater cross-section of field winding and therefore greater amount of field copper. This increased amount of field copper can be accomodated only if the field-pole size is increased. As a consequence of it, the machine diameter increases and hence the overall size, weight and cost of the machine increase. Thus physical size and cost of the synchronous machine are directly proportional to *SCR*.

Another way of explaining the influence of *SCR* on the physical size and cost of the synchronous machine is as under :

Excitation voltage, $E_f = \sqrt{2} \cdot \pi f k_\omega N_{ph} \phi$

For the same armature series turns per phase N_{ph},

$$E_f \propto \text{field flux per pole } \phi \propto \frac{\text{field m.m.f. per pole}}{\text{air-gap reluctance}}$$

Now synchronous inductance, $L_s \propto \dfrac{1}{\text{air-gap reluctance}}$

$$\therefore \quad SCR \propto \frac{1}{L_s} \propto \text{air-gap reluctance or air-gap length.}$$

This shows that if air-gap length is doubled, the value of *SCR* is also doubled. Further, doubling the air-gap length requires double the field m.m.f. for the same E_f. Double the amount of field m.m.f. requires that either field current I_f, or field turns N_f, is doubled; this leads to greater amount of field copper for the field winding. For same field coil depth (as is usually the case), the increased amount of field copper can be accomodated only if height of field coil is increased. But this necessitates an increase in field pole height. As a consequence, overall diameter of the machine increases and this results in bigger size, more weight and cost of the machine. This shows that physical size and cost of the synchronous machine are directly proprtional to *SCR*.

4.7 TRANSIENT ANALYSIS

Investigation of the transient behaviour of a synchronous generator is quite important, because this analysis hepls in determining the shaft stresses, winding and bus-bar stresses, protective-relay settings, circuit-breaker rupturing duties etc. The object of this article is to examine the nature of currents resulting from a sudden three-phase short-circuit at the synchronous generator terminals. The amortisseur circuits are not considered here just to arrive at simpler expressions for the currents. However, if required, the same approach can be applied to investigate the transients of a synchronous generator with amortisseurs. The two assumptions, usually made during transient analysis, are as follows:

(*i*) The machine is running initially on no-load and under steady-state conditions.

(*ii*) Speed before and after the short-circuit remains unchanged from its synchronous speed ω.

Eq. (4.31) gives ths voltage equations for a synchronous motor. These can be modified for generator, merely by putting negative sign before the armature currents i_d and i_q. In view of this, the voltage equations for a synchronous generator are,

$$\left.\begin{aligned} v_f &= (r_f + L_f p)\, i_f - M_d p i_d \\ v_d &= M_d p i_f - (r_a + L_d p)\, i_d + L_q \omega_r i_q \\ v_q &= M_d \omega_r i_f - L_d \omega_r i_d - (r_a + L_q p)\, i_q \end{aligned}\right] \qquad \text{...(4.79)}$$

The use of above equations, for obtaining a solution of the transient problem, involves lengthy manipulations. In order to avoid this, some terms in Eq. (4.79) may by omitted to obtain an easier solution of the transient problem.

(*a*) **All resistances neglected.** With the neglect of resistances of both the field and armature windings and with alternator speed $\omega_r = \omega$, Eq. (4.79) becomes,

$$\left.\begin{aligned} v_f &= L_f p i_f - M_d p i_d \\ v_d &= M_d p i_f - L_d p i_d + L_q \omega i_q \\ v_q &= M_d \omega i_f - L_d \omega i_d - L_q p i_q \end{aligned}\right] \qquad \text{...(4.80)}$$

Before short circuit, *i.e.* at $t = 0-$, the armature currents i_a, i_b, i_c, are zero, therefore both i_{do} and i_{qo} are also zero. The field current before the short circuit is $I_{fo}\left(=\dfrac{V_f}{r_f}\right)$. Here subscript

0 is added to indicate the values before ths short circuit. Since $i_{do} = 0$ and $i_{qo} = 0$, an examination of Eq. (4.80) reveals that before the short circuit, $v_{do} = 0$ and $v_{qo} = M_d \omega I_{fo}$. The effect of a short circuit is to reduce the generator terminal voltages to zero. Here voltage $v_{do} = 0$ both before and afer the short circuit, therefore short circuit has no effect on v_{do}. Voltage $v_{qo} = 0$ after the short circuit but its value before the short circuit is $M_d \omega I_{fo}$. Thus the effect of short circuit is to reduce v_{qo} to zero suddenly and this can be taken as equivalent to the sudden application of a step-function voltage v_{qo} **1** to the q-axis terminals. Both before and after the short-circuit, the voltage applied to field winding is V_f, therefore superimposed voltage v_{ft} for field winding is zero (= voltage after the short circuit – voltage before the short circuit). Here the reader may refer to Art. 3.1.1.

In view of the above discussion, the equations which specify the balanced three-phase short circuit, in terms of superimposed quantities, are

$$0 = L_f p i_{ft} - M_d p i_d \quad \text{...(4.81)}$$

$$0 = M_d p i_{ft} - L_d p i_d + L_q \omega i_q \quad \text{...(4.82)}$$

$$-v_{qo}\mathbf{1} = M_d \omega i_{ft} - L_d \omega i_d - L_q p i_q \quad \text{...(4.83)}$$

No added subscripts are necessary for i_d and i_q because their initial values are zero for an unloaded machine, *i.e.* $i_d = i_{dt}$ and $i_q = i_{qt}$ and both $i_{do} = i_{qo} = 0$. The currents obtained from Eqs. (4.81) to (4.83), flow in the relevant circuit after the short circuit and these must be considered as superimposed on those existing before the short circuit at $t = 0-$. Such currents exist only in the field winding, and armature currents are zero because the machine is assumed to be running initially on no-load.

Now i_{ft} should be eliminated from Eqs. (4.81) to (4.83) to obtain currents i_d and i_q.

From Eq. (4.81),
$$i_{ft} = \frac{M_d}{L_f} i_d \quad \text{...(4.84)}$$

Substitution of i_{ft} in Eq. (4.82) gives

$$0 = \frac{M_d p M_d}{L_f} i_d - L_d p i_d + L_q \omega i_q$$

$$0 = -\left(L_d - \frac{M_d^2}{L_f}\right) p i_d + L_q \omega i_q$$

$$0 = -L_d' p i_d + L_q \omega i_q \quad \text{...(4.85)}$$

where
$$L_d' = L_d - \frac{M_d^2}{L_f} \quad \text{...(4.86)}$$

is the *d-axis transient inductance*. It is an important constant in machine theory. $L_d'\omega = X_d'$ is the *d-axis transient reactance* and can be defined by an equivalent circuit as shown at a later stage in Art. 4.11.

Substitution of i_{ft} in Eq. (4.83) gives,

$$-v_{qo}\mathbf{1} = M_d \omega \frac{M_d}{L_f} i_d - L_d \omega i_d - L_q p i_q$$

$$= -\left(L_d - \frac{M_d^2}{L_f}\right) \omega i_d - L_q p i_q$$

$$-v_{qo}\mathbf{1} = -L_d' \omega i_d - L_q p i_d \quad \text{...(4.87)}$$

Now Eqs. (4.85) and (4.87) are two simultaneous equations in i_d and i_q. From Eq. (4.85),

$$i_q = \frac{L'_d\, p}{\omega L_q}\, i_d \qquad \text{...(4.88)}$$

Substitution of i_q from Eq. (4.88) in Eq. (4.87) gives

$$-v_{qo}\,\mathbf{1} = -L_d'\omega i_d - \frac{L_d p}{\omega L_q} L_d' p i_d = -L_d'\left(\omega + \frac{p^2}{\omega}\right) i_d = -\frac{L_d'}{\omega}(p^2+\omega^2)\, i_d$$

or $$v_{qo}\,\mathbf{1} = \frac{\omega L_d'}{\omega^2}(p^2+\omega^2)\, i_d \qquad \text{or} \qquad i_d = \frac{v_{qo}}{X_d'}\left(\frac{\omega^2}{p^2+\omega^2}\mathbf{1}\right)$$

The above equation in complex frequency domain is

$$I_d(s) = \frac{v_{qo}}{X_d'}\left[\frac{\omega^2}{s(s^2+\omega^2)}\right]$$

Let $$\frac{\omega^2}{s(s^2+\omega^2)} = \frac{A}{s} + \frac{B}{s+j\omega} + \frac{C}{s-j\omega}$$

From above, $$A = 1,\ B = C = -\frac{1}{2}$$

$\therefore$ $$I_d(s) = \frac{v_{qo}}{X_d'}\left[\frac{1}{s} - \frac{1}{2}\left\{\frac{1}{s+j\omega} + \frac{1}{s-j\omega}\right\}\right] = \frac{v_{qo}}{X_d'}\left[\frac{1}{s} - \frac{s}{s^2+\omega^2}\right]$$

Its Laplace inverse is

$$i_d(t) = \frac{v_{qo}}{X_d'}(1-\cos\omega t) \qquad \text{...(4.89)}$$

Note that transient d-axis current $i_d(t)$ consists of a d.c. component v_{qo}/X_d' and a fundamental-frequency component $v_{qo}\cos\omega t/X_d'$.

Substitution of $i_d(t)$ from Eq. (4.89) in Eq. (4.88) gives

$$i_q(t) = \frac{v_{qo}}{X_d'}\cdot\frac{L_d'\omega}{\omega L_q}\cdot\frac{p}{\omega}(1-\cos\omega t)$$

$$= \frac{v_{qo}}{X_d}\cdot\frac{1}{\omega}[0+\omega\sin\omega t]$$

$$= \frac{v_{qo}}{X_d}\sin\omega t \qquad \text{...(4.90)}$$

The transient q-axis current $i_q(t)$ consists of only fundamental frequency component.

Eqs. (4.89) and (4.90) give the variations of $i_d(t)$ and $i_q(t)$ and these are sketched in Fig. 4.18.

The actual phase currents in phases a, b, c can be obtained by means of transformation Eq. (2.11). For phase a,

$$i_a = \left[i_d\cos\theta - i_q\sin\theta\right] \qquad \text{...(4.91)}$$

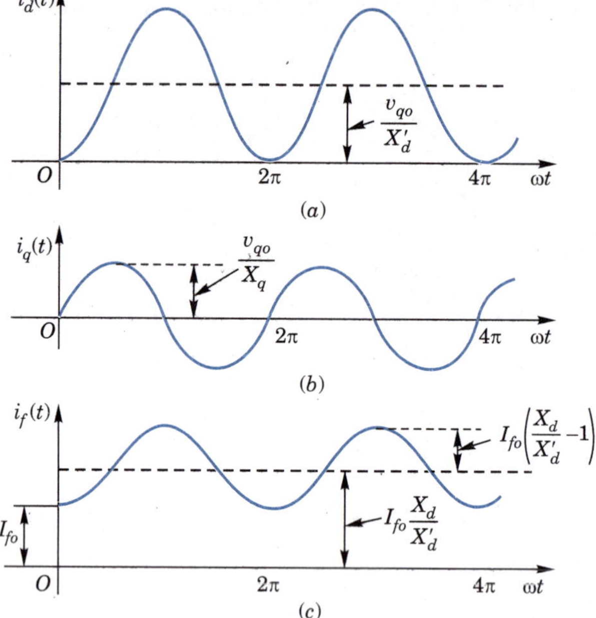

Fig. 4.18: Variations of (a) i_d, (b) i_q and (c) i_f with time, for a sudden three-phase short circuit.

At the instant of short circuit, the axis of phase a is assumed to make an angle of θ_0 with the d-axis, see Fig. 4.19 (a). Since the rotor is running at a synchronous speed of ω rad/sec, the angle θ between d-axis and axis of phase a, after time t seconds, is given by

$$\theta = \omega t + \theta_0$$

This angle $(\omega t + \theta_0)$ is shown in Fig. 4.19 (b).

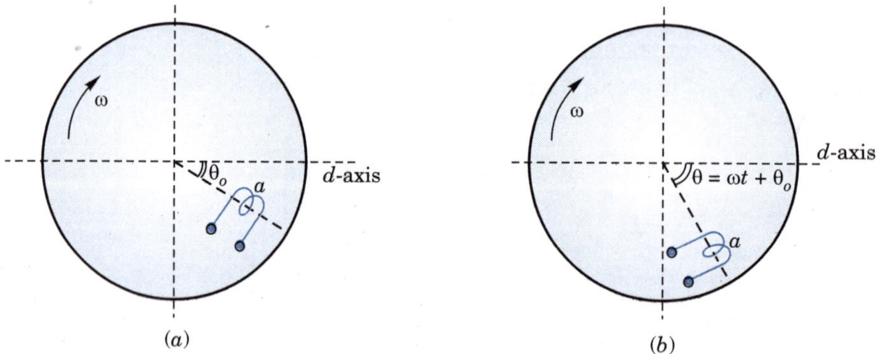

Fig. 4.19: Phase a-axis displaced from d-axis by an angle
(a) θ_0 at the instant of short circuit and (b) $\theta = \omega t + \theta_0$ at any time t.

Substitution of $i_d(t)$ from Eq. (4.89) and $i_q(t)$ from Eq. (4.90) in the transformation Eq. (4.91), gives the value of $i_a(t)$ as

$$i_a(t) = \left[\frac{v_{qo}}{X_d{}'}\cos(\omega t + \theta_o).(1 - \cos\omega t) \;\; - \frac{v_{qo}}{X_d}\sin(\omega t + \theta_o)\sin\omega t\right]$$

This expression can be simplified by making use of the trigonometric relations,

$$\cos A \cos B = \frac{1}{2} [\cos (A - B) + \cos (A + B)]$$

and

$$\sin A \sin B = \frac{1}{2} [\cos (A - B) - \cos (A + B)]$$

$\therefore$

$$i_a(t) = \left[\frac{v_{qo}}{X_d'} \cos (\omega t + \theta_o) - \frac{v_{qo}}{2}\left(\frac{1}{X_d'} + \frac{1}{X_q}\right) \cos \theta_o - \frac{v_{qo}}{2}\left(\frac{1}{X_d'} - \frac{1}{X_q}\right) \cos (2\omega t + \theta_o)\right] \quad ...(4.92)$$

Before the short circuit, *i.e.* at $t = 0-$, $v_{qo} = M_d \omega I_{fo} = \sqrt{2}\, E_{fo}$ and with this, Eq. (4.92) becomes,

$$i_a(t) = \frac{\sqrt{2}\, E_{fo}}{X_d'} \cos (\omega t + \theta_o) - \frac{\sqrt{2}\, E_{fo}}{2}\left(\frac{1}{X_d'} + \frac{1}{X_q}\right) \cos \theta_o - \frac{\sqrt{2}\, E_{fo}}{2}\left(\frac{1}{X_d'} - \frac{1}{X_q}\right) \cos (2\omega t + \theta_o) \quad ...(4.93)$$

The currents in phases b and c can be obtained by replacing θ_o in Eq. (4.93), by $(\theta_o - 120°)$ and $(\theta_o - 240°)$ respectively.

It is seen from Eq. (4.93) that phase current i_a (i_b and i_c also) consists of (*i*) first term as the fundamental frequency component, (*ii*) second term as the d.c. component and (*iii*) third term as the second harmonic component. Eq. (4.93) also reveals that the magnitude of fundamental, d.c. and second harmonic components depend upon the prefault excitation I_{fo}. In addition to this,

(*a*) magnitude of fundamental component depends upon the d-axis transient reactance X_d',

(*b*) the magnitude of d.c. component depends upon θ_o, *i.e.*, the instant at which the short circuit occurs and

(*c*) the magnitude of second harmonic component depends on the term $\left(\frac{1}{X_d'} - \frac{1}{X_q}\right)$, which is called the *transient saliency*.

Note that if short circuit occurs at the instant $\theta_o = 90°$, *i.e.* when phase a-axis is 90° away from d-axis, then d.c. component of current i_a is zero. In spite of this, d.c. component does appear in phase currents i_b and i_c because of 120° phase displacement between phases a, b and c.

It may be observed from Eqs. (4.89) to (4.93) that when dqo variables are transformed to phase variables ;

(*i*) d.c. component of $i_d(t)$ becomes fundamental frequency component of phase current $i_a(t)$ and

(*ii*) fundamental frequency components of $i_d(t)$ and $i_q(t)$ get transformed to d.c. and second-harmonic components of $i_a(t)$.

In the analysis considered above, the neglect of field and armature resistances imply that none of the terms in Eq. (4.93) decays with time. Actually, resistances are present and transients decay exponentially as determinded by their respective time constants. This is illustrated in Fig. 4.20 for phase currents i_a, i_b, i_c and field current i_f.

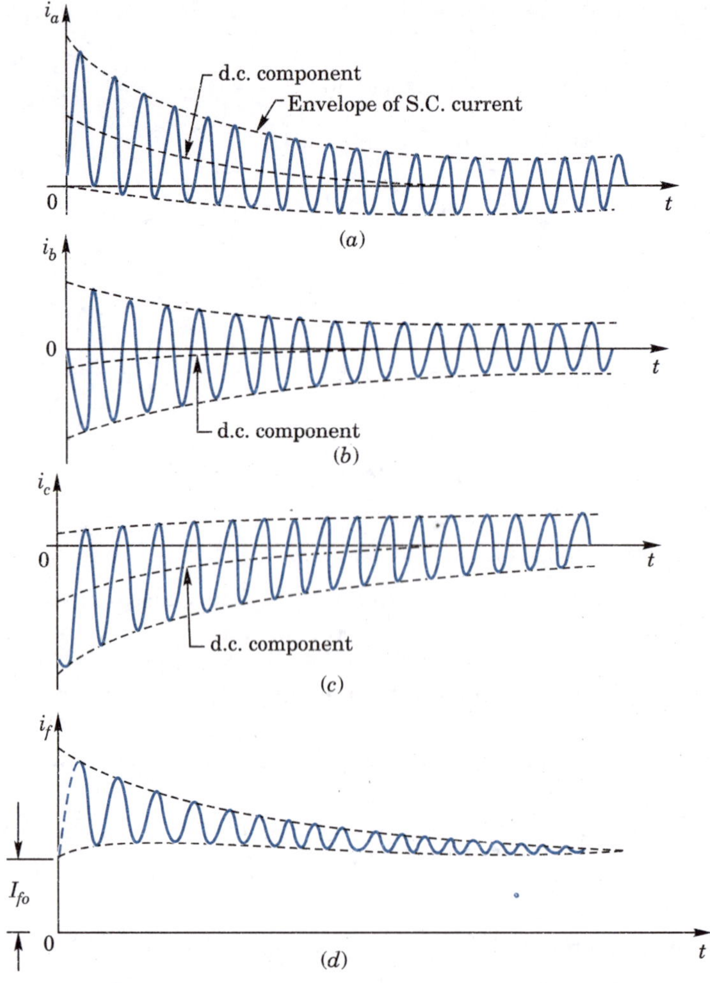

Fig. 4.20: Armature currents and field current of a synchronous generator after the application of sudden three-phase short circuit.

An expression for the transient field current can be obtained by substituting $i_d(t)$ from Eq. (4.89) in Eq. (4.84) for i_{ft}.

$$\therefore \qquad i_{ft}(t) = \frac{M_d}{L_f} \cdot \frac{v_{qo}}{X_d'} (1 - \cos \omega t)$$

Total field current is $\quad i_f(t) = I_{fo} + i_{ft}$

$$= I_{fo} + \frac{M_d}{L_f} \cdot \frac{M_d \omega I_{fo}}{X_d'} (1 - \cos \omega t)$$

$$= I_{fo}\left[1 + \frac{M_d^2}{L_f} \cdot \frac{\omega}{X_d'}(1 - \cos \omega t)\right]$$

Now $$L_d' = L_d - \frac{M_d^2}{L_f} \quad \text{or} \quad \frac{M_d^2}{L_f} = L_d - L_d'$$

$\therefore$ $$i_f(t) = I_{fo}\left[1 + \frac{X_d - X_d'}{X_d'}(1 - \cos \omega t)\right]$$

$$= I_{fo}\left[1 + \left(\frac{X_d}{X_d'} - 1\right)(1 - \cos \omega t)\right]$$

$$= I_{fo}\left[1 + \left(\frac{X_d}{X_d'} - 1\right) - \left(\frac{X_d}{X_d'} - 1\right)\cos \omega t\right]$$

$$= I_{fo}\left[\frac{X_d}{X_d'} - \left(\frac{X_d}{X_d'} - 1\right)\cos \omega t\right] \qquad ...(4.94)$$

It is seen from above that field current $i_f(t)$ consists of a d.c. component and a fundamental frequency component. Its variation with time is shown in Fig . 4.18.

(*b*) **Armature transformer voltages and all resistances neglected.** In the armature voltage equations, the terms containing p are the transformer voltages. Omission of these terms from armature voltages v_d and v_q, results in very simple expressions for the machine currents. With the neglect of armature transformer voltage from Eq. (4.80), the following new voltage equations, specifying the balanced three-phase short-circuit and obtained from Eqs. (4.81) to (4.83), are :

$$0 = L_f p i_{ft} - M_d p i_d \qquad ...(4.95)$$

$$0 = L_q \omega i_q \qquad ...(4.96)$$

$$-v_{qo}\,\mathbf{1} = M_d \omega i_{ft} - L_d \omega i_d \qquad ...(4.97)$$

From Eq. (4.95), $$i_{ft} = \frac{M_d}{L_f}\, i_d$$

From Eq. (4.96), $$i_q = 0$$

From Eq. (4.97), $$-v_{qo}\,\mathbf{1} = M_d\,\omega \frac{M_d}{L_f}\, i_d - L_d\,\omega i_d = -L_d'\,\omega i_d$$

or $$i_d = \frac{v_{qo}}{X_d'}$$

Field current, $$i_{ft} = \frac{M_d}{L_f} \cdot \frac{v_{qo}}{X_d'}$$

Total field current is $$i_f = I_{fo} + \frac{M_d}{L_f} \cdot \frac{M_d \omega I_{fo}}{X_d'} = I_{fo}\left[1 + \frac{M_d^2 \omega}{L_f X_d'}\right]$$

$$= I_{fo}\left[1 + \frac{(L_d - L_d')\omega}{X_d'}\right]$$

$$= I_{fo}\left[1+\frac{X_d - X_d'}{X_d'}\right] = I_{fo}\,\frac{X_d}{X_d'} \qquad ...(4.98)$$

Current in phase a is $i_a = \left[i_d \cos(\omega t + \theta_o) - i_q \sin(\omega t + \theta_o)\right]$

Substitution of the values of i_d and i_q gives

$$i_a(t) = \frac{\sqrt{2}E_{fo}}{X_d'} \cos(\omega t + \theta_o) \qquad ...(4.99)$$

Eq. (4.99) shows that if transformer voltages are neglected from the armature voltage equations, the phase currents consist of only fundamental term ; the d.c. and second harmonic terms are absent. The current i_q is zero, the currents i_d and i_f follow the dashed lines as shown in Fig. 4.18 (*a*) and (*c*) respectively.

Neglect of the transformer voltages in the armature voltage equations implies that the amplitude variation of the armature currents is small as compared to their frequency variation. This assumption is justified in that the field circuits have large time constants and thus the rate of variation of *d-q* axes currents is very slow as compared to the angular frequency ω.

For the analysis of machines, where only fundamental component is required, this assumption of neglecting the transformer voltages in the armature, simplifies the analysis considerably. Further, the average torque of a machine is not appreciably influenced by the d.c. and second harmonic components. In view of this, dynamic analysis of synchronous machines is usually carried out by neglecting the armature transformer voltages.

(*c*) **Armature transformer voltages and its resistances neglected.** Eqs. (4.95) to (4.97) are again suitable here, except that $r_f i_{ft}$ appears on the right hand side of Eq. (4.95). Since the field resistance has been included, the decay of transients can be explored. Now the required voltage equations, under the conditions specified for the three-phase short circuit, are,

$$0 = (r_f + L_f p)\, i_{ft} - M_d p i_d \qquad ...(4.100)$$

$$0 = L_q \omega i_q \qquad ...(4.101)$$

$$-v_{qo}\mathbf{1} = M_d \omega i_{ft} - L_d \omega i_d \qquad ...(4.102)$$

From Eq. (4.100), $$i_{ft} = \frac{M_d p i_d}{r_f + L_f p} \qquad ...(4.103)$$

From Eq. (4.101), $$i_q = 0$$

From Eqn. (4.102), $$-v_{qo}\,\mathbf{1} = -i_d\omega\left(L_d - \frac{M_d^2 p}{r_f + L_f p}\right)$$

$$= -\frac{i_d\omega}{r_f + L_f p}\left[L_d r_f + L_f p\left(L_d - \frac{M_d^2}{L_f}\right)\right]$$

$$= -i_d\omega\left[L_d + \frac{L_f}{r_f}\,.\,pL_d'\right]\frac{r_f}{r_f + L_f p}$$

The ratio $\dfrac{L_f}{r_f} = \tau_f = T_{do}'$ is the field time constant. Since this time constant describes the transient decay with the armature on open circuit, T_{do}' is called the *d-axis open-circuit transient time constant.*

Thus, $$-v_{qo}\,\mathbf{1} = -i_d\omega\,[L_d + \tau_f L_d' p]\,\frac{1}{1+\tau_f p}$$

or $$v_{qo}\,\mathbf{1} = i_d\omega\,[L_d + T_{do}' L_d' p]\,\frac{1}{1+T_{do}' p}$$

$$= i_d\,\omega\left[1 + T_{do}'\frac{L_d'}{L_d}\,p\right]\frac{L_d}{1+T_{do}' p}$$

The term $$T_{do}'\frac{L_d'}{L_d} = T_{do}'\frac{X_d'}{X_d} = T_d' \qquad \text{...(4.104)}$$

is called the *direct-axis short-circuit transient time constant.*

$$\therefore \qquad v_{qo}\,\mathbf{1} = i_d\omega\,L_d\,\frac{1+T_d' p}{1+T_{do}' p} = X_d i_d\left[\frac{1+T_d' p}{1+T_{do}' p}\right]$$

or $$i_d = \frac{v_{qo}\,\mathbf{1}}{X_d}\left[\frac{1+T_{do}' p}{1+T_d' p}\right] \qquad \text{...(4.105)}$$

$$= \frac{v_{qo}\,\mathbf{1}}{X_d}\cdot\frac{1}{(1+T_d' p)} + \frac{v_{qo}\,\mathbf{1}}{X_d}\cdot\frac{T_{do}' p}{(1+T_d' p)}$$

The above equation in s-domain is,

$$I_d(s) = \frac{v_{qo}}{X_d}\cdot\frac{1}{s(1+T_d' s)} + \frac{v_{qo}}{X_d}\cdot\frac{T_{do}'}{1+T_d' s}$$

$$= \frac{v_{qo}}{X_d\cdot T_d'}\cdot\frac{1}{s(s+1/T_d')} + \frac{v_{qo}}{X_d}\cdot\frac{T_{do}'}{T_d'}\cdot\frac{1}{s+\dfrac{1}{T_d'}}$$

$$= \frac{v_{qo}}{X_d}\left[\frac{1}{s} - \frac{1}{(s+1/T_d')}\right] + \frac{v_{qo}}{X_d}\cdot\frac{T_{do}'}{T_d'}\cdot\frac{1}{s+\dfrac{1}{T_d'}}$$

Its solution in time domain is,

$$i_d(t) = \frac{v_{qo}}{X_d}\left(1 - e^{-t/T_d'}\right) + \frac{v_{qo}}{X_d}\cdot\frac{T_{do}'}{T_d'}\cdot e^{-t/T_d'}$$

$$= \frac{v_{qo}}{X_d} + v_{qo}\left(\frac{1}{X_d'} - \frac{1}{X_d}\right)e^{-t/T_d'} \qquad \text{...(4.106)}$$

Substituting the value of i_d from Eq. (4.105) in Eq. (4.103) gives the field current as,

$$i_{ft} = \frac{M_d p}{r_f(1+T_{do}' p)}\cdot\frac{v_{qo}\mathbf{1}}{X_d}\cdot\frac{1+T_{do}' p}{1+T_d' p} = \frac{v_{qo}\,\mathbf{1}}{X_d}\cdot\frac{M_d}{r_f}\cdot\frac{p}{1+T'_d p}$$

In s-domain, $$I_{ft}(s) = \frac{v_{qo}}{X_d}\cdot\frac{M_d}{r_f}\cdot\frac{1}{T_d'}\cdot\frac{1}{s+\dfrac{1}{T_d'}}$$

Its time solution is, $$i_{ft}(t) = \frac{v_{qo}}{X_d}\cdot\frac{M_d}{r_f}\cdot\frac{1}{T_d'}\,e^{-t/T_d'}$$

Substituting the value of T_d' from Eq. (4.104), we get,

$$i_{ft}(t) = \frac{M_d\, \omega I_{fo}}{X_d} \cdot \frac{M_d}{r_f} \cdot \frac{X_d}{T_{do}'} \cdot \frac{1}{X_d'} e^{-t/T_d'}$$

$$= \frac{I_{fo}\, \omega M_d^2}{r_f \cdot X_d'} \cdot \frac{r_f}{L_f} \cdot e^{-t/T_d'}$$

$$= \frac{I_{fo} \cdot \omega \cdot M_d^2}{X_d' L_f} \cdot e^{-t/T_d'} \qquad \text{...(4.107)}$$

From Eq. (4.86), $L_d' = L_d - \dfrac{M_d^2}{L_f}$

or $$\frac{M_d^2}{L_f} = L_d - L_d'$$

Substitution of M_d^2/L_f in Eq. (4.107) gives,

$$i_{ft}(t) = \frac{I_{fo}}{X_d'} (X_d - X_d')\, e^{-t/T_d'} \qquad \text{...(4.108)}$$

Total field current is,

$$i_f(t) = I_{fo} + \frac{I_{fo}}{X_d'} (X_d - X_d')\, e^{-t/T_d'}$$

$$= I_{fo} \left[1 + \frac{X_d - X_d'}{X_d'} e^{-t/T_d'} \right] \qquad \text{...(4.109)}$$

The phase current i_a is given by,

$$i_a = [i_d \cos(\omega t + \theta_o) - i_q \sin(\omega t + \theta_o)]$$

Substituting the value of $i_d\ (t)$ from Eq. (4.106), i_q being zero, we get the armature current for phase a as

$$i_a\,(t) = \frac{\sqrt{2} E_{fo}}{X_d} \cos(\omega t + \theta_o) + \sqrt{2} E_{fo} \left(\frac{1}{X_d'} - \frac{1}{X_d} \right) e^{-t/T_d'} \cdot \cos(\omega t + \theta_o)$$

...(4.110)

On the right hand side of Eq. (4.110), first term is the final steady-state short-circuit current and the second term is the transient current. The effect of including the field resistance r_f is to make the amplitude of short-circuit current equal to $\sqrt{2} E_{fo}/X_d$ after the transients have decayed. Its r.m.s. value is E_{fo}/X_d, which is the normal steady-state short-circuit current.

The equation of the envelope of the short-circuit current, from Eq. (4.110), is

$$i_a(t) = \sqrt{2} \frac{E_{fo}}{X_d} + \sqrt{2} E_{fo} \left(\frac{1}{X_d'} - \frac{1}{X_d} \right) e^{-t/T_d'} \qquad \text{...(4.111)}$$

The r.m.s. value of the short-circuit current as function of time is

$$I_a(t) = \frac{E_{fo}}{X_d} + E_{fo} \left(\frac{1}{X_d'} - \frac{1}{X_d} \right) e^{-t/T_d'} \qquad \text{...(4.112)}$$

At $t = 0+$, *i.e.*, just after the short-circuit, the armature phase current is E_{fo}/X_d' and its final steady-state value is E_{fo}/X_d. Note that the initial amplitude of short-circuit current is limited by d-axis transient reactance X_d' and its final steady-state amplitude by d-axis synchronous reactance X_d. The decay of current from E_{fo}/X_d' to E_{fo}/X_d is exponential and is determined by the time constant T_d'.

A sketch of Eq. (4.112) gives the variation of r.m.s. short-circuit armature current during transients as shown Fig. 4.21. The current E_{fo}/X_d' (= oa) is the short-circuit current just after the short circuit *i.e.* at $t = 0+$ and E_f/X_d (= ob) is the steady short-circuit current. Here $E_{fo}\left(\frac{1}{X_d'} - \frac{1}{X_d}\right)$ is the transient component of the short-circuit current.

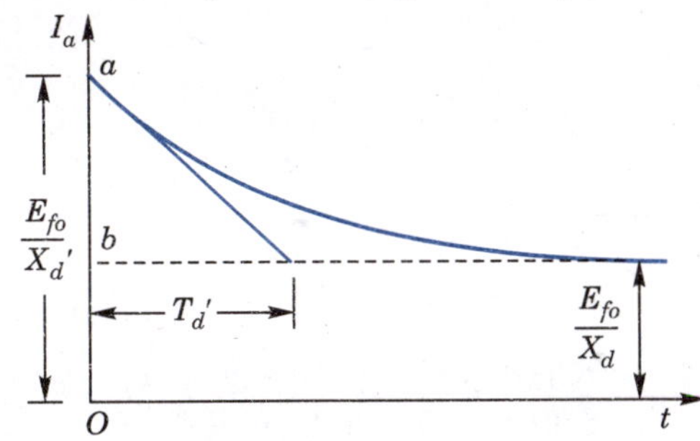

Fig. 4.21: Variation of r.m.s. short-circuit armature current during transients.

(*d*) Same as in (*c*) but amortisseur circuits included. The synchronous machines fitted with damper bars, or amortisseurs, are studied with one coil *KD* in the d-axis and another coil *KQ* in the quadrature axis, as shown in Fig. 1.8 (*b*). Therefore, a synchronous machine with amortisseurs requires five voltage equations for its transient analysis. In addition to the voltage Eqs. (4.100) to (4.102) ; two more voltage equations, one for *KD* coil and the other for *KQ* coil are needed. The solution of these five voltage equations will not be carried out here, but only their results are presented.

Eq. (4.106) reveals that $v_{qo}\left(\frac{1}{X_d'} - \frac{1}{X_d}\right)$ is the transient component of $i_d(t)$. Now with the presence of damper bars, the current $i_d(t)$, just after the fault, would include a subtransient component of current given by a similar expression

$$v_{qo}\left(\frac{1}{X_d''} - \frac{1}{X_d'}\right)$$

This component of current would decay to zero with a time constant T_d'', which is called the *d-axis short-circuit subtransient time constant*. Thus, the expression for current $i_d(t)$, when armature transformer voltages are neglected but with both field and d-axis damper bars present, can be written, similar to Eq. (4.106), as

$$i_d(t) = \frac{v_{qo}}{X_d} + v_{qo}\left(\frac{1}{X_d'} - \frac{1}{X_d}\right)e^{-t/T_d'} + v_{qo}\left(\frac{1}{X_d''} - \frac{1}{X_d'}\right)e^{-t/T_d''}$$

In case the effect of armature transformer voltages is considered, then an examination of Eq. (4.89) reveals that $i_d(t)$, with damper bars present, must include a fundamental frequency component

$$-\frac{v_{qo}}{X_d''}\cos \omega t \qquad ...(4.113)$$

Note that X_d' in Eq. (4.89) is replaced by X_d'' now to take into account the effect of d-axis damper bars. In case armature resistances are also considered, then fundamental frequency component of $i_d(t)$ would decay with armature time constant T_a as explained in Art. 4.10. Thus, the complete expression of current $i_d(t)$ is given by

$$i_d(t) = \frac{v_{qo}}{X_d} + v_{qo}\left(\frac{1}{X_d'} - \frac{1}{X_d}\right)e^{-t/T_d'}$$

$$+ v_{qo}\left(\frac{1}{X_d''} - \frac{1}{X_d'}\right)e^{-t/T_d''} - \frac{v_{qo}}{X_d''}e^{-t/T_a} \cdot \cos \omega t \qquad ...(4.114)$$

With the help of Eqs. (4.90) and (4.113), the effect of q-axis damper bars, armature-circuit resistance and armature transformer voltages can be taken into account by expressing $i_q(t)$ as

$$i_q(t) = \frac{v_{qo}}{X_d''}e^{-t/T_a} . \sin \omega t \qquad ...(4.115)$$

Now $\quad i_a(t) = [i_d \cos (\omega t + \theta_o) - i_q \sin (\omega t + \theta_o)]$

Substitution of the values of $i_d(t)$ and $i_q(t)$ from Eqs. (4.114) and (4.115) respectively and noting that $v_{qo} = \sqrt{2}E_{fo}$, we get,

$$i_a(t) = \sqrt{2}\, E_{fo}\left[\frac{1}{X_d} + \left(\frac{1}{X_d'} - \frac{1}{X_d}\right)e^{-t/T_d'} + \left(\frac{1}{X_d''} - \frac{1}{X_d'}\right)e^{-t/T_d''}\right]$$

$$\cos (\omega t - \theta_o) - \frac{\sqrt{2} . E_{fo}}{2} . e^{-t/T_a'} . \left(\frac{1}{X_d''} + \frac{1}{X_q''}\right) \cos \theta_o$$

$$- \frac{\sqrt{2}\, E_{fo}}{2} . e^{-t/T_a}\left(\frac{1}{X_d''} - \frac{1}{X_q''}\right) \cos (2\omega t + \theta_o) \qquad ...(4.116)$$

In Eq. (4.116), magnitude of second harmonic component (the last term), is usually small and can therefore be neglected. In modern synchronous generators, $X_d'' \approx X_q''$ and therefore subtransient saliency $\left(\frac{1}{X_d''} - \frac{1}{X_q''}\right)$ can be ignored. With these approximations, Eq. (4.116) becomes,

$$i_a(t) = \sqrt{2}\, E_{fo}\left[\frac{1}{X_d} + \left(\frac{1}{X_d'} - \frac{1}{X_d}\right)e^{-t/T_d'} + \left(\frac{1}{X_d''} - \frac{1}{X_d'}\right)e^{-t/T_d''}\right]$$

$$\cos (\omega t + \theta_o) - \sqrt{2}\, E_{fo} \cdot \left[\frac{1}{X_d''}e^{-t/T_a}\right] \cos \theta_o \qquad ...(4.117)$$

The expression for currents i_b and i_c can be obtained by replacing θ_o in Eq. (4.117) by $(\theta_o - 120°)$ and $(\theta_o - 240°)$ respectively. In Eq. (4.117), the fundamental frequency component is the symmetrical component of $i_a(t)$, whereas the d.c. component is assymmetrical component of $i_a(t)$. An examination of Eq. (4.117) reveals that in case the fault occurs at $\theta_o = 0°$, then at the instant of fault ($t = 0$),

$$i_a(t) = \sqrt{2}\, E_{fo}\left[\frac{1}{X_d''}\right] - \sqrt{2}E_{fo}\left[\frac{1}{X_d''}\right] = 0.$$

In the above equation, note that first term $\sqrt{2}E_{fo}\frac{1}{X_d''}$ is the symmetrical, or a.c., component of $i_a(t)$, whereas the second term $\sqrt{2}E_{fo}\frac{1}{X_d''}$ is the asymmetrical or d.c. component of $i_a(t)$. This shows that at $t = 0$ and for $\theta_o = 0°$,

$$\begin{bmatrix}\text{Symmetrical or a.c.}\\ \text{component of } i_a(t)\end{bmatrix} = \begin{bmatrix}\text{Asymmetrical or d.c.}\\ \text{component of } i_a(t)\end{bmatrix}$$

$$= \frac{\sqrt{2}E_{fo}}{X_d''} \qquad ...(4.118)$$

Had there been no decay of either the a.c. component or the d.c. component, then after one-half of cycle, *i.e.* at $\omega t = \pi$, the magnitude of armature current in phase a [from Eq. (4.117)] would be $2 \cdot \frac{\sqrt{2} \cdot E_{fo}}{X_d''}$. Note that this maximum value of armature phase current is possible only if axis of phase a is along d-axis ($\theta_o = 0°$) at the instant of fault and attenuation does not take place.

Because of the rapid decay of current, the maximum possible value of the sudden short-circuit armature current is usually taken as $1.8 \frac{\sqrt{2}E_{fo}}{X_d''}$. Under normal cirumstances, the maximum possible value of current equal to $1.8 \times \sqrt{2} \frac{E_{fo}}{X_d''}$ should not exceed about 15 times the rated peak armature current. If I_r is the r.m.s. rated armature current, then

$$1.8 \times \sqrt{2} \frac{E_f}{X_d''} < 15 \times \sqrt{2} \,.\, I_r$$

In case $E_{fo} = 1.0$ (rated value) and $I_r = 1.00$ (rated value), then

$$X_d'' > \frac{(1.8)\sqrt{2}}{15\sqrt{2}}$$

or

$$X_d'' > 0.12$$

This shows that minimum permissible value of X_d'' is 0.12 per unit.

The symmetrical or a.c. component i_{ac} of the total short-circuit armature current $i_a(t)$, as given by Eq. (4.117), can be written as

$$i_{ac}(t) = \sqrt{2}E_{fo}\left[\frac{1}{X_d} + \left(\frac{1}{X_d'} - \frac{1}{X_d}\right)e^{-t/T_d'} + \left(\frac{1}{X_d''} - \frac{1}{X_d'}\right)e^{-t/T_d''}\right]\cos(\omega t + \theta_o)$$

R.m.s. value of the symmetrical armature short-circuit current is given by

$$I_{ac}(t) = E_{fo}\left[\frac{1}{X_d} + \left(\frac{1}{X_d'} - \frac{1}{X_d}\right)e^{-t/T_d'} + \left(\frac{1}{X_d''} - \frac{1}{X_d'}\right)e^{-t/T_d''}\right] \qquad ...(4.119)$$

Note that the armature current at $t = 0+$, *i.e.* just after the short-circuit, is equal to $\frac{E_{fo}}{X_d''}$ (= oa) as shown in Fig. 4.22. The current changes exponentially from $\frac{E_{fo}}{X_d''}$ to $\frac{E_{fo}}{X_d'}$ with a time constant T_d'' and from $\frac{E_{fo}}{X_d'}$ (= ob) to $\frac{E_{fo}}{X_d}$ (= od) with a time constant T_d' as depicted in Fig. 4.22.

The asymmetrical or d.c. component of the total short-circuit armature current $i_a(t)$ of Eq. (4.117) can be written as

$$I_{dc}(t) = \sqrt{2} \,.\, \frac{E_{fo}}{X_d''} \,.\, e^{-t/T_a} \cos\theta_o \qquad ...(4.120)$$

The r.m.s. or effective value of the total short-circuit armature current I_{sc} at any instant is given by

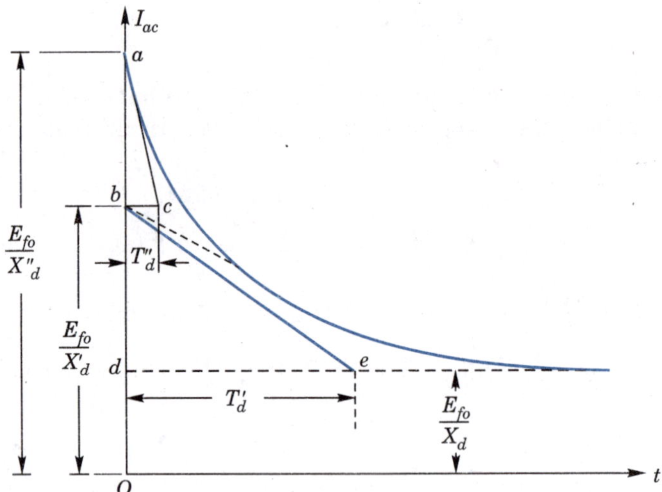

Fig. 4.22: Variation of r.m.s. short-circuit armature current during subtransient conditions.

$$I_{sc} = \sqrt{I_{ac}^2(t) + I_{dc}^2(t)} \quad ...(4.121)$$

It is seen from Eq. (4.119) and Fig. 4.22 that, just after the short circuit, the greatest possible r.m.s. value of symmetrical short circuit armature current is equal to

$$I_{ac \cdot m} = \frac{E_{fo}}{X_d''}$$

Note that this value is achieved with a fully offset wave as shown for phase '*a*' current in Fig. 4.20 (*a*). The greatest possible value of d.c. component at $t = 0$ and with $\theta_o = 0°$, from Eq. (4.120), is

$$I_{dc \cdot m} = \sqrt{2}\,\frac{E_{fo}}{X_d''}$$

Therefore, effective value of the greatest armature current, including a.c. and d.c. components is

$$I_{\max} = \sqrt{I_{ac \cdot m}{}^2 + I_{dc \cdot m}{}^2} = \sqrt{3}\,.\,\frac{E_{fo}}{X_d''} \quad ...(4.122)$$

Example 4.11. *Derive an expression for the transient electrical torque of an unloaded synchronous generator, after the occurrence of a sudden 3-phase short circuit at its terminals. Neglect all the machine resistances.*

Solution. Neglect of all machine resistances permits the use of $i_d(t)$, $i_q(t)$ and $i_f(t)$ as given by Eqs. (4.89), (4.90) and (4.94) respectively. Further, these currents don't decay with time because of the neglect of all resistances.

The expression for the instantaneous torque, from the beginning of Art. 4.5 is

$$T_e = \frac{3}{2}\,[M_d i_q i_f + (L_d - L_q)\, i_d i_q] \quad ...(4.53a)$$

Substitution of the values of i_d, i_q and i_f gives short-circuit torque as,

$$T_{e \cdot sc} = \frac{3}{2} M_d \left(\frac{M_d \omega I_{fo}}{\omega L_q} \sin \omega t \right) I_{fo} \left[1 + \frac{L_d - L_d'}{L_d'} (1 - \cos \omega t) \right]$$

$$+ \frac{3}{2} (L_d - L_q) \frac{M_d \cdot \omega I_{fo}}{\omega L_d'} (1 - \cos \omega t) \frac{M_d \omega I_{fo}}{\omega L_q} \sin \omega t$$

$$= \frac{3}{2} \frac{(M_d I_{fo})^2}{L_q} \sin \omega t \left[1 + \frac{L_d - L_d'}{L_d'} (1 - \cos \omega t) \right]$$

$$+ \frac{3}{2} (L_d - L_q) \left[\frac{(M_d I_{fo})^2}{L_d' L_q} (1 - \cos \omega t) \sin \omega t \right]$$

$$= \frac{3}{2} \frac{(M_d I_{fo})^2}{L_q} \sin \omega t + \frac{3}{2} \frac{(M_d I_{fo})^2}{L_q} \cdot \frac{L_d - L_d'}{L_d'} \sin \omega t$$

$$- \frac{3}{2} \frac{(M_d I_{fo})^2}{L_q} \cdot \frac{L_d - L_d'}{L_d'} (\sin \omega t \cos \omega t) + \frac{3}{2} (L_d - L_q) \frac{(M_d I_{fo})^2}{L_d' L_q} \sin \omega t$$

$$- \frac{3}{2} (L_d - L_q) \frac{(M_d I_{fo})^2}{L_d' L_q} (\sin \omega t \cos \omega t)$$

For convenience, considering first sin ωt terms only, we get,

$$\frac{3}{2} \cdot \frac{(M_d I_{fo})^2}{L_q} \left[1 + \frac{L_d - L_d'}{L_d'} + \frac{L_d - L_q}{L_d'} \right] \sin \omega t$$

$$= \frac{3}{2} \frac{(M_d I_{fo})^2}{L_q L_d'} [L_d' + L_d - L_d' + L_d - L_q] \sin \omega t$$

$$= \frac{3}{2} \frac{(M_d I_{fo})^2}{L_d'} \left[\frac{2L_d}{L_q} - 1 \right] \sin \omega t \qquad \text{...(4.123)}$$

Now considering the (sin ωt cos ωt) terms, we get

$$- \frac{3}{2} \frac{(M_d I_{fo})^2}{L_d' L_q} [L_d - L_d' + L_d - L_q] \sin \omega t \cos \omega t$$

$$= - \frac{3}{2} \frac{(M_d I_{fo})^2}{2L_d'} \left[\frac{2L_d - L_d'}{L_q} - 1 \right] \sin 2\omega t \qquad \text{...(4.124)}$$

Sum of Eqs. (4.123) and (4.124) gives the total electrical torque as,

$$T_{e.sc} = \frac{3}{2} \frac{(M_d I_{fo})^2}{L_d'} \left(\frac{2L_d}{L_q} - 1 \right) \sin \omega t$$

$$- \frac{3}{2} \frac{(M_d I_{fo})^2}{2L_d'} \left(\frac{2L_d - L_d'}{L_q} - 1 \right) \sin 2\omega t \qquad \text{...(4.125)}$$

For a cylindrical-rotor synchronous generator, $L_d = L_q$, therefore Eq. (4.125) becomes,

$$T_{e.sc} = \frac{3}{2} \frac{(M_d I_{fo})^2}{L_d'} \sin \omega t - \frac{3}{2} \frac{(M_d I_{fo})^2}{2L_d'} \left(1 - \frac{L_d'}{L_q} \right) \sin 2\omega t$$

$$= \frac{3}{2}\frac{(M_d I_{fo})^2}{L_d'}\sin\omega t - \frac{3}{2}\frac{(M_d I_{fo})^2}{2}\left(\frac{1}{L_d'} - \frac{1}{L_q}\right)\sin 2\omega t \quad ...(4.126)$$

Now excitation voltage before the short circuit is,

$$E_{fo} = \frac{M_d \cdot \omega \cdot I_{fo}}{\sqrt{2}}$$

$$\therefore \quad T_{e.sc} = \frac{3E_{fo}^2}{\omega X_d'}\sin\omega t - \frac{3E_{fo}^2}{2\omega}\left(\frac{1}{X_d'} - \frac{1}{X_q}\right)\sin 2\omega t \quad ...(4.127)$$

4.8 TRANSIENT TORQUE

The object of this article is not to do the rigorous analysis of torque after sudden 3-phase short circuit, but to calculate the maximum value of torque at the instant of short circuit. In order to do this, the following assumptions are made :

(*i*) $X_d'' = X_q''$.

(*ii*) Field current remains constant at I_{fo}.

(*iii*) Maximum value of i_f, i_q, i_d ; reached after sudden 3-phase short circuit, don't decay.

The torque in a cylindrical-rotor synchronous machine, from Eq. (4.53*a*) is given by

$$T_e = \frac{3}{2} M_d \cdot i_f i_q \quad ...(4.128)$$

From Eq. (4.115), $\quad i_q = \frac{v_{qo}}{X_q''}\sin\omega t = \frac{v_{qo}}{X_d''}\sin\omega t.$

Here e^{-t/T_a} is not included, because value of i_q, after sudden 3-phase short circuit, does not decay as per assumption (*iii*) above.

Therefore, the short-circuit torque is

$$T_{e\cdot sc} = \frac{3}{2}(M_d I_{fo}) \cdot \frac{v_{qo}}{X_d''}\sin\omega t$$

But $\quad E_{fo} = \frac{M_d \cdot \omega I_{fo}}{\sqrt{2}} = \frac{v_{qo}}{\sqrt{2}}$

$$\therefore \quad T_{e.sc} = \frac{3}{2}\left(\frac{\sqrt{2}\,E_{fo}}{\omega}\right) \cdot \frac{\sqrt{2}\,E_{fo}}{X_d''}\sin\omega t$$

$$= \frac{1}{\omega}\frac{3E_{fo}^2}{X_d''}\sin\omega t \quad ...(4.129)$$

Eq. (4.129) shows that initial amplitude of torque, soon after 3-phase sudden short circuit, is $\frac{1}{\omega} \cdot \frac{3E_{fo}^2}{X_d''}$ and it oscillates at fundamental frequency. If effect of damper bars is neglected, then from Eq. (4.129)

$$T_{e\cdot sc} = \frac{1}{\omega} \cdot \frac{3E_{fo}^2}{X_d'}\sin\omega t$$

and this agrees with the fundamental frequency torque component of Eq. (4.127).

If the synchronous machine has V_r and I_r as its rated phase values for voltage and current respectively, then rated torque $T_{e.r}$ is given by

$$T_{e.r} = \frac{3V_rI_r}{\omega} \quad ...(4.130)$$

From Eqs. (4.129) and (4.130), $\dfrac{T_{e.sc}}{T_{e.r}} = \dfrac{E_{fo}^2}{X_d''} \cdot \dfrac{1}{V_rI_r} \sin \omega t$

If per unit system is used, then $V_r = 1.0$ and $I_r = 1.0$. With this,

$$\frac{T_{e.sc}}{T_{e.r}} = \frac{E_{fo}^2}{X_d''} \sin \omega t \quad ...(4.131)$$

In Eq. (4.131), ratio of short-circuit torque to rated torque is maximum, when $\sin \omega t = 1$, *i.e.* $\omega t = 90°$.

$$\therefore \quad \frac{T_{e.scm}}{T_{e.r}} = \frac{E_{fo}^2}{X_d''} \quad ...(4.132)$$

If $E_{fo} = 1.10$ and $X_d'' = 0.2$, then $\dfrac{T_{e.scm}}{T_{e.r}} = \dfrac{(1.1)^2}{0.2} = 6.05$

It is seen from above that maximum value of torque, after sudden 3-phase short circuit, is several times greater than its rated torque. In view of this, the shaft and machine foundations must be suitably designed to withstand jerks caused by such large magnitudes of sudden short-circuit torques.

4.9 SUDDEN REACTIVE LOADING AND UNLOADING

In this article, variation of currents and voltages is investigated when sudden reactive loading, or unloading, of synchronous generators is carried out.

4.9.1 Sudden Reactive Loading

It is assumed that the synchronous generator is initially unloaded and is developing a nominal terminal voltage at synchronous speed. The nature of balanced reactive loading may be inductive or capacitive. Here the transient analysis of synchronous generators, with sudden application of balanced inductive load X_L and then with balanced capacitive load X_C, is considered one after the other.

(*a*) **Sudden inductive loading.** For a sudden inductive loading, the load reactance X_L is taken to be lumped with the alternator internal reactances X_d, X_d' and X_q and then sudden short circuit is assumed to occur at its terminals. Thus, from Eq. (4.112), the r.m.s. value of armature phase current at any time t is

$$I_a(t) = \frac{E_{fo}}{X_d + X_L} + E_{fo}\left[\frac{1}{X_d' + X_L} - \frac{1}{X_d + X_L}\right] e^{-t/T_L'}$$

$$= \frac{E_{fo}}{X_d + X_L}\left[1 + \frac{X_d - X_d'}{X_d' + X_L} e^{-t/T_L'}\right] \quad ...(4.133)$$

where load time constant T_L', from Eq. (4.104), is,

$$T_L' = T_{do}' \frac{X_d' + X_L}{X_d + X_L} \quad ...(4.134)$$

Note that the effect of damper winding is not considered here.

The voltage across the load reactance X_L at any time t is given by, $V_L(t) = I_a(t) \cdot X_L$

$$\therefore \qquad V_L(t) = \frac{E_{fo} X_L}{X_d + X_L}\left[1 + \frac{X_d - X_d'}{X_d' + X_L} e^{-t/T_L'}\right] \qquad \text{...(4.135)}$$

The variation of field current after sudden inductive loading X_L can be obtained from Eq. (4.109). Therefore,

$$i_f(t) = I_{fo}\left[1 + \frac{X_d - X_d'}{X_d' + X_L} e^{-t/T_L'}\right] \qquad \text{...(4.136)}$$

The variation of excitation voltage with time is given as,

$$E_f(t) = \frac{1}{\sqrt{2}} M_d \omega i_f(t)$$

$$= \frac{1}{\sqrt{2}} M_d \omega I_{fo}\left[1 + \frac{X_d - X_d'}{X_d' + X_L} e^{-t/T_L'}\right]$$

$$= E_{fo}\left[1 + \frac{X_d - X_d'}{X_d' + X_L} e^{-t/T_L'}\right] \qquad \text{...(4.137)}$$

Eq. (4.133) can also be obtained, alternatively, from Eq. (4.137) as follows:

The armature current, after sudden inductive loading X_L, is given by,

$$I_a(t) = \frac{E_f(t)}{X_d + X_L}$$

Substitution of $E_f(t)$ from Eq. (4.137) gives,

$$I_a(t) = \frac{E_{fo}}{X_d + X_L}\left[1 + \frac{X_d - X_d'}{X_d' + X_L} e^{-t/T_L'}\right] \qquad \text{...(4.133)}$$

Starting of large induction motors is a fairly good example of sudden inductive loading of synchronous generators.

Examination of Eq. (4.135) shows that just after sudden inductive loading, the terminal voltage at once drops from E_{fo} to $OA = \dfrac{E_{fo} X_L}{X_d' + X_L}$. This value decreases finally to $\dfrac{E_{fo} X_L}{X_d + X_L}$ with a load time constant of T_L', as depicted in Fig. 4.23 (*a*).

In actual practice, voltage regulators are used to maintain a constant voltage at the alternator terminals. The sudden drop in voltage from E_{fo} to OA can't be avoided by regulators. However, depending on its setting, the voltage regulator comes into play and restores the voltage to its original value E_{fo} by automatically increasing the field current of the alternator. The dotted curve in Fig. 4.23 (*a*) illustrates the recovery of voltage with the regulator.

(*b*) **Sudden capacitive loading.** For sudden capacitive loading, the procedure adopted for X_L earlier, is followed. It has been found that wherever X_L appears in the analysis of sudden inductive loading, now $(-X_C)$ takes its place for sudden capacitive loading. In view of this, the behaviour of an alternator for sudden capacitive loading can be obtained simply by replacing X_L with $(-X_C)$.

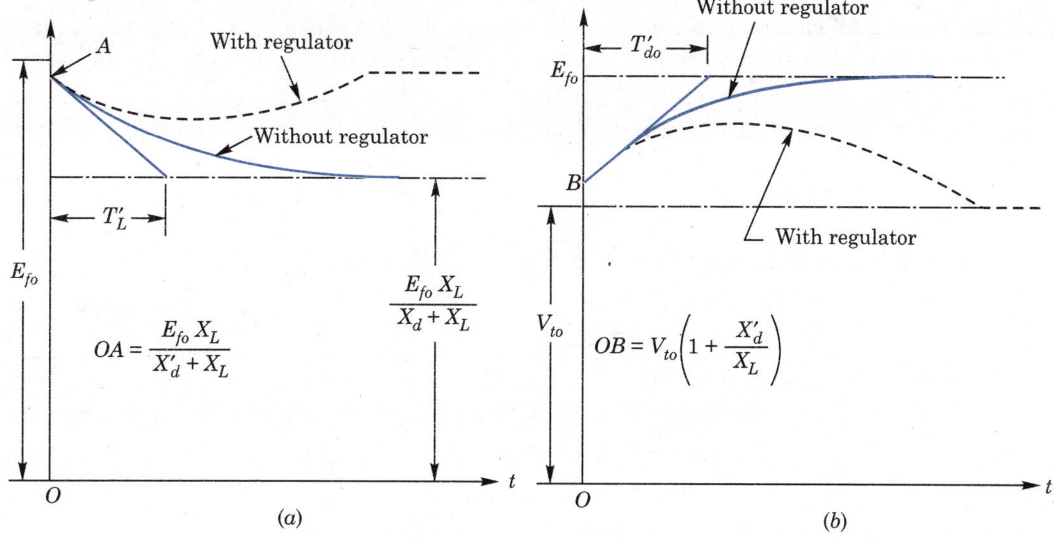

Fig. 4.23: Variation of alternator terminal voltage with (*a*) sudden inductive loading and (*b*) sudden inductive unloading.

From Eq. (4.133), the r.m.s. value of armature current is,

$$I_a(t) = \frac{E_{fo}}{X_d - X_c}\left[1 + \frac{X_d - X'_d}{X'_d - X_c}\, e^{-t/T'_c}\right] \quad ...(4.138)$$

where $$T_c' = T_{do}' \frac{X'_d - X_c}{X_d - X_c} \quad ...(4.139)$$

From Eq. (4.135), the voltage across the load reactance X_c is given by,

$$V_c(t) = \frac{E_{fo}(-X_c)}{X_d - X_c}\left[1 + \frac{X_d - X'_d}{X'_d - X_c}\, e^{-t/T'_c}\right] \quad ...(4.140)$$

From Eq. (4.136), the field current is given as,

$$i_f(t) = I_{fo}\left[1 + \frac{X_d - X'_d}{X'_d - X_c}\, e^{-t/T'_c}\right] \quad ...(4.141)$$

From Eq. (4.137), $$E_f(t) = E_{fo}\left[1 + \frac{X_d - X'_d}{X'_d - X_c}\, e^{-t/T'_c}\right] \quad ...(4.142)$$

Sudden switching on of a long transmisssion line is a common example of sudden capacitive loading on synchronous generators.

Eq. (4.140) reveals that just after the sudden capacitive loading, *i.e.* at $t = 0+$, the voltage at once varies from E_{fo} to $\frac{E_{fo}(-X_c)}{X'_d - X_c}$. This value changes from $\frac{E_{fo}(-X_c)}{X'_d - X_c}$ to its final value $\frac{E_{fo}(-X_c)}{X_d - X_c}$ with a load time constant of T_c'.

4.9.2 Sudden Reactive Unloading

The synchronous generator, running at synchronous speed is initially connected to a reactive load. Here the behaviour of alternator is investigated first with sudden removal of inductive load and then with the sudden removal of capacitive load.

(*a*) **Sudden inductive unloading.** When the generator is supplying a reactive load, its armature current is given by $I_a = \dfrac{E_{fo}}{X_d + X_L}$.

Note that for a purely inductive load (I_a lagging V_t by 90°), $I_a = I_d$, therefore,

$$I_a = I_d = \frac{E_{fo}}{X_d + X_L}.$$

Since the armature current, after the load has been disconnected, is zero, its expression is not of much importance. For the field circuit, the voltage equation, from Eq. (4.79) is

$$v_f = (r_f + L_f p)i_f - M_d p i_d \quad ...(4.143)$$

As per Art. 3.1.1, $\quad v_f = v_{fo} + v_{ft}$

and $\quad i_d = i_{do} + i_{dt}$

Here v_{fo} and i_{do}, before the inductive load is removed, are V_f and $\sqrt{2} I_d$. After the load is removed, v_f and i_d are V_f and zero respectively. In view of this, the superimposed field voltage $v_{ft} = 0$.

As the effect of removal of inductive load is to reduce i_d to zero suddenly, the superimposed current i_{dt} should be taken as a step-function current, *i.e.* $i_{dt} = -i_{do}$. **1**.

But $$\frac{i_{do}}{\sqrt{2}} = I_d = \frac{E_{fo}}{X_d + X_L} \quad ...(4.144)$$

Eq. (4.143), in terms of superimposed quantities, is

$$0 = (r_f + L_f p)\, i_{ft} - M_d p i_{dt}$$

or $$i_{ft} = \frac{M_d p}{r_f + L_f p} i_{dt} = -\frac{M_d p}{r_f + L_f p} i_{do} \cdot \mathbf{1}$$

Substitution of the value of the i_{do} from Eq. (4.144) gives,

$$i_{ft} = -\frac{M_d p \cdot \mathbf{1}}{r_f + L_f p} \cdot \frac{\sqrt{2}\, E_{fo}}{X_d + X_L} = -\frac{M_d p \cdot \mathbf{1}}{r_f + L_f p} \cdot \frac{M_d \omega I_{fo}}{X_d + X_L}$$

or $$i_{ft} = -\frac{I_{fo}\omega}{X_d + X_L} \cdot \frac{M_d^2 p \cdot \mathbf{1}}{r_f (1 + T'_{do} p)}$$

Its Laplace transform is,

$$I_{ft}(s) = -\frac{I_{fo} \cdot \omega}{X_d + X_L} \cdot \frac{M_d^2}{r_f (1 + T'_{do} s)}$$

$$= -\frac{I_{fo} \cdot \omega}{X_d + X_L} \cdot \frac{M_d^2}{r_f \cdot T'_{do} \left(s + \dfrac{1}{T'_{do}} \right)}$$

Its Laplace inverse is,

$$i_{ft}(t) = -\frac{I_{fo}\cdot\omega}{X_d + X_L}\cdot\frac{M_d^2}{L_f}\cdot e^{-t/T'_{do}}$$

Now $$\frac{M_d^2}{L_f} = L_d - L_d'$$

$\therefore$ $$i_{ft}(t) = -\frac{I_{fo}}{X_d + X_L}\cdot(X_d - X_d')\, e^{-t/T'_{do}}$$

$\therefore$ Total field current,

$$i_f(t) = I_{fo} + i_{ft}(t)$$

$$= I_{fo}\left[1 - \frac{X_d - X'_d}{X_d + X_L}\cdot e^{-t/T'_{do}}\right] \quad ...(4.145)$$

After the load is disconnected, excitation voltage and terminal voltage are equal.

$\therefore$ $$E_f(t) = V_t(t) = \frac{1}{\sqrt{2}} M_d\, \omega i_f(t)$$

$$= E_{fo}\left[1 - \frac{X_d - X'_d}{X_d + X_L}\cdot e^{-t/T'_{do}}\right] \quad ...(4.146)$$

If V_{to} is the load terminal voltage before the load is disconnected, then

$$V_{to} = I_d X_L = \frac{E_{fo}\cdot X_L}{X_d + X_L}$$

or $$E_{fo} = V_{to}\left(1 + \frac{X_d}{X_L}\right) \quad ...(4.147)$$

Substituting in Eq. (4.146), the value of E_{fo} from Eq. (4.147), we get

$$V_t(t) = V_{to}\left(1 + \frac{X_d}{X_L}\right)\left[1 - \frac{X_d - X'_d}{X_d + X_L}\cdot e^{-t/T'_{do}}\right] \quad ...(4.148)$$

An examination of Eq. (4.148) shows that just after the inductive load is disconnected, terminal voltage at once rises to $V_{to}\left(1 + \frac{X'_d}{X_L}\right) = OB$. The increase from $V_{to}\left(1 + \frac{X'_d}{X_L}\right)$ to its final value $V_{to}\left(1 + \frac{X_d}{X_L}\right) = E_{fo}$ with a time constant T_{do}', is as shown in Fig. 4.23 (*b*).

In case the effect of voltage regulator action is taken into account, the terminal voltage would vary as shown dotted in Fig. 4.23 (*b*).

(*b*) **Sudden capacitive unloading.** As before, the behaviour of an alternator with sudden capacitive unloading, can be obtained from the equations describing the sudden-inductive unloding, merely by replacing X_L by $(-X_C)$. In view of this, field current from Eq. (4.145) is

$$i_f(t) = I_{fo}\left[1 - \frac{X_d - X'_d}{X_d - X_C}\cdot e^{-t/T'_{do}}\right] \quad ...(4.149)$$

E_{fo} from Eq. (4.147) is,

$$E_{fo} = V_{to}\left(1 - \frac{X_d}{X_c}\right)$$

The terminal voltage, from Eq. (4.148), is

$$V_t(t) = E_{fo}\left[1 - \frac{X_d - X_d'}{X_d - X_c} . e^{-t/T_{do}'}\right]$$

$$= V_{to}\left(1 - \frac{X_d}{X_c}\right)\left[1 - \frac{X_d - X_d'}{X_d - X_c} . e^{-t/T_{do}'}\right] \quad ...(4.150)$$

Example 4.12. *A turbogenerator has the following per unit values :*

$$X_d = 1.00, \qquad X_d' = 0.20, \qquad T_{do}' = 4.0 \text{ sec.}$$

No load terminal voltage is 1.00 and voltage regulator action is disregarded.

(a) For a sudden inductive loading of X_L = 1.50 p.u., find an expression for the terminal voltage as a function of time.

(b) After steady state has reached in part (a), the inductive load is now disconnected. Find an expression for the terminal voltage as a function of time.

For both parts (a) and (b), sketch the variation of armature terminal voltage.

Solution. (*a*) Substitution of the values in Eq. (4.135) gives the expression for the terminal voltage as a function of time for the sudden inductive loading of alternator.

Here $$E_{fo} = 1.00,\ T_L' = T_{do}'\frac{X_d' + X_L}{X_d + X_L} = 4\,\frac{0.2 + 1.5}{1.0 + 1.5} = 2.72 \text{ sec.}$$

$$\therefore \quad V_L(t) = \frac{1.00 \times 1.50}{2.50}\left[1 + \frac{0.8}{1.7}e^{-t/2.72}\right] = 0.6[1 + 0.47e^{-t/2.72}]$$

The terminal voltage, just after the load application, drops to $\dfrac{E_{fo}\,X_L}{X_d' + X_L} = \dfrac{1.5}{1.7} = 0.882$. This variation is sketched in Fig. 4.24 (*a*).

(*b*) The voltage across the load or armature terminals, after steady state is reached in part (*a*), is equal to V_{to} = 0.6. After inductive load is disconnected, the expression for terminal voltage as a function of time is given by Eq. (4.148). Substitution of the values in this equation gives

$$V_t(t) = 0.6\left(1 + \frac{1.00}{1.50}\right)\left[1 - \frac{0.8}{2.5}e^{-t/4.0}\right] = 1\,[1 - 0.32e^{-t/4}]$$

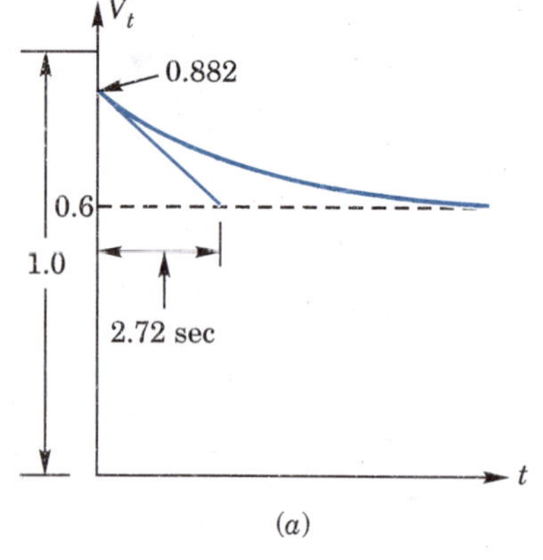

(*a*)

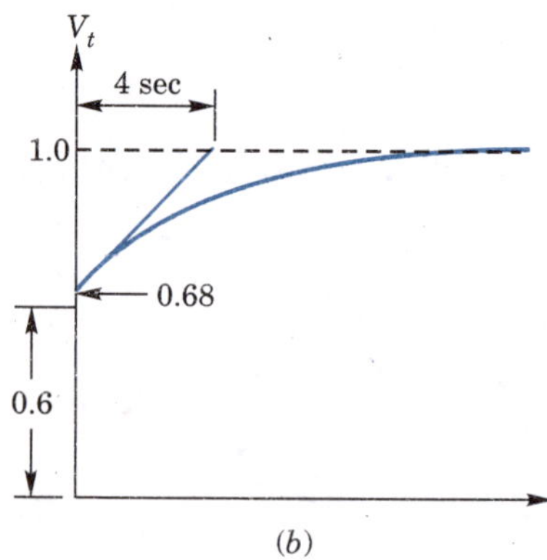

(*b*)

Fig. 4.24: Pertaining to Example 4.12.

Just after X_L is disconnected, the terminal voltage at once rises from 0.6 to $V_{to}\left(1+\frac{X'_d}{X_L}\right)$

$= 0.6 \times \frac{1.7}{1.5} = 0.68$. This variation is sketched in Fig. 4.24 (*b*).

4.10 TRANSIENT ANALYSIS—A QUALITATIVE APPROACH

In Art. 4.7, the transient analysis of synchronous generator is carried out by means of general voltage equations written from its generalized model. In this article, a simple qualitative treatment of the transient behaviour of an alternator, after a sudden three-phase short-circuit, is presented. The results obtained in Eqs. (4.93), (4.94) and (4.119) are explained from a physical consideration of the internal happenings in synchronous machine during the transient process. For simplicity, the synchronous machine resistances are neglected. With this assumption, the total flux linkages with any closed circuit can't change suddenly at the time of any disturbance. In other words, the flux linkages after sudden disturbance in any closed circuit remain constant at their predisturbance value—this fact has come to be known as *constant flux linkage theorem*.

With zero armature resistance, the steady-state armature short-circuit current lags the excitation voltage E_f by 90° as shown in Fig. 4.25*. This figure shows that short-circuit armature m.m.f. F_a is in the *d*-axis of the machine, consequently *d*-axis parameters are mainly involved during the short-circuit analysis. This conclusion is revealed by Eq. (4.119), which shows that the armature short-circuit is affected by *d*-axis parameters X_d, X_d' and X_d''.

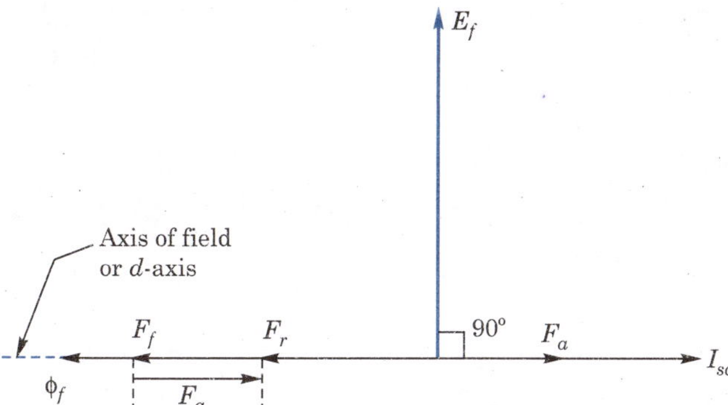

Fig. 4.25: Alternator phasor diagram under short-circuit conditions with negligible armature resistance.

Before the short circuit, the armature is open circuited, therefore the field flux linkages are $\psi_{fo} = L_f I_{fo}$. Just after the three-phase sudden short circuit, the effect of demagnetizing armature m.m.f. F_a must be counterbalanced by a corresponding increase in the field current so that field flux linkages remain constant at ψ_{fo}. This induced component of field current, representing an increase in the field current from its initial value I_{fo}, is given by Eq. (4.84). The combined effect of initial field current I_{fo} and induced field current i_{ft} represents greater field excitation of the alternator. But greater field excitation results in more short-circuit current; this shows that short-circuit armature current during transient is greater than its value during steady-state short circuit. Since the field voltage is constant, there is no additional field voltage to sustain the induced field current. Consequently, the induced field

*Refer to Fig. 5.16 (*b*), Electrical Machinery by the same author.

current decays with a time-constant determined by the field and armature circuit parameters and the corresponding increased short-circuit armature current also decays with the same time constant.

The field poles are usually fitted with damper bars. Then, just after the three-phase short-circuit, the demagnetizing armature m.m.f. is now counteracted not only by the induced field current but also by induced damper-bar currents so that field flux linkages ψ_{fo} remain constant. Now the combined effect of I_{fo}, induced field current i_{ft} and induced damper-bar current, represent still greater excitation of the alternator, this means that short-circuit armature current with damper bars is greater in the subtransient period than its value in transient period as shown in Fig. 4.26. The subtransient period lasts for the first few cycles, whereas the transient period lasts for relatively many more cycles. The envelope of the wave in Fig. 4.26 may be divided into three periods or time regimes, namely subtransient period, transient period and steady-state period. The *subtransient period* is that period during which the effect of I_{fo}, induced field current and induced damper-bar current is present. The *transient period* is that period during which the effect of I_{fo} and induced field current is present. The steady-state period is that period during which the effect of I_{fo} alone is present. The envelopes for three periods, as shown in Fig. 4.26, merge with each other with appropriate exponential decays.

The time constant T_d'' associated with subtransient decrement is much less, because the ratio of appropriate equivalent-inductance to damper-bar resistance is very low as compared to the equivalent inductance to field-circuit resistance defining the transient time constant T_d'.

The armature short-circuit current, as per Eq. (4.93), consists of d.c. and second-harmonic components (in addition to the fundamental frequency component). The physical picture of the internal happenings can also explain the existence of these two components. At the instant of short-circuit, if axis of any phase, say a, is 90° away from field axis, then field flux linkages with phase a are zero. Consequently, for maintaining the flux linkages constant just after the short circuit, no d.c. component is required in phase a current, therefore, the oscillogram of phase a current is symmetrical as shown in Fig. 4.26. If the axis of phase a is along the field axis, then there are maximum flux linkages with phase a, consequently a

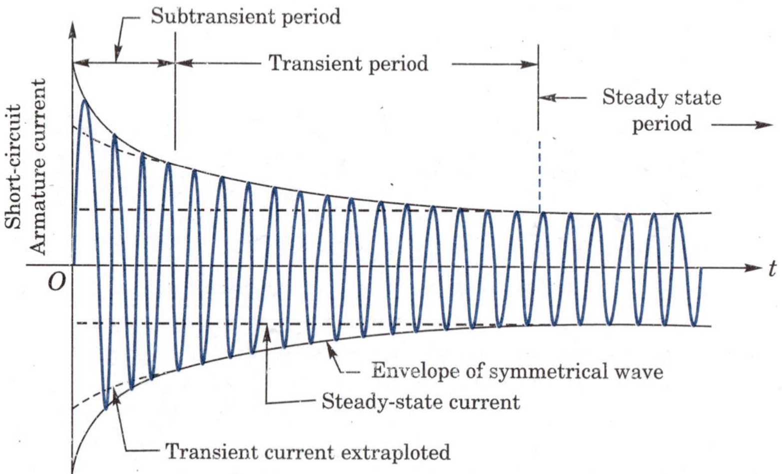

Fig. 4.26: Symmetrical waveform for armature short-circuit current for a 3-phase synchronous generator.

sudden short circuit at this instant would need maximum d.c. component to maintain constancy of flux linkages. For any other angle between phase a and field axis, the d.c. component would have values in between zero and maximum d.c. component. Thus, if short circuit occurs when phase a axis is along the d-axis, then armature short-circuit current wave for phase a is completely offset from zero axis as shown in Fig. 4.20 (a). Since d.c. component in armature current is not supported by any additional armature voltage, it decays with armature time constant T_a. The space angle between three phases a, b, c is 120°, therefore, even if d.c. component is zero in phase a, it would not be zero in phases b and c.

D.C. component of current in the armature produces air-gap field which is stationary with respect to the armature. With armature on the rotor, d.c. produced air-gap field rotates at synchronous speed with respect to stationary field winding and damper bars. As a result of it, fundamental frequency voltages are generated in the field winding and damper bars, Eq. (4.94) shows the existence of fundamental frequency component in the field current. This alternating current of fundamental frequency, in the field and damper-windings, produces a single-phase pulsating field. According to double revolving-field theory, this pulsating field can be resolved into two oppositely rotating components. The forward-field component rotates at synchronous speed in the direction of armature rotation. This forward component is, therefore, stationary with respect to the armature winding and it reacts back on the d.c. component of the armature current.

The backward-field component also rotates at synchronous speed but opposite to the armature rotation. In other words, backward component rotates at double the synchronous speed with respect to the armature. As a result of it, voltages of twice the fundamental frequency are induced in the armature winding. Hence the armature short-circuit current will contain second harmonic current as is revealed by Eq. (4.93). Since second harmonic component is caused by d.c. component of armature current, the time constant for the decay of d.c. as well as second-harmonic component of armature current is the same, *i.e.* armature time constant T_a, see Eq. (4.116).

It may be seen from above that the various components of armature short-circuit current are subtransient, transient, d.c., second-harmonic and steady-state. The components of field current after short circuit are subtransient, transient, fundamental frequency a.c. and prefault current I_{fo}. The time constants T_d'' and T_d' are applicable respectively to the subtransient and transient components of both field and armature currents. The armature time constant T_a is applicable both to the d.c. and second-harmonic components of armature current and also to the fundamental frequency a.c. component of field current.

4.11 REACTANCES AND TIME-CONSTANTS FROM EQUIVALENT CIRCUITS

Expressions for the reactances X_d, X_d', X_d'', X_q, X_q', X_q'' and time-constants T_{do}', T_d', T_{do}'', T_d'', T_{qo}'', T_q'' can be derived from the transformer-type equivalent circuits of a synchronous machine.

4.11.1 Direct-axis Reactances from Equivalent-circuits

The d-axis transient inductance, from Eq. (4.86), is

$$L_d' = L_d - \frac{M_d^2}{L_f} = (M_d + l_d) - \frac{M_d^2}{M_d + l_f} = l_d + \frac{M_d l_f}{M_d + l_f}$$

Multiplying both sides by ω, $X_d' = x_d + \dfrac{X_{md}\, x_f}{X_{md} + x_f}$

Here $X_{md} = \omega M_d$, is the d-axis magnetizing reactance.

D-axis leakage reactance x_d and q-axis leakage reactance x_q are assumed equal.

$$\therefore \qquad x_d = x_q = x_a,$$

the armature leakage reactance. In view of this,

$$X_d' = x_a + \frac{X_{md}\, x_f}{X_{md} + x_f} \qquad \text{...(4.151)}$$

The d-axis synchronous reactance of a synchronous machine is given by

$$X_d = x_d + X_{md} = x_a + X_{md}.$$

The transformer-type equivalent circuit satisfying both the expressions for X_d and X_d' is as shown in Fig. 4.27. Under steady-state operating conditions, the armature currents have no effect on the field-circuit current, this means that in Fig. 4.27, the field circuit should be regarded as open-circuited so that the reactance viewed from the armature terminals is $x_a + X_{md} = X_d$. For sudden disturbance in the armature circuit, a change in armature current is associated with a corresponding change in the field current, so as to maintain constancy of pre-disturbance field-flux linkages as per constant flux linkage theorem. Thus, for sudden changes in the armature circuit, the field terminals can be regarded as short circuited so that the reactance viewed from the armature terminals is d-axis transient reactance X_d' as given by Eq. (4.151).

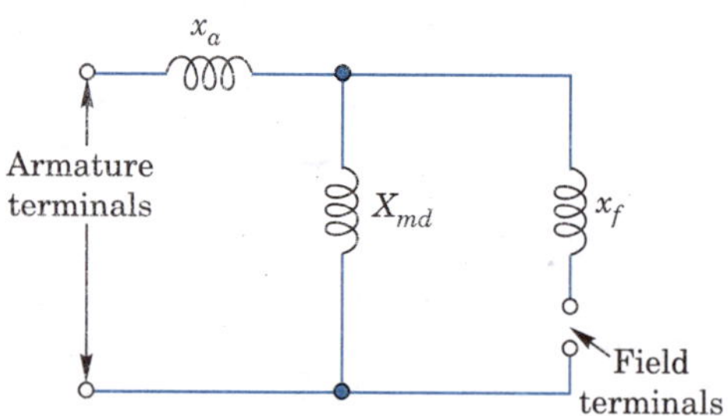

Fig. 4.27: *D*-axis equivalent circuit for a synchronous machine without damper bars.

Suppose, for the time being, that the field circuit is absent but the damper bars are present in the field-pole faces. Under steady state operating conditions, armature currents don't have any effect on the damper bars. However, when a sudden change occurs in the armature circuit, currents are induced in the damper bars so as to maintain constancy of flux linkages. For sudden changes in the armature circuit, the damper bars behave like the short-circuited secondary winding of a transformer with armature winding as its primary. Therefore, equivalent-circuit for sudden armature changes, similar to the transformer equivalent circuit, is as shown in Fig. 4.28. Here x_{kd} is the leakage reactance of the damper winding.

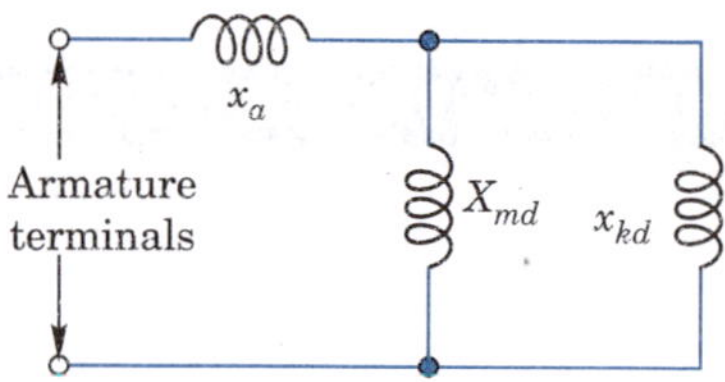

Fig. 4.28: *D*-axis equivalent-circuit with damper bars but with field winding assumed absent.

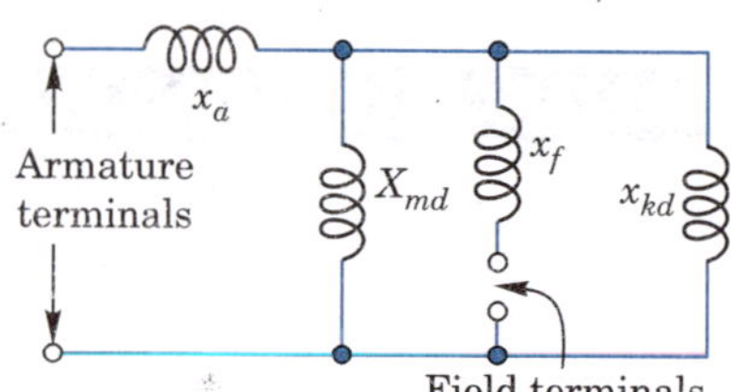

Fig. 4.29: *D*-axis equivalent circuit for a synchronous machine.

Actually, both the field winding and damper bars (or amortisseur circuits) are present, therefore, from the equivalent circuits of Figs. 4.27 and 4.28, equivalent circuit of Fig. 4.29 is obtained. This equivalent circuit is applicable whenever a sudden disturbance occurs in the armature circuit. With both field circuit and damper winding present, for sudden armature circuit changes, the reactance viewed from the armature terminals is the d-axis subtransient reactance X_d''. Therefore, from Fig. 4.29, X_d'', with the field terminals short-circuited, is given by

$$X_d'' = x_a + \frac{1}{\dfrac{1}{X_{md}} + \dfrac{1}{x_f} + \dfrac{1}{x_{kd}}} \qquad ...(4.152)$$

4.11.2 Direct-axis Time Constants from Equivalent-circuits

The time-constants of the synchronous machine can be obtained from the equivalent circuits of Fig. 4.30.

(*a*) **Direct-axis open circuit transient time constant, T_{do}'.** It pertains to the decay of field current with armature open circuited. The reactance viewed from the field terminals, with armature terminals open-circuited, is equal to $X_f = x_f + X_{md}$, see Fig. 4.30 (*a*). The quantity $\frac{x_f + X_{md}}{2\pi f} = L_f$ is the field self-inductance. With a field-circuit resistance r_f, the time constant T_{do}' is given by

$$T_{do}' = \frac{1}{r_f}\frac{x_f + X_{md}}{2\pi f} = \frac{L_f}{r_f} \qquad ...(4.153)$$

(*b*) **Direct-axis short-circuit transient time constant, T_d.** It pertains to the decay of field current with armature terminals short-circuited. The reactance viewed from field terminals, with armature short-circuited, is equal to x_f plus X_{md} and x_a in parallel, see Fig. 4.30 (*b*).

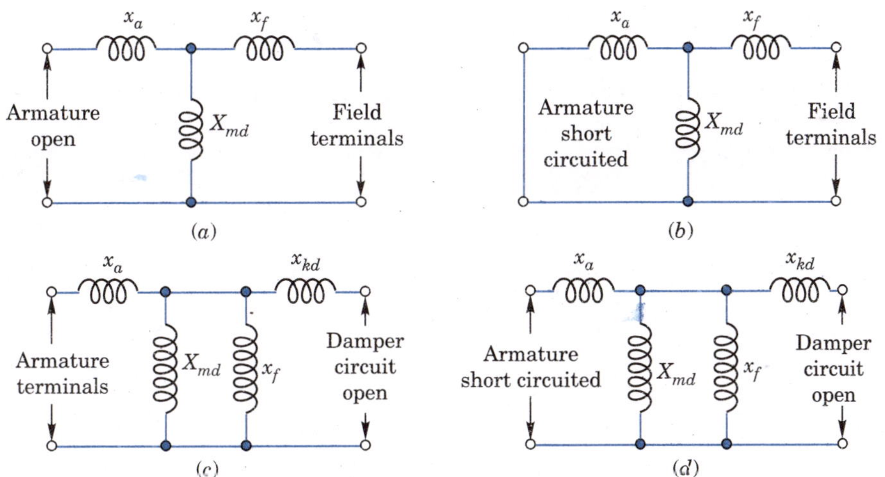

Fig. 4.30: Determination of time-constant T_{do}', T_d', T_{do}'' and T_d''.

$\therefore$ Reactance viewed from field terminals $= x_f + \dfrac{X_{md} \cdot x_a}{X_{md} + x_a}$

Inductance viewed from field terminals $= \dfrac{1}{2\pi f}\left[x_f + \dfrac{X_{md} \cdot x_a}{X_{md} + x_a}\right]$

∴ *D*-axis short-circuit transient time constant

$$T_d' = \frac{1}{r_f} \cdot \frac{1}{2\pi f}\left[x_f + \frac{X_{md} x_a}{X_{md} + x_a}\right] \quad ...(4.154)$$

The relation given in Eq. (4.104) can now be proved from Eq. (4.154) as follows:

$$T_d' = \frac{1}{r_f} \cdot \frac{1}{2\pi f}\left[\frac{x_f X_{md} + x_f x_a + X_{md} x_a}{X_{md} + x_a}\right]$$

$$= \frac{1}{r_f} \cdot \frac{1}{2\pi f} \cdot \frac{1}{X_d} [x_a(x_f + X_{md}) + x_f X_{md}]$$

$$= \frac{1}{r_f} \cdot \frac{1}{2\pi f} \cdot \frac{1}{X_d}\left[x_a + \frac{x_f \cdot X_{md}}{x_f + X_{md}}\right](x_f + X_{md})$$

Now $\frac{1}{2\pi f} \cdot (x_f + X_{md}) = L_f$ and the term within first bracket is X_d'.

$$\therefore \quad T_d' = \frac{L_f}{r_f} \cdot \frac{X_d'}{X_d} = T_{do}' \frac{X_d'}{X_d} \quad ...(4.104)$$

(*c*) **Direct-axis open-circuit subtransient time constant T_{do}''.** It pertains to the decay of *d*-axis damper-bar currents with armature terminals open circuited. The reactance viewed from open-circuited damper circuit in the *d*-axis and with armature terminals open, is given by Fig. 4.30 (*c*) as,

$$x_{kd} + \frac{X_{md} x_f}{X_{md} + x_f}$$

For a damper-circuit resistance of r_{kd} in the *d*-axis, T_{do}'' is given by,

$$T_{do}'' = \frac{1}{r_{kd}} \cdot \frac{1}{2\pi f}\left[x_{kd} + \frac{X_{md} \cdot x_f}{X_{md} + x_f}\right] \quad ...(4.155)$$

(*d*) **Direct-axis short-circuit subtransient time constant T_d''.** It pertains to the decay of *d*-axis damper-bar currents with armature terminals short circuited. The reactance viewed from the open-circuited damper circuit in the *d*-axis and with armature terminals short circuited, is given by Fig. 4.30 (*d*) as,

$$x_{kd} + \frac{1}{\frac{1}{x_a} + \frac{1}{X_{md}} + \frac{1}{x_f}}$$

For a damper-circuit resistance of r_{kd}, T_d'' is given by

$$T_d'' = \frac{1}{r_{kd}} \cdot \frac{1}{2\pi f}\left[x_{kd} + \frac{1}{\frac{1}{x_a} + \frac{1}{X_{md}} + \frac{1}{x_f}}\right] \quad ...(4.156)$$

As in Eq. (4.104), it can be shown that

$$T_d'' = T_{do}'' \frac{X_d''}{X_d'} \quad ...(4.157)$$

4.11.3 Quadrature-axis Reactances and Time Constants

There is no field winding in the *q*-axis of a normal synchronous machine. Thus, the equivalent-circuits for X_q, X_q' and X_q'' are similar to those for X_d, X_d' and X_d'' respectively, except that field-circuit parameters are absent. Fig. 4.31 (*a*) illustrates *q*-axis equivalent circuit for a salient-pole synchronous machine fitted with damper bars in the *q*-axis. For X_q and X_q', the damper-bar circuit is regarded as open-circuited, therefore,

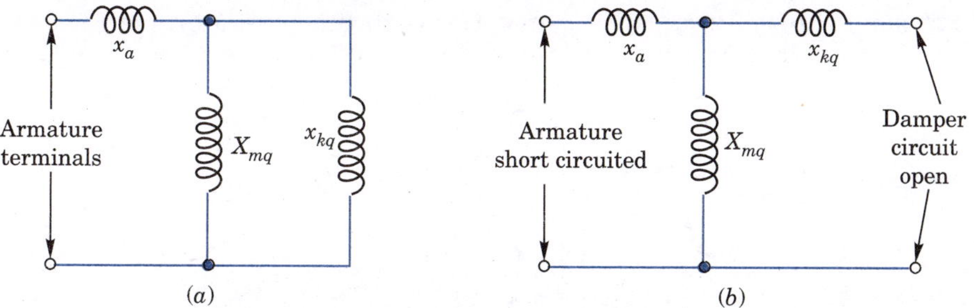

Fig. 4.31: Pertaining to the *q*-axis equivalent circuit.

$$X_q = X_q' = x_q + X_{mq} = x_a + X_{mq} \qquad \text{...(4.158)}$$

Under subtransient conditions, the damper-bar circuit must be considered, therefore, the *q*-axis subtransient reactance X_q'', as viewed from the armature terminals, is

$$X_q'' = x_a + \frac{X_{mq}x_{kq}}{X_{mq} + x_{kq}} \qquad \text{...(4.159)}$$

The *q-axis open circuit subtransient time constant* T_{qo}'' pertains to the decay of *q*-axis damper-bar current with armature terminals open circuited. Therefore, just like T_{do}'',

$$T_{qo}'' = \frac{1}{r_{kq}} \cdot \frac{1}{2\pi f}\,[x_{kq} + X_{mq}] \qquad \text{...(4.160)}$$

The *q-axis short-circuit subtransient time constant* T_q'' pertains to the decay of *q*-axis damper-bar current with armature terminals short circuited. The reactance viewed from the open-circuited damper circuit in the *q*-axis and with armature terminals short circuited is given by Fig. 4.31 (*b*) as,

$$x_{kq} + \frac{x_a X_{mq}}{x_a + X_{mq}}$$

For a *q*-axis damper-circuit resistance of r_{kq}, T_q'' is given by

$$T_q'' = \frac{1}{r_{kq}} \cdot \frac{1}{2\pi f}\left[x_{kq} + \frac{X_{mq}\,x_a}{X_{mq} + x_a}\right] \qquad \text{...(4.161)}$$

Now T_q'' can be expressed in terms of T_{qo}'' as follows:

$$T_q'' - \frac{1}{r_{kq}} \cdot \frac{1}{2\pi f}\left[\frac{x_{kq}\,.\,x_a + x_{kq}\,.\,X_{mq} + X_{mq}\,.\,x_a}{X_{mq} + x_a}\right]$$

$$= \frac{1}{r_{kq}} \cdot \frac{1}{2\pi f} \cdot \frac{1}{X_{mq} + x_a} \cdot [x_a\,(x_{kq} + X_{mq}) + x_{kq}X_{mq}]$$

$$= \frac{1}{r_{kq}} \cdot \frac{1}{2\pi f} \cdot \frac{1}{X_q'} \cdot \left[x_a + \frac{x_{kq}\,.\,X_{mq}}{x_{kq} + X_{mq}}\right](x_{kq} + X_{mq})$$

But, in the above expression, first term in the bracket is X_q'' as per Eq. (4.159).

$$\therefore \qquad T_q'' = \left[\frac{1}{r_{kq}} \cdot \frac{1}{2\pi f} \cdot (x_{kq} + X_{mq})\right] \frac{X_q''}{X_q'} = T_{qo}'' \frac{X_q''}{X_q'} \qquad \text{...(4.162)}$$

If there is an external reactance x_e in series with the generator, both before and after the short-circuit, then its effect can be accounted for by adding x_e to the armature leakage reactance x_a. In view of this, the modified reactances and time-constants including the effect of x_e, are as follows :

$$X_{de} = X_d + x_e, \qquad X_{de}' = X_d' + x_e$$
$$X_{de}'' = X_d'' + x_e, \qquad X_{qe} = X_q + x_e$$
$$X_{qe}' = X_q' + x_e, \qquad X_{qe}'' = X_q'' + x_e$$

The time constants T_{do}', T_{do}'' and T_{qo}', which are defined with the armature open circuited, remain unchanged. However, the time constants which are defined with the armature short circuited are effected as follows:

D-axis short-circuit transient time constant, $T_{de}' = T_{do}' \dfrac{X_d' + x_e}{X_d + x_e}$

D-axis short-circuit subtransient time constant, $T_{de}'' = T_{do}'' \dfrac{X_d'' + x_e}{X_d' + x_e}$

Q-axis short-circuit subtransient time constant, $T_{qe}'' = T_{qo}'' \dfrac{X_q'' + x_e}{X_q' + x_e}$

The armature time-constant T_a pertains to the decay of the d.c. component or second harmonic component of armature short-circuit current. The field produced by d.c. component of armature current is sometimes along *d*-axis and soon after, it is along *q*-axis. In view of this, the reluctance, or inductance, offered to the d.c. produced armature flux is that corresponding to X_d'' and soon after, it is that corresponding to X_q''. Thus the equivalent-armature inductance, pertaining to the decay of d.c. component of armature current, is the mean of X_d'' and X_q'' as is normally the practice. In view of this, armature time constant T_a is given by

$$T_a = \frac{1}{r_a} \cdot \left(\frac{1}{2\pi . f} \frac{X_d'' + X_q''}{2}\right) \qquad \text{...(4.163)}$$

If external impedance $r_e + jx_e$ is present between the armature terminals and the short-circuit, the armature-time constant becomes

$$T_{ae} = \frac{1}{r_a + r_e} \cdot \left[\frac{1}{2\pi . f}\left(\frac{X_d'' + X_q''}{2} + x_e\right)\right]$$

If the various resistances and reactances are expressed in per unit, then $2\pi f$ does not appear in the various time-constants as given by Eqs. (4.153) to (4.156), (4.160), (4.161) and (4.163).

4.12 CONCEPTS OF SYNCHRONOUS MACHINE REACTANCES

The synchronous-machine reactances can be classified into three types, namely, positive-sequence reactance, negative-sequence reactance and zero-sequence reactance. A synchronous machine has only one negative-sequence reactance X_2 and only one zero-sequence reactance

x_0; it has, however, several positive-sequence reactances and these are $X_d, X_q, X_d', X_q', X_d''$ and X_q''. The magnitude of different positive-sequence reactances depends upon :

(*i*) the angular position of the field structure with respect to the armature m.m.f. wave and

(*ii*) whether the armature currents are steady or are varying.

The object of this aricle is to highlight the physical concepts of various synchronous machine reactances.

The armature m.m.f. wave actually consists of a space-fundamental component and many other space-harmonic components. In this article only space-fundamental component of armature m.m.f. wave, travelling at synchronous speed with respect to armature, is considered.

4.12.1 Positive Sequence Reactances

When both the field and armature m.m.f. waves are almost stationary with respect to each other, then the reactances associated with armature are positive sequence reactances. These are now described one after the other.

(*a*) Direct-axis synchronous reactance, X_d. If the peak of steady armature m.m.f. wave is in line with the direct, or polar, axis, then the situation is as illustrated in Fig. 4.32. It is seen from this figure that reluctance, offered to armature flux by two small air-gaps along *d*-axis, is minimum. For given armature currents and therefore for given armature m.m.f., the armature flux has the greatest possible magnitude. Under these conditions the armature flux

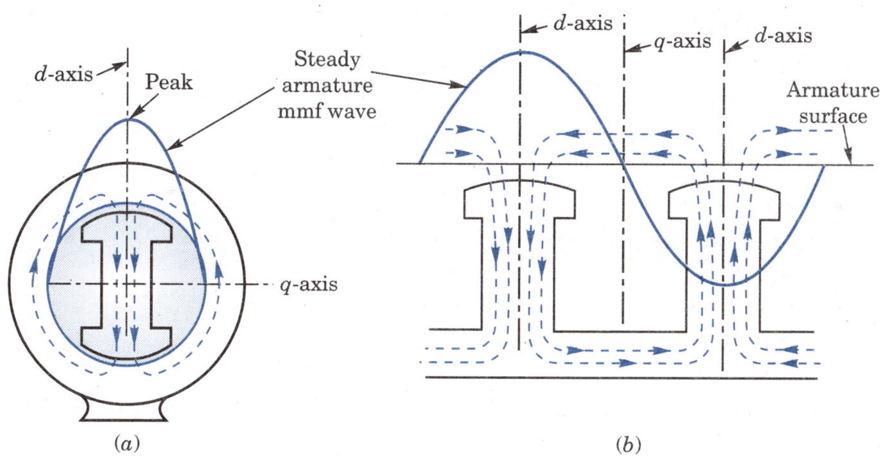

Fig. 4.32: Flux paths for *d*-axis synchronous reactance.

linkages per ampere in the armature winding is called direct axis synchronous inductance L_d. Thus, when peak of steady armature m.m.f. wave coincides with the *d*-axis, then *d*-axis synchronous inductance L_d is given by

$$L_d = \frac{\text{Armature flux} \times \text{Armature phase turns, } N_{ph}}{\text{Armature phase current}}$$

and *d*-axis synchronous reactance $X_d = \omega L_d = 2\pi f L_d$.

Since the relative velocity between field structure and armature m.m.f wave is zero, the field circuit may be open or closed. In Fig. 4.32, figure (*b*) is a developed view of Fig. 4.32 (*a*).

(*b*) Quadrature-axis synchronous reactance, X_q. When the peak of steady armature m.m.f. wave coincides with the quadrature, or interpolar, axis as shown in Fig. 4.33, the reluctance offered by two large air gaps along q-axis is maximum. For given armature currents, armature m.m.f. wave remains constant. For the rotor position shown in Fig. 4.33, constant armature m.m.f. and increased air-gap reluctance results in the lowest possible armature flux. Under these conditions, the armature flux linkages per armature ampere is called the quadrature axis synchronous inductance L_q. Thus, when peak of steady armature m.m.f. wave is in line with the q-axis, then q-axis synchronous inductance L_q is given by

$$L_q = \frac{\text{Armature flux} \times N_{ph}}{\text{Armature phase current}}$$

and q-axis synchronous reactance, $X_q = \omega L_q = 2\pi f L_q$.

Fig. 4.33 (*b*) illustrates the developed view of Fig. 4.33 (*a*).

It can be concluded from above that $X_d > X_q$ for salient-pole synchronous machines.

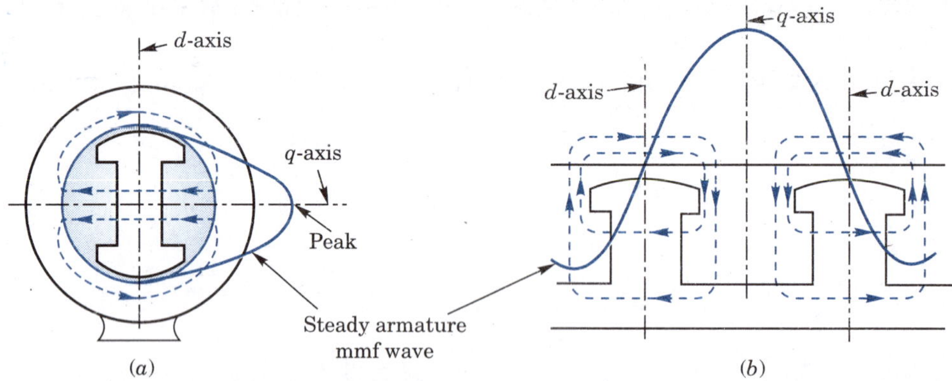

Fig. 4.33: Flux paths for q-axis synchronous reactance.

Since cylindrical rotor machines have uniform air gap, $X_d = X_q = X_s$, where X_s is its synchronous reactance. Strictly speaking, X_q is slightly less than X_d because of the presence of rotor slots along q-axis.

Armature leakage reactance, x_a. Total flux produced by the armature current consists of two components-one component crosses the air-gap whereas the second component does not cross the air gap and links armature only. The component of the total flux that links armature alone, is called the armature leakage flux which gives rise to the armature leakage reactance x_a. All the positive sequence reactances have x_a as one part of it. For example, $X_d = x_a + X_{md}$ and $X_q = x_a + X_{mq}$. Here X_{md} and X_{mq} are the armature magnetizing reactances along d- and q-axes respectively. For convenience, armature leakage reactance x_a is considered equal for both direct and quadrature axes reactances.

(*c*) Direct-axis transient reactance, X_d'. For defining X_d', field structure is assumed to have field winding alone and no other circuit. The field winding is initially unexcited and closed on itself so that field flux linkages are zero. Now armature currents are suddenly applied in such time phase that the peak of varying armature m.m.f. wave is in line with the direct axis. The sudden appearance of varying armature m.m.f. wave along the direct axis, tends to force the flux lines through the pole core. Since the field flux linkages are initially zero, they must remain zero just after the sudden appearance of armature m.m.f. wave as per constant-flux linkages theorem. Hence, in order to maintain the constancy of flux linkages at zero value, currents are induced in the field winding in such a direction that field winding flux opposes the varying armature flux. In view of this, the flux lines due to varying armature m.m.f. wave can't pass through the field poles, therefore the only possible paths are as depicted in Fig. 4.34. Since these paths are largely in air, the reluctance offered is very large and accordingly the armature flux is much less. Under these conditions, the armature flux linkages per armature ampere is called the direct-axis transient inductance L_d' and $X_d' = \omega L_d'$. For a given armature m.m.f., the armature flux linkages in Fig. 4.34 are much less as compared to those in Fig. 4.32 ; consequently $X_d' < X_d$. Fig. 4.34 (*b*) is a developed view of Fig. 4.34 (*a*).

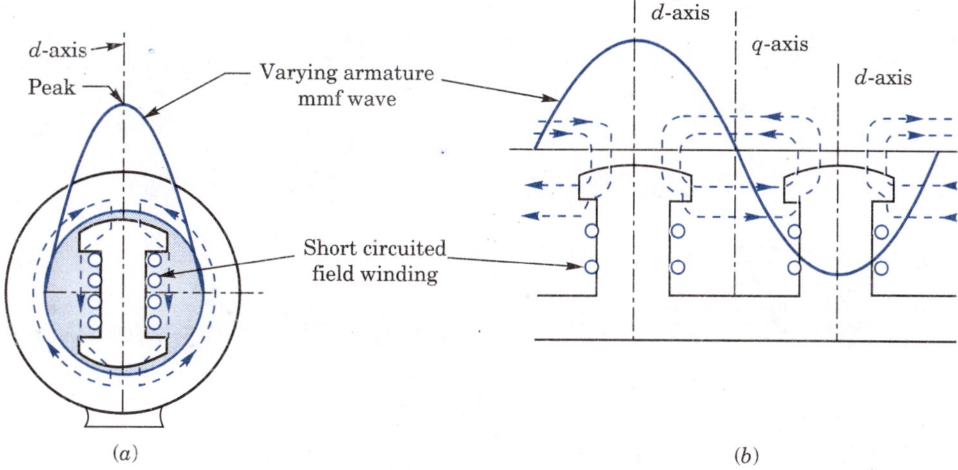

Fig. 4.34: Flux paths for *d*-axis transient reactance.

(*d*) Quadrature-axis transient reactance, X_q'. The assumptions used for defining X_d' are also applicable for defining X_q'. If the armature currents are suddenly applied in such time phase that the peak of varying armature m.m.f. wave stays in line with the *q*-axis, then the paths for the armature flux lines are as shown in Fig. 4.35. Since field flux linkages are initially zero, these must remain zero just after the sudden appearance of armature m.m.f. The armature flux lines shown in Fig. 4.35 pass normal to the field winding axis, there are thus zero flux linkages with the field winding. Examination of Figs. 4.33 and 4.35 shows that the distribution of flux paths in both these figures is identical, showing thereby that for

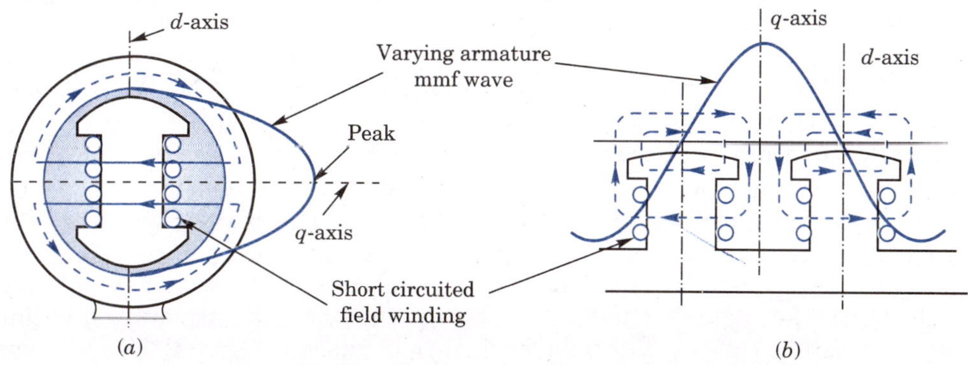

Fig. 4.35: Flux paths for *q*-axis transient reactance.

salient-pole machines without damper bars, $X_q = X_q'$. Further, the reluctance offered in Fig. 4.35 is less than that in Fig. 4.34; in view of this for the same armature m.m.f., armature flux in Fig. 4.35 is more than its value in Fig. 4.34; this leads to the conclusion that $X_q' > X_d'$.

(e) Direct-axis subtransient reactance, X_d''. For defining X_d'', the conditions are the same as used for defining X_d', with the exception that now salient poles are fitted with damper bars also. Solid-rotor iron core of cylindrical-rotor machines also provides eddy-current paths, thus producing the effect similar to damper bars.

Armature currents are suddenly applied in such time phase that the peak of varying armature m.m.f. wave stays in line with the direct axis. Since the flux linkages with the rotor circuits are zero, these must remain zero just after the sudden appearance of armature m.m.f. wave. This is in accordance with constant flux linkage theorem. Thus, in order to maintain the flux linkages zero, currents are induced in damper bars, additional rotor circuits formed by pole-bolts etc. and the field winding.

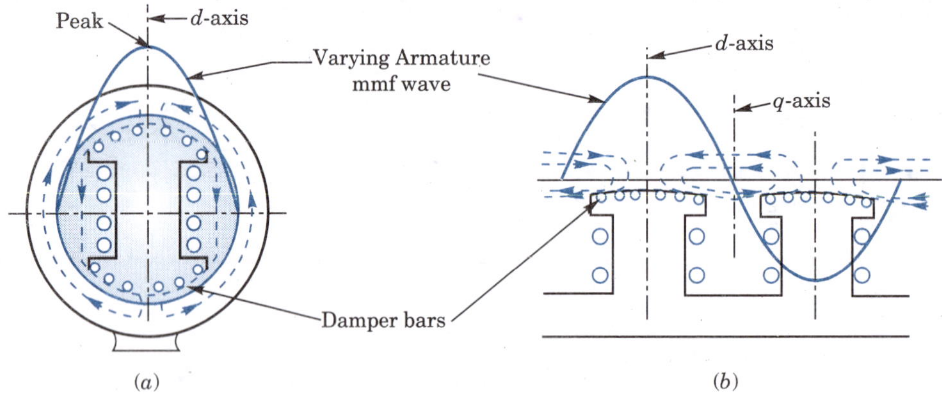

Fig. 4.36: Flux paths for d-axis subtransient reactance.

Since the damper bars are near the air gap, the flux lines due to varying armature m.m.f., are forced to follow the leakage flux path mainly in air as shown in Fig. 4.36. The armature flux linkages per armature ampere, under these conditions, is called direct axis subtransient inductance L_d'' and $X_d'' = \omega L_d''$. A comparison of the leakage flux paths of Figs. 4.34 and 4.36 reveals that for a given m.m.f., the armature flux linkages in Fig. 4.36 are less than in Fig. 4.34 ; consequently $X_d'' < X_d'$. Even if the damper bars are absent, the effect of saturation and additional rotor circuits provided by pole-bolts, field collars etc. causes X_d'' to be less than X_d'.

The effect of damper bars and additional rotor circuits is short-lived, may be at the most for two to three cycles. This short period, called subtransient period, is followed by transient period when the effect of induced field current is still present.

(f) Quadrature axis subtransient reactance, X_q''. This is defined in a manner similar to X_d'', but here the armature currents are applied in such time phase that peak of the varying armature m.m.f. stays in line with the q-axis. The damper bars in the q-axis, force the flux lines of the varying armature m.m.f. to follow the leakage paths as shown in Fig. 4.37. As before, the flux linkages with q-axis damper bars must remain zero, before and after the sudden appearance of armature m.m.f. Under these conditions, the armature flux linkages per armature ampere is called q-axis subtransient inductance L_q'' and $X_q'' = \omega L_q''$, which is much less than X_q'.

In Fig. 4.36, the armature leakage paths consist of a part of pole-face iron and q-axis air space. In Fig. 4.37, the armature leakage paths consist of a part of q-axis air space and whole of the pole-face iron. In view of this, for the same armature m.m.f., armature flux linkages in Fig. 4.37 are more than in Fig. 4.36, consequently X_q'' is slightly higher than X_d''.

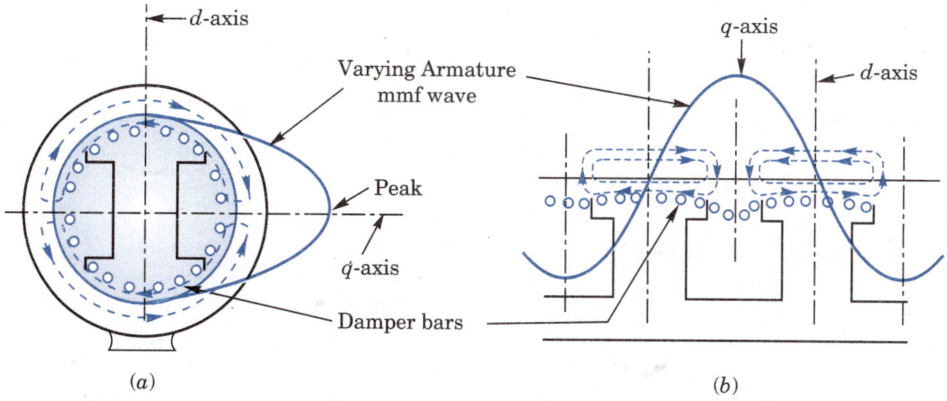

Fig. 4.37: Flux paths for q-axis subtransient reactance.

Out of all the positive sequence reactances, X_d'' and X_q'' have the lowest magnitudes. It is because the damper bars force the armature flux to pass mainly through air (a high reluctance path) and as a consequence, armature flux linkages have the minimum values; therefore X_d'' and X_q'' are the lowest as compared to X_d, X_q, X_d' and X_q'.

4.12.2 Negative-sequence Reactance, X_2

For defining X_2, the unexcited field winding is closed and is assumed on the rotor. The steady 3-phase currents in the armature produce a rotating m.m.f. wave opposite to the rotor rotation. This means that the rotating m.m.f. wave travels at twice the synchronous speed with respect to the rotor. The rotating armature m.m.f. comes in line with d-axis and soon after $\left(= \frac{30}{PN_s} \text{ sec}\right)$ it gets aligned with q-axis and so on. Since the flux linkages with rotor circuit are zero, these must remain zero under the conditions described here. Consequently, the flux paths are mainly through the air gap, similar to those illustrated for X_d'' and X_q''. The armature flux linkages per armature ampere under these conditions is called negative sequence inductance L_2 and $X_2 = \omega L_2$. Since the armature m.m.f. wave experiences d-axis reluctance cooresponding to X_d'' and q-axis reluctance corresponding to X_q'', it is usual to take X_2 as the arithmetic mean of X_d'' and X_q'', *i.e.*

$$X_2 = \frac{X_d'' + X_q''}{2} \qquad \text{...(4.164)}$$

The value of negative sequence reactance is equal to the average of the values of X_d'' and X_q'' as per Eq. (4.164). As X_q'' is only slightly higher than X_d'', the values of X_2 does not differ much from the positive sequence reactances X_d'' and X_q''. The value of X_2, however, is less than the other positive sequence reactances of a synchronous machine.

4.12.3 Zero-sequence Reactance, x_0

If the three-phase armature winding is appropriately connected in series and a single-phase supply is given to this series combination as shown in Fig. 4.42, then the armature leakage flux is produced as illustrated in Fig. 4.38 for full-pitch coils. The armature leakage flux in Fig. 4.38 is stationary (not rotating one) but pulsating. This pulsating armature m.m.f. is opposed by currents induced in the closed circuits on the field structure, consequently air-gap flux produced is very little. The armature flux linkages per armature ampere under these conditions is called zero-sequence inductance L_o and $x_o = \omega L_o$. The zero-sequence reactance x_o is the smallest of all the synchronous machine reactances.

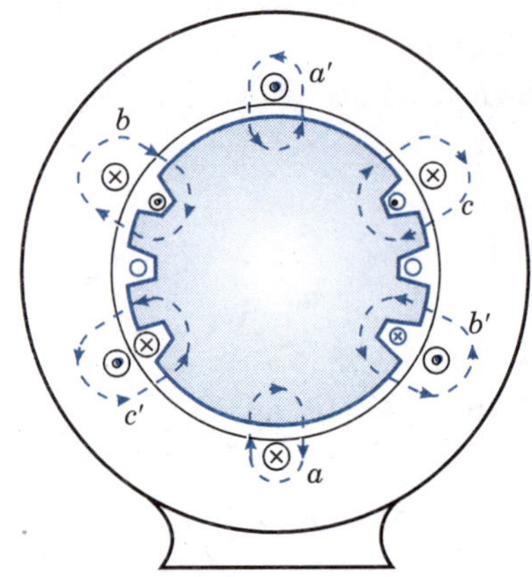

Fig. 4.38: Flux paths for zero-sequence fluxes in a cylindrical rotor synchronous machine.

In a double layer winding, with coil-pitch equal to 2/3 full pitch, x_0 drops to a very low value, because with this coil-pitch the zero-sequence currents, in the top and bottom coil sides in any slot flow in opposite directions.

Typical values of reactances and time-constants of different types of three-phase synchronous machines are given in Table 4.1. Note that reactances are given in per unit with synchronous machine rating as the base and the time-constants are expressed in seconds. The reactances and time-constants for any particular machine may vary on either side of the values given in this table.

Table 4.1 Typical Values of Synchronous Machine Constants

Machine constants	*Turbo-alternators*	*Hydro-generators*	*Salient pole motors*	*Salient pole synchronous condensers*
X_d	1.20	1.10	1.20	1.60
X_q	1.17	0.70	0.90	0.90
X_d'	0.30	0.35	0.46	0.60
X_q'	0.30	0.70	0.90	0.90
X_d''	0.15	0.25	0.30	0.19
X_q''	0.17	0.35	0.40	0.23
X_2	0.15	0.25	0.35	0.21
x_0	0.02	0.10	0.15	0.04
T_{do}'	5.00	5.50	6.00	8.00
T_d'	1.00	1.80	1.40	2.00
T_d''	0.035	0.035	0.035	0.035
T_a	0.15	0.15	0.15	0.15

4.13 MEASUREMENT OF REACTANCES

The methods for the measurement of X_d from open-circuit and short-circuit tests; X_d, X_q from slip test and X_q from maximum lagging current test have been discussed in Art. 5.16*. The object of this article is to describe the methods for measurement of X_d'', X_q'', X_2 and x_o with appropriate experiments.

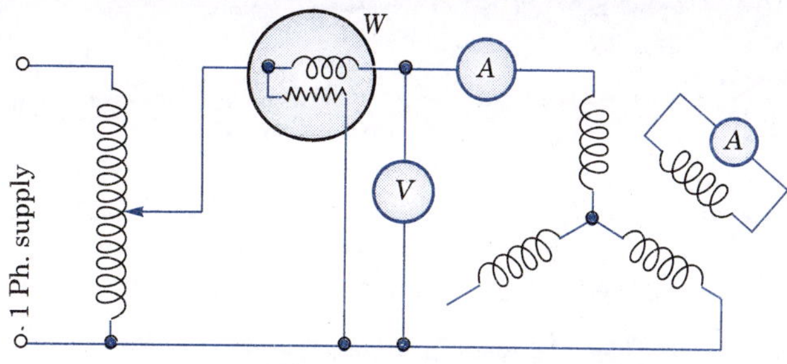

Fig. 4.39: Measurement of X_d'' and X_q''.

(*a*) **Measurement of X_d'' and X_q''.** Any two phases of a three-phase machine are connected in series and a single phase voltage is impressed across them as shown in Fig. 4.39. The rotor is at standstill. The impressed voltage is adjusted to pass sufficient current in the two series-connected armature windings. Now the rotor position is adjusted with hand to get maximum deflection of the ammeter placed in the field winding circuit. Under these conditions, *d*-axis subtransient impedance Z_d'' is given by, $Z_d'' = \dfrac{V}{2I_{max}}$.

Here V and I_{max} are the voltmeter and ammeter readings respectively. If the wattmeter records P watts, then $\cos\theta = \dfrac{P}{VI_{max}}$

$$\therefore \qquad \sin\theta = \sqrt{1-\left(\frac{P}{VI_{max}}\right)^2}$$

∴ *D*-axis subtransient reactance,

$$X_d'' = Z_d'' \sin\theta = \frac{V}{2I_{max}}\sqrt{1-\left(\frac{P}{VI_{max}}\right)^2}$$

$$= \frac{1}{2I_{max}^2}\sqrt{(VI_{max})^2 - P^2} \qquad ...(4.165)$$

Note that induced current in the short-circuited field winding is maximum only when field winding axis (*i.e.* polar or direct axis) is along the direction of resultant armature m.m.f. as shown in Fig. 4.39. Since the resultant armature m.m.f. is pulsating in nature, the conditions illustrated in Fig. 4.39 are identical for which X_d'' has been defined.

If the rotor shaft is rotated by hand through half a pole-pitch (or 90° electrical), then peak of the resultant armature m.m.f. coincides the *q*-axis. These conditions are those for which X_q'' has been defined. Since the field winding axis is 90° away from the resultant armature m.m.f. axis, the ammeter in the field winding should record minimum (sometimes zero) reading. In view of this, for measuring X_q'' the rotor position is adjusted so as to get the

*"Electrical Machinery" by the same author.

minimum value of induced field current. Under these conditions, the instrument readings give,

$$X_q'' = Z_q'' \sin\theta = \frac{V}{2I_{min}}\sqrt{1-\frac{P^2}{(VI_{min})^2}}$$

$$= \frac{1}{2I_{min}^2}\sqrt{(V\,I_{min})^2 - P^2} \qquad ...(4.166)$$

In case resistances are neglected, then

and

$$\left.\begin{aligned} X_d'' &= \frac{V}{2I_{max}} \\ X_q'' &= \frac{V}{2I_{min}} \end{aligned}\right\} \qquad ...(4.167)$$

Here I_{min} is armature current corresponding to minimum induced field current.

(*b*) **Measurement of negative-sequence reactance.** This reactance can be measured by three different methods, which are described here.

(*i*) The subtransient reactances X_d'' and X_q'' have already been measured. As per Eq. (4.164), the negative-sequence reactance per phase is given by

$$X_2 = \frac{1}{2}(X_d'' + X_q'')$$

(*ii*) The second method follows directly from the definition of X_2. In this method, the field winding is short circuited and the rotor is driven at synchronous speed. Balanced three-phase voltages are applied to armature so that constant-amplitude rotating armature m.m.f. wave rotates opposite to the rotor rotation, see Fig. 4.40. The applied voltage is adjusted and the readings of voltmeter, ammeter and wattmeter are recorded. Then, negative-sequence impedance is,

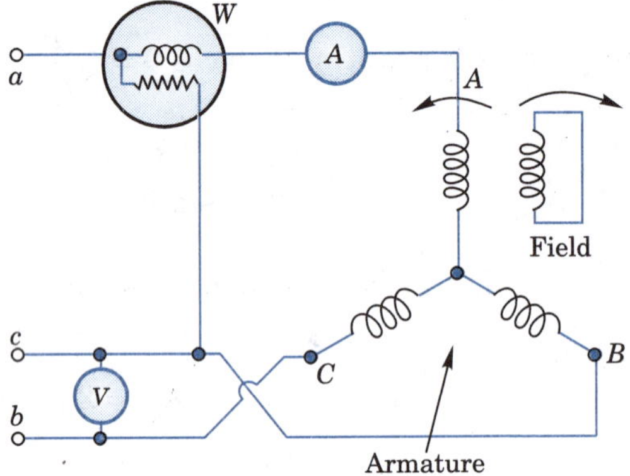

Fig. 4.40: Measurement of X_2.

$$Z_2 = \frac{V}{\sqrt{3}I}$$

and negative-sequence reactance per phase is

$$X_2 = Z_2 \sin\theta = \frac{V}{\sqrt{3}I}\sqrt{1-\frac{P^2}{(\sqrt{3}VI)^2}}$$

$$= \frac{1}{3I^2}\sqrt{3V^2I^2 - P^2} \qquad ...(4.168)$$

If negative-sequence resistance is neglected, then,

$$X_2 = \frac{V}{\sqrt{3}I} \qquad ...(4.169)$$

(*iii*) In the third method, the negative sequence impedance can be measured by referring to the circuit diagram of Fig. 4.41. In this figure, two phases are short circuited through an ammeter and current-coil of a wattmeter. The rotor is driven at synchronous speed, with field winding unexcited and short-circuited. Single phase voltage is applied and instrument readings are recorded from which the negative sequence impedance per phase is,

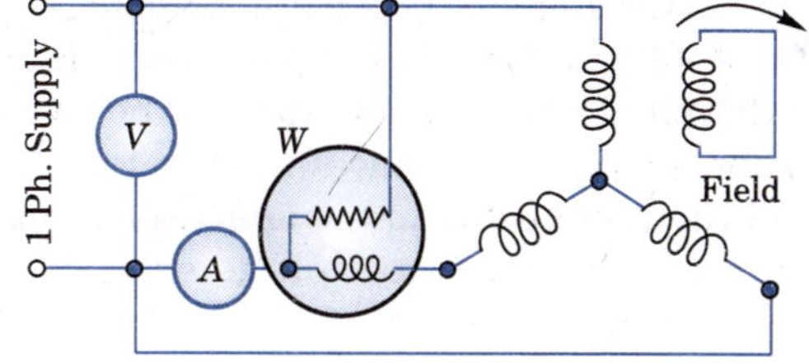

Fig. 4.41: Measurement of X_2.

$$Z_2 = \frac{V}{\sqrt{3}I}$$

For a wattmeter reading P, it can be shown that negative-sequence reactance X_2 is given by,

$$X_2 = \frac{V}{\sqrt{3}I} \cdot \frac{P}{VI} = \frac{P}{\sqrt{3}I^2} \qquad ...(4.170)$$

During this test, the short-circuit current should be kept low in order to avoid undue heating of the field system.

(c) **Measurement of zero sequence reactance.** As per the definition of zero-sequence reactance, the three-phase windings are connected in series as shown in Fig. 4.42. The field winding is short circuited and the rotor is driven at synchronous speed. Single-phase voltage is now applied as shown. If V and I are the voltmeter and ammeter readings respectively then,

$$x_o = \frac{\text{Per phase voltage, } V/3}{I} = \frac{V}{3I}\ \Omega \qquad ...(4.171)$$

In case only three-line and one neutral terminals are available, then x_o can be measured by connecting the three-phase windings in parallel. Care should be taken to ensure that current flows simultaneously from line terminals to neutral or *vice-versa*, as shown in Fig. 4.43. As before, the field terminals are short-circuited and the rotor is driven at synchronous speed. If V and I are the voltmeter and ammeter readings respectively, then zero-sequence reactance per phase is

$$x_o = \frac{V}{I/3} = \frac{3V}{I}\ \Omega \qquad ...(4.172)$$

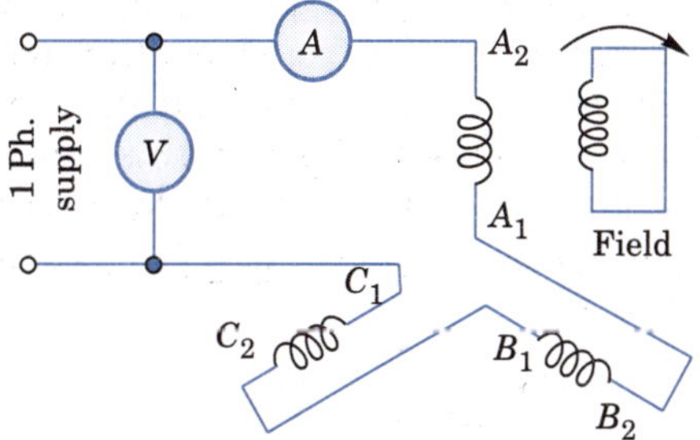

Fig. 4.42: Measurement of x_0.

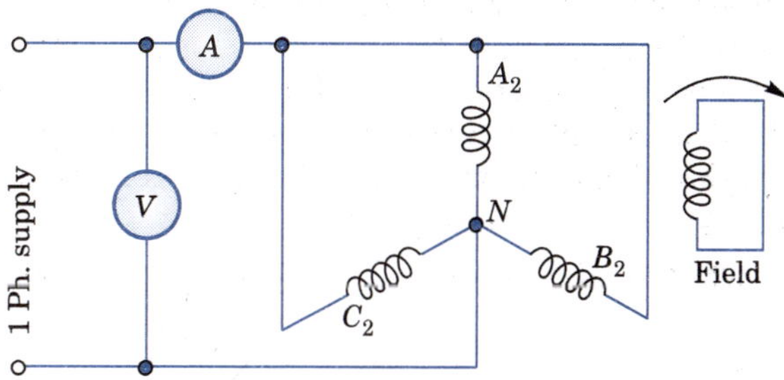

Fig. 4.43: Measurement of x_0.

Another method for measuring x_o is illustrated in Fig. 4.44. The field winding is short circuited and the rotor is driven at synchronous speed. The two output terminals of the synchronous machine armature are short-circuited and then connected to the neutral through an ammeter as shown. If V and I are voltmeter and ammeter readings respectively, then

$$x_o = \frac{V}{I}\ \Omega.$$

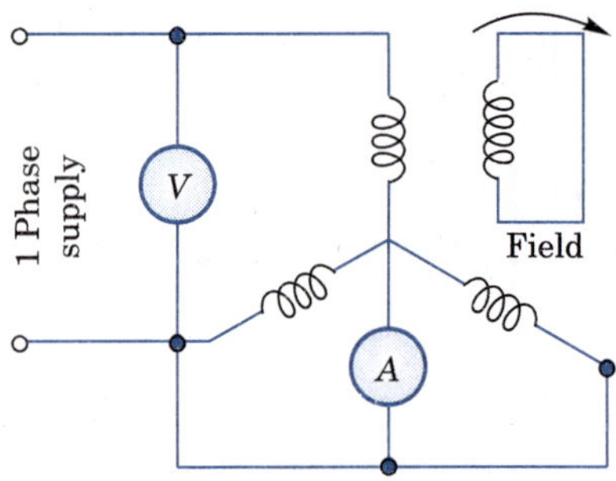

Fig. 4.44: Measurement of x_0.

4.14 REACTANCES AND TIME-CONSTANTS FROM SHORT-CIRCUIT OSCILLOGRAM

The reactances and time constants of a synchronous machine can be determined from the short-circuit armature-current oscillograms recorded after the sudden application of a symmetrical three-phase short circuit at the alternator terminals. In order to perform this test, the alternator is excited to develop a terminal voltage of 30 to 75% of its rated voltage. It should be ensured that the short-circuit switch closes the three terminals simultaneously so as to avoid any error due to single phasing.

The variations of three-phase armature currents and field current, after the sudden application of a symmetrical three-phase short-circuit, are illustrated in Fig. 4.20. The current in each phase consists of d.c. and a.c. components. The d.c. component decays with time constant T_a. Reference to Eq. (4.119) shows that a.c. component consists of (*i*) subtransient component which decays with time constant T_d'', (*ii*) transient component which decays with time constant T_d' and (*iii*) the steady-state short circuit current. From a knowledge of the prefault excitation voltage and the various components of armature current, reactances X_d'', X_d' and X_d can be determined. Logarithmic plots of subtransient, transient and d.c. components help in the calculation of time constants T_d'', T_d' and T_a respectively. The method of determining reactances and time-constants from the short-circuit armature current oscillograms is as follows :

From the oscillographic record of three short-circuit armature currents as illustrated in Fig. 4.20, it is usually preferred to select that oscillogram which has the largest d.c. component in it. Now a smooth line passing through the crest or peak values of this oscillogram is drawn to get the envelope of short-circuit armature current as shown in Fig. 4.20 (*a*). The time can be measured by counting the number of cycles and from the alternator frequency. The current peaks for this envelope are measured quite accurately at suitable time intervals and plotted to get a symmetrical envelope as shown in Fig. 4.45 (*a*). In this figure, note that d.c. component is reduced to zero. The steady-state short-circuit armature current $oa = \sqrt{2}I_{sc}$ is also drawn in Fig. 4.45 (*a*). Extrapolation of the transient envelope *ef* meets the vertical line at *b*. Then X_d'', X_d' and X_d from Fig. 4.45 (*a*) are

$$X_d'' = \frac{\sqrt{2}E_{fo}}{oc}, \qquad X_d' = \frac{\sqrt{2}E_{fo}}{ob}, X_d = \frac{\sqrt{2}E_{fo}}{oa}$$

Here E_{fo} is the prefault r.m.s. excitation voltage.

The difference $\Delta i'$, between the transient envelope and the steady-state short circuit current $\sqrt{2}I_{sc}$, is called the transient component of total short-circuit armature current. A semilog plot of $\Delta i'$ gives a straight line as shown in Fig. 4.45 (*b*).

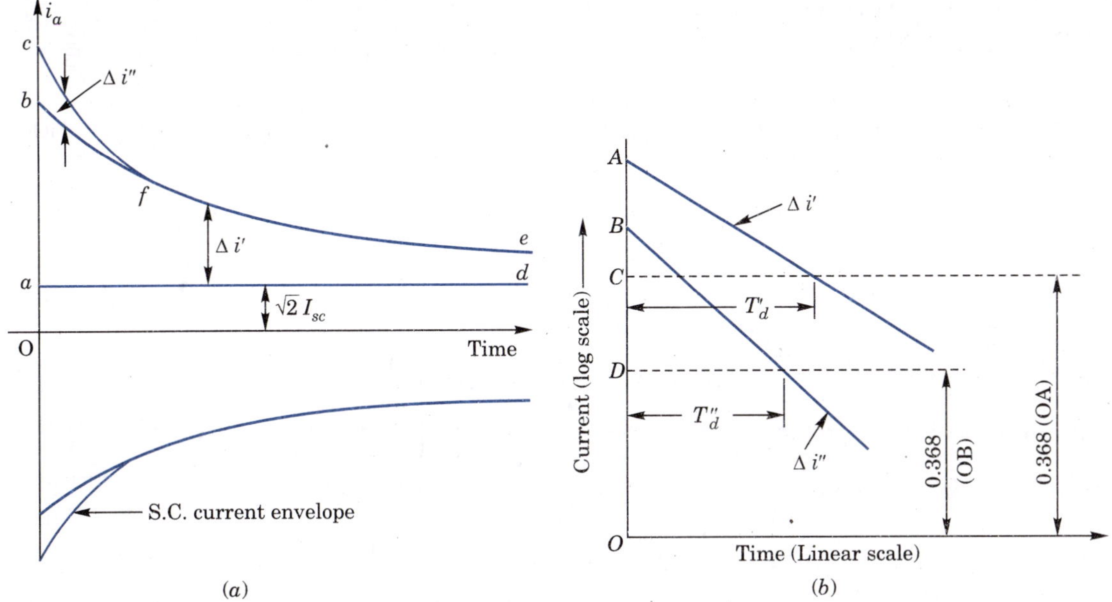

Fig. 4.45: (*a*) Symmetrical envelope of the short-circuit armature current (*b*) Plot of $\Delta i'$ and $\Delta i''$ on semilog graph paper.

The difference $\Delta i''$, between the subtransient envelope and the extrapolated-transient envelope, is called the subtransient component of total short-circuit armature current. A semilog plot of $\Delta i''$ also results in a straight line as shown in Fig. 4.45 (*b*).

Now the *d*-axis short-circuit transient time-constant T_d' is calculated as the time, in which the initial transient component of current *OA* decays to $OC = 0.368\ (OA)$, as shown in Fig. 4.45 (*b*). Similarly the *d*-axis short-circuit subtransient time-constant T_d'' is calculated as the time in which the initial subtransient component of current *OB* decays to $OD = 0.368\ (OB)$ as illustrated in Fig. 4.45 (*b*).

Fig. 4.45 (*a*) reveals that only the positive half envelope of the symmetrical short-circuit armature current is important. Example 4.11 illustrates the method of determining X_d'', X_d', X_d and T_d'' and T_d'. The armature time-constant T_a can also be obtained from a semilog plot of the d.c. component of short-circuit armature current, just like T_d' and T_d''.

Example 4.13. *A 11 kV, 45 MVA, 50 Hz, 3-phase star-connected alternator was run at synchronous speed and its field winding was excited to generate a voltage of 5 kV at no load. A sudden 3-phase symmetrical short-circuit was applied suddenly at the alternator terminals and the armature-current oscillograms were recorded. For the oscillograms having the largest d.c. component, the data pertaining to the peak values of the upper positive-half envelope are as follows :*

S.C. current A	*5571*	*4991*	*4535*	*4299*	*4034*	*3891*	*3766*	*3674*
time, sec	*0*	*0.01*	*0.02*	*0.03*	*0.04*	*0.05*	*0.06*	*0.07*

3601	*3560*	*3481*	*3401*	*3300*	*3190*	*3101*	*3011*	*2921*	*2741*	*2605*	*2451*	*2231*
0.08	*0.10*	*0.12*	*0.15*	*0.20*	*0.30*	*0.4*	*0.50*	*0.6*	*0.80*	*1.0*	*1.20*	*1.60*

For the same excitation voltage of 5 kV, the steady short-circuit current was found to be 800 A r.m.s. Calculate the magnitude of X_d'', X_d', X_d, T_d'' and T_d'.

Solution. (*i*) First of all the upper positive half of the envelope is plotted, with crest values of envelope along vertical axis and time in seconds along horizontal axis, as shown in Fig. 4.46 (*a*). In this plot, peak values of steady-state short-circuit armature current equal to $oa = \sqrt{2}\, I_{sc} = \sqrt{2}(800) = 1131.2$ A is also drawn.

The transient component $\Delta i'$ (= S.C. current $- \sqrt{2}\, I_{sc}$) of the short-circuit current, obtained by taking the difference between short-circuit current envelope and the steady-state short-circuit current of 1131.2 A, is as follows :

$\Delta i'$, A	4440	3860	3404	3168	2903	2760	2635	2543	2470	2360	2300	2270
time, sec	0.0	0.01	0.02	0.03	0.04	0.05	0.06	0.07	0.08	0.10	0.12	0.15

2200	2100	1970	1880	1790	1610	1475	1320	1100
0.20	0.30	0.40	0.50	0.6	0.8	1.00	1.20	1.60

(*ii*) Now $\Delta i'$ is plotted on a semilog paper with $\Delta i'$ along the vertical logarithmic scale and time on the horizontal linear scale as shown in Fig. 4.46 (*b*). It is seen from this plot, that points corresponding to the time greater than about 0.2 sec., lie on a straight line. Draw this line so that it meets the vertical line at *A*. From this graph, initial value of transient component of short circuit current is

$$\Delta i_o = OA = 2440 \text{ A}.$$

According to Fig. 4.45 (*a*),

$$ob = oa + ab = 1131 + 2440 = 3571 \text{ A}.$$

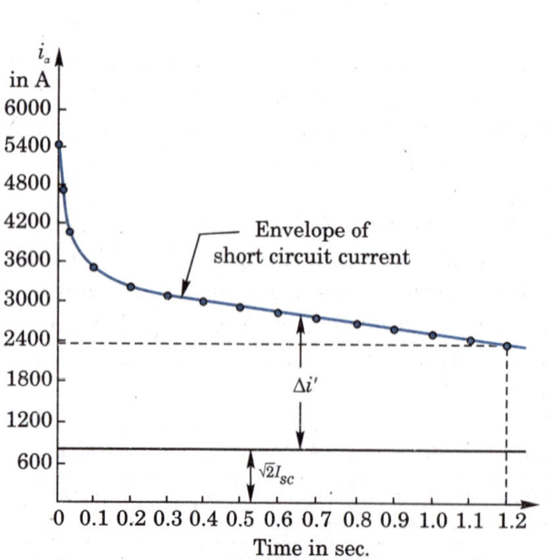

Fig. 4.46: (*a*) Upper positive half of S.C. current envelope, Example 4.13.

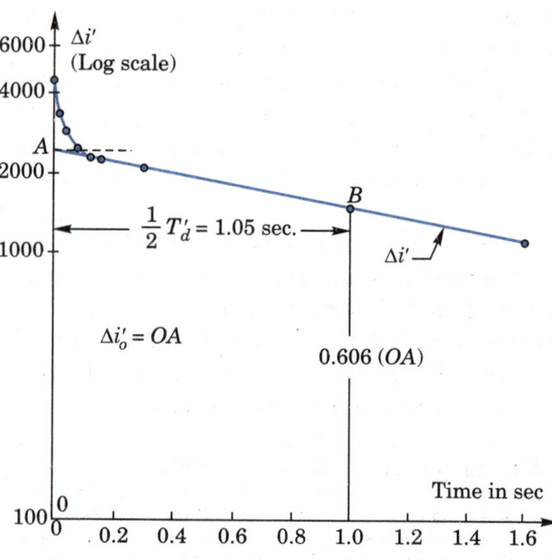

Fig. 4.46: (*b*) Plot of $\Delta i'$ on semilog paper, Example 4.13.

Per-phase prefault excitation voltage,

$$E_{fo} = \frac{5000}{\sqrt{3}} = 2886.8 \text{ V.}$$

$$\therefore \quad X_d' = \frac{E_{fo}}{ob/\sqrt{2}} = \frac{\sqrt{2} \times 2886.8}{3571} = 1.143\ \Omega.$$

T_d' is the time for which the initial transient component of current $\Delta i' = 2440$ A decays to 0.368 (OA). Alternatively, half of T_d' is the time for which the initial value of $\Delta i'$ decays to 0.606 (OA) = 0.606 × 2440 = 1478.6 A, as indicated by point B in Fig. 4.46 (b).

$$\therefore \quad T_d' = 1.05 \times 2 = 2.10 \text{ sec.}$$

(*iii*) The subtransient component of short-circuit armature current $\Delta i''$, obtained by taking the difference between the subtransient envelope and the extrapolated-transient envelope, is as follows :

$\Delta i''$, A	2000	1440	1004	778	523	395	285	208	150
time, sec.	0.0	0.01	0.02	0.03	0.04	0.05	0.06	0.07	0.08

Now $\Delta i''$ is plotted again on another semilog paper, with $\Delta i''$ along the logarithmic scale and time on the linear scale, as shown in Fig. 4.46 (c). A straight line passing through these points meets the vertical axis at C, Fig. 4.46 (c). From this graph, initial value of subtransient component of short-circuit current is

$$\Delta i_o'' = OC = 2000 \text{ A.}$$

For Fig. 4.46 (a),

$$oc = oa + ab + bc$$
$$= 1131 + 2440 + 2000$$
$$= 5571 \text{ A.}$$

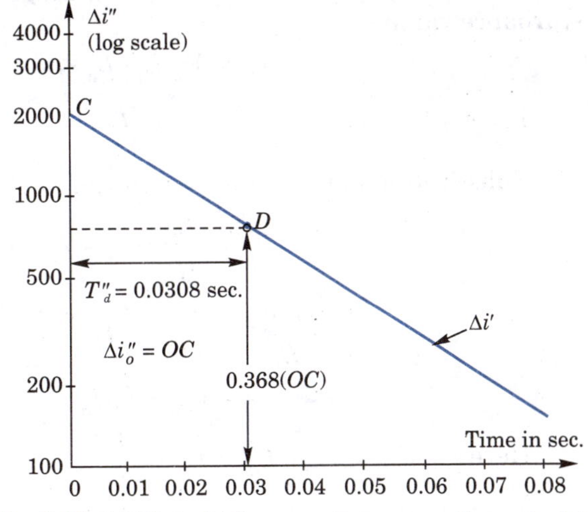

Fig. 4.46: (c) Plot of $\Delta i''$ on semilog paper, Example 4.13.

$$\therefore \quad X_d'' = \frac{\sqrt{2} \times 2886.8}{5571} = 0.733\ \Omega.$$

T_d'' is the time for which the initial subtransient component of current $\Delta i'' = 2000$ A decays to 0.368 (OC) = 0.368 × 2000 = 736 A, as indicated by point D in Fig. 4.46 (c).

$$\therefore \quad T_d'' = 0.0308 \text{ sec.}$$

$$X_d = \frac{E_{fo}}{I_{sc}} = \frac{2886.8}{800} = 3.61\ \Omega$$

$$\text{Base impedance} = \frac{(kV)^2}{MVA} = \frac{(11)^2}{45} = 2.689\ \Omega.$$

$$\therefore \quad X_d = \frac{3.61}{2.689} = 1.343 \text{ p.u.}; \ X_d' = \frac{1.143}{2.689} = 0.425 \text{ p.u.}$$

and

$$X_d'' = \frac{0.733}{2.689} = 0.273 \text{ p.u.}$$

4.15 TRANSIENT POWER-ANGLE CHARACTERISTICS

In this article, a sudden 3-phase short circuit is assumed to occur at the terminals of an alternator which is initially working under loaded conditions. The object is to draw phasor diagram of the alternator under transient state from which transient power-angle characteristics are derived.

Here the constant flux linkage theorem is invoked again according to which the flux linkages with a closed circuit remain constant at their pre-disturbance value. Alternatively, it may be assumed that the voltage regulator action takes place so as to keep the field flux linkages constant at their pre-disturbance value. In view of this constancy of flux linkages, we have,

$$\begin{bmatrix}\text{field flux linkages before} \\ \text{the transient disturbance}\end{bmatrix} = \begin{bmatrix}\text{field flux linkages, just after} \\ \text{the transient disturbance}\end{bmatrix}$$

i.e.,

$$\psi_{fo} = L_f i_f - M_d i_d \quad ...(4.173)$$

Minus sign before $M_d i_d$ is due to the fact that short-circuit armature m.m.f. opposes the field flux. The d-axis armature flux linkages ψ_{do}, also remain constant at their pre-disturbance value.

$$\therefore \quad \psi_{do} = M_d i_f - L_d i_d \quad ...(4.174)$$

From Eq. (4.174),

$$i_f = \frac{\psi_{do} + L_d i_d}{M_d}$$

Substitution of this value of i_f in Eq. (4.173) gives

$$\psi_{fo} = \frac{L_f}{M_d}(\psi_{do} + L_d i_d) - M_d i_d$$

or

$$\frac{\psi_{fo} M_d}{L_f} = \psi_{do} + \left(L_d - \frac{M_d^2}{L_f}\right) i_d$$

$$= \psi_{do} + L_d' i_d \quad ...(4.175)$$

Here

$$L_d' = L_d - \frac{M_d^2}{L_f}$$

is the *d-axis transient inductance*. Multiplication of Eq. (4.175) by ω gives

$$\omega \frac{\psi_{fo} M_d}{L_f} = \omega\psi_{do} + \omega L_d' i_d \quad ...(4.176)$$

or

$$\frac{\omega M_d}{L_f}[L_f i_f - M_d i_d] = \omega\psi_{do} + \omega L_d' i_d$$

or

$$\omega M_d i_f - \omega \frac{M_d^2}{L_f} i_d = \omega\psi_{do} + \omega L_d' i_d \quad ...(4.177)$$

From Eq. (4.79), $v_q = M_d \omega i_f - L_d \omega i_d - (r_a + L_q p)\, i_q$.

From the above expression of v_q, if armature resistance and transformer voltage are neglected, then

$$v_q = \omega\,(M_d i_f - L_d i_d) = \omega\psi_{do}.$$

In view of the above equation, the right hand side of Eq. (4.177) is equal to $v_q + X_d' i_d$.

The left hand side of Eq. (4.177) is equal to

$$\omega M_d i_f - \omega(L_d - L_d')\, i_d.$$

Hence, Eq. (4.177) now becomes

$$\omega M_d i_f - \omega(L_d - L_d')\, i_d = v_q + X_d' i_d$$

Dividing every term of the above equation by $\sqrt{2}$, we get its r.m.s. value as

$$E_f - (X_d - X_d')\, I_d = V_q + X_d' I_d \qquad ...(4.178)$$

Eq. (4.178) is illustrated in the synchronous generator phasor diagram of Fig. 4.47. The voltage $E_f - (X_d - X_d')\, I_d$ lies along the q-axis, it may therefore be designated by E_q'. Thus from Eq. (4.178), $E_q' = V_q + X_d' I_d$ and from Eq. (4.176),

$$E_q' = \frac{\omega}{\sqrt{2}} \frac{M_d}{L_f} \psi_{fo} = V_q + X_d' I_d$$

$$= V_t \cos \delta + X_d' I_d \qquad ...(4.179)$$

Eq. (4.179) shows that when field flux linkages ψ_{fo} are considered constant, the voltage E_q' remains constant during the transient state. The magnitude and phase of E_q' are shown in the phasor diagram of Fig. 4.47, which reveals that E_q' is along the excitation voltage E_f.

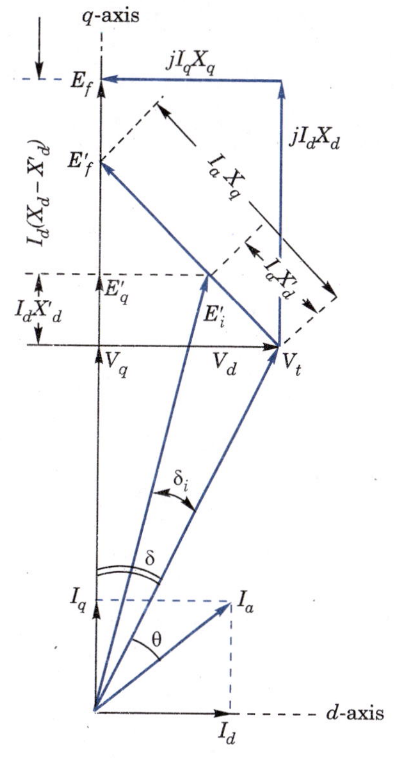

Fig. 4.47: Synchronous generator phasor diagram under transient conditions.

A power-angle expression useful for the analysis of sudden disturbances or sudden-load applications can be obtained from Fig. 4.47, as done before for deriving Eq. (4.58). Note that transient power-angle expression must include X_d' and E_q' in it.

The power for a synchronous machine is given by

$$P = V_t \cos \delta \,.\, I_q + V_t \sin \delta \,.\, I_d$$

But $\quad I_q = \dfrac{V_t \sin \delta}{X_q} \quad$ and $\quad I_d = \dfrac{E_q' - V_t \cos \delta}{X_d'}$

$$\therefore \quad P = \frac{V_t \cos \delta \,.\, V_t \sin \delta}{X_q} + \frac{V_t \sin \delta\,(E_q' - V_t \cos \delta)}{X_d'}$$

$$= \frac{E_q' V_t}{X_d'} \sin \delta + \frac{V_t^2}{2}\left(\frac{1}{X_q} - \frac{1}{X_d'}\right) \sin 2\delta \qquad ...(4.180)$$

The power-angle expression of Eq. (4.180) is applicable for a period of time short as compared with the transient time constant T_d'. This period of time less than T_d', is sufficient to cover the critical period in many transient and dynamic analysis. If the field flux linkages ψ_{fo} are maintained constant, then Eq. (4.180) is applicable till the period of time ψ_{fo} are maintained substantially constant by the voltage regulator action. The power-angle expression for steady state is also applicable to a synchronous machine experiencing sufficiently slow changes.

Fig. 4.48 illustrates steady-state and transient power-angle characteristics of a typical synchronous machine, from which it is seen that the general shape of the two curves is almost similar. Since $\frac{E_q'}{X_d'}$ is greater than $\frac{E_f}{X_d}$, the fundamental term of power has larger magnitude during transient state. Since $X_q > X_d'$, the numerical value of second harmonic term in Eq. (4.180) is negative. The physical reason of the transient amplitude being greater than the steady-state amplitude is that, just after the short-circuit, there is a suddenly induced component of field current which results in greater excitation of the machine. Transient power-angle curve of Fig. 4.48 shows that a synchronous machine in a practical system can withstand a large suddenly applied-power overload, provided its duration is relatively short as compared with T_d'.

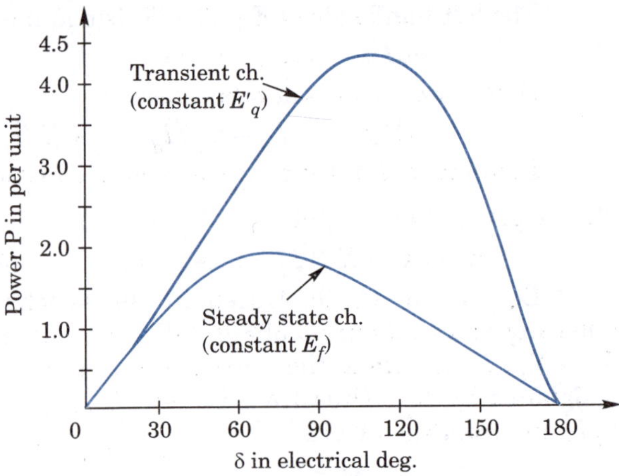

Fig. 4.48: Transient and steady-state power-angle characteristics of a synchronous machine.

The transient power-angle expression of Eq. (4.180) is usually simplified by neglecting the second harmonic term. Examination of Fig. 4.47 shows that $V_t + jI_aX_d' = E_i'$ is almost equal to E_q' in magnitude. Though $\frac{E_i' V_t}{X_d'}\sin\delta_i$ is less than $\frac{E_q' V_t}{X_d'}\sin\delta$, yet it is almost equal to the power given by Eq. (4.180). This is due to the fact that numerical value of second harmonic term in Eq. (4.180) is negative and the total transient power is equal to the difference of first term and the second harmonic term. In view of this, the transient power as given by

Fig. 4.49: Approximate transient equivalent circuit of a synchronous machine. *G*—generator and *M*—motor.

$$P = \frac{E_i' . V_t}{X_d'} \sin\delta_i \qquad ...(4.181)$$

is more accurate than the use of Eq. (4.180) with transient saliency ignored ($X_q = X_d'$). The voltage equation $E_i' = V_t + jI_aX_d'$ leads to the equivalent circuit of Fig. 4.49, which is commonly employed when transients and dynamics of a complex multimachine system are to be investigated even with the help of computers. The voltage E_i' is called the *voltage behind transient reactance*.

Note that use of the equivalent circuit (or model) of Fig. 4.49 is based on two assumptions as under :

(*i*) The voltage behind transient reactance during the transient state is assumed constant. This means that the field flux linkages are maintained constant during the transient time (usually 1 sec. or so) much less as compared to T_d'.

(*ii*) The reactances X_d' and X_q under transient conditions are equal. This assumption only permits the neglect of transient saliency and enables to model the synchronous machine under transient conditions by a single transient reactance of Fig. 4.49.

Example 4.14. *A 3-phase salient-pole synchronous generator has the following constants in per unit system:*

$$X_d = 1.20, \qquad X_q = 0.8, \qquad X_d' = 0.4$$

This generator supplies rated kVA to an infinite bus at rated terminal voltage and at unity power factor.

(*a*) *Find the load angle and then calculate the transient power.*

(*b*) *Repeat part (a) by assuming constant voltage behind transient reactance.*

Solution. For unity power factor, $\cos\theta = 1$, $\therefore \quad \theta = 0°$.

For calculating load angle δ, use Eq. (4.48).

$$\therefore \qquad \tan\delta = \frac{V_t(0) + 1 \times 0.8}{1+0} = 0.8 \qquad \text{and} \quad \delta = 38.66°$$

$$I_d = I_a \sin(\delta + \theta) = 1.00 \sin 38.66° = 0.625.$$

(*a*) From Eq. (4.179),

$$E_q' = V_q + X_d' I_d = V_t \cos\delta + X_d' I_d$$
$$= 1.0 \cos 38.66 + 0.4 \times 0.625 = 1.0308$$

From Eq. (4.108), the transient power P is,

$$P = \frac{1.031 \times 1}{0.4} \sin 38.66° + \frac{1}{2}\left(\frac{1}{0.8} - \frac{1}{0.4}\right) \sin 77.32°$$
$$= 1.6098 - 0.6098 = 1.00.$$

(*b*) From Fig. 4.47, $\quad \bar{E}_i' = \bar{V}_t + j\bar{I}_a X_d'$

With V_t as reference phasor,

$$\bar{E}_i' = (1 + j0.0) + j(1 + j0.0)(0.4) = 1 + j0.40$$

$$\therefore \qquad \bar{E}_i' = \sqrt{(1)^2 + (0.4)^2} \angle\tan^{-1}(0.4) = 1.077 \angle 21.80°$$

$$\therefore \qquad \delta_i = +21.80°$$

Transient power P is given by,

$$P = \frac{E_i' V_t}{X_d'} \sin\delta_i = \frac{1.077 \times 1}{0.4} \sin 21.80° = 1.00$$

This example demonstrates the use of Eq. (4.180) and the equivalent circuit of Fig. 4.49. It also shows that the results obtained from the approximate equivalent circuit of Fig. 4.49 are identical with those obtained from Eq. (4.180).

Example 4.15. *A salient-pole alternator has the following per unit parameters:*

$$X_d = 1.00, \quad X_q = 0.6, \quad X_d' = 0.3$$

If this alternator is delivering rated kVA load directly to an infinite bus at rated terminal voltage and at p.f. of 0.8 lagging, then calculate the steady state and transient power-angle characteristics.

Solution. With terminal voltage as reference,

$$\overline{V}_t = 1 + j0,\ \overline{I}_a = 0.8 - j0.6$$

$$\therefore \quad \overline{E}_f' = \overline{V}_t\ \overline{E}_f' = \overline{V}_t + jI_aX_q = 1 + j0 + j\,(0.8 - j0.6) \times 0.6$$

$$= 1.36 + j0.48 = 1.4422\ \angle 19.44°$$

$$\therefore \quad \text{Load angle } \delta = 19.44°,$$

$$\text{p.f. angle } \theta = \cos^{-1}(0.8) = 36.87°$$

$$\therefore \quad \angle\delta + \theta = 56.31°$$

$$\therefore \quad I_d = I_a \sin(\delta + \theta) = 0.832,\ I_q = I_a \cos(\delta + \theta) = 0.555$$

Excitation voltage, $E_f = E_f' + I_d\,(X_d - X_q) = 1.4422 + 0.832 \times 0.4 = 1.775$ p.u.

From Eq. (4.58), synchronous power P is

$$P = \frac{1.775 \times 1}{1} \sin\delta + \frac{1}{2} \times \frac{0.4}{0.6} \sin 2\delta$$

$$= 1.775 \sin\delta + 0.333 \sin 2\delta = P_1 \sin\delta + P_2 \sin 2\delta$$

The load angle δ at which steady-state power P is maximum is given by the relation (see Problem 4.11),

$$\cos\delta = \frac{-1.775 \pm \sqrt{(1.775)^2 + 32(0.333)^2}}{8 \times 0.333}$$

This gives $\delta = 72.197°$

$$\therefore \quad P_{max} = 1.775 \sin 72.197° + 0.333 \sin 144.394° = 1.884 \text{ p.u.}$$

From Eq. (4.179), $E_q' = V_t \cos\delta + X_d' I_d$

$$= 1.0 \times \cos 19.44° + 0.3 \times 0.832 = 1.1926$$

The transient power, from Eq. (4.180), is,

$$P = \frac{1.1926 \times 1}{0.3} \sin\delta + \frac{1}{2}\left(\frac{1}{0.6} - \frac{1}{0.3}\right) \sin 2\delta$$

$$= 3.975 \sin\delta - 0.833 \sin 2\delta$$

The load angle at which transient power is maximum is given by,

$$\cos\delta = \frac{-3.975 \pm \sqrt{(3.975)^2 + 32(0.833)^2}}{-8 \times (0.833)}$$

This gives $\delta = 109.196°$

$$\therefore \quad P_{max} = 3.975 \sin 109.196 - 0.833 \sin 218.392° = 4.271 \text{ p.u.}$$

The steady-state and transient power-angle characteristics for this example are shown in Fig. 4.48.

4.16 PHASOR DIAGRAMS UNDER TRANSIENT AND SUBTRANSIENT CONDITIONS

For a salient pole alternator working under steady state conditions, the excitation voltage E_f from Eq. (4.44), with negligible armature resistance, is given by,

$$\overline{E}_f = \overline{V}_t + j\overline{I}_d X_d + j\overline{I}_q X_q$$

The phasor sum of V_t, I_dX_d and I_qX_q is shown in Fig. 4.47.

Under transient conditions, the direct-axis transient reactance is X_d' and q-axis transient reactances is $X_q' = X_q$. Fig. 4.47 reveals that under transient conditions,

$$\bar{V}_t + j\bar{I}_d X_d' + j\bar{I}_q X_q = \bar{E}_q' = \bar{V}_q + j\bar{I}_d X_d'$$

Here V_q is the q-axis component of terminal voltage V_t. If V_d is the d-axis component of V_t, so that $\bar{V}_t = \bar{V}_d + j\bar{V}_q$, then under transient conditions,

$$V_d + jI_qX_q = E_d'$$

In magnitude, $V_d = I_qX_q$, therefore $E_d' = 0$.

It is seen from Fig. 4.47 that E_q' is almost equal to E_i', where

$$\bar{E}_i' = \bar{V} + j\bar{I}_a X_d'$$

Here voltage E_i' is called the *voltage behind transient reactance* X_d'.

Under subtransient conditions, the d-axis and q-axis subtransient reactances are X_d'' and X_q'' respectively. The phasor sum of

$$V_q + jI_d X_d'' = E_q'' = oa \quad \text{and} \quad V_d + jI_qX_q'' = E_d'' = ab$$

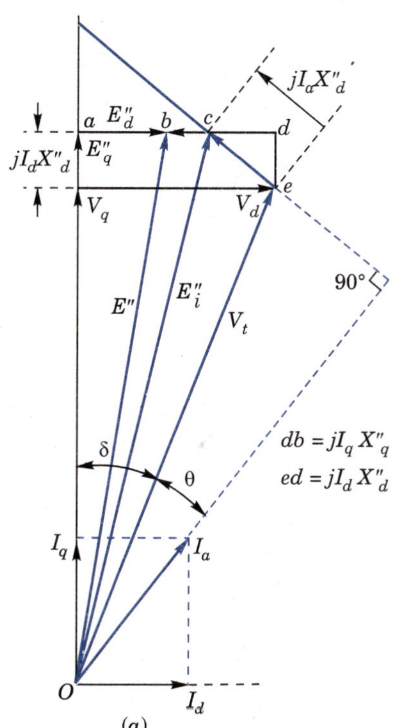

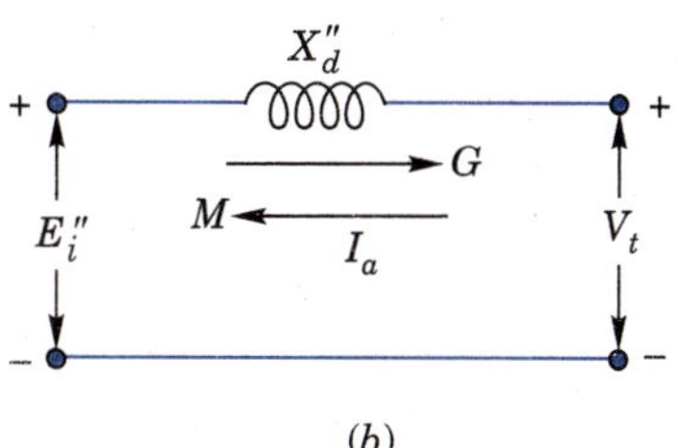

Fig. 4.50: Synchronous generator (*a*) phasor diagram and (*b*) approximate equivalent circuit under subtransient conditions.

is shown in Fig. 4.50 (a). The resultant of E_d'' and E_q'' is equal to $ob = E''$ as shown. It is seen from Fig. 4.50 (a) that $ob = E''$ is almost equal to $oc = E_i''$, where

$$oc = E_i'' = V_t + jI_aX_d'' \qquad \text{...(4.182)}$$

The voltage E_i'' is called the *voltage behind subtransient reactance* X_d''. Eq. (4.182) results in the subtransient equivalent circuit of a synchronous machine as shown in Fig. 4.50 (*b*).

With the help of Figs. 4.47 and 4.50 (*a*), one phasor diagram showing E_i' and E_i'' is as illustrated in Fig. 4.51. The voltage E_i, called voltage behind *d*-axis synchronous reactance X_d, is given by,

$$\bar{E}_i = \bar{V}_t + j\bar{I}_a X_d .$$

Note that E_i and E_f are almost equal in magnitude. This simplified phasor diagram of Fig. 4.51 is used quite often for doing the analysis of a synchronous machine connected to a power system network.

Note that in Fig. 4.51,

for E_i'', $X_d'' = X_q''$, *i.e.*, subtransient saliency is ignored,
for E_i', $X_d' = X_q'$, *i.e.*, transient saliency is ignored,
and for E_i, $X_d = X_q$, *i.e.*, steady-state saliency is ignored.

Under the approximations, the initial current at the instant of short circuit is E_i''/X_d'' as per Fig. 4.50 (*b*). If the effect of damper bars is neglected, then the initial current at the time of short circuit is E_i'/X_d' as per Fig. 4.49. When the effect of damper bars is included, then the initial value of current E_i''/X_d'' decays exponentially to E_i'/X_d' with a time constant T_d'' and current E_i'/X_d' decays to E_i/X_d with a time constant T_d'. As per Eq. (4.119), the r.m.s. value of symmetrical, or a.c. component of short-circuit armature current is

$$I_{ac}(t) = \frac{E_i}{X_d} + \left(\frac{E_i'}{X_d'} - \frac{E_i}{X_d}\right)e^{-t/T_d'} + \left(\frac{E_i''}{X_d''} - \frac{E_i'}{X_d'}\right)e^{-t/T_d''} \qquad ...(4.183)$$

In a power system network, a synchronous machine is represented by

(*i*) Fig. 4.50 (*b*) under subtransient conditions,

(*ii*) Fig. 4.49 under transient conditions,

or (*iii*) X_d in series with E_i under steady-state conditions.

The difference between Eqs. (4.119) and (4.183) must be noted. Eq. (4.119) applies when a sudden 3-phase short circuit occurs across alternator terminals with the machine running initially unloaded and developing an excitation voltage E_{fo}. Eq. (4.183) is applicable when a sudden 3-phase short circuit occurs across the alternator terminals with the machine initially delivering load. In Eq. (4.183), E_i, E_i', E_i'' are the prefault machine voltages behind X_d, X_d', X_d'' respectively with armature current I_a, armature terminal voltage V_t and with known p.f. angle θ.

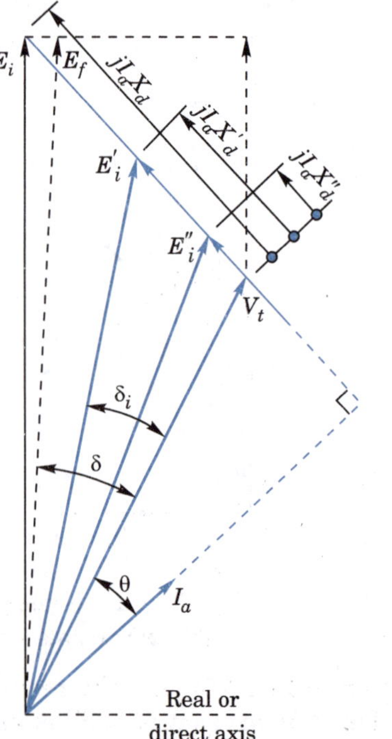

Fig. 4.51: Simplified phasor diagram for the initial current and voltages of a loaded alternator.

4.16.1 Synchronous-machine Representation in a Power System Network

For the problems associated with power-system analysis, a synchronous-machine representation depends upon the type of problem under consideration and the object of this section of the article is to discuss it briefly.

(*a*) **Steady-state analysis.** The term load-flow study means the calculation of system currents when various voltages in the network are known. For such calculations, a synchronous machine is represented by X_q in series with E_f' as per Fig. 4.9 (*a*) or by X_d in series with E_i as per Fig. 4.51. The latter representation is quite accurate when load flow study is to be carried out.

(*b*) **Fault and short-circuit calculations.** For calculating the initial fault and short-circuit currents, a synchronous machine is represented by Fig. 4.50 (*b*). If the effect of damper bars is neglected, then a synchronous machine is represented by Fig. 4.49. For determining the rupturing duties of circuit breakers, settings of the protective relays, bus-bar stresses etc., the effect of power system load is ignored by E_i, E_i' and E_i'' are calculated by taking load currents into consideration. In addition, the effect of d.c. component of fault or short-circuit current is taken into consideration of determining the relay-setting, circuit-breaker rupturing duties and bus-bars stresses.

For determining the torque and power output under transient conditions, the d.c. component of fault or short-circuit current is usually neglected, because it has almost no effect on synchronous power and torques. The calculation of transient torques and power outputs is required for (*i*) determining the shaft stresses (*ii*) designing the machine foundations and (*iii*) examining the flow of synchronizing power for maintaining the sychronization under sudden disturbances.

(*c*) **Transient stability.** The phenomenon during transient stability of a synchronous machine is greatly affected by its mechanical characteristics. During a disturbance, the period of rotor oscillation of a machine is about 1 second or so. The subtransient component of fault, or short circuit, current dies down to zero in a small fraction of a second (2 to 3 cycles or 0.04 to 0.06 second) which is short as compared with the period of rotor oscillations. Therefore, the subtransient component of current is neglected during the transient stability studies. The d.c. component of armature current decays to zero in about 0.15 to 0.3 second for a short circuit at the alternator terminals, but the effect of external resistance greatly reduces this time. Therefore, d.c. component of armature current is also usually ignored during the transient stability analysis of synchronous machines. The transient component of armature current decays to zero after 0.5 to 10 seconds, a time much longer than the period of rotor oscillations. Therefore, only the transient component of armature current is required to be considered during transient stability. A synchronous machine, for such studies, is therefore represented by X_d' in series with E_i' as shown in Fig. 4.49.

For investigating the problems associated with voltage dip at the time of sudden application of load on an unloaded alternator, or voltage rise at the time of sudden removal of load, a knowledge of Art. 4.9 is desirable.

This article brings out clearly the representation of a synchronous machine in a power-system network for handling the system transient problems.

Example 4.16. *A 3-phase, 50 MVA, 11 kV, 50 Hz hydrogenerator has the following reactances in per unit on the generator rating as the base:*

$$X_d = 1.0, \qquad X_d' = 0.4, \qquad X_d'' = 0.25, \qquad T_d' = 2.00 \text{ sec.}$$

This generator supplies a load over two parallel high-voltage transmission lines with transformers at the sending and receiving ends as shown in Fig. 4.52. The transformer and transmission-line reactances in per unit are marked in the figure. The receiving and low-tension bus is assumed an infinite bus with its terminals voltage equal to unity. The generator is initially fully loaded with receiving end p.f. equal to 0.8 lagging.

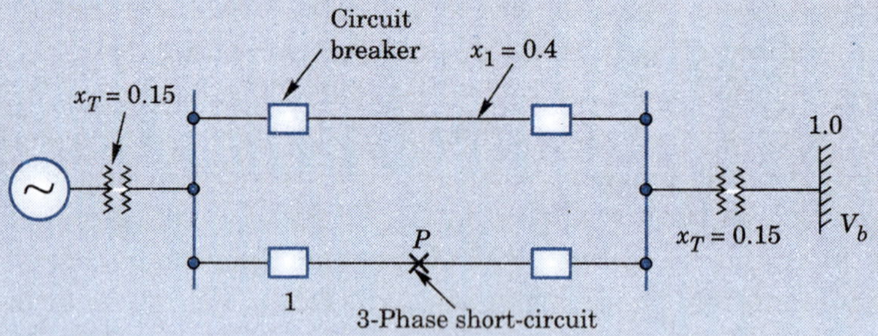

Fig. 4.52: Pertaining to Example 4.16.

A solid 3-phase short circuit occurs at the middle of one of the lines at the point P as shown.

(a) Compute the prefault values of machine voltages behind synchronous, transient and subtransient reactances.

(b) Compute the largest possible initial value of the d.c. component of short circuit current in one phase contributed by both the generator and the infinite bus. Find also the total r.m.s. short-circuit current in that phase just after the short circuit.

(c) The circuit breaker 1 on the sending end of the line opens after 0.15 second. Find the current which one phase of this breaker would have to interrupt in opening its three terminals. Assume that both d.c. and subtransient components of short-circuit current have reached negligible values in 0.15 second.

Solution. (*a*) Let V_b be the infinite bus voltage. Then generator voltage behind X_d is,

$$E_i = V_b + jI_a\left(X_d + 2x_T + \frac{1}{2}x_1\right)$$

With V_b as a reference phasor,

$$V_b = 1.00 \text{ and } I_a = 0.8 - j0.6$$

$$\therefore \quad E_i = 1 + j0.0 + j(0.8 - j0.6)\,(1.5)$$

$$= 1.9 + j1.20 = 2.247\ \underline{/32.276^\circ}$$

Voltage behind X_d' is,

$$E_i' = V_b + jI_a\left(X_d' + 2x_T + \frac{1}{2}x_1\right)$$

$$= 1 + j(0.8 - j0.6)\,(0.9) = 1.54 + j0.72 = 1.7\ \underline{/25.06^\circ}$$

Voltage behind X_d'' is,

$$E_i'' = V_b + jI_a\left(X_d'' + 2x_T + \frac{1}{2}x_1\right)$$

$$= 1 + j(0.8 - j0.6)\,(0.75)$$

$$= 1.45 + j0.6 = 1.57\ \angle 22.48°$$

(*b*) The initial a.c. component of short-circuit current from the generator is,

$$\frac{E_i''}{X_d'' + x_T + \dfrac{0.6 \times 0.2}{0.8}} = \frac{1.57}{0.4 + 0.15} = 2.855.$$

The a.c. component of short-circuit current from infinite bus is

$$\frac{V_b}{x_T + 0.15} = \frac{1.0}{0.3} = 3.333.$$

$\therefore$ Total initial component of symmetrical short-circuit current is 2.855 + 3.333 = 6.188.

As per Eq. (4.120), the largest possible d.c. component of short-circuit current is $\sqrt{2}\,(2.855)$ from the generator and $\sqrt{2}\,(3.333)$ from the infinite bus.

$\therefore$ Total d.c. component having maximum possible value is $\sqrt{2}\,(2.855 + 3.333) = 8.75$

The largest short-circuit current, as per Eq. (4.121), is

$$\sqrt{(6.188)^2 + (8.75)^2} = 10.717.$$

(*c*) Initial component of generator short-circuit current with subtransient ignored is

$$\frac{E_i'}{X_{de}'} = \frac{E_i}{X_d' + x_T + 0.15} = \frac{1.7}{1.55 + 0.15} = 2.429.$$

Final steady-state generator short-circuit current is

$$\frac{E_i}{X_{de}} = \frac{E_i}{X_d + x_T + 0.15} = \frac{2.247}{1.15 + 0.15} = 1.7285.$$

The generator time constant T_{de}' is given by

$$T_{de}' = T_{do}'\,\frac{X_d' + (x_T + 0.15)}{X_d + (x_T + 0.15)} = T_d'\,\frac{X_d}{X_d'}\cdot\frac{X_d' + (x_T + 0.15)}{X_d + (x_T + 0.15)}$$

$$= 2.0 \times \frac{1.0}{0.4}\cdot\frac{0.4 + 0.3}{1 + 0.3} = 2.692 \text{ sec.}$$

The symmetrical short-circuit current decreases from 2.429 to 1.7285 with a time constant of 2.692 seconds.

As per Eq. (4.183) and with subtransient component neglected, the value of symmetrical current at t = 0.15 sec. is,

$$\frac{E_i}{X_{de}} + \left(\frac{E_i'}{X_{de}'} - \frac{E_i}{X_{de}}\right)e^{-t/T_{de}'}$$

$$= 1.7285 + (2.429 - 1.7285)\,e^{-\frac{0.15}{2.692}} = 1.7285 + 0.7e^{-0.05572} = 2.3905$$

One phase of the circuit breaker 1 on the sending end of transmission line has to handle the following symmetrical breaker current

$$= 2.3905 \times \frac{0.6}{0.8} \text{ from generator} + 3.333 \times \frac{0.2}{0.8} \text{ from infinite bus}$$

$$= 2.6261 \text{ per unit.}$$

4.17 SYNCHRONOUS-MACHINE DYNAMICS (OR ELECTRO-MECHANICAL TRANSIENTS)

Under normal running conditions, the relative velocity between stator and rotor fields is zero. Whenever this relative position is disturbed, synchronizing restoring torques tending to maintain this equality come into play. This tendency of the rotor to attain synchronous speed after a slight disturbance, is the basic reason for the analysis of synchronous-machine dynamics. For example, consider a synchronous motor connected to an infinite bus. A sudden increase in the shaft load must reduce the motor speed momentarily so that load angle δ increases to supply the additional load. Before the rotor settles down to a new value of load angle, the rotor oscillates about its final equilibrium position. As a result of it, the rotor speed fluctuates around synchronous speed before finallly attaining synchronous speed. The phenomena involving rotor oscillations about its final equilibrium position is called *hunting*. The nature of synchronous-machine oscillations or hunting can be known only if its electromechanical transients are investigated.

The cause of disturbances in synchronous machines may be any one of the following:

(*i*) A sudden change of load,

(*ii*) A fault in the supply system,

(*iii*) A sudden change in the field current,

(*iv*) Load torque containing harmonic torques in case of motors, or prime-mover torque containing harmonic torques in case of synchronous generators.

The effect of rotor oscillations on the performance of synchronous machines are given below:

(*i*) It increases the mechanical stresses and fatigue of the shaft.

(*ii*) When working as a generator, the output voltage fluctuates which is an undesirable phenomenon.

(*iii*) It increases the machine losses and, therefore, increases its operating temperature.

(*iv*) The rotor oscillations may cause the machine to fall out of step.

The object of this article is to develop the basic electromechanical equation describing the synchronous-machine behaviour under dynamic conditions. This equation is then linearized for small angular oscillations. The forced oscillations arising due to cyclic variations of shaft torque, are also considered.

4.17.1 Electromechanical Equation

Here the basic electromechanical equation is developed first for a motor and then for a generator.

The torque conventions have already been developed in Art. 3.2. From this article, the general torque balance equation is,

$$T_e + T_m = Jp\omega_r + D\omega_r$$

Neglect of the mechanical damping torque $D\omega_r$ gives

$$T_e + T_m = Jp\omega_r$$

or
$$T_e + T_m = T_{iner} \quad \text{...(4.184)}$$

(*a*) **Motor operation.** For a motor, the mechanical torque T_m must flow out of the machine. In view of this,

$$T_m = -T_{sh}$$

where T_{sh} is the shaft load torque.

∴ Eq. (4.184) becomes, $T_e = T_{iner} + T_{sh}$

Multiplying both the sides of above equation by the synchronous speed, we get

$$P_e = P_{iner} + P_{sh} \quad \text{...(4.185)}$$

At time $t = 0$ and at no-load, suppose that the axis of resultant air-gap flux wave coincides with the field-pole axis as shown in Fig. 4.53 (*a*). For a sudden application of shaft load, the rotor must slow down momentarily in order to supply the increased load. As a result of it, the field-pole axis falls back in space from the axis of resultant air-gap flux wave, by an angle δ_m as shown in Fig. 4.53 (*b*). From this diagram it is seen that

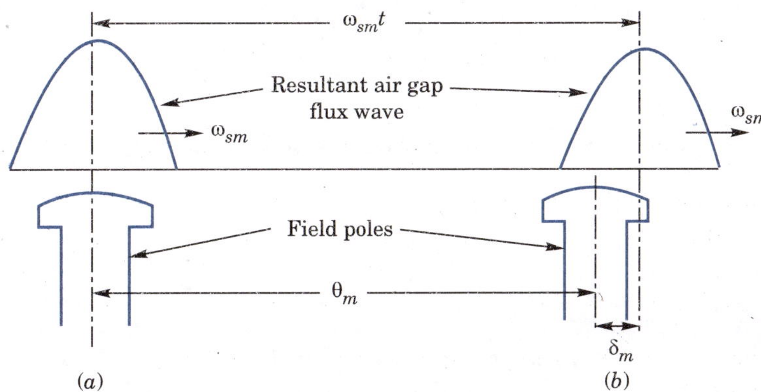

Fig. 4.53: For synchronous motor, the space angle between the axes of resultant air-gap flux and field pole is (*a*) zero at $t = 0$ (*b*) δ_m at any time t after the disturbance.

$$\theta_m = \omega_{sm}t - \delta_m \quad \text{...(4.186)}$$

Here ω_{sm} = synchronous angular velocity in mechanical radians per second,

$\omega_{sm}t$ = space angle travelled by rotating air-gap flux wave, in t seconds after the disturbance,

and θ_m = space angle travelled by field poles, in t seconds after the disturbance.

In Eq. (4.186), θ_m and δ_m are in mechanical degrees.

Had there been no-load suddenly applied to the motor shaft, the angle θ_m would be equal to $\omega_{sm}t$ and the field-pole axis would coincide with the axis of resultant air-gap flux wave.

But 1 mechanical radian $= \dfrac{2}{P}$ (1 electrical radian)

$\therefore$ $$\delta_m = \frac{2}{P}(\delta)$$

Eq. (4.186) now becomes, $\theta_m = \omega_{sm}t - \frac{2}{P}\delta$

$\therefore$ Rotor speed, $$\frac{d\theta_m}{dt} = \omega_{sm} - \frac{2}{P}\cdot\frac{d\delta}{dt}$$

and $$\frac{d^2\theta_m}{dt^2} = -\frac{2}{P}\cdot\frac{d^2\delta}{dt^2}$$

Here $\omega_{sm} - \frac{d\theta_m}{dt} = \frac{2}{P}\cdot\frac{d\delta}{dt}$ is the slip speed, because synchronous speed ω_{sm} is greater than the rotor speed $\frac{d\theta_m}{dt}$.

Now $$T_{iner} = J\frac{d^2\theta_m}{dt^2} = -\frac{2}{P}J\frac{d^2\delta}{dt^2}$$

and P_{iner} = (Rotor speed during oscillations at the instant considered) (T_{iner}).

Since only small oscillations are considered; rotor speed during oscillations = ω_{sm}.

$\therefore$ $$P_{iner} = -\omega_{sm}\frac{2}{P}\cdot J\frac{d^2\delta}{dt^2}$$

$$= -\left(2\pi ns\cdot\frac{2}{P}J\right)\frac{d^2\delta}{dt^2} = -P_j\frac{d^2\delta}{dt^2} \quad ...(4.187)$$

where $P_j = \left(2\pi n_s\cdot\frac{2}{P}J\right)$ is the angular momentum (or inertia power) in watts/electrical radian per sec^2 or in joules/electrical radian per second.

Substituting the value of P_{iner} from Eq. (4.187) in Eq. (4.185), we get

$$P_j\frac{d^2\delta}{dt^2} + P_e = P_{sh} \quad ...(4.188)$$

The quantity P_j can also be expressed conveniently in terms of kinetic energy H of the rotor at synchronous speed. Here H, in joules or watt-secs, is given by

$$H = \frac{1}{2}J\omega_{sm}^2 = \frac{1}{2}J(2\pi n_s)^2 \text{ or } J = \frac{2H}{(2\pi n_s)^2}$$

$\therefore$ $$P_j = 2\pi n_s\cdot\frac{2}{P}\cdot\frac{2H}{(2\pi n_s)^2} = \frac{4H}{2\pi P\cdot n_s}$$

But $n_s = \frac{2f}{P}$. This gives $P_j = \frac{4H}{2\pi P}\cdot\frac{P}{2f} = \frac{H}{\pi f} = \frac{2H}{\omega}$ ...[4.188 (*a*)]

where ω = synchronous angular velocity in electrical radians per second.

(*b*) **Generator operation.** In a generator, electric power flows out of it. Likewise electric torque T_e, corresponding to electric power, flows out of the generator, T_e should, therefore, be treated as negative. In view of this, Eq. (4.184) becomes ;

$$T_{iner} + T_e = T_{sh}$$

Here $T_m = T_{sh}$, is the mechanical torque input to the generator.

Also $$P_{iner} + P_e = P_{sh} \quad ...(4.189)$$

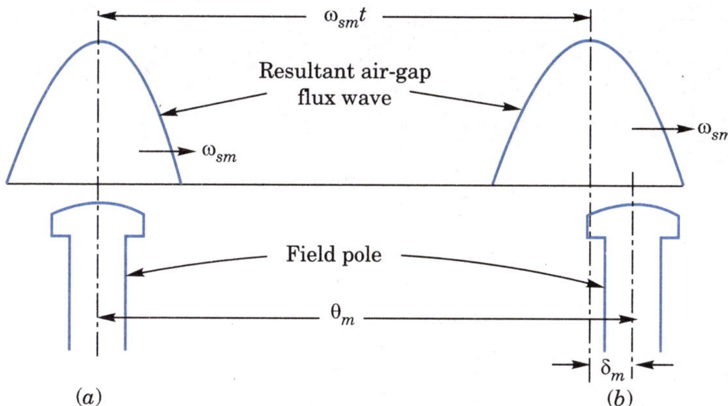

Fig. 4.54: For synchronous generator, the space angle between the axes of resultant air-gap flux wave and field pole is (*a*) zero at $t = 0$ and (*b*) δ_m at any time *t* after the disturbance.

Assume again that at time $t = 0$, the field-pole axis coincides with the axis of resultant air-gap flux wave at no-load, Fig. 4.54 (*a*). A sudden increase in the shaft power input P_{sh}, will take the field-pole axis ahead of the air-gap flux axis, by an angle δ_m, Fig. 4.54 (*b*), such that,

$$\theta_m = \omega_{sm} t + \delta_m$$

or rotor speed, $$\frac{d\theta_m}{dt} = \omega_{sm} + \frac{2}{P}\frac{d\delta}{dt} \quad \text{and} \quad \frac{d^2\theta_m}{dt^2} = \frac{2}{P}\frac{d^2\delta}{dt^2}$$

Here $\dfrac{d\theta_m}{dt} - \omega_{sm} = \dfrac{2}{P}\dfrac{d\delta}{dt}$, is the slip speed, because rotor speed is greater than the synchronous speed ω_{sm}.

Now $$P_{iner} = \omega_{sm} J \frac{d^2\theta_m}{dt^2}$$

$$= \left(2\pi n_s \cdot \frac{2}{P} J\right)\frac{d^2\delta}{dt^2} = P_j \frac{d^2\delta}{dt^2} \qquad \text{...(4.190)}$$

Substituting the value of P_{iner} from Eq. (4.190) in Eq. (4.189), we get

$$P_j \frac{d^2\delta}{dt^2} + P_e = P_{sh} \qquad \text{...(4.191)}$$

Note that Eq. (4.188) for a synchronous motor and Eq. (4.191) for an alternator are identical.

In both the Eqs. (4.188) and (4.191), the electric power P_e has two components. One component, called synchronous power, is due to the presence of load angle δ between E_f and V_t. For a synchronous machine connected with an infinite bus, the synchronous power is given by Eqs. (4.58), (4.62) or (4.72) in the steady state and Eqs. (4.180) or (4.181) in the transient state. The use of any of these equations depends upon the type of synchronous machine and the nature of the electrical network connected to it. For transients of the order of transient-time constant T_d' or shorter, the transient power-angle characteristic given by Eq. (4.180) or (4.181) should be used. When Eq. (4.181) is used, Eq. (4.192) should be written in terms of δ_i. For simplicity the synchronous power as given by Eq. (4.62) is considered here.

The second component of P_e is due to the difference in angular velocities between rotating air-gap flux wave and the rotor. This slip speed gives rise to the production of induction motor torques in such a direction as to minimise the difference in two angular velocities. This induction-motor torque is called the damping torque T_d, since it tends to damp out the rotor oscillations.

For small values of slips, the damping torque is proportional to slip, *i.e.*, from Eq. (5.32),

$$T_d = \frac{mV_e^2}{2\pi n_s}\frac{s}{r_2}$$

But slip speed $= \dfrac{2}{P}\dfrac{d\delta}{dt}$

$$\therefore \qquad \text{slip } s = \frac{1}{\text{Synchronous speed}} \cdot \frac{2}{P}\frac{d\delta}{dt} = \frac{1}{2\pi n_s}\frac{2}{P}\frac{d\delta}{dt}$$

$$\therefore \qquad T_d = \frac{mV_e^s}{(2\pi n_s)^2}\frac{1}{r_2}\frac{2}{P}\frac{d\delta}{dt}$$

The above expression shows that if large damping torque is required, the resistance r_2 of the damper bars must be low, which can be obtained by using thick damper bars.

$$\text{Damping power} = 2\pi n_s T_d = \frac{mV_e^s}{2\pi n_s}\frac{1}{r_2}\frac{2}{P}\frac{d\delta}{dt} = K_d\frac{d\delta}{dt}$$

where
$$K_d = \left(\frac{mV_e^2}{2\pi n_s}\cdot\frac{1}{r_2}\frac{2}{P}\right)$$

is the electrical damping constant in watts per radian per second.

The electromechanical equation for the synchronous-machine dynamics can be obtained either from Eq. (4.188) or from Eq. (4.191), by noting that P_e has two components. Therefore, the required electromechanical equation is,

$$P_j\frac{d^2\delta}{dt^2} + K_d\frac{d\delta}{dt} + P_m \sin\delta = P_{sh} \qquad ...(4.192)$$

where $P_m = \dfrac{E_f V_t}{X_s}$

In Eq. (4.192) note that the synchronous machine is assumed to be connected to an infinite bus.

In Eq. (4.192), $P_m \sin\delta$ is not a linear function of δ, therefore, this equation can't be solved so easily; however, for small angular rotor oscillations, it can be linearized and the analysis can be carried out as illustrated below.

Linearized Analysis. Under steady state, Eq. (4.192) reduces to,

$$P_m \sin\delta_o = P_{sh} \qquad ...(4.193)$$

where δ_o is the load angle at which the synchronous machine is operating under steady-state conditions.

Let the shaft power (shaft power input in case of alternator or shaft loading in case of synchronous motor) be increased from steady value of P_{sh} to $P_{sh} + \Delta P_{sh}$, where ΔP_{sh} is small incremental power on the shaft. Then, for maintaining the power balance, steady load angle δ_o must increase to $\delta_o + \Delta\delta$.

Substituting these changes in Eq. (4.192), we get

$$P_j \frac{d^2(\delta_o + \Delta\delta)}{dt^2} + K_d \frac{d^2(\delta_o + \Delta\delta)}{dt} + P_m \sin(\delta_o + \Delta\delta) = P_{sh} + \Delta P_{sh} \quad ...(4.194)$$

Subtraction of Eq. (4.193) from Eq. (4.194) gives,

$$P_j \frac{d^2(\Delta\delta)}{dt^2} + K_d \frac{d(\Delta\delta)}{dt} + P_m [\sin(\delta_o + \Delta\delta) - \sin\delta_o] = \Delta P_{sh} \quad ...(4.195)$$

In Eq. (4.194), note that

$$P_j \frac{d^2(\delta_o + \Delta\delta)}{dt^2} = P_j \frac{d^2\delta_o}{dt^2} + P_j \frac{d^2\Delta\delta}{dt^2} = 0 + P_j \frac{d^2\Delta\delta}{dt^2}$$

Now $\sin(\delta_o + \Delta\delta) = \sin\delta_o \cos\Delta\delta + \cos\delta_o \sin\Delta\delta$.

For small angular swings ; $\Delta\delta \to 0$

$\therefore$ $\sin\Delta\delta \to \Delta\delta$ and $\cos\Delta\delta \to 1$.

$\therefore$ $[\sin(\delta_o + \Delta\delta) - \sin\delta_o] = (\sin\delta_o + \Delta\delta\cos\delta_o - \sin\delta_o) = \Delta\delta\cos\delta_o$.

$\therefore$ Eq. (4.195) reduces to

$$P_j \frac{d^2(\Delta\delta)}{(dt^2)} + K_d \frac{d(\Delta\delta)}{dt} + \Delta\delta P_m \cos\delta_o = \Delta P_{sh} \quad ...(4.196)$$

For the operating load angle δ_o,

$$\frac{d}{d\delta_o}\left(\frac{E_f V_t}{X_s}\sin\delta_o\right) = P_m \cos\delta_o = P_s,$$

synchronous power per electrical radian

Eq. (4.196) can, therefore, be re-written as,

$$P_j \frac{d^2(\Delta\delta)}{dt^2} + K_d \frac{d(\Delta\delta)}{dt} + P_s \,.\, \Delta\delta = \Delta P_{sh} \quad ...(4.197)$$

Eq. (4.197) is a second order linear differential equation and may be written as,

$$(P_j p^2 + K_{dp} + P_s)\,\Delta\delta = \Delta P_{sh}$$

or

$$\left(p^2 + \frac{K_d}{P_j}p + \frac{P_s}{P_j}\right)\Delta\delta = \frac{\Delta P_{sh}}{P_j} \quad ...(4.198)$$

where $p = \frac{d}{dt}$

It is usually convenient to write Eq. (4.198) as

$$(p^2 + 2\xi\omega_n p + \omega_n^2)\,\Delta\delta = \frac{\Delta P_{sh}}{P_j} \quad ...(4.199)$$

and the reason for doing this is that the quantities involved in this equation have definite physical significance, as will be explained a little later.

A comparison of Eqs. (4.198) and (4.199) gives,

$$\omega_n^2 = \frac{P_s}{P_j} \quad \text{or} \quad \omega_n = \sqrt{\frac{P_s}{P_j}} \quad ...(4.200)$$

and

$$\xi = \frac{1}{2}\frac{K_d}{\sqrt{P_j P_s}} \quad ...(4.201)$$

The solution of Eq. (4.199) consists of two parts, complementary function and the particular integral.

Complementary function. This gives the transient part of the solution and is obtained by solving the equation,

$$(p^2 + 2\xi\omega_n p + \omega_n{}^2)\,\Delta\delta = 0 \qquad ...(4.202)$$

Eq. (4.202) is called a force free equation, since the forcing function ΔP_{sh} is zero. Its solution characterises the natural free oscillations of the synchronous machine.

The solution of Eq. (4.202) is of the type,

$$\Delta\delta = Ae^{p_1 t} + Be^{p_2 t}$$

where p_1, p_2 are the roots of the auxiliary equation,

$P^2 + 2\xi\omega_n p + \omega_n{}^2 = 0$ and these roots are

$$p_1, p_2 = -\xi\omega_n \pm \omega_n\sqrt{\xi^2 - 1}$$

$$\therefore \qquad (\Delta\delta)_{C.F.} = Ae^{p_1 t} + Be^{p_2 t}$$

Particular integral. This gives the steady-state solution and is obtained from Eq. (4.199) by putting $p = 0$.

$$\therefore \qquad \Delta\delta\,.\,\omega_n^2 = \frac{\Delta P_{sh}}{P_j} \qquad \text{or} \qquad (\Delta\delta)_{P.I.} = \frac{\Delta P_{sh}}{P_j}\cdot\frac{1}{\omega_n^2} = \frac{\Delta P_{sh}}{P_s}$$

The complete solution of Eq. (4.198) is

$$\Delta\delta(t) = (\Delta\delta)_{C.F.} + (\Delta\delta)_{P.I.}$$

$$= Ae^{p_1 t} + Be^{p_2 t} + \frac{\Delta P_{sh}}{P_s} \qquad ...(4.203)$$

The constants A and B can be obtained from the initial conditions at $t = 0+$.

$$\text{Damping power} \qquad = K_d\,\frac{d(\Delta\delta)}{dt}$$

Just before the load increment, *i.e.* at $t = 0-$, load angle is δ_o. Just after the load increment, *i.e.* at $t = 0+$, load angle must remain at its initial value δ_o due to inertia of the rotating system. In case load angle at $t = 0+$ increases to $\delta_o + \Delta\delta$, then

$$\frac{\Delta\delta}{[\text{time at } t = 0+] - [\text{time at } t = 0-]}$$

would be infinite and as a result, damping power $K_d\,\dfrac{d(\Delta\delta)}{dt}$ would be infinite which is not feasible. Thus, the load angle both at $t = 0-$ and at $t = 0+$ remains δ_o and the initial condition is that at $t = 0+$, $\Delta\delta = 0$.

$$\text{Inertia power} = P_j\,\frac{d^2(\Delta\delta)}{dt^2} = P_j\,\frac{d}{dt}\left[\frac{d(\Delta\delta)}{dt}\right]$$

Here $d(\Delta\delta)/dt$ represents the departure of rotor speed from synchronous speed. Since a finite change of $\dfrac{d(\Delta\delta)}{dt}$ in zero time (from $t = 0-$ to $t = 0+$) would amount to infinite inertia power which is impossible, the rotor speed can't depart from synchronous speed in the time interval from $t = 0-$ to $t = 0+$. Consequently rotor speed remains constant at synchronous speed at $t = 0+$ also. Thus at $t = 0+$, $\frac{d(\Delta\delta)}{dt} = 0$. Hence the initial conditions are that at $t = 0+$, $\Delta\delta = 0$ and $\frac{d(\Delta\delta)}{dt} = 0$.

The solution of Eq. (4.199) depends upon the value of damping ratio ξ which may be less than, equal to, or greater than unity. For different values of ξ, the solution of Eq. (4.199) is as under :

$0 < \xi < 1$: For ξ more than zero but less than one, $\sqrt{\xi^2 - 1}$ is an imaginary term, therefore the two roots of characteristic or auxiliary equation are

$$p_1, p_2 = -\xi\omega_n \pm j\omega_n\sqrt{1-\xi^2}$$

$$\therefore \quad \Delta\delta(t) = C.F. + P.I. = e^{-\xi\omega_n t}\left[Ae^{j\omega_n t\sqrt{1-\xi^2}} + Be^{-j\omega_n t\sqrt{1-\xi^2}}\right] + \frac{\Delta P_{sh}}{P_s}$$

or

$$\Delta\delta(t) = e^{-\xi\omega_n t}\left[(A+B)\cos(\omega_n t\sqrt{1-\xi^2}) + j(A-B)\sin(\omega_n t\sqrt{1-\xi^2})\right] + \frac{\Delta P_{sh}}{P_s} \quad ...(4.204)$$

Incorporating the initial conditions in Eq. (4.204), the values of $(A + B)$ and $(A - B)$ can be obtained as follows :

At $t = 0$, $\Delta\delta = 0$. This gives $(A + B) = -\frac{\Delta P_{sh}}{P_s}$

Also at $t = 0$, $\frac{d(\Delta\delta)}{dt} = 0$. This gives $j(A - B) = -\frac{\Delta P_{sh}}{P_s}\cdot\frac{\xi}{\sqrt{1-\xi^2}}$

Substitution of these values in Eq. (4.204) gives

$$\Delta\delta(t) = \frac{\Delta P_{sh}}{P_s}\left[1 - e^{-\xi\omega_n t}\left\{\cos(\omega_n t\sqrt{1-\xi^2}) + \frac{\xi}{\sqrt{1-\xi^2}}\sin(\omega_n t\sqrt{1-\xi^2})\right\}\right] \quad ...(4.205)$$

It is well known that

$$A\cos\omega t + B\sin\omega t = \sqrt{A^2 + B^2}\sin\left(\omega t + \tan^{-1}\frac{A}{B}\right)$$

Eq. (4.205) can therefore be written as

$$\Delta\delta(t) = \frac{\Delta P_{sh}}{P_s}\left[1 - \frac{e^{-\xi\omega_n t}}{\sqrt{1-\xi^2}}\left\{\sqrt{1-\xi^2}\,.\cos(\omega_n t\sqrt{1-\xi^2}) + \xi\,.\sin(\omega_n t\sqrt{1-\xi^2})\right\}\right] \quad ...(4.206)$$

If $\tan\phi = \frac{\sqrt{1-\xi^2}}{\xi}$, then $\sin\phi = \sqrt{1-\xi^2}$ and $\cos\phi = \xi$. With this, Eq. (4.206) becomes

$$\Delta\delta(t) = \frac{\Delta P_{sh}}{P_s}\left[1 - \frac{e^{-\xi\omega_n t}}{\sqrt{1-\xi^2}}\left\{\sin\phi\,.\cos(\omega_n t\sqrt{1-\xi^2}) + \cos\phi\sin(\omega_n t\sqrt{1-\xi^2})\right\}\right]$$

$$= \frac{\Delta P_{sh}}{P_s}\left[1 - \frac{e^{-\xi\omega_n t}}{\sqrt{1-\xi^2}}\sin(\omega_n t\sqrt{1-\xi^2} + \phi)\right]$$

Before the disturbance, the load angle is δ_0.

$\therefore$ $$\delta(t) = \delta_0 + \Delta\delta(t)$$

or $$\delta(t) = \delta_0 + \frac{\Delta P_{sh}}{P_s}\left[1 - \frac{e^{-\xi\omega_n t}}{\sqrt{1-\xi^2}} \sin\left(\omega_n t\sqrt{1-\xi^2} + \phi\right)\right] \qquad ...(4.207)$$

For investigating the nature of ω_n, take damping ratio $\xi = 0$ in Eq. (4.207). With this, the value of load angle at any time t is given by,

$$\delta(t) = \delta_0 + \frac{\Delta P_{sh}}{P_s}\left[1 - \sin\left(\omega_n t + \frac{\pi}{2}\right)\right]$$

$$= \delta_0 + \frac{\Delta P_{sh}}{P_s}[1 - \cos \omega_n t] \qquad ...(4.208)$$

Eq. (4.208) gives the variation of load angle δ after a sudden increment of shaft power and this is sketched in Fig. 4.55. This figure reveals that the rotor oscillations continue unbated, since ξ or K_d has been neglected.

The frequency of rotor oscillations (sometimes called hunting) is determined by ω_n and since ξ (or K_d) is zero, ω_n is called the *undamped natural angular frequency* of the synchronous machine. Note that ω_n is associated with the term $\cos \omega_n t$.

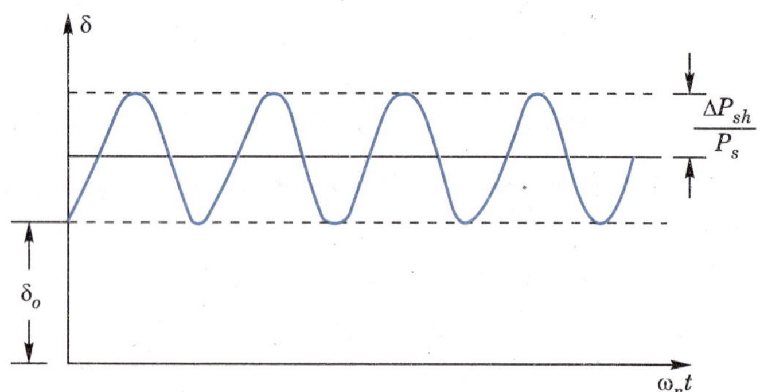

Fig. 4.55: Variation of load angle δ, with sudden increase in shaft power, ξ is neglected.

From Eq. (4.200), $$\omega_n = \sqrt{\frac{P_s}{P_j}}$$

and $$f_n = \frac{1}{2\pi}\sqrt{\frac{P_s}{P_j}} \qquad ...(4.209)$$

where f_n is the undamped nature frequency in Hz. The natural period of rotor oscillation or rotor swing is

$$t_n = \frac{1}{f_n} = 2\pi\sqrt{\frac{P_j}{P_s}} \qquad ...(4.210)$$

$\xi = 1$: $p_1, p_2 = -\omega_n$. The general form of the complementary function is

$$(\Delta\delta)_{C.F.} = (A + Bt)\, e^{-\omega_n t} \quad \text{and} \quad (\Delta\delta)_{P.I.} = \frac{\Delta P_{sh}}{P_s}$$

$\therefore$ $$\Delta\delta(t) = (A + Bt)\, e^{-\omega_n t} + \frac{\Delta P_{sh}}{P_s}$$

Incorporating the initial conditions,

$$A = -\frac{\Delta P_{sh}}{P_s} \quad \text{and} \quad B = -\omega_n \frac{\Delta P_{sh}}{P_s}$$

$$\therefore \qquad \Delta\delta(t) = \frac{\Delta P_{sh}}{P_s}\left[1 - e^{-\omega_n t}(1 + \omega_n t)\right]$$

and

$$\delta(t) = \delta_0 + \frac{\Delta P_{sh}}{P_s}\left[1 - e^{-\omega_n t}(1 + \omega_n t)\right] \qquad ...(4.211)$$

$\xi >> 1$:

$$p_1, p_2 = -\omega_n \xi \pm \omega_n \sqrt{\xi^2 - 1}$$

$$\therefore \qquad \Delta\delta = Ae^{p_1 t} + Be^{p_2 t} + \frac{\Delta P_{sh}}{P_s}$$

With the initial conditions,

$$A = -\frac{\xi + \sqrt{\xi^2 - 1}}{2\sqrt{\xi^2 - 1}} \cdot \frac{\Delta P_{sh}}{P_s} \quad \text{and} \quad B = +\frac{\xi - \sqrt{\xi^2 - 1}}{2\sqrt{\xi^2 - 1}} \cdot \frac{\Delta P_{sh}}{P_s}$$

$$\therefore \qquad \delta(t) = \frac{\Delta P_{sh}}{P_s}\left[1 - \frac{\xi + \sqrt{\xi^2 - 1}}{2\sqrt{\xi^2 - 1}} \cdot \exp\left\{-\omega_n t\left(\xi - \sqrt{\xi^2 - 1}\right)\right\} + \frac{\xi - \sqrt{\xi^2 - 1}}{2\sqrt{\xi^2 - 1}} \exp\left\{-\omega_n t\left(\xi + \sqrt{\xi^2 - 1}\right)\right\}\right] \qquad ...(4.212)$$

Eq. (4.207) reveals that if ξ is present, then the angular frequency of oscillations, as seen from the term

$$\sin\left(\sqrt{1 - \xi^2} \,.\, \omega_n t + \phi\right), \text{ is } \omega_n \sqrt{1 - \xi^2} = \omega_d.$$

This is called the *damped natural angular frequency* of rotor oscillations of the synchronous machine and ξ is known as the *damping ratio*, which is a dimensionless quantity.

Eqs. (4.207), (4.208), (4.211) and (4.212) are plotted in Fig. 4.56 for different values of damping ratio ξ and it is seen that the magnitude of oscillations can be controlled by varying ξ.

The values of ξ (or K_d); as stated before, can be increased by using large cross-sectional damper bars. This will decrease the magnitude of rotor oscillations.

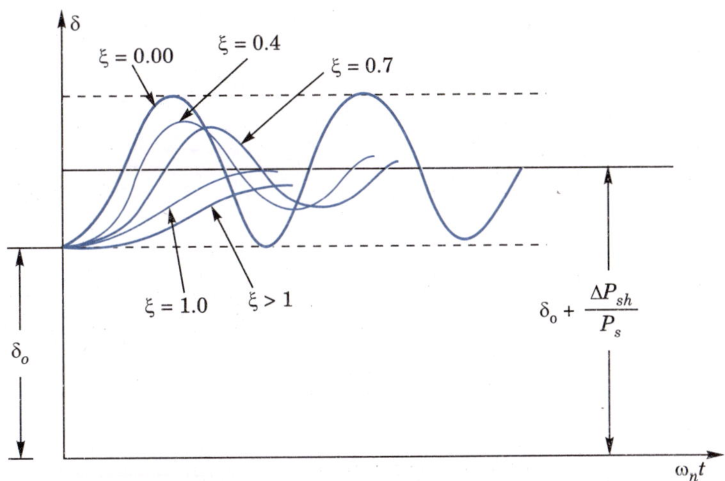

Fig. 4.56: Variation of load angle with different values of ξ, for a sudden increment of shaft power in a synchronous machine.

When there is a slight difference in ω_d and ω_n (for small values of ξ), then an increase of ξ produces only a marginal decrease in ω_d. In such cases, an increase of the inertia (*i.e.*, P_j) will reduce the values of both ω_n and ω_d appreciably. A lower value of ω_d gives reduced frequency of the rotor oscillations.

Thus, rotor oscillations accompanied by a sudden disturbance, can be minimised by (*i*) using thicker damper bars and (*ii*) increasing J, the moment of inertia of the rotating parts. Examination of Eq. (4.200) shows that a suitable value of synchronizing power P_s is also helpful in guarding against the undesirable phenomenon of rotor oscillations, called hunting.

Note that the damper bars have no effect on the steady-state operation of a synchronous machine. These come into play only when rotor speed departs from synchronous speed. The moment of inertia J can be increased by using a flywheel and the synchronizing power P_s can be controlled at the design stage.

4.17.2 Cyclic Variations of Shaft Torque (or Forced Oscillations)

An alternator driven by an internal combustion engine or a synchronous motor driving a reciprocating compressor is subjected to variable shaft torques. The variable torque is equivalent to an average torque plus a large variety of harmonic torques. If any one of the harmonic-torque components has a frequency approaching f_n, the amplitude of rotor oscillations increase and the machine may fall out of step. Such a state of affairs must be carefully investigated. If the frequency f_n differs by more than 25% from the frequency of forced oscillations, it is then assumed that stable operation remains uneffected.

Let the harmonic-torque component of variable shaft torque be represented by $T_{L_m} \sin \omega_L \cdot t$; where T_{L_m} is the maximum amplitude of harmonic torque and its angular frequency is ω_L. Also, (synchronous speed of machine) $(T_{L_m} \sin \omega_L . t) = P_{L_m} \sin \omega_L . t$.

The oscillations in the load angle, caused by this harmonic component of torque, can be obtained from Eq. (4.197). Therefore, the differential equation of motion governing the performance of synchronous machines under forced oscillations is

$$P_j \frac{d^2(\Delta\delta)}{dt^2} + K_d \frac{d(\Delta\delta)}{dt} + P_s \Delta\delta = P_{Lm} \sin \omega_L . t$$

or

$$\frac{d^2(\Delta\delta)}{dt^2} + \frac{K_d}{P_j} \cdot \frac{d(\Delta\delta)}{dt} + \frac{P_s}{P_j} \Delta\delta = \frac{P_{Lm}}{P_j} \sin \omega_L . t$$

or

$$\frac{d^2(\Delta\delta)}{dt^2} + 2\xi\omega_n \frac{d(\Delta\delta)}{dt} + \omega_n^2 \Delta\delta = \frac{P_{Lm}}{P_j} \sin \omega_L . t \qquad ...(4.213)$$

where, as before, $\omega_n = \sqrt{\dfrac{P_s}{P_j}}$ and $\xi = \dfrac{1}{2} \dfrac{K_d}{\sqrt{P_s P_j}}$

Since the harmonic torque persists for a long time, only steady state solution is important, which in phasor form, can be obtained by putting $\dfrac{d}{dt} = j\omega_L$, as it is done in case of a.c. circuits.

The maximum amplitude of oscillation, in phasor form, from Eq. (4.213), is

$$\Delta\delta = \frac{P_{Lm}}{P_j} \frac{1}{(\omega_n^2 - \omega_L^2) + 2j\xi\omega_n\omega_L} \qquad ...(4.214)$$

The amplitude of oscillation is,

$$|\,\Delta\delta\,| = \frac{P_{Lm}}{P_j} \frac{1}{\sqrt{(\omega_n^2 - \omega_L^2)^2 + (2\xi\omega_n\omega_L)^2}} \qquad ...(4.215)$$

If $\omega_n = \omega_L$, the amplitude of swing becomes maximum and the machine may loose synchronism. Under this condition, the amplitude of swing is,

$$|\Delta\delta| = \frac{P_{Lm}}{P_j} \cdot \frac{1}{2\xi\omega_n^2}$$

For a given value of $\Delta\delta$, the corresponding change in synchronous power is $|\Delta\delta| . P_s$ watts.

Example 4.17. *A 1000 kW, 6.6 kV, 50 Hz, 20 pole synchronous motor has the following characteristics:*

Total moment of inertia, $J = 2480$ kg m^2

Synchronizing power co-efficient, $P_s = 40$ kW/elec. degree.

Damping power co-efficient, $K_d = 2$ kW/elec. deg/sec.

(a) Calculate (i) the undamped natural frequency and the natural period of oscillations and (ii) the damped natural frequency of oscillations.

(b) Assume the motor to be running unloaded and under steady state. Investigate the nature of oscillations after a shaft load of 600 kW is suddenly applied.

(c) Now assume the motor to be coupled with a reciprocating compressor, whose first-order harmonic torque component has an amplitude of 10,000 Nm and an angular frequency of 17.15 rad/sec. Under these conditions, calculate the amplitue of swing and the corresponding change in synchronous power.

(d) Repeat part (c) for $J = 4960$ kg m^2 and compare the results.

(e) Repeat part (c) for $K_d = 4$ kW/elec. deg./sec.

Solution. (*a*)
$$n_s = \frac{2f}{P} = \frac{2 \times 50}{20} = 5 \text{ r.p.s.}$$

From Eq. (4.190),
$$P_j = 2\pi n_s \cdot \frac{2}{P} \cdot J$$

$$= 2\pi\,(5)\left(\frac{2}{20}\right)(2480) \text{ watts/elec. rad/sec}^2$$

$$= 2\pi\,(5)\left(\frac{2}{20}\right)(2480)\left(\frac{\pi}{180}\right) = 136 \text{ watts/elec. deg./sec}^2.$$

From Eq. (4.200),
$$\omega_n = \sqrt{\frac{P_s}{P_j}} = \sqrt{\frac{40{,}000}{136}} = 17.15 \text{ rad./sec.}$$

$$f_n = \frac{17.15}{2\pi} \text{ Hz.} \qquad \text{and} \quad t_n = \frac{1}{f_n} = \frac{2\pi}{17.15} = 0.3665 \text{ sec.}$$

From Eq. (4.201),
$$\xi = \frac{K_d}{2\sqrt{P_j P_s}} = \frac{1}{2}\frac{2000}{\sqrt{(136)(40{,}000)}} = 0.429$$

∴ Damped natural frequency of oscillations is,

$$\omega_d = \omega_n\sqrt{1-\xi^2}$$

$$= 17.15\sqrt{1-(0.429)^2} = 15.49 \text{ rad/sec.}$$

(*b*) Since $\xi < 1$, Eq. (4.207) holds good,

$$\frac{\Delta P_{sh}}{P_s} = \frac{600}{40} = 15°,$$

$$\phi = \tan^{-1}\frac{\sqrt{1-\xi^2}}{\xi} = \tan^{-1}(2.11) = 64.6°$$

$$\xi\omega_n = (0.429)\,(17.15) = 7.36.$$

Substitution of these values in Eq. (4.207) gives the nature of rotor oscillations as,

$$\Delta\delta(t) = 15°[1 - 1.107e^{-7.36t} \,.\, \sin(15.49t + 64.6°)]$$

Since the motor is running initially at no load, the power angle δ_0 is taken as zero.

(*c*) From Eq. (4.214), the amplitude of swing is given by,

$$\Delta\delta = \frac{P_{Lm}}{P_j}\,\frac{1}{\omega_n^2 - \omega_L^2 + 2j\xi\omega_n\omega_L}$$

$$= \frac{(10{,}000)\,(2\pi 5)}{136} \cdot \frac{1}{0 + j2\,(0.429)\,(17.15)^2}$$

$\therefore$ $$|\,\Delta\delta\,| = 9.15°.$$

Change in synchronous power = $P_s \,.\, \Delta\delta = 40 \times 9.15 = 366$ kW.

(*d*) Since moment of inertia is now doubled,

$$P_j = 272 \text{ watts/elec. deg./sec}^2.$$

$$\omega_n = \sqrt{\frac{P_s}{P_j}} = \sqrt{\frac{40{,}000}{272}} = 12.12 \text{ rad/sec.}$$

$$\xi = \frac{1}{2}\,\frac{2000}{\sqrt{(272)\,(40{,}000)}} = 0.303.$$

$\therefore$ $$\Delta\delta = \frac{(10{,}000)\,(2\pi 5)}{272} \cdot \frac{1}{\sqrt{[147 - 294]^2 + [2(0.303)\,(17.15)\,(12.12)]^2}}$$

$$= \frac{(10{,}000)\,(2\pi 5)}{(272)\,(193.5)} = 5.97°$$

$\therefore$ Change in synchronous power = $40 \times 5.97 = 238.8$ kW.

It is seen from parts (*c*) and (*d*) that with increased moment of inertia *J*, both the maximum deviation of load angle and the pulsation in synchronous power have decreased, which is advantageous.

(*e*) $$K_d = 4 \text{ kW/elec. deg./sec}^2.$$

$$\omega_n = 17.15 \text{ rad/sec.}$$

$$\xi = \frac{1}{2}\,\frac{4000}{\sqrt{(136)\,(40{,}000)}} = 0.858.$$

$\therefore$ $$\Delta\delta = \frac{(10{,}000)\,(2\pi 5)}{136} \cdot \frac{1}{2(0.858)\,(17.15)^2} = 4.58°$$

Part (*e*) shows that for the same value of *J*, if K_d is doubled, the amplitude of deviation in power angle is halved.

Example 4.18. *A 10 MVA., 11 kV, 3-phase, 8 pole, star-connected alternator is synchronized with an infinite bus. When operating at rated load and at unity power factor, its normal period of oscillations is 1.4 sec. Its synchronous reactance is 20%. Compute the moment of inertia of its rotating parts.*

Solution. Per-phase terminal voltage, $V_t = \frac{11{,}000}{\sqrt{3}} = 6351$ V.

Per-phase armature current,

$$I_a = \frac{10{,}000}{\sqrt{3}(11)} = 524.33 \text{ A.}$$

Percentage reactance, $X_s = \frac{X_s \text{ in ohms}}{\frac{V_t}{I_a}} \times 100.$

$$\therefore \qquad X_s \text{ in ohms} = \frac{20}{100} \times \frac{6351}{524.88} = 2.42\ \Omega$$

With V_t as reference, $\bar{E}_f = \bar{V}_t + j\bar{I}_a X_s$

$$= 6351 + j(524.88)(2.42) = 6351 + j1270.21$$

or

$$E_f = 6476.8 \angle 11.31°$$

Synchronizing power, $P_s = 3\frac{E_f \,.\, V_t}{X_s} \,.\, \cos\delta = 3\ \frac{(6476.8)\,(6351)}{2.42} \cos 11.31°$

$$= 50{,}002{,}497 \text{ watts per elect. rad.}$$

Inertia power, $P_j = 2\pi n_s \frac{2}{P} \,.\, J$

$$= 2\pi\,(12.5)\,\frac{2}{8} \,.\, J = 19.64 \text{ J w/elec. rad/sec}^2.$$

From Eq. (4.210), $t_n = 2\pi\sqrt{\frac{P_j}{P_s}} = 2\pi\sqrt{\frac{19.64 \times J}{50{,}002{,}497}} = 1.4$ sec.

$$\therefore \qquad J = \left(\frac{1.4}{2\pi}\right)^2 \frac{50{,}002{,}497}{19.64} = 126{,}399.6 \text{ kg m}^2.$$

Example 4.19. *A 3-phase cylindrical rotor synchronous machine is connected with an infinite bus. Show that its natural period of oscillations at no-load is given by*

$$t_n = 12.86\sqrt{\frac{Jn_s}{V_t I_{sc} P}}$$

Here V_t and I_{sc} are the per phase terminal voltage and steady-state short-circuit current respectively. J is the moment of inertia, P is the number of poles and n_s is the synchronous speed in r.p.s.

Solution. From Eq. (4.210), the natural period of oscillations is,

$$t_n = 2\pi\sqrt{\frac{P_j}{P_s}}$$

Synchronizing power co-efficient

$$P_s = 3\frac{E_f V_t}{X_s}\cos\delta.$$

Under no-load conditions, load angle δ is very small. In view of this, cos δ → 1.

$$\therefore \qquad P_s = 3\frac{E_f}{X_s}\,.\,V_t = 3I_{sc}V_t \text{ watts/elec. rad.}$$

$$P_j = 2\pi n_s\,.\,\frac{2}{P}\,.\,J \text{ watts/elec. rad./sec}^2$$

Substitution of the values of P_s and P_j in the expression for t_n gives,

$$t_n = 2\pi\sqrt{\frac{2\pi n_s\, 2J}{P\,.\,3I_{sc}V_t}} = 12.86\sqrt{\frac{n_s J}{PI_{sc}V_t}}$$

4.18 LARGE ANGULAR OSCILLATIONS

For small angular oscillations, it is permissible to linearize Eq. (4.192), but for large oscillations it is necessary to deal with Eq. (4.192) in its non-linear form. By the use of analog or digital computers, this non-linear differential equation can be analysed.

If the damping power in a synchronous machine is neglected and the machine is assumed connected to an infinite bus, then the electromechanical differential Eq. (4.192) reduces to

$$P_j\frac{d^2\delta}{dt^2} + P_m\sin\delta = P_{sh} \qquad \text{...(4.216)}$$

Eq. (4.216) is sometimes called the **swing-equation** of a synchronous machine. From this equation,

$$\frac{d^2\delta}{dt^2} = \frac{P_{sh} - P_m\sin\delta}{P_j}$$

Multiplying both sides of above equation by $\frac{d\delta}{dt}$, we get

$$\frac{d^2\delta}{dt^2}\left(\frac{d\delta}{dt}\right) = \left(\frac{P_{sh} - P_m\sin\delta}{P_j}\right)\cdot\frac{d\delta}{dt}$$

or

$$\frac{1}{2}\cdot\frac{d}{dt}\left(\frac{d\delta}{dt}\right)^2 = \left(\frac{P_{sh} - P_m\sin\delta}{P_j}\right)\cdot\frac{d\delta}{dt}$$

or

$$d\left(\frac{d\delta}{dt}\right)^2 = \frac{2(P_{sh} - P_m\sin\delta)}{P_j}\,d\delta$$

On integration, the above equation gives

$$\frac{d\delta}{dt} = \sqrt{\int\frac{2(P_{sh} - P_m\sin\delta)}{P_j}\,d\delta}$$

Here $d\delta/dt$ is the relative velocity between the stator and rotor fields. Since the machine runs at synchronous speed before any disturbance, the relative velocity $d\delta/dt$ must be zero.

After sudden disturbance, the relative velocity $d\delta/dt$ begins to increase from zero. At some time after the disturbance if relative velocity $d\delta/dt$ becomes zero, the rotor attains synchronous speed and the stability is maintained. In other words, when $d\delta/dt$ becomes zero for the first time after the disturbance, δ stops increasing and subsequently it starts to decrease indicating a stable operation. This fact that δ stops increasing (*i.e.*, the relative velocity $d\delta/dt$ becomes zero) for the first time after disturbance, may be taken to indicate stability, though actually the rotor will come to stable equilibrium position only after some oscillations. Thus the condition for stability during large angular oscillations is that,

$$\frac{d\delta}{dt} = 0 \qquad \text{or} \qquad \sqrt{\int \frac{2(P_{sh} - P_m \sin\delta)}{P_j}\, d\delta} = 0$$

or
$$\int (P_{sh} - P_m \sin\delta)\, d\delta = 0 \qquad ...(4.217)$$

Consider the use of Eq. (4.217) specifically for a synchronous motor. In Fig. 4.57, for a shaft load of P_{sho}, the load angle at synchronous speed is δ_0, *i.e.*, $P_m \sin\delta_0 = P_{sho}$. As the shaft load is suddenly increased to P_{sha}, the rotor slows down momentarily and load angle begins to rise from δ_0. Consequently, the load angle swings to a maximum value of δ_b, at which instant the rotor speed is again synchronous. For this system to be stable as per Eq. (4.217), we get

$$\int_{\delta_0}^{\delta_b} (P_{sha} - P_m \sin\delta)\, d\delta = 0$$

or
$$\int_{\delta_0}^{\delta_a} (P_{sha} - P_m \sin\delta)\, d\delta + \int_{\delta_a}^{\delta_b} (P_{sha} - P_m \sin\delta)\, d\delta = 0$$

or
$$\int_{\delta_0}^{\delta_a'} (P_{sha} - P_m \sin\delta)\, d\delta = \int_{\delta_a}^{\delta_b} (P_m \sin\delta - P_{sha})\, d\delta \qquad ...(4.218)$$

Fig. 4.57 shows that $\int_{\delta_0}^{\delta_a} (P_{sha} - P_m \sin\delta)\, d\delta$ represents area A_1 and $\int_{\delta_a}^{\delta_b} (P_m \sin\delta - P_{sha})\, d\delta$ represents area A_2.

In view of this, Eq. (4.218) may be written as,

$$\text{Area } A_1 = \text{Area } A_2$$

Thus for maintaining stability for large angular oscillations, area A_2 should be equal to area A_1. This method of determining the transient stability of a synchronous-machine system is called *equal area criterion of stability*.

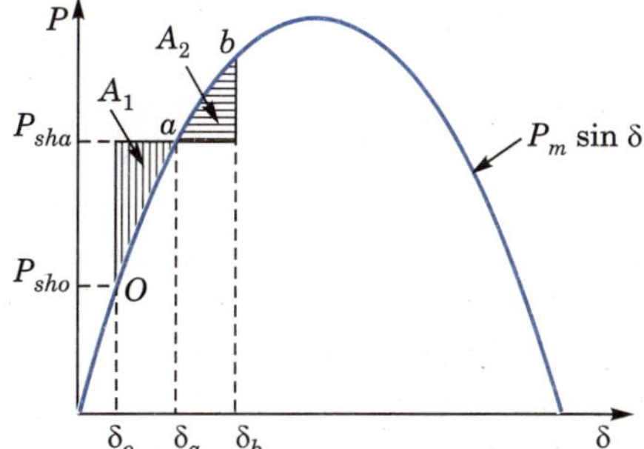

Fig. 4.57: Synchronous motor power-load angle curve and shaft load variation.

Fig. 4.57 can further be analysed to have better appreciation of the conditions prevailing after the sudden increase of shaft load on a synchronous motor connected to an infinite bus.

Initially the motor is operating at synchronous speed with load P_{sho} and load angle δ_0, such that $P_m \sin\delta_0 = P_{sho}$ and relative velocity $\frac{d\delta}{dt} = 0$. Now the shaft load is suddenly increased to a value corresponding to a power output of P_{sha}. To supply this increased power output $\left(E_f, V_t, X_s \text{ assumed constant in } \frac{E_f V_t}{X_s} \sin \delta\right)$, the rotor must momentarily slow down, so that load angle increases beyond δ_0. When load angle first reaches δ_a,

$$P_{sha} = P_m \sin \delta_a$$

and power balance is obtained. But at this operating point a, the speed is still less than synchronous speed. If

$$\int_{\delta_0}^{\delta_a} (P_{sha} - P_m \sin \delta)\, d\delta$$

is divided by synchronous speed, we get

$$\int_{\delta_0}^{\delta_a} (T_{sha} - T_m \sin \delta)\, d\delta$$

Recall that (force) × (linear displacement), *i.e.*, $f_e \cdot dx$ gives the work done and has the units of energy. Similarly for a rotary motion, (torque) × (angular displacement), *i.e.*, $T_e \cdot d\delta$ gives work done and represents energy. Therefore, $\int_{\delta_0}^{\delta_a} (T_{sha} - T_m \sin \delta)\, d\delta$, proportional to $\int_{\delta_0}^{\delta_a} (P_{sha} - P_m \sin \delta)\, d\delta$, gives the total energy extracted from the rotating mass, since in the angular swing $(\delta_a - \delta_0)$ the electrical power is not able to supply the increased output power P_{sha}.

So, at the instant operating point a is reached the speed is less than synchronous speed and at the same time, the rotating mass has suffered a loss of kinetic energy (= area A_1), which of course must be replenished. To do this needful, the operating point travels further and as load angle exceeds δ_a, the electrical power becomes more than P_{sha} and the energy.

$$\int (P_m \sin \delta - P_{sha})\, d\delta$$

gets stored in the rotating mass, the speed increasing at the same time. As soon as the lost kinetic energy is replenished, the synchronous speed is reached and the operating point does not travel further—this is indicated by point b and the load angle δ_b in Fig. 4.57. At the point b, where the rotor speed is synchronous and $d\delta/dt = 0$, the electrical power is greater than P_{sha}, therefore, rotor speed must increase beyond synchronous speed, thereby decreasing the load angle δ. When angle reaches δ_a on its first backward journey from the point b, though power balance is obtained, the speed is more than synchronous speed and, therefore, δ continues to decrease. As soon as δ becomes less than δ_a, the rotor begins to retard (because now P_{sha} is greater than electrical power) and angle δ_0 is reached, where the rotor is again operating at synchronous speed and $d\delta/dt = 0$. This cycle of rotor oscillations continue, at its undamped natural frequency, around the equilibrium load angle δ_a in between angle δ_0 and δ_b. If damping is present, as is usually the case, the subsequent rotor oscillations subside and ultimately the stable equilibrium angle δ_a is reached.

For better physical concepts of the rotor oscillations in a synchronous machine, the pendulum-oscillation analogy must be recalled.

Fig. 4.58 (a) illustrates a pendulum fixed at the pivot and oscillating between the limits o and b. It is obvious that the pendulum velocity is zero at o, b and is maximum at the mid-way point a. Now assume the pivot to coincide with the centre of the rotor shaft rotating clockwise at synchronous speed, Fig. 4.58 (b). When the pendulum moves from o to b, *i.e.*, opposite to the rotor rotation, the resultant speed (= synchronous speed + pendulum speed) is less than the synchronous speed. Keeping the rotor oscillations of Fig. 4.57 in mind, it may be seen that at the points o and b, the resultant speed is synchronous ; from o to a the rotor decelerates to minimum speed at a and from a to b the rotor accelerates to synchronous speed at b. When the pendulum moves from b to o in the direction of rotor rotation, the resultant speed is more than the synchronous speed. Keeping again the rotor oscillations of Fig. 4.57 in mind, it is seen that at the point b and o, the resultant speed is synchronous ; from b to a the rotor accelerates beyond synchronous speed to maximum speed at a and from a to o the rotor decelerates to synchronous speed at the point o. The inherent damping will decrease the subsequent pendulum (*i.e.* the rotor) oscillations about the equilibrium point a.

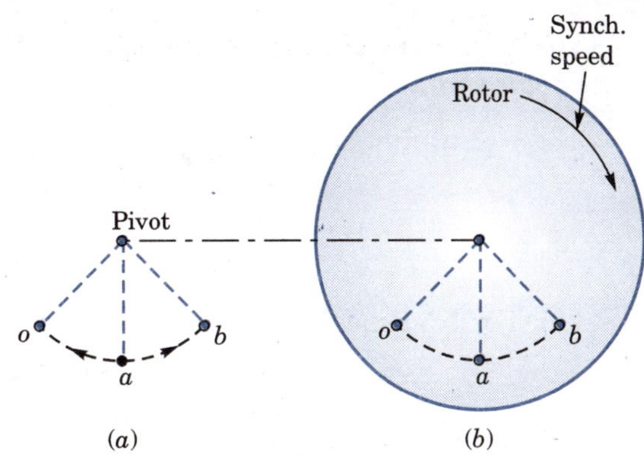

Fig. 4.58: Pendulum-oscillation analogy for rotor oscillations in a synchronous machine.

Suppose the motor to be operating under steady state at a load angle of δ_0 and shaft load of P_{sho}, Fig. 4.59. The shaft load is now suddenly increased to P_{sha} and it is required to find out whether the stability of the system would be maintained or not.

If area A_2 > area A_1, the motor remains in synchronism, *i.e.*, stability is maintained.

If area A_2 = area A_1, the synchronism is just maintained, *i.e.*, it is case of marginal stability.

If area A_2 < area A_1, the motor falls out of step.

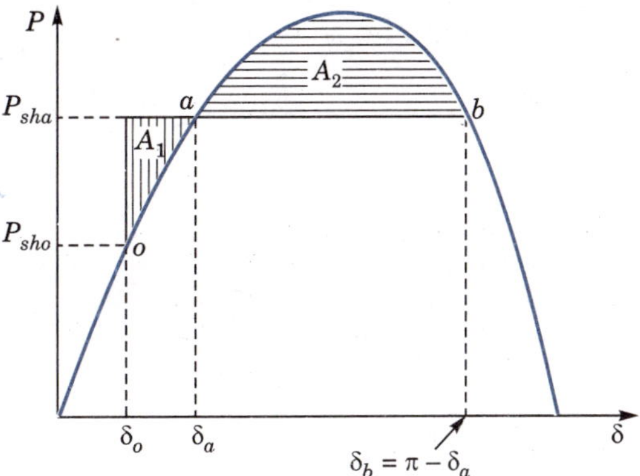

Fig. 4.59: Stability of synchronous motor by equal area criterion.

It may be noted that damping power coefficient K_d has been neglected and hence, if area A_2 is slightly less than area A_1, the motor may not lose synchronism.

Consequently, equal area criterion of transient stability gives pessimistic results.

Example 4.20. *A cylindrical-rotor synchronous motor, connected to an infinite bus, is working under full load conditions with a load angle of 30°.*

(a) If the shaft load is suddenly increased to 1.5 times the full load, determine whether or not the synchronism is maintained.

(b) Determine the maximum additional safe load that can be suddenly thrown on to the motor shaft.

Solution. When working under full-load conditions, from Fig. 4.60 (*a*),

$$P_{sho} = P_m \sin 30° = \frac{P_m}{2}$$

or
$$P_m = 2P_{sho}.$$

(*a*) For 1.5 times full load,

$$1.5P_{sho} = P_m \sin \delta_a = 2P_{sho} \sin \delta_a$$

$\therefore$
$$\delta_a = 48.6°.$$

From Fig. 4.60 (*a*) ;

$$\text{Area } A_1 = \int_{30}^{48.6} (1.5P_{sho} - P_m \sin \delta)\, d\delta$$

$$= P_m \int_{30°}^{48.6°} (0.75 - \sin \delta)\, d\delta = 0.0375\, P_m.$$

$$\text{Area } A_2 = \int_{48.6°}^{\pi - 48.6°} (P_m \sin \delta - 1.5P_{sho})\, d\delta$$

$$= P_m \left[\left| \cos \delta \right|_{\pi - 48.6}^{48.6} - 0.75\,(\pi - 97.2)\frac{\pi}{180} \right] = 0.24P_m.$$

Since area A_2 > area A_1, synchronism is maintained.

(*b*) From Fig. 4.60 (*b*),

$$\text{Area } A_1 = \int_{30°}^{\delta_a} (P_{sha} - P_m \sin \delta)\, d\delta$$

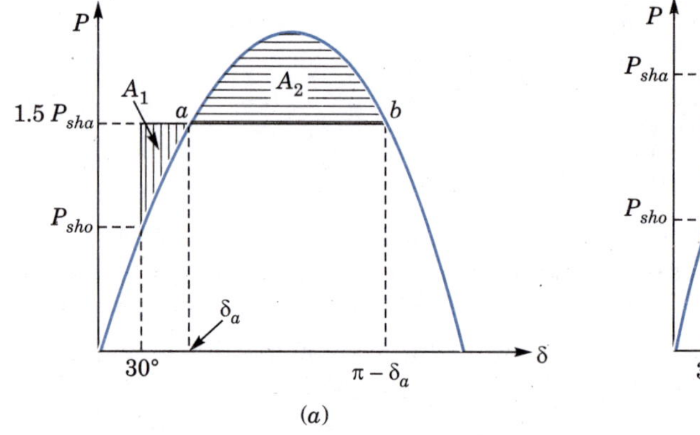

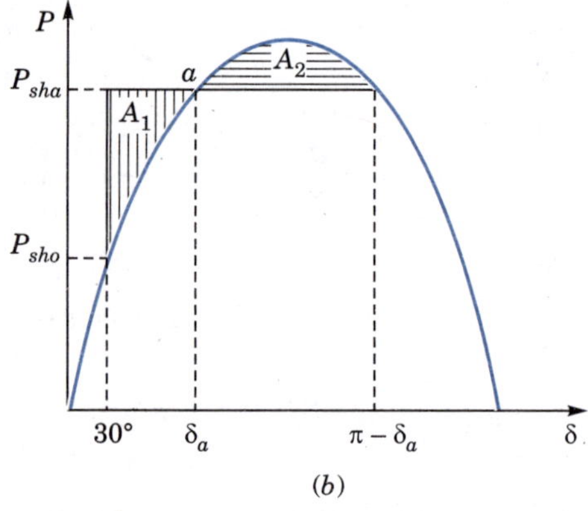

Fig. 4.60: Equal area criterian of stability, Example 4.20.

$$= (\delta_a - 30°)\frac{\pi}{180} P_{sha} + P_m (\cos \delta_a - \cos 30°)$$

But
$$P_{sha} = P_m \sin \delta_a.$$

$\therefore$
$$\text{Area } A_1 = P_m \left[\frac{\pi}{180°} (\delta_a - 30°) \sin \delta_a + (\cos \delta_a - \cos 30°) \right]$$

$$\text{Area } A_2 = \int_{\delta_a}^{\pi - \delta_a} (P_m \sin\delta - P_{sha})\, d\delta$$

$$= P_m \left[(2 \cos\delta_a) - \frac{\pi}{180} (\pi - 2\delta_a) . \sin\delta_a \right]$$

For the synchronous motor to remain in synchronism, the maximum load should be such that

$$\text{Area } A_1 = \text{Area } A_2, \; i.e.,$$

$$\frac{\pi}{180} (\delta_a - 30°) \sin\delta_a + \cos\delta_a - 0.866 = 2 \cos\delta_a - \frac{\pi}{180} (\pi - 2\delta_a) \sin\delta_a$$

or
$$\frac{\pi}{180} (150° - \delta_a) \sin\delta_a = 0.866 + \cos\delta_a$$

The value of load angle δ_a can be obtained by plotting the left hand side function $\frac{\pi}{180}$ $(150 - \delta_a) \sin\delta_a$ and then plotting the right hand side function $0.866 + \cos\delta_a$ on the same graph. The point of intersection of these two curves gives the required value of δ_a.

Alternatively, Newton-Raphson iterative method, for determining δ_a, can be employed as illustrated below:

Here
$$f(\delta_a) = \frac{\pi}{180} (150 - \delta_a) \sin\delta_a - 0.866 - \cos\delta_a$$

$$f'(\delta_a) = \frac{\pi}{180} (150 - \delta_a) \cos\delta_a - \frac{\pi}{180} \sin\delta_a + \sin\delta_a$$

$$= \frac{\pi}{180} (150 - \delta_a) \cos\delta_a$$

δ_a *in radians*	$f(\delta_a)$	$f'(\delta_a)$	$\Delta\delta = -\frac{f(\delta_a)}{f'(\delta_a)}$
0	– 1.866	2.618	0.713
0.713	– 0.3763	1.44094	0.26115
0.97415	– 0.0680	0.924	0.07359
1.04774	– 0.0052	0.7844	0.00663
1.05437			

The value of δ_a is therefore 1.05437 rad = 60.411°

∴ Maximum safe load = $P_m \sin 60.411° = 2P_{sho} \sin 60.411°$

$= 1.7392\, P_{sho}$ = 1.7392 (full load)

∴ Maximum additional safe load = 0.7392 (full load).

4.19 SYNCHRONIZING

Synchronizing is the process of switching on of an alternator to another alternator (or bus-bars) under voltage, without any interruption. This may alternatively be defined as the process of connecting two alternators in parallel, without any interruption. The synchronous machine which is to be synchronized is usually called an *incoming machine.* Certain conditions, which must be fulfilled before synchronization can be carried out, are given below:

(*i*) The terminal voltage of the incoming machine and the already running alternator or bus-bars must be equal.

(*ii*) The frequency of the two voltage sources must be nearly the same.

(*iii*) The two voltages must be in the same phase with respect to the external load. This condition also means that the phase sequence of the two voltages must be the same.

Departure from the above conditions cause the appearance of current and power surges which are accompanied by undesirable electromechanical oscillations of the rotor.

The first condition can be fulfilled by a voltmeter and it is preferable to use the same voltmeter for measuring both the source voltages. In this article, synchronizing process is described first by the use of synchronizing lamps and then with the help of a synchroscope. The use of synchronizing lamps can fulfil both the conditions listed as (*ii*) and (*iii*) above, and can indicate the dark period during which the synchronization switch should be closed. A synchroscope can satisfy condition (*ii*) and can specify the exact moment of closing the synchronizing switch. Since synchroscope is a single phase instrument, for fulfilling condition (*iii*) a synchroscope must be used in association with a phase-sequence indicator.

4.19.1 Synchronizing by Dark-lamp Method

This is the simplest method of synchronizing an incoming machine with another alternator or bus-bars. Fig. 4.61 illustrates the connection scheme, where the lamps are connected across the synchronizing switch S_2.

The incoming machine is brought up to its synchronous speed by the prime-mover and then its field circuit is energised. Now the field current is adjusted till terminal voltage of the incoming machine becomes equal to that of the already running alternator or bus-bar. In this way, first condition of equal voltages is satisfied and switch S_1 is closed. The other two conditions of synchronisation require special considerations.

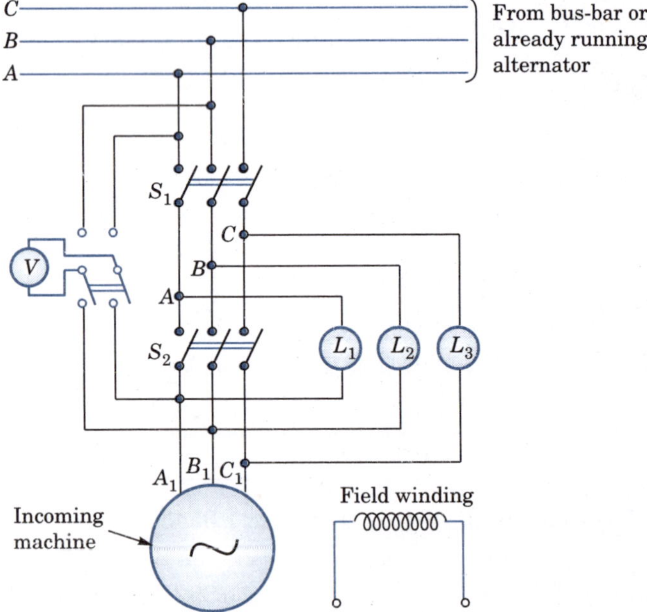

Fig. 4.61: Synchronizing by dark-lamp method.

Suppose the frequencies of the bus-bar and the incoming machine are f and f_1 respectively. Then for equal voltages, the voltage across the synchronizing switch S_2 is

$$v_L = V_m \cos \omega t - V_m \cos \omega_1 t.$$

With the help of trigonometric relation

$$\cos y - \cos x = 2 \sin \frac{x-y}{2} \cdot \sin \frac{x+y}{2}$$

the above equation can be written as

$$v_L = 2V_m \left[\sin \left\{ \frac{f_1 - f}{2} (2\pi t) \right\} \sin \left\{ \frac{f_1 + f}{2} (2\pi t) \right\} \right]$$

The low frequency $\frac{f_1 - f}{2}$ is known as the *beat frequency* and the high frequency $\frac{f_1 + f}{2}$ the *carrier frequency*. An oscillogram, showing the beat and carrier frequencies of the voltage across the synchronizing switch S_2, is illustrated in Fig. 4.62. It is seen from this figure that voltage impressed on the lamp has a frequency equal to the carrier frequency $\frac{f + f_1}{2}$.

The equation for the envelope is $2V_m \sin \frac{f_1 - f}{2} (2\pi t)$.

Since the lamps are bright once in each half of the voltage wave shown in Fig. 4.62, the lamps flicker $(f_1 - f)$ times in one second.

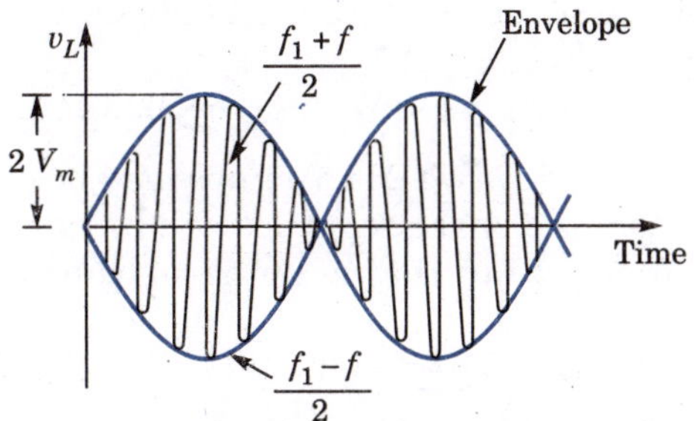

Fig. 4.62: Oscillogram of beat and carrier frequencies of the voltage across synchronizing switch or lamp terminals.

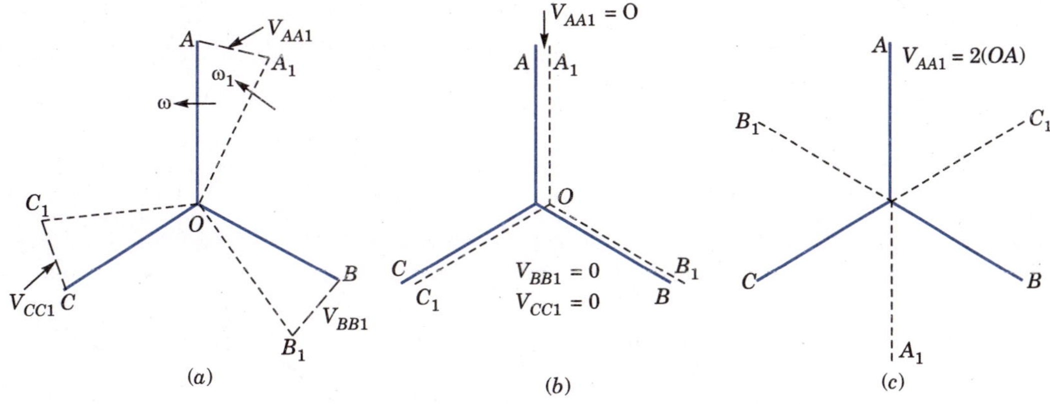

Fig. 4.63: Phasor diagram pertaining to the synchronization of an alternator with another alternator or bus-bar.

In Fig. 4.63 (*a*), 3-phase bus-bar voltage (or voltage of the already running alternator) is represented by phasors *OA*, *OB*, *OC* rotating at angular speed of ω rad/sec. The incoming-machine voltage phasors are OA_1, OB_1, OC_1 and these are shown rotating at speed ω_1. The phasor V_{AA1}, joining the tips *A* and A_1, gives the voltage across lamp 1. Similarly V_{BB1} and V_{CC1} are the voltages across lamps 2 and 3 respectively. When rotating tips *A* and A_1 coincide, Fig. 4.63 (*b*), voltages V_{AA1}, V_{BB1} and V_{CC1} are all equal to zero as indicated by the dark lamps and this is the correct instant for closing the synchronizing switch S_2. However, if the first condition of equal voltages is not fulfilled, even though phasors *OA* and OA_1 overlap V_{AA_1}, V_{BB_1}, V_{CC_1} would not be equal to zero. These small voltages across the lamps 1, 2, 3, can't be seen by the eye. Under these conditions, if the synchronizing switch S_2 is closed, small voltages V_{AA_1}, V_{BB_1}, V_{CC_1} may cause the flow of large current and power surges. In view of this, before synchronizing switch S_2 is closed, the equality of the two source voltages should again be checked.

The frequency of the incoming machine is controlled by varying the speed of its prime-mover. Each time A_1, B_1, C_1 coincide A, B, C ; the three lamps are dark. When A_1, B_1, C_1 are opposite to A, B, C ; the three lamps are the brightest and the voltage across each lamp is $2 \times \frac{V_L}{\sqrt{3}}$, *i.e.*, twice the phase voltage as shown in Fig. 4.63 (*c*). This is the reason why the lamp voltage should be suitably chosen. For example, if the line voltage of the incoming machine (or the bus-bar) is 230 V, then the maximum voltage across each lamp can be $2 \times \frac{230}{\sqrt{3}} = 265.6$ V ; consequently two 230 V lamps may be connected in series. If the three lamps do not flicker in unison, the phase sequence will be improper. This can be rectified by interchanging any two leads either of the incoming machine or of the bus-bars (or already running alternator). Actually, the frequency f_1 is made to differ very slightly from f, so that the beat frequency is considerably low and the flickering subsides, now the synchronizing switch S_2 is closed when the three lamps are in the *middle of their dark period.*

The main advantage of dark-lamp method is that the equipment is quite inexpensive and no phase-sequence indicator is required. Its disadvantages are as follows :

(*i*) The lamps become dark at about one-third of their rated voltage. In view of this, there is a possibility of closing the synchronizing switch even when there is a considerable phase difference between the two source voltages. This voltage across the synchronizing switch will give rise to the flow of large synchronizing current and power accompanied by undesirable rotor oscillations.

(*ii*) The other drawback is that this method does not indicate whether the incoming machine is too fast or too slow. This disadvantage can however be rectified as explained below :

Increase the speed of the incoming machine. If lamp flickering increases, it means that incoming machine is already running faster and this is what is desirable. For synchronizing, decrease the speed of the incoming machine till the lamps flicker very slowly and now close the switch as described before.

With the increase in speed of the incoming machine, if the lamp flickering decreases, it means that the incoming machine is running slower. Now increase the speed of the incoming machine till there is almost no lamp flicker ; this indicates that incoming machine is running at synchronous speed. Now, again increase the speed of the incoming machine very gradually till the lamps flicker slowly and the synchronizing switch is closed as described before.

For high-voltage alternators, lamps can't be used directly—in such cases, the lamps are connected through potential transformers.

4.19.2 Synchronizing by a Synchroscope

A synchroscope is an instrument, fitted with a rotating pointer to indicate the correct instant of closing the synchronizing switch. If the pointer rotates anti-clockwise, the incoming machine is running slow which is not desirable. Clockwise rotation of pointer indicates that the incoming machine is running faster which is desirable. The pointer rotates at a speed proportional to the difference is the two frequencies. For favourable synchronization, the pointer should rotate at a very low speed in the direction of the arrow marked fast, Fig. 4.64 (*a*). When the rotating pointer reaches the vertical position at a slow speed, the synchronizing switch must at once be closed. If the difference in frequencies of the two voltage sources is large, the pointer does not rotate but merely oscillates about some mean position. This state of affairs can be rectified by adjusting the speed of the incoming machine.

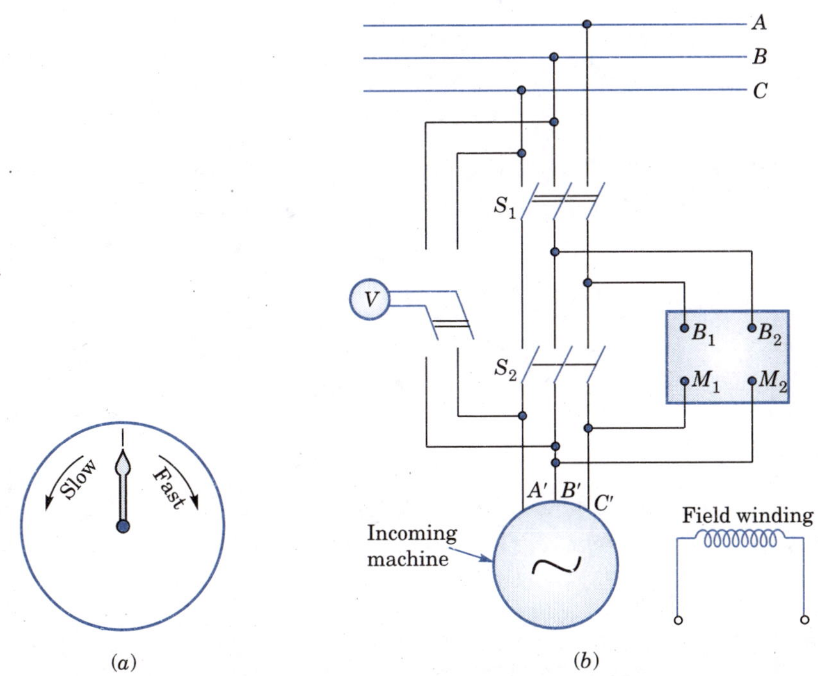

Fig. 4.64: (*a*) Synchroscope and (*b*) synchronizing by means of a synchroscope.

An elementary connection scheme of synchronizing by means of a synchroscope is as shown in Fig. 4.64 (*b*). Synchroscope terminals B_1, B_2 (*B* for bus-bars) should be connected to any two bus-bar lines and its other terminals M_1, M_2 (*M* for machine) are connected to the correspondingly marked lines of the incoming machine. Phase sequence of the voltages, coming from bus-bars and that coming from the incoming machine, must be the same and this can be ascertained only with the help of a phase-sequence indicator, because synchroscope is a single-phase instrument. Bus-bar and incoming-machine voltages should be made equal with the same voltmeter. Now the synchronization is carried out as explained before.

The best synchronization is carried out if both the lamps and synchroscope are used together. Automatic synchronizing devices are also available which perform the entire process of synchronization automatically without the help of any shift engineer. However, the automatic synchronization schemes are more complicated and the time of synchro-nization process may sometimes be much more than that required by a shift engineer.

The effect of wrong synchronization may be illustrated by the following two examples.

Example 4.21. *Two alternators have each a sub-transient reactance of 0.3 p.u. For synchronizing them, their voltages are made equal to their rated values. Calculate the synchronizing current at the time of closing the synchronizing switch, in case their voltages are*

(a) in phase (b) 30° away from each other and (c) 180° away from each other.

Solution. (*a*) When the voltages are in phase, the voltage across the synchronizing switch is zero, consequently the synchronizing current is also zero.

(*b*) When the voltages are 30° away from each other, then voltage across synchronizing switch is equal to 2 sin 15° = 0.5176. Therefore, the synchronizing current at the instant of closing the synchronizing switch is given by

$$\frac{0.5176}{0.3 + 0.3} = 0.863 \text{ p.u.}$$

(*c*) For voltages 180° away from each other, the resultant voltage across the sychronizing switch is equal to 2 p.u. Therefore, the synchronizing current at the time of sychronizing is,

$$\frac{2}{0.3 + 0.3} = 3.33 \text{ p.u.}$$

Such a large current surge may damage both the machines.

Example 4.22. *A 1000 kW, 6.6 kV, 50 Hz, 20 pole alternator has the following constants :*

Total moment of inertia, $J = 2480 \text{ kg m}^2$.

Synchronizing power co-efficient, $P_s = 40 \text{ kW/elec. degree}$.

Damping power co-efficient, $K_d = 2 \text{ kW/elec. deg./sec}$.

This alternator is to be synchronized with an infinite bus. The terminal voltages of the alternator and the bus are made equal, but owing to wrong synchronization, electromechanical oscillations take place which are to be investigated for the following cases:

(a) If the alternator is switched on at proper angle, i.e., when the lamps have zero voltage across them (for dark-lamp method of synchronizing), but its initial speed is 1 Hz fast.

(b) If the alternator is synchronized with correct speed (i.e., frequency), but its phases are 15° ahead of the infinite bus phases.

(c) If the alternator is synchronized when its speed is 1 Hz fast and its phases are leading bus phases by 15 elect. degrees.

Solution. From Example 4.17,

$$P_j = 136 \text{ watts/elec. deg./sec.}^2$$

$$\omega_n = 17.15 \text{ rad./sec.}, \qquad \xi = 0.429$$

and

$$\sqrt{1-\xi^2}\,\omega_n = 15.49 \text{ rad./sec.}$$

The differential equation describing the behaviour of the alternator for this example is given by [refer to Eq. (4.198) with P_{sh} equal to zero],

$$(136p^2 + 2000p + 4 \times 10^4)\,\delta = 0$$

or

$$\left(p^2 + \frac{2000}{136}p + \frac{4 \times 10^4}{136}\right)\delta = 0$$

The solution of this equation, as given by Eq. (4.204), is

$$\delta(t) = e^{-\xi\omega_n t}\,[(A+B)\cos(\sqrt{1-\xi^2}\;\omega_n t) + j\,(A-B)\sin(\sqrt{1-\xi^2}\;\omega_n t)] \quad ...(4.219)$$

The constants A and B can be obtained by employing the initial conditions,

(*a*) Here at $t = 0+$, $\delta = 0$ and from Eq. (4.219), $0 = (A + B)$

At $t = 0+$, $$\frac{d\delta}{dt} = 1 \text{ Hz} = 360° \text{ elec.}$$

$$\therefore \quad 360° = (A+B)(-\xi\omega_n) + j\,(A-B)(\sqrt{1-\xi^2}\,\omega_n)$$

i.e., $$j\,(A-B) = \frac{360°}{\omega_n\sqrt{1-\xi}}.$$

With the values of $(A + B)$ and $j\,(A - B)$ as obtained above, Eq. (4.219) becomes

$$\delta(t) = \frac{360°}{15.49}\,e^{-7.36t}\sin(15.49t) = 23.24e^{-7.36t}\sin(15.49t)$$

(*b*) Here at $t = 0+$, $\delta = 15°$ and from Eq. (4.219).

$$\frac{15\times\pi}{180} = A + B$$

$$A + B = \frac{\pi}{12}$$

Also at $t = 0+$, $$\frac{d\delta}{dt} = 0$$

$$\therefore \quad 0 = (A+B)(-\xi\omega_n) + j(A-B)(\omega_n\sqrt{1-\xi^2})$$

or $$j(A-B) = \frac{\xi}{\sqrt{1-\xi^2}}\,(A+B) = \frac{\pi}{12}\cdot\frac{\xi}{\sqrt{1-\xi^2}}$$

Substitution of these constants in Eq. (4.219) gives

$$\delta(t) = \frac{\pi}{12}\cdot\frac{e^{-\xi\omega_n t}}{\sqrt{1-\xi^2}}\left[\sin(\sqrt{1-\xi^2}\,.\,\omega_n t + \phi)\right]$$

Now $$\phi = \tan^{-1}\frac{\sqrt{1-\xi^2}}{\xi} = 64.6° \quad \text{and} \quad \sqrt{1-\xi^2} = 0.903.$$

$$\therefore \quad \delta(t) = 16.61e^{-7.36t}\,[\sin(15.49t + 64.6°)]$$

(*c*) Here at $t = 0+$, $\delta = 15°$ and this gives,

$$(A+B) = \frac{\pi}{12}.$$

Also at $t = 0+$, $$\frac{d\delta}{dt} = 1 \text{ Hz} = 360° = 2\pi$$

$$\therefore \quad 2\pi = (A+B)(-\xi\omega_n) + j\,(A-B)(\omega_n\sqrt{1-\xi^2})$$

$$= -\frac{\pi}{12}\cdot\xi\omega_n + j\,(A-B)(\omega_n\sqrt{1-\xi^2})$$

$$\therefore \quad j\,(A-B) = \frac{\pi}{12}\left[\frac{24+\xi\omega_n}{\omega_n\sqrt{1-\xi^2}}\right] = \frac{\pi}{12}\,\frac{1.828}{\sqrt{1-\xi^2}}$$

$$\therefore \quad \delta(t) = e^{-\xi\omega_n t} \cdot \frac{\pi}{12}\left[\cos\left(\sqrt{1-\xi^2}\,\omega_n t\right) + \frac{1.828}{\sqrt{1-\xi^2}}\sin\left(\sqrt{1-\xi^2}\,\omega_n t\right)\right]$$

Let
$$\tan\phi = \frac{\sqrt{1-\xi^2}}{1.828} = \frac{0.903}{1.828}$$

$$\therefore \quad \phi = 26.29°$$

$$\therefore \quad \cos\phi = \frac{1.828}{\sqrt{(1.828)^2 + (0.903)^2}} = \frac{1.828}{2.039}$$

and
$$\sin\phi = \frac{0.903}{2.039}$$

$$\therefore \quad \delta(t) = e^{-7.36t}\,\frac{15}{0.903}[0.903\cos(15.49t) + 1.828\sin(15.49t)]$$

$$= \frac{15}{0.903}(2.035)\,e^{-7.36t}\left[\frac{0.903}{2.039}\cos(15.49t) + \frac{1.828}{2.039}\sin(15.49t)\right]$$

$$= 33.8e^{-7.36t}\,[\sin\phi\,(\cos 15.49t) + \cos\phi\,\sin(15.49t)]$$

$$\therefore \quad \delta(t) = 33.8e^{-7.36t}\sin(15.49t + 26.29°).$$

4.20 PARALLEL OPERATION OF TWO ALTERNATORS

The two most important characteristics of a synchronous machine are: (*i*) its constant-speed operation at constant frequency and (*ii*) its ability to operate both at leading and lagging power factors. A synchronous generator is used for converting mechanical energy into electrical energy at the generating stations. A synchronous generator usually operates in parallel with other synchronous generators at these stations. Actually, electricity supply system of a country or a state is fed by a large number of alternators operating in parallel. The generating stations, far away from each other, are interconnected by long transmission lines. The reasons for interconnecting the alternators in parallel are as follows:

(*a*) Operating cost. For a given installed capacity in a generating station, either a single large unit or several small units may be installed. With several units in parallel, the number of alternators operating at a time can be changed depending upon the electricity demand. In this manner, it is possible to operate the alternators near their full-load capacity. Since a machine has maximum efficiency near its full-load, the use of several units in parallel has higher efficiency of operation and, therefore, reduced operating cost. A single unit will have to operate at a reduced load for certain periods of the day, consequently it has lower operating efficiency and, therefore, increased operating costs.

(*b*) Maintenance. For routine maintenance and inspection at the power stations, a unit must be shut down for a certain period. Consequently, the cost of standby unit is much less when several units are installed.

(*c*) Economy and utility. The interconnection of several power stations by a grid is economical and advantageous. This interconnection of thermal and hydroelectric power stations enables the optimum utility of the alternators and the energy sources. Peak-load power stations may be shut down when the electricity demand is less.

(*d*) Continuity of service. Interconnections of the several alternators of different power stations enables better continuity of supply to consumers. In case of a fault on any unit, it can be shut down for repairs and the power supply can still be maintained to the consumers, though at a reduced level.

The process of inter-connection of an alternator with another alternators under voltage or the bus-bar, called synchronizing, has already been explained in Art. 4.19. The object of this article is to examine how the parallel operation of two alternators is effected by a change of either the driving torque or the excitation. Though two alternators rarely operate in parallel in an interconnected system, the aim here is to illustrate the basic features concerning the parallel operation of two alternators.

4.20.1 Effect of Changing Mechanical Torque

The driving torque of an alternator can be varied by controlling the gate-opening in case of hydrogenators or by controlling the throttle-opening in case of turbo-generators. The effect of changing the mechanical torque is considered first with the alternator on no-load and then with the alternator on load. Here cylindrical rotor alternators are assumed for simplicity, but the results obtained are applicable both to the non-salient and salient-pole alternators.

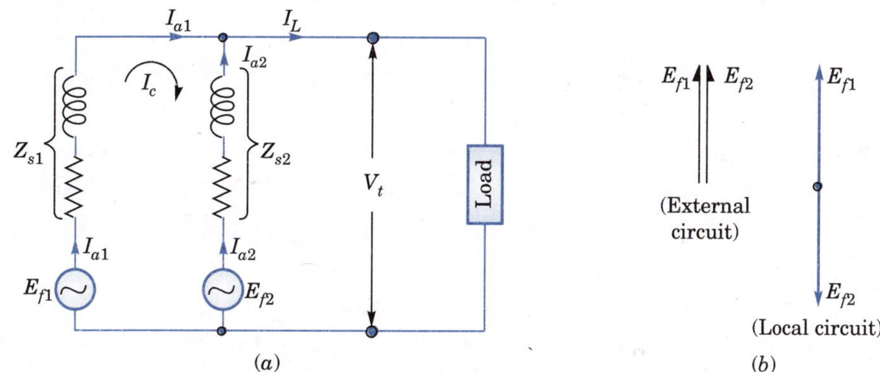

Fig. 4.65: (*a*) Two alternators in parallel and (*b*) phasor diagram of two unloaded a alternators under floating conditions.

(*a*) No-load operation. Consider two unloaded alternators running in parallel as shown in Fig. 4.65 (*a*). Subscripts 1 and 2 are used to indicate alternators 1 and 2 respectively. Here excitation voltages E_{f_1} and E_{f_2} are equal in magnitude and are in phase, so that the resultant voltage in the local circuit formed by E_{f1}, Z_{s1}, E_{f2} and Z_{s2} is zero. It can be stated that excitation e.m.fs. E_{f_1} and E_{f_2} are in phase with respect to the external circuit or are in phase opposition with respect to the local circuit as illustrated in Fig. 4.65 (*b*).

Suppose the driving torque of alternator 1 is increased. This increment in torque tends to accelerate the rotor and as a result of it, e.m.f. E_{f_1} gets ahead of e.m.f. E_{f_2} as shown in Fig. 4.66 (*a*). There now appears a resultant voltage $\overline{E}_c = \overline{E}_{f_1} - \overline{E}_{f_2}$ in the local series circuit, which gives rise to a circulating current

$$\overline{I}_c = \frac{\overline{E}_{f_1} - \overline{E}_{f_2}}{\overline{Z}_{s1} + \overline{Z}_{s2}}$$

through two armatures. The current I_c lags behind E_c by an angle

$$\beta = \tan^{-1}\frac{X_{s1} + X_{s2}}{r_{a1} + r_{a2}} \cong 90°,$$

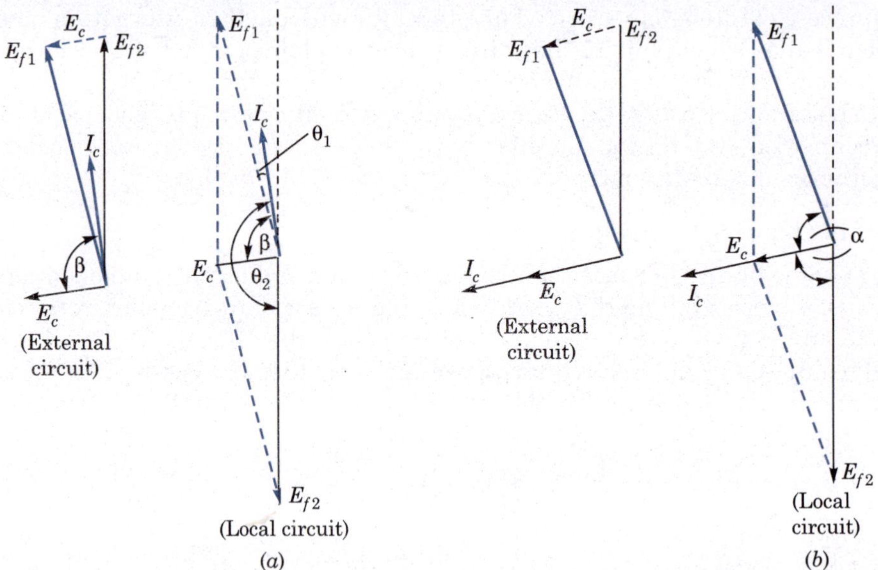

Fig. 4.66: Phasor diagram showing the effect of increase in the driving torque of alternator 1, (*a*) armature impedance mainly reactive (*b*) armature impedance assumed purely resistive.

because Z_{s1} and Z_{s2} are predominantly reactive. In Fig. 4.66 (*a*), the phasor diagram pertaining to the local series circuit gives better physical insight into the internal happenings, therefore, it is preferable to consider this phasor diagram. From Fig. 4.66 (*a*) it is seen that I_c, known as the synchronizing current, is almost in phase with E_{f1} and in phase opposition to E_{f2}. Therefore, alternator 1 generates a power $E_{f1}I_c \cos \theta_1$ which is positive ($\because \theta_1 < 90°$), while alternator 2 generates a power $E_{f2}I_c \cos \theta_2$ which is negative ($\because \theta_2 > 90°$). In other words, alternator 1 experiences a generating action tending to retard it and alternator 2 receives the power generated by 1 (ohmic loss due to I_c neglected) and, therefore, it experiences a motoring action tending to accelerate it. It is thus seen that there is an automatic synchronizing action tending to retard the faster machine and to accelerate the slower machine, in order to maintain the synchronism.

It must be noted that synchronizing power, $E_{f1}I_c \cos \theta_1$ or $E_{f2}I_c \cos \theta_2$, is developed on account of the armature impedance being mainly reactive. If Z_{s1} and Z_{s2} had been purely resistive, I_c would be in phase with E_c as shown in Fig. 4.66 (*b*) and $E_{f1}I_c \cos \alpha = E_{f2}I_c \cos \alpha$. As α is less than 90°, both $E_{f1}I_c \cos \alpha$ and $E_{f2}I_c \cos \alpha$ are positive and as a result, both machines 1 and 2 experience generating action. Therefore, there would be no synchronizing power tending to speed up the slower machine. This shows that the reactance is useful for auto-synchronizing action but is bad for voltage regulation.

(*b*) On-load operation. When two alternators, running in parallel, are loaded, the *division of load* between them is governed mainly by the speed-load characteristics of their prime-movers. In order to illustrate this, refer to Fig. 4.67 (*a*), where alternators 1 and 2 are shown driven by their respective prime-movers 1 and 2. The speed-load characteristics of prime-movers 1 and 2 are shown by solid lines 1 and 2 respectively in Fig. 4.67 (*b*). For the sake of clarity, the slope of speed-load curves 1 and 2 is exaggerated. The total load $2P$ is represented by the horizontal line *ab* and the per unit speed or bus-bar frequency is *f*.

Both the alternators are assumed to be equally loaded, *i.e.* each alternator is sharing a load P. If the mechanical torque of p.m. 1 is increased by its governor setting, its speed becomes more and as a consequence its speed-load curve shifts upward as shown by dotted line 1′. For a constant load of $2P$, the operating points a, b shift to new operating points c, d. Thus the horizontal line cd defines the new operating conditions from which it is seen that load on machine 1 has increased from P to P_1 and that on machine 2 has decreased from P to P_2, such that $P_1 + P_2 = 2P$. Fig. 4.67 (b) also reveals that the bus-bar frequency has increased from f to f'. If it is required to maintain the system frequency constant at f, the mechanical input to prime-mover 2 must be suitably reduced so that its speed-load curve shifts downward as shown by the dotted line 2′. The operating points c and d now shift to the new operating points x and y. The horizontal line xy shows that load on alternator 1 has further increased from P_1 to P_1' and that on alternator 2 has further reduced from P_2 to P_2', such that $P_1' + P_2' = 2P$ again. Thus, the load division between the alternators and the system frequency can be controlled by changing the mechanical torque input to the alternators. The speed-load characteristics of the prime-movers can be shifted up or down by controlling the gate-opening of water-turbines or the throttle-opening of steam-turbines.

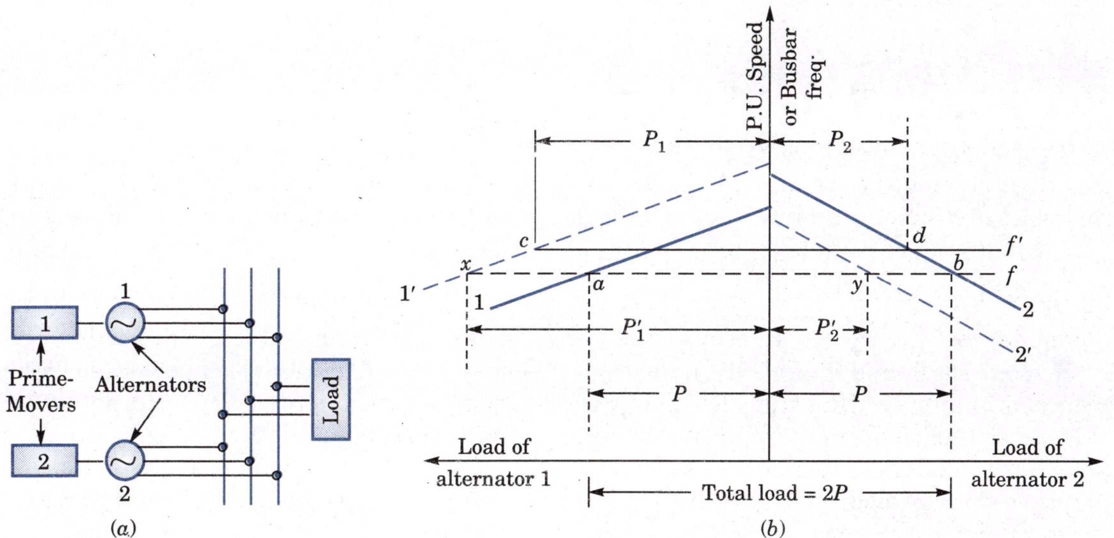

Fig. 4.67: Effect of changing mechanical torque on the load division between two alternators.

The above explanation does not say anything about the internal happenings in the two alternators, when the mechanical torque of one alternator is increased. Their internal behaviour can, however, be understood by referring to their phasor diagrams as described below.

For the two alternators running in parallel, it is first of all assumed, for the sake of simplicity, that their excitation voltages E_{f_1}, E_{f_2} and armature currents I_{a_1}, I_{a_2} are equal such that $E_{f_1} = E_{f_2}$, $I_{a_1} = I_{a_2}$ and load current $I_L = 2I_{a_1} = 2I_{a_2}$. Their terminal voltage V_t is taken to be constant and for equal synchronous reactances, the phasor diagram of Fig. 4.68 is obtained. Each alternator is sharing a load equal to $\dfrac{E_{f_1} V_t}{X_s} \sin \delta = \dfrac{E_{f_2} V_t}{X_s} \sin \delta = P$.

When the mechanical torque of alternator 1 is increased, its electrical output must increase accordingly. Since E_f, V_t and X_s are constant, the electrical power output of alternator 1 can increase only by an increment in load angle from δ to, say, δ_1. In view of this, E_{f_1} becomes ahead of its previous position as shown in Fig. 4.68, so that $\frac{E_{f_1}V_t}{X_s}\sin\delta_1 > P$. Now alternator 1 shares a load greater than P, therefore, load on alternator 2 must be less than P, for a total constant load of $2P$. For a load less than P, E_{f_2} must fall back from its previous position as shown in Fig. 4.68, so that $\frac{E_{f_2}.V_t}{X_s}\sin\delta_2 < P$. But the sum of $\frac{E_{f_1}V_t}{X_s}\sin\delta_1$ and $\frac{E_{f_2}V_t}{X_s}\sin\delta_2$ is again $2P$. With E_{f_1} getting ahead and E_{f_2} falling back their previous position, a voltage AB appears in the local circuit of these two alternators. This voltage AB sends a local current I_c, lagging AB by 90°. An examination of Fig. 4.65 (*a*) reveals that I_c must be added (phasor addition) to I_{a_1} and subtracted from I_{a_2}. As a result of it, alternator 1 carries an increased current I_{a_1}' and alternator 2 shares a decreased current I_{a_2}', but again $\bar{I}a_1' + \bar{I}a_2' = \bar{I}_L$. It is also seen that operating power factor of alternator 1 is improved to cos θ_1 and that of alternator 2 is worsened to cos θ_2, but the load power factor cos θ remains unaltered. Thus the effect of increasing the mechanical torque of an alternator is to (*i*) increase its armature current and (*ii*) improve its operating power factor. As before, it is seen that the effect of increasing the driving torque of an alternator is to make it take an increased share of load, whereas the other alternator operating in parallel with it is relieved of its load by a corresponding amount. In a way, the present discussion supplements the treatment given in Fig. 4.67.

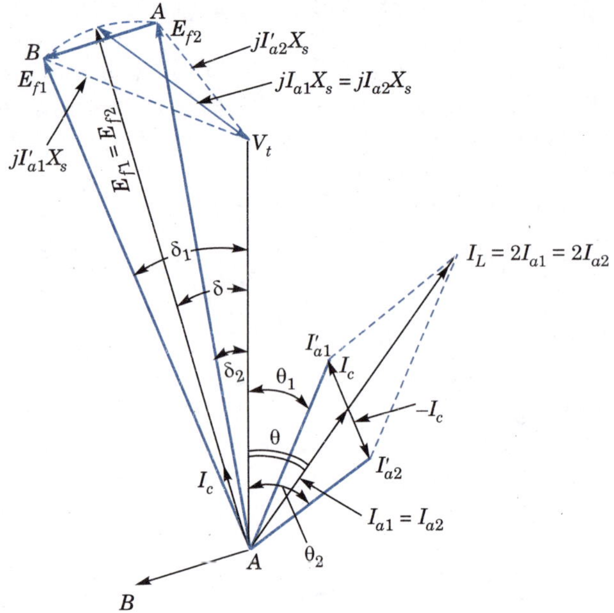

Fig. 4.68: Phasor diagram illustrating the effect of increasing the driving torque of alternator 1.

4.20.2 Effect of Changing Excitation

The field current or excitation of an alternator can be controlled with the help of its field rhcostat. Here again the effect of changing the excitation is considered first on an unloaded alternator and then on loaded alternator. For parallel running alternators, it will be seen that a change in field current effects only the operating power factor of the alternator and has almost no effect on the active power shared by the alternators. Strictly speaking, a change in excitation changes the armature current and, therefore, the armature copper loss. This change in armature ohmic loss will alter the active power output by a very small amount only.

(a) No-load operation. Consider again two alternators running in parallel and at no load. Their excitation e.m.fs. E_{f1} and E_{f2} are equal so that there is no current in their local path. Now if the excitation of alternator 1 is increased, magnitude of E_{f1} becomes more than the magnitude of E_{f2} and consequently, a resultant voltage $\bar{E}_c = \bar{E}_{f1} - \bar{E}_{f2}$ appears in the local circuit as shown in Fig. 4.69 (*a*). Since the synchronous impedances in the local circuit are mainly reactive, local circulating current I_c lags E_c by nearly 90°. For alternator 1, I_c lags E_{f1} by about 90°, its armature reaction is, therefore, demagnetizing and this has the effect of lowering the generated voltage E_{f1}. On the other hand, for alternator 2, I_c leads E_{f2} by nearly 90°, Fig. 4.69 (*a*), its armature reaction is therefore magnetizing and it causes a strengthening of its field, which increases the generated voltage E_{f2}. Thus the circulating current I_c tends to lower the increased generated voltage and to raise the decreased generated voltage. In other words, the circulating current tends to equalize the two generated e.m.fs. at no-load. The power angle δ, however, remains zero.

With an increase in excitation of alternator 1, the terminal voltage changes to a new value as follows :

From Fig. 4.65 (*a*), $\bar{V}_t = \bar{E}_{f1} - \bar{I}_c \bar{Z}_{s1}$ and $\bar{V}_t = \bar{E}_{f2} + \bar{I}_c \bar{Z}_{s2}$

For $Z_{s1} = Z_{s2}$

$$\bar{V}_t = \frac{\bar{E}_{f1} + \bar{E}_{f2}}{2} \qquad \text{...(4.220)}$$

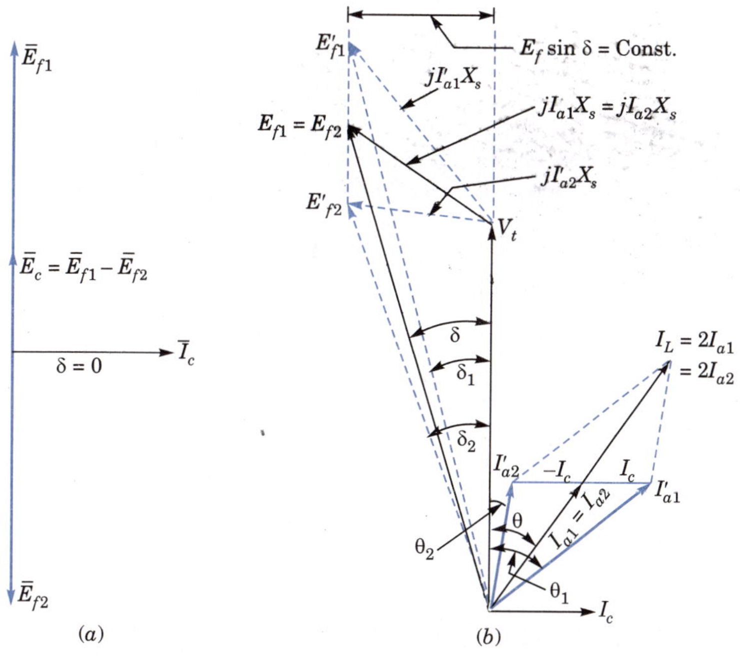

Fig. 4.69: Effect of changing the field excitation of two parallel connected alternators. (*a*) No-load operation and (*b*) On-load operation.

(b) On-load operation. When two alternators, running in parallel, are loaded, it is assumed again that $E_{f1} = E_{f2}$, $I_{a1} = I_{a2}$ and $I_L = 2I_{a1} = 2I_{a2}$. Their operating power factor is $\cos\theta$, terminal voltage is V_t and the phasor diagram of Fig. 4.69 (b) illustrates this.

An increase in the excitation of alternator, say 1, increases its excitation voltage E_{f_1} to a new value E'_{f_1} and this has the effect of raising the terminal voltage V_t as given by Eq. (4.220). However, their terminal voltage can be kept constant by decreasing the excitation of alternator 2. Fig. 4.69 (b) illustrates these changes where increased E'_{f_1} and decreased E'_{f_2} are shown such that $E_f \sin\delta$ remains constant. The voltage $\overline{E}_{f_1}' - \overline{E}_{f_2}'$ gives rise to circulating current $\overline{I}_c$. Reference to Fig. 4.65 (a) reveals that $\overline{I}_c$ must be added to $\overline{I}_{a_1}$ and subtracted from $\overline{I}_{a_2}$. The two new armature currents $\overline{I}_{a_1}'$ and $\overline{I}_{a_2}'$ are shown in Fig. 4.69 (b) where $\overline{E}_{f_1}' = \overline{V}_t + j\overline{I}_{a_1}' X_s$ and $\overline{E}_{f_2}' = \overline{V}_t + j\overline{I}_{a_2}' X_s$. It is seen from Fig. 4.69 (b) that though $\overline{I}_{a_1}'$ has increased in magnitude, its active power component $\overline{I}_{a_1}' \cos\theta_1$ along V_t is unchanged, similarly, $\overline{I}_{a_2}'$ has decreased in magnitude but its active power component $\overline{I}_{a_2}' \cos\theta_2$ along V_t remains the same. The load current I_L, the load terminal voltage V_t and the load power factor have not changed, however, the armature currents, excitation voltages and the operating power factors of individual alternators have altered. Alternator 1, operating at a poor power factor $\cos\theta_1$, is delivering much greater reactive power than alternator 2 which is operating at a better power factor $\cos\theta_2$. Since their mechanical power inputs have not been changed by throttle – or gate opening, their active power outputs ($V_t I_{a_1}' \cos\theta_1 = V_t I_{a_1} \cos\theta$ and $V_t I_{a_2}' \cos\theta_2 = V_t I_{a_2} \cos\theta$) are the same as before. It can be concluded from the foregoing discussion that the distribution of reactive power (VAr) shared by the alternators and their terminal voltage can be controlled by varying the excitations with the help of field rheostats.

Load division. In Fig. 4.65 (a), if Z_L is the load impedance, then

$$\overline{V}_t = (\overline{I}_{a_1} + \overline{I}_{a_2})\overline{Z}_L \qquad \text{...(4.221)}$$

But

$$\overline{V}_t = \overline{E}_{f_1} - \overline{I}_{a_1}\overline{Z}_{s_1} = \overline{E}_{f_2} - \overline{I}_{a_2}\overline{Z}_{s_2}$$

$$\therefore \quad \overline{I}_{a_1} = \frac{\overline{E}_{f_1} - \overline{V}_t}{\overline{Z}_{s_1}} \quad \text{and} \quad \overline{I}_{a_2} = \frac{\overline{E}_{f_2} - \overline{V}_t}{\overline{Z}_{s_2}}$$

Substitution of $\overline{I}_{a_1}$ and $\overline{I}_{a_2}$ in Eq. (4.221) gives

$$\overline{V}_t = \left(\frac{\overline{E}_{f_1} - \overline{V}_t}{\overline{Z}_{s_1}} + \frac{\overline{E}_{f_2} - \overline{V}_t}{\overline{Z}_{s_2}}\right)\overline{Z}_L$$

which on simplification becomes

$$\overline{V}_t\left(\frac{1}{\overline{Z}_{s_1}} + \frac{1}{\overline{Z}_{s_2}} + \frac{1}{\overline{Z}_L}\right) = \frac{\overline{E}_{f_1}}{\overline{Z}_{s_1}} + \frac{\overline{E}_{f_2}}{\overline{Z}_{s_2}} \qquad \text{...(4.222)}$$

Fig. 4.65 (a) also gives

$$\overline{E}_{f_1} - \overline{I}_{a_1}\overline{Z}_{s_1} - (\overline{I}_{a_1} + \overline{I}_{a_2})\overline{Z}_L = 0 \qquad \text{...(4.223)}$$

and

$$\overline{E}_{f_2} - \overline{I}_{a_2}\overline{Z}_{s_2} - (\overline{I}_{a_1} + \overline{I}_{a_2})\overline{Z}_L = 0 \qquad \text{...(4.224)}$$

Eq. (4.223) minus Eq. (4.224) gives

$$\overline{E}_{f_1} - \overline{E}_{f_2} = \overline{I}_{a_1}\overline{Z}_{s_1} - \overline{I}_{a_2}\overline{Z}_{s_2}$$

or
$$\overline{I}_{a_2} = \frac{(\overline{E}_{f_2} - \overline{E}_{f_1}) + \overline{I}_{a_1}\overline{Z}_{s_1}}{\overline{Z}_{s_2}}$$

Substitution of this value of I_{a_2} in Eq. (4.223) gives

$$\overline{I}_{a_1} = \frac{\overline{E}_{f_1}}{\overline{Z}_{s_1} + \overline{Z}_L + \dfrac{\overline{Z}_{s_1}\overline{Z}_L}{\overline{Z}_{s_2}}} + \frac{\overline{E}_{f_1} - \overline{E}_{f_2}}{\overline{Z}_{s_1} + \overline{Z}_{s_2} + \dfrac{\overline{Z}_{s_1}\overline{Z}_{s_2}}{\overline{Z}_L}} \quad ...(4.225)$$

When the two e.m.fs. E_{f_1} and E_{f_2} are unequal in magnitude or are out of phase, then second term of Eq. (4.225) represents the circulating current under loaded conditions. The circulating current under no-load ($Z_L = \infty$) is given by

$$\overline{I}_c = \frac{\overline{E}_{f_1} - \overline{E}_{f_2}}{\overline{Z}_{s_1} + \overline{Z}_{s_2}} \quad ...(4.226)$$

Example 4.23. *Sketch the phasor diagrams of a 3-phase synchronous machine (a) at the moment of synchronizing (b) when working as a motor and (c) when working as a generator, marking the reference directions for voltages and currents in the associated circuit diagrams. Indicate, on the phasor diagrams, the load/torque angle in each case.* *[I.E.S., 1979]*

Solution. Suppose 3-phase synchronous machine is synchronized with 3-phase infinite bus of voltage V_t. Here E_f, the excitation e.m.f. (or no-load generated e.m.f.) of alternator, is assumed to remain constant.

(*a*) At the moment of synchronizing, magnitude of E_f = magnitude of V_t. Both E_f and V_t must be in phase, because no power flow takes place and load angle δ is zero, so that $\frac{E_f . V_t}{X_s}$ sin δ is zero. Armature current is, therefore, also zero. The phasor and circuit diagrams, at the moment of synchronizing are as illustrated in Fig. 4.70 (*a*).

(*b*) When working as a synchronous motor, E_f must lag behind V_t as shown in Fig. 4.70 (*b*). As a result, armature current I_a starts flowing and the motor operates at a lagging *p.f.*, with voltage equation $\overline{V}_t = \overline{E}_f + j\overline{I}_a X_s$. The phasor and circuit diagrams are shown in Fig. 4.70 (*b*). Note that V_t remains vertical, since V_t is the terminal voltage of the infinite bus.

(*c*) When it is made to work as a synchronous generator, E_f must be ahead of V_t as shown in Fig. 4.70 (*c*). The armature current I_a is seen to lead V_t, therefore alternator operates at a leading *p.f.* with voltage equation $\overline{E}_f = \overline{V}_t + j\overline{I}_a X_s$. The phasor and circuit diagrams are illustrated in Fig. 4.70 (*c*). Here again V_t remains fixed along vertical axis.

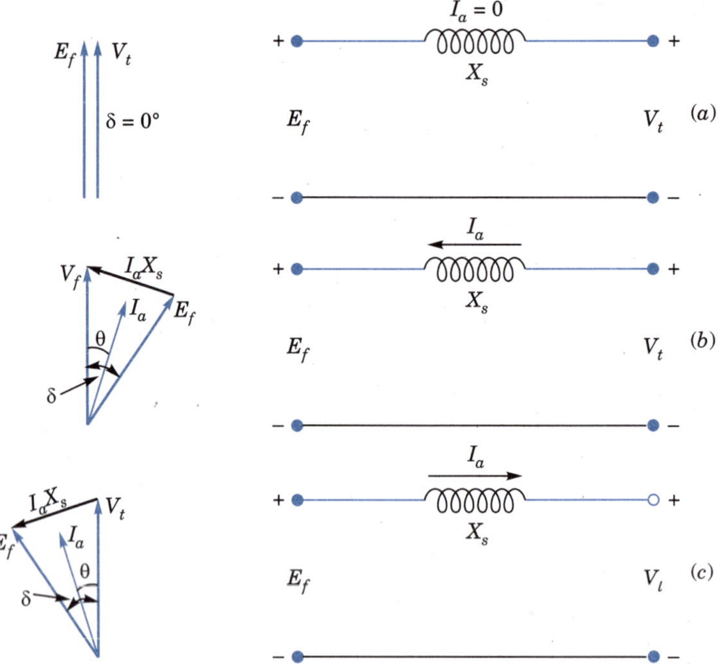

Fig. 4.70: Synchronous machine phasor and circuit diagrams (*a*) at the moment of synchronizing (*b*) when working as a motor and (*c*) when working as a generator.

Example 4.24. *It is desirable that the incoming machine should be a little too fast at the time of synchronizing. Explain.*

Solution. Suppose that an already running alternator 1 is supplying a load current of I_{a_1}. E_{f_1} and E_{f_2} are respectively the excitation voltages for alternator 1 and for the incoming alternator 2. At the time of synchronizing, E_{f_1} and E_{f_2} are opposing each other as shown in Fig. 4.65 (*b*) and the resultant voltage in the local circuit is zero. In case incoming alternator 2 is running slower, then soon after the synchronizing switch is closed, E_{f_2} falls back to the position shown in Fig. 4.71 (*a*). As a consequence of it, a resultant voltage E_c appears in the local circuit, which gives rise to synchronizing current I_c as shown. Total current carried by alternator 1 is now $\bar{I}_{a_1}' = \bar{I}_{a_1} + \bar{I}_c$ and new power developed by it is now $E_{f_1}\bar{I}_{a_1}' \cos(E_{f_1}, I_{a_1}')$ which is much greater than its previous developed power $E_{f_1}I_{a_1} \cos(E_{f_1}, I_{a_1})$—this shows that already loaded alternator gets loaded further. For the incoming alternator 2, $E_{f_2}I_c \cos(E_{f_2}, I_c)$ is negative, showing that it starts working as a synchronous motor soon after the synchronizing switch is closed. Thus, if the incoming alternator is running slower, then soon after the synchronizing switch is closed, the already loaded alternator gets loaded still further and the incoming alternator starts operating as a synchronous motor—this all is an undesirable process.

Let us see what happens if the incoming alternator 2 is running a little too fast. Soon after alternator 2 is connected to alternator 1 (or bus-bar), E_{f_2} gets ahead to the position shown in Fig. 4.71 (*b*). A resultant voltage is again produced and this gives rise to the local synchronizing current I_c as shown. Now $E_{f_2} I_c$ cos $(\overline{E}_{f_2}, I_c)$ is positive. This means that soon after the synchronizing switch is closed, the incoming machine starts operating as an alternator and shares a load proportional to $E_{f_2} I_c$ cos $(\overline{E}_{f_2}, I_c)$ and the already loaded alternator 1 is relieved of its load by a corresponding amount. After the synchronizing switch is closed, the immediate placing of load on the incoming alternator and relieving the already loaded alternator by a corresponding amount is a desirable process. Basically, the object of synchronizing an incoming alternator is to place a load on it soon after the synchronizing switch is closed and this is what happens in case the incoming alternator is a little too fast. In view of this, the incoming machine at the time of synchronizing should be a little too fast than the already running alternator or the bus-bar. In other words, it may be stated that the frequency of the incoming alternator at the time of synchronizing should be a little higher than the frequency of the already running alternator or the bus-bar.

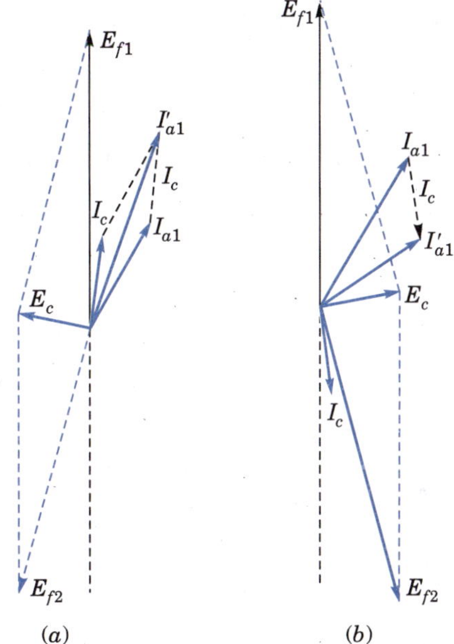

Fig. 4.71: Incoming alternator running (*a*) slower and (*b*) faster.

Example 4.25. *Two similar alternators operating in parallel have the following data:*

Alternator 1—Capacity 700 kW, frequency drops from 50 Hz at no-load to 48.5 Hz at full load.

Alternator 2—Capacity 700 kW, frequency drops from 50.5 Hz at no-load to 48 Hz at full load.

Speed regulation of prime-movers – linear in each case.

(a) Calculate how a total load of 1200 kW is shared by each alternator. Also find the operating bus-bar frequency at this load.

(b) Compute the maximum load that these two units can deliver without overloading either of them.

Solution. The speed-load characteristics of two primemovers or frequency-load characteristics of two alternators are shown by solid lines 1 and 2 in Fig. 4.72. For alternator 1, B is the operating point at no-load and d is the operating point at full load. For alternator 2, A and a are the operating points at no-load and full load respectively. Horizontal line xyz represents the total load of 1200 kW.

$$\therefore \qquad xy + yz = 1200 \text{ kW}.$$

Here oy represents the bus-bar frequency f. Through a and d, draw horizontal lines ab and dc so that ob = 48 Hz and oc = 48.5 Hz. Also ab = 700 kW and dc = 700 kW.

Now from similar triangles Aab and Axy, we get

$$\frac{xy}{Ay} = \frac{ab}{Ab} \qquad \text{or} \qquad \frac{xy}{oA - oy} = \frac{700 \text{ kW}}{oA - ob}$$

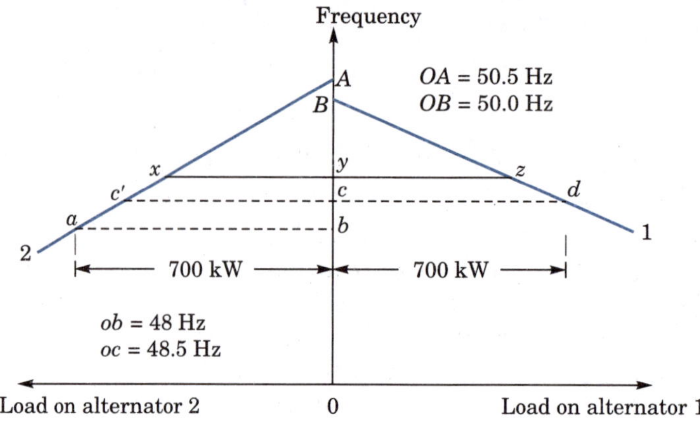

Fig. 4.72: Pertaining to Example 4.25.

$$\therefore \quad \frac{xy}{50.5 - f} = \frac{700}{50.5 - 48.00} \quad \text{or} \quad xy = \frac{700}{2.5}(50.5 - f)$$

From similar triangles Bcd and Byz,

$$\frac{yz}{By} = \frac{cd}{Bc} \quad \text{or} \quad \frac{yz}{oB - oy} = \frac{700 \text{ kW}}{oB - oc}$$

$$\therefore \quad \frac{yz}{50 - f} = \frac{700}{50 - 48.5} \quad \text{or} \quad yz = \frac{700}{1.5}(50 - f).$$

But
$$xy + yz = 1200 = 700\left(\frac{50.5 - f}{2.5} + \frac{50 - f}{1.5}\right)$$

or
$$\frac{12}{7} = \frac{151.50 - 3f + 250 - 5f}{7.5}$$

or
$$f = \frac{388.64}{8} = 48.58 \text{ Hz}.$$

Thus the bus-bar or system frequency at this load is 48.58 Hz.

The load shared by alternator 2 = $xy = \dfrac{700}{2.5}(50.5 - 48.58) = 537.6$ kW.

∴ The load shared by alternator 1 = 1200 – 537.6 = 662.4 kW.

(*b*) An examination of Fig. 4.72 reveals that full load will first come on alternator 1. It is also seen from part (*a*) that alternator 1 shares a much larger load as compared to alternator 2. Full load on alternator 1 is given by cd = 700 kW and occurs at a frequency of 48.5 Hz. Extend dc to c' as shown. Now, for a full load on alternator 1, the load on alternator 2 is given by cc'. From similar triangles, we get

$$\frac{c'c}{oA - oc} = \frac{ab}{oA - ob} \quad \text{or} \quad \frac{c'c}{50.5 - 48.5} = \frac{700 \text{ kW}}{50.5 - 48.0}$$

or
$$c'c = \frac{700}{2.50} \times 2.0 = 560 \text{ kW}.$$

∴ Maximum possible load = 700 + 560 = 1260 kW.

and the operating system frequency at this load is 48.5 Hz.

Example 4.26. *Three alternators, operating in parallel at a bus frequency of 50 Hz, share a load of 140 MW as follows:*

Alternator 1—40 MW, Alternator 2—40 MW, Alternator 3—60 MW.

Each alternator is rated at 100 MW. Their governor settings are so adjusted as to give the following fall in frequency from no-load to rated load:

Alternator 1—1.25 Hz, Alternator 2—1.50 Hz, Alternator 3—2.0 Hz.

How will the three alternators share a total load of 250 MW ? Also calculate the bus frequency at this load.

Solution. In Fig. 4.73, solid lines 1, 2, 3 show the frequency-load characteristics of three alternators 1, 2, 3 respectively. For a bus frequency of 50 Hz, alternators 1 and 2 share a load of 40 MW each and the third alternator shares a load of 60 MW as shown in Fig. 4.73.

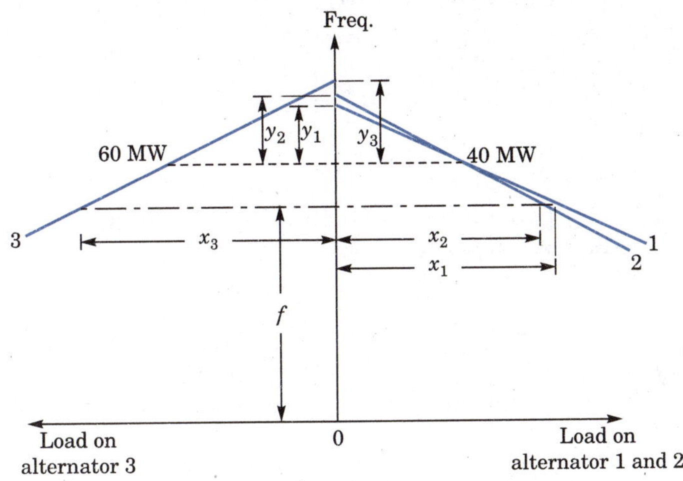

Fig. 4.73: Pertaining to Example 4.26.

For alternator 1, $\frac{y_1}{40 \text{ MW}}$ = Slope of frequency – load curve

$$= \frac{\text{Frequency drop from no-load to full load}}{\text{Full load}} = \frac{1.25 \text{ Hz}}{100 \text{ MW}}$$

or $$y_1 = \frac{1.25}{100} \times 40 = 0.50 \text{ Hz}$$

∴ No-load frequency of alternator 1

$$= 50 + 0.50 = 50.50 \text{ Hz}.$$

For alternator 2, $\frac{y_2}{40}$ = Slope of frequency – load curve = $\frac{1.50}{100}$

or $$y_2 = \frac{1.50}{100} \times 40 = 0.60 \text{ Hz}.$$

∴ No-load frequency of alternator 2 = 50 + 0.6 = 50.6 Hz.

For alternator 3, $\frac{y_3}{60} = \frac{2.00}{100}$ or $y_3 = 1.20$ Hz.

∴ No-load frequency of alternator 3

$$= 50 + 1.2 = 51.2 \text{ Hz.}$$

Out of a total load of 250 MW, let the alternators 1, 2, 3 share a load of x_1, x_2, x_3 MW respectively at a bus frequency of f Hz as shown in Fig. 4.73.

Now for alternator 1,

$$\frac{x_1 \text{ MW}}{50.5 - f} = \frac{100 \text{ MW}}{1.25 \text{ Hz}}$$

∴ $$x_1 = 80\,(50.5 - f)$$

For alternator 2,

$$\frac{x_2}{50.6 - f} = \frac{100}{1.50};$$

∴ $$x_2 = 66.67\,(506 - f)$$

For alternator 3,

$$\frac{x_3}{51.2 - f} = \frac{100}{2.00}$$

∴ $$x_3 = 50\,(51.2 - f)$$

But $$x_1 + x_2 + x_3 = 250$$

∴ $$80\,(50.5 - f) + 66.67\,(50.6 - f) + 50\,(51.2 - f) = 250$$

or $$196.67f = 9723.50 \quad \text{or} \quad f = 49.44 \text{ Hz.}$$

∴ $$x_1 = 80\,(50.5 - 49.44) = 84.8 \text{ MW}$$

$$x_2 = 66.67\,(50.6 - 49.44) = 77.34 \text{ MW}$$

and $$x_3 = 50\,(51.2 - 49.44) = 88.0 \text{ MW}$$

Thus the load shared by alternators 1, 2 and 3 is respectively 84.8 MW, 77.34 MW and 88.0 MW and the bus frequency is 49.44 Hz.

Example 4.27. *Two three-phase alternators, running in parallel and supplying a load of impedance (4 + j2) Ω, have their per phase synchronous impedance of $Z_{s_1} = 0.2 + j\,3.2\ \Omega$ and $Z_{s_2} = 0.25 + j\,4.5\ \Omega$. Their per phase excitation e.m.fs. are 230 V with E_{f_1} leading E_{f_2} by 10°. Compute the terminal voltage, their load currents and power outputs. Also obtain the no-load and full-load circulating currents.*

Solution.

$$\frac{1}{\bar{Z}_{s_1}} + \frac{1}{\bar{Z}_{s_2}} + \frac{1}{\bar{Z}_L} = \frac{1}{0.2 + j3.2} + \frac{1}{0.25 + j4.5} + \frac{1}{4 + j2}$$

$$= \frac{0.2 - j3.2}{10.28} + \frac{0.25 - j4.5}{20.25} + \frac{4 - j2}{20}$$

$$= (0.01945 - j0.3115) + (0.01234 + j0.222) + (0.2 - j0.1)$$

$$= 0.232 - j0.6335 = 0.680\ \underline{/-70.05^\circ}$$

With E_{f_1} as reference,

$$\frac{\bar{E}_{f_1}}{\bar{Z}_{s_1}} = (230 + j0)\,(0.01945 - j0.3115) = 4.47 - j71.6$$

$$\frac{\overline{E}_{f_2}}{\overline{Z}_{s_2}} = \frac{230\,(\cos 10 - j\sin 10)}{\overline{Z}_{s_2}}$$

$$= 230\,(0.985 - j0.174)\,(0.01234 - j0.222) = -\,6.09 - j50.8.$$

$$\therefore \qquad \frac{\overline{E}_{f_1}}{\overline{Z}_{s_1}} + \frac{\overline{E}_{f_2}}{\overline{Z}_{s_2}} = -\,1.62 - j121.4 = 121.4\,\underline{/-90.75}$$

Eq. (4.222) gives,
$$\overline{V}_t = \frac{121.4\;\underline{/-90.75^\circ}}{0.680\;\underline{/-70.05^\circ}} = 178.7\;\underline{/-20.70^\circ}\ \text{V} = (167.1 - j63.15)\ \text{V}$$

$$\overline{I}_{a_1} = \frac{\overline{E}_{f_1} - \overline{V}_t}{\overline{Z}_{s_1}} = \frac{(230 - 167.1 + j63.15)}{\overline{Z}_{s_1}}$$

$$= (62.9 + j63.15)\,(0.01945 + j0.3115)$$

$$= 20.853 - j18.35 = 27.8\;\underline{/-41.5^\circ}\ \text{A}$$

$$\overline{I}_{a_2} = \frac{\overline{E}_{f_2} - \overline{V}_t}{\overline{Z}_{s_2}} = \frac{(226.5 - j40 - 167.1 + j63.5)}{\overline{Z}_{s_2}}$$

$$= (59.4 + j23.5)\,(0.01234 + j0.222)$$

$$= (5.883 - j12.89) = 14.32\,\underline{/-65.7^\circ}.$$

Total load current, $\overline{I}_L = \overline{I}_{a_1} + \overline{I}_{a_2} = (26.74 - j31.24) = 41.15\;\underline{/-49.4^\circ}$ A.

Power delivered by the first machine,

$$= V_t I_{a_1} \cos(41.5^\circ - 20.70^\circ) = (178.7)\,(27.8)\cos(20.80^\circ)$$

$$= 4.64 \text{ kW at p.f. of } 0.935 \text{ lagging.}$$

Power delivered by the second machine,

$$= (178.7)\,(14.32)\cos(65.7^\circ - 20.70^\circ)$$

$$= 1.81 \text{ kW at p.f. of } 0.725 \text{ lagging.}$$

Total power delivered to load,

$$= 4.64 + 1.81 = 6.45 \text{ kW.}$$

Check. Total power delivered to load,

$$= (178.7)\,(41.15)\cos(49.4^\circ - 29.70^\circ)$$

$$= 6.45 \text{ kW at p.f. } 0.877 \text{ lagging.}$$

No-load circulating current,

$$= \frac{\overline{E}_{f_1} - \overline{E}_{f_2}}{\overline{Z}_{s_1} + \overline{Z}_{s_2}} = \frac{230 - (226.5 - j40)}{0.45 + j7.7}$$

$$= 5.2 - j0.15 = 5.202\,\underline{/-1.65^\circ}\ \text{A.}$$

Circulating current under full-load conditions,

$$= \frac{\overline{E}_{f_1} - \overline{E}_{f_2}}{\overline{Z}_{s_1} + \overline{Z}_{s_2} + \dfrac{\overline{Z}_{s_1}.\overline{Z}_{s_2}}{\overline{Z}_L}}$$

$$= \frac{3.5 + j40}{0.45 + j7.7 + \dfrac{(0.2 + j3.2)(0.25 + j4.5)}{4 + j2}}$$

$$= 3.995 - j1.243 = 4.184 \underline{/-17.28^\circ} \text{ A.}$$

The circulating current under no-load is almost in phase with E_{f_1}. The power delivered by machine 1 is 230 (5.202) cos 1.65 = 1195.5 watts per phase and that received by machine 2 is

$$(230)(5.202) \cos(-10^\circ + 1.65^\circ) = 1183.4 \text{ watts per phase}$$

Note that $1195.5 - 1183.4 = I_c^2 (r_{a_1} + r_{a_2}) = (5.202)^2 (0.2 + 0.25) = 12.1$ watts.

Example 4.28. *Two similar 3-phase 6.6 kV star-connected alternators, running in parallel, supply a load of 4000 kW at p.f. 0.8 lagging. The synchronous impedance per phase for the first machine is 0.6 + j10 Ω and for the second machine is 0.5 + j12.0 Ω. The total load is shared equally between the two machines. Without changing their driving torques, the excitation of first alternator is adjusted so that it delivers 200 A at a lagging p.f. Determine the current delivered by the second alternator. Also calculate the power factor, load angle and excitation voltage for each alternator.*

Solution. Total load current,

$$I_L = \frac{4000}{\sqrt{3}\,(6.6)(0.8)} = 437 \text{ A}$$

Taking terminal voltage V_t as reference phasor,

$$\bar{I}_L = 437\,(0.8 - j0.6) = 349 - j262.5 \text{ A}$$

Power factor of first alternator,

$$\cos\theta_1 = \frac{2000}{\sqrt{3}\,(6.6)(200)} = 0.874 \text{ lagging}$$

Now $\theta_1 = 29.0^\circ$ and $\sin\theta_1 = 0.485$.

∴ For first alternator, $\bar{I}_{a_1} = 200\,(0.874 - j0.485) = 174.8 - j97$ A.

For second alternator,

$$\bar{I}_{a_2} = \bar{I}_L - \bar{I}_{a_1}$$
$$= (349 - j262.5) - (174.8 - j97)$$
$$= 174.2 - j165.5 = 240 \underline{/-43.5^\circ} \text{ A.}$$

Power factor of second alternator,

$$\cos\theta_2 = 0.726 \text{ lagging}$$

For first alternator,

$$\bar{E}_{f_1} = \bar{V}_t + \bar{I}_{a_1}\bar{Z}_{s_1}$$
$$= \frac{6.6}{\sqrt{3}} + 10^{-3}(174.8 - j97)(0.6 + j10)$$

$$= 3.81 + 10^{-3}\,(104.9 + j1748 - j58.2 + 970)$$

$$= 4.885 + j1.69 = 5.16\,\angle 18.9°\text{ kV}.$$

∴ Load angle $\delta_1 = 18.9°$ and excitation voltage $E_{f_1} = 5.16$ kV phase voltage or 8.93 kV line voltage.

Also $$\overline{E}_{f_2} = \overline{V}_t + \overline{I}_{a_2}\overline{Z}_{s_2} = \frac{6.6}{\sqrt{3}} + 10^{-3}\,(174.2 - j165.5)\,(0.5 + j12)$$

$$= 5.87 + j2.007 = 6.21\,\underline{/19°}\text{ kV}.$$

For second alternator, load angle δ_2 is 19° and excitation voltage E_{f_2} is 6.21 kV phase voltage or 10.75 kV line voltage.

4.21 SYNCHRONOUS MACHINE ON AN INFINITE BUS

A bus-bar which maintains constant voltage and constant frequency irrespective of the load variations on it, is called an infinite bus. A large number of alternators interconnected together to form a supply system, may be regarded as an infinite bus. In effect, an infinite bus behaves like a voltage source having zero internal impedance and infinite rotational inertia. A synchronous machine switched on to, or off, the infinite bus, does not cause any change in the voltage and frequency of the system.

The behaviour of a synchronous machine connected to an infinite bus is quite different from that when it is connected to another alternator. For example, when two alternators are operating in parallel, a change in the excitation of one alternator changes their terminal voltage and also their operating power factors. On the other hand, for an alternator connected to an infinite bus, any change in its field excitation is going to alter its operating power factor only and not the terminal voltage, which is maintained constant by the bus.

The object of this article is to investigate the effect of varying the field excitation and the driving torque of an alternator connected to an infinite bus. In order to concentrate more on these effects, all losses are assumed to be zero.

4.21.1 Effect of Varying the Excitation

Consider the operation of a cylindrical rotor alternator synchronized with an infinite bus, for which the general voltage equation is, $\overline{E}_f = \overline{V}_b + \overline{I}_a Z_s$

Here E_f is the excitation voltage, V_b is the constant bus voltage, I_a is the armature current and Z_s is the synchronous impedance. If the armature resistance is neglected as shown in Fig. 4.74 (*a*), then the above general voltage equation becomes, $\overline{E}_f = \overline{V}_b + j\overline{I}_a X_s$

As before, the effect of varying the field excitation is considered first with the alternator at no-load and then when it is working on load.

(*a*) **No-load operation.** Since all losses are neglected, load angle δ at no-load is zero. In view of this, power transferred $\left(= \dfrac{E_f . V_b}{X_s}\sin\delta\right)$ either to, or from, the bus is zero. If excitation voltage E_f is equal to the bus voltage V_b, then at no-load, no current flows either to, or from, the bus as illustrated in Fig. 4.74 (*b*). Under these conditions of no current flow, the synchronous machine is said to be *floating* on the bus.

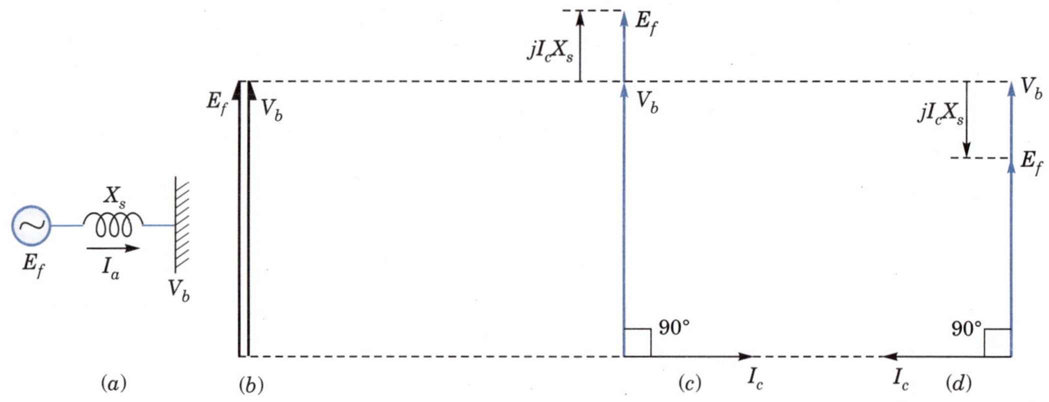

Fig. 4.74: Effect of changing the field excitation of an unloaded alternator connected to an infinite bus.

In case alternator at no-load is over-excited, E_f becomes more than V_b and a circulating current $\bar{I}_c = \dfrac{\bar{E}_f - \bar{V}_b}{jX_s}$ is set up. Load angle δ remains zero, therefore current I_c lags E_f and V_b by 90° as shown in Fig. 4.74 (*c*). Since I_c lags E_f by 90°, it produces demagnetizing armature m.m.f. which nullifies the effect of increased field m.m.f.—this has the effect of maintaining the alternator terminal voltage equal to the constant bus voltage V_b. Now if the alternator is underexcited, E_f becomes less than V_b, circulating current I_c is again set up but this time it leads E_f and V_b, by 90° as illustrated in Fig. 4.74 (*d*). Since I_c leads V_b by 90°, it produces magnetizing m.m.f. which adds to the decreased field m.m.f. thereby making up for the loss of field ampere turns. This has the effect of maintaining the alternator terminal voltage equal to the constant bus voltage V_b.

Note that in both cases illustrated in Fig. 4.74 (*c*) and (*d*), no active power is delivered because I_c is in quadrature with V_b and also load angle δ is zero. However, in Fig. 4.74 (*c*) the alternator is delivering reactive power to the bus because $E_f > V_b$ and in Fig. 4.74 (*d*), it is taking reactive power from the bus because, $E_f < V_b$.

(*b*) **On-load operation.** Now suppose that the alternator is supplying power to an infinite bus with excitation voltage E_f, power angle δ and unity power-factor current I_a as illustrated in Fig. 4.75 (*a*).

If the mechanical power input to alternator is kept constant, then for negligible losses, $\dfrac{E_f V_b}{X_s}$ sin δ must remain constant. An increase of E_f to E_{f_1} causes the load angle to decrease to δ_1, which can be obtained from the relation $E_{f_1} \sin \delta_1 = E_f \sin \delta$ because V_b and X_s are constant. The synchronous reactance drop increases and this has the effect of increasing armature current to I_{a_1}. An examination of Fig. 4.75 (*a*) reveals that the increased current I_{a_1} has a real component I_a and a demagnetizing component I_{c_1}, which results in lagging power factor cos θ_1. If E_f is decreased to E_{f_2}, load angle increases to δ_2 and armature current increases to I_{a_2}. The increased current I_{a_2} has a real component I_a and a magnetizing component I_{c_2}, which results in a leading power factor cos θ_2. Note that the real components of I_{a_1} and I_{a_2} are equal to I_a, *i.e.*,

$$I_{a_1} \cos\theta_1 = I_{a_2} \cos\theta_2 = I_a$$

and as a result of it, $V_b I_{a_1} \cos\theta_1 = V_b I_{a_2} \cos\theta_2 = V_b I_a$

which means that active power delivered to the bus remains unchanged. Thus the adjustment of field rheostat, for changing the alternator excitation, has no effect on the power delivered to the infinite bus. However, a change in the alternator field current alters its operating power factor as shown in Fig. 4.75 (*a*). An examination of Fig. 4.75 (*a*) also reveals that an under-excited alternator operates at a leading power factor, whereas an overexcited alternator operates at a lagging power factor—this is illustrated in Fig. 4.75 (*b*). Note that armature current is minimum at unity power factor. For leading power factor operation, $E_f \cos\delta < V_b$, therefore, the alternator absorbs reactive power from the bus. For lagging power factor operation, $E_f \cos\delta > V_b$, therefore, the alternator delivers reactive power to the bus. In Fig. 4.75 (*a*), so far as the active power fed to the infinite bus is concerned, the currents I_{c_1} and I_{c_2} are undesirable components.

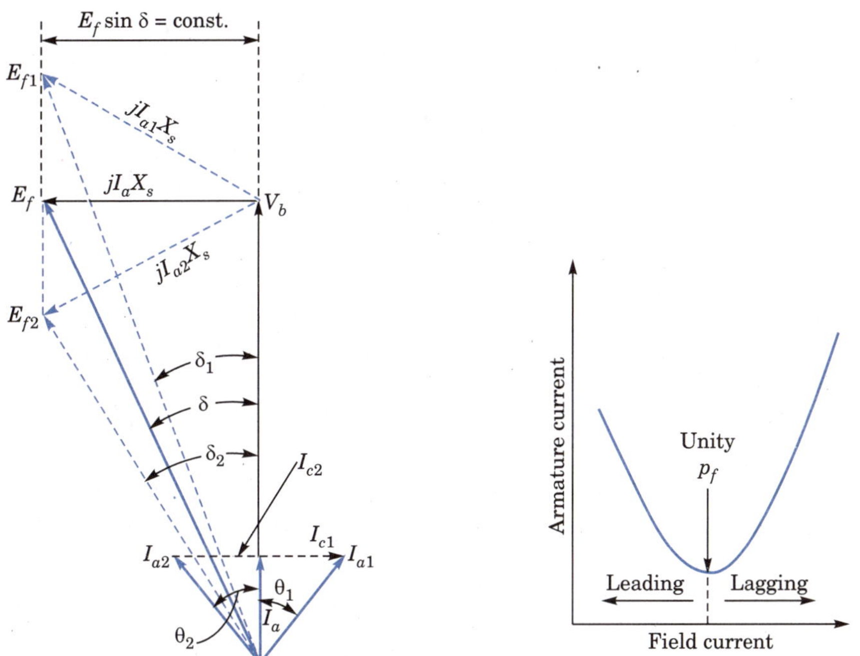

Fig. 4.75: Effect of changing field excitation of a loaded alternator connected to an infinite bus.

4.21.2 Effect of Varying the Driving Torque

As explained before, the driving torque of an alternator can be controlled by the throttle-opening in steam-stations and by gate-opening in case of hydro-stations. For an alternator connected to an infinite bus, the effect of varying the driving torque can be investigated more clearly with the help of its phasor diagram. Fig. 4.76 (*a*) illustrates the alternator phasor diagram for lagging power factor, where $\overline{E}_f = \overline{V}_b + j\overline{I}_a X_s$ and load angle is δ. If the driving torque of the alternator is increased without altering its field current or E_f, the alternator output (neglecting losses) $\frac{E_f V_b}{X_s}$ sin δ must increase. Since E_f is held fixed and V_b and X_s are constant, only δ can increase so as to maintain a balance between increased mechanical

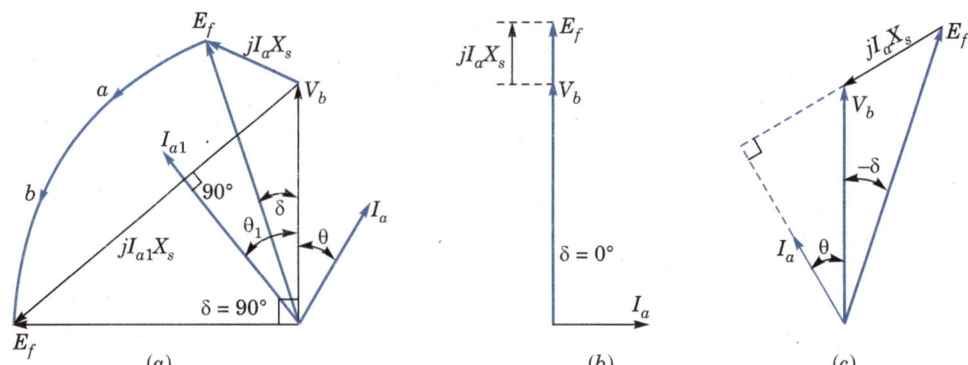

Fig. 4.76: Effect of varying the driving torque of an alternator connected to an infinite bus.

input and $\frac{E_f V_b}{X_s}$ sin δ. As a result of it, tip of phasor E_f follows the curved path *a*, *b*. The maximum stable value of δ is 90°, for which the armature current increases to I_{a_1}, leading the bus voltage V_b by power factor angle θ_1 as shown in Fig. 4.76 (*a*). This figure reveals that with an increase in steam input, the alternator begins to absorb reactive power from the infinite bus the moment p.f. becomes leading. It is obvious that with an increase in steam input, alternator delivers more active power to infinite bus. It should be remembered that alternator frequency and terminal voltage cannot change as it is connected to an infinite bus.

However, if the driving torque is decreased, the angle δ must decrease accordingly. If load angle δ becomes zero as shown in Fig. 4.76 (*b*), no power is transferred to the infinite bus, the prime-mover merely supplies the alternator losses. If the prime-mover driving torque is reversed or else it is de-coupled from the alternator shaft, E_f shifts and lags behind V_b, δ gets reversed and the machine operation alters from synchronous generator ($\overline{E}_f = \overline{V}_b + j\overline{I}_a X_s$) to synchronous motor ($\overline{V}_b = \overline{E}_f + j\overline{I}_a X_s$) as illustrated in Fig. 4.76 (*c*). The synchronous motor now operates at a leading p.f. showing that it is now delivering reactive power to the infinite bus.

Example 4.29. *A 3-phase star-connected cylindrical rotor alternator, with synchronous reactance of 5 Ω per phase, is supplying 240 A at unity power factor to a 11 kV infinite bus.*

(a) If excitation e.m.f. of the alternator is increased by 25% without changing its driving torque, calculate the new values of current, power factor and load angle. Will there be any change in the power supplied to the infinite bus ? Explain.

(b) With the increased excitation of part (a) held fixed, at what power output would the alternator break from synchronism ? Find the corresponding values of current and power factor.

Solution. Per phase infinite bus voltage, $V_b = \frac{11000}{\sqrt{3}} = 6351$ V.

The phasor diagram at unity p.f. is illustrated in Fig. 4.77, from which

$$\bar{E}_f = \bar{V}_b + j\bar{I}_b X_s = 6351 + j240 \times 5$$

$$\therefore \quad E_f = \sqrt{(6351)^2 + (1200)^2} = 6463.4 \text{ V}.$$

(*a*) New value of excitation e.m.f., $E_{f_1} = 1.25 \times 6463.4 = 8079.3$ V

An examination of Fig. 4.77 reveals that $I_{a_1} X_s \cos\theta_1 = I_a X_s$

$$= 240 \times 5 = 1200 \text{ V}.$$

$$\therefore \quad I_{a_1} \cos\theta_1 = \frac{1200}{5} = 240 \text{ A}.$$

$$\therefore \quad E_{f_1} = \sqrt{(V_b + I_{a_1} X_s \sin\theta_1)^2 + (I_{a_1} X_s \cos\theta_1)^2}$$

or $$(8079.3)^2 = (6351 + 5I_{a_1} \sin\theta_1)^2 + (1200)^2$$

or $$I_{a_1} \sin\theta_1 = \frac{7989.7 - 6351}{5} = 327.74 \text{ A}.$$

∴ New armature current,

$$I_{a_1} = \sqrt{(I_{a_1}\cos\theta_1)^2 + (I_{a_1}\sin\theta_1)^2} = \sqrt{(240)^2 + (327.74)^2} = 406.22 \text{ A}.$$

Power factor, $\cos\theta_1 = \dfrac{240}{406.22} = 0.591$ lagging.

The initial angle δ from Fig. 4.77 is

$$\tan\delta = \frac{I_a X_s}{V_b} = \frac{1200}{6351}$$

$$\therefore \quad \delta = 10.7°.$$

Also $$E_f \sin\delta = E_{f_1} \sin\delta_1$$

$$\therefore \quad \sin\delta_1 = \frac{E_f}{E_{f_1}} \sin\delta = \frac{1}{1.25} \sin 10.7° \quad \text{or} \quad \delta_1 = 8.54°.$$

Since the driving torque of the alternator is not changed, mechanical input to alternator is the same as before, consequently the power supplied to infinite bus can't change.

(*b*) With the excitation e.m.f. as in part (*a*), the maximum power output takes place when the load angle between V_b and E_{f_1} is 90° as shown in Fig. 4.77.

∴ Maximum power output

$$= \frac{E_{f_1} V_b}{X_s} \sin 90$$

$$= \frac{8079.3 \times 6351}{5} \times 1$$

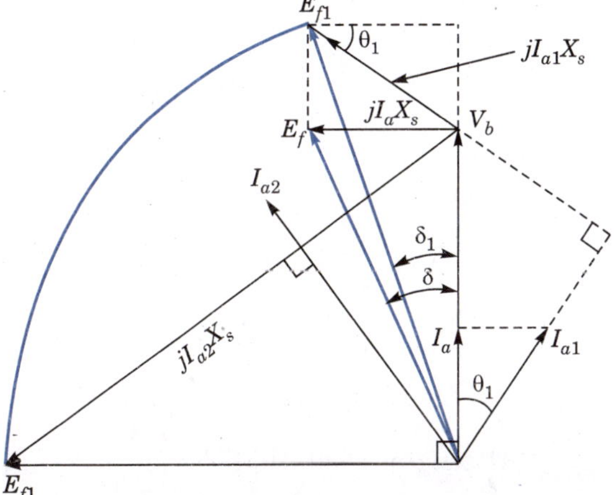

Fig. 4.77: Pertaining to Example 4.29.

$$= 10262.3 \text{ kW per phase} = 30786.9 \text{ kW total.}$$

From Fig. 4.77, $I_{a_2} X_s = \sqrt{E_{f_1}^2 + V_b^2}$

$$= \sqrt{(8079.3)^2 + (6351)^2} = 10276.67.$$

∴ Armature current of alternator under maximum power output is

$$I_{a_2} = \frac{10276.67}{5} = 2055.3 \text{ A.}$$

Fig. 4.77 shows that power factor, under maximum power output, is leading and its value is given by $\frac{10262.3}{6.351 \times 2055.3} = 0.786$ leading.

Example 4.30. *A 3-phase star-connected turbo-generator feeds power to 11 kV infinite bus, through two parallel transmission lines each having a reactance of 4 Ω. The generator synchronous reactance is 3 Ω.*

(a) The mechanical input to alternator and its excitation are adjusted so that the operating power factor at alternator terminals is unity and rated current of 500 A is delivered. Calculate the alternator terminal and excitation voltages. Also determine the active and reactive powers delivered to the infinite bus.

(b) With the excitation fixed as found in part (a), the mechanical input to alternator is adjusted so that no power transfer takes place between alternator and the infinite bus. Calculate the lagging reactive power delivered to the bus and alternator terminal voltage under these conditions.

Solution. Fig. 4.78 (*a*) illustrates the single line diagram for this example and Fig. 4.78 (*b*) gives its phasor diagram, from which it is seen that

$$V_b^2 = V_t^2 + (2I_a)^2.$$

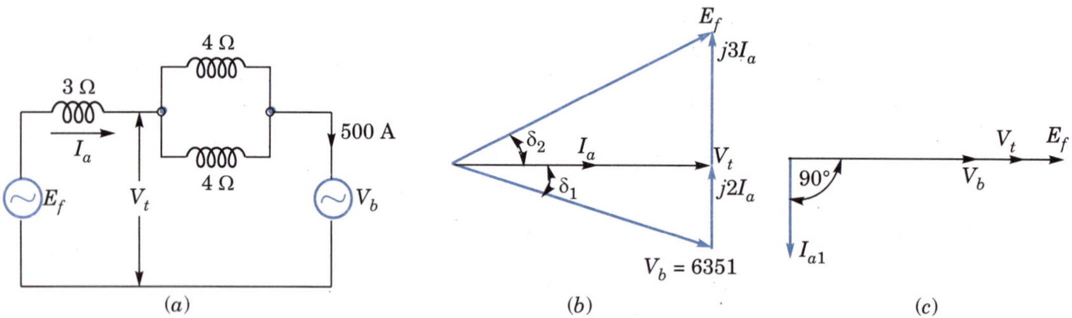

Fig. 4.78: Pertaining to Example 4.30.

Here $$V_b = \frac{11000}{\sqrt{3}} = 6351 \text{ V.}$$

∴ Alternator terminal voltage, $V_t = \sqrt{(6351)^2 - (1000)^2} = 6271.8$ V.

Alternator excitation voltage, $E_f = \sqrt{V_t^2 + (3I_a)^2}$

$$= \sqrt{(6271.8)^2 + (3 \times 500)^2} = 6448.7 \text{ V.}$$

Power angle between V_b and V_t, $\delta_1 = \sin^{-1}\left(\frac{2I_a}{V_b}\right) = \sin^{-1}\frac{1000}{6351} = 9.06°$

Power angle between E_f and V_t, $\delta_2 = \sin^{-1}\frac{3I_a}{E_f} = \sin^{-1}\frac{1500}{6448.7} = 13.45°$

∴ Active power delivered to infinite bus,

$$P = \frac{E_f V_b}{3+2}\sin(\delta_1 + \delta_2)$$
$$= \frac{6448.7 \times 6351}{5}\sin(22.51) = 3135.93 \text{ kW/phase}$$
$$= 9407.79 \text{ kW total.}$$

Check, $P = V_b I_a \cos(\widehat{V_b I_a})$
$$= 6351 \times 500 \cos(9.06) = 3135.88 \text{ kW/phase.}$$

Since I_a leads V_b, the alternator takes reactive power from the infinite bus.

∴ Reactive power taken from the infinite bus $= V_b I_a \sin(\widehat{V_b I_a})$
$$= 6351 \times 500 \sin 9.06° = 500 \text{ kVAr per phase.}$$

or Reactive power delivered to the infinite bus = – 500 kVAr/phase.

(*b*) For the conditions stated in this part, phasor diagram of Fig. 4.78 (*b*) gets modified to that shown in Fig. 4.78 (*c*), from which it is seen that

$$I_{a_1} = \frac{E_f - V_b}{X_s + 2} = \frac{6448.7 - 6351}{5} = 19.54 \text{ A}$$

Alternator terminal voltage, $V_t = V_b + 2I_{a_1} = 6351 + 2 \times 19.54 = 6390.8$ V.

Reactive power delivered to the infinite bus

$$= V_b I_{a_1} = 6351 \times 19.54 = 124.1 \text{ kVAr/phase.}$$

Example 4.31. *A 3-phase, 400 V, 10 kVA, star-connected cylindrical rotor alternator, with synchronous reactance of 7 Ω per phase, is driven by 220 V, 10 kW dc shunt motor. The alternator is synchronized with an infinite bus of 400 V, 50 Hz. All losses are to be ignored.*

(a) Determine the excitation voltage and load angle of the alternator when it delivers rated kVA at unity power factor.

(b) With the driving torque of d.c. shunt motor unaltered, the excitation voltage is increased by 25%. Find the new load angle, current and power factor. Also obtain the maximum stable power output of the alternator and the corresponding values of current and p.f.

(c) With the excitation voltage held constant as obtained in part (a), the driving torque of d.c. shunt motor is decreased till load angle becomes zero. Under these conditions, find the armature currents of both d.c. and a.c. machines.

(d) The driving torque of d.c. machine is now reversed till 10 kW is transferred from infinite bus to d.c. mains. Find the armature current of d.c. shunt machine and a.c. machine. Also obtain the load angle of the synchronous machine.

Solution. (*a*) Phase voltage of the bus, $V_b = \dfrac{400}{\sqrt{3}} = 231$ V

Rated armature current, $I_a = \dfrac{10{,}000}{\sqrt{3}(400)} = 14.43$ A

From Fig. 4.79 (*a*), $\bar{E}_f = \bar{V}_b + j\bar{I}_a X_s$

$= 230 + j(14.43)7 = (231 + j101.01) = 252.12 \angle 23.62°$ V.

∴ Excitation voltage, $E_f = 252.12$ V

and load angle, $\delta = 23.62°$.

(*b*) New excitation voltage, $E_{f_1} = (252.12)\,(1.25) = 315.15$ V.

Since the driving torque remains same, the alternator output with increased excitation voltage is unaltered.

$$\therefore \quad \frac{E_{f_1} V_b}{X_s} \sin \delta_1 = \frac{E_f V_b}{X_s} \sin \delta \qquad \text{or} \qquad E_{f_1} \sin \delta_1 = E_f \sin \delta$$

$$\therefore \quad \sin \delta_1 = \frac{1}{1.25} \sin 23.62° = 0.3205 \text{ and } \delta_1 = 18.69°$$

Fig. 4.79 (*a*) also reveals that,

$$I_{a_1} X_s \sin \theta_1 = E_{f_1} \cos \delta_1 - E_f \cos \delta = (315.15) \cos 18.69° - 231 = 67.5$$

$$\therefore \quad I_{a_1} \sin \theta_1 = \frac{67.5}{7} = 9.64 \text{ A}$$

Also $\quad V_b I_{a_1} \cos \theta_1 = V_b I_a \cos \theta$ = constant alternator output

or $\quad I_{a_1} \cos \theta_1 = 14.43$ A.

∴ New armature current,

$$I_{a_1} = \sqrt{(I_{a_1} \cos \theta_1)^2 + (I_{a_1} \sin \theta_1)^2} = \sqrt{(14.43)^2 + (9.64)^2} = 17.35 \text{ A.}$$

New power factor, $\cos \theta_1 = \dfrac{14.43}{17.35} = 0.832$ lagging.

Maximum power output takes place when the load angle between E_{f_1} and V_b, as shown in Fig. 4.79, is 90°.

∴ Maximum power output

$$= \frac{E_{f_1} V_b}{X_s} \sin 90° = \frac{(315.15)\,(231)}{7} \times 1$$

$= 10.40$ kW per phase $= 31.20$ kW total

From Fig. 4.79 (*a*), $I_{a_2} X_s = \sqrt{(315.15) + (231)^2} = 390.74$ V.

∴ Armature current of synchronous generator for maximum power output is given by

$$I_{a_2} = \frac{390.74}{7} = 55.82 \text{ A}$$

and $\quad \text{p.f.} = \dfrac{10400}{(231)\,(55.82)} = 0.807$ leading.

(*c*) Since the d.c. shunt motor is mechanically coupled with the alternator which is synchronized with an infinite bus, the speed of d.c. shunt motor must always remain constant, equal to the alternator synchronous speed. In view of this, an increase in the field current I_f of d.c. shunt motor causes an increase in its counter, or back, e.m.f. E_a which is given by $k \times I_f \times$ constant synchronous speed. The d.c. motor armature current I_a is given by

$$I_a = \frac{\text{Applied voltage} - E_a}{\text{Armature resistance}}.$$

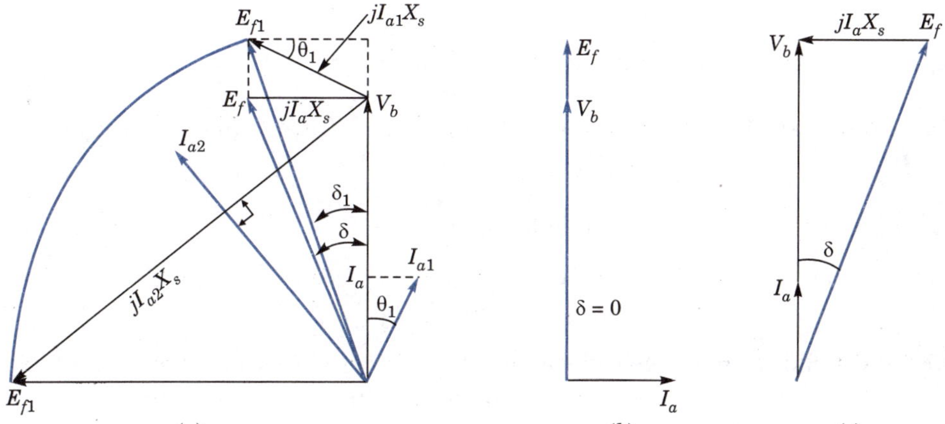

Fig. 4.79: Phasor diagrams pertaining to Example 4.31.

As field current I_f is increased, E_a increases. At some value of I_f, E_a becomes equal to applied d.c. voltage and, therefore, $I_a = 0$. Likewise d.c. motor torque ($\alpha\ I_f\ I_a$) is also zero. Under these conditions, load angle becomes zero and synchronous generator phasor diagram gets modified to that shown in Fig. 4.79 (*b*), from which its armature current is given by

$$\frac{E_f - V_b}{X_s} = \frac{21.12}{7} = 3.02 \text{ A}.$$

(*d*) If field current I_f is increased further, the counter e.m.f. E_a of the d.c. machine becomes greater than the voltage of d.c. mains. As a consequence of it, dc machine armature current reverses and likewise its driving torque ($\alpha\ I_f\ I_a$) is also reversed. In other words, the d.c. machine now operates as a d.c. shunt generator and acts as a mechanical load on the a.c. machine which has now become a synchronous motor as illustrated in Fig. 4.79 (*c*). Thus power is now transferred from a.c. infinite bus to d.c. mains.

In part (*a*), $\dfrac{E_f V_b}{X_s}$ sin δ is 10 kW and now in part (*d*) it is again 10 kW. With all the losses ignored, δ for part (*d*) is again 23.62°. Since $E_f \sin \delta$ is unchanged, $I_a X_s$ is unaltered in Fig. 4.79 (*c*).

∴ Synchronous motor armature current = 14.43 A at unity p.f.

D.C. generator armature current $= \dfrac{10{,}000}{220} = 45.455$ A.

Example 4.32. *A 3-phase star-connected alternator, with $Z_s = 0.5 + j8\ \Omega$, delivers 200 A at p.f. 0.8 lagging to 11 kV infinite bus.*

(*a*) *With steam supply unchanged, find the percentage increase or decrease in the excitation e.m.f. necessary to raise the p.f. to unity. Assume rotational losses to remain constant.*

(*b*) *In case alternator output is unchanged, determine the percentage increase or decrease in the excitation e.m.f. needed to raise the p.f. to unity.*

(*c*) *Repeat part (a) in case $r_a = 0$ and rotational losses are neglected.*

Solution. Bus-bar phase voltage, $V_b = \dfrac{11000}{\sqrt{3}} = 6351$ V

For cylindrical rotor alternator, the excitation voltage E_f is given by [See Fig. 4.10 (*a*)],

$$\bar{E}_f = \bar{V}_b + \bar{I}_a Z_s$$

With V_b as reference, $\bar{I}_a = 200\ (0.8 - j0.6)$

$$\therefore \quad \bar{E}_f = (6351 + j0) + 200\ (0.8 - j0.6)\ (0.5 + j8)$$

$$= 7391 + j1220 = 7491.01\ \angle 9.37^\circ$$

Alternator output power per phase = power delivered to infinite bus per phase

$$= V_b I_a \cos\theta = 6351 \times 200 \times 0.8 = 1016160 \text{ W}$$

Power developed in alternator armature = electromagnetic power

$$= \text{Power delivered to bus bar} + I^2R \text{ losses in armature circuit}$$

$$= V_b I_a \cos\theta + I_a^2 r_a$$

$$= 1016160 + 200^2 \times 0.5 = 1036160 \text{ W}$$

(*a*) Steam power input to alternator = electromagnetic power + rotational losses.

As rotational losses are assumed constant, with steam supply unchanged, the electromagnetic power also remains constant. With p.f. raised to unity, the armature current I_{a_1} can be obtained as under :

Power delivered to infinite bus + I^2R loss = electromagnetic power

$$V_b I_{a_1} + I_{a_1}^2 r_a = 1036160 \text{ W}$$

or $$6351 I_{a_1} + 0.5 I_{a_1}^2 = 1036160 \quad \text{or} \quad 0.5 I_{a_1}^2 + 6351 I_{a_1} - 1036160 = 0$$

Its solution gives $I_{a_1} = 161.1$ A

With V_b as reference, the new excitation voltage E_{f_1}, is

$$E_{f_1} = \bar{V}_{b_1} + \bar{I}_{a_1} Z_s$$

$$= 6351 + 161.1\ (0.5 + j8) = 6559.4\ \angle 11.33^\circ$$

Percentage decrease in excitation e.m.f.

$$= \frac{E_f - E_{f_1}}{E_f} = \frac{7491.01 - 6559.4}{7491.01} \times 100 = 12.436\%$$

(*b*) For no change in alternator output power,

$$V_b I_a \cos\theta = V_b I_{a_2} \times 1 \quad \text{or} \quad I_{a_2} = I_a \cos\theta = 200 \times 0.8 = 160 \text{ A}$$

Here I_{a_2} is the armature current per phase for constant alternator output. Now the excitation voltage E_{f_2} is $\bar{E}_{f_2} = \bar{V}_b + \bar{I}_{a_2} Z_s$ = 6351 + 160 (0.5 + j8) = 6557.15 ∠ 11.26°

$$\text{Percentage decrease in excitation e.m.f.} = \frac{7491.01 - 6557.15}{7491.01} \times 100 = 12.466\%$$

(c) With $r_a = 0$, $\quad \bar{E}_f = \bar{V}_b + j\bar{I}_a X_s = 6351 + j200\,(0.8 - j0.6)8$
$= 7311 + j1280 = 7422.2 \angle 9.93°$

With steam input remaining constant, $V_b I_a \cos\theta = V_b I_{a_3} \times 1$

or $\quad I_{a_3} = 200 \times 0.8 = 160$ A

$$E_{f_3} = \sqrt{V_b^2 + (I_{a_3} X_s)^2} = \sqrt{6351^2 + (160 \times 8)^2} = 6478.7 \text{ V}$$

$$\text{Percentage decrease in excitation e.m.f.} = \frac{7422.2 - 6478.7}{7422.2} \times 100 = 12.12\%.$$

Example 4.33. *With the help of phasor diagram show that power input to a cylindrical-rotor alternator is given by*

$$P = \frac{E_f V_t}{Z_s} \sin(\delta - \alpha_z) + \frac{E_f^2}{Z_s^r} r_a$$

where $\alpha_z = \tan^{-1}\left(\frac{r_a}{X_s}\right)$ *and* $Z_s = (r_a + jX_s)$ *is its synchronous impedance.*

Solution. For a cylindrical-rotor alternator working at a lagging p.f. load, the phasor diagram is as shown in Fig. 4.80. Here the excitation e.m.f. E_f is given by

$$\bar{E}_f = \bar{V}_t + \bar{I}_a \bar{Z}_s$$

or $$\bar{I}_a = \frac{\bar{E}_f}{\bar{Z}_s} - \frac{\bar{V}_t}{\bar{Z}_s} \qquad ...(4.227)$$

The current phasor $\frac{\bar{E}_f}{\bar{Z}_s}$ lags $\bar{E}_f$ by $\theta_z = \tan^{-1}\left(\frac{X_s}{r_a}\right)$ as shown in Fig. 4.80. Similarly, current phasor $\frac{\bar{V}_t}{\bar{Z}_s}$ lags $\bar{V}_t$ by θ_z. The difference of $\bar{E}_f/\bar{Z}_s$ and $\bar{V}_t/\bar{Z}_s$ as per Eq. (4.227) gives the armature current I_a.

Now, per phase power input to alternator is given by

$$P = E_f I_a \cos(\delta + \theta)$$

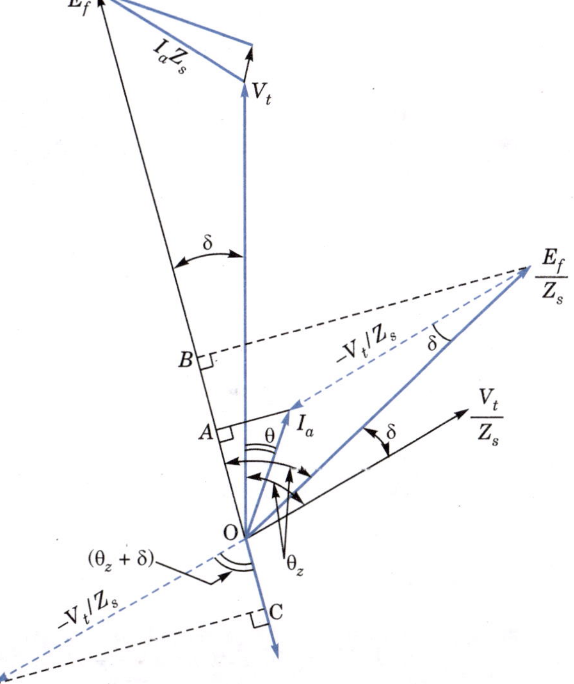

Fig. 4.80: Pertaining to Example 4.33.

In Fig. 4.80, $I_a \cos(\delta + \theta) = OA = OB - AB$. But $OB = \frac{E_f}{Z_s} \cos \theta_Z$

and $$AB = OC = \frac{V_t}{Z_s} \cos(\theta_z + \delta)$$

$$\therefore \quad I_a \cos(\delta + \theta) = \frac{E_f}{Z_s} \cos \theta_z - \frac{V_t}{Z_s} \cos(\theta_z + \delta)$$

$$\therefore \quad P = E_f I_a \cos(\delta + \theta) = \frac{E_f^{\,2}}{Z_s} \cos \theta_z - \frac{E_f \,.\, V_t}{Z_s} \cos(\theta_z + \delta)$$

But $$\cos \theta_z = \frac{r_a}{Z_s} \text{ and } \theta_z = 90 - \alpha_z$$

$$\therefore \quad P = \frac{E_f^2}{Z_s^2} r_a - \frac{E_f \,.\, V_t}{Z_s} \cos[90 + (\delta - \alpha_z)]$$

$$P = \frac{E_f V_t}{Z_s} \sin(\delta - \alpha_z) + \frac{E_f^2}{Z_s^2} r_a \qquad \text{...(4.228)}$$

Example 4.34. *A star-connected turbo-alternator, with $Z_s = (0.5 + j10)$ ohms per phase, delivers 200 A at unity p.f. to an 11 kV infinite bus. If the alternator excitation is increased by 25%, find the current and p.f. at which the machine shall now work. Assume a constant steam supply and unchanged efficiency.*

Solution. Per phase bus-bar voltage, $V_b = \frac{11000}{\sqrt{3}} = 6351$ V

Alternator phasor diagram at unity p.f. gives $E_f = \sqrt{(V_b + I_a r_a)^2 + (I_a X_s)^2}$

$$= \sqrt{(6351 + 200 \times 0.5)^2 + (200 \times 10)^2} = 6753.91 \text{ V}$$

Load angle, $$\delta = \tan^{-1} \frac{2000}{6451} = 17.22°$$

$$\alpha_z = \tan^{-1} \frac{r_a}{X_s} = \tan^{-1} \frac{0.5}{10} = 2.86°$$

$$Z_s = \sqrt{0.5^2 + 10^2} = 10.012\ \Omega$$

New values of excitation voltage, $E_{f_1} = 6753.91 \times 1.25 = 8442.4$ V

As the steam supply and alternator efficiency are unchanged, power input to alternator with E_f = power input to alternator with $1.25E_f$

or $$\frac{E_f \,.\, V_b}{Z_s} \sin(\delta - \alpha_z) + \frac{E_f^2}{Z_s^2} r_a = \frac{1.25E_f \,.\, V_b}{Z_s} \sin(\delta' - \alpha_z) + \frac{(1.25\, E_f)^2}{Z_s^2} r_a$$

Multiplying both sides of above equation by $\frac{Z_s}{E_f \,.\, V_b}$, we get

$$1.25 \sin(\delta' - \alpha_z) + \frac{1.25^2\, E_f}{V_b} \cdot \frac{r_a}{Z_s} = \sin(\delta - \alpha_z) + \frac{E_f}{V_b} \cdot \frac{r_a}{Z_s}$$

or
$$1.25 \sin(\delta' - 2.86) + \frac{1.25^2 \times 6753.91}{6351} \cdot \frac{0.5}{10.012}$$
$$= \sin(17.22 - 2.86) + \frac{6753.91}{6351} \cdot \frac{0.5}{10.012}$$

Its simplification gives $\delta' = 12.91°$

With the excitation increased, let the armature current be I_{a_1}. The alternator phasor diagram, Fig. 4.80, shows that

$$I_{a_1} \cdot Z_s = \sqrt{(1.25E_f)^2 + V_b^2 - 2 \times 1.25E_f \times V_b \cos\delta'}$$

or
$$I_{a_1}(10.012) = \sqrt{8442.4^2 + 6351^2 - 2 \times 8442.4 \times 6351 \times \cos 12.91°}$$

∴
$$I_{a_1} = 265.85 \text{ A}$$

For the same steam input, $1.25E_f I_{a_1} \cos(\delta' + \theta) = E_f I_a \cos\delta$

or
$$1.25 I_{a_1} \cdot \cos(\delta' + \theta) = I_a \cos\delta$$

or
$$\cos(12.91 + \theta) = \frac{200 \cos 17.22}{265.85 \times 1.25} \text{ or } \theta = 42°$$

∴ New p.f. = cos 42° = 0.743 lag.

Example 4.35. *(a) When two alternators are operating in parallel, explain why it is objectionable to operate one at a leading p.f. and the other at a lagging p.f.*

(b) Compare the parallel operation of synchronous generators with those of transformers and d.c. generators.

Solution. (*a*) For the two alternators running in parallel, suppose that E_f and I_a are their excitation voltages and armature currents respectively as shown in Fig. 4.81. Both the alternators are running at unity p.f. and their total output current is $I_L = 2I_a$. Power output by each alternator is $\sqrt{3}V_t I_a$. Now the excitation of alternator 1 is increased and that of alternator 2 is decreased so that their excitation voltages, armature currents and p.fs. are E_{f_1}, I_{a_1}, $\cos\theta_1$ and E_{f_2}, I_{a_2}, $\cos\theta_2$ respectively. Their terminal voltage is again V_t. With this change, output of alternators remain unaltered because nothing has been done to the driving torques of both alternators. The output of alternator 1 is $\sqrt{3}V_t I_{a_1} \cos\theta_1 = \sqrt{3}V_t I_a$ as before and that of second alternator is $\sqrt{3}V_t I_{a_2} \cos\theta_2 = \sqrt{3}\,V_t I_a$ and $I_L = I_{a_1} + I_{a_2}$ as before.

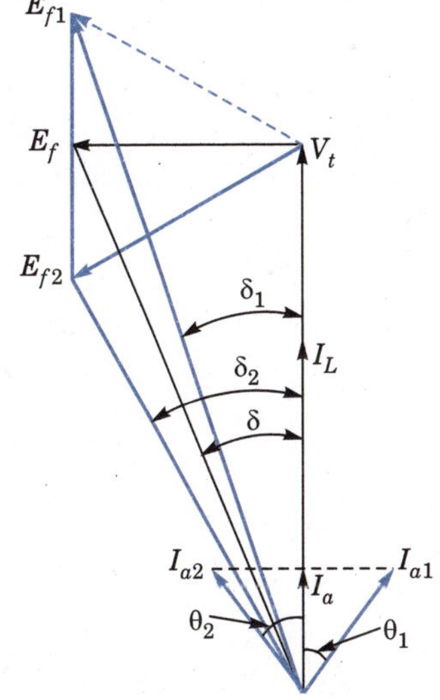

Fig. 4.81: Pertaining to Example 4.35 (*a*).

Examination of Fig. 4.81 reveals that magnitude of both I_{a_1} and I_{a_2} has become more than their previous value I_a. This means that ohmic losses in both the alternators have gone up and this results in decreased output, reduced operating efficiency and undue armature heating.

Fig. 4.81 also reveals that alternator 1 with increased field excitation is capable of delivering more active power without falling out of step as compared to alternator 2 with lower excitation.

It is also seen from this figure that alternator 1 delivers reactive power to the load network which is desirable. But alternator 2 absorbs reactive power from the load network which is undesirable.

It may be summarised from above that the alternator, operating at a leading p.f., absorbs reactive power from the load network, has less pull-out power and has increased ohmic losses which are all undesirable features. In view of this, it is objectionable to operate one alternator at a leading p.f. in parallel with other operating at a lagging p.f.

(*b*) (*i*) First of all, let us compare the parallel operation of synchronous generators with those of transformers.

Transformers. For parallel connected transformers, their primaries are usually fed from the same a.c. source, as a result of it their primary voltages are equal and in phase. In case the primaries are fed from different a.c. sources, then their primary voltages must be equal and in phase and must have the same frequency. For satisfactory parallel operation, their secondary voltages must also be equal and in phase. The loads shared by transformers and their operating power factors (to a lesser degree), depend entirely on their parameters alone. It is because of this reason that transformers must have their parameters inversely proportional to their respective kVA ratings, *i.e.*, their p.u. parameters must be equal both in quantity and quality.

Synchronous generators. The conditions for successful parallel operation of alternators are not so rigid ; since excitation voltages, corresponding to the primary voltages of transformers, need not be equal and in phase. If synchronous impedances are not inversely proportional to their respective alternator ratings, it makes little difference. It is because the kW load can be divided among the alternators in any desired ratio by means of governor settings of the prime-movers. In addition to it, armature currents can be brought into phase by adjusting their field excitations.

(*ii*) A comparison of parallel operation of synchronous generators and those of d.c. generators is now presented here.

(1) Synchronous generators in parallel must run at constant relative speeds with respect to each other so that their frequency is the same. On the other hand, d.c. generators don't have to operate at any fixed relative speed with respect to each other.

(2) If field current of a parallel-connected d.c. generator is increased, its generated e.m.f. E_a increases. As a result of it, its armature current $I_a \left(= \frac{E_a - V_t}{r_a} \right)$ becomes more. Since $E_a I_a$ has become more than the power developed by a prime-mover, the d.c. generator slows down. Now the governor of prime-mover acts accordingly so that its developed power becomes equal to $E_a I_a$ and the set operates at a lower speed.

In case of a parallel connected alternator, an increase in its field current changes its operation p.f. alone. If an alternator is required to carry more load, its governor setting is changed so that its speed-load characteristic is shifted up.

The above comparison between d.c. and synchronous generators may be summarised in tabular form as follows:

D.C. generators	*Synchronous generators*
1. For satisfactory parallel operation, their terminal voltages should be equal.	1. For successful parallel operation, their terminal voltages should not only be equal but should also be in phase.
2. The procedure of connecting a d.c. generator with d.c. mains is easy.	2. The process of connecting a synchronous generator with a.c. mains is more complicated and, therefore, proper synchronization must be carried out carefully.
3. These generators may run at different relative speeds with respect to each other.	3. These must run at constant relative speeds with respect to each other so that their operating frequency is the same.
4. A change in the field current alters the power shared by the generators.	4. A change in field current alters their operating power factor alone.
5. First field current is altered for changing the load shared and then the governor setting adjusts itself to attain the required power balance.	5. The load shared by alternators can be altered by changing their governor settings alone.

Example 4.36. (*a*) *An alternator is supplying power to an infinite bus. Explain how it can be disconnected from the bus.*

(*b*) *Explain how the voltage and frequency of a bus can be controlled.*

(*c*) *Compare the operation of an alternator connected to an infinite bus, with a single alternator supplying its own load.*

(*d*) *A synchronous motor, fed from 50 Hz supply, is mechanically coupled with an alternator. If this alternator is required to generate a voltage of 160 Hz, calculate the least number of poles that the motor-generator set must have.*

Solution. (*a*) For disconnecting an alternator from a bus, first of all the kW load shared by it is reduced to zero by reducing the prime-mover torque—this can be achieved by closing gradually the steam-valve or the water gates. Now reactive power shared by this alternator is brought down to zero by reducing its field current till the alternator just floats on the bus and armature current is zero. The main switch is now opened and the prime-mover is brought to rest.

(*b*) For increasing the bus voltage, the field current of *all* the alternators must be increased accordingly. If field current of only one alternator is increased, the required bus voltage may be attained but then it causes this alternator to supply much more reactive power at an increased armature current. This increased armature current may damage the armature winding by overheating it.

For increasing the bus frequency, the driving torques of *all* the alternators must be increased accordingly. If driving torque of only one alternator is increased, then this alternator would share much more active load by relieving slightly the others operating in parallel with it. Though the required bus frequency may be attained, this alternator would carry an increased armature current which may burn its armature winding.

(*c*) The behaviour of a single alternator connected to its own load is quite different from when it is connected to an infinite bus.

If the field current of an alternator connected to an infinite bus is changed, its operating p.f. changes alone. However, if the field current of the alternator suppling its own load, is changed, it effects its terminals voltage and armature current. For a constant load impedance, its operating power factor will not change with a change in its field current.

If the driving torque of an alternator connected of an infinite bus is changed, the load shared by this alternator changes. In case the driving torque of the alternator supplying its own load is changed, it changes its operating frequency and also the load current carried by it.

When the load on a single alternator is increased, its speed drops because of the drooping speed-load characteristics of the prime-mover. On account of this reduction in speed both the voltage and frequency of this alternator are decreased, its operating power factor at the alternator terminals may however improve.

(*d*) Since the motor and generator are directly coupled, they run at the same speed. Hence, a new frequency can be obtained only if the poles on the alternator are different from the motor poles. If f_m, P_m and f_g, P_g represent frequency and number of poles for the motor and generator respectively, then synchronous speed of the motor is

$$N_s = \frac{120 f_m}{P_m}$$

This is also the speed of the alternator

$$\therefore \qquad N_s = \frac{120 f_g}{P_g}$$

In view of this, $\dfrac{120 f_m}{P_m} = \dfrac{120 f_g}{P_g}$ or $\dfrac{f_m}{f_g} = \dfrac{P_m}{P_g}$

Here $\dfrac{50}{160} = \dfrac{P_m}{P_g}$ or $\dfrac{P_m}{P_g} = \dfrac{5}{16}$

Since a machine can't have 5 poles, the minimum number of poles on motor and generator are 10 and 32 respectively.

4.22 DWR SYNCHRONOUS GENERATOR

Operation of alternators connected to long high-voltage transmission lines and underground cables is quite troublesome, so far as the supply of reactive power is concerned. Long transmission lines and underground cables require a good amount of capacitive current, which has the effect of magnetizing the alternator and thereby increasing its terminal voltage. For maintaining constant system voltage, the generator field current is reduced with a corresponding reduction in excitation voltage E_f. A reduction in E_f results in leading p.f. operation and low values for steady state and transient stability limits particularly when it is lightly loaded. Thus a turbo-generator with a conventionally-wound rotor (cwr) does not operate under favourable conditions when working at a leading p.f. in a lightly loaded energy system. Low values of short circuit ratio used for modern turbo-generators for economic reasons, further add to the problem of maintaining stability under leading power factor operation. The turbo-alternator operation can, however, be improved by using double-wound rotor or divided winding rotor (dwr).

The object of this article is to describe the constructional features of a dwr synchronous generator and to develop its flux and m.m.f. phasors so as to understand the physical concepts of its improved stability and better voltage regulation. Steady state analysis from generalized approach is also presented.

4.22.1 Constructional Features

The 3-phase armature winding in a dwr synchronous generator is on the stator as in a cwr synchronous generator. The rotor of a cwr machine has one winding called exciting, or field, winding ; whereas the rotor of a dwr synchronous machine has two windings, namely *torque winding* and *reactive winding*. The rotor slot arrangements in dwr and cwr generators are identical. But the two windings in dwr machine are so arranged in the rotor slots that the magnetic axes of torque and reactive windings are displaced from each other by about 60°. Fig. 4.82 (*a*) illustrates the 2-pole rotor of a dwr synchronous machine. T_1, T_2 are the two terminals for torque winding and R_1, R_2 are those for the reactive winding. The angle between their magnetic axes is 60°. Actually, the slot conductors in the rotor of a dwr machine are separated by special end connectors into two parts such that the two winding m.m.fs. are displaced from each other by about 60°.

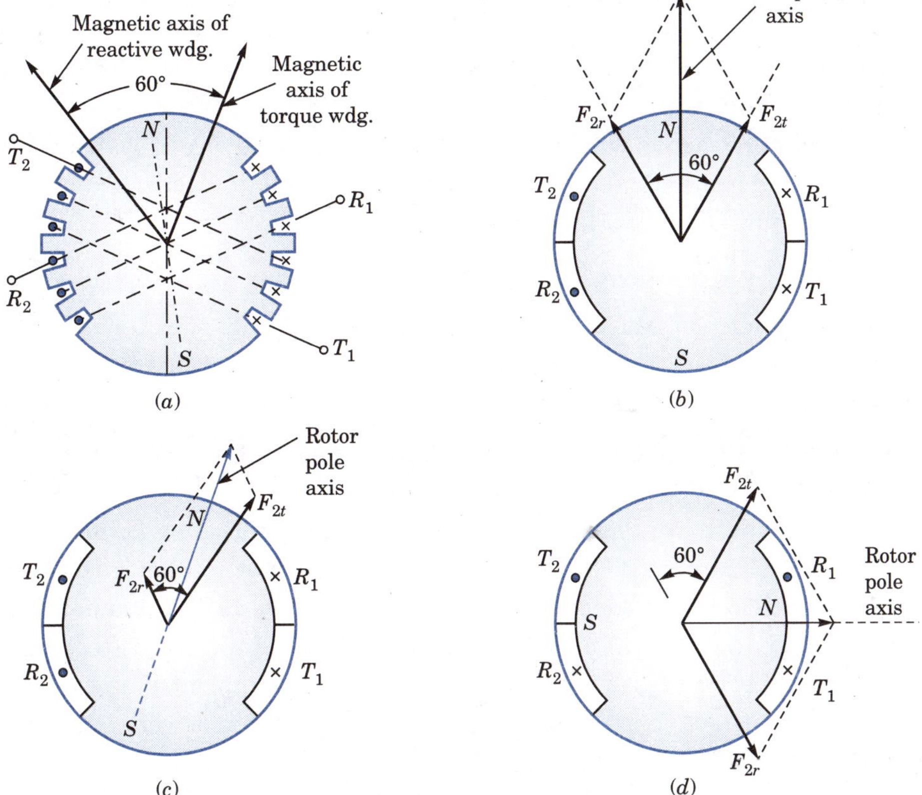

Fig. 4.82: (*a*) Torque and reactive winding arrangements on the rotor of a dwr alternator, (*b*) $F_{2r} = F_{2t}$ and rotor-pole axis is vertical, (*c*) $F_{2r} < F_{2t}$ and rotor-pole axis is shifted, (*d*) F_{2r} is reversed and rotor pole axis is shifted considerably.

The axis of resultant rotor m.m.f., or rotor-pole axis, can be easily varied with respect to the rotor physical position. For example, if the torque winding m.m.f. F_{2t} and reactive winding m.m.f. F_{2r} are equal, the resultant m.m.f., or rotor-pole axis, is as shown in Fig. 4.82 (*b*). If F_{2r} is decreased, Fig. 4.82 (*c*), the rotor-pole axis is shifted from its position of Fig. 4.82 (*b*). In case F_{2r} is reversed, the rotor-pole axis gets shifted considerably from its position of Fig. 4.82 (*b*). This shows that axis of resultant rotor m.m.f., or *rotor-pole axis*, can be conveniently varied with respect to the rotor physical position.

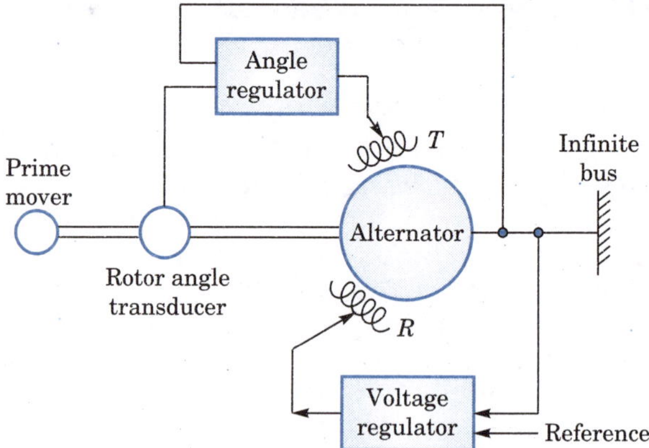

Fig. 4.83: An elementary scheme of dwr synchronous generator.

The m.m.f. of torque winding depends upon the departure of load angle δ from its preset reference value. Consequently, there is a control device which picks up the signal proportional to the variation in load angle δ from its predetermined value and in this manner, m.m.f. of torque winding is controlled. The control device which gives a signal proportional to δ is called *rotor angle regulator*. A rotor angle transducer, driven by alternator shaft, generates a voltage whose phase angle with respect to a reference gives the rotor angle δ ; this is illustrated in Fig. 4.83.

The m.m.f. of the reactive winding depends upon the departure of system voltage from a predetermined reference voltage. An automatic voltage regulator controls the m.m.f. of the reactive winding as illustrated in Fig. 4.83.

4.22.2 Flux and m.m.f. Phasors in dwr Alternators

The object of this section of the article is to develop flux and m.m.f. phasors in a dwr alternator, since it leads to a better physical understanding of this machine. Then its advantages over cwr alternator are presented.

It is worthwhile here to recall the phasor diagram of a cwr alternator, because then it is easier to develop the phasor diagram of a dwr alternator.

(*a*) **Cwr alternator.** It is assumed that cwr generator is feeding power directly to an infinite bus of voltage V_t. In Fig. 4.84, phasor diagrams of a cwr generator are drawn. Here F_f, F_a and F_r are respectively the field m.m.f., armature m.m.f. and resultant m.m.f. E_f, E_r, V_t, I_a and θ are respectively the excitation voltage, air-gap voltage, infinite bus terminal voltage, armature current and pf angle. The alternator operates at a lagging p.f. in Fig. 4.84 (*a*) and at a leading p.f. in Fig. 4.84 (*b*). In both the figures, flux axis is taken as vertical.

In Fig. 4.84 (*a*), if F_f is reduced, E_f decreases, p.f. rises and then becomes leading as shown in Fig. 4.84 (*b*). For an ideal machine, angle between F_f and F_r is load angle δ.

$$\therefore \qquad T_e \propto F_f \,.\, F_r \,.\, \sin \delta.$$

In Fig. 4.84 (*a*), load angle δ is less than 90° and therefore the generator operation is stable. In Fig. 4.84 (*b*), load angle δ is more than 90°, therefore the alternator operation is unstable. This shows that cwr alternator can't operate satisfactorily at leading p.f. loads.

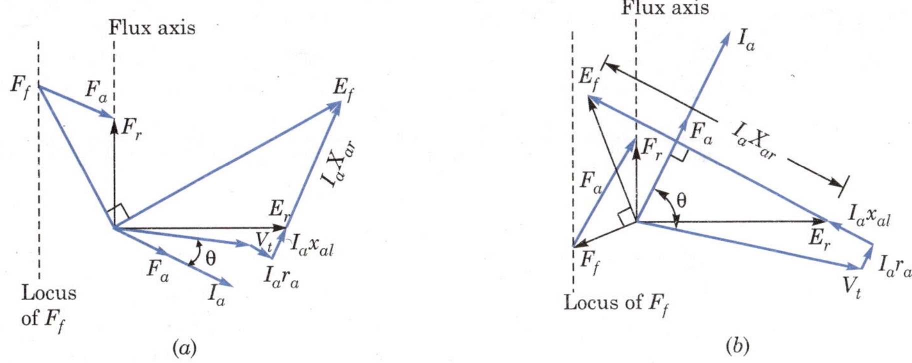

Fig. 4.84: Phasor diagrams for a cwr alternator working at (*a*) lagging p.f. and (*b*) leading p.f.

Now we shall investigate the operation of a dwr synchronous generator both at lagging and leading p.fs.

(*b*) **Dwr alternator.** Phasor diagrams for a dwr alternator are first developed for lagging p.f. operation and then for leading p.f. operation.

(*i*) **Lagging p.f. operation.** For a dwr alternator connected to an infinite bus, the phasor diagram for a lagging p.f. load is as shown in Fig. 4.85 (*a*). Here armature resistance drop $I_a r_a$ and armature leakage reactance drop $I_a x_{al}$ are added to bus bar terminal voltage V_t to get air-gap voltage E_r. This air-gap voltage is generated by air-gap flux ϕ or resultant m.m.f. F_r, therefore ϕ and F_r must lead E_r by 90°. The torque winding m.m.f. F_{2t} and reactive winding m.m.f. F_{2r} are along their respective axis. Armature m.m.f. F_a is in phase with armature current I_a. Resultant of F_{2t} and F_{2r}, displaced from each other by 60°, is F_f and this m.m.f. generates excitation voltage E_f lagging it by 90° as shown. Now the various m.m.fs. acting in the dwr are $F_{2r} = OB$, $F_{2t} = OP$, $F_a = OQ$. These component m.m.fs. combine together to give resultant air-gap m.m.f. $F_r = OD$. Horizontal component of F_a and F_{2t} cancel each other, *i.e.*, $CQ = AP$. Vertical component of F_{2t} is OA, which aids F_{2r} (= OB) to give a total m.m.f. $OK = OB + OA$. Since the vertical component of F_a is demagnetizing in nature, the resultant or air-gap m.m.f. F_r is given by

$$F_r = OK - OC = OK - KD = OD = OA + F_{2r} - OC \qquad ...(4.229)$$

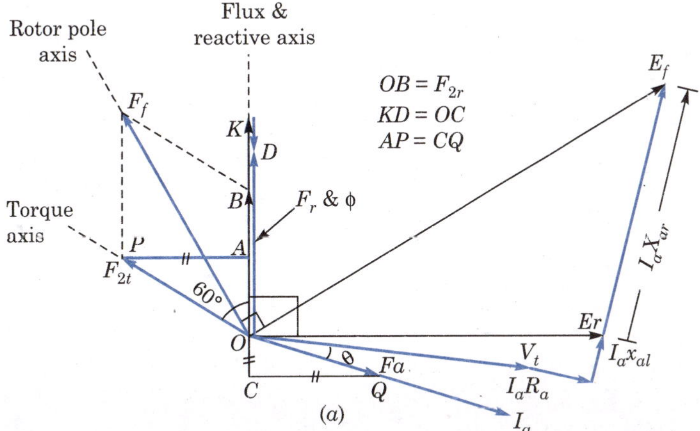

Fig. 4.85: (*a*) Phasor diagram of a dwr alternator working at a lagging p.f..

Note that $F_r = OD$ can also be obtained by the phasor sum of F_f and F_a as in a cwr alternator.

The air-gap m.m.f. F_r generates air-gap voltage E_r lagging it by 90°. The electromagnetic torque is given by, $T_e \propto F_{2t} \cdot F_r \sin 60°$.

Since torque is positive, the dwr alternator is working under stable conditions at lagging p.f. loads as in a cwr alternator.

(*ii*) **Leading p.f. operation.** For a dwr alternator working at a leading p.f. and connected to an infinite bus, the phasor diagram is as illustrated in Fig. 4.85 (*b*). As before, $E_r = V_t + I_a (r_a + jx_{al})$ and $E_f = E_r + jI_a X_{ar}$ are drawn. Armature current I_a leads V_t by p.f. angle θ. The armature m.m.f. F_a has now a magnetizing component QC. Therefore, total m.m.f. is $OK = OA + AK$ where $AK = QC$. The reactive winding m.m.f. is always along the reactive axis and is now demagnetizing in nature for a leading p.f. operation as shown. The resultant air-gap m.m.f. is given by,

$$F_r = OK - F_{2r} = OD = OA + QC - F_{2r} \quad \text{...(4.230)}$$

As before, phasor sum of F_f and F_a is $F_r = OD$.

Air-gap voltage E_r lags F_r by 90°. The resultant of F_{2t} and F_{2r} gives total field m.m.f. F_f and E_f lags this m.m.f. by 90° as shown.

Now $\qquad T_e \propto F_{2t} \cdot F_r \cdot \sin 60°$

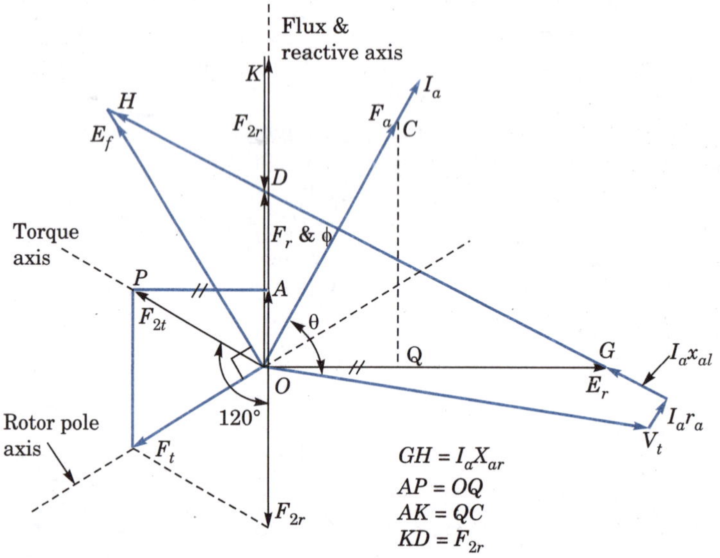

Fig. 4.85: (*b*) Phasor diagram of a dwr alternator working at a leading p.f.

Since this torque is positive, the dwr alternator is stable even on leading p.f. operation, whereas cwr alternator is unstable under leading p.f. operation in case load angle is more than 90°. Thus a dwr alternator has higher steady-state stability limit as compared to a cwr alternator.

Voltage regulation. For a lagging p.f. operation, if reactive winding m.m.f. F_{2r} is increased, Eq. (4.229) reveals that F_r increases and likewise E_r and V_t increase. For leading p.f. operation, Eq. (4.230) reveals that if F_{2r} in reduced, F_r increases and as a result E_r and V_t increase. This shows that voltage regulation of a dwr synchronous generator can be easily regulated by controlling the current in reactive winding.

Transient stability. In cwr alternator, field flux is entirely d-axis flux and q-axis flux is almost zero. As a result, q-axis time constant is zero in cwr machine. In dwr machine, q-axis flux is not zero. Therefore, q-axis time constant of a dwr alternator is quite large and this improves the transient stability of the dwr alternator as compared to a cwr alternator.

It can therefore be concluded from above that a dwr alternator has better voltage regulation and also better steady-state and transient stability limits as compared to a cwr alternator.

4.22.3 Balanced Steady-state Analysis

The schematic diagram of a dwr 3-phase turbo-generator with torque and reactive windings is as shown in Fig. 4.86 (a). In this figure, $\theta_R + \theta_T = 60°$. For analysis purposes, the three-phase armature winding is considered on the rotor and the torque and reactive windings on the stator. The generalized mathematical model for Fig. 4.86 (a) is as shown in Fig. 4.86 (b), where field coils DF and QF are along the d- and q-axes respectively. The two rotor coils D and Q represent the 3-phase armature winding in all respects.

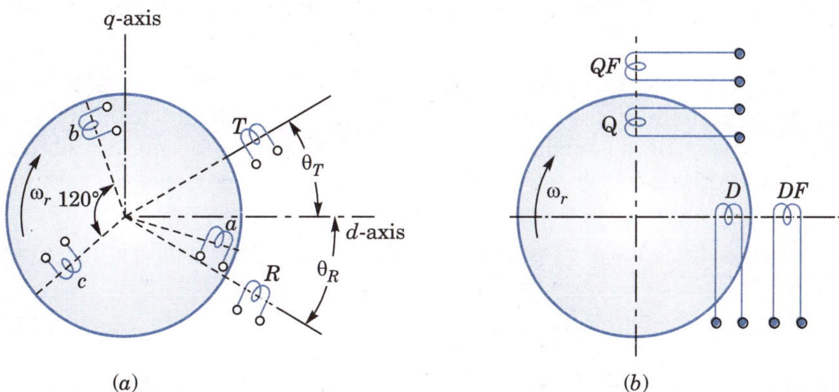

Fig. 4.86: (a) Schematic diagram of a dwr synchronous machine, (b) Its generalized mathematical model.

Assume, for simplicity, that windings R (reactive winding), T (torque winding) and coils DF, QF have equal number of effective turns.

Then, resolving m.m.fs. of R and T along d- and q-axes, we get

$$NI_{df} = NI_R \cos\theta_R + NI_T \cos\theta_T$$

or
$$I_{df} = I_R \cos\theta_R + I_T \cos\theta_T \qquad \text{...(4.231)}$$

Similarly,
$$I_{qf} = I_T \sin\theta_T - I_R \sin\theta_R \qquad \text{...(4.232)}$$

Phasor diagram. The general voltage equations for a dwr machine can be written by referring to Fig. 4.86 (b), which in matrix form are as follows:

$$\begin{bmatrix} v_{df} \\ v_{qf} \\ v_d \\ v_q \end{bmatrix} = \begin{bmatrix} r_{df} + L_{df}p & & M_d p & \\ & r_{qf} + L_{qf}p & & M_d p \\ M_d p & -M_q\omega_r & r_d + L_d p & -L_q\omega_r \\ M_d\omega_r & M_q p & L_d\omega_r & r_q + L_q p \end{bmatrix} \begin{bmatrix} i_{df} \\ i_{qf} \\ i_d \\ i_q \end{bmatrix} \qquad \text{...(4.233)}$$

The armature winding is uniformly distributed and balanced, therefore, $r_d = r_q = r_a$. Also, turbo-generator is a uniform air-gap machine.

$\therefore$ $\quad L_d = L_q = L_s,$ synchronous inductance

and $\quad M_d = M_q = M,$ magnetizing inductance.

With these constraints, Eq. (4.233) can be written as follows:

$$\left.\begin{aligned} v_{df} &= (r_{df} + L_{df}\,p)\,i_{df} + Mp\,i_d \\ v_{qf} &= (r_{qf} + L_{qf}\,p)\,i_{qf} + Mp\,i_q \\ v_d &= Mp\,i_{df} - M\omega_r\,i_{qf} + (r_a + L_s p)\,i_d - L_s\,\omega_r i_q \\ v_q &= M\omega_r\,i_{df} + Mp\,i_{df} + L_s\,\omega_r\,i_d + (r_a + L_s p)\,i_q \end{aligned}\right\} \quad ...(4.234)$$

For obtaining balanced steady state analysis, put $p = 0$ in Eq. (4.234), as done in a cwr machine. Also, the armature can run only at synchronous speed, therefore, $\omega_r = \omega$. Thus the steady state voltage equations for dwr synchronous machine are,

$$\left.\begin{aligned} v_{df} &= r_{df}\,I_{df} \\ v_{qf} &= r_{qf} I_{qf} \\ v_{do} &= -M\omega I_{qf} + r_a i_{do} - L_s\omega i_{qo} \\ v_{qo} &= M\omega I_{df} + L_s\omega i_{do} + r_a i_{qo} \end{aligned}\right\} \quad ...(4.235)$$

The subscript zero indicates constant or d.c. values. The armature voltage equations in Eq. (4.235) are written for a synchronous motor operation. For generator operation, the armature voltage equations can be obtained from Eq. (4.235), merely by reversing the signs of armature currents i_{do} and i_{qo}.

In view of this, the armature voltage equations for a dwr synchronous generator are,

$$\left.\begin{aligned} v_{do} &= -M\omega I_{qf} - r_a i_{do} + X_s\,i_{qo} \\ v_{qo} &= M\,\omega I_{df} - X_s\,i_{do} - r_a\,i_{qo} \end{aligned}\right\} \quad ...(4.236)$$

Now the voltage equation for phase a is given by Eq. (4.36).

$$\therefore \quad \bar{V}_a = \frac{v_{do} + jv_{qo}}{\sqrt{2}}$$

$$= \frac{1}{\sqrt{2}}\,[-M\,\omega\,I_{qf} - r_a\,i_{do} + X_s\,i_{qo} + jM\,\omega\,I_{df} - j\,X_s\,i_{do} - jr_a\,i_{qo}]$$

$$= -\frac{M\omega I_{qf}}{\sqrt{2}} + j\,\frac{M\omega\,I_{df}}{\sqrt{2}} - r_a\left(\frac{i_{do} + ji_{do}}{\sqrt{2}}\right) + X_s I_q - jX_s I_d.$$

In Eq. (4.38), field current I_f along d-axis gave rise to generated e.m.f. E_f along q-axis. Similarly here, field current I_{df} gives rise to generated e.m.f. E_{qf} along q-axis and field current I_{qf} gives rise to generated e.m.f. E_{df} along d-axis. In view of this,

$$\frac{M\omega I_{qf}}{\sqrt{2}} = \frac{X_m I_{qf}}{\sqrt{2}} = E_{df} \quad \text{and} \quad \frac{M\omega I_{df}}{\sqrt{2}} = \frac{X_m\,I_{df}}{\sqrt{2}} = E_{qf}$$

Thus the voltage equation for phase a is given by

$$\bar{V}_a = -E_{df} + jE_{qf} - r_a \bar{I}_a + X_s I_q - jX_s I_d$$

Now $\quad I_d = \bar{I}_d \quad$ and $\quad \bar{I}_q = jI_q$

or $\quad I_q = -j\bar{I}_q$ as shown in Fig. 4.7 (b).

$$\therefore \quad \bar{V}_a = -E_{df} + jE_{qf} - r_a\bar{I}_a - jX_s\bar{I}_q - jX_s\bar{I}_d$$

$$= (-E_{df} + jE_{qf}) - r_a\bar{I}_a - jX_s(\bar{I}_d + \bar{I}_q)$$

$$= (-E_{df} + jE_{qf}) - \bar{I}_a(r_a + jX_s)$$

For negligible armature resistance,

$$\bar{V}_a = (-E_{df} + jE_{qf}) - j\bar{I}_a X_s$$

or $$(-E_{df} + jE_{qf}) = \bar{V}_t + j\bar{I}_a X_s \qquad ...(4.237)$$

Here V_t is written in place of V_a, to denote the terminal voltage V_t.

Eq. (4.237) gives the phasor diagram of Fig. 4.87, where phasor sum of jE_{qf} and $-E_{df}$ is written as E_f.

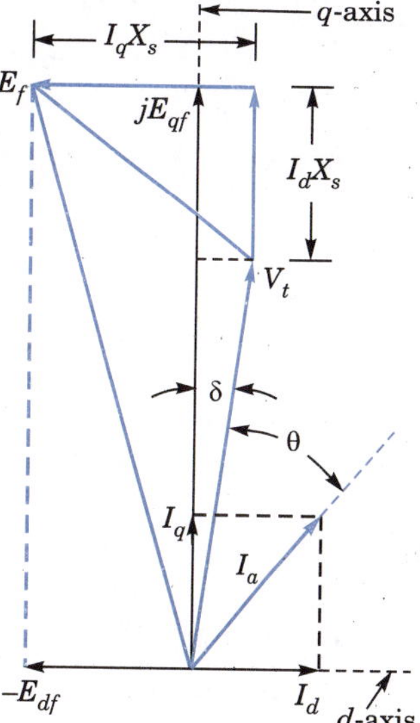

Fig. 4.87: Phasor diagram of a dwr synchronous generator.

The power at the machine terminals is given by

$$P = V_t \cos\delta I_q + V_t \sin\delta I_d \qquad ...(4.238)$$

Fig. 4.87 gives $E_{qf} - V_t\cos\delta = I_dX_s$

or $$I_d = \frac{E_{df} - V_t\cos\delta}{X_s}$$

and $$E_{df} + V_t\sin\delta = I_q X_s$$

or $$I_q = \frac{E_{df} + V_t\sin\delta}{X_s}$$

Substitution of I_d and I_q in Eq. (4.38) gives

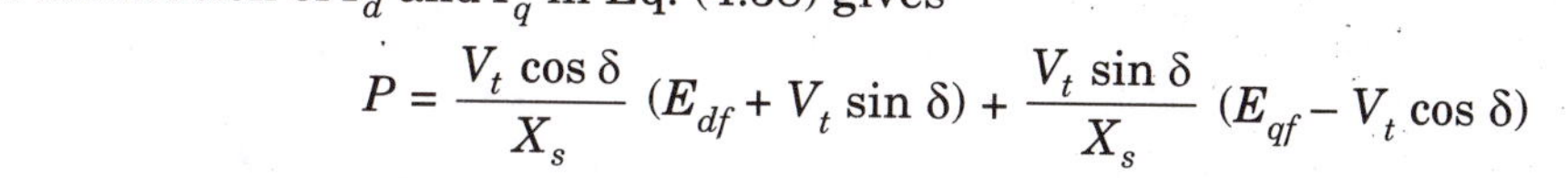

$$P = \frac{V_t\cos\delta}{X_s}(E_{df} + V_t\sin\delta) + \frac{V_t\sin\delta}{X_s}(E_{qf} - V_t\cos\delta)$$

$$= \frac{E_{df}V_t}{X_s}\cos\delta + \frac{V_t^2\sin\delta\cos\delta}{X_s} + \frac{V_tE_{qf}}{X_s}\sin\delta - \frac{V_t^2}{X_s}\sin\delta\cos\delta$$

$$= \frac{V_t}{X_s}(E_{df}\cos\delta + E_{qf}\sin\delta) \qquad ...(4.239)$$

Substitution of the values of E_{df} and E_{qf} in Eq. (4.239) gives,

$$P = \frac{1}{\sqrt{2}}\cdot\frac{V_t}{X_s}(X_m I_{qf}\cos\delta + X_m I_{df}\sin\delta)$$

$$= \frac{1}{\sqrt{2}}\cdot\frac{V_t}{X_s}\cdot X_m [I_{qf}\cos\delta + I_{df}\sin\delta) \qquad ...(4.240)$$

In order to show the effect of I_R and I_T on power P, substitute the values of I_{df} from Eq. (4.231) and I_{qf} from Eq. (4.232) in Eq. (4.240)

$$\therefore \quad P = \frac{1}{\sqrt{2}}\cdot\frac{V_t}{X_s}X_m[(I_T\sin\theta_T - I_R\sin\theta_R)\cos\delta + (I_R\cos\theta_R + I_T\cos\theta_T)\sin\delta]$$

$$= \frac{1}{\sqrt{2}}\cdot\frac{V_t}{X_s}X_m[I_T(\sin\theta_T\cos\delta + \cos\theta_R\sin\delta) + I_R(\cos\theta_R\sin\delta - \sin\theta_R\cos\delta)]$$

$$= \frac{1}{\sqrt{2}}\cdot\frac{V_t}{X_s}X_m[I_T\sin(\delta + \theta_T) + I_R\sin(\delta - \theta_R)] \qquad ...(4.241)$$

The reactive power, from Fig. 4.87, is

$$Q = V_t \cos\delta \,.\, I_d - V_t \sin\delta \,.\, I_q$$

Substitution of the values of I_d and I_q gives,

$$Q = \frac{V_t \cos\delta}{X_s}(E_{qf} - V_t \cos\delta) - \frac{V_t \sin\delta}{X_s}(E_{df} + V_t \sin\delta)$$

$$= \frac{V_t E_{qf}}{X_s}\cos\delta - \frac{V_t^2}{X_s}\cos^2\delta - \frac{E_{df} V_t}{X_s}\sin\delta - \frac{V_t^2}{X_s}\sin^2\delta$$

$$= \frac{V_t}{X_s}[E_{qf}\cos\delta - E_{df}\sin\delta] - \frac{V_t^2}{X_s}$$

or

$$Q = \frac{V_t}{X_s}\cdot\frac{X_m}{\sqrt{2}}[I_{df}\cos\delta - I_{qf}\sin\delta] - \frac{V_t^2}{X_s}$$

$$= \frac{1}{\sqrt{2}}\frac{V_t}{X_s}X_m[I_R\cos\theta_R\cos\delta + I_T\cos\theta_T\cos\delta + I_R\sin\theta_R\sin\delta - I_T\sin\delta_T\sin\delta] - \frac{V_t^2}{X_s}$$

$$= \frac{1}{\sqrt{2}}\frac{V_t}{X_s}X_m[I_R\cos(\delta - \theta_R) + I_T\cos(\delta + \theta_T)] - \frac{V_t^2}{X_s} \quad \text{...(4.242)}$$

If torque winding m.m.f. is so controlled that load angle δ is maintained equal to θ_R, then active power from Eq. (4.241) is

$$P = \frac{1}{\sqrt{2}}\frac{V_t}{X_s}X_m[I_T\sin(\theta_R + \theta_T)] \quad \text{...(4.243)}$$

and reactive power, from Eq. (4.242) is

$$Q = \frac{1}{\sqrt{2}}\frac{V_t}{X_s}X_m[I_R + I_T\cos(\theta_R + \theta_T)] - \frac{V_t^2}{X_s} \quad \text{...(4.244)}$$

Eq. (4.243) reveals that active power P can be controlled by varying the torque-winding exciting current I_T only. Reactive-winding exciting current I_R has no effect on the active power provided $\delta = \theta_R$. Eq. (4.244) shows that the reactive power Q depends on the exciting currents both in torque and reactive windings.

Since active and reactive powers can be controlled without altering the rotor position of $\theta_R = \delta$, both the steady-state and transient stability limits are improved.

4.23 INDUCTOR ALTERNATORS

For generating high-frequency a.c. voltages of the order of 1 kHz, inductor alternators (or inductor generators) are commonly employed. It is because the generation of high frequency voltages by conventional alternators is uneconomical. In addition to it, the main advantage of inductor alternator is that both armature and field windings are on the stator ; and rotor, with no winding on it, is a laminated structure with open slots. The absence of rotor windings and no sliding contacts on the rotor allows the speed to be raised to the maximum possible safe limit for obtaining more output for given machine dimensions.

There are two types of inductor alternators; homopolar inductor alternator and hetropolar inductor alternator. The object of this article is to describe their constructional features and their basic principle of operation.

4.23.1 Homopolar Inductor Alternator

This machine has two stator cores and two rotor cores but they form one single magnetic circuit as shown. The exciting, or field, winding is placed symmetrically in between the two stator cores. Note that field winding axis coincides with the shaft axis. Both stator and rotor cores are slotted. Armature winding consists of coils C wound around each stator teeth as illustrated in Fig. 4.88 (*b*). The number of rotor slots is half of that of the stator slots. The rotor teeth are called *inductors*.

When exciting winding carries current, field flux is produced which completes its path through cast-steel yoke, stator core 1, air gap 1, rotor core 1, cast-iron rotor spider, rotor core 2, air gap 2 and stator core 2. Examination of Fig. 4.88 (*a*) reveals that polarity of all the inductors (or teeth) is the same (S pole) on rotor core 1. For rotor core 2 also, the polarity (N pole) is the same, though opposite to rotor core 1. When the rotor rotates, e.m.fs. are generated in all the armature coils.

When the rotor inductor occupies the position shown in Fig. 4.89 (*a*), the flux linking coil C is *maximum* because of smaller air gap. With the rotor movement, when rotor slot occupies the position shown in Fig. 4.89 (*b*), the flux linking coil C is *minimum* because of

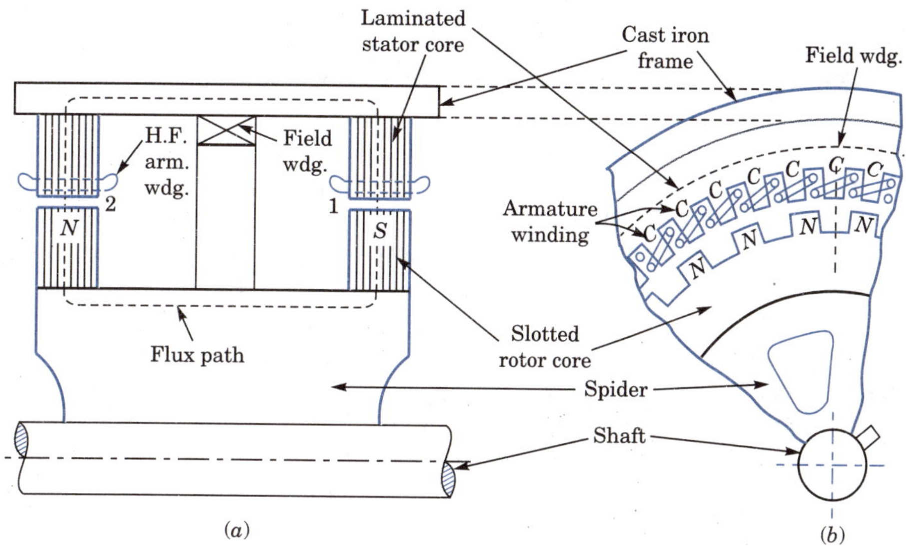

Fig. 4.88: Constructional features of a Homopolar inductor alternator.

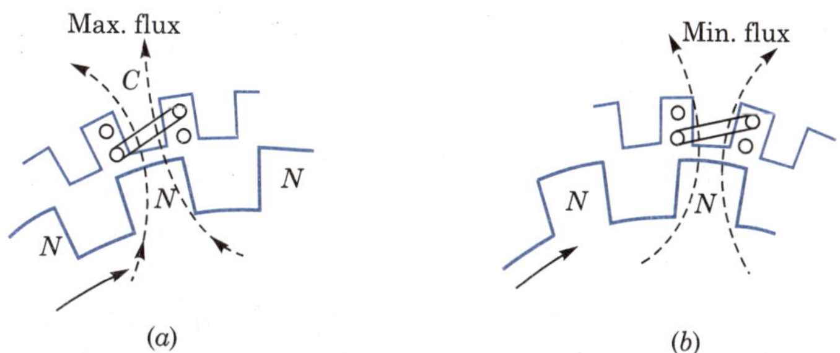

Fig. 4.89: Flux linking coil C is (*a*) maximum and (*b*) minimum.

longer air gap and this shows that flux has changed from maximum to minimum. Note that flux linking the coil does not reverse with the rotor movement as in a conventional alternator and it is this fact that differentiates the two alternators. Since the flux linking the various coils changes from a maximum to a minimum, e.m.fs. are generated in the stator coils. In Fig. 4.89 (*a*), flux through coil C is maximum ; in Fig. 4.89 (*b*), flux through coil C is minimum and when the next inductor occupies the position of Fig. 4.89 (*a*), again maximum flux passes through coil C. This shows that one cycle of e.m.f. is generated for every rotor slot pitch (or tooth pitch) rotation. If there are S_2 rotor slots, then there are S_2 rotor slot pitches and therefore S_2 cycles of e.m.f. generation in one revolution. If rotor speed is in n rps, then frequency of e.m.f. generation is $f = nS_2$ cycles per sec. For example, for generating 2 kHz at 3000 r.p.m., the rotor must have 40 slots. Note that this frequency does not depend on the stator slot arrangement.

4.23.2 Hetropolar Inductor Alternator

The homopolar inductor alternator has many disadvantages given below:

(*a*) It is expensive in construction since it differs considerably from other standard types of electrical machines.

(*b*) The rotor has abnormally large moment of inertia and this imposes severe starting duties on the prime-mover.

(*c*) Bearings must be insulated from the frame, otherwise these may be damaged by heating due to leakage flux through the shaft and frame.

(*d*) The field time constant is very large because there is only one field coil. This causes difficulty in maintaining constant alternator output voltage under fluctuating loads. The field time constant is sometimes as high as 20 seconds.

The hetropolar alternator overcomes some of these disadvantages. It has a single stator core and single rotor core, which are almost similar to those used for squirrel-cage induction motors. As in a homopolar machine, the stator has double the number of rotor slots.

The stator core has deeper as well as shallow slots. The d.c. field winding is housed in deeper slots and the armature winding in both shallow and deeper slots as shown in Fig. 4.90. Note that rotor slots and the high-frequency armature winding on stator are identical to those in homopolar alternator. In homopolar machine, the d.c. flux path is axial ; but in hetropolar machine, the flux path is circumferential as in standard types of machines.

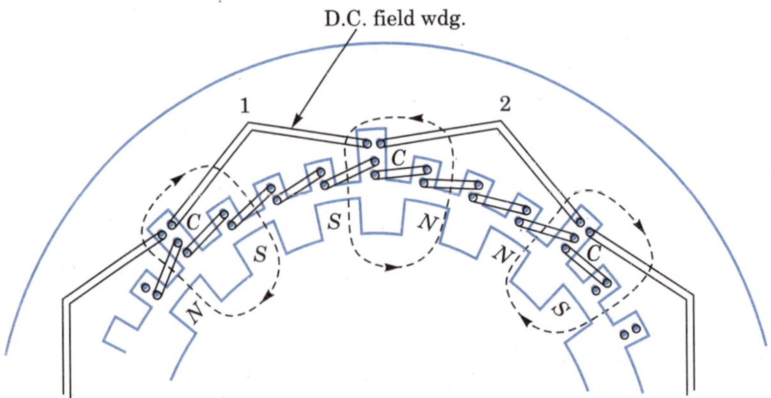

Fig. 4.90: Constructional features of a hetropolar inductor alternator.

Note that rotor slots under field coil 1 have S polarities and those under field coil 2 have N polarities, for the assumed direction of currents in field coils. This means that polarity of rotor teeth goes on changing as they pass from one field coil to the next.

When rotor inductor (or tooth) faces a stator tooth, that coil has maximum flux passing through it. With the rotor movement, when rotor slot comes under stator tooth, that coil has minimum flux passing through it as in a homopolar machine. Note that flux passing through high-frequency coils changes from maximum to minimum but never changes in direction. This changing flux generates high-frequency voltages in the armature winding. As before, one cycle of e.m.f. is generated in each coil for the movement of one rotor slot pitch. As before, the frequency of generated e.m.f. is nS_2 Hz.

Since the flux per pole is small, the stator and rotor core depths are small and this reduces the rotor moment of inertia.

Inductor alternators have small air gap, of the order of 0.125 mm to 1.25 mm. The stator and rotor cores of both the types are made up of very thin laminations, of about 0.175 mm thick, to reduce the eddy current losses. The inductor alternator is usually connected in series with a bank of capacitors to improve the load power factor, such as the p.f. improvement of induction-melting equipment etc.

Inductor generators, or alternators, are used for generating 400 Hz a.c. supply for aircraft. These are also employed for industrial high-frequency heating, *i.e.*, for brazing, hardening, soldering metals, drying and curing of plywood etc. These alternators have been built up to the ratings of about 2 MVA, 300 Hz. The use of inductor alternators for the brushless excitation of large conventional alternators is being investigated.

For a rotor diameter D, the rotor slot pitch is given by

$$y_{s2} = \frac{\pi D}{S_2} = \frac{\pi D n}{n S_2} = \frac{v}{f}.$$

The peripheral speed is usually limited from centrifugal stress considerations. In order to generate very high frequencies, rotor slot pitch must be very small. This is not possible in homopolar and hetropolar machines shown in Figs. 4.88 and 4.90. This limitation can however be overcome by the use of Guy-notched machines ; which, however, would not be discussed here. For small kVA (up to about 5) outputs at frequencies from 1 to 10 kHz, *flux-switch* machines have been developed.

4.24 ELECTRIC BRAKING OF SYNCHRONOUS MOTORS

There are three methods of electric braking of d.c. motors, see Art. 3.10. For the electric braking of 3-phase synchronous motors, however, only one of these three methods can be employed successfully as discussed below.

(*a*) Regenerative braking. In regenerative braking of electric motors, the load forces the motors to run at a speed above its no-load speed.

As synchronous motor is a constant-speed motor, its operating speed can never exceed synchronous speed. Therefore, regenerative braking of synchronous motors is not possible.

(*b*) Plugging. In a synchronous motor, electric torque is developed only when relative speed between stator field and rotor field is zero. During plugging in a 3-phase synchronous motor, when any two supply terminals to the armature are interchanged, the direction of rotating field reverses. As a result, relative velocity between stator and rotor fields will not be zero. There would, therefore, be no braking torque due to synchronous-motor action during plugging. However, some braking torque due to induction-motor action may be produced due to the presence of damper bars in the pole faces.

(c) **Dynamic or rheostatic braking.** In this type of electric braking of a 3-phase synchronous motor, the field current is kept constant and the armature, after being disconnected from 3-phase supply, is connected to a bank of fixed resistors. The synchronous machine, under these conditions, operates as a 3-phase alternator. The kinetic energy of the rotating mass is now converted to electric energy in the alternator which is dissipated as heat in the bank of resistors. As the alternator e.m.f., and therefore the current, depend on speed, the dynamic braking torque T_d is given by, $T_d = K\omega_r$

where K is a constant of proportionality and ω_r is the alternator speed at any time during braking period. As the alternator speed decreases, dynamic braking torque T_d also decreases accordingly.

The nature of braking torque and the load torque influence the time taken by the synchronous-motor drive to come to rest and the number of revolutions made in that time. The expressions for the time and the number of revolutions made by the drive during retardation period can be found as under :

Constant braking torque. In case dynamic braking torque T_d is constant, the total braking torque T_b is given by, $T_b = T_d + T_L = -J\,\dfrac{d\omega_r}{dt}$

where load torque T_L is assumed constant. The negative sign before inertia torque in the above expression is used because the speed during the braking process decreases with time.

From above
$$dt = -\frac{J}{T_b}\,d\omega_r$$

Its integration gives,
$$t = -\frac{J}{T_b}\omega_r + A$$

where A is a constant of integration.

Before the dynamic braking is applied, *i.e.*, at $t = 0$, $\omega_r = \omega_s$ (synchronous speed of motor).

$$\therefore \qquad A = \frac{J}{T_b}\,\omega_s$$

or
$$t = \frac{J}{T_b}\,[\omega_s - \omega_r] \qquad \text{...(4.245)}$$

Angular speed in radians per second is given by $\omega_r = \dfrac{d\theta}{dt}$

where θ is the total angular rotation in time t seconds.

But $\theta = 2\pi r$, where r is the number of revolutions made by the drive before it stops in time t seconds.

$$\therefore \qquad \omega_r = \frac{d}{dt}(2\pi r) \qquad \text{or} \qquad r = \frac{1}{2\pi}\int \omega_r\,dt$$

From Eq. (4.245),
$$\omega_r = \omega_s - \frac{T_b}{J}t$$

$$\therefore \qquad r = \frac{1}{2\pi}\int\left(\omega_s - \frac{T_b}{J}t\right)dt = \frac{1}{2\pi}\left[\omega_s t - \frac{T_b}{J}\frac{t^2}{2}\right] + B$$

At time $t = 0$, number of revolutions, $r = 0 \quad \therefore \quad B = 0$

Thus total number of revolutions made in time t sec before the drive stops are

$$r = \frac{1}{2\pi}\left[\omega_s t - \frac{T_b}{J}\frac{t^2}{2}\right] \qquad \text{...[4.246 (a)]}$$

When the motor stops, $\omega_r = 0$. Therefore, from Eq. (4.245),

$$t = \frac{J}{T_b}\omega_s \quad \text{or} \quad \omega_s = \frac{T_b}{J}t$$

Substitution of this value of ω_s in Eq. (4.246 a) gives

$$\left.\begin{aligned} r &= \frac{1}{4\pi}\frac{T_b}{J}t^2 \\ \text{or} \qquad r &= \frac{1}{4\pi}.\omega_s t \end{aligned}\right\} \qquad \text{...[4.246 (b)]}$$

Braking torque proportional to speed. In case dynamic braking torque T_d is proportional to speed, then its value at any speed ω_r can be written as $T_d = K\omega_r$. Thus, total braking torque T_b is given by, $T_b = T_d + T_L = K\omega_r + T_L = -J\dfrac{d\omega_r}{dt}$

As before, T_L is assumed constant.

$$\therefore \qquad dt = -\frac{J}{T_L + K\omega_r}.d\omega_r$$

Its integration gives, $\quad t = -\dfrac{J}{K}\ln(T_L + K\omega_r) + C$

Before the dynamic braking, synchronous motor is running at synchronous speed ω_s. Therefore, at $t = 0$, $\omega_r = \omega_s$. This gives

$$C = \frac{J}{K}\ln(T_L + K\omega_s)$$

$$\therefore \qquad t = \frac{J}{K}\ln\left[\frac{T_L + K\omega_s}{T_L + K\omega_r}\right] \qquad \text{...(4.247)}$$

As before, the number of revolutions r is given by, $\quad r = \dfrac{1}{2\pi}\displaystyle\int \omega_r\, dt$

From Eq. (4.247), $\quad \dfrac{T_L + K\omega_r}{T_L + K\omega_s} = e^{-\frac{K}{J}t}$

$$\text{or} \qquad \omega_r = \frac{1}{K}\left[(T_L + K\omega_s)e^{-\frac{K}{J}t} - T_L\right]$$

Substitution of ω_r gives the number of revolutions as

$$r = \frac{1}{2\pi K}\int\left[(T_L + K\omega_s)e^{-\frac{K}{J}t} - T_L\right]dt$$

$$= \frac{1}{2\pi K}\left[-\frac{J}{K}(T_L + K\omega_s)\,e^{-\frac{K}{J}t} - T_L.t\right] + C$$

At $t = 0$, $r = 0$

and
$$C = \frac{1}{2\pi K}\left[\frac{J}{K}(T_L + K\omega_s)\right]$$

$\therefore$
$$r = \frac{1}{2\pi K}\left[\frac{J}{K}(T_L + K\omega_s)(1 - e^{-\frac{K}{J}t}) - T_L t\right] \quad ...(4.248)$$

Example 4.37. *A 3-phase 375 r.p.m. synchronous motor and its driven equipment have a total moment of inertia of 500 kg m² and a constant frictional torque of 150 Nm. Calculate the time taken by this electric drive to come to rest and the number of revolutions made during the retardation process when it is braked by the following methods:*

(a) Braked by plugging with a constant braking torque of 1500 Nm.

(b) Braked by rheostatic braking with field current and braking resistances held constant at a value that gives an initial dynamic braking torque of 6 kNm.

Solution. (*a*) Constant frictional torque, $T_f = 150$ Nm

Constant braking torque by plugging, $T_p = 1500$ Nm

During dynamic braking, frictional torque adds to the braking torque.

$\therefore$ Total constant braking torque, $T_b = T_f + T_p = 1650$ Nm

Synchronous speed, $\omega_s = \dfrac{2\pi \times 375}{60} = 39.27$ rad/sec

From Eq. (4.245), the time for stopping the drive ($\omega_r = 0$) is

$$t = \frac{500}{1650}[39.27 - 0] = 11.90 \text{ sec}$$

The number of revolutions made before the drive stops, from Eq. (4.246), are

$$r = \frac{1}{2\pi}\left[39.27 \times 11.9 - \frac{1650}{500} \times \frac{(11.90)^2}{2}\right] = 37.18 \text{ revolutions.}$$

(*b*) Initial dynamic braking torque, $T_d = 6000$ Nm. As the initial speed at the time of dynamic braking is synchronous speed ω_s, $K\omega_s = 6000$ Nm. This gives $K = 6000/39.27 = 152.79$ Nm-sec/rad.

Here constant friction torque can be treated as $T_L = T_f = 150$ Nm.

Time for stopping the drive, from Eq. (4.247) is

$$t = \frac{500}{152.79}\ln\left[\frac{150 + 152.79 \times 39.27}{150 + 0}\right] = 12.153 \text{ sec.}$$

Then number of revolutions made during the braking process, from Eq. (4.248), are,

$$r = \frac{1}{2\pi \times 152.79}\left[\frac{500}{152.79}(150 + 152.79 \times 39.27)\left(1 - e^{-\frac{152.79}{500} \times 12.153}\right) - 150 \times 12.153\right]$$

$= 18.55$ revolutions.

When rotor speed falls below $\omega_r = 150/152.79 = 0.982$ rad/sec, the electric braking torque becomes less than the frictional torque. In other words, below $\omega_r = 0.982$ rad/sec, frictional torque dominates and the rotor is stopped by frictional torque alone.

Example 4.38. *A 3300 V, 200 kW, 500 r.p.m., star-connected synchronous motor drives a fertilizer mill having a total moment of inertia of 800 kg.m². Synchronous reactance of motor is 15 Ω. When the mill is running at full load, dynamic braking is employed by switching the armature to a bank of star-connected resistors of 20 Ω per phase and field current is kept constant. Estimate the time taken and the number of revolutions made before the motor stops. The motor has an efficiency of 92% and its operating p.f. was unity before electric braking was applied.*

Solution. Motor full load torque $= \dfrac{200 \times 1000 \times 60}{2\pi \times 500} = 3819.7$ Nm

Motor full load current $= \dfrac{200 \times 1000}{\sqrt{3} \times 3300 \times 1 \times 0.92} = 38.03$ A

Per phase terminal voltage $= \dfrac{3300}{\sqrt{3}} = 1905.3$ V

∴ Per phase excitation voltage,

$$\bar{E}_f = \bar{V}_t - j\bar{I}_a X_s$$

or

$$E_f = \sqrt{V_t^2 + (I_a X_s)^2}$$

$$= \sqrt{1905.3^2 + (38.03 \times 15)^2} = 1988.9 \text{ V}$$

Per phase armature current when dynamic braking is employed

$$= \frac{E_f}{\sqrt{R_b^2 + X_s^2}} = \frac{1988.9}{\sqrt{20^2 + 15^2}} = 79.56 \text{ A}$$

Per phase current of 38.03 A gives a torque of 3819.7 Nm

Per phase current of 79.56 A would produce an initial braking torque of

$$\frac{3819.7}{38.03} \times 79.56 = 7990.9 \text{ Nm}$$

Total initial braking torque

= Load torque (assumed constant) + initial dynamic braking torque

= 3819.7 + 7990.9 = 11810.6 Nm

Also, initial dynamic braking torque $= K\omega_r = 7990.9$

$$\therefore \qquad K = \frac{7990.9 \times 60}{2\pi \times 500} = 152.61 \text{ Nm-sec/rad.}$$

Time for stopping the mill, from Eq. (4.247), is

$$t = \frac{800}{152.61} \ln\left[\frac{3819.7 + 7990.9}{3819.7 + 0}\right] = 5.917 \text{ sec}$$

The number of revolutions before the drive stops, from Eq. (4.248), are

$$r = \frac{1}{2\pi \times 152.61}\left[\frac{800}{152.61}(3819.7 + 7990.9)\left(1 - e^{-\frac{152.61}{800} \times 5.917}\right) - 3819.7 \times 5.917\right]$$

= 20.11 revolutions.

Below $\omega_r = 3819.7/152.61 = 25.03$ rad/sec, electric torque is less than the frictional torque. Therefore, eventually frictional torque stops the drive.

4.25 SPEED CONTROL OF SYNCHRONOUS MOTORS

A polyphase synchronous motor runs at constant synchronous speed, called rated speed, given by

$$\left.\begin{aligned} N_s &= \frac{120\,f}{P} \quad \ldots rpm \\ \text{or} \quad \omega_s &= \frac{4\pi\,f}{P} \quad \ldots \text{rad/sec} \end{aligned}\right\} \qquad \ldots(4.249)$$

where f is the rated frequency of the applied voltage.

Eq. (4.249) shows that the simplest means of speed control of a polyphase synchronous motor is to vary the frequency of the voltage applied to the armature winding of a synchronous motor. One such converter scheme used for the speed control of a synchronous motor is shown in Fig. 4.91. In this figure, 3-phase utility supply at 50 (or 60) Hz is converted to dc and then dc is converted to variable voltage and variable frequency (VVVF) by means of pulse-width modulated inverter. This adjustable votage and frequency when applied to polyphase synchronous motor controls its operating speed. The speed of a synchronous motor can be controlled below as well as above the rated speed as discussed below.

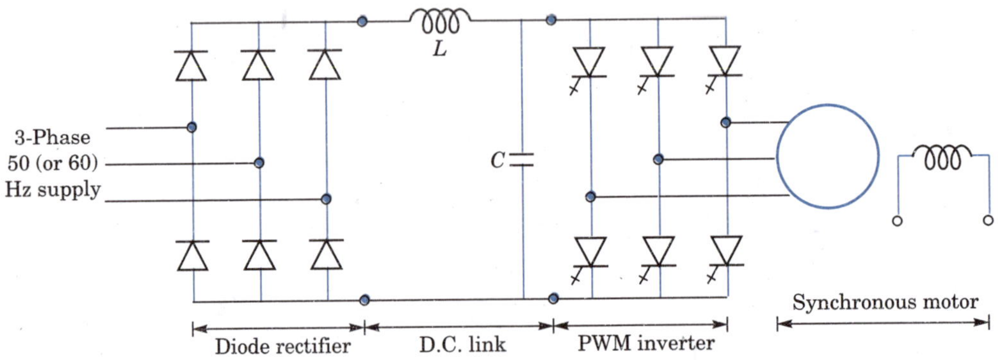

Fig. 4.91: A three phase VSI feeding a polyphase synchronous motor.

4.25.1 Speed Control Below Rated Speed

At rated voltage and rated frequency operation, a polyphase synchronous motor runs at rated speed, base speed or rated synchronous speed as given by Eq. (4.249). In case leakage impedance of synchronous motor is neglected, then

$$V_t = \sqrt{2}\;\pi f \phi N k_w$$

where V_t = motor terminal voltage,

f = frequency of motor terminal voltage.

and other symbols have their usual meanings.

When operating frequency is decreased, motor begins to run at a speed less than rated speed. But operation at constant source voltage and reduced frequency results in increased air-gap flux and therefore more air-gap flux density. Increased value of flux density leads to more core losses and at the same time, more machine current would be needed to create more flux. Therefore, with constant voltage and reduced frequency operation, a synchronous motor has more core and ohmic losses resulting in reduced efficiency, more heating and therefore reduced life of motor.

In case V_t/f is kept constant, flux density remains constant and normal operation of synchronous motor at adjustable speed is obtained. Thus optimum operation of synchronous motor results if both V_t and f are decreased together so that ratio V_t/f is kept constant. Maintaining of constant ratio of armature voltage to frequency is called **constant volt/hertz control.** This shows that speeds below rated speed in a synchronous motor are best obtained by decreasing applied voltage and frequency so that V_t/f remains constant. For a polyphase synchronous motor,

$$\text{power, } P = \frac{E_f \, . V_t}{X_s} \sin \delta$$

and

$$\text{torque, } T_e = \frac{1}{\omega_s} \frac{E_f \, . V_t}{X_s} \sin \delta$$

For $\delta = 90°$, pull-out power P_{mx} and pull-out (or maximum) torque T_{em} are obtained as under,

$$P_{mx} = \frac{E_f \, . V_t}{X_s} \quad \text{and} \quad T_{e\,.\,m} = \frac{1}{\omega_s} \frac{E_f \, . V_t}{X_s}$$

Now

$$\omega_s = \frac{4\pi f}{P} \quad \text{and} \quad E_f = \sqrt{2}\,\pi f N \phi k_w$$

$\therefore$

$$T_{e.m} = \frac{P}{4\pi f} \cdot \frac{\sqrt{2}\pi f N \phi k_w}{2\pi f L_s} \, . V_t$$

$$= \left[\frac{\sqrt{2}}{8.\pi} \frac{P . N \phi k_w}{L_s} \right] . \frac{V_t}{f} \qquad \text{...(4.250)}$$

The terms inside the bracket in Eq. (4.250) are constant for a given synchronous motor. Therefore, if applied voltage and frequency are decreased below rated value by keeping V_t/f constant, Eq. (4.250) shows that maximum torque remains constant for speeds less than rated speed.

$$P_{mx} = \frac{4\pi f}{P} \, . T_{em} \qquad \text{...(4.251)}$$

As V_t/f is varied below rated value, Eq. (4.251) shows that pull-out power P_{mx} varies linearly with speed, though maximum torque T_{em} remains constant, Fig. 4.92. Speed control below rated speed is usually referred to as **constant torque region.**

In constant torque region, low value of practical operating frequency is obtained when armature-resistance drop is quite a large percentage of the applied voltage.

4.25.2 Speed Control above Rated Speed

For obtaining speeds above rated value, Eq. (4.249) shows that frequency of the applied voltage should be increased above rated frequency. Again if (V_t/f) is kept constant at frequencies above rated frequency, applied voltage would have to be increased beyond rated value. But voltages above rated value would cause deterioration of insulation and shorter life of motor. Therefore, for frequencies above rated value, applied voltage is kept constant at its rated value V_r and only applied frequency is increased.

Now

$$P_{mx} = \frac{E_f \, . V_t}{X_s} = \frac{\sqrt{2} \, . \pi f \phi N k_w}{2\pi f L_s} \, . V_t = \left[\frac{\phi N k_w}{\sqrt{2} \, L_s} \right] . V_t \qquad \text{...(4.252)}$$

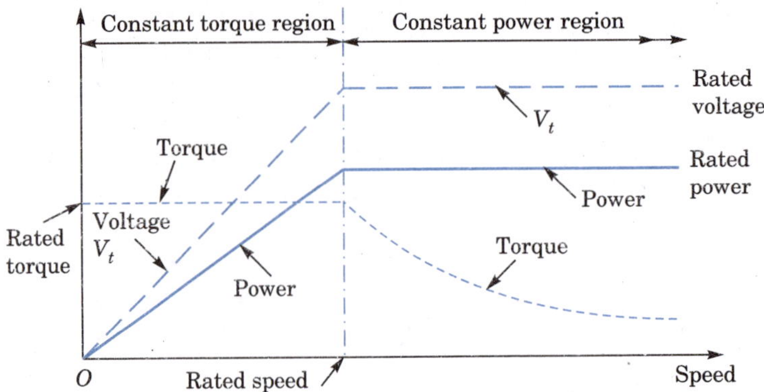

Fig. 4.92: Different operating regions for a polyphase synchronous motor under VVVF control.

Eq. (4.252) is seen to be independent of frequency. Therefore, if V_t is kept constant at rated value V_r and applied frequency is increased above rated value, then maximum power = rated power = $V_r I_r$ would remain constant. However, $T_{e.m} = \dfrac{P}{4\pi f} . P_{mx}$ would decrease as applied frequency is raised, Fig. 4.92. Operation of synchronous motor above rated speed is called **constant-power region.**

In constant power region, the upper speed limit of synchronous motor is usually limited by

(*i*) the maximum frequency that can be derived from PWM inverter and

(*ii*) the stress considerations at higher speeds that the shaft can withstand without any damage to the mechanical system.

The speed control of a polyphase synchronous motor by *V/f* control is not much used in industrial applications. It is due to the fact that with change of frequency, rotating field speed changes and for the rotor to track these changes is a difficult task [4]. This problem can, however, be tackled by means of *field-oriented control* or vector control of synchronous motors. This technique, being a bit involved, has not been discussed here.

Example 4.39. *A 15 MVA, 6.6 kV, 50 Hz, three-phase, four-pole synchronous motor is fed from VVVF, 3-phase source with V/f constant. Motor synchronous reactance is 1.1 pu. The synchronous machine generates rated open-circuit voltage for a field current of 25 A.*

(*a*) *Calculate rated speed and rated current of synchronous motor.*

(*b*) *If the motor operates under rated values of voltage, frequency and power, calculate the field current required to operate the motor at unity power factor.*

(*c*) *If the applied frequency is reduced to 40 Hz and load torque to 75% of rated torque, calculate the motor speed and field current to obtain unity power factor operation of the sychronous motor.*

(*d*) *With field current raised to 32.5 A and applied frequency reduced to 40 Hz, calculate the power factor at which the synchronous motor would operate. Load torque is held fixed at rated value.*

Solution. (*a*) Rated speed = $\dfrac{120 \times 50}{4}$ = 1500 rpm.

Rated motor current, $I_a = \dfrac{1500}{\sqrt{3} \times 6.6} = 131.22$ A

(*b*) Under unity pf operation, phasor diagram is drawn in Fig. 4.93 (*a*), where V_t, E_f and I_a are rated per phase values.

Per phase, $V_t = \dfrac{6600}{\sqrt{3}} = 3810.6$ V, Per-phase, $I_a = 131.22$ A

Base impedance, $Z_b = \dfrac{kV_B^2}{MVA_B} = \dfrac{6.6^2}{1.5} = 29.04\ \Omega$

$\therefore$ X_s in ohms = X_s is pu × Z_b = 1.1 × 29.04 = 31.944 Ω

From the phasor diagram, $E_f = \sqrt{V_t^2 + (I_a X_s)^2}$

$$= \sqrt{3810.6^2 + (131.22 \times 31.944)^2} = 5664.9 \text{ V}$$

Now $E_f = \sqrt{2}\pi f \phi N k_w$ or $E_f \propto f \,.\, I_f$

It is given that $3810.6 \propto 50 \times 25$

$5664.9 \propto 50 \times$ new field current

or $\dfrac{5664.9}{3810.6} = \dfrac{50 \times \text{new field current}}{50 \times 25}$

$\therefore$ New field current $= \dfrac{5664.9 \times 25}{3810.6} = 37.165$ A

(*c*) Motor speed $= \dfrac{120 \times 40}{4} = 1200$ rpm

Torque $\propto \phi I_a$. As *V*/*f* is constant, ϕ is constant, $\therefore$ $T_L \propto I_a$

Also $0.75\, T_L \propto I_{a1}$

$\therefore$ $I_{a1} = 0.75\, I_a = 0.75 \times 131.22 = 98.415$ A

New terminal voltage $= \dfrac{40}{50} V_t = \dfrac{4}{5} \times 3810.6 = 3048.48$ V

New synchronous reactance drop $= 0.75\, I_a \times \dfrac{40}{50} X_s$

$$= 98.415 \times \frac{4}{5} \times 31.944 = 2515.02 \text{ V}$$

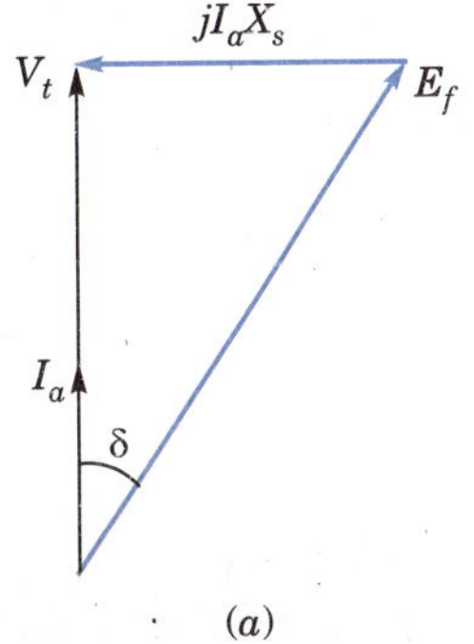

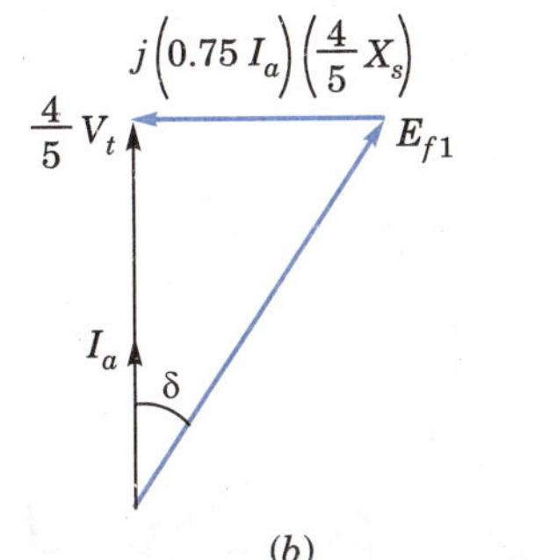

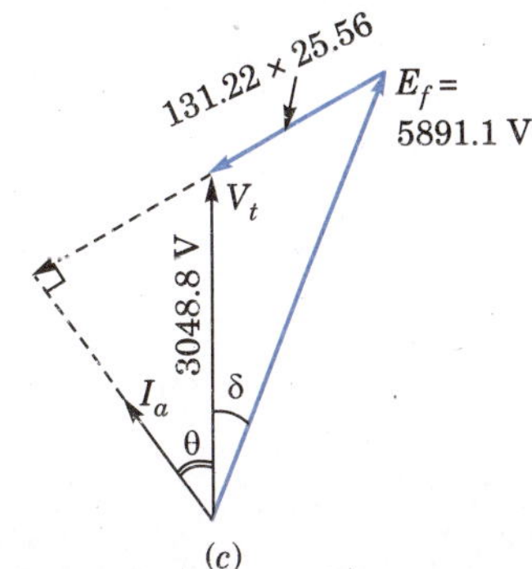

Fig. 4.93: Pertaining to Example 4.39.

Under new operating conditions at unity *pf*, the phasor diagram is as shown in Fig. 4.93 (*b*). From this diagram, new excitation voltage E_{f1} is

$$E_{f1} = \sqrt{3048.48^2 + 2515.02^2} = 3952.032 \text{ V}$$

But $\quad E_f \propto f I_f \quad$ or $\quad 3810.6 \propto 50 \times 25$

$$3952.032 \propto 40 \times I_{f1}$$

$\therefore$ $$I_{f1} = \frac{3952.032 \times 50 \times 25}{3810.6 \times 40} = 32.41 \text{ A}$$

(*d*) Here $E_f \propto f I_f \quad \therefore \quad$ New $E_f = 5664.9 \times \frac{40}{50} \times \frac{32.5}{25} = 5891.5$ V

New $$V_t = \frac{40}{50} \times 3810.6 = 3048.48 \text{ V}$$

As load torque is held fixed, armature current remains unaltered.

$\therefore$ $$I_a = 131.22 \text{ A.}$$

New $$X_s = \frac{40}{50} \times 31.944 = 25.56\ \Omega$$

With changed parameters, phasor diagram is now as shown in Fig. 4.93 (*c*). From the triangle made up of E_f, V_t and $I_a X_s$, we get $(I_a X_s)^2 = E_f^2 + V_t^2 - 2E_f \cdot V_t \cos \delta$

$$(131.22 \times 25.56)^2 = 5891.5^2 + 3048.48^2 - 2 \times 5891.5 \times 3048.48 \times \cos \delta$$

Its solution gives $\quad \delta = 24.238°$

With no armature resistance, $V_t I_a \cos \theta = \frac{E_f \cdot V_t}{X_s} \sin \delta$

or $$3048.48 \times 131.22 \times \cos \theta = \frac{5891.5 \times 3048.48}{25.56} \sin 24.238°$$

or $$\cos \theta = \frac{5891.5}{131.22 \times 25.56} \cdot \sin 24.238° = 0.7211$$

Since $E_f \cos \delta = 5891.5 \times \cos 24.238° = 5372.5$ V is more than $V_t = 3048.48$ V, the synchronous motor is operating at a leading power factor of 0.7211.

5.26 PERMANENT MAGNET SYNCHRONOUS MACHINES

Evolution of new permanent-magnetic materials has generated interest in the development of new rotating electrical machines; permanent magnet synchronous machines (PMSMs) is one of them. In PMSMs, the field windings are replaced by permanent magnets. A conventional synchronous machine (CSM) with field winding permits the control of its excitation emf, reactive power flow and its power factor. But this is not feasible in PMSMs. In spite of this, PMSMs are being built because of the following reasons.

(*i*) Since modern permanent magnet materials produce high flux densities, size of the machine gets reduced.

(*ii*) There is no field-resistance loss in PMSMs. This leads to high efficiency (95 to 97%) of PMSMs.

Permanent magnet synchronous motors, also called *permanent magnet ac motors,* are of two types, (*i*) trapezoidal type and (*ii*) sinusoidal type. PMS motors consist of permanent magnets on the rotor, rotor speed and position sensor and power-electronic converters. PMS motors are discussed in detail in chapter 9.

Permanent magnet synchronous machines can be analysed with the techniques already known to the reader for the analysis of conventional synchronous machines.

Example 4.40. *A 8 kVA, 440 V, 50 Hz, four-pole star-connected permanent magnet synchronous generator develops rated voltage on open circuit when driven at rated speed. At rated load of 0.8 pf lag, its terminal voltage is found to be 390 V. Armature resistance of this PMSG is assumed negligible.*

(*a*) *Calculate the alternator synchronous reactance in ohms and also in per unit.*

(*b*) *If alternator is loaded to 6 kW at unity power factor, calculate the terminal voltage at the alternator terminals.*

Solution. (*a*) Excitation emf, $E_f = \dfrac{440}{\sqrt{3}} = 254.04$ V

Alternator terminal voltage, $V_t = \dfrac{390}{\sqrt{3}} = 225.17$ V

Rated armature current, $I_a = \dfrac{8000}{\sqrt{3} \times 440} = 10.498$ A

Alternator phasor diagram at lagging *pf* gives

$$E_f^2 = (V_t \cos\theta)^2 + V_t \sin\theta + I_a \,.\, X_s)^2$$

$$254.04^2 = (225.17 \times 0.8)^2 + (225.17 \times 0.6 + 10.498 \,.\, X_s)^2$$

$\therefore$ Synchronous reactance, $X_s = \dfrac{179.1294 - 225.17 \times 0.6}{10.498} = 4.194 \simeq 4.2\ \Omega$

Base impedance, $Z_b = \dfrac{V_B^2}{(VA)^2} = \dfrac{440^2}{8000} = 24.2\ \Omega$

$\therefore$ X_s in pu $= \dfrac{4.2\ \Omega}{24.2\ \Omega} = 0.1736$ pu

(*b*) Let V_t be the alternator terminal voltage tube calculated. This gives $I_a = \dfrac{8000}{\sqrt{3} \,.\, V_t}$

Alternator phasor diagram at unity power factor gives,

$$E_f^2 = V_t^2 + (I_a X_s)^2$$

$$254.04^2 = V_t^2 + \left(\frac{8000}{\sqrt{3}\, V_t} \times 4.2\right)^2$$

$$V_t^2 - 64536.32\, V_t^2 + \frac{64 \times 10^6}{3} \times 4.2^2 = 0$$

$$V_t^2 = \frac{64536.32 \pm 51571.86}{2}$$

$\therefore$ $V_t = 80.512$ V or 240.944 V

The plausible value of V_t = 240.944 (phase value)

or $$V_t = \sqrt{3} \times 240.944 = 417.315 \text{ V (line value)}$$

Example 4.41. *Two identical synchronous machines of rating 100 MW, 50 Hz operating in parallel have the following characteristics :*

Machine 1 : Speed droop R = 4%

Speed changer set to give 50% rated load at rated speed.

Machine 2 : Speed droop R = 4%

Speed changer set to give 75% rated load at rated speed.

(a) Determine the load taken by each machine for a total load of 150 MW and the frequency of operation.

(b) What adjustments should be made by the speed changers of the machines to share the load as in (a) but with a frequency of 50 Hz ? [*I.E.S., 1990*]

Solution. In Fig. 4.94, Ob is the rated speed corresponding to 50 Hz = 100 so that load on machine 1 is 0.5 × 100 = 50 MW = ab and load on machine 2 is 0.75 × 100 = 75 MW = bc. Also bA is the percentage speed drop = 4%. This means that

$$\frac{bA}{\text{Rated speed }(Ob)} = \text{speed drop} \quad \text{or} \quad \frac{bA}{100} = 0.4 \quad \text{or} \quad bA = 4$$

∴ No load speed = $OA = Ob + bA = 100 + 4 = 104 = 50.2$ Hz.

In Fig. 4.94, xy and yz represent the load on machine 1 and 2 respectively so that $xy + yz$ = 150 MW and $oy = f$, the new operating frequency.

(*a*) For machine 1, similar triangles abA and xyA give,

$$\frac{xy}{yA} = \frac{ab}{bA}, \quad \therefore \quad \frac{xy}{104 - f} = \frac{50}{4} \quad \text{or} \quad xy = (104 - f)\,\frac{50}{4}$$

Similarly, for machines 2, $yz = (104 - f)\,\dfrac{75}{4}$

$$\therefore \quad (xy + yz) = 150 = (104 - f)\left[\frac{50}{4} + \frac{75}{4}\right].$$

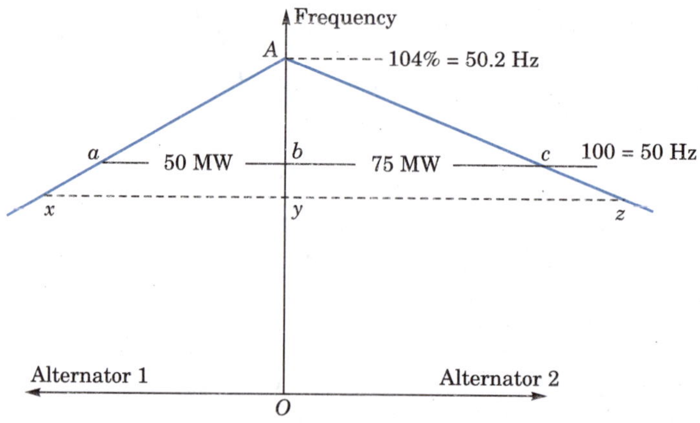

Fig. 4.94: Pertaining to Example 4.41.

Its solution gives $f = 99.2\%$

or $f = 0.992 \times 50 = 49.6$ Hz

$\therefore$ Load on machine 1 $= (104 - 99.2) \times \dfrac{50}{4} = 60$ MW

and load on machine 2 $= (104 - 99.2) \times \dfrac{75}{4} = 90$ MW

(*b*) Machine 1, Speed droop $R = 4\%$

Speed changer should be set to give 60% rated load at rated speed.

Machine 2, Speed droop $R = 4\%$

Speed changer should be set to give 90% rated load at rated speed.

PROBLEMS

4.1. What are the various basic parameters of a synchronous machine ? Derive expressions for armature to field mutual inductances and armature self inductances for a salient-pole synchronous machine. How are these inductance expressions modified for a cylindrical-rotor synchronous machine ? What is the advantage of resolving armature m.m.f. into *d-q* axes components ?

4.2. (*a*) Derive expressions for armature mutual inductances of a salient-pole synchronous machine from a consideration of its basic parameters.

(*b*) Explain how Park's transformations transform equations in *a*, *b*, *c* variables to *d*, *q*, 0 variables.

4.3. Write the impedance matrix for a 3-phase salient-pole synchronous machine fitted with amortisseurs. Hence obtain an expression for the instantaneous electromagnetic torque and identify the various terms in it.

4.4. Starting from the impedance matrix of a 3-phase salient pole synchronous machine without amortisseurs, derive the phasor voltage equation under balanced steady-state operation. Hence draw the phasor diagrams for both motor and generator.

4.5. A 2-pole, 3-phase 50 Hz, star-connected uniform air gap synchronous machine has the following data:

Armature winding: synchronous inductance = 0.01 H per phase, resistance is negligible.

Field winding : self-inductance = 30 H, resistance = 20 Ω.

Motional inductance between field winding and any one coil of two-axis model = 0.5 H.

This synchronous machine, working as a generator at rated speed, delivers power to a balanced load at 1.0 p.f. Field winding is energised from 200 V d.c. source. If terminal voltage across the load terminals is 900 V perphase, compute the electrical power output of the generator in kW.

$\left[\textbf{Hint.}\text{ From Eq. (4.40), } E_f = \dfrac{0.5 \times 100\pi \times 10}{\sqrt{2}} \text{ etc.}\right]$ **[Ans.** 559.69 kW]

4.6. A 3-phase, 50 Hz cylindrical-rotor synchronous machine has the following parameters :

Self-inductance for phase a = 3.15 mH

Armature leakage inductance = 0.35 mH

For this machine, calculate the mutual inductance between armature phases and its synchronous reactance. **[Ans.** (– 1.4) mH, 1.4294 Ω]

4.7. A 3-phase star-connected, 4-pole, 50 Hz alternator develops an open-circuit voltage of 12.5 kV for an applied field voltage of 400 V. For a field circuit resistance of 10 Ω, calculate the magnitude of motional inductance and the amplitude of armature-field mutual inductance.

[**Ans.** 1.6244 H, 1.083 H]

4.8. (*a*) From the torque matrix of a 3-phase salient-pole alternator and its phasor diagram, obtain an expression for synchronous power in terms of the load angle.

(*b*) A salient-pole synchronous generator has

$$X_q = 0.8 \text{ pu.} \quad \text{and} \quad r_a = 0.02 \text{ pu.}$$

If this generator delivers rated kVA at 0.8 p.f. lagging and at rated voltage, compute the load angle. [**Ans.** $\delta = 22.77°$]

4.9. (*a*) From the phasor diagram of a salient-pole alternator working at a leading p.f., but with p.f. angle θ less than load angle δ, obtain the following relations :

(*i*) $$\tan(\delta - \theta) = \frac{I_a X_q - V_t \sin\theta}{V_t \cos\theta + I_a r_a}$$

(*ii*) $$E_f = V_t \cos\delta + I_a r_a \cos(\delta - \theta) + I_d X_d.$$

(*b*) Find excitation voltage of an alternator when delivering rated output at 0.8 p.f. leading and at rated voltage. For this alternator,

$$X_d = 1.25 \text{ p.u.} \quad \text{and} \quad X_q = 1.00 \text{ p.u.}$$ [**Ans.** (*b*) 1.006]

4.10. (*a*) From the phasor diagram of a salient-pole synchronous motor working at a leading p.f., obtain the following relations :

(*i*) $\tan(\delta + \theta) = \dfrac{V_t \sin\theta + I_a X_q}{V_t \sin\theta - I_a r_a}$ and (*ii*) $E_f = V_t \cos\delta - I_q r_a + I_d X_d$

(*b*) A salient-pole synchronous motor delivers rated mechanical output at rated voltage and takes rated current at 0.8 p.f. leading. Compute the motor excitation voltage if

$$X_d = 1.25 \text{ p.u.} \quad \text{and} \quad X_q = 1.00 \text{ p.u.}$$ [**Ans.** (*b*) 2.0115]

4.11. (*a*) For a salient-pole synchronous machine, P_1 and P_2 are the maximum values of electromagnetic power and reluctance power respectively. Show that the load angle δ, at which resultant power is maximum, can be obtained from the relation,

$$\cos\delta = \frac{-P_1 \pm \sqrt{P_1^2 + 32P_2^2}}{8P_2}$$

(*b*) If amplitude of reductance power is 20% of that of the electromagnetic power, compute the load angle at which steady-state power limit is reached.

[**Hint.** (*a*) $P = P_1 \sin\delta + P_2 \sin 2\delta$ etc.] [**Ans.** (*b*) $\delta = 71.4138°$]

4.12. A 3-phase, 50 Hz, 6.6 kV, star-connected salient-pole synchronous motor is operating at 0.8 p.f. leading and taking 400 A from the mains. For this motor,

$$X_d = 4\ \Omega \quad \text{and} \quad X_q = 2.5\ \Omega$$

Calculate the maximum power that the motor can develop if its excitation is maintained constant. [**Ans.** 15.30 MW]

4.13. (*a*) A synchronous machine is synchronized with an infinite bus and now, without changing its field current, it is made to operate as

(*i*) a motor and

(*ii*) a generator. Explain, in each case, whether the machine is delivering or absorbing reactive power.

(*b*) Synchronizing power P_s is defined as the rate at which synchronous power P varies with load angle δ.

A cylindrical-rotor synchronous machine, connected to an infinite bus, is operating at unity p.f. Show that its per phase synchronizing power P_s is given by $\frac{V_t^2}{X_s}$.

[**Hint.** (*a*) At the time of synchronizing, $E_f = V_t$

(*b*) Find $\frac{dP}{d\delta}$ and take the help of its phasor diagram.]

[**Ans.** (*a*) For both parts, reactive power is absorbed.]

4.14. (*a*) From the phasor diagram of a cylindrical-rotor synchronous motor, show that its per phase power output is given by

$$P = \frac{E_f V_t}{Z_s} \sin(\delta + \alpha_z) - \frac{E_f^2}{Z_s^2} r_a$$

where $\alpha_z = \tan^{-1} \frac{r_a}{X_s}$.

(*b*) From part (*a*), find an expression for the maximum per phase power output of the synchronous motor.

[**Hint.** (*a*) $P = E_f I_a \cos(\theta - \delta)$ for a lagging p.f. operation.] $\left[\textbf{Ans. } (b) \left(\frac{E_f V_t}{Z_s} - \frac{E_f^2}{Z_s^2} r_a\right)\right]$

4.15. (*a*) Define the short-circuit ratio of a synchronous generator. Show that *SCR* is equal to the reciprocal of per unit value of direct-axis synchronous reactance X_d.

(*b*) Explain the influence of *SCR* on the operating characteristics and the physical size of a synchronous machine.

4.16. (*a*) Why is it important to investigate the transient behaviour of synchronous generators ?

(*b*) A 3-phase salient-pole synchronous generator (without damper bars) is developing rated voltage at its terminals, when running at sychronous speed and at no-load. A three-phase balanced short circuit suddenly occurs at alternator terminals. If all the synchronous machine resistances and armature transformer voltages are neglected, develop expressions for the armature and field currents as functions of time. Explain the nature of these currents.

How is the expression for armature current effected in case armature transformer voltages are included ?

4.17. A 3-phase salient-pole synchronous generator (without amortisseurs) is developing rated voltage at its terminals, when running at synchronous speed and at no-load. A three-phase balanced short circuit occurs suddenly at alternator terminals. Derive an expression for the current in any one phase as a function of time and identify its various terms. All the synchronous machine resistances may be neglected.

4.18. A symmetrical sudden 3-phase short circuit is applied to the terminals of an excited salient-pole synchronous generator (without damper bars) running at rated speed. Develop an expression for the armature current at any instant of time following the short circuit, in case armature transformer voltages and armature resistances are neglected.

Hence, find an expression for the r.m.s. short-circuit armature current in case salient poles are fitted with damper bars. Sketch this current and mark clearly the subtransient and transient time constants.

4.19. A 3-phase salient-pole synchronous machine is running at synchronous speed, with its field winding unexcited. Effect of field resistance is included but armature resistances are neglected.

(*a*) If alternator terminals are open circuited and a voltage V_f is suddenly applied across its field winding at $t = 0$, derive expressions for d, q components of armature voltages as functions of time. Find also the instantaneous phase voltages.

(*b*) Repeat part (*a*), if armature transformer voltages are also neglected.

[**Hint.** (*a*) $V_t\, 1 = (r_f + L_f p)\, i_f$

$v_d = M_d\, p\, i_f$ and $v_q = M_d\, \omega\, i_f$ etc.]

Ans. (*a*)
$$v_d = \frac{M_d V_f}{L_f}\, e^{-t/T_{d0}'}\ ;\ v_q = \frac{M_d\, \omega\, V_f}{r_f}\,(1 - e^{-t/T_{d0}'})$$

$$v_a = \left[\frac{M_d V_f}{L_f}\, e^{-t/T_{d0}'} \cos(\omega t + \theta_0) - \frac{M_d\, .\, \omega V_f}{r_f}(1 - e^{-t/T_{d0}'}) \sin(\omega t + \theta_0)\right]$$

For v_b, v_c replace θ_0 by $(\theta_0 - 120°)$ and $(\theta_0 - 240°)$ respectively.

(*b*) $v_d = 0$, v_q = same as in part (*a*).

$$v_a = \left[-\frac{M_d\, .\, \omega\, V_f}{r_f}(1 - e^{-t/T_{d0}'}) \sin(\omega_t + \theta_0) \text{ etc.}\right]$$

4.20. A 3-phase, 11 kV, 125 MVA, star-connected turbo-alternator has the following p.u. constants.

$$X_d = 1.00\ ;\ X_d' = 0.25\ ;\ T_d' = 1.00 \text{ sec.}$$

This alternator is operating at no-load with its rated terminal voltage. Now a sudden three-phase short circuit occurs across its terminals. Armature transformer voltages are neglected for parts (*a*), (*b*), (*c*), (*d*) and not for part (*e*). Express the currents both in p.u. and in amperes.

(*a*) Find the current in phase *a* as a function of time. Assume that the short circuit occurs when phase *a* axis is 90° away from field axis.

(*b*) Write an equation for the envelope of the short circuit current wave as a function of time.

(*c*) Write the equation giving the r.m.s. value of the symmetrical short-circuit current as a function of time.

(*d*) Find the r.m.s. value of symmetrical current in phase *a*, just after the three-phase short circuit.

(*e*) If armature transformer voltages are not neglected, then phase *a* current must include d.c. and second harmonic components. Find the maximum possible magnitude of d.c. component just after the 3-phase short circuit.

[**Hint.** (*a*) Use Eq. (4.110).

(*e*) Maximum d.c. component = $\sqrt{2}$ × r.m.s. value of symmetrical sc current.]

[**Ans.** (*a*) $\sqrt{2}(1 + 3e^{-t}) \sin \omega t$. (*b*) $\sqrt{2}\,(1 + 3e^{-t})$ (*c*) $(1 + 3e^{-t})$ (*d*) 4.00 p.u. (*e*) $\sqrt{2}$ (4). p.u. armature current = 6561 A]

4.21. The alternator in Prob. 4.20 has additional constants as under :

$$X_d'' = 0.1,\ T_d'' = 0.3 \text{ s}$$

Work prob. 4.20 for all its parts.

[**Ans.** (*a*) $\sqrt{2}\,[1 + 3e^{-t} + 6e^{-3.33t}] \sin \omega t$

(*b*) $\sqrt{2}\,[1 + 3e^{-t} + 6e^{-3.33t}]$

(*c*) $1 + 3e^{-t} + 6e^{-3.33t}$

(*d*) 10 p.u. (*e*) $\sqrt{2}$.10 p.u.]

4.22. (*a*) For a sudden inductive loading $\dot{X}_L$ on a 3-phase alternator developing a voltage E_{f0}, show that the terminal voltage at once falls from E_{f0} to $\dfrac{E_{f0}\,X_L}{X_d' + X_L}$, with its final value equal to $\dfrac{E_{f0}\cdot X_L}{X_d + X_L}$.

(*b*) If the inductive load X_L is suddenly disconnected, show that the terminal voltage at once rises from its initial value V_{t0} to $V_{to}\left(1+\dfrac{X_d'}{X_L}\right)$ with its final value equal to

$$V_{t0}\left(1+\frac{X_d}{X_L}\right) = E_{f0}.$$

4.23. A balanced three-phase short circuit on a 3-phase salient-pole alternator is performed at rated speed so that rated armature current flows under steady state short circuit conditions. If the armature short circuit is now suddenly removed, derive expressions for the field current and armature terminal voltage as a function of time. The effect of damper bars on both direct and quadrature axes is neglected.

Find also the magnitude of field current and armature terminal voltage at the instant short-circuit is removed.

[**Hint.** Follow Art. 4.9.2 for sudden inductive unloading but with $X_L = 0$]

$$\left[\textbf{Ans. } i_f(t) = I_{f0}\left[1-\frac{X_d - X_d'}{X_d}\,e^{-t/T_d'}\right],\; V_t(t) = E_{f0}\left[1-\frac{X_d - X_d'}{X_d}\,e^{-t/T_d'}\right]\right.$$

$$\left.\text{At } t = 0,\; i_f(t) = I_{f0}\,\frac{X_d'}{X_d} \text{ and } V_t(t) = E_{f0}\cdot\frac{X_d'}{X_d}.\right]$$

4.24. A 4-pole, 50 Hz, star-connected salient-pole alternator has the following parameters:

$$X_d = 5\ \Omega,\ X_q = 3\ \Omega,\ X_d' = 1\ \Omega,\ T_{d0}' = 4s,\ r_f = 1\ \Omega,\ r_a = 0,\ M_d = 0.176\ \text{H}$$

(*a*) With the field winding unexcited and armature terminals open-circuited, the machine is run at rated speed by a prime-mover. If a voltage of 400 V is suddenly applied to the field winding, find (*i*) the field current as a function of time and (*ii*) the armature terminal voltage as a function of time.

(*b*) With 400 V applied to field winding, a 3-phase steady-state short-circuit exists across the armature terminals. Find the steady state values of field and armature currents.

(*c*) If the steady-state short circuit is suddenly removed, then find (*i*) the field current and armature terminal voltage as a function of time and (*ii*) the field current and armature terminal voltage soon after the removal of short circuit.

[**Ans.** (*a*) (*i*) $400\,(1 - e^{-0.25t})$ A, (*ii*) $7820.66\,(1 - e^{-0.25t})$ V
(*b*) 400 A, 1564.132 A
(*c*) (*i*) $400\,(1 - 0.8e^{-0.25t})$, $7820.66\,(1 - 0.8e^{-0.25t})$
(*ii*) 80 A, 1564.132 V]

4.25. (*a*) During the balanced 3-phase short-circuit analysis, explain why *d*-axis parameters are mainly involved.

(*b*) Just after the short-circuit, the induced field current and increased armature current decay with the same time constant. Explain.

(*c*) The effect of damper bars, just after the sudden short circuit, is to increase the amplitude of short-circuit current. Explain.

4.26. (*a*) Draw the symmetrical waveform for the armature short-circuit current for a 3-phase synchronous generator. Indicate the three periods into which its envelope may be divided.

(*b*) Explain why the d.c. component of armature short-circuit current in phase *a*, for a sudden 3-phase short circuit, is

(*i*) zero if phase-*a* axis is 90° away from *d*-axis and

(*ii*) maximum if phase-*a* axis is along the *d*-axis.

4.27. For a 3-phase synchronous generator, explain from physical considerations,

(*a*) the presence of d.c. and second harmonic components in its armature short-circuit current and

(*b*) the presence of fundamental frequency a.c. component in its field current.

4.28. (*a*) Explain the various reactances and time-constants from the *d*-axis equivalent circuits of a 3-phase synchronous machine.

(*b*) Show that $T_d'' = T_{d0}'' \dfrac{X_d''}{X_d'}$.

4.29. (*a*) Explain the various reactances and time constants from the *q*-axis equivalent circuits of a 3-phase synchronous machine.

(*b*) If there is an external reactance x_e in series with the generator, find its effect on T_{d0}', T_{d0}'', T_{q0}'', T_d', T_d'' and T_q''.

(*c*) Explain the armature time constant T_a.

4.30. The following parameters, expressed in per unit, relate to a particular salient-pole synchronous machine:

D-axis magnetizing reactance,	$X_{md} = 1.06$
Armature leakage reactance,	$x_a = 0.14$
Field winding leakage reactance,	$x_f = 0.14$
Field winding resistance,	$r_f = 0.30$
Q-axis magnetizing reactance,	$X_{mq} = 0.76$
Damper-winding resistance,	$r_{kd} = 2.00$
Damper-winding leakage reactance,	$x_{kd} = 0.02$

(*a*) Determine X_d, X_d', X_d'' and X_q.

(*b*) Determine T_{d0}', T_d', T_{d0}'' and T_d''.

(*c*) Show that (*i*) $X_d' = \dfrac{T_d'}{T_{d0}'} \cdot X_d$ and (*ii*) $X_d'' = \dfrac{T_d''}{T_{d0}''} \cdot X_d'$

[**Ans.** (*a*) 1.20, 0.2637, 0.1572, 0.90. All in p.u. (*b*) 4, 0.879, 0.07183, 0.042832. All in seconds.]

4.31. Give the physical concepts of X_d'', X_d' and X_d. Explain why $X_d'' < X_d' < X_d$.
In cylindrical-rotor synchronous machines, X_d is a little higher than X_q. Explain.

4.32. Give the physical concepts of X_q'', X_q' and X_q.
Explain why $X_q = X_q'$ and $X_q'' < X_q'$.
Why is X_q'' greater than X_d'' ? Explain.

4.33. Give the physical concepts of negative sequence reactance and zero-sequence reactance. Explain how these can be measured in the laboratory.

4.34. (*a*) Distinguish between X_d', X_d'' and between X_q, X_q'' parameters of a salient-pole synchronous machine. Give the corresponding flux linkage diagrams, as also the electrical equivalent circuits for these parameters.

(*b*) Explain how X_d, X_d' and X_d'' can be determined from the armature-current oscillograms obtained after a sudden symmetrical 3-phase short circuit at the alternator terminals.

4.35. A 230 V, 8 kVA, star-connected salient-pole synchronous machine gave the following data for the measurement of X_d'' and X_q''.

For X_d'' : 28 V, 10 A, 23 watts

For X_q'' : 28 V, 7 A, 16 watts.

Find X_d'', X_q'' and negative sequence reactance in ohms and also in per unit values.

Derive the expressions used for the measurement of X_d'' and X_q''.

[**Ans.** 1.3953 Ω, 1.9933 Ω, 1.6943 Ω, 0.211 p.u., 0.3014 p.u., 0.2562 p.u.]

4.36. Draw the sketches of 3-phase armature currents showing their variation with time, after a sudden 3-phase symmetrical short circuit is suddenly applied at the alternator terminals. Explain why they differ from each other.

How can the reactances X_d'', X_d', X_d and time constants T_d'', T_d' be determined from these oscillograms ?

4.37. A steady-state short-circuit is to be performed on a 3-phase alternator. For this purpose, the alternator is driven at rated speed and a large resistance is inserted in series with its field winding.

If its field winding is energised first and then the switch that short circuits the three terminals is closed, there is invariably a sudden jerk on the machine. If the switch that short circuits the three terminals, is closed first and then its field winding is energised, there is no jerk on the machine. Explain why this happens.

[**Hint.** When field winding is energised first, a field current does exist even if there is a large resistance in series with it. This field current gives rise to some voltage at the alternator terminals, which may cause the flow of large short-circuit currents when these terminals are short circuited. These large sc currents cause the appearance of power surges accompanied by a jerk on the machine. When the switch that short circuits ... etc.].

4.38. Develop the three phase synchronous generator phasor diagram under transient conditions and hence derive its transient power-angle characteristics. Explain the effect of neglecting the transient saliency.

4.39. (*a*) What are the causes of disturbances in synchronous machines ?

Discuss the effect of rotor oscillations on the performance of a synchronous machine.

(*b*) Derive and show that the electromechanical equation for the synchronous-machine dynamics is given by $P_j \dfrac{d^2\delta}{dt^2} + K_d \dfrac{d\delta}{dt} + P_m \sin \delta = P_{sh}$

Here P_j, K_d and P_{sh} are the inertia power, electrical damping constant and shaft power respectively. P_m is equal to $\dfrac{E_f V_t}{X_s}$.

4.40. (*a*) Explain what you know about undamped natural angular frequency ω_n, damped natural angular frequency ω_d and damping ratio ξ in case of synchronous machines.

For a sudden increment of shaft power on a synchronous motor, draw the curves depicting the variation of load angle δ with different values of ξ. Assume the initial value of load angle to be zero.

(*b*) A 500 kW, 10 pole, 50 Hz synchronous motor operates with a load angle of 25° on full load. Total moment of inertia of rotating parts is 1150 kg-m^2. Determine the natural frequency of rotor oscillations. Neglect armature resistance and saliency.

[**Hint.** (*b*) $500{,}000 = 3 \dfrac{E_f V_t}{X_s} \sin 25°$.

$\therefore \quad P_s = \dfrac{500{,}000}{\tan 25°}$ etc.]

[**Ans.** (*b*) 1.371 Hz]

4.41. (*a*) Show that the natural period of oscillations for a cylindrical-rotor synchronous machine operating at no-load, is given by

$$t_n = 9.10\, n_s \sqrt{\frac{J}{f I_{sc}\, V_t}}$$

The symbols used have their usual meanings.

(*b*) A 10 MVA, 11 kV, 3-phase, 6 pole, 50 Hz star-connected alternator is connected to an infinite bus. Its short-circuit current is three times the full-load current and the moment of inertia of rotating parts is 30,000 kg-m^2. Calculate its natural period of oscillations at no-load. [**Ans.** (*b*) 1.175 sec.]

4.42. (*a*) Explain what you know about forced oscillations in synchronous machines ?

Find an expression giving the magnitude of maximum deviation in load angle when the synchronous machine is subjected to a harmonic torque component of $T_{Lm} \sin \omega_L \,.\, t$.

(*b*) A 1500 kW, 6600 volt, 3-phase, 50 Hz, 16-pole synchronous motor is directly fed from a large power system network. The motor has the following data:

Total moment of inertia, J = 8200 kg-m^2

Synchronizing-power coefficient, P_s = 560 kW/elec. rad.

Damping torque coefficient = 4000 Nm/elec. rad/sec.

If this motor drives a reciprocating compressor whose first order harmonic-torque component has an amplitude of 1000 Nm at an angular frequency of 2.5 rad/sec., then calculate the maximum deviation in load angle and the corresponding pulsation of synchronous power. [**Ans.** (*b*) 4.51°, 44.08 kW]

4.43. (*a*) Show that the condition for stability for large angular oscillations in synchronous machines is given by $\frac{d\delta}{dt} = 0$.

(*b*) What is equal-area criterion of stability ?

Explain how it is used to determine the transient stability of synchronous machine systems ?

4.44. A 50 kVA, 3-phase, star-connected, 381 volts, 6-pole, 50 Hz alternator has a synchronous reactance of 25% and is running in parallel with an infinite bus. Calculate the sychronizing power and the corresponding synchronizing torque per mechanical degree of phase displacement on full load at 0.8 p.f. leading. Neglect resistance of the alternator.

[**Ans.** 8843.3 W, 84.45 Nm]

4.45. A cylindrical rotor synchronous motor, connected to an infinite bus, is running on no-load. If the power-angle equation for this motor is 3 sin δ, then find the maximum shaft load that can be suddenly applied to the motor shaft without loss of synchronism. Neglect all losses and damping.

[**Hint.** Since losses are neglected, load angle at no-load is zero. If P_{sh} is the maximum safe load that can be suddenly applied to the motor shaft without loss of synchronism, then

$$\text{Area } oabo = \int_0^{\delta_a} (P_{sh} - 3 \sin \delta)\, d\delta = P_{sh}\, \delta_a + 3 \cos \delta_a - 3.$$

$$\text{Area } acda = \int_{\delta_a}^{\pi - \delta_a} (3 \sin \delta - P_{sh})\, d\delta$$

$$= 6 \cos \delta_a - \pi P_{sh} + 2P_{sh}\, \delta_a.$$

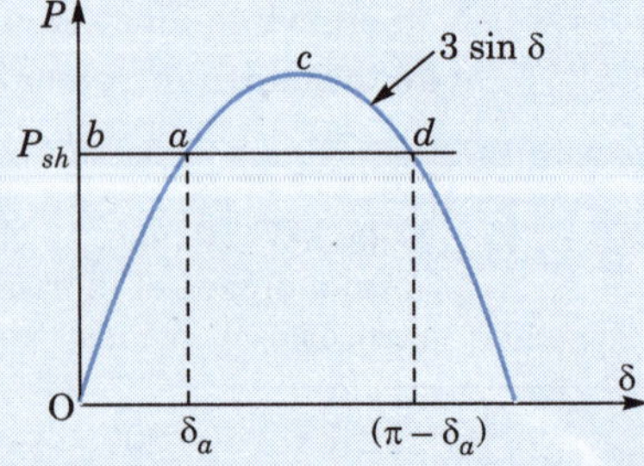

Fig. 4.95: Pertaining to Prob. 4.45.

For the synchronous motor to remain in synchronism,

Area *oabo* = area *acda*

$$P_{sh} \cdot \delta_a + 3 \cos \delta_a - 3 = 6 \cos \delta_a - \pi P_{sh} + 2P_{sh} \cdot \delta_a$$

Substituting the value of $P_{sh} = 3 \sin \delta_a$, we get

$$(\pi - \delta_a) \sin \delta_a = \cos \delta_a + 1$$

or $f(\delta_a) = 1 + \cos \delta_a - (\pi - \delta_a) \sin \delta_a$ etc. **[Ans.** 2.1737 (full-load)]

4.46. For a cylindrical rotor synchronous machine, P_m is the maximum power that it can deliver.

(*a*) This machine is initially supplying a load of $0.4P_m$. If the load is suddenly increased to $0.9P_m$, determine whether or not synchronism is maintained.

(*b*) In case machine loses synchronism in part (*a*), what should be the initial value of load so that the sudden increase of load to $0.9\ P_m$ does not destabilise the machine.

[Ans. (*a*) The machine loses synchronism. (*b*) $0.6126\ P_m$]

4.47. (*a*) What is synchronizing ? What conditions must be fulfilled before an alternator can be connected to an infinite bus ?

(*b*) Describe the dark-lamp method of synchronizing one 3-phase alternator with another. What should be the voltage rating of synchronizing lamps as compared to the system voltage ?

4.48. (*a*) What are the disadvantages of dark-lamp method of synchronizing ? Explain how this method can be used to indicate that incoming machine is running a little too fast ?

(*b*) What is a synchroscope ? Explain how it is used for synchronizing an alternator with an infinite bus ?

(*c*) Phase sequence indicator is essential for synchronizing with a synchroscope, but it is not required for dark-lamp method. Explain.

(*d*) Why is synchronizing by a synchroscope, superior to the dark-lamp method of synchronizing ?

4.49. (*a*) What are the effects of wrong synchronization ?

(*b*) Define the terms incoming machine and infinite bus.

(*c*) What do you know about beat and carrier frequencies ?

An alternator, running at 50.5 Hz, is to be synchronized with 50 Hz infinite bus. How many times will the synchronizing lamps light up in one minute ?

Derive the formula used. **[Ans.** (*c*) 30]

4.50. (*a*) An alternator is to be connected with an infinite bus. When its synchronizing switch is closed, the incoming machine experiences a jerk on account of wrong synchronization. Explain the cause of this jerk.

(*b*) Two 3-phase, 45 MVA, star-connected alternators have each a subtransient reactance of 0.73 Ω per phase. Calculate the synchronizing current at the time of closing the synchronizing switch, in the following cases :

(*i*) Both the e.m.fs. are equal to 11 kV, but are displaced from each other by 30°.

(*ii*) Both the e.m.fs. are in phase but one e.m.f. is 11 kV and the other is 10 kV.

(*iii*) One e.m.f. is 11 kV, the other is 10 kV and both are displaced from each other by 30°.

[Ans. (*a*) Jerk is due to the synchronizing torque associated with the synchronizing current and the corresponding power surge. (*b*) 2251.73 A, 395.45 A, 2183.06 A]

4.51. (*a*) What are the two characteristics of a polyphase synchronous machine that distinguish it from other rotating machines ?

(*b*) Explain the reasons for running the alternators in parallel.

(c) If driving torque of one of the two unloaded alternators operating in parallel is increased, show that there is an automatic synchronizing action. Hence show that reactance is useful for autosynchronizing action, whereas resistance is not.

4.52. (a) Show that for alternators running in parallel, the division of load between them is governed mainly by the speed-load characteristics of their prime-movers.

(b) For two alternators running in parallel, show with the help of a phasor diagram that the effect of increasing the driving torque of one alternator is to make it take an increased share of load.

4.53. (a) The field current of one of the two alternators running in parallel is changed. Show that this change afters their operating p.fs. only and not the division of active power between them.

(b) For two alternators running in parallel, derive the equations giving the load currents shared by each.

4.54. Two similar alternators operating in parallel have the following data :

Alternator 1 : Capacity 2 MW, frequency drops from 50 Hz at no-load to 48.0 Hz at full load.

Alternator 2 : Capacity 2 MW, frequency drops from 50.5 Hz at no-load to 48.5 Hz at full load.

Prime-mover speed regulation is linear.

(a) Calculate how a total load of 3.6 MW is shared by each alternator. Also find the operating bus frequency at this load.

(b) Compute the maximum load that these two units can deliver without overloading either of them. [**Ans.** (a) 1.55 MW, 2.05 MW, 48.45 Hz (b) 3.5 MW, 48.5 Hz]

4.55. (a) "At the time of synchronizing, the frequency of the incoming machine should be slightly higher than that of the infinite bus." Justify this statement.

(b) Two similar 3-phase star-connected alternators supply in parallel a load of 1000 kW at 10 kV at a p.f. of 0.8 lagging, sharing the load equally. The synchronous impedance of each machine is $4 + j50$ ohms per phase. The field excitation of the first machine is so adjusted that its armature current is 50 A lagging. Determine the armature current and p.f. of the second machine and the excitation of the first machine.

[**Ans.** (b) 28.98 A, 0.996 lagging, 8.033 kV]

4.56. A turbo-alternator having a per phase reactance of 10 Ω, is supplying 220 A at unity p.f. to 11 kV infinite bus.

(a) What will be the current and p.f. if the excitation of the machine is increased by 20% without changing its steam admission ? Will there be any change in power output ? Explain.

(b) With the increased excitation, at what power output would the alternator break from synchronism ? [**Ans.** (a) 261.25 A, 0.842 lagging (b) 15367.5 kW]

4.57. A synchronous generator with a synchronous reactance of 1.3 p.u. is connected to an infinite bus whose voltage is 1.0 p.u. through an equivalent reactance of 0.2 p.u. The maximum permissible output is 1.2.

(a) Compute the excitation voltage.

(b) The power output is gradually reduced to 0.7 p.u. with fixed field excitation as in part (a). Find the new current, power angle and the p.f. [*GATE, 1990*]

[**Hint.** (b) $I_a (X_s + x_e) = [E_f^2 + V_b^2 - 2E_f V_b \cos \delta]^{1/2}$ etc.]

[**Ans.** (a) 1.8 p.u. (b) 0.76476, 35.6585°, 0.9153 lag]

4.58. A synchronous machine is connected to an infinite bus. Its excitation voltage leads the bus voltage by 30° and the phase current lags the terminal voltage by 30°. The phase resistance is negligible.

(a) Is the machine working as a generator or a motor ? Explain.

(*b*) The excitation is now increased. Explain its effect on power angle, power output and p.f. of the machine. Under these conditions, is the reactive power absorbed or delivered by the machine ?

[**Ans.** (*a*) Generator, because E_f is leading V_t. (*b*) Power angle decreases, power output remains unchanged and p.f. decreases. Reactive power is delivered.]

4.59. A synchronous machine is connected to an infinite bus. Its excitation voltage E_f leads the bus voltage V_b, but E_f is less than V_b. Phase resistance is negligible. Answer the following with the help of phasor diagrams wherever possible:

(*a*) Is the machine working as a generator or motor ?

(*b*) Is the machine working at a leading or lagging p.f. ?

(*c*) Is the machine delivering or absorbing reactive power ?

(*d*) How can this machine be made to operate at unity p.f. ?

[**Ans.** (*a*) Generator (*b*) leading p.f. (*c*) absorbing reactive power (*d*) by increasing field excitation.]

4.60. (*a*) A synchronous machine, connected to an infinite bus, is working at unity p.f. An increase in its excitation causes it to operate at a leading p.f. Is this machine working as a generator or a motor ? Illustrate your answer with a phasor diagram.

(*b*) A synchronous machine is connected to an infinite bus. Its armature current is leading the terminal voltage. An increase in its field current causes a decrease in its armature current. Is this machine working as a generator or a motor ? Illustrate your answer with a phasor diagram.

(*c*) A salient-pole alternator, connected to an infinite bus, is supplying about 15% of its rated power. What happens to this alternator if its excitation fails ? Explain.

(*d*) An alternator fitted with damper bars is supplying its rated power to an infinite bus. Explain what happens if its field circuit gets open circuited accidently.

[**Ans.** (*a*) Synchronous motor (*b*) Synchronous generator (*c*) It works as a reluctance generator with increased I_a and δ. (*d*) It works as an induction generator with large I_a and therefore, armature may become overheated.]

4.61. (*a*) A turbo-generator is delivering power to an infinite bus at a lagging p.f. If steam supply to the turbine of this generator stops accidently, explain what happens to the synchronous machine.

(*b*) Synchronous generators in a hydro-station are interconnected to a large power-system network. If these hydrogenerators start working as synchronous motors, what would be the reason for this maloperation ?

(*c*) Two identical alternators, one with a higher field current as compared to the other, are connected to an infinite bus. Explain which one of these two, is capable of delivering more power to the bus without losing synchronism.

[**Ans.** (*a*) It becomes synchronous motor and works at a leading p.f. (*b*) Water-admission to turbine fails or reduces to such an extent that mechanical input can't even supply the rotational losses. (*c*) One with a higher excitation.]

4.62. A shunt-wound d.c. machine is coupled to a synchronous machine. The synchronous machine is connected to a constant voltage a.c. supply mains and the d.c. machine to a constant voltage d.c. mains. Both the machines are provided with field rheostats. Explain what happens when (*i*) the excitation of d.c. machine is varied and (*ii*) the excitation of a.c. machine is varied. Assume the set to be floating without any change of power initially and neglect losses. Explain your answer with relevant phasor diagrams. [*I.A.S., 1987*]

[**Hint.** Read Example 4.31.]

4.63. A star-connected synchronous machine is synchronized with an 11 kV infinite bus ; its steam input is then increased till its output power is 10 MW. Now, when its excitation voltage is increased to 120%, the machine starts operating at a p.f. of 0.8 lagging. Compute synchronous reactance of the machine. Neglect armature circuit resistance.

Find also the load angle and p.f. of the machine before the excitation voltage is increased. [**Hint.** Find I_a = 656.1 A and use alternator phasor diagram with r_a = 0. Before the excitation voltage is increased, p.f. angle $\theta = \frac{1}{2}\ \delta$ etc.]

[**Ans.** X_s = 2.85 Ω, δ = 13.623°, p.f. = 0.993 leading]

4.64. A number of alternators are working in parallel with their terminal voltage equal to the rated value. One of the machines, which has a synchronous reactance of 50% and a resistance of 1%, delivers a power output in kW equal to 70% of its rated kVA. If the e.m.f. of this unit equals 1.2 times the terminal voltage, find out the power factor at which the machine is operating. (*I.A.S., 1989*)

[**Hint.** From the alternator phasor diagram,

$$E_f^2 = (1.2V_t)^2 = V_t^2\left[\left(\cos\theta + \frac{I_a r_a}{V_t}\right)^2 + \left(\sin\theta + \frac{I_a X_s}{V_t}\right)^2\right]$$

or $\qquad 0.014 \cos\theta + 0.7 \sin\theta = 0.317451$ etc.] [**Ans.** p.f. = 0.9002 lag]

4.65. An alternator is supplying 60% of its rated power to an infinite bus at rated voltage and frequency. The excitation voltage is made equal to the rated voltage. The per unit reactance is 0.8.

(*a*) Determine the power angle, armature current and p.f. of the machine.

(*b*) If the excitation is increased by 40% with prime-mover driving torque unchanged, find the new values of power angle, armature current and p.f.

[**Hint.** (*a*) $\bar{I}_a = \dfrac{\bar{E}_f - \bar{V}_b}{jX_s}$. With V_b as reference phasor,

$$\bar{I}_a = \frac{1\angle\delta - 1\angle 0°}{j(0.8)} = 1.25\ [\sin\delta + j\,(1 - \cos\delta)\ \text{etc.}]$$

[**Ans.** (*a*) 28.69°, 0.6194, 0.9687 leading (*b*) 20.05°, 0.7177, 0.836 lagging].

4.66. (*a*) What are the major problems concerning the operation of a cwr turbo-alternator connected to a lightly loaded supply system ?

(*b*) What is dwr synchronous machine ?

Explain its constructional features.

(*c*) Generalized mathematical model of a synchronous machine assumes field winding on the stator and armature winding on rotor. Why ?

4.67. (*a*) Describe the constructional features of a dwr synchronous machine with suitable diagrams. Explain how the rotor pole axis can be varied with respect to the rotor physical position.

(*b*) Explain, with phasor diagrams, how dwr synchronous generator operators better than cwr synchronous generator so far as voltage regulation and stability limits are concerned.

4.68. Develop the phasor diagram of a dwr synchronous generator and hence derive the expressions for active and reactive power outputs. Show that its active power can be controlled by the exciting current of torque-winding alone provided $\delta = \theta_R$; but reactive power depends on the exciting currents of both the torque and reactive windings.

4.69. (*a*) What is an inductor alternator ? Give the constructional features of one type of alternators. Explain the principle of working of this alternator.

(*b*) Give the advantages of one alternator over the other.

(*c*) A 400 Hz inductor alternator is driven at 1500 r.p.m. What must be the number of its rotor slots ? [**Ans.** (*c*) 16]

4.70. A 3-phase, 14-pole, 50 Hz synchronous motor, coupled with a load, has a total moment of inertia of 450 kg-m^2 and a constant frictional torque of 100 Nm. Find the time taken for this synchronous-motor drive to come to rest and the number of revolutions executed during the braking period when it is braked by the following methods :

(*a*) Braked by plugging which gives a constant braking torque of 1350 Nm.

(*b*) Braked by dynamic braking with field current and braking resistances held constant at a value that gives an initial braking torque of 5.5 kNm.

Derive the formulae used. [**Ans.** (*a*) 13.93 sec, 49.47 rev. (*b*) 14.78 sec, 24.31 rev.]

4.71. A 3-phase alternator having a reactance of 10 ohms has an armature current of 220 A at unity power factor when running on 11 kV constant frequency bus-bars. If the steam admission be unchanged and the e.m.f. raised by 25%, determine graphically or otherwise the new value of machine current and power factor. [*I.E.S., 1990*]

[**Ans.** 281.582 A, 0.7813 lag]

4.72. A synchronous motor is receiving 30 percent of the power that is capable of receiving from an infinite bus. If the load on it is doubled, calculate the maximum value of the rotor angle during swinging of the motor around its new equilibrium position. [*I.E.S., 1991*]

[**Ans.** 58.1°]

4.73. Define and distinguish the following terms :

'Transient reactance', 'synchronous reactance' and 'subtransient reactance' as applicable to a synchronous generator.

Show how the armature-current oscillograms look like in the event of a symmetrical short-circuit fault on the generator. Discuss the nature of these oscillograms for salient and non-salient pole machines. [*I.A.S., 1983*]

4.74. (*a*) Explain the various reactances associated with an alternator and how they are caused. [*I.A.S., 1985*]

(*b*) A synchronous motor is connected to an infinite bus and suddenly a load is added to the shaft of the motor. Using equal-area criterion, analyse the transient stability of the system. [*I.A.S., 1991*]

4.75. A 3-phase synchronous machine, energised from a constant voltage, constant frequency supply, is rigidly coupled to a separately excited d.c. machine, the armature of which is connected to a constant voltage d.c. supply. Initially, the field current of the d.c. machine is adjusted such that its armature current is zero. What changes do you expect on the synchronous machine side when (*i*) the field current of the d.c. machine is increased, (*ii*) the field current of the d.c. machine is decreased ? Explain. [*I.A.S., 1987*]

[**Hint.** Read Example 4.31]

4.76. A 30 kVA, 440 V, 50 Hz, 6-pole, 3-phase, star-connected synchronous machine needs a field current of 3 A for generating an open-circuit voltage of 440 V. Its synchronous reactance is 0.85 pu. This motor is driven by VVVF three-phase VSI that keeps *V*/*f* constant.

(*a*) If the motor operates at rated values of voltage, frequency and power and at unity *pf*, find the motor speed and its field current.

(*b*) If the applied frequency is reduced to 40 Hz at rated torque, calculate the motor speed and the field current to obtain unity power-factor operation.

[**Ans.** (*a*) 1000 rpm, 3.9374 A (*b*) 800 rpm, 3.9374 A]

4.77. Two generators rated 400 MW and 600 MW are operating in parallel. The drop characteristics of their governors are 3% and 4% respectively from no-load to full-load. Assuming that the generators are operating at 50 Hz at no load, how would a load of 1000 MW be shared between them? What will be the system frequency at this load? Assume linear governor operation. [*I.E.S., 1981*]

[**Ans.** Alt. 1 : 468.132 MW, Alt. 2 : 531.668 MW; *f* = 48.296 Hz]

5 Polyphase Induction Machines

In polyphase induction machines, both the stator and rotor windings carry alternating currents. The stator-produced flux rotates at synchronous speed with respect to stator. The currents induced in the rotor also produce a field that rotates at synchronous speed with respect to stator. Thus, under steady-state conditions, the relative speed between stator and rotor fields is zero. Note that the rotor receives energy from stator by electromagnetic induction. The object of this chapter is to develop the analytical techniques for carrying out the induction machine analysis under dynamic, transient and steady state conditions.

5.1 TRANSFORMATIONS

A schematic diagram of a three-phase induction motor is shown in Fig. 5.1. (*a*). In this figure, three-phase stator winding is represented by three coils *A*, *B*, *C* and rotor winding by three coils *a*, *b*, *c*. In order that rotating magnetic field is produced in the reference direction of rotation, the stator phase order is taken *ABC* clockwise.

The generalized, or two-axis, model of three-phase induction machine is given in Fig. 5.1. (*b*). In this figure, 3-phase stator winding is represented by two coils *DS*, *QS* on stator and three-phase rotor, or squirrel-cage, winding by two pseudo-stationary coils *DR*, *QR* on rotor. For convenience, the axis of stator coil *DS* is taken to coincide the axis of stator phase *A*. In Fig. 5.1, three-phase stator winding is transformed to two-phase stator winding represented by two fixed coils *DS*, *QS* on stator.

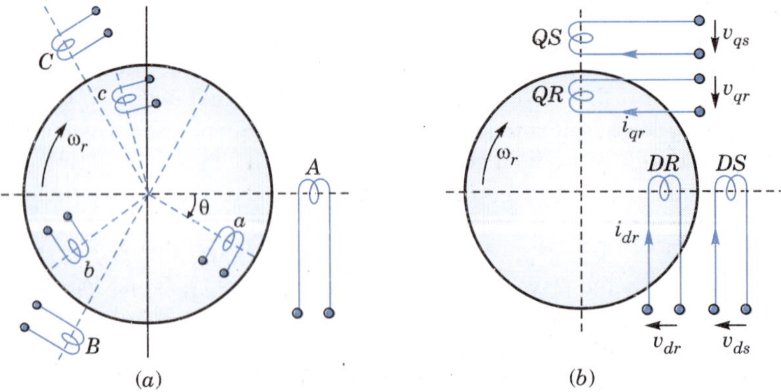

Fig. 5.1: Three-phase induction machine, (*a*) its schematic diagram and (*b*) its generalized model.

The transformation from 3-phase stator variables A, B, C to two-phase stator variables DS, QS ; when $\theta = 0$; is repeated here as under.

$$\begin{bmatrix} i_{ds} \\ i_{qs} \\ i_{os} \end{bmatrix} = \frac{2}{3} \begin{bmatrix} 1 & -\frac{1}{2} & -\frac{1}{2} \\ 0 & -\frac{\sqrt{3}}{2} & \frac{\sqrt{3}}{2} \\ \frac{1}{2} & \frac{1}{2} & \frac{1}{2} \end{bmatrix} \begin{bmatrix} i_A \\ i_B \\ i_C \end{bmatrix} \qquad \text{...(I)}$$

As stated before, rotor cage winding, or rotor 3-phase winding, can be represented by two pseudo (or quasi)-stationary coils DR, QR on the rotor.

For rotor, three-phase a, b, c transformation to d, q, o variables ; given by Eq. (2.12) ; is repeated here as under.

$$\begin{bmatrix} i_{dr} \\ i_{qr} \\ i_{or} \end{bmatrix} = \frac{2}{3} \begin{bmatrix} \cos\theta & \cos\left(\theta - \frac{2\pi}{3}\right) & \cos\left(\theta - \frac{4\pi}{3}\right) \\ -\sin\theta & -\sin\left(\theta - \frac{2\pi}{3}\right) & -\sin\left(\theta - \frac{4\pi}{3}\right) \\ \frac{1}{2} & \frac{1}{2} & \frac{1}{2} \end{bmatrix} \begin{bmatrix} i_a \\ i_b \\ i_c \end{bmatrix} \qquad \text{...(II)}$$

In Eqs. (I) and (II), voltages are related by identical expressions.

In Eq. (I), subscript s stands for stator quantities and subscript r in Eq. (II) denotes rotor quantities. Inverse of Eq. (II) is given by Eq. (2.11). As DR, QR are pseudo-stationary coils and rotor winding rotates, angle θ is variable angle. Frequency of emfs in actual three-phase rotor winding is slip frequency sf. Since the d-q axes windings on rotor are pseudo-stationary, frequency of emfs in DR, QR coils is the line frequency f.

The model of three-phase induction machine given in Fig. 5.1 (b) is usually referred to as generalized model, two-axis model, *Stanley's model* or *stator-reference frame model.*

5.2 ELECTRICAL PERFORMANCE EQUATIONS

The primitive machine diagram or generalized mathematical model for a polyphase induction machine requires four coils as illustrated in Fig. 5.1 (b). Two coils DS and QS on the stator represent polyphase stator windings of both 3-phase and 2-phase induction machines. Two coils DR and QR on the rotor represent the wound-rotor as well as the squirrel-cage rotor. For cage rotor machines, the two coils DR and QR may be thought of as equivalent to all the squirrel-cage bars.

The general voltage equations, for Fig. 5.1 (b) are written on the next page, Eq. (5.1).

A knowledge of the induction machine construction gives the various constraints as follows :

Stator and rotor both have balanced winding configuration.

$\therefore \qquad r_{ds} = r_{qs} = r_s$ = resistance of each stator coil

and $\qquad r_{dr} = r_{qr} = r_r$ = resistance of each rotor coil.

$$
\begin{array}{c}
\\ ds \\ qs \\ dr \\ qr
\end{array}
\begin{bmatrix} v_{ds} \\ v_{qs} \\ v_{dr} \\ v_{qr} \end{bmatrix}
=
\begin{array}{c|cccc}
 & ds & qs & dr & qr \\ \hline
ds & r_{ds}+L_{ds}p & & M_d p & \\
qs & & r_{qs}+L_{qs}p & & M_q p \\
dr & M_d p & -M_q\omega_r & r_{dr}+L_{dr}p & -L_{qr}\omega_r \\
qr & M_d\omega_r & M_q p & L_{dr}\omega_r & r_{qr}+L_{qr}p
\end{array}
\begin{bmatrix} i_{ds} \\ i_{qs} \\ i_{dr} \\ i_{qr} \end{bmatrix}
\qquad \text{...(5.1)}
$$

The air gap is uniform, thus

$$L_{ds} = L_{qs} = L_s = \text{self-inductance of each stator coil}$$

and $$L_{dr} = L_{qr} = L_r = \text{self-inductance of each rotor coil.}$$

Coils DS, DR and QS, QR are identical.

$$\therefore \qquad M_d = M_q = M$$

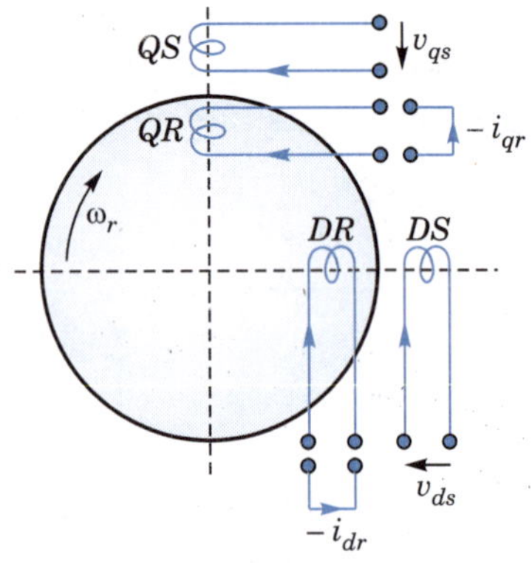

Fig. 5.2: Rotor coils short-circuited, currents i_{dr}, i_{qr} get reversed.

Further, the rotor windings are short circuited, therefore $v_a = v_b = v_c = 0$ for the 3-phase rotor winding and $v_\alpha = v_\beta = 0$ for the 2-phase rotor winding Fig. 2.4 (a). Now voltages v_{dr}, v_{qr} are given by Eq. (2.8) in terms of v_α, v_β and by Eq. (2.12) in terms of v_a, v_b, v_c. Since $v_a = v_b = v_c = 0$ and $v_\alpha = v_\beta = 0$, the coil voltages v_{dr}, v_{qr} are also equal to zero, *i.e.* $v_{dr} = v_{qr} = 0$.

The rotor is short-circuited, therefore, the direction of currents i_{dr} and i_{qr} shall get reversed see Fig. 5.2 and this must be considered while writing down the general voltage equations.

With all these constraints, the general voltage equations become :

$$
\begin{bmatrix} v_{ds} \\ v_{qs} \\ 0 \\ 0 \end{bmatrix}
=
\begin{bmatrix}
r_s + L_s p & & -Mp & \\
& r_s + L_s p & & -Mp \\
Mp & -M\omega_r & -(r_r + L_r p) & L_r\omega_r \\
M\omega_r & Mp & -L_r\omega_r & -(r_r + L_r p)
\end{bmatrix}
\begin{bmatrix} i_{ds} \\ i_{qs} \\ i_{dr} \\ i_{qr} \end{bmatrix}
\qquad \text{...(5.2)}
$$

$$
T_e = \begin{bmatrix} i_{ds} & i_{qs} & i_{dr} & i_{qr} \end{bmatrix}
\begin{bmatrix}
 & & & \\
 & & & \\
 & -M & & -L_r \\
M & & L_r &
\end{bmatrix}
\begin{bmatrix} i_{ds} \\ i_{qs} \\ i_{dr} \\ i_{qr} \end{bmatrix}
$$

$$
\begin{bmatrix} Mi_{qr} & -Mi_{dr} & L_r i_{qr} & -L_r i_{dr} \end{bmatrix} \quad \text{Written below}
$$

The negative sign before i_{dr} and i_{qr} has been taken into consideration in the corresponding columns.

The electromagnetic torque at any instant is obtained from the speed voltage terms of matrix (5.1). Therefore,

$$T_e = M(i_{ds}i_{qr} - i_{dr}i_{qs}).$$

Since i_{dr}, i_{qr} get reversed, the rotor being short-circuited, the instantaneous torque becomes :

$$T_e = M\,(i_{qs}i_{dr} - i_{ds}i_{qr}).$$

The above torque expression agrees with the concepts of torque production due to interacting magnetic fields. The q-axis stator flux Mi_{qs}, interacts with d axis rotor current i_{dr} and d-axis stator flux Mi_{ds} interacts with q-axis rotor current i_{qr}. Since the d-and q-axis are space-displaced by 90°, the sine of the space-displacement angle is unity. In the above torque expression, the first term is positive indicating it to be a motoring term; whereas the second term, being negative, is a generating term.

5.2.1 Steady-state Analysis

With polyphase supply given to stator windings, the resultant air-gap flux rotates at synchronous speed with respect to stator. In view of this, steady-state voltage equations in phasor form can be obtained by replacing p by $j\omega$ in matrix Eq. (5.2).

Also $\omega_r = v\omega$

where $$v = \frac{\text{Actual rotor speed}}{\text{Synchronous speed}} = (1 - s)$$

Here s is the slip. So in phasor form, the matrix Eq. (5.2) becomes :

$$\begin{bmatrix} \bar{V}_{ds} \\ \bar{V}_{qs} \\ 0 \\ 0 \end{bmatrix} = \begin{bmatrix} r_s + j\omega L_s & & -j\omega M & \\ & r_s + j\omega L_s & & -j\omega M \\ j\omega M & -Mv\omega & -(r_r + j\omega L_r) & L_r v\omega \\ Mv\omega & j\omega M & L_r v\omega & -(r_r + j\omega L_r) \end{bmatrix} \begin{bmatrix} \bar{I}_{ds} \\ \bar{I}_{qs} \\ \bar{I}_{dr} \\ \bar{I}_{qr} \end{bmatrix} \quad ...(5.3)$$

There is no difference in the d- and q- phases except one of time. For obtaining a clockwise rotating field, the current in coil DS must lag that in coil QS, as shown in Fig. 5.3 (a). At the instant marked $t = 0$,

$$id_s = 0 \text{ and } i_{qs} = I_m.$$

Thus the m.m.f. is set up along q-axis [Fig. 5.3. (b)].

At the instant marked $t = t_2$, $i_{ds} = i_{qs} = \frac{I_m}{\sqrt{2}}$ and the m.m.f. is set up along an axis, which has traversed an angular distance of 45° clockwise from the q-axis [Fig. 5.3 (b)].

At the instant marked $t = t_3$; $i_{ds} = I_m$ and $i_{qs} = 0$ and the m.m.f. is establishes along the d-axis, as shown in Fig. 5.3 (b).

Thus for obtaining a clockwise rotating field, the following relations can be written by referring to Fig. 5.3 (a).

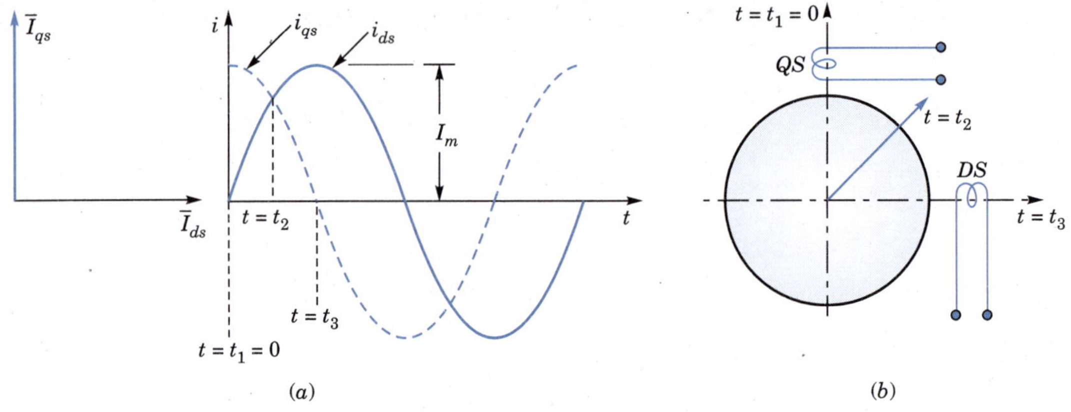

Fig. 5.3: Distribution of currents in the two stator coils.
The orientation of stator m.m.f. at the instants considered.

In magnitude I_{qs} and I_{ds} are equal, but I_{qs} leads I_{ds} by 90°.

$\therefore$ $$I_{qs} = jI_{ds}$$

Let $$\bar{I}_{ds} = \bar{I}_s \quad \text{then} \quad \bar{I}_{qs} = j\bar{I}_s$$

Similarly $$\bar{I}_{dr} = \bar{I}_r \quad \text{and} \quad \bar{I}_{qr} = j\bar{I}_r$$

For voltage, identical relations are $\bar{V}_{ds} = \bar{V}_s$ and $\bar{V}_{qs} = j\bar{V}_s$

The transformation matrix relating the old currents $\bar{I}_{ds}, \bar{I}_{qs}, \bar{I}_{dr}, \bar{I}_{qr}$ and the new currents $\bar{I}_s$ and $\bar{I}_r$ is

$$\begin{bmatrix} \bar{I}_{ds} \\ \bar{I}_{qs} \\ \bar{I}_{dr} \\ \bar{I}_{qr} \end{bmatrix} = \begin{bmatrix} 1 & \\ j & \\ & 1 \\ & j \end{bmatrix} \begin{bmatrix} \bar{I}_s \\ \bar{I}_r \end{bmatrix} \quad \text{or} \quad [I] = [C][I']$$

The new impedance matrix is $[Z'] = [C_t^*][Z][C]$

$$[Z'] = \begin{bmatrix} 1 & -j & & \\ & & 1 & -j \end{bmatrix} \begin{bmatrix} r_s + jX_s & & -jX_m & \\ & r_s + jX_s & & -jX_m \\ jX_m & vX_m & -(r_r + jX_r) & vX_r \\ vX_m & jX_m & -vX_r & -(r_r + jX_r) \end{bmatrix} \begin{bmatrix} 1 & \\ j & \\ & 1 \\ & j \end{bmatrix}$$

$$= \begin{bmatrix} 1 & -j & & \\ & & 1 & -j \end{bmatrix} \begin{bmatrix} r_s + jX_s & -j(r_s + X_s) & -jX_m & -X_m \\ +jX_m(1-v) & X_m(1-v) & -(r_r + jX_r) + jvX_r & vX_r + j(r_r + jX_r) \end{bmatrix} = \text{Written below}$$

$$= 2 \begin{bmatrix} r_s + jX_s & -jX_m \\ jX_m(1-v) & -r_r - jX_r(1-v) \end{bmatrix}$$

The new voltage matrix is $[V'] = [C_t^*][V]$

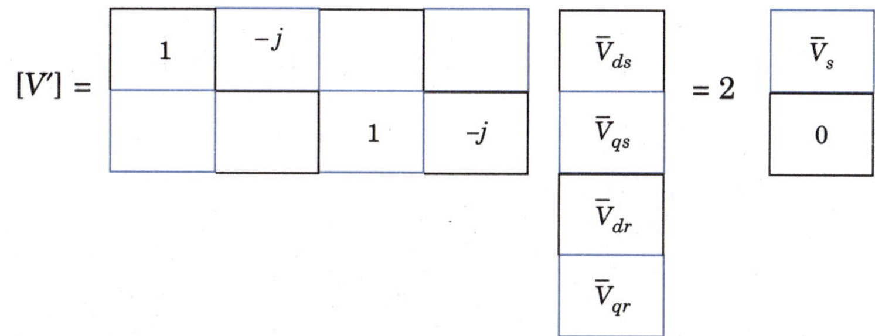

$$[V'] = \begin{bmatrix} 1 & -j & & \\ & & 1 & -j \end{bmatrix} \begin{bmatrix} \bar{V}_{ds} \\ \bar{V}_{qs} \\ \bar{V}_{dr} \\ \bar{V}_{qr} \end{bmatrix} = 2 \begin{bmatrix} \bar{V}_s \\ 0 \end{bmatrix}$$

Thus the new voltage equations are

$$[V'] = [Z'] \; [I']$$

$$\begin{bmatrix} \bar{V}_s \\ 0 \end{bmatrix} = \begin{bmatrix} r_s + jX_s & -jX_m \\ j_s \cdot X_m & -r_r - j_s \cdot X_r \end{bmatrix} \begin{bmatrix} \bar{I}_s \\ \bar{I}_r \end{bmatrix} \qquad \text{...(5.4)}$$

where, $s = 1 - v$

The impedance matrix (5, 4) is not symmetric and it is not possible, therefore, to construct an equivalent circuit. However, this matrix can be made symmetric by dividing the second row elements by $(-s)$. Therefore,

$$\begin{bmatrix} \bar{V}_s \\ 0 \end{bmatrix} = \begin{bmatrix} r_s + jX_s & -jX_m \\ -jX_m & \frac{r_r}{s} + jX_r \end{bmatrix} \begin{bmatrix} \bar{I}_s \\ \bar{I}_r \end{bmatrix} \qquad \text{...(5.5)}$$

For convenience, the quantities pertaining to stator would now be indicated by subscript 1 and those of rotor by subscript 2, just like a transformer. In view of this, Eq. (5.5) can be re-written as

$$\begin{bmatrix} \bar{V}_1 \\ 0 \end{bmatrix} = \begin{bmatrix} r_1 + jX_1 & -jX_m \\ -jX_m & \frac{r_2}{s} + jX_2 \end{bmatrix} \begin{bmatrix} \bar{I}_1 \\ \bar{I}_2 \end{bmatrix} \qquad \text{...(5.6)}$$

Equations of matrix (5.6) result in the induction motor equivalent circuit of Fig. 5.4.

From the equations of matrix (5.4),

$$\bar{V}_1 = r_1\bar{I}_1 + j\omega L_1\bar{I}_1 - j\omega M\bar{I}_2 \qquad \text{...(5.7)}$$

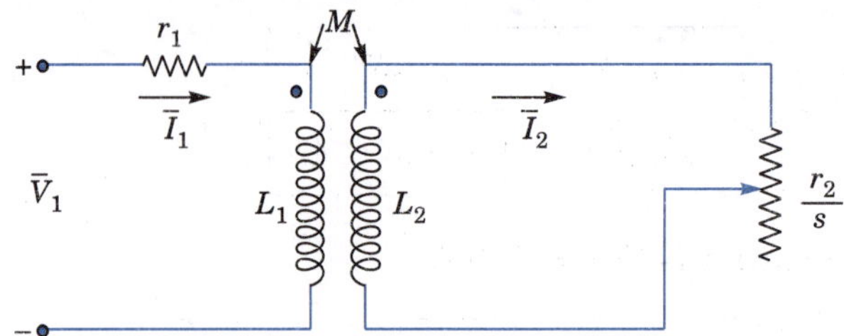

Fig. 5.4: Induction motor equivalent circuit with mutual inductance.

and
$$0 = -\ j\omega M\bar{I}_1 + \frac{r_2}{s}\bar{I}_2 + j\omega L_2\bar{I}_2 \qquad ...(5.8)$$

Eq. (5.7) may be rewritten as,

$$\bar{V}_1 = r_1\bar{I}_1 + j\omega(L_1 - M)\,\bar{I}_1 + j\omega M(\bar{I}_1 - \bar{I}_2)$$
$$= r_1\bar{I}_1 + j\omega l_1\bar{I}_1 + j\omega M(\bar{I}_1 - \bar{I}_2)$$

or
$$\bar{V}_1 = r_1\bar{I}_1 + jx_1\,\bar{I}_1 + jX_m\,(\bar{I}_1 - \bar{I}_2) \qquad ...(5.9)$$

Eq. (5.8) may be re-written as,

$$0 = \frac{r_2}{s}\bar{I}_2 + j\omega(L_2 - M)\bar{I}_2 - j\omega M(\bar{I}_1 - \bar{I}_2)$$
$$= \frac{r_2}{s}\bar{I}_2 + j\omega l_2\bar{I}_2 - j\omega M(\bar{I}_1 - \bar{I}_2)$$

or
$$0 = \frac{r_2}{s}\bar{I}_2 + jx_2\bar{I}_2 - jX_m(\bar{I}_1 - \bar{I}_2) \qquad ...(5.10)$$

Note that here

$\omega(L_1 - M) = \omega l_1 = x_1$ = stator leakage reactance per phase

$\omega(L_2 - M) = \omega l_2 = x_2$ = rotor leakage reactance per phase

and $\omega M = X_m$ = Magnetizing reactance per phase.

With the help of Eqs. (5.9) and (5.10) and with all rotor quantities referred to stator, induction motor equivalent circuit of Fig. 5.5 is obtained. In this circuit same symbols for the referred rotor quantities have been used just to avoid the complicated notation. Bars over V_1, I_1 etc. have been dropped in the equivalent circuit. As in a transformer, the phasor sum of stator current I_1 and rotor current I_2 gives the induction motor magnetizing current I_ϕ.

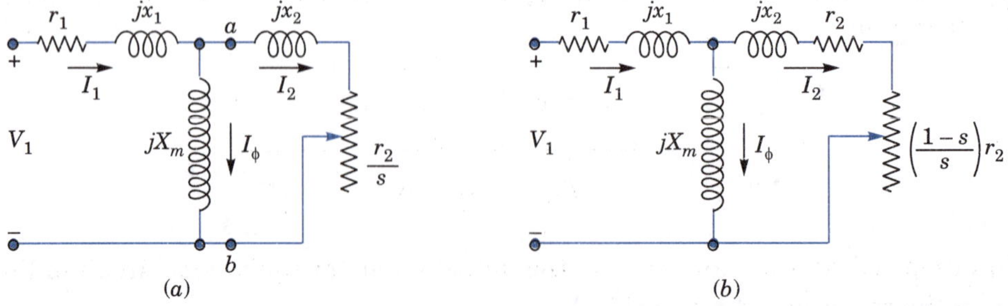

Fig. 5.5: Equivalent circuit for a polyphase induction motor. All values are per phase.

Equivalent circuit of Fig. 5.5 may also obtained from Fig. 5.4 and this is left here as an exercise for the reader.

In Fig. 5.5 (*b*), resistance $\frac{r_2}{s}$ has been split into r_2 and $r_2\left(\frac{1-s}{s}\right)$, merely to emphasise the presence of rotor ohmic loss $I_2{}^2\, r_2$ and the internal mechanical power developed $I_2{}^2\, r_2 \left(\frac{1-s}{s}\right)$ $(= P_m)$ in the rotor.

In Fig. 5.5 (*b*), if $s = 1$ as at standstill, the circuit becomes the equivalent circuit of a short circuited 2-winding transformer and if $s = 0$ (at synchronous speed), the circuit becomes the equivalent circuit of an open-circuited 2-winding transformer. This shows the similarity between the transformers and the induction machines.

Resistance $\frac{r_2\,(1-s)}{s}$ is the electrical representation of the variable mechanical load.

Steady State Torque Analysis. From the transient impedance matrix, given in matrix (5.1), the rotational-inductance matrix (or torque matrix) is obained from the speed-voltage terms. In view of this, the torque matrix G from Eq. (5.1), is

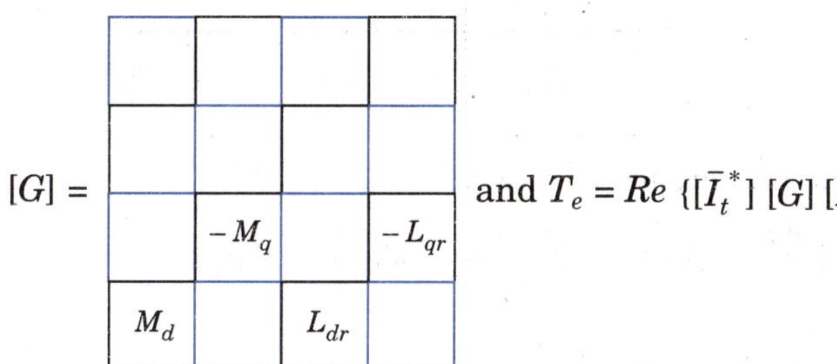

$$[G] = \begin{bmatrix} & & & \\ & & & \\ & -M_q & & -L_{qr} \\ M_d & & L_{dr} & \end{bmatrix} \quad \text{and } T_e = Re\,\{[\bar{I}_t^{\,*}]\,[G]\,[\bar{I}]\}$$

$$\therefore \qquad T_e = Re \begin{bmatrix} \bar{I}_{ds}^{*} & \bar{I}_{qs}^{*} & \bar{I}_{dr}^{*} & \bar{I}_{qr}^{*} \end{bmatrix} \begin{bmatrix} & & & \\ & & & \\ & -M_q & & -L_{dr} \\ M_d & & L_{dr} & \end{bmatrix} \begin{bmatrix} \bar{I}_{ds} \\ \bar{I}_{qs} \\ \bar{I}_{dr} \\ \bar{I}_{qr} \end{bmatrix}$$

$M_d\,\bar{I}_{qr}^{*}$	$-M_q\,\bar{I}_{dr}^{*}$	$L_{dr}\,\bar{I}_{qr}^{*}$	$-L_{qr}\,\bar{I}_{dr}^{*}$	Written below

$$= Re\,[M_d\,\bar{I}_{qr}^{*}\,\bar{I}_{ds} - M_q\,\bar{I}_{dr}^{*}\,\bar{I}_{qs} + L_{dr}\,\bar{I}_{qr}^{*}\,\bar{I}_{dr} - L_{dr}\,\bar{I}_{dr}^{*}\,\bar{I}_{qr}] \qquad \text{...(5.11)}$$

But $M_d = M_q = M$ and $L_{dr} = L_{qr} = L_r$. Also the direction of rotor currents gets reversed and this must be accounted for in Eq. (5.11). With these constraints, Eq. (5.11) reduces to

$$T_e = Re[-M\bar{I}_{qr}^{*}\,\bar{I}_{ds} + M\bar{I}_{dr}^{*}\,\bar{I}_{qs} + L_r\bar{I}_{qr}^{*}\,\bar{I}_{dr} - L_r\bar{I}_{dr}^{*}\,\bar{I}_{qr}] \qquad \text{...(5.12)}$$

Also $\bar{I}_{ds} = \bar{I}_s$; $\bar{I}_{qs} = j\bar{I}_s$ and $\bar{I}_{dr} = \bar{I}_r$; $\bar{I}_{qr} = j\bar{I}_r$

Substitution of these in Eq. (5.12) gives

$$T_e = Re\, [j2M\bar{I}_r^*\, \bar{I}_s - j2L_r\bar{I}_r^*\bar{I}_r]$$

But $\bar{I}_r^*\, \bar{I}_r = I_r^2$ is a real quantity and when multiplied by j, becomes imaginary. Thus

$$T_e = Re\, [2jM\bar{I}_r^*\bar{I}_s] \qquad \text{...(5.13)}$$

or

$$T_e = Re[2jM\bar{I}_2^*\bar{I}_1] \qquad \text{...(5.14)}$$

In abbreviated form, Eq. (5.6) may be written as,

$$[V'] = [Z'][I'] \quad \text{or} \quad [I'] = [Z']^{-1}\, [V'] = [Y']\, [V']$$

where,

$$[Y'] = [Z']^{-1}$$

$$= \text{Inverse of impedance matrix } [Z'].$$

This demonstrates that the currents $\bar{I}_1$ and $\bar{I}_2$ can be obtained by inverting the impedance matrix $[Z']$. Thus, inverting the matrix given by Eq. (5.6), we get

$$\begin{bmatrix} \bar{I}_1 \\ \bar{I}_2 \end{bmatrix} = \frac{1}{\Delta} \begin{bmatrix} \frac{r_2}{s} + jX_2 & jX_m \\ jX_m & r_1 + jX_1 \end{bmatrix} \begin{bmatrix} \bar{V}_1 \\ 0 \end{bmatrix} \qquad \text{...(5.15)}$$

where Δ = determinant of the impedance matrix $[Z]$

$$= \left(\frac{r_1 r_2}{s} - X_1 X_2 + X_m^2\right) + j\left(X_1\frac{r_2}{s} + X_2 r_1\right)$$

Also

$$\bar{I}_1 = \frac{\bar{V}_1}{\Delta}\left(\frac{r_2}{s} + jX_2\right)$$

$$\bar{I}_2 = \frac{jX_m\bar{V}_1}{\Delta} \quad \text{and} \quad \bar{I}_2^* = \frac{-jX_m\bar{V}_1^*}{\Delta^*}$$

Use of these values in Eq. (5.14) gives

$$T_e = Re\left[2jM\frac{-jX_m\bar{V}_1^*}{\Delta^*}\cdot\frac{\bar{V}_1}{\Delta}\left(\frac{r_2}{s} + jX_2\right)\right]$$

$$= \left[\frac{2X_m^2}{\omega}\cdot\frac{\bar{V}_1}{\Delta}\cdot\frac{\bar{V}_1^*}{\Delta^*}\frac{r_2}{s}\right] \quad \text{But} \quad \bar{I}_2\bar{I}_2^* = \frac{\bar{V}_1}{\Delta}\cdot\frac{\bar{V}_1^*}{\Delta^*}X_m^2.$$

In view of this, $T_e = \dfrac{2}{\omega}\cdot\dfrac{r_2}{s}\left(\bar{I}_2\, \bar{I}_2^*\right) = \dfrac{2}{\omega}\bar{I}_2^{\,2}\dfrac{r_2}{s} = \dfrac{2}{\omega}(|I_2|)^2\dfrac{r_2}{s}$

The total electromagnetic torque is thus the power dissipated in $\dfrac{2r_2}{s}$ divided by the synchronous angular velocity ω. Since the analysis pertains to the two phase (d-q phases) induction machine, the torque per phase is given by

$$T_e = \frac{1}{\omega}I_2^{\,2}\frac{r_2}{s} \qquad \text{...(5.16)}$$

For any number of poles, the total torque in newton-metres is

$$T_e = (\text{pole pairs}) \frac{m}{\omega} I_2^2 \frac{r_2}{s} \quad \text{...(5.17)}$$

where m is the number of induction machine stator phases and $\omega = 2\pi f$ is the synchronous angular velocity for a 2-pole machine.

Also, $$T_e = m \frac{1}{\omega_s} I_2^2 \frac{r_2}{s} \quad \text{...(5.18)}$$

where, $$\omega_s = \frac{\omega}{\text{pole-pairs}} = \frac{4\pi f}{\text{poles}} = 2\pi n_s$$

is the synchronous angular velocity in mechanical radians per second for P poles and n_s is synchronous speed in r.p.s.

5.3 ANALYSIS OF THE EQUIVALENT CIRCUIT

In the induction motor equivalent circuit, the stator iron losses can be represented by a suitable resistance connected across jX_m, as in the equivalent circuit of a transformer. But, since core loss is generally constant if voltage and frequency are constant, it has not been shown in the induction motor equivalent circuit and is, therefore, accounted for separately. That is, for calculating the shaft power output P_{sh}, the core loss is subtracted from the internal mechanical power developed at the same time when friction, windage and stray load losses are subtracted.

The second voltage equation of matrix (5.6), for the short-circuited rotor phase, is repeated here as,

$$0 = -\, jX_m \bar{I}_1 + \bar{I}_2 \frac{r_2}{s} + jX_2 \bar{I}_2$$

Multiplying the above equation by $\bar{I}_2^*$ gives

$$j\omega M \bar{I}_1 \bar{I}_2^* = \bar{I}_2 \bar{I}_2^* \frac{r_2}{s} + jX_2 \bar{I}_2 \bar{I}_2^* \quad \text{...(5.19)}$$

Air-gap power per phase, $P_g = \omega \times$ torque per phase

$$= \omega \times \frac{1}{2} \times \text{torque in 2-phase motor given by Eq. (5.14)}$$

$$= \omega \times \frac{1}{2} \times Re\,[2jM\bar{I}_1\bar{I}_2^*] = Re[j\omega M\bar{I}_1\bar{I}_2^*]$$

Thus, from Eq. (5.19), we get $Re[j\omega M\bar{I}_1\bar{I}_2^*] = P_g = Re\left[\bar{I}_2^2 \frac{r_2}{s} + j\bar{I}_2^2 X_2\right]$

$\therefore$ Power per phase, $P_g = I_2^2 \frac{r_2}{s}$

Alternatively, P_g can also be obtained as follows.

Voltage across magnetizing reactance jX_m, in Fig. 5.5, is given by

$$\bar{E}_2 = jX_m(\bar{I}_1 - \bar{I}_2) = jX_m \bar{I}_\phi$$

where, $\bar{I}_\phi = (\bar{I}_1 - \bar{I}_2)$ is the magnetizing current.

The power input to rotor per phase is, $P_g = E_2 I_2 \cos\theta_2$

where, θ_2 is the time-phase angle between E_2 and I_2.

But $\cos \theta_2$ = rotor power factor = $\dfrac{r_2/s}{z_2}$

$$\therefore \quad P_g = \frac{E_2}{z_2} . I_2 \frac{r_2}{s} = I_2^{\,2} \frac{r_2}{s} \qquad ...(5.20)$$

P_g is also called the power transferred across the air gap from stator to rotor.

Also, air-gap power,

$$P_g = I_2^{\,2} \frac{r_2}{s} = I_2^{\,2} r_2 + I_2^{\,2} r_2 \left(\frac{1-s}{s} \right)$$

or P_g = Rotor ohmic loss + Internal mechanical power developed (P_m)

$$\therefore \quad P_g = sP_g + (1-s)\,P_g \qquad ...(5.21)$$

It is seen from Eq. (5.21) that

$$P_g : P_m : \text{Rotor } I^2R \text{ loss} = 1 : (1-s) : s.$$

Fixed losses, *i.e.* core losses, friction, and windage losses must be taken into consideration for computing the power and torque available at the shaft. Note that air-gap power P_g for an induction motor is given by,

P_g = Stator power input P_1 – Stator core loss – Stator ohmic loss

The power P_{sh}, available at the shaft is,

P_{sh} = (P_g – Rotor ohmic loss) – F and W losses

= P_m – F and W losses.

Motor efficiency is given by $\eta = \dfrac{P_{sh}}{P_1}$

Since the rotor frequency under normal operating conditions is very low (1 to 3 Hz), the rotor core losses are very small and these losses are, therefore, usually neglected.

Sometimes P_g is also called the torque in synchronous watts.

$\therefore$ Torque in synchronous watts = P_g

$$= I_2^{\,2} \frac{r_2}{s} = \frac{\text{Rotor ohmic loss}}{\text{Slip}}$$

Electromagnetic torque (or internal electrical torque) developed per phase is

$$T_e = \frac{\text{Mechanical power developed, } P_m}{\text{Rotor speed in mechanical rad./sec.}}$$

$$= \frac{P_g\,(1-s)}{\omega_s\,(1-s)} = \frac{P_g}{\omega_s} = \frac{\text{Rotor ohmic loss}}{\omega_s(\text{slip})}$$

$$= \frac{\text{Rotor ohmic loss}}{2\pi n_s(\text{slip})} \qquad ...(5.22)$$

Output shaft torque is given by, $T_{sh} = \dfrac{P_{sh}}{\text{Rotor speed}} = \dfrac{P_{sh}}{\omega_s(1-s)}$.

Example 5.1. *When running on full load at 400 V, a 3-phase delta-connected induction motor takes an input current of 60 A at 0.85 p.f. When running light at 400 V, the motor input current and power are 16 A and 2200 watts respectively. Its friction and windage losses are 800 watts. If stator resistance per phase is 0.6 Ω, calculate the shaft power and its efficiency at a full-load slip of 0.04.*

Solution. No load stator ohmic loss $= 3\left(\dfrac{16}{\sqrt{3}}\right)^2 \times 0.6 = 153.6$ watts.

$\therefore$ Stator core loss $= 2200 - 800 - 153.6 = 1246.4$ W

Full-load power input $= \sqrt{3}\ (400) \times 60 \times 0.85 = 35332.8$ W

Full-load stator ohmic loss $= 3\left(\dfrac{60}{\sqrt{3}}\right)^2 \times 0.6 = 2160$ W

$\therefore$ Air-gap power, $P_g = 35332.8 - 1246.4 - 2160 = 31926.4$ W

Mechanical power developed, $P_m = (1 - s)\, P_g = 0.96 \times 31926.4 = 30649.3$ W

$\therefore$ Shaft power, $P_{sh} = 30649.3 - 800 = 29849.3$ W

Motor efficiency $= \dfrac{\text{Shaft power}}{\text{Motor input}} \times 100 = \dfrac{29849.3}{35332.8} \times 100 = 84.48\%.$

5.4 TORQUE-SLIP CHARACTERISTICS

Torque-slip or power-slip characteristics of a 3-phase induction motor can be obtained from its equivalent circuit of Fig. 5.5 (*a*). Simplification of this equivalent circuit by Thevenin's theorem leads to easier computation of these characteristics.

Consider two points *a*, *b* in this induction-motor equivalent circuit of Fig. 5.5 (*a*). Apply Thevenin's theorem viewing from the points *a* and *b* towards the voltage source. Then the circuit consisting of r_1, x_1, X_m and source voltage V_1 can be replaced by an equivalent voltage source V_e and an equivalent series impedance $Z_e = R_e + jX_e$ as shown in Fig. 5.6, where

$$\overline{V}_e = \frac{V_1 (jX_m)}{r_1 + j\,(x_1 + X_m)} \qquad ...(5.23)$$

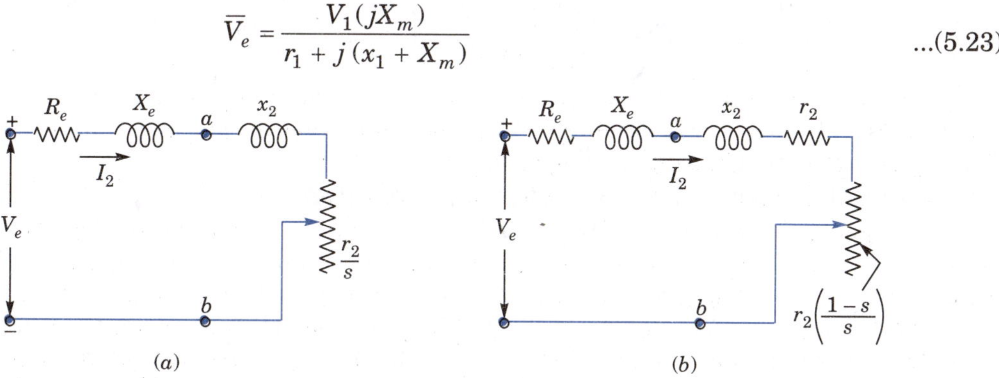

Fig. 5.6: Thevenin's equivalent circuits of an induction motor.

and
$$\overline{Z}_e = \frac{(r_1 + jx_1)\,(jX_m)}{r_1 + j(x_1 + X_m)} \qquad ...(5.24)$$

Here $\overline{V}_e$ is the voltage appearing across terminals *a*, *b* with the rotor circuit disconnected from the two points. Equivalent stator impedance $\overline{Z}_e$ is the impedance viewed from terminals *a*, *b* towards the voltage source but with the source voltage short circuited.

For most induction motors, $(x_1 + X_m)$ is much greater than r_1.

In view of this, r_1 can be neglected in the denominator of both Eqs. (5.23) and (5.24), without causing any noticeable error. Thus

$$V_e = \frac{V_1 X_m}{x_1 + X_m} = \frac{V_1 X_m}{X_1} \qquad ...(5.25)$$

and

$$\bar{Z}_e = R_e + jX_e = \frac{r_1 X_m}{x_1 + X_m} + \frac{jx_1 X_m}{x_1 + X_m}$$

$$= \frac{r_1 X_m}{X_1} + j\frac{x_1 X_m}{X_1} \qquad ...(5.26)$$

Here $X_1 = x_1 + X_m$ is the stator self-reactance per phase.

From the equivalent circuit of Fig. 5.6. (*a*),

$$\bar{I}_2 = \frac{\bar{V}_e}{\left(R_e + \frac{r_2}{s}\right) + j\,(x_2 + X_e)}$$

and from Eq. (5.18), the total torque is

$$T_e = \frac{m}{\omega_s} \cdot \frac{V_e^{\,2}}{\left(R_e + \frac{r_2}{s}\right)^2 + (x_2 + X_e)^2} \cdot \frac{r_2}{s} \text{ Nm} \qquad ...(5.27)$$

Here m is the number of stator phases.

For convenience, Eq. (5.27) is re-written as,

$$T_e = \frac{K_t}{\left(R_e + \frac{r_2}{s}\right)^2 + X^2} \frac{r_2}{s} \text{ Nm} \qquad ...(5.28)$$

where,

$$K_t = \frac{m\,V_e^2}{\omega_s} = \frac{mV_e^2}{2\pi n_s} \quad \text{and} \quad X = x_2 + X_e$$

The various points on the torque-slip (or speed) characteristics for an induction motor can be plotted from Eq. (5.27) for different values of slip s and the general shape is as shown in Fig. 5.7. The induction machine will operate as,

(*i*) a motor when $0 < s \le 1$, *i.e.*, when slip is positive,

(*ii*) a generator when $s < 0$, *i.e.*, when slip is negative. For obtaining negative slip, the induction machine must be driven above synchronous speed by a prime mover. If $s > 1$, the braking action, called plugging takes place. For obtaining $s > 1$ or for obtaining plugging, any two stator leads are interchanged—with this the phase sequence is reversed and, therefore, the direction of rotating magnetic field becomes suddenly opposite to that of the rotor rotation. The electromagnetic torque T_e, now acting opposite to rotor rotation, produces the braking action. Thus the motor can be quickly brought to rest by plugging, but the stator must be disconnected from the supply before the rotor can start in the reversed direction. All the three region of operation (braking region, s = 2.0 to s = + 1.0; motor region, s = 1.0 to s = 0 and generator region, s = 0 to s = – 1) are illustrated in Fig. 5.7.

Maximum internal torque. This is also referred to as the stalling torque, pull-out torque or breakdown torque T_{em}. The internal torque T_e is proportional to $I_2^2 \frac{r_2}{s}$ (= torque in synchronous watts) and it will be maximum when power delivered to $\frac{r_2}{s}$ is a maximum. Applying the general theorem for maximum power transfer ($Z_{load} = Z_{source}$) to Fig. 5.6 (*a*), the maximum torque will occur when

$$\frac{r_2}{s_{mT}} = \sqrt{R_e^2 + (x_2 + X_e)^2} = \sqrt{R_e^{\,2} + X^2}$$

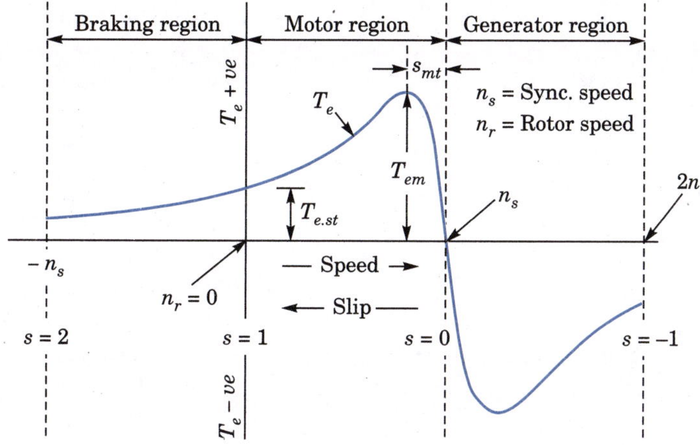

Fig. 5.7: Torque-slip curve for a polyphase induction machine in braking region, motor region and generator region.

where, $$X = x_2 + X_e$$

Thus the slip s_{mT}, at which maximum torque occurs, is given by

$$s_{mT} = \frac{r_2}{\sqrt{R_e^{\,2} + X^2}} \quad \text{...(5.29)}$$

Corresponding to s_{mT}, the maximum torque, from Eq. (5.28), is

$$T_{em} = \frac{K_t}{\left(R_e + \dfrac{r_2}{s_{mT}}\right)^2 + X^2} \cdot \frac{r_2}{s_{mT}}$$

Substitution of $\dfrac{r_2}{s_{mT}}$ in the above equation gives T_{em} as

$$T_{em} = \frac{K_t\left[\sqrt{R_e^{\,2} + X^2}\right]}{\left[R_e + \sqrt{R_e^{\,2} + X^2}\right]^2 + X^2}$$

$$= \frac{K_t\left[\sqrt{R_e^{\,2} + X^2}\right]}{R_e^{\,2} + R_e^{\,2} + X^2 + 2R_e\sqrt{R_e^{\,2} + X^2} + X^2}$$

$$= \frac{K_t\left[\sqrt{R_e^{\,2} + X^2}\right]}{2.\sqrt{R_e^{\,2} + X^2}\left[R_e + \sqrt{R_e^{\,2} + X^2}\right]}$$

$$\therefore \quad T_{em} = \frac{K_t}{2\left[R_e + \sqrt{R_e^{\,2} + X^2}\right]} \quad \text{...(5.30)}$$

Eq. (5.29) shows that the slip at which maximum torque occurs is directly proportional to the rotor resistance r_2, but Eq. (5.30) reveals that the maximum torque T_{em} is independent of r_2. Now K_t ($\propto V_e^2$) is proportional to the square of stator voltage V_1, R_e is proportional to stator resistance r_1 and X is proportional to x_1 and x_2. In view of these facts, an examination of Eq. (5.30) reveals that

(*i*) T_{em} is directly proportional to the square of the stator applied voltage.

(*ii*) T_{em} is reduced by an increase in stator resistance r_1 (*i.e.*, R_e) and

(*iii*) T_{em} is reduced by an increase in stator leakage reactane x_1 and rotor leakage reactance x_2.

(*iv*) T_{em} is independent of rotor-circuit resistance r_2, but note that s_{mT} is directly proportional to r_2.

Typical torque-slip curves for an induction motor with variable rotor-circuit resistance are shown in Fig. 5.8. For the load torque T_L as shown, the speed is n_1 for a rotor-circuit resistance of r_2; speed is reduced to n_2 for $r_2' > r_2$ etc. From the torque-slip curves of Fig. 5.8, it can be concluded for a wound-rotor motor only, that

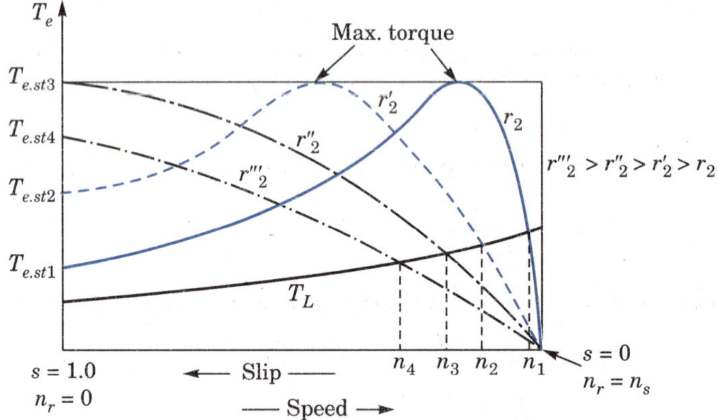

Fig. 5.8: Induction motor torque-slip curves with variable rotor-circuit resistance.

(*i*) the speed of motor can be controlled by varying the rotor-circuit resistance ;

(*ii*) the starting torque can be varied by changing the rotor-circuit resistance ; and

(*iii*) the line current taken by the motor shall also vary with rotor-circuit resistance, though it is not depicted in Fig. 5.8.

In order to get better performance of the induction motor, starting torque $T_{e.st}$ is increased by inserting a suitable external resistance in the rotor circuit at starting and as the motor accelerates, it is cut out in steps, till finally external resistance is reduced to zero.

Starting torque. At starting, slip s = 1.00. Starting torque $T_{e.st}$ from Eq. (5.28), is given by

$$T_{e.st} = \frac{K_t}{(R_e + r_2)^2 + X^2} \cdot r_2 \qquad \text{...(5.31)}$$

Starting torque $T_{e.st}$ can be controlled by varying rotor-circuit resistance, as illustrated in Fig. 5.8. In order to get maximum starting torque, the rotor-circuit resistance must be increased to $\sqrt{R_e^2 + X^2}$ as per Eq. (5.29), where s_{mT} = 1.00. This new value of rotor-circuit resistance can be obtained by inserting external resistance equal to $(\sqrt{R_e^2 + X^2} - r_2)$ in the rotor circuit at the time of starting.

Motor operation near synchronous speed. When slip s is small, $\frac{r_2}{s}$ becomes quite large as compared to other denominator terms of Eq. (5.28) and consequently these can be ignored. Thus from Eq. (5.28),

$$T_e \cong \frac{K_t}{\left(\frac{r_2}{s}\right)^2}\frac{r_2}{s} = \frac{sK_t}{r_2} \quad ...(5.32)$$

$$= sK \quad ...(5.33)$$

An examination of Fig. 5.8 (with rotor-circuit resistance r_2) also reveals that under normal operating region of small slips, the torque-slip characteristic is almost a linear one.

If terminal voltage is variable, then form Eq. (5.32),

$$T_e = K' V_1^2 s \quad ...(5.34)$$

where, $K = \left(\frac{K_t}{r_2}\right)$ and K' are constants.

Motor torque in terms of T_{em}. The torque expression of an induction motor can also be expressed in terms of maximum torque T_{em} and the dimensionless ratio $\frac{s}{s_{mT}}$. In order to get a simple and approximate expression, stator resistance r_1, or the stator equivalent resistance R_e, is neglected.

Division of Eq. (5.28) by Eq. (5.30) gives

$$\frac{T_e}{T_{em}} = \frac{2[R_e + \sqrt{R_e^{\,2} + X^2}\,]}{\left(R_e + \frac{r_2}{s}\right)^2 + X^2}\cdot\frac{r_2}{s}$$

Since r_1 or R_e is neglected,

$$\frac{T_e}{T_{em}} = \frac{2X}{\left(\frac{r_2}{s}\right)^2 + X^2}\cdot\frac{r_2}{s} \quad ...(5.35)$$

From Eq. (5.29), $r_2 = s_{mT}X$ $\quad [\because \ R_e = 0]$

Substitution of this value of r_2 in Eq. (5.35) gives

$$\frac{T_e}{T_{em}} = \frac{2X}{\left(\frac{s_{mT}\,X}{s}\right)^2 + X^2}\cdot\frac{s_{mT}X}{s}$$

or

$$\frac{T_e}{T_{em}} = \frac{2}{\frac{s_{mT}}{s} + \frac{s}{s_{mT}}}$$

or

$$T_e = \frac{2T_{em}}{\frac{s_{mT}}{s} + \frac{s}{s_{mT}}} \quad ...(5.36)$$

In Eq. (5.36), note that T_e is the torque at any slip s. For example, if $T_e = T_{e.fl}$, then $s = s_{fl}$; if $T_e = T_{est}$, then $s = 1.00$ and so on.

5.4.1 Power-slip Characteristics

The total internal mechanical power developed is $P_m = m\,(1 - s)\,P_g$

$$= m\, I_2^2\, r_2 \left(\frac{1-s}{s}\right) \text{ watts}$$

or
$$P_m = \frac{mV_e^2}{\left[R_e + r_2 + \dfrac{r_2\,(1-s)}{s}\right]^2 + X^2} \cdot r_2 \left(\frac{1-s}{s}\right) \qquad ...(5.37)$$

Maximum power transfer theorem is invoked again to obtain maximum value of internal mechanical power developed. Since P_m per phase is the power delivered to $r_2\left(\frac{1-s}{s}\right)$, internal mechanical power developed is maximum, refer to Fig. 5.6 (*b*), when

$$\frac{r_2\,(1-s_{mP})}{s_{mP}} = \sqrt{(R_e + r_2)^2 + X^2}$$

or
$$s_{mP} = \left[\frac{r_2}{r_2 + \sqrt{(R_e + r_2)^2 + X^2}}\right] \qquad ...(5.38)$$

Corresponding to s_{mP}, the maximum power P_{mm}, from Eq. (5.37), is given by

$$P_{m.m} = \frac{mV_e^2}{\left[R_e + r_2 + \dfrac{r_2(1-s_{mP})}{s_{mP}}\right]^2 + X^2} \cdot \frac{r_2(1-s_{mP})}{s_{mP}}$$

Substitution of $r_2\dfrac{(1-s_{mP})}{s_{mP}}$ in the above equation gives $P_{m.m}$ as

$$P_{m.m.} = \frac{mV_e^2\sqrt{(R_e + r_2)^2 + X^2}}{[R_e + r_2 + \sqrt{(R_e + r_2)^2 + X^2}]^2 + X^2}$$

or
$$P_{m.m} = \frac{mV_e^2}{2[R_e + r_2 + \sqrt{(R_e + r_2)^2 + X^2}]} \qquad ...(5.39)$$

Note that the denominator of Eq. (5.39) can be obtained from the denominator of Eq. (5.30), if R_e is replaced by $(R_e + r_2)$.

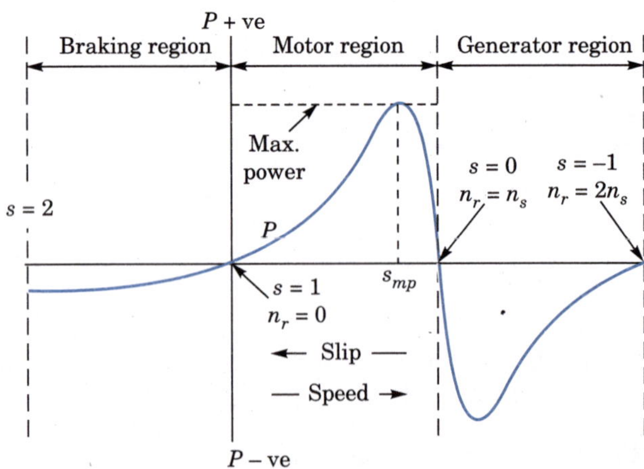

Fig. 5.9: Power-slip curve for an induction machine in braking region, motor region and generator region.

It is observed from Eq. (5.39) that P_{mm} depends on rotor resistance r_2, whereas T_{em} does not.

Eq. (5.37) reveals that at starting, internal mechanical power developed P_m is zero. The variation of mechanical power developed P_m with slip s is illustrated in Fig. 5.9.

At starting, though the internal mechanical power developed is zero, the starting torque $T_{e.st}$ is not zero. This is due to the fact that when slip s = 1, the air-gap power transferred from stator to rotor is $I_2{}^2 r_2$ and this all appears as ohmic loss in the rotor circuit and, therefore, the mechanical power developed P_m is zero. However,

$$T_{e.st} = \frac{1}{\omega_s} I_2^2 \, r_2 \text{ is not zero.}$$

In order to get maximum power output from an induction generator, reference to Fig. 5.9 reveals that the rotor must be driven at a speed above the synchronous speed n_s. This speed is given by

$$n_s \left[1 + \frac{r_2}{\sqrt{(R_e + r_2)^2 + X^2} + r_2} \right]$$

Example 5.2. *A 3-phase star-connected, 400 V, 50 Hz, 4 pole induction motor has the following constants in ohms per phase referred to stator :*

$$r_1 = 0.15,\ x_1 = 0.45,\ r_2 = 0.12,\ x_2 = 0.45,\ X_m = 28.5$$

Fixed losses (core, friction and windage losses) = 400 watts.

Compute

(a) the stator current, output torque and efficiency at a slip of 0.04 ;

(b) the slip at which maximum torque occurs, the maximum torque and the corresponding power output ;

(c) the rotor current and torque at starting ; and

(d) the external resistance to be inserted in the rotor circuit to produce maximum torque at starting. Stator to rotor effective turns ratio is 1.2.

Solution. From the equivalent circuit of the induction motor as shown in Fig. 5.10 (*a*) the impedance offered to the voltage source is

$$\overline{Z}_{AB} = 0.15 + j0.45 + \frac{\left(\dfrac{0.12}{0.04} + j0.45\right)(j\,28.5)}{3 + j28.95}$$

$$= 3.02 + j1.188 = 3.25 \angle 21.47°$$

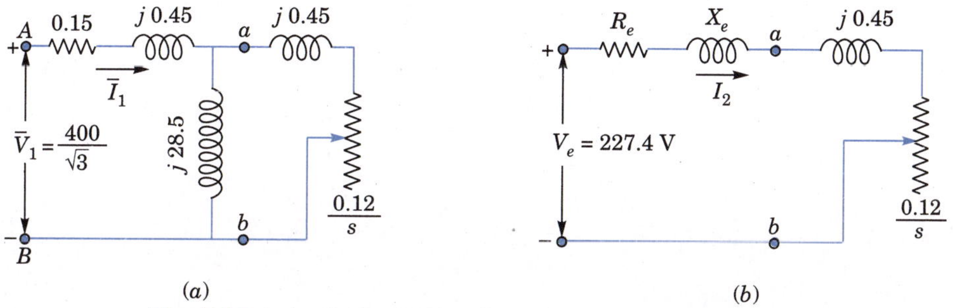

(*a*) (*b*)

Fig. 5.10: Induction motor equivalent circuits, Examples 5.2.

Stator current $\bar{I}_1 = \dfrac{400 \angle 0°}{\sqrt{3}\,(3.25 \angle 21.47°)} = 71.06 \angle -21.47°$

Power factor $= \cos 21.74° = 0.93$

Stator ohmic loss $= 3\,(71.06)^2\,(0.15) = 2272.3$ watt

Stator input $= \sqrt{3}\,(400)\,(71.06)\,(0.93) = 45.784$ kW.

Power from stator to rotor = Rotor input power or air-gap power

or $$P_g = 45.784 - 2.272 = 43.512 \text{ kW}$$

Mechanical power developed, $P_m = (1 - s)\,P_g$

$$= (0.96)\,(43.512) = 41.77 \text{ kW}$$

∴ Power output, $P_{sh} = P_m$ – Fixed losses $= 41.77 - 0.40 = 41.37$ kW

Output torque $= \dfrac{P_{sh}}{\omega_r} = \dfrac{41370}{(1-s)\omega_s} = \dfrac{41370}{(0.96)\,(50\pi)} = 274.34$ Nm

Efficiency $= 1 - \dfrac{\text{Losses}}{\text{Input}} = 1 - \dfrac{45.784 - 41.37}{45.784}$

$$= 1 - 0.09632 = 0.90368 = 90.37\%$$

(*b*) Reduce the circuit of Fig. 5.10 (*a*) to Thevenin's equivalent circuit of Fig. 5.10 (*b*), in which

$$\bar{Z}_e = \frac{(0.15 + j0.45)\,(j28.5)}{(0.15 + j28.95)} \cong \frac{(0.15 + j0.45)\,(j28.5)}{j28.95}$$

∴ $$R_e = \frac{(0.15)\,(j28.5)}{j28.95} = 0.1476\ \Omega$$

and $$X_e = \frac{(0.45)\,(j28.5)}{j28.95} = 0.443\ \Omega$$

From Fig. 5.10 (*b*), torque is maximum when

$$\frac{0.12}{s_{mT}} = 0.1476 + j0.893$$

or $$s_{mT} = \frac{0.12}{\sqrt{(0.1476)^2 + (0.893)^2}} = \frac{0.12}{0.905} = 0.1326$$

$$V_e = \frac{V_1}{\sqrt{3}} \cdot \frac{28.5}{28.95} = \frac{400}{\sqrt{3}}\,\frac{28.5}{28.95} = 227.4 \text{ V}$$

From Eq. (5.30), the maximum internal torque is

$$T_{em} = \frac{3\,(227.4)^2}{(50\,\pi)\,2\,[0.1476 + \sqrt{(0.1476)^2 + (0.893)^2}\,]} = 469.1 \text{ Nm}$$

Corresponding mechanical power developed,

$$= 469.1\,(1 - 0.1326)\,(50\pi) = 63915.3 \text{ W}$$

∴ Output, or shaft, power, $P_{sh} = 63915.3 - 400 = 63515.3$ W

∴ Maximum shaft torque $= \dfrac{63515.3}{(50\pi)\,(0.8674)} = 466.2$ Nm (*c*) At starting $s = 1$. From Thevenin's equivalent circuit, the rotor current at starting is

$$I_{2\cdot st} = \frac{227.4}{\sqrt{(0.2676)^2 + (0.893)^2}} = 243.94 \text{ A}$$

Starting torque, $$T_{e.st} = 3\,(243.94)^2 \left(\frac{0.12}{1}\right)\frac{1}{50\,\pi} = 136.4 \text{ Nm}$$

(*d*) From Fig. 5.10 (*b*), for maximum torque at starting, we have

$$\frac{r_2 + R}{1} = 0.1476 + j0.893$$

or $$r_2 + R = \sqrt{(0.1476)^2 + (0.893)^2} = 0.9051$$

$\therefore$ External resistance (referred to stator), which must be inserted in rotor circuit

$$= 0.9051 - 0.12 = 0.7851\ \Omega$$

Actual external resistance that must be inserted in the rotor circuit

$$= \frac{0.7851}{(1.2)^2} = 0.5452\ \Omega.$$

Example 5.3. *A 10 kW, 400 V, 3-phase, 4-pole, 50 Hz slipring induction motor develops rated output at rated voltage and frequency and with its slip rings short-circuited. The maximum torque, equal to twice the full-load torque, occurs at a slip of 10% with zero external resistance in the rotor circuit. Stator resistance and rotational loss are neglected. Determine:*

(*i*) *slip and rotor speed at full load torque,*

(*ii*) *rotor ohmic loss at full-load torque,*

(*iii*) *starting torque at rated voltage and frequency*

(*iv*) *full-load efficiency,*

The rotor resistance is now trebled by inserting external resistance in the rotor circuit. Find:

(*v*) *the slip at maximum torque* (*vi*) *full-load slip and rotor speed*

(*vii*) *starting torque* (*viii*) *rotor I^2R loss at full-load torque and*

(*ix*) *developed power at full-load torque and efficiency.*

Solution. (*i*) Maximum torque,

$$T_{em} = 2\text{ (full-load torque)} = 2\,T_{e.fl}$$

Here $$s_{mT} = 0.10$$

From Eq. (5.36), $$\frac{T_{e.fl}}{T_{e.m}} = \frac{2}{\dfrac{s_{mT}}{s_{fl}} + \dfrac{s_{fl}}{s_{mT}}}$$

or $$\frac{1}{2} = \frac{2}{\dfrac{0.1}{s_{fl}} + \dfrac{s_{fl}}{0.1}} \quad \text{or} \quad s_{fl}^2 - 0.4\,s_{fl} + 0.01 = 0$$

Its solution gives full-load slip, $s_{fl} = 0.0268$ or 2.68%

Rotor speed, $$N_r = 1500\,(1 - 0.0268) = 1459.8 \cong 1460 \text{ rpm}$$

(*ii*) Since rotational losses (*i.e.*, fixed losses) are neglected, the mechanical power developed is P_m = shaft power of 10,000 watts.

$\therefore$ Air-gap power, $$P_g = \frac{P_m}{1 - s_{fl}} = \frac{10,000}{1 - 0.0268} = 10275.4 \text{ W}$$

Rotor ohmic loss at full-load torque = $sP_g = 0.0268 \times 10275.4 = 275.4$ watts.

Alternatively, rotor ohmic loss = $P_g - P_m$ = 10,275.4 – 10,000 = 275.4 watts.

(*iii*) Full-load torque $T_{e.fl}$ is given by

$$T_{e.fl} = \frac{P_g}{2\pi n_s} = \frac{10,275.4}{2\pi(25)} = 65.42 \text{ Nm}$$

Now $$\frac{T_{e.st}}{T_{em}} = \frac{2}{\dfrac{s_{mT}}{1} + \dfrac{1}{s_{mT}}}$$

$$\therefore \qquad T_{e.st} = \frac{2T_{em}}{\dfrac{0.1}{1} + \dfrac{1}{0.1}} = \frac{(4T_{e.fl})}{10.1} = \frac{4}{10.1}(65.42) = 25.91 \text{ Nm}$$

(*iv*) $$\text{Efficiency} = \frac{\text{Output}}{\text{Input}} \times 100 = \frac{10.000}{10275.4} \times 100 = 97.32\%$$

(*v*) Before the external resistance is inserted in the rotor circuit, Eq. (5.29) with $r_1 = 0$ gives

$$\frac{r_2}{s_{mT}} = \sqrt{(x_2 + X_e)^2} = \sqrt{X^2} = X$$

$$\therefore \qquad \frac{r_2}{X} = s_{mT} = 0.10$$

When rotor-circuit resistance is trebled, then $\dfrac{3r_2}{X} = s_{mT1}$

$\therefore$ New value of slip at which maximum torque occurs is given by

$$s_{mT1} = 3(0.10) = 0.3 \text{ or } 30\%.$$

(*vi*) From Eq. (5.36), $$\frac{1}{2} = \frac{2}{\dfrac{s_1}{0.3} + \dfrac{0.3}{s_1}}$$

Its solution gives full-load slip, $s_1 = 0.0804$.

Rotor speed = 1500 (1 – 0.0804) = 1279.4 rpm.

(*vii*) $$\frac{T_{e.st}}{T_{em}} = \frac{2}{\dfrac{1}{0.3} + \dfrac{0.3}{1}}$$

$$\therefore \qquad T_{e.st} = \frac{2}{3.63}(2T_{e.fl}) = \frac{4}{3.63}(65.42) = 72.09 \text{ Nm}$$

(*viii*) Rotor ohmic loss at full-load torque,

$$= \left(\frac{P_m}{1 - s_1}\right)s_1 = \frac{10000}{1 - 0.0804} \times 0.0804 = 874.3 \text{ W}$$

(*ix*) Power developed at full-load torque,

$$P_{m1} = (1 - s_1) P_g = (1 - 0.0804) (10275.4) = 9449.26 \text{ W}$$

$$\therefore \qquad \text{Efficiency} = \frac{9449.26}{10275.4} \times 100 = 91.66\%$$

This example illustrates that the effect of introducing external resistance in the rotor circuit is

(*a*) to decrease the rotor speed, output power and efficiency and

(*b*) to increase the slip at which maximum torque occurs, rotor ohmic loss and starting torque.

5.5 EFFECT OF VOLTAGE AND FREQUENCY VARIATIONS ON THE INDUCTION MOTOR PERFORMANCE

When constant voltage and constant frequency is applied to a three-phase induction motor, it runs at constant speed. Sometimes, there may be inadvertent variations in supply voltage and frequency above or below their rated values. All these variations in the supply modify the operating characteristics of 3-phase induction motors. The object of this article is to examine qualitatively the effect of these variations.

5.5.1 Variable Voltage, Constant Frequency

When a three-phase induction motor operates from a source of constant voltage V_1 and constant frequency f_1, it has torque-speed characteristic as indicated by V_1 in Fig. 5.11. Here, starting torque T_{est1}, maximum torque T_{em1} and slip at maximum torque s_{mT1} are also shown for V_1 characteristic.

In a three-phase induction motor, if stator impedance is neglected, then starting torque $T_{est} \propto \frac{3}{w_s} \cdot \frac{V_1^2}{r_2^2 + x_2^2} \cdot r_2$, maximum torque $T_{em} \propto \frac{3}{w_s} \cdot \frac{V_1^2}{2x_2}$ and slip at maximum torque $s_{mT} = \frac{r_2}{x_2}$.

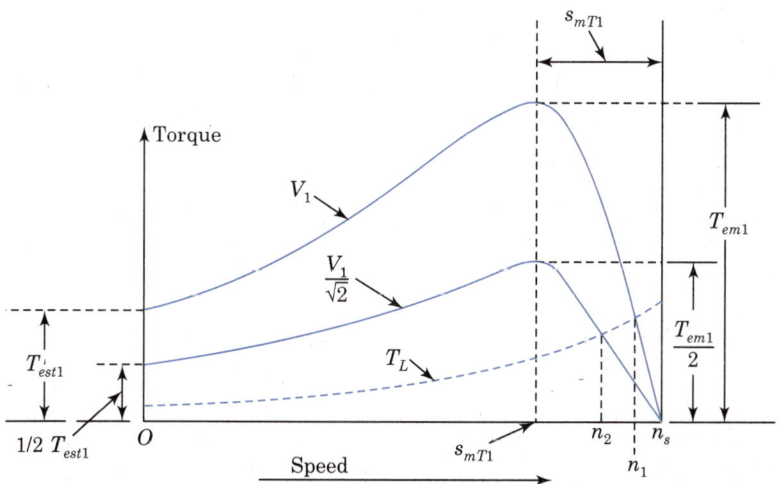

Fig. 5.11: Effect of supply voltage variation on torque-speed characteristics.

It is seen from above that in a 3-phase induction motor, torque is proportional to supply voltage squared. Therefore, if supply voltage reduces from V_1 to $V_1/\sqrt{2}$ with constant frequency f_1, then starting torque reduces to $T_{est2} = \frac{1}{2} T_{est1}$, maximum torque also reduces to $T_{em2} = \frac{1}{2} T_{em1}$. But slip at maximum torque remains s_{mT} because voltage has no effect on r_2 and x_2.

For load torque T_L, the motor operating speed is n_1 for voltage V_1 and n_2 ($< n_1$) for reduced voltage $V_1/\sqrt{2}$. Since supply frequency remains constant at f_1, synchronous speed is n_s for both voltages V_1 and $V_1/\sqrt{2}$.

Thus, a reduction in supply voltage only would mean reduced magnitudes of starting torque, maximum torque and operating speed, slip at maximum torque remains unchanged.

5.5.2 Constant Voltage, Variable Frequency

For constant voltage and frequency V_1 and f_1 respectively, the torque-speed characteristic marked f_1 is shown in Fig. 5.12. For source frequency f_1, synchronous speed is $n_{s1} = \frac{2f_1}{P}$ *rps*, maximum torque is T_{em1}, slip at maximum torque is s_{mT1} and starting torque is T_{est1}. Here n_{s1}, T_{em1}, T_{est1}, s_{mT1} are shown on the characteristic marked f_1 in Fig. 5.12.

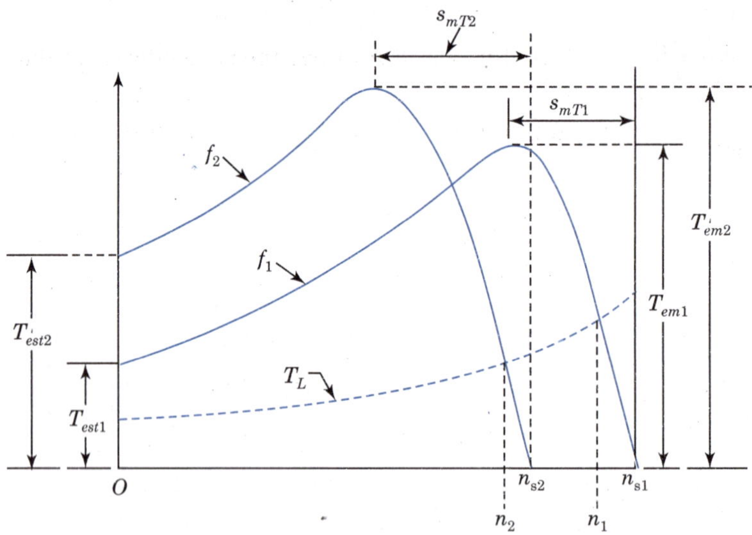

Fig. 5.12: Effect of supply frequency variation on torque-speed characteristics.

In case supply frequency reduces from f_1 to f_2, then synchronous speed $n_{s2} = \frac{2f_2}{P}$ rpm gets reduced from n_{s1}.

It has already been stated above that if stator impedance is neglected in a 3-phase induction motor, then $T_{em} \propto \frac{3}{w_s} \cdot \frac{V_1^2}{2x_2}$, $T_{est} \propto \frac{3}{w_s} \cdot \frac{V_1^2}{r_2^2 + x_2^2} \cdot r_2$ and $s_{mT} = \frac{r_2}{x_2}$. Here, with reduced frequency f_2, both x_2 and synchronous speed are reduced. As a result, maximum torque T_{em2}, starting torque T_{est2} and slip at maximum torque s_{mT2} at reduced frequency f_2 are more than their respective magnitudes T_{em1}, T_{est1} and s_{mT1} at higher frequency f_1. Here, T_{est2}, T_{em2} and s_{mT2} are also indicated in Fig. 5.12. For load torque T_L, operating speed at frequency f_1 is n_1 and at frequency f_2 ; it is $n_2 < n_1$.

Thus, a reduction in supply frequency only would mean increased magnitudes of T_{est}, T_{em}, s_{mT}; however operating speed gets reduced.

5.5.3 Variable Voltage, Variable Frequency

If voltage and frequency are varied in such a manner so as to keep V_1/f a constant value, then the air-gap flux ϕ remains substantially constant. The ratio V_1/f can be maintained constant in case the 3-phase induction motor is fed from a synchronous-generator set, in which a change in the prime-mover speed alters the voltage and frequency by the same ratio. The ratio V_1/f can also be kept constant by the use of dc-link inverter, which is used extensively for the speed control of three-phase induction motors. The induction motor performance under the constant V_1/f ratio is illustrated by Example 5.4.

Example 5.4. *A 3-phase, star connected, 400 V, 50 Hz, 4-pole induction motor, has the following constants in ohms per phase referred to stator.*

$$r = 0.8;\ r_2 = 0.3,\ x_1 = x_2 = 2.0,\ X_m = 48.00$$

If this motor is operated at a reduced voltage and frequency of 200 V, 25 Hz ; compute

(a) the current and pf at the instant of starting and under maximum torque conditions ; compare the results with normal values ;

(b) starting and maximum (pull-out) torques and compare with normal values.

Under normal operation and at rated load, the motor has a slip of 0.03. Find the value of slip, if the motor is now operated at half the voltage and half the frequency at the original rated load.

Solution. Applying Thevenin's theorem at the points a, b in Fig. 5.13 (a), we get

$$\overline{Z}_e = R_e + jX_e = \frac{(r_1 + jx_1)(jX_m)}{j(x_1 + X_m)}$$

$$\therefore \quad R_e = \frac{r_1 \cdot X_m}{x_1 + X_m} = \frac{0.8 \times 48}{50.0} = 0.768\ \Omega$$

$$X_e = \frac{x_1 \cdot X_m}{x_1 + X_m} = \frac{2 \times 48}{50.0} = 1.92\ \Omega$$

$$V_e = \frac{V_1 \cdot X_m}{x_1 + X_m} = \frac{(400/\sqrt{3}) \times 48}{50.0} = 222\ \text{V}$$

The Thevenin's equivalent circuit for this 3-phase induction motor is shown in Fig. 5.13 (b).

The subscripts n and d are introduced for normal operation and reduced-voltage reduced-frequency operation respectively.

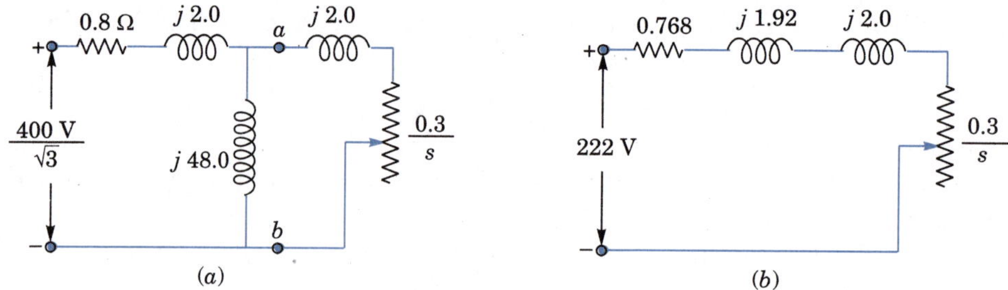

Fig. 5.13: (*a*) Induction motor equivalent circuit (*b*) Its Thevenin's equivalent ; Example 5.4.

(*a*) Starting current :

$$I_n = \frac{222}{\left[\left(0.768 + \dfrac{0.3}{1}\right)^2 + (1.92 + 2)^2\right]^{1/2}} = 54.7 \text{ A}$$

$$I_d = \frac{\dfrac{222.0}{2}}{\left[\left(0.768 + \dfrac{0.3}{1}\right)^2 + \left(\dfrac{3.92}{2}\right)^2\right]^{1/2}} = 49.7 \text{ A}$$

$$(\cos\theta)_n = \frac{1.068}{[(1.068)^2 + (3.92)^2]^{1/2}} = 0.263$$

$$(\cos\theta)_d = \frac{1.068}{\left[(1.068)^2 + \left(\dfrac{3.92}{2}\right)^2\right]^{1/2}} = 0.476$$

(*b*) Starting torque :

$$T_{e.n.} = \frac{3}{\omega_s} . I_n^2 . \frac{r_2}{s} = \frac{3}{50\pi} \cdot (54.7)^2 \times \left(\frac{0.3}{1}\right) = 17.16 \text{ Nm.}$$

$$T_{e.d} = \frac{3}{25\pi}(49.7)^2 \left(\frac{0.3}{1}\right) = 28.32 \text{ Nm.}$$

At reduced voltage and reduced frequency, it is seen that,

(*i*) starting current is decreased which is advantageous ;

(*ii*) power factor at starting is improved and therefore more power input to rotor ;

(*iii*) though the starting current in decreased, yet the starting torque is increased from 17.16 Nm to 28.32 Nm.

It can be concluded from above that with reduced voltage and frequency (keeping voltage/frequency constant), the performance of induction motor at starting is improved.

Maximum torque. The slip at which maximum torque occurs, is given by

$$\frac{0.3}{s_{mT.n}} = \sqrt{(0.768)^2 + (3.92)^2} \cong 4.00$$

$$\therefore \quad s_{mT.n} = \frac{0.3}{4.00} = 0.075$$

$$I_n = \frac{222.00}{\left[\left(0.768 + \frac{0.3}{0.075}\right)^2 + (3.92)^2\right]^{1/2}} = 35.96 \text{ A.}$$

At reduced voltage and frequency,

$$\frac{0.3}{s_{mT \cdot d}} = \sqrt{(0.768)^2 + \left(\frac{3.92}{2}\right)^2} = 2.105$$

$$\therefore \quad s_{mT \cdot d} = \frac{0.3}{2.105} = 0.1425$$

$$I_d = \frac{111.00}{\left[\left(0.768 + \frac{0.3}{0.1425}\right)^2 + \left(\frac{3.92}{2}\right)^2\right]^{1/2}} = 31.9 \text{ A.}$$

$$(\cos\theta)_n = \frac{4.768}{6.18} = 0.772 \quad \text{and} \quad (\cos\theta)_d = \frac{2.873}{3.48} = 0.826$$

$$T_{em.n} = \frac{3}{50\pi}(35.9)^2 \times 4 = 98.6 \text{ Nm.}$$

$$T_{em.d} = \frac{3}{25\pi}(31.9)^2 \times 2.105 = 81.82 \text{ Nm.}$$

At reduced voltage and frequency it is thus seen that

(*i*) current is decreased and power factor is improved under maximum torque conditions ;

(*ii*) the maximum torque is decreased from 98.6 Nm to 81.82 Nm.

Under normal operation, at a full-load slip of 0.03,

$$T_{e.n.} = \frac{3}{50\pi} \cdot \frac{(222)^2}{\left[\left(0.768 + \frac{0.3}{0.03}\right)^2 + (3.92)^2\right]} \times \left(\frac{0.3}{0.03}\right)$$

At reduced voltage and reduced frequency, at any slip s,

$$T_{e.d} = \frac{3}{25\pi} \cdot \frac{(111)^2}{\left[\left(0.768 + \frac{0.3}{s}\right)^2 + \left(\frac{3.92}{2}\right)^2\right]} \times \left(\frac{0.3}{s}\right)$$

$$\therefore \quad \frac{T_{e.n}}{T_{e.d}} = \frac{25\pi}{50\pi} \cdot \left(\frac{222}{111}\right)^2 \times \frac{\left[\left(0.768 + \frac{0.3}{s}\right)^2 + 3.84\right]}{[(10.768)^2 + (3.92)^2]} \times \frac{s}{0.03} = 1$$

or

$$1 = \frac{2\left[\left(0.768 + \frac{0.3}{s}\right)^2 + 3.84\right]}{131.4} \times \left(\frac{s}{0.03}\right)$$

or

$$s^2 - 0.3415\, s + 0.0203 = 0$$

or

$$s = 0.0757 \text{ and } 0.265.$$

The required value of slip for stable operation is 0.0757.

Example 5.5. *A 400 V, 50 Hz, 6 pole, star-connected induction motor has the following parameters in ohms per phase referred to stator.*

$$r_1 = 0.4,\ r_2 = 0.5,\ x_1 = x_2 = 1.6,\ X_m = 28.4$$

This motor is driving a load requiring an electromagnetic power of 10 kW. Calculate the slip and the motor operating speed. Neglect rotational losses.

Solution. The equivalent circuit for this motor is shown in Fig. 5.13A. Applying Thevenin's theorem at the points a, b in this fig., we get

$$Z_e = R_e + jX_e = \frac{(r_1 + jx_1)(jX_m)}{j(x_1 + X_m)}$$

$$\therefore \quad R_e = \frac{r_1 . X_m}{x_1 + X_m} = \frac{0.4 \times 28.4}{1.6 + 28.4} = 0.3787\ \Omega$$

$$X_e = \frac{x_1 . X_m}{x_1 + X_m} = \frac{1.6 \times 28.4}{30} = 1.5147\ \Omega$$

$$V_e = \frac{V_1 . X_m}{x_1 + X_m} = \frac{400}{\sqrt{3}} \times \frac{28.4}{30.0} = 218.63\ \text{V}$$

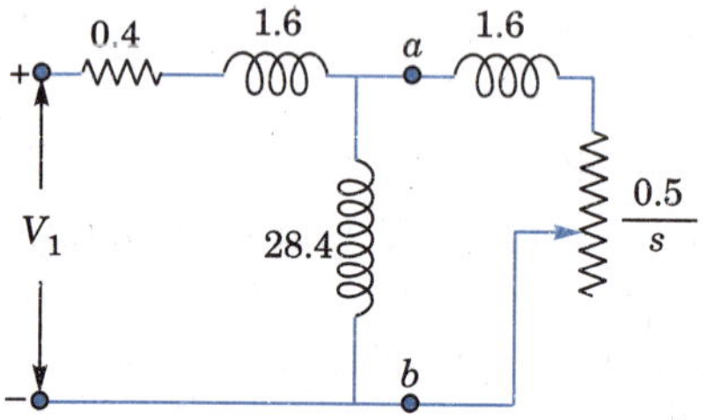

(a)

Fig. 5.13A: Induction motor equivalent circuit, Example 5.5

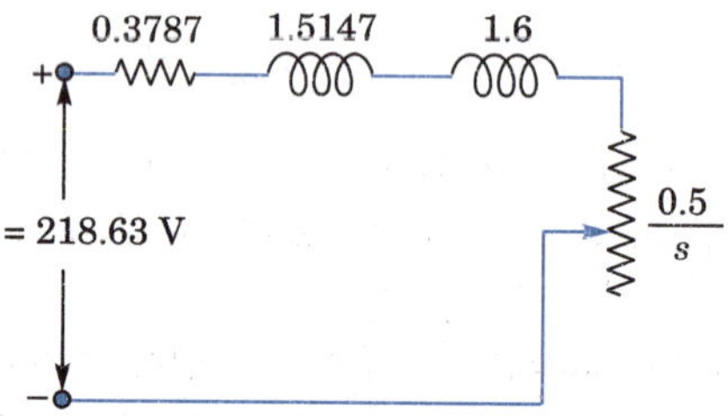

(b)

Fig. 5.13B: Thevenin's equivalent circuit for Fig. 5.13A.

Thevenin's equivalent circuit is shown in Fig. 5.13B. From Eq. (5.24) and Fig. 5.13B, the electromagnetic torque is

$$T_e = \frac{3}{w_s}\left[\frac{V_e^2}{\left(R_e + \frac{r_2}{s}\right)^2 + (x_2 + x_2)^2}\right] \times \frac{r_2}{s}$$

$$= \frac{3}{w_s} \times \left[\frac{218.63^2}{\left(0.3787 + \frac{0.5}{s}\right)^2 + (1.5147 + 1.6)^2}\right] \times \frac{0.5}{s}$$

or

$$T_s . w_s = 10{,}000 = 3\left[\frac{218.63^2}{\left(0.3787 + \frac{0.5}{s}\right)^2 + (3.1147)^2}\right] \times \frac{0.5}{s}$$

$$\left[\left(0.3787 + \frac{0.5}{s}\right)^2 + (3.1147)^2\right] s = \frac{3 \times 218.63^2 \times 0.5}{10{,}000} = 7.17$$

or

$$9.843s^2 - 6.7913s + 0.25 = 0$$

It solution gives slip $s = 0.039$

$\therefore$ Motor operating speed $= N_s(1-s) = \dfrac{120 \times 50}{6}(1-0.039) = 961$ rpm

5.5.4 Constant Current, Constant Frequency

In some drives, the induction motor is fed from a controlled-current source such as current-source inverter. The behaviour of a three-phase induction motor, when connected to a current-limited source, is different from when the motor is fed from a constant-voltage source. In this part of the article, performance of a three-phase induction motor under constant-current mode is discussed briefly.

In Fig. 5.5 (a), consider that a constant current I_1 is fed to stator winding of a 3-phase induction motor. So far as rotor current I_2 is concerned, $(r_1 + jx_1)$ plays no role. Therefore, when machine working under constant-current mode is studied, effect of $(r_1 + jx_1)$ is omitted. However, $(r_1 + jx_1)$ does influence the magnitude of applied stator voltage V_1. For stator current I_1, the rotor current I_2, from Fig. 5.5 (a), is given by

$$I_2 = I_1 \frac{jX_m}{\dfrac{r_2}{s} + j(x_2 + X_m)} \quad \text{...(5.41)}$$

The internal electromagnetic torque T_e is

$$T_e = \frac{m}{\omega_s} . I_2^2 \frac{r_2}{s}$$

$$= \frac{m}{\omega_s} \cdot \frac{I_1^2 \cdot X_m^2}{\left(\dfrac{r_2}{s}\right)^2 + (x_2 + X_m)^2} \cdot \frac{r_2}{s} \quad \text{...(5.42)}$$

Invoking the principle of maximum power transfer, the equivalent circuit of Fig. 5.5 (a), with $(r_1 + jx_1) = 0$, gives.

$$\frac{r_2}{s_{mT}} = x_2 + X_m$$

or

$$s_{mT} = \frac{r_2}{x_2 + X_m} \quad \text{...(5.43)}$$

This is the slip at which maximum torque occurs when 3-phase induction motor is fed from current-limited source.

Maximum torque $T_{e.m}$ is obtained by substituting $\dfrac{r_2}{s_{mT}} = x_2 + X_m$ in Eq. (5.42).

$$\therefore \quad T_{e.m} = \frac{m}{\omega_s} \cdot \frac{I_1^2 X_m^2}{2(x_2 + X_m)^2} \cdot (x_2 + X_m)$$

$$= \frac{m}{\omega_s} \cdot \frac{(I_1 X_m)^2}{2(x_2 + X_m)} \quad \text{...(5.44)}$$

Eq. (5.44) shows that maximum torque does not depend upon the rotor resistance as before.

The starting torque, from Eq. (5.42), is given by

$$T_{e.st} = \frac{m}{\omega_s} \cdot \frac{(I_1 X_m)^2}{r_2^2 + (x_2 + X_m)^2} \cdot r_2 \quad \text{...(5.45)}$$

Example 5.6. *A 400 V, 4-pole, 50 Hz, 3-phase, star-connected induction motor has $r_1 = 0$, $x_1 = x_2 = 1\ \Omega$, $r_2 = 0.4\ \Omega$, $X_m = 50\ \Omega$. This induction motor is fed from*

(i) a constant-voltage source = 231 V per phase

(ii) a constant-current source with current equal to that occuring at a slip of 0.05 in part (i).

For both parts (i) and (ii), calculate

(a) torque at a slip of 0.05 and the slip for maximum torque

(b) the starting and maximum torques

(c) the supply voltage required to sustain the constant current at maximum torque.

Solution. The equivalent circuit for this motor is shown in Fig. 5.14 (*a*). Its Thevenin's equivalent circuit is drawn in Fig. 5.14 (*b*) where X_e and V_e are given by

$$X_e = \frac{1 \times 50}{51} = 0.9804\ \Omega \quad \text{and} \quad V_e = \frac{231 \times 50}{51} = 226.5\ \text{V}$$

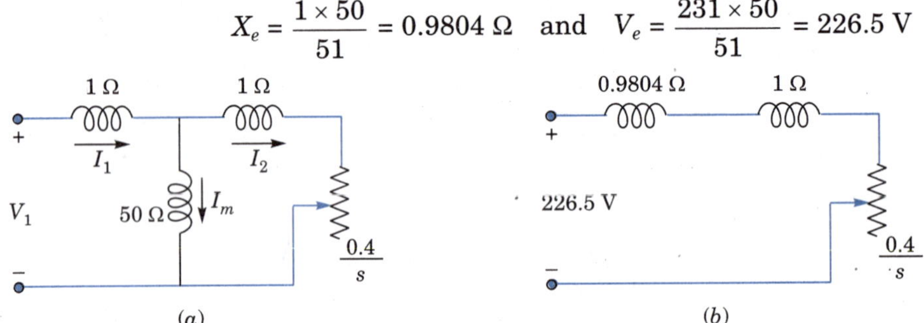

Fig. 5.14: Induction motor equivalent circuit, Example 5.6.

(*a*) (*i*) Synchronous speed,

$$\omega_s = \frac{4\pi f}{P} = \frac{4\pi \times 50}{4} = 50\ \text{rad/sec.}$$

From Eq. (5.27), the torque at slip $s = 0.05$ is

$$T_e = \frac{3}{50\pi} \cdot \frac{(226.5)^2}{\left(\frac{0.4}{0.05}\right)^2 + (1.9804)^2} \times \frac{0.4}{0.05} = 115.403\ \text{Nm}$$

From Fig. 5.14 (*b*), $s_{mT} = \dfrac{0.4}{1.9804} = 0.202$

(*a*) (*ii*) From the equivalent circuit of Fig. 5.14 (*a*),

$$Z_1 = j1.0 + \frac{j50\left(\frac{0.4}{0.05} + j1.0\right)}{\frac{0.4}{0.05} + j51} = j1.0 + 7.808\ \underline{/\ 16.05^\circ}$$

$$= 8.148\ \underline{/\ 23.26^\circ}$$

$\therefore$ Stator current, $I_1 = \dfrac{V_1}{Z_1} = \dfrac{231}{8.148} = 28.35\ \text{A}$

$$I_2 = 28.35\ \frac{50}{\left[\left(\frac{0.4}{0.05}\right)^2 + (51)^2\right]^{1/2}} = 27.46\ \text{A}$$

From Eq. (5.42), torque at a slip of 0.05 is

$$T_e = \frac{3}{50\pi} \cdot (27.46)^2 \frac{0.4}{0.05} = 115.211 \text{ Nm}$$

From Eq. (5.43), $s_{mT} = \dfrac{4.0}{51} = 0.00784$

(*b*) (*i*) For constant voltage input, $T_{e.st}$ from Eq. (5.27) is

$$T_{e.st} = \frac{3}{50\pi} \cdot \frac{(226.5)^2}{(0.4)^2 + (1.9804)^2} \times 0.4 = 96.012 \text{ Nm}$$

$T_{e.m}$ from Eq. (5.30) is

$$T_{e.m} = \frac{3}{50\pi} \cdot \frac{(226.5)^2}{2(1.9804)} = 247.37 \text{ Nm}$$

(*b*) (*ii*) For constant current input, T_{est} from Eq. (5.45), is

$$T_{e.st} = \frac{3}{50\pi} \cdot \frac{(28.35 \times 50)^2}{0.4^2 + 51^2} \times 0.4 = 5.901 \text{ Nm}$$

From Eq. (5.44), maximum torque is

$$T_{e.m.} = \frac{3}{50\pi} \cdot \frac{(28.35 \times 50)^2}{2 \times 51} = 376.225 \text{ Nm.}$$

It is seen from above that for constant-current mode, $T_{e.st}$ is much smaller (5.901 Nm) as compared to $T_{e.st}$ for constant-voltage mode (96.012 Nm). But maximum torque for constant-current mode is much more (376.225 Nm) than its value for constant voltage mode (247.37 Nm). Also, the slip at which maximum torque occurs is very low (0.00784) for constant-current mode as compared to its value for constant-voltage mode (0.202). Typical torque-slip characteristics for a 3-phase induction motor operating under these modes are sketched in Fig. 5.15.

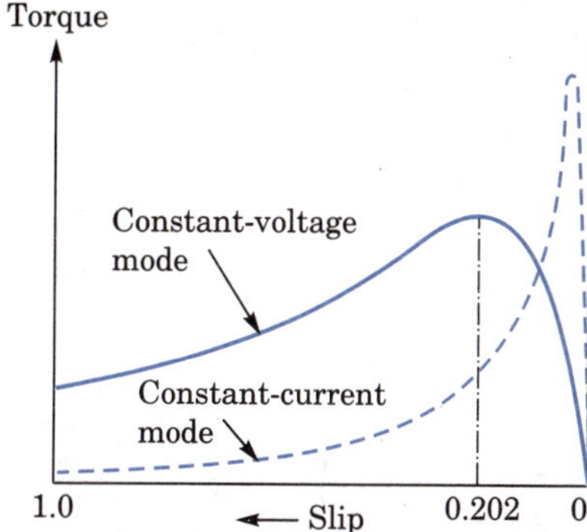

Fig. 5.15: Three-phase induction motor torque-slip characteristics for constant voltage and constant-current modes.

(*c*) At maximum torque, $s_{mT} = 0.00784$. From the equivalent circuit of Fig. 5.14 (*a*), magnetizing current I_m is

$$I_m = I_1 \cdot \frac{\dfrac{r_2}{s} + jx_2}{\dfrac{r_2}{s} + j(x_2 + X_m)} = 28.35 \frac{\dfrac{0.4}{0.00784} + j1}{\dfrac{0.4}{0.00784} + j51}$$

$$= 20.055 \angle -43.87°$$

∴ Supply voltage required to sustain constant current of 28.35 A is given by

$$V_1 = \sqrt{3}\ (20.055)\ (50) = 1736.3 \text{ V}$$

This shows that maximum torque at low value of slip necessitates a large value of source voltage which is much higher than the rated source voltage. But acquiring such a large voltage is not feasible. Thus, a large value of maximum torque at low slip is not a practical possibility.

In actual practice, the saturation occurs and the magnitude of X_m is reduced. As a consequence, the value of maximum torque under constant current mode has a much lower value than computed here.

5.6 HIGH-TORQUE CAGE MOTORS

It has been shown in the previous articles of this chapter that an increase of rotor-circuit resistance gives higher starting torque and lower starting line current at an improved power factor. However, if the increased rotor circuit resistance is retained, it results in a reduction of the full-load speed, poor speed regulation from no load to full load, more rotor ohmic losses and, therefore, a reduced efficiency. On the other hand, low rotor resistance results in almost constant-speed operation from no load to full load, low operating slip, less rotor ohmic losses and, therefore, high-operating efficiency. But a low rotor resistance has the disadvantage of reduced starting torque and high starting current at low power factor.

It can, therefore, be concluded from above that high rotor resistance at starting and low rotor resistance at normal-operating speed, are the desirable features of a polyphase induction motor.

In wound-rotor induction motors, these features are incorporated by inserting external resistance in the rotor circuit at the time of starting. As the rotor speeds up, the external resistance is cut out in steps, till finally slipring brushes are short-circuited at the normal operating speed.

In cage-rotor induction motors, the desirable features of high starting torque and low operating slip, can be achieved by the use of deep-bar or double-cage rotors. Both the deep-bar and double cage rotors make use of the skin-effect phenomenon, according to which the current distribution in rotor conductors is governed by the inductive effect of rotor slot-leakage flux. At standstill, rotor frequency is equal to the stator frequency ; whereas at normal operating speed, rotor frequency is quite small (may be 2 to 3 Hz). Thus, the skin-effect phenomenon which depends on frequency, is mush more predominant at standstill than at the low-operating slip. Consequently, the rotor resistance at standstill is several times higher than its value at low-operating slip.

5.6.1 Deep-Bar Rotor

The stator of deep-bar induction motor is similar to the stator of an ordinary induction motor. The deep bars are short circuited by two end-rings one on each side, just like a squirrel-cage rotor. On the left hand side, of Fig. 5.16 (*a*), one deep and narrow bar of rectangular cross-section is shown. Deep bars of other shapes, as shown in Fig. 5.16 (*b*), are also used but the rectangular bars are more common.

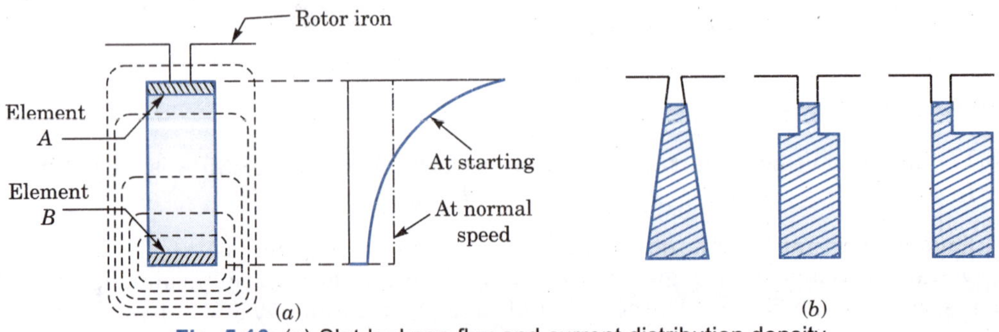

Fig. 5.16: (*a*) Slot-leakage flux and current distribution density in a deep-bar rotor (*b*) Different deep-bar rotor shapes.

For the rectangular bars of Fig. 5.16 (*a*), the general nature of slot-leakage flux is as shown. Since the permeability of rotor iron is very high, slot-leakage flux tends to crowd at the bottom of the slot. An element *B* at the bottom of rotor bar is linked by the greatest number of leakge-flux lines [5 lines in Fig. 5.16 (*a*)]. In view of this element *B* has much greater leakage inductance than the top bar element *A* which is linked by the least number of leakage-flux lines [one line in Fig. 5.16 (*a*)]. At the time of start, the rotor frequency is equal to the stator frequency, therefore, the leakage reactance of element *B* is the highest and the current in it is the least. The element *A* has the least leakage reactance and, therefore, current in it is the greatest. In other words, at the time of start, most of the bar current is forced towards the top element *A* as shown by the current-density distribution curve in Fig. 5.16 (*a*). This non-uniform distribution of bar current, due to skin effect, decreases the effective bar area, therefore, the effective rotor-bar resistance is increased and consequently higher-starting torque is developed.

Since the leakage reactance is proportional to frequency, non-uniform distribution of current depends upon the rotor frequency. This shows that skin effect, resulting in current distortion, is maximum with the rotor at standstill. As the rotor speeds up, rotor frequency decreases and likewise, the skin effect also decreases. Under normal operating speed, the rotor frequency is quite small, therefore, skin-effect is almost negligible and current distribution in the bar is uniform as shown in Fig. 5.16 (*a*). Thus, effective bar resistance at normal rotor speeds is almost equal to its d.c. value. This shows that the skin-effect has the effect of increasing rotor resistance at starting and cutting it out automatically as the rotor accelerates. In this manner, deep-bar rotors possess better performance characteristics both at standstill and at normal-operating speeds.

Equivalent circuit for deep bar motor. The equivalent circuit of Fig. 5.5 (*a*) is also applicable to the deep-bar rotor induction motor, but now suitable values of r_2 and x_2 should be used in determining the motor performanace. For determining the starting performance, r_2 and x_2 should correspond to their effective values at stator frequency. For computing the running performance in the normal range of small slips, the rotor resistance and leakage reactance should correspond to their effective values at low rotor frequency.

5.6.2 Double-cage Rotor

The stator of a double-cage rotor induction motor is similar to that of an ordinary induction motor, but its rotor consists of two cages as the name suggests. A typical slot-section of a double-cage rotor is shown in Fig. 5.17. The top bar, being of lower cross section, has higher resistance than that of the bottom bar. In case the cross-sectional areas of the two cages are equal, then top bars are made up of high-resistance material like brass, aluminium, bronze etc. and the bottom bars from low resistance copper material. The top and bottom bars are separated by narrow *slit* as shown in Fig. 5.17.

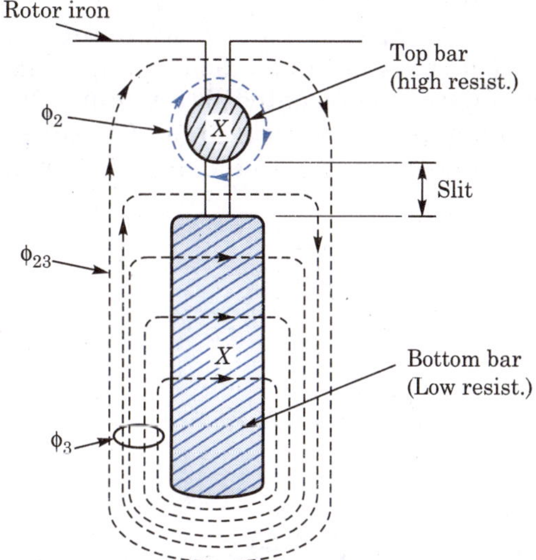

Fig. 5.17: Rotor slot of a double cage induction motor and the slot leakage flux.

In Fig. 5.17, flux ϕ_2 is the leakage flux of top bar, flux ϕ_3 is the leakage flux of bottom bar and flux ϕ_{23} is the mutual flux linking both the top and bottom bars. Note that ϕ_{23} is also the rotor leakage flux since it does not link the stator winding. An examination of the flux in the slit shows that ϕ_2 and ϕ_3 are opposing each other, this has the effect of reducing the top-bar leakage flux to a very low value. For very high rotor iron permeability, the slot leakage flux tends to crowd at the bottom of inner bar and the general nature of the leakage flux is as shown in Fig. 5.17. The bottom, or inner, bar is seen to have much higher leakage flux and the top bar a negligible value of leakage flux. In other words, the leakage inductance of top cage is negligibly small whereas the leakage inductance of bottom cage is relatively much higher.

At the time of starting, rotor frequency is equal to the supply frequency. The rotor current, shared by the top and bottom cages, is inversely proportional to their leakage impedances. At starting, leakage reactance of bottom cage is very high ; its leakage impedance is, therefore, several times greater than that of the high resistance top cage whose leakage reactance is negligibly small. Therefore, most of the rotor current at starting flows in the top cage having much lower leakage impedance. Since the top cage, sharing most of the rotor current at starting, has higher resistance, it results in higher starting torque, and low starting current at an improved power factor.

As the rotor speeds up, rotor frequency decreases and this has the effect of decreasing the leakage reactance of bottom cage and a corresponding increase of current in it. At normal operating speed, rotor frequency is very low and the leakage reactance of bottom cage becomes negligibly small as compared to its resistance. Thus, at normal operating speed, reactances become unimportant and the total rotor-current division between the two cages is governed mainly by their resistances. Since resistance of the top cage is considerably higher (5 to 6 times) than that of the bottom cage, total rotor current is shared mostly by the bottom cage. Hence, under normal operating speed, torque is developed mainly by a low-resistance bottom winding resulting in good operating characteristics.

Double squirrel-cage motors are also constructed with die-cast aluminium rotor windings with appropriate slots. The slit, separating the top and bottom cages, is also filled with aluminium and this provides electrical contact between the two cages along their axial length. Analysis of this type of die-cast rotor construction is similar to that adopted for double-cage rotor given above. The heat of the bottom cage is transferred to the top cage by the aluminium filled slit from where it is dissipated to the cooling medium.

Equivalent circuit for double-cage motor. The generalized mathematical model of a double-cage induction motor is as illustrated in Fig. 5.18 (*a*). Three-phase stator winding is represented by two coils DS and QS, Coils DR_1, DR_1 represent the top-cage winding in all respects. Similarly coils DR_2, QR_2 represent the bottom cage winding. Its procedure of analysis is the same as that adopted for an ordinary squirrel-cage induction motor.

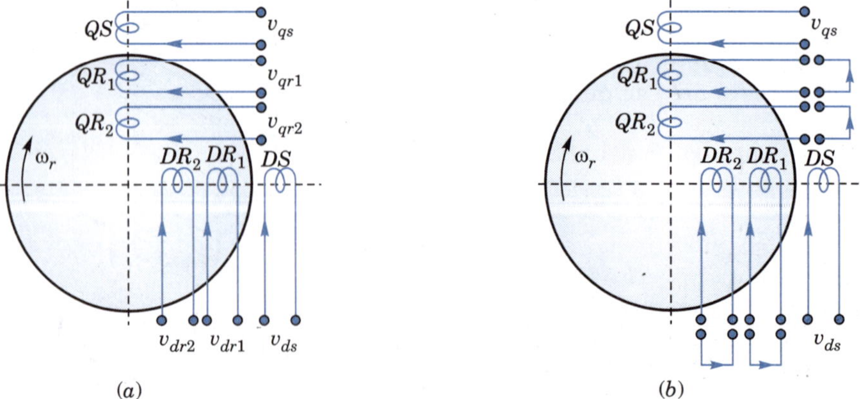

Fig. 5.18: (*a*) Generalized mathematical model of double-cage induction motor (*b*) Equivalent rotor coils short circuited.

The voltage equations in matrix form, from Fig. 5.18 (a), are

$$
\begin{bmatrix} v_{ds} \\ v_{qs} \\ v_{dr1} \\ v_{qr1} \\ v_{dr2} \\ v_{qr2} \end{bmatrix}
=
\begin{array}{c|cccccc}
 & ds & qs & dr\,1 & qr\,1 & dr\,2 & qr\,2 \\ \hline
ds & r_{ds}+L_{ds}p & & M_dp & & M_dp & \\
qs & & r_{qs}+L_{qs}p & & M_qp & & M_qp \\
dr\,1 & M_dp & -M_q\omega_r & r_{dr1}+L_{dr1}p & -L_{qr1}\omega_r & M_dp & -M_q\omega_r \\
qr\,1 & M_d\omega_r & M_qp & L_{dr1}\omega_r & r_{qr1}+L_{qr1} & M_d\omega_r & M_qp \\
dr\,2 & M_dp & -M_q\omega_r & M_dp & -M_q\omega_r & r_{dr2}+L_{dr2}p & -L_{qr2}\omega_r \\
qr\,2 & M_d\omega_r & M_qp & M_d\omega_r & M_qp & L_{dr2}\omega_r & r_{qr2}+L_{qr2}p
\end{array}
\begin{bmatrix} i_{ds} \\ i_{qs} \\ i_{dr1} \\ i_{qr1} \\ i_{dr2} \\ i_{qr2} \end{bmatrix}
\quad \ldots(5.46)
$$

The various constraints given below are similar to those for an ordinary 3-phase squirrel cage induction motor.

$$r_{ds} = r_{qs} = r_s \qquad L_{ds} = L_{qs} = L_s$$

$$r_{dr_1} = r_{qr_1} = r_{r_1} \qquad L_{dr_1} = L_{qr_1} = L_{r_1}$$

$$r_{dr_2} = r_{qr_2} = r_{r_2} \qquad L_{dr_2} = L_{qr_2} = L_{r_2}$$

$$M_d = M_q = M$$

$$v_{dr_1} = v_{qr_1} = 0$$

and $$v_{dr_2} = v_{qr_2} = 0.$$

The direction of currents $i_{dr_1}, i_{qr_1}, i_{dr_2}$ and i_{qr_2} shall get reversed and this must be accounted for while writing down the general voltage equations.

Incorporating these constraints in matrix (5.46), the voltage equations become :

$$
\begin{bmatrix} v_{ds} \\ v_{qs} \\ 0 \\ 0 \\ 0 \\ 0 \end{bmatrix}
=
\begin{bmatrix}
r_s+L_sp & & -Mp & & -Mp & \\
 & r_s+L_sp & & -Mp & & -Mp \\
Mp & -M\omega_r & -(r_{r1}+L_{r1}p) & L_{r1}\omega_r & -M & M\omega_r \\
M\omega_r & Mp & -L_{r1}\omega_r & -(r_{r1}+L_{r1}p) & -M_d\omega_r & -Mp \\
Mp & -M\omega_r & -Mp & M\omega_r & -(r_{dr2}+L_{r2}p) & L_{r2}\omega_r \\
M\omega_r & Mp & -M\omega_r & -Mp & -L_{r2}\omega_r & -(L_{r2}+L_{r2}p)
\end{bmatrix}
\begin{bmatrix} i_{ds} \\ i_{qs} \\ i_{dr1} \\ i_{qr1} \\ i_{dr2} \\ i_{qr2} \end{bmatrix}
\quad \ldots(5.47)
$$

5.6.3 Steady State Analysis

Steady state voltage equations in phasor form are obtained by replacing p by $j\omega$. Put $\omega_r = \upsilon\omega$.

So the voltage equations in phasor form, from matrix Eq. (5.47) are :

$$\begin{bmatrix} \overline{V}_{ds} \\ \overline{V}_{qs} \\ 0 \\ 0 \\ 0 \\ 0 \end{bmatrix} = \begin{bmatrix} r_s + jX_s & & -jX_m & & -jX_m & \\ & r_s + jX_s & & -jX_m & & -jX_m \\ jX_m & -\upsilon X_m & -(r_{r1} + jX_{r1}) & \upsilon X_{r1} & -jX_m & \upsilon X_m \\ \upsilon X_m & jX_m & -\upsilon X_{r1} & -(r_{r1} + jX_{r1}) & -\upsilon X_m & -jX_m \\ jX_m & -\upsilon X_m & -jX_m & \upsilon X_m & -(r_{r2} + jX_{r2}) & \upsilon X_{r2} \\ \upsilon X_m & jX_m & -\upsilon X_m & -jX_m & -\upsilon X_{r2} & -(r_{r2} + jX_{r2}) \end{bmatrix} \begin{bmatrix} \overline{I}_{ds} \\ \overline{I}_{qs} \\ \overline{I}_{dr1} \\ \overline{I}_{qr1} \\ \overline{I}_{dr2} \\ \overline{I}_{qr2} \end{bmatrix}$$

The connection matrix, transforming the currents $\overline{I}_{ds}, \overline{I}_{qs}, \overline{I}_{dr_1}, \overline{I}_{qr_1}, \overline{I}_{dr_2}, \overline{I}_{qr_2}$ into new currents $\overline{I}_s, \overline{I}_{r_1}, \overline{I}_{r_2}$ is

$$\begin{bmatrix} \overline{I}_{ds} \\ \overline{I}_{qs} \\ \overline{I}_{dr1} \\ \overline{I}_{qr1} \\ \overline{I}_{dr2} \\ \overline{I}_{qr2} \end{bmatrix} = \begin{bmatrix} 1 & & \\ j & & \\ & 1 & \\ & j & \\ & & 1 \\ & & j \end{bmatrix} \begin{bmatrix} \overline{I}_s \\ \overline{I}_{r1} \\ \overline{I}_{r2} \end{bmatrix}$$

or $$[I] = [C]\,[I']$$

The new impedance matrix $[\overline{Z}']$ is obtained by the product $[C_t^*][\overline{Z}][C]$. This product is done on the next page.

The new voltage matrix is

$$[V'] = [C_t^*][V] = \begin{bmatrix} 2\overline{V}_s \\ 0 \\ 0 \end{bmatrix}$$

Thus the new voltage equations, with $s = (1 - v)$ are :

$$\begin{bmatrix} \bar{V}_s \\ 0 \\ 0 \end{bmatrix} = \begin{bmatrix} r_s + jX_s & -jX_m & -jX_m \\ jsX_m & -r_{r1} - jsX_{r1} & -jsX_m \\ jsX_m & -jsX_m & -r_{r2} - jsX_{r2} \end{bmatrix} \begin{bmatrix} \bar{I}_s \\ \bar{I}_{r1} \\ \bar{I}_{r2} \end{bmatrix} \qquad \text{...(5.48)}$$

The impedance matrix in Eq. (5.48) can be made symmetric by dividing the elements of second and third rows by $(-s)$. This symmetric matrix is written further in Eq. (5.49)

$$\begin{array}{|c|c|c|c|c|c|c|c|c|} \hline r_s + jX_s & & -jX_m & & -jX_m & & 1 & & \\ \hline & r_s + jX_s & & -jX_m & & -jX_m & j & & \\ \hline jX_m & -vX_m & -(r_{r1} + jX_{r1}) & -vX_{r1} & -jX_m & vX_m & & 1 & \\ \hline vX_m & jX_m & -vX_{r1} & -(r_{r1} + jX_{r1}) & -vX_m & -jX_m & & j & \\ \hline jX_m & -vX_m & -jX_m & vX_m & -(r_{r2} + jX_{r2}) & vX_{r2} & & & 1 \\ \hline vX_m & jX_m & -vX_m & -jX_m & -vX_{r2} & -(r_{r2} + jX_{r2}) & & & j \\ \hline \end{array}$$

$$[Z'] = \begin{array}{|c|c|c|c|c|c|} \hline 1 & -j & & & & \\ \hline & & 1 & -j & & \\ \hline & & & & 1 & -j \\ \hline \end{array} \; \begin{array}{|c|c|c|c|c|c|c|c|c|} \hline r_s + jX_s & -j(r_s + jX_s) & -jX_m & -X_m & -jX_m & -X_m & 2(r_s + jX_s) & -2jX_m & -2jX_m \\ \hline \dfrac{jX_m}{(1-v)} & \dfrac{X_m}{(1-v)} & -\left[r_{r1} + \dfrac{jXr_1}{(1-v)}\right] & \dfrac{jr_1 - Xr_1}{(1-v)} & \dfrac{-jX_m}{(1-v)} & \dfrac{-X_m}{(1-v)} & \dfrac{2jX_m}{(1-v)} & -2\left[r_{r1} + \dfrac{jXr_1}{(1-v)}\right] & \dfrac{-2jX_m}{(1-v)} \\ \hline \dfrac{X_m}{(1-v)} & \dfrac{X_m}{(1-v)} & \dfrac{-jX_m}{(1-v)} & \dfrac{-X_m}{(1-v)} & \dfrac{-r_{r2} - jX_{r2}}{(1-v)} & \dfrac{-jr_2 - X_{r2}}{(1-v)} & \dfrac{2jX_m}{(1-v)} & \dfrac{-2jX_m}{(1-v)} & -2\left[r_{r2} + \dfrac{jXr_2}{(1-v)}\right] \\ \hline \end{array}$$

$$\begin{bmatrix} \bar{V}_s \\ 0 \\ 0 \end{bmatrix} = \begin{bmatrix} r_s + jX_s & -jX_m & -jX_m \\ -jX_m & \dfrac{r_{r1}}{s} + jX_{r1} & jX_m \\ -jX_m & jX_m & \dfrac{r_{r2}}{s} + jX_{r2} \end{bmatrix} \begin{bmatrix} \bar{I}_s \\ \bar{I}_{r1} \\ \bar{I}_{r2} \end{bmatrix} \qquad \text{...(5.49)}$$

For convenience, the subscripts s, r_1 and r_2 are replaced by 1, 2 and 3 respectively. With this change in the subscripts, Eq. (5.49) is re-written as follows :

$$\begin{bmatrix} \bar{V}_1 \\ 0 \\ 0 \end{bmatrix} = \begin{bmatrix} r_1 + jX_1 & -jX_m & -jX_m \\ -jX_m & \dfrac{r_2}{s} + jX_2 & jX_m \\ -jX_m & jX_m & \dfrac{r_3}{s} + jX_3 \end{bmatrix} \begin{bmatrix} \bar{I}_1 \\ \bar{I}_2 \\ \bar{I}_3 \end{bmatrix} \qquad \text{...(5.50)}$$

Equations of matrix Eq. (5.50) give the equivalent circuits of Fig. 5.19 (*a*), 5.19 (*b*) and 5.19 (*c*). In Fig. 5.19 (*b*) and (*c*), the rotor parameters must be referred to stator. Here the same symbols have been used for the referred rotor parameters so as to avoid the complicated notation.

The equivalent circuit of Fig. 5.19 (*c*) can be simplified by applying Thevenin's theorem at the terminals *a*, *b*. The resulting circuit will consist of two impedances in parallel. This simplified equivalent circuit can be used to obtain the performance analysis of a double-cage induction motor.

As in a single-cage induction motor, per phase air-gap power for both cages is

$$P_g = I_2^2 \frac{r_2}{s} + I_3^2 \frac{r_3}{s} \qquad \text{...(5.51)}$$

Total electromagnetic torque T_e is

$$T_e = \frac{3}{2\pi n_s}\left[I_2^2 \frac{r_2}{s} + I_3^2 \frac{r_3}{s}\right] \qquad \text{...(5.52)}$$

Equivalent circuit of Fig. 5.19 (*c*) can also be obtained qualitatively. If only top bars are present, the equivalent circuit is similar to that of a polyphase induction motor of Fig. 5.5 (*a*). If only bottom bars are present, the equivalent circuit of Fig. 5.5. (*a*) is again obtained but with rotor quantities I_2, r_2, x_2 replaced by I_3, r_3, x_3 respectively. Superposition of these two equivalent circuits results in the double-cage induction motor equivalent circuit of Fig. 5.19 (*c*). Note that the effect of mutual flux between top and bottom bars ϕ_{23} in Fig. 5.17 is assumped negligible and it, therefore, not shown in Fig. 5.19 (*c*).

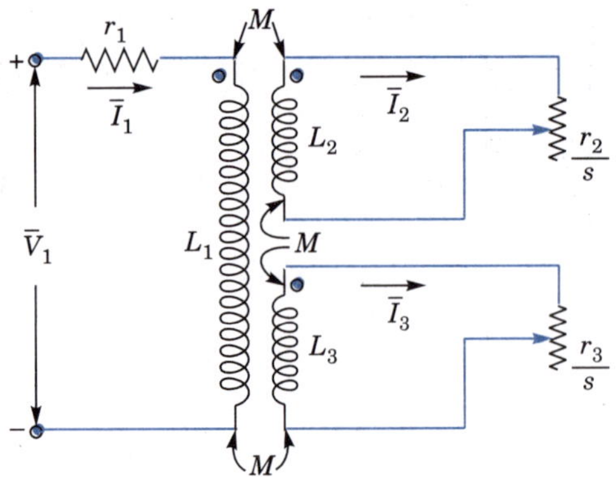

(*a*) With mutual inductance

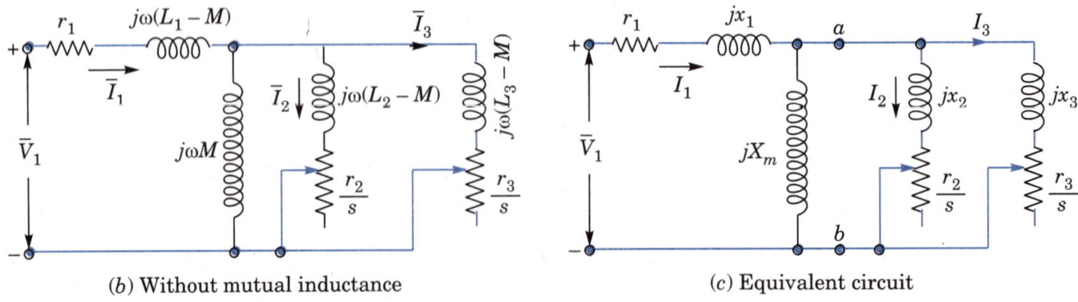

(*b*) Without mutual inductance (*c*) Equivalent circuit

Fig. 5.19: Equivalent circuit of a double-cage polyphase induction motor. All values are per phase values.

Torque-slip characteristics of double-cage induction motor can be obtained by assuming that each cage is quite independent and produces torque as if the other cage were absent. The torque-slip curves for high-resistance outer cage and low-resistance inner cage are as shown in Fig. 5.20. The total torque of the machine is, therefore, the sum of the two cage torques as illustrated in Fig. 5.20.

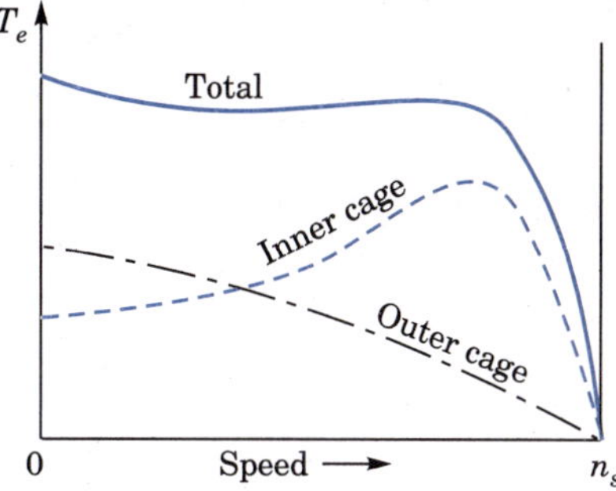

Fig. 5.20: Torque-speed curves of a double-cage induction motor.

If a comparison of the torques due to top and bottom cages is required, then

$$\frac{T_{e.t}}{T_{e.b}} = \frac{I_2^2\, r_2/s}{I_3^2\, r_3/s} = \left(\frac{I_2}{I_3}\right)^2 \frac{r_2}{r_3} \qquad ...(5.53)$$

It is seen from the equivalent circuit of Fig. 5.19 (*c*) that

$$I_2 = \frac{\text{Rotor voltage}}{\frac{r_2}{s} + jx_2} \quad \text{and} \quad I_3 = \frac{\text{Rotor voltage}}{\frac{r_3}{s} + jx_3}$$

$$\therefore \qquad \frac{T_{e.t}}{T_{e.b}} = \frac{\left(\frac{r_3}{s}\right)^2 + (x_3)^2}{\left(\frac{r_2}{s}\right)^2 + (x_2)^2} \cdot \frac{r_2}{r_3} \qquad ...(5.54)$$

Here the subscripts t and b along with T_e denote torques due to top and bottom cages respectively.

Comparison between single-cage and double-cage motors. For comparison purposes, circle diagrams for both single-cage and double-cage induction motors are drawn in the same figure.

The current locus (circle diagram) for double cage induction motor can be drawn by first considering the two cages electrically and magnetically separate and then adding the two current-loci.

The bottom cage has high leakage reactance, its circle has, therefore, smaller diameter ; whereas the top cage having a lower leakage reactance has greater circle diameter as shown in Fig. 5.21. The points corresponding to slip $s = 1$ (*i.e.* short circuit) on the circle diagrams are also shown. For top cage, the short-circuit point d_2 is near the creast of circle because this cage has high resistance. For bottom cage, the short-circuit point d_3 is quite lower, because this cage has lower resistance. The phasor sum of od_2 and od_3 gives the total starting current as od for the double-cage motor. Other points on the current locus of the double-cage motor can be obtained similarly. For comparison purposes, the current locus for a corresponding single-cage induction motor is also drawn in Fig. 5.21.

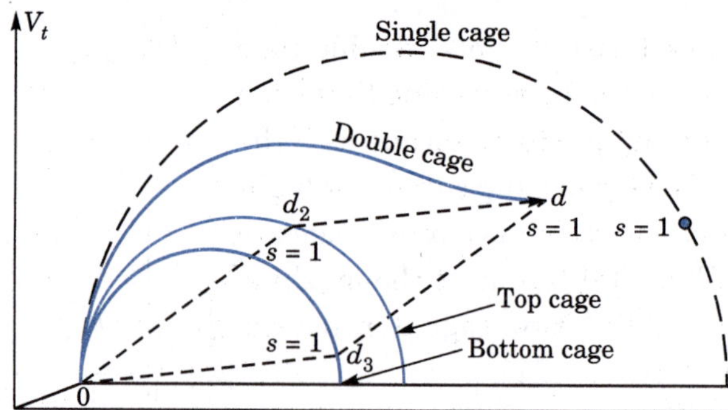

Fig. 5.21: Current locus for a double-cage and single-cage induction motors of the same rating.

Now a single-cage motor and a double-cage motor of the same rating can be compared as follows :

(i) Starting performance. A double-cage motor develops higher starting torque for low starting currents-in view of this, it is more suitable for direct-on-line starting. Since effective rotor resistance for a double-cage motor is higher, there is more rotor heating during starting as compared to a single-cage motor.

(ii) Full-load performance. A double-cage induction motor has higher effective rotor leakage reactance-in view of this, it has lower breakdown torque and lower full-load power factor. Since effective rotor resistance in a double cage motor is higher, it has lower efficiency as compared to a single-cage induction motor. Full load slip of double-cage motor may be lower than the single-cage motor.

(iii) Torque-slip characteristics. With double-cage motors, a wide range of torque-slip characteristics can be obtained by a proper choice of top and bottom cage resistances and the slit in between them; this, however, is not possible in an ordinary squirrel-cage induction motor.

Example 5.7. *A 3-phase, 420 V, double-cage induction motor has standstill per-phase leakage impedances of 3 + j1 Ω and 0.5 + j6.0 Ω for its two cages. If stator impedance and magnetizing current are neglected, then for a full-load slip of 5%, calculate the starting torque in terms of full-load torque with direct-on-line starting.*

Solution. Note that $3 + j1\ \Omega$ is the per phase standstill leakage impedance of top cage and $0.5 + j\,6.00\ \Omega$ that for the bottom cage.

Therefore, $r_2 + jx_2 = 3 + j1\ \Omega$ and $r_3 + j\,x_3 = 0.5 + j\,6\ \Omega$.

From Eq. (5.52), the starting torque is given by

$$T_{e.st} = \frac{3}{2\pi n_s}\,[I_2^2\,r_2 + I_3^2\,r_3]$$

$$= \frac{3}{2\pi n_s}\left[\frac{V^2}{3^2+1}\times 3 + \frac{V^2}{(0.5)^2+6^2}\times 0.5\right] = \frac{3V^2}{2\pi n_s}\,(0.3138)$$

Full-load torque is given by

$$T_{e.fl} = \frac{3}{2\pi n_s}\left[\frac{V^2}{\left(\frac{3}{0.05}\right)^2+1}\times\frac{3}{0.05}+\frac{V^2}{\left(\frac{0.5}{0.05}\right)^2+6^2}\times\frac{0.5}{0.05}\right]$$

$$= \frac{3V^2}{2\pi n_s}\left[\frac{1}{3601}\times 60+\frac{1}{136}\times 10\right] = \frac{3V^2}{2\pi n_s}\,[0.0902]$$

$$\therefore \qquad \frac{T_{e.st}}{T_{e.fl}} = \frac{0.3138}{0.0902} = 3.48.$$

Example 5.8. *A 3-phase, 400 V, double cage induction motor has per-phase standstill leakage impedance of 2 + j2.0 Ω and 0.5 + j10 Ω for its two cages. Find the relative values of torques given by each cage ; (a) at starting and (b) at 5% slip.*

Solution. From Eq. (5.54), the ratio of top and bottom-cage torques at starting is given by,

$$\frac{T_{e.t}}{T_{e.b}} = \frac{\left(\frac{r_3}{1}\right)^2+(x_3)^2}{\left(\frac{r_2}{1}\right)^2+(x_2)^2}\cdot\frac{r_2}{r_3} = \frac{(0.5)^2+(10)^2}{(2)^2+(2)^2}\cdot\frac{2}{0.5} = 50.125$$

$$\therefore \qquad T_{e.t.} : T_{e.b.} :: 50.125 : 1.$$

(*b*) From Eq. (5.54), the ratio of top and bottom-cage torques, at a slip 5%, is given by

$$\frac{T_{e.t}}{T_{e.b}} = \frac{\left(\frac{0.5}{0.05}\right)^2+(10)^2}{\left(\frac{2}{0.05}\right)^2+(2)^2}\times\frac{2}{0.5} \cong 0.5$$

$$\therefore \qquad T_{e.t} : T_{e.b} :: 0.5 : 1.$$

Example 5.9. *At standstill, the ratio of resistance to leakage reactance is 4 for the top-cage and 0.3 for the bottom cage. At standstill, the top-cage current is twice the bottom-cage current. For a full-load slip of 6%, determine the relative magnitudes of (a) bar currents and (b) the electromagnetic torques.*

Solution. Here $\frac{r_2}{x_2} = 4$ and $\frac{r_3}{x_3} = 0.3$

At standstill, $$\frac{I_2}{I_3} = \frac{\sqrt{(r_3/1)^2+(x_3)^2}}{\sqrt{(r_2/1)^2+(x_2)^2}}$$

$$= \frac{x_3}{x_2}\cdot\sqrt{\frac{(0.3)^2+1}{(4)^2+1}} \quad \text{or} \quad 2 = \frac{x_3}{x_2}\cdot\sqrt{\frac{1.09}{17}}$$

$$\therefore \qquad \frac{x_3}{x_2} = 2\sqrt{\frac{17}{1.09}} = 7.898.$$

(*a*) At full-load slip of 6%,

$$\frac{I_2}{I_3} = \frac{\sqrt{(r_3/0.06)^2 + x_3{}^2}}{\sqrt{(r_2/0.06)^2 + x_2{}^2}} = \frac{x_3}{x_2}\,\frac{\sqrt{(0.3/0.06)^2 + 1}}{\sqrt{(4/0.06)^2 + 1}}$$

$$= 7.898\sqrt{\frac{26}{4445.4}} = 0.604.$$

(*b*) At full-load slip of 6%,

$$\frac{T_{e.t}}{T_{e.b}} = \frac{\left(\dfrac{r_3}{0.06}\right)^2 + x_3^2}{\left(\dfrac{r_2}{0.06}\right)^2 + x_2^2}\cdot\frac{r_2}{r_3}$$

$$= \left(\frac{x_3}{x_2}\right)^2 \times \frac{26}{4445.4}\cdot\frac{r_2}{r_3} = \frac{x_3}{x_2}\cdot\frac{26}{4445.4}\times\frac{4}{0.3}$$

$$= 7.898\left(\frac{26}{4445.4}\right)\times\frac{4}{0.3} = 0.616.$$

Example 5.10. *A 4-pole, 50 Hz double cage induction motor has the following per phase parameters referred to stator.*

Stator ;	$r_1 = 0.5\ \Omega$	$x_1 = 1.5\ \Omega$
Rotor ; top-cage,	$r_2 = 2\ \Omega$	$x_2 = 0.6\ \Omega$
bottom cage,	$r_3 = 0.4\ \Omega$	$x_3 = 3.4\ \Omega$

The primary in delta is energised from 400 V. Calculate the starting torque and full-load torque at 4% slip using the approximate equivalent circuit. Find also the pf at starting and at full-load.

Solution. For this example, refer to Fig. 5.19 (*c*). Here X_m is zero. The total impedance at the input terminals at starting is given by

$$Z = 0.5 + j\,1.5 + \frac{(2 + j\,0.6)\,(0.4 + j\,3.4)}{2.4 + j\,4}$$

$$= 0.5 + j\,1.5 + 1.157 + j\,1.0043$$

$$= 1.657 + j\,2.5043 = 3.003\,\underline{/\,56.51}°.$$

Synchronous speed, $\omega_s = 2\pi \times 25 = 50\,\pi$ rad/sec

Stator starting current,

$$I_1 = \frac{400}{3.003}\ \text{A}$$

$\therefore$ Starting torque $= \dfrac{3}{\omega_s}(I_1)^2 \times$ Equivalent rotor resistance

$$= \frac{3}{50\,\pi}\left(\frac{400}{3.003}\right)^2 \times 1.157 = 392.052\ \text{Nm}.$$

Power factor at starting

$$= \cos 56.51° = 0.5518\ \text{lag}.$$

The input impedance at full-load is given by

$$Z = 0.5 + j\,1.5 + \frac{\left(\dfrac{2}{0.04} + j\,0.6\right)\left(\dfrac{0.4}{0.04} + j\,3.4\right)}{\left(\dfrac{2.4}{0.04} + j\,4\right)}$$

In $\dfrac{2}{0.04} + j\,0.6$, or $50 + j\,0.6$, 50 is much greater than 0.6, therefore, 0.6 may be neglected without any appreciable error.

$$\therefore \qquad Z = 0.5 + j\,1.5 + \frac{(50)\,(10 + j\,3.4)}{60 + j4}$$

$$= 0.5 + j\,1.5 + 8.485 + j\,2.269$$

$$= 8.985 + j\,3.769 = 9.743\,\underline{/\,22.76°}$$

Full-load stator current $= \dfrac{400}{9.743}$ A

Full-load torque $= \dfrac{3}{50\pi}\left(\dfrac{400}{9.743}\right)^2 \times 8.485 = 273.142$ Nm.

Full-load $pf = \cos 22.76° = 0.9221$ lag.

In this example, starting torque is higher than full-load torque, but full-load *pf* is better than starting *pf*.

5.7 INDUCTION MACHINE DYNAMICS

For some industrial applications, induction motors are frequently started, braked or reversed. For such applications, the time required for starting, braking or reversing is quite important, because if effects the rotor heating and the motor temperature rise. Sometimes, the normal operation of a polyphase induction motor is effected by a sudden disturbance in the load or the supply voltage. For example, a momentary reduction in the supply voltage would decrease the induction motor speed and electrical torque and this would effect the normal operation of the induction motor. Under certain circumstances ; depending upon the time, extent of reduction in supply voltage and the nature of load torque, the induction motor may stall and come to rest. The sudden voltage dip in the supply may occur due to the starting of a large induction motor in the neighbourhood or due to a fault in the supply system. Single-phase or 3-phase welding transformers connected to the lines feeding the polyphase induction motors, also cause wide and rapid fluctuations in the system voltage which is detrimental to the normal operation of induction motors. All these problems associated with the starting, braking or reversing of induction motors and their behaviour under sudden disturbance in load or the supply voltage, are the most common dynamic problems of the induction motors.

In induction motors, the electrical transients are of very short duration as compared to the motional transients. In view of this, electrical transients during the analysis of induction-machine dynamics can be neglected. This assumption simplifies greatly the induction motor analysis under dynamic conditions ; and permits the use of steady-state equivalent circuit of Fig. 5.5 and torque-slip curve of Fig. 5.7. The object of this article is to study the induction machine dynamics during starting, braking, reversing and the normal operation.

5.7.1 Induction-Machine Dynamics During Starting and Braking

Here, first the rotor energy loss responsible for its heating and then, the time required for motor starting, stopping and its reversal is considered. After this, the magnitude of rotor circuit resistance is determined so as to obtain optimum time for starting, braking or reversing of the polyphase induction motors.

(a) Rotor energy loss. Energy losses, responsible for rotor heating, can be determined by a consideration of Eq. (5.20).

∴ Air-gap power, $P_g = mI_2^2\frac{r_2}{s} = \frac{1}{s}$ (total rotor ohmic loss, P_r).

But $P_g = \omega_s T_e$

∴ Total rotor ohmic loss, $P_r = sP_g = s\omega_s T_e$ ...(5.55)

The motor torque balance equation is, $T_e = Jp\omega_r + D\omega_r + T_L$.

Assume that the motor is connected to a pure inertia load whose total moment of inertia, including motor and load, is J kgm^2. Load torque T_L is taken as zero and for simplicity, rotational losses *i.e.* friction torque $D\omega_r$ is neglected. With these assumptions, the torque balance equation becomes

$$T_e = Jp\omega_r = J\frac{d}{dt}\,[\omega_s\,(1-s)]$$

$$= -\,\omega_s\,J\frac{ds}{dt} \qquad ...(5.56)$$

Substitution of T_e from Eq. (5.56) in Eq. (5.55) gives, $P_r = -\,\omega_s^2\,Js\frac{ds}{dt}$

Total energy dissipated in the rotor circuit, as slip change from s_1 to s_2, is given by

$$W_r = \int_{t_1}^{t_2} P_r \cdot dt = \int_{s_1}^{s_2} (-\,\omega_s^2 J)\;s\,ds$$

$$= \frac{J\omega_s^2}{2}\,(s_1^2 - s_2^2) \text{ Joules} \qquad ...(5.57)$$

At starting, the rotor frequency is equal to the supply frequency f. At normal rotor speed, the rotor frequency, equal to sf, is very small. At the instant of plugging ; the rotor frequency equal to $(2 - s)\,f$, is quite large. At these different frequencies, the current distribution in rotor conductors is different due to the skin-effect phenomenon. At small frequency sf, the rotor current is almost uniformly distributed and at rotor frequency of $(2-s)f$, the current is not distributed uniformly. On this account, the rotor resistance does not remain constant at starting, at normal rotor speed and at the instant of plugging. However, the above expression for rotor energy loss is derived on the assumption of a constant rotor resistance.

During acceleration from $s_1 = 1$ (standstill) to negligible slip $s_2 = 0$ (ideal case), the total energy loss appearing as heat in the rotor is equal to $\frac{1}{2}J\omega_s^2$ joules and it is seen to be independent of the accelerating time. Also, $\frac{1}{2}J\omega_s^2$ is the kinetic energy stored in the rotating mass. Thus, total energy taken by an induction motor from the a.c. source is equal to $J\omega_s^2$ and this gives an energy efficiency of 50%.

If the motor, running at normal speed, is brought to rest by means of plugging (reversing phase sequence of the supply voltage), the energy lost in the rotor can be obtained from Eq. (5.57). At the instant phase sequence is reversed, slip $s_1 = 2$ (ideal case) and when the induction motor stops, slip $s_2 = 1$.

∴ Rotor energy loss from normal speed to rest, by plugging

$$= \frac{j\omega_s^2}{2}(4-1) = \frac{3}{2} J\omega_s^2 \text{ Joules.}$$

If the motor is reversed by plugging, then $s_1 = 2$ and $s_2 = 0$ (ideal case) and the rotor energy loss with reversal from forward normal speed to backward normal speed is equal to

$$\frac{J\omega_s^2}{2}(4-0) = 2J\omega_s^2 \text{ Joules.}$$

At the time of starting, breaking or reversing, large currents flow in a three-phase induction motor. In order to limit these large currents and to control the starting, braking or reversing times external resistances are inserted in the rotor circuit of wound-rotor induction motors. In view of this, most of the rotor energy loss is dissipated in the external resistors ; this, however, is not the case in squirrel-cage induction motors. Consequently, rotor heating in wound-rotor motors during starting or plugging is much lower than in the case of squirrel-cage motors.

Stator heating during starting or plugging, approximately equal to $\frac{r_1}{r_2}$ (W_r), can be reduced by designing the stator winding with minimum possible resistance.

(b) Accelerating, braking and reversing times. If stator resistance is neglected, then the electrical torque T_e can be expressed by Eq. (5.56) ; which, for convenience, is repeated here as

$$T_e = T_{em} \frac{2}{\dfrac{s}{s_{mT}} + \dfrac{s_{mT}}{s}}$$

The time taken by the motor to change its slip from s_1 to s_2 can be obtained by substituting the value of T_e given in Eq. (5.56). Therefore,

$$-J\omega_s \frac{ds}{dt} = \frac{2T_{em}}{\dfrac{s}{s_{mT}} + \dfrac{s_{mT}}{s}}$$

or, $$\int_0^t dt = -\frac{J\omega_s}{2T_{em}}\left[\int_{s_1}^{s_2} \frac{s}{s_{mT}}\, ds + \int_{s_1}^{s_2} \frac{s_m T}{s}\, ds\right] \quad ...[5.58(a)]$$

or, $$t = \frac{J\omega_s}{2T_{em}}\left[\frac{s_1^2 - s_2^2}{2s_{mT}} + s_{mT} \ln \frac{s_1}{s_2}\right] \quad ...(5.58)$$

The accelerating time from $s_1 = 1$ (standstill) to any slip $s_2 = s$, from Eq. (5.58), is given by

$$t = \frac{J\omega_s}{2T_{em}}\left[\frac{1-s^2}{2s_{mT}} + s_{mT} \ln \frac{1}{s}\right] \quad ...(5.59)$$

The time required to stop the motor (running at any slip s) by plugging can be obtained from Eq. 5.58. At the instant phase squence is reversed, s_1 becomes equal to

$$2 - s \left[= \frac{n_s + n_s(1-s)}{n_s}\right]$$

and s_2 becomes equal to 1 (at standstill). Thus, the time required to stop the motor, *i.e.* the braking time from Eq. (5.58) is

$$t = \frac{J\omega_s}{2T_{em}}\left[\frac{(2-s)^2 - 1}{2s_{mT}} + s_{mT} \ln (2-s)\right] \quad ...(5.60)$$

The time required for the reversal by plugging gives the limits of integration from $(2 - s)$ $(= s_1)$ to s $(= s_2)$. Therefore, the reversing time, from Eq. (5.58), is

$$t = \frac{J\omega_s}{2T_{em}}\left[\frac{(2-s)^2 - s^2}{2s_{mT}} + s_{mT}\ \ln\frac{2-s}{s}\right] \quad ...(5.61)$$

(c) Rotor circuit resistance for optimum times. If induction motor is to be designed so as to bring the pure inertia load from slip s_1 to slip s_2 in the minimum possible time, the value of rotor circuit resistance to do so can be determined from Eq. (5.58). Differentiating Eq. (5.58) with respect to that value of slip which depends on the rotor resistance, *i.e.* s_{mT} and equating it to zero, we get

$$\frac{dt}{ds_{mT}} = \frac{J\omega_s}{2T_{em}}\left[-\frac{s_1^2 - s_2^2}{2s_{mT}^2} + \ln\frac{s_1}{s_2}\right] = 0$$

$$\therefore \qquad s_{mT} = \left[\frac{s_1^2 - s_2^2}{2\ln\frac{s_1}{s_2}}\right]^{1/2} \quad ...(5.62)$$

From the above expression

$$s_{mT}^2 = \frac{s_1^2 - s_2^2}{2\ln\frac{s_1}{s_2}} \quad \text{or} \quad (s_1^2 - s_2^2) = 2\,s_{mT}^2 \ln\frac{s_1}{s_2}.$$

Substituting this value of $(s_1^2 - s_2^2)$ in Eq. (5.58), we get minimum time t_{min} for the slip to change from s_1 to s_2.

$$\therefore \qquad t_{min} = \frac{J\omega_s}{2T_{em}}\left[\frac{2\,s_{mT}^2 \ln\frac{s_1}{s_2}}{2s_{mT}} + s_{mT}\ \ln\frac{s_1}{s_2}\right] = \frac{J\omega_s}{2T_{em}}\left[(s_{mT})\,2\ln\frac{s_1}{s_2}\right]$$

Substitution of s_{mT} from Eq. (5.62) in the above expression gives

$$t_{min} = \frac{J\omega_s}{2T_{em}}\left[\sqrt{\frac{s_1^2 - s_2^2}{2\ln\frac{s_1}{s_2}}}\cdot 2\ln\frac{s_1}{s_2}\right]$$

$$= \frac{J\omega_s}{2T_{em}}\left[2\,(s_1^2 - s_2^2)\ln\frac{s_1}{s_2}\right]^{1/2} \quad ...(5.63)$$

Now $\qquad \frac{r_2}{s_{mT}} = X, \quad \text{where } X = x_2 + X_e$

$\therefore$ Rotor circuit resistance, from Eq. (5.62), is

$$R_2 = Xs_{mT} = X\left[\frac{s_1^2 - s_2^2}{2\ln\frac{s_1}{s_2}}\right]^{1/2} \quad ...(5.64)$$

Here R_2 is equal to rotor circuit resistance r_2 plus the external resistance.

For bringing the pure inertia load from rest ($s_1 = 1$) to any slip s ($s_2 = s$) in the minimum possible time ; the required rotor circuit resistance, from Eq. (5.64), is

$$R_2 = X\left[\frac{1-s^2}{2\ln\frac{1}{s}}\right]^{1/2} \qquad ...(5.65)$$

and the minimum time, from Eq. (5.63), is

$$t_{min} = \frac{J\omega_s}{2T_{em}}\left[2(1-s^2)\ln\frac{1}{s}\right]^{1/2} \qquad ...(5.66)$$

For stopping the motor (running at a slip s) by plugging in the minimum possible time ; the required rotor circuit resistance, from Eq. (5.64), is

$$R_2 = X\left[\frac{(2-s)^2-1}{2\ln(2-s)}\right]^{1/2} \qquad ...(5.67)$$

and the minimum time, from Eq. (5.63), is

$$t_{min} = \frac{J\omega_s}{2T_{em}}\,[2\,\{(2-s)^2-1\}\ln(2-s)]^{1/2} \qquad ...(5.68)$$

For minimum time reversal by plugging, the rotor circuit resistance, from Eq. (5.64), is

$$R_2 = X\left[\frac{(2-s)^2-s^2}{2\ln\frac{2-s}{s}}\right]^{1/2} \qquad ...(5.69)$$

and the minimum time is $t_{min} = \frac{J\omega_s}{2T_{em}}\left[2\left\{(2-s)^2-s^2\right\}\ln\frac{2-s}{s}\right]^{1/2}$ ...(5.70)

Example 5.11. *A 400 V, 3-phase, 50 Hz, 4-pole, 15 A, 0.88 pf squirel-cage induction motor has a full-load speed of 1455 rpm. The stator losses total 150 watts. Total inertial of motor plus load is 0.0563 kgm^2.*

(a) Calculate the number of starts and stops (by plugging) per minute that this motor can make without exceeding the permissible temperature rise.

How many starts and stops can be made if the motor has 8 poles, all other conditions remaining unchanged.

(b) Also calculate the number of reversals per minute that the motor can make by plugging, without exceeding the designed temperature.

Solution. (*a*) Power input from stator to rotor = air-gap power,

$$P_g = \sqrt{3}\,(400)\,(15)\,(0.88) - 150 = 9000 \text{ W}$$

Total rotor ohmic loss = $sP_g = \left(\frac{1500-1455}{1500}\right) \times 9000 = 270$ watts.

The rotor is designed to dissipate 270 watts, without exceeding the permissible temperature rise. Therefore, the permissible amount of energy that can be dissipated by rotor in one minute is given by

$$(270)\,(60) = 16200 \text{ watt-sec or joules.}$$

Energy dissipated in rotor during acceleration from slip 1 to slip s, from Eq. (5.57), is

$$\frac{1}{2} J\omega_s^2 (1 - s^2).$$

Energy dissipated in rotor during plugging, from slip $(2 - s)$ to slip 1, is

$$\frac{1}{2} J\omega_s^2 [(2 - s)^2 - 1].$$

∴ Total energy dissipated in rotor during acceleration and braking (by plugging) is

$$= \frac{1}{2} J\omega_s^2 [(1 - s^2) + (2 - s)^2 - 1] = 2J\omega_s^2 (1 - s) \text{ Joules}$$

$$= 2 (0.0563) (50\pi)^2 (0.97) = 2700 \text{ Joules.}$$

∴ Total number of starts and stops per minute $= \frac{16{,}200}{2700} = 6$

With 8 poles, total number of starts and stops per minute

$$= \frac{16{,}200}{2 (0.0563) (25\pi)^2 (0.97)} = 24$$

During acceleration and braking, the average rotor speeds are low, consequently the rotor heat dissipated by ventilation is decreased. Thus the results obtained above for starts and stops are optimistic.

(*b*) Energy dissipted in rotor during reversal by plugging from slip $2 - s$ to slip s is

$$= \frac{1}{2} J\omega_s^2 [(2 - s)^2 - s^2]$$

$$= \frac{1}{2} (0.0563) (50\pi)^2 [(1.97)^2 - (0.03)^2] = 2700 \text{ watt-sec.}$$

∴ Total number of reversals for 4 and 8 poles are 6 and 24 respectively. The results obtained for reversals are also optimistic, because the motor cooling by ventilation is impaired considerably as the rotor speed crosses zero during each reversal.

Example 5.12. *A 400 V, 3-phase, 50 Hz, 4-pole star-connected induction motor has the following per phase constants :*

$$r_1 = 0 \,;\, x_1 = x_2 = 1.2\ \Omega \,;\, X_m = 38.8\ \Omega.$$

The magnitude of total rotor-circuit resistance is to be determined so that the motor can be

(a) brought to a slip of 0.05 from standstill, in the minimum possible time and

(b) brought to rest by plugging in the quickest possible time, from a slip of 0.05.

Direct-on-starting is used and the total inertia of motor and load is 4.00 kgm². Find also the minimum time of acceleration and braking.

Solution. (*a*) The rotor circuit resistance required to bring the motor from rest to any slip s is given by Eq. (5.65), *i.e.*,

$$R_2 = X \left[\frac{1 - s^2}{2 \ln \frac{1}{s}} \right]^{\frac{1}{2}}$$

Now $X = x_2 + X_e.$

The Thevenin's equivalent reactance,

$$X_e = \frac{x_1 \,.\, X_m}{X_m + x_1} = \frac{1.2 \times 38.80}{40} = 1.164\ \Omega$$

$\therefore$ $X = 1.2 + 1.164 = 2.364\ \Omega$

$\therefore$ Rotor circuit resistance required is

$$R_2 = X\, s_{mT} = X \left[\frac{1 - s^2}{2 \ln \frac{1}{s}}\right]^{\frac{1}{2}}$$

$$= 2.364 \left[\frac{1 - (0.05)^2}{2 \ln \frac{1}{0.05}}\right]^{\frac{1}{2}} = 2.364\ (0.408) = 0.965\ \Omega$$

From Eq. (5.30), the maximum torque with $R_e = 0$ is given by

$$T_{em} = \frac{3\, V_e^{\,2}}{2\, \pi n_s\, (2X)}$$

where, $$V_e = \frac{V_1 \,.\, X_m}{x_1 + X_m} = \frac{(400/\sqrt{3})\,(38.8)}{40} = 224\ \text{V}$$

$\therefore$ $$T_{em} = \frac{3\,(224)^2}{(50\pi)\,(2)\,(2.264)} = 202.684\ \text{Nm}$$

Substitution of the values of $T_{e.m} = 202.684$ Nm, $s = 0.05$, $\omega_s = 50\pi$ rad/sec and $J = 4.00$ kgm^2 in Eq. (5.66) gives the minimum time of acceleration as

$$t_{min} = \frac{(4.00)\,(50\pi)}{2\,(202.684)} \left[2\,(0.9975) \ln \frac{1}{0.05}\right]^{\frac{1}{2}} = 3.789\ \text{sec.}$$

(*b*) The rotor circuit resistance required to bring the motor to stop by plugging from any slip s is given by Eq. (5.67), *i.e.*,

$$R_2 = X \cdot s_{mT} = X \left[\frac{(2 - s)^2 - 1}{2 \ln (2 - s)}\right]^{\frac{1}{2}} = (2.364) \left[\frac{(1.95)^2 - 1}{2 \ln 1.95}\right]^{\frac{1}{2}}$$

$$= (2.364)\,(1.4485) = 3.4243\ \Omega.$$

From Eq. (5.68), the minimum time for braking is

$$t_{min} = \frac{(4.00)\,(50\pi)}{2\,(202.684)} \left[2\,\{(1.95)^2 - 1)\ln 1.95\}\right]^{\frac{1}{2}}$$

$$= \frac{(4.00)\,(50\pi)}{2\,(202.684)}\,[1.9347] = 2.999\ \text{sec.}$$

5.7.2 Accelerating Time

The accelerating time given by Eq. (5.59) is correct only if the motor is coupled with a pure inertia load and load torque T_L is zero. Electromagnetic torque developed by induction motor is a function of the slip or motor speed. Even if the load torque is constant, the accelerating torque (T_e–T_L) is not constant from standstill to rated speed. In other words, the accelerating torque is a non-linear function of the motor speed. For such drive problems, the accelerating time can be obtained graphically.

The dynamic equation for the motor-load combination is

$$T_e = T_L + J\,\frac{d\omega}{dt}$$

or

$$T_e - T_L = J\,\frac{d\omega}{dt} \qquad \text{...(5.71)}$$

In Eq. (5.71), the torque difference ($T_e - T_L$) as shown in Fig. 5.22 (*a*) is available for speeding up the motor and the load. From Eq. (5.71),

$$dt = J\,\frac{d\omega}{T_e - T_L} \quad \text{or} \quad t = J\int_{\omega_1}^{\omega_2} \frac{d\omega}{T_e - T_L}$$

Here t is the time required for the speed to change from ω_1 to ω_2. When initial speed $\omega_1 = 0$ and the final speed $\omega_2 = \omega_0$, then the accelerating time t is given by

$$t = J\int_{0}^{\omega_0} \frac{d\omega}{T_e - T_L} \qquad \text{...(5.72)}$$

The value of the integral in Eq. (5.72) is the area under the curve relating $\left(\dfrac{1}{T_e - T_L}\right)$ and ω. For a typical motor-load combination, whose speed-torque characteristics are shown in Fig. 5.22 (*a*), the reciprocal of the accelerating torque ($T_e - T_L$), *i.e.*, $1/(T_e - T_L)$ is plotted as a function of speed in Fig. 5.22 (*b*). The shaded area is the value of the integral in question and when multiplied by the total inertia J gives the accelerating time.

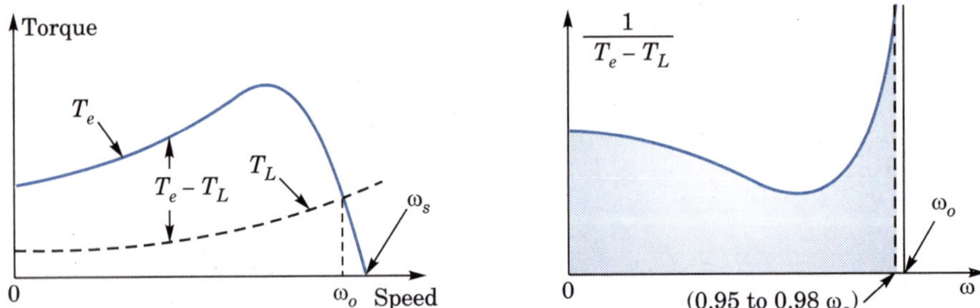

Fig. 5.22: (*a*) Typical motor and load torque curves (*b*) Plot of $1/(T_e - T_L)$ versus speed.

∴ Accelerating time = J (shaded area) (scale of x-axis) (scale of y-axis)

As speed approaches steady state value ω_0, ($T_e - T_L$) tends to zero and this would lead to an infinite accelerating time. This difficulty can, however, be overcome in practice by computing the time required to reach say 95 to 98% of the final steady speed. Any desired value of accelerating time can be attained by appropriately modifying the speed-torque characteristic of the induction motor.

Another method of computing the accelerating time is as under :

From Eq. (5.71), $$\Delta t = \frac{J}{T_e - T_L}\,.\,\Delta\omega \qquad \text{...(5.73)}$$

For known values of T_e and T_L at different values of speeds, the magnitude of $(T_e - T_L)$ is plotted against speed as shown in Fig. 5.23. Here $(T_e - T_L)$ is called the accelerating torque or dynamic torque of the drive.

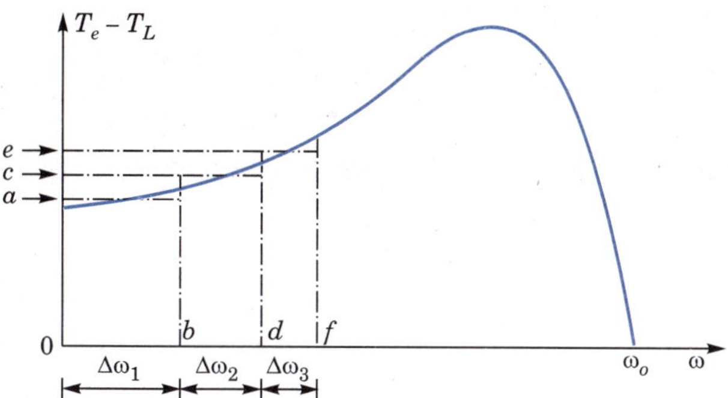

Fig. 5.23: Pertaining to the computation of accelerating time.

Now the dynamic-torque versus speed curve is divided into a series of well defined steps of speed as shown in Fig. 5.23. The width of each speed-step should be so chosen that dynamic-torque variation over each step is small. For each step, torque is considered constant and equal to the average value over a given increment in speed. For each step, Eq. (5.73), is applicable.

In Fig. 5.23, first step of speed is $\Delta\,\omega_1 = ob$. Average value of torque over speed increment ob is $(T_e - T_L) = oa$. Then the time for the first speed increment is

$$\Delta t_1 = J\,\frac{\Delta\,\omega_1}{T_e - T_L} = J\,\frac{ob}{oa}\ \text{sec}$$

For the second speed increment $\Delta\omega_2$,

$$\Delta t_2 = J\,\frac{\Delta\omega_2}{T_e - T_L} = J\,\frac{bd}{oc}\ \text{sec}$$

Similarly,

$$\Delta\,t_3 = J\,\frac{\Delta\omega_3}{T_e - T_L} = J\,\frac{df}{oe}\ \text{sec}$$

$$\Delta t_n = J\,\frac{\Delta\omega_n}{T_e - T_L}$$

$\therefore$ Total accelerating time

$$= (\Delta t_1 + \Delta t_2 + \Delta t_3 + \ldots + \Delta t_n)\ \text{sec.}$$

Example 5.13. *A 3-phase, 4-pole, 50 Hz, squirrel cage induction motor has the following torque-speed characteristic at rated voltage and frequency :*

Speed, rpm	*1500*	*1425*	*1350*	*1200*	*1125*	*1050*	*900*	*750*	*600*	*450*	*300*	*150*	*0*
Torque, Nm	*0*	*31.5*	*55*	*80*	*78*	*73.5*	*62*	*53*	*45*	*37.5*	*35*	*32*	*30*

This motor is coupled with a fan whose torque requirement is proportional to square of the speed. The fan takes a torque of 31.5 Nm at 1425 rpm. Determine the time taken by the fan to reach its rated speed when DOL starter is used. The combined moment of inertia of motor and load is 2 kgm^2.

Solution. The fan torque is 31.5 Nm at 1425 rpm. The torque required by the fan at other speeds is given by the relation

$$T_L = 31.5\left(\frac{\text{operating speed in rpm}}{1425}\right)^2 \text{Nm}$$

Fan torque at different speeds is computed and tabulated as under :

Speed, rpm	1425	1350	1200	1125	1050	900	750	600	450	300	150	0
T_L, *Nm*	31.5	28.3	22.3	19.6	17.1	12.6	8.7	5.6	3.1	1.6	0.4	0
$(T_e - T_L)$, *Nm*	0	26.7	57.7	58.4	56.4	49.4	44.3	39.4	34.4	33.4	31.6	30

From the above table, the magnitude of $(T_e - T_L)$ is plotted against speed in rpm in Fig. 5.24. Here ten steps are taken as shown.

For first step, oa = 31.6 Nm and ob = 300 rpm

$\therefore$ Time for first step, $\Delta t_1 = J\,\dfrac{ob}{oa} = 2.0\,\dfrac{300 \times 2\pi}{31.6 \times 60}$ sec

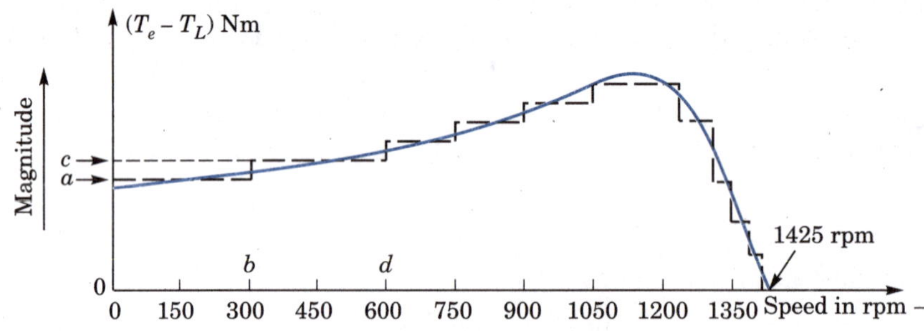

Fig. 5.24: Pertaining to Example 5.12.

For second step, oc = 36 Nm and bd = 300 rpm

$\therefore$ Time for second step, $\Delta t_2 = J\,\dfrac{bd}{oc} = 2.0\,\dfrac{300 \times 2\pi}{36 \times 60}$ sec

In this manner ; Δt_3, Δt_4, ... Δt_{10} are calculated.

$\therefore$ Total accelerating time, $t = \Delta t_1 + \Delta t_2 + ... + \Delta t_{10}$

or

$$t = 2.0\,\frac{2\pi}{60}\left[\frac{300}{31.8} + \frac{300}{36} + \frac{150}{42} + \frac{150}{46.8} + \frac{150}{53} + \frac{187.5}{57} + \frac{75}{47.5} + \frac{37.5}{30} + \frac{37.5}{20} + \frac{27.5}{10}\right]$$

$= 7.99581 \cong 8$ sec.

5.8 SPEED CONTROL OF INDUCTION MOTORS

Ordinarily, a plain induction motor runs at a substantially constant speed as the load is varied. Some industrial drives, however, require several different speeds or even continuously variable speeds. The induction motor, being the most rugged motor with almost negligible maintenance, has been and is even now the centre of interest for electrical engineers to make it run successfully at different discreet or continuously variable speeds.

The operating speed of a three-phase induction motor is given by $\dfrac{120f}{P}(1 - s)$. This expression reveals that speed of a 3-phase induction motor can be controlled by varying the supply frequency f, number of stator poles P or the slip s. The main important basic methods of speed control of a three-phase induction motor are as under.

(*a*) Pole-changing control
(*b*) Supply frequency control
(*c*) Line voltage control
(*d*) Rotor resistance or reactance control
(*e*) Rotor voltage injection control.

Method (*a*) is applicable to squirrel-cage induction motor (SCIM) only, methods (*b*) and (*c*) are applicable to both SCIMs and slip-ring induction motors (SRIMs). Methods (*d*) and (*e*) can be used for SRIMs only. It can also be stated that methods (*a*), (*b*) and (*c*) are carried out from stator side whereas methods (*d*) and (*e*) from the rotor side. These methods are now described one after the other.

(a) Pole-changing Control. A change in the number of poles, alters the synchronous speed $N_s \left(= \dfrac{120f}{P} \text{ rpm} \right)$ and therefore, the induction motor operating speed. Since the number of poles can be changed only by even numbers, the speed control is not continuous but a stepped one. This method can be effectively applied to SCIM only. It is because the cage winding adjusts itself automatically to any number of stator poles.

Variation in the number of poles in the stator winding of a three-phase induction motor can be achieved by three methods, namely : (*i*) use of multiple stator winding (*ii*) use of consequent-pole technique and (*iii*) use of pole-amplitude modulation.

I. Multiple Stator Winding. In this method, stator is provided with separate windings, each wound for different number of poles. For example, for a two-speed motor, a motor may have one 3-phase winding for 4 poles and the second 3-phase winding for 6 poles. For 50 Hz supply and a slip of 4%, 4-pole winding would give an operating speed of $\dfrac{120 \times 50}{4}$ $(1 - 0.04) = 1440$ rpm. But 6-pole winding would result in an operating speed of $\dfrac{120 \times 50}{6}$ $(1 - 0.04) = 960$ rpm. In this manner, two different operating speeds can be obtained. Three terminals from one winding are designated as low-speed terminals and the other three from the second winding as high-speed terminals. Change from one to another speed is made by a TPDT switch.

Only one winding is energized at a time. The idle winding is kept open-circuited so as to avoid the flow of circulating current and its heating.

II. Consequent-pole Technique. In this technique, stator is provided with one winding or with two independent windings. But, in each case, coils of each winding can be reconnected so as to produce stator poles in the ratio of 2 : 1. Here only one 3-phase stator winding is considered.

Fig. 5.25 (*a*) shows a single-layer winding for one phase of a 3-phase stator winding. It consists of two coils I and II. For coil I, terminals are *a*, *b* and for coil II, terminals are *c*, *d*. Current directions in the two coils are shown. If the terminals *b*, *d* are connected together, Fig. 5.25 (*a*) and (*b*), two coils become in series. With current in these two coils, two poles as shown in Fig. 5.25 (*a*), are produced giving a synchronous speed of 3000 rpm for a 50 Hz system. Figure on the right side of Fig. 5.25 (*a*) indicates current directions by crosses and dots in coils I and II. These two coils create 2 poles on stator as shown in Fig. 5.25 (*a*). If terminal a is connected to *d* and *b* to *c*, coils I and II become in parallel as shown in Fig. 5.25 (c). Since the direction of current in both coils in Fig. 5.25 (*c*) is the same as that in Fig. 5.25 (*b*), again two poles are created as shown in Fig. 5.25 (*a*). Thus, two-pole connection scheme of Fig. 5.25 (*a*) gives high-speed operation of 3000 rpm.

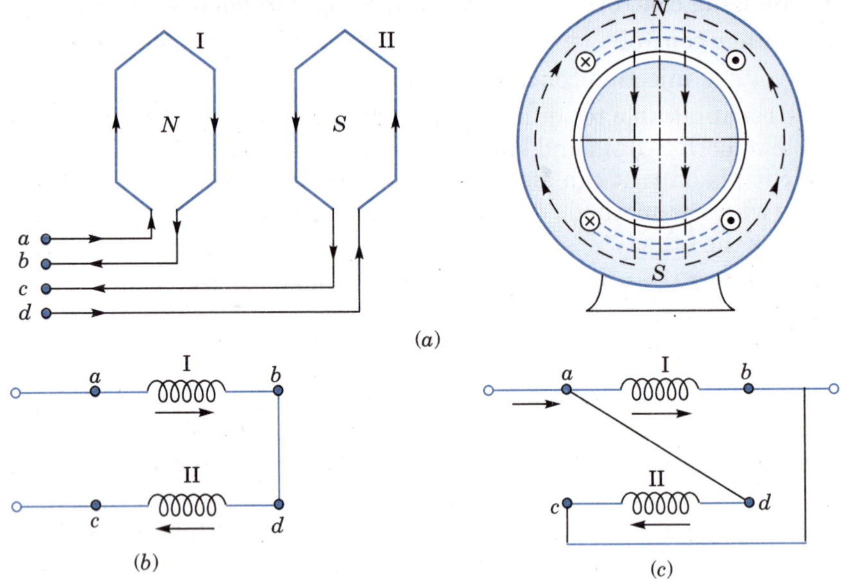

Fig. 5.25: High speed (*a*) production of two poles (*b*) coils in series and (*c*) coils in parallel.

If the direction of current in coil II is reversed as shown in Fig. 5.26 (*a*), two north poles are produced. Magnetic flux from these two north poles must complete their magnetic circuit, Fig. 5.26 (*a*). In doing so, two south poles are automatically created in the interpolar space as shown in the right-hand side of Fig. 5.26 (*a*). These induces poles are called *consequent-poles*. This four-pole connection of Fig. 5.26 (*a*) gives low speed operation at 1500 rpm.

As before, terminals *b*, *c* can be connected together, Fig. 5.26 (*b*), giving series connection of coils I and II. Also, terminals *a* to *c* and *b* to *d* can be connected together giving parallel connection of coils *I* and *II* as shown in Fig. 5.26 (*c*).

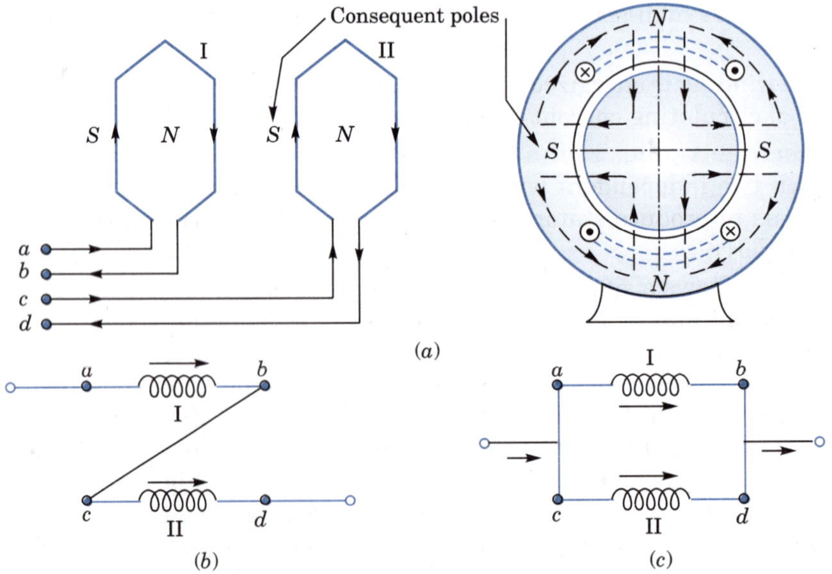

Fig. 5.26: Low speed (*a*) production of four poles (*b*) coils in series and (*c*) coils in parallel.

It may be concluded from Fig. 5.25 and 5.26 that

(*i*) if the current, in the two coils, flows *from a to b* and then *from d to c*, *high-speed* operation is obtained and

(*ii*) if the current, in the two coils, flows *from a to b* and then *from c to d*, *low-speed* operation is obtained.

The above basic principle can be extended to all the three phases of an induction motor. The connections amongst the three phases can be in delta or in star. Further, the coils of individual phases may be connected in series or parallel. With series or delta connections and series or parallel combination of coils, two-speed operation having constant-torque, constant-power or variable-torque characteristics can be obtained. For these connections shown in Figs. 5.27 to 5.29, let

$$V = \text{line to line voltage}$$
$$I = \text{rated current for each coil}$$
$$n_l, n_h = \text{efficiencies at LS and HS respectively.}$$
$$\cos\theta_l, \cos\theta_h = \text{power factors at LS and HS respectively.}$$

Here LS and HS stand for low-speed and high-speed operations respectively. Three-phase supply is applied to the three terminals *A*, *B* and *C*.

(*i*) Constant-torque connections. In Fig. 5.27 (*a*), the current flows *a* to *b* and then from *c* to *d*, therefore, series-delta connection results in *LS* operation. In Fig. 5.27 (*b*), the current flows from *a* to *b* and then from *d* to *c*, consequently this parallel-star connection results in HS operation. The term series-delta means that the two coils *a*, *b* and *c*, *d* are in series with the 3-phases in delta. Similarly, the term parallel-star means that the two coils *a*, *b* and *c*, *d* are in parallel with 3-phases in star.

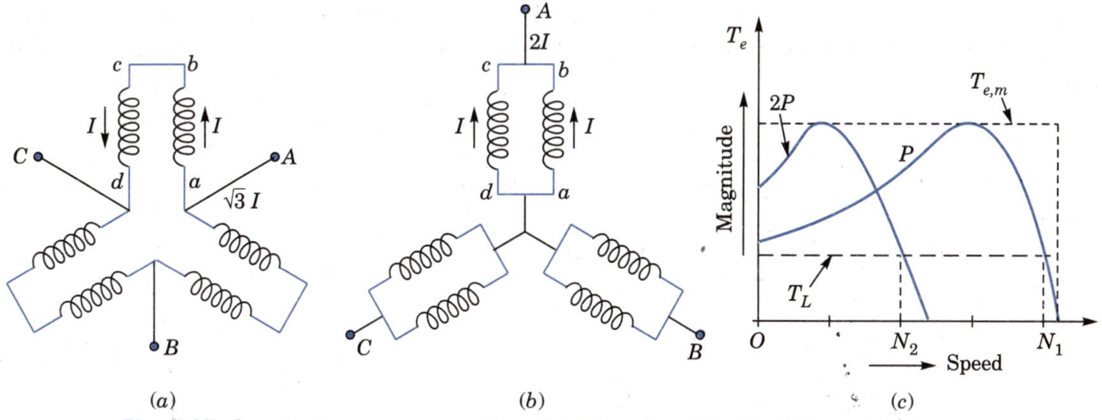

Fig. 5.27: Constant-torque connections (*a*) LS series delta (*b*) HS parallel star and (*c*) torque-speed characteristics.

In Fig. 5.27 (*a*), phase current is *I* and the line current is $\sqrt{3}I$. In Fig. 5.27 (*b*), line-current is 2*I*. From these two figures,

$$\frac{\text{LS output}}{\text{HS output}} = \frac{\sqrt{3}\,V(\sqrt{3}I)\,\eta_l \cos\theta_l}{\sqrt{3}V\,(2I)\,\eta_h \cos\theta_h} = 0.866\,\frac{\eta_l \cdot \cos\theta_l}{\eta_h \cdot \cos\theta_h}$$

With large number of poles, the magnetic leakage is increased and this gives poor power factor at low speeds. Also, efficiency of a *LS* speed machine is less. Thus the ratio $\dfrac{\eta_l \cdot \cos\theta_l}{\eta_h \cdot \cos\theta_h}$ is much less than unity. This ratio is of the order of 0.68, therefore

$$\frac{\text{LS output}}{\text{HS output}} = (0.866)\ (0.68) = 0.588$$

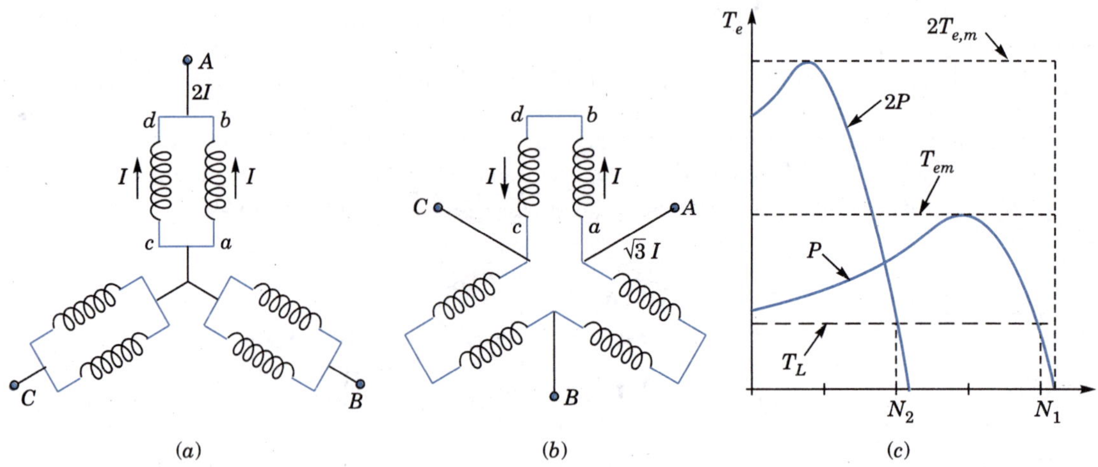

Fig. 5.28: Constant-power connections (*a*) LS parallel star (*b*) HS series delta and (*c*) torque-speed characteristics.

and
$$\frac{\text{LS torque}}{\text{HS torque}} = (0.588)\ \frac{\text{high speed}}{\text{low speed}} = (0.588)\ (2) = 1.176$$

Now, 1.176 is almost nearer to unity, thus giving approximately the same torque at both the speeds. Constant-torque drive is applicable to loads requiring the same torque at high as well as low speeds ; *e.g.* the loads in which friction is dominant like reciprocating pumps, air-compressors etc.

(ii) **Constant-power connections.** In Fig. 5.28 (*a*), the current flows from *a* to *b* and from *c* to *d* ; this results in *LS* parallel star scheme. In Fig. 5.28 (*b*), the current flows from *a* to *b* and then from *d* to *c* ; this results in *HS* series delta scheme. If may be seen from this fig. that

$$\frac{\text{LS output}}{\text{HS output}} = \frac{\sqrt{3}\ V\ (2I)\ \eta_l \cdot \cos\theta_l}{\sqrt{3}\ V\ (\sqrt{3}I)\ \eta_h \cdot \cos\theta_h} = \frac{2}{\sqrt{3}}\ (0.68) = 0.786.$$

If 0.786 is assumed close enough to unity, then this connection can be termed as a constant-power drive.

Also,
$$\frac{\text{LS torque}}{\text{HS torque}} = 0.786\ \frac{\text{high speed}}{\text{low speed}} = 0.786\ (2) = 1.572.$$

The torque at LS is approximately twice (if 1.572 is assumed close enough to 2) of that on HS. This scheme is used for machine tools, winches etc., *i.e.,* for the drives requiring constant power.

(iii) **Variable-torque connections.** Fig. 5.29 gives the connection scheme for obtaining variable-torque induction motor. An examination of this fig. shows that

$$\frac{\text{LS output}}{\text{HS output}} = \frac{\sqrt{3}\ V\ (I)\ \eta_l \cdot \cos\theta_l}{\sqrt{3}\ V\ (2I)\ \eta_h \cdot \cos\theta_h} = (0.5)(0.68) = 0.34$$

and
$$\frac{\text{LS torque}}{\text{HS torque}} = 0.34 \times \frac{\text{High speed}}{\text{Low speed}} = 0.34 \times 2 = 0.68$$

Since the motor torque at LS is much different from that at high speed, the scheme of connections shown in Fig. 5.29 can be designated as a variable-torque drive. This scheme is used to drive loads whose maximum torque requirement is less at low speeds and more at high speeds. A few example of such loads are fans, blowers, centrifugal pumps etc.

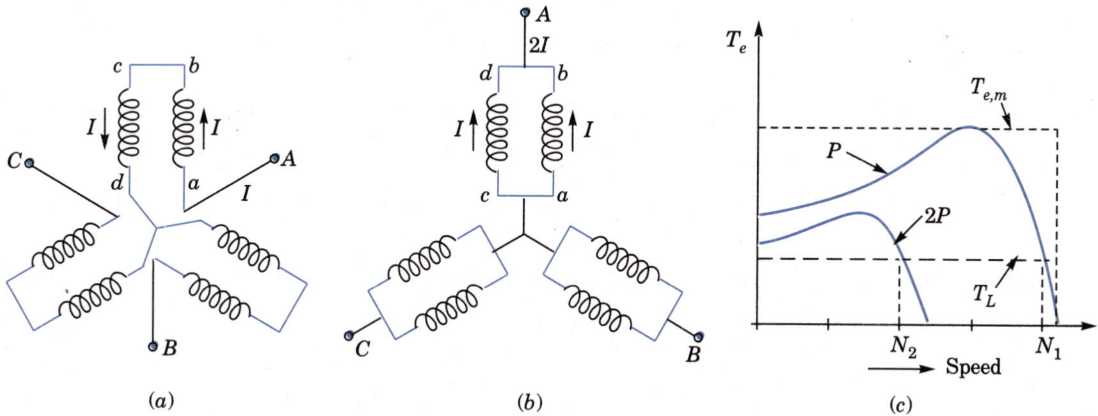

Fig. 5.29: Variable-torque connections (*a*) LS series star (*b*) HS parallel star and (*c*) torque-speed characteristics.

For comparison purposes, torque-speed curves, for the three types of connection schemes discussed above, are illustrated in Fig. 5.30. Here *OA* is the synchronous speed for lower number of poles and *OB* for the higher number of poles. This fig. shows that the electromagnetic torque for lower operating speed is the highest for constant power drive. In view of this, constant-power drive is the largest in physical size and is, therefore, the most expensive arrangement.

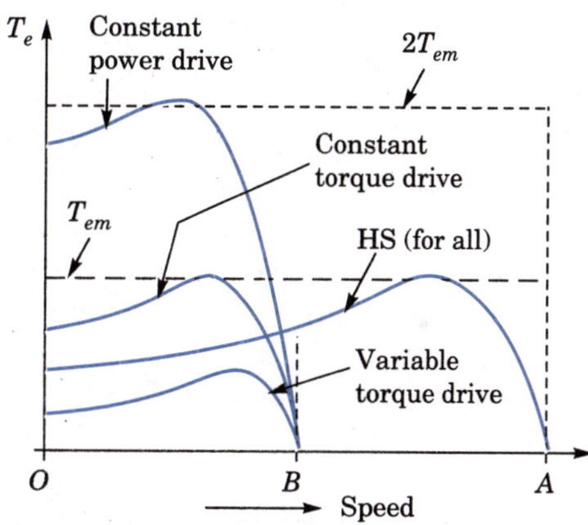

Fig. 5.30: Torque-speed curves for a pole-changing 3-phase induction motor.

(iv) **Pole-amplitude Modulation.** In consequent-pole technique, the speed control of induction motor is possible in the ratio 2:1. But in pole-amplitude modulation technique, speed control in the ratio other than 2:1 is possible.

For understanding pole-amplitude modulation, consider sinusoidally distributed mmf waves produced by three-phase stator winding.

$$\left.\begin{aligned} &\text{For phase } a, \quad && F_a = F_m \sin \frac{P.\theta}{2} \\ &\text{For phase } b, \quad && F_b = F_m \sin \left(\frac{P.\theta}{2} - \frac{2\pi}{3}\right) \\ &\text{For phase } c, \quad && F_c = F_m \sin \left(\frac{P.\theta}{2} - \frac{4\pi}{3}\right) \end{aligned}\right\} \quad ...(5.74)$$

where, P = number of stator poles and θ is the mechanical angle.

Let the three-phase mmfs of Eq. (5.74) be modulated by another three-phase sinusoidal mmf wave having P_m poles.

Modulating mmf wave of phase a,

$$\left.\begin{aligned} F_{ma} &= F \sin \frac{P_m . \theta}{2} \\ F_{mb} &= F \sin \left(\frac{P_m . \theta}{2} - \frac{2\pi}{3}\right) \\ \text{and} \quad F_{mc} &= F \sin \left(\frac{P_m . \theta}{2} - \frac{4\pi}{3}\right) \end{aligned}\right\} \quad ...(5.75)$$

Equations of the modulated mmf waves are obtained by the product of appropriate terms in Eqs. (5.74) and (5.75). Therefore, modulated mmf wave F_a' of phase 'a' is given by

$$F_a' = F_a \times F_{ma} = F_m F \sin \frac{P . \theta}{2} . \sin \frac{P_m . \theta}{2}$$

But $\quad \sin A \sin B = \frac{1}{2}[\cos (A - B) - \cos (A + B)]$

$$\left.\begin{aligned} \therefore \quad F_a' &= \frac{F_m F}{2}\left[\cos\left(\frac{P - P_m}{2}\right)\theta - \cos\left(\frac{P + P_m}{2}\right)\theta\right] \\ \text{Similarly,} \quad F_b' &= \frac{F_m F}{2}\left[\cos\left(\frac{P - P_m}{2}\right)\theta - \cos\left\{\left(\frac{P + P_m}{2}\right)\theta + \frac{2\pi}{3}\right\}\right] \\ \text{and} \quad F_c' &= \frac{F_m F}{2}\left[\cos\left(\frac{P - P_m}{2}\right)\theta - \cos\left\{\left(\frac{P + P_m}{2}\right)\theta + \frac{4\pi}{3}\right\}\right] \end{aligned}\right\} \quad ...(5.76)$$

It is seen from Eq. (5.76) that first term is co-phasol in all the three phases, therefore, net three-phase mmf produced by first terms having $(P - P_m)$ number of poles would be zero.

The second terms of Eq. (5.76) are displaced from each other by 120°, therefore, net mmf produced by $(P + P_m)$ *poles* would produce a field rotating in opposite direction to that produced by the unmodulated mmf wave of Eq. (5.74).

Now let the three-phase modulating mmf wave, different from Eq. (5.75), be given by

$$\left.\begin{aligned} F_{ma} &= F \sin \frac{P_m . \theta}{2} \\ F_{mb} &= F \sin \left(\frac{P_m . \theta}{2} + \frac{2\pi}{3}\right) \\ \text{and} \quad F_{mc} &= F \sin \left(\frac{P_m . \theta}{2} + \frac{4\pi}{3}\right) \end{aligned}\right\} \quad ...(5.77)$$

Now the modulated mmf waves for each phase, as before, would be given by

$$F_a' = F_a \times F_{ma} = \frac{F . F_m}{2}\left[\cos\left(\frac{P - P_m}{2}\right)\theta - \cos\left(\frac{P + P_m}{2}\right)\theta\right] \quad ...(5.78a)$$

$$F_b' = F_m \sin\left(\frac{P\theta}{2} - \frac{2\pi}{3}\right) F . \sin\left(\frac{P_m . \theta}{2} + \frac{2\pi}{3}\right)$$

$$= \frac{FF_m}{2}\left[\cos\left\{\left(\frac{P - P_m}{2}\right)\theta - \frac{4\pi}{3}\right\} - \cos\left(\frac{P + P_m}{2}\right)\theta\right] \quad ...(5.78b)$$

Similarly, $\quad F_c' = \frac{FF_m}{2}\left[\cos\left\{\left(\frac{P - P_m}{2}\right)\theta - \frac{2\pi}{3}\right\} - \cos\left(\frac{P + P_m}{2}\right)\theta\right] \quad ...(5.78c)$

Eqs. (5.78) show that the second terms are co-phasol, therefore net three-phase mmf produced by second terms having $(P + P_m)$ number of poles would be zero. The first terms of Eq. (5.78*a*) are displaced from each other by 120°; therefore, these would produce net mmf of $(P - P_m)$ number of poles rotating at synchronous speed in a direction opposite to that produced by the unmodulated mmf wave of Eq. (5.74).

It is seen from above that, depending upon the modulating mmf wave, the modulated mmf wave is equivalent to two rotating mmf waves, one having $(P - P_m)$ number of poles and the other having $(P + P_m)$ number of poles.

The modulation can be achieved by dividing each phase winding into P_m groups with alternate groups reverse connected.

Fig. 5.31 (*a*) shows $P = 8$ poles of one phase winding. Rectangular modulating poles are $P_m = 2$, Fig. 5.31 (*b*). These are two methods of achieving modulation.

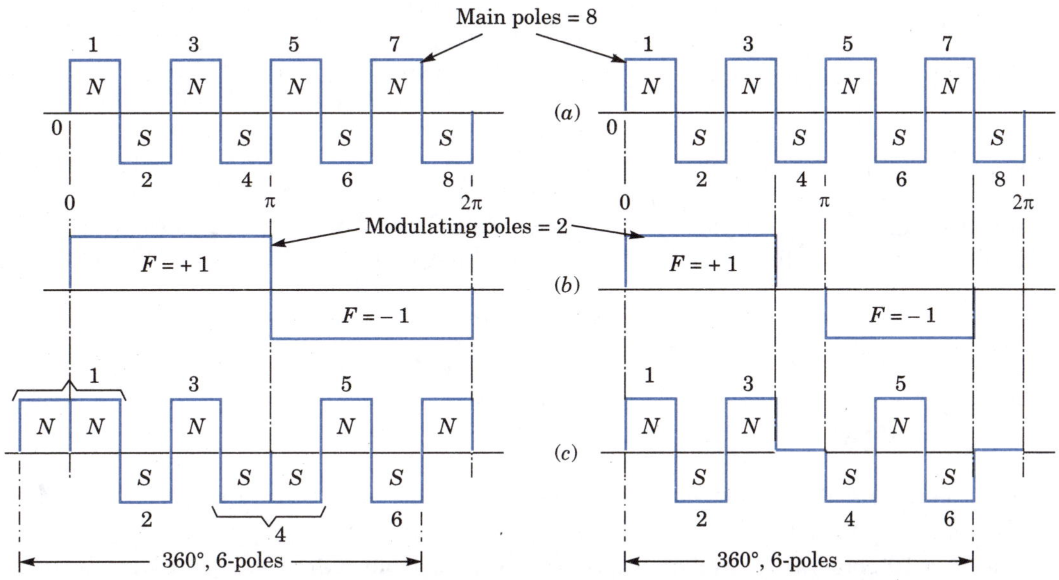

Fig. 5.31: Each phase has 8-pole winding with 2-pole rectangular modulation.

(*i*) In one method, the second half of each phase winding is reversed with respect to the first half, see left of Fig. 5.31 (*b*). Here $F = -1$ means reverse connection of pole groups 5, 6, 7 and 8. Multiplication of the original 8-pole wave with the modulating wave having $P_m = 2$ poles gives the resultant modulated wave as shown in the left of Fig. 5.31 (*c*). Two adjacent poles constitute one pole, there are therefore $P_1 = P - P_m = 6$ poles which are clearly visible, but $P_2 = P + P_m = 10$ poles cannot be made evident.

(*ii*) In the second method, a portion from each half of modulating wave is first omitted and then the second half is reversed as shown in the right of Fig. 5.31 (*b*). Multiplication of $P = 8$-pole wave with modulating wave gives right of Fig. 5.31 (*c*). Here also $P_1 = 6$ poles are evident but $P_2 = 10$ poles are not obvious. For this purpose, Eq. (5.76) or Eq. (5.78) has to be used. As stated above, this motor can run with original 8 poles and modulated 10 poles, see Eq. (5.76).

For basic P-pole three-phase winding, let the angle between place axes be $r\left(\frac{2\pi}{3}\right)$ where r is an integer but not a multiple of 3.

Thus, for P poles, electrical spaces angle $= r\left(\frac{2\pi}{3}\right)$ rad and for $(P \pm P_m)$ modulated poles, electrical space angle

$$= \left(\frac{P \pm P_m}{P}\right) r.\left(\frac{2\pi}{3}\right) \quad \text{...(5.79)}$$

Out of the two modulated pole numbers $(P + P_m)$ or $(P - P_m)$, one of the pole numbers must be suppressed. This is possible if electrical phase spacing for either $(P + P_m)$ poles or $(P - P_m)$ poles, is multiple of 2π rad, *i.e.* $2\pi m$ rad where $m = 0, 1, 2, 3, 4, ...$ From Eq. (5.79), we get

$$\frac{P \pm P_m}{P} \times r \times \frac{2\pi}{3} = 2\pi m \quad \text{or} \quad \frac{m}{r} = \frac{1}{3}\left(1 \pm \frac{P_m}{P}\right) \quad \text{...(5.80)}$$

For suppressing pole number $P_1 = P - P_m$, relation $\frac{m}{r} = \frac{1}{3}\left(1 - \frac{P_m}{P}\right)$ must be satisfied and for suppressing pole number $P_2 = P + P_m$, relation $\frac{m}{r} = \frac{1}{3}\left(1 + \frac{P_m}{P}\right)$ must hold good.

For example, for main poles $P = 8$, let the number of modulating poles be $P_m = 2$ as shown in Fig. 5.31. Therefore, number of modulated poles are $P_1 = P - P_m = 8 - 2 = 6$ or $P_2 = P + P_m = 8 + 2 = 10$.

For $P_1 = 6$ poles, $\quad \frac{1}{3}\left(1 - \frac{2}{8}\right) = \frac{1}{4} = \frac{m}{r}$ and

For $P_2 = 10$ poles, $\quad \frac{1}{3}\left(1 + \frac{2}{8}\right) = \frac{5}{12} = \frac{m}{r}$

It is seen from above that for $P_1 = 6$ poles, $m = 1$ and $r = 4$. Since r is not a multiple of 3, poles $P_1 = 6$ get suppressed.

For $P_2 = 10$ poles, $m = 5$ and $r = 12$. Since r is a multiple of 3, poles $P_2 = 10$ are developed. Therefore, 8-pole motor is modulated to 10 poles and can therefore, run at two different speed of $\frac{120 \times 50}{8} = 750$ rpm and $\frac{120 \times 50}{10} = 600$ rpm.

With pole-amplitude modulation, two speeds need not be in the ratio of 2 : 1. Since only one winding is used for the stator for pole-amplitude modulation, size and cost of induction motor does not increase.

Example 5.14. *A three-phase, 50 Hz induction motor, wound for pole-amplitude modulation, has 20 main poles and 4 modulating poles. Find the possible motor speeds.*

Solution. Here $P = 20$ and $P_m = 4$

For $\quad P_1 = P - P_m = 20 - 4 = 16$, $\frac{m}{r} = \frac{1}{3}\left(1 - \frac{4}{20}\right) = \frac{4}{15}$. $\quad \therefore \quad m = 4$ and $r = 15$

For $\quad P_2 = P + P_m = 20 + 4 = 24$, $\frac{m}{r} = \frac{1}{3}\left(1 + \frac{4}{20}\right) = \frac{2}{5}$. $\quad \therefore \quad m = 2$ and $r = 5$

For $P_2 = 24$, $m = 2$ and $r = 5$. Since r is not a multiple of 3 , poles $P_2 = 24$ get suppressed. For $P_1 = 16$, $m = 4$ and $r = 15$. Since r is a multiple of 3, poles $P_1 = 16$ can develop. Therefore, the motor can run with original poles $P = 20$ and modulated poles $P_1 = 16$.

$$\therefore \quad \text{Motor speed} \quad (P = 20) \quad = \frac{120 \times 50}{20} = 300 \text{ rpm}$$

$$\text{Other motor speed } (P_1 = 16) \quad = \frac{120 \times 50}{16} = 375 \text{ rpm}$$

(a) Supply-Frequency Control. A change in the supply frequency alters the synchronous speed of the induction motor and thus its operating speed. Its earlier application was in the electrically propelled ships, where a change in the speed of the turbine (prime-mover) would alter both the voltage and frequency of the supply given to induction motors. At present, static frequency changers, making use of thyristors, are becoming more common for the speed control of three-phase induction motors.

Solid-state converters are of two types : (*a*) rectifier-inverted type and (*b*) cyclo-converter-type. In the former type, the supply frequency input is first converted into d.c. by using diode or thyristor bridge. The direct voltage, after being filtered, is then converted into desired frequency a.c. output using static inverters. In the latter type, *i.e.*, in a cycloconverter, supply frequency input is directly converted into the desired frequency output. In cycloconverter type, the power is handled once, it is, therefore, more efficient than the rectifier-inverter type in which power is handled twice. The only drawback of the cycloconverter type is that its output frequency range is from zero to about one-half of the supply frequency. For the rectifier-inverter (or d.c. link inverter) type, a wide frequency range from zero to about 2 to 3 kHz can be obtained.

The starting torque, from Eq. (5.27), is

$$T_{e.st} = \frac{m}{2\pi n_s} \cdot \frac{V_e^2}{(R_e + r_2)^2 + (X_e + x_2)^2} \cdot r_2 \qquad \text{...(5.81)}$$

The reactance $(X_e + x_2)$ is usually much greater than $(R_e + r_2)$. Therefore, if $(R_e + r_2)$ is ignored, then Eq. (5.81) becomes

$$T_{e.st} = \frac{m}{2\pi} \cdot \frac{P}{2f} \cdot \frac{V_e^2}{(2\pi f)^2 (L_e + l_2)^2} \cdot r_2$$

$$= \frac{mP}{16\pi^3} \cdot \left(\frac{V_e}{f}\right)^2 \frac{1}{f} \cdot \frac{1}{(L_e + l_2)^2} \cdot r_2 \qquad \text{...(5.82)}$$

The maximum torque, from Eq. (5.30), is

$$T_{em} = \frac{m}{2\pi n_s} \cdot \frac{V_e^2}{2[R_e + \sqrt{R_e^2 + X^2}]} \qquad \text{...(5.82A)}$$

If stator resistance is neglected, then R_e is zero and Eq. (5.82A) becomes

$$T_{e.m} = \frac{m}{2\pi} \cdot \frac{P}{2f} \cdot \frac{V_e^2}{2(2\pi f)(L_e + l_2)}$$

$$= \frac{mP}{16\pi^2} \cdot \left(\frac{V_e}{f}\right)^2 \cdot \frac{1}{L_e + l_2} \qquad \text{...(5.83)}$$

Eq. (5.82) shows that if supply voltage V_1 or V_e is kept constant, then the starting torque is inversely proportional to f^3. Eq. (5.83) shows that with constant V_1 or V_e, the maximum torque is inversely proportional to f^2. The torque-speed curves, when only frequency f is varied with constant V_1, are illustrated in Fig. 5.32 (*a*). With reduction in frequency for constant V_1, the air-gap flux increases and the induction-motor magnetic circuit gets saturated. As a result, core losses in induction motor increase leading to more temperature rise which is highly undesirable. In view of this, induction motor speed control with constant supply voltage and variable frequency is rarely used in practice.

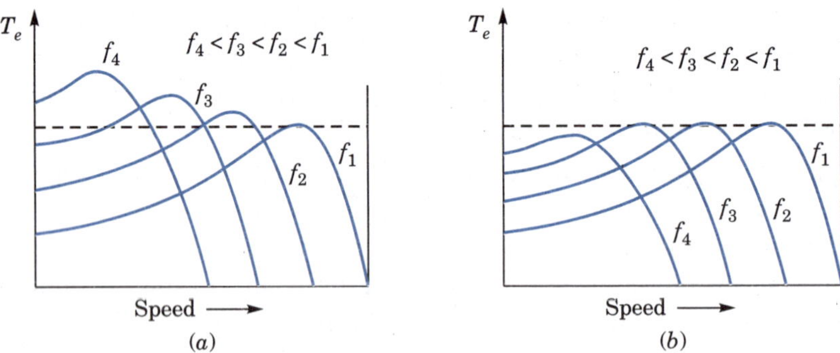

Fig. 5.32: Induction motor torque-speed curves (*a*) with variable frequency and constant V_1 and (*b*) with constant ratio V_1/f.

In case the ratio V_1/f or V_e/f is kept constant, then Eq. (5.82) reveals that starting torque is inversely proportional to f, but Eq. (5.83) shows that maximum torque remains unaltered. However, at lower values of frequencies, the effect of stator resistances cannot be neglected as compared to the reactances. This has the effect of reducing the magnitude of maximum torque at lower frequencies as shown in Fig. 5.32 (*b*). An examination of *Example 5.4* verifies the conclusions drawn here.

Torque-speed characteristics with constant V_1/f are more desirable, because this results in constant flux and saturation does not occur.

(*b*) Line Voltage Control. The speed of a 3-phase induction motor can be controlled by varying its supply voltage. Fig. 5.11 shows that torque developed in a 3-phase induction motor is proportional to square of the supply voltage. Eq. (5.43) shows that the slip at which maximum torque occurs does not depend on the supply voltage. Also note that variation of the supply voltage does not alter the motor synchronous speed. Based on these facts, the torque-speed characteristics of a 3-phase induction motor are drawn in Fig. 5.33 (*a*) for supply voltage V_1 and $V_1/2$. In this figure is also shown torque speed characteristic T_L for a fan-type load. The intersection of motor and load torque curves gives the two operating speeds n_1 for voltage V_1 and n_2 for voltage $V_1/2$. This method of speed control is not so important because of the following disadvantages.

(*i*) Magnetic saturation does not allow speed control above rated voltage.

(*ii*) Range of speed control is limited.

(*iii*) Low operating efficiency.

(*iv*) Poor speed regulation with change in load.

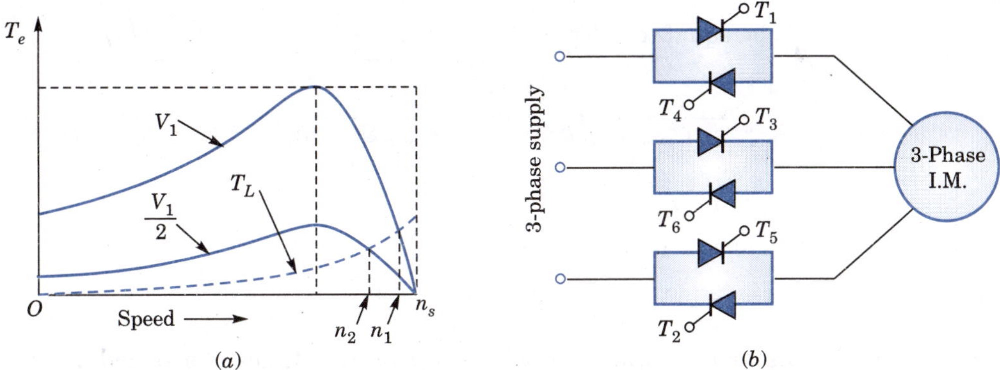

Fig. 5.33: (*a*) Torque-speed characteristics under stator voltage control and (*b*) 3-phase ac voltage controller feeding a 3-phase induction motor.

For stator voltage control, a 3-phase ac voltage controller is usually employed. Fig. 5.33 (*b*) shows this controller feeding a 3-phase induction motor. By controlling the firing angle of thyristors connected in antiparallel in each phase, the rms value of stator voltage is regulated. As a consequence, the motor torque and speed of motor is controlled. Since the waveform of the voltage applied to stator winding does not remain sinusoidal, there are increased losses in the induction motor and this method is, therefore, limited to small induction motors only.

(*c*) Rotor Resistance or Reactance Control. Here first the rotor-resistance control and then the rotor-reactance control are discussed.

(*i*) Rotor-resistance control. Under normal operating conditions, the torque-slip relation for small values of slips, as given by Eq. (5.32), is

$$s = \frac{T_e}{K_t} \cdot r_2 \qquad \text{...(5.32)}$$

Eq. (5.32) shows that for a constant torque, the slip is directly proportional to the rotor resistance. If resistance in the rotor circuit is increased, the slip increases (*i.e.* speed decreases) and vice-versa. This method is applicable to wound-rotor induction motors. Fig. 5.8 shows clearly how the speed varies with variable rotor resistance. It is seen from this figure that (*i*) the maximum torque remains constant and does not depend on rotor circuit resistance (*ii*) slip, at which maximum torque occurs, increases with rotor circuit resistance (*iii*) starting torque rises with rotor circuit resistance (*iv*) synchronous speed remains the same and (*v*) speed below rated speed can only be obtained.

The disadvantages of this method are (*i*) speeds below rated speed can only be obtained (*ii*) reduced efficiency at low speeds due to more rotor circuit resistance and (*iii*) speed regulation is very poor. This method of speed control is used when drop in speed is required only for a short time as for example in overhead cranes, in load equalization etc.

A simple analysis for rotor-resistance control method can be carried out with the help of Eq. (5.36), which is repeated here as,

$$\frac{T_e}{T_{em}} = \frac{2}{\dfrac{s}{s_{mT}} + \dfrac{s_{mT}}{s}}$$

Let the ratio, $\frac{T_{em}}{T_e}$ be equal to k. Then,

$$\frac{2}{\frac{s}{s_{mT}} + \frac{s_{mT}}{s}} = \frac{1}{k} \quad \text{or} \quad \frac{2 . s . s_{mT}}{s_{mT}^2 + s^2} = \frac{1}{k}$$

or,
$$s_{mT}^2 - 2s_{mT} . sk + s^2 = 0$$

This equation is quadratic in s_{mT}.

$$\therefore \qquad s_{mT} = \frac{2sk \pm \sqrt{4s^2k^2 - 4s^2}}{2} = s\ [k \pm \sqrt{k^2 - 1}] \qquad \text{...(5.84A)}$$

With negligible stator resistance and with external resistance R inserted in the rotor circuit, s_{mT} from Eq. (5.29) is $s_{mT} = \frac{R_2}{X}$

where, $R_2 = r_2$ + external resistance R and $X = x_2 + X_e$

$$\therefore \quad R_2 = s.X\ [k \pm \sqrt{k^2 - 1}] \qquad \text{...(5.85)}$$

Eq. (5.85) gives two values of R_2 of which only one value is feasible whereas the other is not practicable. If the torque-slip relation is a straight line as it is in the normal operating region, then electromagnetic torque relation may be used.

$$T_e = \frac{K_t}{r_2} . s = \frac{K_1 . V_1^2}{r_2} . s$$

For rotor resistance r_2, let the operating slip be s_1 and the load torque be T_{L1}. Then

$$T_{L1} = \frac{K_1 . V_1^2}{r_2} . s_1$$

For rotor resistance R_2 (= r_2 + external resistance) and load torque T_{L2}, let the operating slip be s_2. Then the ratio of T_{L1} and T_{L2} gives

$$\frac{T_{L1}}{T_{L2}} = \frac{s_1}{r_2} . \frac{R_2}{s_2}$$

or
$$R_2 = r_2 \left[\frac{s_2}{s_1}\right]\left[\frac{T_{L1}}{T_{L2}}\right] \qquad \text{...(5.86)}$$

***(ii)* Reactance control.** Reactance variation for the speed control of three-phase induction motors is not much used in industry. However, the effect of reactance variation can be examined as under.

The developed torque is

$$T_e = \frac{m}{2\pi n_s} . \frac{V_e^2}{\left(R_e + \frac{r_2}{s}\right)^2 + (x_2 + X_e)^2} \times \frac{r_2}{s}$$

where, $X_e = \frac{x_1 . X_m}{x_1 + X_m}$

From Eq. (5.29), the slip at maximum torque is

$$s_{mT} = \frac{r_2}{\sqrt{R_e^2 + (X_2 + X_e)^2}}$$

From above, $$T_e = \frac{3}{2\pi n_s} \cdot \frac{V_e^2}{\left[\left(R_e + \frac{r_2}{s}\right)^2 + X^2\right]} \cdot \frac{r_2}{s} \quad ...(5.86A)$$

where, $X = x_2 + \dfrac{x_1 \,.\, X_m}{x_1 + X_m}$

From Eq. (5.29), the slip at maximum torque is

$$s_{mT} = \frac{r_2}{\sqrt{R_e^2 + X^2}} \quad ...(5.86B)$$

It is seen from Eq. (5.86A) that if the equivalent reactance X of the motor is increased by inserting external reactance in the (*i*) stator circuit or (*ii*) rotor circuit or (*iii*) both, the starting and maximum torques would decrease. At the same time, Eq. (5.86B) shows that the slip at which maximum torque occurs decreases. The torque-speed curves, as affected by the variation of equivalent reactance X are shown in Fig. 5.34. The intersection of load torque and motor torque curves gives the operating speeds n_1, n_2 and n_3. It is observed that (*i*) speeds below rated speed can only be obtained and (*ii*) the range of speed control is very narrow. In order to achieve better speed control characteristics below synchronous speed, a saturable reactor in the rotor circuit of SRIM can be used. But this will not be discussed here.

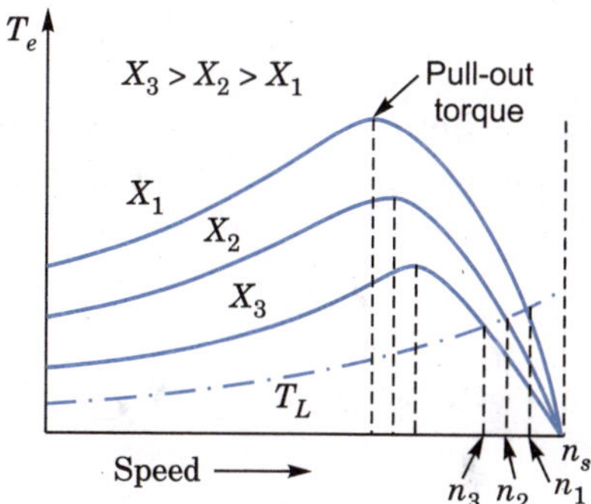

Fig. 5.34: Induction motor characteristics with variable equivalent reactance X.

(d) Rotor slip-power control. It has already been discussed that a slip-ring induction motor can be operated at reduced speeds by inserting suitable external resistances in its rotor circuit. In this method, rotor power at slip frequency is lost as heat in external resistances. This leads to reduced operating efficiency. A better method of speed control of SRIM is based on the efficient use of slip-power through suitable sip-power converters. In this section, the effective use of slip-frequency-power by cascading two induction motors is considered. Then, the rotor voltage injection for recovering the slip-power is discussed for the speed control of SRIM.

(i) Cascading of induction motors. This scheme is sometimes called tandem control and, though not used now-a-days, is discussed here merely for its historical importance.

In speed control by cascading of two induction motors, the slip power of main induction motor is effectively utilized by feeding it to the auxiliary induction motor which converts it into mechanical power and then adds to the main motor output.

Two induction machines are coupled electrically in cascade and also mechanically, either direct or through gears or belts. The stator of main induction motor is connected to supply lines and its rotor exports slip-power at a frequency $f_2 = s_1 f_1$ to the stator of the second motor (squirrel-cage or wound-rotor type) as shown in Fig. 5.35 (*a*). The arrangement of Fig. 5.35 (*b*) is more suited ; since with this scheme, the slip rings of both the motors can be dispensed with and the power can flow from motor 1 to motor 2 along the shaft or through a hollow shaft.

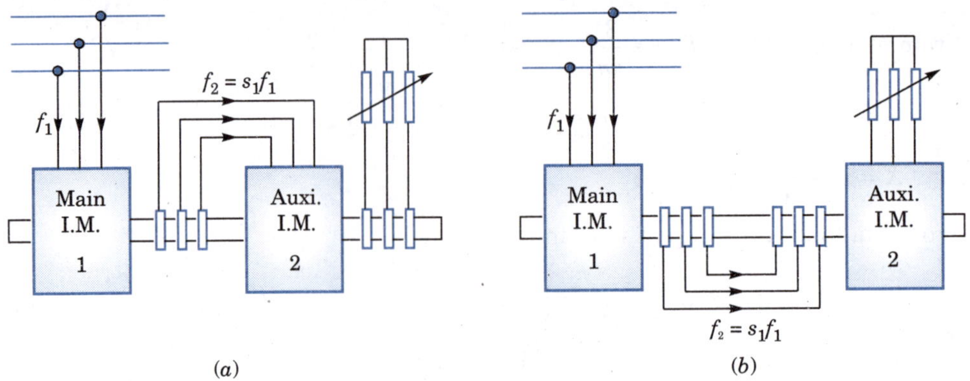

Fig. 5.35: Cascade connections.

Let P_1, P_2 and s_1, s_2 be the number of poles and slips respectively for main and auxiliary induction motors. Then, for the main motor, the synchronous speed is given by

$$= \frac{120\, f_1}{P_1}$$

and its actual speed $= n_{r1} = \dfrac{120\, f_1}{P_1}\,(1 - s_1).$

For the auxiliary motor, the synchronous speed is $\dfrac{120\, f_2}{P_2}$

and its actual speed $= n_{r2} = \dfrac{120\, s_1\, f_1}{P_2}\,(1 - s_2).$

Neglecting the small value of the slip s_2 and taking the motors to be directly coupled,

$$\frac{n_{r1}}{n_{r2}} = 1 = \frac{\dfrac{120\, f_1}{P_1}(1 - s_1)}{\dfrac{120\, f_1\, s_1}{P_2}} = \frac{(1 - s_1)\, P_2}{s_1\, P_1} \quad \text{or} \quad s_1 = \frac{P_2}{P_1 + P_2}$$

The actual speed of the main motor and hence of the cascaded arrangement is

$$n_r = \frac{120\, f_1}{P_1}\,(1 - s_1) = \frac{120\, f_1}{P_1}\left(1 - \frac{P_2}{P_1 + P_2}\right) = \frac{120\, f_1}{P_1 + P_2}.$$

In other worlds, the speed of the cascaded set is same as that of a single motor with $(P_1 + P_2)$ poles. The torques of the two motors are in the same direction and the scheme is called cumulatively cascaded.

If the phase sequence of the voltages applied to second motor is changed by interchanging any of the two leads, then auxiliary motor develops torque in a direction opposite to that developed by the main motor. This scheme is then called a differentially cascaded arrangement. Under these conditions,

$$n_{r3} = -\frac{120\, f_1 s_1}{P_2}\,(1 - s_3) = \frac{120\, f_1}{P_1}\,(1 - s_1)$$

If s_3 is neglected again, then $s_1 = \dfrac{P_2}{P_2 - P_1}$

The actual speed of the cascaded arrangement is

$$n_r = \frac{120 f_1}{P_1}(1 - s_1) = \frac{120 f_1}{P_1}\left[1 - \frac{P_2}{P_2 - P_1}\right] = \frac{120 f_1}{P_1 - P_2}$$

and this speed is possible only if $P_1 \neq P_2$.

Let the electrical power taken from the supply by the main motor stator be P.

Then, assuming no losses, mechanical power developed by first motor.

$$= (1 - s_1)\, P = \left[\frac{P_1}{P_2 + P_1}\right] . P$$

The slip power of the first motor, *i.e.* s_1P, is fed into the stator of the auxiliary motor, which develops a mechanical output power equal to $(1 - s_2)\, s_1P$. If s_2 is neglected, as done earlier, then

$$\text{Mechanical power developed by auxiliary motor} = s_1P = \left(\frac{P_2}{P_1 + P_2}\right)P.$$

$$\therefore \quad \frac{\text{Mech. power developed by main I.M.}}{\text{Mech. power developed by auxiliary I.M.}} = \frac{(1 - s_1)\, P}{s_1P} = \frac{P_{main}}{P_{aux}}$$

i.e.,

$$\frac{P_{main}}{P_{aux}} = \frac{1 - s_1}{s_1} = \frac{P_1}{P_2}$$

This shows that the mechanical power developed by the two machines are directly proportional to their number of poles.

Consider two induction motors with 6 poles and 4 poles connected in cascade. At 50 Hz supply system, the various possible speeds are 3000 rpm (differentially cascade, $P_{main} - P_{aux}$) ; 1500 rpm (main motor alone, P_{main}) ; 1000 rpm (auxiliary motor alone, P_{aux}) and 600 rpm (cumulatively cascaded, $P_{main} + P_{aux}$).

If $P_1 = P_2$ in the differential cascade, output is zero and no rotation takes place.

For stable operation, mechanical coupling is essential.

The disadvantages of this scheme are (*i*) a second induction motor is required ; (*ii*) the scheme works at a poor power factor since the magnetizing current for both machines is drawn from the supply mains.

However, the arrangement is suitable for regenerative braking and it is for this reason that it was earlier used for traction purposes.

(ii) Rotor voltage injection. Here, the basic concepts regarding the voltage injection into the rotor circuit of a slip-ring induction motor (SRIM) for its speed control are described.

It is given in Eq. (5.21) that power transferred from stator to rotor is

$$P_g = sP_g + (1 - s)\, P_g. \qquad \text{...(5.86C)}$$

Here $(1 - s)\, P_g$ represents the mechanical power developed in the rotor and slip power sP_g appears as rotor ohmic loss $(I_2^2 r_2)$ if rotor is short-circuited. However, instead of wasting the slip frequency power sP_g in the rotor circuit, it can be converted by various schemes to useful power which is either returned to the supply or added to the motor shaft.

The most useful method of recovering the slip power sP_g and controlling the speed thereby, involves the injection of an emf into the rotor circuit from some suitable external sources. It should be understood that the injected emf must be at slip frequency at all the rotor speeds. Note that when the emf is injected in the rotor circuit, the wound-rotor induction motor becomes a doubly-excited induction machine.

The effect of an injected emf into the rotor circuit of an induction motor, can be better understood with the help of its phasor diagrams.

Fig. 5.36 (*a*) shows the phasor diagram of a 3-phase induction motor running at slip *s* and with its rotor short-circuited. In this phasor diagram, the stator voltage and current are not shown so as to concentrate more on the effects of emf injection. Here, normal rotor speed is n_r rps. If load torque on the induction motor is assumed constant and no-load rotational losses are neglected, then per-phase electromagnetic torque T_e is given by

$$T_e = \frac{E_2}{\omega_s} . I_2 \cos \theta_2 = \left[\frac{E_2}{2\pi n_s}\right] . I_2 \cos \theta_2 = \text{load torque.}$$

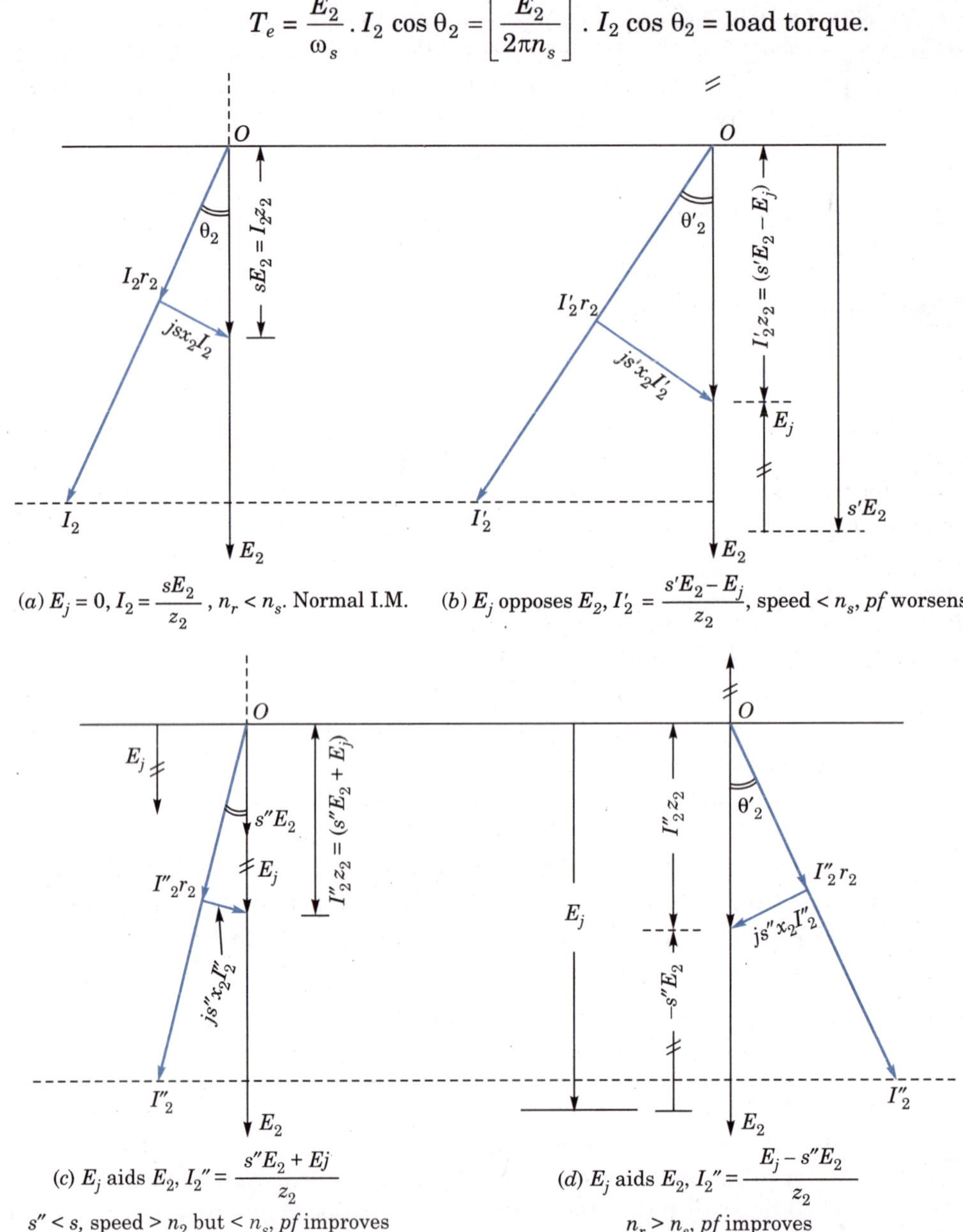

Fig. 5.36: Effect of rotor injected emf in a slip-ring induction motor.

Since E_2 and n_s are constant, $I_2 \cos \theta_2$ must remain constant for a constant torque load. Here E_2 is the emf induced at standstill in the rotor phase winding by the main air-gap flux and sE_2 is its magnitude at any slip s. Synchronous speed n_s is in rps. Rotor current I_2 lags sE_2 due to rotor leakage reactance x_2. Motor, therefore, operates at a lagging power factor, Fig. 5.36(a).

Now an emf E_j is injected in phase opposition to standstill rotor emf E_2, Fig. 5.36 (b). Since the speed and, therefore, slip cannot change suddenly due to rotor inertia, the immediate effect of voltage injection is to decrease the rotor current from $\frac{sE_2}{z_2}$ to $\frac{sE_2 - E_j}{z_2}$.

The decreased rotor current reduces the electrical torque developed. Since the load torque is constant and the developed electrical torque has decreased, the speed drops and slip emf sE_2 increases. As a result of increase in slip emf, the rotor current rises till again the electrical torque has become equal to the constant load torque. Fig. 5.36 (b) illustrates this condition. The resultant of new rotor emf $s'E_2$ and the injected emf E_j must be equal to $I_2'z_2$. Here I_2' is more than I_2. The operating speed is less than normal speed n_r and the power factor worsens.

If an emf $E_j < I_2z_2$ is injected in phase with E_2, the rotor current and hence the electrical torque tend to become more. For a constant land torque, an increased electrical torque has the effect of increasing the speed or decreasing the slip. As a result of it ; slip emf, rotor current and electrical torque decrease till torque balance is obtained. This shows that speeds above normal operating speed of Fig. 5.36 (a) can be obtained by injecting an emf in phase with the rotor voltage E_2. This is illustrated in Fig. 5.36 (c). Here s'' is the reduced slip, rotor current I_2'' (less than I_2) $= \frac{s'' E_2 + E_j}{z_2}$, rotor speed is more than normal speed n_r but less than n_s and power factor improves.

Now an emf $E_j > I_2z_2$ is injected in phase with E_2 as shown in Fig. 5.36 (d). Since E_j is more than I_2z_2, new rotor emf $s''E_2$ must oppose E_2. This is possible only if $s''E_2$ is negative for $E_j > I_2z_2$. The slip s'' can be negative in case rotor speed is above synchronous speed. In Fig. 5.36 (d), the negative slip is s'', speed is more than synchronous, rotor current $I_2'' = \frac{E_j - s''E_2}{z_2}$ and rotor power factor is leading. This shows that the speeds above synchronous speed can be obtained by injecting an emf $E_j > I_2 z_2$ and in phase with E_2.

Rating of the auxiliary equipment. The auxiliary equipment injects a voltage E_j in the rotor circuit and the rotor current I_2 flows through the electrical circuit of the auxiliary equipment. In view of this, the slip power P_{sp} handled by the auxiliary equipment is given by

$$P_{sp} = m \,.\, E_j \,.\, I_2 \cos (\overline{E_j, I_2}) \qquad ...(5.87)$$

where, m is the number of phases.

If the angle between E_j and I_2 is 90°, then the auxiliary equipment supplies the reactive power only.

Torque-speed characteristics. The effect of rotor voltage injection on the torque-speed characteristics of an induction motor is now investigated.

When the injected voltage E_j is zero, then $s\overline{E}_2 = \overline{I}_2\overline{z}_2$.

When the voltage is injected in the rotor circuit, the speed and slip change. Let the new value of slip be s'. The resultant of rotor circuits emfs $s'\overline{E}_2$ and $\overline{E}_j$ is equal to $\overline{I}_2\overline{z}_2$, which can be written as

$$s'\overline{E}_2 + \overline{E}_j = \overline{I}_2\overline{z}_2$$

With zero injected voltage, $s\overline{E}_2 = \overline{I}_2\overline{z}_2$

$$\therefore \quad s'\overline{E}_2 + \overline{E}_j = s\overline{E}_2$$

or

$$s' = s - \frac{\overline{E}_j}{\overline{E}_2} \qquad \text{...(5.88)}$$

If E_j and E_2 are in the same phase, then E_j and E_2 have the same signs and, therefore, s' decreases or the speed increases, Fig. 5.36 (*c*). In case E_j and E_2 oppose each other, then E_j and E_2 have opposite signs and therefore s' increases or the speed decreases, Fig. 5.36 (*b*).

The induction motor speed, after emf injection, is given by

$$n_r = n_s\,(1 - s')$$

Substitution of the value of s' from Eq. (5.88) gives

$$n_r = n_s\left[1 - s + \frac{\overline{E}_j}{\overline{E}_2}\right] \qquad \text{...(5.89)}$$

Eq. (5.89) verifies the conclusions derived from Eq. (5.88).

With E_j and E_2 in the same phase, if $\dfrac{E_j}{E_2} > s$ or $E_j > sE_2$ $(= I_2z_2)$, then rotor speed n_r becomes more than synchronous speed n_s, Fig. 5.36 (*d*).

For a given injected voltage, $\dfrac{E_j}{E_2}$ is constant. At no load, slip s is very small and if it is assumed zero, then the rotor speed at no load is $n_s\left[1 + \dfrac{\overline{E}_j}{\overline{E}_2}\right]$. When E_j aids E_2, the no-load speed is $n_s\left(1 + \dfrac{E_j}{E_2}\right)$; when E_j opposes E_2, the no-load speed is $n_s\left(1 - \dfrac{E_j}{E_2}\right)$ and when $E_j = 0$, the no-load speed is synchronous, this is illustrated in Fig. 5.37. The intersection of the torque-speed curves of motor and load gives the operating point. Fig. 5.37 reveals that the operating speeds below and above synchronous speed are possible by voltage injection into the rotor circuit of a 3-phase wound-rotor induction motor.

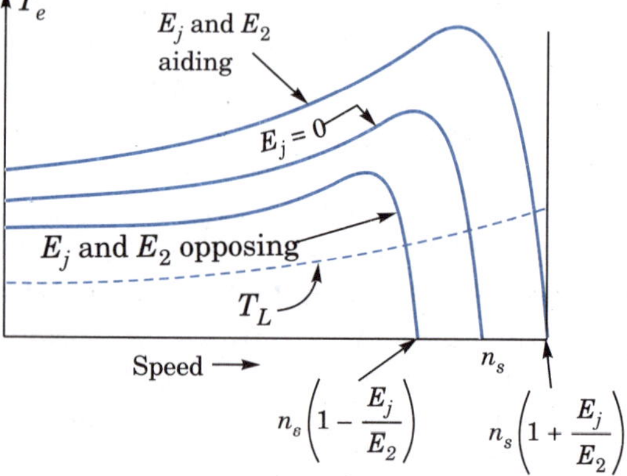

Fig. 5.37: Effect of rotor voltage injection on the torque-speed characteristics of an induction motor.

Substituting the value of $s = \dfrac{\bar{I}_2\bar{z}_2}{\bar{E}_2}$, Eq. (5.89) may now be written as

$$n_s = n_s\left[1+\frac{\bar{E}_j}{\bar{E}_2}-\frac{\bar{I}_2\bar{z}_2}{\bar{E}_2}\right] \quad \text{...(5.90)}$$

With the increase in load on the induction motor, rotor current I_2 increases accordingly. Since I_2z_2 is much smaller in magnitude than E_2, there is only a marginal decrease in speed as the load is increased and in view of this, the induction motor torque-speed characteristics of Fig. (5.37) are obtained.

Eq. (5.90) may also be re-written as

$$n_r = n_s\left[1+\frac{1}{\bar{E}_2}(\bar{E}_j - \bar{I}_2\bar{z}_2)\right] \quad \text{...(5.91)}$$

The conclusions drawn from the phasor diagrams may also be arrived at from Eq. 5.91 as under.

(*i*) If $E_j = 0$, normal rotor speed $n_r = n_s\left[1-\dfrac{\bar{I}_2\bar{z}_2}{\bar{E}_2}\right]$ is obtained.

(*ii*) If E_j opposes E_2, then $n_r = n_s\left[1+\dfrac{1}{\bar{E}_2}(-\bar{E}_j - \bar{I}_2\bar{z}_2)\right]$

$$= n_s\left[1-\frac{1}{\bar{E}_2}(\bar{E}_j + \bar{I}_2\bar{z}_2)\right]. \text{ So here}$$

rotor speed is less than normal rotor speed of an ordinary induction motor.

(*iii*) If $\bar{E}_j = \bar{I}_2\bar{z}_2$ and E_j aids E_2, $n_r = n_s$

(*iv*) If $E_j > I_2z_2$ and E_j aids E_2, then $(\bar{E}_j - \bar{I}_2\bar{z}_2)$ is positive and therefore rotor speeds is more than synchronous speed n_s.

Torque-speed characteristics. The effect of rotor voltage injection on the torque-speed characteristics of an induction motor is now investigated.

For a given injected voltage, $\dfrac{E_j}{E_2}$ is constant. At no load, slip s is very small and if it is assumed zero, then the rotor speed at no load in $n_s\left(1+\dfrac{\bar{E}_j}{\bar{E}_2}\right)$. When E_j aids E_2, the no-load speed is $n_s\left(1+\dfrac{E_j}{E_2}\right)$; when E_j opposes E_2, the no-load speed is $n_s\left(1-\dfrac{E_j}{E_2}\right)$ and when $E_j = 0$, the no-load speed is synchronous, this is illustrated in Fig. 5.37. The intersection of the torque-speed curves of motor and load gives the operating point and Fig. 5.37 reveals that the operating speeds below and above synchronous speed are possible by voltage injection into the rotor circuit of a 3-phase wound-rotor induction motor.

Example 5.14. *A 440 V, 3-phase, 4-pole, 50 Hz squirrel cage induction motor develops a maximum torque of 3 times the full-load torque at a speed of 1200 rpm and at rate voltage and frequency. If this motor is now connected to a 400 V, 40 Hz a.c. source ; then, neglecting the stator resistance effect, compute*

(a) the magnitude of maximum torque and

(b) the speed at which maximum torque would now occur.

Solution. (*a*) From Eq. (5.30), the maximum torque is

$$T_{em} = \frac{m}{2\pi n_s} \cdot \frac{V_e^2}{[R_e + \sqrt{R_e^2 + X^2}]}$$

With negligible stator resistance, $R_e = 0$

$$\therefore \qquad T_{em} = \frac{m}{2\pi n_s} \cdot \frac{V_e^2}{2X}$$

Both X and n_s are proportional to supply frequency f, therefore,

$$T_{em} \propto \left(\frac{V_e}{f}\right)^2 \quad \text{or} \quad T_{em} = K\left(\frac{V_1}{f}\right)^2$$

where, K is the proportionality constant.

For 440 V, 50 Hz source, $T_{em1} = 3T_{e.fl} = K\left(\frac{440}{50}\right)^2$

For 400 V, 40 Hz source, $T_{em2} = K\left(\frac{440}{40}\right)^2$

$$\therefore \qquad \frac{T_{em1}}{T_{em2}} = \frac{3T_{e.fl}}{T_{em2}} = \left(\frac{440}{50}\right)^2 \times \left(\frac{40}{400}\right)^2$$

or

$$T_{em2} = 3T_{e.fl}\left(\frac{50}{440}\right)^2 \times \left(\frac{400}{40}\right)^2 = 3.874\ T_{e.fl}.$$

(*b*) At 50 Hz operation,

$$s_{mT1} = \frac{1500 - 1200}{1500} = 0.2 \quad \text{and} \quad \frac{r_2}{s_{mT1}} = X = 2\pi\,(50)\,L$$

$$\therefore \qquad \frac{r_2}{2\pi L} = (50)\,(0.2) = 10$$

At 40 Hz operation,

$$\frac{r_2}{s_{mT2}} = 2\pi\,(40)\,L \qquad \therefore \qquad s_{mT2} = \frac{r_2}{2\,\pi\,L} \times \frac{1}{40} = \frac{10}{40} = 0.25$$

For 400 V, 40 Hz operation, therefore, the speed at which maximum torque would occur is given by

$$\frac{120\,f}{P}(1 - s_{mT2}) = \frac{120 \times 40}{4}(1 - 0.25) = 900 \text{ rpm.}$$

Example 5.15. *A 20 kW, 3-phase, 400 V, 4-pole, 50 Hz squrrel cage induction motor, when working at rated voltage and frequency, develops a full-load torque at 1470 rpm. If the motor is fed from 40 Hz source, with its voltage adjusted to give the same air-gap flux as at 50 Hz, then calculate*

(*a*) *the magnitude of the 40 Hz voltage source and*

(*b*) *the speed at which the motor would now run so that the same full-load torque, as at 50 Hz, is developed.*

Solution. (*a*) For an induction motor, the air-gap flux is given by

$$\phi \propto \frac{\text{Voltage}}{\text{Frequency}} \quad \text{or} \quad \phi = k\,\frac{V}{f}$$

For 50 Hz source, $\phi = k\,\dfrac{400}{50}$

For 40 Hz source, $\phi = k\,\dfrac{V_2}{40}$

$$\therefore \quad k\frac{V_2}{40} = k\,\frac{400}{50} \quad \text{or} \quad V_2 = \left(\frac{400}{50}\right)(40) = 320 \text{ V.}$$

(*b*) Slip $s_1 = \dfrac{1500 - 1470}{1500} = 0.02.$

At small values of slips, the electromagnetic torque from Eq. (5.32) is given by

$$T_e = \frac{m\,V_e^2}{2\pi n_s}\,\frac{s}{r_2} = K\frac{V^2}{f}\,s$$

Now $T_{e1} = K\dfrac{V_1^2}{f_1}\,s_1 = K\dfrac{(400)^2}{50} \times 0.02$

and $T_{e2} = K\dfrac{V_2^2}{f_2}\cdot s_2 = K\dfrac{(320)^2}{50}\,.\,s_2$

From above, $\dfrac{T_{e1}}{T_{e2}} = 1 = \left(\dfrac{400}{320}\right)^2 \times \left(\dfrac{40}{50}\right) \times \left(\dfrac{0.02}{s_2}\right)$

$$\therefore \quad \text{Slip } s_2 = \left(\frac{400}{320}\right)^2 \times \left(\frac{40}{50}\right) \times (0.02) = 0.025$$

∴ The motor speed, when fed for 40 Hz source is

$$\frac{120\,f_2}{P}(1 - s_2) = \frac{120 \times 40}{4}(1 - 0.025) = 1170 \text{ rpm.}$$

Example 5.16. *A 400 V, 4-pole, 50 Hz, 3-phase squirrel cage induction motor develops full-load torque at 1470 rpm and has full-load pf of 0.85. Its magnetizing current and rotational losses may be neglected. If the supply voltage reduces to 340 V, with the load torque remaining constant, then compute,*

(*a*) *the motor speed*

(*b*) *the percentage increase in rotor ohmic losses and*

(*c*) *the motor full-load power factor.*

Solution. Full-load slip, $s_1 = \dfrac{1500 - 1470}{1500} = 0.02.$

(*a*) From Eq. (5.34), $T_e = K'V_1^2 s$

$$\therefore \quad T_{e1} = K' (400)^2 \times 0.02$$

and
$$T_{e2} = K' (340)^2 \times s_2$$

$$\therefore \quad \frac{T_{e2}}{T_{e1}} = 1 = \frac{K' (340)^2 \cdot s_2}{K' (400)^2 \times 0.02} \quad \text{or} \quad s_2 = \left(\frac{400}{340}\right)^2 \times 0.02 = 0.0277.$$

∴ The motor speed at reduced voltage of 340 V is

$$\frac{120 f}{P}(1 - s_2) = \frac{120 \times 50}{4}(1 - 0.0277) = 1458.5 \text{ rpm}$$

(*b*) Rotor ohmic loss,

$$P_{o1} = s_1 P_g = s_1 (\omega_s T_{e1})$$

Also,
$$P_{o2} = s_2(\omega_s T_{e1}) = s_2 (\omega_s T_{e1})$$

∴ Percentage increase in rotor-ohmic losses

$$= \frac{P_{o2} - P_{o1}}{P_{o1}} \times 100 = \frac{s_2 - s_1}{s_1} \times 100$$

$$= \frac{0.0277 - 0.02}{0.02} \times 100 = 38.5\%.$$

(*c*) Motor p.f.,
$$0.85 = \frac{r_2}{\sqrt{r_2^2 + (s_1 x_2)^2}} = \frac{r_2}{\sqrt{r_2^2 + (0.02\, x_2)^2}}$$

or $(0.85)^2 [r_2^2 + (0.02\, x_2)^2] = r_2^2$

$$\therefore \quad x_2^2 = 960\, r_2^2.$$

∴ Motor p.f. at a slip of 0.0277

$$= \frac{r_2}{\sqrt{r_2^2 + (s_2 x_2)^2}} = \frac{r_2}{\sqrt{r_2^2 + (0.0277)^2 (960\, r_2^2)}} = 0.759.$$

Example 5.17. *An induction motor runs at a slip frequency of 2 Hz when supplied from a three-phase, 400 V, 50 Hz supply. For the same developed torque, find the slip frequency at which it will run when supplied from a 3-phase, 340 V, 40 Hz system. Slip at which the machine develops maximum torque using 50 Hz supply is 0.1. Neglect the stator impedance and assume linear torque-slip characteristic between zero torque and maximum torque in the working region.*

Solution. Slip,
$$s = \frac{f_2}{f_1} = \frac{2}{50} = 0.04$$

With negligible stator impedance, maximum torque is

$$T_{e.m.} = \frac{m}{2\pi n_s} \cdot \frac{V_e^2}{2X} \quad \text{or} \quad T_{em} \propto \frac{V_1^2}{f^2} = k\left(\frac{V_1}{f}\right)^2$$

$$\therefore \qquad T_{em1} = k\left(\frac{400}{50}\right)^2 \text{ and } T_{em2} = k\left(\frac{340}{40}\right)^2$$

or
$$\frac{T_{em2}}{T_{em1}} = \left(\frac{340}{40}\right)^2 \times \left(\frac{50}{400}\right)^2 = 1.129 \quad \text{or} \quad T_{em2} = 1.129\, T_{em1}$$

Slip at maximum torque is

$$s_{mT} = \frac{r_2}{X} \quad \text{or} \quad s_{mT} \propto \frac{1}{f}$$

$$\therefore \qquad \frac{s_{mT1}}{s_{mT2}} = \frac{f_2}{f_1} \quad \text{or} \quad \frac{0.1}{s_{mT2}} = \frac{40}{50} \quad \text{or } s_{mT2} = 0.125$$

For linear torque-slip relation between zero torque and maximum torque, the slope of torque-slip line is T_{em}/s_{mT}. Thus, torque at any slip s is given by

$$T_e = \frac{T_{em}}{s_{mT}} \cdot s$$

$$\therefore \qquad T_e = \frac{T_{em1}}{0.1} \times 0.04 = \frac{T_{em2}}{s_{mT2}} \cdot s_2 = \frac{1.129\, T_{em1}}{0.125} \times s_2$$

or
$$s_2 = \frac{0.04}{0.1} \times \frac{0.125}{1.129} = 0.04429$$

$\therefore$ Slip frequency $= s_2 \times f_1 = 0.4429 \times 40 = 1.772$ Hz.

Example 5.18. *A 7.5 kW, 3-phase, 4-pole, 50 Hz, 415 V induction motor is delivering rated torque at 5% slip driving a pump load. The motor delivers maximum torque at 10% slip. The pump load is such that the demanded torque is proportional to the square of speed. A power electronic controller controls the rms supply voltage (below the rated value) to effect a limited speed control. Assume the torque-speed characteristics of the motor in the stable region to be linear. Calculate the rms voltage at which the motor runs at 1350 rpm.*

Solution. Synchronous speed $= \dfrac{120 \times 50}{4} = 1500$ rpm.

Rotor speed, $\quad N_r = 1500\,(1 - 0.05) = 1425$ rpm.

For linear torque-speed characteristic, the electromagnetic torque can be written as

$$T_e = kV_1^2\, s$$

For 1350 rpm speed, the slip $= \dfrac{1500 - 1350}{1500} = 0.1$

It is given that load torque $T_L \propto (\text{speed})^2$

$$\therefore \qquad T_{L1} = T_{e1} \propto (1425)^2 \propto k\,(415)^2 \times 0.05$$

and
$$T_{L2} = T_{e2} \propto (1350)^2 \propto k\,(V_2)^2 \times 0.1$$

or
$$\left(\frac{1425}{1350}\right)^2 = \frac{k\,(415)^2 \times 0.05}{k\,(V_2)^2 \times 0.10} \quad \text{or} \quad V_2 = 415 \times \frac{1350}{1425} \times \sqrt{0.5} = 278 \text{ V}$$

$\therefore$ rms Voltage required = 278 V.

Example 5.19. *A 3-phase, 6-pole, 50 Hz, 400-V induction motor develops maximum torque at a slip of 10%. In a particular application, it runs at 5% slip at rated voltage, driving a load whose torque demand is proportional to square of the speed. What is the minimum value to which the supply voltage can drop, if the speed of the motor is not to decrease below 900 rpm ? Neglect stator impedance drop.*

Solution. $s_{mT1} = 0.1, \quad N_s = 1000$ rpm, slip $s_1 = 0.05$

Rotor speed, $N_1 = 1000\,(1 - 0.05) = 950$ rpm

$$\therefore \quad \frac{T_{e1}}{T_{em1}} = \frac{2}{\dfrac{0.1}{0.05} + \dfrac{0.05}{0.1}} = 0.8 \quad \text{or} \quad T_{e1} = 0.8\, T_{em1}$$

Now $T_{e1} = T_{L_1} \propto N_1^2$ and $T_{em1} \propto (\text{voltage})^2$

$$\therefore \quad N_1^2 \propto 0.8\, V_1^2 \qquad \ldots(i)$$

At 900 rpm, slip $s_2 = \dfrac{1000 - 900}{1000} = 0.1$

$$\therefore \quad \frac{T_{e2}}{T_{em2}} = \frac{2}{\dfrac{0.1}{0.1} + \dfrac{0.1}{0.1}} = 1$$

$$\therefore \quad T_{e2} = T_{em2} \quad \text{or} \quad (N_2)^2 \propto V_2^2 \qquad \ldots(ii)$$

From (*i*) and (*ii*), $\left(\dfrac{N_1}{N_2}\right)^2 = 0.8\left(\dfrac{V_1}{V_2}\right)^2$ or $V_2 = \sqrt{0.8}\left(\dfrac{900}{950}\right) \times 400 = 338.941$ V.

Example 5.20. *A 3-phase, 500 kW, 50 Hz induction motor has a full-load slip of 2.1%. The rotor circuit has standstill impedance of 0.3 + j1.8 Ω per phase. If an external resistance of 1.5 Ω per phase is inserted in each of the rotor circuit, determine the slip and power output when the stator current has its full load value. Neglect stator impedance and rotational losses.*

Solution. For full-load value of current at both slips,

$$\frac{V_1}{\left[\left(\dfrac{0.3}{0.021}\right)^2 + 1.8^2\right]^{1/2}} = \frac{V_1}{\left[\left(\dfrac{1.8}{s}\right)^2 + (1.8)^2\right]^{1/2}} \quad \text{or} \quad \frac{0.3}{0.021} = \frac{1.8}{s}$$

$$\therefore \quad \text{Slip,} \quad s = \frac{1.8}{0.3} \times 0.021 = 0.126 \text{ or } 12.6\%$$

As rotational losses are neglected, mechanical power developed, $P_m = 500$ kW

$$\therefore \quad \text{Air-gap power} = \frac{500}{1 - 0.021}\ \text{kW}$$

Power output at a slip of 0.126 is $P = \left(\dfrac{500}{1 - 0.021}\right)(1 - 0.126) = 428.012$ kW.

Example 5.21. *A 50 kW, 400 V, 3-phase, 4-pole, 50 Hz wound-rotor induction motor develops a maximum internal torque of 240% at a slip of 20% when working under rated voltage and frequency conditions and with slip rings short circuited. Determine (a) full-load slip (b) rotor I^2R loss at full load and (c) starting torque in Nm. Neglect stator resistance and rotational losses.*

The rotor resistance is now doubled. Calculate the slip and the torque when the stator current has its full-load value.

Solution. (*a*) Here $T_{em} = 2.4\ T_{e.fl}$, $s_{mT} = 0.20$, full-load slip = s_1. From Eq. (5.36),

$$\frac{T_{e.fl}}{T_{e.m}} = \frac{2}{\dfrac{0.2}{s_1} + \dfrac{s_1}{0.2}} = \frac{1}{2.4} \quad \text{or} \quad s_1^2 - 0.96\, s_1 + 0.04 = 0$$

Its solution gives full-load slip $s_1 = 0.044$ or 4.4%

(*b*) As rotational losses are neglected, mechanical power developed, $P_m = 50$ kW.

$$\therefore \quad \text{Air-gap power,} \quad P_g = \frac{P_m}{1-s} = \frac{50}{1-0.044}\ \text{kW}$$

$$\therefore \quad \text{Rotor } I^2R \text{ loss} = sP_g = 0.044\ \frac{50{,}000}{0.956} = 2301.26\ \text{W}$$

(*c*)
$$\frac{T_{e.st}}{T_{e.m}} = \frac{2}{\dfrac{0.2}{1} + \dfrac{1}{0.2}} = 0.3846$$

$$\therefore \quad T_{e.st} = 0.3846 \times 2.40\ T_{e.fl}$$

$$\text{Synchronous speed } \omega_s = \frac{4\pi f}{P} = \frac{4\pi \times 50}{4} = 50\pi \text{ rad/sec}$$

$$\therefore \quad T_{e.fl} = \frac{P_m}{\omega_r} = \frac{50{,}000}{50\pi\,(1-0.044)} = 332.96\ \text{Nm}$$

Starting torque, $T_{e.st} = 0.3846 \times 2.40 \times 332.96 = 307.33$ Nm

(*d*) Stator full-load current

$$= \frac{E_2}{\left[\left(\dfrac{r_2}{0.044}\right)^2 + x_2^2\right]^{1/2}} = \frac{E_2}{\left[\left(\dfrac{2r_2}{s}\right)^2 + x_2^2\right]^{1/2}}$$

or
$$\frac{r_2}{0.044} = \frac{2r_2}{s}$$

$$\therefore \quad \text{Slip} \quad s = 0.088$$

As ratio $\dfrac{r_2}{s}$ is unaltered, the torque at full-load stator current is equal to $T_{e.fl} = 332.96$ Nm.

Example 5.22. *A 3-phase, 100 kW, 415 V, 50 Hz, 20-pole, slip ring induction motor has resistance of 0.06 Ω measured between each pair of its slip rings. Both stator and rotor are star-connected. The turns ratio from stator to rotor is 1.2. This motor drives a fan which requires 100 kW at full-load slip of 0.03. The torque demand of the fan varies as the square of the speed. What resistance should be inserted in series with each slip ring so that the fan will run at 210 rpm.*

Assume the torque-slip curve to be straight line from no-load to full-load speed of the motor.

Solution. For star-connected rotor, resistance of rotor per phase

$$= \frac{0.06}{2} = 0.03 \text{ W.}$$

Rotor resistance referred to stator per phase = $0.03 \times 1.2^2 = 0.0432\ \Omega$

Synchronous speed $= \dfrac{120 \times 50}{20} = 300$ rpm

Rotor speed at full-load $= 300\ (1 - 0.03) = 291$ rpm

Speed of 210 rpm gives a slip of 0.3. Load torque $T_L \propto (\text{speed})^2$

or $$T_{L1} \propto (291)^2$$

As torque-slip curve is linear from no-load to full load, the motor torque can be expressed as

$$T_{e1} \propto \frac{s}{r_2} \quad \text{or} \quad T_{L1} = K\frac{s}{r_2} \text{ as } T_{e1} = T_{L1}$$

$$\therefore \qquad (219)^2 \propto K\frac{0.03}{0.0432}$$

Also $$(291)^2 \propto K\frac{0.3}{R_2} \quad \text{or} \quad \left(\frac{291}{210}\right)^2 = \left(\frac{0.03}{0.0432}\right)\left(\frac{R_2}{0.3}\right)$$

or $$R_2 = \left(\frac{291}{210}\right)^2 \times \frac{0.0432}{0.03} \times 0.3 = 0.8295\ \Omega$$

R_2 when referred to rotor $= \dfrac{0.8295}{1.2^2} = 0.576\ \Omega$

External resistance required in each rotor phase = $0.576 - 0.03 = 0.546\ \Omega$.

Example 5.23. *Repeat Example 5.22 in case torque-slip curve is not a straight line from no-load to full-load speed of the motor. But now neglect stator leakage impedance and rotational losses.*

Solution. As rotational losses are neglected, $P_m = 100$ kW

Torque at full load $= \dfrac{100{,}000 \times 60}{2\pi \times 300\ (1 - 0.03)} = 3281.55$ Nm

Also $$T_{e.fl} = \frac{3}{\omega_s} \cdot \frac{V_1^2}{\left(\frac{r_2}{s}\right)^2 + x_2^2} \cdot \frac{r_2}{s}$$

or $$3281.55 = \frac{3}{10\pi} \cdot \frac{(415/\sqrt{3})^2}{\left(\frac{0.0432}{0.03}\right)^2 + x_2^2} \times \frac{0.0432}{0.03} \quad \text{or} \quad x_2^2 = 0.332$$

Now load torque $T_{L1} = T_{e1} \propto N_1^2$ and $T_{L2} = T_{e2} \propto N_2^2$

$$\therefore \qquad \left(\frac{291}{210}\right)^2 = \frac{3}{\omega_s} \cdot \frac{V_1^2}{(1.44)^2 + 0.332} \times \frac{0.0432}{0.03} \times \frac{\omega_s}{3V_1^2} \cdot \frac{\left(\frac{R_2}{0.3}\right)^2 + x_2^2}{1} \times \frac{0.3}{R_2}$$

or $$1.92 = \frac{1.44}{2.4056} \cdot \frac{\left(\frac{R_2}{0.3}\right)^2 + 0.332}{R_2/0.3} \quad \text{or} \quad R_2{}^2 - 0.962\,R + 0.0298 = 0$$

$$\therefore \quad R_2 = 0.032\ \Omega \quad \text{or} \quad R_2 = 0.93\ \Omega$$

As the value of $R_2 = 0.032\ \Omega$ is less than r_2, this value is redundant. Therefore, the other value of $R_2 = 0.93\ \Omega$ is possible.

$\therefore$ External resistance required in each rotor phase $= \dfrac{0.93 - 0.0432}{(1.2)^2}$ = **0.6158 Ω.**

Example 5.24. *At standstill, the voltage across two slip rings of a star-connected rotor of a 6 kW induction motor is 400 V. Its full-load slip is 2%. Calculate the resistance to be inserted in the rotor circuit to reduce the full-load speed by 25%. The torque of the drive varies as the speed-squared. Neglect rotational losses.*

Solution. Since rotational losses are ignored, mechanical power developed,

$$P_m = \frac{6}{3} = 2\ \text{kW}.$$

$\therefore$ Air-gap power, $$P_g = \frac{P_m}{1-s} = \frac{2000}{1-0.02} = 2040.8\ \text{W}.$$

Also $$P_g = I_2{}^2\,\frac{r_2}{s} = \frac{E_2^2}{\left(\frac{r_2}{s}\right)^2 + x_2^2} \cdot \frac{r_2}{s}$$

For small values of slips, x_2 is much smaller as compared to r_2/s.

$$\therefore \quad P_g = \frac{E_2^2}{r_2}\,s \quad \text{or} \quad 2040.8 = \left(\frac{400}{\sqrt{3}}\right)^2 \times \frac{0.02}{r_2}$$

$$\therefore \quad r_2 = \frac{(400/\sqrt{3})^2 \times 0.02}{2040.8} = 0.523\ \Omega.$$

New speed $= 0.75 \times 0.98 = 0.735$

$\therefore$ Slip $s_2 = 1 - 0.735 = 0.265$

Slip $s_1 = 0.02.$

From Eq. (5.86), $$R_2 = r_2\left(\frac{s_2}{s_1}\right)\left(\frac{T_{L1}}{T_{L2}}\right)$$

Here $T_{L1} = \propto n_1^2$ or $T_{L1} \propto (0.98)^2$

and $T_{L2} \propto (0.735)^2$

$$\therefore \quad R_2 = 0.523\left(\frac{0.265}{0.02}\right)\left(\frac{0.98}{0.735}\right)^2 = 12.32\ \Omega.$$

$\therefore$ External resistance that must be inserted in the rotor circuit

$$= 12.32 - 0.523 = 11.797\ \Omega.$$

Example 5.25. *A 3-phase, 50 Hz, 12 pole, induction motor has star connected rotor and the resistance measured across any two slip rings is 0.04 Ω. Its full-load slip is 0.02. Calculate the resistance to be inserted in the rotor circuit to reduce the full-load speed to 350 rpm. The torque required by the load varies as the speed-squared. Assume the torque-slip curve to be a straight line in the normal operating region.*

Solution. Per phase rotor resistance, $r_2 = \dfrac{0.04}{2} = 0.02\ \Omega$

Full-load slip, $s_1 = 0.02$

New slip, $s_2 = \dfrac{500 - 350}{500} = 0.30$

Now load torque, $T_L \propto n^2$

$\therefore$ $T_{L1} \propto [(1 - 0.02)\ 500]^2$ or $T_{L1} \propto (490)^2$

and $T_{L2} \propto (350)^2$.

From Eq. (5.86), $R_2 = r_2 \left(\dfrac{s_2}{s_2}\right)\left(\dfrac{T_{L_1}}{T_{L_2}}\right) = 0.02\left(\dfrac{0.30}{0.02}\right)\left(\dfrac{490}{350}\right)^2 = 0.588\ \Omega.$

$\therefore$ External resistance that must be inserted in each rotor phase

$= 0.588 - 0.02 = 0.568\ \Omega$

Example 5.26. *Discuss the effect of injecting voltage E_j in the rotor circuit of 3-phase slip-ring induction motor in case E_j leads the standstill rotor emf E_2 by 90°.*

Solution. The effect of injecting voltage E_j at an angle 90° leading the standstill rotor emf E_2 is shown in Fig. 5.38. It is seen from this figure that the phasor orientation of the resultant rotor circuit voltage $(\overline{E}_j + s\overline{E}_2)$ and the rotor current I_2 has changed from its orientation when $E_j = 0$, Fig. 5.36 (*a*). The effect of rotor current on the stator, or primary side, is to improve the motor power factor considerably. In Fig. 5.38, stator power factor is shown to be cos θ_1 leading. It may be seen that E_j is neither assisting nor opposing E_2, but actually pf improvement is accompanied by a change in speed also. This is revealed by Example 5.27.

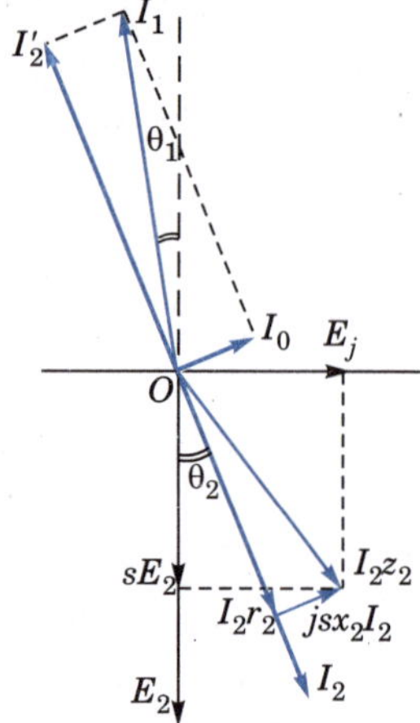

Fig. 5.38: Power factor control by injecting E_j leading E_2 by 90°.

Example 5.27. *A 30 kW, 50 Hz, 6-pole, 400 V, 3-phase induction motor has standstill rotor impedance of (0.04 + j 0.30) Ω per phase and stanstall rotor phase e.m.f. is 50 V. If the rotor current is maintained constant at 50 A per phase, then calculate the slip, rotor power factor and motor speed when.*

(a) rotor is short circuited.
(b) 10 V per phase is injected in phase opposition to rotor emf
(c) 10 V per phase is injected in phase with rotor emf and
(d) 1.5 V per phase is injected at 90° leading the rotor emf.

Solution. (*a*) The voltage equation for a short-circuited rotor is

$$\bar{I}_2\bar{z}_2 = s\bar{E}_2$$

Substituting the values,

$$50\,(0.04 + j\,0.3\,s) = s\,(50) \quad \text{or} \quad 0.0016 + 0.09\,s^2 = s^2$$

$$\therefore \qquad s = \pm\sqrt{0.00175824} = \pm\,0.0419.$$

$$\text{Rotor power factor} = \frac{r_2}{\sqrt{{r_2}^2 + (sx_2)^2}} = \frac{0.04}{\sqrt{(0.04)^2 + (0.0419 \times 0.3)^2}}$$

$$= 0.954 \text{ lagging.}$$

$$\text{Motor speed,} \qquad N_r = N_s\,(1 - s) = \frac{120 \times 50}{6}\,(1 - 0.0419) = 958.1 \text{ rpm.}$$

(*b*) Since $E_j = 10$ V is injected in phase opposition to E_2, we get an algebraic relation as

$$s'E_2 - E_j = I_2 z_2$$

$$\therefore \qquad s'\,50 - 10 = 50\,(0.04 + j\,0.3\,s')$$

or

$$(s' - 0.2)^2 = 0.0016 + 0.09\,s'^2 \quad \text{or} \quad s'^2 - 0.439\,s' + 0.0422 = 0.$$

Its solution gives $\quad s' = 0.297$ or 0.142

From Eq. (5.90), for E_j in phase opposition to E_2, the operating speed is given by

$$n_r = n_s\left(1 - \frac{E_j}{E_2}\right) = n_s\left(1 - \frac{10}{50}\right) = 0.8\,n_s.$$

If $I_2\,z_2$ drop is not neglected, then n_r would be less than $0.8\,n_s$. Therefore, operating speed would be less than $0.8\,n_s$ and the operating slip more than 0.2. This shows that the required operating slip is 0.297.

$$\therefore \quad \text{Rotor power factor} = \frac{0.04}{\sqrt{(0.04)^2 + (0.297 \times 0.3)^2}} = 0.41 \text{ lagging.}$$

$$\text{Motor speed,} \qquad = 1000\,(1 - 0.297) = 703 \text{ rpm}$$

(*c*) The algebraic equation for this part is $s'E_2 + E_j = I_2 z_2$

$$\therefore \qquad s'50 + 10 = 50\,(0.04 + j\,0.3\,s')$$

$$s'^2 + 0.439\,s' + 0.0422 = 0$$

Its solution gives $\quad s' = -\,0.297$ or $-\,0.142$

From Eq. (5.90), for E_j in phase with E_2, the operating speed is given by

$$n_r = n_s\left[1 + \frac{E_j}{E_2}\right] = n_s\left[1 + \frac{10}{50}\right] = 1.2\,n_s.$$

If $I_2\,z_2$ drop is included, n_r would be less than $1.2\,n_s$ and therefore operating slip would be less than $-\,0.2$. It may, therefore, be concluded that the required operating slip is $-\,0.142$.

$\therefore$ Rotor power factor $= \dfrac{0.04}{\sqrt{(0.04)^2 + (0.142 \times 0.3)^2}} = 0.6845$ leading.

$$\text{Motor speed} = 1000\,(1 + 0.142) = 1142 \text{ rpm}$$

(*d*) Since $E_j = 1.5$ V

$$(50\, z_2)^2 = (1.5)^2 + (s'50)^2$$

$$[50\,(0.04 + j0.3\, s')]^2 = (1.5)^2 + (s'.\, 50)^2$$

$$0.0016 + 0.09\, s'^2 = 0.0009 + s'^2$$

$\therefore$ $s' = \pm\, 0.0277.$

$$\text{Rotor power factor} = \frac{0.04}{\sqrt{(0.04)^2 + (0.027 \times 0.3)^2}} = 0.9791; \text{ leading}$$

$$\text{Motor speed} = 1000\,(1 - 0.0277) = 972.3 \text{ rpm.}$$

This example demonstrates that with rotor emf injected at 90° leading E_2, power factor has improved considerably from 0.954 lagging to 0.9791 leading and motor speed has also increased from 958.1 rpm to 972.3 rpm.

Example 5.28. *A 440 V, 3-phase, star-connected wound-rotor induction motor has a ratio of transformation from stator to rotor as 2.5. At full-load operation, the slip e.m.f. is 4 volts per phase. If the load torque varies as the square-root of slip, then compute the value of injected voltage required to increase the slip to 40%. Neglect rotational losses and rotor leakage reactance.*

Solution. Per phase rotor e.m.f. at standstill, $E_2 = \dfrac{440}{\sqrt{3}} \cdot \dfrac{1}{2.5} = 101.62$ V.

Now slip e.m.f., $s_1 E_2 = 4$ V

$\therefore$ Full-load slip, $s_1 = \dfrac{4}{101.62} = 0.0394.$

For negligible rotational losses, $T_e \propto \phi\, I_2$. For torque balance, T_e = load torque T_L. Therefore, $T_L \propto \phi\, I_2$. It is given

$$\text{that load torque} \propto \sqrt{\text{slip}} \quad \text{or} \quad \phi\, I_2 \propto \sqrt{s_1} \quad \text{and} \quad \phi\, I_2' \propto \sqrt{s_2}$$

$$\therefore \quad \frac{I'_2}{I_2} = \sqrt{\frac{s_2}{s_1}} = \sqrt{\frac{0.40}{0.0394}} = 3.186 \quad \text{or} \quad I'_2 = 3.186\, I_2.$$

Now the voltage equation for the rotor circuit is

$$s'\,\overline{E}_2 + \overline{E}_j = \overline{I}_2{}'\, r_2$$

$$\therefore \quad 0.4\, \overline{E}_2 + \overline{E}_j = 3.186\, \overline{I}_2 r_2$$

But $\overline{I}_2 r_2 = s_1 \overline{E}_2 = 4$ V

$$\therefore \quad 0.4 \times 101.62 + E_j = 3.186 \times 4$$

$$\therefore \quad E_j = -\,27.904 \text{ V.}$$

Since E_j has turned out to be negative, the injected voltage must be in phase opposition to rotor voltage E_2.

Example 5.29. (*a*) *A 400 V, 3-phase induction motor is developing an electromagnetic torque of 80 Nm for a rotor current of 20 A. With the help of rotor voltage injection, if the rotor current is increased to 5 times its initial value, then find the new value of electromagnetic torque*

(*b*) *A 3-phase wound-rotor induction motor drives a constant torque load and its slip e.m.f. is 10 volts. If the rotor leakage reactance is neglected, then find the voltage that must be injected in the rotor circuit to develop twice this torque at five times the slip.*

Solution. (*a*) A polyphase induction motor is almost a constant-flux machine, therefore,

$$T_e \propto \phi I_2$$

Here $\quad T_{e1} \propto \phi I_2 \quad \text{or} \quad 80 \propto \phi\,(20) \quad \text{and} \quad T_{e2} \propto \phi\,(5 \times 20)$

$\therefore \quad \dfrac{T_{e2}}{80} = \dfrac{\phi\,(100)}{\phi\,(20)} \quad \text{or} \quad T_{e2} = 80 \times 5 = 400 \text{ Nm.}$

(*b*) Let the initial values of slip and rotor current be s_1 and I_2 respectively, then

$$I_2 r_2 = 10 \text{ V}, \quad \therefore \quad I_2 = \frac{10}{r_2}$$

Also $\quad s_1 E_2 = 10 \text{ V}, \quad \therefore \quad s_1 = \dfrac{10}{E_2}$

For developing twice the torque ($\propto \phi\, I_2$), the rotor current I_2' must be equal to $2I_2$, because induction motor is a constant flux machine.

$\therefore \quad I_2' = \dfrac{20}{r_2}$

New slip, $\quad s_2 = 5\, s_1 = \dfrac{50}{E_2}$

The voltage equation for the rotor circuit is

$$s_2 \overline{E}_2 + \overline{E}_j = \overline{I}_2'\, r_2$$

$\therefore \quad \dfrac{50}{\overline{E}_2}\overline{E}_2 + \overline{E}_j = \dfrac{20}{r_2}\, r_2 \quad \text{or} \quad \overline{E}_j = -\,30 \text{ V}$

Since E_j is negative, the injected voltage should oppose the rotor e.m.f. E_2.

Example 5.30. *A 50 Hz, 3-phase wound-rotor induction motor is running with a slip of 0.03. The per phase rotor e.m.f. and leakage impedance at standstill are 200 V and 0.3 + j 0 Ω respectively. For obtaining slips of 0.4, 0 and – 0.4, calculate the magnitude, frequency and phase of the injected voltage in the rotor circuit, when*

(*a*) *the load torque is constant and*

(*b*) *the load torque is proportional to speed.*

Solution. Electromagnetic torque, $T_e \propto E_2 I_2 \cos \theta_2$.

Since rotor circuit is purely resistive, $\cos \theta_2 = 1$.

$\therefore \quad T_e \propto E_2 I_2.$

The standstill rotor voltage E_2 remains substantially constant ; in view of this, $T_e \propto I_2$.

For torque balance, $T_e = T_L$

$\therefore \quad$ Load torque $\propto I_2$

(*a*) For a constant-torque load, the rotor current I_2 must remain constant at all the rotor speeds.

Under normal operation and with the rotor short-circuited,

$$I_2 r_2 = sE_2 \quad \text{or} \quad I_2 = \frac{sE_2}{r_2} = \frac{(0.03)(200)}{0.3} = 20 \text{ A.}$$

Voltage equation for the rotor circuit is $\bar{I}_2 r_2 = s\bar{E}_2 + \bar{E}_j$

For slip $s = 0.4$,

$$(20)(0.3) = (0.4)(200) + \bar{E}_j$$

$$\bar{E}_j = -74 \text{ V.}$$

Since E_j is negative, 74 volts at a frequency of 20 Hz (= *sf*) must be injected in phase opposition to E_2. The same conclusion can be arrived at from physical considerations. For obtaining larger *sf* or speeds less than the normal one, the injected voltage should be in phase opposition to the rotor voltage E_2.

For slip $s = 0$, $(20)(0.3) = 0 + \bar{E}_j$ or $\bar{E}_j = 6$ V.

Since E_j is positive the injected voltage at zero frequency should be in phase with E_2.

For slip $s = -0.4$,

$$\bar{E}_j + (-0.4)(200) = (20)(0.3) \quad \text{or} \quad \bar{E}_j = 86 \text{ V.}$$

Here E_j is positives, therefore, 86 V at a frequency of 20 Hz must be in phase with E_2.

(*b*) Here load torque $T_L \propto n_r$. But $T_e \propto I_2$

For torque balance, $T_e = T_L$ or $I_2 \propto n_r \propto n_s(1 - s)$,

At normal speed, $20 \propto n_s(1 - 0.03)$.

For slip $s = 0.4$, $I_2' \propto n_s(1 - 0.4)$

$$\therefore \quad \frac{I_2'}{20} = \frac{n_s(0.6)}{n_s(0.97)} \quad \text{or} \quad I_2' = \left(\frac{0.6}{0.97}\right)(20) = 12.88 \text{ A.}$$

$$\therefore \quad \bar{E}_j + s\bar{E}_2 = \bar{I}_2' r_2 \quad \text{or} \quad \bar{E}_j + (0.4)(200) = (12.88)(0.3)$$

$$\therefore \quad \bar{E}_j = -76.136 \text{ V.}$$

$\therefore$ E_j should be in phase opposition to E_2.

For slip $s = 0$, $\dfrac{I_2'}{20} = \dfrac{n_s}{0.97\, n_s}$ or $I_2' = \dfrac{20}{0.97} = 20.62$ A

Now $\bar{E}_j + 0 = \bar{I}_2' r_2 = (20.62)(0.3)$ or $\bar{E}_j = 6.186$ V.

$\therefore$ E_j should be in phase with E_2.

For slip $s = -0.4$, $\dfrac{I_2'}{20} = \dfrac{1.4\, n_s}{0.97\, n_s}$ or $I_2' = \left(\dfrac{1.4}{0.97}\right)(20) = 28.88$ A

$\therefore$ $E_j + (-0.4)(200) = (28.88)(0.3)$ or $E_j = 88.664$ V.

$\therefore$ E_j should be in phase with E_2.

Example 5.31. *A 10 kW, 50 Hz, 4-pole, 3-phase induction motor has a rotor leakage impedance of (0.2 + j 1.5) Ω per phase at standstill. When delivering full-load torque, the motor runs at 1440 rpm. Standstill rotor emf per phase is 60 V. Determine the magnitude of emf injected at the rotor terminals for a speed of (a) 1000 rpm and (b) 1800 rpm, for a constant-torque load.*

Also calculate the slip power flowing through the auxiliary equipment and its rating in kVA.

Solution. Synchronous speed $= \dfrac{120\,f}{P} = 1500$ rpm

Full-load slip, $$s = \frac{1500 - 1440}{1500} = 0.04$$

Rotor leakage impedance at full load, $\bar{z}_2 = [0.2 + j\,(0.04)\,(1.5)] = 0.2 + j\,0.06$

$$z_2 = 0.2085\ \Omega$$

Rotor pf at full-load, $$\cos\theta_2 = \frac{r_2}{z_2} = \frac{0.2}{0.2085} = 0.958 \text{ lagging.}$$

∴ Full-load rotor current, $$I_2 = \frac{sE_2}{z_2} = \frac{0.04 \times 60}{0.2085} = 11.5 \text{ A.}$$

(*a*) Slip, $$s_1 = \frac{1500 - 1000}{1500} = \frac{1}{3}$$

∴ $$\bar{z}_{21} = (0.2 + j\,1.5 \times \frac{1}{3}) \text{ or } z_{21} = 0.538\ \Omega$$

$$\cos\theta_{21} = \frac{r_2}{z_{21}} = \frac{0.2}{0.538} = 0.372 \text{ lagging.}$$

For constant-torque load,

$$I_{21}\cos\theta_{21} = I_2\cos\theta_2$$

∴ $$I_{21} = \frac{11.5 \times 0.958}{0.372} = 29.6 \text{ A.}$$

With injected voltage, the voltage equation for the rotor circuit is,

$$s_1\bar{E}_2 + \bar{E}_j = \bar{I}_{21}\,\bar{z}_{21} \quad \text{or} \quad \bar{E}_j = (29.6)\,(0.538) - \frac{1}{3}\,(60) = -\,4.08 \text{ V.}$$

Thus $E_j = 4.08$ V should be injected in phase opposition to E_2. The slip power P_{sp} handled by the auxiliary equipment is given by

$$P_{sp} = 3\,E_j\,I_{21}\cos\,(E_j, I_{21})$$

Fig. 5.36 (*b*) shows that the angle between E_j and I_{21} is $180 + \theta_{21}$

∴ $$P_{sp} = 3\,(4.08)\,(29.6)\cos\,(180 + \theta_{21})$$
$$= -\,3\,(4.08)\,(29.6)\,(0.372) = -\,135 \text{ watts.}$$

The slip power has turned out to be negative. This means that slip power of 135 watts flows from the rotor winding to the auxiliary equipment.

kVA rating of the auxiliary equipment

$$= 3\,(4.08)\,(29.6)\,10^{-3} = 0.362 \text{ kVA.}$$

(*b*) Slip $$s_2 = \frac{1500 - 1800}{1500} = -\frac{1}{5}$$

$$\therefore \quad z_{22} = \left(0.3 - j\,1.5 \times \frac{1}{5}\right), \quad \text{or} \quad z_{22} = 0.36\ \Omega$$

$$\cos\theta_{22} = \frac{r_2}{z_{22}} = \frac{0.2}{0.36} = 0.556 \text{ leading}$$

For constant-torque load, $I_{22}\cos\theta_{22} = I_2\cos\theta_2$

$$\therefore \quad I_{22} = \frac{11.5 \times 0.958}{0.556} = 19.82 \text{ A.}$$

For the rotor circuit,

$$\bar{E}_j + s_2\,\bar{E}_2 = \bar{I}_{22}\,\bar{z}_{22} \quad \text{or} \quad \bar{E}_j = (19.82)\,(0.36) - 60\left(-\frac{1}{5}\right) = 19.14 \text{ V.}$$

Thus E_j = 19.14 V should be in phase with E_2. Slip power handled by the auxiliary equipment

$$= 3E_j\,I_{22}\cos(\bar{E}_j, I_{22}) = 3\,(19.14)\,(19.82)\,(0.556) = 633 \text{ watts.}$$

Positive sign for slip power indicates that the auxiliary equipment gives 633 watts to the rotor winding.

kVA rating of the auxiliary equipment = 3 (19.14) (19.82) 10^{-3} = 1.138 kVA

Since the auxiliary equipment must be capable of handling higher kVA, the rating of the auxiliary equipment must be 1.138 kVA.

5.9 SLIP-POWER-RECOVERY SCHEMES FOR INDUCTION MOTOR SPEED CONTROL

The slip power sP_g for an induction motor is positive for subsynchronous speeds, because slip s is positive ; but it is negative for super-synchronous speeds. Various schemes have been invented for recovering the slip-frequency-power. In all these schemes, slip-frequency-adjustable voltages are injected into the rotor circuit for induction motor speed control. The slip-power can either be returned to, or taken from, the supply mains. Also, the slip power can be added to, or subtracted from, the main-motor shaft output. The slip-power recovery schemes offer wide range of induction motor speed control more economically and efficiently.

Slip-power recovery schemes can be classified into two types of drives, depending upon whether the slip-power is returned to, or taken from, the line; or added to, or taken from, the shaft power of the main induction motor. The object of this article is to discuss the basic principles of these two types of drives and in the presentation that follows; the main induction motor, auxiliary machine and slip-power converter are assumed to have no losses.

5.9.1 Constant-torque Drive

For obtaining a constant-torque drive, the slip-power sP_g is either returned to, or taken from, the supply mains. In order to illustrate this, assume that the power input to motor is P and its synchronous speed ω_s. As all losses are ignored, P = power input to motor = air-gap power, P_g.

Subsynchronous Speed. For speeds below synchronous speed, slip s is positive, slip power sP_g appears at the slip rings and the remaining power $(1-s)P_g$ appears as shaft output. Slip power sP_g at slip frequency sf_1 is converted by slip-power converter to line frequency f_1. Power output sP_g at f_1 is fed to the line so that net power taken from source is $(1-s)P_g$, Fig. 5.39 (*a*).

Shaft speed, $\omega_r = \omega_s(1-s)$

Shaft output power, $P_m = P_g(1-s)$

$$\text{Torque} = \frac{\text{Shaft power}}{\text{Shaft speed}} = \frac{(1-s)P_g}{(1-s)\omega_s} = \frac{P_g}{\omega_s} \qquad ...(i)$$

As all losses are ignored, Fig. 5.39 (*a*) shows that shaft power output = power taken from source = $(1-s)P_g$; this is as expected.

Supersynchronous speed. For speeds above synchronous speed, slip s is negative. Therefore, direction of slip-power flow gets reversed from that when slip is positive. Stator input power P_g flows directly to motor shaft. Slip power sP_g at frequency f_1 is now withdrawn from source, slip-power converter converts this line frequency slip power to sP_g at slip frequency sf_1. This is then injected into rotor through three rotor slip rings as shown in Fig. 5.39 (*b*).

Shaft power output, $P_m = (1+s)P_g$

Shaft speed, $\omega_r = [1-(-s)]\,\omega_s = (1+s)\,\omega_s$

$$\text{Torque} = \frac{(1+s)\,P_g}{(1+s)\,\omega_s} = \frac{P_g}{\omega_s} \qquad ...(ii)$$

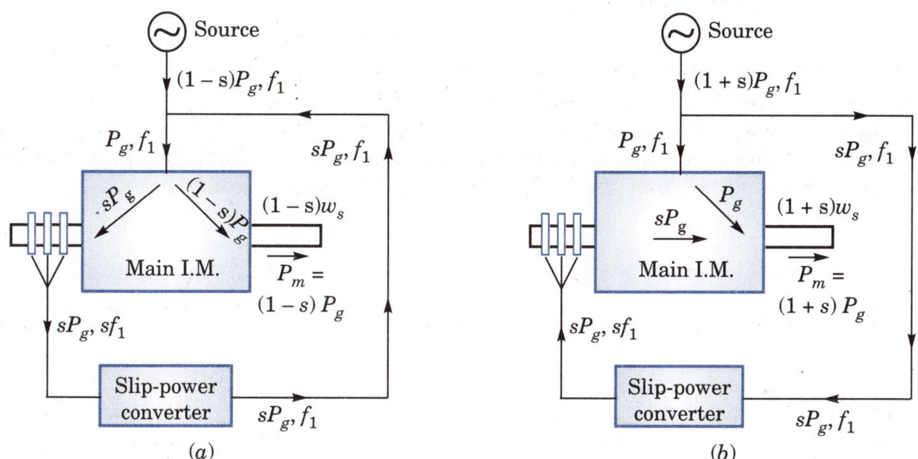

Fig. 5.39: Constant-torque drive: slip power (*a*) returned to source (*b*) taken from source.

Since all losses are neglected, shaft power output

= power input from source = $(1+s)P_g$.

Eqs. (*i*) and (*ii*) reveal that Figs. 5.39 (*a*) and (*b*) give constant-torque drive as shown in Fig. 5.40 (*a*). Therefore, when slip-frequency power sP_g is either returned to, or taken from the supply source, a *constant-torque* drive is obtained. However, the power available at the shaft = (constant torque × speed) varies linearly with speed as shown in Fig. 5.40 (*a*).

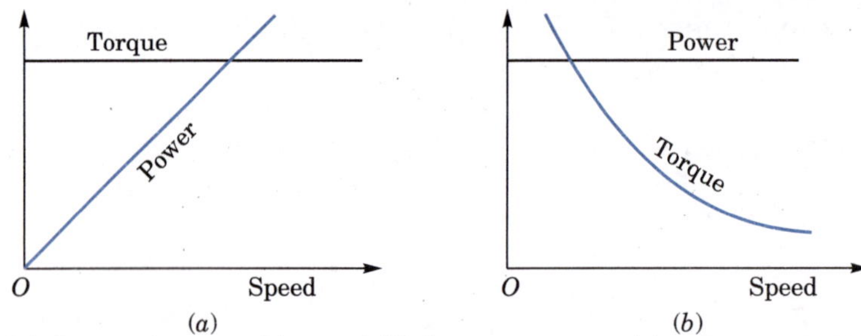

Fig. 5.40: (*a*) Constant-torque drive and (*b*) Constant-power drive, for constant motor input.

5.9.2 Constant-power Drive

For obtaining a constant-power drive, slip power is either added to, or taken from, the shaft output of the main induction motor. Power input to main motor is again assumed to be P = air-gap power, P_g (as all losses are neglected).

Subsynchronous Speed. For subsynchronous speed operation, slip s is positive. Slip power sP_g at slip frequency sf_1 is converted by slip-power converter to a frequency suitable for the auxiliary machine. Then, this power sP_g is fed to auxiliary machine, which converts the input power sP_g at a suitable frequency f_1 to mechanical power sP_g. The auxiliary machine is, therefore, working as a motor in Fig. 5.41 (*a*).

Net shaft power output = shaft power output from main motor, $(1 - s)\, P_g$ + shaft power output from auxiliary motor, $sP_g = P_g$.

Shaft speed, $\omega_r = (1 - s)\omega_s$

$$\text{Torque} = \frac{P_g}{\omega_s(1 - s)}$$

$$\text{Net shaft power} = P_g \qquad \text{...}(iii)$$

Supersynchronous speed. As slip at super synchronous speed is negative, the flow of slip-power gets reversed from that shown in Fig. 5.41(*a*). Slip power at any frequency f_1 is taken from the auxiliary machine, converted to sP_g at slip frequency sf_1 by slip-power converter and then fed to main induction motor through three rotor slip rings. Shaft power output from main motor is $(1 + s)P_g$ and from auxiliary machine, electrical power output is sP_g so that net shaft power from the set is P_g. The auxiliary machine is, therefore, working as a generator in Fig. 5.41 (*b*).

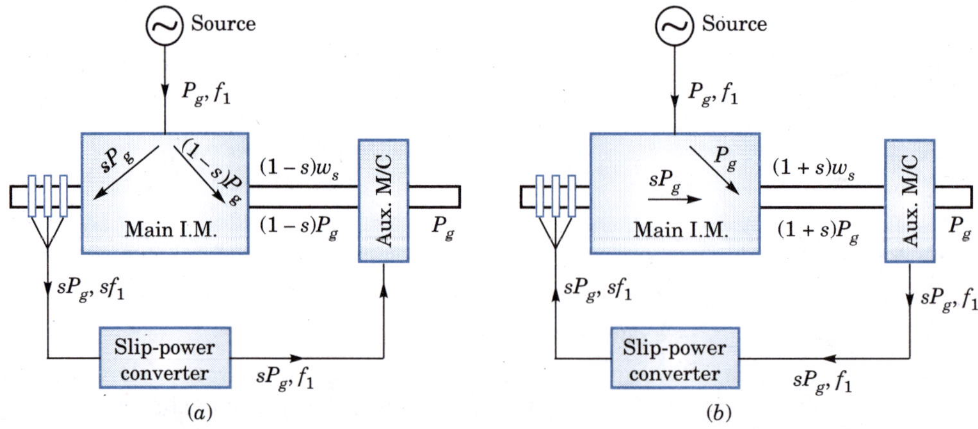

Fig. 5.41: Constant-power drive, Slip-power (*a*) added to motor shaft and (*b*) taken from the motor shaft.

Net shaft power output = Shaft power from main motor, $(1 + s) P_g$ – mechanical power converted to electrical power $sP_g = P_g$

$$\text{Shaft speed, } \omega_r = [1 - (-s)]\,\omega_s = (1 + s)\,\omega_s$$

$$\text{Torque} = \frac{P_g}{(1+s)\omega_s}$$

$$\text{Net shaft power} = P_g \qquad ...(iv)$$

It is seen from Eqs. (*iii*) and (*iv*) that as shaft speed increases from $\omega_s(1 - s)$ to $\omega_s(1 + s)$, the net shaft power output remains constant but shaft torque = (constant power/speed) decreases. This is shown in Fig. 5.40 (*b*). Therefore, when slip power is utilized in an auxiliary machine coupled with the main SRIM, *a constant-power drive* is obtained. Note that the auxiliary machine may be a dc machine or an ac machine.

The constant-power drive is simpler and is used for low-speed drives. The constant-torque drive is well suited to high-speed drives because no auxiliary machine is to be coupled with main induction motor. Both the schemes are used for the speed control of large loads whose torque requirement is proportional to speed-squared. These schemes are, therefore, used for driving (*i*) large centrifugal pumps, as for sewerage and drainage purposes and (*ii*) mine-ventilating fans.

The slip-power converter for induction motor speed control may be a system of rotating electrical machines or of power-electronic devices, or a combination of both rotating machines and power-electronic devices. The present trend is towards the use of power-electronic control systems.

The rating of slip-power converter is usually much smaller as compared to the main induction motor, since it has to handle only s times the stator power of the main SRIM.

Example 5.32. *A 3-phase, 50 Hz, 10 pole, wound rotor induction motor has its slip rings directly connected to a slip-power converter. This induction motor controls the speed of a load requiring torque proportional to the cube of its speed. The speed is to be adjusted over a range from 50 to 570 rpm and the load requires a power of 4000 kW at 570 rpm. For negligible losses, find the power handled by the slip-power converter in terms of slip, when*

(i) the slip power is returned to the supply

(ii) the slip power is added to the output of main motor shaft.

Determine the value of slip-power and motor input at 50 and 570 rpm in each case.

Find also the maximum power that the slip-power converter should be capable of carrying in both the cases.

Solution. The load torque $T_L \propto \omega^3$ or $T_L = k\omega^3$

$\therefore$ Load power, $P_L = \omega T_L = k\omega^4 = k\omega_s^4 (1 - s)^4$

Now slip $$s = \frac{600 - 570}{600} = 0.05$$

For $s = 0.05$, the load power P_L is 4000 kW.

$$\therefore \qquad 4000 = k\omega_s^4 (0.95)^4$$

or $$k\omega_s^4 = \frac{4000}{(0.95)^4} = 4911 \text{ kW}, \qquad P_L = 4911 (1 - s)^4.$$

(*i*) When the slip power is returned to the supply, then from Fig. 5.39 (*a*),

$$P_L = \text{motor input } (1 - s)$$

$\therefore$ Motor input, $\quad P_g = \dfrac{P_L}{1-s} = 4911\,(1-s)^3.$

$\therefore$ Slip-power as a function of slip, $P_{sp} = sP_g = 4911\,s\,(1-s)^3.$

For 50 rpm speed, the slip $= \dfrac{600-50}{600} = \dfrac{11}{12}$

$\therefore$ The motor input at 50 rpm, $P_g = 4911\left(\dfrac{1}{12}\right)^3 = 2.842$ kW.

$\therefore$ Slip power at 50 rpm $= sP_g = \dfrac{11}{12}(2.842) = 2.605$ kW

The motor input at 570 rpm, $P_g = 4911\left(\dfrac{19}{20}\right)^3 = 4210.6$ kW.

Slip power at 570 rpm, $= sP_g = 0.05\,(4210.6) = 210.53$ kW.

Now slip power, $\quad P_{sp} = 4911\,s\,(1-s)^3.$

The slip at which P_{sp} would be maximum, can be obtained by differentiating P_{sp} with respect to s and equating it to zero.

$$\therefore \quad \frac{dP_{sp}}{ds} = 4911\,[(1-s)^3 - s\,.\,3(1-s)^2] = 0 \quad \text{or} \quad s = \frac{1}{4}$$

$\therefore$ Maximum slip-power, $P_{sp} = 4911 \times \dfrac{1}{4}\left(\dfrac{3}{4}\right)^3 = 517.96$ kW.

(*ii*) When the slip power is added to the output of motor shaft, then from Fig. 5.41 (*a*),

Load power $\quad P_L = P_g$, and slip power $P_{sp} = sP_g$.

$\therefore$ Slip power, $\quad P_{sp} = sP_L = 4911\,s\,(1-s)^4.$

and motor input, $\quad P_g = P_L = 4911\,(1-s)^4$

Motor input at 50 rpm $= 4911\left(\dfrac{1}{12}\right)^4 = 0.237$ kW.

Slip power at 50 rpm $= sP_g = \dfrac{11}{12}(0.237) = 0.217$ kW

Motor input at 570 rpm $= 4911\,(0.95)^4 = 4000$ kW.

Slip power at 570 rpm $= sP_g = 0.05\,(4000) = 200$ kW.

Now, $\quad P_{sp} = 4911\,s\,(1-s)^4$

$$\therefore \quad \frac{dP_{sp}}{ds} = 4911\,[(1-s)^4 - s\,.\,4\,(1-s)^3] = 0 \quad \text{or} \quad s = \frac{1}{5}$$

$\therefore$ Maximum slip power $= 4911 \times \dfrac{1}{5}\left(\dfrac{4}{5}\right)^4 = 402.31$ kW.

5.10 FREQUENCY CONVERTERS (OR CHANGERS)

The object of this article is to describe the various types of rotating-frequency converters. First of all, the working principle and construction of the commutator-frequency converter is presented. Then synchronous-synchronous frequency converter and the induction-frequency converter are described.

5.10.1 Commutator-Frequency Converter

Here first of all, the working principle of the frequency converter is described. For this purpose, consider the schematic diagram of Fig. 5.42 (*a*) for a two-pole d.c. machine. The rotation of the armature in the field flux gives rise to rotational emf E across the q-axis brushes. Now let the field poles be rotated clockwise through 90°, to the position shown in Fig. 5.42 (*b*). In this figure, emf E is reduced to zero. A further rotation through 90°, as shown in Fig. 5.42 (*c*), reverses the polarity of E but without effecting its magnitude as obtained in Fig. 5.42 (*a*). If field poles are rotated 90° ahead of the position shown in Fig. 5.42 (*c*), the emf

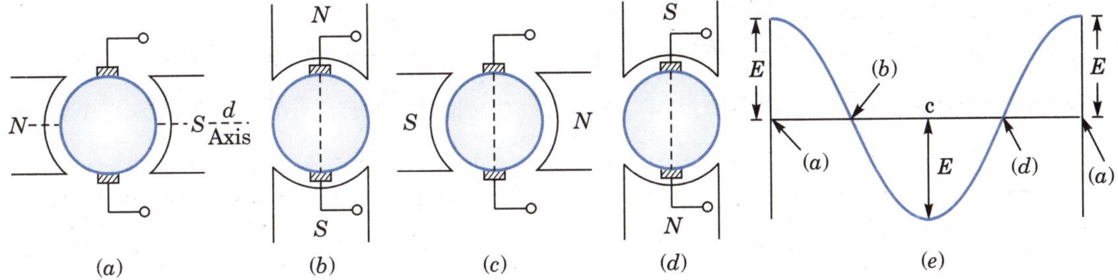

Fig. 5.42: Principle of a rotating frequency-converter.

E is again reduced to zero in Fig. 5.42 (*d*) and a further 90° movement brings the field poles back to their initial position of Fig. 5.42 (*a*) and the emf E is again generated. Fig. 5.42 (*e*) illustrates a plot of this variation of emf E as the field poles are rotated clockwise. An examination of Fig. 5.42 reveals that for a 2-pole machine, with one revolution of the field poles, one cycle of emf $\left(f_b = \frac{nP}{2} = 1\frac{2}{2} = 1\right)$ is generated. This emf variation can be observed by a voltmeter connected across the brushes. If the field poles make 2 (= n) revolutions per second, then 2 cycles of emf $\left(f_b = \frac{P.n}{2} = \frac{2 \times 2}{2} = 2\right)$ are generated in one second. Likewise if the field poles are made to rotate at speed, say n_r rps, then the number of cycles per second, *i.e.*, the frequency of the emf at the bruches would be given by

$$f_b = \frac{Pn_r}{2} = \frac{2 \times n_r}{2} = n_r \text{ Hz for a 2-pole machine.}$$

From the foregoing discussion, it can be concluded that the speed of the field flux with respect to the stationary bruches, determines the frequency of the brush emf. If the brushes were made to rotate in the direction of field flux and at the speed of the latter, the relative speed between the two would be zero and the frequency of the brush emf would, therefore, be zero, *i.e.*, d.c.

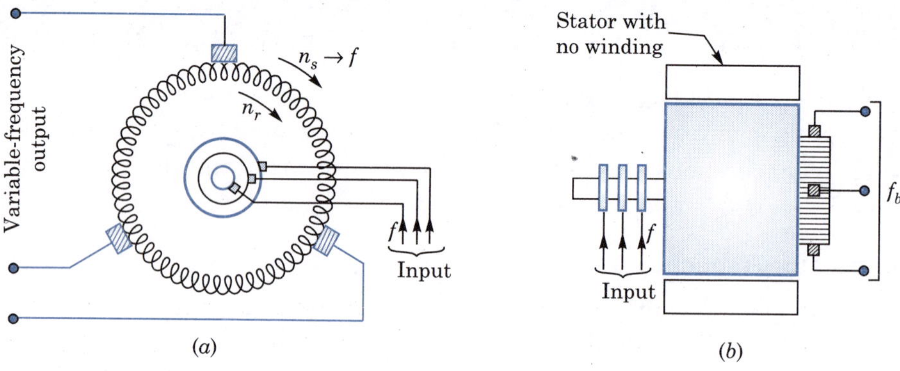

Fig. 5.43: Rotating frequency converter.

A simple rotating frequency converter, with no stator winding, is illustrated in Fig. 5.43. The stator iron is present merely to provide a low-reluctance path to the magnetic flux. Also, no electromechanical energy conversion can take place because the stator carries no winding. The d.c. armature winding on the rotor is fitted with both slip rings at one end and commutator at the other end as shown in Fig. 5.43 (*b*).

Polyphase currents of frequency *f*, fed to the slip rings, set up a rotating magnetic field. The speed of this rotating field is $n_s = \dfrac{2f}{P}$ rps relative to the armature conductors, whatever the speed of the armature may be. If the armature is stationary, then field speed in space is n_s. In other words, the field speed relative to the fixed brushes is n_s and the frequency of the emf at the brushes is

$$f_b = \frac{Pn_s}{2} = f.$$

The term 'field speed in space' must be clearly understood. For this, the reader should imagine himself seated on the stator tooth. Now speed of the air-gap field relative to the reader is called field speed in space.

Suppose the armature is rotated at speed n_r against the direction of rotation of the revolving field. Then the field speed in space or relative to the fixed brushes is $n_s - n_r$, so the frequency of the brush emf is

$$f_b = \frac{P(n_s - n_r)}{2}.$$

If the armature is made to revolve at speed n_r, in the direction of the rotating field, then the field speed in space, or relative to the fixed brushes, is $n_s + n_r$ and

$$f_b = \frac{P(n_s + n_r)}{2}.$$

Note that whatever the armature speed may be, its conductor emfs and currents remain at supply frequency, since these conductors are fed directly *via* the slip rings. Thus the frequency changer converts the supply frequency *f* at the slip rings to frequency.

$$f_b = \frac{P(n_s \pm n_r)}{2}. \qquad ...(5.92)$$

at the fixed brushes.

For a constant slip ring voltage, the brush emf is fixed and is independent of the armature speed. In order to change the magnitude of brush emf, therefore, slip ring voltage must be varied by means of an auto-transformer or tapped transformer.

The phase angle of the brush emf relative to the slip ring voltage can be varied, merely by rocking around all the commutator brushes together, to a new spatial position. This is proved in chapter 7.

5.10.2 Synchronous-Synchronous Frequency Converter

In this type of converter, two synchronous machines are coupled together so that their rotor speeds are the same. If the synchronous machines have P_1 and P_2 poles and operate at frequencies of f_1 and f_2 respectively ; then since their speeds are equal,

$$n = \frac{2f_1}{P_1} = \frac{2f_2}{P_2} \quad \text{or} \quad \frac{f_1}{f_2} = \frac{P_1}{P_2} \qquad \text{...(5.93)}$$

Eq. (5.93) shows that each machine has a frequency that is proportional to the number of poles for which its armature winding is designed.

Example 5.33. *Two directly coupled synchronous machines are used for converting 50 to 20 Hz. Find the mimimum number of poles that the two machines must have. At what speed will the set operate ?*

Solution. From Eq. (5.93), $\frac{P_1}{P_2} = \frac{f_1}{f_2} = \frac{50}{20} = \frac{5}{2}$

This means that if machine 1 has 5 poles, machine 2 must have 2 poles. Now a machine can't have odd number of poles, therefore, machine 1 must have 10 poles while machine 2 must have 4 poles.

$$\text{Speed of the set} = \frac{120f}{P} = \frac{120 \times 50}{10} = 600 \text{ rpm.}$$

5.10.3 Induction-Frequency Converter

Induction-frequency converter is essentially a wound-rotor induction machine driven by a synchronous motor or a d.c. motor. The stator of the induction-frequency converter is fed from supply frequency f_1, which sets up a magnetic field rotating at synchronous speed of

$$N_s = \frac{120f_1}{P} \text{ rpm}$$

The frequency f_2, of the emf at the slip-ring terminals of the induction-frequency converter, is given by

$$f_2 = \frac{P\,(\text{relative speed in rpm between rotor and rotating field})}{120} \qquad \text{...(5.94)}$$

When the rotor is driven at N_r rpm in the direction of rotating field, the relative speed between rotor and rotating field is $N_s - N_r$ rpm. In case rotor is driven at N_r rpm against the direction of rotating field the relative speed between rotor and roatging field becomes $N_s + N_r$ rpm. Therefore, the output, frequency of the frequency-converter is,

$$f_2 = \frac{P\,(N_s \pm N_r)}{120} \qquad \text{...(5.95)}$$

Substitution of, $N_s = \frac{120 f_1}{P}$ in Eq. (5.95) gives,

$$f_2 = f_1 \pm \frac{P}{120} N_r \quad \text{...(5.96)}$$

Substitution of, $P = \frac{120 f_1}{N_s}$ in Eq. (4.95) gives

$$f_2 = \frac{(N_s \pm N_r)}{N_s} f_1 = \left(1 \pm \frac{N_r}{N_s}\right) f_1 \quad \text{...(5.97)}$$

Note that plus sign is to be used when the rotor is driven against the direction of rotating field and negative sign when the rotor rotates in the direction of rotating field.

The power output available at the rotor terminals of freqnency converter consists of two parts, namely (*i*) the power P_{sr} transferred from its stator to rotor by transformer action as in any induction motor and (*ii*) the power transferred mechanically from the coupled motor.

If exciting current, losses and leakage impedance voltage drops are neglected and stator to rotor turns ratio is assumed unity, then

Stator phase current I_1 = rotor phase current I_2.

For per phase stator voltage V_1 and load p.f. cos θ, the power transferred from stator to rotor is

$$P_{sr} = V_1 I_1 \cos \theta.$$

Power output from rotor of frequency converter, P = slip power

$$\therefore \quad P = s \,.\, P_{sr} = s V_1 I_1 \cos \theta.$$

Since s is usually greater than 1, $P > P_{sr}$. The power $P - P_{sr}$ must be supplied mechanically from the driving motor.

∴ Power delivered by the driving motor $= P - P_{sr} = (V_1 I_1 \cos \theta)(s - 1)$

$$\therefore \quad \frac{\text{Driving motor power}}{\text{Power transferred from stator to rotor}} = (s - 1) \quad \text{...(5.98)}$$

The output voltage from the induction-frequency converter depends upon the relative speed between rotor conductors and the rotating field. This means that output voltage and frequency of the frequency-converter vary in the same ratio. For example, if the output voltage and frequency at the rotor terminals are 200 V and 50 Hz, then these values would be 300 V at 75 Hz, 400 V at 100 Hz etc. In other words, the ratio of output voltage to output frequency of the induction-frequency converter remains constant. In view of this ; a squirrel cage induction motor, fed from an induction-frequency converter, can operate satisfactorily without any magnetic saturation since flux ϕ remains constant. For example, if squirrel cage motor is designed for 200 V, 50 Hz, 1500 rpm, then it can operate satisfactorily at 100 V, 25 Hz, 750 rpm ; 400 V, 100 hz, 3000 rpm ; 600 V, 150 Hz, 4500 rpm with the maximum torque remaining substantially constant.

Induction-frequency converters are widely used where high-speed operation is desirable for getting better quality of the finished products, such as in wood-working and furniture industries, metal-working industries etc.

5.10.4 Synchronous-induction Frequency Converter

In the previous article, induction-frequency converter has been described when the induction machine has coupled with it either an ac machine or a dc machine. In this part of the article, a general study of induction machine coupled with a synchronous machine has been presented.

Frequency converters employing a synchronous machine coupled with an induction machine are called *synchronous-induction frequency converters*. For the purpose of frequency conversion, rotor of both induction and synchronous machines must be mechanically coupled. Depending upon how the stator or rotor of induction machine is electrically connected to stator (or armature) of synchronous machine, there are two possible configurations of synchronous-induction frequency converter.

I. *Synchronous machine stator and induction-machine rotor connected together.* When 3 phase stator of the synchronous machine and 3-phase rotor of the induction machine are connected together to the same 3-phase supply system and the stator of induction machine to another 3-phase source, the connection scheme is as shown in Fig. 5.44. The power distribution in the two machines depends upon the value of slip at which induction machine operates.

Slip < 1. When slip is less than 1, *i.e.* rotor frequency f_2 (= sf_1) is less than stator frequency f_1 of the induction machine, the power distribution in the two machines is as shown in Fig. 5.44 (*a*), Here P is the power input to induction machine stator, sP is the slip power available at the rotor slip rings. As $sP < P$, the rest of the power, *i.e.,* $P - sP = (1 - s)P$ must flow to the synchronous machine along the shaft. As electrical power output from synchronous machine is $(1 - s)P$, it is working as a synchronous generator.

For no loss in the system, input power = output power = P

Power handled by synchronous machine, $P_{sy} = (1 - s)P$

Power handled by induction machine, $P_{im} = P$

$$\therefore \qquad \frac{P_{sy}}{P_{im}} = (1 - s)$$

Slip > 1. When slip is more than 1, slip power sP is more than P. As rotor output sP is more than stator input P, the difference $(s - 1)P$ must flow from synchronous machine along the shaft as shown in Fig. 5.44 (*b*). For power balance, $(s - 1)P$ flows from rotor output to synchronous machine. As synchronous machine has electric power input $(s - 1)P$, it is working as a synchronous motor.

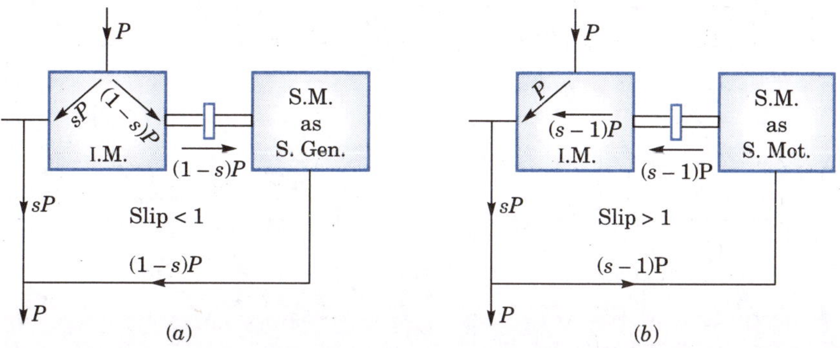

Fig. 5.44 Synchronous-induction frequency converter with synchronous machine stator and induction motor rotor connected together.

Here $P_{sy} = (s - 1)\,P$ and $P_{im} = P$

$$\therefore \quad \frac{P_{sy}}{P_{im}} = (s - 1)$$

Note that for slip $s < 1$, synchronous machine acts as a synchronous generator and for slip $s > 1$, it acts as a synchronous motor.

II. *Stators of both machines connected together.* When stators of both induction and synchronous machines are connected together to the same 3-phase ac source and the rotor of induction machine to a separate 3-phase ac source, Fig. 5.45, the power distribution again depends upon the value of slip.

Slip < 1. With P_1 as the input to stator of induction machine, the rotor output is $sP_1 = P$. As $s < 1$, $sP_1 < P_1$; the difference $P_1 - sP_1 = (1 - s)P_1$ must flow to synchronous machine along the shaft as shown in Fig. 5.45 (*a*). Synchronous machine is therefore acting as a synchronous generator. Power output of synchronous generator $(s - 1)\,P$ adds to P at node A to give P_1 as the input to induction machine. At the node A,

$$P + (1 - s)\,P_1 = P$$

$$\therefore \quad P = sP_1 = \text{Total input power}$$

$$P_{sy} = (1 - s)\,P_1 = \frac{1 - s}{s}\,P$$

$$P_{im} = P_1 = \frac{P}{s} \quad \therefore \quad \frac{P_{sy}}{P_{im}} = (1 - s)$$

Slip > 1. With P_1 as the input to stator of induction machine, the rotor output is $sP_1 = P$. As $s > 1$, $sP_1 > P_1$. Therefore, stator input power P_1 directly flows to slip rings and the remaining power $sP_1 - P_1 = (s - 1)\,P_1$ must flow along the shaft from the synchronous machine as shown in Fig. 4.45 (*b*). Therefore, power input to synchronous machine has to be $(s - 1)\,P_1$; it therefore works as a synchronous motor, Fig. 5.45 (*b*). At node A, $P = (s - 1)\,P_1 + P_1$ or $P = sP_1$ as in Fig. 5.45 (*b*).

$$P_{sy} = (s - 1)\,P_1 = \frac{s - 1}{s}\,P\,;\; P_{im} = P_1 = \frac{P}{s}$$

$$\therefore \quad \frac{P_{sy}}{P_{im}} = (s - 1)$$

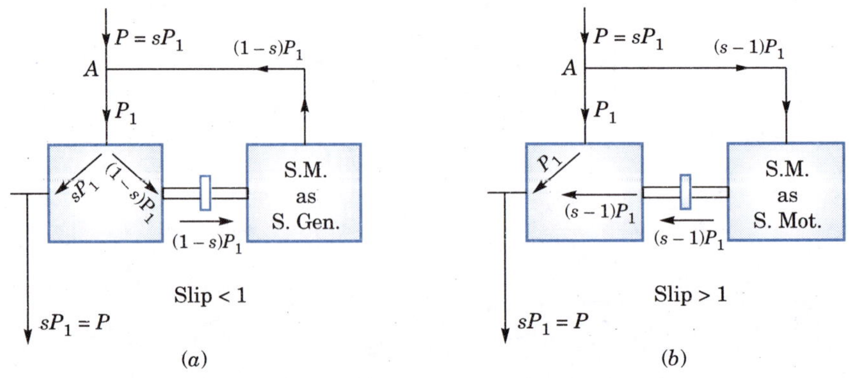

Fig. 5.45: Synchronous-induction frequency converter with stators of both induction and synchronous machines connected together.

As before, for $s < 1$, synchronous machine acts as a synchronous generator with power $= \frac{1-s}{s} P (1-s) P_1$ and for $s > 1$, it acts as a synchronous motor with power $= \frac{s-1}{s} P = (s-1) P_1$ where P is the input power to the whole set and P_1 is the input to induction machine.

Example 5.34. *An 8-pole 3-phase induction machine fed from 40 Hz source is mechanically coupled with an 8-pole 3-phase synchronous machine fed from a separate 50 Hz source. Discuss how power will be transferred.*

Solution. For induction machine, rotating field speed $= \frac{120 \times 40}{8} = 600$ rpm

For synchronous machine, rotating field speed $= \frac{120 \times 50}{8} = 750$ rpm

It is the synchronous machine that decides the combined speed of the set. The coupled set, therefore, runs at 750 rpm. For induction machine, rotor rotates at a speed of 750 rpm which is more than its rotating field speed of 600 rpm. The induction machine, therefore, acts as an induction generator and the other machine as a synchronous motor. Power is, therefore, transferred from 50 Hz system to 40 Hz system through the induction generator.

Example 5.35. *Two possible schemes for frequency conversion from 50 Hz to 30 Hz system are as shown in Fig. 5.46. For both these schemes, find*

(a) the minimum number of poles on each 3-phase machine,

(b) the power distribution between them. Neglect losses and take power input as 300 kW.

Solution. (*a*) For obtaining rotor frequency lower than stator frequency, the rotor of induction machine must be driven in the direction of rotating field so that relative speed between stator field and the rotor is equal to the difference of the two speeds.

If P_i = number of poles on 3-phase induction motor

and P_s = number of poles on 3-phase synchronous machine, then for Fig. 5.46 (*a*), Eq. (5.94) gives

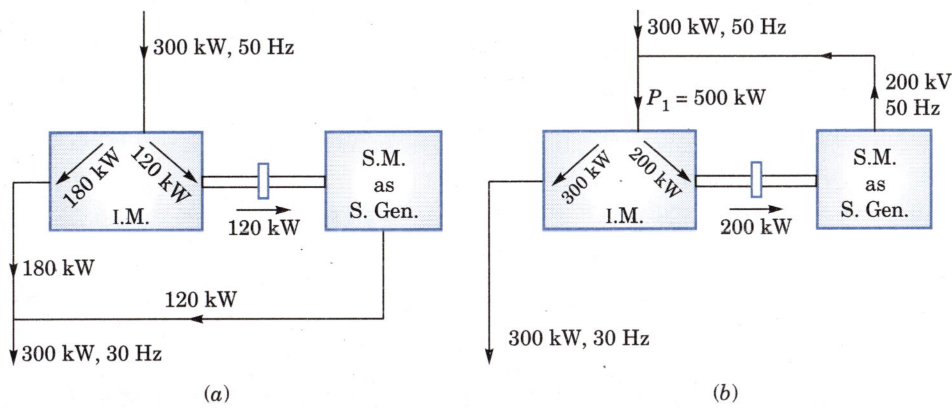

Fig. 5.46: Pertaining of Example 5.35.

$$f_2 = \frac{P_i\left[\dfrac{120 \times 50}{P_i} - \dfrac{120\,0 \times 30}{P_s}\right]}{120} = 30 \text{ Hz}$$

or $$6000 - \frac{3600}{P_s}\,.\,P_i = 3600 \quad \text{or} \quad \frac{P_i}{P_s} = \frac{2}{3} = \frac{4}{6}$$

This gives $P_i = 4$ poles and $P_s = 6$ poles

For Fig 5.46 (*b*), $$30 = \frac{P_i\left[\dfrac{120 \times 50}{P_i} - \dfrac{120 \times 50}{P_s}\right]}{120}$$

or $$3600 = 6000 - 6000\,\frac{P_i}{P_s} \quad \text{or} \quad \frac{P_i}{P_s} = \frac{2}{5} = \frac{4}{10}$$

∴ $P_i = 4$ poles and $P_s = 10$ poles

(*b*) Here slip $$s = \frac{f_2}{f_1} = \frac{30}{50} = 0.6$$

For Fig. 5.46 (a) : As slip < 1, the slip power $= \frac{3}{5} \times 300 = 180$ kW flows out of rotor terminals as shown. The remaining 120 kW must flow along the shaft to synchronous machine making it a synchrnous generator as shown.

∴ Power handled by synchronous generator = 120 kW

Power handled by induction motor = 300 kW

The power distribution in the two machines is as shown in Fig. 5.46 (*a*).

For Fig. 5.46 (b) : Power input to induction motor

$$= P_1 = \frac{P}{s} \quad \text{or} \quad P_1 = \frac{300 \times 5}{3} = 500 \text{ kW}$$

With P_1 known, the power distribution in the two machines is as shown in Fig. 5.46 (*b*). The synchronous machine is working as a synchronous generator and is supplying 200 kW as shown. The power input to induction motor is 500 kW, see Fig. 5.46 (*b*).

Example 5.36. *Fig. 5.47 (a) shows a scheme of interconnection between two 3-phase systems of frequencies 50 Hz and 60 Hz. The windings of the induction machine and synchronous machine are so arranged that the stator mmf rotates in opposite directions in the two. Deduce the minimum number of poles on each machine for the operation to be feasible. Assuming the losses in the machines to be negligible, determine the power developed by the sysnchronous motor when the set transfers P kW from the 50 Hz system to the 60 Hz system.*

Solution. Rotor frequency $f_2 = sf_1$

∴ $$\text{slip } s = \frac{60}{50} = 1.2$$

Speed of rotating field in induction motor $= \dfrac{120 \times 50}{P_i}$ rpm

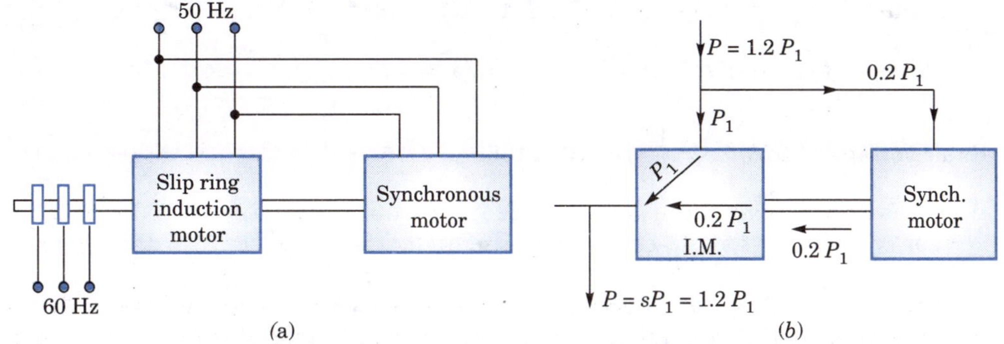

Fig. 5.47: (*a*) Pertaining to Example 5.36, (*b*) Pertaining to Example 5.36.

Speed of rotating field in synchronous motor $= \dfrac{120 \times 50}{P_s}$ rpm

where, P_i = No. of poles in induction motor

P_s = No. of poles in synchronous motor

With the two stator mmfs rotating in opposite directions, the relative speed between the rotating field and rotor conductors of induction motor is $\dfrac{6000}{P_i} + \dfrac{6000}{P_s}$

∴ Rotor frequency in 3-phase induction motor

$$= \frac{P_i\left[\dfrac{6000}{P_i} + \dfrac{6000}{P_s}\right]}{120} = 60 \text{ (given)} \quad \text{or} \quad \frac{P_i}{P_s} = \frac{1200}{6000} = \frac{1}{5} = \frac{2}{10}$$

∴ Minimum number of poles on I.M. = 2 and on S.M. = 10.

For determining the power distribution in the two machines, a single line diagram as shown in Fig. 5.47 (*b*) is drawn. With P_1 as the power input to stator of 3-phase induction motor, the rotor output is $sP_1 = P = 1.2\ P_1$ = total power input.

For $s > 1$, entire P_1 flows to the slip rings and the remaining power $0.2\ P_1$ has to come along the shaft from the synchronous machine. With no losses, power input to synchronous machine is $0.2\ P_1$; it is therefore acting as a synchronous motor.

∴ Power developed by the synchronous motor,

$$P_{sy} = 0.2\ P_1 = 0.2 \times \frac{P}{1.2} = \frac{1}{6} P \text{ kW}.$$

Example 5.37. *A 16-pole, 3-phase induction-frequency converter is driven at 2250 rpm and its stator is connected to a 50 Hz system. If rotor terminal voltage at standstill is 15 V, then find what voltages and frequencies can be obtained from this frequency-converter.*

Solution. Synchronous-speed of induction-frequency converter

$$= \frac{120\ f_1}{P} = \frac{120 \times 50}{16} = 375 \text{ r.p.m.}$$

From Eq. (5.97), the output frequency is,

$$f_2 = \left(1 \pm \frac{2250}{375}\right) \times 50 = 350 \text{ Hz or } 250 \text{ Hz}$$

At standstill, rotor voltage is 15 V and its frequency is 50 Hz.

$\therefore$ Rotor voltage at 250 Hz $= \frac{15}{50} \times 250 = 75$ V.

Rotor voltage at 350 Hz $= \frac{15}{50} \times 350 = 105$ V.

If rotor is driven against the direction of rotating field, the output is 105 V at 350 Hz. In case the rotor is driven in the direction of rotating field, the output is 75 V at 250 Hz.

Example 5.38. *A 3-phase induction-frequency converter, with its stator fed from 50 Hz, is required to give an output frequency range from 120 to 480 Hz. Its rotor is to be driven at 2600 rpm by a d.c. motor and the output from the converter is 40 kW at 0.8 p.f., 480 Hz and 10 kW at 0.8 p.f., 120 Hz.*

If the exciting current, losses and leakage impedance drops of the induction-frequency converter are neglected, then determine

(a) its possible number of poles,

(b) its minimum and maximum rotor speeds,

(c) kVA rating of its stator winding and

(d) power rating of the d.c. motor.

Solution. From Eq. (5.96), output frequency is

(*a*) $$f_2 = f_1 \pm \frac{P}{120} N_r.$$

For higher frequency outputs, the rotor is driven usually opposite to the direction of rotating field.

$$\therefore \quad f_2 = f_1 + \frac{P}{120} N_r$$

Now $$120 = 50 + \frac{P}{120} \times 2600$$

or $$P = \frac{70 \times 120}{2600} = 3.23, \quad \therefore \quad P = 4 \text{ poles.}$$

Also, $$480 = 50 + \frac{P}{120} \times 2600$$

$$\therefore \quad P = \frac{430 \times 120}{2600} = 19.84, \quad \therefore \quad P = 20 \text{ poles.}$$

Since 480 Hz, 20 poles require rotor speed N_r to be high, the induction-frequency converter must have 20 poles.

(*b*) Now $$480 = 50 + \frac{20}{120} N_r \quad \text{or} \quad N_r = \frac{430 \times 120}{20} = 2580 \text{ rpm.}$$

Also, $$120 = 50 + \frac{20}{120} N_r \quad \text{or} \quad N_r = \frac{70 \times 120}{29} = 420 \text{ rpm.}$$

$\therefore$ Minimum and maximum speeds of the induction-frequency converter are 420 and 2580 rpm respectively.

(*c*) and (*d*) Power output from the rotor of frequency converter is

$$sV_1I_1 \cos\theta = 40 \text{ kW}$$

For 480 Hz, the slip $s = \dfrac{N_s + N_r}{N_s} = \dfrac{\dfrac{120 \times 50}{20} + 2580}{300} = 9.6$

$$\therefore \quad V_1I_1 = \frac{40{,}000}{0.8 \times 9.6} = 5210 \text{ VA} = 5.21 \text{ kVA.}$$

Power delivered by the d.c. motor = $(V_1I_1 \cos\theta)(s - 1)$

$$= (5.21)(0.8)(9.6 - 1) = 35.845 \text{ kW}$$

For 120 Hz, $s = \dfrac{420 + 300}{300} = 2.4.$

$$\therefore \quad V_1I_1 = \frac{10{,}000}{0.8 \times 2.4} = 5208 \text{ VA} \cong 5.21 \text{ kVA.}$$

Power delivered by d.c. motor

$$= (5.21)(0.8)(1.4) = 5.835 \text{ kW.}$$

Therefore, kVA rating of the stator winding is $V_1I_1 = 5.21$ kVA and the d.c. motor power rating is 35.845 kW.

5.11 STATIC SLIP-POWER SPEED CONTROL

As stated before, slip-power recovery offers two schemes for the speed control of SRIM; constant-torque drive and constant-power drive. In constant-torque drive, slip-power is either returned to, or taken from, the supply. In the constant-power drive, an auxiliary machine to be coupled with the shaft of main SRIM is essential. Out of the two schemes, constant-torque drive employing static slip-power converter has become more popular. A static slip-power converter usually consists of rectifier-inverter scheme. One scheme, giving speed control below synchronous speed only is known as *static Kramer drive* and the other, permitting speed control both below and above synchronous speed is called *static Scherbius drive.* These are discussed below briefly.

5.11.1 Static Kramer Drive

A static Kramer drive scheme is shown in Fig. 5.48. It consists of SRIM, a rectifier bridge, a filter, an inverter bridge and a transformer.

In this scheme of speed control, slip power is recovered from the rotor of SRIM and is fed back to the supply line through rectifier, inverter and transformer. The slip-frequency alternating voltage is first rectified by diode bridge and this unidirectional voltage is smoothed by a filter circuit after which it is fed to the 3-phase inverter. This inverter is line commutated. The slip power returned to the supply depends upon the inverter firing angle, direct voltage at the inverter terminals and the 3-phase supply voltage. The function of the three-phase transformer is to match the inverter output voltage with the 3-phase supply voltage. The speed control is achieved by varying the firing angle of the inverter. The usual range of firing angle is from 90° to 160° for a wide-speed range. The power flow through the rectifier is unidirectional, therefore, only sub-synchronous speed below the normal value are obtainable. Since the slip power is returned to the supply, the scheme illustrated in Fig. 5.48 results in a constant-torque drive.

The converter components of the scheme of Fig. 5.48 have to handle only slip power, therefore, converter power ratings are low. In addition, this drive system possesses speed control characteristics similar to a dc motor. Static Kramer drive, therefore, offers an adjustable speed drive which is more efficient, less costly and has simple control circuitry.

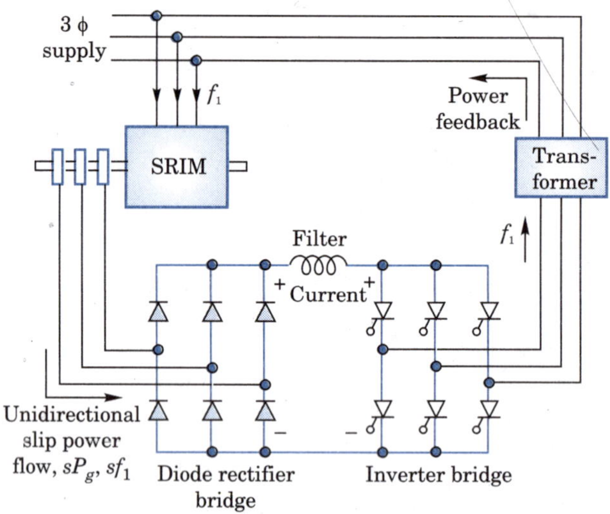

Fig. 5.48: Static Kramer drive for the speed control of 3-phase SRIM.

As stated before, static Kramer drive is popular in large pump and compressor-type drives where the speed-control range below synchronous speed is usually limited.

5.11.2 Static Scherbius Drive

In Fig. 5.48, speed can be controlled only below synchronous speed, because rectifier bridge restricts the power flow from rotor circuit to the supply line. In other words, for subsynchronous speed control, the slip-power flow is unidirectional. For subsynchronous and supersynchronous speed control, slip-power flow must be bidirectional. This type of control is realizable by two schemes, namely (*i*) dc-link static Scherbius drive and (*ii*) cycloconverter static Scherbius drive. These are now discussed briefly.

5.11.2.1 DC link Static Scherbius Drive

A dc-link Scherbius drive, shown in Fig. 5.49, allows both subsynchronous and supersynchronous speed control. It consists of main SRIM, two-phase controlled bridges requiring twelve thyristors, smoothing inductor and a transformer.

For subsynchronous speed control, bridge 1 has firing angle less than 90° whereas bridge 2 has firing angle more than 90°. In other words, bridge 1 works as rectifier and bridge 2 as line-commutated inverter for subsynchronous motor control. The slip power flows from rotor circuit to bridge 1, bridge 2, transformer and to the supply.

For supersynchronous motor control, bridge 1 is made to work as line-commutated inverter with firing angle more than 90° and bridge 2 as a rectifier with firing angle less than 90°. The power flow is now from the supply to transformer, bridge 2, bridge 1 and to the rotor circuit.

This scheme requires twelve thyristors and the associated firing circuitry, its cost is, therefore, more. At the same time, slip-frequency emfs near synchronous speed are insufficient to commutate the thyristors naturally. Therefore, special circuit schemes for forced commutation are necessary for passing through the synchronous speed. This complicates the static Scherbius drive system of Fig. 5.49. The advantages of lower cost and simplicity inherent in static Kramer drive are no longer present in the static Scherbius drive. This scheme of Fig. 5.49 offers constant-torque drive.

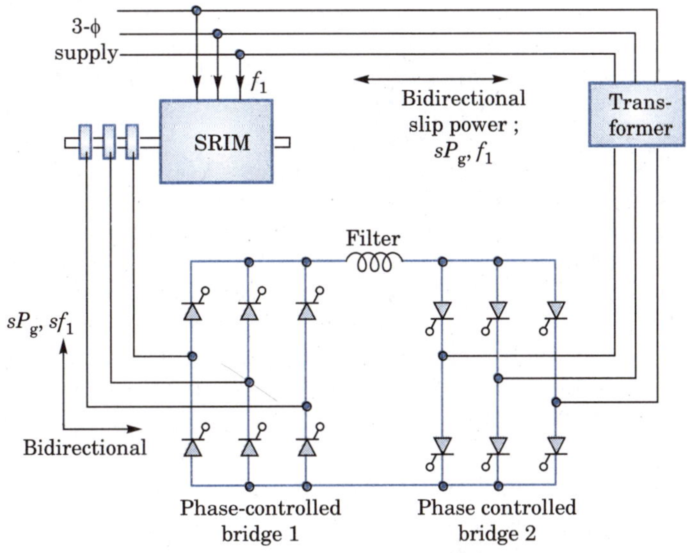

Fig. 5.49: DC-link static Scherbius drive.

5.11.2.2 Cycloconverter Static Scherbius Drive

The dual controlled converter system used in dc link Scherbius drive, Fig. 5.49, is now replaced by one phase-controlled line-commutated cycloconverter as shown in Fig. 5.50. Such schemes are used for very high-power pumps and blower-type drives. Cycloconverter permits the slip-power flow in either direction and the machine can, therefore, be controlled in both subsynchronous and supersynchronous ranges with motoring and regeneration features. As slip power is either returned to, or taken from, the supply mains, cycloconverter static Scherbius drive offers constant-torque drive scheme.

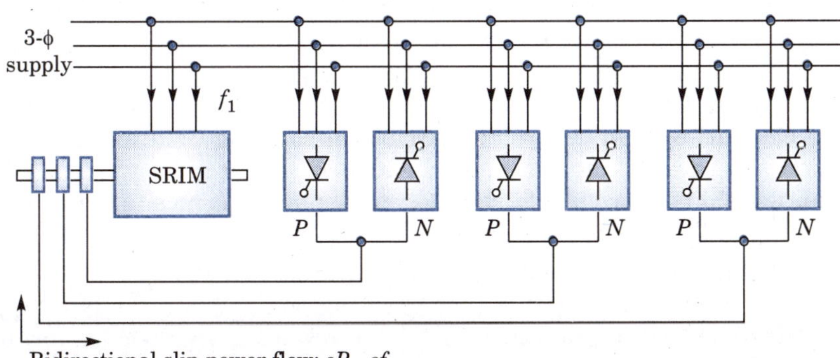

Fig. 5.50: Cycloconverter static Scherbius drive.

5.12 ELECTRICAL BRAKING OF INDUCTION MOTORS

In many applications, it becomes necessary to stop an induction motor and its coupled load quickly. A motor, during electrical braking conditions, operates under severe duty cycle. Therefore electrical braking is employed only when it is highly desirable to control the braking time, deceleration etc. There are three important methods for electrical braking of polyphase induction motors. These are regenerative braking, plugging and dynamic braking. The object of this article is to discuss these three methods of braking and to examine the speed-torque characteristics of polyphase induction motors for a particular method of braking. When frequent starting and braking of polyphase induction motors is required, it is preferable to use low-speed machines in order to avoid its undue heating during acceleration and deceleration.

(a) Regenerative braking. Regenerative braking takes place when the load forces the motor to run above synchronous speed. When the rotor speed, as when lowering of load in a crane or a hoist, becomes more than rotating field speed, the slip becomes negative. A negative slip means that the induction machine now operates as an induction generator in the second quadrant as shown in Fig. 5.51 and returns power to the supply line. The power delivered to the supply is given by the product of regenerative braking torque and the corresponding rotor speed. Fig. 5.51 shows that the amount of power returned to the supply line, depends upon how far is the rotor speed above synchronous speed. When rotor speed falls to synchronous speed, the regenerative braking comes to an end.

Regenerative braking range can be increased if the motor has pole-changing winding. For example, in Fig. 5.51, A is the operating point for 4 pole operation for a load torque T_L. When the number of poles are suddenly increased to 8 poles the operating point shifts from A to B and regenerative braking takes place, because now slip $= \dfrac{Ob - Oa}{Ob}$ becomes negative. The operating point B travels to the new operating point C along the arrows as shown in Fig. 5.51. The regenerative braking ceases when the new synchronous speed Ob, corresponding to 8 poles, is reached. This techniques is useful only in squirrel cage motors, because in wound-rotor motors the stator and rotor poles must be changed simultaneously.

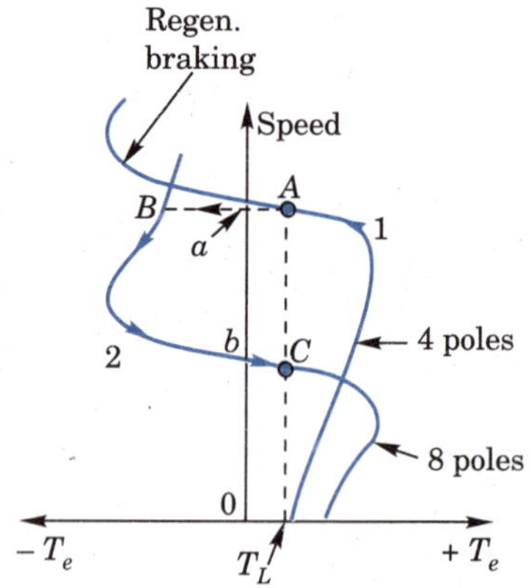

Fig. 5.51: Regenerative braking of polyphase induction motors.

(b) Plugging. In this method, any two supply leads are interchanged so that the direction of rotating field gets reversed. A forward rotating field is one that rotates in the direction of rotor and soon after the interchange of any two leads, this field becomes backward-rotating field. In a polyphase induction motor, electromagnetic torque is developed in the direction of rotating field. Therefore, backward-rotating field torque T_1 is opposite to the rotor rotation and the braking torque so developed brings the rotor to stop quickly. The supply terminals should be disconnected as soon as the motor comes to stop, otherwise motor would start running in the backward direction.

Fig. 5.52 (*a*) shows the speed-torque characteristics of a squirrel-cage induction motor during plugging. For load torque T_L, A is the operating point. When the two supply leads are interchanged, the initial braking torque is T_b = load torque T_L + backward torque T_1 and the operating point A shift at once to point B in the second quadrant of Fig. 5.52 (*a*). Braking action now takes place along the curve BC. At point C, the supply should be disconnected to stop the motor. In case supply is not disconnected, the motor starts accelerating in the reversed direction along the curve *CD* and point *D* in the third quadrant is the final operating point. If any two supply leads are again reversed, the operation shifts from point *D* to point *E* in the fourth quadrant. Braking action now takes place along the curve *EG*. If the supply is not switched off at point *G*, the final operating point is *A* as before.

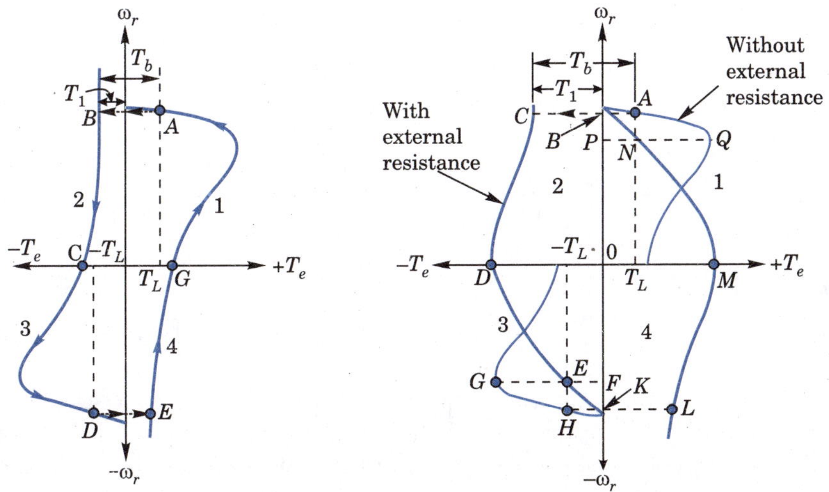

Fig. 5.52: Speed-torque characteristics during plugging of (*a*) squirrel-cage motor and (*b*) wound-rotor motor.

Fig. 5.52 (*b*) illustrates the speed-torque characteristics of a wound-rotor induction motor during plugging. At the time of plugging, an external resistance is inserted in the rotor circuit for current limitation and also to increase the backward rotating torque T_1. For load torque T_L, *A* is the operating point with *OB* as the rotor speed. When two supply leads are interchanged and at the same time an external resistance is inserted in the rotor circuit, the initial braking torque is T_b = load torque T_L + backward torque T_1 and the operating point *A* shifts to point *C* in the second quadrant. Braking action now takes place along the curve *CD*. At point *D*, the supply should be disconnected to stop the motor. In case the supply is not switched off the motor starts accelerating in the reversed direction along the curve *DE* and *E* is the final operating point in the third quadrant. If the external rotor circuit resistance is now removed, point *E* shifts at once to point *G* and then to point *H* along the curve *GH*. Point *H* corresponds to the induction motor rotation in the reversed direction with rotor speed *OK* = *OB* and load torque T_L. If any two supply leads are reversed again, with simultaneous introduction of external resistance in the rotor circuit, point *H* shifts to point *L* in the fourth quadrant and then motor operates along the curve *LM*. If supply is not disconnected at point *M*, the motor operation continues along the curve *MN*, with final operating point at *N* in the first quadrant and with motor speed equal to *OP*. If now the external rotor circuit resistance is removed, point *N* shifts to point *Q* and then to point *A* along the curve *QA*. In this manner, electric braking by plugging and the four-quadrant operation of squirrel-cage and wound-rotor induction motors can be achieved.

Plugging involves heavy loss of power, but the motor can be brought to rest quickly.

(c) Dynamic (or rheostatic) braking. Dynamic braking of an induction motor is achieved if its stator winding, after being disconnected from three phase supply, is switched on to a d.c. source. Under normal operating conditions, the stator field moves faster than the rotor conductors by slip speed sn_s.

In Fig. 5.53 (a), a 3-phase induction motor is shown running under normal conditions with slip s. The direction of rotor induced emf is indicated by dots and crosses. Stator poles N, S rotate at synchronous speed n_s clockwise. Rotor must rotate at speed n_r clockwise so that relative speed between stator field and rotor is $(n_s - n_r) = sn_s$ and the rotor frequency is $f_2 = sf_1$.

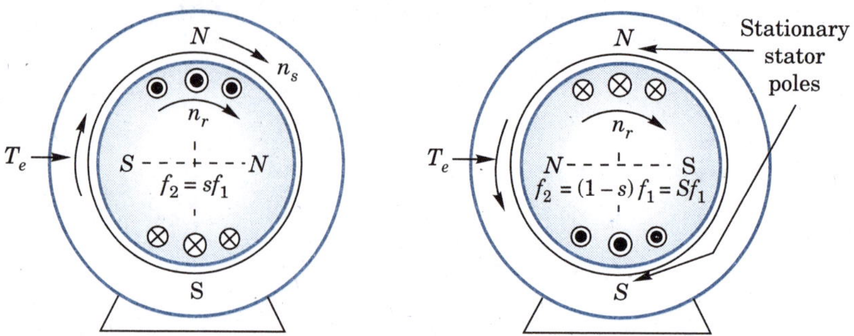

Fig. 5.53: Induction machine under (a) normal motor operation and (b) dynamic braking conditions.

When induction motor stator is energised with dc, stator field becomes stationary in space, Fig. 5.53 (b). With stator field at rest, rotor now moves clockwise at a relative speed of $n_r = n_s (1 - s)$ with respect to stator poles so that rotor frequency is $f_2 = (1 - s) f_1 = Sf_1$. If the stator field in Fig. 5.53 (a) is assumed at rest, the rotor moves anticlockwise at slip speed $(n_s - n_r) = sn_s$. If Fig. 5.53 (b), with stator poles at rest, rotor moves clockwise at slip speed $n_r = (1 - s)\, n_s = Sn_s$. As the rotor speed with respect to stator field is opposite in Fig. 5.53 (b), the induced emf in rotor conductors is also opposite to that shown in Fig. 5.53 (a); this is indicated by crosses under N pole and dots under S pole. As a consequence poles created on the rotor interact with stator poles to produce anticlockwise torque which is called dynamic braking torque.

It is seen from above that under normal running, the rotor frequency is sf_1 and at the instant dynamic braking is applied, the rotor frequency becomes $(1 - s) f_1 = Sf_1$. This shows that induction motor performance during dynamic braking can be obtained by using the induction motor equivalent circuit of Fig. 5.5 (a) merely replacing s by $(1 - s) = S$.

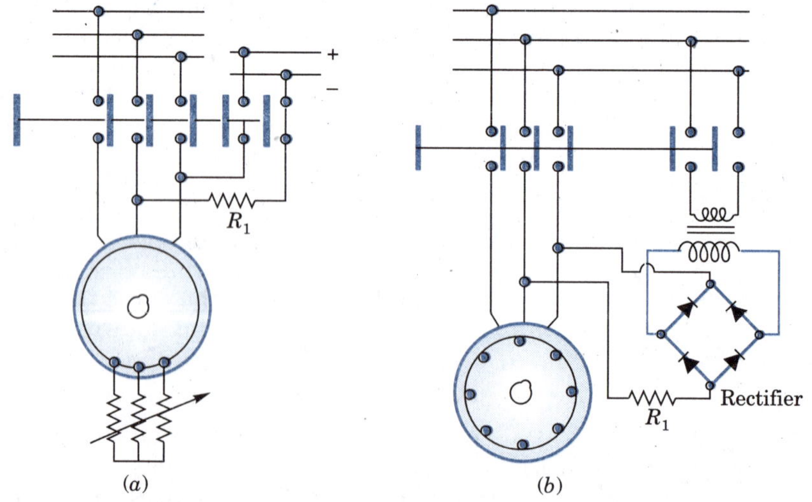

Fig. 5.54: D.C. dynamic braking of polyphase induction motors.

The direct current supply, for applying to the stator for dynamic braking, can be obtained from a separate dc source Fig. 5.54 (*a*), or from the same ac source through a transformer-rectifier unit as shown in Fig. 5.54 (*b*). A series resistor R_1 helps to limit the stator current. For a slip-ring induction motor, additional resistance is inserted in the rotor circuit so as to obtain higher dynamic braking torque.

When rotor is running at synchronous speed and stator is excited with d.c., the relative speed between stator field and rotor is synchronous and slip $s = 1$. This condition resembles a polyphase induction motor with rotor at standstill. When rotor is at rest in dynamic braking, stationary stator flux induces no rotor emf ; this condition resembles a polyphase induction motor with rotor running at synchronous speed. It may be concluded from this that

(*i*) conditions with the rotor at rest during dynamic braking are similar to the conditions with rotor at synchronous speed during induction motor operation ;

(*ii*) conditions with rotor at synchronous speed during dynamic braking are similar to the conditions with rotor at rest during induction motor operation.

In view of the above observation, the induction motor operation during dynamic braking conditions, can be analysed replacing s by $1 - s$ $(= S)$ in the polyphase induction-motor equivalent circuit. This conclusion is already arrived at from Fig. 5.53. Further, since d.c. is given to stator, its leakage reactance x_1 is of no interest except during transients. The stator resistance is required only to know the d.c. excitation voltage for a given value of stator current. There is no stator iron loss and the rotor iron loss merely increases the rotor circuit resistance. This shows that the equivalent circuit of Fig. 5.5 (*a*) for a polyphase induction motor can be drawn as shown in Fig. 5.55 (*a*) for the dynamic braking analysis of an induction motor. This equivalent circuit, modified by dividing throughout by S $(= 1 - s)$, is as shown in Fig. 5.55 (*b*).

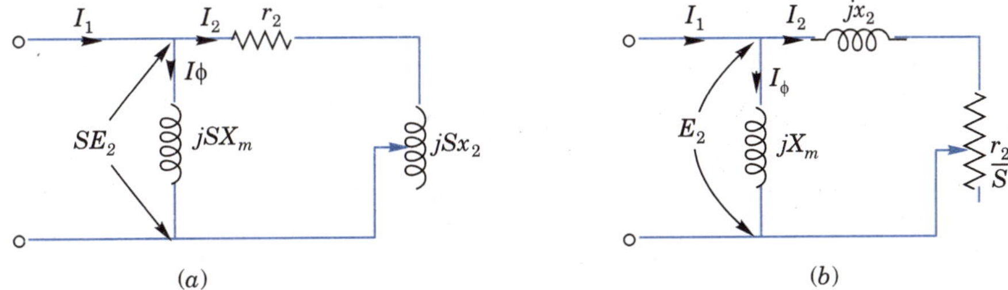

Fig. 5.55: Equivalent circuits during the dynamic braking of a polyphase induction motor.

Stator winding under dynamic braking conditions, carriers d.c. But for analysis purposes, it may be assumed that stator carries alternating current I_1 which produces the same magnitude of m.m.f. as produced by direct current I_{dc}. The relation between I_1 and I_{dc} depends upon the stator-winding connections during the dynamic braking. The m.m.f. produced by a 3-phase stator-winding, carrying an alternating current of I_1 rms is given by $\frac{3}{2}(\sqrt{2}I_1)\ N_1$. Here N_1 is the effective stator series turns per phase.

For stator connections of Fig. 5.56 (*a*), the m.m.f. produced by phase A is $I_{dc}\,N_1$ directed vertically downward as shown in the figure. Mmf produced by phase C is $I_{dc}\ N_1$ but it is displaced by 60° from phase A m.m.f. as depicted in Fig. 5.56 (*a*). Resultant m.m.f. due to phases A and C is seen to be $\sqrt{3}\,I_{dc}\ N_1$. Therefore, for stator winding connections of Fig. 5.56 (*a*); the equivalent stator current I_1, producing the same m.m.f. as developed by I_{dc}, is given by the relation,

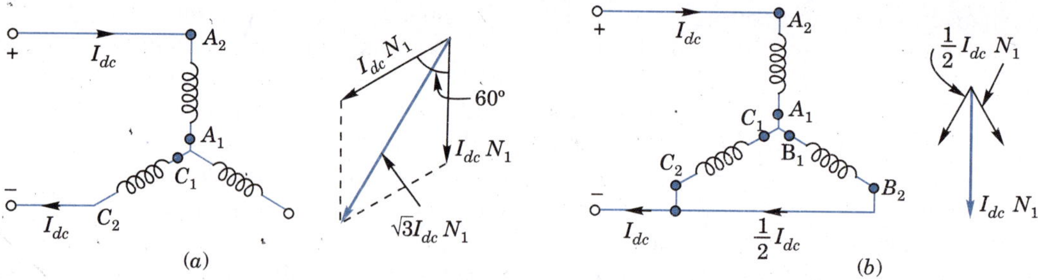

Fig. 5.56: Connection schemes for the stator windings of a polyphase induction motor during dynamic braking.

$$\tfrac{3}{2}(\sqrt{2}I_1)\, N_1 = \sqrt{3}\, I_{dc} N_1$$

or
$$I_1 = \sqrt{\frac{2}{3}}\, I_{dc} \qquad \text{...(5.99)}$$

An examination of Fig. 5.56 (*b*) reveals that $\frac{3}{2}(\sqrt{2}I_1)N_1 = \frac{3}{2} I_{dc}\, N_1$

or
$$I_1 = \frac{1}{\sqrt{2}} I_{dc} \qquad \text{...(5.100)}$$

These two connection schemes of Fig. 5.56 are more common in drive systems, mainly because these result in simple arrangement of the switching connections. However, there are other possible connections for the stator winding during dynamic braking of induction motors, but these will not be considered here.

The induction motor phasor diagram under dynamic braking conditions is as shown in Fig. 5.57 (*a*). Rotor m.m.f. I_2N_2 must be balanced by stator m.m.f. I'_2N_1, so that $I_\phi N_1$ produces the required air-gap flux ϕ.

During dynamic braking, the entire power developed in the rotor is dissipated in the rotor-circuit resistance. In view of this, the electromagnetic torque T_{ed} developed during dynamic braking is given by

$$T_{ed} = \frac{3}{\omega_s} I_2^{\,2} \frac{r_2}{S} \text{ Nm.}$$

But I_2 in terms of I_1, from Fig. 5.55 (*b*), is

$$\bar{I}_2 = \bar{I}_1 \frac{jX_m}{\dfrac{r_2}{S} + j(X_m + x_2)} \qquad \text{...(5.101)}$$

$$\therefore \quad T_{ed} = \frac{3}{\omega_s} \cdot \frac{I_1^{\,2}\, X_m^{\,2}}{\left(\dfrac{r_2}{S}\right)^2 + (X_m + x_2)^2} \cdot \frac{r_2}{S} \qquad \text{...(5.102)}$$

As in a polyphase induction motor, the dynamic braking torque is maximum when power delivered to $\frac{r_2}{S}$ is maximum in Fig. 5.55 (*b*).

$$\therefore \quad \frac{r_2}{S_{mT}} = (x_2 + X_m)$$

Thus the slip at which maximum braking torque occurs is given by

$$S_{mT} = \frac{r_2}{(x_2 + X_m)} \qquad ...(5.103)$$

Note that here $S = 1 - s$ and likewise $S_{mT} = 1 - s_{mT}$.

In order to obtain the value of maximum braking torque, substitute the value of $\frac{r_2}{S_{mT}}$ in Eq. (5.102).

$$\therefore \quad T_{ed.m} = \frac{3}{\omega_s} \frac{I_1^2 X_m^2}{(X_m + x_2)^2 + (X_m + x_2)^2} (X_m + x_2)$$

$$= \frac{3}{\omega_r} \cdot \frac{I_1^2 X_m^2}{2(X_m + x_2)} \qquad ...(5.104)$$

The speed-torque curves of Fig. 5.57 (*b*) are similar to those of an induction motor, but with slip scale reversed. For example, the slip at which maximum braking torque occurs is $S_{mT} = 1 - s_{mT}$ where s_{mT} is the slip for induction motor maximum torque. The effect of rotor-circuit resistance on the braking torque is also depicted in Fig. 5.57 (*b*). For load torque T_L, A is the operating point in first quadrant.

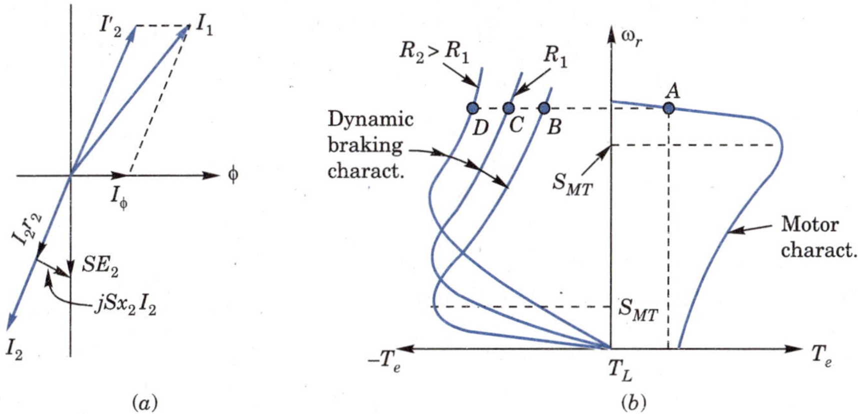

Fig. 5.57: (*a*) Phasor diagram and (*b*) speed-torque curves pertaining to the dynamic braking of polyphase induction motors.

As soon as the stator is disconnected from a.c. source, and is switched on to d.c. source for dynamic braking, the point A shifts to second quadrant point B for no external resistance in rotor, to point C for R_1 and to point D for R_2. This shows that the initial braking torque can be controlled by varying the rotor-circuit resistance. In fact, by properly adjusting rotor-circuit resistance, the maximum braking torque $T_{ed.m}$ can be obtained from slip S to slip S_{mT}.

Since X_m varies with rotor speed, care should be taken regarding the use of Eq. (5.102). For zero rotor speed, there is no rotor current to neutralize the stator m.m.f. In view of this ; the entire stator current is, in effect, a magnetizing current. Thus at zero rotor speed, there is maximum flux and saturation is greatest, therefore, value of X_m would be the least. At higher values of rotor speeds, X_m would be more.

Dynamic braking of induction motors gives smooth stop, results in less rotor-circuit loss and has no tendency to reverse. This method is however less quick than plugging.

Example 5.39. *A 400 V, 50 Hz, 4-pole, 3-phase star-connected induction motor has the following data :*

Stator leakage impedance per phase

$= 0.5 + j\,1.2\ \Omega$

Standstill rotor leakage impedance per phase referred to stator

$= 0.3 + j\,1.0\ \Omega$

Full-load slip = 0.05

No-load current is assumed negligible.

(a) Determine the initial braking torque soon after plugging.

(b) Determine the initial dynamic braking torque when d.c. is fed to the two phases in series to produce the same air-gap flux.

If an external resistance of 1.2 Ω per phase and referred to stator is inserted in the rotor circuit, find how the magnitude of dynamic braking torque is effected.

Find the magnitude of d.c. excitation for both the above cases of dynamic braking.

Solution. Per phase voltage, $V_1 = \dfrac{400}{\sqrt{3}} = 230.95$ V.

Synchronous speed, $\omega_s = 2\pi \left(\dfrac{2 \times 50}{4}\right) = 50\,\pi$ rad/sec.

Since no-load current of the induction motor is neglected, the rotor current I_2 from Fig. 5.5 (a) is given by

$$I_2 = \frac{V_1}{\left(r_1 + \dfrac{r_2}{s}\right) + j(x_1 + x_2)}$$

The electromagnetic torque T_e, from Eq. (5.18), is

$$T_e = \frac{3}{\omega_s} \cdot \frac{V_1^2}{\left(r_1 + \dfrac{r_2}{s}\right)^2 + (x_1 + x_2)^2} \cdot \frac{r_2}{s}$$

∴ Full-load torque $T_{e.fl}$ at slip 0.05 is given by

$$T_{e.fl} = \frac{3}{50\pi} \cdot \frac{(230.95)^2}{\left(0.5 + \dfrac{0.3}{0.05}\right) + (1.2 + 1.0)^2} \cdot \frac{0.3}{0.05} = 129.8 \text{ Nm.}$$

(a) As soon as any two stator terminals are interchanged for plugging, the slip becomes

$2 - s = 2 - 0.05 = 1.95$

∴ Plugging torque,

$$T_1 = \frac{3}{50\pi} \cdot \frac{(230.95)^2}{\left(0.5 + \dfrac{0.3}{1.95}\right)^2 + (1.2 + 1.0)^2} \cdot \frac{0.3}{1.95} = 29.74 \text{ Nm.}$$

∴ Total initial braking torque

$= T_1 + T_{e.fl} = 29.74 + 129.8 = 159.54$ Nm.

(*b*) For negligible no-load current, the air-gap flux is proportional to E_2, which is given by

$$\overline{E}_2 = \frac{\overline{z}_2}{\overline{z}_1 + \overline{z}_2} . \overline{V}_1$$

Here $\overline{z}_1 = r_1 + j\,x_1 = 0.5 + j\,1.2\ \Omega$

and $\overline{z}_2 = \frac{r_2}{s} + j\,x_2 = \frac{0.3}{0.05} + j\,1.00 = 6 + j\,1.00\ \Omega.$

$$\overline{z}_1 + \overline{z}_2 = 6.5 + j\,2.2.\ \Omega$$

$\therefore$ $\overline{E}_2 = \frac{6 + j\,1.00}{6.5 + j\,2.2} \times 230.95$

or $E_2 = \sqrt{\frac{6^2 + 1^2}{(6.5)^2 + (2.2)^2}} \times 230.95 = 204.72\ \text{V}.$

From Fig. 5.55 (*b*), rotor current under dynamic braking is given by

$$I_2 = \frac{E_2}{\sqrt{(r_2/S)^2 + (x_2)^2}} = \frac{204.72}{\sqrt{(0.3/0.95)^2 + 1^2}} = 195.22\ \text{A}$$

Here $I_1 = I_2$, because no-load current is neglected.

From Eq. (5.99), d.c. excitation is given by

$$I_{dc} = \sqrt{\frac{3}{2}}\, I_2 = \sqrt{\frac{3}{2}} \times 195.22 = 239.095\ \text{A}.$$

Dynamic braking torque $= \frac{3}{\omega_s} . I_2^{\,2}\, \frac{r_2}{S} = \frac{3}{50\pi} (195.22)^2 \times \frac{0.3}{0.95} = 120.3$ Nm.

When external resistance of 1.2 Ω is inserted in rotor circuit, then rotor current during dynamic braking is $I_2 = \frac{204.72}{\sqrt{[(0.3 + 1.2)/0.95]^2 + 1^2}} = 109.54$ A.

$\therefore$ Dynamic braking torque $= \frac{3}{50\pi} \cdot (109.54)^2\, \frac{1.5}{0.95} = 361.84$ Nm.

This shows that initial dynamic braking torque has increased from 229.85 to 361.84 Nm, when an external resistance of 1.2 Ω is inserted in the rotor circuit at the time of dynamic braking.

D.C. excitation, $I_{dc} = \sqrt{\frac{3}{2}} \cdot I_2 = \sqrt{\frac{3}{2}}\ (109.54) = 134.16$ A.

Example 5.40. *A 3 phase star-connected squirrel-cage induction motor has a full-load torque of 6 Nm at 960 r.p.m. If this motor is subjected to dynamic braking with a direct current of 30 A supplied between any two of its stator terminals, then compute the initial braking torque. Neglect stator impedance and rotational losses.*

This motor has per phase standstill rotor leakage impedance of 0.2 + j 0.5 Ω referred to stator and a magnetizing reactance of 20 Ω. For dynamic braking, one stator phase is connected in series with the other two in parallel.

Solution. When one stator phase is connected in series with the other two in parallel as shown in Fig. 5.56 (*b*), then from Eq. (5.100).

$$I_1 = \frac{1}{\sqrt{2}} I_{dc} = \frac{1}{\sqrt{2}}(30) = 21.22 \text{ A.}$$

For a full-load rotor speed of 960 r.p.m., the synchronous speed must be 1000 r.p.m. This gives $s = 0.04$. From Eq. (5.101), the rotor current is

$$I_2 = I_1 \frac{X_m}{\sqrt{(r_2/S)^2 + (X_m + x_2)^2}}$$

$$= 21.22 \frac{20}{\sqrt{(0.2/0.96)^2 + (20 + 0.5)^2}} = 20.70 \text{ A.}$$

Now,
$$\omega_s = 2\pi \times \frac{1000}{60} = \frac{100\pi}{3} \text{ rad/sec.}$$

$\therefore$ Dynamic braking torque, $T_{ed} = \frac{3}{\omega_s} . I_2^2 \frac{r_2}{S} = \frac{3}{\frac{100\pi}{3}} (20.70)^2 \times \frac{0.2}{0.96} = 2.557$ Nm.

$\therefore$ Total initial braking torque = $T_{e.fl} + T_{ed} = 8.557$ Nm.

5.13 OPERATION ON UNBALANCED SUPPLY VOLTAGE

The analysis of a 3-phase induction motor has been carried out till now by assuming that the supply voltage is balanced. The three-phase winding of induction motors are usually symmetrical as a result of proper design and construction. However, on account of accidental short-circuit between coils etc., the 3-phase windings may not remain symmetrical, but this aspect will not be considered here.

The voltages obtainable from 3-phase systems are usually balanced. But sometimes, the unbalanced phase voltages do exist due to the presence of unbalanced loads on the system or due to some line disturbances. Many a time, the supply to an induction motor is deliberately unbalanced to get modified speed-torque curves. This asymmetrical voltage control is used for cranes, even though the operating efficiency is reduced. In this article, the effect of unbalanced supply voltage on the operation of a polyphase induction motor is examined at an elementary level only.

When the supply voltage is unbalanced, the analysis of induction-motor operation can be carried out best by the method of symmetrical components. According to this method, the unbalanced voltages are resolved into two sets. One set consists of symmetrical voltages having positive sequence and the second set of symmetrical voltages having negative sequence. Since the induction motors with symmetrical star or delta windings are only considered, the zero-sequence set of voltages is absent. The positive and negative sequences of balanced voltages are assumed to act separately. Each set produces its own balanced currents and its own electromagnetic torque. The net electromagnetic torque is obtained by the superposition of positive and negative sequence torques.

Let the unbalanced supply voltage be resolved into positive sequence per phase voltage V_p and negative-sequence per phase voltage V_n. Here the subscripts p and n are used to denote positive and negative sequence quantities respectively. The rotor runs in the direction of rotating field produced by positive-sequence voltage V_p. For convenience, the field produced by the positive-sequence voltage V_p produces a forward rotating field. The negative sequence voltage V_n produces a backward rotating magnetic field. With respect to stator (or primary), the speeds of both forward and backward rotating fields are equal to synchronous speed n_s. If n_r is the rotor speed, then the relative speed between rotor and forward rotating field is $n_s - n_r$ and, therefore, the slip s_p is

$$s_p = \frac{n_s - n_r}{n_s} \quad \text{or} \quad n_r = n_s\,(1 - s_p).$$

The relative speed between rotor and the backward rotating field is $n_s + n_r$, therefore, slip s_n is

$$s_n = \frac{n_s + n_r}{n_s} = \frac{n_s + n_s(1 + s_p)}{n_s} = 2 - s_p.$$

The behaviour of the motor to the positive sequence voltage is identical with that obtained already for an ordinary induction motor. In view of this, the equivalent circuit of Fig. 5.58 (*a*) is also applicable to the positive sequence voltage V_p and this is redrawn in Fig. 5.58 (*a*) for convenience. The equivalent circuit, applicable to the conditions under negative-sequence voltage, is as shown in Fig. 5.58 (*b*), where r_2 is divided by $s_n = 2 - s_p$. From these equivalent circuits, the internal power developed per phase is given by

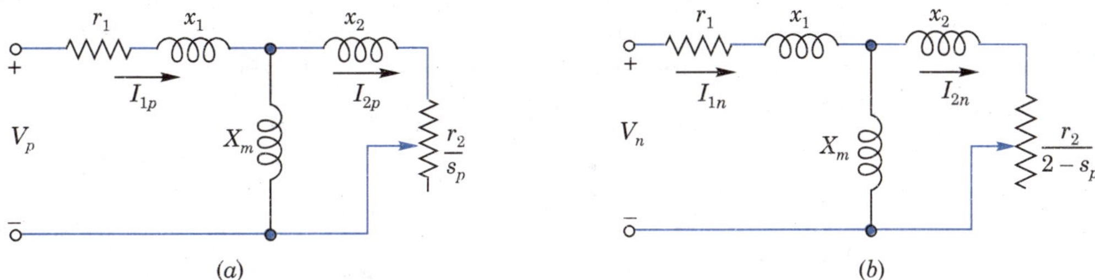

Fig. 5.58: Induction motor equivalent circuit for (*a*) positive-sequence voltage and (*b*) negative sequence voltage.

$$P_g = I_{2p}^2 \frac{r_2}{s_p} - I_{2n}^2 \frac{r_2}{2 - s_p} \qquad \text{...(5.105)}$$

The power output per phase is

$$P = I_{2p}^2 r_2 \frac{1 - s_p}{s_p} - I_{2n}^2 r_2 \frac{1 - s_p}{2 - s_p}$$

The electromagnetic torque developed in the motor is

$$T_e = \frac{3}{2\pi n_s} \cdot r_2 \left[\frac{I_{2p}^2}{s_p} - \frac{I_{2n}^2}{2 - s_p} \right] \qquad \text{...(5.106)}$$

Since the rotating fields produced by the positive and negative sequence voltages are in opposite directions, the effect of negative sequence voltage is to reduce both the power output P and the electromagnetic torque T_e. With the unbalanced voltages usually encountered in the 3-phase systems, V_n should not exceed about 10 percent of V_p so that percentages reduction in P and T_e is not appreciable. Since the backward field runs at about twice (= $2 - s_p$) the synchronous speed with respect to rotor, there are increased core losses and ohmic losses in the rotor, this gives rise to excessive heating of the induction motor. In view of this, it is preferable to have the system voltage as much balanced as is possible. Some protective relays may be used which should disconnect the induction motor from the supply mains in case the degree of voltage unbalance is more than a preset allowable value.

The equivalent circuits of Fig. 5.58 can be simplified by applying, Thevenin's theorem as done in Fig. 5.58 (*a*) and then electromagnetic torque T_e can be computed accordingly.

Single-phasing. The term single-phasing means the operation of a 3 phase induction motor when one of its supply line gets disconnected from the a.c. source. The most common cause of the single-phasing of a 3-phase induction motor is the burning of fuse wire in any one phase. A faulty contact on the 'run' side of a star delta or auto-transformer starter may also be the cause of single phasing. If single-phasing occurs in a fully-loaded 3-phase induction motor, then the motor starts taking much more current and as a result of it both stator and rotor get seriously overheated. If stator is star-connected, two phases get overheated and if delta-connected, only one phase experiences marked temperature rise. Sometimes, single-phasing in a fully-loaded motor may even stall the motor. Single-phasing is the major cause for the burning of stator windings of 3-phase induction motors.

Single-phasing causes the appearance of backward rotating field, therefore, net electromagnetic torque is reduced. In case single-phasing occurs in a 3-phase induction motor carrying half its rated load then the motor may continue operating satisfactorily.

Example 5.41. *A 3-phase, star-connected, 50 Hz, 4-pole induction motor is connected to unbalanced supply voltage with positive and negative sequence voltages of 370 V and 80 V respectively. Its parameter in ohms, referred to stator, are as under :*

$r_1 = 0.15,\ x_1 = x_2 = 0.45,\ r_2 = 0.12$, *neglect* X_m.

Calculate the net torque developed at a slip of 0.04. In case friction and windage losses are ignored, determined the net shaft power.

Solution. Positive-sequence calculations

Per-phase voltage, $V_p = \dfrac{370}{\sqrt{3}} = 213.63$ V

Per-phase rotor circuit,

$$I_{2p} = \frac{V_p}{\sqrt{\left(r_1 + \dfrac{r_2}{s}\right)^2 + (x_1 + x_2)^2}} = \frac{213.63}{\sqrt{\left(0.15 + \dfrac{0.12}{0.04}\right)^2 + (0.45 + 0.45)^2}}$$

$= 65.21$ A

Synchronous speed, $\omega_s = \dfrac{4\pi f}{P} = \dfrac{4\pi \times 50}{4} = 50\,\pi$ rad/sec

Total torque, $T_{ep} = \dfrac{3}{\omega_s} . I_{2p}^2 \dfrac{r_2}{s_p} = \dfrac{3}{50\pi} \times 65.21^2 \times \dfrac{0.12}{0.04} = 243.64$ Nm

Negative-sequence Calculations

Per-phase voltage, $V_n = \dfrac{80}{\sqrt{3}} = 46.19$ V

Per-phase rotor current,
$$I_{2n} = \frac{V_n}{\sqrt{\left(r_1 + \dfrac{r_2}{2-s}\right)^2 + (x_1 + x_2)^2}} = \frac{46.19}{\sqrt{\left(0.15 + \dfrac{0.12}{1.96}\right)^2 + (0.9)^2}}$$

$= 49.965$ A

$$\text{Total torque, } T_{en} = \frac{3}{\omega_s} \cdot I_{2n}^2 \frac{r_2}{(2-s)} = \frac{3}{50\pi} = 49.965^2 \times \frac{0.12}{1.96}$$

$$= 2.92 \text{ Nm}$$

$$\text{Net torque, } T_e = T_{ep} - T_{en} = 243.64 - 2.92 = 240.72 \text{ Nm}$$

$$\text{Net shaft power} = w_s(1-s)\, T_e = 50\,\pi\,(0.96) \times 240.72 = 36.299 \text{ kW.}$$

5.14 SLOT HARMONICS

They are also called tooth harmonics, slot ripples or tooth ripples. These higher order harmonics in rotating electrical machines are caused by the slot-openings. When the slot-openings are large compared with the tooth width and air gap length, their effect is more pronounced. Higher order harmonics in the flux wave travel at the same speed as the fundamental flux wave with respect to the conductors. However, note that slot harmonics (always of higher order) do not travel with respect to the conductors but are always present opposite the slots and teeth which cause their existence. The object of this article is to give a brief account of the slot harmonics.

Consider an ideal case of smooth surfaces for both stator and rotor so that uniform air gap is obtained as shown in Fig. 5.59 (*a*). Assume the stator to be excited and producing a sine m.m.f. wave as shown. Since the air-gap reluctances is uniform, the flux $= \dfrac{\text{mmf}}{\text{reluctance}}$ has the same waveform as that of the stator mmf wave as shown in Fig. 5.59 (*c*).

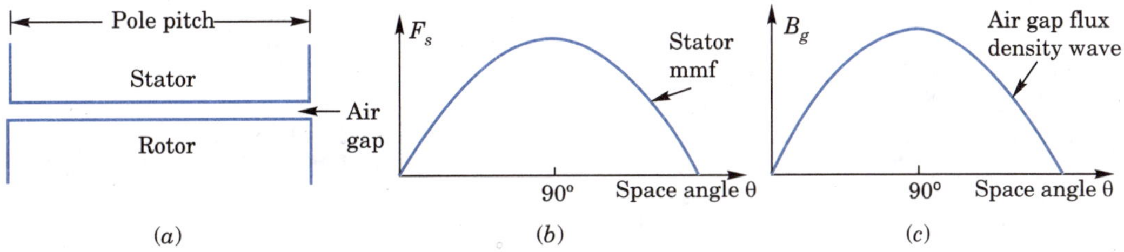

Fig. 5.59: Air-gap flux density wave for uniform air gap.

Now consider the rotor air-gap periphery to be slotted as shown in Fig. 5.60 (*a*). Here again the stator is assumed to produce a sine mmf wave. For this case, air gap is not uniform, the air-gap reluctance is not constant and therefore the flux density wave would not be a sine wave. Air-gap length over the slot width is more, therefore reluctance here is more and flux density is less. Over the tooth width, air gap is less, reluctance is less and consequently flux density here is more. This resultant flux density waveform is illustrated in Fig. 5.60 (*c*). This resultant waveform can be resolved into fundamental and higher order harmonics as shown respectively in Fig. 5.60 (*d*) and (*e*). These higher order harmonics of Fig. 5.60 (*e*), caused by teeth and slot-openings, are called tooth ripples, tooth harmonics, slot ripples or slot harmonics.

An examination of Fig. 5.60 (*d*) and (*e*) reveals that for half-cycle of fundamental frequency component, there are 8 half cycles of slot harmonics or for one cycle of fundamental-frequency component, there are 8 cycles of slot harmonics. This means that slot harmonics have a frequency of 8 × f where f is the fundamental frequency. But note that here 8 is equal to the number of slots (or teeth) per pair of poles. This thought process leads to the following relation :

Slot-harmonic frequency,

$$f_s = (\text{fundamental frequency}, f) \times \left(\text{number of slots per pole-pair}, \frac{S}{P/2}\right)$$

or
$$f_s = f \times \frac{2S}{P} \qquad ...(5.107)$$

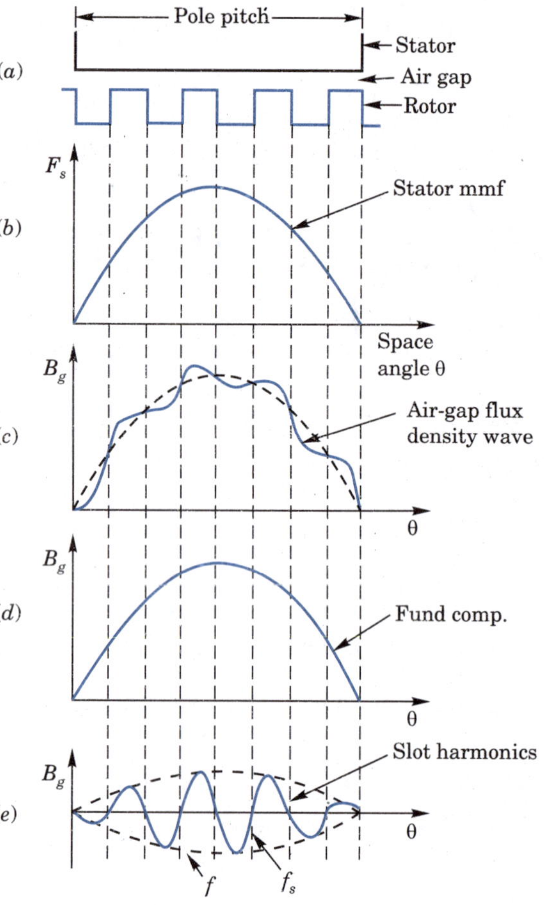

Fig. 5.60: Air-gap flux density wave for non-uniform air gap.

Now let the flux per pole produced by stator be resolved into ϕ_1 and ϕ_s, where ϕ_1 is the peak value of fundamental component and ϕ_s, the peak value of slot-harmonic flux. The total flux produced by stator can be written as

$$\phi = \phi_1 \cos \omega t + \phi_s \sin \omega_s t \cos \omega t.$$

Here ωt is measured from the peak of fundamental component, therefore cos ωt must appear with ϕ_1. The frequency of the slot-harmonic flux is ω_s (= $2\pi f_s$), but their envelope has a frequency of ω (= $2\pi f$) as shown in Fig. 5.60 (*e*) ; therefore sin $\omega_s t$ and cos ωt must be associated with ϕ_s.

The emf generated in one N-turn coil is given by

$$e = -N\frac{d\phi}{dt} = -N\frac{d}{dt}\,[\phi_1 \cos \omega t + \phi_s \sin \omega_s t \cos \omega t]$$

$$= -N\frac{d}{dt}\left[\phi_1 \cos \omega t + \frac{\phi_s}{2}\{\sin(\omega_s + \omega)t + \sin(\omega_s - \omega)t\}\right]$$

$$= N\omega\,\phi_1 \sin \omega t - \frac{N\phi_s}{2}[(\omega_s + \omega)\cos(\omega_s + \omega)\,t + (\omega_s - \omega)\cos(\omega_s - \omega)\,t] \qquad ...(5.108)$$

In Eq. (5.108), first emf term has fundamental frequency ω or f, whereas second and third emf terms have frequencies of $(\omega_s + \omega)$ and $(\omega_s - \omega)$ respectively.

Here
$$\omega_s + \omega = 2\pi f_s + 2\pi f = 2\pi f\left(\frac{2S}{P} + 1\right)$$

Similarly
$$\omega_s - \omega_s = 2\pi f\left(\frac{2S}{P} - 1\right)$$

This shows that slot harmonics of frequency ω_s in the field flux have generated emfs in the winding whose frequency is

$$\left(\frac{2S}{P} \pm 1\right) f \text{ Hz} \qquad \text{...(5.109)}$$

Also, $\frac{2S}{P} = 2\,mq = 2Q$, where Q = slots per pole, q = slots per pole per phase and m is the number of phases. For a 3-phase machine, $m = 3$ and $\frac{2S}{P} = 6q$. This shows frequency of slot-harmonic emfs in rotor windings is $(6q \pm 1)\,f$ or $(2Q \pm 1)\,f$. If both stator and rotor are slotted, then stator slots S_1 produce harmonic emfs of order $\left(\frac{2S_1}{P} \pm 1\right)$ and rotor slots S_2 of order $\left(\frac{2S_2}{P} \pm 1\right)$.

5.14.1 Skewed Slots

The skew means angular twist of the slot away from the shaft axis, by a suitable angle θ_s, as shown in Fig. 5.61 (*c*). The basic principle of eliminating slot harmonics is illustrated in Fig. 5.61. In Fig. 5.61 (*a*), coil-span is equal to one pole pitch. If 5 V are generated in each coil-side, resultant output voltage per coil is 10 V. In Fig. 5.61 (*b*), coil-span is equal to 2 pole-pitches, *i.e.* if one coil-side is under *N* pole then its other coil side is also under *N*-pole. Here the resultant output emf is zero, because emfs of 5 V in each coil-side are opposing each other. From this, it follows that if slots are skewed by 2 harmonic pole-pitches, then the effect of slot harmonics can be eliminated. The skew through 2 harmonic pole-pitches is illustrated in Fig. 5.61 (*c*), where one bar-end is under one harmonic pole and its other bar-end is under the next but similar harmonic pole. Thus the skewing should be done through one slot pitch or through 2 harmonic pole-pitches. For example, for a 4-pole machine if 17th harmonic is to be eliminated, then this machine would have 17 × 4 = 68 harmonic poles and therefore,

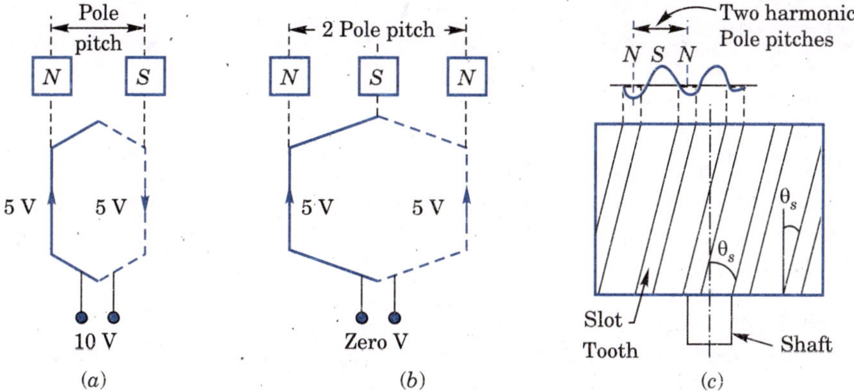

Fig. 5.61: Pertaining to the elimination of slot harmonics.

$$\text{harmonic pole-pitch} = \frac{360°}{4 \times 17} \text{ mech}$$

$$\therefore \quad \text{Angle of skew, } \theta_s = 2 \text{ harmonic pole-pitches} = \frac{2 \times 360°}{4 \times 17} \text{ mech}$$

In general, angle of skew,

$$\theta_s = \frac{720°}{P \times n} \text{ mech}$$

where, P = number of poles and n = order of slot harmonics

Angle of skew in electrical degrees is given by

$$\theta_s = \frac{720}{Pn} \times \frac{P}{2} = \frac{360°}{n} \text{ elect} \quad ...(5.110)$$

5.14.2 Winding Factor

With skewed slots, the rotating flux cuts one bar-end first and then gradually proceeds across the length to cut other bar-end. Therefore, a skewed rotor bar is, in effect, spread over the angle θ_s, and winding factor k_{dn} is accordingly introduced in the emf induced by it. The winding factor k_{dn} is given by

$$k_{dn} = \frac{\sin \frac{n\theta_s}{2}}{\frac{1}{2} n\theta_s} \quad ...(5.111)$$

Other effects of skewing the rotor slots are as follows :

(*a*) Since the skewed rotor slot is not parallel to stator slot in an induction motor, there is more leakage reactance. As a result, induction motor has lower starting and maximum torques.

(*b*) The skewed rotor bar develops an axial force which puts more load on the thrust bearings.

(*c*) It prevents cogging.

(*d*) With skewed rotor bars ; the revolving flux, in effect, encounters an air gap of uniform reluctance and this results in a uniform torque and quieter operation.

(*e*) With skewed slots, rotor bar length is more, therefore rotor resistance is also increased. This gives more I^2R losses in rotor circuit.

In summary, the advantages of using skewed slots are (*i*) the elimination of parasitic torques so as to obtain a uniform torque-speed curve and (*ii*) reduction in vibration and noise so as to result in a quieter motor.

The disadvantages are (*i*) more rotor conductor material and, therefore, more I^2R losses and less efficiency (*ii*) more leakage reactance and, therefore less starting and maximum torques and (*iii*) axial force developed puts more load on thrust bearings. The advantages gained by using skewed slots are far more important than the disadvantages, therefore, it is usual to use skewed slots in 3-phase induction motors.

Example 5.42. *A 3-phase, 6 pole alternator has 36 slots. What slot harmonics do you expect in output voltage wave ? If it is desired to eliminate lower order harmonic, find the angle of skew. Investigate the effect of this skew on the higher order harmonic.*

Solution. The order of slot harmonics in the output voltage wave, form Eq. (5.109), is given by

$$\frac{2S}{P} \pm 1 = \frac{2 \times 36}{6} \pm 1 = 11 \text{ and } 13.$$

Angle of skew for eliminating lower order harmonic, from Eq. (5.110), is

$$\theta_s = \frac{360°}{11} = 32.727° \text{ elect}$$

Here $$k_{d11} = \frac{\sin \frac{n\theta_s}{2}}{\frac{1}{2} . n\,\theta_s} = \frac{\sin 180°}{\pi} = 0.$$

This shows that 11th harmonics are eliminated from the output voltage wave.

$$k_{d13} = \frac{\sin\left(13 \times \frac{360°}{11 \times 2}\right)}{13 \times \frac{2\pi}{11 \times 2}} = -\,0.145616.$$

Since k_{d13} is very small, the effect of skewing by 32.727° elect is to reduce the 13th harmonic considerably.

Example 5.43. *A 3-phase, 12-pole, 50 Hz, star-connected alternator has 180 slots with 5 conductors per slot. The fundamental component of total flux per pole is 0.02 Wb. The air-gap flux contains 10% of third harmonic flux and 4% tooth harmonic flux. Calculate per phase and line e.m.fs. for full-pitch coils.*

Solution. Slots per pole per phase,

$$q = \frac{180}{12 \times 3} = 5. \qquad k_{d1} = \frac{\sin \frac{60}{2}}{5 \sin \frac{60}{5 \times 2}} = 0.957 = k_{\omega 1}$$

$$k_{d3} = \frac{\sin \frac{3 \times 360}{2}}{5 \sin \frac{3 \times 60}{5 \times 2}} = 0.647 = k_{\omega 3}$$

Turns per phase, $N_{Ph} = \frac{180 \times 5}{2 \times 3} = 150$

$$\therefore \qquad E_{Ph1} = \sqrt{2}\,\pi f\, N_{Ph}\, \phi_1 k_{\omega 1}$$

$$= \sqrt{2}\ .\ \pi \times 50 \times 150 \times 0.02 \times 0.957 = 637.68 \text{ V}$$

$$E_{Ph3} = \sqrt{2}\ .\ \pi \times 150 \times 150 \times 0.002 \times 0.647$$

$$= \frac{3}{10} \times 637.68 \times \frac{0.647}{0.957} = 129.34 \text{ V}$$

Order of slot harmonic in the generated e.m.f.

$$= \frac{2S}{P} \pm 1 = \frac{2 \times 180}{12} \pm 1 = 29 \text{ and } 31.$$

$$k_{d.29} = k_{d.31} = k_{d1} = 0.957$$

Examination of Eq. (5.108) shows that flux ϕ_s of 4% generates e.m.fs. of 2% each for 29th and 31st harmonics. Since the winding factors for fundamental, 29th and 31st harmonics are equal,* a tooth harmonic flux of 4% generates harmonic e.m.fs. of 2% of the fundamental-frequency e.m.fs.

$$\therefore \qquad E_{Ph29} = \frac{2}{100} \times 637.68 = 12.754 \text{ V}$$

$$E_{Ph31} = \frac{2}{100} \times 637.68 = 12.754 \text{ V}$$

$$\therefore \qquad E_{Ph} = \sqrt{\text{sum of the squares of Ist, 3rd, 29th and 31st harmonic e.m.fs.}}$$

$$= \sqrt{637.68^2 + 129.34^2 + 2 \times 12.754^2} = 650.915 \text{ V}.$$

$$E_l = \sqrt{3}\,\sqrt{637.68^2 + 2 \times 12.754^2} = 1104.90 \text{ V}.$$

5.15 EFFECT OF SPACE HARMONICS ON 3-PHASE INDUCTION-MOTOR PERFORMANCE

Harmonics in the time variation of the impressed voltage wave do have some effect on the induction motor performance. These effects are considered in detail in Art. 5.17.

When the space distribution of flux wave along the air-gap periphery is sinusoidal, torque-speed curve of the polyphase induction motor is a smooth curve as shown in Fig. 5.7. When the air-gap flux wave contains odd harmonics (5th, 7th, 11th etc.), then the torque-speed curve at low speeds is not smooth. The space harmonics in the air-gap flux wave are caused by

(*i*) the distribution of stator winding and

(*ii*) the variation of air-gap reluctance due to stator and rotor slots.

The space harmonics caused by the variation of air-gap reluctance are called tooth, or slot, harmonics. The effect of these harmonic, in the air-gap flux-wave, is to give birth to unwanted torques, called parasitic torques, vibration and noise. The object of this article is to discuss the effect of space harmonics on the behaviour of 3-phase induction motors.

5.15.1 Harmonic Induction (or Asynchronous) Torques

Even if the stator currents are sinusoidal, the stator mmf wave is not a sine wave because the stator winding, even in large machines, can't have more than 3 or 4 slots per pole per phase. The analysis of stator mmf wave, by Fourier series, shows it to consist of fundamental mmf wave and other odd-numbered (3rd, 5th, 7th etc.) harmonic mmf waves. The third harmonic flux waves produced by each of the three phases neutralize one another, therefore resultant air gap flux is free from third and triplen harmonics ; this is because the third harmonics in the flux wave of all the three phases are in space phase but differ in time phase by 120°. The fundamental mmf wave produces flux rotating at synchronous speed $n_s = \frac{2f_1}{P}$ rps, where f_1 is the supply frequency and P is the number of poles for which stator winding is wound. The fifth harmonic m.m.f. wave travels at $\frac{2f_1}{5P} = \frac{n_s}{5}$ rps and in a direction opposite to the fundamental

* See Art. 3.5 "Electrical Machinery" by the same author.

m.m.f. wave. The seventh harmonic m.m.f. wave travels at $\frac{2f_1}{7P} = \frac{n_s}{7}$ rps and in the direction of fundamental m.m.f. wave. The fifth and seventh harmonic m.m.f. waves may be assumed to be produced by $5P$ and $7P$ poles respectively. Summarising the above, it may be stated that harmonic m.m.f. waves travel at speeds $\frac{1}{k}$ times the fundamental speed and (*i*) in the same direction if $k = 6m + 1$ (*i.e.* 7th, 13th harmonic etc.) and (*ii*) in the reversed direction if $k = 6m - 1$ (*i.e.* 5th, 11th harmonic etc.). Here m is any integer 1, 2, 3 ... The most predominant space harmonics are fifth and 7th ; attention will, therefore, be confined to the effect of these harmonics only.

For the development of electromagnetic torque in an induction motor, the relative speed between stator and rotor fields must be zero. For example, in a 4-pole, 50 Hz induction motor, the stator field rotates at 1500 rpm. If rotor runs at some speed, say 1460 rpm, then speed of rotor field with respect to rotor is 40 rpm. Consequently, the speed of rotor field with respect to rotor is equal to rotor speed plus the speed of rotor field with respect to rotor. Thus the speed of rotor field with respect to stator is 1460 + 40 = 1500 rpm *i.e.,* the relative speed between stator and rotor fields is zero for the development of torque in an induction motor. In general, if the speed of stator field is n_s, then speed of the rotor field with respect to stator = speed of rotor field with respect to rotor, sn_s + rotor speed, $n_s(1 - s) = n_s$. Note that whatever the rotor speed may be, the relative speed between stator and rotor fields is zero and asynchronous (or induction) torque is developed. Let us now extend this physical concept to 5th and 7th harmonics, rotating in the air-gap in opposite directions.

The fifth harmonic field rotates at $n_s/5$ *rps* and in a direction opposite to the rotor movement. Therefore, slip of rotor with respect to fifth harmonic field is

$$s_5 = \frac{\text{5th harmonic field speed} - \text{rotor speed}}{\text{5th harmonic field speed}}$$

$$= \frac{-\frac{n_s}{5} - n_r}{-\frac{n_s}{5}} = \frac{-\frac{n_s}{5} - n_s(1-s)}{-\frac{n_s}{5}} = 1 + 5(1-s) = 6 - 5s.$$

Since the fifth-harmonic field rotates opposite to rotor, negative sign has been put before $n_s/5$. Slip s corresponds to the rotor slip with respect to the fundamental field. The frequency of the rotor currents induced buy the 5th harmonic rotating field is

$$f_{2.5} = \text{Stator frequency} \times s_5$$
$$= f_1(6 - 5s).$$

Now speed of 5th harmonic rotor field with respect to the rotor is given by

$$\frac{2\,(\text{rotor frequency}, f_{2.5})}{5P} = \frac{2}{5P} \cdot f_1(6 - 5s) = \frac{n_s}{5}(6 - 5s)$$

As before, speed of 5th harmonic rotor field with respect to stator = speed of 5th harmonic rotor field with respect to rotor + rotor speed

$$= -\frac{n_s}{5}(6 - 5s) + n_r = -\frac{6}{5}n_s + sn_s + n_s(1 - s) = -\frac{n_s}{5} \text{ rps.}$$

Negative sign before $n_s/5\ (6-5s)$ is used because 5th harmonic field rotates opposite to rotor movement. Recall that the speed of 5th harmonic stator field with respect to stator is also $-n_s/5$ rps. This shows that speed of 5th harmonic stator field is equal to the speed of 5th harmonic rotor-induced fields, *i.e.*, the relative speed between the 5th harmonic stator and rotor fields is zero. In view of this, stator and rotor 5th harmonic fields are stationary with respect to each other, they can therefore interact to produce 5th harmonic induction motor torque just like the torque produced by the fundamental component.

The 7th harmonic field rotates at $n_s/7$ rps in the direction of rotor rotation. Therefore, slip of the rotor with respect to 7th harmonic field is

$$s_7 = \frac{\dfrac{n_s}{7} - n_r}{n_s/7} = \frac{\dfrac{n_s}{7} - n_s(1-s)}{n_s/7} = 7s - 6.$$

Frequency of the rotor currents induced by the 7th harmonic rotating field is

$$f_{2.7} = \text{stator frequency} \times s_7 = f_1 \cdot (7s-6)$$

Speed of 7th harmonic rotor field with respect to rotor is given by

$$\frac{2\,(\text{rotor frequency}, f_{2.7})}{7P} = \frac{2}{7P} \cdot f_1 (7s-6) = \frac{n_s}{7}(7s-6).$$

Speed of 7th harmonic rotor field with respect to stator

$$= \frac{n_s}{7}(7s-6) + n_r = \frac{n_s}{7}(7s-6) + n_s(1-s) = \frac{n_s}{7} \text{ rps.}$$

But $n_s/7$ rps is the speed of the 7th harmonic stator field with respect to stator. Therefore, 7th harmonic stator and rotor fields rotate at the same speed of and interaction between them gives rise to 7th harmonic induction motor torque.

It may be concluded from above that each space harmonic (excluding the third and its multiples) of the stator mmf wave produces its own asynchronous torque. In view of this, a polyphase induction motor may be considered as equivalent to a number of induction motors mechanically coupled and with different number of poles. Their stators are assumed to be connected in series in such a manner that phase sequence of the supply voltage changes alternately. Up to 7th harmonic, a polyphase induction motor is equivalent to three mechanically coupled motors with poles P, $5P$ and $7P$. The torque produced by fundamental component of stator mmf wave of synchronous speed n_s is shown in Fig. 5.62. The torque produced by second motor with $5P$ poles *i.e.*, the torque produced by 5th harmonic component of stator mmf wave of synchronous speed $n_s/5$ is also shown. Since 5th harmonic field rotates opposite to the rotor rotation, 5th harmonic torque opposes fundamental component torque and acts as a brake on the induction motor as shown in Fig. 5.62. The 7th harmonic field rotates in the direction of rotor movement, therefore, 7th harmonic asynchronous torque aids the fundamental component torque as shown. Note that 5th harmonic braking torque is zero at $-n_s/5$ rps and 7th harmonic motoring torque is zero at $+n_s/7$ rps. The sum of the ordinates of fundamental, 5th and 7th harmonic torques gives the resultant torque-speed curve as shown in Fig. 5.62. The resultant torque has two dips, one near the slip 1.2 and the other near the slip 6/7. The dip near $s = 6/7$ is more important. The resultant torque-speed curve is stable in the neighbourhood of $s = 6/7$; since, here, the torque decreases with increase in speed. If load torque curve T_L is as shown, then motor will run at about $1/7\ n_s$ and the operating point would be A. This stable operation near sub-synchronous sped $n_s/7$ is called *crawling* or *asynchronous crawling*. The crawling is accompanied by much higher stator current and sometimes noise and vibrations is also observed.

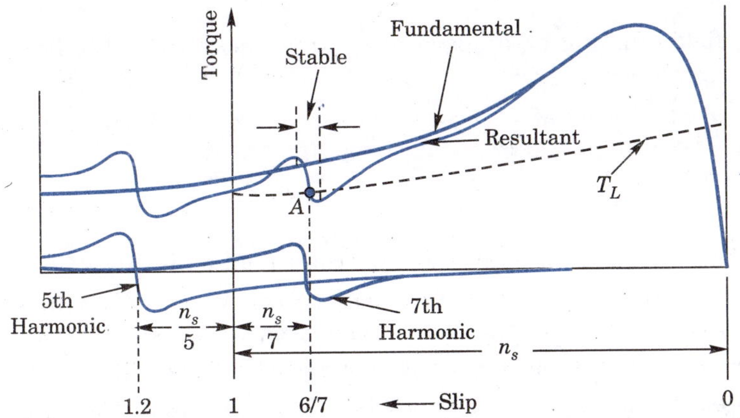

Fig. 5.62: Torque-speed characteristics of a polyphase induction motor showing the influence of space harmonics.

Every effort is made at the design stage to eliminate crawling. In spite of this, if a motor crawls, then it can be overcome by applying a sudden external torque to the driven load in the direction of rotor rotation. In case the supply voltage decreases ; the induction motor torque also decreases because $T_e \propto V_1^2$. Therefore, asynchronous crawling may also be observed in 3-phase induction motors (though not present under rated voltage conditions), when these are started under reduced supply voltage conditions.

5.15.2 Harmonic Synchronous Torques

The difference between harmonic asynchronous (or induction) torque and the harmonic synchronous torque must be understood at the outset. An asynchronous torque is developed when stator harmonic mmf produces a rotor harmonic mmf of the same number of poles and both the stator and rotor harmonic mmfs are stationary with respect to each other *at all possible rotor speeds.* Recall that in a synchronous motor, the synchronous torque is developed only at one rotor speed. Two harmonic fluxes of the same order, one produced by stator and the other by rotor, may interact with each other *at one particular speed only* to produce harmonic synchronous torque. These harmonic synchronous torques are caused by the tooth harmonics.

The stator-slotting produces its tooth harmonics of order $\frac{2S_1}{P} \pm 1$ and rotor-slotting produces its tooth harmonics of order $\frac{2S_2}{P} \pm 1$ as explained in Art. 5.14. Here S_1 and S_2 are the stator and rotor slots respectively. The plus sign refers to the harmonic-field rotation in the direction of rotor movement.

In order to illustrate the concepts of harmonic-synchronous torque, consider a 4-pole induction motor with $S_1 = 24$ and $S_2 = 28$. The stator and rotor produce tooth harmonics of order $\frac{2 \times 24}{4} \pm 1$ and $\frac{2 \times 28}{4} \pm 1$ respectively. That is, the stator produces 11th backward and 13th forward harmonics, rotor produces 13th backward and 15th forward harmonics. Thus, two harmonic fluxes of order 13 are produced by both stator and rotor but rotating in opposite directions.

Consider, for the time being, that rotor produced 13th harmonic field is only present. This 13th harmonic field produces 13th harmonic currents in the rotor. These currents give rise to rotating field running at a speed of $\frac{n_s}{13}$ rps backward. This field will cause rotor rotation backward at a speed of $\frac{n_r}{13}$ rps, so that relative speed between backward rotating field and rotor structure is equal to slip-speed $= -\left(\frac{n_s - n_r}{13}\right)$ rps. Here negative sign before $(n_s - n_r)/13$ is used because speed of 13th harmonic rotor field with respect to rotor is backward.

Actually, rotor runs at a speed of n_r rps forward. When only fundamental frequency rotating field is present, we know that rotor-field speed with respect to (w.r.t.) stator

$$= \text{actual rotor speed } n_r + \text{speed of rotor field w.r.t. rotor, } sn_s = n_s.$$

A similar expression can be written when 13th harmonic backward rotating field is present in addition to the forward rotor rotation at speed n_r rps.

∴ 13th harmonic rotor field speed w.r.t. stator = actual rotor speed n_r + speed of 13th harmonic backward rotating field w.r.t. rotor, $\left(-\frac{n_s - n_r}{13}\right)$

$$= n_r - \left(\frac{n_s - n_r}{13}\right)$$

But the speed of forward 13th harmonic stator field is $n_s/13$ with respect to stator. These two harmonic fields would be stationary with respect to each other only when

$$n_r - \left(\frac{n_s - n_r}{13}\right) = \frac{n_s}{13} \quad \text{or} \quad n_r = \frac{n_s}{7}.$$

The interaction between the two oppositely rotating harmonic fields will, therefore, produce harmonic synchronous torque only at one-seventh of synchronous speed as shown in Fig. 5.63 by a vertical line. For these number of stator and rotor slots, the motor would run at sub-synchronous speed $n_s/7$. This stable operation at subsynchronous speed, caused by slot harmonics, is also called crawling or more precisely *synchronous crawling* Three-phase induction motor operation under synchronous crawling is associated with noise and vibration.

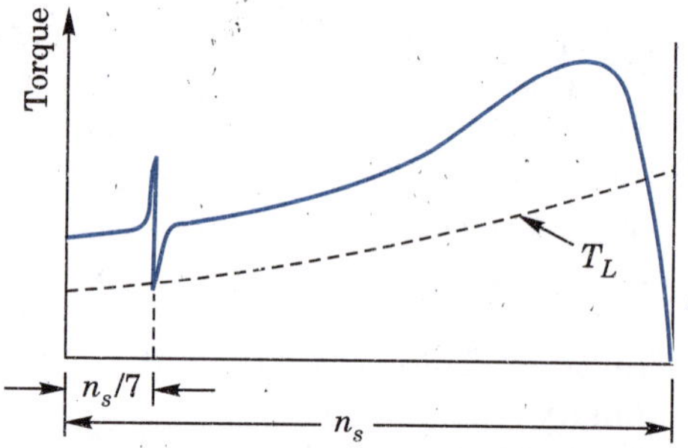

Fig. 5.63: Torque-speed characteristics of a polyphase induction motor with harmonic synchronous torque at $n_s/7$.

If the motor has $S_1 = S_2 = 24$, then both stator and rotor slot harmonics are given by

$$\frac{2 \times 24}{4} \pm 1 = 11 \text{ or } 13.$$

For both stator and rotor, harmonics of order 11 produce backward rotating field and harmonics of order 13 produce forward rotating field. For harmonics of the same order, say 11th harmonic, the two harmonic fields would be stationary with respect to each other only when

$$n_r - \left(\frac{n_s - n_r}{11}\right) = -\frac{n_s}{11} \quad \text{or} \quad n_r = 0$$

The negative sign before $n_s/11$ is used because harmonic field due to 11th harmonic rotates backward with respect to stator.

Similarly, for 13th harmonic, $\frac{n_s - n_r}{13} + n_r = \frac{n_s}{13}$ or $n_r = 0$.

This shows that harmonic synchronous torque is developed at zero rotor speed. From physical considerations, it can be stated that the two 11th harmonic fields produced by both stator and rotor are stationary with respect to each other, harmonic synchronous torque at zero rotor speed is, therefore, developed. Same is true for 13th harmonic field. In view of this, rotor remains at rest. This phenomenon of the induction motor to remain at rest, when connected to a 3-phase source, is called *cogging*. Stator-tooth harmonics of order $\frac{2S_1}{P} \pm 1$ may interact at sub-synchronous speeds with rotor harmonics of order $\frac{2S_2}{P} \pm 1$ to produce the harmonic-synchronous torques. Therefore,

$$\frac{2S_1}{P} \pm 1 = \frac{2S_2}{P} \pm 1 \quad \text{or} \quad S_1 = S_2$$

Also
$$\frac{2S_1}{P} - 1 = \frac{2S_2}{P} + 1 \quad \text{or} \quad S_1 - S_2 = P.$$

Thus, when $S_1 = S_2$, $S_1 - S_2 = P$ or when S_1 is an integral multiple of S_2, cogging is sure to occur.

The harmonic parasitic torques are normally of no importance for the wound-rotor induction motors, because these motors can be started with its maximum torque at starting, by inserting external resistances in the rotor circuit.

The asynchronous (or induction) harmonic torques can't be avoided, but can be reduced (*i*) by a proper choice of coil-span and (*ii*) by skewing as explained in Art. 5.14. The synchronous harmonic torques can be avoided entirely by a proper slot-combination of stator and rotor slots.

5.15.3 Vibration Torques and Noise

When a rotor runs, its teeth move with respect to the stator teeth. At a particular position, stator and rotor teeth have one value of flux density, but after a little rotor movement, the flux density in stator and rotor teeth varies. This variation of flux density in stator and rotor teeth causes noise like humming, whistling etc. In addition to it, when the axis of stator and rotor teeth coincide, rotor teeth are attracted by stator teeth. In this manner, a unidirectional pull is exerted on the rotor. When the rotor revolves this unidirectional pull moves around the air-gap at a particular speed and causes the rotor to vibrate. At a certain speed of the rotor, frequency of these vibrations may become equal to the frequency of natural mechanical rotor oscillations. Under these conditions, rotor vibrations increase considerably and this may make the rotor running impossible. Analysis reveals that if vibration torques are to be avoided, then

$$S_1 - S_2 \neq \pm 1 \pm P, \quad S_1 - S_2 \neq \pm 2 \pm 2P.$$

5.15.4 Reduction of Harmonic Torques and Vibrations

As stated before, harmonic asynchronous torques can't be avoided but can be reduced, but the harmonic synchronous torque can be eliminated entirely.

(*a*) *Proper choice of coil-span.* An appropriate choice of coil span helps in the reduction of stator mmf harmonics. The windings are usually short-pitched by a suitable chording angle. Thus, fractional-pitch windings are preferable for 3-phase induction motors so as to reduce the stator harmonic mmf waves and therefore to reduce the harmonic asynchronous torques.

(*b*) *Integral-slot windings.* If slot per pole per phase is not a whole number in 3-phase induction motors, then space distribution of stator mmf wave is not symmetrical around the air-gap periphery. This condition is favourable to the production of noise and vibrations in induction motors. Therefore, fractional-pitch, integral-slot windings (stator slots per pole per phase a whole number) should only be used for stator windings of 3-phase induction motors so as to reduce the noise and vibrations.

(*c*) *Choice of stator and rotor slots.* The number of stator and rotor slots should be so chosen as to reduce vibrations and noise a nd to avoid the harmonic synchronous torques.

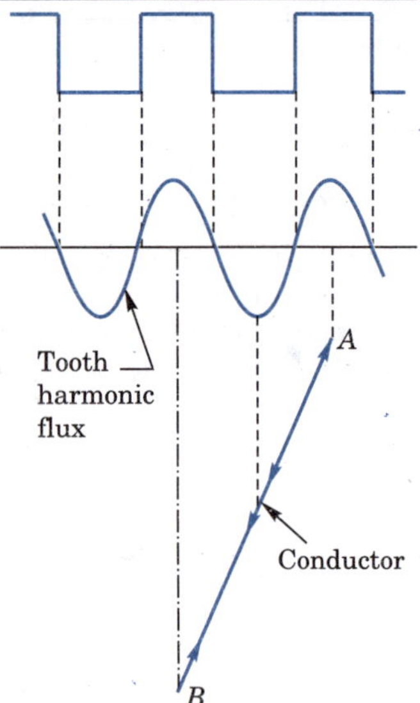

Fig. 5.64: Pertaining to skewing.

(*d*) *Skewing.* The stator or rotor slots are skewed usually by one slot-pitch as shown in Fig. 5.64. Both ends *A* and *B* of the conductor are cutting positive half of the tooth harmonic flux. Therefore resultant emf. induced in the conductor by tooth-harmonic flux is zero. In this manner, harmonic torques due to tooth-harmonic flux are eliminated. Since slots are skewed, either of the stator or of the rotor, skewing also reduces vibration torques and noise.

5.15.5 Crawling due to Unsymmetrical Rotor Circuits

In 3-phase induction motors, rotor circuit is more likely to be unbalanced than the stator circuit. In a squirrel-cage motor, the rotor circuit may become unbalanced, or unsym-metrical, due to any one or all of the following reasons.

(*a*) A rotor bar may be broken.

(*b*) The end-ring may become open circuited.

The rotor circuit of a slip-ring induction motor may become unbalanced due to any one or all of the following reasons.

(*a*) The phase impedances are unequal.

(*b*) Any one or two phases become open circuited.

The object of this part of the article is to investigate qualitatively the effect of unbalanced rotor circuits on induction-motor operation.

With three-phase voltages applied to stator of a 3-phase induction motor, a rotating magnetic field is produced. Assume that this field rotates in the clockwise (cw) direction. Since the rotor circuit is unsymmetrical, this rotating field generates unbalanced emfs and currents in the secondary at standstill. These unbalanced rotor currents can be resolved into positive sequence and negative sequence currents. Positive sequence currents produce a forward rotating field (frf) in the direction of polyphase field, *i.e.*, in the cw direction ; whereas negative sequence currents produce a backward rotating field (brf) against the direction of polyphase field. With the rotor at standstill, the speed of both the frf and brf is synchronous with respect to rotor. When the rotor starts running, the speed of both frf and brf becomes less than synchronous with respect to rotor.

The frf and polyphase field run in the same direction (*i.e.,* cw) and at the same speed just like rotor and stator fields in a balanced polyphase induction motor. Therefore, this field produces a forward torque similar to that produced in a polyphase motor. Consequently, the torque-speed curve for frf is as shown in Fig. 5.65 (*a*).

Now give attention only to brf running in counter-clockwise (ccw) direction. Assume for the purpose of physical understanding, that brf is produced by a primary winding on the rotor. It should be kept in mind that this primary winding has slip frequency (= slip × supply frequency f_1) voltages induced in it. Recall that when the primary is on the rotor, the rotor must run against the direction of its rotating field. Here brf is rotating ccw, therefore, at standstill this field produces a cw torque which aids the torque due to frf. The effect of brf can be studied in steps as follows :

(*i*) At standstill, rotor speed $n_r = 0$ slip $s = 1$, rotor (or primary) frequency = supply frequency f_1, stator (or secondary) frequency = f_1.

$$\therefore \quad \text{Brf speed w.r.t. rotor} = \frac{12f_1}{P} = n_s, \text{ ccw.}$$

Brf speed w.r.t. stator $= n_s - n_r = n_s$, ccw

Since speed of brf w.r.t. stator is ccw, starting torque is developed in cw direction and this augments the starting torque produced by frf.

(*ii*) At $n_r = 0.2\ n_s$, cw (say) ; slip = 0.8

Rotor frequency = slip × f_1 = $0.8\ f_1$.

$$\therefore \quad \text{Brf speed w.r.t. rotor} = \frac{120 \times 0.8f_1}{P} = 0.8\ n_s, \text{ ccw.}$$

Brf speed w.r.t. stator $= 0.8\ n_s - n_r = 0.8\ n_s - 0.2\ n_s = 0.6\ n_s$, ccw.

Since brf speed w.r.t. stator is ccw, this field produces cw torque, *i.e.,* motoring torque.

(*iii*) At $n_r = 0.5\ n_s$, cw ; slip = 0.5, rotor frequency = $0.5\ f_1$.

$$\therefore \quad \text{Brf speed w.r.t. rotor} = \frac{120 \times 0.5f_1}{P} = 0.5\ n_s, \text{ ccw.}$$

Brf speed w.r.t. stator $= 0.5\ n_s - n_r = 0.5\ n_s - 0.5\ n_s = 0$.

Since brf is stationary with respect to stator, or secondary, winding; no emf is induced in the secondary and therefore torque developed at rotor speed $n_r = 0.5\ n_s$ is zero. This is illustrated in Fig. 5.65 (*a*).

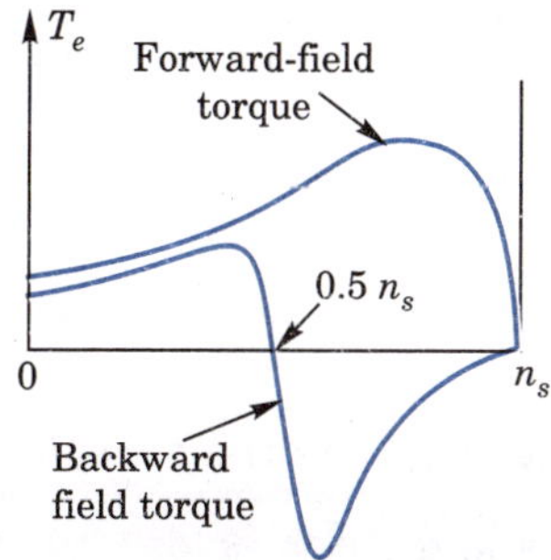

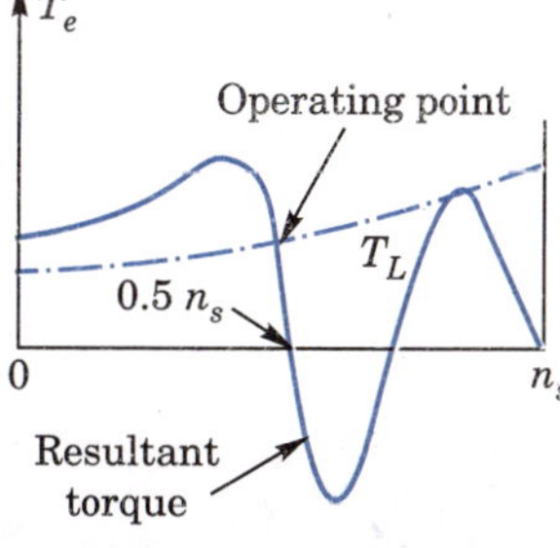

Fig. 5.65: Polyphase induction motor, torque-speed characteristics with rotor circuit unbalanced.

(*iv*) At $n_r = 0.6\ n_s$, cw ; slip = 0.4, rotor frequency = $0.4\ f_1$.

$$\therefore \quad \text{Brf speed w.r.t. rotor} = \frac{120 \times 0.4 f_1}{P} = 0.4\ n_s, \text{ ccw}$$

$$\text{Brf speed w.r.t. rotor} = 0.4\ n_s - n_r$$

$$= 0.4\ n_s - 0.6\ n_s = -\ 0.2\ n_s, \text{ ccw} = 0.2\ n_s, \text{ cw.}$$

This shows that with rotor speed above $0.5\ n_s$, the rotor is running faster (cw) than the brf in the same direction (here $0.2\ n_s$ cw). Recall that with rotor running faster than the rotating field in the same direction, induction motor becomes induction generator. Therefore, the torque developed by brf is negative or a generating torque is developed. This negative torque-speed characteristic is somewhat similar to that below $0.5\ n_s$. When rotor speed equals n_s, no torque is developed because then the relative speed between rotor and polyphase field becomes zero and no emfs are induced in the rotor circuit. The torque-speed characteristic due to brf is shown in Fig. 5.65 (*a*). The resultant torque in a 3-phase induction motor with unbalanced rotor circuit is obtained by adding the ordinates of the two torques in Fig. 5.65 (*a*). The resultant torque speed characteristic is illustrated in Fig. 5.65 (*b*). The nature of this characteristic may vary depending upon the cause of unbalance and the type of motor.

For a load torque T_L as shown, the motor crawls near half the synchronous speed as shown. This shows that a polyphase induction motor may crawl near half the synchronous speed if the rotor, or secondary, winding is unbalanced. This phenomenons is also referred to as *George's phenomenon.*

Example 5.44. *A 3-phase, 4-pole, 50 Hz squirrel-cage induction motor has 48 stator and 52 rotor slots. Find the rotor speed at which harmonic synchronous torque would be developed.*

Solution. Order of the tooth harmonics produced by stator slotting.

$$= \frac{2S_1}{P} \pm 1 = \frac{2 \times 48}{4} \pm 1 = 23 \text{ and } 25.$$

Order of tooth harmonics produced by rotor-slotting

$$= \frac{2S_2}{P} \pm 1 = \frac{2 \times 52}{4} \pm 1 = 25 \text{ and } 27.$$

It is seen here that stator-produced 25th harmonic field rotates forward and rotor-produced 25th harmonic field rotates backward.

The rotor speed is n_r rps. The speed of 25th harmonic backward rotating field with respect to rotor is $-\left(\frac{n_s - n_r}{25}\right)$ rps. Since the rotor speed is n_r rps, forward, the speed of 25th harmonic backward rotor field with respect to stator is $n_r - \left(\frac{n_s - n_r}{25}\right)$ rps. But the stator-produced 25th harmonic forward field rotates at $+\frac{n_s}{25}$ rps. The harmonic synchronous torque would be developed only when 25th harmonic stator and rotor fields are stationary with respect to each other, *i.e.*, when

$$n_r - \left(\frac{n_s - n_r}{25}\right) = +\frac{n_s}{25} \quad \text{or} \quad n_r = \frac{n_s}{13} \text{ rps.}$$

Thus the speed, at which harmonic synchronous torque is developed

$$= \frac{n_s}{13} \text{ rps.} = \frac{120 \times 50}{4} \times \frac{1}{13} = 115.4 \text{ rpm.}$$

Example 5.45. *A 3-phase, 4-pole, 50 Hz induction motor has 36 stator and 40 rotor slots. If it exhibits a crawling tendency at about 150 rpm, what are the precise causes of it ?*

Solution. Synchronous speed $= \dfrac{120 \times 50}{4} = 1500$ rpm.

Let us first investigate whether the crawling at 150 rpm is due to harmonic induction torque. The harmonic fields produced by the winding are of the order $k = 6m \pm 1$

For $m = 1$, $k = 5$ or 7.

This shows that stator winding produces 5th harmonic backward rotating field and 7th harmonic forward rotating field. Since the motor crawls at 150 rpm in the forward direction, it may crawl due to 7th harmonic only.

But speed of 7th harmonic field, $= \dfrac{n_s}{7} = \dfrac{1500}{7} = 214.3$ rpm.

This shows that 7th harmonic field is not responsible for the crawling at 150 rpm.

For $m = 2$, $k = 11$ or 13

Speed of 13th harmonic forward field $= \dfrac{n_s}{13} = \dfrac{1500}{13} = 115.4$ rpm.

Since 115.4 rpm. is far different from 150 rpm, it can't crawl due to 13th harmonic forward field. It can, therefore, to be concluded that this induction motor does not crawl at 150 rpm. due to harmonic induction torque.

Let us now investigate the effect of harmonics produced by stator and rotor slotting.

Order of harmonic produced by stator slotting $= \dfrac{2S_1}{P} \pm 1 = \dfrac{72}{4} \pm 1 = 17b, 19f.$

Order of harmonic produced by rotor slotting $= \dfrac{2S_2}{P} \pm 1 = \dfrac{80}{4} \pm 1 = 19b, 21f.$

Note that synchronous crawling can take place with the same order of stator and rotor harmonics. Speed of backward 19th harmonic rotor field is $-\left(\dfrac{n_s - n_r}{19}\right)$ with respect to rotor.

$\therefore$ Speed of backward 19th harmonic rotor field with respect to stator

$$= n_r - \left(\frac{n_s - n_r}{19}\right)$$

For the production of harmonic synchronous torque,

$$n_r - \left(\frac{n_s - n_r}{19}\right) = \text{speed of forward 19th harmonic stator}$$

$$\text{field} = \frac{n_s}{19} \qquad \therefore \qquad n_r = \frac{n_s}{10} = 150 \text{ rpm.}$$

This shows that the motor crawls at 150 rpm due to the harmonic fields produced by stator and rotor slotting. Thus harmonic synchronous torque is responsible for its crawling at 150 rpm.

5.16 LINEAR ELECTRIC MOTORS

A linear motion can be mechanically obtained from a rotating electric motor. However, linear electric motors (LEMs) have been developed which can provide linear motion much more economically and efficiently. By *linear motion* we mean motion in a horizontal direction. A force producing linear motion is called thrust, propulsion force or traction force.

In principle, every rotating electric machine can have its counterpart in the form of LEM. However, only linear induction machines and linear synchronous machines have been found economically viable machines. Furthermore, only linear motors, rather than generators, have found applications so far. Therefore, only linear induction motors (LIMs) and linear synchronous motors (LSMs) require consideration in this article. The object of this article is to discuss LEMs at their introductory level only.

5.16.1 LIM and its Principle of Operation

Fig. 5.66 (*a*) shows a polyphase rotary induction motor. If this induction motor is cut at X and laid out flat as shown in Fig. 5.66 (*b*), a linear induction motor is obtained. In this figure, rotor is shown in the form of conducting sheet. Henceforth, stator and rotor would be called primary and secondary respectively. In Fig. 5.66 (*b*), the primary, consisting of core and windings, has a finite length called active length of LIM.

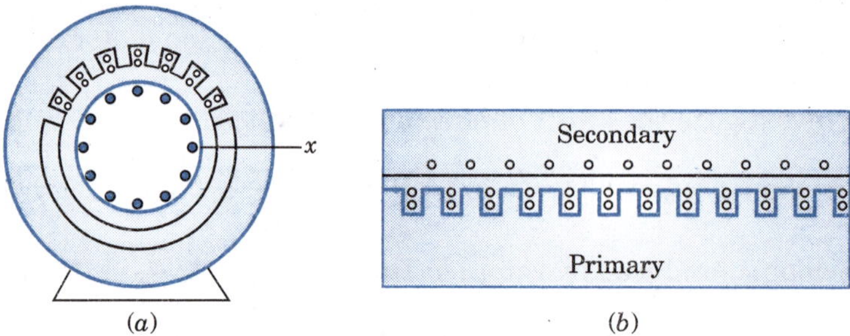

Fig. 5.66 Deriving a LIM from rotary polyphase induction motor.

In a rotary 3-phase induction motor, a rotating magnetic field is produced. When the 3-phase winding of Fig. 5.66 (*b*) is energised from 3-phase supply, a linear travelling field is produced. The velocity of this travelling field is

$$v_s = 2f\,(\text{pole-pitch}) = f(\lambda)^* \text{ m/sec} \qquad ...(5.112)$$

Here λ is the wavelength of the travelling field and is equal to two pole-pitches.

This linear travelling field induces currents in the secondary. The interaction between primary and secondary fields results in the production of linear force. As in an ordinary induction motor, the speed of the secondary in LIM is less than v_s and is given by

$$v_r = v_s\,(1 - s) \text{ m/sec} \qquad ...(5.113)$$

* See Art. 3.7. "Electrical Machinery" by the same Author.

Unlike a rotary induction motor, a LIM may have moving primary and fixed secondary or moving secondary with fixed primary.

Depending on their use, a LIM may have short primary, Fig. 5.67 (*a*) ; or a short secondary Fig. 5.67 (*b*). LIM may have two primaries to obtain a double-sided LIM (DSLIM) as shown in Fig. 5.67 (*a*). In case LIM has one primary, then it is called single-sided LIM (SLIM).

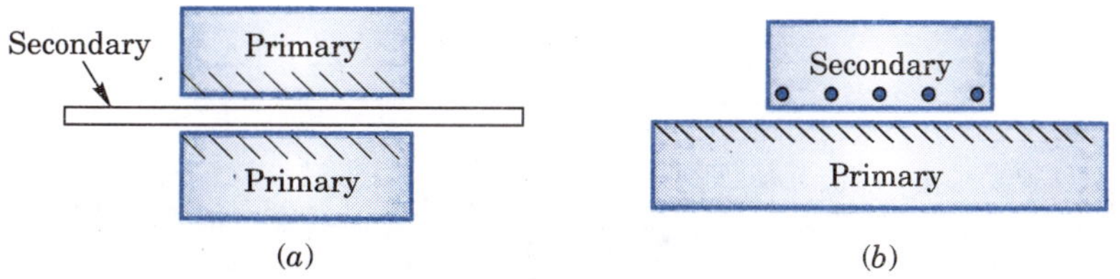

Fig. 5.67 (*a*) Short primary, DSLIM (*b*) Short secondary, SLIM.

Linear force. An approximate expression for the linear force developed in a LIM can be obtained in terms of its main dimensions, just like an ordinary induction motor.

Neglecting magnetizing current and primary losses, the power across the air gap is

$$P_g = 3E_1 I_1 \cos \theta_1$$

where, E_1 = per phase emf induced in primary winding

$$= \sqrt{2}\, \pi f k_\omega N_{ph}\, \phi$$

I_1 = per phase primary current

$\cos \theta_1$ = primary p.f.

The specific electric loading $\overline{ac}$ is defined as the primary ampere conductors per metre length of field system.

$$\therefore \qquad \overline{ac} = \frac{3 \times N_{ph} I_1 \times 2}{L} \qquad \text{...(5.114)}$$

where, $L = P \cdot Y$, is the total length of the field system along the direction of linear motion, see Fig. 5.68. Here Y is the pole pitch.

The specific magnetic loading B_{av} is defined as the average air-gap flux density in Tesla.

$$\therefore \qquad B_{av} = \frac{P\phi}{LW}$$

or

$$P\phi = B_{av} . LW \qquad \text{...(5.115)}$$

Here W is the width of the field system of linear motor as shown in Fig. 5.68. Substituting the values of E_1, I_1 in P_g, we get

$$P_g = 3 \cdot \sqrt{2}\, \pi k_\omega N_{Ph}\, \phi \cdot f \, \frac{\overline{ac} \cdot L}{3 \cdot N_{Ph} \cdot 2} \cdot \cos \theta_1$$

From Eq. (5.112), $f = \dfrac{v_s}{2Y}$

$$\therefore \qquad P_g = 3 \cdot \sqrt{2}\, \pi k_\omega \cdot \phi \cdot \frac{v_s}{2Y} \frac{\overline{ac} \cdot L}{6} \cos \theta_1$$

Now $$\phi = \frac{B_{av} \cdot LW}{P}$$

$\therefore$ $$P_g = \frac{\pi}{2\sqrt{2}} \cdot k_\omega \cdot \frac{B_{av} \cdot LW}{P} \cdot \frac{v_s}{Y} \cdot \overline{ac} \cdot L \cdot \cos\theta_1$$

But $L = PY$ and assuming an efficiency of η, the thrust, or linear force, developed is

$$F = \eta \frac{\text{Air-gap power}}{\text{Linear synchronous velocity}}$$

$$= \eta \frac{P_g}{v_s} = \eta \frac{\pi}{2\sqrt{2}} B_{av}\, \overline{ac}\, .\, LW\, k_\omega \cos\theta_1, \text{ Newton} \qquad ...(5.116)$$

Phenomena peculiar to LEM. The presentation given above for LIM is only approximate. For doing the rigorous analysis, electromagnetic field theory must be employed.

Certain phenomena peculiar to LEM must be investigated for better understanding of this motor. The phenomena which need consideration are (*i*) transverse edge effects and (*ii*) end-effects. These are now described briefly.

(i) Transverse edge-effects. In an ordinary induction motor, the rotor winding provides well defined paths for the currents induced in it. In LIM, the secondary consists of a solid conducting plate. Therefore, there, are no well defined paths for the currents induced in the secondary. These paths are shown in Fig. 5.68, for LIM. The current paths perpendicular to the direction of motion, such as *ab* and others parallel to *ab*, contribute to the production of useful linear force or thrust. The current paths along the direction of motion, such as *bc, BD* etc. contribute towards losses.

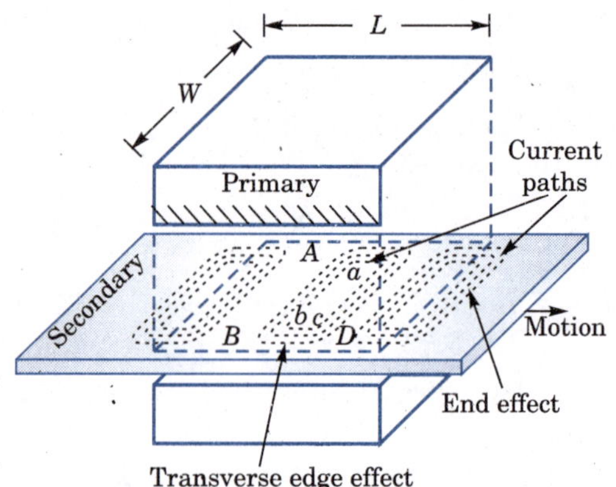

Fig. 5.68: Transverse edge effect and end effect in LEM.

In conventional electrical motor, the width W is equal to core length. In LIM or LEM, the length of current path nearer to the pole centre is less. For example, in Fig. 5.68, the length of current *ab* nearer to the pole centre is less than *AB* away from the pole centre. As a result, the effective width W of the LEM is less and this has the effect of reducing the output, see Eq. (5.116).

Summarising, the main consequences of transverse edge effects in LEM are as follows :

(*a*) Current paths along the direction of motion add only to the losses of LEM.

(*b*) The effective width W of LEM is reduced.

(*c*) Both the above effects deteriorate the LEM performance.

(ii) End effects. Since the primary winding and primary core are of finite length, the end effects appear in LEM. For example, the field flux nearer the ends has different configuration than at the middle. The currents induced in the secondary nearer each end go beyond the field structure length L as shown in Fig. 5.68. These currents may be termed end-effect currents and they produce additional forces causing braking action specially at lower values of slip.

Summarising, the consequences of end effects are the production of braking forces in the low-slip operation. This has the effect of reducing the efficiency, power factor and output thrust of the LEM.

5.16.2 Linear Synchronous Motors (LSM)

In principle, LSM is similar to conventional synchronous motor. It became important only very recently as a traction motor for high-speed ground transportation (HSGT). LSM has polyphase armature winding and d.c. field winding just as in a conventional synchronous motor. LSM may have conventional field winding or superconducting field winding. From practical consideration, LSM with movable field winding is more suitable.

5.16.3 Linear Levitated Machines (LLM)

In LEM, normal (perpendicular to ground) forces are also developed in addition to linear forces. The existence of normal forces have been put to use for the development of LLMs. For HSGT, the vehicle should not make any contact with the track, whereas linear force provides the required linear velocity to the vehicle. In this manner, LLMs are being developed at present. There are two types of LLMs, attraction type LLM and repulsion type LLM.

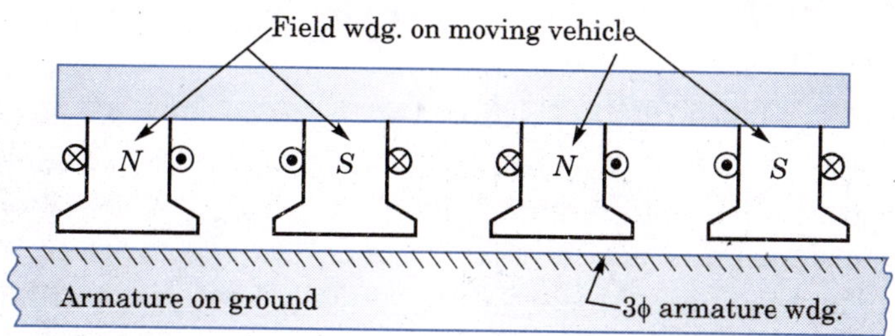

Fig. 5.69: An elementary salient-pole LSM.

5.16.4 Applications

From application view-point, LEMs can be divided into three types, namely (*a*) force machines (*b*) power machines and (*c*) energy machines.

(a) Force machines. These are short-duty machines and operate usually at low speeds. In these machines, efficiency is not a major consideration, because these are most useful in small sizes. Examples of the use of force machines are for shuttle propulsion, for stop valves, as induction stirrers for molten metals etc.

(b) Power machines. These are continuous-duty machines and often operate at medium and high speeds. Power machines must have high operating efficiency. These have been used for conveyors, haulers, electromagnetic pumps, travelling cranes and high-speed rail traction.

Overhead travelling crane. A LIM for overhead travelling crane consists of a travelling primary and a fixed secondary. A simple arrangement of this scheme is shown in Fig. 5.70 (*a*). In this figure, one-sided primary is on the travelling gantry and the secondary is fixed. Note that the *T*-section secondary serves as a supporting track for the wheels to travel on it. The speed control and linear thrust are controlled by varying the voltage. The advantages of using this scheme using LIM are (*i*) simple construction with no rotating parts (*ii*) elimination of gears, clutches and coupling shafts and (*iii*) easy control.

High-speed trains. Rotary motors can run the trains up to speeds of above 250-300 km/hr. For speeds above 300 km/hr or so, rotary motors usually offer a poor choice because of limited adhesion (between wheel and rail) and other mechanical considerations. On the other had, a linear motor offers an attractive alternative method of propulsion for speeds exceeding 300 km/hr. One possible futuristic system using LIM is illustrated in Fig. 5.70 (*b*). In this figure, double-sided primary is mounted on the moving vehicle and a *T*-section aluminium plate serves as the secondary of LIM.

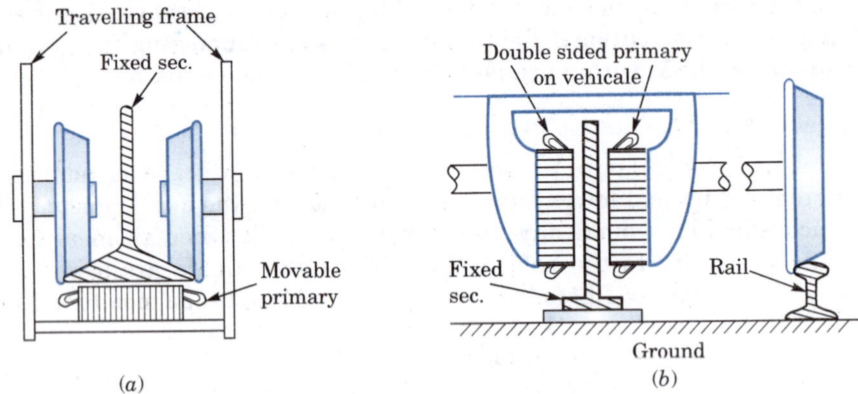

Fig. 5.70: Use of LIM for (*a*) crane (*b*) railway.

For high-speed trains without wheels and in which mechanical contact is undesirable, LLMs have been proposed. For both propulsion and suspension of HSGT vehicles, prototypes of LLMs have been designed and partially tested in U.S., Great Britain, West Germany and Japan. Japan has given the name "Maglev" (magnetically levitated) to LLMs.

(*c*) *Energy Machines.* These are also short-duty machines. One of the earliest applications of LIM as an energy machine was to launch an aircraft. This LIM, called electropult, was developed in U.S. Other modern applications of LIMs as energy machines are as follows :

(*i*) Accelerators for very high velocity projectiles, for example for accelerating cars or lorries for indoor crash tests.

(*ii*) Actuators for h.v. circuit breakers.

(*iii*) Impact extruders for metals.

5.17 NON-SINUSOIDAL SUPPLY VOLTAGE

The power supply from utility undertakings is usually sinusoidal. The performance of three-phase induction motors considered so far is on the assumption of sinusoidal supply voltage. However, in inverter-controlled three-phase induction motors, the supply voltage may not be sinusoidal. The performance of induction motors, when fed from non-sinusoidal voltage waveforms, gets modified. The purpose of this article is to study this changed behaviour.

If V_s = dc source voltage input to 3-phase inverter, then the inverter line to neutral output voltage, fed to 3-phase induction motor, can be expressed as under.

$$V_a = \frac{2V_s}{\pi}\left[\sin \omega t + \frac{1}{5}\sin \omega t + \frac{1}{7}\sin 7\omega t + \frac{1}{11}\sin 11\omega t + \frac{1}{13}\sin 13\omega t + \ldots\right] \quad \ldots(5.117)$$

Here $\omega = 2\pi f$ is the fundamental frequency. In addition to fundamental, other voltage components have harmonic frequency of order $n = 5, 7, 11, 13, ...,$ *i.e.* $6k \pm 1$ where k is any positive integer. Also, the amplitude of harmonic voltage is $\frac{1}{n}$ times the amplitude of fundamental voltage. Phase voltages v_b, v_c can be obtained by substituting $\left(\omega t - \frac{2\pi}{3}\right)$ and $\left(\omega t - \frac{4\pi}{3}\right)$ in place of ωt in Eq. (5.117).

When three-phase complex voltage waveforms, as given by Eq. (5.117) for phase a, are impressed on the stator of a 3-phase induction motor, the performance for each order of frequency is determined. The final behaviour of motor is then obtained by superimposing the effects of each harmonic components on the fundamental component.

Fundamental frequency performance. When fundamental frequency voltages are applied, positive phase sequence (pps) of currents are established. These currents set up an mmf wave rotating at synchronous speed $\omega_s = 2\pi n_s = \frac{4\pi f}{P}$ rad/sec. The motor runs at speed $\omega_r < \omega_s$ and fundamental frequency slip s_1 is given by

$$s_1 = \frac{\omega_s - \omega_r}{\omega_s} \qquad ...(5.118)$$

Harmonic order $n = 6k + 1$. Voltages of harmonic order $6k + 1$, *i.e.* 7, 13 etc. are pps voltages. These voltages establish pps currents in the stator winding. As a result, pps travelling mmf wave, travelling in the direction of fundamental mmf wave, is set up and its speed is given by $\frac{120(nf)}{P} = n \cdot \omega_s$ rad/sec.

Note that stator winding is would for P poles. Even for supply frequency nf, stator winding would develop P poles only.

The pps rotating mmf and rotor run in the same direction, therefore, the slip s_n for harmonic order n is given by

$$s_n = \frac{n\omega_s - \omega_r}{n\omega_s} = \frac{n\omega_s - \omega_s(1 - s_1)}{n\omega_s} = \frac{(n-1) + s_1}{n}$$

These order of harmonics would produce torque in the direction of fundamental-frequency torque.

Harmonic order n = 6k – 1. Voltages of harmonic order $6k - 1$, *i.e.* 5, 11, ... etc. form negative sequence of voltages. Therefore, negative phase sequence (nps) currents, established by these voltages, would develop mmf wave rotating at speed $n\omega_s$ in opposite direction to the fundamental mmf wave. Now the slip s_n is given by

$$s_n = \frac{-n\omega_s - \omega_r}{-n\omega_s} = \frac{(n+1) - s_1}{n}$$

In general, $$s_n = \frac{(n \mp 1) \pm s_1}{n} \qquad ...(5.119)$$

Equivalent circuits. For fundamental frequency, equivalent circuit is as shown in Fig. 5.71 (a). This equivalent circuit can be modified for nth harmonic also. For harmonic frequency nf, r_1 and r_2 are assumed constant, but reactances are multiplied by n. Therefore, harmonic equivalent circuit for frequency nf is as shown in Fig. 5.71 (*b*). Since $n(x_1 + x_2) >> (r_1 + r_2)$, resistances r_1 and r_2 can be ignored. Also $n X_m$ is much greater than $n(x_1 + x_2)$. Therefore, an approximate equivalent circuit for harmonics of order n can be drawn as shown in Fig. 5.71 (*c*). It is seen from approximate equivalent circuit that harmonic current is limited mainly by harmonic leakage reactance $n(x_1 + x_2)$.

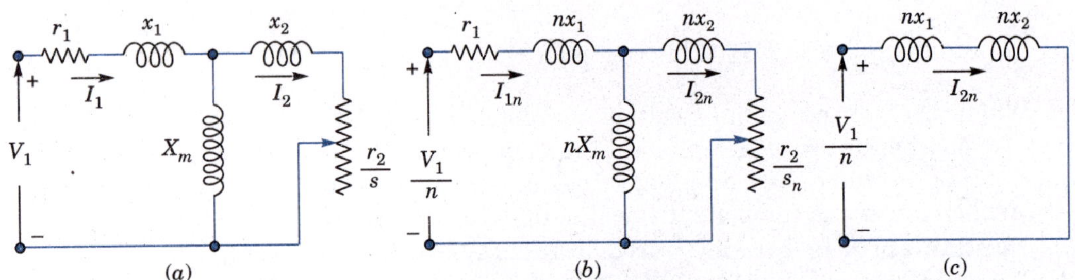

Fig. 5.71: Three-phase induction motor equivalent circuit at (*a*) fundamental frequency (*b*) harmonic frequency $n\omega$ and (*c*) approximate equivalent circuit at frequency $n\omega$.

Steady harmonic torques. Analysis for fundamental-frequency operation is already carried out. Therefore, fundamental-frequency electro-magnetic torque, from Eq. (5.18), is

$$T_{e1} = \frac{mP}{4\pi f} \cdot I_2^2 \frac{r_2}{s_1}$$

for nth harmonic currents, the torque is given by

$$T_{en} = \frac{mP}{4\pi nf} (I_{2n})^2 \frac{r_{2n}}{s_n}$$

$$\therefore \quad \frac{T_{en}}{T_{e1}} = \frac{1}{n}\left(\frac{I_{2n}}{I_2}\right)^2 \frac{r_{2n}}{r_n} \cdot \frac{s_1}{s_n} \quad \text{...(5.120)}$$

Assuming $r_{2n} = r_2$,

$$\frac{T_{en}}{T_{e1}} = \frac{1}{n} \cdot \left(\frac{I_{2n}}{I_2}\right)^2 \frac{s_1}{s_n} \quad \text{...(5.121)}$$

Full-load torque. From Eq. (5.119), $s_n = \dfrac{(n \mp 1) \pm s_1}{n}$

Under normal running conditions, fundamental frequency slip s_1 is small,

$\therefore \quad s_n = \dfrac{n \mp 1}{n}$. From Eq. (5.121),

$$\frac{T_{en}}{T_{e1}} = \frac{1}{n} \cdot \left(\frac{I_{2n}}{I_2}\right)^2 \frac{n \cdot s_1}{n \mp 1} = \left(\frac{I_{2n}}{I_2}\right)^2 \frac{s_1}{n \mp 1}$$

From the approximate equivalent circuit of Fig. 5.71 (*c*), we get

$$I_2 = \frac{V_1}{x_1 + x_2} \quad \text{and} \quad I_{2n} = \frac{V_1/n}{n(x_1 + x_2)} = \frac{V_1}{n^2(x_1 + x_2)}$$

$$\therefore \quad \frac{T_{en}}{T_{e1}} = \left[\frac{V_1}{n^2(x_1 + x_2)} \cdot \frac{x_1 + x_2}{V_1}\right]^2 \frac{s_1}{n \mp 1} = \frac{1}{n^4} \cdot \frac{s_1}{(n \mp 1)}$$

As n is large, we may write $(n \mp 1)$ as n in the above expression.

$$\therefore \quad \frac{T_{en}}{T_{e1}} = \frac{s_1}{n^5} \quad \text{...(5.122)}$$

In case $r_{2n} \neq r_n$ and $(n \pm 1)$ is not equal to n, then from Eq. (5.120) and approximate equivalent circuit,

$$\frac{T_{en}}{T_{e1}} = \frac{1}{n^4} \cdot \frac{r_{2n}}{r_2} \cdot \frac{s_1}{(n \mp 1)} \quad \text{...(5.123)}$$

For 5th harmonic torque, $n = 5$ and if r_{2n} is taken equal to $3r_2$ and full-load slip $s_1 = 0.04$, then from Eq. (5.123), we get

$$\frac{T_{e5}}{T_{e1}} = -\frac{1}{5^4} \cdot \frac{3}{1} \cdot \frac{0.04}{5+1} = -0.32 \times 10^{-4}.$$

This shows that fifth harmonic torque is only 0.32×10^{-4} times the fundamental-frequency torque at full load.

For 7th harmonic torque, $n = 7$. Let (r_{2n}/r_2) be 3 as before. For full-load slip of 0.04, from Eq. (5.123), we get

$$\frac{T_{e.7}}{T_{e.1}} = +\frac{1}{7^4} \cdot \frac{3}{1} \cdot \frac{0.04}{7-1} = 0.083 \times 10^{-4}$$

Therefore, seventh harmonic torque is only 0.083×10^{-4} times the fundamental full-load torque.

Starting torque. From Eq. (5.120),

$$\frac{T_{en}}{T_{e1}} = \frac{1}{n}\left(\frac{I_{2n}}{I_2}\right)^2 \frac{r_{2n}}{r_2} \cdot \frac{s_1}{s_n} \quad \text{...(5.124)}$$

Also $\quad s_n = \dfrac{(n \mp 1) \pm s_1}{n}$. At starting, $s_1 = 1.0$, $\therefore \quad s_n = \dfrac{(n \mp 1) \pm 1}{n} = 1$

$$\therefore \quad \frac{T_{st.n}}{T_{st.1}} = \frac{1}{n}\left(\frac{I_{2n}}{I_2}\right)^2 \cdot \frac{r_{2n}}{r_2} = \frac{1}{n^5} \cdot \frac{r_{2n}}{r_2} \quad \text{...(5.125)}$$

For 5th harmonic, starting torque from Eq. (5.125) is

$$\frac{T_{st.5}}{T_{st.1}} = -\frac{1}{5^5} \cdot \frac{3}{1} = -0.96 \times 10^{-3}$$

For 7th harmonic, From Eq. (5.125), $\dfrac{T_{st.7}}{T_{st.1}} = \dfrac{1}{7^5} \times \dfrac{3}{1} = 0.1784 \times 10^{-3}$

Net full-load harmonic torque due to combined effect of 5th and 7th harmonics

$$= (-0.32 + 0.083) \times 10^{-4}. T_{e1} = -0.237 \times 10^{-4}. T_{e1}$$

Similarly, net starting harmonic torque

$$= (-0.96 + 0.1784) \times 10^{-3} . T_{st.1} = -0.7816 \times 10^{-3} . T_{st.1}$$

It is seen from above that the combined effect of 5th and 7th harmonics is to reduce both full-load and starting torques by a negligible amount. Same logic applies to eleventh and thirteenth harmonics. Since overall effect of time-harmonic torques is negligible in steady state torque, these are usually ignored during the normal analysis of three-phase induction motors.

5.17.1 Pulsating Harmonic Torques

In a 3-phase induction motor, steady state torque is developed by the interaction of stator rotating air-gap flux with rotor rotating mmf of the *same* order. Pulsating torque is, however, produced by the interaction of stator harmonic rotating flux with rotor harmonic mmf of *different* order. Harmonic air-gap fluxes are usually small; their contribution towards the production of pulsating toque is, therefore, negligible. It is only the fundamental rotating air-gap flux that produces noticeable pulsating torques.

Fifth harmonic currents have negative phase sequence, these currents, therefore, produce air-gap flux rotating at speed 5 ω_s opposite to the fundamental air-gap flux. The fifth harmonic field induces rotor currents at frequency $5f$ and this further creates rotor rotating mmf at speed $- 5\omega_s$. Relative speed between this rotor mmf wave and fundamental air-gap flux is 6 ω_s. Therefore, pulsating torque is developed at six times the fundamental frequency by the fifth time-harmonic voltage.

Seventh harmonic currents have positive phase sequence, these currents creates mmf rotating at speed $7\omega_s$ in the direction of fundamental field. This seventh harmonic field induces rotor currents at frequency $7f$. These rotor currents at seventh harmonic create rotor mmf rotating at seven times the synchronous speed in the direction of fundamental field. The relative speed between this rotor harmonic mmf wave and the fundamental stator field is again $6\omega_s$. Therefore, pulsating torque, as before, is developed at six times the fundamental frequency by the seventh time-harmonic voltage. The two pulsating torques at six times the fundamental frequency combine together to cause a fluctuation in the steady torque developed by the motor.

Similarly, eleventh and thirteenth time harmonics in the supply voltage wave would produce twelfth harmonic pulsating torques. However, sixth harmonic pulsating torques are more dominant when the three-phase induction motor is fed from six-step inverters.

The pulsating torques may lead to vibration of the motor, particularly at low-supply frequency operation of the three-phase induction motor.

5.17.2 Losses

Non-sinusoidal supply voltage to a 3-phase induction motor produces additional losses. Time harmonic voltage will cause additional harmonic-current flow in the windings leading to more I^2R loss. It is reported that I^2R loss with non-sinusoidal supply current is 1.04 to 1.2 times the normal I^2R loss. Harmonic I^2R loss depends upon the degree of harmonic content in the non-sinusoidal supply and does not depend on the load.

5.18 DOUBLY-FED INDUCTION MACHINES

A doubly-fed induction machine (DFIM) is a slip-ring induction machine (SRIM) with its stator and rotor windings connected to separate sources at different voltages and frequencies. DFIM can be used as a motor for the speed control of large pumps. It can also operate as an induction generator (IG). A SCIM and SRIM can work as induction generators when their rotor speed exceeds synchronous speed. A salient feature of DFIM is that it can operate as an induction generator even at speeds below synchronous speed. The object of this article is to discuss the basic principles of DFIM operation as a DFI motor and also as a DFI generator.

5.18.1 Doubly-Fed Induction Motor

Fig. 5.72 shows a 3-phase SRIM being fed from two different voltage sources. Stator is connected to voltage source V_1, f_1 and rotor to another voltage source V_2, f_2. Power to stator at V_1, f_1 will create stator rotating flux and power to rotor at V_2, f_2 will create rotor rotating flux.

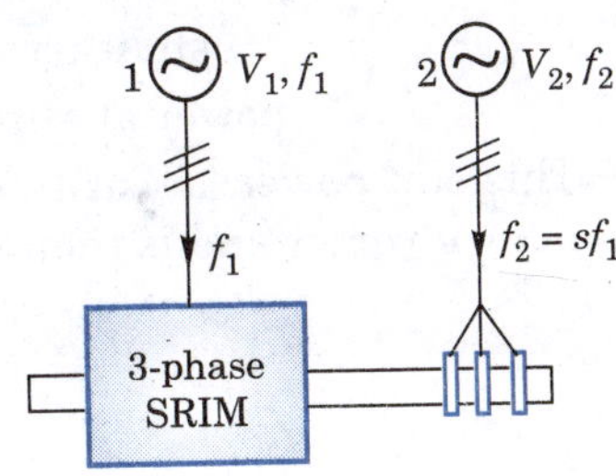

Fig. 5.72: Doubly-fed induction motor fed from two separate voltage sources.

$$\text{Speed of stator produced flux} = \frac{120 f_1}{P} \text{ rpm}$$

(say, clockwise)

$$\text{Speed of rotor produced flux} = \frac{120 f_2}{P} \text{ rpm}$$

A steady electromagnetic torque would develop when relative speed between stator field and rotor field is zero. In case rotor produced flux rotates in the direction of stator produced flux, *i.e.*, clockwise, then

$$\text{Speed of rotor} = \frac{120 f_1}{P} - \frac{120 f_2}{P}$$

$$= \frac{120 f_1}{P}\left(1 - \frac{f_2}{f_1}\right) = \frac{120 f_1}{P}(1 - s) \quad \text{...(5.126)}$$

Under the conditions stated above, the rotor runs at subsynchronous speed given by Eq. (5.126).

Let us now interchange any two leads feeding power to rotor. With this change, rotor produced flux would start rotating anticlockwise at speed $\frac{120 f_2}{P}$ rpm. Now the torque can develop only when

$$\text{Rotor speed} = \frac{120 f_1}{P} + \frac{120 f_2}{P} = \frac{120 f_1}{P}\left(1 + \frac{f_2}{f_1}\right) = \frac{120 f_1}{P}(1 + s) \quad \text{...(5.127)}$$

Under the conditions stated here, the rotor must run at supersynchronous speed given by Eq. (5.127).

From above, it can be stated, in general, that rotor of DFI motor runs at

(*i*) subsynchronous speed for positive sequence rotor currents and

(*ii*) supersynchronous speed for negative sequence rotor currents.

5.18.1.1 Power Flow in DFI Motor

Here the power flow in a DFI motor is examined when it runs at subsynchronous as well as supersynchronous speeds.

Subsynchronous speed. Fig. 5.73 shows the power flow in a DFI motor when running at subsynchronous speed. With f_1 = stator frequency and f_2 = rotor frequency, the slip $s = \frac{f_2}{f_1}$ is fixed. Therefore, rotor speed $= \frac{120 f_1}{P}\left(1 - \frac{f_2}{f_1}\right) = \frac{120 f_1}{P}(1 - s)$ is also fixed. In a way, DFI motor now runs as a special type of synchronous motor at constant speed given by Eq. (5.126). As in a SRIM, see Fig. 5.41 (*a*),

$$\text{shaft power, } P_m = (1-s)P_g$$
$$\text{power at slip rings, } = sP_g$$

This slip power sP_g at frequency $f_2 = sf_1$ is converted to power sP_g at frequency f_1 by frequency converter and is then fed to source 2 as shown in Fig. 5.73.

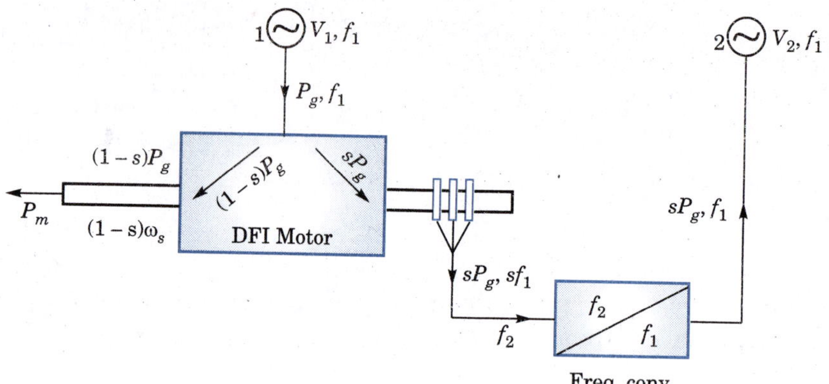

Fig. 5.73: Power flow during subsynchronous operation of DFI motor.

$$\text{Shaft speed} = \omega_s(1-s)$$
$$\text{Torque} = \frac{P_g}{\omega_s} \text{ Nm}$$

Net power input to DFI motor from both sources $= P_g - sP_g = (1-s)\,P_g$

Also, shaft power output $= (1-s)\,P_g$

As all losses are ignored, net power input = shaft power output, and therefore, efficiency of the drive scheme is 100%.

The scheme of DFI motor shown in Fig. 5.73 can also be re-arranged as shown in Fig. 5.74. If output voltage of frequency converter differs from V_1, a suitable transformer (not shown), with a proper turns ratio, can be interposed between frequency converter and supply source.

As before, in Fig. 5.74, power input from source $V_1, f_1 = (1-s)\,P_g$ shaft power output.

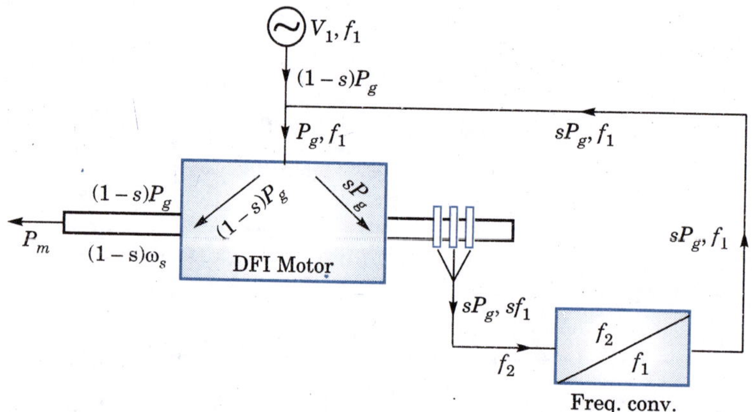

Fig. 5.74: Power flow in DFI motor running at subsynchronous speed.

Super-synchronous speed. Fig. 5.75 shows the power flow in a DFI motor running at supersynchronous speed. Reference to Fig. 5.41 (*b*) gives

$$\text{shaft power output, } P_m = (1 + s)\, P_g$$

$$\text{shaft speed, } \omega_r = (1 + s)\omega_s$$

$$\text{Torque} = \frac{P_g}{\omega_s}$$

$$\text{Power fed into slip ring} = sP_g$$

Net power taken from source $V_1, f_1 = P_g + sP_g = (1 + s)\, P_g$ = shaft power output.

It is seen from above that motor torque at both subsynchronous and super-synchronous speeds remain the same.

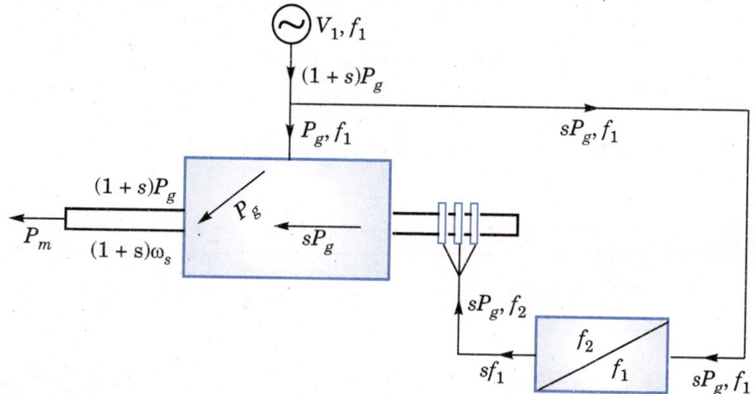

Fig. 5.75: Power flow in DFI motor running at supersynchronous speed.

5.18.1.2 Power Flow in DFI Generator

Power flow in DFI motor has been discussed at both subsynchronous and super-synchronous speeds. The basic principle of conversion from DFI motor to DFI generator would be discussed in the next article. Here, we would discuss merely the power flow in a DFI generator at speeds below and above synchronous speed.

Subsynchronous speed. When mechanical power, as for example from a wind mill, flows into the shaft of induction machine, it begins to operate as an induction generator. The direction of power flow in DFIG can be obtained by reversing the direction of power flow in DFI motor of Fig. 5.74; it is now as shown in Fig. 5.76.

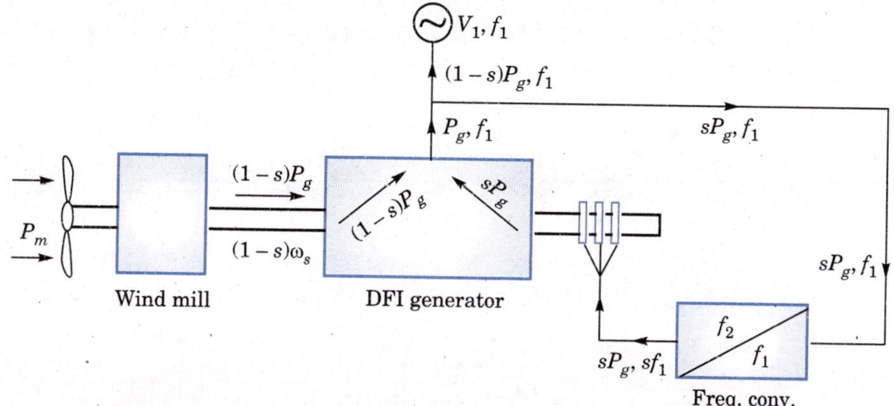

Fig. 5.76: Power flow in a DFI generator at subsynchronous speed.

$$\text{shaft power input, } P_m = (1 - s)\, P_g$$
$$\text{power input at slip rings} = sP_g$$
$$\text{stator power output} = P_g$$
$$\text{Power input to source } V_1, f_1 = (1 - s)\, P_g = \text{shaft power input}$$
$$\text{Torque} = \frac{P_g}{\omega_s} \text{ Nm.}$$

Supersynchronous speed. With mechanical power flowing into the shaft and rotor running at supersynchronous speed, the power flow in DFI generator can be obtained by reversing the power flow in DFI motor of Fig. 5.75; it is shown in Fig. 5.77.

$$\text{shaft power input, } P_m = (1 + s)\, P_g$$
$$\text{power output at slip rings} = sP_g$$
$$\text{stator power output} = P_g$$
$$\text{Power input to source } V_1, f_1 = (1 + s)\, P_g = \text{shaft power input}$$
$$\text{Torque} = \frac{P_g}{\omega_s} \text{ Nm}$$

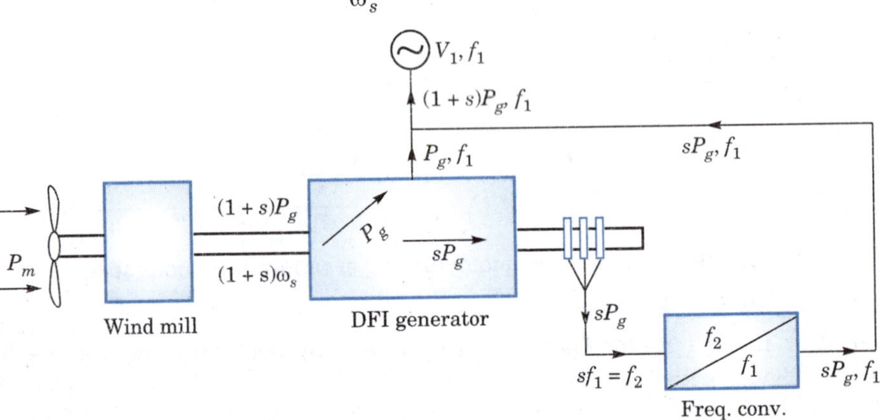

Fig. 5.77: Power flow in a DFI generator running at supersynchronous speed.

A SCIM can run as induction generator when rotor speed exceeds synchronous speed. However, a DFI machine can operate as induction generator even at speeds less than synchronous speed (and also at supersynchronous speeds). This feature of DFIG has made it popular these days for wind-power-generation applications. This shows a DFIG can conveniently harness low-wind speeds (less than synchronous speed) as well as high-wind speeds (above synchronous speed).

5.19 CONVERSION OF DFI MACHINE FROM MOTORING MODE TO GENERATING MODE

When three-phase supply at frequency f_1 is given to stator, a rotating magnetic field is produced. This rotating flux creates two poles N_1, S_1 on the stator as shown in Fig. 5.78. Rotor is also fed from a separate 3-phase source at frequency f_2. Rotor creates its own rotating flux and it produces two poles N_2, S_2 on the rotor as shown in Fig. 5.78. Since stator poles N_1, S_1 and rotor poles N_2, S_2 rotate in the same direction and at the same speed, relative speed between these two fields is zero. Thus, electromagnetic torque is developed. Stator poles N_1,

S_1 attract respectively the rotor poles S_2, N_2 and therefore, a clock-wise torque T_e is developed. Accordingly, rotor runs in clockwise direction at speed $\frac{120f_1}{P}\left(1-\frac{f_2}{f_1}\right)$ $= \frac{120f_1}{P}$ $(1 - s)$ as given by Eq. (5.126).

Under steady state, motor torque = load torque $T_L = K\,\phi_s\,.\,\phi_r\,\sin\delta$, where ϕ_s = stator flux, ϕ_r = rotor flux, δ = torque angle and K = constant.

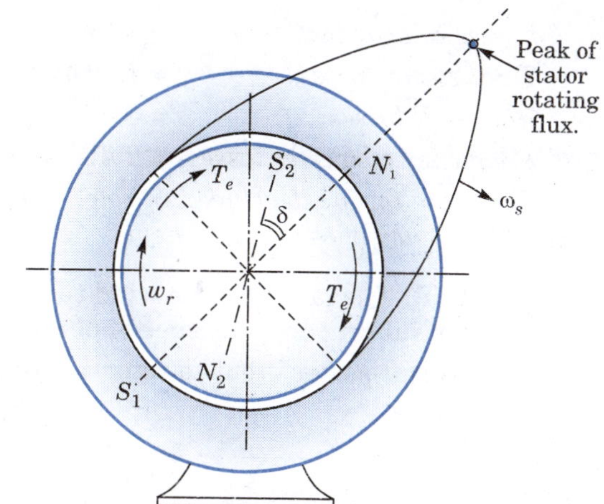

Fig. 5.78: Development of induction motor torque in DFI machine.

Supposing load torque is reduced, T_e would reduce and therefore torque angle δ would reduce. When $T_L = T_e = 0$, $\delta = 0$ and therefore, no torque is developed. Now, with the help of wind-mill (or any other prime-mover), let mechanical power input be applied to motor shaft in clockwise direction. This mechanical input torque T_{sh} would force the rotor poles S_2, N_2 to move ahead of stator poles N_1, S_1, Fig. 5.79, so that mechanical input torque T_{sh} = electrical torque ($= K\,\phi_s\,\phi_r\,\sin\delta$). As speed of stator and rotor fields is synchronous, a steady torque T_e is developed. As before, stator poles N_1, S_1 attract respectively the rotor poles S_2, N_2 in Fig. 5.79 and now electrical torque developed is in anti-clockwise direction. But mechanical input torque is clockwise. Since electrical torque developed opposes the applied mechanical torque, DFI machine begins to operate as DFI generator. Note that rotor subsynchronous speed $= \frac{120f_1}{P}\left(1-\frac{f_2}{f_1}\right)$ has not changed during machine transition from motoring mode to generating mode. It is because stator frequency f_1 and rotor frequency f_2 remain constant.

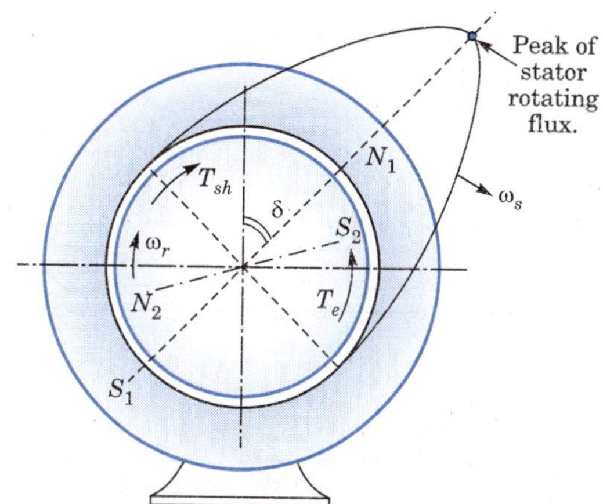

Fig. 5.79: Development of induction generator torque in DFI machine.

During motoring mode, power flow is shown in Fig. 5.74 and during generating mode, power flow is given in Fig. 5.76 for subsynchronous speed operation. Description for the conversion of DFI machine from motoring mode to generating mode at supersynchronous speed is similar to the explanation presented here for subsynchronous speed.

Example 5.46. *The stator of a three-phase, 4-pole, 500 kW doubly-fed induction generator is fed from 50 Hz source whereas its rotor is connected to 20 Hz through a frequency converter. The DFIG is driven by wind turbine which develops 400 kW at subsynchronous speed. Other data for the drive scheme is as under :*

Losses in gear box $= 8$ *kW*
Total stator losses $= 12$ *kW*
Rotor I^2R *losses* $= 3$ *kW*
Frequency converter losses $= 2$ *kW.*

Calculate torque developed in rotor, power delivered to main source at 50 Hz and the overall efficiency of the drive scheme.

Solution. The layout of the wind turbine and DFI generator is shown in Fig. 5.80. The power flow for subsynchronous speed operation is also indicated in Fig. 5.80.

Mechanical power input to rotor = Wind-turbine power – (gear-box losses)

$$= 400 - 8 = 392 \text{ kW} = P_m$$

$$\text{Slip, } s = \frac{f_2}{f_1} = \frac{20}{50} = 0.4$$

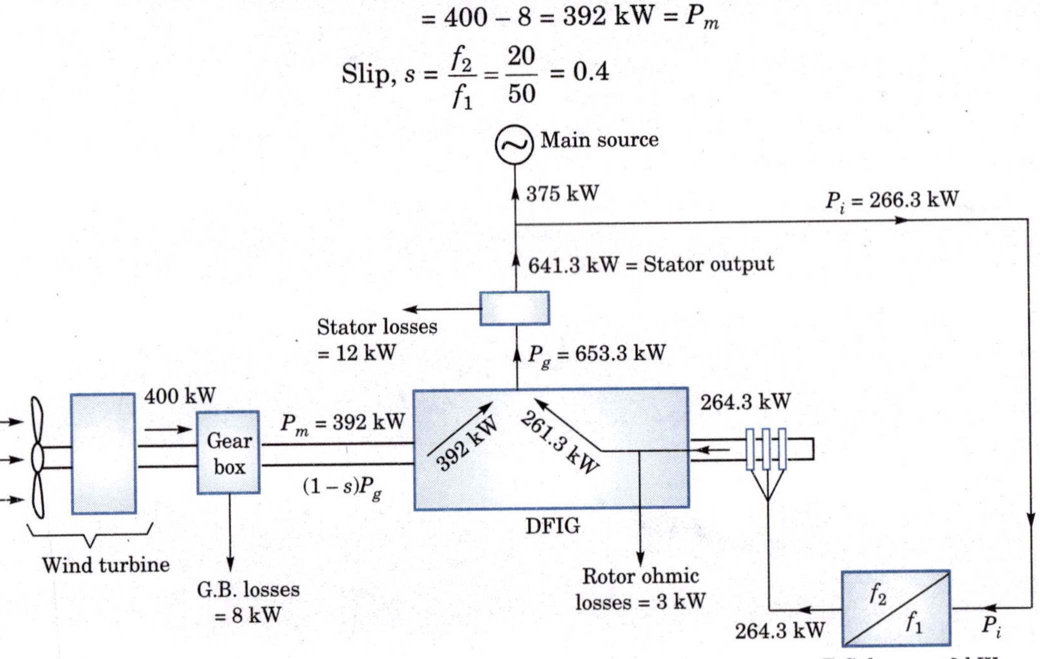

Fig. 5.80: Pertaining.

Here $P_m = (1 - s)\, P_g = 392$ kW

$$\therefore \quad \text{Air-gap power flow, } P_g = \text{power input from rotor to stator} = \frac{392}{1 - 0.4} = 653.3 \text{ kW}$$

$$\text{Synchronous speed, } \omega_s = \frac{4\pi f_1}{P} = \frac{4 \times 50}{4} = 50\,\pi \text{ rad/sec.}$$

$$\therefore \quad \text{Mechanical torque developed in rotor} = \frac{P_g}{\omega_s} = \frac{653.3 \times 10^3}{50\pi} = 4159.04 \text{ Nm.}$$

Electrical power input to rotor $= sP_g = 0.4 \times 653.3 = 261.3$ kW.
Rotor ohmic losses = 3 kW
Electrical power output of frequency converter = 261.3 + 3 = 264.3 kW
Electrical power input to frequency converter, $P_i = 264.3 + 2 = 266.3$ kW

Electrical power output from stator

$= P_g$ – stator losses = 655.3 – 12 = 641.3 kW

Net power delivered to main source

= stator output – power input to freq. conv. P_i

= 641.3 – 266.3 = 375 kW

$$\text{Overall efficiency of the scheme} = \frac{375}{400} \times 100 = 93.75\%$$

Note. Here, air-gap power P_g = 653.3 kW is more than the power input = 400 kW from the wind turbine. An examination of Fig. 5.80 reveals that rotor of DFIG in the subsynchronous operating mode takes in two powers; (*i*) one electrical power from the frequency converter and (*ii*) the other mechanical power from the wind turbine.

Example 5.47. *Repeat Example 5.46 in case DFIG runs at supersynchronous speed.*

Solution. The layout of the scheme and power flow at supersynchronous speed are shown in Fig. 5.81. Calculations are left as an exercise to the reader.

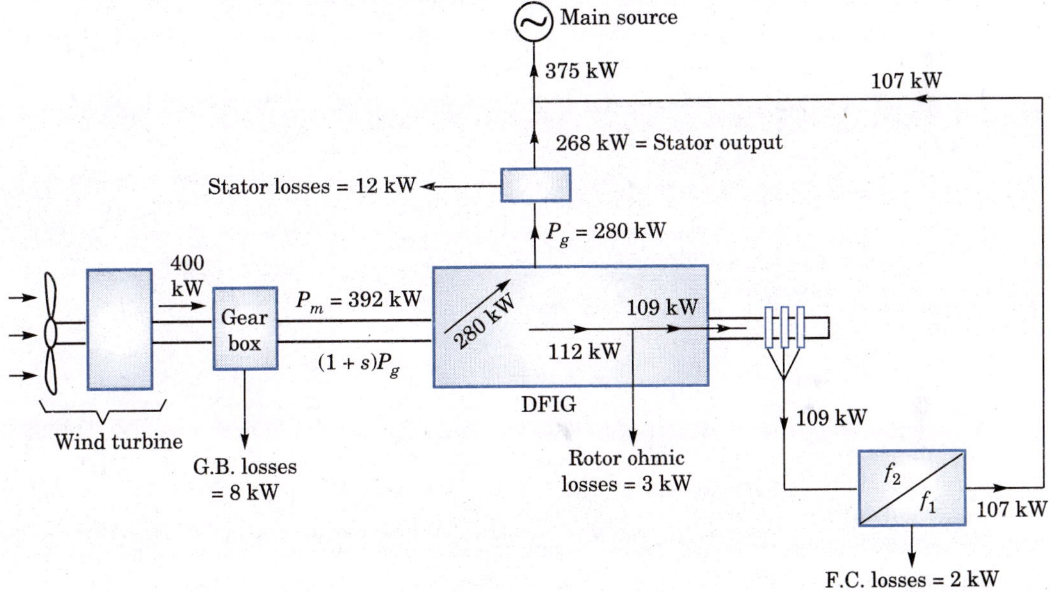

Fig. 5.81: Pertaining.

It is seen from Fig. 5.81 that power input from rotor to stator P_g = 280 kW is less than the mechanical power input = 400 kW from the wind turbine. It is because DFIG in the supersynchronous mode (*i*) takes in mechanical power from the wind turbine but (*ii*) delivers electrical power to the frequency converter and then to the main source.

PROBLEMS

5.1. Draw the generalized mathematical model of a polyphase induction machine. Write down the voltage equations for this model and obtain therefrom the equivalent circuit for a polyphase induction motor.

5.2. Write down the voltage equations for the two-axis model of a polyphase induction machine and hence obtain an expression for the steady-state torque when balanced three-phase supply is impressed on the stator.

5.3. (*a*) Draw the equivalent circuit for a polyphase induction motor and state what is represented by the various parameters involved in this circuit.

(*b*) From the equivalent circuit for a polyphase induction motor, derive an expression for the air-gap power in terms of rotor resistance, slip etc.

5.4. (*a*) Explain the similarities between the induction-motor and transformer equivalent circuits.

(*b*) What advantage is gained if core loss is not represented in the equivalent circuit of a polyphase induction motor ? Explain, how core loss is accounted for in computing the shaft power from the mechanical power developed.

(*c*) Under normal operating speeds, rotor core loss is usually neglected. Explain the reason.

(*d*) For a polyphase induction motor, show that

P_g : rotor ohmic loss : $P_m = 1 : s : (1 - s)$.

Here P_g is the air-gap power, P_m is the internal mechanical power developed and s is the operating slip.

5.5. (*a*) Explain the terms air-gap power P_g, internal mechanical power developed P_m and shaft power P_{sh}. How are these terms related with each other ?

(*b*) A 10 kW, 50 Hz, 6-pole, polyphase induction motor has a full-load slip of 0.04. If its friction and windage losses are 4% of the output, then compute

(*i*) rotor ohmic loss at full load,

(*ii*) full-load electromagnetic torque.

and (*iii*) rotor efficiency (= rotor output/rotor input). [**Ans.** (*b*) 433.3 W, 103.45 Nm, 92.31%]

5.6. (*a*) If the stator resistance of a polyphase induction motor is neglected, show that its torque can be expressed as

$$T_e = T_{em} \cdot \frac{2}{\dfrac{s_{mT}}{s} + \dfrac{s}{s_{mT}}}$$

(*b*) A 3-phase, 6-pole, squirrel cage induction motor has a maximum torque of 2.5 times the full-load torque at a slip of 30%, when balanced rated voltage at rated frequency of 50 Hz is applied to the stator terminals. Stator winding resistance may be neglected. Sketch the torque-speed curve for this induction motor.

5.7. If the stator impedance of a 3-phase induction motor is neglected, then show from its equivalent circuit that the maximum torque per phase is given by

$$T_{em} = \frac{1}{2\pi n_s} \cdot \frac{V_1^2}{2x_2}$$

and hence show that, $\dfrac{T_e}{T_{em}} = \dfrac{2s \cdot s_{mT}}{s_{mT}^2 + s^2}$

For small values of slips, occurring in the sable operating region prove that

$$T_e = \frac{T_{em}}{s_{mT}} s.$$

5.8. (*a*) Sketch a typical torque-slip curve of a 3-phase induction motor. How is this curve modified,

(*i*) if rotor-circuit resistance is increased ?

(*ii*) if the rotor-circuit reactance is increased ?

(b) A 3-phase induction motor develops a maximum torque of 5 times the full-load torque at a slip of 0.30. Rotor resistance is 0.05 Ω per phase. The stator resistance and rotational losses are negligible. Compute

(i) the slip at full-load torque and

(ii) the starting torque in terms of full-load torque. [**Ans.** (b) 0.03, 2.755 $T_{e.fl}$]

5.9. (a) From the equivalent circuit of a 3-phase induction motor and with stator resistance neglected, show that

$$\frac{I_{2.st}}{I_2} = \sqrt{\frac{1+(s_{mT}/s)^2}{1+s_{mT}^{\ 2}}}$$

where, I_{2st} = rotor current at starting

I_2 = rotor current at any slip s

and, s_{mT} = slip at maximum torque.

(b) A 3-phase squirrel-cage induction motor has a rotor starting current of 6 times the full-load value. The motor has a full-load slip of 5%. Determine

(i) starting torque in terms of full-load torque,

(ii) slip at maximum torque and

(iii) maximum torque in terms of full-load torque.

[**Hint :** (i) $T_{e.st} = \frac{1}{\omega_s} \cdot I_{2.st}^{\ 2}\, \frac{r_2}{1}$ and $T_e = \frac{1}{\omega_s} \cdot I_2^{\ 2} \cdot \frac{r_2}{s}$

$\therefore \quad \frac{T_{e.st}}{T_{e.fl}} = \ldots$] [**Ans.** (b) 1.8 $T_{e.fl}$, 0.31, 3.18, $T_{e.fl}$]

5.10. (a) A 4-pole, 400 V, 3-phase induction motor has a standstill rotor emf of 100 V per phase. The rotor has a resistance of 50 milli ohms per phase and a standstill reactance of 0.5 ohms per phase.

Calculate the maximum torque developed by the motor and the slip at which it occurs. Neglect stator impedance drop.

(b) A 3-phase induction motor at rated voltage and frequency has a maximum torque of 275 percent and a starting torque of 125% of full-load torque. Determine the slip (i) at maximum torque and (ii) at full load torque. Assume constant rotor resistance and neglect stator resistance and rotational losses.

[**Ans.** (a) 190.986 NM, 0.1 (b) 0.2404, 0.0453]

5.11. The maximum torque of a 3-phase squirrel cage induction motor is 3 times the full-load torque and starting torque is 1.5 times the full-load torque. For negligible stator resistance, compute,

(a) slip at maximum torque. (b) full-load slip, and

(c) starting current in terms of full-load current. [**Ans.** (a) 0.268, (b) 0.045, (c) 5.833]

5.12. (a) Show that the maximum electromagnetic torque in a polyphase induction motor is independent of rotor-circuit resistance.

(b) Show, from the polyphase induction-motor equivalent circuit, that the slip at maximum torque is given by

$$s_{mT} = \frac{r_2}{\sqrt{R_e^{\ 2} + (x_2 + X_e)^2}}$$

where, $R_e + j\,X_e$ is the Thevnin's equivalent-circuit impedance.

5.13. Sketch a typical torque-speed characteristic of a polyphase induction motor under rated voltage and frequency conditions. On the same diagram, sketch how this torque speed characteristic gets modified with the following changes :

(*a*) With rated supply frequency,
   (*i*) supply voltage is decreased,
   (*ii*) supply voltage is increased.

(*b*) With rated supply voltage,
   (*i*) supply frequency is decreased,
   (*ii*) supply frequency is increased.

(*c*) The ratio of supply voltage V_1 to supply frequency f.
   (*i*) is decreased so that V_1/f remains constant,
   (*ii*) is increased so that V_1/f remains constant.

5.14. A 3-phase induction motor, driving a constant-torque load, is connected to constant-frequency voltage source. For this induction motor, explain the following :

(*a*) With the reduction in supply voltage, the stator current increases.

(*b*) With a small increment in supply voltage, the supply current may decrease but with large increments, the supply current increases.

5.15. A 3-phase, 400 V, 50 Hz induction motor is fed from 400 V, 45 Hz source. If the induction motor is driving a constant torque load, then determine the following in terms of their rated values,

(*a*) change in air-gap flux,

(*b*) change in rotor current assuming same power factor and

(*c*) change in synchronous speed. [**Ans.** (*a*) 0.11, (*b*) 0.1, (*c*) 0.1]

5.16. (*a*) In deep-bar rotor polyphase induction motors, explain how the skin-effect phenomenon is helpful in attaining desirable features of high-starting torque and low-operating slip. Assume rectangular cross-section of the rotor bar.

(*b*) Explain, how the equivalent circuit of an ordinary polyphase induction motor is also applicable to deep-bar induction motors.

5.17. (*a*) In double-cage polyphase induction motors, explain how the desirable features of high-starting torque and low-operating slip are attained.

(*b*) A 4-pole, 50 Hz, double-cage, 3-phase induction motor has per phase leakage impedances of $0.05 + j\,0.4\ \Omega$ and $0.5 + j\,0.1\ \Omega$ for the two cages at supply frequency. Calculate the relative values of torques developed by the two cages (*i*) at starting and (*ii*) at a full-load slip of 5%. [**Ans.** (*b*) 6.25, 0.116]

5.18. Discuss the relative merits and disadvantages of single-cage and double-cage induction motors.

If the standstill impedance of the outer cage of a double cage machine is $0.3 + j\,0.4$ ohm and of the inner cage is $0.1 + j\,1.5$ ohm, compare the relative currents and torques of the two cages

(*a*) at standstill (*b*) at a slip of 5%

[**Ans.** (*a*) 3.007, 27.12 ; (*b*) 0.41574, 0.51853]

5.19. Derive the equivalent circuit of a double-cage polyphase induction motor with the help of its generalized mathematical model.

5.20. (*a*) Compare single-cage and double-cage induction motors in so far as their starting performance, full-load performance and torque-slip characteristics are concerned.

(*b*) The ratio of resistance to standstill reactance is 3 for the top cage and 0.3 for the bottom cage of a double-cage induction motor. The ratio of reactances of the two cages is 5 and full-load slip is 8%. For the two cages, compute the relative magnitudes of currents and torques at full-load. [**Ans.** (*a*) 0.5173, 0.5352]

5.21. A double cage 4-pole induction motor has the following parameters referred to stator.

Stator,	$r_1 = 1\ \Omega$,	$x_1 = 3\ \Omega$
Rotor ;	cage 1, $r_2 = 3\ \Omega$,	$x_2 = 1\ \Omega$
	cage 2, $r_3 = 0.6\ \Omega$,	$x_3 = 5\ \Omega$.

The primary is delta connected and rated for 440 V. Calculate the starting and full-load torques at 4% slip using the approximate equivalent circuit. Find also the starting and full-load power factors. [**Ans.** 223.244 Nm., 204.55 Nm., 0.5079 lag, 0.9035 lag]

5.22. (*a*) Enumerate the most common problems concerning the dynamics of induction motors.

(*b*) With the induction motor coupled with a pure inertia load, derive an expression for the total energy dissipated in the rotor circuit as the slip changes form s_1 to s_2.
Hence show that the energy efficiency during starting, from rest to a negligible slip, is equal to 50%.

(*c*) Does the rotor-circuit resistance remain constant at the instants of starting, normal operation and plugging ? Explain.

(*d*) Rotor heating during starting, braking and reversing is much less in wound-rotor induction motors than in squirrel-cage induction motors. Explain.

5.23. For a polyphase induction motor driving a pure inertia load, find the time taken for the slip to change from s_1 to s_2. Neglect stator resistance.
Hence show that the minimum time required for the slip to change from s_1 to s_2 is given by

$$t_{min} = \frac{J \cdot \omega_s}{2T_{em}} \left[2\,(s_1^2 - s_2^2) \ln \frac{s_1}{s_2} \right]^{\frac{1}{2}}$$

where J, ω_s and T_{em} are the moment of inertia, synchronous speed and maximum torque respectively.

5.24. In a 4-pole, 50 Hz, 3-phase induction motor, the ratio of maximum to starting torque is 3 and the power output at maximum torque is 12 kW. Determine the time required to accelerate this motor from rest to 1440 rpm in case inertia of rotating parts is 2 kgm^2, the shaft is unloaded and direct-on-line starting is employed. [**Ans.** 5.896 sec]

5.25. As 5 kW, 3-phase, 4-pole, 50 Hz induction motor has full-load efficiency of 85%. The total moment of inertia of rotor and connected load is 0.094 kgm^2. The total losses of motor may be assumed 2.25 times the rotor ohmic losses. Assuming full-load slip to be negligibly small, estimate

(*a*) the total energy loss in rotor during starting,

(*b*) the total energy loss in rotor during reversing if the motor is plugged,

(*c*) the number of times per minute that the motor can be reversed without exceeding its allowable temperature rise. [**Ans.** 1159.68 watt-sec ; 4638.72 watt-sec ; 5]

5.26. A 400 V, 3-phase, 50 Hz, 6-pole, star-connected induction motor has the following per phase parameters :

$$r_1 = 0\ ;\ x_1 = x_2 = 1.0\ \Omega;\ r_2 = 0.2\ \Omega;\ X_m = 36\ \Omega.$$

Find the magnitude of external resistance that must be inserted in the rotor circuit, so that the motor can be accelerated from rest to a slip of 0.04 in minimum possible time. Direct-on-starting is used and the total inertia of motor and load is 10 kgm^2. Also, compute the minimum time of acceleration. [**Ans.** 0.5774 Ω, 3.62 sec.]

5.27. A 3-phase, 6-pole, 400 V, 50 Hz, induction motor has a torque-speed characteristic given below :

Torque, Nm	0	65	117	154	170	164	150	127	112	92	85	80
Speed, rpm	1000	950	900	850	800	750	700	600	500	300	150	0

This motor drives a load requiring a constant torque of 50 Nm. Calculate the accelerating time from rest to rated speed if the total inertia of the motor-load combination is 2.8 kgm^2.

[**Ans.** 5.5811 sec.]

5.28. (*a*) Enumerate the main important basic methods for the speed control of 3-phase induction motors.

(*b*) Name the three methods by which number of poles in the stator winding of a 3-phase induction motor can be varied.

(*c*) Bring out clearly the difference between multiple stator winding technique and consequent-pole technique for the speed control of a three-phase induction motor.

(*d*) Explain how the three different torque-speed characteristics are obtained by consequent-pole technique and by suitable connections amongst the three phases. Sketch these characteristics on the same diagram.

5.29. (*a*) Bring out the difference between consequent-pole technique and pole-amplitude modulation technique.

(*b*) Explain the pole-amplitude modulation technique for the speed control of a three-phase induction motor. Illustrate your answer with appropriate derivations and waveforms.

(*c*) A three-phase, 50 Hz induction motor, wound for pole-amplitude modulation, has 10 main poles and 2 modulating poles. Find the possible motor speeds.

[**Ans.** (*c*) 600 rpm, 750 rpm]

5.30. (*a*) Sketch a typical torque-speed curve of a polyphase induction motor working under rated supply voltage *V* and frequency *f*. On the same diagram, sketch the torque-speed curve for the following voltages and frequencies but with rotor resistance remaining constant:

(*i*) $\frac{V}{2}$ and f (*ii*) $\frac{V}{2}$ and $f/2$ (*iii*) V and $f/2$.

Describe the nature of these curves briefly.

(*b*) A 440 V, 60 Hz, 3 phase, 6-pole, squirrel-cage induction motor develops a maximum torque of 2.5 times the full-load torque at a speed of 1020 rpm when fed from the rated voltage and frequency source. If this motor is now operated from 400 V, 50 Hz source, then with negligible stator resistance, compute

(*i*) the magnitude of maximum torque and

(*ii*) the speed at which maximum torque occurs. [**Ans.** (*b*) 2.975 $T_{e.fl}$; 820 rpm]

5.31. A 3-phase, 400 V, 50 Hz, squirrel-cage induction motor, when working at rated voltage and frequency, can develop full-load torque at a speed of 970 rpm and pf of 0.86. The magnetizing current and rotational losses are to be neglected. If the supply voltage reduces to 350 V, with the supply frequency remaining unchanged, then for a constant-torque load, calculate

(*a*) the speed at which motor would run,

(*b*) the percentage increase in rotor ohmic losses and

(*c*) the motor full-load pf. [**Ans.** 960.8 rpm, 30.67%, 0.7903 lagging]

5.32. A 150 kW, 2.2 kV, 50 Hz, 3-phase, 8-pole, star-connected stator induction motor has the following per phase parameters referred to stator :

$$r_1 = 0,\ r_2 = 0.40\ \Omega,\ x_1 = x_2 = 2.5\ \Omega,\ X_m = 57.5\ \Omega.$$

At rated voltage and frequency, the motor has a full-load slip of 0.025. Neglect rotational losses. Compute the value of external resistance to be inserted in the rotor circuit so as to reduce the speed to 375 rpm, if the motor drives.

(*a*) a constant-torque load,

(*b*) a load whose torque requirement is proportional to speed,

(*c*) a load whose torque requirement is proportional to speed squared.

[**Ans.** 13.696 Ω, 27.83 Ω, 55.27 Ω]

5.33. (*a*) Explain, how the speed varies with the load when resistance is inserted in the rotor circuit of an induction motor.

(*b*) The standstill voltage across two slip rings of a star-connected rotor of a 15 kW induction motor is 450 V and full-load slip is 3%. Calculate the resistance to be inserted in the rotor circuit to reduce the full-load speed by 20%. The torque of the driven load is proportional to the speed. Neglect rotational losses. [**Ans.** 3.275 Ω]

5.34. A 3-phase, 50 Hz, 10 pole, induction motor has star-connected rotor and the resistance measured across any two slip rings is 0.06 Ω. Its full-load slip is 0.025. Calculate the resistance to be inserted in the rotor circuit to reduce the full-load speed to 480 rpm. The torque required by the load is

(*a*) constant, (*b*) proportional to the speed,

(*c*) proportional to the speed-squared and

(*d*) proportional to the cube of speed. [**Ans.** 0.21 Ω; 0.2625 Ω; 0.326 Ω; 0.4045 Ω]

5.35. (*a*) A 3-phase, 400 V, 4-pole, slip-ring induction motor runs at a speed of 1440 rpm and develops rated torque with slip rings short circuited. When an additional resistance of 1 Ω is inserted in series with each rotor phase, the motor is found to develop rated torque at a speed of 1410 rpm. Find the inherent per-phase resistance of the rotor circuit of the motor.

(*b*) Repeat Example 5.18 in case torque-speed characteristic in the stable region is not assumed linear. [**Ans.** (*a*) 2 Ω (*b*) 334.07 V]

5.36. A 3-phase, 6-pole, 50 Hz, wound-rotor induction motor has per phase rotor leakage impedance of $0.3 + j\,2.00\ \Omega$ at supply frequency. Its full-load speed is 970 rpm and the standstill rotor emf is 80 V per phase.

For a constant-torque load, determine the magnitude of emf to be injected in the rotor circuit for a speed of (*a*) 500 rpm and (*b*) 1500 rpm.

Also, calculating rating of the slip-power converter. [**Ans.** (– 12.05 V) ; 67.95 V ; 5.457 kVA]

5.37. (*a*) Explain how the speed of a polyphase induction motor can be controlled by injecting a voltage in the rotor circuit of a polyphase induction motor.

Draw the torque-speed curves showing the effect of rotor voltage injection.

(*b*) A 3-phase wound rotor induction motor has a full-load slip of 0.04. The per phase rotor emf and leakage impedance at standstill are 300 V and $0.8 + j\,0\ \Omega$ respectively. For a constant torque load, calculate the magnitude and phase of the injected voltage for obtaining a slip of 0.5. [**Ans.** (*b*) 138 V opposite to E_2]

5.38. (*a*) Explain the terms 'constant power drive' and 'constant torque drive' schemes. For both the schemes, give the power distribution between the main induction motor and the auxiliary equipments for speeds above and below synchronous speed.

(*b*) A 3-phase, 50 Hz, 8-pole, wound-rotor induction motor has its slip rings directly connected to a slip-power converter. This induction motor controls the speed of a load requiring torque proportional to speed. Find the power handled by the slip-power converter at 500 rpm. The load requires a power of 200 kW at 705 rpm. **[Ans.** (*b*) 50.30 kW]

5.39. A 3-phase, 50 Hz, 16 pole wound-rotor induction motor is coupled with a load, whose torque requirement is proportional to speed-squared. The speed is to be adjusted over a range of 30 to 345 rpm, with load power of 30 MW at a speed of 345 rpm. If the speed control is carried out by a slip power recovery scheme, then find the power handled by the slip-power converter in terms of slip when

(*a*) slip power is returned to the supply,

(*b*) slip power is added to the motor shaft.

Determine, in each case, the motor input and slip power at 30 and 345 rpm.

Find also the maximum power carried by the slip-power converter in each case.

[Ans. (*a*) 38526 $s(1-s)^2$. At 30 rpm – 246.57 kW, 226.84 kW. At 345 rpm – 32608.4 kW, 2608.7 kW. 5707.6 kW.
(*b*) 38526 $s(1-s)^3$. At 30 rpm – 19.53 kW, 18.19 kW. At 345 rpm – 30 MW., 2.4 MW. 4063.3 kW.]

5.40. A 3-phase, 50 Hz, 10 pole induction motor has its slip rings directly connected to slip-power converter. Load requires a power of 540 kW at 600 rpm. Determine the maximum power that slip-power converter should be able to handle over the range from full speed to standstill. Load torque is proportional to (speed)^2. Slip power is returned to the supply. **[Ans.** 80 kW]

5.41. (*a*) Explain the principle of a commutator-frequency converter and show that frequency f_b of the brush emf is given by

$$f_b = \frac{P(n_s \pm n_r)}{2}$$

(*b*) A 3-phase induction-frequency converter, with its stator connected to 50 Hz supply, is required to give a frequency range from 100 to 400 Hz. If its rotor is to be driven at 2800 rpm, find the possible number of poles on the induction-frequency converter.

[Ans. 16 poles]

5.42. (*a*) For an induction-frequency converter, show that the output frequency f_2 is given by

$$f_2 = \left(1 \pm \frac{n_r}{n_s}\right) f_1$$

where n_r and n_s are the rotor and synchronous speeds in rps respectively and f_1 is the supply frequency.

Explain how a squirrel-cage induction motor can operate satisfactorily when fed from induction-frequency converter.

(*b*) Explain the working of a synchronous-synchronous frequency converter.

Two synchronous machines are directly coupled for converting 50 to 35 Hz. Find the minimum number of poles that the two machines should have. Also find the speed of the set. **[Ans.** (*b*) 20, 14 ; 300 rpm]

5.43. A 3-phase induction-frequency converter, with its stator fed from 50 Hz, is required to give an output frequency range from 130 to 450 Hz. Its rotor is driven at 2500 rpm by a dc motor. The output required by the load from the rotor terminals of this converter, remains constant at 80 kW at 0.8 pf for the entire frequency range.

For negligible values of exciting current, losses and leakage impedance drops of the induction-frequency converter, determine

(*a*) its possible number of poles

(*b*) its maximum and minimum rotor speeds,

(*c*) kVA rating of its stator winding and

(*d*) power rating of dc machine. [**Ans.** 20 poles ; 2400 and 480 rpm ; 38.46 kVa ; 71.04 kW]

5.44. (*a*) A 10-pole induction machine fed from 50 Hz system is mechanically coupled with a 16-pole synchronous machine fed from 60 Hz-system. Discuss how power will be transferred.

(*b*) A 4-pole, 3-phase, 50 Hz synchronous machine has its rotor directly coupled to that of a 3-phase slip-ring induction motor. Stators of both machines are connected to the same 3-phase, 50 Hz supply. It is desired to use such an arrangement to generate 150 Hz across the rotor terminals of the induction motor. Determine the number of poles for which the induction machine should be wound. Give all possibilities.

[**Ans.** (*a*) From 50-Hz system to 60-Hz system (*b*) 8 poles or 16 poles]

5.45. Repeat Example 5.36 in case the stator mmfs produced in the two machines rotate in the same direction. [**Ans.** (*a*) $P_i = 22$ poles, $P_s = 10$ poles, $P_{sy} = \frac{P}{6}$ kW]

5.46. (*a*) What are the two types of static slip-power recovery schemes for the speed control of SRIM? Which of the two is popular and why?

(*b*) Describe static Kramer and static Scherbius drives for the speed control of SRIMs with appropriate circuit diagrams.

5.47. (*a*) Explain the need for electrical braking of polyphase induction motors.

(*b*) When frequent starting and stopping is required, low speed machines are preferable. Why ?

(*c*) Explain regenerative braking of polyphase induction motors. Discuss how regenerative-braking range can be increased for a pole-changing induction motor.

5.48. Discuss how electric braking by plugging can be achieved in polyphase induction motors? Explain four-quadrant operation of both squirrel-cage and wound-rotor polyphase induction motors.

5.49. (*a*) During dynamic braking, the direction of rotor currents becomes opposite to its direction during normal motor operation. Explain.

(*b*) Draw the equivalent circuit during the dynamic braking of a polyphase induction-motor and explain how it can be derived from the polyphase induction-motor equivalent circuit.

5.50. (*a*) Give two important connection schemes for the stator windings of a polyphase induction-motor during dynamic braking. For these two schemes, drive the relation between alternating and direct currents in the stator.

(*b*) Show that the maximum torque $T_{ed.m}$, developed during dynamic braking, is given by

$$T_{ed.m} = \frac{3}{\omega_s} \frac{I_1^2 \cdot X_m^2}{2\,(x_2 + X_m)}$$

(*c*) Draw and explain the speed-torque curve of a polyphase induction motor during its dynamic braking.

5.51. A 3-phase, 8-pole, 50 Hz, squirrel cage induction motor has the following data :

Standstill rotor leakage impedance = 0.4 + *j* 2.0 Ω per phase

Maximum torque = 150 Nm

Full-load output = 6 kW at slip 0.05.

If stator impedance, magnetizing current and rotational losses are neglected, then compute

(a) initial plugging torque,

(b) total initial braking torque if motor is plugged at full-load.

$$\left[\textbf{Hint. } T_{em} = \frac{3}{\omega_s} \cdot \frac{V_1^2}{2x_2} = 150 \text{ Nm}\right.$$

$$\therefore \quad \frac{3}{\omega_s} V_1^2 = 300\,(x_2) = 600$$

$$\left.\text{Plugging torque} = \frac{3}{\omega_s} \cdot \frac{V_1^2}{\left(\frac{r_2}{2-s}\right)^2 + x_2^2} \cdot \frac{r_2}{2-s} = \frac{600}{\left(\frac{r_2}{2-s}\right)^2 + x_2^2} \cdot \frac{r_2}{2-s} \text{ etc.}\right]$$

[**Ans.** 30.45 Nm, 110.87 Nm]

5.52. (a) A 3-phase wound-rotor induction motor has a maximum braking torque at 85% slip during dynamic braking. Determine the external resistance, in terms of the inherent rotor resistance, that must be inserted in the rotor circuit to obtain the same maximum dynamic braking torque at a slip of 5%.

(b) A 400 V, 50 Hz, 6-pole, 3-phase delta connected induction motor has the following data:

$$r_1 + j\,x_1 = 0.4 + j\,1.00\ \Omega \text{ per phase}$$

$$r_2 + j\,x_2 = 0.2 + j\,0.6\ \Omega \text{ per phase}$$

Full-load slip = 0.04.

If no-load current is neglected, then compute the initial braking torque soon after plugging. [**Ans.** (a) 5.33 r_2 (b) 888.85 Nm]

5.53. A 30 kW, 400 V, 3-phase, 4-pole, 50 Hz induction motor has full-load slip of 5%. If the ratio of standstill reactance to resistance per rotor phase is 4, estimate the plugging torque at full-load speed. Neglect rotational losses and stator impedance. Find also the maximum torque.

[**Hint :** $P_g\,(1 - s) = 30{,}000$ watts.

$$P_g = \frac{3V_1^2}{r_2} \cdot \frac{20}{(20)^2 + 4^2} \quad \therefore \quad \frac{3V_1^2}{r_2} = 656842.1 \text{ etc.}\Bigg]$$

[**Ans.** 131.858 Nm, 522.698 Nm]

5.54. A 415 V, 3-phase, 50 Hz, 6-pole star-connected induction motor has stator impedance of $0.8 + j\,2\ \Omega$ and rotor impedance of $0.3 + j\,0.6\ \Omega$. Per-phase turns ratio from stator to rotor is 2. Motor inertia is 2 kgm^2. When running on no load at 960 rpm, it is brought to rest by plugging. Determine the time to stop the motor. Neglect magnetizing reactance. [**Ans.** 3.6765 sec]

5.55. A 20 kW, 960 rpm, 3-phase induction motor has stored energy per kW of 3000 Nm. Determine the time taken to start the motor if the maximum torque is twice the rated torque. Rotational losses are neglected. [**Ans.** 5.9753 sec]

5.56. A 4-pole, 50 Hz, 3-phase induction motor runs at 1440 rpm. Determine under these conditions :

(a) Speed of rotation of the stator field relative to the rotor conductors.

(b) Speed of rotation in the air-gap of the fifth space harmonic component of the stator mmf.

(c) Speed of rotation of rotor mmf in air-gap. (*I.A.S., 1989*)

[**Ans.** (a) 60 rpm; in the direction of rotor rotation

(b) 300 rpm, opposite to rotor rotation

(c) 1500 rpm, in the direction of rotor rotation]

5.57. Sketch the torque-speed curve of a conventional induction motor and indicate how this will change when

(a) rotor resistance is doubled, keeping stator voltage and frequency unchanged;

(*b*) the applied voltage is halved, the frequency and rotor resistance remaining unchanged;

(*c*) Both the applied voltage and frequency are halved, rotor resistance remaining unchanged.

5.58. A 10 hp, 400 V, 3-phase, 50 Hz, 6-pole squirrel-cage motor operates at 4% slip at full-load when rated voltage and frequency is applied. Assuming a linear relationship between torque and slip in the operating region, calculate the no-load speed of the motor when the supply voltage is reduced to half its rated value. The no-load torque is 6 Nm.

$\left[\textbf{Hint. } \dfrac{7460 + 6 \cdot \omega_s (1 - s_0)}{0.96\, \omega_s} \propto (0.04)(400)^2 \,;\, 6 \propto s_0 (200)^2 \text{ etc.}\right]$ **[Ans.** – 988.06 rpm]

5.59. A 30 kW, 400 V, 3-phase, 4-pole, 50 Hz induction motor has full-load slip of 4%. If the ratio of standstill reactance to resistance per phase of the rotor is 4, estimate the plugging torque at rated speed. Find also the starting torque. Neglect stator impedance.

[Ans. 160.053 Nm ; 300.054 Nm]

5.60. The rotor of a 3-phase, 50 Hz, 4-pole slip-ring induction motor has a standstill open-circuit voltage of 50 volts per phase. A 3-phase variable frequency voltage is impressed on the rotor for speed control. Calculate the frequency and magnitude of the impressed voltage to make the motor run at 1000, 1200 and 1800 rpm under no-load conditions.

Discuss briefly any practical scheme which incorporates the above principle for speed control of slip ring induction machines.

[Ans. 16.67 V in phase opposition to E_2 at 16.67 Hz
10 V in phase opposition to E_2 at 10 Hz
10 V in phase with E_2 at 10 Hz.]

5.61. (*a*) A 3-phase induction motor is connected to an unbalanced supply voltage. Under this condition, derive its equivalent circuits and show that the net electromagnetic torque is reduced.

(*b*) What do you understand by the term 'single-phasing' of 3-phase induction motors ? Explain how the operation of a 3-phase induction motor is effected when single-phasing occurs.

(*c*) The regenerative braking, up to speed $n_s/3$, can be obtained in a 3-phase induction motor when fed from single-phase supply. Explain.

5.62. (*a*) Explain the presence of slot harmonics in rotating electrical machines. Show that frequency of the e.m.f. generated due to slot-harmonic flux is $\left(\dfrac{2S}{P} \pm 1\right) f$ Hz.

(*b*) Describe how skewed slots eliminate slot harmonics. Give the merits and demerits of skewing the slots.

5.63. (*a*) What are the causes of space harmonics in the air-gap flux wave of 3-phase induction motors?

(*b*) Explain how the space harmonics in the air-gap flux wave introduce harmonic asynchronous torques and give rise to crawling.

5.64. (*a*) State clearly the difference between harmonic asynchronous and harmonic-synchronous torques.

(*b*) Explain how space harmonics in the air-gap flux wave cause the appearance of harmonic synchronous torques in 3-phase induction motors. How can these harmonic torques be avoided ?

(*c*) Explain the production of vibration torques and noise in 3-phase induction motors.

5.65. (*a*) Explain the method of speed control of induction motors using variable frequency technique. Bring out the relevant merits and demerits of this method.

(*b*) Explain why some induction motors have double-cage rotors and indicate the situations where they are preferred for use.

(*c*) Explain any one technique by which the speed of a three-phase induction motor can be varied continuously over a wide range. (*I.A.S., 1982*)

(*d*) Identify whether the following statement is correct or not. Give a brief justification for your answer :

Skewing the rotor bars of an induction motor results in large starting torque.

(*e*) Explain the technique of varying the speed of a 3-phase induction motor by injecting an appropriate emf in the rotor circuit. Indicate the merits, if any, of this method.

(*f*) Explain with the help of neat diagrams variable voltage variable frequency speed control of induction motors. What happens if the frequency is smaller than or greater than the normal frequency ?

5.66. (*a*) Give the methods of reducing harmonic torques and vibrations in 3-phase induction motors.

(*b*) A 3-phase, 6-pole, induction motor has 42 stator and 48 rotor slots. Find the rotor speed at which harmonic synchronous torque would be developed. [**Ans.** 125 rpm]

5.67. What are the probable causes for the rotor-circuit unbalance in a 3-phase induction motor ? Explain qualitatively how the operation of a 3-phase induction motor is effected in case the rotor circuit is unsymmetrical.

5.68. (*a*) A 3-phase squirrel-cage induction motor, when switched on across supply, fails to start. Give the probable causes for this failure.

(*b*) A 3-phase squirrel-cage induction motor, when started from rest, does not accelerate to normal speed but to a speed approximately 1/7 of synchronous speed. Give the causes.

(*c*) A 3-phase induction motor crawls near half synchronous speed. Give the reasons.

(*d*) Explain whether the motors using pole-changing windings on the stator always employ a squirrel-cage or wound-rotor type of rotor construction.

[**Ans.** (*a*) Cogging, Load-torque > starting-torque of motor, single-phasing,

(*b*) Asynchronous crawling due to 7th harmonic or synchronous crawling with a particular stator-slot and rotor-slot combination.

(*c*) Rotor circuit is unbalanced or $\dfrac{dT_L}{dn} < \dfrac{dT_e}{dn}$ at $\dfrac{1}{2}n_s$.

(*d*) Squirrel-cage rotor.]

5.69. (*a*) "A 3-phase induction motor with semiclosed slots gives less noisy operation than one with closed slots". State whether this statement is true or false and briefly justify your answer.

(*b*) "A polyphase induction motor may crawl near half synchronous speed if the secondary winding is unsymmetrical". Justify whether this statement is right or wrong.

(*c*) Discuss the phenomenon of "single-phasing" when applied to the three-phase induction motors, designed for continuous working. Explain the difference in behaviour when the single-phasing occurs in the primary and the secondary windings.

5.70. (*a*) What are linear electrical machines ? Give the principle of operation of LIM.

(*b*) For LIM, derive an expression for the linear force in terms of specific loadings and linear dimensions.

(*c*) Give the applications of linear-force machines and energy machines.

5.71. (*a*) What phenomena are peculiar to LEM ? Discuss their consequences with a suitable diagram.

(*b*) Describe briefly LSM and LLM.

(*c*) Discuss the applications of LIM for overhead travelling cranes and high-speed trains.

5.72. Explain how the performance of a 3-phase induction motor gets modified when fed from non-sinusoidal supply voltage. Illustrate your answer with equivalent circuits. Derive a general expression for the *n*th harmonic torque in terms of fundamental torque.

5.73. (*a*) How are pulsating-harmonic torques developed in a three-phase induction motor? Discuss the development of sixth harmonic and twelfth harmonic pulsating torques in a three phase induction motor.

(*b*) How do the losses get affected by non-sinusoidal supply voltage? Discuss.

5.74. Stator of a three-phase SRIM is fed from source V_1, f_1 and its rotor from source V_2, f_2. Discuss the two possible speeds at which rotor of this motor can run. How can the speed be changed from subsynchronous to supersynchronous or vice-versa?

5.75. A DFI machine has its stator connected to source V_1, f_1 and rotor to source V_2, f_2. Show, on a relevant diagram, the power flow when the machine runs as a motor at subsynchronous speed. Is it possible to connect this scheme to one source V_1, f_1? Discuss.

5.76. A DFI machine is running as a motor when its stator is fed from source V_1, f_1 and rotor from source V_2, f_2. Explain how this machine can be altered from motoring mode to generating mode at subsynchronous as well as supersynchronous speeds.

5.77. A doubly-fed induction machine is running at subsynchronous speed. Is the rotor delivering power to, or absorbing power from, the slip-power (or frequency) converter if it acts as (*a*) motor and (*b*) generator. **[Ans.** (*a*) delivers power (*b*) absorbs power**]**

5.78. The stator of a 6-pole DFIG is fed from 50 Hz source. The generator runs at 1300 rpm. The power flow from rotor to stator is 600 kW.

(*a*) Calculate the slip-power frequency

(*b*) Find the magnitude of power being delivered, or absorbed, by the rotor.

(*c*) If stator losses are 20 kW and rotor I^2R plus frequency converter losses are 10 kW, calculate overall efficiency of the system. **[Ans.** (*a*) 15 Hz (*b*) 180 kW (*c*) 96.154%**]**

6 Single Phase Motors

A large number of fractional-kW a.c. motors are designed to operate from a single-phase supply. Although three-phase motors can be designed and built in small sizes, their initial cost precludes their common use. In addition, wherever fractional kW a.c. motors are required to do the useful work, as for example in homes, offices, business premises etc., only single-phase supply is usually available. The annual production of fractional-kW a.c. motors may be as high as 80% of the total numerical annual production of all types of both single-phase and three-phase machines. It is because of this fact that the study of single-phase motors forms an essential part of electrical machinery course.

Numerous types of fractional-kW a.c. motors have been developed to meet the requirements of the various applications. For example, single-phase induction motor is needed where constant speed drive is required, single-phase series motor is used where high-starting torque is required and so on. In this chapter, single phase induction and synchronous motors will only be discussed. Single-phase commutator motors are dealt with in Chapter 7 on a.c. commutator machines.

6.1 SINGLE-PHASE INDUCTION MOTORS

When 3-phase supply is given to a polyphase induction motor, a rotating air-gap field is produced and starting torque is developed. If a 3-phase induction motor, carrying less than half-rated load, has its one supply line disconnected, the motor continues running though at a slightly reduced speed and with increased stator current. With one supply line disconnected; the two remaining phases constitute, in effect, a single-phase supply and, therefore, only pulsating stator mmf wave is produced. The single phase motor so obtained from a 3-phase motor has proof pf, lower capacity and reduced efficiency. As is already known, a 3-phase induction motor with rotating air-gap field is self-starting one. But a single phase induction motor with pulsating air-gap field is not a self-starting motor. In this article are described the constructional features of single phase induction motors.

Constructional Features. The rotor of a single phase induction motor is exactly similar to the squirrel cage rotor of a 3-phase induction motor. A wound rotor with slip rings is rarely used in these motors because it increases cost of the machine and, is therefore, seldom in demand.

The stator of a single phase induction motor carries two windings, namely, main (or running) winding and auxiliary (or starting) winding. Both windings are of the single layer concentric type. The main winding is distributed along the stator periphery in about two-thirds of the total slots, because no advantage is achieved if all the stator slots are wound.

Since the stator periphery is not fully utilised, a single phase induction motor has lower power output than a 3-phase induction motor of the same size in which all the stator slots are wound.

Fig. 6.1 illustrates both main and auxiliary windings for a 4-pole, single-phase induction motor with 24 stator slots. In this figure, 16 slots are utilized by the main winding and the auxiliary winding is housed in the remaining 8 slots. In actual practice, however, some slots may contain coil-sides belonging to both the main and auxiliary windings. If the main winding is traversed from S_M to F_M, it is seen that movement of concentric coils is first clockwise, then anti-clockwise and so on. Same is true for auxiliary winding S_A, F_A. Examination of Fig. 6.1 also reveals that concentric coils in one coil-group are traversed from outside to inside, in the adjacent coil group from inside to outside and so on. Same is also true for auxiliary winding having more than one coil in the one coil group. It must be noted that the space angle between S_M and S_A is 90°, *i.e.* the magnetic axes of main and auxiliary windings are in space quadrature.

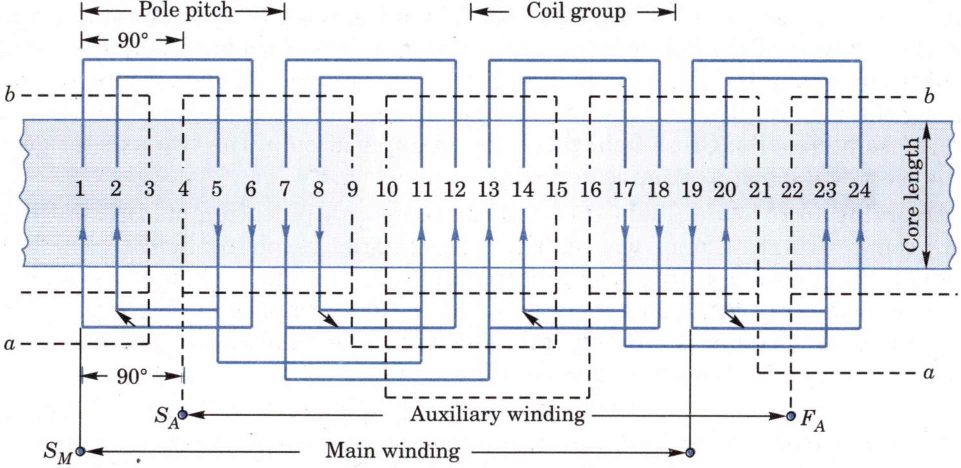

Fig. 6.1: Main and auxiliary windings of a single-phase induction motor.

Split-phase single-phase induction motors have centrifugal switch mounted on the motor shaft and connected in series with the auxiliary winding. In these motors, both the main and auxiliary windings are in circuit at the time of starting and the purpose of centrifugal switch is to disconnect the auxiliary winding when rotor attains 70 to 80 per cent of synchronous speed.

6.2 REVOLVING FIELD THEORY OF SINGLE-PHASE INDUCTION MOTORS

In this article, first a qualitative examination of induction motor behaviour at starting is presented and then revolving field theory is explained.

(a) Qualitative examination. A single-phase induction motor with its main winding alone, can be represented schematically as illustrated in Fig. 6.2. With the rotor at standstill, the conditions are similarly to those in a transformer with its secondary short-circuited. An alternating current in the main winding produces a stator mmf wave which is stationary in space but pulsating in magnitude. As a result of it, the stator field ϕ_s, produced by the main winding mmf, is alternating in polarity but varying sinusoidally with time. By transformer

action, alternating flux ϕ_s induces large rotor currents which, for any instant, are as shown in Fig. 6.2. For the assumed direction of pulsating stator flux ϕ_s, the direction of induced rotor currents is indicated by crosses and dots. These rotor currents set up rotor mmf which opposes the stator mmf at all instants of time. Since the stator and rotor mmf waves are along the same axis, the torque angle between ϕ_s and ϕ_r is 180° and no starting torque is, therefore, developed. This shows that a single-phase induction motor has no inherent starting torque. But once started by auxiliary means in any one direction, it continues running in that direction.

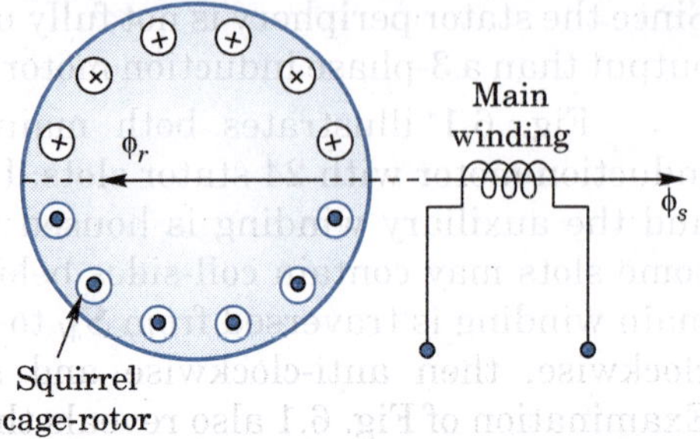

Fig. 6.2: Single-phase induction motor at standstill.

The behaviour of single-phase induction motor, with its rotor at standstill and main winding excited, is simple as described above. When the rotor is made to rotate by auxiliary means, the analysis of the single-phase induction motor performance is not so simple. Two different theories, namely, the *cross-field theory* and *revolving field theory,* may be adopted for explaining the running performance of a single-phase induction motor. Both these theories lead to the same results. Cross-field theory is an application of the two-axis, or generalized theory of electrical machines and is described in article 6.4.

According to revolving field theory, the stationary, pulsating stator mmf is resolved into two counter-rotating mmf waves. The advantage of revolving field theory is that the analytical techniques of rotating-field concepts in polyphase induction motors can be recalled and used conveniently for determining the running performance of single-phase induction motors. Since the reader is already familiar with the analysis of polyphase induction machines, revolving field theory is discussed here in this article.

(b) Revolving-field theory. In the revolving-field theory, the pulsating, stationary stator mmf wave is resolved into two counter-rotating mmf waves of equal amplitude and moving at synchronous speeds. Assuming the stator pulsating mmf wave to be sinusoidally distributed along the air-gap periphery, the space mmf wave can be expressed as

$$F_s = F_{sp} \cos \alpha \quad \text{....(6.1)}$$

where, α = electrical space angle, measured from the stator winding axis, along the air-gap periphery,

F_s = magnitude of stator mmf at any space angle α and

F_{sp} = peak value of mmf corresponding to any value of stator current.

If stator current is zero, $F_{sp} = 0$ and if stator current is maximum, F_s is also maximum ($= F_{s\,.\,max}$). If stator current is constant, F_{sp} does not vary with time. The peak value of F_{sp}, for any stator current, is alway aligned along the stator winding axis.

In case stator current is taken as $i = I_m \cos \omega t$, then peak value of stator pulsating mmf wave at any time, shown in Fig. 6.3, can be expressed as

$$F_{sp} = F_{s\,.\,max} \cos \omega t \quad \text{...(6.2)}$$

Substitution of Eq. (6.2) in Eq. (6.1) gives stator mmf wave pulsating in nature as

$$F_s = F_{s\,.\,max} \cos \omega t \cos \alpha \quad \text{...(6.3)}$$

In Eq. (6.3), the term cos ωt indicates that the mmf variation is co-sinusoidal with time and the term cos α signifies its co-sinusoidal distribution in space along the air-gap periphery.

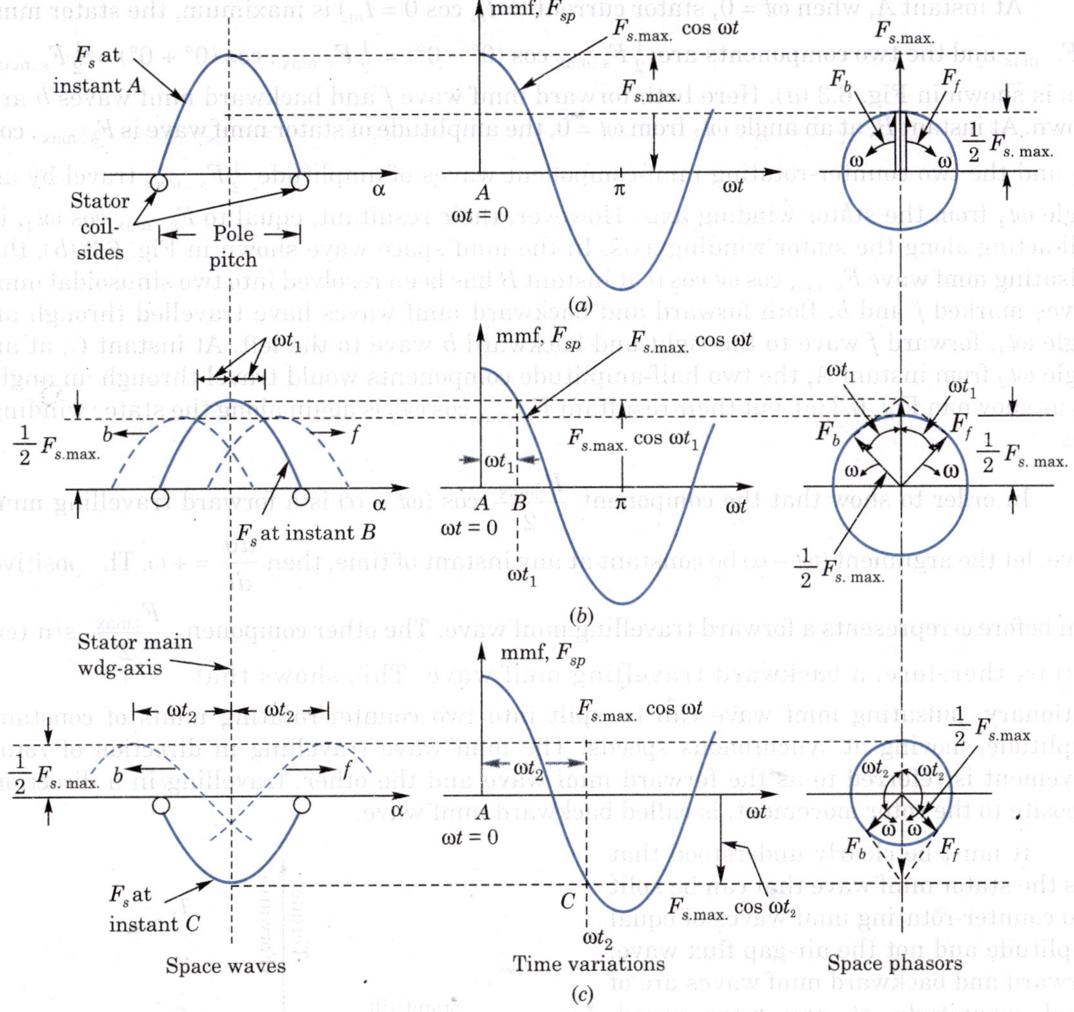

Fig. 6.3: Stator mmf wave split into two counter-rotating mmf waves of constant amplitude $\frac{1}{2} F_{s.max}$.

With the help of trigonometric relation

$$\cos a \cos b = \frac{1}{2} [\cos (a - b) + \cos (a + b)],$$

Eq. (6.3) can be expressed as

$$F_s = \frac{1}{2} \cdot F_{s\,.\,max} \cos (\omega t - \alpha) + \frac{1}{2} F_{s\,.\,max} \cos (\omega t + \alpha) \qquad ...(6.4)$$

Eq. (6.4) shows that the pulsating, stationary mmf wave of amplitude $F_{s\,.\,max}$, as given by Eq. (6.3), can be resolved into two counter-rotating mmf component waves of equal amplitudes. The maximum value of each counter-travelling mmf wave is $\frac{1}{2} F_{s\,.\,max}$, which is half the amplitude of the original pulsating mmf wave. These two counter-rotating mmf waves are illustrated in Fig. 6.3. In this figure, left hand diagrams pertain to the space mmf waves, middle diagrams show the time variations of mmf wave and in the right-hand diagrams, space phasors are drawn at different instants of time.

At instant A, when $\omega t = 0$, stator current ($= I_m \cos 0 = I_m$) is maximum, the stator mmf is $F_{s\,.\,\max}$ and the two components are $\frac{1}{2} F_{s\,.\max} \cos (0° - 0°) = \frac{1}{2} F_{s\,.\max} \cdot \cos (0° + 0°) = \frac{1}{2} F_{s\,.\max}$, this is shown in Fig. 6.3 (a). Here both forward mmf wave f and backward mmf waves b are shown. At instant B, at an angle ωt_1 from $\omega t = 0$, the amplitude of stator mmf wave is $F_{s\,.\,\max} \cdot \cos \omega t_1$ and the two counter-rotating mmf-component waves of amplitude $\frac{1}{2} F_{s\,.\,\max}$ travel by an angle ωt_1 from the stator winding axis. However, their resultant, equal to $F_{s\,.\,\max} \cos \omega t_1$, is still acting along the stator winding axis. In the mmf space wave shown in Fig. 6.3 (b), the pulsating mmf wave $F_{s\,.\,\max} \cos \omega t \cos \alpha$ at instant B has been resolved into two sinusoidal mmf waves marked f and b. Both forward and backward mmf waves have travelled through an angle ωt_1, forward f wave to the right and backward b wave to the left. At instant C, at an angle ωt_2 from instant A, the two half-amplitude components would travel through an angle ωt_2 as shown in Fig. 6.3 (c), but their resultant $F_{s\,.\,\max} \cos \omega t_2$ is again along the stator winding axis.

In order to show that the component $\frac{F_{s.\max}}{2} \cos (\omega t - \alpha)$ is a forward travelling mmf wave, let the argument $(\omega t - \alpha)$ be constant at any instant of time, then $\frac{d\alpha}{dt} = +\,\omega$. The positive sign before ω represents a forward travelling mmf wave. The other component $\frac{F_{s.\max}}{2} \sin (\omega t + \alpha)$ is, therefore, a backward travelling mmf wave. This shows that stationary, pulsating mmf wave can be spilt into two counter-rotating mmfs of constant amplitude, moving at synchronous speeds. The mmf wave travelling in direction of rotor movement is referred to as the forward mmf wave and the other, travelling in a direction opposite to the rotor movement, is called backward mmf wave.

It must be clearly understood that it is the stator mmf wave that can be split into counter-rotating mmf waves of equal amplitude and not the air-gap flux wave. Forward and backward mmf waves are of equal magnitude at any rotor speed, whereas forward and backward flux waves are equal only at standstill. At all other rotor speeds, the forward flux wave is much larger than the backward flux wave (proved in the end of this article). In other words, as the rotor speed builds up, the forward flux wave increases whereas the backward flux wave decreases. However, the sum of these flux waves must remain almost constant, since this flux has to induce counter-emf in stator winding, almost equal to the supply voltage.

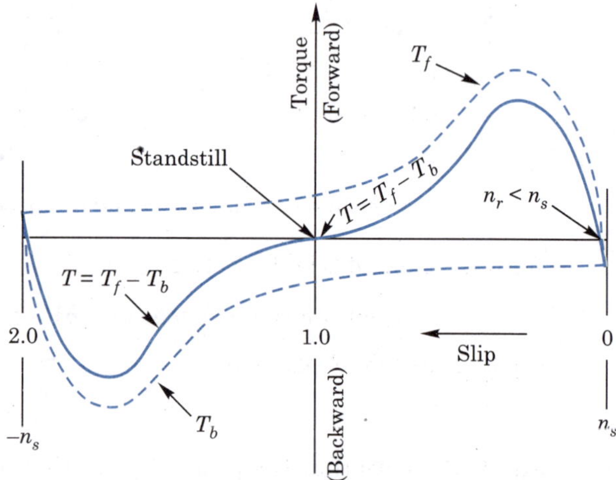

Fig. 6.4: Torque-speed characteristics of a single-phase induction motor.

The two rotating flux waves produce their own torques, similar to the production of torque in polyphase induction motor. Forward and backward fields produce induction-motor torques T_f and T_b respectively, but these torques, in opposite directions, are shown by dashed curves in Fig. 6.4. The superposition of the two torques T_f and T_b gives the required torque-slip curve of a single-phase induction motor as illustrated in Fig. 6.4. An examination of this figure reveals that motor torque T is zero when rotor speed is (*i*) zero and (*ii*) slightly less than synchronous speed n_s. Fig. 6.4 also reveals that single-phase induction motor can run in either direction if an external torque, greater than friction and load torque, is applied to its shift.

If the rotor runs at a speed n_r, then the rotor speed relative to the forward field is $(n_s - n_r)$ rps, just as in a polyphase induction motor.

$\therefore$ Slip speed with respect to the forward field = $n_s - n_r$ and slip of the rotor currents is given by

$$s_f = \frac{n_s - n_r}{n_s} = s$$

The rotor speed relative to the backward field is $n_s + n_r$, *i.e.*, slip speed with respect to the backward field is $(n_s + n_r)$ rps.

$\therefore$ Slip of rotor currents due to the backward field is

$$s_b = \frac{n_s + n_r}{n_s} = 2 - s.$$

Therefore, the forward field induces rotor currents of frequency sf and the backward field, of frequency $(2 - s)f$ in the same rotor conductors. An oscillogram of the rotor current, shown in Fig. 6.5 verifies these results.

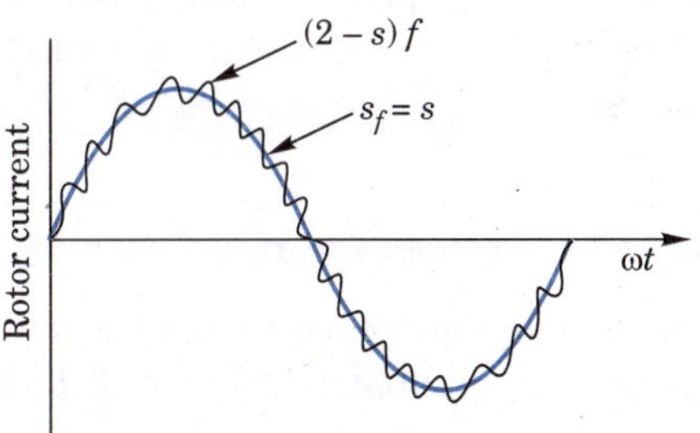

Fig. 6.5: Single-phase induction motor oscillogram for the rotor current.

The forward and backward rotating fields are equal only at standstill ; at all other rotor speeds the forward flux wave is larger than the backward flux wave. This can be explained from an examination of the induction-motor equivalent circuit, but here the qualitative explanation is only presented.

At standstill, both forward and backward fields rotate at synchronous speed n_s with respect to rotor conductors. Both these fields, therefore, induce equal rotor emfs, equal rotor currents and give rise to equal rotor mmfs. These equal rotor mmfs react with their corresponding equal counter-rotating stator mmfs and, therefore, both forward and backward rotating fields are equal with the rotor at standstill.

When the rotor rotates at speed n_r, the speed of backward field becomes $n_s + n_r$ with respect to the rotor conductors. In view of this, backward field induces large rotor emf, large rotor current and, therefore, large rotor mmf as compared to their standstill values. The rotor frequency is $(2 - s)f$, therefore, rotor pf is poor. This large rotor mmf component at a poor pf is much greater than its value at standstill and it opposes the constant backward rotating mmf wave. As a result of it, backward flux wave is reduced considerably from its magnitude at standstill.

With the rotor at speed n_r, the speed of forward flux wave is $(n_s - n_r)$ with respect to rotor conductors. This reduced relative speed induces small rotor emf, small rotor current and, therefore, small rotor mmf as compared to their values at standstill. The rotor frequency is sf and it results in less rotor leakage reactance and, therefore, a better rotor pf. This reduced rotor mmf component at a better pf is much smaller than its magnitude at standstill and it opposes the constant forward mmf wave. Consequently, the forward flux wave becomes higher than its value at standstill. This shows that with the rise in speed from standstill, the backward flux wave decreases and forward flux wave increases. However, the sum of forward and backward fields must remain approximately constant at all the rotor speeds ; because this air-gap flux must induce counter emf in the stator, almost equal to the supply voltage if stator leakage impedance is small. Therefore, under running condition, forward-field torque T_f is greater than the backward-field torque T_b and the net torque (= $T_f - T_b$) is in the direction of rotor rotation. In the normal working region, where the slip is quite small, the forward flux wave is several times greater than the backward flux wave and the resultant air-gap field is not much different from its value had it been a polyphase induction motor. This shows that in the normal working region, the torque-speed curve of single-phase induction motor is not far inferior to that a polyphase induction motor having the same dimensions and the same amplitude of air-gap flux density.

The relative speed between forward and backward rotating fields is double the synchronous speed. These two oppositely rotating fields interact with each other and produce torque pulsating at double the line frequency. The time average value of this pulsating torque is zero, but it makes a single-phase induction motor, more noisier than a polyphase induction motor. This unwanted pulsating torque can't be avoided in a single-phase induction motor because single-phase instantaneous power is inherently pulsating in nature. The effect of pulsating torque *i.e.*, the noise can, however, be reduced by mounting this motor on an elastic base.

6.3 EQUIVALENT CIRCUIT FOR A SINGLE-PHASE INDUCTION MOTOR

For developing the equivalent circuit for a single-phase induction motor, it is convenient to consider it as consisting of two 3-phase stators and two cage rotors as shown in Fig. 6.6 (*b*).

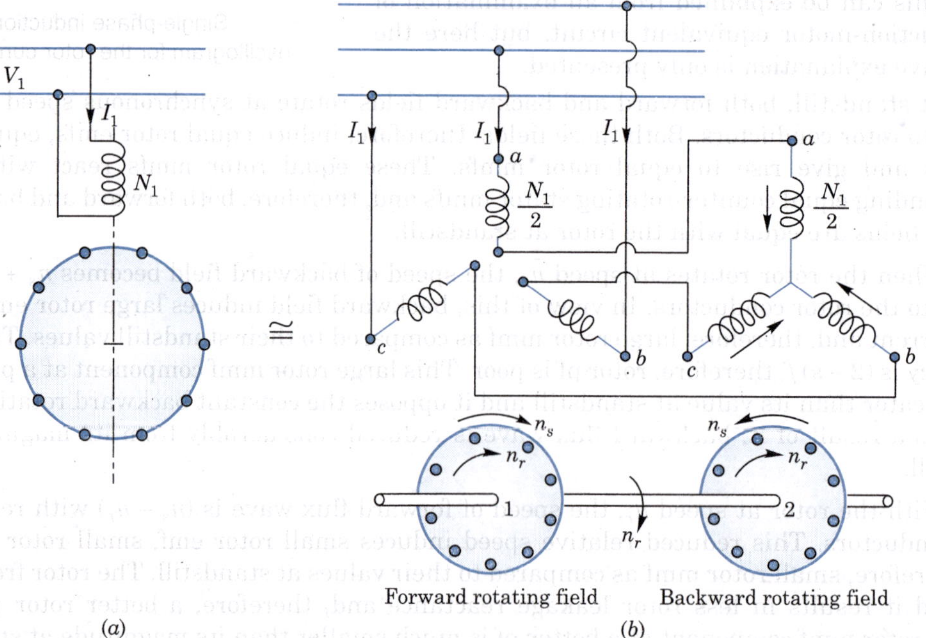

Fig. 6.6: Single-phase induction motor equivalent to two three-phase motors.

The two rotors are mechanically coupled by a common shaft. Both the stator windings are connected in series so that the same current is flowing in them. Also, the direction of currents in 3-phase stator windings are such that the two fields are rotating in opposite directions. In other words, one stator winding produces forward rotating field, whereas the other produces backward rotating field as shown in Fig. 6.6 (*b*). Each stator has half the number of turns as possessed by the single-phase stator of Fig. 6.6 (*a*). At standstill, the forward and backward rotating flux waves are equal and the resulting torque is zero.

When the rotor is stationary, the behaviour of the single phase motor of Fig. 6.6 (*a*), is similar to 1-phase transformer on short circuit. Therefore, the equivalent circuit of a single-phase induction motor at standstill resembles the equivalent circuit of a single-phase short-circuited transformer, this is shown in Fig. 6.7. In this equivalent circuit, $(r_1 + jx_1)$ is the stator leakage impedance, $(r_2 + jx_2)$ is the standstill rotor leakage impedance referred to stator and X_m is the magnetizing reactance. The core loss is omitted and would be considered along the friction and windage losses. E is counter-emf induced in the main stator winding, by the stationary, pulsating flux wave produced by the combined action of both stator and rotor mmfs. It must be noted that the equivalent circuit of Fig. 6.7 is drawn, when only main winding is considered.

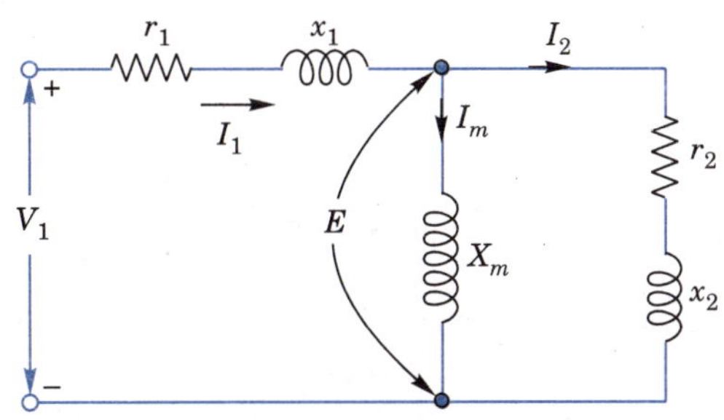

Fig. 6.7: Single-phase induction motor equivalent circuit at standstill.

Now recall the double revolving field theory and Fig. 6.6 (*b*). At standstill, both the forward and backward rotating flux waves are equal to half the amplitude of the stationary, pulsating air-gap flux wave. If the forward rotating flux wave were only present (*i.e.*, the rotor 1 alone), then the equivalent circuit of Fig. 6.8 (*a*) would be obtained with the rotor stationary. Had there been only backward rotating flux wave present (*i.e.*, rotor 2 alone), then the equivalent circuit of Fig. 6.8 (*b*) would be obtained at standstill. Both the equivalent circuits of Fig. 6.8 have been drawn by keeping in mind the equivalent circuit of a polyphase induction motor at standstill. In Fig. 6.7, the standstill impedance $r_2 + jx_2$ in parallel with jX_m represents the effect of pulsating air-gap flux wave as viewed from the stator. According to double revolving field theory, both the forward and backward rotating flux waves at standstill have their amplitudes equal to half the amplitude of the pulsating field. Consequently, when viewed from the stator, the effect of equal forward and backward

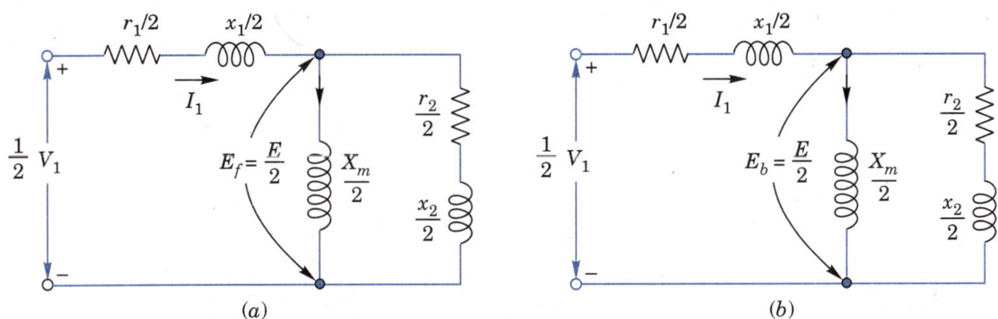

Fig. 6.8: Single-phase induction motor equivalent circuit at standstill, (*a*) when only forward field is present and (*b*) when only backward field is present.

rotating flux waves at standstill can be represented by an impedance $\frac{1}{2}(r_2 + jx_2)$ in parallel with $\frac{1}{2}\,jX_m$ as shown in Fig. 6.8 (a) and (b) respectively. The stator constants are also halved because each stator carries $\frac{N_1}{2}$ turns. Since both the forward and backward rotating flux waves and rotors 1 and 2 are present, at the same time, the two stators are in series, the equivalent circuits of Fig. 6.8 (a) and (b) can be connected in series to obtain single-phase induction motor equivalent circuit at standstill, this is illustrated in Fig. 6.9 (a). It should also be understood that all rotor-circuit quantities when referred to stator, are at the stator frequency.

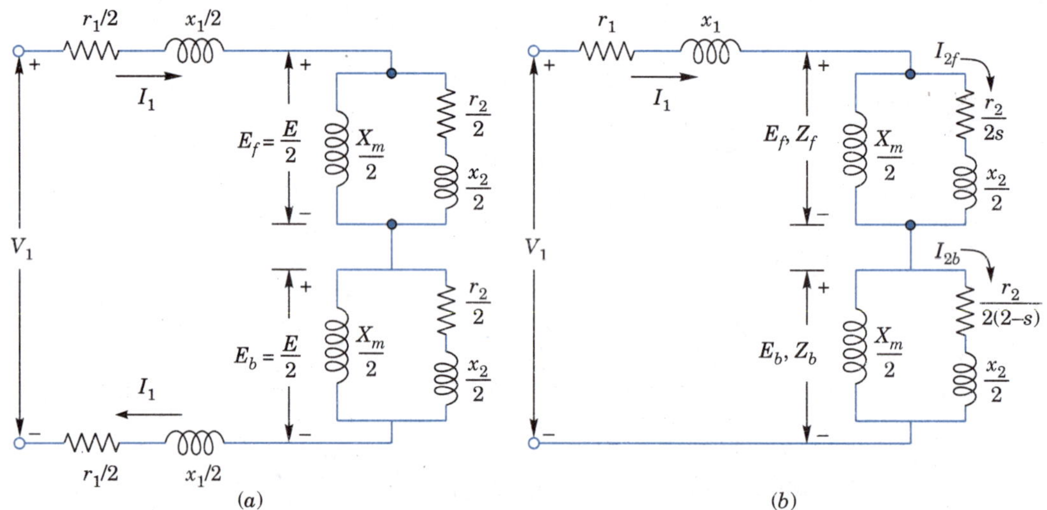

Fig. 6.9: Equivalent circuits for a single-phase induction motor (a) with the rotor blocked and (b) with the rotor running.

Now consider that the motor has been started by auxiliary means and the rotor is running with only main winding in circuit. Under these conditions, the rotor operates with slip s with respect to forward flux wave and with slip $(2 - s)$ relative to the backward flux wave. Just like a polyphase induction motor, slips s and $(2 - s)$ will be associated with the corresponding resistance terms and the equivalent circuit of Fig. 6.9 (b) is obtained for any rotor speed. Note that r_2 associated with the backward field is much larger than r_2 associated with the forward field, due to skin effect at higher frequency of $(2 - s)f$. The impedance Z_f, given by $\frac{1}{2}\left(\frac{r_2}{s} + j\,x_2\right)$ in parallel with $\frac{1}{2}\,jX_m$, represents the reflected effect of rotor as viewed from the stator forward field, just as in a polyphase induction motor. Similarly, the impedance Z_b, given by $\frac{1}{2}\left(\frac{r_2}{2-s} + j\,x_2\right)$ in parallel with $\frac{1}{2}\,jX_m$, represents the reflected effect of rotor as viewed from the stator backward field. Here Z_f and Z_b are called forward-field and backward-field impedances respectively.

The rotor currents induced by the forward field are at slip frequency sf. These rotor currents set up a forward rotating field, moving at slip speed $= \frac{2sf}{P} = sn_s$ with respect to rotor.

Since the rotor is running at speed $n_r = n_s(1 - s)$, the speed of rotor field with respect to stator is equal to rotor speed n_r plus the rotor-field speed with respect to rotor $= n_s(1 - s) + sn_s = n_s$. Thus the forward stator and rotor fields are at rest with respect to each other. The combination of both forward stator and rotor mmf waves gives the resultant forward air-gap flux wave. The emf E_f in Figs. 6.8 and 6.9 is the counter-emf generated in the main winding by the resultant forward air-gap flux wave. The rotor currents induced by backward field are at slip frequency $(2 - s)f$. These rotor currents, set up a backward rotating field, moving at speed

$$= \frac{2f}{P}(2 - s) = (2 - s)\, n_s$$

with respect to rotor. Since the rotor is running at speed $n_r = n_s(1 - s)$, the speed of rotor field with respect to stator is equal to forward rotor speed—backward rotating field speed with respect to rotor $= n_s(1 - s) - (2 - s)\, n_s = -\, n_s$, *i.e.*, the synchronous speed in the backward direction. This shows that backward stator and rotor fields are at rest with respect to each other. The resultant of backward rotating stator and rotor mmf waves gives the resultant backward air-gap flux wave. The emf E_b in Figs. 6.8 and 6.9 is the counter-emf generated in the main winding by the resultant backward air-gap flux wave.

Consideration of the equivalent circuit of Fig. 6.9 (*b*) shows that at small values of slips, $\frac{r_2}{2s}$ is much larger than $\frac{r_2}{2(2 - s)}$. In other words, at small values of slips, the forward-field impedance Z_f is much higher than the backward-field impedance Z_b. This amounts to the increase of E_f and decrease of E_b at small values of slips, though at standstill $E_f = E_b$. Therefore, the forward flux wave, proportional to E_f, increases and the backward flux wave, proportional to E_b, decreases, as the rotor speed increases. It can, therefore, be expressed as

$$\frac{\phi_f}{\phi_b} = \frac{E_f}{E_b} = \frac{Z_f}{Z_b} \qquad \text{...(6.3)}$$

where, ϕ_f = magnitude of forward flux

and, ϕ_b = magnitude of backward flux.

The equivalent circuit of Fig. 6.9 (*b*) can be used for the determination of stator current, motor output, operating pf etc., for any value of slip in the running conditions. But this equivalent circuit can't be used for computing the starting torque of the motor. This is due to the fact that the equivalent circuit of Fig. 6.9 (*b*) is derived when only main winding is excited, which gives zero starting torque.

Now the power and torque developed in a single-phase induction motor can be computed by recalling the power and torque relations developed for a polyphase induction motor.

The air-gap power P_{gf}, delivered from stator winding to forward field is given by,

$$P_{gf} = I_{2f}^2 \frac{r_2}{2s} \text{ watts.}$$

∴ Forward-field torque T_f is

$$T_f = \frac{1}{\omega_s} \cdot P_{gf} = \frac{1}{\omega_s} \cdot I_{2f}^2 \frac{r_2}{2s} \text{ Nm.}$$

The air-gap power P_{gb}, delivered from stator winding to the backward field is given by

$$P_{gb} = I_{2b}^2 \frac{r_2}{2(2-s)} \text{ watts.}$$

$\therefore$ Backward-field torque T_b is

$$T_b = \frac{1}{\omega_s} \cdot P_{gb} = \frac{1}{\omega_s} \cdot I_{2b}^2 \frac{r_2}{2(2-s)} \text{ Nm.}$$

Here ω_s is the synchronous angular velocity in mechanical radians per second. It is given by

$$\omega_s = 2\pi \times \frac{2(\text{Stator frequency})}{\text{Stator poles}}.$$

Since the backward field torque opposes the forward-field torque, the net developed torque, or internal torque, T is given by

$$T = T_f - T_b = \frac{1}{\omega_s}[P_{gf} - P_{gb}]$$

$$= \frac{1}{\omega_s}\left[I_{2f}^2 \frac{r_2}{2s} - I_{2b}^2 \frac{r_2}{2(2-s)}\right] \text{Nm} \quad \text{...(6.4)}$$

The net developed power, or internal power, P_m converted to mechanical form is given by

$$P_m = \text{Rotor speech in rad/sec} \times \text{Net developed torque in Nm}$$

$$= [(1-s)\,\omega_s]\left[\frac{1}{\omega_s}(P_{gf} - P_{gb})\right]$$

$$= (1-s)(P_{gf} - P_{gb}) \quad \text{...(6.5)}$$

Forward-field rotor ohmic losses $= sP_{gf}$ ...(6.6)

Backward-field rotor ohmic losses $= (2-s)\,P_{gb}$ ...(6.7)

Total rotor ohmic losses $= sP_{gf} + (2-s)\,P_{gb}$ ...(6.8)

Since core losses have not been shown in the equivalent circuit of Fig. 6.9 (*b*), the shaft, or output, power is equal to internal power P as given by Eq. (6.5), minus the rotational losses (= Core losses + Friction and windage losses).

Shaft, or output, torque

$$= \frac{\text{Shaft power in watts}}{\text{Shaft speed in rad/sec.}} = \frac{P_m - \text{Rotational losses}}{(1-s)\,\omega_s} \text{ Nm.}$$

The rotational losses are assumed to remain constant, because change in operating speed from no-load to full load is small.

If Z_f and Z_b are the forward and backward field impedances respectively, then

$$Z_f = R_f + jX_f = \frac{j\dfrac{X_m}{2}\left[\dfrac{r_2}{2s} + j\dfrac{x_2}{2}\right]}{\dfrac{r_2}{2s} + j\left(\dfrac{x_2}{2} + \dfrac{X_m}{2}\right)}$$

and

$$Z_b = R_b + jX_b = \frac{j\dfrac{X_m}{2}\left[\dfrac{r_2}{2(2-s)} + j\dfrac{x_2}{2}\right]}{\dfrac{r_2}{2(2-s)} + j\left(\dfrac{x_2}{2} + \dfrac{X_m}{2}\right)}$$

Since the resistance $\frac{R_m}{2}$ representing the core loss has been neglected in the equivalent circuit of a single-phase induction motor, $I_{2f}^2 \frac{r_2}{2s}$ must be equal to $I_1^2 R_f = P_{gf}$.

Similarly, $\qquad I_{2b}^2 \frac{r_2}{2(2-s)} = I_1^2 R_b = P_{gb}$.

Resultant air-gap power $= P_{gf} - P_{gb} = I_1^2 (R_f - R_b)$

Internal mechanical power developed,

$$P_m = (1 - s)\, I_1^2 (R_f - R_b) \qquad \text{...(6.9)}$$

The use of these relations is illustrated in Example 6.1.

Example 6.1. *A 230 V, 4-pole, 50 Hz, single-phase induction motor has the following constants and losses :*

$r_1 = 2.3\ \Omega$ $\qquad x_1 = 3.2\ \Omega$

$r_2 = 4.2\ \Omega$ $\qquad x_2 = 3.2\ \Omega$

$X_m = 74\ \Omega$

Core loss = 98 watts.

Friction and windage loss = 30 watts.

If this motor is running with a slip 0.05 at rated voltage and frequency, then compute the stator current, pf, power output, torque and efficiency with its auxiliary winding open.

Solution. Forward-field impedance is,

$$Z_f = R_f + jX_f = \frac{j\frac{X_m}{2}\left[\frac{r_2}{2s} + j\frac{x_2}{2}\right]}{\frac{r_2}{2s} + j\frac{1}{2}(x_2 + X_m)}$$

$$= \frac{j37\,(42 + j1.6)}{42 + j38.6} = 27.23\ \angle 49.64°$$

$$= 27.23\,(\cos 49.64 + j \sin 49.64) = (17.66 + j\,20.75)\ \Omega.$$

Backward-field impedance is

$$Z_b = R_b + jX_b = \frac{j\frac{X_m}{2}\left[\frac{r_2}{2(2-s)} + j\frac{x_2}{2}\right]}{\frac{r_2}{2(2-s)} + j\frac{1}{2}(x_2 + X_m)}$$

$$= \frac{j(37)\,(1.077 + j1.6)}{1.077 + j38.6} = 1.85\ \angle 57.6° = (0.99 + j\,1.562)\ \Omega.$$

Total motor impedance $= (r_1 + R_f + R_b) + j\,(x_1 + X_f + X_b)$

$= (20.95 + j25.5)\ \Omega = 33.1\ \angle 50.4°$.

$\therefore$ Stator current, $I_1 = \frac{230}{33.1} = 6.95$ A.

Power factor $= \cos 50.4° = 0.637$ lagging.

Power input $= V_1 I_1 \cos\theta = (230)(6.95)(0.637) = 1020$ watts.

Power delivered to forward field, $P_{gf} = I_1^2 R_f = (6.95)^2\,(17.66) = 854$ watts

Power delivered to backward field, $P_{gb} = I_1^2 R_b = (6.95)^2\,(0.99) = 47.8$ watts.

$\therefore$ Total electrical power developed = power input to rotor = 854 – 47.8 = 806.2 watts.

Total mechanical power developed = $(1 - s)\,(P_{gf} - P_{gb}) = (0.95)(806.2) = 765$ watts.

Core loss + Friction and windage losses = rotational losses = 98 + 30 = 128 watts.

$\therefore$ Power output = 765 – 128 = 637 watts.

$$\text{Synchronous speed, } \omega_s = 2\pi\,\frac{2\times 50}{4} = 50\pi \text{ rad/sec.}$$

$$\therefore \text{ Rotor speed, } \omega_r = (1 - s)\,\omega_s = (0.95)(50\pi) = 149.2 \text{ rad/sec.}$$

$$\therefore \text{Torque} = \frac{\text{Power output}}{\text{Rotor speed}} = \frac{637}{149.2} = 4.27 \text{ Nm.}$$

$$\text{Efficiency} = \frac{637}{1020} \times 100 = 62.5\%.$$

P_{gf} and P_{gb} obtained above from R_f and R_b, can alternatively be obtained from I_{2f} and I_{2b}. From Fig. 6.9 (*b*).

$$I_{2f} = \frac{I_1\left(j\dfrac{X_m}{2}\right)}{\dfrac{r_2}{2s} + j\dfrac{1}{2}(x_2 + X_m)}$$

$$= \frac{I_1\dfrac{X_m}{2}}{\dfrac{1}{2}(x_2 + X_m) - j\dfrac{r_2}{2s}} = \frac{(6.95)\,(37)}{38.6 - j42} = 4.51 \text{ A}$$

$$\therefore \quad P_{gf} = I_{2f}^2\,\frac{r_2}{2s} = (4.51)^2\,(42) = 854 \text{ watts.}$$

Now

$$I_{2b} = \frac{I_1\cdot\dfrac{X_m}{2}}{\dfrac{1}{2}(x_2 + X_m) - j\dfrac{r_2}{2(2-s)}} = \frac{(6.95)\,(37)}{38.6 - j1.077} = 6.66 \text{ A.}$$

$$\therefore \quad P_{gb} = I_{2b}^2\,\frac{r_2}{2\,(2-s)} = (6.66)^2\,(1.077) = 47.8 \text{ watts.}$$

Thus the same values for P_{gf} and P_{gb} are obtained, though the computational work has increased considerably. So it is preferable to compute P_{gf} and P_{gb} from R_f and R_b respectively.

Example 6.2. *For the single-phase induction motor of Example 6.1, determine the ratio of forward-field flux to the backward-field flux at slips of 0.05 and 0.1. For slip 0.1, choose zero time at the instant the two flux phasors are in space phase and draw a diagram showing the component flux phasors and their resultant for the instants of time corresponding to ωt = 0, 30, 60, 90, 120, 150 and 180°. Sketch the locus of the tip of the resultant flux phasor and identify the nature of the curve so obtained.*

Solution. From Example 6.1, for

$$s = 0.05,\ Z_f = 27.23\ \Omega \text{ and } Z_b = 1.85\ \Omega$$

From Eq. (6.3), $\frac{\phi_f}{\phi_b} = \frac{Z_f}{Z_b} = \frac{27.23}{1.85} = 14.719.$

For slip, $s = 0.1$, $Z_f = \frac{j37\,(21 + j1.6)}{21 + j38.6} = 17.735 \angle 32.9°$

$$Z_b = \frac{j37\,(1.105 + j1.6)}{1.105 + j38.6} = 1.8626 \angle 57.01°$$

$$\therefore \quad \frac{\phi_f}{\phi_b} = \frac{Z_f}{Z_b} = \frac{17.735}{1.8626} = 9.52$$

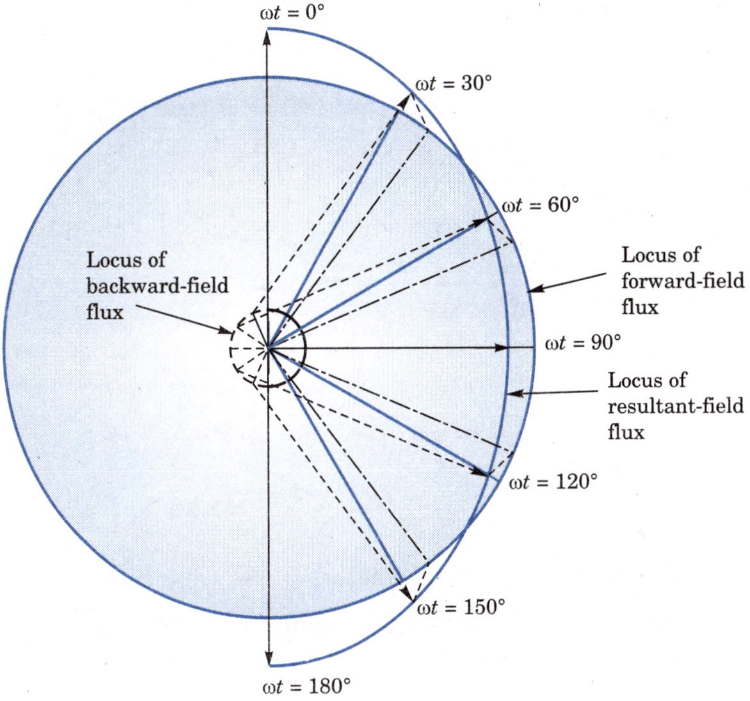

Fig. 6.10: Pertaining.

It is seen from above that at slip 0.1, the magnitude of forward field flux is 9.52 times the magnitude of backward-field flux. In Fig. 6.10, locus of backward-field flux ϕ_b is represented by a small circle whereas the locus of toward-field flux ϕ_f is represented by a bigger circle whose radius is 9.52 times the radius of smaller circle. At instant $\omega t = 0°$, both backward-field and forward-field fluxes are in space phase, their resultant is therefore their arithmetic sum, Fig. 6.10. At $\omega t = 30°$, ϕ_f travels by 30° in the forward direction (assumed clockwise) and ϕ_b travels by 30° in the backward direction. Their phasor sum then gives the resultant flux at $\omega t = 30°$ as shown. In this manner, the resultant flux is plotted at different instants of ωt, as shown in Fig. 6.10. Now the tips of the resultant flux phasors are joined. It is found that locus of the tip of the resultant flux forms an ellipse.

(*b*) At $s = 1.0$, *i.e.*, with the rotor at standstill, $\phi_f = \phi_b$. Both ϕ_f and ϕ_b and their resultant can be plotted as done in Fig. 6.10. It will be found that locus of the tip of resultant-flux phasor is a straight line.

Example 6.3. *A single-phase, 4-pole, induction motor takes a line current of 60 ∠– 70° A at standstill with its main winding excited from 230 V, 50 Hz source. Neglecting stator impedance, magnetizing current and rotational loss, compute the torque at a slip of 0.05.*

Solution. As stator leakage impedance $r_1 + jx_1$ and magnetizing reactance are neglected, single-phase induction motor equivalent circuit at standstill gives

$$z_2 = r_2 + jx_2 = \frac{230}{60 \angle -70°} = 3.833 \angle 70° = 1.311 + j3.602 \ \Omega$$

$\therefore$ $$r_2 = 1.311 \ \Omega \quad \text{and} \quad x_2 = 3.602 \ \Omega$$

Now $$R_f + jX_f = \frac{r_2}{2s} + j\frac{x_2}{2} = \frac{1.311}{2 \times 0.05} + j\frac{3.602}{2} = 13.11 + j1.801 \ \Omega$$

$$R_b + jX_b = \frac{r_2}{2(2-s)} + j\frac{x_2}{2} = \frac{1.311}{2 \times 1.95} + j\frac{3.602}{2} = 0.3362 + j1.801 \ \Omega$$

Total input impedance at a slip of 0.05 is

$$Z_1 = R_f + jX_f + R_b + jX_b = 13.4462 + j3.602 = 13.92 \angle 15° \ \Omega$$

Stator current, $$I_1 = \frac{V_1}{Z_1} = \frac{230}{13.92 \angle 15°} = 16.523 \angle -15° \text{ A}$$

Mechanical power developed = $(1 - s)\, I_1^2 (R_f - R_b)$

$$\text{Torque} = \frac{(1-s) I_1^2 \, (R_f - R_b)}{(1-s)\, \omega_s}$$

$$= \frac{(16.523)^2 [13.11 - 0.3362]}{50\pi} = \mathbf{22.2 \ Nm}$$

6.3.1 Measurement of Equivalent-Circuit Parameters

As in a polyphase induction motor, the equivalent-circuit parameters of a single-phase induction motor can be measured from no-load and blocked-rotor test and from stator winding resistance r_1.

(a) Blocked-rotor test. With the rotor at rest, single-phase voltage, applied to the stator main winding, is increased gradually from zero so that rated current flows in the main winding. Under these conditions ; voltmeter, ammeter and wattmeter readings respectively denoted by V_{sc}, I_{sc} and W_{sc} are recorded. Measure d.c. resistance of main stator winding soon after this test by ammeter-voltameter method. This d.c. resistance should be multiplied by a factor 1.1 to 1.3, so as to obtain effective a.c. resistance r_1 at the line frequency. With the rotor stationary, the slip s = 1 and the voltage required to circulate full-load current is very low. Therefore, the flux is small and the magnetizing current flowing through X_m is also very low. In view of this, magnetizing reactance can be neglected modifying the equivalent circuit of Fig. 6.9 (*b*) to that of Fig. 6.11 (*a*). From the test data, the equivalent impedance referred to stator is

$$Z_{sc} = \frac{V_{sc}}{I_{sc}} \qquad ...(6.10)$$

The equivalent resistance R_{sc}, from Fig. 6.11 (*a*), is given by

$$R_{sc} = r_1 + \left(\frac{r_2}{2}\right)2 = \frac{W_{sc}}{I_{sc}^2} \quad ...(6.11)$$

Since resistance of main stator winding r_1 is already measured, effective rotor resistance r_2 at line frequency is

$$r_2 = R_{sc} - r_1 = \frac{W_{sc}}{I_{sc}^2} - r_1 \quad ...(6.12)$$

From Fig. 6.11 (*a*), $X_{sc} = x_1 + \left(\frac{1}{2}x_2\right)2 = x_1 + x_2$.

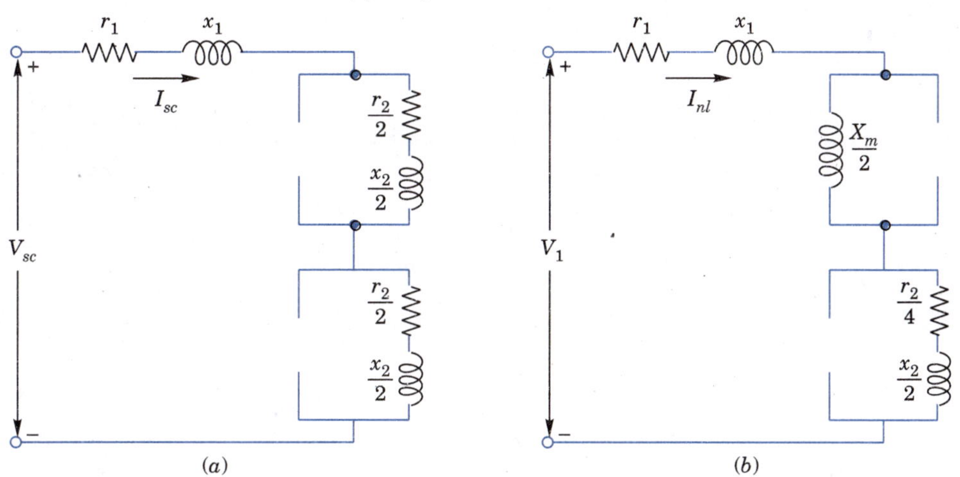

Fig. 6.11: Simplified equivalent circuit for a single-phase induction motor (*a*) for blocked-rotor test and (*b*) for no-load test.

Since the leakage reactances x_1 and x_2 can't be separated out, it is a common practice to assume

$$x_1 = x_2$$

$$\therefore \quad x_1 = x_2 = \frac{1}{2} X_{sc}$$

or
$$x_1 = x_2 = \frac{1}{2}\sqrt{Z_{sc}^2 - R_{sc}^2} \quad ...(6.13)$$

In blocked-rotor test, note that only main winding is excited, the auxiliary winding is left open.

Thus, from blocked-rotor test, parameters r_2, x_1 and x_2 can be determined if r_1 is known.

(b) No-load test. The single-phase induction motor, under no-load conditions, is run at rated voltage and frequency. With the motor running at no-load, the slip is very close to zero, it may, therefore, be assumed that $s \cong 0$. Under these conditions, $\frac{r_2}{2s}$ becomes infinity and $\frac{r_2}{2(2-s)} = \frac{r_2}{4}$ becomes several times smaller than $\frac{X_m}{2}$. In view of these approximations, $\frac{r_2}{2s} + j\frac{x_2}{2}$ and $\frac{X_m}{2}\left(\text{across } \frac{r_2}{4} + j\frac{x_2}{2}\right)$ may be neglected giving the equivalent circuit of Fig. 6.11 (*b*).

Under no-load test, let the voltmeter, ammeter and wattmeter readings be V_1, I_{nl} and W_{nl} respectively. Then, no-load pf is.

$$\cos \phi_{nl} = \frac{W_{nl}}{V_1 I_{nl}}$$

No-load equivalent impedance is, $Z_{nl} = \dfrac{V_1}{I_{nl}}$

$$\therefore \qquad X_{nl} = Z_{nl}\sqrt{1-\cos^2 \theta_{nl}} = Z_{nl} \sin \phi_{nl}.$$

From Fig. 6.11 (*b*), $Z_{nl} = R_{nl} + jX_{nl} = \left(r_1 + \dfrac{r_2}{4}\right) + j\left[x_1 + \dfrac{1}{2}(x_2 + X_m)\right]$

$$\therefore \qquad x_1 + \frac{1}{2}(x_2 + X_m) = X_{nl} \qquad ...(6.14)$$

Since x_1 and x_2 are already known from blocked-rotor test, magnetizing reactance X_m can be calculated from Eq. (6.14). Thus, from no-load test, only magnetizing reactance X_m is determined provided x_1 and x_2 are known.

Note. Under normal running conditions, the slip s with respect to forward field is small and rotor frequency is sf; therefore, rotor resistance for this field approaches the d.c. resistance r_{2dc}. In view of this, r_2 obtained from Eq. (6.12) at line frequency should be divided by a suitable factor 1.2 to 1.4 to get r_{2dc}.

$$\therefore \qquad r_{2dc} = \frac{r_2}{1.2 \text{ to } 1.4} = r_{2f}$$

The slip with respect to backward field, under normal running conditions, is $2 - s$ and rotor frequency is $(2 - s)f$. At this higher frequency, effective rotor resistance r_{2b} is high, usually 1.5 to 1.8 r_{2dc}.

$$\therefore \qquad r_{2b} = (1.5 \text{ to } 1.8)\, r_{2dc} = (1.5 \text{ to } 1.8)\, r_{2f}$$

In view of the above, r_{2dc} should be associated with forward-field impedance and r_{2b} with backward-field impedance ; for an accurate estimation of the induction motor running performance. Therefore, Z_f should be calculated with r_2 replaced by r_{2f}. Similarly, Z_b should be obtained by replacing r_2 with r_{2b}.

Example 6.4. *The following data relates to tests on a 110-volt, 150 watt, 50 Hz, 6-pole single-phase induction motor :*

No-load test : 110 volts, 63 watts, 2.7 amps.

Blocked-rotor test : 55 volts, 212 watts, 5.8 amps.

The stator winding resistance is 2.5 ohms and during the blocked rotor test, the starting winding is open. Determine the equivalent circuit parameters. Also, find the core, friction and windage losses.

Solution. Blocked-rotor test :

From Eq. (6.10), $Z_{sc} = \dfrac{55}{5.8} = 9.48\ \Omega$

From Eq. (6.11), $R_{sc} = r_1 + 2\left(\dfrac{r_2}{2}\right) = \dfrac{212}{(5.8)^2} = 6.3\ \Omega$

$$\therefore \qquad X_{sc} = x_1 + x_2 = \sqrt{(9.48)^2 - (6.3)^2} = 7.08\ \Omega.$$

From Eq. (6.13), $x_1 = x_2 = \frac{1}{2} X_{sc} = 3.54\ \Omega$

Now $r_1 = 2.5\ \Omega.$

$\therefore$ $r_2 = 6.3 - 2.5 = 3.8\ \Omega$

No-load test

No-load pf, $\cos \theta_{nl} = \frac{63}{110 \times 2.7} = \frac{7}{33}$

$$\sin \theta_{nl} = \sqrt{1 - \left(\frac{7}{33}\right)^2} = \frac{323}{330}. \quad Z_{nl} = \frac{110}{2.7}\ \Omega$$

$\therefore$ $$X_{nl} = Z_{nl} \sin \theta_{nl} = \frac{110}{2.7} \times \frac{323}{330} \cong 40\ \Omega.$$

Also $x_1 + \frac{1}{2}(x_2 + X_m) = 40$

$\therefore$ $X_m = 69.38\ \Omega.$

The values of the various parameters in ohms are indicated in the equivalent circuit of Fig. 6.12.

The power input to single-phase induction motor at no-load is equal to the core, friction and windage losses and small $I^2 R$ loss.

An examination of Fig. 6.11 (*b*) shows that the core, friction and windage losses are given by $W_{nl} - I_{nl}^2 \left(r_1 + \frac{r_2}{4}\right)$.

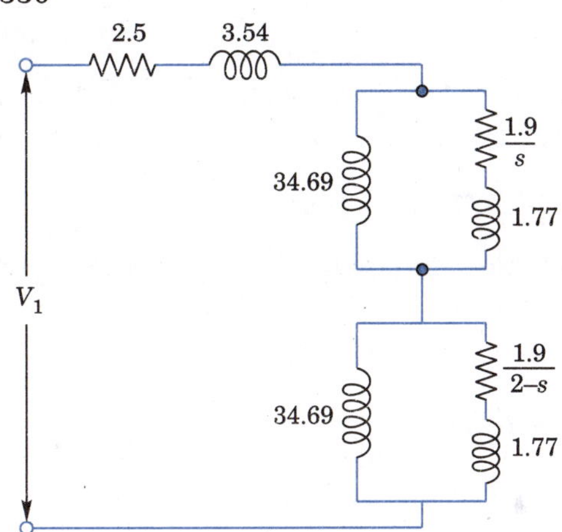

Fig. 6.12: Single-phase induction motor equivalent circuit, Example 6.4. All values are in ohms.

$\therefore$ Rotational losses $= 63 - (2.7)^2 \left[2.5 + \frac{3.8}{4}\right] = 63 - 25.15 = 37.85$ watts.

6.3.2 Approximate Equivalent Circuit

An approximate equivalent circuit of a single-phase induction motor is quite useful, in case its behaviour over the normal operating range of slip is to be investigated. The full-load slip, under normal running region, is around 5 to 10%. In view of this, the value of backward field resistance $\frac{r_2}{2(2-s)}$ varies from $\frac{r_2}{3.9}$ to $\frac{r_2}{3.8}$ and this may approximately be taken as $\frac{r_2}{4}$. With this approximation, equivalent circuit of Fig. 6.13 (*b*) becomes that as shown in Fig. 6.13 (*a*).

Since $\frac{X_m}{2}$ is several times greater than $\sqrt{\left(\frac{r_2}{4}\right)^2 + \left(\frac{x_2}{2}\right)^2}$, the shunting effect of $\frac{1}{2} X_m$ on the backward-field impedance Z_b may be neglected, hence, $Z_b \cong \frac{r_2}{4} + j\frac{x_2}{2}$.

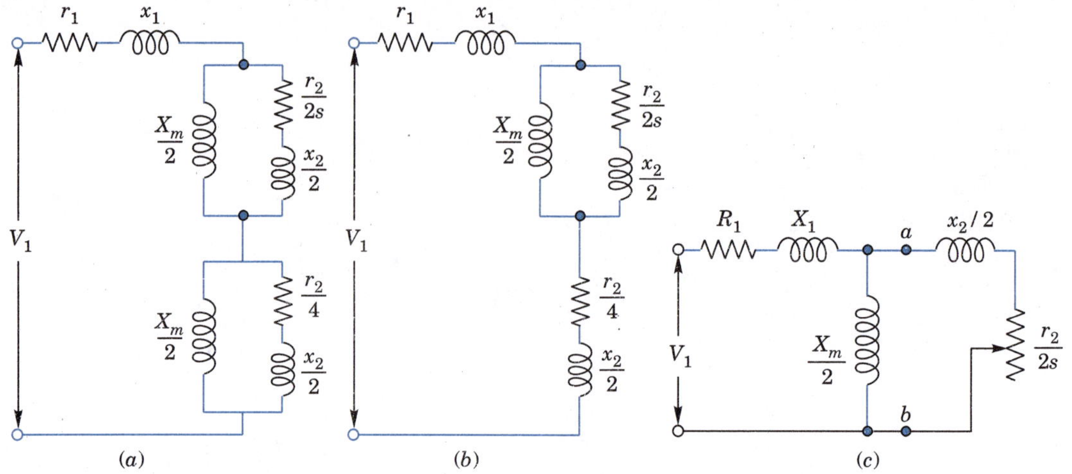

Fig. 6.13: Approximate equivalent circuits for a single-phase induction motor.

With this approximation, equivalent circuit of Fig. 6.13 (*b*) is obtained and it is redrawn in Fig. 6.13 (*c*) in a more convenient form, where $R_1 = r_1 + \frac{r_2}{4}$ and $X_1 = x_1 + \frac{x_2}{2}$. As done in a polyphase induction motor, the equivalent circuit of Fig. 6.13 (*c*) can be modified by applying Thevenin's theorem at the terminals *a*, *b*. The Thevenin's equivalent circuit is drawn in Fig. 6.14 (*a*), in which

$$Z_e = R_e + jX_e = \frac{(R_1 + jX_1)\left(j\frac{X_m}{2}\right)}{R_1 + j\left(X_1 + \frac{X_m}{2}\right)}$$

and
$$V_e = \frac{V_1\left(j\frac{X_m}{2}\right)}{R_1 + j\left(X_1 + \frac{X_m}{2}\right)}$$

If R_1 in the denominator is neglected, then,

$$Z_e = R_e + jX_e = \frac{\frac{1}{2}R_1X_m}{X_1 + \frac{1}{2}X_m} + \frac{\frac{1}{2}jX_1X_m}{X_1 + \frac{1}{2}X_m}$$

and
$$V_e = \frac{1}{2}\frac{V_1X_m}{X_1 + \frac{1}{2}X_m}$$

The slip at which maximum torque occurs is given by,

$$\frac{r_2}{2s_{mT}} = \sqrt{R_e^2 + \left(X_e + \frac{x_2}{2}\right)^2}$$

or
$$s_{mT} = \frac{r_2}{2\sqrt{R_e^2 + (X_e + 1/2\,x_2)^2}} \qquad \text{...(6.15)}$$

The maximum torque is given by

$$T_{e.m} = \frac{V_e^2}{2\pi n_s} \cdot \frac{1}{2[R_e + \sqrt{R_e^2 + (X_e + \frac{1}{2}x_2)^2}\,]} \qquad \text{...(6.16)}$$

Note that Thevenin's equivalent resistance R_e is dependent on R_1 and, therefore, on rotor circuit resistance, but this is not so in a polyphase induction motor as per Eq. (5.26).

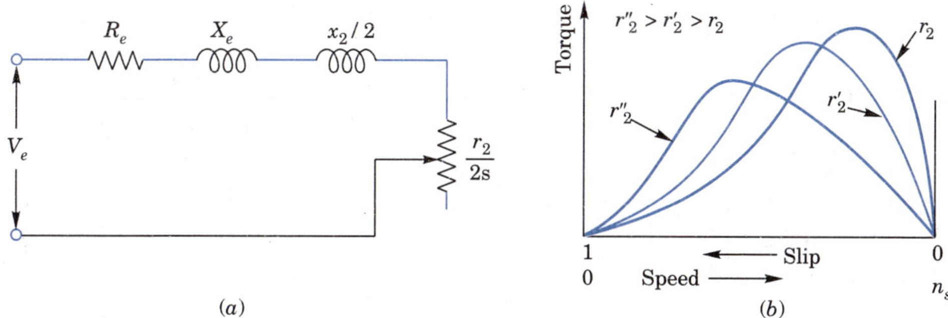

Fig 6.14: (*a*) Thevenin's equivalent circuit for a single-phase induction motor.
(*b*) Effect of rotor resistance on torque-speed curve of a single-phase induction motor.

The slip at which maximum torque occurs is effected by r_2, both in single-phase and 3-phase induction motors. The maximum torque T_{em} in a 3-phase induction motor does not depend on rotor resistance r_2 as per Eq. (5.30). But in a single-phase induction motor, the maximum internal torque $T_{e.m}$ decreases with increase in rotor resistance as illustrated in Fig. 6.14 (*b*). The induction motor performance obtained with these approximations is not very accurate, however these approximations do highlight the general behaviour of a single-phase induction motor in the normal running region.

6.3.3 Comparison between Single-phase and Polyphase Induction Motors

In this section of the article, a comparison between single-phase and polyphase induction motors, having the same speed and the same stator and rotor core dimensions, is presented.

(*i*) Rotor core losses in single-phase induction motor are more because of the backward rotating field, as compared to those in a 3-phase induction motor.

(*ii*) Rotor ohmic loss, because of the double-frequency currents induced by the backward field, is also higher in single-phase motors.

(*iii*) For the same load torque, single-phase induction motor requires more stator current and operates at a higher slip. In view of this, single-phase motor has more stator ohmic losses.

(*iv*) For the same size, single-phase induction motor output is less, because backward field torque opposes the forward field torque. As has been stated in (*i*), (*ii*) and (*iii*) above, single-phase motor has more losses. In view of this, for the same size, single-phase motor has higher temperature rise and lower efficiency as compared to a polyphase induction motor.

(*v*) The stator winding of a single-phase motor carries magnetizing current for both the forward and backward fields. As a result of it, the ratio of magnetizing current to the active component of stator current is much greater in a single-phase induction motor than the ratio of the same currents in a polyphase induction motor. In view of this, single-phase induction motor operates at a poor pf as compared to a polyphase induction motor.

For the same power and speed rating, single-phase motor requires larger frame size than a polyphase induction motor. Therefore, single-phase induction motors require more iron and the necessity of providing auxiliary windings, makes them costlier as compared to 3-phase induction motors of the same power rating and speed. However, large scale production of fractional-kW single-phase induction motors may decrease their cost, almost comparable with the cost of polyphase induction motors of the same power rating and speed.

6.4 CROSS-FIELD THEORY OF SINGLE-PHASE INDUCTION MOTORS

This theory is an application of two-axis, or generalized, theory of electrical machines. In this article, cross-field theory is applied to the analysis of a single-phase induction motor during its normal running conditions.

The main stator winding of the single-phase induction motor is taken along the d-axis as DS. The squirrel-cage rotor winding is effectively equivalent to two coils DR and QR on the rotor as shown in Fig. 6.15. The procedure of analysis is similar to that adopted for a polyphase induction motor.

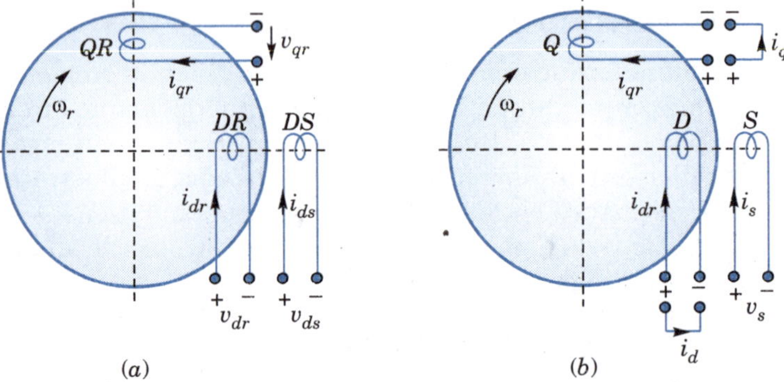

Fig. 6.15: Single-phase induction motor (*a*) its generalized model and (*b*) the rotor constraints.

Fig. 6.15 (a) gives the primitive machine diagram for a single phase induction motor and the voltage equations obtained from this figure are :

$$\begin{bmatrix} v_{ds} \\ v_{dr} \\ v_{qr} \end{bmatrix} = \begin{bmatrix} r_{ds} + L_{ds}p & M_d p & \\ M_d p & r_{dr} + L_{dr}p & -L_{qr}\omega_r \\ M_d\omega_r & L_{dr}\omega_r & r_{qr} + L_{qr}p \end{bmatrix} \begin{bmatrix} i_{ds} \\ i_{dr} \\ i_{qr} \end{bmatrix} \quad \text{...(6.17)}$$

Constraints. Rotor winding in the form of damper bars is uniformly distributed over the rotor surface *i.e.*, the rotor winding is balanced. This gives

$$r_{dr} = r_{qr} = r_r \text{ (say)}$$

The machine has a uniform air gap

$$\therefore \quad L_{dr} = L_{qr} = L_r \text{ (say)}$$

Since the rotor bars are short-circuited

$$v_{dr} = v_{qr} = 0 \quad \text{and} \quad i_{dr} = -\,i_d\,;\, i_{qr} = -\,i_q.$$

By imposing these constraints on matrix (6.17), the general voltage equations become :

$$\begin{bmatrix} v_s \\ 0 \\ 0 \end{bmatrix} = \begin{bmatrix} r_s + L_{sp} & -M_{dp} & \\ M_{dp} & -(r_r + L_r p) & \omega_r L_r \\ M_d\omega_r & -\omega_r L_r & -(r_r + L_r)p \end{bmatrix} \begin{bmatrix} i_s \\ i_d \\ i_q \end{bmatrix} \qquad \text{...(6.18)}$$

Coil DS has been designated by S and the negative sign before i_d and i_q have been accounted for in the impedance matrix.

The electromagnetic torque at any instant from matrix (6.17) is, $T_e = [i_t]\,[G]\,[i]$.

						i_{ds}
					$-L_{qr}$	i_{dr}
			M_d	L_{dr}		i_{qr}
$T_e =$ i_{ds}	i_{dr}	i_{qr}	$M_d i_{qr}$	$L_{dr} i_{qr}$	$-L_{qr} i_{dr}$	Written below

$$T_e = [M_d i_{qr} i_{ds} + L_{dr} i_{qr} i_{dr} - L_{qr} i_{dr} i_{qr}].$$

Use of the constraints for electromagnetic torque T_e gives

$$T_e = -\,M_d i_s i_q.$$

Steady state analysis. The steady state voltage equations, obtained from matrix (6.18), in phasor form are :

$$\begin{bmatrix} \bar{V}_s \\ 0 \\ 0 \end{bmatrix} = \begin{bmatrix} r_s + jX_s & -jX_{md} & \\ jX_{md} & -(r_r + jX_r) & vX_r \\ vX_{md} & -\,vX_r & -(r_r + jX_r) \end{bmatrix} \begin{bmatrix} \bar{I}_s \\ \bar{I}_d \\ \bar{I}_q \end{bmatrix}$$

or $$[\bar{V}] = [\bar{Z}][\bar{I}] \qquad \text{...(6.19)}$$

Let $[A] = [Z]$;

$$\therefore \quad [A_t] = \begin{bmatrix} r_s + jX_s & jX_{md} & vX_{md} \\ -\,jX_{md} & -\,(r_r + jX_r) & -\,vX_r \\ & vX_r & -\,(r_r + jX_r) \end{bmatrix}$$

$$\therefore \qquad Z]^{-1} = \frac{1}{\Delta}\begin{bmatrix} (r_r + jX_r)^2 + v^2X_r^{\,2} & & \\ jX_{md}(r_r + jX_r) + v^2X_{md}X_r & & \\ vX_{md}r_r & & \end{bmatrix}$$

Thus the inverse of the matrix (6.19) can be written as

$$\begin{bmatrix} \bar{I}_s \\ \bar{I}_d \\ \bar{I}_q \end{bmatrix} = \frac{1}{\Delta}\begin{bmatrix} (r_r + jX_r)^2 + v^2X_r^{\,2} & & \\ jX_{md}(r_r + jX_r) + v^2X_{md}X_r & & \\ vX_{md}r_r & & \end{bmatrix}\begin{bmatrix} \bar{V}_s \\ 0 \\ 0 \end{bmatrix} \qquad \text{...(6.20)}$$

where Δ is the determinant of the impedance matrix in Eq. (6.19).

$$\therefore \qquad \Delta = (r_s + jX_s)\,[r_r^2 - X_r^2 + 2j\, r_r X_r + v^2 X_r^2] - jX_{md}\,[(r_r + jX_r) \times jX_{md} + v^2 X_r X_{md}]$$

$$= [\{r_r^2 - X_r^2 (1 - v^2)\}\, r_s - 2r_r X_r X_s + X_{md}^2\, r_r] + j\,[\{r_r^2 - X_r^2 (1 - v^2)\}\, X_s + 2r_s r_r X_r + (1 - v^2)\, X_r X_{md}] \qquad \text{...(6.21)}$$

The value of Δ may also be expressed as

$$\Delta = Z_s\,[Z_r^2 + v^2X_r^2] - jX_{md}\,[Z_r j\, X_{md} + v^2\, X_r X_{md}]$$

$$= Z_s\,[Z_r^2 + v^2X_r^2] - jX_{md}^2[jZ_r + v^2X_r] \qquad \text{...(6.22)}$$

Steady state torque. It is given by

						i_{ds}
					$-L_{qr}$	i_{dr}
			M_d	L_{dr}		i_{qr}
$T_e =$ i_{ds}	i_{dr}	i_{qr}	$M_d I_{qr}^*$	$L_{dr} i_{qr}$	$-L_{qr} I_{dr}^*$	Written below

$$T_e = Re\,[M_d \bar{I}_{qr}^* \bar{I}_{ds} + L_{dr} \bar{I}_{qr}^* \bar{I}_{dr} - L_{qr} \bar{I}_{dr}^* \bar{I}_{qr}] \qquad \text{...(6.23)}$$

Use of the constraints in Eq. (6.23) gives

$$T_e = Re\;[- M_d \bar{I}_q^* \bar{I}_d + L_r (\bar{I}_q^* \bar{I}_d - \bar{I}_d^* \bar{I}_q)]$$

Let $\quad \bar{I}_d = a + jb \quad$ and $\quad \bar{I}_q = c + jd,$

then $\quad \bar{I}_q^* \bar{I}_d - \bar{I}_d^* \bar{I}_q = 2j\,(bc - ad).$

Thus $(\bar{I}_q^* \bar{I}_d - \bar{I}_d^* \bar{I}_q)$ is an imaginary term and torque is, therefore, given by,

$$T_e = Re\;[- M_d \bar{I}_q^* \bar{I}_s] \qquad [\because\; \bar{I}_d = \bar{I}_s] \qquad \text{...(6.24)}$$

From matrix Eq. (6.20)

$$\bar{I}_s = \frac{\bar{V}_s}{\Delta}[(r_r + jX_r)^2 + v^2X_r^2]$$

$$\bar{I}_q = \frac{\bar{V}_s}{\Delta}[vX_{md}r_r] \quad \text{and} \quad \bar{I}_q^* = \frac{\bar{V}_s^*}{\Delta^*}[vX_{md}r_r].$$

Substitution of the values $\bar{I}_s$ and $\bar{I}_q^*$ in Eq. (6.24) gives

$$T_e = Re\left[\frac{\bar{V}_s}{\Delta}\{r_r^2 - X_r^2(1-v^2) + 2jr_rX_r\}(-M_d)\cdot\frac{\bar{V}_s^*}{\Delta^*}\{vX_{md}r_r\}\right]$$

$$= \frac{\bar{V}_s\bar{V}_s^*}{\Delta\Delta^*}\cdot\frac{vX_{md}^2r_r}{\omega}[X_r^2(1-v^2) - r_r^2]$$

$$= \left|\frac{\bar{V}_s}{\Delta}\right|^2\cdot\frac{vX_{md}^2r_r}{\omega}[X_r^2(1-v^2) - r_r^2] \qquad \text{...(6.25)}$$

At zero speed, $v = 0$ and $T_e = 0$.

At synchronous speed, $v = 1$

and $$T_e = -\frac{\bar{V}_s\bar{V}_s^*}{\Delta\Delta^*}\cdot\frac{X_{md}^2}{\omega}r_r^3 = -\left|\frac{\bar{V}_s}{\Delta}\right|^2\cdot\frac{X_{md}^2}{\omega}r_r^3.$$

So at synchronous speed torque becomes negative. This shows that there must be a speed at which $T_e = 0$ (in addition to $v = 0$) and this is obtained by equating T_e in Eq. (6.25) to zero. This gives

$$v = \sqrt{1 - \frac{r_r^2}{X_r^2}} \qquad \text{...(6.26)}$$

$$\text{Slip speed} = (1 - v)\,\omega = \omega\left[1 - \sqrt{1 - \left(\frac{r_r}{X_r}\right)^2}\right].$$

∴ Non-zero rotor speed, at which internal torque is zero, is given by

$$\omega_r = v\omega = \omega\sqrt{1 - \left(\frac{r_r}{X_r}\right)^2} = \frac{4\pi f}{P}\sqrt{1 - \left(\frac{r_r}{X_r}\right)^2} \qquad \text{...(6.26a)}$$

The magnitude of currents $\bar{I}_s$, $\bar{I}_d$ and $\bar{I}_q$ can be obtained from matrix (6.20) and then

Stator ohmic losses = $(\bar{I}_s)^2(r_s)$

and rotor ohmic losses = $\sqrt{(\bar{I}_d^2 + \bar{I}_q^2)^2}\,(r_r)$,

In this article, symbols V_s, I_s, r_s, r_r, X_{md}, X_r $(= X_{md} + x_r)$, X_s $(= X_{md} + x_s)$, x_r and x_s have been used in place of the previously used symbols V_1, I_1, r_1, r_2, X_m, X_2 $(= X_m + x_2)$, X_1 $(= X_m + x_1)$, x_2 and x_1 respectively, just for the sake of convenience.

Example 6.5. *A 230 V, 4 pole, 50 Hz, single-phase induction motor has the following constants and losses :*

Stator resistance and leakage reactance : 2.3 Ω, 3.2 Ω. Rotor resistance and leakage reactance : 4.2 Ω, 3.2 Ω (referred to stator).

Magnetizing reactance : 74 Ω.

Core loss = 98 watts. Friction and windage loss = 30 watts.

Determine the stator current, p.f., power output, torque and efficiency at a slip of 0.05, with the auxiliary winding open.

Find also non-zero rotor speed at which torque is zero.

Solution. First of all, the value of the determinant Δ given by Eq. (6.21) is computed.

For this $r_s = 2.3\ \Omega$, $r_r = 4.2\ \Omega$

$X_s = 3.2 + 74 = 77.2\ \Omega$, $X_r = 3.2 + 74 = 77.2\ \Omega$

$X_{md} = 74\ \Omega$

Substitution of these values of the constants in Eq. (6.21) gives

$$\Delta = [\{(4.2)^2 - (77.2)^2 (1.95)(0.05)\}2.3 - 2(4.2)(77.2)^2 + (74)^2 (4.2)] + j[\{(4.2)^2 - (77.2)^2 (1.95)(0.05)\}]77.2 + 2(2.3)(4.2)(77.2) + (1.95)(0.05)(74)^2] = -29{,}649 - j709.$$

Also $(r_r + jX_r)^2 + v^2 X_r^2 = [r_r^2 - (1 - v^2) X_r^2 + j2r_r X_r] = -564.8 + j648$

From matrix (6.20),

$$\bar{I}_s = \frac{\bar{V}_s[(r_r + jX_r)^2 + v^2 X_r^2]}{\Delta} = \frac{230(-564.8 + j648)}{-29649 - j709}$$

$$= \frac{(230)(860)\angle 131.1^\circ}{29650\angle 181.30} = 6.67\angle -50.2^\circ$$

$$\text{pf} = \cos 50.2^\circ = 0.64 \text{ lagging.}$$

Power input = 230 × 6.67 × 0.64 = 982 watts.

Now $X_{md}[jr_r - X_r(1 - v^2)]$

$$= 74[j4.2 - 77.2(1.95)(0.05)] = 74(j4.2 - 7.52)$$

$$\therefore \quad I_d = \frac{230 \times 74(j4.2 - 7.52)}{29{,}650} = \frac{230 \times 74 \times 8.6}{29{,}650} = 4.95 \text{ A}$$

$$I_q = \frac{230(0.95)(74)(4.2)}{29{,}650} = 2.29 \text{ A.}$$

Thus, stator ohmic losses

$= (6.67)^2 \times 2.3 = 102.2$ watts.

Rotor ohmic losses $= 4.2[(4.95)^2 + (2.29)^2] = 125.0$ watts

Total losses = 102.2 + 125.0 + 98 + 30 = 355.2 W.

Power output = 982 – 355.2 = 626.80 watts.

Rotor speed, $\omega_r = (1 - s)\,\omega_s = 0.95 \times 2\pi \times \frac{1500}{60} = 149.2$ rad/sec.

Torque $= \dfrac{\text{Power output}}{\text{Rotor speed in rad/sec.}} = \dfrac{626.8}{149.2} = 4.2$ Nm

Efficiency $= \dfrac{626.8}{982} \times 100 = 63.8\%$

From Eq. (6.26 *a*), non zero rotor speed at which torque is zero is

$$\omega_r = \pi\, 50 \sqrt{1 - \left(\frac{4.2}{77.2}\right)^2} = 156.847 \text{ rad/sec or } 1497.8 \text{ r.p.m.}$$

The results obtained here agree with those obtained in Example 6.1.

6.5 STARTING METHODS OF SINGLE-PHASE INDUCTION MOTORS

As already stated, a single-phase induction motor with main stator winding has no inherent starting torque, since main winding produces only stationery, pulsating air-gap flux wave. For the development of starting torque, rotating air-gap field at starting must be produced. Several methods which have been developed for the starting of single-phase induction motors, may be classified as follows :

(*a*) Split-phase starting. (*b*) Shaded-pole starting.

(*c*) Repulsion-motor starting and (*d*) Reluctance starting.

A single-phase induction motor is commonly known by the method employed for its starting. The selection of a suitable induction motor and choice of its starting method, depend upon the following :

(*i*) torque-speed characteristics of load from standstill to the normal operating speed,

(*ii*) the duty cycle and

(*iii*) the starting and running line-current limitations as imposed by the supply authorities.

In this article, the starting methods and the associated torque-speed characteristics of single-phase induction motors are discussed qualitatively.

6.5.1 Split-phase Starting

Single-phase induction motors employing this method of starting are called *split-phase motors*. All the split-phase motors have two stator windings, a main (or running) winding and an auxiliary (or starting) winding. Both these windings are connected in parallel but their magnetic axes are space displaced by 90° electrical as illustrated in Fig. 6.1.

(a) Resistor-split-phase motors. A resistor-split-phase motor, many a time, is simply called *split-phase motor*. A schematic diagram of this motor, with two stator windings in quadrature is shown in Fig. 6.16(*a*). Fig. 6.16 (*b*) represents the circuit diagram for the two windings of the split-phase motor. Subscripts m and a are used to denote the main and auxiliary winding quantities respectively. CS is the centrifugal switch.

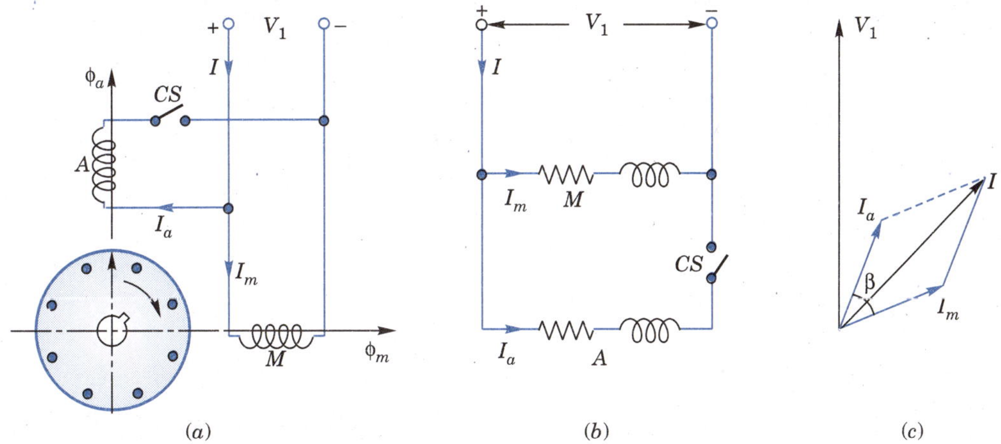

Fig. 6.16: Resistor-split phase motor, (*a*) its schematic diagram (*b*) circuit for the two windings and (*c*) phasor diagram at starting.

If the two winding currents are shifted in time phase, a rotating field is created which is necessary for the production of starting torque. In order to achieve this, main winding M is designed to have lower resistance (thick wire) and higher leakage reactance, whereas the auxiliary winding is made to possess higher resistance (thin wire) and lower leakage reactance. The use of thin wire for auxiliary winding is permissible because this winding is in circuit during starting only and the use of thick wire for main winding is essential because it has to be permanently in the circuit. Since reactance is proportional to the square of turns, the auxiliary winding has less number of turns as compared to those in the main winding. In addition, the leakage reactance of main winding is increased somewhat by placing it in the bottom of slots and that of auxiliary winding is reduced slightly by placing it in the top of the slots. Since main winding has higher leakage reactance as compared to that of the auxiliary winding, the main-winding current I_m lags the auxiliary winding current I_a as shown in phasor diagram of Fig. 6.16 (*c*). This phasor diagram, representing the conditions at starting, reveals that current I_a reaches its maximum first and after some time, determined by the angle β (30° to 40°) in Fig. 6.16 (*c*), the current I_m reaches maximum. As a result of this, stator field reaches it maximum first along the auxiliary-winding axis and after sometime it becomes maximum along the main-winding axis, *i.e.*, field rotates in the clockwise direction in Fig. 6.16 (*a*). This means that the stator field is first directed along the auxiliary winding axis and sometime later, along the main winding axis. In this manner, a rotating field is produced and rotor starts rotating from the auxiliary winding to main winding, provided the poles of the same polarity are created. If the direction of rotation is to be reversed, interchange two terminals either of the auxiliary winding as shown in Fig. 6.17 (*a*), or of the main winding. The two windings are in space quadrature but the two currents are not in time quadrature, therefore, the motor at the time of starting behaves as an unbalanced 2-phase induction motor.

The starting winding is disconnected automatically by means of a centrifugal switch *CS*, at about 70% to 80% of synchronous speed. If the centrifugal switch fails to operate, auxiliary winding will remain in circuit and noisy performance is observed. Since the auxiliary winding is short-time rated, it may become overheated and burn out. A typical torque-speed characteristics for this type of motor is illustrated in Fig. 6.17 (*b*).

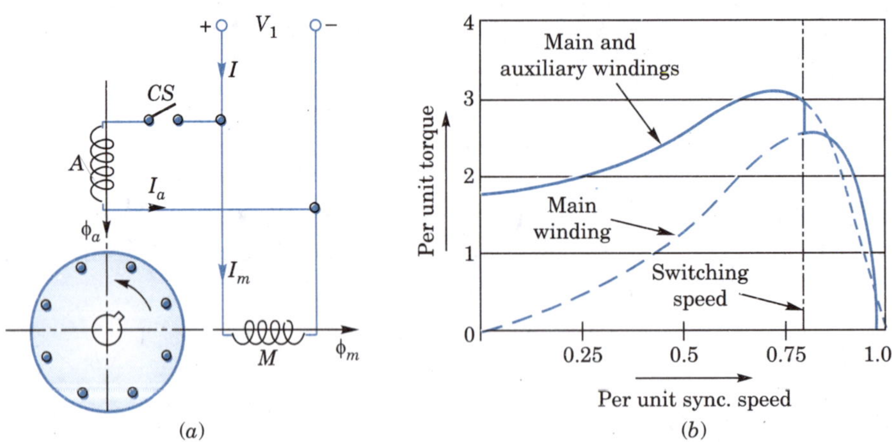

Fig. 6.17: (*a*) Resistor-split-phase motor and (*b*) its typical torque-speed characteristics.

Typical applications of these motors are for the fans, blowers, centrifugal pumps and refrigerators. A refrigerating unit for domestic use is commonly called a refrigerator in which the resistor-split phase motor and the reciprocating compressor are hermetically sealed into one unit. Their economical power ratings are from about 10 to 250 watts.

(b) Capacitor split-phase motors. The schematic diagram for a capacitor split phase motor is shown in Fig. 6.18. (*a*) and (*b*). The main winding is designed by taking into consideration the required performance of this motor. The time phase displacement between auxiliary winding current I_a and the main winding current I_m is obtained by putting a suitable capacitor in series with the auxiliary winding. The centrifugal switch CS disconnects the auxiliary winding at about 70 to 80% of synchronous speed.

An examination of Figs. 6.16 (*c*) and 6.18 (*c*) reveals that the line current with capacitor split phase motor is less than for a resistor split-phase motor. Since the starting torque is proportional to $I_a I_m \sin \beta$, capacitor split-phase motors have high starting torque as compared to resistor split phase motors for the same line current. By the use of a suitable starting capacitor, angle β can be made 90° at standstill and this results in the highest possible starting torque. But size and hence cost of the starting capacitor ; then, would be quite high. In view of this, it is usual to make angle β slightly less than 90° so as to obtain a best compromise between the starting torque, starting current and the cost.

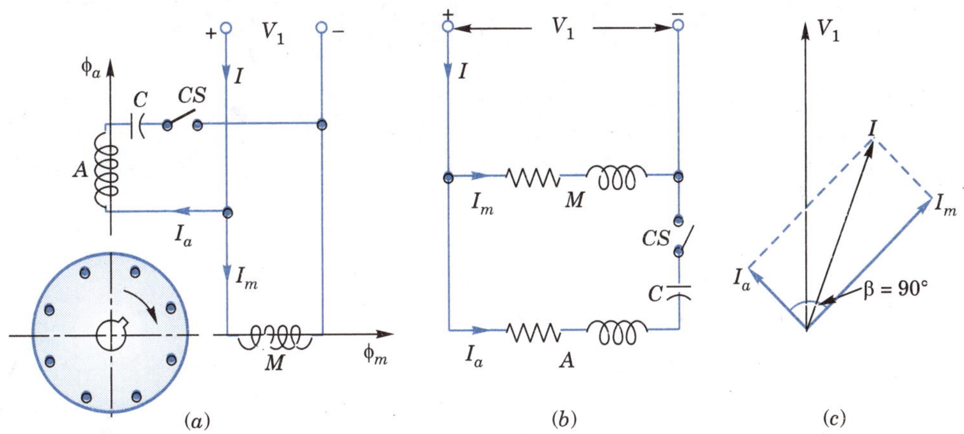

Fig. 6.18: (*a*) and (*b*) Capacitor split-phase motor and (*c*) its phasor diagram.

The auxiliary winding and starting capacitor are in circuit for a short time only, these can, therefore, be designed for a minimum cost. A capacitor split phase motor has high starting torque as is shown in its typical torque speed curve of Fig. 6.19.

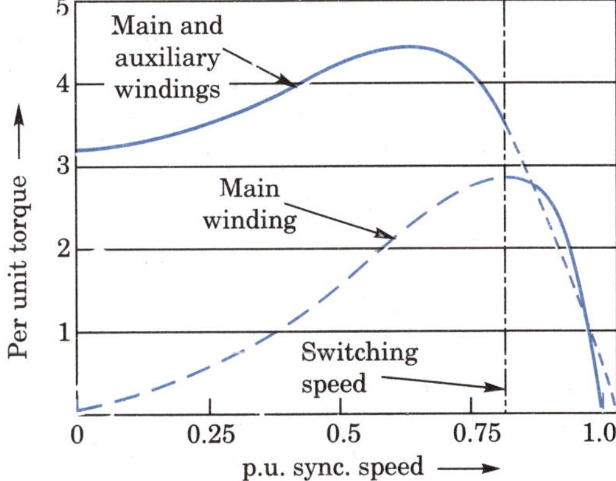

Fig. 6.19: Typical torque-speed characteristic of a capacitor split-phase motor.

These motors have typical power ratings of 100 to 800 watts. The value of starting capacitor varies from 20 to 30 μF for 100 W motors and from 60 to 100 μF for 750 W motors. A.C. electrolytic capacitors are more economical. But the motor should not be started too frequently, otherwise the electrolytic capacitor may become overheated and get damaged. Since the motors posses high-starting torque, these are used for refrigeration and air-conditioning equipment, compressors, reciprocating pumps and other loads requiring high-starting torques.

(c) Capacitor start and run motors. Fig. 6.20 (*a*) illustrates the schematic diagram of this type of motor. A large capacitor C_1 is connected in parallel with capacitor C_2 at the time of starting only. The centrifugal switch disconnects C_1 automatically at about 75% of synchronous speed ; leaving behind C_2 a small capacitance in series with the auxiliary winding. Thus, best starting with a high capacitance, and best running performance with a low capacitance, are obtained with this type of motor. Since C_2 and auxiliary winding are permanently in circuit, C_2 can be so designed as to result in a balanced 2-phase motor under running conditions. In this way, torque pulsations are reduced and a quiet motor is obtained. Power factor and efficiency are also improved.

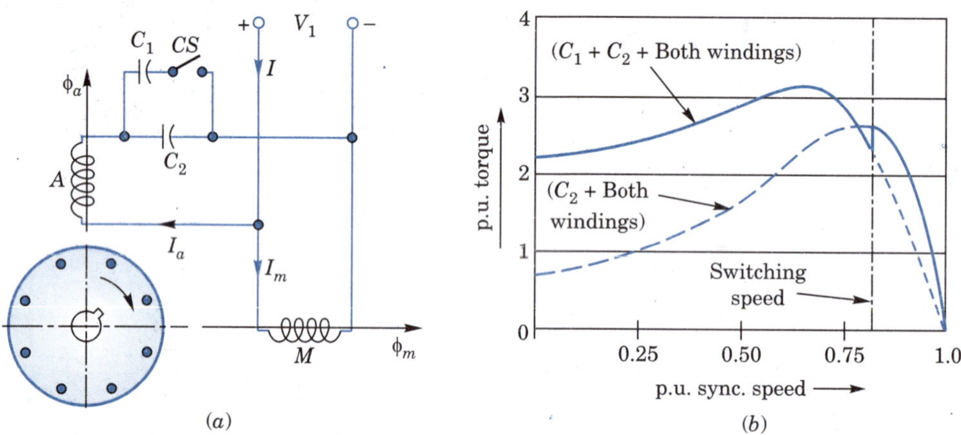

Fig. 6.20: (*a*) Capacitor-start-and-run motor and (*b*) its typical torque-speed characteristic.

These motors have typical power ratings of 100 to 400 watts. The starting capacitor C_1 is of the a.c. electrolytic type, but permanent capacitor C_2 should be a.c. paper, foil and oil type capacitor. These motors are used for office equipment, fans etc., where a quiet operation is important. For optimum operating conditions both at starting and running, C_2 should be less than 1/2 $(C_1 + C_2)$.

(d) Capacitor-run motors. This motor is also called *permanent split capacitor motor.* The same capacitor is kept permanently in series with auxiliary winding both at starting and under running conditions as illustrated in Fig. 6.21 (*a*). There is, therefore, no need of centrifugal switch. At a particular desired load, the capacitor and auxiliary winding can be so designed as to result in 90° time-phase displacement between the two winding currents. In such a case, the motor would operate as a balanced two phase induction motor, backward rotating flux would, therefore, be absent and the motor would have improved efficiency and better operating power factor. Since backward rotating field can be reduced to zero, the pulsating torque due to interaction between forward and backward rotating fields is absent and this results in a quiet motor.

In these motors, the value of permanent capacitor is so chosen as to obtain a compromise between the best starting and running conditions. A typical torque-speed characteristic is shown in Fig. 6.21 (*b*).

These motors are used where quiet operation is essential, as in offices, class rooms, theaters etc. The ceiling fans are invariably of the permanent-split-capacitor type, in which the value of capacitance varies from 2 to 3 μF.

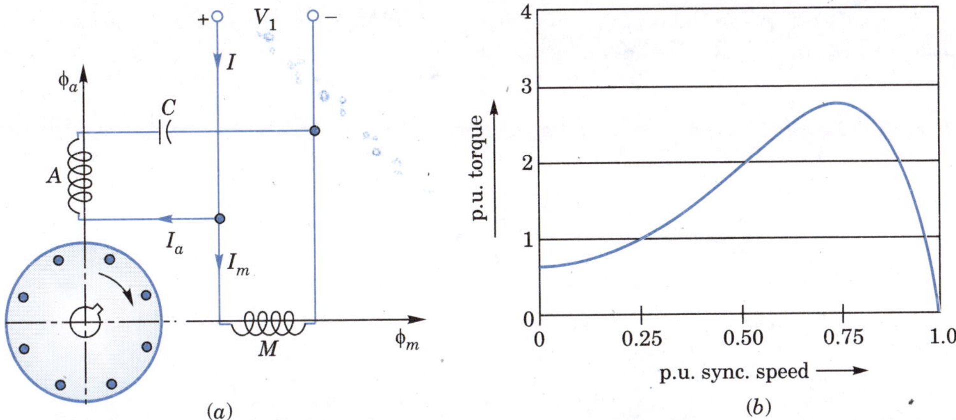

Fig. 6.21: (*a*) Capacitor-run motor and (*b*) its typical torque-speed characteristic.

6.5.2 Shaded-pole-starting

Fig. 6.22 (*a*) gives the schematic diagram of a shaded-pole motor. These motors employ salient pole construction and cage type rotor with skewed slots. A part of each pole carries a short-circuited ring of copper (or aluminium), called a *shading coil*. The main winding flux ϕ_m is alternating in nature, it therefore induces emf E_{sc} in the shading coil by transformer action as shown in Fig. 6.22 (*b*). The magnitude of the ring current I_{sc} and its angle of lag behind E_{sc}, depend upon the impedance of the short-circuited shading coil. The current I_{sc} produces shading coil flux ϕ_{sc} in phase with it. Now the shaded pole carries both ϕ_m and ϕ_{sc}, so that their phasor sum gives the total flux ϕ_{sp} in the shaded pole. Since main-pole flux ϕ_m and shaded-pole flux ϕ_{sp} are having time phase displacement as shown in Fig. 6.22 (*b*), a rotating field is produced giving rise to a starting torque.

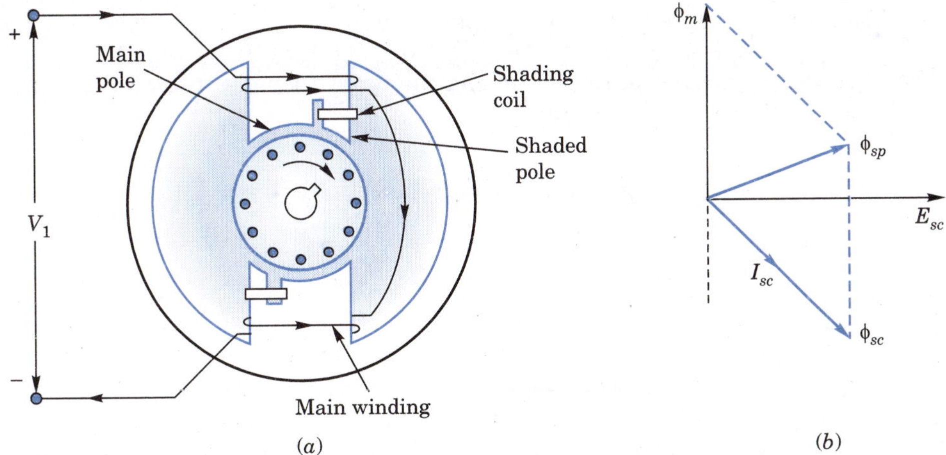

Fig. 6.22: (*a*) Shaded-pole motor (*b*) its phasor diagram for fluxes ϕ_m—main winding flux ; ϕ_{sc}—shading coil flux ; ϕ_{sp}—shaded-pole flux.

The main pole flux leads the shaded pole flux. In view of this, ϕ_m reaches maximum first and a little time latter determined by the time angle between ϕ_m and ϕ_{sp}, the shaded-pole flux ϕ_{sp} also reaches maximum. In other words, the rotating flux always rotates from unshaded pole to shaded pole. Therefore, the rotor direction of rotation is from the unshaded to shaded pole as shown in Fig. 6.22 (*a*). A typical torque-speed characteristic for this type of motor is illustrated in Fig. 6.23 (*a*).

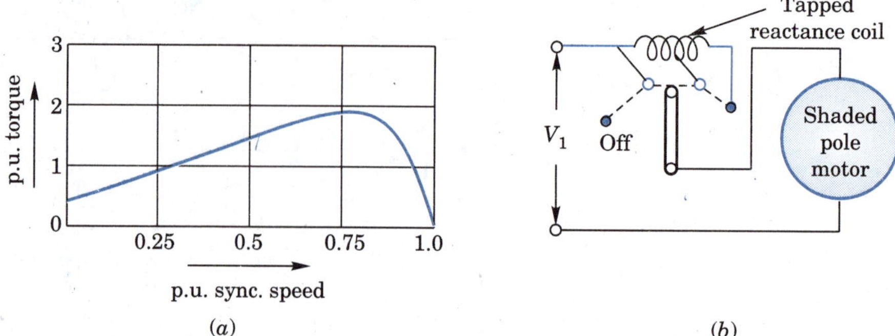

Fig. 6.23: (*a*) Typical torque-speed characteristic of a shaded pole motor. (b) Speed control of shaded-pole motor by tapped reactance coil.

The efficiency of this type of motor is low (20% to 50%). In spite of this fact, shaded-pole motors are widely used in very small sizes, *e.g.* in small domestic fans, record-player motors, tape-recorders, movie-projectors, blowers, heaters etc. Shaded-pole motors possess very simple construction, these are, therefore, very cheap and are built up to power ratings of about 50 watts. Even if this motor gets stalled, its locked rotor current is only slightly more than its full-load current.

The speed of a shaded-pole motor can be controlled by three methods, but the one that is commercially employed is the tapped reactance-coil method illustrated in Fig. 6.23 (*b*) which is self explanatory.

6.5.3 Repulsion-motor-starting

The rotor carries a d.c. armature winding. The brushes are short circuited and the brush axis is displaced from the stator field axis by a suitable angle, Fig. 6.24 (*a*). This motor possesses series characteristics and, therefore, at the time of switching in, a high-starting torque is developed, Fig. 6.24 (*b*). In view of this, repulsion-motor starting is employed for large inertia or frictional, loads, requiring high-starting torques.

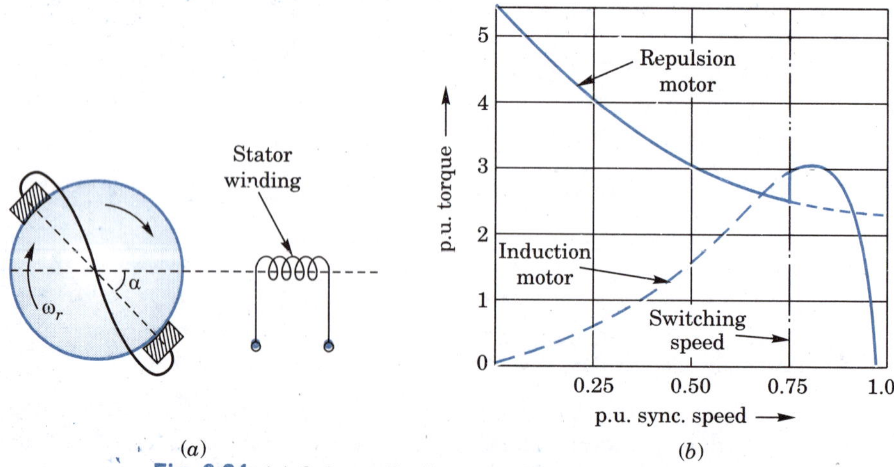

Fig. 6.24: (*a*) Schematic diagram of repulsion motor and (*b*) a typical torque-speed characteristics for repulsion-induction motor.

When motor speed is about 75% of synchronous speed, a centrifugal mechanism short circuits all the commutator segments. After this, the armature winding behaves like a squirrel cage winding and the motor becomes a single-phase induction motor. In some cases, the brushes are lifted as soon as the commutator bars are short circuited. This reduces wear and noise of the motor.

Direction of rotation can be reversed by shifting the brushes to the other side of the stator field axis. This method of starting is now rarely used, because capacitor-start induction motor has taken over the repulsion-induction motor. Therefore, most of the induction motor manufacturers have stopped making repulsion-start induction motors.

6.5.4 Reluctance-starting

Another motor, in which the non-uniform air gap is used to produce a rotating magnetic field in a manner similar to that in a shaped-pole motor, is called *reluctance-start motor*. Fig. 6.25 (*a*) illustrates the typical constructional details of a 2-pole reluctance start induction motor. The air gap under the salient poles is non-uniform.

If an air-cored coil is excited by an alternating current, then the flux is in phase with the exciting current. In case an iron-cored coil is excited by a.c., then flux lags behind the exciting current in time. The conditions in the wide and narrow air gaps are somewhat similar to those in air-cored and iron-cored coils respectively. Keeping these two elementary facts in mind, it may be concluded that flux ϕ_1 in the wide air gap is in phase with the exciting current I_1 and the flux ϕ_2 in the narrow air gap lags the existing current I_1 by some angle β as shown in Fig. 6.25 (*b*). This means that ϕ_1 reaches maximum first and some times later, determined by angle β, ϕ_2 also reaches maximum. Thus, a rotating magnetic field from wide to narrow air gap is produced. Consequently, the rotor rotates always from wide to narrow air gap as shown.

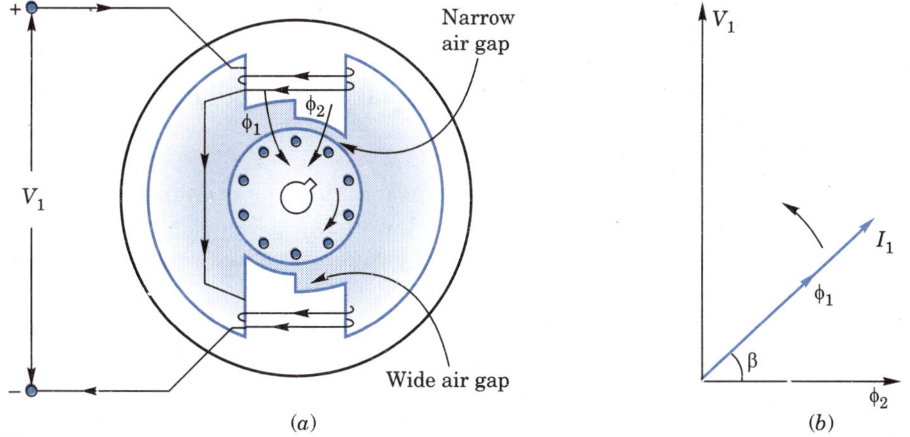

Fig. 6.25: (*a*) Schematic diagram of a 2-pole reluctance-start induction motor (*b*) its phasor diagram.

This motor should not be confused with a reluctance motor, in which the reluctance as seen by the working flux must change with the rotor movement. The motor described here is a reluctance start induction motor, because rotor receives its energy from stator by induction. Its operating characteristics are similar to those of a shaded-pole motor.

For small electric drives, shaded-pole motors are usually preferred however, reluctance-start induction motors may be used where the starting torque requirements are low. The methods adopted for speed control of shaded-pole motor are also applicable to this motor.

6.6 MAXIMUM STARTING TORQUE CONDITIONS IN SINGLE PHASE INDUCTION MOTORS

In split-phase motors, the starting torque is produced by the combined action of both the main and auxiliary windings ; but the torque at normal operating speed is produced by the main winding alone. In view of this, the main winding is designed for optimum running characteristics. The object of this article is to find the value of resistance in resistor-split-phase motors or the capacitance in case of capacitor-split phase motors, so that maximum starting torque is produced. Since the main-winding design is fixed for obtaining optimum running performance, its current I_m is constant and lags V_1 by a constant angle θ_m at the time of starting.

6.6.1 Resistor Split-phase Motors

The schematic diagram for the resistor split-phase motors is as shown in Fig. 6.26 (*a*). Main-winding current I_m lags supply voltage V_1 by an angle θ_m, where

$$\theta_m = \tan^{-1} \frac{X_m}{r_m}$$

Here r_m and X_m are the main winding resistance and reactance respectively.

If auxiliary winding resistance r_a is zero, then

$$I_a = \frac{V_1}{X_a} = oa$$

and it lags V_1 by 90° as shown in Fig. 6.26. (*b*). Here X_a is the auxiliary winding reactance. When r_a is equal to infinity, I_a is zero and this is indicated by point *o* itself. When both r_a and X_a are present, current I_a lags V_1 by some angle less than 90°. Thus, as r_a is increased from zero to infinity, tip of phasor I_a follows a semi-circular current locus as shown in Fig. 6.26 (*b*). The centre of this locus is *f*, where $of = \frac{V_1}{2X_a}$. If phasor I_m, lagging V_1 by θ_m, is extended, it meets the semi-circle at the point *c*.

The starting torque in a single-phase induction motor is proportional to

$$I_m I_a \sin \beta = I_m \times (\text{Perpendicular component of } I_a).$$

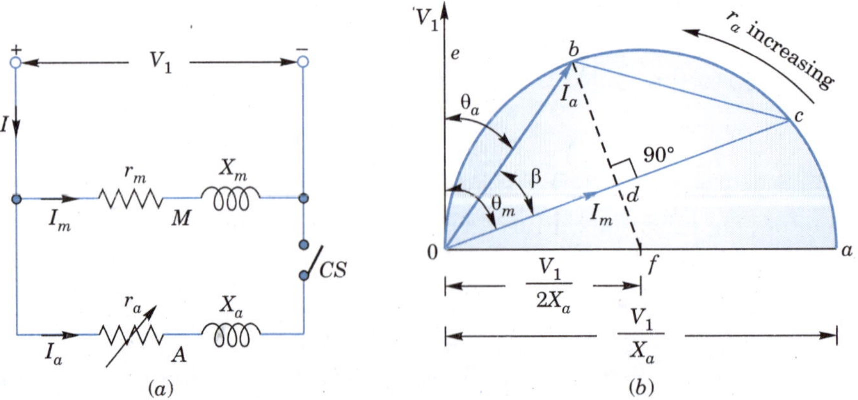

Fig. 6.26: (*a*) Resistor slip-phase motor and (*b*) its phasor diagram under maximum starting-torque conditions.

Fig. 6.26 (*b*) reveals that $I_a \sin \beta$ would have maximum value only when $I_a \sin \beta = bd$. This gives $ob = I_a$. Since bd is maximum, $ob = bc$ and $od = dc$. Note that bd, when extended, must pass through f, the centre of the semi-circle. In other words, when a perpendicular is drawn from centre f of the semi-circular locus, on to the extended phasor I_m, then point b is obtained. The line joining b and o, then gives the required starting current I_a in the auxiliary winding so that maximum starting torque is obtained.

Now V_1 or oe is the tangent to the circle at o and $ob = cb$. As per the relations of a circle, we have

$$\angle bco = \angle boe = \theta_a \qquad \text{But} \quad \angle bco = \angle bod = \beta = \theta_a$$

$$\therefore \qquad \theta_m = \angle doe = \theta_a + \beta = 2\theta_a \qquad \text{or} \quad \theta_a = \frac{1}{2}\theta_m.$$

Thus, under maximum starting torque conditions, $\theta_a = \dfrac{1}{2}\theta_m$.

Taking tangent of both the sides, $\tan \theta_a = \tan \dfrac{\theta_m}{2} = \dfrac{\sin \dfrac{\theta_m}{2}}{\cos \dfrac{\theta_m}{2}} = \dfrac{2 \sin \dfrac{\theta_m}{2} \cos \dfrac{\theta_m}{2}}{2 \cos^2 \dfrac{\theta_m}{2}}$

$$= \frac{\sin \theta_m}{\left(\sin^2 \dfrac{\theta_m}{2} + \cos^2 \dfrac{\theta_m}{2}\right) + \left(\cos^2 \dfrac{\theta_m}{2} - \sin^2 \dfrac{\theta_m}{2}\right)} = \frac{\sin \theta_m}{1 + \cos \theta_m} \qquad \text{...(6.27)}$$

Now $\qquad \tan \theta_a = \dfrac{X_a}{r_a}$, $\sin \theta_m = \dfrac{X_m}{Z_m}$ and $\cos \theta_m = \dfrac{r_m}{Z_m}$.

Here $r_a + jX_a = Z_a$ is the auxiliary winding impedance at standstill and $r_m + jX_m = Z_m$ is the main winding impedance at standstill, across their respective terminals.

Substitution of the values of $\tan \theta_a$, $\sin \theta_m$ and $\cos \theta_m$ in Eq. (6.27) gives

$$\frac{X_a}{r_a} = \frac{X_m / Z_m}{1 + \dfrac{r_m}{Z_m}} = \frac{X_m}{r_m + Z_m}$$

Therefore, the resistance for obtaining the maximum starting torque is

$$r_a = \left(\frac{X_a}{X_m}\right)(r_m + Z_m) \qquad \text{...(6.28)}$$

Since X_a and X_m are proportional to the square of their respective number of effective turns N_a and N_m, Eq. (6.28) can be rewritten as

$$r_a = \left(\frac{N_a}{N_m}\right)^2 (r_m + Z_m) \qquad \text{...(6.29)}$$

The value of r_a as given by Eq. (6.29) is the total resistance required in the auxiliary winding for obtaining maximum torque at starting. Therefore, the external resistance to be inserted in series with auxiliary winding is equal to r_a as given by Eq. (6.29) minus the auxiliary winding resistance.

6.6.2 Capacitor Split-Phase Motors

Schematic diagram for capacitor split-phase motors is illustrated in Fig. 6.27 (*a*). As before, main-winding current I_m is constant and lags V_1 by a constant angle θ_m. The starting-capacitor C, in series with the auxiliary winding, is assumed lossless. Now when $C = 0$,

$x_c\left(=\dfrac{1}{2\pi fC}\right)=\infty$ and, therefore, I_a is zero giving the operating point o in Fig. 6.27 (b). When $C=\infty$, $x_c=0$ and $I_a=V_1/Z_a$ and when capacitive reactance x_c = inductive reactance X_a, I_a is given by $V_1/r_a = oa$. When C is increased from zero, x_c starts becoming less than infinity and as x_c is more than X_a, I_a leads V_1. The locus of the tip of phasor I_a is therefore, a circle as shown in Fig. 6.27 (b). For some value of C, I_a leads V_1 by some angle θ_a. The extension of phasor I_m, lagging V_1 by ϕ_m, meets the circle at point c.

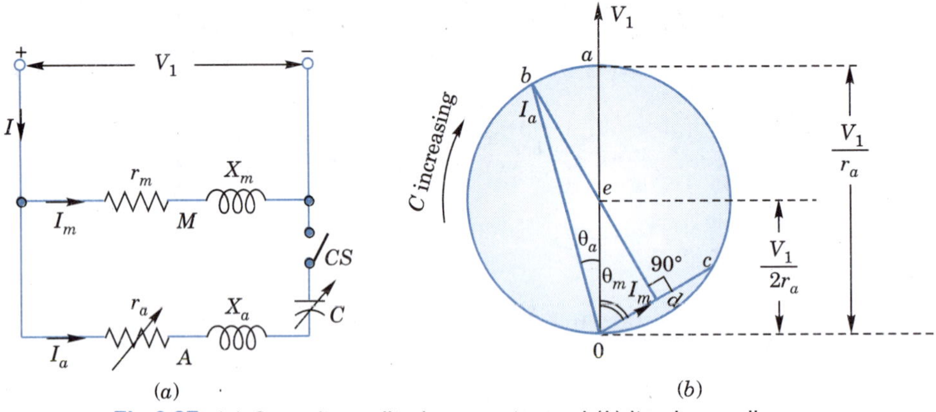

Fig.6.27: (a) Capacitor split-phase motor and (b) its phasor diagram under maximum starting-torque conditions.

As stated before, the starting torque is maximum when component of I_a[$= I_a \sin(\theta_a + \theta_m)$] perpendicular to phasor I_m is maximum. Now draw bd normal to oc. The perpendicular bd on to the phasor I_m must pass through e, the centre of the current locus. In other words when a perpendicular is drawn from centre e of the circular locus, on the extended phasor I_m, the point b is obtained. The line joining b with o, then gives the required starting current I_a in the auxiliary winding so that maximum starting torque is obtained. Since $oe = eb$ = radius of the circle, $\angle eob = \angle ebo = \theta_a$.

In the right angled triangle odb, $\angle dob + \angle obd = 90°$

or $$(\theta_a+\theta_m)+\theta_a = 90° \quad \text{or} \quad \theta_a = \frac{90-\theta_m}{2}$$

Now $$\tan\theta_a = \frac{\sin\theta_a}{\cos\theta_a}$$

Use of the trigonometric relations

$$\sin\theta_a = \sqrt{\frac{1-\cos 2\theta_a}{2}} \quad \text{and} \quad \cos\theta_a = \sqrt{\frac{1+\cos 2\theta_a}{2}}$$

gives $$\tan\theta_a = \left(\frac{1-\cos 2\theta_a}{1+\cos 2\theta_a}\right)^{\frac{1}{2}}$$

Substitution of the value of $\theta_a = \dfrac{90-\theta_m}{2}$ in the above equation gives

$$\tan\theta_a = \left[\frac{1-\cos(90-\theta_m)}{1+\cos(90-\theta_m)}\right]^{\frac{1}{2}} = \left[\frac{1-\sin\theta_m}{1+\sin\theta_m}\right]^{\frac{1}{2}} \quad ...(6.30)$$

Since I_a has been taken as leading V_1.

$$\tan \theta_a = \frac{x_c - X_a}{r_a} \quad \text{Also} \quad \sin \theta_m = \frac{X_m}{Z_m}$$

Substitution of $\tan \theta_a$ and $\sin \theta_m$ in Eq. (6.30) gives,

$$\frac{x_c - X_a}{r_a} = \left[\frac{Z_m - X_m}{Z_m + X_m}\right]^{\frac{1}{2}} \qquad \text{...(6.31)}$$

Now, $$Z_m^2 = r_m^2 + X_m^2$$

or, $$Z_m^2 - X_m^2 = r_m^2 \quad \text{or} \quad Z_m - X_m = \frac{r_m^2}{Z_m + X_m}$$

Substitution of the value of $(Z_m - X_m)$ in Eq. (6 31) gives

$$\frac{x_c - X_a}{r_a} = \left[\frac{r_m^2}{(Z_m + X_m)^2}\right]^{\frac{1}{2}} = \frac{r_m}{Z_m + X_m}$$

$$\therefore \quad x_c = X_a + \frac{r_a r_m}{Z_m + X_m} \qquad \text{...(6.32)}$$

The value of capacitance to be inserted in series with the auxiliary winding for obtaining maximum torque at starting is given by, $C = 1/\omega x_c$

where ω is the angular frequency of supply voltage.

Example 6.6. *The following data pertains to a 230 V, 50 Hz, capacitor-start single-phase induction motor at standstill.*

Main-winding excited alone : 100 V, 2 A, 40 W

Auxiliary-winding excited alone : 80 V, 1 A, 50 W.

Determine the value of capacitance for obtaining the maximum starting torque.

Solution. For main winding,

$$Z_m = \frac{100}{2} = 50\ \Omega, \quad r_m = \frac{40}{(2)^2} = 10\ \Omega$$

$$\therefore \quad X_m = \sqrt{(50)^2 - (10)^2} = 48.99\ \Omega$$

For auxiliary winding,

$$Z_a = \frac{80}{1} = 80\ \Omega, \quad r_a = \frac{50}{1^2} = 50\ \Omega$$

$$\therefore \quad X_a = \sqrt{(80)^2 - (50)^2} = 62.45\ \Omega.$$

From Eq. (6.32), the value of x_c for obtaining the maximum starting torque is

$$x_c = 62.45 + \frac{50 \times 10}{50 + 48.99} = 67.50\ \Omega$$

$\therefore$ Capacitance C for maximum starting torque is

$$C = \frac{10^6}{2\pi \times 50 \times 67.50} = 47.16\ \mu\text{F}.$$

Example 6.7. (*a*) *Derive an expression for the starting-capacitor reactance* x_c, *so that the auxiliary-winding current leads the main winding current by 90° at the time of start.*

(*b*) *For Example 6.6, compute the value of starting capacitance so that main and auxiliary winding currents are in quadrature at the time of start.*

(*c*) *Repeat part (b) of this example by using basic circuit theory.*

Solution. (*a*) In Fig. 6.18 (*c*), auxiliary winding current I_a is shown leading I_m by 90°. If I_a leads V_1 by θ_a and I_m lags V_1 by θ_m, then, $\theta_m + \theta_a = 90°$

or $$\theta_a = 90 - \theta_m \quad \text{or} \quad \tan\theta_a = \tan(90 - \theta_m) = \cot\theta_m.$$

Since I_a leads V_1 by θ_a,

$$\tan\theta_a = \frac{x_c - X_a}{r_a} \quad \text{and} \quad \tan\theta_m = \frac{X_m}{r_m}$$

$$\therefore \quad \frac{x_c - X_a}{r_a} = \frac{r_m}{X_m} \quad \text{or} \quad x_c = X_a + \frac{r_a r_m}{X_m} \qquad ...(6.33)$$

(*b*) From Example 6.6,

$$X_a = 62.45\ \Omega,\ r_a = 50\ \Omega$$

$$r_m = 10\ \Omega \text{ and } X_m = 48.99\ \Omega$$

From Eq. (6.33), $$x_c = 62.45 + \frac{50 \times 10}{48.99} = 72.66\ \Omega$$

Therefore, the starting capacitance C that would make I_a and I_m in time quadrature at starting, is given by

$$C = \frac{10^6}{2\pi \times 50 \times 72.66} = 43.81\ \mu\text{F}.$$

(*c*) The applied voltage is taken as reference phasor.

Phasor diagram for a capacitor-start single-phase induction motor, at the time of start, is shown in Fig. 6.18(*c*). This fig. reveals that main winding current I_m lags the applied voltage V_1 while the auxiliary-winding current leads V_1.

Phase angle of lag, θ_m, of the main-winding current is given by

$$\theta_m = \tan^{-1}\frac{X_m}{r_m} = \tan^{-1}\frac{48.99}{10} = 78.463°$$

Phase angle of lead, θ_a, of the auxiliary-winding current, with capacitor in series, is given by

$$\theta_a = \tan^{-1}\left(\frac{x_c - X_a}{r_a}\right) = \tan^{-1}\left(\frac{x_c - 62.45}{50}\right)$$

The angle between I_a and I_m has to be 90°.

$$\therefore \quad \theta_a + \theta_m = 90°$$

$$\tan^{-1}\left(\frac{x_c - 62.45}{50}\right) + 78.463° = 90°$$

or $$\frac{x_c - 62.45}{50} = \tan(11.537) = 0.204125$$

$$\therefore \quad x_c = \frac{1}{\omega C} = 0.204125 \times 50 + 62.45 = 72.6563$$

or $$C = \frac{10^6}{2\pi \times 50 \times 72.6563} = 43.81\ \mu\text{F}$$

Example 6.8. *A 230 V, 50 Hz, 1-phase induction motor has the following impedances for the main and auxiliary windings :*

Main winding, $Z_m = 28 \angle 70^\circ \ \Omega$

Auxiliary winding, $Z_a = 42 \angle 45^\circ \ \Omega$

(a) Compute the input current at starting.

(b) Now a capacitor is connected in series with the auxiliary winding so that maximum starting torque is obtained. Find the value of this capacitance.

Compare also the input starting current, input auxiliary winding current and the starting torque with and without the capacitor in auxiliary winding circuit.

Solution. (*a*) Main winding current,

$$I_m = \frac{230}{28 \angle 70^\circ} = 8.214 \angle -70^\circ = 2.809 - j7.719 \text{ A}$$

Auxiliary winding current,

$$I_a = \frac{230}{42 \angle 45^\circ} = 5.476 \angle -45^\circ = 3.872 - j3.872 \text{ A}$$

Input line current at starting,

$$I = I_m + I_a = 6.681 - j11.591 = 13.378 \angle -60.04^\circ \text{ A.}$$

(*b*) $$Z_m = 28 \angle 70^\circ = 9.576 + j26.311 \ \Omega$$

$$Z_a = 42 \angle 45^\circ = 29.698 + j29.698 \ \Omega$$

From Eq. (6.32),

$$x_c = 29.698 + \frac{9.576 \times 29.698}{28 + 26.311} = 34.934 \ \Omega$$

$$\therefore \quad C = \frac{10^6}{2\pi (50) (34.934)} = 91.12 \ \mu\text{F}$$

Now $Z_a + x_c = 29.698 - j5.236 = 30.156 \angle -10^\circ$

With C in series with auxilry winding,

$$I_a = \frac{V_1}{Z_a + x_c} = \frac{230}{30.156 \angle -10^\circ} = 7.627 \angle 10^\circ \text{ A}$$

$$= 7.511 + j1.324 \text{ A}$$

$\therefore$ Input starting current $= 7.511 + j\, 1.324 + 2.809 - j\, 7.719$

or $$I = 10.320 - j6.395 = 12.141 \angle -31.785^\circ \text{ A}$$

Starting torque without capacitor,

$$T_{e1} = KI_a I_m \sin (I_a, I_m) = K\, 5.476 \times 8.214 \sin 25^\circ$$

Starting torque with capacitor,

$$T_{e2} = K\, 7.627 \times 8.214 \sin 80^\circ$$

$$\therefore \quad \frac{T_{e2}}{T_{e1}} = \frac{7.627 \sin 80^\circ}{5.476 \sin 25^\circ} = 3.2456$$

$$\frac{\text{Input starting current with } C}{\text{Input starting current without } C} = \frac{12.141}{13.378} = 0.9075$$

$$\frac{\text{Auxiliary winding current with } C}{\text{Auxiliary winding current without } C} = \frac{7.627}{5.476} = 1.393$$

This example demonstrates that though auxiliary winding current has increased, the input line current at starting has gone down. Also, there is a substantial increase in the starting torque.

6.7 SINGLE-PHASE SYNCHRONOUS MOTORS

For very low-power drives requiring constant speed operation, single-phase synchronous motors are widely used. These motors are named depending upon their rotor construction or on their principle of operation. The object of this article is to describe the reluctance motors, sub-synchronous motors and hysteresis motors operating from single-phase supply. It should be noted that all single phase synchronous motors are singly-excited machines.

6.7.1 Single-Phase Reluctance Motors

The stator of a single-phase reluctance motor is similar to the stator of any one of the single-phase induction motors described in Art. 6.5. Any type of rotor construction may be used, but the essential condition is that the air-gap reluctance should vary as the rotor position is changed with respect to the stator field axis. For single-phase reluctance motors, salient poles on the rotor are created by removing some of the rotor teeth ; one such lamination with 4 poles is illustrated in Fig. 6.28 (*a*). The rotor construction is completed just like squirrel-cage rotor. The bare bars are present even in the space from where the teeth are removed as shown in Fig. 6.28 (*b*). The two end-rings short-circuit these bars as in a cage rotor.

When the stator is energised with single-phase supply, the motor starts as a single-phase induction motor. At comparatively light loads, the rotor speeds up to near about synchronous speed. The tendency of the rotor to align itself in the minimum reluctance position of the synchronously rotating forward flux wave, gives rise to reluctance torque. At a small slip, this reluctance torque consists of a constant torque component and a superimposed alternating torque component as shown in Fig. 6.28 (*c*). During the positive half cycle of this alternating torque component, the rotor is accelerated ; but during the negative half cycle, the rotor gets decelerated. Under favourable conditions, the rotor pulls into synchronism during the positive half cycle of this torque and continues running at synchronous speed. The effect of backward rotating field is to decrease the forward-field torque.

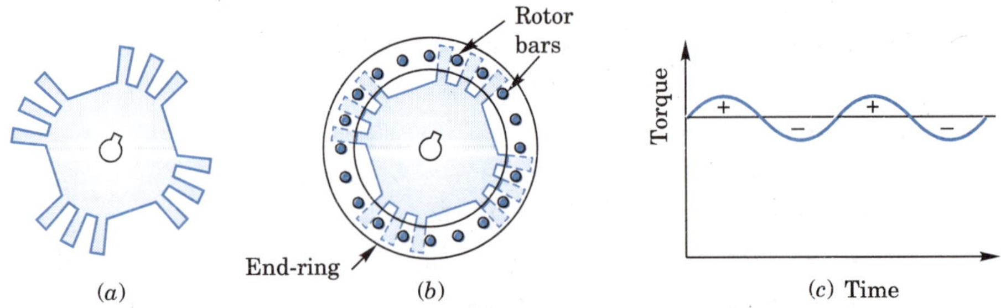

Fig. 6.28: Single-phase reluctance motor (*a*) 4-pole rotor laminations (*b*) 4-pole rotor laminations with bars and end rings (*c*) reluctance torque pulsations at small slip.

A typical torque-speed characteristic of a single phase reluctance motor is shown in Fig. 6.28 (*d*). On account of salient-pole rotor, these motors exhibit 'cogging' at the time of starting as induction motors. As a result, the starting torque varies considerably with the rotor position as shown in Fig. 6.28 (*d*). The cogging is minimised by skewing the rotor bars and by having the rotor slots not exact multiple of the number of poles.

For reliable operation, power rating of reluctance motors is approximately one-third to one-half of the power rating as single-phase induction motors with cylindrical rotor structure. This is the primary reason for high starting torque in Fig. 6.28 (*d*).

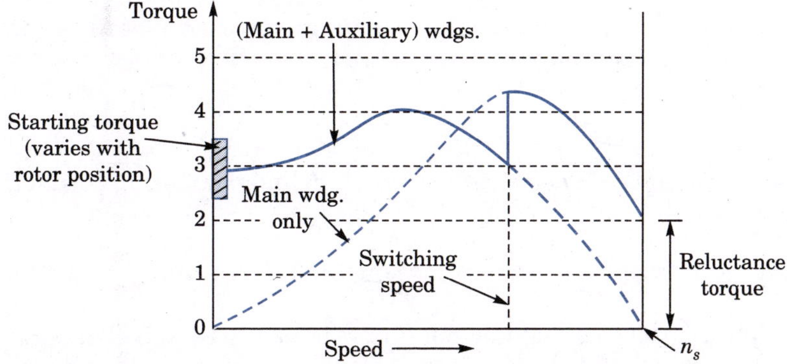

Fig. 6.28: (*d*) Torque-speed characteristics of a 1-phase reluctance motor.

These motors operate at poor pf and lower efficiency as compared to equivalent single-phase induction motors. In spite of all this, single phase reluctance motors are used for constant speed drives like recording instruments, phonograph turntables, control equipment and other timing devices.

6.7.2 Sub-synchronous Motors

A schematic diagram of a sub-synchronous motor is shown in Fig. 6.29. It consists of two-pole stator and the rotor has large even-number of poles. In Fig. 6.29, rotor is shown to have 8 poles.

This motor possesses no inherent starting torque, it is, therefore, brought up to synchronous speed by spinning it with hand. When the rotor is running at synchronous speed ; then, as the stator-field is increasing, it attracts two diametrically opposite rotor poles. On account of inertia, the rotor poles go beyond the stator poles. In the mean time the stator flux passes through zero, reverses and as it is increasing in the reversed direction it attracts next pair of diametrically opposite rotor poles. In this manner stator and rotor poles lock in and synchronous speed operation is maintained. Since a pair of rotor poles passes the two stator poles in every half cycle, rotor speed is determined by the number of rotor poles and is given by the relation.

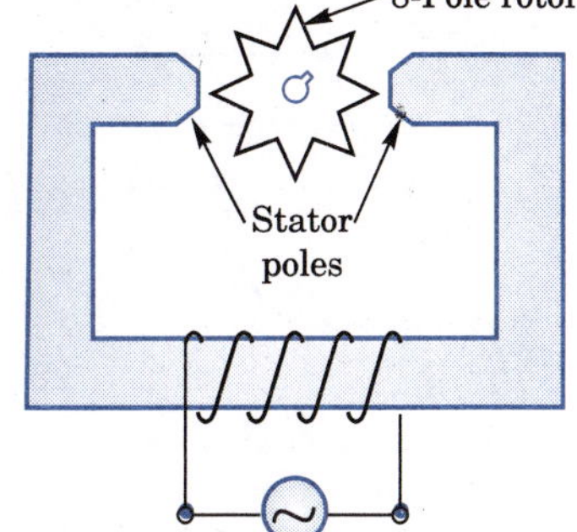

Fig. 6.29: Schematic diagram of a sub-synchronous motor.

$$\text{Rotor speed} = \frac{120\,(\text{Supply frequency})}{\text{Rotor poles}}\ \text{rpm}$$

Since the rotor speed is much less than that corresponding to synchronous speed determined by the stator poles, this motor has come to be called a sub-synchronous motor. The eight-pole rotor shown in Fig. 6.29 would run at 750 rpm for a 50 Hz supply. If the rotor speed is brought by hand to half the synchronous speed, then rotor and stator poles may lock-in at this reduced speed. This occurrence at half the synchronous speed should, however, be avoided. Note that here the synchronous speed refers to that speed which is determined by the stator poles and supply frequency.

The rotor of a sub-synchronous motor is provided with considerable flywheel effect in order to prevent hunting and to have a smoother rotation.

6.7.3 Hysteresis Motors

These motors may operate from single-phase or three phase source, but the essential requirement is that a rotating magnetic field should be produced by the stator. For a single phase hysteresis motor, the stator winding is of the permanent split-capacitor type or of the shaded-pole type for very small sizes. For the permanent split-capacitor type, the value of capacitor is so chosen as to result in almost a balanced 2-phase operation at the synchronous speed.

Hysteresis-motor rotor consists of a smooth cylinder made up of magnetically hard chrome, or cobalt, steel having very large hysteresis loop as illustrated in Fig. 6.30 (*a*). The smooth cylinder is mounted on a non-magnetic spider such as aluminium to make the rotor light, Fig. 6.31 (*a*). The periphery of the rotor is without any slots and therefore without any winding.

The principle of hysteresis motor operation is based on the B-H loop of a magnetic material. It may be recalled that the B-H loop is traversed always in the direction of arrows as indicated in Fig. 6.30 (*a*). Since time is implied as the loops are traversed, induced flux density B lags the inducing magnetizing force H, Fig. 6.30 (*b*). In other words, when H is zero, B is finite but negative at instant 1. Further, when H is finite and positive, B is zero at instant 2 and so on, Fig. 6.30 (*b*). This shows that induced flux density B lags the inducing magnetizing force H by an angle δ. Therefore, if the stator winding produces rotating mmf wave F_s, then the induced flux density B_r in the rotor iron, must lag behind the inducing mmf wave F_s by an angle δ.

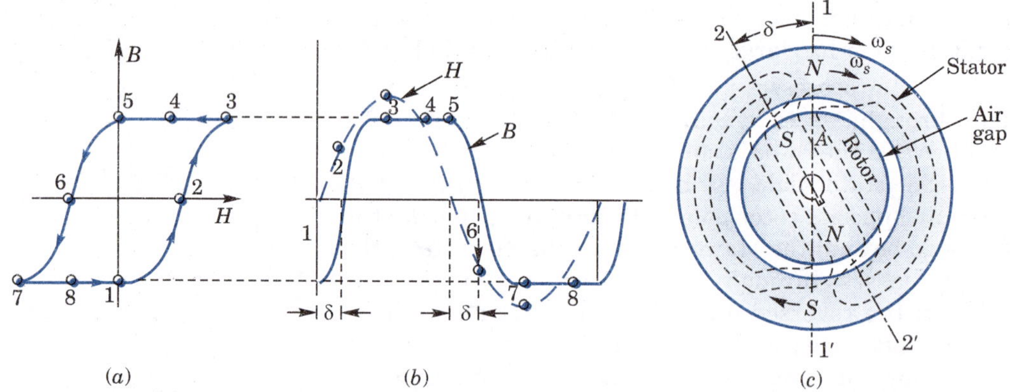

Fig. 6.30: Hysteresis motor (*a*) its B-H loop (*b*) B lags H by hysteretic angle δ (*c*) the distribution of magnetic field in the stator, air gap and rotor of a 2-pole motor.

Suppose the inducing mmf wave F_s produced by 2-pole stator, is revolving at a synchronous speed of ω_s radians per second. In Fig. 6.30 (*c*) the axis of the inducing mmf wave F_s is taken as vertical along 11′. This mmf wave F_s causes the appearance of N, S poles on the stator as shown. Now S-pole on the rotor should have been induced at the point A, just near the inducing stator N-pole, had there been no hysteresis. But because of hysteresis, the induced S-pole on the rotor lags behind the position A by hysteretic angle δ. Same is true for rotor induced N-pole. Note that angle δ depends upon the nature of hysteresis loop and not on the rotor speed or the rate at which it is traversed. In view of this, the torque developed by a hysteresis motor, proportional to the product of fundamental components of stator mmf, rotor flux and sine of the torque angle δ, is constant from standstill up to synchronous speed. Strictly speaking, the total starting torque is due to the combined action of hysteresis torque as explained above and the induction motor torque produced by eddy currents in the rotor iron. Though magnetic material of the smooth cylinder is made from high resistivity material to reduce the eddy-current loss, even then some eddy current torque is produced during the starting process. If the developed torque (hysteresis torque + eddy-current torque) is more than the load torque, the rotor gets accelerated from standstill. When the rotor speed is nearing synchronous speed, the rotor induced poles pull into step with the stator poles and synchronous speed operation of the hysteresis motor is obtained. At synchronous speed, the relative speed between stator field and rotor is zero, therefore no eddy currents are induced in the rotor and thus there is no eddy-current torque at synchronous speed. This shows that at synchronous speed, the motor operation is exclusively by hysteresis torque.

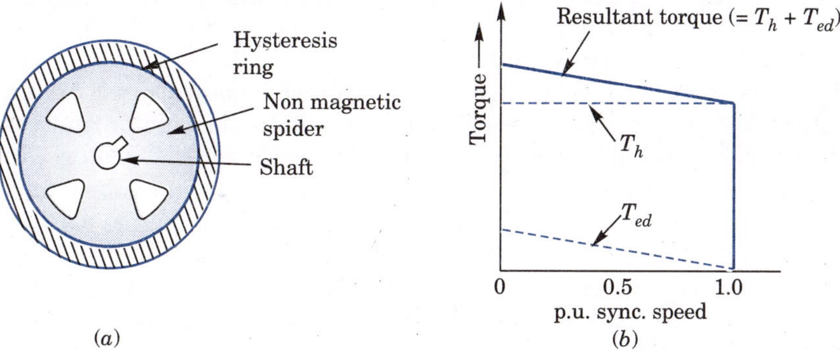

Fig. 6.31: (*a*) Rotor of hysteresis motor (*b*) Torque-speed characteristics of hysteresis motor.

At standstill, the rotor iron undergoes hosteresis loop at line frequency, *i.e.*, the hysteresis loop is traversed at line frequency, but angle δ remains constant. As the rotor accelerates, the rotor iron undergoes hysteresis cycle at slip frequency ; but angle δ, representing the hysteretic angle, remains unaltered. For constant stator inducing mmf F_s, the induced rotor flux is constant, in view of this, the developed hysteresis torque proportional to (F_s) (rotor flux) sin δ, remains constant from standstill up to its synchronous speed as shown in Fig. 6.31 (*b*). The conclusion that torque developed by hysteresis motor remains constant, can also be explained as follows.

At standstill, the rotor iron is subjected to magnetic reversals at a frequency f. Let the hysteresis loss in the rotor at standstill be P_{ho}. As the rotor accelerates, the frequency of magnetic reversals decreases. Since the hysteresis loss is proportional to the frequency of hysteresis cycle to which the rotor is subjected, the hysteresis loss at any slip frequency sf is $P_h = sP_{ho}$.

In a polyphase induction motor the rotor ohmic loss results in the development of electromagnetic torque.

$$T_e = \frac{1}{\omega_s} \frac{\text{rotor-ohmic loss}}{s} = \frac{1}{\omega_s} \cdot \frac{I_2^2 r_2}{s}$$

Similarly, the rotor hysteresis loss given rise to hysteresis torque given by

$$T_h = \frac{1}{\omega_s} \frac{\text{rotor hysteresis loss}}{s} = \frac{1}{\omega_s} \frac{sP_{ho}}{s} = \frac{1}{\omega_s} \cdot P_{ho}.$$

The slip does not appear in the above expression for T_h, therefore, for constant stator mmf, P_{ho} is constant and hence the hysteresis torque remains constant from standstill up to synchronous speed as shown in Fig. 6.31 (*b*). Similar to the development of hysteresis torque due to rotor hysteresis loss, there is eddy-current torque present due to rotor eddy-current loss.

Let the eddy current loss in the rotor iron at standstill be P_{eo} at rotor frequency *f*. As the rotor speeds up, the frequency of eddy currents in the rotor decreases from *f* to lower frequency *sf* where *s* is the slip. Since eddy-current loss is proportional to frequency squared, the eddy-current loss P_e at slip frequency is given by $P_e = s^2 P_{eo}$. Eddy-current loss gives rise to the production of eddy-current torque given by

$$T_{ed} = \frac{1}{\omega_s} \cdot \frac{\text{eddy-current loss}}{\text{slip}} = \frac{1}{\omega_s} \cdot \frac{s^2 P_{eo}}{s} = \frac{1}{\omega_s} \cdot sP_{eo}$$

At standstill, eddy-current loss and therefore eddy-current torque is the highest because $s = 1$. As the rotor accelerates, *s* decreases and likewise T_{ed} decreases. At synchronous speed, eddy-current torque is zero. This shows that during the accelerating time of the rotor, both hysteresis and eddy-current torques are present. But at synchronous speed, only hysteresis torque is operating the motor as a hysteresis motor. Fig. 6.31 (*b*) shows the torque-speed characteristics of a hysteresis motor.

The difference between reluctance and hysteresis motors must be understood. In reluctance motors, the motor starts as a single-phase induction motor and rotor pulls into synchronism under favourable conditions. But in a hysteresis motor, any load gets synchronized with stator poles provided hysteresis torque is able to accelerate it. In a reluctance motor, there is a tendency for the rotor to oscillate before synchronism, but in a hysteresis motor, rotor and stator poles lock with each other without any oscillation.

Since the rotor periphery is smooth and without any slots, the motor is not subjected to magnetic and mechanical vibrations and is, therefore, extremely quiet. The most common application of hysteresis motor is for electric clocks and other timing devices. These motors are also used for driving gyros. Since these motors are noiseless, these are used for sound-recording and sound-producing equipments like record-players, tape recorders etc. If stator is wound with pole-changing winding, then multispeed synchronous motor operation of the hysteresis motor is possible.

6.8 TWO-PHASE SERVOMOTORS

These motors are widely used as actuating motors in feedback control systems. A schematic diagram of a 2-phase servomotor is illustrated in Fig. 6.32. Stator has two-phase windings in space quadrature and rotor is squirrel-cage type. One stator phase winding, called *reference winding*, is energised with fixed rated voltage called reference voltage V_r. The other stator phase winding, called *control winding*, is in space quadrature with the reference winding and is energised from a servoamplifier. The voltage V_c, applied to control winding, is usually adjusted to be exactly 90° out of phase with V_r. At the same time, the voltages V_r and V_c must have the same frequency which means these voltages must be derived from the same power source.

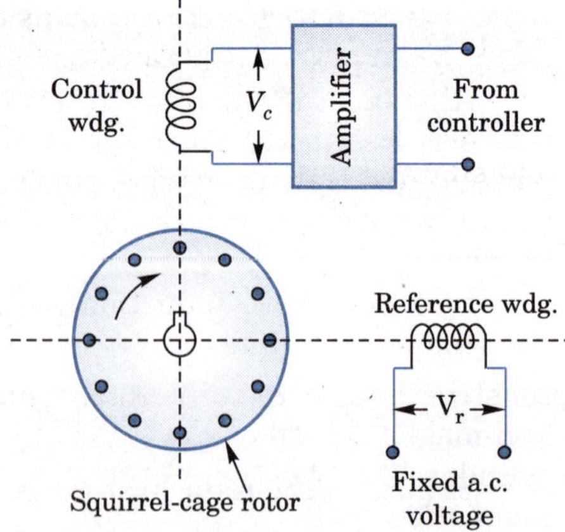

Fig. 6.32: Schematic diagram of two-phase servomotor.

The 2-phase servomotor has the advantage that its direction of rotation can be reversed merely by reversal of phase sequence of the applied voltages. For example, when V_c leads V_r by about 90°, rotation is in one direction ; when V_c lags V_r rotation is in the other direction. Since torque depends on both V_r and V_c and V_r is a constant-frequency rated voltage, the developed torque can be controlled in magnitude and direction by changing the control voltage V_c.

When a conventional 2-phase motor is energised from balanced 2-phase voltages, the torque-speed curve 1, similar to that of a 3-phase induction motor, is obtained, see Fig. 6.33. Such a torque-speed curve is undesirable in control systems, because it has positive torque-speed slope over most of the operating speed region. A positive slope in control systems means negative damping which can lead to unstable operation. This means that for control system applications, 2-phase motor design must be modified so as to obtain negative torque-speed curve (or positive damping) over the full speed range. A simple way to achieve this is to design the rotor with high rotor circuit resistance so that torque-speed curve marked 3 in Fig. 6.33 is obtained. For curve 3, the maximum torque occurs at a slip between 1.5 and 2, about 10 times the slip that obtained for curve 1. An ordinary 2-phase induction motor designed with a high rotor circuit resistance becomes a 2-phase servomotor. For this motor, normal working region is around zero speed (slip = 1), where the torque-speed curve is almost rectilinear, *i.e.*, straight line. Since the torque-speed slope is negative around zero speed, the motor operating to the right of maximum torque point (Point K in Fig. 6.33) is in the stable region. An important factor is that motor torque should be zero for zero error signal across control winding. This can be achieved by careful building of the motor and by the use of a high-resistance rotor. Sometimes, in actual situations, the rotor may keep on running even with zero voltage across control winding due to single-phasing. This problem is usually avoided by designing the motor with equal positive and negative sequence impedances over a wide speed range.

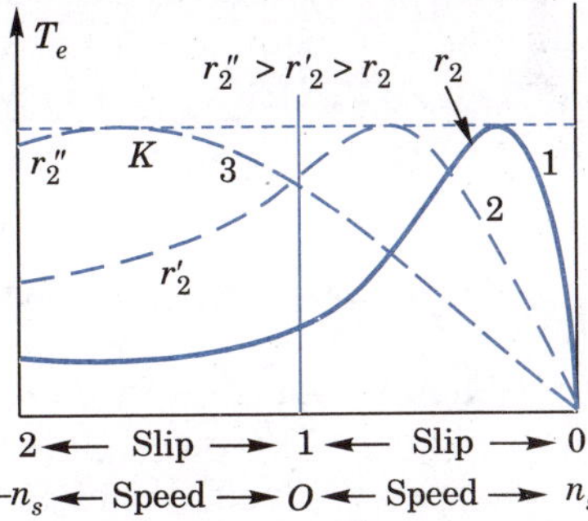

Fig. 6.33: Torque-speed curve of a balanced 2-phase motor with different rotor circuit resistances.

The rotor slots are usually skewed in order to reduce the effect of slot-harmonics.

Two-phase servomotors have the following merits and demerits as compared to other servomotors.

Advantages :

(*i*) It possesses simple and rugged construction.

(*ii*) It is economical and technically more suitable as a servomotor.

(*iii*) It requires negligible inspection and maintenance because of the absence of brushes and sliding contacts.

(*iv*) Since rotor requires no insulation, higher rotor temperatures can be tolerated than in other types of motors.

(*v*) The inertia of this motor is less as compared to a d.c. motor of the same rating.

(*vi*) The inertia of this motor can be reduced even further by using *drag-cup rotor* construction shown in Fig. 6.34. The drag-cup rotor is a hollow thin-walled cylinder of some non-magnetic material (usually aluminium). A stationary rotor core, placed inside the hollow cylinder, is a stack of steel laminations and its function is to reduce the reluctance of the magnetic circuit. Note that drag-cup rotor construction has two air gaps in series as compared to one air gap in ordinary cage-rotor construction. Low rotor inertia for a servomotor is very important from the view point of quick response to the control signal voltage V_c.

The main disadvantage of the two-phase control motor is its low efficiency. But not much significance is attached to the efficiency and p.f. in two phase servomotors, though these terms are very important in industrial power drives.

The two-phase servomotors have ratings upto about 1 kW. Above this rating, d.c. motors are more satisfactory. A high-frequency (usually 400 Hz) servomotor, as compared to a low-frequency (50 Hz) servomotor, has less volume and weight and therefore less cost and low rotor inertia.

Performance analysis. In order to simplify the performance analysis of two-phase servomotor, it is assumed that stator has identical 2-phase stator windings operated from an unbalanced sinusoidal 2-phase source. The two-phase voltages are V_r across the reference winding and V_c across the control winding. These unequal voltages are in time quadrature as shown in Fig. 6.35 (*a*). According to the method of symmetrical components, V_r and V_c are resolved into positive and negative sequence components as shown in Fig. 6.35 (*b*) and (*c*) respectively. It is seen from this Fig. 6.35.

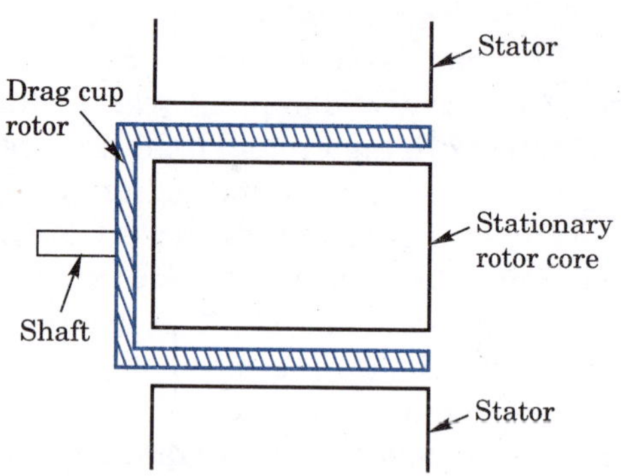

Fig. 6.34: Two-phase drag-cup rotor servomotor.

$$\bar{V}_r = \bar{V}_{r1} + \bar{V}_{r2} \quad \text{...[6.34 (a)]}$$

and

$$\bar{V}_c = \bar{V}_{c1} + \bar{V}_{c2} \quad \text{...[6.34 (b)]}$$

where additional subscripts 1 and 2 are added to denote positive and negative sequence components respectively. Note that V_{c1}, V_{r1} constitute one set of balanced voltages and V_{c2}, V_{c2} another set. V_{c1} leads V_{r1} by 90° and V_{c2} lags V_{r2} by 90°.

$$\therefore \quad \bar{V}_{c1} = j\bar{V}_{r1} \quad \text{...[6.35 (a)]}$$

$$\bar{V}_{c2} = -j\bar{V}_{r2} \quad \text{...[6.35 (b)]}$$

From Eq. [6.34 (*b*)], $\bar{V}_c = j(\bar{V}_{r1} - \bar{V}_{r2})$ ...[6.35 (*c*)]

or

$$-j\bar{V}_c = (\bar{V}_{r1} - \bar{V}_{r2})$$

From Eq. [6.34 (*a*)], $\bar{V}_r = \bar{V}_{r1} + \bar{V}_{r2}$

Addition and subtraction of above two voltage equations give

$$\bar{V}_{r1} = \frac{1}{2}(\bar{V}_r - j\bar{V}_c) \quad \text{...[6.36 (a)]}$$

and

$$\bar{V}_{r2} = \frac{1}{2}(\bar{V}_r + j\bar{V}_c) \quad \text{...[6.36 (b)]}$$

In Fig. 6.35 (*a*), $\bar{V}_r$ is horizontal and $\bar{V}_c$ leads it by 90°. In phasor form, these voltages can be written as

$$\bar{V}_r = V_r + j0 \quad \text{and} \quad \bar{V}_c = 0 + jV_c \quad \text{or} \quad -j\bar{V}_c = V_c$$

Substitution of these values in Eqs. (6.36 (*a*)) and (6.36 (*b*)) gives

$$\bar{V}_{r1} = \frac{1}{2}(V_r + V_c) + j0 \qquad \text{...[6.37 (a)]}$$

and

$$\bar{V}_{r2} = \frac{1}{2}(V_r - V_c) + j0 \qquad \text{...[6.37 (b)]}$$

Difference between Eqs. (6.36) and (6.37) must be noted. Eqs. (6.36) give positive and negative sequence components of voltages in terms of known voltages V_r and V_c, which may or may not be in time quadrature. Eqs. (6.37), however, give the positive-sequence and negative-sequence components of voltages for known voltages V_r and V_c, which are in *time quadrature* for the 2-phase servomotor under consideration.

Reference-winding current I_r and control-winding current I_c can also be resolved into positive and negative sequence components. Therefore, as per Eqs. (6.36 (*a*)) and (6.36 (*b*)), we have

$$\bar{I}_{r1} = \frac{1}{2}(\bar{I}_r - j\bar{I}_c) \qquad \text{...[6.38 (a)]}$$

and

$$\bar{I}_{r2} = \frac{1}{2}(\bar{I}_r + j\bar{I}_c) \qquad \text{...[6.38 (b)]}$$

From Eq. (6.34 (*a*)), $\bar{I}_r = \bar{I}_{r1} + \bar{I}_{r2}$ ....[6.39 (*a*)]

From Eq. [6.35 (*c*)], $\bar{I}_c = j(\bar{I}_{r1} - \bar{I}_{r2})$ ....[(6.39 (*b*)]

Positive-sequence components in each phase, $\bar{V}_{r1}$ and $\bar{V}_{c1}(= j\bar{V}_{r1})$ in Fig. 6.35 (*b*), combine to produce a positive-sequence (or forward) rotating field which interacts with rotor winding to produce positive-sequence torque T_1. Similarly, negative-sequence components in each phase, $\bar{V}_{r2}$ and $\bar{V}_{c2}(= -j\bar{V}_{r2})$ in Fig. 6.35 (*c*), co-operate in producing a negative-sequence (or backward) rotating field which give rise to negative-sequence torque T_2. Since two torques are opposing each other, the resultant torque is $T_1 - T_2$. In view of this, a 2-phase motor with unbalanced supply voltages can be replaced by two balanced 2-phase motors mechanically coupled as shown in Fig. 6.36. The positive-sequence voltages V_{r1}, $j\,V_{r1}$ and corresponding currents I_{r1}, $j\,I_{r1}$ produce torque T_1 in the direction of rotor rotation. Therefore T_1 is treated as positive. The negative-sequence voltages V_{r2}, $-V_{r2}$ and corresponding currents I_{r2}, $-j\,I_{r2}$ produce torque T_2 against the rotor rotation. Therefore T_2 is treated as negative and thus the output torque is $T_1 - T_2$.

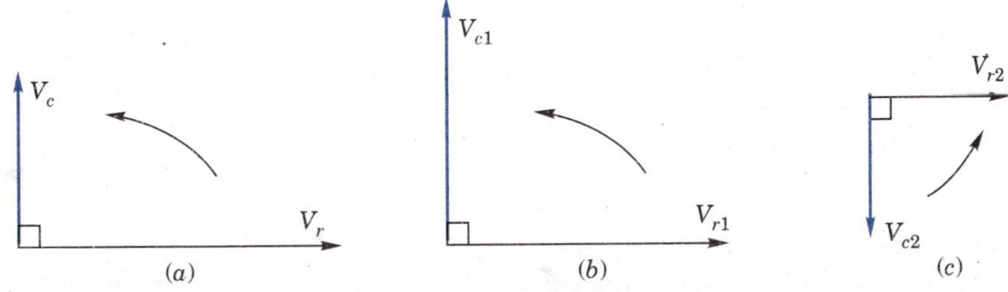

Fig. 6.35: (*a*) Two-phase unbalanced voltage (*b*) positive sequence voltages and (*c*) negative-sequence voltages.

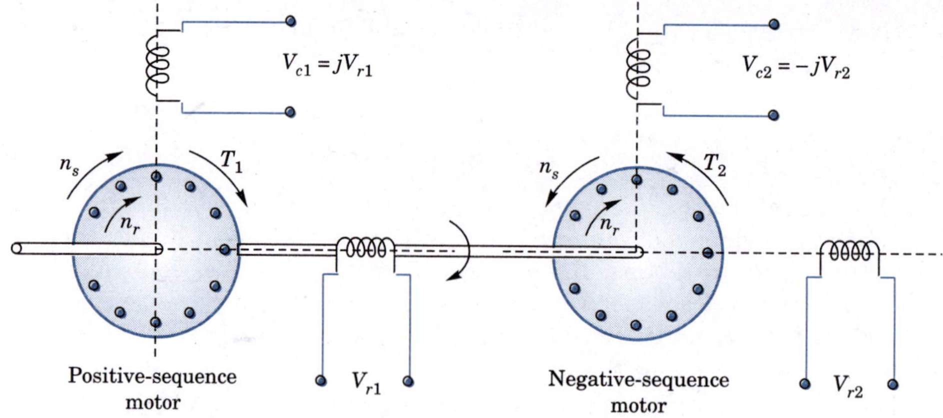

Fig. 6.36: Positive and negative sequence motors coupled together to represent a two-phase servomotor.

The rotor of the positive-sequence motor runs at n_r with slip s. The negative-sequence motor runs with slip $(2 - s)$. Since positive-sequence motor produces forward rotating field, just like a 3-phase induction motor, its positive-sequence equivalent circuit is shown in Fig. 6.37 (*a*). The equivalent circuit of servomotor for balanced negative-sequence set is depicted in Fig. 6.37 (*b*). The performance calculations can be done for both positive-sequence and negative-sequence equivalent circuits as done in a 3-phase induction motor.

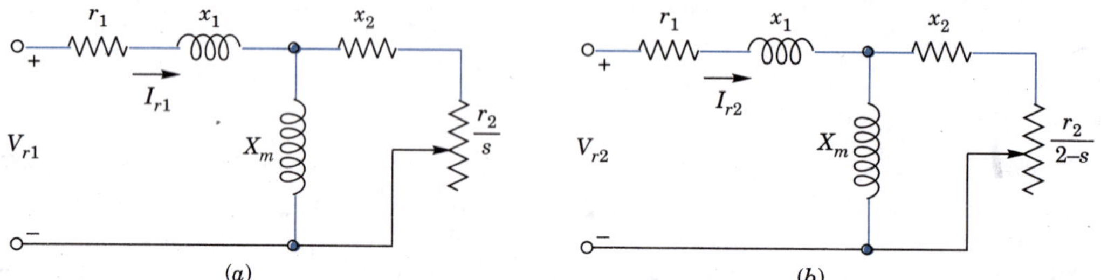

Fig. 6.37: Two-phase servomotor, (*a*) Positive-sequence (*b*) negative-sequence equivalent circuits.

From positive-sequence equivalent circuit, the input impedance is

$$\bar{Z}_1 = r_1 + j\,x_1 + R_1 + j\,X_1 \qquad \text{...(6.40)}$$

where, $R_1 + j\,X_1 = j\,X_m$ in parallel with $\left(\frac{r_2}{s} + j\,x_2\right)$ ...(6.41)

$$\therefore \quad \text{Positive-sequence current, } \bar{I}_{r_1} = \frac{\bar{V}_{r1}}{\bar{Z}_1} \qquad \text{...(6.42)}$$

The air-gap power, delivered to positive-sequence rotating field, by 2 stator phases is,

$$P_{g_1} = 2\,.\,I_{r1}^2\,.\,R_1 \qquad \text{...(6.43)}$$

Positive-sequence rotating field torque,

$$T_1 = \frac{P_{g_1}}{\omega_s} \text{ Nm} \qquad \text{...(6.44)}$$

where, $\omega_s = 2\pi n_s = 2\pi \frac{2f}{P}$ rad/sec.

From negative-sequence equivalent circuit, the input impedance is

$$\bar{Z}_2 = r_1 + j\,x_1 + R_2 + jX_2 \quad \text{...(6.45)}$$

where, $R_2 + jX_2 = jX_m$ in parallel with $\left(\frac{r_2}{2-s} + jx_2\right)$ ...(6.46)

$\therefore$ Negative-sequence current, $\bar{I}_{r2} = \frac{\bar{V}_{r2}}{\bar{Z}_2}$ ...(6.47)

The air-gap power, delivered to negative-sequence rotating field, by the 2 stator phases is,

$$P_{g2} = 2I_{r2}^2 \cdot R_2 \quad \text{...(6.48)}$$

Negative-sequence rotating field torque, $T_2 = \frac{P_{g_2}}{\omega_s}$ Nm ...(6.49)

The resultant-torque produced by the combined effect of positive and negative-sequence voltages is given by, $T = T_1 - T_2 = \frac{1}{\omega_s}(P_{g1} - P_{g2})$ ...(6.50)

The resultant line current in the reference winding, similar to Eq. [6.34 (*a*)], is

$$\bar{I}_r = \bar{I}_{r1} + \bar{I}_{r2} \quad \text{....(6.51)}$$

and in control winding, similar to Eq. (6.35 (*c*)), is $\bar{I}_c = j(\bar{I}_{r1} - \bar{I}_{r2})$ ...(6.52)

Example 6.9. *A 2-phase, 4-pole servomotor has the following parameters at 50 Hz.*

$r_1 = 360\ \Omega,\quad r_2 = 250\ \Omega,\quad x_1 = x_2 = 50\ \Omega,$

$X_m = 900\ \Omega.$

This motor is operated with 115 V across the reference winding and 75 V across the control winding, the latter leading the former by 90°.

Calculate the stator currents, output power and motor torque at a slip of 0.5. The rotational losses under conditions given above are 0.7 watt. Both the windings have equal number of turns.

Solution. Positive-sequence component of applied voltage, from Eq. (6.37 (*a*)), is

$$\bar{V}_{r1} = \frac{1}{2}(115 + 75) + j0 = 95 + j0 \text{ volts}$$

Negative-sequence component of applied voltage, from Eq. (6.37 (*b*)), is

$$\bar{V}_{r2} = \frac{1}{2}(115 - 75) + j0 = 20 + j0 \text{ volts}$$

Input impedance offered to positive-sequence voltage, from Eq. 6.40), is

$$Z_1 = 360 + j50 + \frac{j900\left(\frac{200}{0.5} + j50\right)}{\frac{250}{0.5} + j950}$$

$$= 360 + j50 + 351.47 + j232.28$$

$$= 711.47 + j282.28 = 765.42 \angle 21.64^\circ$$

$$\therefore \quad \bar{I}_{r1} = \frac{95 + j0}{765.42 \angle 21.64} = 0.124 \angle -21.64^\circ = 0.1153 - j\,0.046.$$

Input impedance offered to negative-sequence voltage, from Eq. (6.45), is

$$\bar{Z}_2 = 360 + j50 + \frac{j900\left(\dfrac{250}{1.5} + j50\right)}{\dfrac{250}{1.5} + j950}$$

$$= 360 + j50 + 145.11 + j72.82$$

$$= 505.11 + j122.82 = 519.83 \angle 13.7^\circ.$$

$$\therefore \quad \bar{I}_{r2} = \frac{20 + j0}{519.83 \angle 13.70} = 0.0385 \angle -13.7^\circ$$

$$= 0.0374 - j\,0.00912$$

Phase current in reference winding, from Eq. (6.51), is

$$\bar{I}_r = 0.1153 - j\,0.046 + 0.0374 - j\,0.00912$$

$$= 0.1527 - j\,0.05512 = 0.1623 \angle -19.85^\circ$$

Phase current in control winding, from Eq. (6.52), is

$$\bar{I}_c = j\,(0.0779 - j\,0.03688) = 0.03688 + j\,0.0779 = 0.0862 \angle 64.67^\circ$$

Positive-sequence gap power, from Eq. (6.43), is

$$P_{g1} = 2\,(0.124)^2 \times 351.47 = 10.808 \text{ watts}$$

Negative-sequence gap power, from Eq. (6.48), is

$$P_{g2} = 2\,(0.0385)^2 \times 145.11 = 0.4302 \text{ watts.}$$

Resultant gap power = 10.808 – 0.4302 = 10.3778 W

Internal mechanical power developed is

$$P = (1 - s)\,(P_{g1} - P_{g2}) = 0.5 \times 10.3778 = 5.189 \text{ W}$$

Power output = 5.189 – 0.7 = 4.489 W

$$\therefore \quad \text{Shaft torque} = \frac{4.489}{0.5 \times 2\pi \times 25} = 0.05716 \text{ Nm.}$$

Example 6.10. *A 200 W, 120/120 V, 2-phase, 4-pole, 50 Hz balanced squirrel-cage induction motor, when energised from balanced 2-phase, 120 V, 50 Hz supply, gave the following data for its internal-torque and slip characteristic :*

Slip	0	0.2	0.4	0.6	0.8	1.0	1.2	1.4	1.6	1.8	2.0
Internal torque, Nm	0	3.8	6.6	8.6	10.32	11.4	11.9	12.27	12.30	12.10	11.3

This motor is used as a 2-phase servomotor with constant voltage 120 V applied to its reference winding and variable applied to its control winding. The control-winding voltage leads the reference voltage by 90°. For control voltages of 96, 72, 48, 24 and 0 V, plot a family of internal torque versus slip characteristics, for a slip range of zero to 2.

Solution. The data given in this example are for the positive sequence component at rated voltage, because this characteristic is obtained under balanced rated 2-phase voltages. Note that a balanced supply voltage constitutes a positive-sequence voltage.

The torque for the negative-sequence voltage can be obtained easily. Slip s for positive-sequence field is $(2 - s)$ for negative-sequence field. Therefore, positive-sequence torque at rated voltage for any slip s (say, 0.4), is also the negative-sequence torque at rated voltage for slip $2–s$ *i.e.*, 1.6. Based on this fact, Table 6.1 gives the negative-sequence components T_2' of internal torque.

Table 6.1: Negative-sequence component of internal torque

$2-s$	0	0.2	0.4	0.6	0.8	1.0	1.2	1.4	1.6	1.8	2.0
T_2'	11.3	12.1	12.3	12.27	11.9	11.4	10.32	8.6	6.6	3.8	0.0

For $V_r = 120$ V and $V_c = 96$ V and from Eqs. [6.37 (*a*) and (*b*)]

$$\bar{V}_{r1} = \frac{1}{2}(V_r + V_c) = \frac{1}{2}(120 + 96) = 108 \text{ V}$$

$$\bar{V}_{r2} = \frac{1}{2}(V_r - V_c) = \frac{1}{2}(120 - 96) = 12 \text{ V}$$

Recall that internal torque developed in a polyphase induction motor is proportional to the square of voltage.

Therefore, positive-sequence component T_1 of internal torque at any slip $s = 0.2$ is

$$T_1 = 3.8\left(\frac{108}{120}\right)^2 = 3.078 \text{ Nm}$$

Negative-sequence component of internal torque T_2 at slip $s = 0.2$ $(2 - s = 1.8)$ is

$$T_2 = 12.1\left(\frac{12}{120}\right)^2 = 0.121 \text{ Nm}$$

Hence, net torque at a slip $s = 0.2$ is

$$T = T_1 - T_2 = 3.078 - 0.121 = 2.957 \text{ Nm}$$

For $s = 0.2$, internal torque for other control voltages is calculated in tabular form as given in Table 6.2.

Table 6.2: Internal torque calculations for $s = 0.20$

s	T_1'	T_2'	V_c	V_{r1}	V_{r2}	T_1	T_2	T, Nm
			0	60	60	0.95	3.025	−2.075
			24	72	48	1.368	1.936	−0.568
0.2	3.8	12.1	48	84	36	1.862	1.089	0.773
			72	96	24	2.432	0.484	1.948
			96	108	12	3.078	0.121	2.957
			120	120	0	3.80	0.0	3.80

Now take $s = 0.4$ and calculate internal torque for all control voltages as illustrated in Table 6.2. Repeat this for $s = 0$ and for $s = 0.6$ to $s = 2.0$ and plot internal-torque versus slip characteristics as shown in Fig. 6.38.

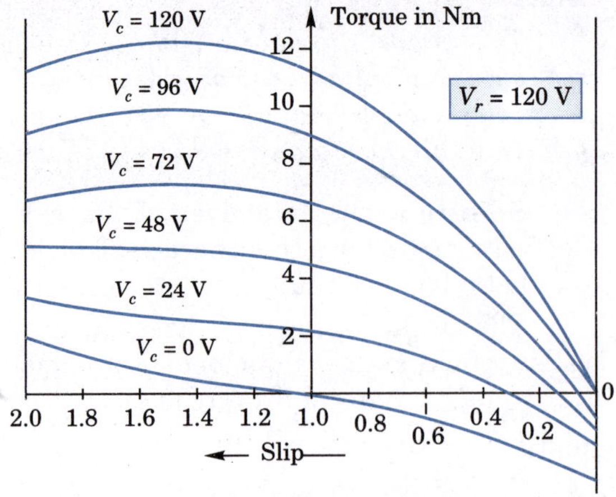

Fig. 6.38: Internal torque-slip curves of a two-phase servomotor of Example 6.10.

Example 6.11. *Torque-slip characteristics of Fig. 6.38 for a 2-phase servomotor may be assumed as straight lines parallel to each other for different control voltages as illustrated in Fig. 6.39. Under these assumptions, determine the transfer function of this motor relating,*

(a) motor shaft position and the control voltage,

(b) motor shaft velocity and the control voltage.

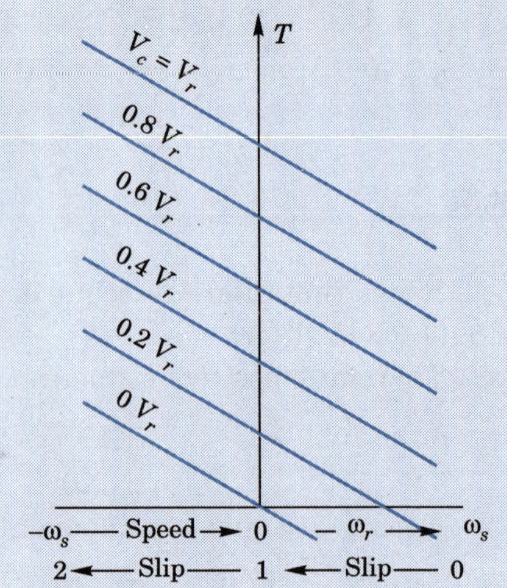

Fig. 6.39: Linearized torque-speed characteristics of a 2-phase servomotor.

Solution. For constant reference voltage V_r, torque is proportional to control voltage V_c. In addition, $dT/d\omega_r$ is negative. Both these facts can also be included in the torque-speed equation of 2-phase servomotor by the relation.

$$T = AV_c - B\omega_r \qquad \text{....(6.53)}$$

The constants A and B can be obtained from torque-speed characteristics. With rotor speed ω_r equal to synchronous speed ω_s and $V_c = V_r$, torque $T = 0$ (torque at synchronous speed with balanced polyphase voltages).

$$\therefore \qquad 0 = AV_c - B\omega_s$$

or

$$\frac{A}{B} = \frac{\omega_s}{V_c} \qquad \text{...(6.54)}$$

When $\omega_r = 0$ and $V_c = V_r$, $T = T_s$ (stalling torque)

$$\therefore \qquad T_s = AV_r$$

or
$$A = \frac{T_s}{V_r} = \frac{\text{Stalling torque}}{\text{Rated reference voltage, } V_r}$$

From Eq. (6.54), $B = \dfrac{AV_c}{\omega_s} = \dfrac{AV_r}{\omega_s} = \dfrac{T_s}{\omega_s} = \dfrac{\text{Stalling torque}}{\text{Synchronous speed}}$

Eq. (6.53) now becomes $T = T_s\left(\dfrac{V_c}{V_r} - \dfrac{\omega_r}{\omega_s}\right)$ ...(6.55)

(*a*) When the motor is coupled with inertia J and friction load D, then torque balance equation in terms of shaft-position angle θ is

$$J\frac{d^2\theta}{dt^2} + D\frac{d\theta}{dt} = AV_c - B\frac{d\theta}{dt} \quad \text{or} \quad [Jp^2 + (D + B)p]\,\theta = AV_c$$

Here
$$\frac{d\theta}{dt} = \omega_r$$

$\therefore$ The required transfer function is

$$\frac{\theta}{V_c} = \frac{A}{p[Jp + (D + B)]} = \frac{A}{p(D + B)[1 + T_m p]}$$

where, $T_m = \dfrac{J}{D + B}$, is motor time constant in seconds

In case V_c is sine wave of frequency ω, then the transfer function is

$$\frac{\bar{\theta}}{\bar{V}_c} = \frac{A}{J(j\omega)^2 + j\omega\,(D + B)} = \frac{A}{-J\omega^2 + j\omega\,(D + B)}$$

(*b*) The differential equation in terms of shaft angular velocity ω_r is

$$J\frac{d\omega_r}{dt} + D\omega_r = AV_c - B\omega_r \quad \text{or} \quad \omega_r[(D + B) + Jp] = AV_c$$

$$\therefore \qquad \frac{\omega_r}{V_c} = \frac{A}{(D + B) + Jp} = \frac{A}{(D + B)(1 + T_m p)}$$

Also
$$\frac{\bar{\omega}_r}{V_c} = \frac{A}{(D + B) + j\omega J}.$$

Example 6.12. *A two-phase induction motor with stator voltages V_r and V_c, which are unequal but in space quadrature, produces some starting torque. Show that the same starting torque is produced by 2-phase balanced voltages of magnitude $\sqrt{V_r V_c}$.*

Solution. At standstill, slip $s = 1$ and both positive and negative sequence impedances are equal.

$\therefore$ Positive sequence current. $I_{r1} = \dfrac{V_{r1}}{Z_1}$

and negative sequence current, $I_{r2} = \dfrac{V_{r2}}{Z_1}$

∴ Resultant starting torque, $T = \frac{2}{\omega_s}[I_{r1}^2 R_1 - I_{r2}^2 R_1] = \frac{2R_1}{\omega_s}[I_{r1}^2 - I_{r2}^2]$

$$= \frac{2R_1}{\omega_s} \cdot \frac{1}{Z_1^2}[V_{r1}^2 - V_{r2}^2]$$

Substituting the values of V_{r1} and V_{r2} in terms of V_r and V_c from Eqs. (6.37) ; we get

$$T = \frac{2R_1}{\omega_s} \cdot \frac{1}{Z_1^2} \cdot \frac{1}{4}[(V_r + V_c)^2 - (V_r - V_c)^2]$$

$$= \frac{2R_1}{\omega_s} \cdot \frac{1}{Z_1^2}[V_r V_c] \quad \text{...(6.56)}$$

If 2-phase balanced voltages have a magnitude of V_1 per phase, then starting torque produced by it, from equivalent circuit of Fig. 6.37 (*a*), is given by

$$T = 2 \times \text{torque per phase}$$

$$= \frac{2}{\omega_s}(I_1^2 R_1) = \frac{2}{\omega_s}\left(\frac{V_1}{Z_1}\right)^2 R_1 = \frac{2R_1}{\omega_s} \cdot \frac{1}{Z_1^2} \cdot V_1^2 \quad \text{...(6.57)}$$

From Eqs. (6.56) and (6.57), we have $V_1 = \sqrt{V_r V_c}$

This proves the required result.

Example 6.13. *An induction motor, with negligible stator resistance, develops a maximum torque of 10 Nm at a negative slip of 0.5 when balanced 2-phase, 220-V are applied to its symmetrical 2-phase stator windings.*

This motor is now used as a 2-phase control motor with reference voltage of 220 V in time quadrature with control voltage of (a) 220 V and (b) 110 V. Find the torques at a slip of 0.6.

Solution. When running as a balanced two-phase motor, Eq. (5.36) is valid

$$\therefore \quad \frac{T_e}{T_{e.m}} = \frac{2}{\frac{s_{mT}}{s} + \frac{s}{s_{mT}}}$$

Here $s_{mT} = 1.5$ and $T_{e.m} = 10$ Nm.

(*a*) When control voltage is 220 V, the control motor runs as a balanced 2-phase motor. For a slip of $s = 0.6$, we have

$$\frac{T_e}{10} = \frac{2}{\frac{1.5}{0.6} + \frac{0.6}{1.5}} = 0.6896, \quad \text{or} \quad T_e = 6.896 \text{ Nm}$$

(*b*) When $V_c = 115$ V, then

From Eq. [6.37 (*a*)], positive sequence voltage, $V_{r1} = \frac{1}{2}(220 + 110) = 165$ V

and from Eq. [6.37 (*b*)], negative sequence voltage, $V_{r2} = \frac{1}{2}(220 - 110) = 55$ V

For a positive sequence voltage of 165 V, torque T_1 at a slip of 0.6 is given by

$$T_1 = 6.896\left(\frac{165}{220}\right)^2 = 3.879 \text{ Nm}$$

The slip for positive sequence flux is 0.6. The slip for the negative sequence flux or backward flux is $2 - s = 2 - 0.6 = 1.4$. Negative sequence torque T_2' at slip 1.4 for 220 V as the control voltage is

$$T_2' = \frac{2 \times 10}{\frac{1.5}{1.4} + \frac{1.4}{1.5}} = 9.976 \text{ Nm}$$

$\therefore$ T_2 at negative sequence voltage of 55 V is given by,

$$T_2 = 9.976 \left(\frac{55}{220}\right)^2 = 0.6235 \text{ Nm.}$$

Net torque at $s = 0.6$ is $T = T_1 - T_2 = 3.879 - 0.6235 = 3.255$ Nm.

6.9 AC TACHOMETERS

An a.c. tachometer is a device used for the measurement of angular velocity of a shaft in the form of an alternating voltage of constant frequency. Its use in automatic control systems is more common. A small 2-phase induction motor can be used to work as an a.c. tachometer. It consists of a squirrel cage rotor and a pair of phase windings in space quadrature as shown in Fig. 6.40. One stator phase winding is called *fixed field* or *reference field winding* r and the other stator phase winding is referred to as *auxiliary* or *control winding* C. The reference winding is energized from a constant voltage and constant frequency source. As a result, emf of the same line frequency is generated in the control winding C. The magnitude of generated emf in winding C is, however, proportional to rotor speed. As control winding is connected to a high impedance amplifier, winding C can be considered as open circuited. It means that winding C does not effect winding r in any way. Thus, the tachometer as viewed from the reference winding r is equivalent to a single-phase induction motor and therefore equivalent circuit of Fig. 6.9 (*b*), based on double-revolving field theory, can be employed for its analysis.

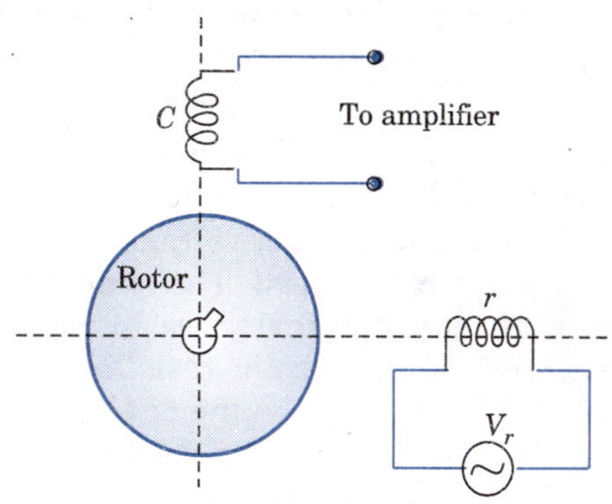

Fig. 6.40: Schematic diagram of a 2-phase ac tachnometer.

In Fig. 6.9 (*b*), emfs E_f and E_b are generated in winding r by the forward and backward flux waves respectively. As these flux waves come across winding C, emfs are also generated in this winding C. If

$$\frac{\text{effective turns in winding } C}{\text{effective turns in winding } r} = a,$$

then
$$\frac{\text{emf generated in winding } C, E_{cf}}{\text{emf generated in winding } r, E_{rf}} = a$$

or
$$E_{cf} = a \cdot E_{rf} \qquad ...(6.58)$$

In Fig. 6.40, forward field is assumed to rotate clockwise. This means that forward field comes across winding C first and a quarter cycle of time later, it comes across winding r. Thus emf $\overline{E}_{cf}$ generated by the forward field in winding C leads by 90° the corresponding emf $\overline{E}_{rf}$

generated in winding r by the forward field, Fig. 6.41 (*a*). In complex notation, with the help of Eq. (6.58) and Fig. 6.41 (*a*), it can be expressed as

$$\overline{E}_{cf} = ja\,\overline{E}_{rf} = ja\,\overline{I}_1 Z_f \qquad \text{...(6.59)}$$

where I_1 is the phasor current in winding r and can be determined from the equivalent circuit of Fig. 6.9 (*b*). The backward field revolves in the opposite direction. Therefore, emf $\overline{E}_{rb}$ generated in the reference winding by backward field leads by 90° the emf $\overline{E}_{cb}$ generated in the control winding C by the same backward field, Fig. 6.41 (*b*). In complex notation,

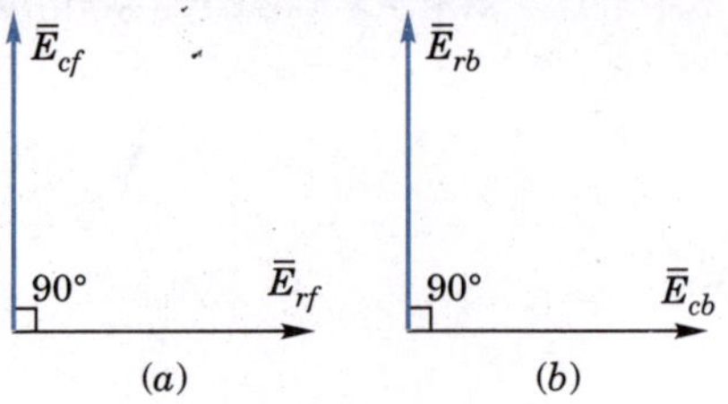

Fig. 6.41: Emfs generated in 2-phase tachometer.

$$\overline{E}_{cb} = -\,ja\overline{E}_{rb} = -jaI_1 Z_b \qquad \text{...(6.60)}$$

Thus the total voltage $\overline{E}_c$ generated in control winding C, as per Fig. 6.9 (*b*), is

$$\overline{E}_c = \overline{E}_{cf} + \overline{E}_{cb} = ja\,(E_{rf} - E_{rb}) = jaI_1\,(Z_f - Z_b) \qquad \text{...(6.61)}$$

At standstill, the magnitudes of forward and backward fields are equal or the magnitudes of forwards-field and backward-field impedances are equal. Therefore, emf E_c generated in winding C is zero, Eq. (6.61). When the rotor revolves, forward-field impedance Z_f increases whereas backward-field impedance Z_b decreases ; the difference $(Z_f - Z_b)$ is therefore a function of rotor speed. As a result, emf in winding C is generated which is proportional to rotor speed. The phase of the voltage in control winding is reversed with the reversal of direction of rotor rotation.

The ideal characteristics of a.c. tachometer are : (*i*) emf in control winding C is linearly proportional to rotor speed and (*ii*) the phase of voltage across winding C is fixed with respect to the phase of voltage applied to reference winding r.

The variation of voltage from control winding and its phase angle can be plotted as a function of rotor speed. The shapes of these curves depend upon the speed range and on the ratio of rotor self-reactance to rotor resistance, *i.e.*, on $Q_2 = X_2/r_2$, where X_2 = rotor self-reactance and r_2 = rotor resistance. It can be proved that either a low value of Q_2 (less than about 0.1) or a high value of Q_2 (more than about 10) will provide almost a constant phase angle and nearly a linear relation between control-winding voltage and speed.

In order that a.c. tachometer produces minimum effect on the system in which it is inserted, its torque requirement should be low as compared to other torques acting in the system. Also, its rotor inertia should be small if rapid response is required in the control system. The rotor inertia can be minimized by making a.c. tachometer with drag-cup rotor construction as shown in Fig. 6.34. A.C. tachometers are often used in 400 Hz systems.

Example 6.14. *Motor of Example 6.1 is used as an a.c. tachogenerator with auxiliary and main windings acting respectively as control and reference windings. If the effective turns ratio from control winding to reference winding is 1.5, then determine the emf generated in control winding when the rotor speed is 1425 rpm. The reference winding is energized from 20 V, 50 Hz. Neglect stator leakage impedance.*

Solution. From the solution of Example 6.1,
forward field impedance, $Z_f = 17.66 + j20.75\ \Omega$
and backward field impedance, $Z_b = 0.99 + j1.562\ \Omega$

$$\therefore \quad Z_f + Z_b = 18.65 + j22.312 = 29.08 \angle 50.11° \ \Omega$$

$$Z_f - Z_b = 16.67 + j19.138 = 25.38 \angle 48.94° \ \Omega$$

$$\therefore \quad I_1 = \frac{V_1}{Z_f + Z_b} = \frac{20}{29.08} \text{A}$$

From Eq. (6.61), the magnitude of emf generated in control winding is

$$E_c = aI_1 (Z_f - Z_b) = 1.5 \times \frac{20}{29.08} \times 25.38 = \mathbf{26.183 \ V}$$

Example 6.15. *When main winding is excited alone in a single-phase induction motor, internal torque is also zero at nonzero rotor speed. Derive an expression for this nonzero rotor speed in terms of* $Q_2 = \dfrac{x_2 + X_m}{r_2} = X_2 r_2$.

Solution. It is seen from Eq. (6.9) that internal torque T_e is given by

$$T_e = \frac{I_1^2 (R_f - R_b)}{\cdot \omega_s}$$

This torque would be zero when $R_f = R_b$. Expression for R_f and R_b can be obtained from forward and backward field impedances. From Art. 6.3, forward-field impedance is given by

$$Z_f = R_f + jX_f = \frac{j\dfrac{X_m}{2}\left[\dfrac{r_2}{2s} + j\dfrac{x_2}{2}\right]}{\dfrac{r_2}{2s} + j\left[\dfrac{x_2}{2} + \dfrac{X_m}{2}\right]}$$

$$= \frac{jX_m\left[\dfrac{r_2}{s} + jx_2\right]}{\dfrac{r_2}{s} + j[x_2 + jX_m]} \times \frac{\dfrac{r_2}{s} - j[x_2 + X_m]}{\dfrac{r_2}{s} - j[x_2 + X_m]}$$

Taking only the real terms from both sides, we get,

$$R_f = \frac{-x_2 X_m \dfrac{r_2}{s} + x_2 X_m \dfrac{r_2}{s} + \dfrac{X_m^2 r_2}{s}}{\left(\dfrac{r_2}{s}\right)^2 + (x_2 + X_m)^2}$$

$$= \frac{X_m^2}{s/r_2} \frac{1}{\left(\dfrac{r_2}{s}\right)^2 + (x_2 + X_m)^2}$$

$$= \frac{X_m^2}{X_2} \cdot \frac{1}{\dfrac{r_2}{sX_2} + \dfrac{s \cdot X_2}{r_2}} = \left(\frac{X_m^2}{X_2}\right) \frac{1}{\dfrac{1}{sQ_2} + sQ_2} \qquad \text{...}(i)$$

where, $Q_2 = \dfrac{X_2}{r_2}$

Similarly, backward-field impedance is given by

$$Z_b = R_b + j\,X_b = \frac{j\,\dfrac{X_m}{2}\left[\dfrac{r_2}{2(2-s)} + j\,\dfrac{x_2}{2}\right]}{\dfrac{r_2}{2(2-s)} + j\left[\dfrac{x_2}{2} + \dfrac{X_m}{2}\right]}$$

$$= \frac{j\,X_m\left[\dfrac{r_2}{2-s} + j\,X_2\right]}{\dfrac{r_2}{(2-s)} + j\,[x_2 + X_m]} = Z_f \text{ with } s \text{ replaced by } (2-s).$$

$$\therefore \qquad R_b = \left(\frac{X_m^2}{X_2}\right)\cdot\frac{1}{\dfrac{1}{(2-s)\,Q_2} + (2-s)\,Q_2} \qquad ...(ii)$$

For zero internal torque, $R_f = R_b$. From Eqs. (*i*) and (*ii*), we get

$$\frac{X_m^2}{X_2}\cdot\frac{1}{\dfrac{1}{sQ_2} + sQ_2} = \frac{X_m^2}{X_2}\cdot\frac{1}{\dfrac{1}{(2-s)\,Q_2} + (2-s)\,Q_2}$$

$$(2-s)\,Q_2 + \frac{1}{(2-s)\,Q_2} = s\,Q_2 + \frac{1}{s\,Q_2},\quad (2-2s)\,Q_2 = \frac{2-2s}{s(2-s)}\cdot\frac{1}{Q_2}$$

$$s\,Q_2 = \frac{1}{Q_2\,(2-s)}$$

$$s^2 - 2s + \frac{1}{Q_2^2} = 0,\quad s = 1 \pm \sqrt{1 - \frac{1}{Q_2^2}}$$

$$\therefore \quad \text{Nonzero rotor speed} = (1-s)\,n_s = \mp\, n_s\sqrt{1 - \frac{1}{Q_2^2}} = n_s\sqrt{1 - \left(\frac{r_2}{X_2}\right)^2}$$

This relation agrees with that already derived in Eq. (6.26*a*).

PROBLEMS

6.1. (*a*) What happens to a 3-phase induction motor if one of its three supply-leads gets disconnected?

(*b*) Give the constructional features of a single-phase induction motor.

Draw a diagram illustrating both the main and auxiliary windings for a 4-pole, 24-slot single-phase induction motor. Show that the two windings are space displaced by 90°.

6.2. For a single-phase induction motor, give qualitative explanation for the following :

(*a*) Behaviour of the motor with its rotor at standstill and with only main winding excited.

(*b*) The forward flux wave is several times greater than the backward flux wave at normal rotor speed, but they are equal at standstill.

6.3. (*a*) Explain how the stationary, pulsating m.m.f. wave of a single-phase induction motor can be considered as equivalent to two equal but oppositely rotating m.m.f. waves.

(*b*) A 4-pole, 50 Hz, single-phase induction motor has an effective standstill rotor resistance of 5.00 Ω referred to stator. The full-load slip of the motor is 5%. The forward and backward components of currents referred to stator are 2.5 A and 4.0 A respectively. Determine the full-load torque in Nm. [**Ans.** 1.86 Nm]

6.4. (*a*) Explain the double revolving-field theory as applied to a single-phase induction motor.

(*b*) A 4-pole, 50 Hz, single-phase induction motor has an effective rotor resistance referred to stator as 2.4 Ω at slip frequency. At about twice the mains frequency, this resistance should be increased by 50%. The forward and backward components of current at a slip of 5% are 2.6 A and 3.8 A respectively. Assuming mechanical loss as 5% of the internal power developed, compute the output power and torque of the motor.

[**Hint.** Forward field rotor resistance referred to stator is $\frac{1}{2}$ (2.4) Ω and backward field rotor resistance referred to stator is $\frac{1}{2}$ (2.4 × 1.5) = 1.8 Ω.

$$\therefore \text{ Internal power developed} = 0.95\left[(2.6)^2 \frac{3.4}{2 \times 0.05} - (3.8)^2 \frac{3.6}{2 \times 1.95} \text{ etc.}\right]$$

[**Ans.** 134.39 watts, 0.9006 Nm]

6.5. (*a*) Derive the equivalent circuit of a single-phase induction motor with the help of double revolving field theory.

(*b*) A 6-pole, 50 Hz, single-phase induction motor, when running at normal speed, has forward field and backward field resistances of 60 Ω and 1.4 Ω respectively. The stator current at a full-load slip of 5% is 3 A. Determine the full-load torque in Nm. Assume rotational losses to be 4% of the internal power developed.

[**Hint.** Here R_f = 60 Ω and R_h = 1.4 Ω] [**Ans.** 4.835 Nm]

6.6. A 3-phase induction motor continues to run if one of the line fuses blows off but does not start under one line off condition. How is this feature explained with the help of two revolving field theory ? Hence explain the operation and develop an equivalent circuit for a single-phase induction motor.

6.7. (*a*) Draw the equivalent circuit for a single-phase induction motor based on the two revolving field theory and identify the various parameters involved in it. With this equivalent circuit, prove that forward flux wave is several times greater than the backward flux wave at normal rotor speed.

(*b*) Develop an expression for the resultant torque of a single-phase induction motor when running with slip *s*. Explain how the core losses are accounted for in determining the shaft power output.

6.8. A 230-V, 4-pole, 50 Hz, capacitor-start single-phase induction motor has the following constants and losses :

r_1 = 2.10 Ω x_1 = 3.00 Ω

r_2 = 4.00 Ω x_2 = 3.00 Ω

X_m = 70 Ω

Core loss = 48 watts. Friction and windage loss = 20 watts.

For a slip of 0.05, compute the stator current, pf, power output, torque and efficiency when this motor is running at rated voltage and frequency with its auxiliary winding open.

[**Ans.** 7.36 A, 0.632, 743.4 W, 4.982 Nm, 69.486%]

6.9. (*a*) A single-phase a.c. induction motor usually has two distributed windings on the stator one of which is connected to the main supply. The principal use of the second winding is to provide a starting torque for normal motor operation but further applications are to be found in practice. Discuss the application in which the second winding facilitates the operation of the machine as an a.c. tachogenerator. Give circuit diagram and brief theory underlying the above mode of operation. [*I.A.S., 1981*] (*b*) If motor of problem 6.8 is used as an a.c. tachometer, with effective turns ratio of 2 from control winding to reference winding, then determine the emf generated in control winding when rotor speed is 1425 rpm. The reference winding is energised from 20 V, 50 Hz source. Stator leakage impedance is neglected. **[Ans.** 34.993 V]

6.10. (*a*) Explain how the equivalent circuit parameters of a single-phase induction motor can be determined experimentally. State various assumptions made.

(*b*) A 230 V, 380 watts, 50 Hz, 4-pole, single-phase induction motor gave the following test results :

No-load test : 230 V, 84 W, 2.8 A

Blocked-rotor test : 110 V, 460 W, 6.2 A.

The stator winding resistance is 4.6 Ω and during the blocked rotor test, the auxiliary winding is open. Determine the equivalent circuit parameters.

[Ans. $r_1 = 4.6\ \Omega$, $x_1 = x_2 = 6.551\ \Omega$, $r_2 = 7.367\ \Omega$, $X_m = 143.23\ \Omega$]

6.11. A single-phase, 230 V, 50 Hz, 4-pole induction motor, when connected to a.c. source gave voltmeter, ammeter and wattmeter readings as 230 V, 2 A and 10 W respectively with the rotor driven at synchronous speed. Neglecting stator leakage impedance and rotational losses, estimate the torque at a slip of 0.05 at rated voltage and frequency. The motor has a magnetizing reactance of 220 Ω. **[Ans.** 3.09 Nm]

6.12. A 6-pole, 50 Hz, 1-phase induction motor gave the following data under loaded conditions with only main winding in circuit.

Applied voltage = 230 V, input power = 628 W, input current = 4.8 A, operating slip = 0.05.

The stator winding resistance is 3.0 Ω and no-load rotational losses are 82 W. Under the above operating conditions, if resistive component of forward field impedance is 20 times that of the backward field impedance, then compute.

(*a*) power delivered to forward and backward fields,

(*b*) power output, total losses and efficiency,

(*c*) shaft torque.

[**Hint.** $I_1^2 (r_1 + 21R_b) = 628$ W etc.]

[Ans. (*a*) 532.22 W, 26.61 W (*b*) 398.33 W, 229.62 W, 63.43% (*c*) 4.004 Nm]

6.13. The following data relates to a 185 watt, 110 V, 50 Hz, 4-pole single-phase induction motor :

Running winding resistance	3.8 Ω
Running winding leakage reactance	4.5 Ω
Rotor winding resistance	4.0 Ω
Rotor winding leakage reactance	4.6 Ω
Magnetizing reactance	50.0 Ω

All these values are referred to the running winding.

If a blocked-rotor test is performed on the motor, with 55 volts applied to the running winding and with starting winding left open, compute the expected data (input current and power). If the no-load speed is 1470 r.p.m., calculate the no-load current at rated voltage.

[Ans. 4.59 A, 164.345 W, 3.42 A]

6.14. (*a*) Draw the equivalent circuit of a single-phase induction motor and obtain therefrom its approximate equivalent circuit stating the various assumptions made.

(*b*) Compare single-phase induction motor with a polyphase induction motor having the same size and speed.

6.15. (*a*) A single-phase induction motor, coupled with a prime-mover, is driven at synchronous speed. Explain what happens to forward torque, backward torque and the resultant torque.

(*b*) A 2-pole, 50 Hz, single-phase induction motor has an effective rotor resistance and standstill leakage reactance of 0.6 Ω and 1.00 Ω respectively. If the motor is running at 2700 r.p.m., then determine the frequencies of the two rotor-current components and the relative magnitudes of the forward and backward fluxes. Neglect magnetizing current and stator leakage impedance. **[Ans.** 5 Hz, 95 Hz, 5.8004]

6.16. (*a*) Explain why a single-phase induction motor, as compared to a 3-phase induction motor, has larger slip, less efficiency and more noise.

(*b*) When single-phase induction motor behaviour is to be investigated over the normal operating values of slips from its equivalent circuit, the backward impedance Z_b is usually treated constant. Justify the statement.

[Hint. (*b*) Refer to Art 6.3.2]

6.17. (*a*) Classify single-phase induction motors in accordance with the methods of starting. Discuss the capacitor—split phase type of motor with circuit diagram, phasor diagram at starting and a typical torque speed characteristic.

(*b*) A 400 watt, 230 V, 50 Hz capacitor start single-phase induction motor has the following standstill constants for the main and auxiliary windings :

Main winding, $Z_m = 8 + j6.8\ \Omega$

Auxiliary winding, $Z_a = 17 + j6.0\ \Omega$

Find the value of starting capacitance that will place the main and auxiliary winding currents in quadrature at starting. **[Ans.** 122.43 μF]

6.18. State and describe the methods of starting single phase induction motors. Explain, how a rotating field is produced in each one of them at the time of starting.

6.19. (*a*) A single-phase capacitor start induction motor has 120 and 150 effective number of turns in the main and auxiliary windings respectively. The two stator windings are in space quadrature. At standstill, the main winding current is 10 A. Calculate the magnitude and phase of the auxiliary winding current at standstill, so that only forward stator m.m.f. wave is produced.

(*b*) In a single-phase capacitor start induction motor, it is required that the auxiliary winding current should lead the main winding current by 90°, at the time of start. Find the value of capacitive reactance x_c in series with the auxiliary winding, in terms of two winding constants. **[Ans.** (*a*) 8 A, 90° leading main winding current.

(*b*) $x_c = X_a + \dfrac{r_a r_m}{X_m}\ \Omega$]

6.20. A 230 V, 50 Hz, single phase split-phase induction motor has the following data at standstill :

Main winding impedance, $Z_m = 5.2 + j10.1\ \Omega$

Auxiliary winding impedance, $Z_a = 12.7 + j9.2\ \Omega$

Find the value of external resistance that should be inserted in series with the auxiliary winding so that maximum torque at starting is obtained.

Derive the formula used. **[Ans.** 2.38 Ω]

6.21. A single-phase capacitor start induction motor has 200 and 250 effective turns for main and auxiliary windings respectively. The two windings are in space quadrature. The value of capacitance in series with the auxiliary winding is such that at the time of start, auxiliary winding current of 4 A leads the main winding current of 10 A by 70°. At the time of start, compute.

(*a*) the amplitude of forward and backward stator m.m.f. waves.

(*b*) the ratio of the amplitudes of forward and backward air gap flux waves,

(c) the ratio of forward torque to backward torque and

(d) the ratio of forward torque to the net starting torque.

[**Hint.** Refer to Eq. (6.1)].

(a) For main winding, $F_{s.m} = \sqrt{2} \times 2000 \cos \omega t \cos \alpha$

For auxiliary winding, $F_{s.a} = \sqrt{2} \times 1000 \cos (\omega t + 70) \cos (\alpha + 90°)$

The above two equations can be expanded as

$$F_{s.m} = \sqrt{2} \times 1000 \cos (\omega t - \alpha) + \sqrt{2} \times 1000 \cos (\omega t + \alpha)$$

and
$$F_{s.a} = \sqrt{2} \times 500 \cos (\omega t - \alpha - 20°) + \sqrt{2} \times 500 \cos (\omega t + \alpha + 160°)$$

Note that the forward m.m.f. wave components of main and auxiliary windings are displaced by 20°.

∴ The magnitude of forward m.m.f. wave is

$$F_f = \sqrt{(\sqrt{2}.1000 + \sqrt{2}.500 \cos 20)^2 + (\sqrt{2}.500 \sin 20)^2} = 2092.58 \text{ ATs}$$

$$F_b = \sqrt{(\sqrt{2}.1000 + \sqrt{2}.500 \cos 160)^2 + (\sqrt{2}.500 \sin 160)^2} = 787.87 \text{ ATs}$$

[**Ans.** (a) 2092.58 ATs, 787.87 ATs (b) 2.656 (c) 7.054 (d) 1.165]

6.22. (a) Give the constructional features, working and applications of single phase reluctance motors.

(b) Describe the working of single phase sub-synchronous motor. Why should its rotor possess considerable flywheel effect ?

6.23. (a) Give the constructional features, principle of operation, working and applications of single phase hysteresis motors.

(b) Explain, from the analogy of a polyphase induction motor, that hysteresis motor torque remains constant from standstill upto synchronous speed.

(c) Describe the difference between reluctance and hysteresis motors.

6.24. Describe, with reasons, the type of motor that would be used for the following applications :

Compressors, centrifugal pump, refrigerator, ceiling fan, record-player, table fan, tape-recorder, pedestal fan, clock, for driving gyros, movie-projector, a 200 W fan for hospital room, a hi-fi turntable.

[**Ans.** 1. Capacitor-split IM ; 2, 3 : split-phase IM ; 4 : capacitor-run IM ; 5, 6, 7, 8 : shaded-pole motor ; 9, 10 : hysteresis M ; 11 : shaded-pole M ; 12 : capacitor-run IM ; 13 : hysteresis motor.]

6.25. (a) Give the constructional features of a 2-phase servomotor.

(b) Explain how the performance analysis of this motor is done by resolving the stator supply voltages into positive and negative sequence voltages.

Derive an expression for the resultant torque in terms of currents, synchronous speed etc.

6.26. (a) What is the advantage of having low rotor inertia for a 2-phase servomotor ?

(b) Explain the requirement of negative slope for the torque speed curve of an a.c. servomotor. What would happen if this slope were positive ?

(c) Enumerate the merits and demerits of an a.c. servomotor as compared to other servomotors.

(d) How can the direction of rotation of a 2-phase servomotor be reversed ? Explain.

(e) What are the advantages of using high-frequency a.c. servomotors ?

6.27. (a) Efficiency and p.f. are important parameters in industrial drives but not for a.c. servomotors. Justify the statement.

(*b*) A small 2-phase, 2-pole induction motor has the following constants at 50 Hz,
$r_1 = 350\ \Omega$, $r_2 = 240\ \Omega$, $x_1 = x_2 = 40\ \Omega$, $X_m = 860\ \Omega$.
This motor is used as a 2-phase control motor with 110 V across the reference winding and 70 V across the control winding leading the reference by 90° (both voltages at 50 Hz). Calculate the internal mechanical power at a slip of 0.80. [**Ans.** 1.99654 W]

6.28. A 2-phase control motor, with balanced 2-phase voltages of 100 V applied to its symmetrical stator windings produces a torque of 4 Nm at standstill.

This motor and load have a total moment of inertia of 0.02 kgm^2 and negligible friction. It is required that this motor should produce an acceleration of 50 rad/sec^2 in this motor-load combination at zero rotor speed. Find the voltage to be applied to control winding with reference winding-voltage remaining at 100 V in time quadrature.

[**Hint.** Read Example 6.11] [**Ans.** 25 V]

6.29. (*a*) Explain the function of two stator windings in a single-phase induction motor. [*I.A.S., 1989*]

(*b*) Draw the torque-speed characteristics of single-phase and three-phase induction motors and explain the reasons for which significant differences in their performance are noticed. [*I.A.S., 1983*]

(*c*) Explain, with neat diagrams, the operation of a single-phase capacitor-start capacitor-run induction motor. Which capacitor has a higher value, the start-or run-capacitor ? Give reason. [*I.A.S., 1991*]

6.30. Comment with justification on the correctness of the following statements, restricting your answer within 200 words for each :

(*a*) A single-phase induction motor, if provided with a three-phase slip-ring type rotor connected to a starting resistance, results in a large starting torque. [*I.A.S., 1983*]

(*b*) Single-phase induction motors must have two stator windings. [*I.A.S., 1987*]

(*c*) Reversal of rotation of single-phase induction motors is never a problem. [*I.A.S., 1988*]

[**Ans.** (*a*) correct (*b*) correct (*c*) correct]

7

A.C. Commutator Machines

When the choice of an electric motor is to be made for any given electric drive, an induction motor is usually the first preference ; because of its simplicity, low cost, minimum maintenance and ruggedness. But induction motors have constant-speed characteristics and low operating power factors. On account of this, induction motors are not used where wide-speed range and improved pf performance are required. Since d.c. distribution is completely discarded, the role of d.c. motors for wide-speed control can be met to some extent, by a.c. commutator motors. In addition, a.c. commutator motors can be made to operate nearer unity p.f. so as to achieve an economy in their running cost.

In view of the above, a.c. commutator machines are used only in special cases where the desired performance can't be realised by other electromechanical-energy converters. For example, in electric traction, a single-phase series motor possesses best operating characteristics, therefore, it is still in use on low-frequency rail systems in Europe. For speed control and p.f. improvement of low-speed large electric motors, a.c. commutator machines are widely used.

There is a great variety of a.c. commutator machines, but in this chapter only those machines are discussed which have proved commercially successful. Two-axis, or generalized approach is also given for single-phase series motor and for the Schrage motor.

7.1 E.M.FS. INDUCED IN COMMUTATOR WINDINGS

In the armature of an a.c. commutator machine, two kinds of e.m.fs. are generally induced. These two e.m.fs. are (*i*) rotational e.m.f. due to armature rotation in the main field, as in d.c. machines and (*ii*) the transformer e.m.f., since the armature winding is linked by an alternating field. For transformer e.m.f., the field and armature windings may be considered respectively as the primary and secondary windings of a transformer. The object of this article is to consider these e.m.fs., first for single-phase commutator machines having alternating field and then for polyphase commutator machines having rotating field.

7.1.1 E.m.fs. Produced by Pulsating Field

Pulsating, or alternating, field is produced in single-phase commutator machines. Here rotational and transformer e.m.fs. are considered as they are produced by the pulsating field.

(*a*) **Rotational e.m.f.** Fig. 7.1. (*a*) illustrates the schematic diagram of a d.c. machine. A rotational e.m.f. E_r is developed across brushes *AB*, due to the armature rotation in the *d*-axis flux ϕ.

The field flux ϕ is assumed sinusoidally distributed along the air-gap periphery. The magnitude of rotational voltage E_r in a d.c. machine is given by

$$E_r = \frac{\phi ZnP}{a} \text{ volts} \qquad \text{...(7.1)}$$

where, n = armature speed in r.p.s.,

Z = total number of armature conductors,

P = number of field poles, and

a = number of parallel armature circuits.

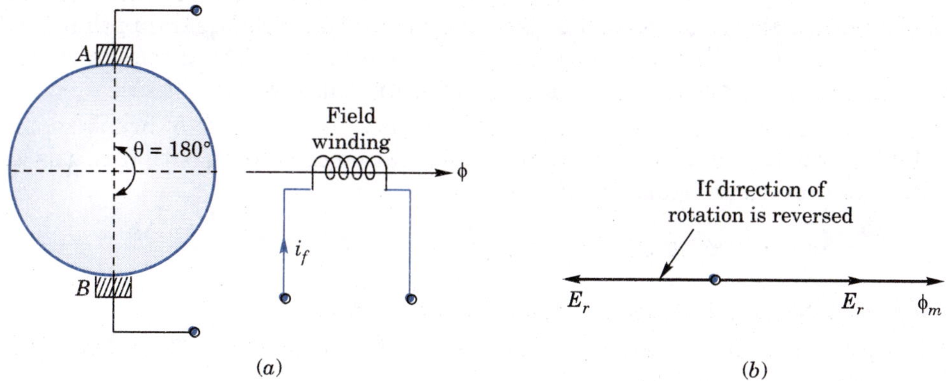

Fig. 7.1: (*a*) Schematic diagram for a d.c. machine
(*b*) Rotational voltage E_r, in phase with, or anti-phase with the main flux *f*.

With constant speed and negligible saturation; if ϕ is decreased, E_r decreases proportionally; if ϕ is zero, E_r (neglecting residual voltage) is zero and if ϕ is reversed, E_r is also reversed in polarity. It means that rotational voltage E_r varies in accordance with field flux ϕ and on account of this fact, both E_r and ϕ are in time phase. If polarity of field flux ϕ is reversed ten times per second, then polarity of E_r is also reversed ten times per second. It follows therefore that if field flux ϕ is an alternating quantity, then E_r is also alternating quantity and whatever is the frequency of the field current or field flux, same is the frequency of E_r.

Let the flux ϕ be an alternating quantity given by $\phi_m \sin \omega t$. This pulsating flux gives rise to rotational e.m.f. across brushes *AB* and its instantaneous value, from Eq. (7.1), is given by

$$e_r = \frac{ZnP}{a} \phi_m \sin \omega t = E_{rm} \sin \omega t$$

where, $E_{rm} = \dfrac{ZnP}{a} \phi_m$ volts.

The r.m.s. value of rotational e.m.f. is

$$E_r = \frac{1}{\sqrt{2}} E_{rm} = \frac{Z\phi_m}{\sqrt{2}} \cdot \frac{Pn}{a}$$

$$= \sqrt{2} \cdot \frac{Z\phi_m}{a} \cdot \left(\frac{Pn}{2}\right) \qquad \text{...(7.2)}$$

Now $\frac{Pn}{2} = f_r$ is called the rotational, or speed frequency, because it depends on the speed of armature rotation. Note the difference between f_r and f, the former depends on the armature speed only and the latter on the supply frequency given to the exciting field.

$$\therefore \qquad E_r = \sqrt{2}\, f_r \phi_m \frac{Z}{a} \qquad ...(7.3)$$

If N is the total number of armature turns, then

$$N = \frac{Z}{2} \quad \text{and} \quad E_r = 2\sqrt{2} f_r \phi_m \frac{N}{a} \qquad ...(7.4)$$

The frequency of rotational e.m.f. E_r is equal to the pulsating field frequency f and is independent of the armature speed. In other words, if armature speed changes, f_r and therefore the magnitude of E_r changes as per Eq. (7.3), but the frequency of E_r remains equal to the pulsating field frequency f. Also E_r is in time phase with the field flux that produces it as shown in Fig. 7.1 (*b*). With no change in the field current, if the direction of rotation is reversed, E_r becomes antiphase to the flux ϕ_m as illustrated in Fig. 7.1 (*b*).

Angle of brush separation θ in Fig. 7.1 (*a*) is 180°. When angle of brush separation is less than 180°, but with the centre line of brush separation coinciding with flux axis as shown in Fig. 7.2 (*a*), the rotational e.m.f. E_r is given by

$$E_r = \sqrt{2}\, f_r \phi_m \frac{Z}{a} \sin\frac{\theta}{2} \qquad ...(7.5)$$

When $\theta = 180°$ as in Fig. 7.1 (*a*), Eq. (7.3) is obtained.

If the centre line of brush separation is displaced from field axis by an angle β as shown in Fig. 7.2 (*b*), then E_r is given by

$$E_r = \sqrt{2}\, f_r \phi_m \frac{Z}{a} \sin\frac{\theta}{2} \cdot \cos\beta \qquad ...(7.6)$$

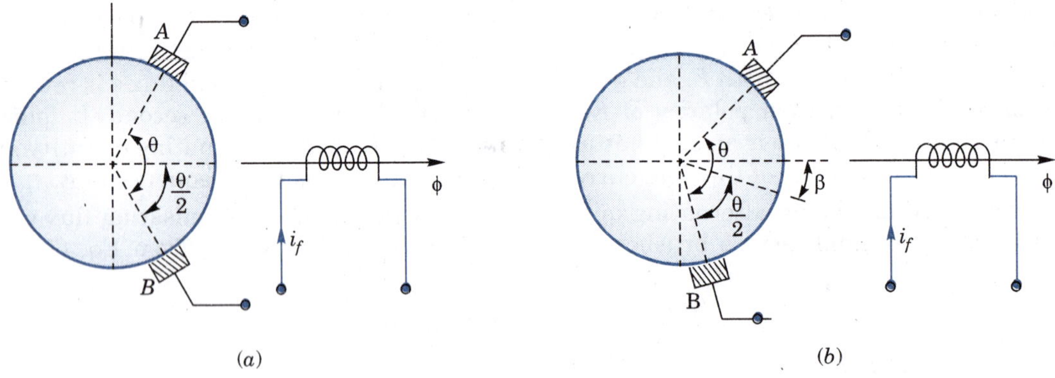

Fig. 7.2: Centre line of brush separation (*a*) along the field axis and (*b*) displaced by angle β from field axis.

In Eq. (7.6), note that field-flux component $\phi_m \cos\beta$, along the centre line of the brush separation is only effective in producing rotational voltage E_r.

(*b*) **Transformer e.m.f.** In Fig. 7.1 (*a*), the armature magnetic axis or brush axis *AB* is 90° away from the axis of pulsating field flux ϕ. Therefore, no transformer e.m.f. appears across brushes *AB* and only rotational e.m.f. E_r is present. Assume that the brushes *AB* are shifted by 90°, so that brush axis AB coincides with the field axis as shown in Fig. 7.3 (a). Now a transformer e.m.f. E_t, of frequency equal to the pulsating-field frequency f, appears across brushes AB in Fig. 7.3 (a) and the rotational e.m.f. E_r is zero. The transformer e.m.f. E_t is always independent of the armature or rotor speed.

The ordinary formula for the e.m.f. induced in a transformer winding is

$$E_t = \sqrt{2}\,\pi f \phi_m N \text{ volts.}$$

In a rotating machine, the armature turns are distributed symmetrically over the armature periphery. In view of this, the winding factor k_ω must be introduced in the transformer e.m.f. across the brushes AB in Fig. 7.3 (a). In addition to it, N in the transformer e.m.f. equation must be replaced by armature series turns N/a between the two brushes AB. Thus the magnitude of transformer e.m.f. E_t across the brushes AB is given by

$$E_t = \sqrt{2}\,\pi f \phi_m \frac{N}{a} \cdot k_\omega$$

where, $k_\omega = k_p \cdot k_d$.

For full-pitch turns, pitch-factor $k_p = 1$. For uniformly distributed winding, the distributed factor k_d is given by

$$k_d = \frac{\sin \sigma^{*}/2}{\sigma/2} = \frac{\sin \pi/2}{\pi/2} = \frac{2}{\pi}$$

∴ The transformer e.m.f. across brushes AB is

$$E_t = \sqrt{2}\,\pi f \phi_m \frac{N}{a} \cdot \frac{2}{\pi} = 2\sqrt{2} f \phi_m \frac{N}{a} \qquad \text{...(7.7)}$$

Since $N = \frac{Z}{2}$, Eq. (7.7) becomes

$$E_t = \sqrt{2} f \phi_m \frac{Z}{a} \qquad \text{...(7.8)}$$

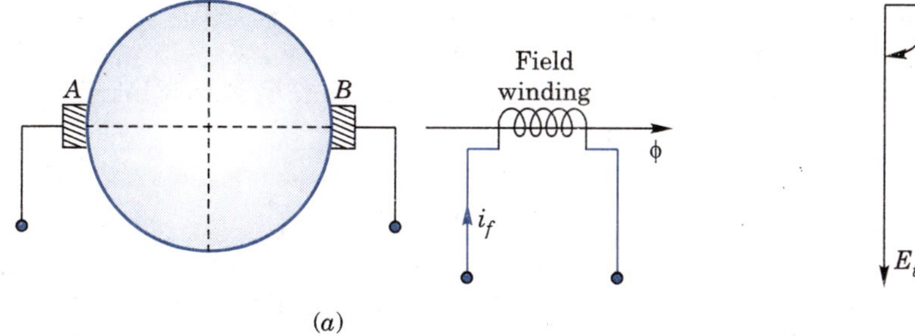

Fig. 7.3: (a) D.C. machine with brush axis along field axis
(b) Transformer e.m.f. E_t lags ϕ_m by 90°

The magnitude of transformer e.m.f. E_t depends on the supply frequency f and is independent of rotational frequency f_r. Also, the transformer e.m.f. is in time-quadrature lagging the flux inducing it as shown in Fig. 7.3 (b).

It may be noted from Eqs. (7.3) and (7.8) or from Eqs. (7.4) and (7.7) that transformer e.m.f. E_t differs from speed e.m.f. E_r only in that f replaces f_r.

* The commutator machines with diametrically placed brushes have a phase spread of π radians.

Again from Eqs. (7.3) and (7.8) or from Eqs. (7.4) and (7.7).

$$\frac{\text{Transformer e.m.f., } E_t}{\text{Rotational e.m.f., } E_r} = \frac{f}{f_r} = \frac{\text{Field-flux frequency}}{\text{Rotational frequency}}$$

$$= \frac{n_s \cdot \frac{P}{2}}{\frac{n \cdot P}{2}} = \frac{n_s}{n} = \frac{\text{Synchronous speed}}{\text{Armature speed of rotation}}$$

(*c*) **General case.** If the brush axis is displaced from the neutral axis by an angle α as shown in Fig. 7.4 (*a*), both rotational and transformer e.m.fs. are present across brushes *AB*. The field flux, ϕ_m, alternating at frequency *f* can be resolved into two components ; one along the brush axis *AB*, *i.e.*, $\phi_t = \phi_m \cdot \sin \alpha$,

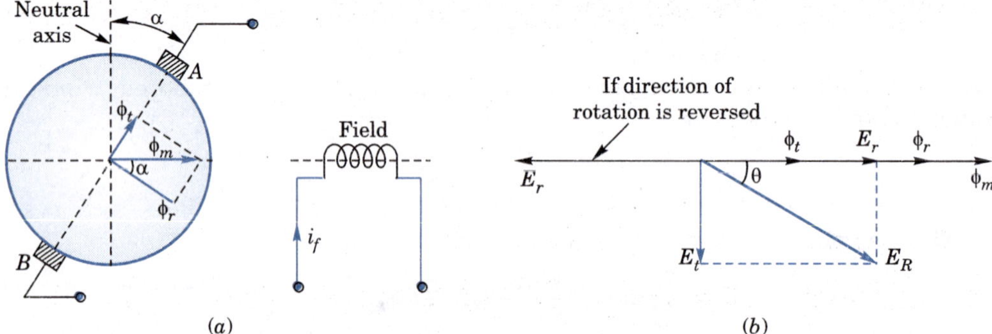

Fig. 7.4: (*a*) Space and (*b*) time phasor diagrams of fluxes and e.m.fs. $\phi_t = \phi_m \sin \alpha$

and the other in space quadrature with brush axis *i.e.*, $\phi_r = \phi_m \cos \alpha$.

Note that if ϕ_m is decreasing, both ϕ_t and ϕ_r are also decreasing ; if ϕ_m is zero both ϕ_t and ϕ_r are zeros and in case ϕ_m is increasing both ϕ_t and ϕ_r are also increasing. In other words, though ϕ_t and ϕ_r are in space-quadrature, both ϕ_t and ϕ_r are in time-phase with ϕ_m as shown in Fig. 7.4 (*b*).

The flux components ϕ_t, in time phase with ϕ_m, induces e.m.f. E_t across brushes *AB*, due to transformer action. Its magnitude is given by

$$E_t = \sqrt{2}\, f\, \phi_m \frac{Z}{a} \sin \alpha \qquad \text{...(7.9)}$$

This transformer e.m.f. E_t is in time quadrature lagging ϕ_t, as shown in Fig. 7.4 (*b*) and its frequency is the same as that of the field flux *i.e.*, *f*. The other flux component ϕ_r, in time phase with ϕ_m, causes rotational e.m.f. E_r to appear across brushes *AB*. Its magnitude is given by

$$E_r = \sqrt{2}\, f_r\, \phi_m \frac{Z}{a} \cos \alpha \qquad \text{...(7.10)}$$

This rotational e.m.f. E_r is in time phase with ϕ_r. However, if the direction of armature rotation is reversed, E_r becomes antiphase to ϕ_r as shown Fig. 7.4 (*b*). The frequency of E_r is equal to the field-flux frequency *f*.

It is, therefore, seen that e.m.fs. E_t and E_r, as given by Eqs. (7.9) and (7.10) respectively, have the same frequency *f* and are present across the brushes *AB*. Their resultant E_R across brushes *AB*, as given by Fig. 7.4 (*b*), is

$$E_R = \sqrt{E_t^2 + E_r^2} = \sqrt{2}\ \phi_m \frac{Z}{a} \sqrt{f^2 \sin^2 \alpha + f_r^2 \cos^2 \alpha} \qquad \text{...[7.11 (a)]}$$

or,

$$E_R = 2\sqrt{2}\ \phi_m \frac{N}{a} \sqrt{f^2 \sin^2 \alpha + f_r^2 \cos^2 \alpha} \qquad \text{...[7.11 (b)]}$$

The time-phase angle θ between E_R and ϕ_m is $\tan \theta = \frac{E_t}{E_r} = \frac{f}{f_r} \tan \alpha$

If the armature runs at synchronous speed, then $f_r = f$ and

$$E_R = \sqrt{2}\ \phi_m \frac{Z}{a} f \quad \text{or} \quad = 2\sqrt{2}\ \phi_m f \frac{N}{a}$$

and time-phase angle θ = space-angle α.

This shows that at synchronous speed, E_R is independent of α; *i.e.*, whatever the brush shift from neutral axis may be, the magnitude of E_R is unaltered at synchronous speed. At the same time, the time-phase angle of E_R, *i.e.* θ, is equal to the space-angle α through which the brushes are displaced from the neutral axis. Thus, an a.c. commutator machine at synchronous speed can act as a *phase-shifter*, with the magnitude of E_R remaining constant.

7.1.2 E.m.fs. Produced by Rotating Field

In d.c. machines, the total flux per pole ϕ is constant and stationary in space and the rotational e.m.f. at the brushes has zero frequency, with its magnitude given by Eq. (7.1). Now consider a rotating flux which is sinusoidally distributed in space and has a constant amplitude of ϕ_m. If the field flux rotates in the direction of rotor rotation, then relative velocity between conductors and rotating flux becomes $(n_s - n)$ r.p.s. Here n is the rotor speed in r.p.s. and n_s is rotating field speed in r.p.s. This relative velocity of $(n_s - n)$ r.p.s. is responsible for the generation of e.m.f. E_{RT} in the armature conductors. Its r.m.s. value at the brushes, as per Eq. (7.2), is given by

$$E_{RT} = \sqrt{2}\ \frac{Z\phi_m}{a} \frac{P(n_s - n)}{2} \qquad \text{...[7.12 (a)]}$$

$$= \sqrt{2}\ (f - f_r)\ \phi_m \frac{Z}{a} \qquad \text{...[7.12 (b)]}$$

where,

$$f = \frac{n_s P}{2} \quad \text{and} \quad f_r = \frac{nP}{2}$$

The frequency of the e.m.f. in the armature conductors is $(f - f_r)$ Hz, because it depends upon the relative speed between armature conductors and the rotating field. Reference to Art. 5.10 shows that the brush frequency f_b depends on the rotating field speed with respect to the stationary brushes. In the present case, the rotating-field speed with respect to the stationary brushes is constant at n_s r.p.s. whatever the rotor speed may be. Therefore brush frequency $f_b = f$ at all the possible rotor speeds.

In case the field flux ϕ_m is revolving opposite to the armature movement then the relative speed between armature conductors and rotating flux becomes $(n_s + n)$ r.p.s. and the r.m.s. resultant e.m.f., as per Eq. (7.2), is given by

$$E_{RT} = \sqrt{2}\ \frac{\phi_m Z}{a} \cdot \frac{P(n_s + n)}{2} \qquad \text{...[7.13 (a)]}$$

or,

$$E_{RT} = \sqrt{2}\ (f + f_r)\ \phi_m \frac{Z}{a} \qquad \text{...[7.13 (b)]}$$

The frequency of the e.m.f. in armature conductors is now $(f + f_r)$ Hz. But the brush frequency remains f Hz, because the relative speed between brushes and the rotating field is again n_s r.p.s. at all the speeds.

Eqs. (7.12) and (7.13) may be combined in one equation as

$$E_{RT} = \sqrt{2}\,(f \pm f_r)\,\phi_m \frac{Z}{a} \text{ volts} \qquad ...(7.14)$$

In case brush separation angle θ is less than 180° as shown in Fig. 7.2 (*a*), then Eq. (7.14) becomes,

$$E_{RT} = \sqrt{2}\,(f \pm f_r)\,\phi_m \frac{Z}{a} \sin\frac{\theta}{2} \qquad ...(7.15)$$

Note that if rotor is rotating at synchronous speed in the direction of rotating field, then relative speed between rotor and rotating field becomes zero and no e.m.f. is, therefore, generated in the armature conductors and across the brushes. In Eqs. (7.14) and (7.15) plus sign is used when rotor is rotating opposite to the rotating field and negative sign when rotor is rotating in the direction of rotating field.

Example 7.1. *A 2-pole a.c. commutator machine has the following data :*

Armature turns = 300 ;

Armature speed = 1800 r.p.m.

Frequency and maximum value of pulsating flux

= 50 Hz and 0.02 Wb respectively.

Find the magnitude and frequency of the e.m.f. appearing at the brushes ; if the brush axis is

(a) 90° away from the field axis *(b) aligned along the field axis and*

(c) 30° away from the field axis.

Solution. (*a*) When the brush axis is 90° away from the field or d-axis, rotational e.m.f. alone appears across the brushes and transformer e.m.f. is zero. The magnitude of rotational e.m.f., from Eq. (7.3), is given by $E_r = \sqrt{2}\, f_r\, \phi_m \frac{Z}{a}$ volts.

Here rotational frequency,

$$f_r = \frac{nP}{2} = \frac{1800 \times 2}{2 \times 60} = 30 \quad \text{and} \quad Z = 300 \times 2 = 600.$$

$$\therefore \qquad E_r = \sqrt{2}\,(30)\,(0.02) \times \frac{600}{2} = 254.52 \text{ V}$$

The frequency of E_r is equal to the field-flux frequency, *i.e.*, 50 Hz.

(*b*) If the brush axis coincides with field axis, only transformer e.m.f. is induced and its magnitude, as given by Eq. (7.8), is

$$E_t = \sqrt{2}\, f\, \phi_m \frac{Z}{a} = \sqrt{2}\,(50)\,(0.02)\,\frac{600}{2} = 424.2 \text{ V at 50 Hz.}$$

(*c*) When brush axis is displaced from the neutral axis, both rotational and transformer e.m.fs. appear across the brushes. For this part, brush axis is 30° away from field axis, therefore $\alpha = 60°$. The magnitude of resultant voltage E_R, from Eq. [7.11 (*a*)], is

$$E_R = \sqrt{2}\ \phi_m \frac{Z}{a} \sqrt{f^2 \sin^2 \alpha + f_r^2 \cos^2 \alpha}$$

$$= \sqrt{2}\ (0.02) \frac{600}{2} \sqrt{(50 \sin 60)^2 + (30 \cos 60)^2}$$

$$= \sqrt{2}\ (60) \sqrt{20.99} = 388.74 \text{ V at 50 Hz.}$$

Example 7.2. *A 2-pole commutator machine, with 100 armature turns, is running at 1200 r.p.m. clockwise. The stationary flux of 0.12 Wb per pole is sinusoidally distributed in space. The brushes are separated by an angle $\theta = 60°$ and the centre line of brush separation coincides with field axis.*

(*a*) *Find the magnitude of e.m.f. across the two brushes.*

(*b*) *If the field flux of constant amplitude 0.12 Wb, is assumed to be rotating at 1800 r.p.m. in the (i) clockwise direction and (ii) anti-clockwise directions ; then compute the magnitude and frequency of the brush e.m.f. when $\theta = 60°$. Also, calculate the frequency of the conductor e.m.fs. in both the cases.*

(*c*) *The armature at the other end of the commutator is tapped and connected to balanced 3-phase voltages, so that a rotating field is produced. The speed of this rotating field is 3000 r.p.m. (i) clockwise and (ii) anti-clockwise. The stator is left open and the armature is driven at 2400 r.p.m. clockwise for this part of the example. Find the frequency of the brush e.m.f. in the two cases.*

Solution. (*a*) Since the flux is stationary, just as in a d.c. machine, only rotation e.m.f. $\frac{\phi ZnP}{a}$, would appear across the brushes along the neutral axis, *i.e.*, when $\theta = 180°$.

For any other value of brush separation, the e.m.f. across the brushes is given by

$$E_r = \frac{\phi ZnP}{a} \sin \frac{\theta}{2} \qquad \text{...(7.16)}$$

$$= \frac{(0.12)\ (200)\ (20) \times 2}{2} . \sin \frac{60°}{2} = 240 \text{ V.}$$

(*b*) (*i*) When the field flux is rotating in the direction of armature rotation, then e.m.f. across brushes as per Eq. (7.15) is $E_r = \sqrt{2}\ (f - f_r)\ \phi_m\ (Z/a) \sin \frac{\theta}{2}$

Here $$f = \frac{n_s P}{2} = \frac{1800 \times 2}{60 \times 2} = 30 \text{ Hz}$$

and $$f_r = \frac{nP}{2} = \frac{1200 \times 2}{60 \times 2} = 20 \text{ Hz}$$

∴ $$E_r = \sqrt{2}\ (30 - 20)\ (0.12) \frac{200}{2} \sin \frac{60°}{2} = 84.84 \text{ V.}$$

Frequency of conductor e.m.fs. $= f - f_r = 30 - 20 = 10$ Hz.

The brush frequency f_b depends on the field speed relative to the brushes. Since the revolving-field speed is constant at 1800 r.p.m., f_b remains constant at $1800 \times 2/60 \times 2$, *i.e.*, 30 Hz and it is independent of armature speed and its direction of rotation.

(*ii*) When the field flux is revolving opposite to the armature rotation, magnitude of e.m.f., as per Eq. (7.15), is given by

$$E_r = \sqrt{2}\,(f + f_r)\,\phi_m \frac{Z}{a} \sin\frac{\theta}{2}$$

$$E_r = \sqrt{2}\,(30 + 20)\,(0.12)\,\frac{200}{2} \sin\frac{60^\circ}{2} = 424.2 \text{ V}.$$

Frequency of conductor e.m.fs $\quad = f + f_r = 50$ Hz

and brush frequency, $\quad f_b = 30$ Hz.

(*c*) This part of the example pertains to the commutator-frequency converter. A review of art 5.10 is, therefore, helpful.

(*i*) The armature is running clockwise at a speed of 2400 r.p.m. When the armature field is also rotating clockwise at a speed of 3000 r.p.m., then the field speed relative to the fixed brushes is $(3000 + 2400) = 5400$ r.p.m. This gives,

$$f_b = \frac{2 \times 5400}{2 \times 60} = 90 \text{ Hz}$$

(*ii*) When the field is rotating at 3000 r.p.m. anti-clockwise, the field speed relative to the brushes is $(3000 - 2400) = 600$ r.p.m.

$$\therefore \qquad f_b = \frac{2 \times 600}{2 \times 60} = 10 \text{ Hz}.$$

Example 7.3. *A 4-pole rotor carries a lap-connected winding with full-pitched coils. The armature, with 360 turns, rotates in a constant sine-distributed d-axis flux of 0.01 Wb. One end of the winding is tapped at 6 equidistant points and connected to 6 slip rings. At the other end, a pair of commutator brushes is placed in the q-axis. Compute the magnitude and frequency of the e.m.fs. appearing across the q-axis brushes and between adjacent slip rings if the armature rotates at*

(a) 2400 r.p.m. (b) 1200 r.p.m. (c) 400 r.p.m.

Solution. (*a*) Since flux is constant as in a d.c. machine, the brush e.m.f. is given by

$$E_r = \frac{\phi ZnP}{a} = \frac{0.01 \times 720 \times 40 \times 4}{4}$$

$$= 288 \text{ V at zero Hz}.$$

For 6 equidistant taps, the winding is equivalent to 6-phase winding with a phase spread of $\sigma = 2\pi/6 = 60^\circ$.

$$\therefore \text{ Distribution factor, } k_d = \frac{\sin \sigma/2}{\sigma/2} = \frac{\sin 30^\circ}{\pi/6} = \frac{3}{\pi}$$

For full-pitched winding, the winding factor is $k_\omega = \frac{3}{\pi} \times 1 = \frac{3}{\pi}$

$\therefore$ E.m.f. $E_{ph,}$ appearing between adjacent slip rings, is

$$E_{ph} = \sqrt{2}\ \pi f_r N_{Ph}\ \phi\ k_\omega$$

$$= \sqrt{2}\pi \left[\frac{4 \times 2400}{120}\right] \times \frac{360}{6} \times 0.01 \times \frac{3}{\pi} = 203.62 \text{ V.}$$

Frequency of slip-ring e.m.f.

$$= \frac{P.n}{2} = \frac{4 \times 2400}{2 \times 60} = 80 \text{ Hz.}$$

(*b*) When the armature rotates at 1200 r.p.m., then brush e.m.f. is

$$E_r = 144 \text{ V at zero Hz} \quad \text{and} \quad E_{Ph} = 101.81 \text{ V at 40 Hz.}$$

(*c*) For armature speed of 400 r.p.m.,

$$E_r = 48 \text{ V at zero Hz} \quad \text{and} \quad E_{Ph} = 33.94 \text{ V at 13.33 Hz.}$$

It may be seen from parts (*a*), (*b*) and (*c*) that $\frac{E_r}{E_{Ph}} = \sqrt{2}$.

This can also be proved as follows :

For voltage across *q*-axis brushes, $E_r = \frac{\phi ZnP}{a} = 2 f_r \phi \frac{Z}{a}$

For voltage across adjacent slip rings,

$$E_{Ph} = \sqrt{2}\pi f_r N_{Ph}\ \phi\ k_\omega$$

$$= \sqrt{2}\pi f_r \cdot \left[\frac{Z}{2 \times 6}\right] \cdot \phi \cdot \frac{3}{\pi} = \frac{1}{2\sqrt{2}} f_r Z\phi$$

$$\therefore \quad \frac{E_r}{E_{Ph}} = \frac{4\sqrt{2}}{a} = \frac{4\sqrt{2}}{4} = \sqrt{2}.$$

7.2 TORQUE

Fig. 7.5 shows a stator winding producing a sinusoidal m.m.f. F_s and therefore a sinusoidal distribution of stator flux along its periphery. The currents in the rotor, as assumed in this figure, give rise to rotor m.m.f. F_r and therefore the rotor flux, in quadrature with F_s. Their interaction results in the development of torque *T*/4 in each of the four quadrants (according to left hand rule) as shown in Fig. 7.5. The four-quadrant torques act in clockwise direction

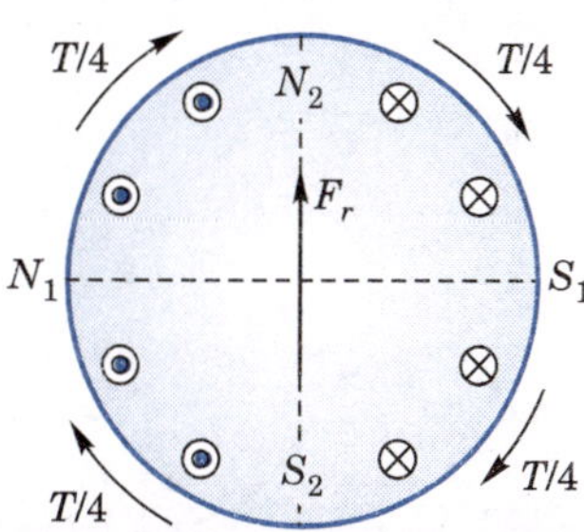

Fig. 7.5: Illustrating the production of torque.

thereby giving a resultant torque T. Another way of describing this is that the stator m.m.f. F_s gives rise to 2 poles N_1S_1 on the stator and rotor m.m.f. F_r causes the appearance of 2 poles N_2S_2 on the rotor as shown in Fig. 7.5. The interaction between stator and rotor poles gives rise to torque T in clockwise direction.

In Fig. 7.6, the assumed rotor currents gives rise to m.m.f. F_r in line with stator m.m.f. F_s and the net torque is found to be zero. Alternatively, the stator produced poles N_1S_1 and rotor produced poles N_2S_2 are along the same axis, therefore torque angle is 180° and no electromagnetic torque is developed.

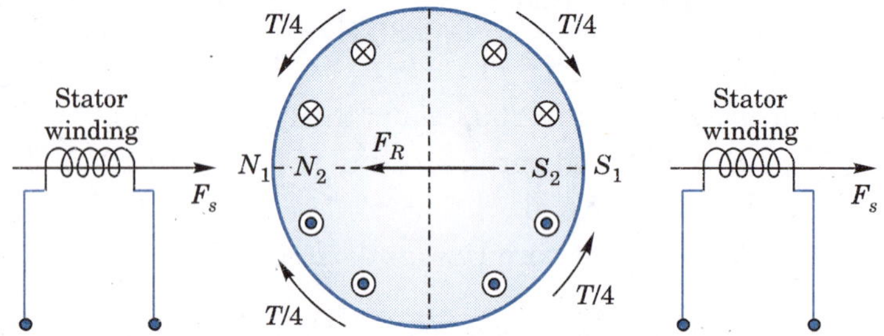

Fig. 7.6: Illustrating the production of zero torque.

It may thus be concluded from above that if the two windings, one on stator and the other on rotor, have their m.m.fs. (or fluxes), or their components, at right angles to each other, electromagnetic torque is developed.

Consider the simple arrangement of an a.c. commutator machine as shown in Fig. 7.7. The brush axis AB is displaced by an angle α from the d-axis. The field flux ϕ is sinusoidally distributed in space and varying sinusoidally with time. As stated above, the component $\phi \cos \alpha$ only will give rise to the production of torque, because it is normal to the armature magnetic axis, *i.e.*, the brush axis.

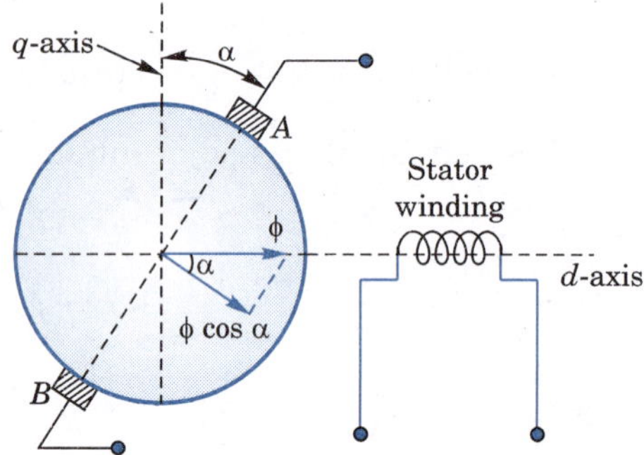

Fig. 7.7: Torque production in a single-phase commutator motor.

This instantaneous torque $T_{e.inst}$ is proportional to $i\ \phi \cos \alpha$, where i is the armature current.

In a d.c. machine, the electromagnetic torque developed is given by

$$T_e = \frac{\text{Electrical power developed}}{\omega_r}$$

$$= \frac{\text{(Rotational e.m.f. in armature) (current)}}{\omega_r}$$

$$= \frac{E_a I_a}{\omega_r} = \frac{\phi ZnP}{(2\pi n)a} \cdot I_a = \frac{ZP}{2a\pi} \phi I_a$$

or
$$T_e = \frac{ZP}{2a\pi} \text{(field flux) (armature current)}$$

For an a.c. commutator machine shown in Fig. 7.7, the instantaneous torque is given by

$$T_{e.inst} = \frac{ZP}{2a\pi} (\phi \cos \alpha)(i) \qquad ...(7.17)$$

Let the field flux ϕ be given by $\phi = \phi_m \sin \omega t$ and the corresponding armature current be given by

$$i = I_m \sin (\omega t \pm \psi).$$

Here ψ is the angle of time phase displacement between flux and current. The plus sign indicates current leading flux by an angle ψ and negative the reverse.

Substitution of ϕ and i in Eq. (7.17) gives

$$T_{e.inst} = \frac{ZP}{2a\pi} \cdot \phi_m \sin \omega t \cos \alpha \cdot I_m \sin (\omega t \pm \psi)$$

$$= \frac{ZP}{2a\pi} \cdot \phi_m \cos \alpha \cdot I_m [\sin \omega t \cdot \sin (\omega t \pm \psi)]$$

Since $\sin A \sin B = 1/2 [\cos (A - B) - \cos (A + B)]$

$$T_{e.inst} = \frac{ZP}{2a\pi} \cdot \frac{1}{2} \cdot \phi_m \cos \alpha \, (\sqrt{2} I) \, [\cos \psi - \cos (2\omega t \pm \psi)]$$

$$= \frac{\sqrt{2}}{4\pi} \cdot \frac{ZP}{a} \phi_m I \cos \alpha [\cos \psi - \cos (2\omega t \pm \psi)] \qquad ...(7.18)$$

Eq. (7.18) shows that the instantaneous torque consists of (*i*) one component which is constant and (*ii*) second component which alternates at double the supply frequency, its average value being zero over the complete cycle.

Therefore, the average torque or steady torque for the single-phase commutator motor shown in Fig. 7.7 is

$$T_s = 0.11254 \frac{ZP}{a} \cdot \phi_m I \cos \alpha \cos \psi \text{ Nm} \qquad ...(7.19)$$

The torque is, therefore, maximum when $\psi = 0$, *i.e.* when the flux and current are in time phase. Torque is also maximum when $\alpha = 0$, *i.e.* when armature magnetic axis and field axis are in quadrature.

7.3 SINGLE-PHASE SERIES MOTORS

If an alternating voltage is applied to on ordinary d.c. series motor, then for one half cycle, the field flux ϕ_d and armature flux ϕ_q may be as shown in Fig. 7.8 (*a*). Their interaction results in the development of torque in the clockwise direction. For the other half of the cycle, the direction of current in both field and armature is reversed simultaneously, because they are in series. As a result of this, both the field and armature fluxes are reversed as shown in Fig. 7.8 (*b*) and torque is developed again in the clockwise direction. Thus an ordinary d.c. series motor, if energised from an a.c. source, would develop unidirectional torque and the armature would rotate. The electromagnetic torque T_e, proportional to the product of field flux ϕ_d and armature current i, as per Eq. (7.19) is unidirectional but pulsating at double the supply frequency as illustrated in Fig. 7.8 (c). Here time-phase angle between ϕ_d and i is assumed zero. The average torque is positive and the motor rotates. However, an ordinary d.c. series motor when energised from a.c. source, would operate inefficiently because of inferior commutation, poor p.f. and increased iron losses in poles and yoke which are usually unlaminated.

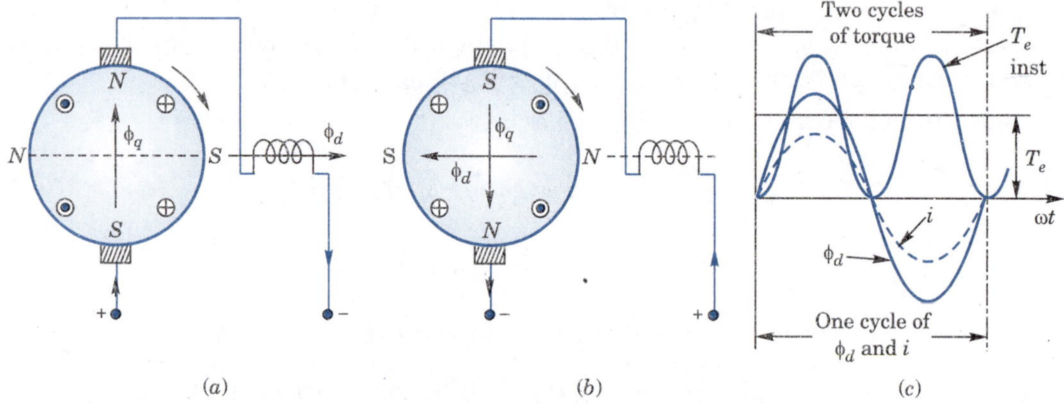

Fig. 7.8: Pertaining to the development of torque in d.c. series motor when fed from a.c. source.

It may be concluded from above that single-phase series motors are similar to d.c. series motors, except that their poles and yokes are made up of thin laminations having better magnetic properties. Fractional-kW a.c. series motors make use of salient pole construction. But for large-size motors, salient-pole (non-uniform air gap) construction is now given up, in favour of uniform air-gap machines. The rotor slots are usually skewed to obtain a quiet operation of the single-phase series motors.

The performance and characteristics of an a.c. series motors can be understood better by taking up its phasor diagram.

Phasor diagram and operating characteristics : In a single-phase series motor, the applied voltage has to overcome (*i*) the voltage drops across field and armature windings and (*ii*) emf generated in the armature winding. These voltages are discussed below one after the other.

(*i*) Voltage drop across field winding V_f is given by

$$V_f = (r_f + j\,x_f)\,I + j\,X_{md}\,I$$

where, I = motor current

$(r_f + j\,x_f)$ = leakage impedance of field winding

and, X_{md} = magnetizing reactance of field (or d-axis) winding.

Here X_{md} accounts for the d-axis field flux. The equation for voltage drop across field winding is similar to primary emf equation ($V_1 = (r_1 + j\,x_1)\,I_1 + j\,X_m\,I_1$) for a transformer.

(*ii*) Voltage drop across armature winding V_a is given by

$$V_a = (r_a + j\,x_a)\,I + j\,X_{mq}\,I$$

where, $(r_a + j\,x_a)$ = leakage impedance of armature winding

and, X_{mq} = magnetizing reactance of armature (*q*-axis) winding

Here X_{mq} accounts for the armature reaction flux.

(*iii*) Rotational emf in armature winding = E_r

Emf E_r is generated in the armature winding of ac series motor due to field flux ϕ, just like the back emf generated in a dc motor.

From above, the applied voltage V_t can be expressed as, $V_t = V_f + V_a + E_r$

or $$V_t = (r_f + j\,x_f)\,I + j\,X_{md}\,I + (r_a + j\,x_a)\,I + j\,X_{mq}\,I + E_r \qquad ...(7.20)$$

Rotational, or speed, emf E_r can also be expressed in terms of armature current I as under.

From Eq. (7.3), rotational emf E_r is $E_r = \sqrt{2}\,.\,f_a\,.\,\phi_m\,.\,\dfrac{Z}{a}$

Also, $$\phi_m = \text{maximum value of field flux}$$

$$= \frac{\text{Effective field turns } N_f \times I_{\max}}{\text{Reluctance}} = \frac{N_f\,(\sqrt{2}\,I)}{\text{Reluctance}}$$

$\therefore$ $$E_r = \sqrt{2}\,.\,\frac{P\,.\,n}{2}\,,\,\frac{N_f\,(\sqrt{2}\,I)}{\text{Rel}}\,.\,\frac{Z}{a} \text{ volts}$$

$$= \frac{P\,.\,N_f\,.\,Z}{a}\,.\,\frac{1}{\text{Rel}}\,.\,In \;= CIn$$

where, constant $C = \dfrac{P\,.\,N_f\,.\,Z}{a\,.\,\text{Reluctance}}$

Now, voltage equation for 1-phase series motor (uncompensated), from Eq. (7.20), can be written as

$$\bar{V_t} = \bar{I}\,[(r_a + r_f) + j\,(x_a + x_f) + j\,(X_{md} + X_{mq})] + C\bar{I}n$$

$$= \bar{I}\;[r + j\,(x + X_m)] + C\bar{I}n$$

$$= \bar{I}\;[r + j\,X] + C\bar{I}n \qquad ...(7.21)$$

where, $r = r_a + r_f$ = total resistance of field F and armature A windings

$x = x_a + x_f$ = total leakage reactance of F and A windings

$X_m = X_{md} + X_{mq}$ = total magnetizing reactance of F and A windings

$X = x + X_m$ = total reactance of motor circuit.

On the basis of Eq. (7.21), phasor diagram of a single-phase series motor is as shown in Fig. 7.9, where current I is taken as horizontal reference phasor. Field flux ϕ and current I producing this flux are in phase. This implies that core loss, friction and windage loss have not been included in the phasor diagram. These losses should be deducted from mechanical power developed in order to obtain motor shaft power.

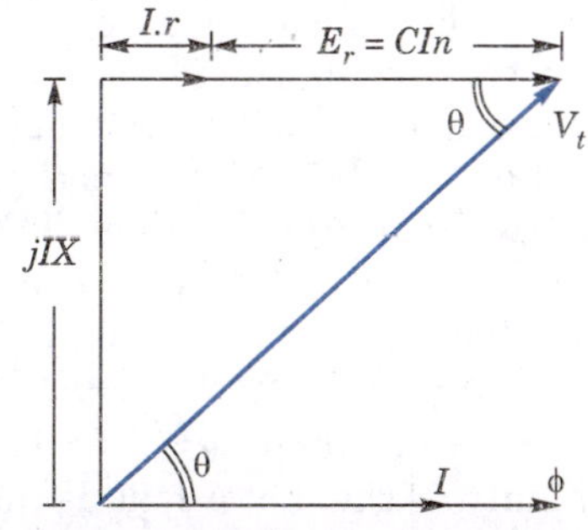

Fig. 7.9: Phasor diagram of a single-phase series motor.

In the phasor diagram, speed voltage $E_r = CIn$ is in phase with the current I.

From Eq. (7.21), speed n can be obtained as

$$n = \frac{1}{C}\left[\sqrt{\left(\frac{V_t}{I}\right)^2 - X^2} - r\right] \quad ...(7.22)$$

Electromagnetic power developed, P_e = (rotational emf in armature) × (armature current)

$$\therefore \qquad P_e = E_r \,.\, I = CI^2 n$$

$$\text{Electromagnetic torque, } T_e = \frac{P_e}{\omega_s} = \frac{CI^2 n}{2\pi n} = \frac{C}{2\pi} I^2 = kI^2$$

Eq. (7.22) can be re-written to include T_e as

$$n = \frac{1}{C}\left[\sqrt{\frac{kV_t^2}{T_e} - X^2} - r\right] \quad ...(7.23)$$

or

$$T_e = \frac{k \,.\, V_t^2}{(r + Cn)^2 + X^2} \quad ...(7.24)$$

It is seen from Eq. (7.23) that with the increase in load torque ($T_L = T_e$), the speed drops as shown in Fig. 7.10. For a given load torque T_L or T_e, Eq. (7.23) indicates that motor operating speed on lower-operating frequencies is higher. On dc operation, motor speed is given by [$X = 0$ in Eq. (7.22)]

$$n = \frac{1}{C} \cdot \frac{V_t - rI}{I}$$

It is also seen from Fig. 7.9 that $V_t \cos\theta - Ir = E_r = CIn$

$$\therefore \qquad \cos\theta = \frac{I\,(Cn + r)}{V_t} \quad ...(7.25)$$

Eq. (7.25) indicates that as the speed n rises, the power factor of motor gets improved.

The starting torque can be obtained from Eq. (7.24) by putting $n = 0$.

$$\therefore \qquad T_{e.st} = \frac{kV_t^2}{r^2 + X^2} \quad ...(7.26)$$

Eq. (7.26) shows that the starting torque is low at higher operating frequencies as illustrated in Fig. 7.10.

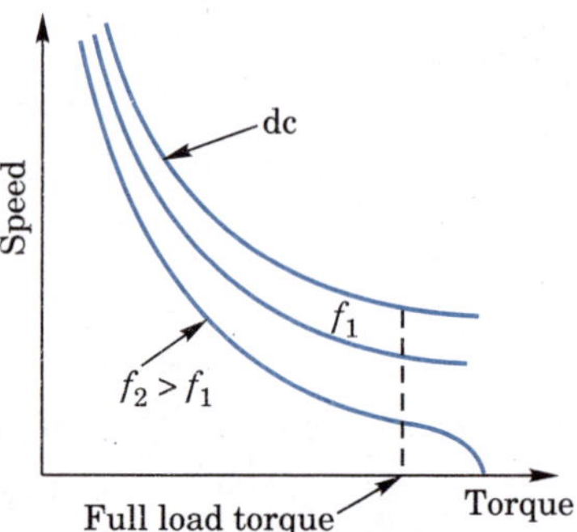

Fig. 7.10: Speed-torque curves of a series motor.

The uncompensated, or plain, series motor is usually constructed in fractional-kW sizes. Small single-phase ac series motors, which can operate satisfactorily both on dc and ac, are called *universal motors*. These motors are built up to about 200 W range. The main advantages of universal motors are their high no-load speed, high starting torque and light weight. These merits have made these motors popular for their use in vacuum cleaners, food mixers, sewing machines, mechanical computing machines and portable tools like electric saw, electric drill, electric tile-cutter etc.

No-load speeds of universal motors vary from 5000 to 15000 rpm. But the speed drops rapidly as the motor load is increased, the power demand remaining almost constant. In case single-phase series motor is required to operate at constant speed, then a mechanical governing device can be used. This governing device inserts a resistor in series with the motor so that speed is held constant.

7.3.1 Compensated A.C. Series Motors

In small a.c. series motors, the commutating difficulties are not of much importance, since these motors operate at lower currents. In addition, these motors run at high speeds and, therefore, their operating p.f. is relatively good. In view of this, small a.c. series motors are usually uncompensated. But for larger series motors, a compensating winding is necessary to get better p.f., better speed-torque characteristics and improved commutation.

The functions of compensating windings in both a.c. and d.c. series motors are similar. Phasor diagram of plain series motor of Fig. 7.9 reveals that its low p.f. is mainly due to voltage drop $I.\ X_m = I(X_{md} + X_{mq})$. The q-axis magnetizing reactance X_{mq} accounts for the armature reaction flux along brush axis. If ampere-turns of compensating winding, placed along brush axis, neutralizes armature reaction mmf completely, then X_{mq} would be zero and this would improve pf the motor and its other operating characteristics.

There are two methods of connecting the compensating windings. In Fig. 7.11 (*a*), the compensating winding is connected in series with the armature and this arrangement is called *conductively compensated* machine. An alternative arrangement called an *inductively compensated* machine, is given in Fig. 7.11 (*b*), where the compensating winding is disconnected from the main circuit and short-circuited on itself. The compensating winding now acts as the short-circuited secondary of a transformer, the armature winding acting as its primary.

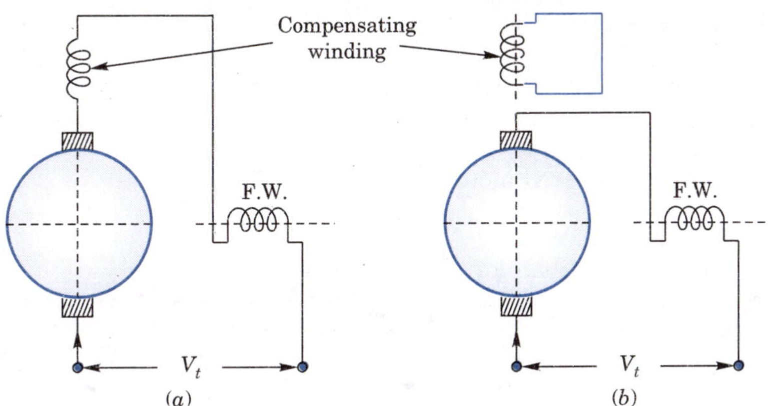

Fig. 7.11: A.C. series motor (*a*) conductively compensated and (*b*) inductively compensated. *FW* is field winding.

For a compensated series motor, if armature reaction mmf along brush axis is completely neutralized by compensating winding mmf, then, as stated above, q-aixs magnetizing reactance X_{mq} would be zero. As a result, phasor diagram of Fig. 7.9 gets modified to that shown in Fig. 7.12, where X_{mq} is taken as zero. But in this phasor diagram, leakage impedance $(r_c + j\ x_c)$ of compensating winding must be taken into consideration. For the inductively-compensated motor, resistance r_c and leakage reactance x_c must be referred to the armature, as in a transformer.

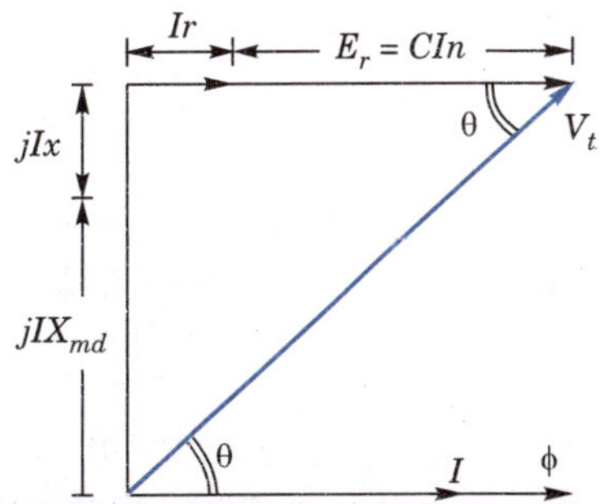

Fig. 7.12: Phasor diagram of a compensated A.C. series motor.

In Fig. 7.12, $r = r_a + r_f + r_c$ and $x = x_a + x_f + x_c$,

From Fig. 7.12, $\overline{V_t} = I\,(r + jx + jX_{md}) + E_r$

$$= \overline{I}\,(r + j\,(x + X_{md})) + C\overline{I}n \quad \text{or} \quad \overline{V_t} = \overline{I}\ (r + Cn) + j\overline{I}\ (x + X_{md})$$

or $$n = \frac{1}{C}\left[\sqrt{\left(\frac{V_t}{I}\right)^2 - (x + X_{md})^2} - r\right] \qquad \text{...(7.26a)}$$

As already explained, $T_e = kI^2$,

$$\therefore \quad n = \frac{1}{C}\left[\sqrt{\frac{kV_t^2}{T_e} - (x + X_{md})^2} - r\right] \qquad \text{...(7.27)}$$

Eq. (7.27) shows that if the torque increases, speed decreases giving again series characteristics.

From Eq. (7.27), the electromagnetic torque T_e is given by

$$T_e = \frac{kV_t^2}{(r + Cn)^2 + (x + X_{md})^2} \qquad \text{...(7.28)}$$

The starting torque can be obtained by putting $n = 0$ in Eq. (7.28).

$$\therefore \quad T_{e.st} = \frac{kV_t^2}{r^2 + (x + X_{md})^2} \qquad \text{...(7.29)}$$

It is seen from Eqs. (7.24) and (7.28) that for a given V_t and speed n, torque for a compensated series motor is higher ($\because$ $X_{md} < X$), thus giving better speed-torque characteristics. From Eqs. (7.26) and (7.29), starting torque is also higher for a compensated series motor.

Power factor of compensated motor, $$= \frac{r + Cn}{\sqrt{(r + Cn)^2 + (x + X_{md})^2}}$$

and p.f. of uncompensated motor, $$= \frac{r + Cn}{\sqrt{(r + Cn)^2 + (x + X)^2}}$$

It is also seen from Fig. 7.12 that $\sin\theta = \dfrac{I\,(x + X_{md})}{V_t}$

$\therefore$ Pf of compensated motor, $$\cos\theta = \sqrt{1 - \left(\frac{I\,(x + X_{md})}{V_t}\right)^2}$$

and pf of uncompensated motor, $$= \sqrt{1 - \left(\frac{I\,(x + X)}{V_t}\right)^2}$$

The above expressions for pfs indicate that for a given speed, compensated motor has better p.f., because X_{md} is less than X.

As in a dc motor the mechanical power developed in the armature of an a.c. series motor is

$$P_a = I \times E_{rad}$$

$\therefore$ Shaft power output,

$$P_{sh} = P_a - (\text{core loss + mechanical loss})$$

$$P_{sh} = P_a - \text{stray-power loss.}$$

For a single-phase series motor, typical speed, torque and power factor characteristics as a function of motor current are shown in Fig. 7.13. It is seen from this figure that speed and power factor decrease whereas the electric torque increases as the motor is loaded.

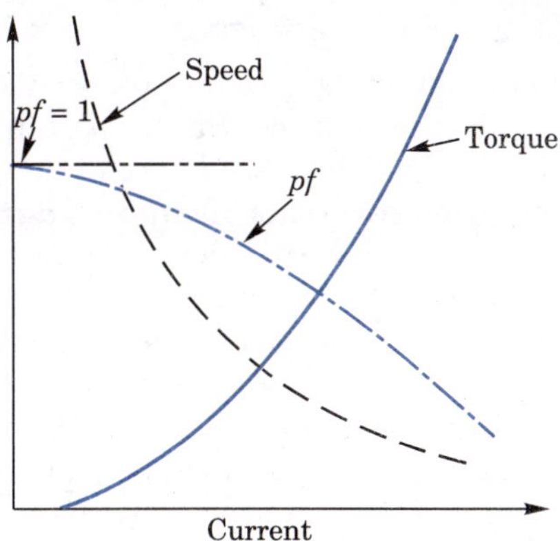

Fig. 7.13: Typical characteristics of a 1-phase series motor.

In the commutating zone, the compensating winding neutralizes the armature reaction flux. As a consequence, emf induced in the coil undergoing commutation is reduced. This results in better commutation in compensated ac series motors.

Thus, series motors fitted with compensating windings have better speed-torque characteristics, better pf and improved commutation as compared to uncompensated motors.

Large single-phase ac series motors are widely used for railway traction purposes in some countries of the world.

Starting. The various methods of starting series motors are as follows :

(*i*) Direct-on-line starting for a.c. series motors of fractional-kW ratings.

(*ii*) Resistance starters as in the case of d.c. series motors.

(*iii*) Auto-transformer with a number of tappings on its windings. This method is used for large series motors.

Speed Control. A synchronous machine runs at a constant speed determined by the number of poles and supply frequency f. Induction motor speed depends on the number of poles, frequency and the slip. But the speed of electrical machines fitted with commutator and brushes is not governed by the number of poles and frequency. It is because the brush and commutator arrangement can act as a frequency converter for both input and output voltages and currents. As a result, commutator machines can be built to operate over wide speed ranges. For example, the brush voltage in a d.c. motor has zero-frequency. This zero frequency voltage is converted by means of commutator and brushes to speed frequency ($= nP/2$) voltage in the rotor conductors for any rotor speed n r.p.s. Same is true for a.c. series motors. The line frequency voltage at the brushes is converted to speed frequency voltage in the rotor conductors and the rotor can therefore, run at any speed depending upon its design. This shows that synchronous speed has no significance for a.c. series motors.

The speed of a.c. series motors becomes quite high when load is removed, but in small motors friction and windage losses limit the no-load speed to safe values. The maximum speed of a single-phase a.c. series motor is governed by its satisfactory communication.

The methods adopted for the speed control of d.c. series motors, are also applicable to a.c. series motors. These are:

(*i*) Armature resistance or reactance control.

(*ii*) Field-flux control and ;

(*iii*) Armature voltage control.

Method (*i*) is used for small motors. For large size motors, method (*iii*) is most common.

7.3.2 Radio Interference

When 1-phase series motors are used for domestic applications, these may cause interference with the normal operation of radios or even TV sets. It is because the commutating period (time for which the coils are under going commutation) in series motors is usually very small. The rapid reversals of cuurent during commutation and sparking at the brushes, may cause high-frequency voltages to appear at the armature terminals. These voltages of random frequency send high-frequency currents in the supply lines, which then act as transmitting aerials. The radio receivers operating in the neighbourhood may pick up these random-frequency signals and then cause their noisy operation.

Radio interference can be checked effectively by short circuiting the random high-frequency voltages. This is achieved by connecting a small capacitor (0.005 to 0.05 microfarad), across the two brushes. It has been found that the best results are attained, when two capacitors in series across the brushes have their mid-points connected to the properly-earthed motor frame. Small a.c. commutator motors used for domestic appliances, must be fitted with capacitor suppressors to avoid radio interference.

Example 7.4. *Will a d.c. shunt motor operate when energised from an alternating voltage ? Explain.*

Solution. In a d.c. shunt motor, field and armature windings have their magnetic axes in space quadrature as shown in Fig. 7.14 (*a*). When alternating voltage V_t is applied, the armature current I_a lags V_t by small angle θ, because armature inductance is less. Since field inductance is relatively very high, the field current lags V_t by almost 90°. Consequently, the field flux ϕ lags V_t by about 90° as shown in Fig. 7.14 (*b*). Use of Eq. (7.19), gives torque in a single-phase shunt motor as

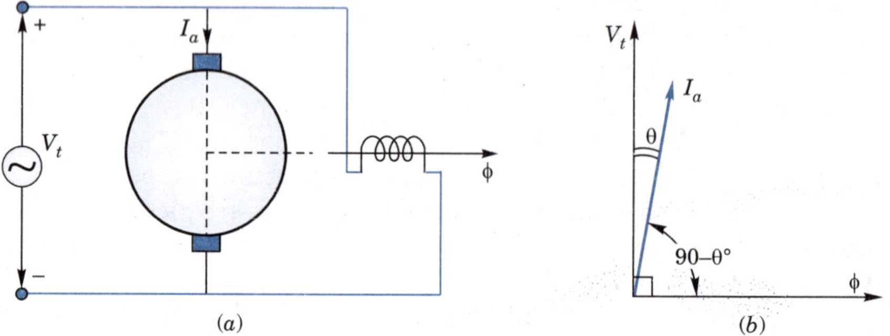

Fig. 7.14: (*a*) D.C. shunt motor fed from A.C. source and (*b*) its phasor diagram for part (*a*).

$$T_e = 0.11254 \frac{ZP}{a} \cdot \phi_m \cdot I_a \cdot \cos 0° \cdot \cos (90 - \theta)$$

$$= 0.11254 \frac{ZP}{a} \phi_m I_a \cos (90 - \theta).$$

Since field and armature winding axes are in space quadrature, space angle $\alpha = 0$. The angle θ being quite small, time angle $\psi = (90 - \theta)$ is nearer to 90° and as a result only a small amount of electromagnetic torque is developed in a d.c. shunt motor fed from alternating voltage source.

Time-phase angle correction can be applied by putting a capacitor in series with field winding, but a single-phase shunt motor with suitable characteristics needs additional equipment and has, therefore, not proved commercially successful.

Example 7.5. *A 2-pole, 50 Hz, 300 V, single-phase series motor has 800 armature turns and 350 field turns. The total effective resistance is 6 Ω and total leakage reactance is 14 Ω. For a power input of 350 watts, the motor draws 2A and the speed is 3600 r.p.m.*

(a) Compute the peak value of field flux per pole.

(b) If the motor is conductively compensated and draws the same amount of current, find the p.f. and speed. The motor has full compensation and the leakage impedance of compensating winding is 1 + j 2 Ω.

Also, determine the speed if the motor is energised from 300 V d.c. and takes the same current.

Solution. (*a*) From Fig. 7.9,

$$V_t \cos\theta = E_r + Ir \quad \text{or} \quad V_t I \cos\theta = I(E_r + Ir)$$

$$\therefore \quad 350 = 2(E_r + 2 \times 6) \quad \text{or} \quad E_r = 163 \text{ volts.}$$

But $$E_r = \sqrt{2}\, f_r\, \phi_m \frac{Z}{a} = 163 \quad \text{or} \quad \sqrt{2}\,(60)\, \phi_m \frac{800 \times 2}{2} = 163$$

∴ Peak value of field flux per pole, $\phi_m = 2.4$ mWb.

(*b*) When the motor is fully-compensated, $E_{taq} = I \cdot X_{mq}$ in Fig. 7.9 is reduced to zero.

Now $$I X_{md} = \sqrt{2}\pi f N_f \phi_m = \sqrt{2}\pi\,(50)\,(350)\,(2.4 \times 10^{-3})$$
$$= 186.6 \text{ volts.}$$

From Fig. 7.12, $V_t \sin\theta = I X_{md} + Ix = 186.8 + 2\,(16)$ or $\sin\theta = \dfrac{218.8}{300} = 0.729$

∴ p.f. of the compensated motor, $\cos\theta = 0.683$.

Also, $$E_r + Ir = V_t \cos\theta = 300\,(0.683) = 204.9$$

$$\therefore \quad E_r = \sqrt{2}\, f_r\, \phi_m \frac{Z}{a} = 204.9 - 2\,(7)$$

or $$f_r = \frac{190.9 \times 2}{\sqrt{2}\,(2.4 \times 10^{-3}) \times 800 \times 2} = 70.2 \text{ Hz.}$$

∴ Rotor speed in r.p.m. $= \dfrac{120 f_r}{P} = \dfrac{124 \times 70.2}{2} = 4212$ r.p.m.

For a.c. series motor, $E_r = CIn$

$$190.9 = CI\,(4212)$$

$$\therefore \quad CI = \frac{190.9}{4212} \text{ V/r.p.m.}$$

For d.c. series motor, $V_t = E_a + Ir_a = CIn + Ir_a$

or $$300 - 2 \times 7 = CIn = \frac{190.9}{4212} \times n$$

$$\therefore \quad n = \frac{286 \times 4212}{190.9} = 6310.28 \text{ r.p.m.}$$

Example 7.6. *A universal series motor when operating on 220 V d.c., draws 10 A and runs at 1400 r.p.m. Find the new speed and p.f., when connected to 220 V, 25 Hz supply, the motor current remaining the same. The motor has total resistance of 1 Ω and total inductance of 0.1 H.*

Solution. When working on d.c.,

$$V_t = Ir + CIn \quad \text{or} \quad 220 = 10 \times 1 + CI\,(1400)$$

$$\therefore \qquad CI = \frac{210}{1400} = \frac{3}{20} \text{ V/r.p.m}$$

When working on a.c., $V_t = I\,(r + jX) + CIn$

where, X = total reactance of the motor = $2\pi\,(25)\,(0.1) = 15.7\ \Omega$

For a.c. operation of the motor, $220 = 10\,(1 + j\,15.7) + CIn$

or $$(220)^2 = (CIn + 10)^2 + (157)^2 \quad \text{or} \quad CIn = 154.11 - 10 = 144.11$$

$$\therefore \qquad n = \frac{144.11}{CI} = \frac{144.11}{3} \times 20 = 960.7 \text{ r.p.m.}$$

$$\text{p.f.} = \frac{CIn + Ir}{V_t} = \frac{154.11}{220} = 0.7005 \text{ lagging.}$$

Example 7.7. *A 230 V, 500 W, 4000 rpm, 50 Hz single-phase series motor has total resistance of 3 Ω and total reactance of 20 Ω. For a stray-power loss of 40 W, determine the current and pf when working under rated conditions.*

Solution. Internal mechanical power developed in the armature,

$$P_a = P_{sh} + \text{stray-power loss}$$

or $$P_a = 500 + 40 = 540 \text{ W} = E_r I \quad \text{or} \quad E_r = \frac{P_a}{I}$$

It is seen from Fig. 7.9 that $V_t^2 = (IX)^2 + (rI + E_r)^2 = (IX)^2 + \left(rI + \frac{P_a}{I}\right)^2$

or $$I^4\,(X^2 + r^2) - (V_t^2 - 2\,P_a r)\,I^2 + P_a^2 = 0$$

Substituting the values, we get

$$I^4\,(20^2 + 3^2) - (230^2 - 2 \times 540 \times 3)\,I^2 + 540^2 = 0 \quad \text{or} \quad I^4 - 121.42\,I^2 + 712.96 = 0$$

Its solution gives $\quad I^2 = 115.24$ A or 6.19 A

Higher value of current is not feasible, therefore, motor current

$$I = \sqrt{6.19} = 2.488 \text{ A.} \quad \sin\theta = \frac{IX}{V_t} = \frac{2.488 \times 20}{230}$$

$$\text{Power factor} = \cos\theta = \sqrt{1 - \sin^2\theta} = 0.9763 \text{ lag.}$$

Example 7.8. *A single-phase series motor, when connected to 230 V, 50 Hz mains, takes rated current I at pf 0.88 and runs at rated speed n. If the supply frequency is reduced to $16\frac{2}{3}$ Hz, then calculate the supply voltage and pf for the same current I and speed n.*

Solution. For the same current I and speed n, $(rI + E_r) = A$ in Fig. 7.9 remains constant. It is also seen from this figure that for

$$V_t = 230 \text{ V and } pf = 0.88,$$

$$\cos\theta = 0.88 = \frac{A}{V_t} = \frac{A}{230} \quad \text{or} \quad A = 230 \times 0.8 = 202.4$$

Also $V_t^2 = A^2 + (IX)^2$ or $(IX)^2 = (230)^2 - (202.4)^2 = 11934.24$

When supply frequency is reduced to $16\frac{2}{3}$ Hz, then new

$$(\text{reactance drop})^2 = \frac{1}{9}(IX)^2 = \frac{1}{9}(11934.24) = 1326.03. \text{ From Fig. 7.9,}$$

$$V_t = \sqrt{\frac{1}{9}(IX)^2 + A^2} = \sqrt{1326.03 + (202.4)^2} = 205.65 \text{ V}$$

$$\text{pf } \cos\theta = \frac{A}{V_t} = \frac{202.4}{205.65} = 0.9842 \text{ lag}$$

Example 7.9. *A universal motor gave the following test results :*

	Input current	*Voltage across field winding*	*Voltage across armature winding*	E_r/ω_r
DC test	*2A*	*16 V*	*10 V*	*0.34 V-s/rad*
AC test	*2A*	*110 V*	*20 V*	*0.28 V-s/rad*

In case motor current is 2 A at 220 V, estimate the motor speed and torque when it is energized from (a) dc source and (b) ac source.

Solution. (*a*) DC operation :

$$V_t = I(r_a + r_f) + E_r \quad \text{or} \quad 220 = 10 + 16 + 0.34 \times \omega_r$$

where, ω_r = motor operating speed in rad/sec

$$\therefore \quad \omega_r = \frac{220 - 26}{0.34} = 570.88 \text{ rad/sec} = 5448.7 \text{ rpm}$$

$$\text{Torque} = \frac{E_r}{\omega_r} \cdot I = 0.34 \times 2 = 0.68 \text{ Nm}$$

(*b*) AC operation : $I.r_a = 10$ V, $\therefore \quad r_a = \frac{10}{2} = 5$ W

$I.r_f = 16$ V, $\therefore \quad r_f = \frac{16}{2} = 8$ W

Voltage across armature winding

$$= I\sqrt{r_a^2 + X_a^2} = 20 \text{ V}, \quad \therefore \quad X_a = \sqrt{10^2 + 5^2} = 8.66 \,\Omega$$

Voltage across field winding $= I\sqrt{r_f^2 + X_f^2} = 110$ V,

$$\therefore \quad X_f = \sqrt{55^2 - 8^2} = 54.42 \,\Omega$$

From the phasor diagram of Fig. 7.9, $V_t^2 = [E_r + I]\,(r_a + r_f)]^2 + [I\,(X_a + X_f)]^2$

or $$220^2 = [0.28 \times \omega_r + 2 \times 13]^2 + [2\,(8.66 + 54.42)]^2$$

or $$\omega_r = \frac{180.23 - 26}{0.28} = 550.83 \text{ rad/sec or 5260 rpm.}$$

$$\text{Torque} = 0.28 \times 2 = 0.56 \text{ Nm.}$$

7.3.3 Generalized Theory

In this section of the article, the analytical treatment of a single-phase series motor is carried out by generalized (or two-axis) theory.

The two-axis model for a.c. series motor is similar to that of a d.c. series motor. In view of this, voltage Eq. (3.34) for a d.c. series motor is also applicable to a.c. series motor, which is repeated here for convenience.

$$\therefore \quad v = [(r_f + r_a) + (L_f + L_a)p + M_d\, \omega_r]\, i \qquad \text{...(7.30)}$$

For steady state a.c. operation, put $p = j\omega$ in Eq. (7.30) to obtain the phasor equation for the series motor.

$$\therefore \quad \bar{V} = [R + j\omega L + M_d v\omega]\, \bar{I}$$

where, $R = r_f + r_a$; $L = L_f + L_a$ and $\omega_r = v\omega$.

From the voltage equation in phasor form, current $\bar{I}$ is given by

$$\bar{I} = \frac{\bar{V}}{(R + vX_{md}) + j\omega L} \qquad \text{...(7.31)}$$

Power factor of the motor at any speed

$$= \frac{R + vX_{md}}{[(R + vX_{md})^2 + X^2]^{1/2}} \qquad \text{...(7.32)}$$

At starting, $v = 0$ and p.f. becomes $\dfrac{R}{(R^2 + X^2)^{1/2}}$

Usually, total reactance X (= ωL) is far greater than total resistance R. In view of this, the p.f. of the series motor is very poor at starting. As the motor speeds up, vX_{md} starts increasing in Eq. (7.32) and therefore the motor operating p.f. improves.

The phasor current, after rationalisation, is

$$\bar{I} = \frac{\bar{V}[(R + vX_{md}) - jX]}{(R + vX_{md})^2 + X^2}$$

The torque matrix, from Eq. (7.30), is $[G] = [M_d]$.

Thus the steady state torque is, $T_e = Re\,\{[\bar{I}_t{*}][G][\bar{I}\,]\} = Re\,[M_d \bar{I}^* \bar{I}\,]$

Substitution of $\bar{I}$ of and $\bar{I}^*$ gives

$$T_e = Re\left[M_d \frac{\bar{V}^*[(R + vX_{md}) + jX]}{(R + vX_{md})^2 + X^2} \cdot \frac{\bar{V}[(R + vX_{md}) - jX]}{(R + vX_{md})^2 + X^2}\right]$$

$$= \frac{M_d \bar{V}\bar{V}^*}{(R + vX_{md})^2 + X^2} = \frac{X_{md}|\bar{V}\,|^2}{\omega\,[(R + vX_{md})^2 + X^2]} \qquad \text{...(7.33)}$$

For any number of poles,

$$T_e = (\text{Pole pairs}) \frac{X_{md}|\bar{V}\,|^2}{\omega[(R + vX_{md})^2 + X^2]} \qquad \text{...(7.34)}$$

If the same motor is now operated on d.c., the torque, from Eq. (7.33) become :

$$T_e = \frac{M_d V^2}{(R + M_d \omega_r)^2} \qquad \text{...(7.35)}$$

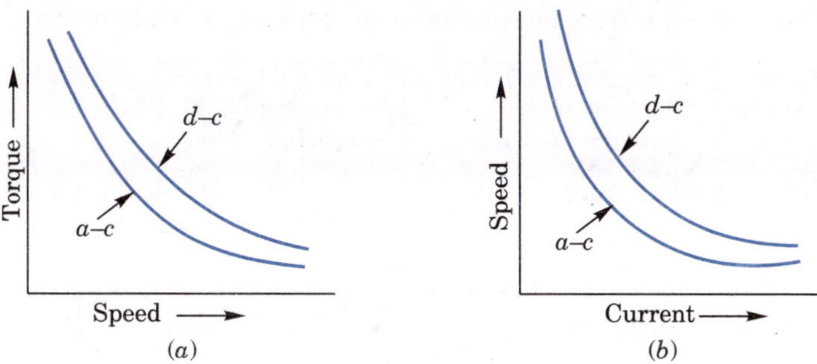

Fig. 7.15: Series motor characteristics for d.c. and a.c. operation. (*a*) T_e *versus* ω_r (*b*) ω_r *versus* I.

The denominator of Eq. (7.35) is less than that of Eq. (7.33). This shows that for a particular voltage and speed, the motor develops more torque when connected to d.c. than when connected to a.c. Fig. 7.15 illustrates the variation of torque *versus* speed and speed *versus* current, both for d.c. and a.c. motor operations.

Single Phase Series Motors (inductively compensated). The primitive machine diagram for this motor is shown in Fig 7.16 (*a*), where coil *QS* represents the compensating winding.

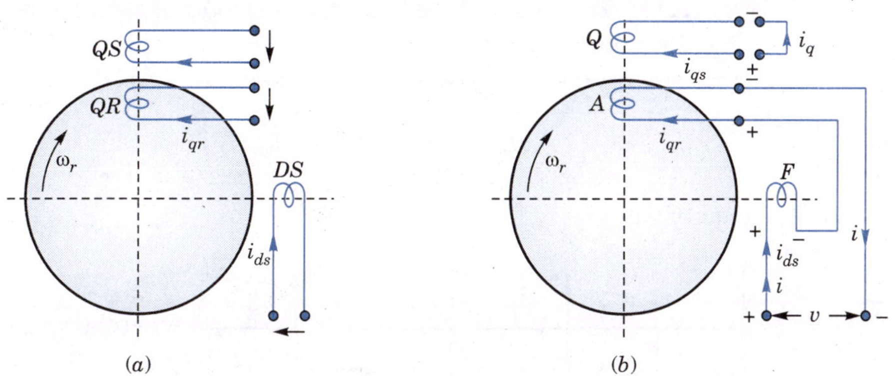

Fig. 7.16: Inductively compensated single-phase series motor. (*a*) Its primitive representation. (*b*) Interconnection between the coils.

The voltage equations in matrix form, Fig. 7.16 (*a*), are :

$$\begin{bmatrix} v_{ds} \\ v_{qs} \\ v_{qr} \end{bmatrix} = \begin{array}{c} ds \\ qs \\ qr \end{array} \overset{\begin{array}{ccc} ds & qs & qr \end{array}}{\begin{bmatrix} r_{ds} + L_{ds}p & & \\ & r_{qs} + L_{qs}p & M_q p \\ M_d \omega_r & M_q p & r_{qr} + L_{qr}p \end{bmatrix}} \begin{bmatrix} i_{ds} \\ i_{qs} \\ i_{qr} \end{bmatrix} \quad ...(7.36)$$

Coils *DS*, *QR* and *QS* are designated now as *F*, *A* and *Q* respectively. The interconnection between field and armature, and the short-circuit of compensating winding is shown in Fig. 7.16 (*b*). The possible constraints are :

$$i_{ds} = i_{qr} = i \text{ (say)} ; i_{qs} = - i_q. \quad v_{qs} = 0.$$

The matrix connecting new and old currents can now be written as

$$\begin{bmatrix} i_{ds} \\ i_{qs} \\ i_{qr} \end{bmatrix} = \begin{bmatrix} 1 & \\ & -1 \\ 1 & \end{bmatrix} \begin{bmatrix} i \\ i_q \end{bmatrix}$$

The new impedance matrix is

$$\begin{array}{cc} & \begin{array}{ccc|cc} r_f + L_{fp} & & & 1 & \\ & r_q + L_q p & M_q p & & -1 \\ M_d \omega_r & M_q p & r_a + L_a p & 1 & \end{array} \\ [Z'] = \begin{array}{ccc} 1 & & 1 \\ & -1 & \end{array} & \begin{array}{ccc|c} r_f + L_f . p + M_d \omega_r & M_q p & r_a + L_a p & \text{Written} \\ & -(r_q + L_q p) & -M_q p & \text{below} \end{array} \end{array}$$

$$= \begin{bmatrix} r_a + r_f + (L_a + L_f)p + M_d \omega_r & -M_q p \\ -M_q p & r_q + L_q p \end{bmatrix}$$

The new voltage matrix is

$$[v'] = \begin{bmatrix} 1 & & 1 \\ & -1 & \end{bmatrix} \begin{bmatrix} v_f \\ 0 \\ v_a \end{bmatrix} = \begin{bmatrix} v \\ 0 \end{bmatrix} \quad \text{where, } v = v_f + v_a$$

The required voltage matrix is

$$\begin{bmatrix} v \\ 0 \end{bmatrix} = \begin{bmatrix} r_a + r_f + (L_a + L_f)p + M_d \omega_r & -M_q p \\ -M_q p & r_q + L_q p \end{bmatrix} \begin{bmatrix} i \\ i_q \end{bmatrix}$$

From the above voltage matrix, the two voltage equations are

$$v = [r_a + r_f + (L_a + L_f)\, p + M_d \omega_r] i - M_q p i_q$$

$$0 = -M_q p i + (r_q + L_q p)\, i_q.$$

Eliminating i_q from the above two voltage equations, we get

$$v = \left[r_a + r_f + M_d \omega_r + p(L_f + L_a) - \frac{M_q^2 p}{r_q + L_q p} \right] i.$$

If r_q is neglected,

$$v = \left[r_a + r_f + M_d \omega_r + L_f p + \left(L_a - \frac{M_q^2}{L_q} \right) p \right] i$$

$\left(L_a - \dfrac{M_q^2}{L_q} \right) = L_a'$ may be called, by analogy with synchronous machine transients, as armature transient inductance. Thus

$$v = [r_a + r_f + M_d \omega_r + (L_f + L_a')\, p]\, i \qquad \text{...[7.37]}$$

The steady stage voltage equation is obtained by putting $p = j\omega$.

$$\therefore \qquad \overline{V} = (r_a + r_f + vX_{md}) + j\,(X_f + X_a')\,\overline{I}$$

or

$$\overline{I} = \frac{\overline{V}}{(r_a + r_f + vX_{md}) + j\,(X_f + X_a')} \qquad \text{...(7.38)}$$

Total effective reactance for compensated series motor is $X_f + X_a'$, which is considerably less than $X_f + X_a$, the total effective reactance of uncompensated series motor. Thus the power factor of the compensated series motor is better and the current is greater for a particular voltage and speed. This would result in greater torque as well.

The steady state torque is obtained with the help of G matrix the latter being taken from matrix (7.36).

							$\overline{I}_{ds}$
							$\overline{I}_{qs}$
				M_d			$\overline{I}_{qr}$
$T_e = Re$	$\overline{I}_{ds}^*$	$\overline{I}_{qs}^*$	$\overline{I}_{qr}^*$	$M_d \overline{I}_{qr}^*$			$M_d \overline{I}_{qr}^* \overline{I}_{ds}$

$$= Re\,[M_d\, \overline{I}_{qr}^* \overline{I}_{ds}]$$

Using the constraints for the currents,

$$T_e = Re\,[M_d\, \overline{I}^*\, \overline{I}\,] \qquad \text{...(7.39)}$$

From Eq. (7.38) the phasor current after rationalisation, is

$$\overline{I} = \frac{\overline{V}\,[(r_a + r_f + vX_{md}) - j\,(X_f + X'_a)]}{(r_a + r_f + vX_{md})^2 + (X_f + X'_a)^2}$$

Substitution of $\overline{I}^*$ and $\overline{I}$ in Eq. (7.39) gives

$$T_e = \frac{M_d \overline{V}\overline{V}^*}{(r_a + r_f + vX_{md})^2 + (X_f + X'_a)^2}$$

$$= \frac{X_{md} \, |\overline{V}\,|^2}{\omega\,[(r_a + r_f + vX_{md})^2 + (X_f + X_a{}')^2]} \qquad ...(7.40)$$

Examination of Eqs. (7.33) and (7.40) shows that compensated series motor develops more torque as compared to uncompensated motor, for the same voltage V.

Example 7.10. *The constants of a single phase series motor (universal motor, usable both for d.c. and a.c.) obtained from tests with rotor at standstill are :*

Total resistance = 20 Ω

Total reactance = 100 Ω

When 200 V d.c. is given to the motor, it runs at 9000/π r.p.m., and draws a no load current of 1 ampere. Find the speed, power factor and output when the motor is connected to 200 V a.c. and takes 1 ampere again.

If iron, friction and windage loss is assumed to be equal to 40 watts, find its efficiency also.

Solution. D.C. Operation :

$$V = I\,(R + M_d\omega_r)$$

where, $$\omega_r = \frac{2\pi N}{60} = \frac{2\pi\,(9000)}{(60)\,(\pi)} = 300 \text{ rad/sec.}$$

Thus $$200 = 1.00\,(20 + M_d\, 300).$$

This gives $$M_d = 0.6 \text{ H.}$$

A.C. Operation :

$$\overline{V} = (R + M_d\omega_r + j\,X)\,\overline{I}$$

Thus $$200 = (20 + 0.6\,\omega_r + j\,100)\,1.00$$

or $$(200)^2 = (20 + 0.6\,\omega_r)^2 + (100)^2$$

or $$(20 + 0.6\,\omega_r) = \sqrt{(200)^2 - (100)^2} = 173.21$$

∴ $$\omega_r = \frac{153.21}{0.6} = 255.35 \text{ rad/sec.}$$

and $$N = \frac{255.35 \times 60}{2\pi} = 2440.3 \text{ r.p.m.}$$

$$\text{Power factor} = \frac{R + vX_{md}}{\sqrt{(R + vX_{md})^2 + X^2}} \qquad \text{[From Eq. (7.32)]}$$

$$= \frac{173.09}{(173.09)^2 + (1.0)^2} = 0.8654 \text{ lag}$$

$$\text{Torque} = M_d \cdot I^2 = 0.6\,(1) = 0.6 \text{ Nm.}$$

$$\text{Output} = \text{Torque} \times \omega_r = 0.6 \times 255.15 = 153.09 \text{ watts.}$$

This is the available output, had there been no other losses. The presence of iron, friction and windage losses reduces the output. Thus the net output now is

$$(153.09 - 40) = 113.06 \text{ watts.}$$

$$\text{Efficiency} = \frac{113.06}{200 \times 1 \times 0.8654} = 62.5\%$$

Example 7.11. *A single-phase 230 V, 50 Hz, 2-pole inductively compensated series motor has the following constants :*

Series field winding,

$r_f = 5\ \Omega \qquad L_f = 0.05\ H$

Armature winding,

$r_a = 2\ \Omega \qquad L_a = 1.00\ H$

Compensating winding,

$r_q = 0\ \Omega \qquad L_q = 2\ H, \qquad M_q = 1.4\ H.$

(a) At full load speed of 4800 r.p.m., the motor takes 2 amperes. Find the p.f., power output and torque developed at the same speed.

(b) With the value of M_d found in part (a) and assuming the speed to remain at 4800 r.p.m., compute current, pf, torque and power developed with zero compensation.

Solution. (*a*) Synchronous speed

$$= \frac{120 \times 50}{2} = 3000 \text{ r.p.m.}$$

$$\therefore \qquad v = \frac{4800}{3000} = 1.6$$

$$L_a' = \left(L_a - \frac{M_q^2}{L_q}\right) = 1 - \frac{1.96}{2} = 0.02 \text{ H.}$$

Substitution of the values in Eq. [7.37] gives

$$230 = 2[7 + 1.6\, M_d\omega] + j\,(314 \times 0.07)].$$

Solving for M_d, we get

$$M_d = 0.2105 \text{ H.}$$

$$\text{p.f.} = \frac{7 + (1.6)\,(2\pi 50)\,(0.2105)}{\sqrt{[7 + (1.6)\,(2\pi 50)\,(0.2105)]^2 \times [314 \times 0.07]^2}} = \frac{112.8}{115} = 0.981.$$

Torque developed $= M_d I^2 = (0.2105)\,(4) = 0.8420$ N-m.

Power output $= T_e \cdot \omega_r = T_e \cdot v\omega = (0.8420)\ 1.6 \times 314 = 423$ watts

(*b*)
$$\bar{I} = \frac{\bar{V}}{(R + vX_{md}) + j\omega L}$$

$$\therefore \qquad I = \frac{230}{[(112.8)^2 + (314 \times 1.05)^2]^{1/2}} \quad \text{or} \quad I = \frac{230}{348.5} = 0.660 \text{ A.}$$

$$\text{p.f.} = \frac{112.8}{348.5} = 0.3237$$

$$T_e = M_d I^2 = (0.2105)\,(0.66)^2 = 0.0878 \text{ N-m.}$$

Power output $= (0.0878)\,(1.6)\,(314) = 44.11$ watts.

This example illustrates that with zero compensation ; p.f., torque and power output are considerably reduced.

7.4 SCHRAGE MOTOR

It has been shown in Chapter 5 that by injecting voltage in the rotor circuit of a wound rotor induction motor (WRIM), its speed and pf can be controlled. For injecting voltage of appropriate frequency in the rotor circuit, a separate frequency-converter is essential. In 1911, K.H. Schrage of Sweden combined elegantly a WRIM and a frequency-converter into a single unit. This machine is now known as Schrage motor.

For understanding the working of a Schrage motor, the reader is advised to go through the commutator-frequency converter discussed in Art 5.10.1 in Chapter 5. It is shown there that frequency of the emf at the brushes is given by

$$f_b = \frac{P\,(n_s \pm n_r)}{2}$$

Schrage motor is basically an inverted polyphase induction motor, with primary winding on the rotor and secondary winding on the stator. As in a polyphase induction motor, the primary winding on the rotor is fed through three slip rings and brushes at line frequency ; secondary winding on the stator has slip frequency voltages induced in it. In addition to these two windings, there is a third winding called *tertiary* or *adjusting* winding, which is housed in the same rotor slots as the primary—this is illustrated in Fig. 7.17 (*b*). The tertiary winding is connected to commutator on which there are three sets of movable brush pairs, to collect the required e.m.f. for injection into the secondary circuit for speed and p.f. control. Note that the three separate phase windings on the stator are not connected to each other, but are connected to brushes *a*, *b*, *c*, *d*, *e*, *f* as shown. Alternate brushes *a*, *c*, *e*, 120 electrical degrees apart, are mounted on one brush rocker and brushes *b*, *d*, *f* on the second brush rocker. The groups of alternate brushes can be moved in opposite directions by means of rack and pinion arrangement and one handwheel provided outside the motor frame. The Schrage motor incorporates, in a single machine, the functions of a polyphase induction motor and a frequency converter.

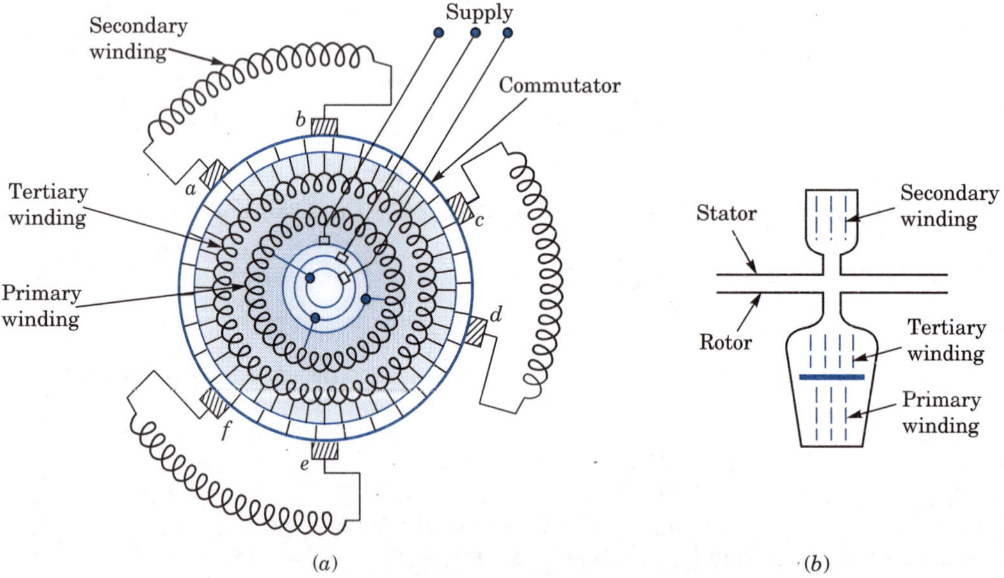

Fig. 7.17: Schrage motor (*a*) Schematic diagram
(*b*) Arrangement of three windings in stator and rotor slots.

The difference in the construction of Schrage motor and an ordinary induction motor must be noted. The primary winding of Schrage motor is on the rotor and is fed through 3 slip rings, whereas the primary winding of induction motor is on the stator. The secondary winding of Schrage motor is on stator, whereas that of the induction motor is on the rotor. In induction motor, the secondary winding is usually star-connected for wound-rotor motors and in squirrel-cage motors, the bars are short circuited. In Schrage motor, the three secondary phase windings have no interconnection amongst them, but two ends of each phase winding are connected to two brushes riding on the commutator. In an induction motor, if the primary and secondary windings are interchanged, the performance of the motor is uneffected. But in a Schrage motor, it is essential to have the primary winding on the rotor, as explained below.

At standstill, three phase currents in the primary and secondary windings of Schrage motor produce a rotating field, just as in ordinary induction motor. This rotating field, with the rotor at standstill, is running at synchronous speed n_s with respect to the primary and secondary conductors. Now induction-motor action requires that the rotor of Schrage motor must revolve in such a direction as to induce slip frequency e.m.fs. in the secondary windings on the stator. In view of this, the rotor must start running at speed, say n_r, in a direction opposite to the synchronously rotating field. As a result of it, the rotating field speed in the air gap becomes $(n_s - n_r)$ *i.e.* slip speed. This air-gap flux rotating at slip speed with respect to stator, induces slip-frequency e.m.fs. in the stator winding. It has already been shown in Art. 5.10.1 that frequency of the e.m.fs. at the stationary brushes is proportional to the speed of the rotating field relative to these brushes. In the present case, the rotating field speed with respect to the brushes is slip speed, therefore, slip-frequency e.m.fs. are picked up by these brushes. This shows that brush e.m.fs. are always suitable for voltage injection into the secondary winding on stator. In a Schrage motor, if the primary winding were on the stator, then speed of the rotating field in the air gap and therefore, relative to the fixed brushes would always be synchronous at all rotor speeds. Consequently, the e.m.f. collected by the brushes would be at line frequency, which is not suitable for voltage injection into the secondary winding having slip-frequency e.m.fs. in it.

The tertiary and primary windings, being in the same slots, are mutually coupled. Therefore, the e.m.fs induced in the tertiary winding are by transformer action and are always at line frequency f, at all the rotor speeds.

Speed Control. Let us assume in the beginning that the brushes are in contact with the same commutator segment as shown in Fig. 7.18 (*a*). The secondary winding is therefore, short circuited by the brushes and commutator segment and consequently, the Schrage motor operates as an ordinary induction motor at subsynchronous speed almost equal to synchronous speed. The operation under these conditions is illustrated in Fig. 5.36 (*a*). Now the brushes *a, b* are separated by a positive angle θ such that the centre line (or axis) of the tertiary winding between angle θ is coincident with centre line of corresponding secondary winding. Standstill secondary-winding e.m.f. E_2 and the tertiary winding (or injected) e.m.f. E_j are induced by the same rotating flux and are shown by arrows directed from right to left. Further, the e.m.fs. E_2 and E_j reach their maximum values at the same time, because their respective centre lines are coincident. Trace of the circuit *BAabB* in Fig. 7.18 (*b*) shows that the e.m.f. E_j is injected in phase opposition to E_2, giving the speed below synchronous speed. The operation under these conditions is shown in Fig. 5.36 (*b*). If the brush positions *a, b* of Fig. 7.18 (*b*) are interchanged to those shown in Fig. 7.18 (*c*), the e.m.fs. E_2 and E_j reach their maximum values at the same time, because their respective centre lines are even now coincident. The circuit *BAabB* when traced in Fig. 7.18 (*c*) shows that E_j is in phase with E_2.

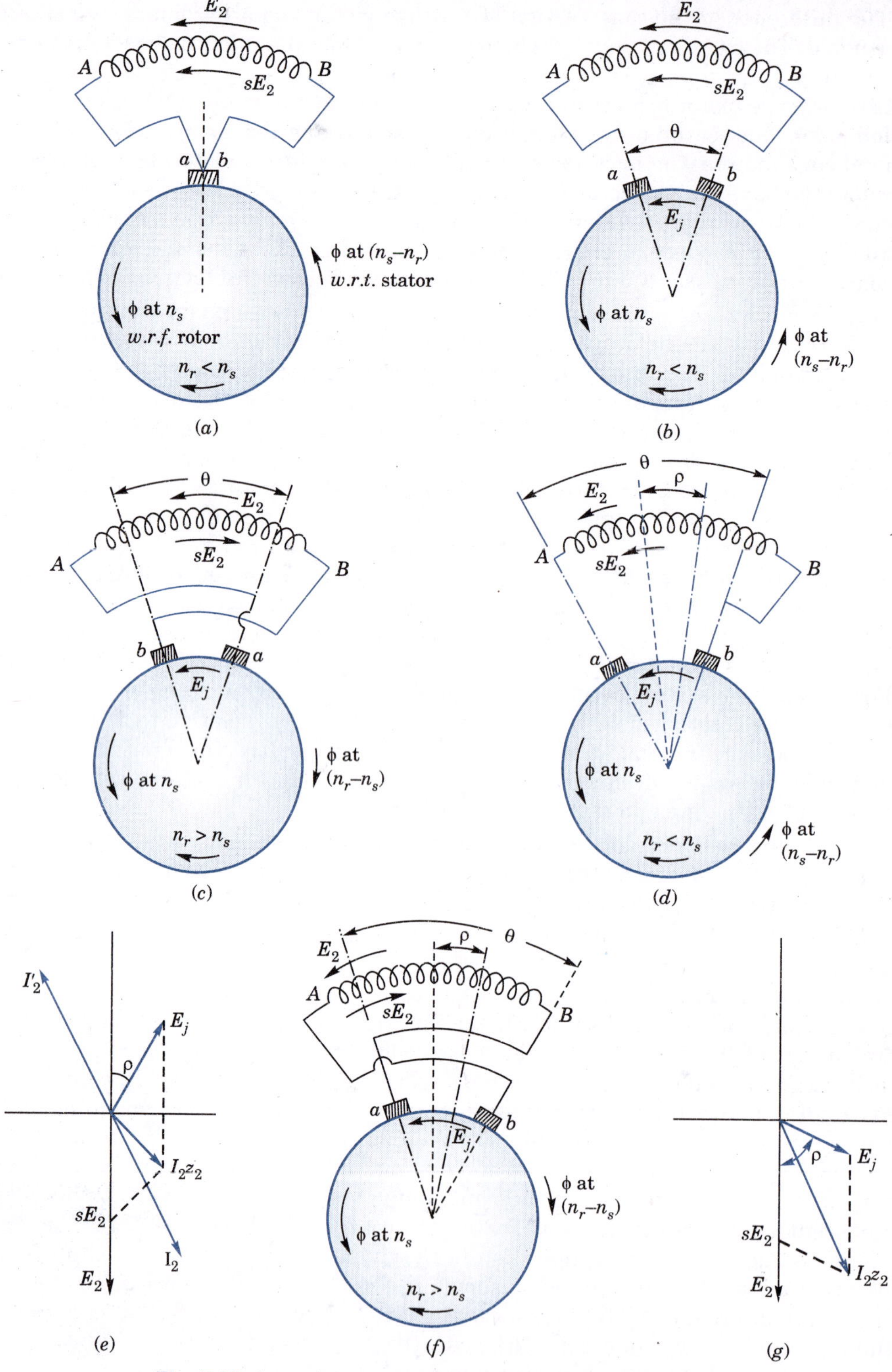

Fig. 7.18: Speed and power factor control of Schrage motor.

Under these conditions, the motor must operate at super-synchronous speed if $E_j > I_2 z_2$ [(see Fig. 5.36 (*d*))], and consequently slip *s* in negative and sE_2 is opposite to E_2 as shown in Fig. 7.18 (*c*). It should be noted that the magnitude of E_j, collected by the brushes, depends on the brush separation angle θ. In Fig. 7.18 (*c*) brush separation angle θ is negative.

Now let the brushes of Fig. 7.18 (*b*), be moved bodily against the direction of rotor rotation and occupy the position shown in Fig. 7.18 (*d*), such that the two centre lines are not coincident and have an angle ρ between them. The flux ϕ rotating at speed n_s relative to the rotor, reaches the centre line of tertiary-winding conductors between the angle θ, at a later moment determined by the *brush shift* ρ. Therefore, e.m.f. E_j of Fig. 7.18 (*d*) with brush shift ρ lags the e.m.f. E_j of Fig. 7.18 (*b*), where ρ is zero. This is illustrated in Fig. 7.18 (*e*) and it is seen that both-p.f. and speed can be controlled by varying the angle θ and ρ. Components E_j cos ρ and E_j sin ρ, are assumed to effect the speed and p.f. respectively. A careful examination of Fig. 7.18 (*e*) reveals that if brush-shift is against the direction of rotor rotation, the speed decreases but the power factor is improved.

If the centre line of the tertiary winding between the angle θ is moved in the direction of rotor rotation by an angle ρ as shown in Fig. 7.18 (*f*), then E_j as illustrated in Fig. 7.18 (*g*) would lead the e.m.f. E_j of Fig. 7.18 (*c*), where brush shift ρ is zero. Here again E_j cos ρ and E_j sin ρ components effect speed and p.f. respectively. An examination of Fig. 7.18 (*g*) shows that with brush-shift in the direction of rotor rotation, the speed increases and the power factor is improved.

Characteristics Curves of Schrage motor. The rotating field in Schrage motor induces the following e.m.fs. in the three windings.

(*i*) E.m.f. E_1 in the primary winding on the rotor. It differs from the applied voltage by the primary leakage impedance drop, as in the case of a polyphase induction motor.

(*ii*) Standstill e.m.f E_2 in the secondary winding on the rotor, as in a polyphase induction motor.

(*iii*) E.m.f. E_j in the regulating or tertiary winding. Let its magnitude be $E_{j.max}$ when the brushes are space displaced by θ = 180 electrical degrees. Then for any brush separation angle θ, the e.m.f. E_j at the brushes is given by

$$E_j = E_{j\,max} \sin \theta/2$$

Note that when rotor revolves, the magnitude of e.m.fs. E_2 and E_j (for fixed θ) remains constant, while the secondary e.m.f. changes to sE_2, as in a polyphase induction motor.

The voltage equation for the circuit *BAabB* is given by

$$sE_2 \pm E_{j\,max} \sin \theta/2 = I_2 z_2 \qquad \text{...(7.41)}$$

Here plus sign is to be used when the injected e.m.f. E_j is in phase with e.m.f. E_2 and minus sign when E_j is in phase opposition to E_2. Note that Eq. (7.41) is not a phasor equation.

At no load, I_2 is very small and, therefore, the secondary leakage impedance drop $I_2 z_2$ may be ignored.

$$\therefore \qquad s_o E_2 = \mp E_{j.\,max} \sin \theta/2$$

or

$$\text{no-load slip, } s_o = \mp \frac{E_{j.max}}{E_2} \sin \frac{\theta}{2} \qquad \text{...(7.42)}$$

Now the transformer e.m.f. in commutator winding, as per Eq. (7.8), is given by

$$E_{j.max} = \sqrt{2}\, f \phi_m Z/a$$

Here *Z* is the total number of tertiary winding conductors. Note that tertiary winding is d.c. type double-layer winding connected to the commutator.

The transformer e.m.f. induced in the secondary winding on the stator, like the rotor winding of an ordinary induction motor, is given by

$$E_2 = \sqrt{2}\,\pi f \phi_m N_2 k_\omega.$$

Here N_2 is the actual number of secondary series turns per phase and k_ω is their winding factor.

Substitution of the values of $E_{j.max}$ and E_2 in Eq. (7.42) gives,

$$s_0 = \mp \frac{\sqrt{2} f \phi_m \dfrac{Z}{a}}{\sqrt{2}\pi f \phi_m N_2'} \sin\frac{\theta}{2}$$

Here $N_2' = N_2 k_\omega$, is the effective number of secondary series turns per phase.

$$\therefore \qquad s_0 = \mp \frac{Z}{a\pi N_2'} \sin\frac{\theta}{2} \qquad ...(7.43)$$

or

$$s_0 = \mp k \sin\frac{\theta}{2}, \text{ where } k = \frac{Z}{a\pi N_2'} = \frac{E_{j.max}}{E_2}$$

Thus, no-load rotor speed is

$$n_{ro} = n_s (1 - s_o) = n_s \left(1 \pm k \sin\frac{\theta}{2}\right) \qquad ...(7.44)$$

Plus and minus in Eq. (7.44) indicate speeds above and below n_s respectively. For a particular motor, k is constant.

Therefore, the lowest possible no-load speed is $n_{ro.min} = n_s (1 - k)$ and is obtained when positive angle θ = 180 electrical degrees, *i.e.* when the brushes are one pole-pitch apart.

If the brush positions are now interchanged, so that negative angle $\theta = -180°$, then maximum no-load speed is

$$n_{ro.max} = n_s (1 + k).$$

The curve showing the variation of no-load speed with brush separation is illustrated in Fig. 7.19 (*a*) and is obtained from Eq. (7.44).

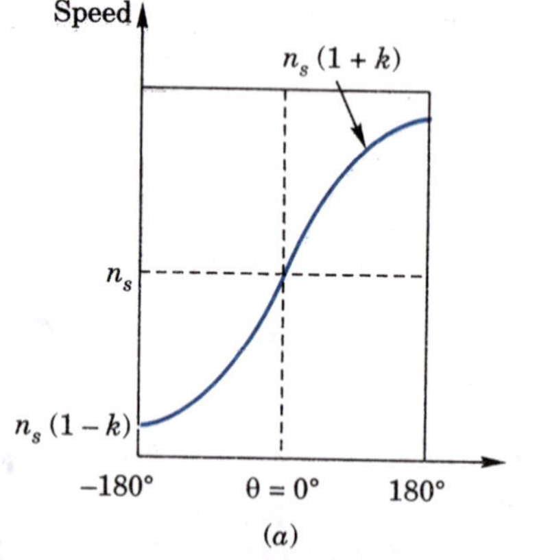

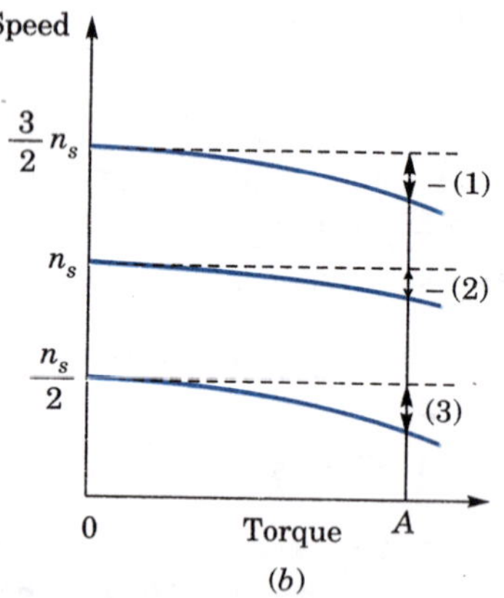

Fig. 7.19: (*a*) Variation of no-load speed with brush separation and (*b*) speed-torque characteristics at different speeds.

The usual speed range is from $3n_s/2$ to $n_s/2$, *i.e.*, 3 : 1. With this speed range,

$$n_{r.\,min} = \frac{n_s}{2}(1-k)$$

and
$$n_{r.max} = \frac{3n_s}{2}(1+k)$$

or
$$\frac{1+k}{1-k} = 3 \quad \text{or} \quad k = \frac{1}{2}.$$

This shows that a Schrage motor with a speed range of 3 : 1 should have

$$k = \frac{Z}{a\pi N_2'} = \frac{1}{2}.$$

The speed-torque characteristics can be obtained by referring to Eq. (7.41). From this equation,

$$s = \mp \frac{E_{j.max} \sin\frac{\theta}{2}}{E_2} + \frac{I_2 z_2}{E_2}$$

$$= \text{no-load slip for a given brush separation} + I_2 z_2/E_2 \quad ...[7.45\ (a)]$$

Now
$$\text{torque} \propto I_2 \text{ or } I_2 = CT_e,$$

$\therefore$
$$s = \text{no-load slip} + \frac{CT_e}{E_2} z_2 \quad ...[7.45\ (b)]$$

Secondary leakage impedance drop I_2z_2 is much smaller than E_2, or in other words $CT_e z_2 << E_2$, and speed-torque characteristics of shunt type as shown in Fig. 7.19 (*b*) are obtained. For any given torque *OA* in Fig. 7.19 (*b*) ; the speed drop (2) is much less than the speed drops (1) and (3). This is due to the increased values of z_2, at speeds far differing from n_s.

In Fig. 7.18 (*b*), note that voltage $E_{j.max} \sin \theta/2$ is in phase opposition to E_2 and is fully utilized for change. In Fig. 7.18 (*d*) and (*e*) or in Figs. 7.18 (*f*) and (*g*), the component $E_{j.max} \sin \theta/2 \cos \rho$ is the speed-regulating component and $E_{j.max} \sin \theta/2 \sin \rho$ is the phase-compensating component. Taking into consideration the speed-regulating component of E_j in Fig. 7.18 (*d*), (*e*), (*f*) and (*g*) ; the no-load speed from Eq. (7.44) can be written as

$$n_{ro} = n_s \left(1 \pm k \sin\frac{\theta}{2}\cos\rho\right) \quad ...(7.46)$$

Slip-power and efficiency. The torque developed by Schrage motor is proportional to the product of secondary current and the air-gap flux, as in a polyphase induction motor. Since the primary leakage impedance drop is a small percentage of the applied voltage, the air-gap flux in a Schrage motor remains approximately constant for a given applied voltage. For maximum allowable secondary current, therefore, the developed torque is substantially constant over the entire speed range. Schrage motor can, therefore, be termed as a *constant-torque drive motor* and the power developed varies in direct proportion to speed. For example, a Schrage motor developing 4 kW at synchronous speed of 1000 r.p.m., will develop 7.2 kW at 1800 r.p.m. and 2.4 kW at 600 r.p.m.; the torque remaining constant at all the rotor speeds.

That the Schrage motor is a constant torque motor can alternatively be explained as follows. At sub-synchronous speed, the current in the tertiary winding is almost opposite to the injected e.m.f. E_j [refer to Fig. 5.36 (*b*)]. The power handled by the tertiary winding is $E_j I_2 \cos(180 + \theta_2)$ or $-E_j I_2 \cos\theta_2$. The negative sign before the power, indicates the power flow from secondary winding to the tertiary winding which is then transferred to the primary winding by transformer action. Therefore, at sub-synchronous speeds the power taken from the supply is reduced. At super-synchronous speed, the tertiary winding current is nearly in phase with e.m.f. E_j induced in it [refer to Fig. 5.36 (*d*)]. The power $E_j I_2 \cos \theta_2$ handled by tertiary winding is now positive and corresponds to the power flow from tertiary winding to the secondary winding. Further the tertiary winding receives this power $E_j I_2 \cos \theta_2$ by transformer action from the primary winding, resulting in an increased power taken from the supply mains. Thus it is seen for Schrage motor that at sub-synchronous speed, the power developed is decreased, while at super-synchronous speed, the power developed is increased, resulting in almost constant torque.

This also explains for the increased efficiency at higher speeds than at lower speeds, because for a constant-torque motor, the power developed increases with the rise in speed. Losses in Schrage motor, though enlarged at higher speeds, are only a fraction of the increased output and consequently the efficiency increases with the rise in speed. The power factor, as is evident from Fig. 5.36, improves with the rise in speed. For a given Schrage motor, typical efficiency and p.f. curves are shown respectively in Fig. 7.20 (*a*) and (*b*), for two different speeds. Curve I corresponds to lower speed and curve II corresponds to high speed. Power factor at higher operating speeds may become even leading as shown by curve II in Fig. 7.20 (*b*).

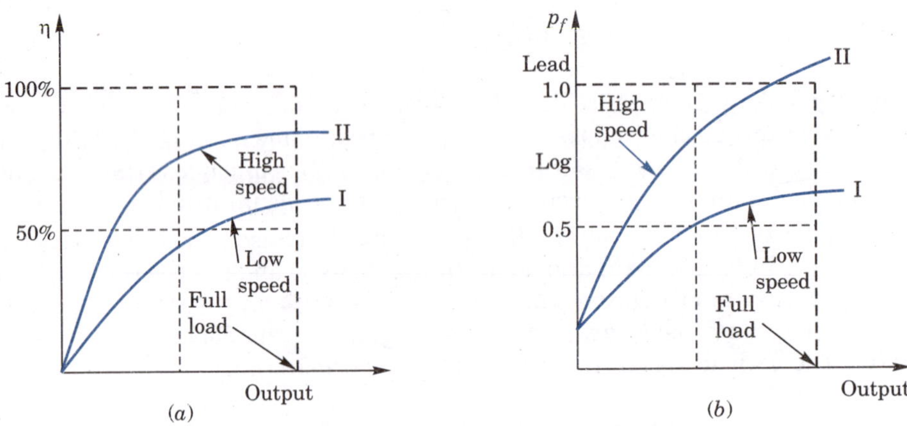

Fig. 7.20: Typical performance characteristics for a Schrage motor. (*a*) Efficiency-output curves and (*b*) pf-output curves.

The secondary and tertiary windings have to deal with only the slip power sP_g. For a speed control of 50% above and 50% below synchronous speed, the speed range is 3 : 1 and the slip power is 0.5 P_g. If the speed range is increased to 9 : 1, the slip power becomes 0.8 P_g. In other words, for a wide speed range, the slip power to be handled by the secondary and tertiary windings would be more and accordingly, cost of the Schrage motor would increase.

Starting. At the time of starting, when $s = 1$, Eq. (7.41) becomes,

$$I_{2.st} z_2 = E_2 \pm E_{j.max} \sin \frac{\theta}{2} \qquad ...(7.47)$$

If e.m.f. $E_{j\ max} \sin \frac{\theta}{2}$ is injected in phase opposition to E_2, then speeds below synchronous speed are obtained as shown in Fig. 7.18 (*b*) and Eq. (7.47) becomes,

$$I_{2.st} z_2 = E_2 - E_{j\ max} \sin \frac{\theta}{2}$$

$$\therefore \quad \text{Starting current,} \quad I_{2.st} = \frac{E_2 - E_{j\,max} \sin \dfrac{\theta}{2}}{z_2} \qquad \text{...(7.48)}$$

Eq. (7.48) shows that the starting current in a Schrage motor can be kept within safe limits if the brushes are spaced to their maximum possible separation of positive angle θ = 180°, *i.e.* a pole pitch. Thus no special starting devices are required for a Schrage motor. This maximum brush separation of pole pitch also gives minimum possible speed, increasing the starting torque at the same time. In view of the above, the brushes should be set to the minimum-speed position, before a Schrage motor is directly switched on to the supply mains. Starting torque equal to about 1.5 times the full load value are available with 1.5 to 2 times the rated current.

Uses. Schrage motor is suitable for electric drives requiring adjustable-speed control. Its specific applications, where it has proved quite successful, are printing presses, textile mills, paper making machinery, fans, centrifugal pumps, cranes and hoists.

The main disadvantage of Schrage motor is that its primary is fed through slip rings and can, therefore, work reliably for supply voltages up to about 600 V. Its power rating was limited to about 20 kW per pole-pair on account of commutation difficulties and design considerations. However, with improved techniques of total optimisation and better quality material used now-a-days, its power rating has been increased to about 30 kW per pole-pair. Four standard speed ranges are generally available with the manufactures. These speed ranges are 3 : 1, 6 : 1, 10 : 1, and 20 : 1 with their corresponding maximum and minimum speeds in r.p.m. as 1925 : 640, 2100 : 350, 2250 : 225 and 2375 : 120. In order to meet the demand of modern industrial applications, other speed ranges are also available. The efficiency of a Schrage motor is a little lower than a polyphase induction motor of the same size, because of the additional losses in the tertiary winding and at the brush contacts.

Sometimes, the secondary winding of a Schrage motor has more than three phases. It is proved in literature that if Schrage motor has more number of phases, then the reactance e.m.f. in the coil undergoing commutation decreases. This results in improved commutation and better operation of the Schrage motor.

Example 7.12. *Examine the Schrage motor operation at synchronous speed.*

Solution. When a Schrage motor runs at synchronous speed, the air-gap flux becomes stationary with respect to secondary winding on stator. There is, therefore, zero e.m.f. induced in stator winding by this stationary field. But there must be some injected e.m.f. available from tertiary winding in order to overcome the secondary-circuit impedance drop. Accordingly, the brushes must be displaced from each other by some negative angle θ. The tertiary winding conductors between angle θ are synchronously running in stationary field. Since the relative speed between brushes and stationary air-gap field is zero, the tertiary e.m.f. has zero frequency at the brushes, *i.e.* the brush e.m.f. is direct e.m.f. This brush e.m.f. sends direct current in the secondary winding when the rotor speed is synchronous.

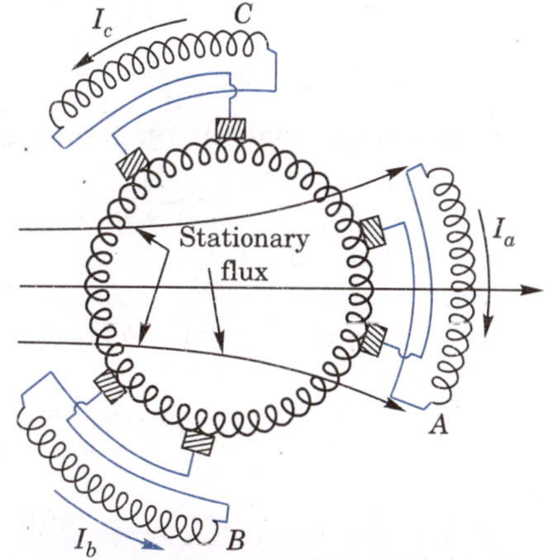

Fig. 7.21: Pertaining to Schrage motor operation at synchronous speed.

Note that air-gap field becomes stationary in any one position depending on the moment of brush shift. In Fig. 7.21, the stationary air-gap field is shown horizontal. This figure reveals that tertiary conductors supplying phase *A* are cutting the maximum flux while those supplying phases *B* and *C* are cutting much less flux. It may be noted that tertiary winding conductors supplying phases *B* and *C* are cutting negative flux with respect to those of phase *A*. Since different tertiary e.m.fs. are generated, the direct currents in the stator phases have unequal magnitudes. If, at the moment of attaining synchronous speed by brush shift, the stationary air-gap field is vertical in Fig. 7.21, the phase *A* would have zero direct current whereas brushes *B* and *C* would have equal magnitudes of direct current.

These unequal currents don't have any effect on primary, as a result primary currents are balanced.

There is no tendency of a Schrage motor to remain at synchronous speed, just like a synchronous motor. If brush shift is changed from synchronous-speed position, the air-gap flux starts rotating at slip speed and Schrage motor runs at sub- or super-synchronous speed depending on the brush shift. This shows that it is possible to operate a Schrage motor at synchronous speed and speed adjustment from sub- to super-synchronous is a smooth one.

Example 7.13. (*a*) *Explain whether a Schrage motor can be operated as a Schrage generator.*

(*b*) *Explain what happens to the Schrage motor, if fuse in one of the supply lines blows while it is running.*

Solution. (*a*) For a given brush separation, *i.e.*, for any no-load speed setting *n*, if the rotor speed is increased by a prime-mover above *n*, Schrage motor starts operating as a Schrage generator, or induction generator. With the prime-mover speed more than the no-load speed setting *n*, the secondary currents gets reversed as in the case of induction generator. The Schrage motor can work as a generator only when it is connected to a 3-phase source for supplying its magnetizing current as in a 3-phase induction generator.

(*b*) With the Schrage motor running under steady speed, if fuse in one of the supply lines blows it will not stop. The motor will continue running from single-phase supply, though at a reduced speed. It will, however, draw more current from the supply. It has been found that the motor makes more noise under single-phasing.

7.4.1 Generalized Theory

Schrage motor analysis by generalized theory, being more involved, is not done here.

Example 7.14. *A 4 pole, 50 Hz Schrage motor, running at no-load, gives minimum and maximum speeds of 500 and 2500 r.p.m. respectively, for brush separation of 180 electrical degrees (i.e. one pole pitch). Find the brush separation in electrical and mechanical degrees for no load speed of (a) 1000 r.p.m. and (b) 1800 r.p.m.*

Solution. From Eq. (7.44), $n_{ro} = n_s \left(1 \pm k \sin\frac{\theta}{2}\right)$

$$\therefore \qquad n_{ro.min} = 500 = 1500\,(1 - k) \quad \text{and} \quad n_{ro.\,max} = 2500 = 1500\,(1 + k)$$

or
$$\frac{2500}{500} = \frac{1+k}{1-k}$$

This gives $k = \frac{2}{3}$

(*a*) When rotor speed is 1000 r.p.m. *i.e.,* less than synchronous speed of 1500 r.p.m.,

then from Eq. (7.44), $1000 = 1500\left(1 - \frac{2}{3}\sin\frac{\theta}{2}\right)$

This gives $\theta = 60°$ electrical.

Now $\theta_{mech} = \frac{2}{P}, \theta_{elec} = 30°.$

(*b*) When speed is 1800 r.p.m., *i.e.,* above synchronous speed, then from Eq. (7.44),

$$1800 = 1500\left(1 + \frac{2}{3}\sin\frac{\theta}{2}\right)$$

This gives $\theta = 34.92°$ electrical and 17.46° mechanical.

Example 7.15. *In case of 4 pole, 50 Hz Schrage motor, the e.m.f. available across the brushes one pole-pitch apart is 48 V. The secondary e.m.f. at standstill is 60 V. Find the no-load speed range.*

Solution. Here maximum voltage available across the brushes, $E_{j\,max} = 48$ V.

Secondary e.m.f. at standstill, $E_2 = 60$ V,

$$\therefore \quad k = \frac{E_{j\,max}}{E_2} = \frac{48}{60} = \frac{4}{5}$$

Now, $n_{ro} = n_s\left(1 \pm k\sin\frac{\theta}{2}\right)$

$$\therefore \quad n_{ro.\,min} = 1500\left(1 - \frac{4}{5}\sin 90°\right) = 300 \text{ r.p.m.}$$

and $n_{ro.\,max} = 1500\left(1 + \frac{4}{5}\right) = 2700$ r.p.m.

∴ Speed range is 2700 : 300 or 9 : 1.

Example 7.16. *A 4 pole, 400 V, 50 Hz, 3-phase star-connected Schrage motor has the following data :*

Effective secondary series turns per phase = 80.

Total lap-connected tertiary turns = 300.

Calculate the minimum and maximum no-load speeds of this motor for a brush separation tangle of 60° electrical.

Solution. From Eq. (7.44),

$$n_{ro} = n_s\left(1 \pm k\sin\frac{\theta}{2}\right)$$

Here, $Z = 300 \times 2 = 600, \quad N_2' = 80, a = P = 4,$

Now, $k = \frac{Z}{a\pi N_2'} = \frac{600}{4\pi\,(80)} = 0.597$

and, $n_s = \frac{120f}{P} = 1500$ r.p.m.

For a brush separation angle of $\theta = 60°$ electrical.

$$n_{ro} = 1500\left(1 \pm 0.597 \sin \frac{60°}{2}\right) = 1500\ (1 \pm 0.2985).$$

For $\theta = 60$, the motor runs at minimum speed when the injected e.m.f. is in phase opposition to the secondary standstill e.m.f. E_2

$$\therefore \quad n_{ro.\ min} = 1500\ (1 - 0.2985) = 1062.75 \text{ r.p.m.}$$

Maximum motor speed is obtained when the injected e.m.f. is in phase with the standstill secondary e.m.f.

$$\therefore \quad n_{ro.\ max} = 1500\ (1 + 0.2985) = 1947.75 \text{ r.p.m.}$$

Thus, the minimum and maximum no-load speeds, for a brush separation angle of 60° electrical, are 1062.75 r.p.m. and 1947.75 r.p.m. respectively.

7.5 SUMMARY

Wide-speed control of three-phase induction motors can be obtained by frequency-control techniques employing power-electronic components. Three-phase commutator motor, like Schrage motor, also offers wide speed control of three-phase ac drives. Commutator-motor drives, however, possess certain advantages over adjustable-frequency solid-state drives as enumerated below :

(*i*) For speed range up to 4 : 1 or so, three-phase commutator motors offer a cheaper electric drive system.

(*ii*) Commutator-motor drive does not distort the supply voltage and current waveforms. But in frequency-controlled techniques, the supply system is polluted by the harmonic generation and this effects the operation of other equipment working on the same supply line.

(*iii*) Commutator-motor drive offers simple and reliable speed control.

(*iv*) Commutator-motor drives can withstand overload without any harm to the drive components. But in frequency-control techniques, the overload is restricted by the power-switching devices.

The main drawback of commutator motors is the need for their frequent maintenance.

PROBLEMS

7.1. (*a*) What are the two kinds of e.m.fs. induced in the armature of a.c. commutator machines ? Derive expressions for these e.m.fs. in case field flux is pulsating.

(*b*) A 4-pole lap-connected armature has 450 turns and rotates at 1200 r.p.m. in a sine-distributed pulsating flux of frequency 50 Hz and of amplitude 0.018 Wb per pole.

Calculate the voltage and frequency of the e.m.f. at the brushes, if the brush axes are,

(*i*) 90° away from the field axes

(*ii*) aligned along the field axes and

(*iii*) 30° away from the field axes.

[**Ans.** 229.10 V, 50 Hz ; 286.38 V, 50 Hz ; 273.18 V, 50 Hz]

7.2. (*a*) Derive expressions for the brush e.m.fs. produced by rotating field in case of a.c. commutator machines. How can the same e.m.f. expressions be obtained by resolving the rotating field into its two pulsating field components ?

(*b*) A 4-pole commutator machine, with 160 armature turns, is running at 1800 r.p.m. clockwise. The constant-amplitude flux of 0.05 Wb is rotating at 2400 r.p.m. (*i*) clockwise and (*ii*) anticlockwise. Compute the magnitude and frequency of the brush e.m.f. for $\theta = 70°$. Also, calculate the conductor e.m.f. frequencies in both the cases.

[**Ans.** (*i*) 64.853 V, f_b = 80 Hz, 20 Hz (*ii*) 454.25 V, f_b = 80 Hz, 140 Hz]

7.3. A 2-pole rotor has a double-layer winding with full-pitched coils. The armature, with 180 turns, rotates in a constant sine-distributed *d*-axis flux of 0.01 Wb. One end of the winding is tapped at three-equidistant points and connected to three slip rings. At the other end, a pair of commutator brushes is placed in the *q*-axis. Compute the magnitude and frequency of the e.m.fs. appearing across *q*-axis brushes and between adjacent slip rings if the armature totates at 3000 r.p.m.

Show that the ratio of brush e.m.f. to the slip-ring e.m.f. equal to 1.633, is independent of the armature conductors, its speed and the field flux. [**Ans.** 180 V at zero Hz, 110.23 V at 50 Hz]

7.4. A 2-pole commutator machine, with full-pitched coils, has constant-amplitude rotating flux of 0.02 Wb. The armature has 360 turns. the rotating flux revolves at 1500 r.p.m. clockwise. Compute the brush e.m.f. and frequency, in case there are

(*a*) two diametrically spaced brushes and rotor rotates at 900 r.p.m. (*i*) clockwise (*ii*) anti-clockwise.

(*b*) three brushes spaced at 120° and rotor rotates at 900 r.p.m. (*i*) clockwise (*ii*) anti-clockwise.

[**Hint.** (*b*) Use Eq. (7.15) with $\theta = 120°$.]

[**Ans.** (*a*) 101.823 V and 407.29 V ; f_b = 25 Hz (*b*) 88.18 V and 352.72 V ; f_b = 25 Hz]

7.5. (*a*) Explain the operation of a d.c. series motor when connected to an a.c. source. What measures may be adopted to improve the performance of d.c. series motor when fed with a.c.?

(*b*) A single-phase a.c. series motor has a resistance of 30 Ω and a total inductance of 0.5 H. When connected to 250 V d.c. supply and loaded to take 0.8 ampere, it runs at 2000 r.p.m. Estimate the speed and p.f. when connected to 250 V, 50 Hz. a.c. supply and loaded to the same current. [**Ans.** (*b*) 1700.19 r.p.m., 0.8645 lagging]

7.6. (*a*) Draw and explain the phasor diagram of a single-phase series motor.

(*b*) A series motor has a total resistance of 25Ω and a total inductance of 0.2 H. The motor runs at 1000 rpm. when it draws 1 A from 220 V d.c. source. Calculate the speed and pf when it draws the same current from 220 V, 50 Hz source.

[**Ans.** (*b*) 953.01 rpm., 0.9584 lagging]

7.7. (*a*) Show with the help of phasor diagrams that a compensated series motor possesses better speed-torque characteristics better pf operation and improved commutation as compared to an uncompansated series motor.

(*b*) Explain how radio interference can be supressed in 1-phsae series motors.

7.8. (*a*) Give the applications of compensated and uncompensated single-phase series motors. Enumerate their methods of starting and speed control.

(*b*) For a universal motor, prove the following relation :

$$\frac{n_{ac}}{n_{dc}} = \frac{\sqrt{(V_t/I)^2 - X^2} - r}{\dfrac{V_t}{I} - r} = \frac{\cos\theta - \dfrac{I.r}{V_t}}{1 - \dfrac{I.r}{V_t}}$$

where V_t is the applied voltage, r is the total resistance and X is the total reactance, Motor p.f. is cos θ.

7.9. Derive an expression for the electromagnetic torque of a.c. series motor in which the armature current i and the field flux ϕ_d are not in time phase. Assume the brush axis to be along the geometrical neutral axis.

[**Hint.** The effect of core losses and commutated-coil current causes ϕ_d to lag behind i. Let this angle of lag be ψ, If $i = I_{max} \sin \omega t$, the $\phi_d = \phi_{dm} \sin (\omega t - \psi)$. Now follow the article 7.2].

[**Ans.** 0.11254 $ZP/a\ \phi_{dm}\ I \cos \psi$ Nm]

7.10. A 220 V, 600 W, 5000 rpm, 50 Hz single-phase series motor has total resistance of 2Ω and total reactance of 20 Ω. For stray power loss of 40 W, determine,

(*a*) current and power factor under rated conditions and

(*b*) speed, power factor and efficiency at half rated load.

[**Ans.** (*a*) 3.127 A, 0.9587 lag, (*b*) 10338.7 rpm., 0.9896 lag, 86.94%]

7.11. A 6-pole, lap-connected single phase series motor has 300 turns. For an armature current of 15 A, the amplitude of the sine-flux wave is 0.04 Wb per pole. The field flux lags the current by an angle of 10° due to hysteresis. Calculate the magnitude of the torque developed. Also, derive the torque expression used here.

If the load torque is equal to $(2 + 0.04\ \omega_r)$ Nm, find the motor speed in r.p.m. Here ω_r is the rotor speed in rad/second. [**Ans.** 39.899 Nm, 9047.7 r.p.m.]

7.12. Write the impedance matrix of a conductively compensated single-phase series motor and obtain therefrom, an expression for the electromagnetic torque in terms of the terminal voltage and other constants.

7.13. (*a*) Sketch the speed-torque characteristics of d.c. and a.c. series motors in one figure and discuss their nature. How can the speed of an a.c. series motor be reversed ?

(*b*) A universal series motor has total resistance of 1 Ω and total inductance of 0.05 H. When connected to 220 V d.c., the motor draws 10 A and runs at 1400 rpm. Calculate the speed and power factor when the motor draws the same current from

(*i*) 220 V, 50 Hz source and

(*ii*) 220 V, $16\frac{2}{3}$ Hz source. [**Ans.** (*i*) 960.2 rpm, 0.7 lag (*ii*) 1357.86 rpm, 0.9713 lag.]

7.14. (*a*) Give a scheme commonly employed for obtaining four speeds in a universal motor for a mixer.

(*b*) A single-phase series motor drives a constant-torque load at 3000 r.p.m. and takes a current of 2 A at a p.f. of 0.7 lagging from 230 V a.c. mains. Its armature circuit resistance is 0.3 Ω. If its supply voltage reduces to 200 V, calculate the

(*i*) motor current, (*ii*) motor speed and (*iii*) motor p.f.

Neglect magnetic saturation and losses.

[**Hint.** (*b*) Refer to Fig. 7.9

$V_t \cos \theta = Ir + CIn, \quad \therefore \quad C = ...$

Also $\quad V_t \sin \theta = IX \quad \therefore \quad X = ...$

From Eq. (7.23), calculate n etc.]

[**Ans.** (*a*) By tapping the field coils. (*b*) (*i*) 2A (*ii*) 2123 rpm (*iii*) 0.5705 lagging]

7.15. (*a*) Explain the constructional features of a Schrage motor. How does it differ from an ordinary induction motor ?

(*b*) A 4-pole, 50 Hz. Schrage motor can run at minimum and maximum no-load speeds of 600 and 1800 rpm respectively, for a brush separation of one pole pitch. Find the brush separation angle for no-load speed of

(*i*) 1000 rpm and (*ii*) 1600 rpm [**Ans.** (*b*) 83.62°, 15.324°]

7.16. (*a*) Explain why the primary winding in a Schrage motor is provided on the rotor.

(*b*) a 3-phase, 400 V, 50 Hz, 6-pole Schrage motor has the following data :

Secondary effective series turns per phase = 40

Lap-connected total tertiary turns = 252.

Estimate the approximate no-load speed of the motor with brush separation angle of 120° electrical, with the injected emf directly,

(*i*) helping,

(*ii*) opposing the standstill secondary emf. **[Ans.** 1579 rpm, 421 rpm]

7.17. (*a*) Explain, with neat diagrams, how it is possible to obtain the speeds both below and above synchronous speed in a Schrage motor.

(*b*) A 4-pole, 50 Hz Schrage motor has minimum and maximum no-load speeds of 500 and 2000 r.p.m, for brush separation of one pole pitch. What is the brush frequency at these two speeds ? **[Ans.** (*b*) 33.3 Hz, 16.67 Hz]

7.18. (*a*) Show that a Schrage motor is a constant-torque drive motor.

(*b*) No special starting devices are required for a Schrage motor. Explain.

(*c*) The speed of a 6-pole, 50 Hz Schrage motor is to be raised to 1500 r.p.m. at no-load. Find the phase and magnitude of the injected tertiary voltage in terms of the standstill secondary e.m.f. E_2. **[Ans.** (*c*) + 0.5 E_2]

7.19. A 6-pole, 50 Hz Schrage motor, with normal voltage applied to its primary, gave a voltage of 42 V across brushes 180° (elect.) apart, with secondary winding connections opened. If the stator per phase voltage can be either 36 or 72 V per phase, estimate for each case the total possible range of speed control. The tertiary and stator winding axes are coincident.

[Ans. – 166.7 to 2166.7 rpm, 416.7 to 1583.3 r.p.m]

7.20. (*a*) Explain the constructional features and principle of working of a Schrage motor.

(*b*) A 6-pole, 50 Hz Schrage motor has a standstill secondary e.m.f. of 100 V per phase. What must be the e.m.f. induced between the brushes to give a no-load speed of 1500 r.p.m.? Under these conditions at what speed the air-gap flux would be rotating with respect to the stator ? If the maximum brush voltage is 80 V, calculate the angular displacement between the brushes.

[**Hint.** For the air-gap flux speed with a respect to stator, refer to Fig. 7.18 (*c*)]

[Ans. + 50 V, 500 r.p.m in the direction of rotor rotation, 77.36°]

7.21. (*a*) Sometimes the secondary windings of a Schrage motor have more than three phases. Why ?

(*b*) For a 6-pole, 50 Hz Schrage motor, calculate the air-gap flux speed with respect to rotor and stator, the injected emf in terms of secondary standstill emf E_2 and brush frequency, for the following rotor speeds at no-load.

(*i*) Zero, (*ii*) 600 r.p.m and (*iii*) 1100 r.p.m.

[Ans. (*b*) (*i*) 1000 r.p.m, 1000 r.p.m ; – E_2 50 Hz

(*ii*) 1000 r.p.m, 400 r.p.m against rotor rotation; – 0.4 E_2, 20 Hz.

(*iii*) 1000 r.p.m, 100 r.p.m in the direction of rotor rotation; + 0.1 E_2, 5 Hz]

8 Transformers

The basic concepts of single-phase transformers have been dealt with in detail in the companion volume.* In addition to the subject matter presented in the above mentioned book, some other topics like parallel operation of three-phase transformers, transformer phasor groups, excitation phenomenon in transformers, phase conversion, multicircuit transformers etc. are also important from engineering considerations. The object of this chapter is to discuss most of these topics.

8.1 THREE-PHASE TRANSFORMERS

In modern power systems, almost the entire electrical energy is generated in three-phase generators, which is then transmitted and distributed over three-phase circuits. From generating station to the consumers, the voltage is raised and lowered several times for economic reasons. Each time the voltage is stepped up or stepped down, a three-phase transformer is required. There are, thus, a large number of three-phase transformers used in three-phase power systems. For each voltage transformation from one value to another, three units of single-phase transformers or one unit of three phase transformer may be used. When three identical units of single-phase transformers are used, the arrangement is commonly called a bank of three transformers or a *three-phase transformers bank,* for the sake of distinguishing it from a three-phase transformer. Fig. 8.1 illustrates a three-phase transformer bank with both primary and secondary windings connected in star.

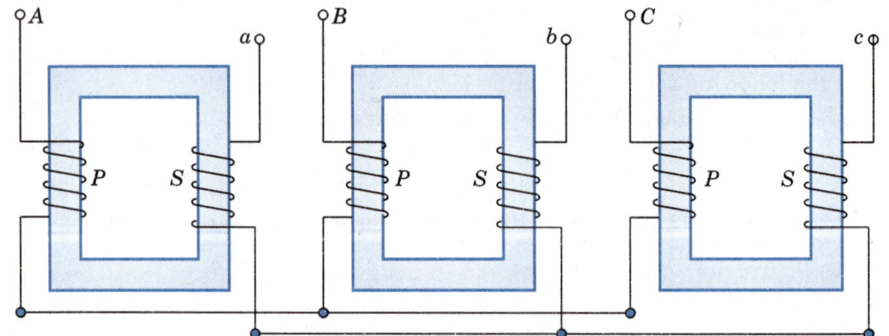

Fig. 8.1: Three-phase transformer bank consisting of three units of single phase transformers.

*"Electrical Machinery" by the same author.

A three-phase transformer may be of core type or shell type, as in single phase transformers. It is interesting, at this stage, to know about the evolution of a three-phase core-type transformer. Fig. 8.2 (*a*) displays three single-phase transformers, with their yokes placed 120° apart. The primary and secondary windings are wound over the limbs I, II, III and the three unwound limbs (or legs) are brought in close contact. Three phase currents in three primaries produce three-phase fluxes mutually time-displaced by 120°. These fluxes flow through their respective yokes and then through the central limbs placed together. The resultant flux in the three central limbs must be zero, since the phasor sum of three equal fluxes time displaced by 120° is zero, just as the phasor sum of three-phase balanced currents meeting at a point is zero. Alternatively, if we look Fig. 8.2 (*a*) from top, then the three yokes appear to be in star and the resultant flux at the star point, made up by the three central limbs, is zero. Since the central leg carries no flux, it can be eliminated as shown in Fig. 8.2 (*b*), without disturbing any of the existing conditions. The flux produced in any one leg, would return through the other two legs or limbs; similar to a 3-phase system, where current in one wire at any instant returns through the other two wires. The construction of a transformer with such type of core would be very expensive and it is, therefore, more practicable to construct a transformer core as depicted in Fig. 8.2 (*c*). Note that Fig. 8.2 (*c*) is obtained from Fig. 8.2 (*b*) by reducing the yoke of transformer II to zero and arranging the cores I, II, III in the same plane.

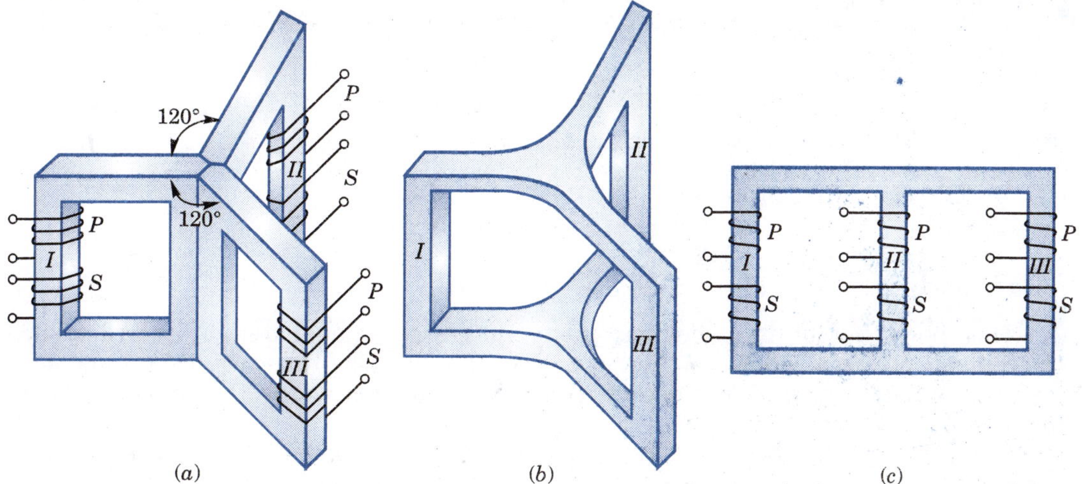

Fig. 8.2: Pertaining to the evolution of three-phase core-type transformer from three single-phase units.

An examination of the magnetic circuit of Fig. 8.2 (*c*) would reveal that the reluctance offered to the flux of central limb II is less than the reluctance offered to the outer two fluxes produced in legs I and III. Consequently, the exciting current for the phase winding on the central limb is less than it is for the outer two phase windings. However, the difference in the exciting currents is so small that it does not have any material effect on the operation of a 3-phase core-type transformer.

A three-phase shell type transformer is obtained if three single-phase shell type cores are placed side by side as shown in Fig. 8.3 (*a*). In the magnetic circuits marked 2 and 3, the resultant flux is seen to be equal to the phasor difference of the component fluxes. For example, in the section marked 2, the resultant flux ϕ_2 is the phasor difference of $\phi_A/2$ and $\phi_B/2$ as illustrated in Fig. 8.3 (*b*).

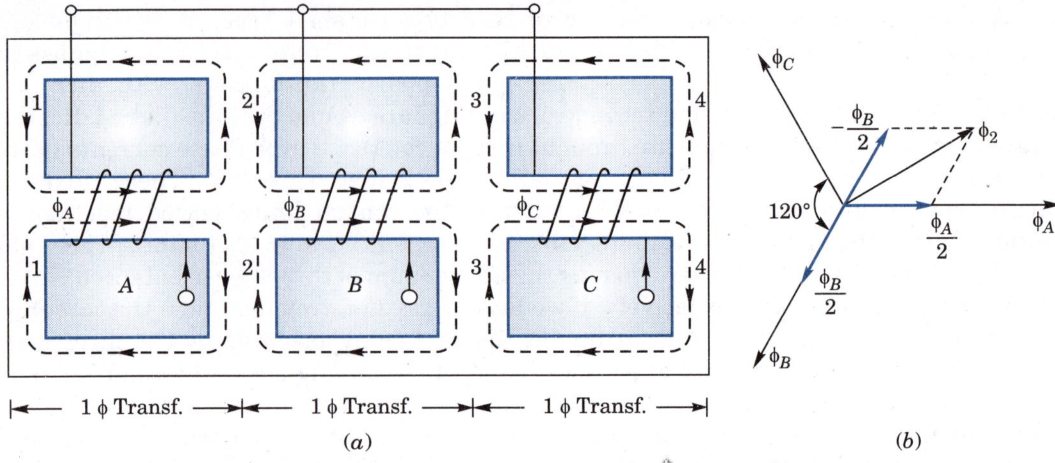

Fig. 8.3: Three-phase shell type transformer with three windings wound in the same direction.

$$\therefore \qquad \bar{\phi}_2 = \frac{\bar{\phi}_A}{2} - \frac{\bar{\phi}_B}{2}$$

With ϕ_A as the reference phasor,

$$\bar{\phi}_2 = \frac{1}{2}[\phi \angle 0° - \phi \angle -120°] = \frac{1}{2}\,[\phi - \phi\,(\cos 120° - j \sin 120°]$$

$$= \frac{1}{2}\left[\phi + \frac{\phi}{2} + j\frac{\sqrt{3}}{2}\phi\right] = \frac{\phi}{2}\left[\frac{3}{2} + j\frac{\sqrt{3}}{2}\right]$$

$$\therefore \quad \text{The magnitude of } \phi_2 = \frac{\phi}{2}\sqrt{\left(\frac{3}{2}\right)^2 + \left(\frac{\sqrt{3}}{2}\right)^2} = \frac{\sqrt{3}}{2}\phi.$$

$$\text{Similarly} \qquad \phi_3 = \frac{\sqrt{3}}{2}\phi.$$

This shows that for the same flux density, the cross-sectional areas at 2 and 3 are 86.6% of the central core area, where the flux is $\phi = \phi_A = \phi_B = \phi_C$. The flux carried by 1 and 4 is ϕ_2, therefore, their areas are 50% of the central core area. In other words, the area at 2 and 3 are 1.732 times the areas at 1 and 4.

If the winding *B* is wound in the reversed direction as shown in Fig. 8.4(*a*), then the resultant flux ϕ_2 for the section marked 2 would be the phasor sum of $\phi_A/2$ and $\phi_B/2$, Fig. 8.4 (*b*). For balanced operation,

$$\bar{\phi}_2 = \frac{\bar{\phi}_A}{2} + \frac{\bar{\phi}_B}{2}$$

With ϕ_A as the reference phasor,

$$\bar{\phi}_2 = \frac{1}{2}\,[\phi \angle 0° + \phi \angle -120°] = \frac{\phi}{2}\left[1 - \frac{1}{2} - j\frac{\sqrt{3}}{2}\right] = \frac{\phi}{2}\left[\frac{1}{2} - j\frac{\sqrt{3}}{2}\right]$$

$$\therefore \qquad \phi_2 = \frac{\phi}{2}\sqrt{\left(\frac{1}{2}\right)^2 + \left(\frac{\sqrt{3}}{2}\right)^2} = \frac{\phi}{2}$$

$$\text{Similarly} \qquad \phi_3 = \frac{\phi}{2}.$$

Thus, with the winding B wound in the reversed direction, the area of cross-section of the portions marked 1, 2, 3 and 4 is the same and is equal to one-half of the central limb area. In this manner, a considerable economy is effected in the core material. It may be seen from Fig. 8.4 (*a*) that the magnetic circuits for fluxes ϕ_A, ϕ_B and ϕ_C are in parallel and, therefore, independent of each other. In view of this, the analysis of a three-phase shell-type transformer is similar to the analysis of a bank of three transformers whose magnetic circuits are clearly separate as shown in Fig. 8.1. The effect of reducing the cross-sectional area at 2 and 3 is to cause slight unbalance in the exciting currents of the three phases. This, however, has little effect on the operation of this transformer, as in the case of a three-phase core type transformer of Fig. 8.2 (*c*).

A three-phase shell type transformer is not in much use.

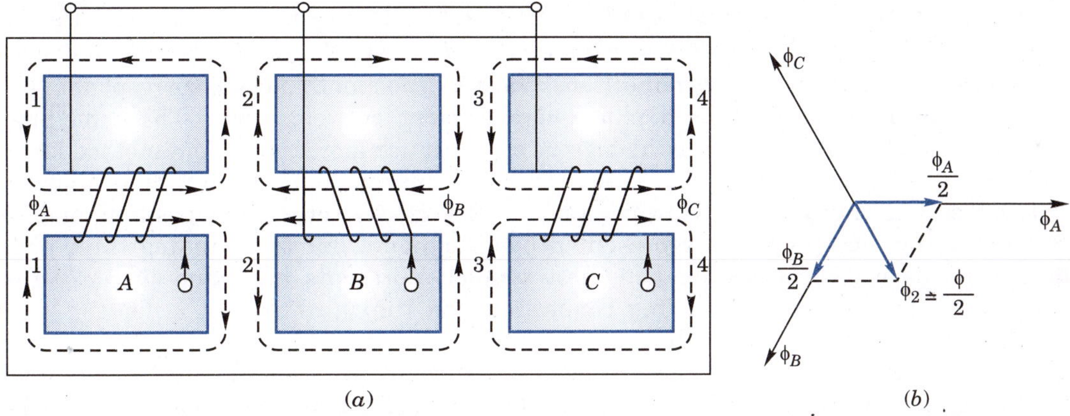

Fig. 8.4: Three-phase shell type transformer with middle winding wound in the reversed direction.

8.2 THREE-PHASE TRANSFORMER CONNECTIONS AND PHASOR GROUPS

A bank of three transformers or a three-phase transformer, may have its primary and secondary windings connected in star, delta or zig-zag. The choice of particular connections depends upon the service conditions. The commonly employed connections are star, delta, zig-zag and these are designated by the symbols Y, D, Z respectively. Zig-zag connection is also called *interconnected star* or *inter star*. The object of this article is to discuss these connections for three-phase transformers and the four phasor groups.

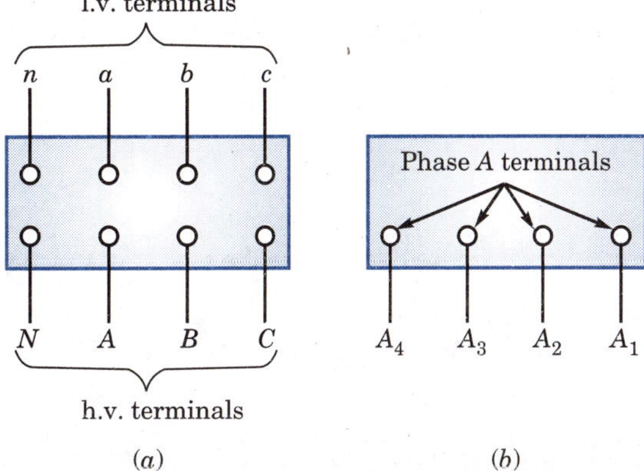

Fig. 8.5: Pertaining to the terminal markings of three phase transformers.

There is a standard method of marking the transformer terminals. As per IS, the transformer terminals are brought out in rows. The h.v. and l.v. terminals are mounted on opposite sides of the tank. The h.v. terminals have capital letters A, B, C for three phases and l.v. terminals have correspondingly lower case letters a, b, c. Tertiary winding, where provided, have its terminals lettered with $3A$, $3B$ and $3C$ for its three phases. When viewing from h.v. side, both sets of h.v. and l.v. terminals are lettered alphabetically from left to right for the phase terminals as shown in Fig. 8.5 (*a*). If neutral is provided, it is fitted on the extreme left, see Fig. 8.5 (*a*). Further, the letters are assigned numbers to serve as subscripts. For example, if four terminals are brought out for phase *A*, then symbol A_1 is used for the extreme right terminal, A_2 for the second right terminal, A_3 for the next in sequence, *i.e.,* second from A_4 for the extreme left terminal, the main output terminals being A_1 and A_4 as shown in Fig. 8.5 (*b*). In general, the main terminals are A_1 and the last numbered letter. The winding numbers are so arranged that when A_1 is positive with respect to A_2 at any instant, then a_1 is positive with respect to a_2 and $3A_1$ is positive with respect to $3A_2$ at the same instant.

In representing a three-phase transformer, the h.v. winding is indicated by a capital letter (*e.g., Y* for star, *D* for delta etc.) and l.v. winding by a lower case letter (*e.g., y* for star, *d* for delta etc.). The symbol "*Yd*" represents a 3-phase transformer with h.v. in star and l.v. in delta.

In the various transformer connections, the h.v. line e.m.f. and the corresponding l.v. line e.m.f. may or may not have a phase displacement between them. This time-phase displacement can be expressed either in degrees or by a much more convenient method known as *clock method* of angle designation. According to this method, the h.v. line phasor is considered as the minute hand always set at 12 O'clock (zero hour) position and the corresponding l.v. line phasor is represented by hour hand. For two winding three-phase transformers, as per the clock method, first symbol represents h.v. winding connection, second symbol represents l.v. winding connection and the third symbol is for the phase displacement between h.v. and l.v. line e.m.fs. expressed as clock hour number. For example, symbol "*Yd* 11" represents a polyphase transformer with h.v. winding in star, l.v. winding in delta and the l.v. line phasor at 11 O'clock, *i.e.,* 30° ahead of the zero hour position of the h.v. line phasor as shown in Fig. 8.6 (*a*). For three-winding three-phase transformers, the first letter pertains to the highest voltage winding connection and the next two letters pertain to the other two winding connections in order of decreasing voltage. In addition, the last two letters are associated with clock hour number of the corresponding winding, the phasor of h.v. winding taken as reference along the zero-hour position. For example, symbol *Dy*1*y*1 represents a three phase transformer (h.v. in delta/l.v. in star/tertiary in star) with both secondary and tertiary line emfs at 1 O'clock (– 30° or 30° lag) position and h.v. line emf at zero hour position as shown in Fig. 8.6 (*b*). Symbol *Yy*0*d*1 represents a poly-phase transformer with h.v. in star, secondary winding in star with its line emf in phase with h.v. line emf and tertiary winding of lowest emf in delta with its line emf 30° lagging the h.v. line e.m.f.

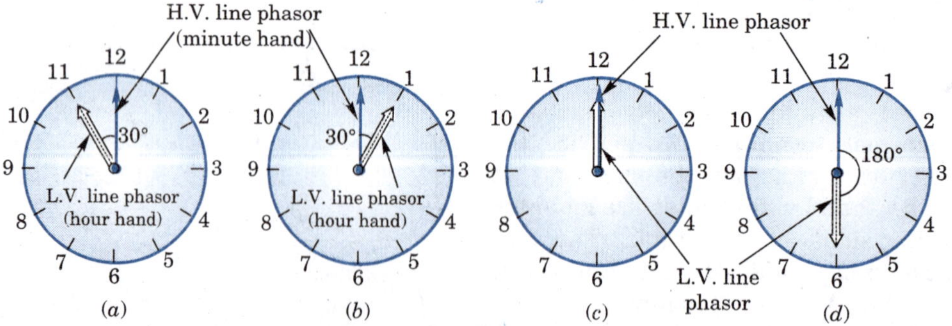

Fig. 8.6: The minute hand (long hand) represents the h.v. line phasor and is treated as fixed. The hour hand (short hand) represents l.v. line phasor, (*a*) Group No. 4 (*b*) Group No. 3 (*c*) Group No. 1 (*d*) Group No. 2.

The phase angle between h.v. and l.v. line emfs, depends upon the direction in which the windings are wound and the method of connecting the three phases. Thus for three-phase transformers, in addition to the knowledge of h.v. and l.v. connections (star, delta or interstar), the phase angle between the h.v. and l.v. line emfs must be known. Depending upon the type of connections and phase displacement between the h.v. and l.v. line emfs, there are four phasor groups. Each group is characterised by a different phase displacement and for understanding their phasor diagrams, the following points should be kept in mind.

In the phasor diagrams, the phasors rotate in the counter clockwise direction as usual. The phasors representing the induced emfs in the h.v. and l.v. windings for a particular phase, are drawn parallel to each other. For example, for phase A, the l.v. phasor a_1a_2 must be drawn parallel to the h.v. phasor A_1A_2. The h.v. winding is assumed to be the primary and l.v. winding the secondary. The position of h.v. terminals A_2, B_2, C_2 is assumed fixed, for convenience, in the top, bottom right and bottom left corners respectively, of the equilateral triangle A_2, B_2, C_2. In view of this, phasors for star and delta connections on h.v. side must be drawn in different positions.

8.2.1 Phasor Groups

The four phasor groups are now discussed in detail.

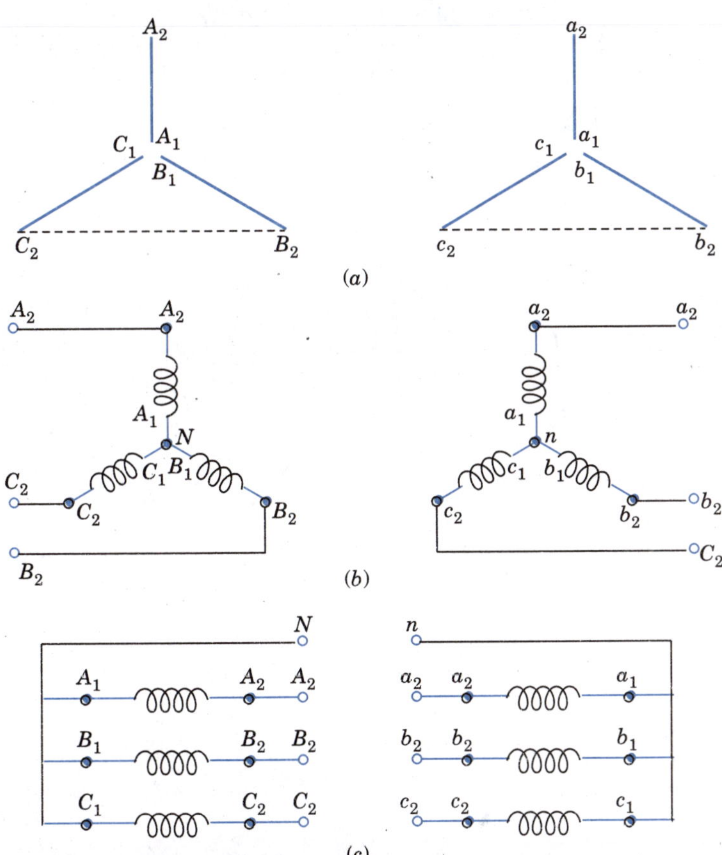

Fig. 8.7: Yy0 arrangement, group No. 1.

(*a*) **Group No. 1 (Zero degree phase displacement).** The phase displacement between the h.v. and l.v. line emfs for group number 1 is zero as shown in Fig. 8.6 (*c*). For *Yy* arrangement, $A_1 A_2$ and $a_1 a_2$ for phase *A* are drawn parallel to one another. Similarly $b_1 b_2$ and $c_1 c_2$ are drawn parallel to $B_1 B_2$ and $C_1 C_2$ respectively as shown in Fig. 8.7 (*a*). If c_2 of the l.v. side is made of coincide C_2 of the h.v. side, then it would be seen that l.v. line phasor $c_2 b_2$ overlaps the h.v. line phasor C_2B_2. There is thus no phase angle between the h.v. and l.v. line emfs and star-star connection is designated as *Yy*0. Zero after *y* indicates zero phase displacement. For h.v. and l.v. windings, the connection diagrams illustrated in Fig. 8.7 (*b*) or Fig. 8.7 (*c*) may be used.

For *Dd*0 connection, if the h.v. phasors are drawn in the position of Fig. 8.7 (*a*), then phasor diagram of Fig. 8.8 (*a*) is obtained. Since the reference position of A_2, B_2, C_2, as assumed before, has been altered, the three h.v. phasors must be drawn to have different positions. If the three phasors are drawn as indicated in Fig. 8.8 (*b*), the reference position of A_2, B_2, C_2, is maintained. An examination of phasor diagram for *Dd*0 in Fig. 8.8 (*b*) reveals that l.v. line emf $a_2 b_2$ is in phase with h.v. line emf $A_2 B_2$. The connection diagrams are as illustrated in Fig. 8.8 (*c*) and (*d*).

For *Dz*0, the phasor diagram for h.v. side is as shown in Fig. 8.8 (*b*). The l.v. winding, for convenience in drawing the l.v. phasor diagram, is indicated in Fig. 8.9 (*a*) in sectionalised form. Terminals $a_2 b_2 c_2$ are joined together to form the neutral *n*. Further, join c_1 with a_3, a_1 with b_3 and b_1 with c_3 to obtain the l.v. zigzag phasor diagram, which also helps in drawing the connection diagram of Fig. 8.9 (*c*). The l.v. line phasor $c_4 b_4$ is parallel to the corresponding h.v. line phasor C_2B_2 of Fig. 8.8 (*b*), there is, therefore, no phase displacement between h.v. and l.v. line e.m.fs.

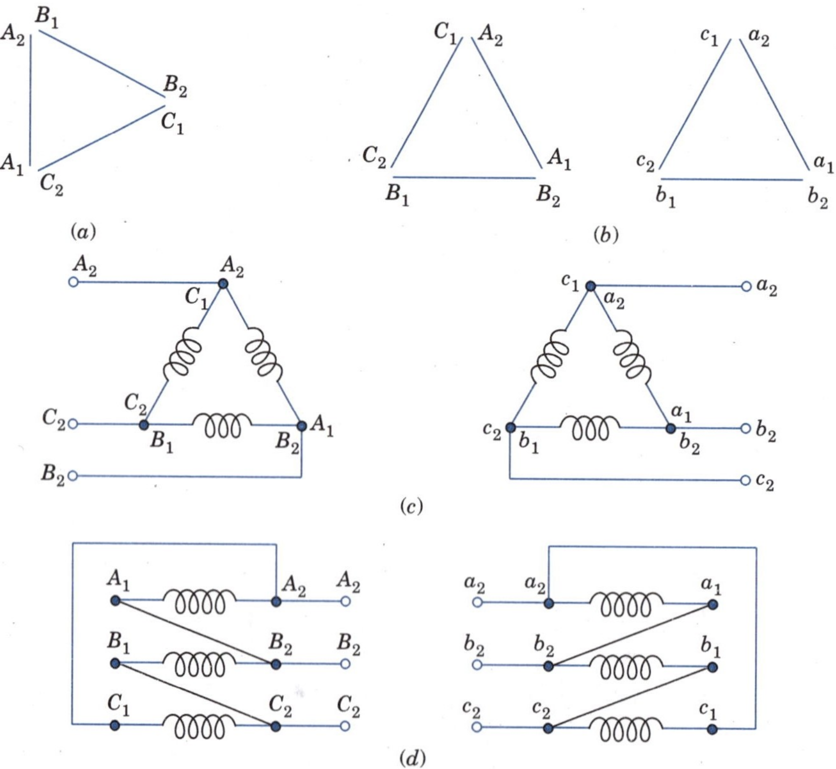

Fig. 8.8: *Dd*0 arrangement, Group No. 1.

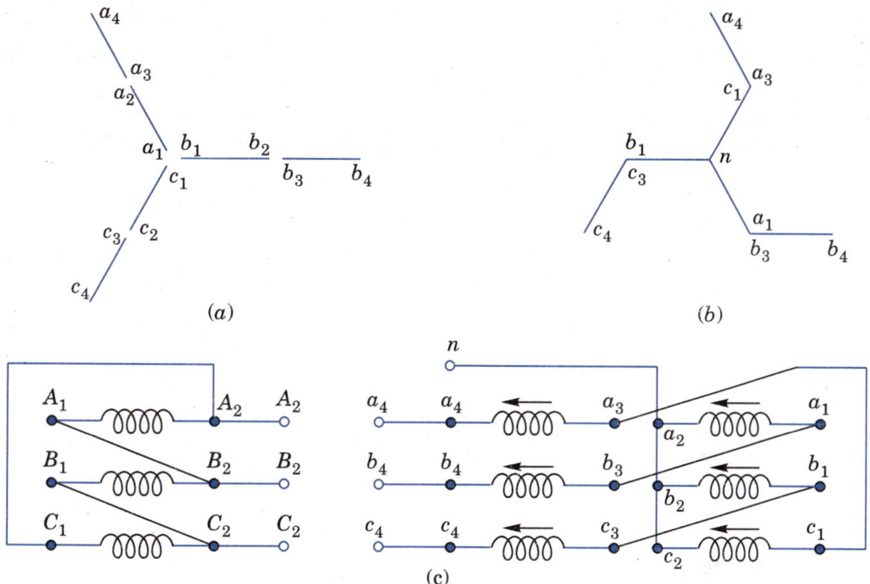

Fig. 8.9: *Dz*0 arrangement, Group No. 1.

Zigzag, or *interstar*, connection is primarily used to suppress the third harmonic e.m.f.s between line and neutral. The third harmonic e.m.fs. are all directed in the same direction, *i.e.* from a_1, b_1, c_1 to a_4, b_4, c_4 as illustrated in Fig. 8.9 (*c*). If the winding is traversed from neutral along the path $n\ c_2 c_1 a_3 a_4$, it is seen that e.m.f. in $c_2 c_1$ is $(-E_3)$ and in $a_3 a_4$, it is E_3; where E_3 is the third harmonic e.m.f. induced in each half l.v. section. The resultant third harmonic emf between neutral and line is, therefore, zero. If E_1 is the fundamental-frequency voltage of each half l.v. section, then the magnitude of line to neutral voltage is found to be $\sqrt{3}E_1$ from the phasor diagram of Fig. 8.9 (*b*). Had the l.v. winding been in star, the line to neutral voltage would be $2E_1$. Therefore, the phase voltage (or line voltage) in inter-star is reduced to $\sqrt{3}E_1/2E_1 = 0.866$ of its value in star. If the voltage $2E_1$ is to be retained in inter-star, then the l.v. turns must be increased to 1.15 $(= 2/\sqrt{3})$ times their value in star. When this is done, interstar connection becomes expensive, because it involves extra copper, additional insulation, more iron etc. A *Yy* transformer cannot supply a line to neutral load, whereas *Yz* transformer can do so as explained in Art. 8.5.

Inter-star connections are used for rectifier circuits. The direct current, after entering the neutral n in the Fig. 8.9 (*c*), divides equally in all the three secondary phases. Since each half of the secondary winding carries direct current in opposite direction, their magnetic effects cancel each other. As a result of it, the core flux and, therefore, core loss and temperature rise remain uneffected. Had the secondary been star connected instead of zigzag, the direct current would divide equally in three phases. The flux produced by direct current would add to the alternating flux, thereby increasing the core flux, core loss and temperature rise of the transformer.

(*b*) **Group No. 2 (180° phase displacement).** The phase displacement between the h.v. and l.v. line e.m.fs for group number 2 is 180° as shown in Fig. 8.6 (*d*). For this group, the connections of all the secondary terminals are reversed with respect to the primary connections. For example, in a star-star transformer, the primary terminals A_1, B_1, C_1 are joined together to form neutral N, whereas on the secondary side, terminals a_2, b_2, c_2 must be joined together to form the neutral n as shown in Fig. 8.10. The h.v. side has A_2, B_2, C_2 as the input terminals and l.v. side has a_1, b_1, c_1 as the output terminals. If b_1 is made to coincide B_2, then the phase angle between h.v. line phasor $B_2\,C_2$ and l.v. line phasor $b_1\,c_1$ is 180°, giving *Yy*6 arrangement. The connection arrangement is illustrated in Fig. 8.10 (*b*).

For *Dd*6, the h.v. terminals A_1 and B_2 are joined together as before. For reversing the secondary connections, a_2 and b_1 should be joined together as shown in Fig. 8.11 (*a*). The input terminals on the h.v. side are A_2, B_2, C_2 and the l.v. output terminals are a_1, b_1, c_1. The phase angle between B_2C_2 and b_1c_1 is seen to be 180°. The connection arrangement is as shown in Fig. 8.11 (*b*).

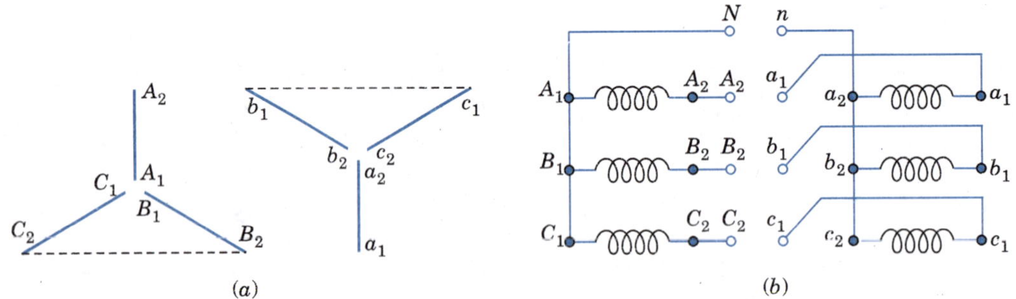

Fig. 8.10: *Yy*6 arrangement, Group No. 2.

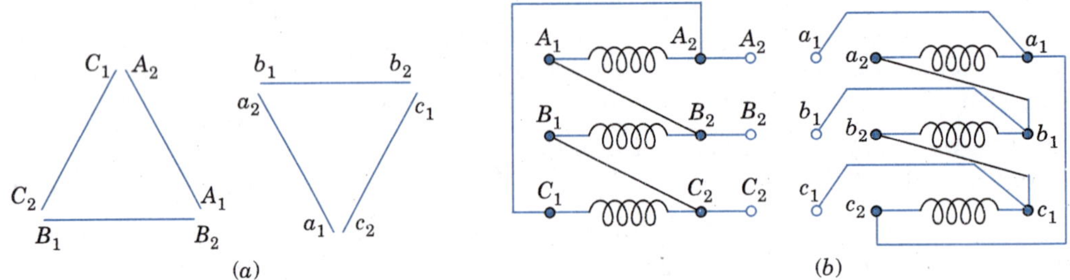

Fig. 8.11: *Dd*6 arrangement, Group No. 2.

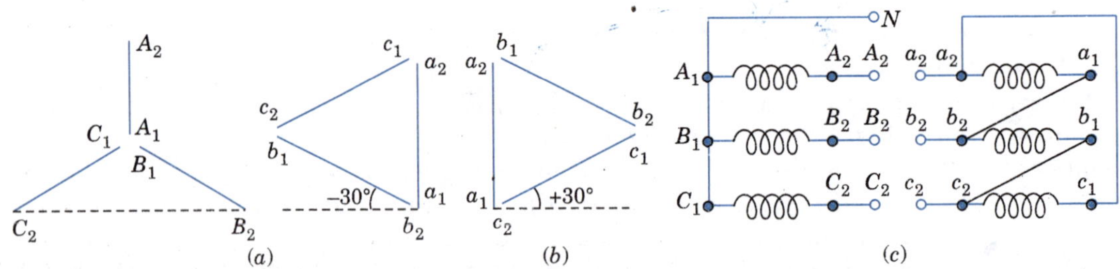

Fig. 8.12: *Yd*1 arrangement, Group No. 3.

(*c*) **Group No. 3 (Minus 30° phase displacement).** A phase displacement of minus 30° means that the l.v. line phasor lags the corresponding h.v. line phasor by 30° as shown in Fig. 8.6 (*b*). For star-delta transformer, the phasor diagram is as shown in Fig. 8.12 (*a*). When B_2 is coinciding b_2, the l.v. line phasor $b_2\,c_2$ lags the h.v. line phasor $B_2\,C_2$ by 30°. If phasor B_2 C_2 is assumed along the zero hour position of the clock, then phasor $b_2\,c_2$ occupies 1 O'clock position, thereby showing it to be a $Yd1$ arrangement. If the secondary connections are made as shown in Fig. 8.12 (b) $Yd11$ arrangement of group number 4 is obtained per chance.

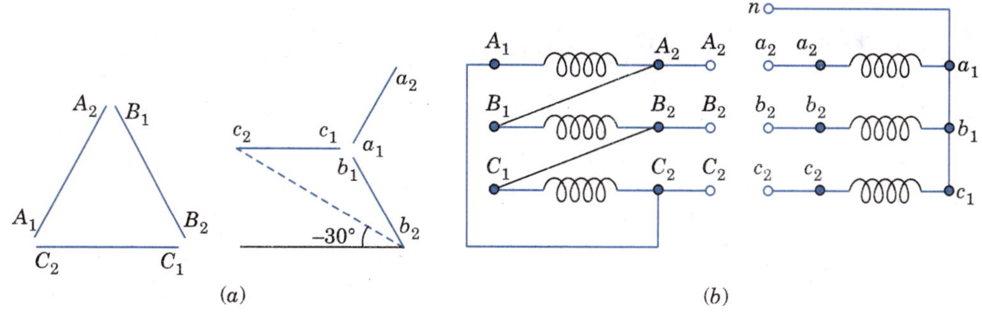

Fig. 8.13: $Dy1$ arrangement, Group No. 3.

For delta-star, the phasor orientation of h.v. line voltages A_1A_2, B_1B_2 and C_1C_2 have been changed to get $Dy1$ arrangement as shown in Fig. 8.13.

The connection schemes for $Yd1$ and $Dy1$ arrangements are as shown in Figs. 8.12 (c) and 8.13 (b) respectively.

Group No. 4 (Plus 30° phase displacement). For group numbers 3 and 4, h.v. and l.v. windings must be connected differently to get a suitable phase displacement. Plus 30° phase displacement means that the l.v. line phasor leads the corresponding h.v. line phasor by 30° as shown in Fig. 8.6 (a). For $Dy11$ arrangement, the phasor diagram is drawn in Fig. 8.14 (a). When C_2 coincides c_2, l.v. phasor c_2b_2 is seen to lead h.v. phasor C_2B_2 by 30° and this proves it to be $Dy11$ arrangement. The connection scheme for $Dy11$ is drawn in Fig. 8.14 (b).

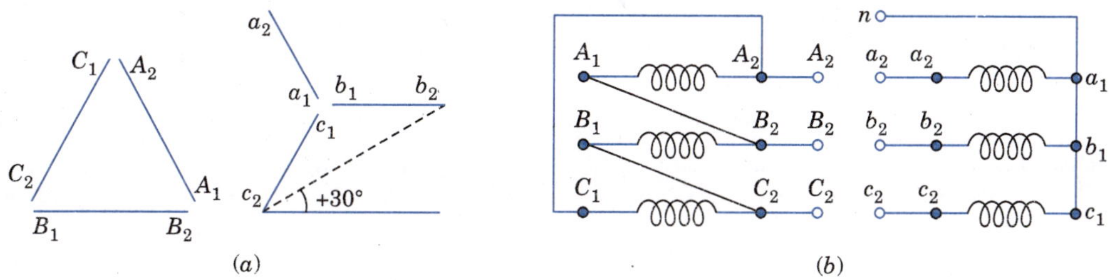

Fig. 8.14: $Dy11$ arrangement, Group No. 4.

The phasor diagram for the l.v. side of $Yd11$ is already shown in Fig. 8.12 (b), for which the connection diagram can be drawn accordingly.

It is suggested that the reader should have sufficient practice for drawing the phasor diagrams for group numbers 3 and 4.

8.2.2 Effect of Polarity Markings and Phase Sequence

In making three-phase transformer connections, proper attention must be given to the polarity markings. If the primary or the secondary connections are done with wrong-polarity markings, the transformer operation will be unsatisfactory and in some cases it may even burn. The importance of polarity markings can be appreciated by considering a transformer connected with wrong-polarity markings.

Let a transformer with $Yy0$ connection be considered for this purpose. The connection diagram and the phasor diagram with proper polarity markings, though already illustrated in

Fig. 8.7 are repeated in Fig. 8.15 for convenience. Line voltages are indicated by dotted lines joining A_2B_2, B_2C_2 etc. in Fig. 8.15 (*b*).

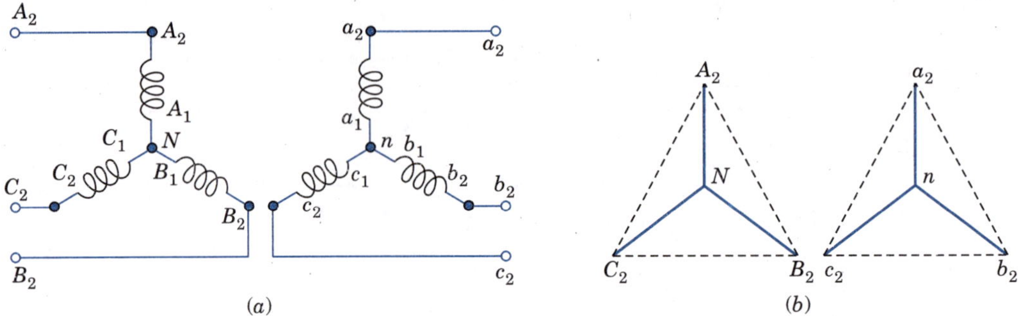

Fig. 8.15: *Yy*0 arrangement with correct polarity markings.

Now suppose the l.v. (secondary) winding connection a_1 and a_2 are reversed without altering h.v. winding connections A_1 and A_2 as shown in Fig. 8.16 (*a*). With this change, l.v. phasor diagram of Fig. 8.15 (*b*) gets modified to that shown in Fig. 8.16 (*b*). Note that phasor a_2a_1 is reversed from the position it occupied in Fig. 8.15 (*b*). The secondary line voltages are indicated by dotted lines in the phasor diagram of Fig. 8.16 (*b*). In order to show the line voltages clearly, the phasor diagram of Fig. 8.16 (*c*) is drawn. The three line voltages $V_{a_1b_2}$, $V_{b_2c_2}$ and $V_{c_2a_1}$ on the l.v. side are seen to be unbalanced. The line voltages $V_{a_1b_2}$ and $V_{c_2a_1}$ have their maginitudes equal to the phase voltage and these are time displaced from each other by 60°. The line voltage $V_{b_2c_2}$ is $\sqrt{3}$ times the phase voltage, but is time displayed by 150° from other two line voltages $V_{a_1b_2}$ and $V_{c_2a_1}$. The same effect, as explained above, can be obtained if phase *A* terminals A_1, A_2 instead of its secondary terminals a_1, a_2, are reversed.

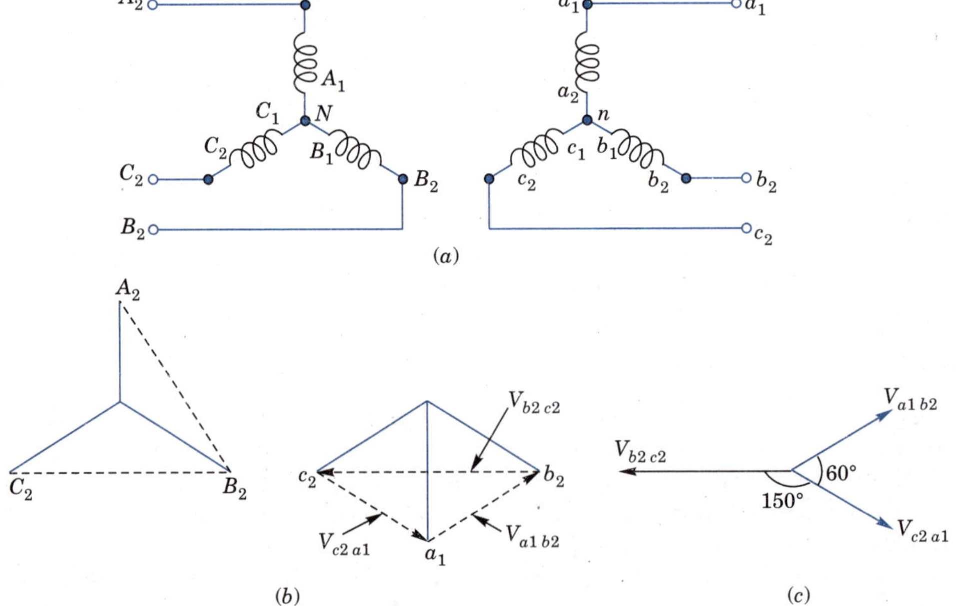

Fig. 8.16: Pertaining to the effect of connecting three, secondary windings inaccurately.

For investigating the effect of change in the phase sequence, consider again *Yy*0 arrangement, for simplicity. The connection arrangement and phasor diagram, with proper phase sequence, are illustrated in Fig. 8.17. After a cyclical interchange of the primary (*i.e.* h.v.) leads from A_2, B_2, C_2 to C_2, A_2, B_2; the connection diagram is as shown in Fig. 8.17 (*a*). Since the primary voltages are those obtained from the supply, their phase orientation cannot change. Now C_2 is connected to A_2, therefore l.v. phasor nc_2 occupies the position of na_2 of Fig. 8.15 (*b*) and so on. In view of this, the l.v. line voltages are displaced by a time-phase angle of 120° clockwise, from the position they occupied before this change as shown in Fig. 8.15 (*b*). This can be ascertained from the phasor orientation of l.v. phasor a_2b_2 of Fig. 8.15 (*b*) and l.v. phasor a_2b_2 of Fig. 8.17 (*b*).

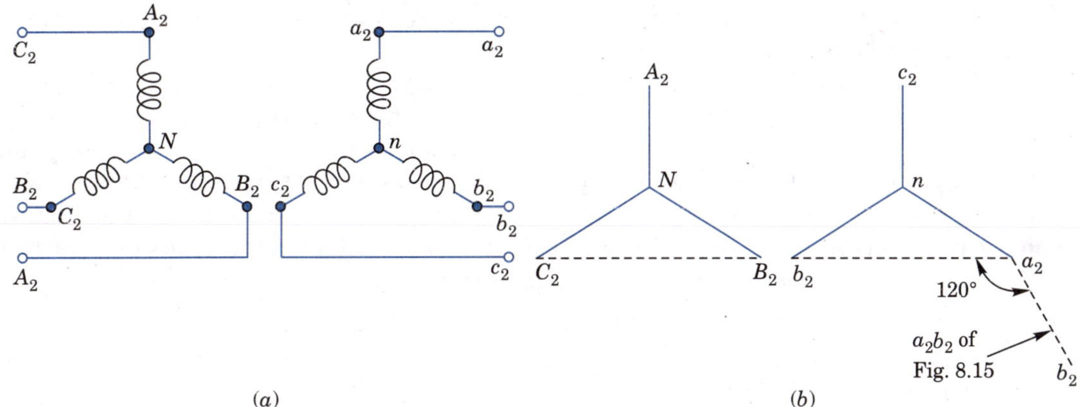

Fig. 8.17: Illustrating the effect of change in phase sequence.

If the h.v. (or primary) leads are changed cyclically from $A_2B_2C_2$ to $B_2C_2A_2$, the connection arrangement and phasor diagram are as shown in Fig. 8.18. From the change also, it is seen that the l.v. line voltages are time-displaced by 120° anti-clockwise from the position they occupied before this change. Hence, it may be concluded from above that if the primary leads are interchanged cyclically once, the secondary line phasors are rotated through a time-phase angle of 120°.

In case the primary leads are interchanged cyclically twice, for example from $A_2B_2C_2$ to $C_2A_2B_2$ and then from $C_2A_2B_2$ to $B_2C_2A_2$ in Fig. 8.17 the secondary line phasors are rotated through a time phase angle of 240°. This is left as an exercise to the reader.

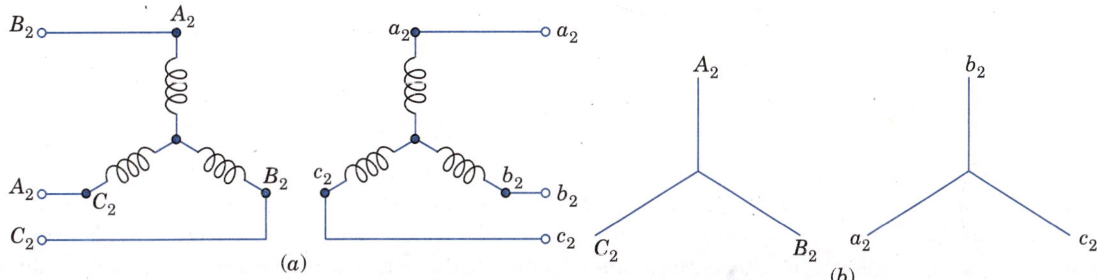

Fig. 8.18: Illustrating the effect of change in phase sequence.

8.3 PARALLEL OPERATION OF THREE-PHASE TRANSFORMERS

The need for parallel operation of three-phase transformers arises more frequently, since the generation, transmission and distribution of power is almost always three phase. The advantages of using two or more transformers in parallel, over the use of one large unit, are described in Art 1.13.* Basic relations pertaining to the behaviour of parallel operation of single-phase transformers are also given there. In view of this, a review of this article is of considerable importance.

The various conditions that must be fulfilled, for the successful parallel operation of 3-phase transformers, are as follows:

(*a*) The line voltage ratios of the transformers must be the same.

(*b*) The transformers should have equal per unit leakage impedances.

(*c*) The ratio of equivalent leakage reactance to equivalent resistance should be same for all the transformers.

(*d*) The transformers should have the same polarity.

The above four conditions are also applicable for the successful parallel operation of single-phase transformers. In addition to these four conditions, two more *essential* conditions that must be fulfilled for the parallel operation of three-phase transformers are as follows:

(*e*) **Relative-phase displacement.** The relative-phase displacement between the secondary line voltage of all the transformers must be zero; *i.e.*, the transformers to be connected in parallel, must belong to the same group number. For example *Yy*0 and *Dd*0 belong to group number 1, these can, therefore, be operated in parallel.

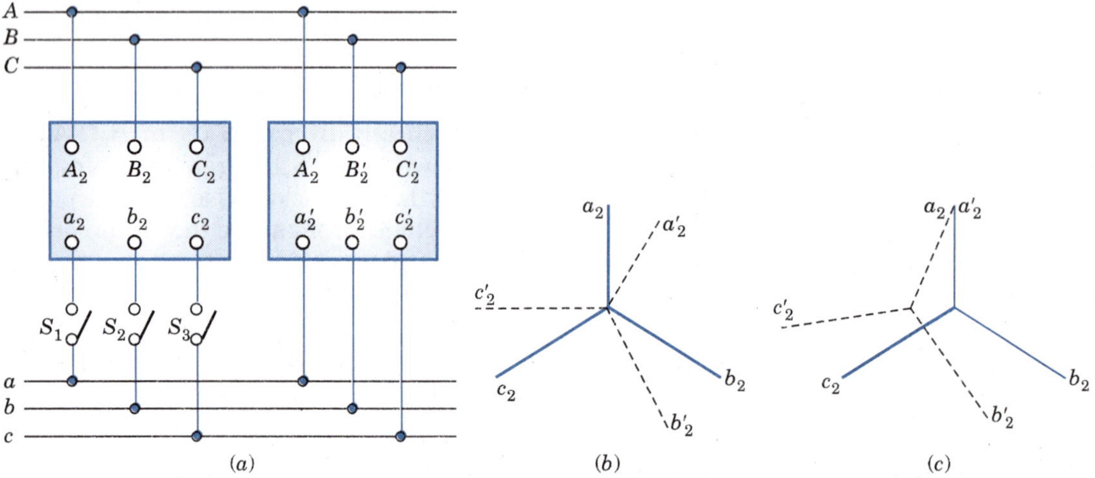

Fig. 8.19: Parallel operation of three-phase transformers with different group numbers.

What would happen if transformers of different group numbers are connected in parallel? In order to examine this, consider two, 3-phase transformers of different group numbers connected to the same source of supply as shown in Fig. 8.19 (*a*). The secondary line voltages of these two tranformers are not in phase as shown in Fig. 8.19 (*b*). In this fig., the phasors joining a_2, a_2' ; b_2, b_2' and c_2, c_2' represent the voltages across switches S_1, S_2 and S_3 respectively. Any one of the three switches can be closed without any danger. For example, if

*"Electrical Machinery" by the same author.

S_1 is closed, there will be no circulating current because the secondary circuit is not complete. The effect of closing the switch S_1 is to bring a_2 and a_2' together so that these overlap each other as shown in Fig. 8.19 (*c*). Now the voltage across switches S_2 and S_3 will be equal to the phasors joining b_2b_2' and c_2c_2' respectively in Fig. 8.19 (*c*). After closing S_1, if S_2 is also closed, voltage b_2b_2' would send a large circulating current in phases *A* and *B* which may be damaged. Hence, for successful parallel operation, the voltage across switches S_1, S_2 and S_3 (or across S_2 and S_3 if S_1 is closed), should be zero. In other words, it is essential that the transformers belong to the same group number so that the relative-phase displacement between the secondary line voltages is zero. However, transformers of group numbers 3 and 4 can be successfully operated in parallel as explained in Example 8.1.

(*f*) **Phase-sequence.** If the secondary line voltages are of the same phase sequence as shown in Fig. 8.20 (*a*), then the voltage across switches S_1, S_2 and S_3 of Fig. 8.19 (*a*) would be zero and the parallel operation is possible. However, an improper phase sequence as shown in Fig. 8.20 (*b*), would give zero voltage across switch S_1 and line voltages across switch S_2 and S_3. Conseqently the parallel operation is not possible. Hence, it is essential that the secondary line voltages are of proper phase sequence.

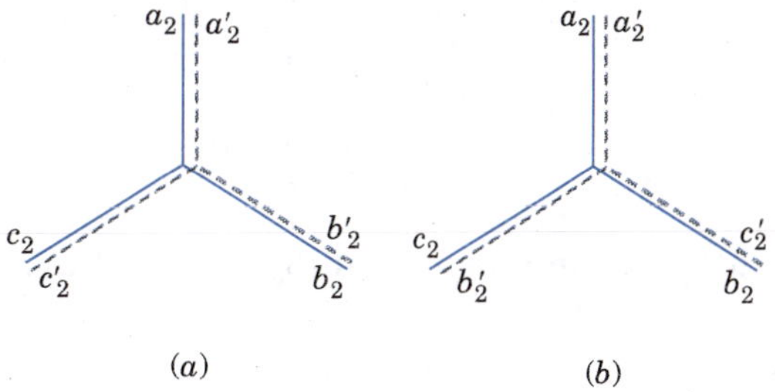

Fig. 8.20: Pertaining to the phase sequence of three-phase transformers.

The computations, pertaining to the parallel operation of three-phase transformers under balanced conditions, can be carried out by reducing a 3-phase problem to an equivalent single-phase problem. For this purpose, equivalent circuits and various relations, derived for the parallel operation of single-phase transformers, can be used.

Example 8.1. *Explain clearly how a three-phase transformer Yd11 of group number 4, can be successfully operated in parallel with another transformer Dy1 of group number 3.*

Solution. The phasor diagrams for *Yd*11 and *Dy*1 are illustrated in Fig. 8.21, from which it is seen that the secondary line voltages, say c_2a_2 for *Yd*11 and *Dy*1, are having a phase displacement of 60°. Fig. 8.21 (*b*) also reveals that secondary line voltage c_2a_2 of *Dy*1 lags 60° behind the secondary line voltage c_2a_2 of *Yd*11. Same is true for all other line voltages. It is, however, possible to bring the secondary line voltages in phase with each other as described below:

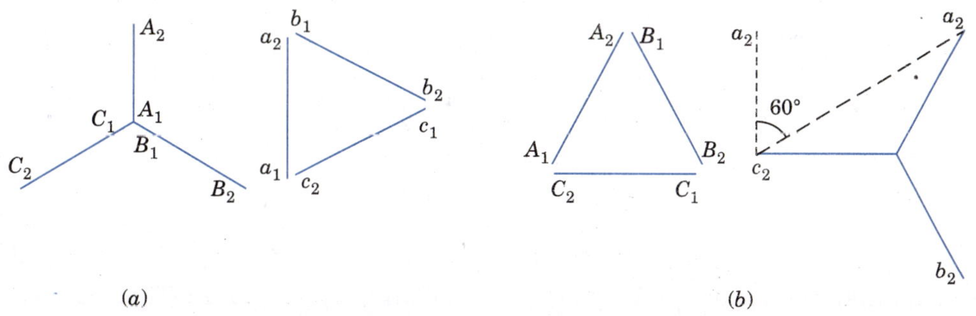

Fig. 8.21: Phasor diagrams for (*a*) *Yd* 11 and (*b*) *Dy*1.

The supply terminals $Dy1$ are cyclically interchanged from Fig. 8.22 (a) to (b), *i.e.*, from $A_2\ B_2\ C_2$ to $C_2\ A_2\ B_2$. This change has the effect of rotating the secondary voltages of $Dy1$ through 120° clockwise as indicated in Fig. 8.23 (a), (refer to Figs. 8.17 and 8.18). Now reverse the three-phase-winding terminals of either the primary or the secondary of $Dy1$. Fig. 8.22 (c) shows the reversal of the primary terminals of $Dy1$, where A_1B_2 etc. are connected together instead of A_2B_1 etc of Fig. 8.22 (a). This reversals has the effect of reversing the secondary line voltages, thereby bringing the secondary line phasors of $Dy1$ and $Yd11$ into coincidence as shown in Fig. 8.21 (a) and 8.23 (b).

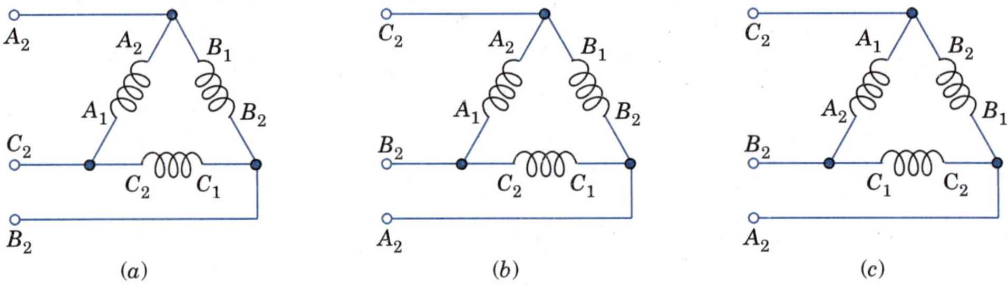

Fig. 8.22: Pertaining to the parallel operation of $Yd11$ and $Dy1$.

Thus the three-phase transformers $Yd11$ and $Dy1$ can be successfully operated in parallel by adopting the procedure outlined above.

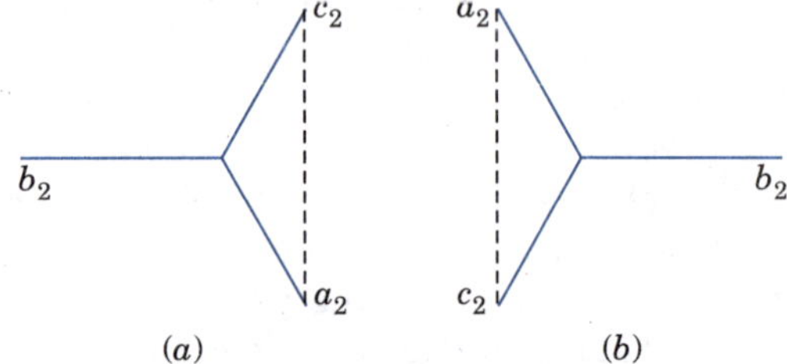

Fig. 8.23: Pertaining to the parallel operation of $Yd11$ and $Dy1$.

Example 8.2. *Two delta-star 11000/400 V transformers are to be operated in parallel. Their primaries in delta are energised from the same supply mains of 11 kV. The secondary terminals are marked $a_2 b_2 c_2$ for one transformer and $a_2' b_2' c_2'$ for the second transformer.*

(a) If terminals a_2 and a_2' are connected together, then the voltmeters connected across b_2b_2', c_2c_2', c_2b_2' and b_2c_2' give the following readings:

$$V_{b_2b'_2} = V_{c_2c'_2} = 800 \text{ V and } V_{c_2b'_2} = V_{b_2c'_2} = 693 \text{ V}.$$

Their secondary neutrals are not connected. Explain by means of phasor diagrams, how this happens.

(b) Now a_2 and a_2' are disconnected but their neutrals are joined together. Calculate the voltages $V_{a_2a'_2}$, $V_{b_2b'_2}$ and $V_{c_2c'_2}$.

(c) Explain how these transformers can be operated in parallel.

Solution. (a) If the phasor diagrams of voltages $a_2\ b_2\ c_2$ and $a_2'\ b_2'\ c_2'$ are as shown in Fig. 8.24 (a), then voltage $V_{a_2 a'_2}$, $V_{b_2 b'_2}$, $V_{c_2 c'_2}$ would all be equal to zero. This, however, is not the case in the present example. When a_2a_2' are connected together, $V_{a_2a'_2}$ is forced to become zero. Note that the neutrals are not connected. It is given that voltage $V_{b_2b'_2} = V_{c_2c'_2} = 800$ V $(= 2 \times 400 = 2 \times \sqrt{3} \times 231)$ and voltage $V_{c_2b'_2} = V_{b_2c'_2} = 693$ V $(= \sqrt{3} \times 400 = \sqrt{3} \times \sqrt{3} \times 231)$, where 231 V is the per phase voltage. This can happen only if the two secondary stars are opposite to each other so that the phasors are oriented as depicted in Fig. 8.24 (*b*). In this figure, star a_2', b_2', c_2' is shown inverted with respect to star $a_2\, b_2\, c_2$. Note that line voltage a_2b_2, $a_2'b_2'$ and a_2c_2, $a_2'c_2'$ are along the same line. The line voltages $V_{a_2c_2}$ and $V_{a'_2b'_2}$ are 120° away from each other.

(*b*) When their neutrals are joined together, the two neutrals n and n' must overlap as illustrated in Fig. 8.24 (*c*). It is obvious from this figure that

$$V_{a_2a'_2} = V_{b_2b'_2} = V_{c_2c'_2} = 231 + 231 = 462 \text{ V}.$$

(*c*) For parallel operation, reverse the star of any one transformer. If the star $a_2'\, b_2'\, c_2'$ is reversed, that phasor diagram of Fig. 8.24 (*c*) gets changed to Fig. 8.24 (*d*), from which it is seen that $V_{a_2a'_2} = V_{b_2b'_2} = V_{c_2c'_2} = 0$. Hence, the two transformers can now be operated in parallel.

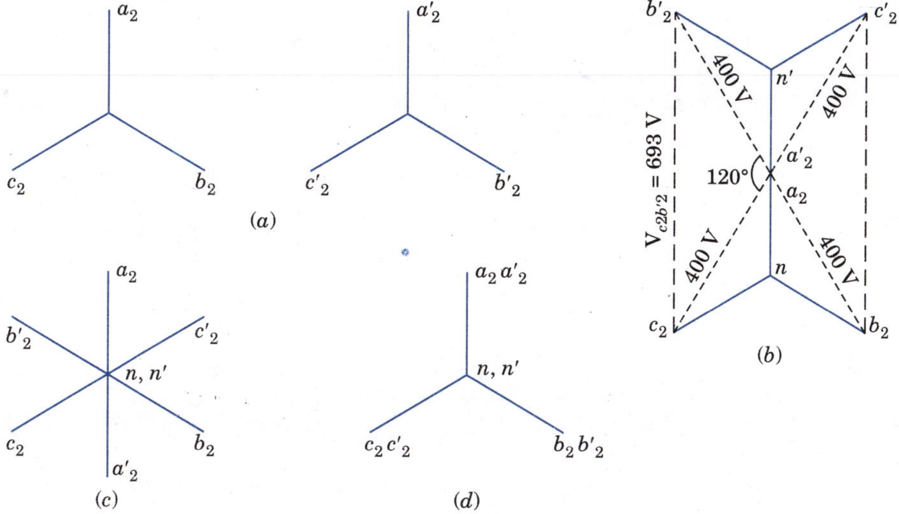

Fig. 8.24: Pertaining to Example 8.2.

Example 8.3. *Two 3-phase transformers, rated at 500 kVA and 450 kVA respectively, are connected in parallel to supply a load of 1000 kVA at 0.8 p.f. lagging. The per phase resistance and per phase leakage reactance of the first transformer are 2.5% and 6% respectively and of the second transformer 1.6% and 7% respectively. Calculate the kVA load and power factor at which each transformer operates.*

Solution. Here subscripts 1 and 2 are used for 500 kVA and 450 kVA transformers respectively. Now $\bar{z}_{e_1} = (2.5 + j6)$ per cent and $\bar{z}_{e2} = (1.6 + j7)$ per cent. When using percentage or per unit values, z_{e_1} and z_{e_2} must be referred to the common base kVA. Here choosing 500 kVA base arbitrarily, we get,

$$\bar{z}_{e_1} = \frac{500}{500}(2.5 + j6) = (2.5 + j6) \text{ per cent} = 6.5 \angle 67.38 \text{ percent}$$

$$\bar{z}_{e2} = \frac{500}{450}(1.6 + j7) = (1.78 + j7.78) \text{ per cent} = 7.98 \angle 77.11° \text{ percent}$$

$$\bar{z}_{e1} + \bar{z}_{e2} = 4.28 + j13.78 = 14.43 \angle 72.75° \text{ percent}$$

Load kVA, $\bar{S} = 1000 \angle -\cos^{-1} 0.8 = 1000 \angle -36.9°$

As in single-phase transformers, the load shared by transformer 1 is given by

$$\bar{S}_1 = \bar{S}\frac{\bar{z}_{e2}}{\bar{z}_{e1} + \bar{z}_{e2}} = 1000 \angle -36.9° \frac{7.98 \angle 77.11°}{14.43 \angle 72.75°} = 553.01 \angle -32.54° \text{ kVA}$$

$\therefore$ $S_1 = 553.01$ kVA, at pf cos 32.54° or at pf 0.843 lagging.

Load shared by transformer 2 is given by

$$\bar{S}_2 = \bar{S}\frac{\bar{z}_{e2}}{\bar{z}_{e1} + \bar{z}_{e2}} = 1000 \angle -36.9° \frac{6.5 \angle 67.38°}{14.43 \angle 72.75°} = 450.45 \angle -42.27°$$

$\therefore$ $S_2 = 450.45$ kVA, at pf cos 42.27° or at pf 0.74 lagging.

Check : Total load = 553.01 × 0.843 + 450.45 × 0.74 = 799.52 kW ≅ 800 kW

Example 8.4. *Two 3-phase transformers have the following per phase parameters, referred to secondary :*

$$r_{e1} = 0.004\ \Omega,\ x_{e1} = 0.018\ \Omega$$

$$r_{e2} = 0.002\ \Omega,\ x_{e2} = 0.012\ \Omega$$

Subscripts 1 and 2 refer to 500 kVA and 1000 kVA transformers. These two transformers are connected for parallel operation. How will they share a load of 1500 kVA at 0.8 pf lagging ?

Solution. Per-phase leakage impedance of transformer 1,

$$\bar{z}_{e1} = 0.004 + j0.018 = 0.01844 \angle 77.47°$$

Per-phase leakage impedance of transformer 2,

$$\bar{z}_{e2} = 0.002 + j0.012 = 0.01216 \angle 80.54°$$

$$\therefore \quad \bar{z}_{e1} + \bar{z}_{e2} = 0.006 + j0.03 = 0.03059 \angle 78.69°$$

Since z_{e1} and $z_{e1}$are given in ohms, their values should not be referred to the common base kVA. For the two transformers operating in parallel, the load shared by transformer 1 is given by

$$\bar{S}_1 = \bar{S}\frac{\bar{z}_{e2}}{\bar{z}_{e1} + \bar{z}_{e2}} = 1500 \angle -36.9° \frac{0.01216 \angle 80.54°}{0.03059 \angle 78.69°}$$

$$= 596.27 \angle -35.05°$$

$\therefore$ $S_1 = (596.27) \cos 35.05°$ kW, at pf of cos 35.05 lagging

$= 488.11$ kW, at 0.8186 lagging pf.

Load shared by second transformer is given by

$$\bar{S}_2 = 1500 \angle -36.9° \frac{0.01844 \angle 77.47°}{0.03059 \angle 78.69°} = 905.4 \angle -38.12°$$

$\therefore$ $S_2 = (905.4) \cos 38.12°$, at lagging pf of cos 38.12°

$= 712.55$ kW, at 0.787 pf lagging.

Check: Total load = 488.11 + 712.55 = 1200.66 kW.

Example 8.5. *Two 6600/440 V transformers have ratings of 250 kVA and 600 kVA respectively. On short-circuit test, the 250 kVA transformer requires 5% of normal voltage to circulate full-load current, the power factor being 0.23. The corresponding figures for the 600 kVA transformer are 4% and 0.16. How will they share a load of 680 kW at 0.8 pf lagging?*

Solution. Base current I_B = rated current = 1.0. Under short-circuit test, $I_{sc} \cdot z_{e1} = V_{sc}$

Here I_{sc} = rated current = 1.0 p.u.

$\therefore$ $1 \,.\, z_{e1} = 0.05$ or $z_{e1} = 0.05$ p.u.

As short-circuit power factor is $0.23 = \cos \theta_{sc}$, z_{e1} in complex notation is given by

$$\bar{z}_{e1} = 0.05\,(\cos \theta_{sc} + j \sin \theta_{sc}) = 0.05\,(0.23 + j0.9732) = 0.0115 + j0.0487$$

Similarly, $\bar{z}_{e2} = 0.04\,(0.16 + j0.987) = 0.0064 + j0.0395$

Choosing a base of 600 kVA arbitrarily, we get

$$\bar{z}_{e1} = \frac{600}{250}(0.0115 + j0.0487) = 0.0276 + j0.1169 = 0.1201\,\angle 76.72°$$

$$\bar{z}_{e2} = \frac{600}{600}(0.0064 + j0.0395) = 0.0064 + j0.0395 = 0.04\,\angle 80.797°$$

Total leakage impedance,

$$z_e = z_{e1} + z_{e2} = 0.034 + j0.1564 = 0.16\,\angle 77.74°$$

Total load, $\bar{S} = \dfrac{680}{0.8}\angle -36.9° = 850\,\angle -39.9°$ kVA

Load shared by transformer 1 of 250 kVA,

$$S_1 = 850\,\angle -36.9 \times \frac{0.04\,\angle 80.797°}{0.16\,\angle 77.74°} = 212.5\,\angle -33.843°$$

Load shared by transformer 2 of 600 kVA

$$S_2 = 850\,\angle -36.9° \times \frac{0.1201\,\angle 76.72°}{0.16\,\angle 77.74°} = 638.03\,\angle -37.92°$$

Transformer 1 shares 212.5 kVA at pf = cos 33.843° = 0.8306 lag or 176.503 kW at pf 0.8306 lag. Transformer 2 shares 638.03 kVA at pf = cos 37.92° = 0.789 lag or 503.406 kW at pf 0.789 lag.

Check : $176.503 + 503.406 \cong 680$ kW.

8.4 EXCITATION PHENOMENA IN TRANSFORMERS

While studying the behaviour of three-phase transformers, some of the questions, outlined below, cannot be answered unless excitation phenomena in transformers is investigated.

(*i*) In three-phase power and distribution transformers, why one of the two windings is always connected in delta?

(*ii*) Why is the tertiary winding in three-phase three-winding transformers always connected in delta ?

(*iii*) Why is the voltage across the open-circuited delta not zero in a star-delta transformer?

(*iv*) What is the purpose of using earthing transformers in 3-phase circuits.

The answers to such questions are possible if one has understood the excitation phenomena in transformers. In addition, a knowledge of this phenomena leads to a better understanding of the internal behaviour of transformers having independent and interlinked magnetic circuits.

In an ideal transformer, it is assumed that the magnetic saturation does not occur. When the phasor diagram and the equivalent circuit of a trransformer are developed, the magnetic linearity is assumed even then. The reason for doing so is that the effect of magnetic non-linearity cannot be represented in the equivalent circuit and phasor diagram of a transformer.

For linear magnetization curve, the flux is proportional to magnetizing current and their waveforms are identical. In practice, the magnetic saturation does occur and the waveforms of the flux and magnetizing current are different from each other. The object of this article is to study the excitation phenomena both in single-phase and three-phase transformers.

The current required to establish the flux in a magnetic circuit is called the *exciting current.* The study of the excitation phenomena in transformers means the study of the nature of exciting current, voltage and flux when the transformer primary is energised with secondary winding open.

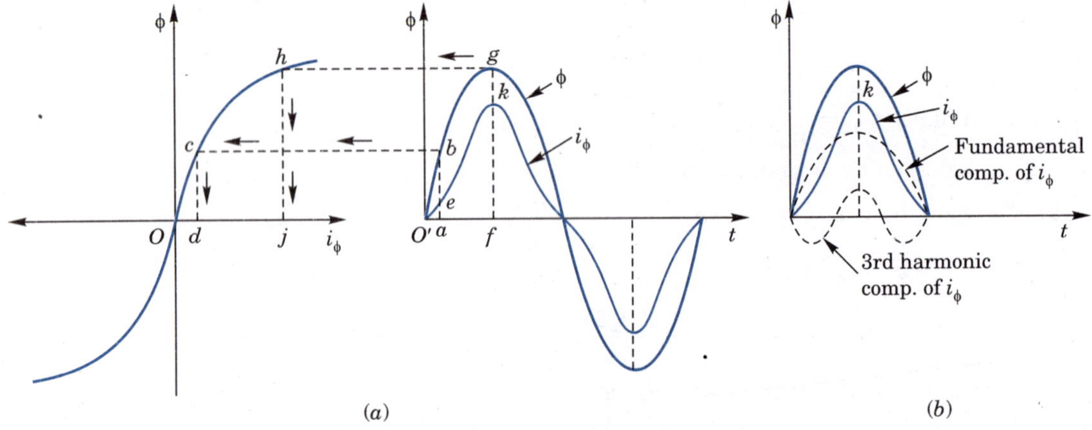

Fig. 8.25: (*a*) Waveform of magnetizing current i_ϕ when hysteresis is ignored and (*b*) fundamental and third harmonic components of i_ϕ.

First of all, consider, for simplicity, the magnetization curve for the core having no hysteresis, Fig. 8.25 (*a*). Here the magnetization curve is represented by flux ϕ (= B × Area) and magnetizing current i_ϕ (= Hl/N), instead of the usual flux density B and the megnetic field intensity H. This is done in order to read the value of i_ϕ directly, for a given value of flux ϕ. The applied voltage V_1 is assumed sinusoidal. The primary leakage impedance drop at no load is small, it may, therefore, be ignored. Consequently, the flux set up in the iron core can be obtained from the relation $V_1 = \sqrt{2}\ \pi f N_1 \phi_m$ and since V_1 is a sine wave, the flux ϕ must also be a sine wave. Now for a sinusoidal flux, the exciting-current waveform is to be obtained. For any flux equal to *ab*, draw *bc* parallel to *oo*′ and *cd* perpendicular to *oo*′, Fig. 8.25 (*a*). Then *od* = *ae* is the magnetizing current for setting up the flux *ab*. For peak flux equal to *fg*, proceed along the arrows *gh* and *hj*. The current *oj* = *fk* sets up the peak flux *fg*. The points *e* and *k* lie on the required waveform of the magnetizing current. This procedure is repeated till a sufficient number of points of the current waveform are obtained. A curve passing through these points gives the required current waveform as shown in Fig. 8.25 (*a*). The distinctive features of this current waveform are that

(*i*) it is peaked in nature and is symmetrial about its maximum value and

(*ii*) the flux and the current have their maximum values at the same time.

The Fourier analysis of this waveform shows that the magnetising current consists of a fundamental sine component and a series of odd harmonics ; the predominant of these being the third harmonic as shown in Fig. 8.25 (*b*). This fundamental component of i_ϕ is seen to be in phase with ϕ and since ϕ lags V_1 by 90°, the fundamental component of i_ϕ also lags V_1 by 90°. Consequently, the power obtained from source is zero, because of the 90° time-phase angle between V_1 and fundamental component of i_ϕ. The power associated with fundamental-frequency voltage V_1 and odd harmonics of i_ϕ is always zero. This shows that the magnetic saturation (without hysteresis) does not result in any power loss, it merely distorts the current waveform.

Consider now the hysteresis loop for the transformer core material as shown in Fig. 8.26 (*a*). As before, *B-H* loop is plotted in terms of core flux ϕ and no-load current i_0. A graphical procedure for determining the waveshape of current i_0 for sinusoidal flux is as shown in Fig. 8.26.

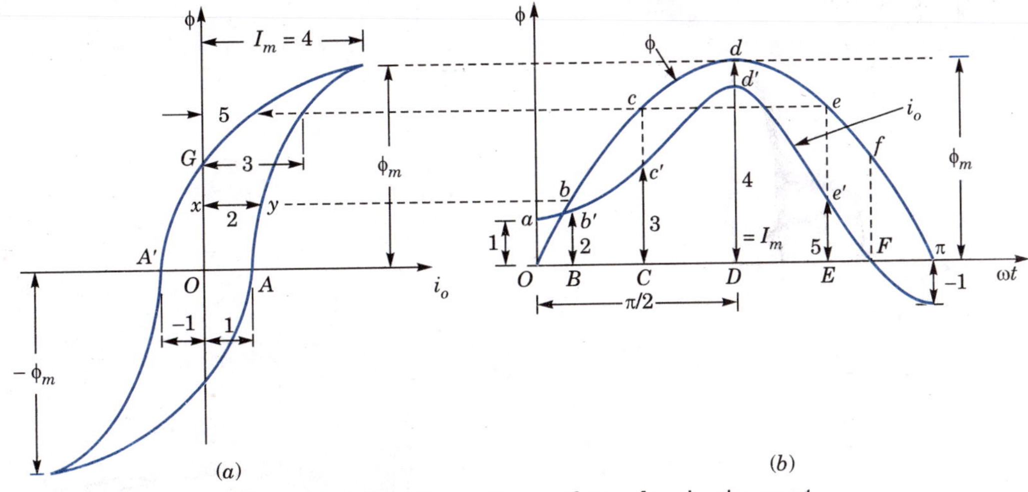

Fig. 8.26: (*a*) *B-H* loop (*b*) waveform of no-load current.

At instant $\omega t = 0$ of the flux-time curve in Fig. 8.26 (*b*), flux is zero. The corresponding current for zero flux seen from hysteresis loop of Fig. 8.26 (*a*) is $OA = 1$. This current OA is plotted in Fig. 8.26 (*b*) as $Oa = 1$ at instant $\omega t = 0$. At the instant $\omega t = OB$ in Fig. 8.26 (*b*), core flux is $Bb = Ox$ and the corresponding current in Fig. 8.26 (*a*) is $xy = 2$. It is plotted as $Bb' = xy = 2$ in Fig. 8.26 (*b*) at instant OB. Similarly, at instant $\omega t = OC$, flux is Cc, i_0 is $Cc' = 3$ in Fig. 8.26 (*b*). At instant $\omega t = OD = \pi/2$ in Fig. 8.26 (*b*), flux is maximum ϕ_m and no-load current is also maximum I_m. This is plotted as $Dd' = 4 = I_m$ in Fig. 8.26 (*b*).

Afer instant $\omega t = OD = \pi/2$, the flux begins to decrease from ϕ_m. At instant $\omega t = OE$, flux is Ee, current from Fig. 8.26 (*a*) is denoted by 5 and is plotted in Fig. 8.26 (*b*) as $Ee' = 5$. When flux is Ff in Fig. 8.26 (*b*) and OG in Fig. 8.26 (*a*), current is zero, this is indicated by point F in Fig. 8.26 (*b*). Now when the flux decreases to zero at $\omega t = \pi$ in Fig. 8.26 (*b*), the current is negative and equal to $OA' = -1$. This negative current equal to 1 is also shown below the reference line in Fig. 8.26 (*b*). In this manner, other points for the no-load current i_0 can be obtained and a curve passing through them, gives the required waveform of the no-load current i_0.

The procedure outlined above can be followed to plot the current-time curve for the entire full cycle. In Fig. 8.26 (*b*), only positive half cycle of no-load current wave is plotted just for convinience.

It is seen from Fig. 8.26 (*b*) that

(*i*) the flux waveform is symmetrical about its peak and is sinusoidal.

(*ii*) the no-load current waveform is unsymmetrical about its peak and is non-sinusoidal.

(*iii*) the flux and current waveforms have their maximum values at the same instant.

The analysis of the no-load current waveform shows that it consists of fundamental component and third, fifth and higher order odd harmonics. The amplitude of harmonic currents decreases as the order of harmonics increases. Out of various harmonic components, third harmonic is the most dominant. Sometimes, the third harmonic may be as high as 40% of the fundamental component.

The total primary current is the phasor sum of load component of current and the no-load current. Since no-load current is quite small (2 to 6% of rated current), the total primary current is almost sinusoidal under loaded conditions.

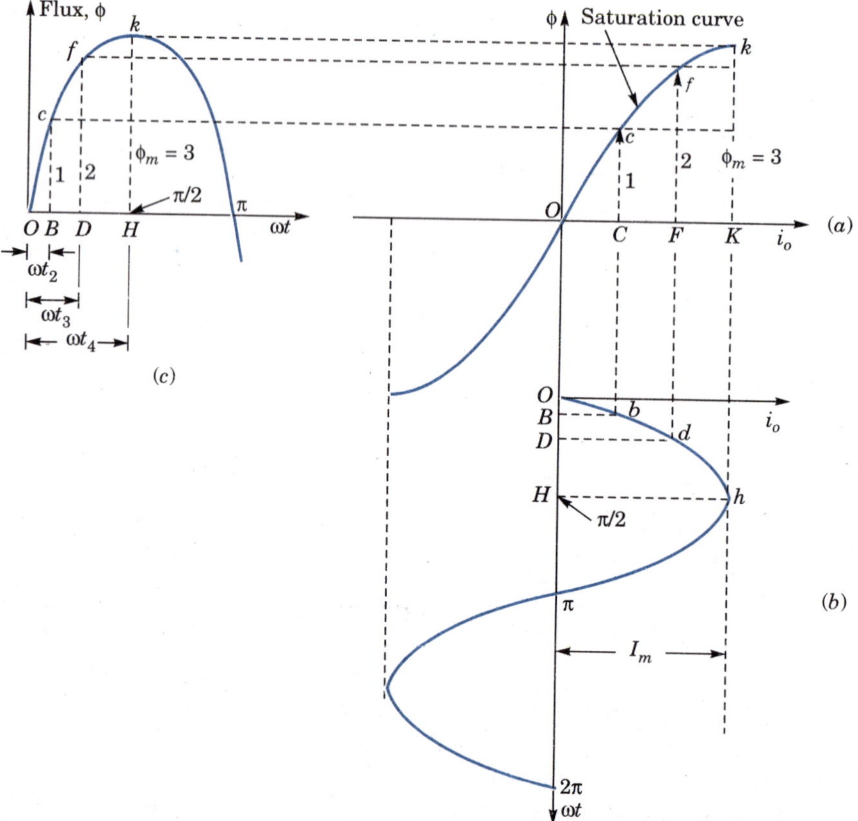

Fig. 8.27: (*a*) Magnetization curve (*b*) sinusoidal no-load current and (*c*) waveform of magnetic flux.

Sinusoidal no-load current: If the no-load, or exciting, current is constrained to vary sinusoidally (*e.g.*, by putting a large series resistance in the primary circuit), then the flux variation with respect to time can be obtained as explained below.

Consider again the magnetization curve without hysteresis as shown in Fig. 8.27 (*a*). In Fig. 8.27 (*b*) is shown the sinusoidal variation of no-load current i_0.

At instant $\omega t_1 = 0$ in Fig. 8.27 (*b*), current i_0 is zero. For zero i_0, flux is also zero in Fig. 8.27 (*a*). This flux is plotted as zero in Fig. 8.27 (*c*) at $\omega t_1 = 0$. At instant $\omega t_2 = OB$, current is Bb in Fig. 8.27 (*b*). From b, draw vertical line meeting saturation curve at c showing that flux is $Cc = 1$ in Fig. 8.27 (*a*). This flux is plotted as $Bc = 1$ at $\omega t_2 = OB$ in Fig. 8.27 (*c*).

At instant $\omega t_3 = OD$, current $i_0 = Dd$. From d, draw vertical line meeting magnetization curve at f showing that flux for $i_0 = OF = Dd$ is Ff. Plot this flux as $Df = Ff = 2$ at $\omega t_3 = OD$ in Fig. 8.27 (c). At $\omega t_4 = \pi/2 = OH$, current is $Hh = I_m$ in Fig. 8.27 (*b*). From h, draw vertical line meeting saturation curve at k so that flux is $Kk = \phi_m = 3$ for $i_0 = OK$. This is plotted in Fig. 8.27 (*c*) as $Hk = Kk = 3 = \phi_m$ at $\omega t = \pi/2 = OH$. In this manner, other points on flux waveform can be obtained. When all these points are joined together, waveform of flux with respect to ωt for sinusoidal no-load current is obtained.

It is observed from Fig. 8.27 (*c*) that a sinusoidal no-load current i_0 produces a **flat-topped flux wave**.

8.4.1 Harmonics in Single-phase Transformers

Excitation phenomena considered above is applicable to any magnetic circuit that is excited with alternating voltage. As excitation phenomena in single-phase transformers is more important, in this part of the article, this phenomena is described in greater detail.

For a sinusoidal supply voltage, the flux is also sinusoidal but the magnetizing current must contain a strong third harmonic current. The triplen (multiples of three) frequency currents in a transformer winding can exist only if there appears a triplen frequency emf. But a triplen frequency emf can be induced only by a triplen frequency flux. Therefore, the actual waveform of the flux is the combination of sine flux wave and the third harmonic flux wave. The departure of the resultant flux wave from a sine wave depends upon the value of flux density in the core. If the transformer is worked at a higher flux density, there will be more pronounced third harmonic current (see Fig. 8.25) and therefore, a large third harmonic emf E_3 is required to circulate it. A large value of E_3 can be induced only by a correspondingly large value of third harmonic flux ϕ_3. As a consequence, the resultant flux wave (sine flux ϕ_1 + large third harmonic flux ϕ_3) at higher flux densities departs noticeably from its ideal sine wave. At lower value of flux densities, the third harmonic current decreases; E_3 and, therefore, ϕ_3 decrease and the resultant flux approaches almost a sine wave.

It should be noted that with constant voltage applied to a single-phase transformer, the operating flux is constant and therefore the magnitude of third harmonic current is also constant. If the third harmonic impedance Z_3 of the transformer primary is small, then $I_3Z_3 = E_3$ is small and therefore ϕ_3 (which induces E_3) is also small. As a result, the resultant flux wave approaches almost a sine wave. In case Z_3 is large, E_3 $(= I_3Z_3)$ is large and therefore ϕ_3 is large. As a consequence, the resultant flux wave $(\phi_1 + \phi_3)$ departs appreciably from sine wave.

(*a*) A Fourier analysis of the flat-topped flux wave of Fig. 8.27 may be written as

$$\phi = \phi_{m1} + \sin \omega t + \phi_{m3} \sin 3\omega t + \phi_{m5} \sin \omega t + \ldots \qquad \ldots[8.1\ (a)]$$

where ϕ_{m1}, ϕ_{m3}, ϕ_{m5} ..... are respectively the maximum values of the fundamental, third, fifth ... harmonic components of flux ϕ. The emf per turn in both primary and secondary windings is given by

$$e = -\frac{d\phi}{dt} = -\omega[\phi_{m1} \cos \omega t + 3\phi_{m3} \cos 3\omega t + 5\phi_{m5} \cos 5\omega t + ...] \quad ...[8.1\ (b)]$$

The emf as given by Eq. 8.1 (*b*) is plotted in Fig. 8.28 (*a*), sinusoidal no-load current in Fig. 8.28 (*b*) and flat-topped flux wave in Fig. 8.28 (*c*). It is seen from this figure that a flat-topped flux induces emfs E_1 in primary winding and E_2 in the secondary winding which are peaky in nature. Note that in Fig. 8.28 (*a*), only fundamental and third harmonic emfs are shown and fifth harmonic emf is not plotted for the sake of clarity.

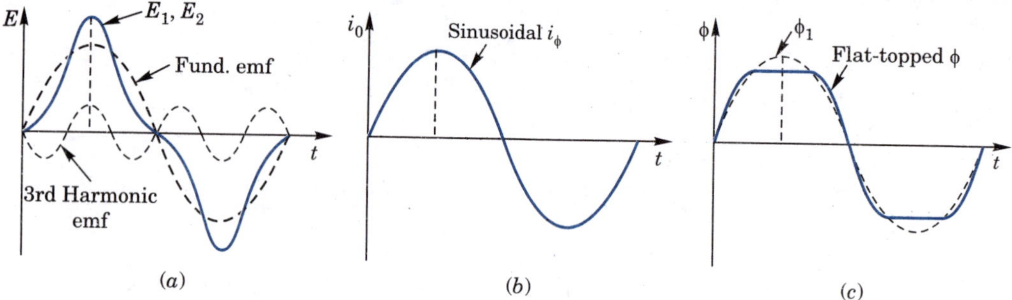

Fig. 8.28: Waveforms of emf and flux for sinusoidal magnetizing current i_ϕ.

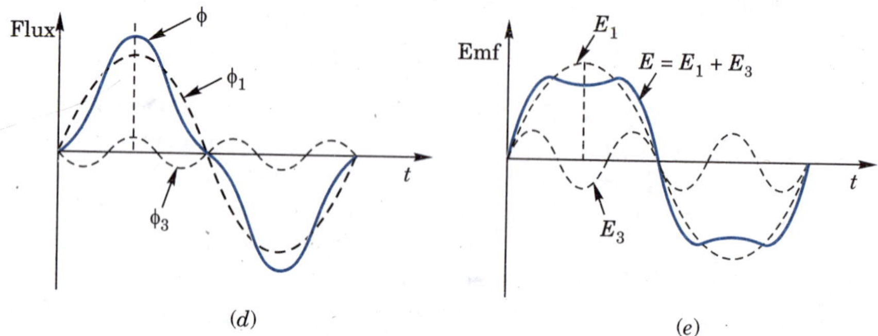

Fig. 8.28: Waveform for emf for peaky flux.

(*b*) In case flux is peaky in nature as shown in Fig. 8.28 (*d*), its Fourier analysis would give

$$\phi = \phi_{m1} \sin \omega t - \phi_{m3} \sin 3\omega t - \phi_{m5} \sin 5\omega t - ... \quad ...[8.2\ (a)]$$

The emf per turn in both primary and secondary windings is given by

$$e = -\frac{d\phi}{dt} = -\omega[\phi_{m1} \cos \omega t - 3\phi_{m3} \cos 3\omega t - 5\phi_{m5} \cos 5\omega t - ...] \quad ...[8.2\ (b)]$$

The emf as given by Eq. 8.2 (*b*) is plotted in Fig. 8.28 (*e*). A peaky flux is seen to induce a flat-topped (saddle-shaped) emf in both primary and secondary windings. As in Fig. 8.28 (*a*), only fundamental and third harmonic components are shown in Fig. 8.28 (*d*) and (*e*).

Examination of Eqs. (8.1) and (8.2) reveal that the third harmonic components of induced emfs in Eqs. 8.1 (*b*) and 8.2 (*b*) are three times as great as the third harmonic component of flux in Eqs. 8.1 (*a*) and 8.2 (*a*). Similarly, fifth harmonic component of induced emf is five times as great as the fifth harmonic component of flux. For example, if third and fifth harmonic components of fluxes are respectively 10% and 3% of the fundamental flux, then third and fifth harmonic components of induced emfs would be respectively 30% and 15% of the fundamental induced emf. This shows that even a small departure of the flux from sine wave introduces readily the third and fifth harmonic emfs in the induced emf waveforms of both primary and secondary windings.

If I_1, I_3, I_5 etc are respectively the effective values of the fundamental, third and fifth harmonic components of the no-load current I_0, then

$$I_0 = \sqrt{I_1^2 + I_3^2 + I_5^2 + \ldots}$$

For the e.m.fs, $$E = \sqrt{E_1^2 + E_3^2 + E_5^2 + \ldots\ldots}$$

The resultant of the harmonic emfs E_1, E_3, E_5 ..... is independent of the signs of harmonic emfs and the phase angles between them.

Core loss in a transformer is approximately proportional to the square of maximum flux density. Thus, the core loss in a flat-topped flux wave is less than for a sine flux wave. In practice, applied voltage is sine wave, exciting current is peaky, flux is therefore also peaky. So the effect of harmonics is to increase the core loss in a transformer.

From the above, it may be summarised that

(*a*) for a sinusoidal applied voltage, the flux is a sine wave and the magnetizing current due to saturation is peaky containing a pronounced third harmonic current, Fig. 8.25; and

(*b*) for a sinusoidal no-load current, the flux wave is flat-topped and the induced emfs both in primary and secondary windings are peaky containing a strong third harmonic emf, Fig. 8.28.

If the transformer permits the flow of harmonic magnetizing currents, the conditions described above in (*a*) hold good. If, for some reason, the harmonic magnetizing currents cannot flow in the transformer winding, the conditions described in (*b*) above hold good.

Out of the various higher order harmonics, the fifth, seventh, ... harmonics are much less pronounced as compared with the third harmonic. In view of this, the effect of higher order harmonics is always ignored, while that of the third harmonic is considered in detail.

The harmonics can be reduced or even eliminated by operating the transformers at very low flux densities. But this is not an economical proposition. The transformers are usually operated somewhere near the knee of the magnetization curve and, therefore, harmonics do exist in the exciting currents of the transformers.

Example 8.6. *The voltage applied to the primary winding of an unloaded single phase transformer is given by* $v = 400 \cos \omega t + 100 \cos 3\omega t$.

The primary has 500 turns and frequency of the fundamental component of the applied voltage is 50 Hz.

(*a*) *Find the maximum value of the flux in mWb.*

(*b*) *If the no-load current is found to be* $i_0 = 0.43 \cos (\omega t - 40°) + 0.08 \cos (3\omega t - 10°)$ *find the total core loss. Neglect primary winding resistance.*

(*c*) *If the primary voltage is free of third harmonic voltage, find the percentage change in eddy-current loss.*

Solution. (*a*) The applied voltage

$$v = -e = N\frac{d\phi}{dt}$$

$$\therefore \qquad d\phi = \frac{1}{N}(vdt) \quad \text{or} \quad \phi = \frac{1}{N}\int vdt$$

But $$v = 400 \cos \omega t + 100 \cos 3\omega t$$

$$\therefore \qquad \phi = \frac{1}{500}\int (400 \cos \omega t + 100 \cos 3\omega t)\, dt$$

$$= \frac{100}{500}\left[\frac{4}{\omega}\sin \omega t + \frac{1}{3\omega}\sin 3\omega t\right]$$

$$= \frac{1}{5\,(2\pi \times 50)}\left[4 \sin \omega t + \frac{1}{3}\sin \omega t\right] \text{Wb}$$

or $$\phi = \frac{1000}{500\pi}\left[4 \sin \omega t + \frac{1}{3}\sin \omega t\right] \text{mWb}$$

A plot of ϕ, as given by above equation, will indicate that the flux wave is flat-topped.

Maximum value of ϕ occurs at $\omega t = 90°$

$\therefore$ Maximum value of flux, $\phi_m = \frac{2}{\pi}\left[4 - \frac{1}{3}\right] = 2.334$ mWb.

(*b*) $$i_0 = 0.43 \cos (\omega t - 40°) + 0.08 \cos (3\omega t - 10°)$$

The applied voltage is, $v = 400 \cos \omega t + 100 \cos 3\omega t$.

For negligible primary winding resistance, the no-load power given to the transformer is equal to the total core loss. In the expression for power = voltage × current × cos θ, the voltage and current must be of the same frequency.

$$\therefore \qquad \text{Core loss} = \frac{1}{2}V_{m1}I_{m1}\cos \theta_1 + \frac{1}{2}V_{m3}I_{m3}\cos \theta_3$$

$$= \frac{1}{2}(400)\,(0.43)\cos 40° + \frac{1}{2}(100)\,(0.80)\cos 10°$$

$$= 65.88 + 3.94 = 69.82 \text{ watts.}$$

(*c*) When third-harmonic voltage is absent, then the applied voltage is 400 cos ωt. It is already known that

Eddy-current loss $\propto (B_m f)^2 \propto (V)^2$

Now $$V = \sqrt{\left(\frac{V_{m1}}{\sqrt{2}}\right)^2 + \left(\frac{V_{m3}}{\sqrt{2}}\right)^2} = \sqrt{\left(\frac{400}{\sqrt{2}}\right)^2 + \left(\frac{100}{\sqrt{2}}\right)^2} = \sqrt{\frac{170{,}000}{2}}$$

With no third harmonic,

$$V' = \frac{V_{m1}}{\sqrt{2}} = \frac{400}{\sqrt{2}}.$$

Since the voltage V' is less than V, there is reduction in the eddy-current loss.

$\therefore$ Percentage reduction in eddy current loss

$$= \frac{V^2 - V'^2}{V^2} \times 100 = \frac{\dfrac{170{,}000}{2} - \dfrac{160{,}000}{2}}{\dfrac{170{,}000}{2}} \times 100 = 5.882\%.$$

8.4.2 Harmonics in Three-phase Transformers

In power and distribution transformers, the exciting currents are only a small percentage (2 to 6%) of the rated currents. In single-phase transformers, the harmonics in the exciting currents do not have any appreciable effect on their operation. In view of this, harmonics in single-phase transformers are usually neglected. But harmonic phenomena in 3-phase transformers are quite important. It is because under certain conditions, the exciting current harmonics may cause inadvertent operation of the protective equipment and may also cause interference with communication circuits. In view of this, energy-system and communication engineers should be able to investigate and avert such situations. The object of this section of the article is to discuss the harmonics in 3-phase transformers.

The harmonic phenomena in three-phase transformers are dependent upon the following :

(*i*) The type of transformer winding connection, *i.e.,* whether the transformer winding is connected in star, delta or inter-star and

(*ii*) whether the magnetic circuits of the three phases are separate or interlinked.

The effect of these two factors would be investigated at a later stage.

First of all, the three-phase applied voltages are assumed to be symmetrical, with the fundamental frequency voltages mutually displaced by 120°. Since only odd harmonics can be present in the voltage, the voltage equations for the three-phases can be written as :

$$v_A = V_{m1} \sin \omega t + V_{m3} \sin 3\omega t + V_{m5} \sin 5\omega t + ...$$

$$v_B = V_{m1} \sin (\omega t - 120°) + V_{m3} \sin 3(\omega t - 120°) + V_{m5} \sin 5(\omega t - 120°) + ...$$

$$v_C = V_{m1} \sin (\omega t - 240°) + V_{m3} \sin 3(\omega t - 240°) + V_{m5} \sin 5(\omega t - 240°) + ...$$

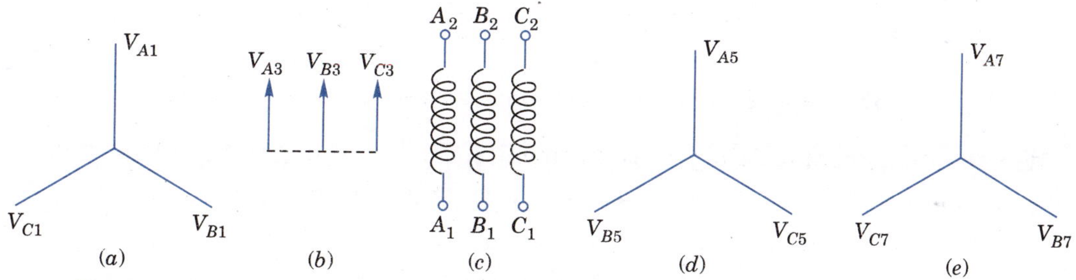

Fig. 8.29: Phasor diagrams for fundamental, third, fifth and seventh harmonic voltages.

Here V_{m1}, V_{m3} ... are the maximum values of the fundamental, third harmonic... components of the applied voltage. From these equations, it is seen that the fundamental components of voltages form a three-phase balanced system with phase sequence *ABC* as shown in Fig. 8.29 (*a*).

The third harmonic voltages are

$$v_{A3} = V_{m3} \sin 3\omega t \quad \text{for phase } A$$

$$v_{B3} = V_{m3} \sin (3\omega t - 360°) = V_{m3} \sin 3\omega t V_{m3} \quad \text{for phase } B$$

and

$$v_{C3} = V_{m3} \sin (3\omega t - 720°) = V_{m3} \sin 3\omega t \quad \text{for phase } C.$$

It is seen from above that the third harmonic voltages v_{A3}, v_{B3}, v_{C3} in the three voltages are in time phase as shown in Fig. 8.29 (*b*). In other words, the triplen harmonic voltages act either from A_1, B_1, C_1 to A_2, B_2, C_2 or from A_2, B_2, C_2 to A_1, B_1, C_1 at the same instant of time in the three windings shown in Fig. 8.29 (*c*).

The fifth harmonic voltages are

$$v_{A5} = V_{m5} \sin 5\omega t \quad \text{for phase } A$$

$$v_{B5} = V_{m5} \sin (5\omega t - 600°) = V_{m5} \sin (5\omega t - 240°) \quad \text{for phase } B$$

and

$$v_{C5} = V_{m5} \sin (5\omega t - 1200°) = V_{m5} \sin (5\omega t - 120°) \quad \text{for phase } C.$$

The fifth harmonic voltages are, therefore, time displaced by 120°, but have the phase sequence *ACB* [(as shown in Fig. 8.29 (*d*)], opposite to the fundamental phase sequence *ABC*.

The seventh harmonic voltages can be shown to have the phase sequence *ABC*, Fig. 8.29 (*e*).

Now the effect of connecting the three-phase winding of a transformer in star and delta would be examined.

Star connection. For obtaining star connection, the terminals with the same polarity are joined together as illustrated in Fig. 8.7 (*b*). The line voltage V_{AB} may be obtained from the relation.

$$\overline{V}_{AB} = \overline{V}_A - \overline{V}_B.$$

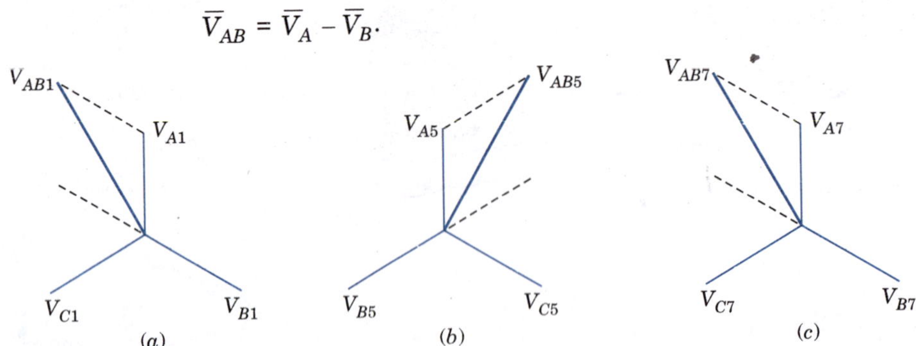

Fig. 8.30: Fundamental, 5th and 7th harmonic phasor diagrams for voltages.

For the fundamental, 5th and 7th harmonics, the line voltages V_{AB1}, V_{AB5} and V_{AB7} are as shown in Fig. 8.30. For the third harmonic emf, the line voltage is,

$$v_{AB3} = v_{A3} - v_{B3} = V_{m3} \sin 3\omega t - V_{m3} \sin 3\omega t = 0.$$

Therefore, for a star connection arrangement, the line voltages are free from triplen harmonics, even though the phase voltages contain them. At any instant, the third harmonic phase emfs in a star connection may be represented as illustrated in Fig. 8.31. From line to star point, there is a voltage drop and from star point to line, there is an equal voltage rise; therefore, the third harmonic voltages across any two line terminals are zero. This agrees with the conclusion already obtained.

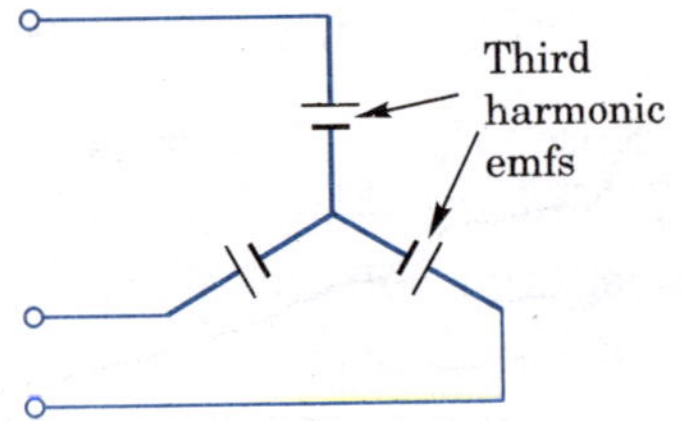

Fig. 8.31: Representation of third harmonic emf for star connection at any instant.

Delta Connection. For obtaining a delta connection, the terminals of different polarities are joined as shown in Fig. 8.32 (*a*). If the three windings in delta are opened at one point and a voltmeter is connected as shown in Fig. 8.32 (*b*), then the voltmeter reading would be zero, if there were only fundamental, 5th and 7th harmonic emfs in the three phases. There are, however, triplen harmonic emfs acting simultaneously from $A_1 B_1 C_1$ to $A_2 B_2 C_2$ or *vice versa*. At any instant, these triplen emfs are represented in a simple manner as illustrated in Fig. 8.32 (*c*).

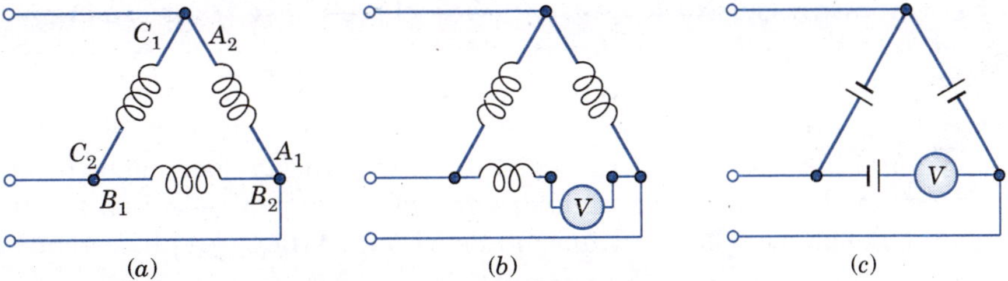

Fig. 8.32: Pertaining to the third harmonics in delta-connection.

If the magnitudes of triplen emfs in each phase are E_3, E_9 etc., then the voltmeter reading in Fig. 8.32 (*b*) would be equal to

$$V_3 = 3\sqrt{E_3^2 + E_9^2} + \ldots$$

If the voltmeter is taken out and an ammeter is inserted in its place, then the third harmonic current I_3 (neglecting I_9 etc.) can be measured. It should be noted that third harmonic current cannot exist in the lines of a delta-connected transformer. In order to prove this, let the third harmonic currents in the 3-phases of a delta-connected transformer be given by

$$i_{A3} = I_{m3} \sin 3\omega t$$

$$i_{B3} = I_{m3} \sin 3(\omega t - 120°) = I_{m3} \sin 3\omega t$$

and

$$i_{C3} = I_{m3} \sin 3(\omega t - 240°) = I_{m3} \sin 3\omega t\,.$$

For a delta connection, the line current can be found from the relation,

$$i_{AB3} = i_{A3} - i_{B3} = I_{m3} \sin 3\omega t - I_{m3} \sin 3\omega t = 0.$$

It can be concluded from the above that the third-harmonic magnetizing current can flow in the closed delta, but not in the lines.

It should also be noted that the triplen harmonic emfs don't appear between the lines even in delta-connected windings. This is due to the fact that triplen e.m.f.s. are fully balanced by the corresponding impedance drops due to triplen currents. For example, if each phase has E_3 as the third harmonic emf and Z_3 as the third harmonic impedance, then the third harmonic circulating current I_3 in the closed delta is given by

$$I_3 = \frac{3E_3}{3Z_3} = \frac{E_3}{Z_3} \quad \text{or} \quad E_3 = I_3 Z_3.$$

$\therefore$ Third harmonic emf across any phase of the closed delta is

$$E_3 - I_3 Z_3 = E_3 - \frac{E_3}{Z_3} \times Z_3 = 0$$

This shows that in each phase, third harmonic e.m.f. E_3 is fully balanced by the third harmonic impedance drop $I_3 Z_3$. Same is true for other triplen harmonics.

A transformer in a 3-phase circuit may be a three-phase core-type, 3-phase shell-type or a bank of three single-phase transformers. From the magnetic circuit view-point, the three-phase transformers can be sub-divided into two, namely.

(*i*) those having independent magnetic circuits for the three-phases and

(*ii*) those having interlinked or coupled magnetic circuits for the three-phases.

The various three-phase connections are now described in detail.

(*a*) Yy connection (without neutral). The three-phase transformers with separate and interlinked magnetic circuits are discussed here.

(*I*) Transformers with independent magnetic systems. Three-phase shell-type transformer and a bank of three single-phase transformers have independent magnetic circuits as shown in Figs. 8.4 and 8.1 respectively. It has already been shown that the third-harmonic voltages in star-connected transformers do not appear between the lines, though they are present in the phase. The third harmonic currents in the three phases can be written as

$$i_{A3} = I_{m3} \sin 3\omega t$$

$$i_{B3} = I_{m3} \sin 3\omega t \quad \text{and} \quad i_{C3} = I_{m3} \sin 3\omega t\,.$$

These currents are directed either towards the star point or away from it. Therefore, no third-harmonic current can flow in the star connected transformers without neutral and in the lines connected to their terminals. This fact can alternatively be explained as follows:

In a star connection, if the neutral is provided, then the current in the neutral wire is

$$i_n = i_{A3} + i_{B3} + i_{C3} = 3I_{m3} \sin 3\omega t$$

If the neural is not provided, then i_n must be zero.

$$\therefore \qquad i_n = 3I_{m3} \sin 3\omega t = 0 \quad \text{or} \quad I_{m3} = 0.$$

Since *Yy* without neutral is being studied here, third harmonic currents cannot flow in the lines and phases of star-connected transformer. Consequently, the no-load magnetizing current taken from the supply is free of third harmonic current, but higher order harmonics may be present. Thus, for a star connection, the magnetizing current is almost a sine wave (neglecting higher order harmonics). But a sine wave of magnetizing current requires the flux wave to be flat-topped, which consists of pronounced third harmonic flux ϕ_3. Since the transfomers under consideration have separate magnetic circuits, the reluctance offered to ϕ_3 is very low. The magnitude of ϕ_3 is, therefore, quite a large percentage of the fundamental flux ϕ_1 and consequently, flux wave-form departs much more from the sine wave. In some cases, ϕ_3 may be about 20% of ϕ_1 or even more, depending upon the saturation. A 20% of ϕ_3 at a frequency of 3*f*, gives rise to triplen induced emfs equal to 60% of the fundamental-emf, see Eq. (8.1). As a result of it, the phase emfs, induced in the primary and secondary windings are peaked having their amplitudes (maximum values) equal to 160% of the fundamental emf amplitude. These peak voltages may be injurious to insulation. Hence, a *Yy* transformer connection, with independent magnetic circuits, should not be used in h.v. systems. The line voltages remain sinusoidal, since they are free from third harmonic voltages.

It may also be noted that the rms value of the resultant phase voltage is equal to $\sqrt{1^2 + 0.6^2} = 1.17$ times the fundmental component of the phase voltage when $\phi_3 = 20\%$ of ϕ_1. Therefore, the relation, line voltage= $(\sqrt{3})$ phase voltage, does not hold good for transformers connected in *Yy* without neutral.

Another effect of third-harmonic emfs is to oscillate the neutral at 3*f* as shown in Fig. 8.33. In this figure, fundamental and third harmonic emfs are combined at three different instants of time. In the phasor diagrams of this figure, third-harmonic voltage v_3 is cophasal in all the three-phase voltages. The resultant of fundamental and third harmonic voltages is shown dotted on the right hand side of Fig. 8.33 at $\omega t = 0$, $\omega t = \frac{\pi}{12}$ and $\omega t = \frac{\pi}{2}$. Note that the phasor v_3 rotates at 3ω rad/sec, whereas the fundamental phasors rotate at ω rad/sec. This means that if fundamental phasors rotate through 30°, the phasor v_3 rotates through 3 × 30° = 90° as shown in Fig. 8.33 (*b*).

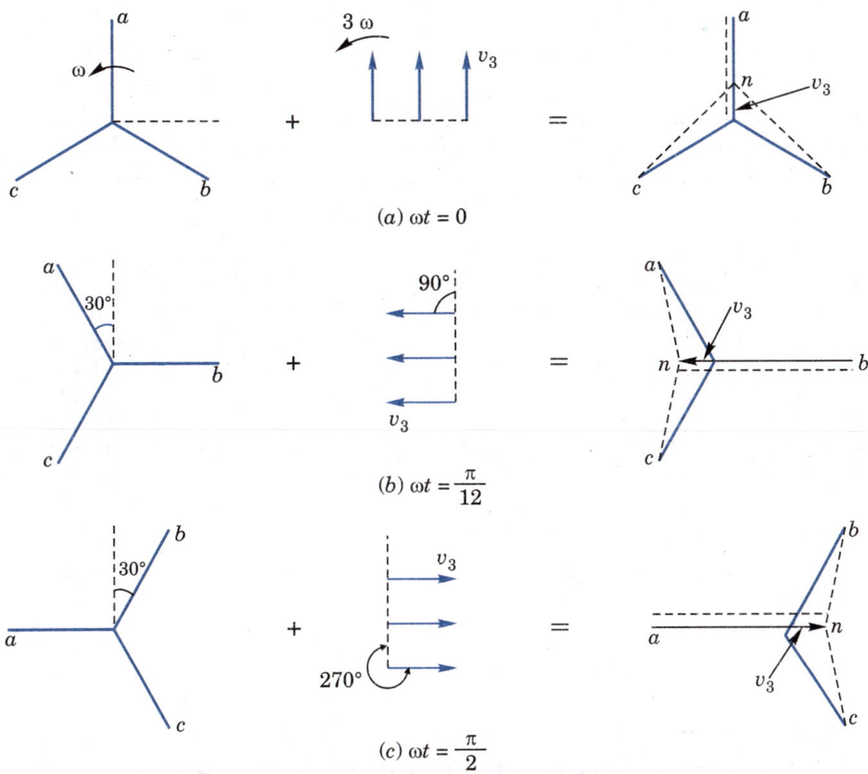

Fig. 8.33: Pertaining to the oscillations of the neutral point.

Since the transformer is connected to a large 3-phase power network, the tips *a*, *b*, *c* of the fundamental phasors cannot change their positions. It is the neutral that shifts its position at frequency 3*f* as shown in Fig. 8.33. The effect of this oscillating neutral is to cause the fluctuations in the line to star-point voltages. An examination of Fig. 8.33 reveals the following :

(*i*) The maximum voltage across a phase winding is equal to $V_{m1} + V_{m3}$, depending upon the relative positions of V_1 and V_3. For example, in Fig. 8.33 (*b*) maximum voltage occurs across phase *B* winding; at some other instant of time in Fig. 8.33 (*c*), maximum voltage appears across phase *A* winding. This shows that the phase windings are subjected to additional strain which may be injurious to insulation.

(*ii*) The line voltages remain uneffected, but the line to neutral voltage is $\sqrt{V_1^2 + V_3^2}$. This shows that line voltage is not equal to $\sqrt{3}$ times the phase voltage for a *Yy* transformer with separate magnetic circuits and without neutral.

(II) Transformers with interlinked, or coupled, magnetic system. The three phase core type transformer, which is much more commonly employed, is a three-legged transformer and the magnetic circuits of the three phases are interlinked. In other words, the magnetic flux of one phase on one leg completes its magnetic path through the other two legs and the yoke.

The triplen harmonic fluxes, like the triplen emfs or currents, are all directed either upwards or downwards in all the three legs. At any instant, triplen fluxes are equal in magnitude. Further, the triplen flux in one leg cannot return through the other two legs, because it is being opposed by the triplen fluxes of the same magnitudes. Consequently, the only return path for the triplen flux is through the air or oil around the core as shown in Fig. 8.34. Since the air has high reluctance, the triplen fluxes and, therefore, the triplen phase emfs are small. The phase voltages now contain only a small magnitude of third harmonic emfs and in view of this, the phase voltages may approach sine waves if higher order harmonics are absent.

The triplen fluxes would have a tendency to return through the least reluctance path offered by the steel tank, channels, bolts etc. The triplen frequency flux may, therefore, give rise to large eddy current losses in these parts, thereby reducing the transformer efficiency considerably. In view of this, every effort should be made to suppress the triplen harmonic fluxes, one of the methods being to use a conducting ring around the whole transformer. The triplen frequency induced currents in this ring oppose the third harmonic flux to a large extent.

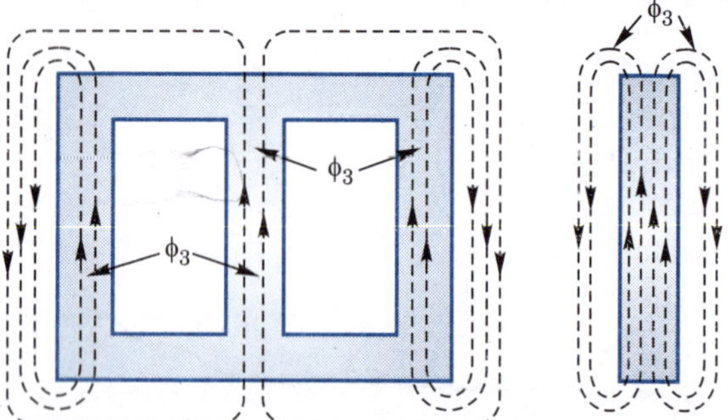

Fig. 8.34: Path for the third (or triplen) harmonic fluxes in 3-phase core-type transformer.

If the tank is made up of aluminium instead of steel, then the reluctance offered to triplen flux by aluminium tank, is more than that offered by steel tank. As a result of it, the triplen flux is small and therefore the triplen-frequency currents induced in the aluminium tank are much less. These triplen-frequency currents in the aluminium tank would oppose the third harmonic flux more effectively than a conducting ring in the steel tank. A transformer with an aluminium tank would have, therefore, more efficiency and consequently less temperature rise as compared to the transformer with a conducting ring in the steel tank. It is because of this reason that aluminium tanks for a 3-phase core type transformers may be preferred these days.

(b) Yy with neutral. If the alternator and the primary of the *Yy* transformer have their neutrals grounded, then third-harmonic currents can return through the ground. Therefore, the third harmonic magnetizing current can exist in the lines as well as in the phase windings of the transformer. As a result of it, the flux and, therefore, the phase voltages are sine waves. The line voltage is equal to $\sqrt{3}$ times the phase voltage and the neutral is stabilised. Further, the third harmonic current, passing through the ground, is equal to three times the magnetizing current in the lines or phase windings as proved in Eq. (8.2).

The main disadvantage of the third harmonic currents flowing in the lines is that these may cause considerable interference with the communication circuits, running parallel to the transmission lines.

(c) Dy connection. The sinusoidal supply voltage applied to a *Dy* connected transformer provides a sinusoidal magnetizing current in the lines. This sinusoidal magnetizing current also flows in the transformer windings which gives rise to flat-topped flux wave, containing a pronounced third harmonic flux. The triplen-frequency flux induces triplen-frequency emfs acting in the same direction in all the three phases of the delta winding. The resultant of these emfs establishes third harmonic current in the closed delta. Hence it can be concluded that the transformer-winding current consists of a sinusoidal magnetizing current plus a third-harmonic magnetizing current, the resultant current wave being similar to that illustrated in Fig. 8.25. But the presence of third harmonic in the magnetizing current requires sine flux wave, therefore, the emfs induced both in the primary and secondary windings are almost sinusoidal. The higher order harmonics operate just like the fundamental component. Thus with *Dy* connection, the magnetizing current in the lines contains fundamental component (plus 5th and 7th harmonics if present). But the magnetizing current in the closed delta contains fundamental plus third harmonic components (plus 5th and 7th harmonics, if present).

It may be noted that the third harmonic magnetizing current in the closed delta can flow only due to third harmonic emf and, therefore, presence of third-harmonic flux ϕ_3 is essential. This flux ϕ_3 links the secondary winding also. Consequently, a very small amount of third harmonic e.m.f. (1% of rated phase voltage or even less) is induced in the secondary phases. But, as before, the output line voltages are free from third harmonic e.m.f.s. Therefore, the line voltage on the secondary side is almost equal to $\sqrt{3}$ times the phase voltage and the secondary-star point is now stabilized at earth potential.

The above treatment is for the transformers having separate magnetic circuits.

(d) Yd connection. Since the third-harmonic current cannot flow in the star-connected windings of a *Yd* transformer, the magnetizing current derived from the supply must be a sine wave (in case higher order harmonics are absent). But a sinusoidal magnetizing current requires flat-topped flux wave having a pronounced third-harmonic flux. This third harmonic flux induces third harmonic e.m.f.s both in the primary and secondary windings. Since the secondary is connected in delta, third harmonic e.m.f.s give rise to third harmonic current. In view of this, the magnetizing current in the secondary delta consists of third harmonic current only. The combined action of fundamental frequency current in the primary and third harmonic current in the secondary closed delta produces the resultant flux in the core.

But it has already been established that if the magnetizing current consists of fundamental and third harmonic currents, then the flux must be a sine wave. Thus in the *Yd* connection, the magnetic flux linking both the primary and secondary windings is a sine wave. As a result of it, the primary and secondary phase e.m.f.s. are free of third harmonic e.m.f.s. and their waveforms are almost sine waves.

As explained in the *Dy* connection, the primary phase voltage in *Yd* connection may contain third harmonic e.m.f.s. of the order of 1% of rated phase voltage or even less. The primary and secondary line voltages are of course, free of third harmonic voltages.

(e) Dd connection. For *Dd* connected transformer, the line current is sinusoidal, but the third harmonic magnetizing currents can flow both in the primary and secondary deltas as described above for *Yd* to *Dy* connection. It should be noted that the required third harmonic flux is established by the combined effects of circulating currents both in primary and secondary deltas. Therefore, the third harmonic magnetizing current, in the primary delta of *Dd* connection, must be less than the third harmonic magnetizing current in the primary delta of *Dy* connection. Actually, the third harmonic magnetizing currents are divided between primary and secondary deltas in a manner inversely proportional to their triple-frequency leakage impedances, with the third-harmonic current and impedances referred to the same side. The resultant flux in *Dd* is very nearly a sine wave, since the third harmonic flux is very small.

Note that the discussion in parts (*b*), (*c*), (*d*) and (*e*) of Art. 8.4.2, is applicable to transformers having separate magnetic circuits.

8.4.3 Disadvantages of Harmonics in Transformers

The harmonics currents and harmonics e.m.f.s. have different effects on the operation of 3-phase transformers. These bad effects are now described below.

(*a*) **Current harmonics**

(*i*) **Effect on I²R loss.** The presence of harmonic circulating currents in the transformer windings results in additional ohmic losses and, therefore, greater temperature rise and reduced efficiency.

(*ii*) **Electromagnetic interference with communication circuits.** The harmonic currents produce harmonic fluxes of corresponding frequencies around the transmission line conductors. These harmonic magnetic fluxes induce e.m.f.s. in the communication circuits running parallel to them and thereby the interference is caused. For example, in a star/star transformer with four wire supply (or with primary and alternator neutrals grounded), the triplen harmonic currents can flow in the transmission lines and, therefore, interference in the nearby communication circuits is produced. This inductive interference may also cause the faulty operation of the protective devices, when pilot wires* are used.

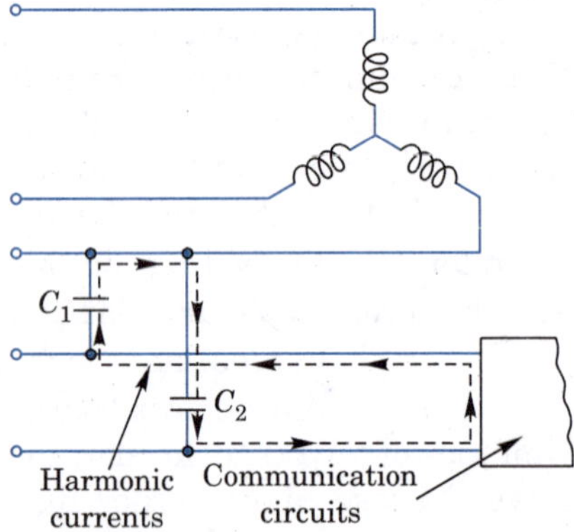

Fig. 8.35: Electrostatic interference with communication circuits.

(*iii*) **Effect on core loss.** When the e.m.f. is peaked, the flux wave is flat-topped. Therefore the hysteresis loss, approximately proportional to $(\text{flux})^2$, is reduced. But the eddy current loss, proportional to $(\text{e.m.f.})^2$, is increased. Since the hysteresis loss forms a major part of the core loss, there is an overall reduction in the core loss. If the e.m.f. is flat-topped, the core loss is increased. Note that the flux is flat-topped when the third harmonic currents are not flowing in the transformer windings.

(*b*) **Voltage harmonics**

(*i*) **Voltage strain on insulation.** In some cases the voltage across the windings may increase their rated voltages. If this happens, the transformer insulation is subjected to higher voltage strains, resulting in increased dielectric losses. The life of the insulation is shortened and the transformer efficiency is decreased. For example, in star/star transformer (without neutral), the phase voltages are more than the rated voltages and contain predominant third-harmonic e.m.f.s. Therefore, life of the insulation is shortened and the transformer efficiency is decreased in star/star transformers without neutral.

* Wires running parallel to the transmission lines or cables for protection purposes are called pilot wires.

(*ii*) **Electrostatic interference with communication circuits.** A communication circuit, running parallel to the transmission lines, may be capacitively coupled as indicated in Fig. 8.35. Capacitance $(C_1 + C_2)$ forms a series circuit with inductance of the communication circuit. If the capacitive reactance of $C_1 + C_2$ becomes equal to the inductive reactance at some harmonic frequency, the series resonance takes place. As a result of it, increased harmonic current flows, giving rise to interference with the communication circuits.

(*iii*) **Large resonant voltages.** If a star/star transformer, with its secondary neutral grounded, is connected to long transmission lines or cables, then the resonance phenomenon may occur. The transformer inductances and the transmission line or cable capacitances form series circuit as shown in Fig. 8.36. If the magnetizing reactances of the transformer at $3f$ becomes equal to the capacitive reactances from line to ground at $3f$, then series resonance occurs. Therefore, the third harmonic e.m.f., present between line to ground, circulates large third-harmonic exciting currents due to series resonance. These amplified third-harmonic exciting currents cause the third harmonic voltage, between line to neural, to become dangerously high. In addition, the large third harmonic currents, caused by the series resonance, increase the ohmic losses and the high third harmonic voltages augment the core and dielectric losses. In view of the above discussion, the occurrence of such cases should be carefully investigated.

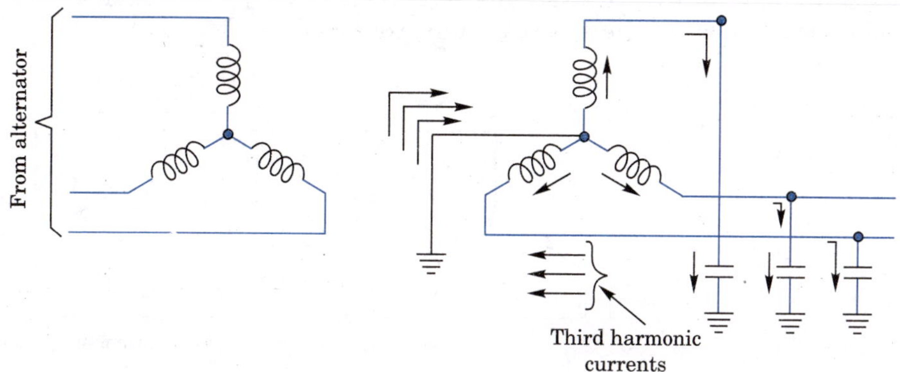

Fig. 8.36: Series resonance phenomena in a star/star transformer (secondary grounded), connected to long transmission line or cable.

8.4.4 Suppression of Harmonics

The harmonics in the transformers can be suppressed as follows :

(*i*) **Lower flux densities.** Harmonics can be reduced by using lower core flux densities. But this results in large core area (for the same voltage), more conductor material and, therefore more cost. Hence it is not economical to design and work transformers at lower flux densities.

(*ii*) **Type of connections.** Triplen harmonic currents and voltages in the lines are suppressed by the use of star (3-wire supply) or delta connections of the transformers.

(*iii*) **Primary or secondary winding in delta.** Harmonic voltages have more nuisance value than the harmonic currents. Therefore, every effort should be made to suppress the third harmonic voltages.

It has already been shown that when one of the transformer windings is delta connected, the triplen harmonic voltages are suppressed considerably. In view of this, one of the transformer windings (either primary or secondary) must be connected in delta, in order to suppress triplen harmonic voltages.

(*iv*) **Use of tertiary winding.** If it is not possible to connect the primary or secondary winding in delta, then the three-phase transformer must be designed to have an additional winding, called the third winding. It is more common to call the third winding as tertiary winding, and it is connected in delta. This closed delta formed by the tertiary winding, provides a path for the third harmonic currents; therefore, the flux and emfs become almost sine waves. Note that the tertiary winding has no effect on the fundamental component of voltage, because the phasor sum of three emfs, mutually displaced by 120°, is zero in the closed tertiary delta.

(*v*) **Star-delta earthing transformer.** The third harmonic voltages in a two-winding star/star transformer can also be suppressed by using a star-delta earthing transformer, as illustrated in Fig. 8.37. The closed delta provides the path for third harmonic currents, therefore, the flux and emf waves remain sine waves. The potential of the star point is stabilized and the oscillating neutral is avoided.

For a star/star transformer, the third harmonic voltages can also be suppressed by using a 4-wire supply (or earthing the transformer neutral point if the alternator neutral is grounded). The neutral wire provides the path for the third harmonic current, therefore, the flux and emfs are sine waves. But the interference caused by the triplen currents, in the nearby communication circuits must be carefully examined.

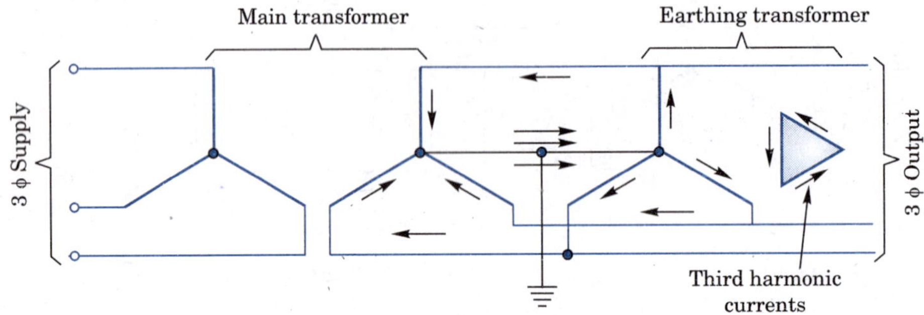

Fig. 8.37: Star-delta earthing transformer for the suppression of triplen harmonic emfs.

8.4.5 Tertiary or Stabilizing Windings

In addition to the primary and secondary windings, the transformers are sometimes provided with third winding, called the tertiary or stabilizing winding. Therefore, the transformers, furnished with tertiary windings are the three-winding transformers and are discussed in detail in Art. 8.11.

The tertiary winding is usually delta connected and many a times, its terminals are not brought outside the tank. In such a case, its various functions in star-star transformers are as follows :

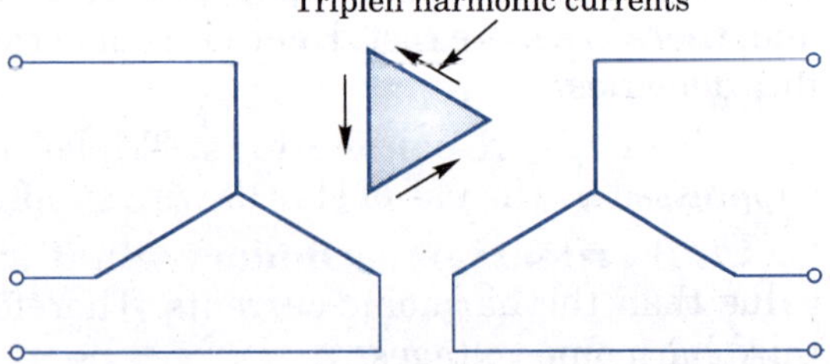

Fig. 8.38: Pertaining to tertiary winding.

(*i*) The third harmonic magnetizing current can flow in the delta connected tertiary winding as shown in Fig. 8.38. As a result of this, the core flux and the emfs are almost sine waves.

(*ii*) The single phase load, between line and neutral, can be supplied by a bank of star/star transformer having tertiary winding. This is explained in Art. 8.5.

(*iii*) For a line to earth fault, the tertiary winding permits the flow of sufficient fault current, in order to operate the protective devices, see Art. 8.5.

When the tertiary winding terminals are brought outside the tank, it may be used to supply power to any other equipment, such as power-factor correction apparatus, supply to power house or substation auxiliaries etc.

Like any other apparatus, the rating of the tertiary winding is also decided by the permissible temperature rise. The design of the tertiary winding is usually based on the fault conditions, because these have more adverse effects on the tertiary winding.

Example 8.7. *A three-phase star-delta transformer has its delta open-circuited as shown in Fig. 8.39. A voltmeter placed across phase winding AB reads 260 V and when placed in open-circuited delta, it reads 300 V. Find the reading of the voltmeter if it is placed across terminals BC and BD. The odd harmonics, upto seventh harmonic, are only to be considered.*

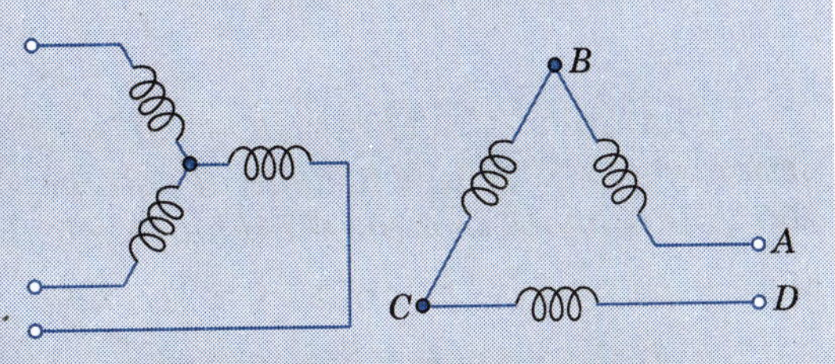

Fig. 8.39: Pertaining to Example 8.7.

Solution. Since, the delta is open-circuited, the voltage across phase winding AB is the resultant of fundamental, third, fifth and seventh harmonic voltages.

$$\therefore \quad E_{AB} = \sqrt{E_1^2 + E_3^2 + E_5^2 + E_7^2} \quad \text{or} \quad (260)^2 = E_1^2 + E_3^2 + E_5^2 + E_7^2$$

The voltage across AD is the resultant of third harmonic e.m.fs E_3 in the 3-phase windings. Since E_3 in the three-phase windings act in the same direction, $3E_3 = 300$ or $E_3 = 100$ V. Thus

$$(260)^2 = E_1^2 + (100)^2 + E_5^2 + E_7^2$$

or
$$E_1^2 + E_5^2 + E_7^2 = (260)^2 - (100)^2 = 57,600$$

The voltage across the phase winding BC is the same as that across phase winding AB.

$$\therefore \quad E_{BC} = 260 \text{ V.}$$

The voltage across BD is the resultant E_1, E_5, E_7 and twice of third harmonic e.m.f E_3

$$\therefore \quad E_{BD} = \sqrt{E_1^2 + (2E_3)^2 + E_5^2 + E_7^2}$$

$$= \sqrt{(57,600) + (200)^2} = 312.41 \text{ volts.}$$

Example 8.8. *The transformer secondary in star supplies power to a purely resistive load, with one ammeter and wattmeter connected as shown in Fig. 8.40. The readings on the ammeter and wattmeter are 9 A and 810 W respectively. The line to line voltages are balanced. Find the value of the resistor R. Consider harmonics up to third harmonic only.*

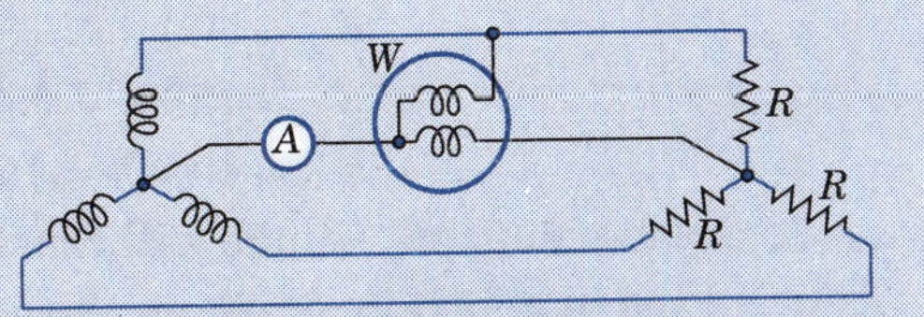

Fig. 8.40: Pertaining to Example 8.8.

Solution. The third harmonic currents I_3 flow through the resistors and add arithmetically to $3I_3$ in the neutral wire.

∴ The ammeter reading = $3I_3 = 9$ A or $I_3 = 3$ A.

Since the load is purely resistive, the load power factor is unity. Now for the wattmeter.

$$\begin{bmatrix}\text{3rd harmonic voltage}\\\text{across voltage coil}\end{bmatrix} \times \begin{bmatrix}\text{3rd harmonic current}\\\text{in the current coil}\end{bmatrix} \times [\text{pf}] = \text{Wattmeter reading}$$

or $$(V_3)(3I_3)(1) = 810$$

∴ $$V_3 = \frac{810}{9} = 90 \text{ volts.}$$

∴ Value of the resistor $R = \frac{V_3}{I_3} = \frac{90}{3} = 30\ \Omega$.

Example 8.9. *Three identical single-phase transformers are connected in star on primary side. The line to neutral voltage, due to the fundamental component of flux ϕ_1, is 200 V. It is found that the third harmonic flux ϕ_3 and fifth harmonic flux ϕ_5 are 20% and 4% of ϕ_1 respectively. The primary to secondary turns ratio of each transformer is $\frac{1}{4}$.*

(a) If the secondary is connected in star, calculate

(i) line to neutral voltages and (ii) line to line voltages on the secondary side.

(b) If the secondary is connected in delta, calculate

(i) the voltage across the open-circuited delta and (ii) line to line voltage when delta is closed.

(c) If the primary neutral is connected to the source neutral and the secondary is in star, calculate the secondary line and phase voltages.

(d) In part (c), if the secondary winding is arranged in delta, find the voltage across the secondary open-circuited delta.

Solution. Fundamental component of voltage $E_1 = 200$ V

Examination of Eq. (8.1) reveals that if ϕ_3 is 20% of ϕ_1, then the e.m.f induced due to third harmonic flux ϕ_3 is 60% (= 3 × 20%) of that induced due to ϕ_1.

∴ $$E_3 = \frac{60}{100} \times 200 = 120 \text{ V.}$$

Similarly, the fifth harmonic e.m.f E_5 is 20% (= 4 × 5%) of E_1.

∴ $$E_5 = \frac{4 \times 5}{100} \times 200 = 40 \text{ V.}$$

(*a*) Emfs, E_1, E_3 and E_5 when referred to the secondary side are

$$E_1' = 200 \times 4 = 800 \text{ V}$$
$$E_3' = 120 \times 4 = 480 \text{ V}$$
$$E_5' = 40 \times 4 = 160 \text{ V.}$$

(*i*) Line to neutral voltage will consist of E_1', E_3' and E_5'.

∴ Line to neutral voltage on the secondary side

$$= \sqrt{E'^2_1 + E'^3_3 + E'^2_5} = \sqrt{(800)^2 + (480)^2 + (160)^2}$$

= 946.57 volts.

(*ii*) Line to line voltages are free of third harmonic voltages.

∴ Line to line voltage on secondary side

$$= \sqrt{3}\sqrt{E_1'^2 + E_5'^2} = \sqrt{3}\sqrt{(800)^2 + (160)^2} = 1413.04 \text{ volts.}$$

(*b*) (*i*) The voltage across the open-circuited delta is due to the third harmonic emfs only and, therefore, its magnitude is equal to $3E_3' = 3\,(480) = 1440$ V.

(*ii*) When the delta is closed; the line to line voltage, free of third harmonic e.m.f.s., is given by

$$\sqrt{E'_1{}^2 + E'_5{}^2} = \sqrt{(800)^2 + (160)^2} = 815.84 \text{ V.}$$

(*c*) When the primary and source neutrals are connected, the third harmonic magnetizing current can flow, making the core flux almost a sine wave. Therefore, the secondary phase voltage is free of third harmonics.

∴ Secondary phase voltage $= \sqrt{E'_1{}^2 + E'_5{}^2} = 815.84$ V.

Secondary line voltage $= \sqrt{3}\ (815.84) = 1413.04$ V.

(*d*) Since the flux is a sine wave, as explained in part (*c*), the third harmonic e.m.f.s. are absent. Hence the voltage across the open-circuited delta would be zero.

Example 8.10. *Three identical single-phase transformers have their rated voltages of 200, 150 and 100 V respectively for the primary, secondary and tertiary windings. The primary is connected in star to 3-phase sinusoidal supply of 433 volts. The secondary is also connected in star. The voltmeter, when connected across the open-circuited delta of the tertiary winding gave a reading of 120 V.*

Determine the line and phase voltages on the secondary if the tertiary delta is (a) open-circuited and (b) closed.

Solution. The voltmeter across the open-circuited delta reads $3E_3$.

∴ The third harmonic voltage in the tertiary winding, $E_3 = 120/3 = 40$ V.

Phase voltage on the primary side $= 433/\sqrt{3} = 250$ V.

The transformer primary winding is rated for 200 V. Therefore, the applied voltage is 250/200 = 1.25 times the rated voltage.

(*a*) When tertiary delta is open-circuited, the third harmonic current cannot flow, the flux is flat-topped and the third harmonic emfs appear in the phase emfs. A third-harmonic voltage of 40 V in tertiary winding is equivalent to third harmonic voltage of 40 × 150/100 = 60 V on the secondary side.

∴ Phase voltage on secondary side

$$= 1.25\sqrt{E_1^2 + E_3^2} = 1.25\,[\sqrt{(150)^2 + (60)^2}\,] = 201.94 \text{ V.}$$

Line voltage on the secondary side is free of third harmonic voltage.

∴ Secondary line voltage $= 1.25\,[\sqrt{3}\,E_1] = 1.25\,[\sqrt{3} \times 150] = 324.75$ V.

(*b*) When the tertiary delta is closed, third harmonic magnetizing current can flow, resulting in sine flux wave. Hence no third harmonic voltage will appear across the secondary phase voltage.

∴ Secondary phase voltage $= 1.25 \times 150 = 187.5$ V

and secondary line voltage $= 1.25\,(\sqrt{3}) \times 150 = 324.75$ V.

Example 8.11. *A bank of delta / star power transformer is connected to a bank of star / star distribution transformer as illustrated in Fig. 8.41. The secondary of the power transformer is solidly grounded and the secondary line voltages are sinusoidal. The two neutrals of the distribution transformer are not grounded.*

A voltmeter connected between ground and the primary neutral of the distribution transformer gave a reading of 3000 V. Calculate the effective values of line and phase voltages across the secondary of the distribution transformer, for which the primary to secondary turns ratio is 30.

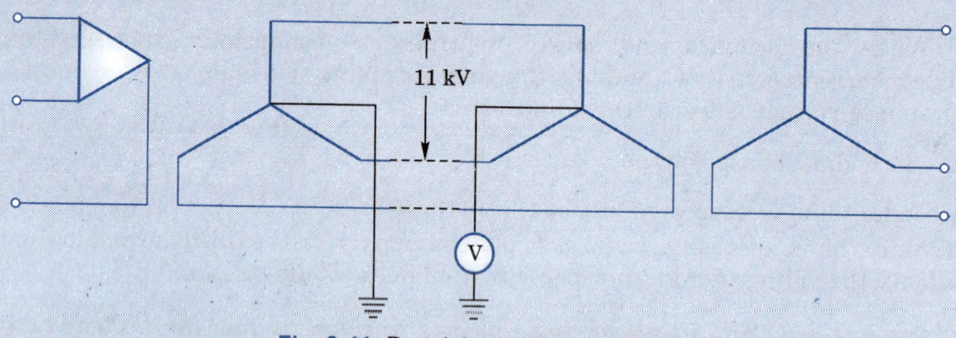

Fig. 8.41: Pertaining to Example 8.11.

Solution. Here 3000 V, present between transformer neutral and ground is due to the third harmonic voltages in the primary phase of the distribution transformer.

∴ Its component in the secondary phase winding is given by

$$\frac{3000 \times N_2}{N_1} = \frac{3000}{30} = 100 \text{ V}.$$

For distribution transformer :

Fundamental component of primary phase voltage $= \dfrac{11{,}000}{\sqrt{3}} = 6351$ V

∴ Fundamental component of secondary phase voltage, $E_1 = \dfrac{6351}{30} = 211.70$ V.

∴ Effective secondary phase voltage $= \sqrt{{E_1}^2 + {E_3}^2} = \sqrt{(211.70)^2 + (100)^2} = 234.13$ V.

The line to line voltage is not effected by the presence of third harmonic content in the phase voltages.

∴ Line to line effective voltage $= \sqrt{3}\,(211.70) = 366.66$ V.

Example 8.12. *A bank of three identical unity-ratio transformers is connected as shown in Fig. 8.42. At no-load, the readings on ammeter A_1 and A_2 are 0.75 A and 0.46 A respectively.*

(a) If the secondary is also connected in delta, what will happen to the readings of ammeter A_1 and A_2.

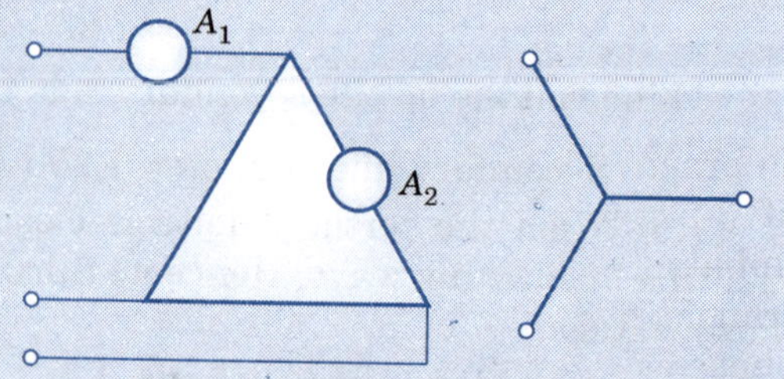

Fig. 8.42: Pertaining to Example 8.12.

(*b*) *If the transformer is connected in star/delta, find the currents in the primary star and the secondary closed delta.*

(*c*) *If the transformer is connected in star/star with four wire supply, calculate the current in the line and in the neutral wire.*

Solution. The ammeter reading A_2 in Fig. 8.42 records the resultant of the component currents I_1, I_3, I_5 and I_7.

$$\therefore \qquad \sqrt{I_1^2 + I_3^2 + I_5^2 + I_7^2} = 0.46 \text{ A.}$$

The third harmonic current and its multiples can flow in the delta, but not in the lines.

$$\therefore \qquad I_{line} = \text{Reading of ammeter } A_1$$

or $$\sqrt{3}\cdot\sqrt{I_1^2 + I_5^2 + I_7^2} = 0.75 \text{ A.} \quad \text{or} \quad \sqrt{I_1^2 + I_5^2 + I_7^2} = \frac{0.75}{\sqrt{3}} = 0.433 \text{ A.}$$

$$\therefore \qquad I_3 = \sqrt{(0.46)^2 - (0.433)^2} = 0.1553 \text{ A.}$$

(*a*) When the secondary is also closed in delta, the third harmonic current can flow both in the primary and secondary deltas. Since the third harmonic flux, necessary to permit the mutual flux to be sinusoidal, is now produced by the combined effect of these third harmonic primary and secondary currents, the reading of ammeter A_2 will be reduced. However, the reading of ammeter A_1 will remain uneffected.

(*b*) When the primary is connected in star, then the ammeter A_1 will record the resultant of I_1, I_5 and I_7.

$\therefore$ Current in the primary star

$$= \sqrt{I_1^2 + I_5^2 + I_7^2} = \frac{0.75}{\sqrt{3}} = 0.433 \text{ A.}$$

In the secondary closed delta, the resultant of E_1, E_5 and E_7 is zero. But the resultant of third harmonic emfs E_3 is equal to $3E_3$. Hence, only the third harmonic currents can flow in the closed delta on the secondary side.

$\therefore$ Current in the secondary closed delta = I_3 = 0.1553 A.

(*c*) With the transformer in star/star with four wire supply, the neutral wire will carry three times I_3.

$\therefore$ Current in the neutral wire = $3I_3$ = 3 (0.1553) = 0.4659 A.

The current in the line now is the resultant of the components I_1, I_3, I_5 and I_7, because the path for third harmonic current is existing through the neutral wire.

$\therefore$ The line current $= \sqrt{I_1^2 + I_3^2 + I_5^2 + I_7^2} = 0.46$ A.

8.5 UNBALANCED OPERATION OF THREE-PHASE TRANSFORMERS

In practice, single-phase loads to the consumers are invariably supplied from the secondaries of 3-phase transformers. Though every effort is made to keep the phase loads equal, unbalanced conditions do exist in three-phase transformers. In addition to it, three-phase transformers may operate under unbalanced conditions on account of dissymmetry in the phase windings or due to single-phase loads or single-phase short circuits. Unbalanced operation of transformers is an undesirable phenomenon, because unequal currents in 3-phase windings have the following adverse effects on their operation.

(*i*) There are additional core and ohmic losses which reduce the transformer efficiency. These losses further give rise to more heating, thereby reducing the transformer life.

(*ii*) Line and phase voltages become distorted and unbalanced.

(*iii*) The transformer rating is reduced.

The unbalanced phase or line voltages have detrimental effect on the operation of electrical apparatus connected to these transformers. For example, a three-phase induction motor working from an unbalanced supply system would have reduced starting and running torques, low operating speed and an impaired efficiency.

In order to investigate accurately the transformer behaviour under unbalanced conditions, the method of symmetrical components must be employed. The object of this article, however, is not to do the rigorous analysis, but merely to present an approximate picture of the unbalanced operation of 3-phase transformers. In this article, first the behaviour of three-phase transformers for single-phase loads is discussed and then their operation under single phasing is examined. The effect of using tertiary winding, in *Yy* transformers with separate magnetic circuits and supplying line to neutral load, is also discussed.

8.5.1 Single-phase Load on Three-phase Transformers

The single-phase load between line to neutral or between two lines causes the worst unbalanced conditions in 3-phase transformers. In addition, an unbalanced polyphase load is equivalent to a polyphase balanced load plus single-phase load between line to neutral or between two lines. In view of this, it is usually important to investigate the behaviour of 3-phase transformers for single-phase loads.

In the various types of connections discussed in this article, the mmf balance on the primary and secondary sides, helps in the determination of winding currents. The primary and secondary windings of the same phase are drawn parallel to each other and phase-turns ratio, for simplicity, is assumed unity. In the various figures, arrows have been marked to give the direction of current flow and the numbers along with the arrows indicate the magnitudes of the currents.

(*a*) In Fig. 8.43 (*a*), neutral may or may not be present on the primary side of the star-star transformer. One phase winding and one line wire on the primary side do not carry any current.

(*b*) In Fig. 8.43 (*b*), neutral wire on the primary side must be present in order to supply single-phase load between line and neutral in a star-star transformer.

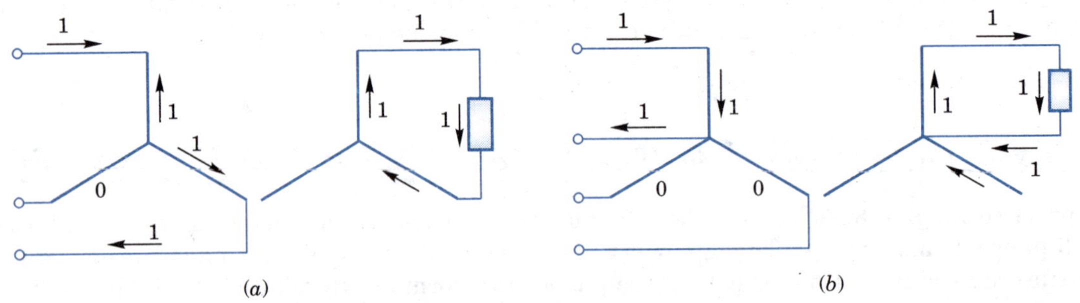

Fig. 8.43: Single-phase load on three-phase transformers.

(*c*) In Fig. 8.43 (*c*), one phase winding carries zero current and one line wire carries double the current as shown.

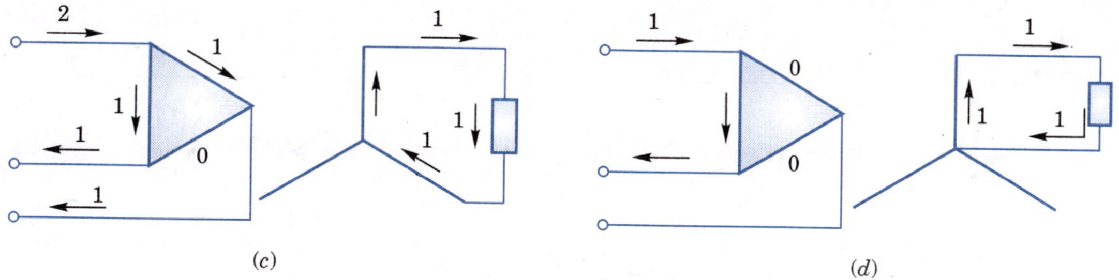

Fig. 8.43: Single-phase load on three-phase transformers.

(d) In Fig. 8.43 (d), two phase windings and one line wire carry zero current as shown.

(e) In Fig. 8.43 (e), let the magnitude of secondary current $I_{bc} = I_{ca}$ be equal to 1. For mmf balance, the secondary currents I_{bc}, I_{ca} cause the flow of primary currents $I_{CN} = 1$,

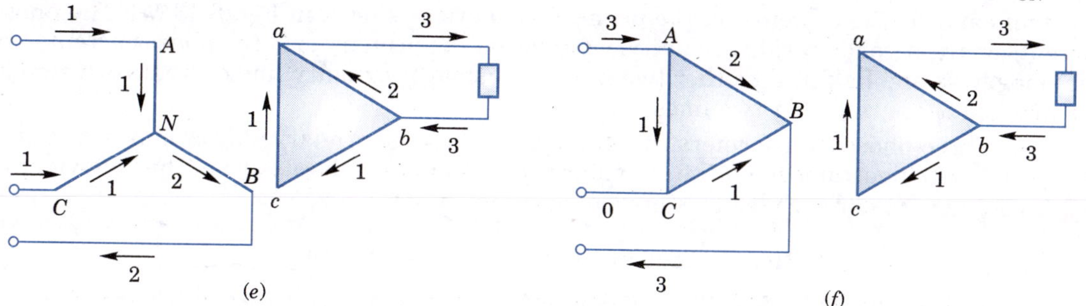

Fig. 8.43: Single-phase load on three-phase transformers.

$I_{AN} = 1$ respectively. Consequently $I_{NB} = I_{CN} + I_{AN} = 2$ and, therefore, $I_{ba} = 2$ for mmf balance. In this manner, the current distribution in the various phase windings is determined. On the primary side, one line and one phase winding have current of magnitude 2, whereas the other two lines and two phase windings have current of magnitude 1 in each.

(f) In Fig. 8.43 (f), the current distribution in the delta-delta can be determined as follows:

On the secondary side, *ba* is in parallel with the series combination of *bc* and *ca*.

∴ $$z_{ba} I_{ba} = (z_{bc} + z_{ca})\, I_{bca}$$

Here $$I_{bca} = I_{bc} = I_{ca}$$

∴ $$I_{bca} = \frac{z_{ba}}{z_{bc} + z_{ca}} I_{ba}$$

If the transformer leakage impedances are equal, *i.e.*, $z_{ba} = z_{bc} = z_{ca}$, then

$$I_{bca} = \frac{1}{2} I_{ba}.$$

If $I_{ba} = 2$, then $I_{bca} = 1$ and $I_{bc} = I_{ca} = 1$.

Now mark $I_{bc} = I_{ca} = 1$ and $I_{ba} = 2$ on the seconadary side. Mmf balance gives $I_{AC} = I_{CB} = 1$ and $I_{AB} = 2$. Note that one primary line carries zero current.

(g) In a star/zigzag transformer, the current distribution is shown in Fig. 8.43 (g), for a line to neutral load on the secondary side. Note that, for mmf balance, the primary current is half of that on the secondary side.

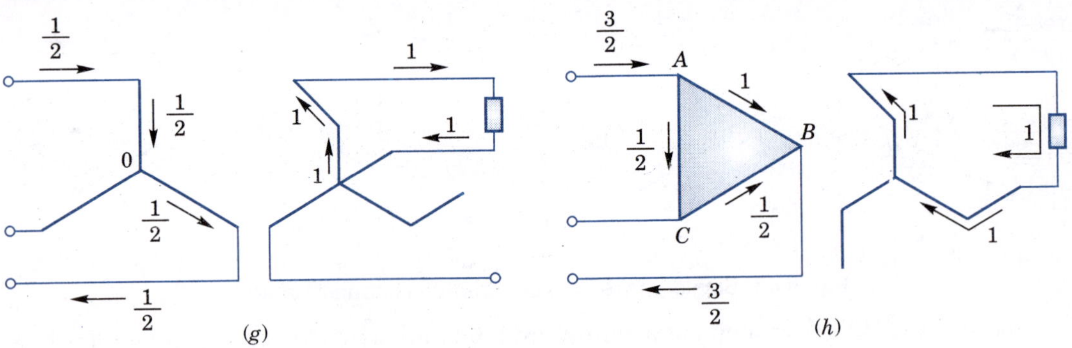

Fig. 8.43: Single-phase load on 3-phase transformers.

(*h*) For delta/zigzag connection, the load is assumed between the two secondary lines. For mmf balance, the currents on the primary side are as shown in Fig. 8.43 (*h*). The phase currents on the secondary side are unity, whereas on the primary side the phase currents are 1 in one phase and half in the other two phases as shown. Primary line currents are zero in one line and 3/2 in the other two lines.

(*i*) Three-phase transformers without a neutral on the primary may or may not be able to supply line to neutral load on the secondary side. A detailed discussion of the behaviour of *Yy* transformers under such loads is presented below in Art. 8.5.2.

8.5.2 Single-phase Line to Neutral Load on Three-phase Transformers

As stated before, single-phase line to neutral load causes worst unbalanced loading of three-phase transformers. In this section of the article, this unbalanced loading is considered for

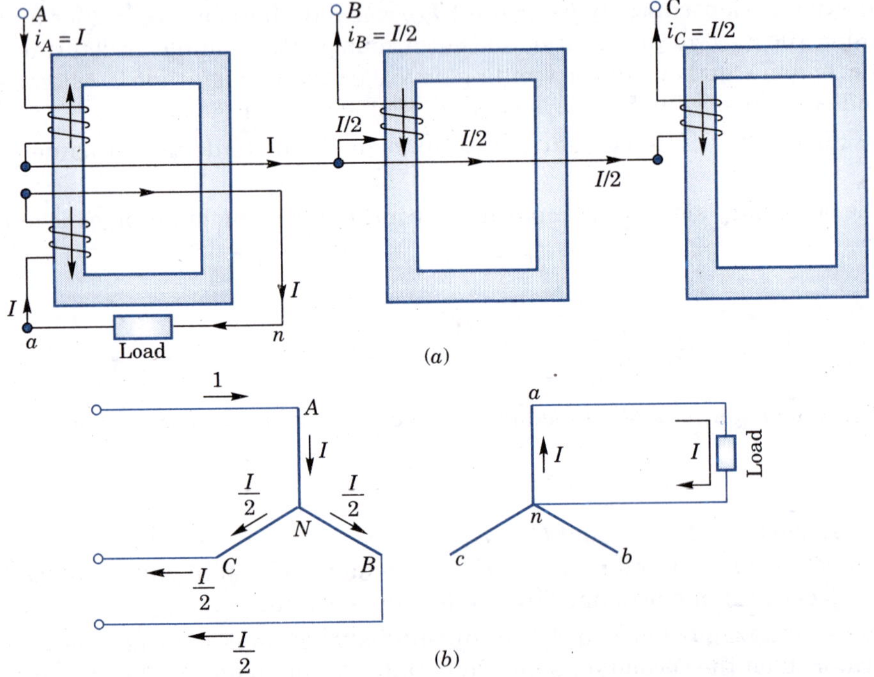

Fig. 8.44: Single-phase load between line to neutral on *Yy* bank without a neutral.

three-phase transformers with separate magnetic circuits then for those having interlinked magnetic circuits.

(a) **Bank of three-phase transformers.** Fig. 8.44 illustrates a *Yy* bank without a neutral on the primary side. A line to neutral load on the secondary of phase *A* causes a current *I* to flow through the secondary phase and the load as shown. For phase turns ratio equal to unity, a current *I* must flow in the primary of phase *A*, in order to balance the mmf in the corresponding secondary phase. This can also be ascertained by referring to Fig. 8.44 *(a)*. For the loaded phase *A*, the mmfs produced by secondary current *I* and primary current i_A must oppose each other and in view of this,

$$[i_A N \text{ (upward mmf)} - IN \text{ (downward mmf)}] = 0$$

or $$i_A = I$$

Further note that the primary current i_A in phase *A* must return to the source through the primary phases *B* and *C*. In other words, primary phases *B* and *C* are forced to carry a current *I*/2 as shown in Fig. 8.44. The corresponding secondaries of phases *B* and *C*, however, can't carry any compensating current, because these are open circuited. Therefore, the currents of magnitude *I*/2 in the primaries of phases *B* and *C* must be exciting currents* and consequently the cores of transformers *B* and *C* may get saturated considerably if these currents are of sufficient magnitude. As a result of it, abnormally high voltages ($= \frac{1}{2} I \times$ exciting impedance** of phase *B* or *C*) are developed across phases *B* and *C*. Therefore, the line to neutral voltages become unbalanced as illustrated in Fig. 8.44 *(c)*. In this figure, triangle *ABC* represents the primary line voltages and *N* is the neutral of both the primary and secondary emfs. Since the transformer is assumed to be connected to a large power source, the supply voltage triangle *ABC* remains uneffected. It is only the neutral that is effected. The voltage across phase *A* collapses from V_{AN} to $V_{AN'}$, whereas that across identical phases *B*, *C* rises from V_{BN}, V_{CN} to $V_{BN'}$, $V_{CN'}$ respectively. If *I*/2, in phase *B* or *C*, is less than or equal to their exciting currents, then phase voltages remain balanced. This means that single-phase load current equal to two times their exciting currents can be delivered without any collapse of the loaded phase voltage. Note that phasor diagram of Fig. 8.44 *(c)* is true only if both the transformers *B* and *C* have the same magnitude of exciting currents. In case transformer *B*, for example, has less exciting current (and therefore more exciting impedance) as compared to transformer *C*, then voltage developed across transformer *B* would be more than that across transformer *C* as shown in Fig. 8.44 *(d)*.

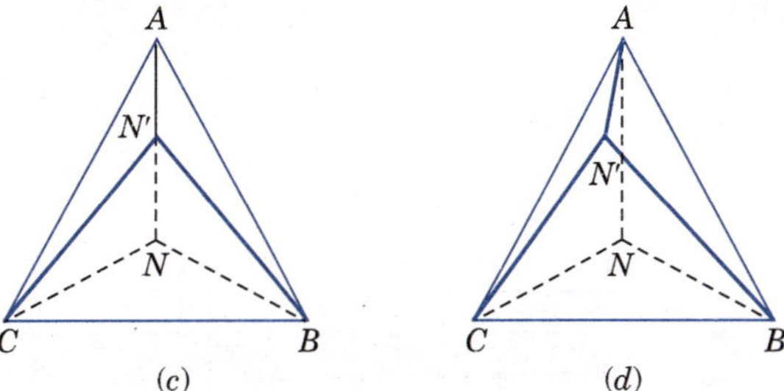

Fig. 8.44: Pertaining to line to neutral load of phase *A* of *Yy* bank.

In case of 3-phase variable ratio auto-transformers, the connection of single-phase load between any line and neutral also causes the collapse of loaded phase-voltage, because these transformers have their three-phase windings wound on three toroidal cores having

* An exciting current flows in one winding only and its mmf is not balanced by a current in any other winding.

** Exciting impedance, or shunt impedance, of a transformer is the resultant of R_c (core-loss resistance) and X_ϕ (magnetizing reactance) in parallel.

independent magnetic circuits. In view of this, whenever single-phase load is to be connected across a three-phase variable ratio transformer, line to line terminals should only be used.

(*b*) **Three-legged and five-legged three-phase transformers.** Figs. 8.45 (*a*) and (*b*) illustrate three-legged and five-legged transformers respectively. A single-phase line to neutral load is assumed to be connected across the secondary of phase *A*. Secondary phase current is designated by i_a as shown. As before, the secondary mmf i_aN must oppose the primary mmf i_AN in leg *A*. For the assumed directions of currents i_A, i_B, i_C; the magnetic flux in legs *A*, *B*, *C* is upwards as shown. Now traversing the magnetic circuits of legs *A* and *B* in both the Figs. 8.45 (*a*) and (*b*),

$$i_AN - i_BN - i_aN = 0 \quad \text{or} \quad i_A - i_B = i_a \qquad \text{...(8.3)}$$

For the magnetic circuits of legs *B* and *C* in both the Figs. 8.45 (*a*) and (*b*),

$$i_BN - i_CN = 0 \quad \text{or} \quad i_B = i_C \qquad \text{...(8.4)}$$

Since currents are flowing towards the isolated neutral,

$$i_A + i_B + i_C = 0$$

$$\therefore \qquad i_A = -(i_B + i_C) = -2i_B$$

or

$$i_B = -\frac{i_A}{2} \qquad \text{...(8.5)}$$

From Eqs. (8.3), (8.4) and (8.5),

$$i_A - \left(-\frac{i_A}{2}\right) = i_a \quad \text{or} \quad i_A = \frac{2}{3}i_a \qquad \text{...(8.6)}$$

and

$$i_B = i_C = -\frac{1}{3}i_a \qquad \text{...(8.7)}$$

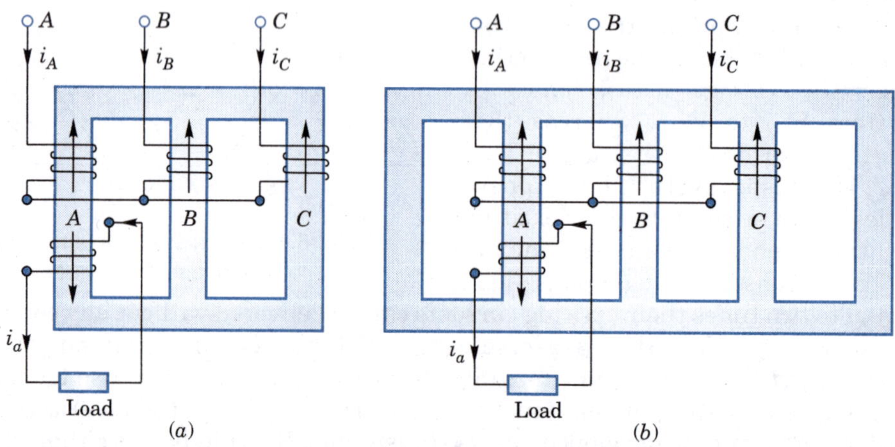

Fig. 8.45: Single-phase line to neutral load on three-phase (*a*) three-legged and (*b*) five-legged transformers.

In Eq. (8.7), i_B and i_C turn out to be negative, this means that the core flux set up by currents i_B and i_C in legs *B* and *C* respectively is opposite to that shown in Figs. 8.45 (*a*) and (*b*); *i.e.*, it is downward as shown in Figs. 8.45 (*c*) and (*d*) at the instant considered. At the same instant, the core flux set up in leg *A* is also downward, because i_A $(= \frac{2}{3} i_a)$ is less than secondary current i_a. In other words, the downward core flux in all the three legs *A*, *B*, *C* has the same magnitude as it is produced by the same mmf $\frac{1}{3} i_a N$. The nature of this flux is that of third-harmonic flux. Let this unbalanced flux be ϕ_0. In three-lagged transformer, ϕ_0, *i.e.* the third harmonic flux has to complete its magnetic path largely through air of high reluctance as shown in Fig. 8.45 (*c*). In Figs. 8.45 (*c*) and (*d*), the phase windings are not shown for the sake of clarity. Since the reluctance offered to unbalanced flux in Fig. 8.45 (*c*) is large, the flux ϕ_0 is relatively small. But in five-legged transformer, the conditions are different. Examination of Fig. 8.45 (*d*) reveals that the unbalanced flux completes its return path through low reluctance two outer legs and consequently flux ϕ_0 is quite large. It can therefore be concluded from above that for a given value of secondary current i_a, the unbalanced flux ϕ_0 is quite small in three-legged transformer of Fig. 8.45 (*c*) and is quite large in five-legged transformer of Fig. 8.45 (*d*). This inequality in flux ϕ_0 affects the operation of three-legged and five-legged transformers as follows.

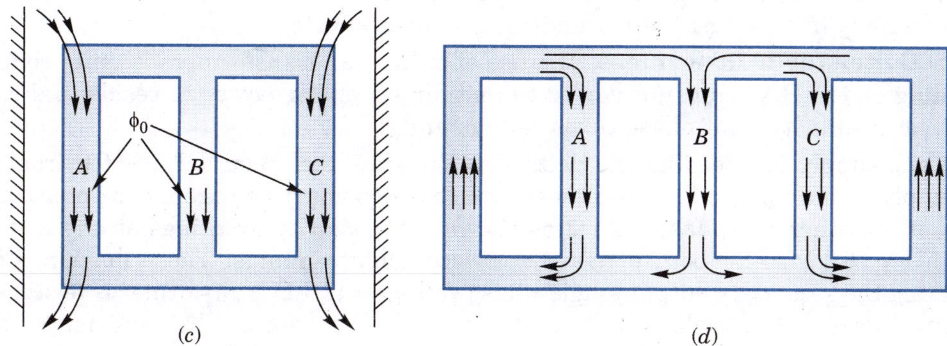

Fig. 8.45: Path of the unbalanced magnetic flux in (*a*) three-legged and (*b*) five-legged transformers.

Assume that single-phase load on the secondary side of phase A is inductive in nature. This means that the secondary current I_a would lag phase voltage V_{NA} by an angle θ as shown in Fig. 8.46. Here cos θ is the *pf* of the inductive load. The unbalanced flux ϕ_0, produced by the resultant mmf $\frac{1}{3} I_a N$ in leg A, is in phase with current I_a (neglecting hysteresis). This flux ϕ_0 induces in each phase an emf E_0 lagging ϕ_0 by 90°. Since the potentials of points A, B, C can't change, the neutral gets shifted. In three-lagged core type transformer of Fig. 8.45 (*c*), the unbalanced flux ϕ_0 and therefore E_0 are relatively small; as a result of it, the shift of the neutral from position N to N' is rather small and the phase voltages $V_{AN'}$, $V_{BN'}$, $V_{CN'}$ remain practically balanced as shown in Fig. 8.46 (*a*). In five-legged transformer of Fig. 8.45 (*d*), the unbalanced flux ϕ_0 and therefore E_0 are quite large, as a consequence of it, the shift of the neutral from position N to N' is appreciable and the phase

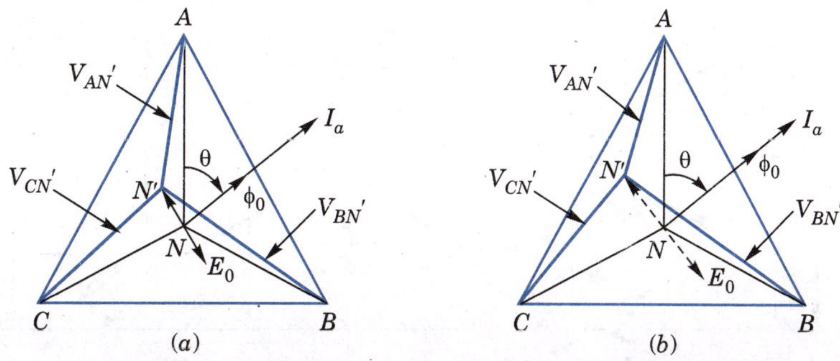

Fig. 8.46: Effect of single-phase line to neutral load on three-phase (*a*) three-legged and (*b*) five-legged transformers.

voltages V_{AN}', V_{BN}', V_{CN}' are considerably unbalanced as shown in Fig. 8.46 (*b*). This figure also shows that voltage of the loaded phase is reduced considerably but that for other phases *B* and *C* is increased to more than their rated values, which is an undesirable phenomenon.

It can be concluded from the foregoing that transformers with independent magnetic circuits, like three-phase banks, five-legged and shell-type transformers should not be connected in *Yy*. But a three legged core type transformer can be connected in *Yy* without neutral and a single-phase line to neutral load, equal to several percent of its three-phase rating, can be delivered without seriously unbalancing the phase voltages.

8.5.3 Single-phasing in 3-phase Transformers

The object of this section of the article is to discuss the behaviour of 3-phase transformers when one supply line feeding their primaries gets disconnected.

(*a*) **Delta-star transformers.** The use of delta-star transformers is quite common at the sending end of H.V. transmission lines and for supplying power to residential colonies. Assume, for simplicity, that phase turns ratio is unity.

If one supply line feeding the delta gets disconnected, then delta is fed from single-phase supply of line voltage *V*. Under these conditions, primary voltage for one phase is *V* and for each of the other two phases is *V*/2 as shown. The polarity markings at any instant are shown in Fig. 8.47 (*a*) for both primary and secondary windings. These markings help in determining the secondary output single-phase voltages. If this transformer is feeding power to a colony, then only one feeder supplies rated voltage *V* between one line and neutral and the other two have output voltage of *V*/2 between the neutral and each of the remaining two lines. The secondary line voltages are single-phase voltages of magnitude 1.5 V, 1.5 V and zero, instead of 3-phase balanced line to line voltages of magnitude 1.732 V.

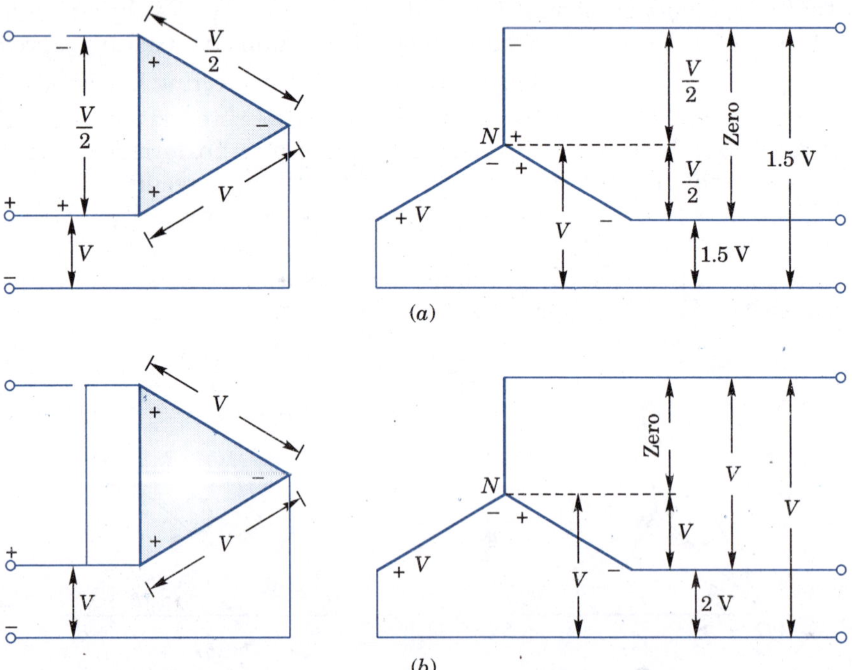

Fig. 8.47: Single-phasing in Dy transformers.

When one supply line gets disconnected, sometimes the connections of the primary delta are made in such a manner that voltage across one primary phase is reduced to zero as shown in Fig. 8.47 (*b*). In this case, two feeders supply rated line to neutral voltage V to the consumers, whereas the third feeder output voltage is zero. The transformer polarities at any instant are as shown. The secondary line voltages are single-phase and their magnitudes are V, V, $2V$ instead of 3-phase balanced line to line voltage of 1.732 V.

(*b*) **Star-delta transformers.** A star-delta transformer is used at the receiving end of a H.V. transmission line for stepping down the voltage. Fig. 8.47 (*c*) shows a *Yd* transformer fed from 3-wire three-phase supply. In case one supply line gets disconnected, the secondary line voltages become single phase with their magnitudes equal to $V/2$, $V/2$, 0 as shown in Fig. 8.47 (*c*), instead of 0.578 V for 3-phase balanced voltages. The polarity markings are also depicted in this figure and these help in determining the output secondary voltages.

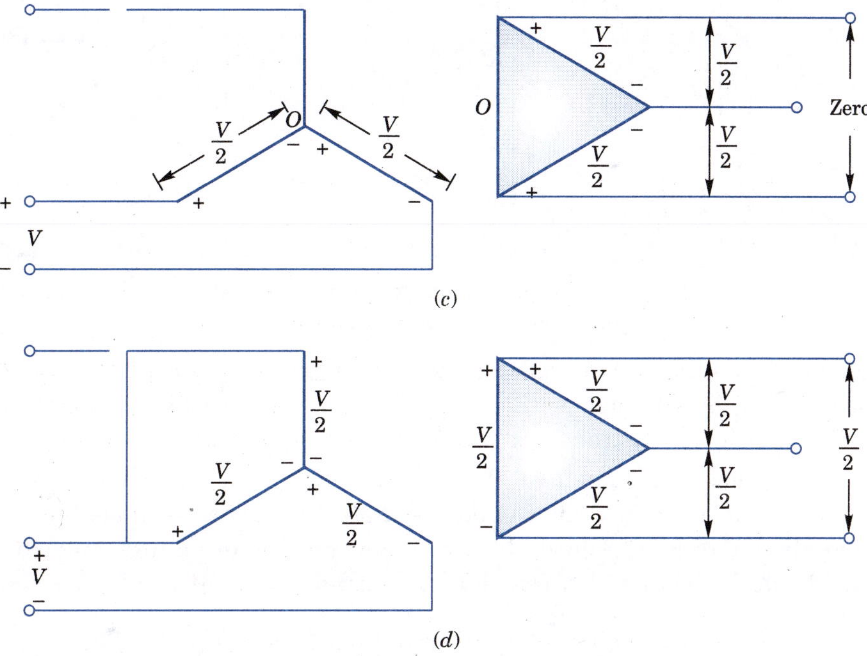

Fig. 8.47: Single-phasing in *Yd* transformers.

In case the disconnnected tranformer wire is connected with live terminal on primary side as shown in Fig. 8.47 (*d*), voltages of primary phase winding are reduced to $V/2$. The output line voltages are now $V/2$ amongst all the three terminals as shown.

8.5.4 Effect of Using Tertiary Winding

If the third (or tertiary) winding is used in *Yy* transformers having separate magnetic circuits, then the single-phase load between line to neutral can be supplied. In order to prove this, let the single-phase load current in the secondary of phase A be $I_2 = I$ as shown in Fig. 8.48. Current I_1 in the primary of phase A, opposes I_2 in the secondary and this current I_1 divides equally in phase B and C, *i.e.*, $I_B = I_C = \frac{1}{2} I_1$. Current $I_1/2$ in the primary of phase B causes the appearance of current I_3 in the tertiary of phase B (secondary of phase B can't carry any current because it is open), so that mmf balance is achieved. Note that I_3 in the tertiary of phase B must oppose $I_1/2$ in the primary of phase B. Similarly, current $I_1/2$ in the primary of phase C forces the tertiary of phase C to carry I_3 but in opposite direction as shown in Fig. 8.48. Consequently, the current in the tertiary of phase A must be in the direction of I_3 *i.e.,* downward as shown. For unity turns ratio, the examination of Fig. 8.48 reveals that for phase A,

Primary mmf + Tertiary mmf = secondary mmf

or $$I_1 + I_3 = I_2 = I \quad \text{...(8.8)}$$

For phase B, $\dfrac{I_1}{2} = I_3$ and for phase C, $\dfrac{I_1}{2} = I_3$, $I_1 = 2I_3$

From Eq. (8.8), $2I_3 + I_3 = I$ or $I_3 = \dfrac{1}{3}I$ and $I_1 = \dfrac{2}{3}I$.

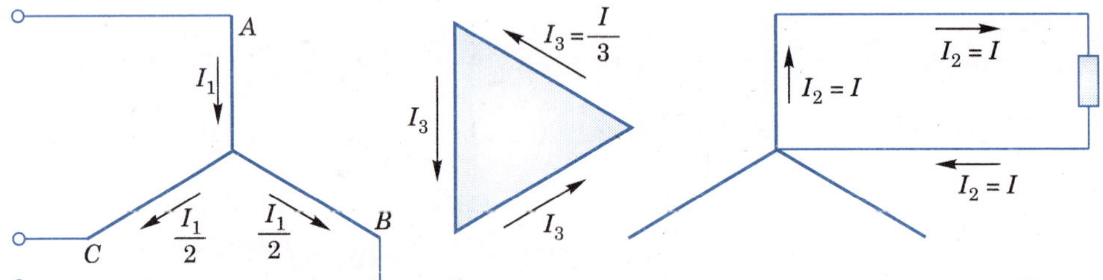

Fig. 8.48: Single-phase load between line to neutral on *Yy* transformer with independent magnetic circuit but having a tertiary in dalta.

Since there is complete mmf balance, the single-phase load between line to neutral of *Yy* transformers can be supplied without any collapse of the voltage, provided a tertiary winding in delta is used in *Yy* transformers having separate magnetic circuits.

For a single-phase line to neutral short circuit, the tertiary winding permits the flow of large fault currents as explained above and the protective devices can operate. The tertiary winding currents due to line to neutral short circuit may be quite high and, therefore, this winding must be designed to withstand all these currents without getting overheated.

Example 8.13. *Single-phase loads are connected across the secondaries of three-phase transformers as shown in Fig. 8.49. If single phase load, in each case, is VI voltamperes, then for equal primary and secondary line voltages, determine the currents in the phase windings and in the primary lines. Neglect the transformer exciting currents.*

Solution. (*a*) In Fig. 8.49 (*a*), the load current is I for load voltameres equal to VI. In this figure, the per phase secondary load is $V/\sqrt{3} \cdot I$ voltamperes. According to the transformer principle, primary per phase voltamperes VI_1 = secondary per phase voltamperes, $V/\sqrt{3} \cdot I$. This gives primary phase current as $1/\sqrt{3}\ I = 0.577I$. Similarly, for the other phase, the primary current is $0.577I$ as shown in Fig. 8.50 (*a*). Since these currents are single-phase currents, one primary line current is $1.154I$ and the other two line currents are $0.577I$ as shown.

(*b*) In Fig. 8.49 (*b*), line to neutral secondary voltage is $V/\sqrt{3}$. Since load is connected across line to neutral, the load current is $\sqrt{3}I$ so that load voltamperes are $\sqrt{3}I \times V/\sqrt{3} = VI$ as given in this example. For secondary zigzag, voltage of each half section is $V/3$. For equal

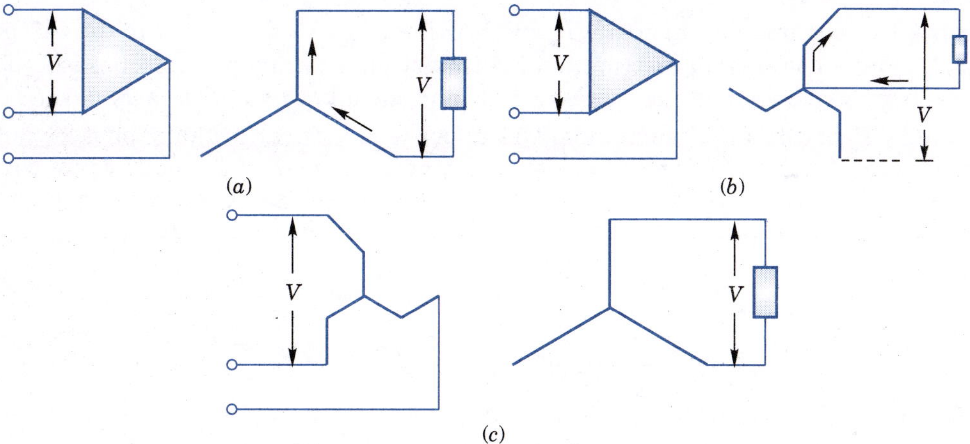

Fig. 8.49: Pertaining to Example 8.13.

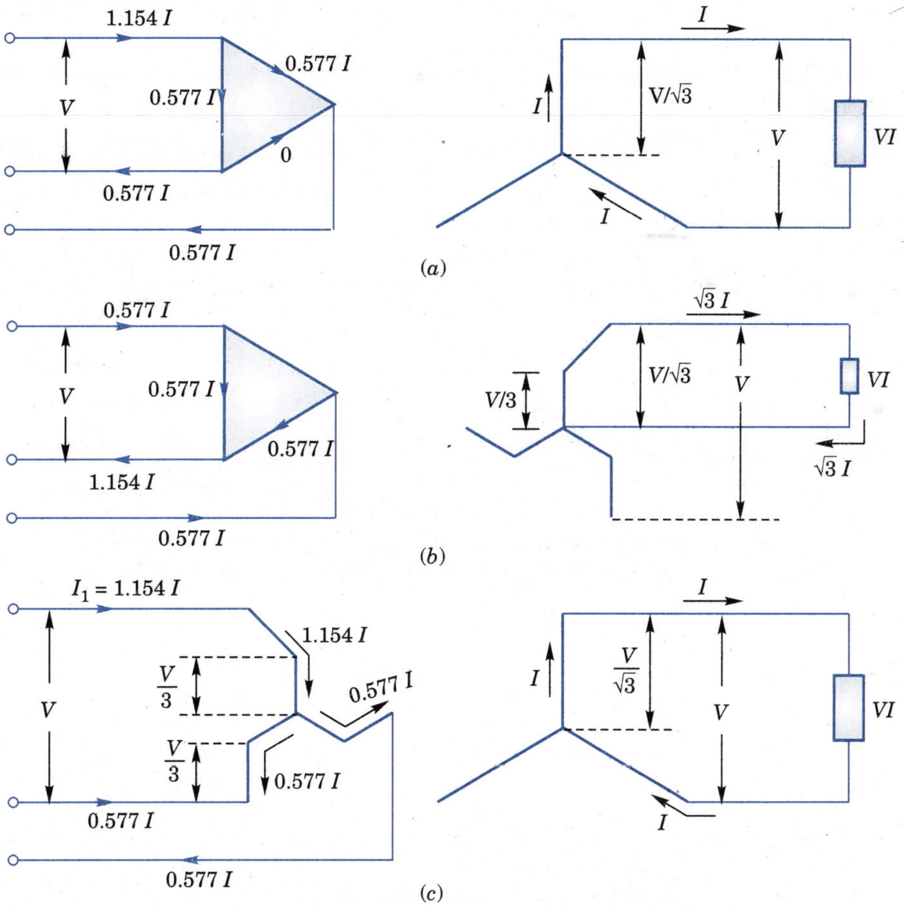

Fig. 8.50: Pertaining to the solution of Example 8.13.

primary and secondary voltamperes, $VI_1 = V/3(\sqrt{3}I)$ or $I_1 = 1/\sqrt{3} = 0.577I$ in the two primary phases as shown. The current distribution in primary phase windings and lines is as depicted in Fig. 8.50 (*b*). One primary line carries $1.154I$ and the other two lines carry $0.577I$.

(*c*) Let I_1 be the input current in the upper-half vertical primary phase winding as shown in Fig. 8.50 (*c*). This current divides equally at the primary star point so that current in the lower-half vertical primary winding is $\frac{1}{2} I_1$. Now, for phase windings drawn vertical in Fig. 8.50 (*c*), per-phase primary voltampers = per-phase secondary voltamperes

$$\therefore \qquad \frac{V}{3} \cdot I_1 + \frac{V}{3} \cdot \frac{I_1}{2} = \frac{V}{\sqrt{3}} \cdot I$$

$$\frac{V}{3} I_1 \left[1 + \frac{1}{2}\right] = \frac{V}{\sqrt{3}} I \quad \text{or} \quad I_1 = \frac{2}{\sqrt{3}} I = 1.154\, I$$

Therefore, current in the upper-vertical half is $1.154\, I$ and in the lower-vertical half is $\frac{1.154}{2} I = 0.577\, I$ as shown in Fig. 8.50 (*c*).

Same is done to the other primary phase winding parallel to the loaded secondary phase winding. Note that both half sections of the primary phase winding, pertaining to the unloaded secondary phase winding, are carrying current in opposite directions so that net mmf is zero. In Fig. 8.50 (*c*), both phase and line currents in the primary are shown.

Example 8.14. *A delta-star, 6.6/0.4 kV bank of three identical single phase transformers supplies a three-phase balanced load of 600 kVA at 0.8 p.f. lagging and a single-phase load of 80 kW at unity p.f. between one line and neutral. Determine the magnitude of currents in each primary phase winding and in each input line. Mark thier values in a relevant circuit diagram. Ignore internal voltage drops and their no-load current.*

Solution. Single-phase load is assumed to be connected across the secondary phase *a* as shown in Fig. 8.51.

$$\text{Secondary phase voltage} = \frac{400}{\sqrt{3}} = 231 \text{ V}$$

Current in the secondary phase a due to single-phase load

$$= I_{as} = \frac{80{,}000}{231 \times 1} = 346.32 \text{ A.}$$

But $\qquad I_{bs} = I_{cs} = 0.$

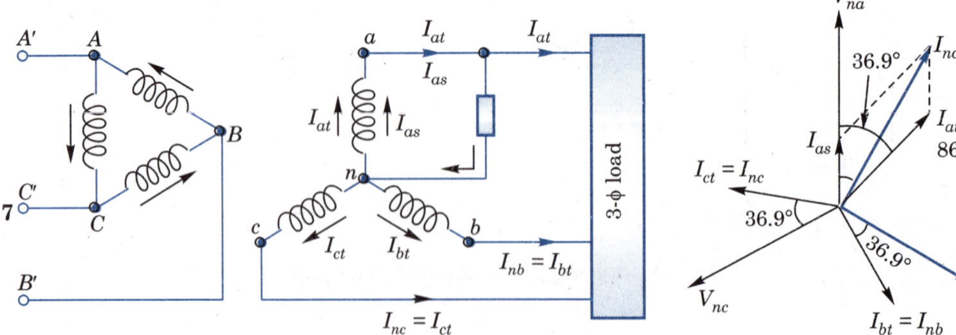

Fig. 8.51: Pertaining to Example 8.14.

Here subscripts s stands for the single-phase load. For three phase load, current in each secondary phase winding $= \dfrac{600}{\sqrt{3}(0.4)} = 866$ A.

The circuit and phasor diagrams for this example are illustrated in Fig. 8.51. With voltage V_{na} as reference phasor, the three phase currents can be expressed as follows :

$$\bar{I}_{at} = 866 \angle -36.9° \qquad [\because \ \theta = \cos^{-1}(0.8) = 36.9°]$$

$$\bar{I}_{bt} = 866 \angle -36.9° - 120° = 866 \angle -156.9°$$

$$\bar{I}_{ct} = 866 \angle -36.9° - 240° = 866 \angle -276.9°$$

Here subscript t is used to denote three phase load.

The single phase load current, with V_{na} as reference phasor, is $\bar{I}_{as} = 346.32 \angle 0°$. Also $\bar{I}_{bs} = \bar{I}_{cs} = 0$.

The currents in the secondary phase windings, due to the combined single-phase and three-phase loads, are given below.

$$\bar{I}_{na} = \bar{I}_{as} + \bar{I}_{at} = 346.32 \angle 0° + 866 \angle -36.9°$$
$$= 346.32 + j0 + 866\,(0.8 - j0.6) = 1039.12 - j519.6$$

$$\bar{I}_{nb} = 866 \angle -156.9° = 866\,(\cos 156.9° - j \sin 156.9°)$$
$$= -796.6 - j339.76$$

$$\bar{I}_{nc} = 866 \angle -276.9° = 866\,(\cos 276.9° - j \sin 276.9°)$$
$$= 104.04 + j859.73.$$

Turns ratio for each transformer $= \dfrac{6600}{400/\sqrt{3}} = 28.58.$

The currents on the primary side, obtained by referring to Fig. 8.51, are as follows :

$$\bar{I}_{BA} = \frac{1}{28.58}(\bar{I}_{nb}) = -27.87 - j11.89$$

$$\bar{I}_{CB} = \frac{1}{28.58}(\bar{I}_{nc}) = 3.64 + j30.08$$

$$\bar{I}_{AC} = \frac{1}{28.58}(\bar{I}_{na}) = 36.36 - j18.18$$

$\therefore$ $\quad I_{BA} = \sqrt{(27.87)^2 + (11.89)^2} = 30.30$ A.

Similarly, $\quad I_{CB} = 30.30$ A and $I_{AC} = 40.65$ A.

The primary line currents are,

$$\bar{I}_{A'A} = \bar{I}_{AC} - \bar{I}_{BA} = 36.36 - j18.18 + 27.87 + j11.89 = 64.23 - j6.29$$

$\therefore$ $\quad \bar{I}_{A'A} = \sqrt{(64.23)^2 + (6.29)^2} = 64.54$ A.

$$\bar{I}_{B'B} = \bar{I}_{BA} - \bar{I}_{CB} = -27.87 - j11.89 - 3.64 - j30.08 = -31.51 - j41.97$$

$\therefore$ $\quad I_{B'B} = 52.48$ A

$$\bar{I}_{C'C} = \bar{I}_{CB} - \bar{I}_{AC} = 3.64 + j30.08 - 36.36 + j18.18 = 32.72 + j48.26$$

$\therefore \qquad I_{C'C} = 58.31$ A.

Check. The currents I_{CB} and I_{BA} should be equal to 866/28.58 = 30.30 A and further current $I_{B'B}$ must be equal to $\sqrt{3} \times 30.2 = 52.48$ A. These values agree with those calculated above.

Example 8.15. *A 11/0.4 kV star-delta transformer is connected to 3-phase balanced load of 300 kVA at unity p.f. and also to a single-phase load of 60 kVA at unity p.f. Calculate the values of the currents on the primary star. The no-load current and the internal leakage impedance drops are neglected.*

Solution. Fig. 8.52 illustrates the circuit and phasor diagrams for this example, where subscripts *s* and *t* denote single-phase and three-phase loads respectively.

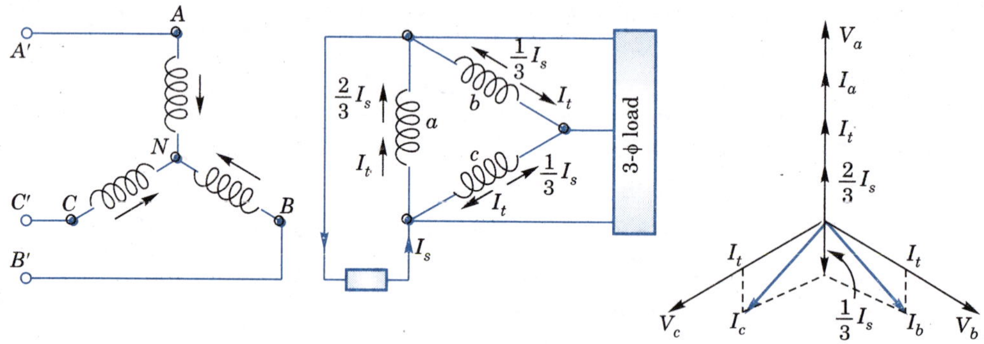

Fig. 8.52: Pertaining to Example 8.15.

Current due to single-phase load, $I_s = \dfrac{60{,}000}{400} = 150$ A.

Current I_s divides in the three-phase delta winding as illustrated in Fig. 8.52. For this refer to Fig. 8.43 (*e*). The currents $\frac{2}{3}\,I_s$ and I_t in secondary phase *a* must flow in the same direction, because the single-phase load is connected across this phase.

Current in secondary phase winding due to 3-phase load. $I_t = \dfrac{300}{3(0.4)} = 250$ A.

From the phasor diagram, the currents in the secondary phase winding *a* are seen to be in the same phase.

$$\therefore \qquad I_a = I_t + \tfrac{2}{3} I_s = 250 + \tfrac{2}{3}(150) = 350 \text{ A.}$$

The phasor and circuit diagrams reveal that the currents in phase windings *b* and *c* are equal to the phasor difference of I_t and $\frac{1}{3}$.

$$\therefore \qquad \bar{I}_b = \bar{I}_c = \bar{I}_t - \tfrac{1}{3}\bar{I}_s .$$

As per the above expression, $\frac{1}{3}I_s$ is reversed and added to I_t to obtain I_b and I_c. Since the angle between I_t and $\frac{1}{3}I_s$ is 60°, the magnitude of currents I_b and I_c is given by

$$I_b = I_c = \sqrt{I_t^2 + \left(\frac{1}{3}I_s\right)^2 + 2(I_t)\left(\frac{1}{3}I_s\right)\cos 60^\circ}$$

$$= \sqrt{(250)^2 + (50)^2 + 2(250)\,(50)\frac{1}{2}} = 278.4 \text{ A.}$$

$$\text{Turns ratio for each phase} = \frac{11{,}000}{\sqrt{3} \times 400} = 15.88$$

$\therefore$ The currents on the primary side are

$$I_{A'A} = I_{AN} = \frac{1}{15.88}(I_a) = \frac{1}{15.88}(350) = 22.4 \text{ A.}$$

$$I_{B'B} = I_{BN} = \frac{1}{15.88}(I_b) = \frac{1}{15.88}(278.4) = 17.53 \text{ A}$$

$$I_{C'C} = I_{CN} = \frac{1}{15.88}(I_c) = 17.53 \text{ A.}$$

Example 8.16. *Three similar single phase transformers have the primary and secondary windings connected in star and the tertiary winding in delta. In each transfomer, secondary and tertiary turns are equal and ratio of primary to secondary turns is 2. The primary is fed at rated voltage by three wires.*

(a) A single-phase load, taking 24 A at unity p.f., is connected between one line and neutral of the secondary. Calculate the currents in each winding of the three transformers.

(b) In addition to the single-phase load of part (a), the secondary is now connected to a 3-phase balanced load requiring a line current of 40 A at 0.8 p.f. lag. Determine the currents in each winding of the three transformers.

Solution. (*a*) For a single-phase load between one line and neutral, the secondary mmf I_2N_2 set up by $I_2 = 24$ A, must be balanced by the combined action of primary mmf I_1N_1 and tertiary mmf I_3N_3 as shown in Fig. 8.53 (*a*). In view of this,

$$I_1N_1 + I_3N_3 = I_2N_2 \quad \text{or} \quad I_1 + I_3\frac{N_3}{N_1} = I_2\frac{N_2}{N_1}$$

Here $\quad \dfrac{N_1}{N_2} = \dfrac{N_1}{N_3} = 2$

$$\therefore \quad I_1 + \frac{I_3}{2} = I_2\left(\frac{1}{2}\right) = 24\left(\frac{1}{2}\right) = 12 \qquad \text{...(8.9)}$$

Current I_1 in phase A must divide equally in phases B and C. Since secondary phase b cannot carry any current, the mmf set up by primary phase B must be balanced by a current I_3 in the corresponding tertiary phase. Therefore, for mmf balance.

Primary mmf, $\dfrac{I_1}{2}N_1 = \text{tertiary mmf}, I_3N_3 \quad \text{or} \quad I_1 = 2I_3\dfrac{N_3}{N_1} = I_3.$

From Eq. (8.9), $I_3 + \dfrac{I_3}{2} = 12 \quad \text{or} \quad I_3 = 8 \text{ A}$

$$\therefore \quad I_1 = I_3 = 8 \text{ A.}$$

(*b*) When the secondary, in addition to the single-phase load of 24 A, carries a 3-phase balanced load, then the tertiary winding currents remain uneffected. An examination of Fig. 8.53 (*a*) reveals that secondary current I_{na} is equal to the phasor sum of 24 A at unity p.f. and 40 A at 0.8 p.f. lagging. Therefore, with V_{na} as reference,

$$\bar{I}_{na} = 24\angle 0° + 40\angle -36.9°$$

$$= 24 + j0° + 32 - j24 = 56 - j24$$

$$\therefore \quad I_{na} = \sqrt{(56)^2 + (24)^2} = 60.93 \text{ A}, \quad I_{nb} = I_{nc} = 40 \text{ A.}$$

Three-phase balanced current of 40 A in the secondary winding causes a balanced current of $I'_1 = 20$ A in the primary winding for the required mmf balance. Fig. 8.53 (*a*) reveals that I_{AN} is the phasor sum of 8 A at unity pf and 20 A at pf of 0.8 lagging.

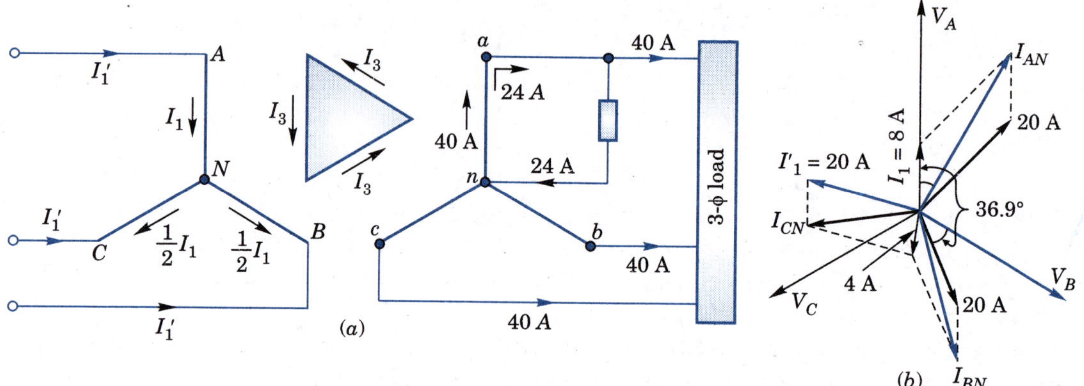

Fig. 8.53: Pertaining to Example 8.16.

$$\therefore \quad \bar{I}_{AN} = 8\angle 0° + 20\angle -36.9° = 8 + j0 + 16 - j12 = 24 - j12$$

$$\therefore \quad I_{AN} = \sqrt{(24)^2 + (12)^2} = 26.83 \text{ A.}$$

It is seen from Fig. 8.53 (*a*) that in phases *B* and *C*, I'_1 and $\frac{1}{2}I_1$ oppose each other, therefore, $I_{BN} = I_{CN} = I'_1 - \frac{1}{2}I_1$. This means that $I_1/2$ must be reversed and added to I'_1 to get I_{BN} and I_{CN}. This is illustrated in Fig. 8.53 (*b*).

For I_{CN}, the angle between 20 A and 4 A is 60° + 36.9° = 96.9°

$$\therefore \quad I_{CN} = \sqrt{20^2 + 4^2 + 2 \times 20 \times 4 \cos 96.9°} = 19.92 \text{ A.}$$

Similarly $$I_{BN} = \sqrt{20^2 + 4^2 + 2 \times 20 \times 4 \cos (60 - 36.9°)} = 23.73 \text{ A.}$$

Example 8.17. *Fig. 8.54 (a) shows a Δ-Y connected three-phase distribution transformer used to step down the voltage from 11000 V to 415 V line-to-line. It has two switches S_1 and S_2. Under normal conditions, S_1 is closed and S_2 is open. Under certain special conditions, S_1 is open and S_2 is closed. In such a case, the magnitude of the voltage across the LV terminals a and c is*

(a) 240 V *(b) 480 V* *(c) 415 V* *(d) 0 V* [GATE 2003]

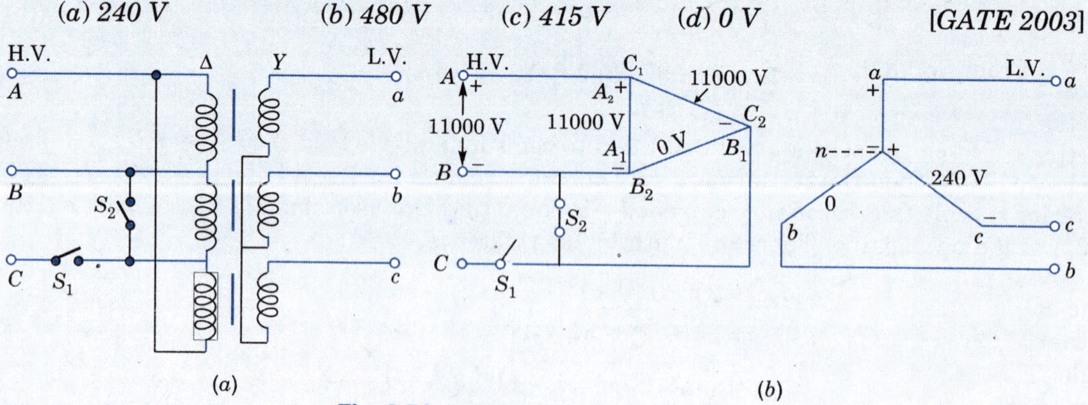

Fig. 8.54: Pertaining to Example 8.17.

Solution. Per-phase primary voltage = 11000 V

$$\text{Per-phase secondary voltage} = \frac{415}{\sqrt{3}} = 240 \text{ V}$$

Such problems can be solved more conviniently by drawing the primary and secondary windings in star or delta as the case may be. So here, with S_1 open and S_2 closed, Fig. 8.54 (*a*) gets modified to that shown in Fig. 8.54 (*b*).

Here single-phase voltage of V_{AB} = 11000 V appears as $V_{A2A1} = V_{C2C1}$ = 11000 V with $V_{B2B1} = 0$. Terminal A_2 has positive polarity whereas A_1 has negative polarity on primary side. Therefore, secondary winding *an*, parallel to A_2A_1, has secondary voltage v_{an} = 240 V with terminals *a* positive and *n* negative. Similarly, secondary voltage v_{cn} = 240 V with polarities as shown in Fig. 8.54 (*b*). Voltage $V_{B2B1} = V_{bn} = 0$.

Voltage across L.V. terminals *a* and *c* is

$$v_{ac} = v_{an} + v_{nc} = -240 - 240 = -480 \text{ V}$$

Thus, magnitude of voltage across L.V. terminals *a* and *c* is 480 V. $\therefore$ **Ans.** (*b*)

8.6 OPEN-DELTA OR V-CONNECTION

When a three-phase transformer bank, connected in delta/delta, supplies three-phase balanced load, then each transformer carries one third of the total load as in any symmetrical arrangement of connections. Any one transformer, if accidently damaged due to some reason or the other, can be removed and three-phase power can still be supplied, though at a reduced level. The resulting connection obtained, after the removal of one transformer from *Dd* connection, is called *open-delta* or *V-connection* as shown in Fig. 8.55 (*a*).

The supply mains *A′B′C′* are assumed to form a three-phase symmetrical system. Therefore, the phasor sum of the line to line supply voltages, taken in a cyclic order, must be zero, *i.e.*,

$$\overline{V}_{A'B'} + \overline{V}_{B'C'} + \overline{V}_{C'A'} = 0.$$

The supply terminals *A′B′C′* are directly connected to the transformer terminals *ABC* as shown in Fig. 8.55 (*a*). Therefore, the above voltage expression can also be written in terms of the primary phase voltage of the transformer as

$$\overline{V}_{AB} + \overline{V}_{BC} + \overline{V}_{CA} = 0 \qquad \text{...(8.10)}$$

As per Eq. (8.10), the phasors representing the line or phase voltages V_{AB}, V_{BC}, V_{CA} can be drawn in the form of an equilateral triangle as shown in Fig. 8.55 (*b*). The secondary line voltages V_{bc} and V_{ca} are directly available at the transformer secondary terminals *bc* and *ca* respectively. At no-load, voltages V_{bc} and V_{ca} are in phase with voltages V_{BC} and V_{CA} respectively and their magnitudes are given by

$$\frac{V_{bc}}{V_{BC}} = \frac{V_{ca}}{V_{CA}} = \frac{\text{Secondary phase turns}}{\text{Primary phase turns}}$$

The secondary line voltages V_{bc} and V_{ca} are shown by solid lines in Fig. 8.55 (*c*). The voltage across the open-delta terminals *ab* is indicated in Fig. 8.55 (*c*) by the dotted line V_{ab}. Note that the secondary line voltage V_{ab} forms the closing side of the secondary line-voltage triangle. This shows that the secondary line-voltage triangle is similar to the primary line-voltage triangle and it is almost correct to write.

$$\overline{V}_{ab} + \overline{V}_{bc} + \overline{V}_{ca} = 0 \qquad ...(8.11)$$

Hence, two transformers in open-delta can be used to supply 3-phase power, though at a reduced load capacity.

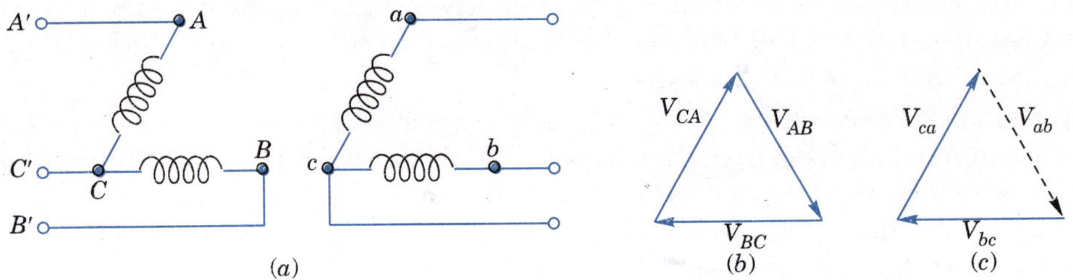

Fig. 8.55: (*a*) Transformers connected in open delta. Phasor diagram for (*b*) Primary line voltages and (*c*) Secondary line voltages.

The voltage across the open-delta terminals *ab* can be found with the help of Eq. (8.11).

$$\therefore \qquad \overline{V}_{ab} = -(\overline{V}_{bc} + \overline{V}_{ca}).$$

For equal secondary-line voltages, let $V_{bc} = V_{ca} = V$. Then, with V_{ca} as reference, Fig. 8.55 (*c*) shows that

$$\overline{V}_{ca} = V \angle 0° \quad \text{and} \quad \overline{V}_{bc} = V \angle 120°$$

$$\therefore \qquad \overline{V}_{ab} = -[V \angle 120° + V \angle 0°]$$

$$= -[V(\cos 120 + j \sin 120°) + V]$$

$$= -V[-\frac{1}{2} + j0.866 + 1] = V\left[-\frac{1}{2} - j0.866\right] = V \angle -120°$$

It is seen from above that V_{ab} is equal in magnitude to the other secondary voltages and is displaced from both V_{bc} and V_{ca} by 120°. This shows that at no load, the secondary line voltages form a balanced 3-phase system of voltages.

kVA delivered by open delta. Let the rated phase voltage and rated phase current be V_{ph} and I_{ph} respectively, for each of the three transformer secondaries. When these are connected in closed delta then

Line voltage, $\qquad V_l$ = phase voltage, V_{ph}

and line current, $\qquad I_l = \sqrt{3}\, I_{ph}$.

$\therefore$ VA rating of the bank of three transformers in delta

$$= \sqrt{3} V_l I_l = \sqrt{3}\, V_{ph} (\sqrt{3}\, I_{ph}) = 3\, V_{ph}\, I_{ph}.$$

When one transformer is entirely removed from the closed delta, one may have the impulse to say that volt-ampere rating of the open-delta transformers becomes $2V_{ph}\, I_{ph}$, but this is not true. Note from Fig. 8.55 (*a*) that for an open-delta,

Line voltage, $\qquad V_l$ = phase voltage V_{ph} as before

and line current, $\qquad I_l$ = phase current I_{ph}

The relation $I_l = I_{ph}$ for an open-delta is true, since the current entering at terminal *a* or *b* is equal to the current leaving the corresponding terminal in Fig. 8.55 (*a*). Further, the secondary line voltages form a balanced three-phase system as shown in Fig. 8.55 (*c*).

$\therefore$ VA rating of the open-delta connection $= \sqrt{3}V_l\, I_l = \sqrt{3}V_{ph}I_{ph}$.

It is thus seen that the VA rating of open-delta is $\sqrt{3}V_{ph}I_{ph}$ and not $2V_{ph}I_{ph}$.

$$\therefore \quad \frac{\text{Open–delta VA or kVA rating}}{\text{Closed–delta VA or kVA rating}} = \frac{\sqrt{3}V_{ph}I_{ph}}{3V_{ph}I_{ph}} = 0.577.$$

For example, if each transformer is rated at 100 kVA, then the closed delta kVA rating is 300 kVA. The rating of the open-delta, consisting of only two transformers is not 200 kVA but 173.2 kVA.

It may be noted that open-delta operates at a lower kVA capacity $(= \sqrt{3}V_{ph}I_{ph} \cdot 10^{-3})$ compared with the sum of the individual transformer kVA capacities $(= 2V_{ph}I_{ph} \cdot 10^{-3})$. The ratio $\frac{\text{Actual available kVA rating}}{\text{Sum of the kVA ratings of the transformers installed}}$ is called the *utilisation, or rating, factor* for a particular type of connections. For open-delta connection, the utilisation factor is

$$\frac{\sqrt{3}V_{ph}I_{ph}}{2V_{ph}I_{ph}} = 0.866.$$

and for a closed delta, the utilization factor is unity.

Suppose three transformers in delta-delta supply rated load with line current I_L and phase winding current $1/\sqrt{3}\ .\ I_L$. When this D-D connection is made to operate as V-V transformer, current in each phase winding becomes equal to I_L, see Fig. 8.55 (*a*). This shows that with load remaining constant, each transformer in *V-V* connection is now overloaded by

$$\left(I_L - \frac{1}{\sqrt{3}} I_L\right) \text{ or by } \frac{I_L - \frac{1}{\sqrt{3}} . I_L}{\frac{1}{\sqrt{3}} . I_L} \times 100 = 73.2\%.$$

Thus, load in open-delta connection must be reduced to $1/\sqrt{3}$ times the original load in delta-delta connection. Otherwise, the transformer phase windings may be damaged due to overloading.

8.6.1 Power Delivered to Purely Resistive Load

The three-phase resistive load will be assumed to be connected first in star and then in delta.

(*a*) **Star-connected load.** Fig. 8.56 (*a*) illustrates two transformers in open-delta delivering power to three-phase balanced resistive load connected in star. The line to neutral voltages across the star are $V_{a'0}$, $V_{b'0}$, $V_{c'0}$ and the corresponding load currents I_a, I_b, I_c are in phase with their respective voltages as shown in Fig. 8.56 (*b*).

The Kirchchoff's voltage law for circuit $c\ a\ a'\ o\ c'\ c$ is

$$\overline{E}_{ca} = \overline{V}_{a'c'} = \overline{V}_{a'o} + \overline{V}_{oc'} = \overline{V}_{a'o} - \overline{V}_{c'o}.$$

Therefore E_{ca} is obtained by substracting $V_{c'0}$ from $V_{a'o}$ as illustrated in Fig. 8.56 (*b*).

The Kirchchoff's voltage law for circuit $b\ c\ c'\ o\ b'\ b$ is

$$\overline{E}_{bc} = \overline{V}_{c'b'} = \overline{V}_{c'o} + \overline{V}_{ob'} = \overline{V}_{c'o} \quad \overline{V}_{b'o}$$

and this is also shown in Fig. 8.56 (*b*).

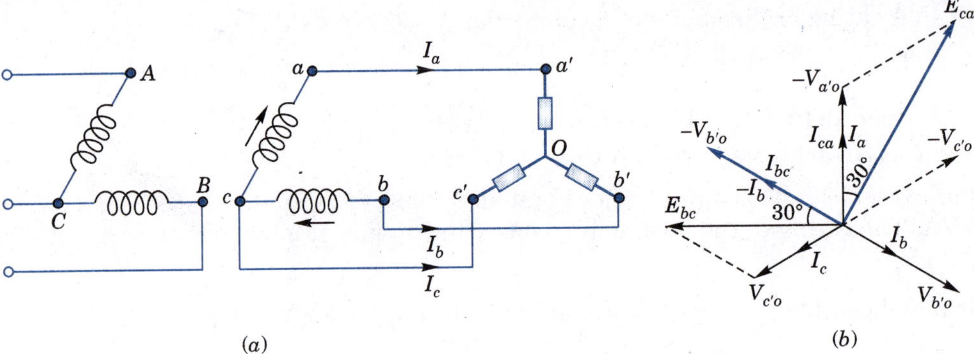

Fig. 8.56: (*a*) Open-delta supplying power to star-connected load and (*b*) Its phasor diagram.

In a closed delta, currents are taken to flow, in a cyclic order, from a to b, b to c and c to a and same is done in Fig. 8.56 (*a*). The currents I_a, I_b, I_c are shown flowing to the three-phase load. Therefore, the Kirchchoff's current law at the point a is $I_{ca} = I_a$ and at the point b is $I_{bc} = -I_b$.

Total power delivered by the transformer to the load given by

$$P_L = E_{ca} I_{ca} \cos (E_{ca}, I_{ca}) + E_{bc} I_{bc} \cos (E_{bc}, I_{bc})$$
$$= E_{ca} I_{ca} \cos (+30°) + E_{bc} I_{bc} \cos (-30°)$$

Note that transformer between terminals ca operates at a leading pf of cos 30° = 0.866 and other transformer between bc operates at a lagging pf of cos 30° = 0.866. Further, let

$$E_{bc} = E_{ca} = E \text{ and } I_{bc} = I_{ca} = I.$$

$$\therefore \quad P_L = EI \cos 30° + EI \cos (-30°) = \sqrt{3}EI = \sqrt{3}$$

(per phase power at unity pf)

(*b*) **Delta-connected load.** A delta-connected load across the secondary of transformer in open-delta is illustrated in Fig. 8.57 (*a*). The load is assumed to be resistive, for which the phasor diagram is drawn in Fig. 8.57 (*b*).

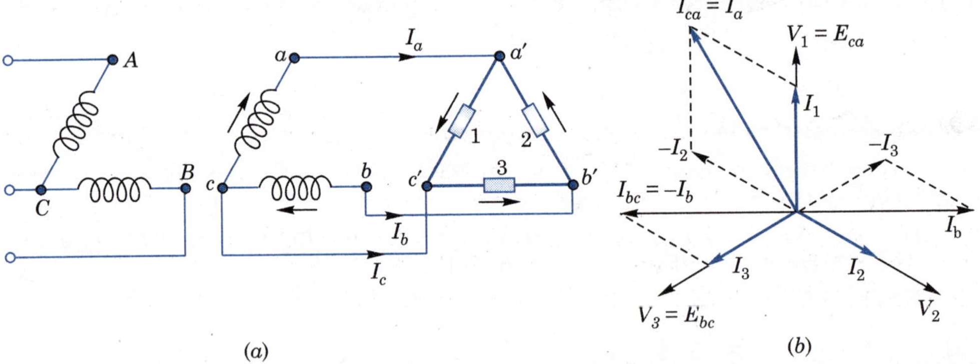

Fig. 8.57: (*a*) Delta-connected resistive load across open-delta transformer and (*b*) its phasor diagram.

The Kirchchoff's current law,

at point a' is, $\quad \bar{I}_a = \bar{I}_1 - \bar{I}_2$ ...[8.12 (*a*)]

at point b' is $\quad \bar{I}_b = \bar{I}_2 - \bar{I}_3$ ...[8.12 (*b*)] at point a is, $\quad I_{ca} = \bar{I}_a = \bar{I}_1 - \bar{I}_2$ ...[8.12 (c)]

and at point b is, $\quad \bar{I}_{bc} = -\bar{I}_b = -(\bar{I}_2 - \bar{I}_3)$ ...[8.12 (d)]

The currents $I_{ca} = I_a$ and $I_{bc} = -I_b$ are obtained from load currents I_1 and I_2 with the help of Eq. (8.12) and this is illustrated in Fig. 8.57 (b). In this diagram, V_1, V_2, V_3 are the load voltages and the corresponding load currents I_1, I_2, I_3 are in phase with their respective voltages.

The Kirchchoff's voltage law gives,

$$E_{ca} = V_1, \text{ voltage across load 1}$$

and

$$E_{bc} = V_3, \text{ voltage across load 3.}$$

∴ Total power delivered to the load

$$P_L = E_{ca}\, I_{ca} \cos(E_{ca}\, I_{ca}) + E_{bc}\, I_{bc} \cos(E_{bc}\, I_{bc})$$

$$= E_{ca}\, I_{ca} \cos(30°) + E_{bc}\, I_{bc} \cos(-30°).$$

As before, let $\quad E_{bc} = E_{ca} = E$ and $I_{bc} = I_{ca} = I$.

$$\therefore \quad P_L = 2EI \cos 30° = \sqrt{3}EI = \sqrt{3} \text{ (per phase power at unity pf).}$$

Thus the power delivered to star or delta connected balanced resistive load is $\sqrt{3}EI$.

From the foregoing discussion, it can be concluded that for unity p.f load, one transformer operates at 0.866 p.f leading and the other operates at 0.866 pf lagging.

8.6.2 Power Delivered to Inductive Load

Let the V-V bank of transformers supply a balanced three-phase load operating at a lagging power factor of cos θ. For this type of load, one transformer would operate at a lagging p.f of cos (θ – 30°) and the other at a leading pf of cos (θ + 30°). Therefore, power supplied by each transformer is

$$P_1 = E_L I_L \cos(\theta - 30°) \quad \text{and} \quad P_2 = E_L I_L \cos(\theta + 30°)$$

where, E_L and I_L are line values for the load.

Total power delivered by the two transformers

$$P = P_1 + P_2 = E_L I_L \cos(\theta - 30°) + E_L I_L \cos(\theta + 30°)$$

$$= 2\, E_L I_L \cos\theta \cos 30° = \sqrt{3}\, E_L I_L \cos\theta = \sqrt{3} \text{ (per-phase power)}$$

For a load of p.f = 0.5, θ = 60°.

∴ Power shared by one transformer $= E_L\, I_L \cos(60° - 30°)$

$$= \frac{\sqrt{3}}{2} E_L I_L = 0.866\, E_L I_L$$

Power shared by second transformer $= E_L I_L \cos(60° + 30°) = 0$

This shows that for lead p.f = 0.5, one transformer shares zero power whereas the second transformer shares the entire power required by the load.

For a load of p.f 0.866, θ = 30°.

∴ Power shared by one transformer $= E_L I_L \cos(30 - 30) = E_L I_L$

Power shared by second transformer $= E_L I_L \cos(30 + 30) = \frac{1}{2} E_L I_L$

This shows that for load p.f = 0.866, one transformer shares double the power shared by the other transformer.

Uses: An open-delta connection may be used as under.

1. For maintaining the continuity of supply to 3-phase loads, though at a reduced level, in the case of damage to one transformer in closed delta.

2. The open-delta system may be used in newly developing areas. The use of V-connection of two-transformers reduces the initial cost. When the need arises to meet the increased power demand, a third transformer is added for closed-delta operation. The addition of third transformer increases the capacity of the system from $\sqrt{3}\ V_{ph}I_{ph}$ to $3\ V_{ph}I_{ph}$. There is thus an increases of

$$\frac{3V_{ph}I_{ph} - \sqrt{3}\,V_{ph}I_{ph}}{\sqrt{3}\,V_{ph}I_{ph}} \times 100 = 73.2\%$$

3. In some cases, a large 1-phase load and smaller 3-phase loads may be supplied from open-delta connection. In such a case, transformer feeding additional 1-phase load is bigger in size.

Example 8.18. *Four 25 kW, 3-phase, 400 V induction motors are to be supplied by transformers connected in open-delta from an 11 kV line. At full load, each motor has an efficiency of 95% and operates at a pf of 0.866 lagging.*

(*a*) *Determine kVA rating of each of the two transformers and their turns ratio.*

(*b*) *Determine the line currents on the l.v. and h.v. sides. At what power factor is each transformer operating ?*

(*c*) *What is the real power supplied by each transformer ?*

(*d*) *What would be the available capacity, if a third transformer of the same rating is used to form the closed delta ?*

Solution. Total induction motor load = 4 × 25 = 100 kW.

$$\text{Total load on transformers in kVA} = \frac{100}{(0.95)\,(0.866)} = 121.55\ \text{kVA}$$

The open delta must be able to supply 121.55 kVA to the load. In other words, the available capacity of open-delta transformers must be 121.55 kVA.

(*a*) It has already been shown that the ratio

$$\frac{\text{Available capacity in kVA}}{\text{Sum of the kVA ratings of the transformers installed}} = 0.866.$$

$$\therefore \quad \text{Sum of the kVA ratings of the two transformers installed} = \frac{121.55}{0.866} = 140.34\ \text{kVA}.$$

$$\therefore \quad \text{Rating of each transformer} = \frac{140.34}{2} = 70.17\ \text{kVA}.$$

$$\text{Primary to secondary phase turns-ratio} = \frac{11{,}000}{400} = 27.5$$

$$(b)\ \text{Secondary line current} = \frac{70.17}{400} \times 1000 = 174.43\ \text{A}$$

$$\text{Alternatively, secondary line current} = \frac{100}{\sqrt{3}\,(0.4)\,(0.866)\,(0.95)} = 174.43\ \text{A}.$$

$\therefore$ H.v., *i.e.*, primary line current $= \dfrac{174.43}{27.5} = 6.34$ A.

Load power-factor angle, $\theta = \cos^{-1}(0.866) = 30°$

p.f of one transformer $= \cos(30° - 30°) = 1$

p.f of second transformer $= \cos(30° + 30°) = 0.5$

(*c*) Real power supplied by one $= 70.17 \times 1 = 70.17$ kW

Real power supplied by second $= 70.17 \times 1/2 = 35.085$ kW

Total power supplied by open-delta $= 70.17 + 35.085 \approx 105.26$ kW

Check. Total power input to the four induction motors $= \dfrac{100}{0.95} = 105.26$ kW.

(*d*) When a third transformer of the same rating is installed to form a closed delta, then available capacity becomes equal to $70.17 \times 3 = 210.51$ kVA.

Example 8.19. *Three identical single-phase transformers, connected in delta/delta, supply a balanced three-phase load. Each transformer carries rated current at rated voltage. One transformer develops fault and is removed from the circuit.*

(a) For the same load kVA, find the percentage increase in losses and reduction in efficiency. Each transformer has a core loss of 0.01 p.u. and an ohmic loss of 0.02 p.u. at rated voltage and rated current. Assume load pf to be unity.

(b) For the same temperature rise, determine the percentage reduction in kVA capacity of the open-delta.

Solution. *Delta/delta.* Total losses $= 3\,(0.01 + 0.02) = 0.09$ p.u.

Total output $= 3$ p.u.

$$\therefore \quad \text{Efficiency} = 1 - \frac{\text{Losses}}{\text{Input}} = 1 - \frac{0.09}{3.09} = 0.9709 \text{ or } 97.09\%.$$

(*a*) *Open-delta.* When one transformer is removed, the resulting connection is open delta. For the same kVA, the current carried by each transformer in open-delta is $\sqrt{3}$ p.u. Now core losses in each transformer remain unchanged.

$\therefore$ Total core losses $= 2\,(0.01) = 0.02$

$$\text{Total ohmic losses} = 2\left(\frac{\sqrt{3}}{1}\right)^2 (0.02) = 0.12$$

Total losses $= 0.02 + 0.12 = 0.14$

$$\therefore \quad \text{Percentage increase in losses} = \frac{0.14 - 0.09}{0.09} \times 100 = 55.56\%.$$

Total input $= 3 + 0.14 = 3.14$.

$$\therefore \quad \text{Efficiency} = 1 - \frac{0.14}{3.14} = 0.9554 \text{ or } 95.54\%.$$

$$\text{Percentage reduction in efficiency} = \frac{0.9709 - 0.9554}{0.9709} \times 100 = 1.596\%.$$

(*b*) Core losses remain unaltered. Therefore, for the same temperature rise, the ohmic losses must be lowered, *i.e.*, the current in the transformer winding must be reduced to rated current from $\sqrt{3}$ p.u.

∴ Available capacity for open-delta

= (0.866) (sum of kVA rating of the two transformers installed)

= (0.866) (1 + 1) = 1.732 p.u.

The available capacity for open-delta is also equal to $\sqrt{3}\, V_{rated} I_{rated} = \sqrt{3}$ p.u.

Original capacity when in delta/delta = 3

$$\therefore \quad \text{Percentage reduction in kVA capacity} = \frac{3 - 1.732}{3} \times 100 = 42.3\%.$$

8.7 TESTING OF 3-PHASE TRANSFORMER BANK FOR PROPER CONNECTIONS

Since a three-phase transformer bank has independent magnetic circuits ; its primary, in star or delta, can be connected at random and energied from 3-phase supply. The object of this article is to discuss the method of testing their secondaries for proper connection, with the help of a voltmeter only.

8.7.1 Primary in Star

If the transformer primary is connected in star, then its neutral must be connected to the source neutral so as to avoid the presence of third harmonic voltages on the secondary side.

(*a*) **Secondary in star.** In order to connect the transformer secondaries in star, connect one terminal of one secondary with one terminal of the other secondary. Then connect a voltmeter across the two free terminals of these two connected secondaries. If the voltmeter reads $\sqrt{3}\, V_2$ (here V_2 is voltage of one secondary), then the two secondaries are connected properly. In case voltmeter reads V_2, the secondaries are wrongly connected. This wrong connection can, however, be corrected by reversing the terminal connections of either of the two secondaries.

When two secondaries are properly connected, then their common junction is connected to any one terminal of the remaining thrd secondary. Now a voltmeter, across the free terminal of third secondary and the free terminal of either of the two already connected secondaries, should read $\sqrt{3}V_2$. In case voltmeter reads V_2 as shown in Fig. 8.58 (*a*), then reverse the connections of the third secondary so that voltmeter reads $\sqrt{3}V_2$. In this manner, three secondaries have their three terminals connected together to form the neutral and the remaining three terminals to serve as the output terminals.

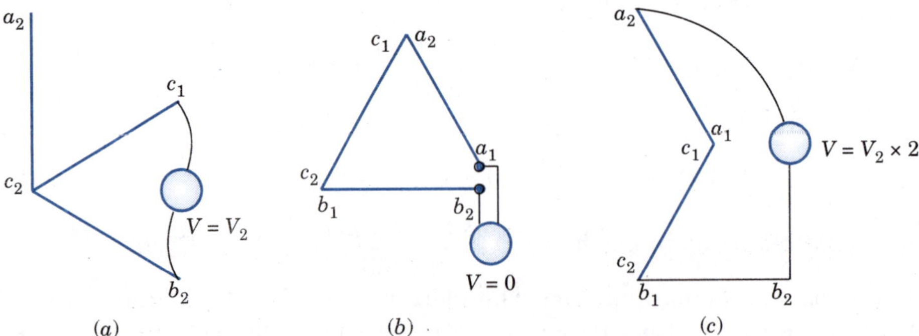

Fig. 8.58: Pertaining to the testing of 3-phase transformer bank.

(*b*) **Secondady in delta.** In order to connect the transformer secondaries in delta, one terminal of one secondary is connected to one terminal of the other secondary. The two free terminals so obtained are connected to a voltmeter. If the voltmeter reads V_2, then the secondaries are properly connected. In case the voltmeter reads $\sqrt{3}V_2$, then reverse the connections of any one secondary so that voltmeter reads V_2.

After two secondaries are properly connected, then connect one terminal of the third secondary to one of the free terminals of the already connected two secondaries. The two free terminals so obtained are connected to voltmeter. If the voltmeter reads zero as shown in Fig. 8.58 (*b*), the polarities are correct and these two terminals can be joined together to form the closed delta. In case the voltmeter reads $2V_2$ as shown in Fig. 8.58 (*c*), then the third secondary is wrongly connected. It can, however, be corrected by reversing the terminal connections of the third secondary so that voltmeter reads zero as shown in Fig. 8.58 (*b*).

8.7.2 Primary in Delta

If the primary is connected in delta, the third harmonic magnetizing current can flow in the closed delta and in view of this, the secondary voltages are free of third harmonic voltages as explained in Art. 8.4.2. The secondaries can now be connected in star or delta as explained above.

In practice, the terminal markings are already indicated on the single-phase transformers and they can be connected accordingly in star or delta to achieve the proper connections.

Example 8.20. *A three-phase 11/0.4 kV transformer has its low voltage winding connected in delta as shown in Fig. 8.59 (a), where d, e, f are the mid taps of the transformer windings ab, bc, ca respectively. Determine the magnitude of the voltages ab, bc, ca, de, ef, fd, ae, bf, cd and show them on a relevant phasor diagram. Find the time-phase angle between voltages V_{de}, V_{ab} and V_{bf}, V_{bc}.*

Solution. In the phasor diagram 8.59 (*b*), phase (or line) voltages V_{ab}, V_{bc}, V_{ca} are drawn mutually displaced by a time phase angle of 120° and their magnitude is 400 V. For the sake of clarity, the phasors V_{ab}, V_{bc}, V_{ca} are shown in star.

Since *d, e, f* are the mid-taps of the transformer l.v. side,

$$V_{ad} = V_{db} = V_{be} = V_{ec} = V_{cf} = V_{fa} = 400/2 = 200 \text{ V}$$

and these voltages are indicated in the phasor diagram accordingly.

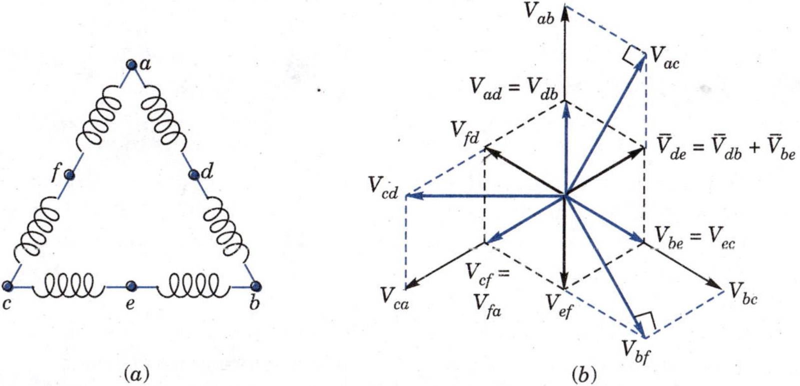

Fig. 8.59: Pertaining to Example 8.20.

The voltage between the mid-taps *d, e, f* are given by

$$\bar{V}_{de} = \bar{V}_{db} + \bar{V}_{be}$$

$$\overline{V}_{ef} = \overline{V}_{ec} + \overline{V}_{cf} \quad \text{and} \quad \overline{V}_{fd} = \overline{V}_{fa} + \overline{V}_{ad}.$$

These voltages are shown in the fig. and their magnitude is seen to be equal to 200 V. The voltage V_{de} lags V_{ab} by 60°.

The voltages V_{ae}, V_{bf} and V_{cd} are given by

$$\overline{V}_{ae} = \overline{V}_{ab} + \overline{V}_{be}$$

$$\overline{V}_{bf} = \overline{V}_{bc} + \overline{V}_{cf} \quad \text{and} \quad \overline{V}_{cd} = \overline{V}_{ca} + \overline{V}_{ad}.$$

These voltages are indicated in the phasor diagram and their magnitude is given by

$$V_{ae} = V_{bf} = V_{cd} = \sqrt{400^2 - 200^2} = 364.4 \text{ V}.$$

The voltage V_{bf} lags V_{bc} by 30° as shown in the fig.

8.8 CHOICE OF TRANSFORMERS FOR THREE-PHASE CIRCUITS

The choice between a bank of three single-phase transformers and a three-phase core type transformer of equivalent capacity, may be based on the comparison of merits and demerits given in tabular form below:

Bank of three single-phase transformers	*Three-phase core-type transformer*
1. It is more costly because it requires more iron, more auxiliary apparatus, three separate tanks and therefore more oil.	1. It is less costly because it has shorter magnetic path, less volume of iron, smaller tank and therefore, less oil.
2. For star or delta connection on h.v. side, six high voltage leads must be brought out. There are thus six h.v. bushings and the transformer cost is high.	2. In a three-phase transformer, the windings can be connected in star or delta inside the tank. In view of this, only three bushings are required and the transformer cost is low.
3. It requires more floor space and for indoor substations, the building cost is increased considerably.	3. It requires less floor space and for indoor substations, the building cost is less.
4. It offers greater flexibility in installation.	4. It does not have any flexibility in installation.
5. If one transformer is damaged, it can be easily replaced by a spare single-phase unit.	5. If any one phase-winding is damaged, the whole transformer must be replaced. Therefore, the cost of spare parts and its maintenance is high.
6. Only one single-phase unit is required as a standby, therefore, cost of standby unit is less.	6. One complete three-phase unit is required as a standby, therefore, cost of standby unit is more.
7. The three units being separate, their repair is comparatively easy.	7. It is somewhat more difficult to repair.
8. Because of more iron, it has more losses. Therefore, it is less efficient.	8. Because of less iron, losses are less, it is therefore more efficient.
9. A transformer in star/star without neutral, can't supply a single phase load between line to neutral, because it causes considerable unbalance of the phase voltages.	9. A transformer in star/star without neutral, can supply a single phase load between line and neutral without appreciable unbalance of the three phase voltages.

It may be seen from the above comparison that a 3-phase core-type transformer is more efficient, less costly and is, therefore, more commonly used as compared to a bank of three single-phase units.

However, in hilly areas, mines etc. where the transportation is a problem, a bank of three single-phase transformers should be preferred. Since the transformer repair workshops are at a few places only ; if a three-phase core type transformer is to be repaired, its transportation to the workshop and back is more costly and troublesome than that of single-phase units.

So far as the choice between star and delta connections is concerned, it should be noted that

(*i*) in star connection, the neutral can be solidly grounded and the maximum voltage between windings and core (or frame) is only $1/\sqrt{3}$ times the line voltage, the insulation required is, therefore, less.

(*ii*) in delta connection, if one line is grounded by fault, the maximum voltage between windings and core becomes the full-line voltage, the transformer, therefore, requires more insulation.

It may, therefore, be concluded that the star connection is relatively cheaper than the delta connection.

However, from technical considerations, it is essential to have one winding in delta.* In view of this, delta/star transformers are used as step-up transformers at the sending end of h.v. transmission lines. Star/delta transformers are used as step-down transformers at the receiving ends of h.v. transmission lines. The delta/delta transformer can be used for medium voltages and possess the following advantages.

(*a*) If the load is small, two transformers in open-delta can be installed. As the load demand increases, the transformers can be connected in delta.

(*b*) If a fault develops in one transformer, it can be removed from the circuit and continuity of supply can be maintained. For three-legged core-type transformer, the damaged phase windings must be open-circuited by opening the tank.

(*c*) A delta/delta transformer can be re-connected as delta/star. In this manner, the transmission line voltage can be increased by 73.2%, though the power transmitted remains the same. The disadvantage of *Dd* connection is the lack of neutral for grounding and other purposes.

It has already been discussed in Art. 8.5 that single-phase line to neutral load can't be delivered by *Yy* bank; but single-phase line to neutral load ; up to about 10% of the three-phase rating, can be delivered by a three-legged *Yy* transformer. A *Dy* transformer can however, supply line to neutral load conveniently. In *Yy* transformer, the third harmonic flux and the unbalanced flux (due to unequal phase loadings) have to complete its path through tank, channels, bolts etc. Consequently, the iron and stray load losses are more in a *Yy* three-legged transformer, as compared to *Dy* or *Yd* three-legged transformer. In view of the above, a *Yy* connection is not preferred even for three-phase three-legged transformers. However, *Yy* with tertiary winding in delta or *Yy* with both transformer and system neutrals grounded may be used.

---

* A closed delta provides path for third harmonic magnetizing currents, thus permitting the flux to be sine wave. Accordingly, the phase voltages are also sine waves, which is a desirable feature.

For distribution purposes, the delta/star connection is essential, since single-phase loads between line to neutral and three-phase loads across the three lines can be supplied conveniently. When the primary winding is in delta, then each primary phase winding can receive power from the source without effecting the other two windings and in this manner, primary can receive any current from the source to balance the secondary load ampere turns.

Example 8.21. *A three-phase step-down transformer is energised from 11 kV, 50 Hz source. If it takes a line current of 20 A from the supply mains, then calculate the output voltage, output current and output kVA for each of the following connections:*

(a) star / star *(b) star / delta* *(c) delta / star*

(d) delta / delta *(e) delta / zigzag.*

The magnetizing current and losses are ignored. Per phase turns ratio is 44.

Solution. (*a*) **Star/star**

$$\text{Per phase primary voltage} = \frac{11000}{\sqrt{3}} = 6351 \text{ V}$$

$$\text{Per phase secondary voltage} = \frac{6351}{44} \text{ V}$$

$$\therefore \quad \text{Secondary line voltage} = \frac{6351}{44} \times \sqrt{3} = 250 \text{ V} = \text{output voltage}$$

Primary phase current = 20 A.

$\therefore$ Secondary phase current = 20 × 44 = 880 A.

= secondary line current or the output current.

$$\text{Output in kVA} = \sqrt{3} V_l I_l \times 10^{-3}$$

$$= \sqrt{3}(250)(880)\, 10^{-3} = 381.04 \text{ kVA}.$$

(*b*) **Star/delta**

Primary phase voltage = 6351 V

$$\therefore \quad \text{Secondary phase voltage} = \frac{6351}{44} = 144.341 \text{ V} = \text{output voltage}.$$

Primary phase current = 20 A.

Secondary phase current = 20 × 44 = 880 A

$\therefore$ Secondary line current $= 880\,(\sqrt{3}) = 1524.16$ A = output current.

$$\text{Output in kVA} = \sqrt{3}\, V_l I_l \times 10^{-3}$$

$$= \sqrt{3}\,(144.341)\,(1524.16) \times 10^{-3} = 381.04 \text{ kVA}.$$

(*c*) **Delta/star**

Primary phase voltage = 11000 V

$$\text{Secondary phase voltage} = \frac{11000}{44} = 250 \text{ V}$$

$\therefore$ Secondary line voltage $= 259\,(\sqrt{3}) = 433$ V = output voltage

$$\text{Primary phase current} = \frac{20}{\sqrt{3}} = 11.547 \text{ A}.$$

∴ Secondary phase current $= (11.547)(44) = 508.07$ = Output current

∴ Output in kVA $= \sqrt{3}\,(433)\,(508.07)\,10^{-3} = 381.03$ kVA.

(*d*) **Delta/delta**

Primary phase voltage $= 11000$ V.

Secondary phase voltage $= \dfrac{11000}{44} = 250$ V = Output voltage.

Primary phase current $= \dfrac{20}{\sqrt{3}}$ A

Secondary phase current $= \dfrac{20}{\sqrt{3}} \times 44 = \dfrac{880}{\sqrt{3}}$ A

∴ Secondary line current $= \dfrac{880}{\sqrt{3}} \times \sqrt{3} = 880$ A.

Output in kVA $= \sqrt{3}\, V_l I_l \times 10^{-3}$

$= \sqrt{(250)}\,(880) \times 10^{-3} = 381.04$ kVA.

(*e*) **Delta/zigzag**

Primary phase voltage $= 11{,}000$ V.

It hase been shown in Art. 8.2 that phase voltage in zigzag is 0.866 times its value in star.

∴ Secondary phase voltage $= 0.866\left(\dfrac{11{,}000}{44}\right) = 216.5$ V

Secondary line voltage $= \sqrt{3} \times 216.5 = 374.98$ V = Output voltage.

Primary phase current $= \dfrac{20}{\sqrt{3}} = 11.547$ A

Secondary phase current $= 11.547 \times 44 = 508.07$ A = Output current

∴ Output in kVA $= \sqrt{3}\,(374.98)\,(508.07) \times 10^{-3} = 329.97$ kVA

Note that first primary phase values are calculated, then the secondary phase values by using the phase turns ratio and then the secondary line values are determined.

Example 8.22. *A 400 V, 3-phase factory load of 100 kW at 0.8 pf is to be supplied from 11 kV line through three identical single-phase step-down transformers. Determine the voltage, current and kVA rating of each of the three transformers if they are connected.*

(*a*) *delta / delta* (*b*) *star / star* (*c*) *star / delta*

(*d*) *delta / star and* (*e*) *open-delta.*

Solution. Factory load in kVA $= \dfrac{100}{0.8} = 125$ kVA

(*a*) **Delta/delta**

Per phase secondary voltage $= 400$ V

Per phase primary voltage $= 11000$ V

∴ Voltage rating of each transformer is 11/0.4 kV.

Per phase secondary current $= \dfrac{125}{3 \times 0.4} = 104.167$ A

Per phase primary current $= \dfrac{125}{3 \times 11} = 3.788$ A.

∴ Current rating of each transformer is 3.788/104.167 A. kVA rating of each transformer

$$= V_{ph} I_{ph} \cdot 10^{-3} = 400 \times 104.167 \times 10^{-3} = 41.67 \text{ kVA}.$$

(*b*) **Star/star**

Per phase secondary voltage $= \dfrac{400}{\sqrt{3}} = 231$ V

Per phase primary voltage $= \dfrac{11000}{\sqrt{3}} = 6351$ V

∴ Voltage rating of each transformer is 6351/231 V.

Per phase secondary current $= \dfrac{125}{3 \times 0.231} = 180.38$ A

Per phase primary current $= \dfrac{125}{3 \times 6.351} = 6.56$ A.

∴ Current rating of each transformer is 6.56/180.38 A.

kVA rating of each transformer is 41.67 kVA.

(*c*) **Star/delta.** For secondary in delta, per phase voltage and current are 400 V and 104.167 A. For primary in star, per phase voltage and current are 6351 V and 6.56 A. Therefore, each transformer rating is 6351/400 V, 6.56/104.167 A, 41.67 kVA.

(*d*) **Delta/star.** For secondary in star, per phase voltage and current are 231 V and 180.38 A. For primary in delta, per phase voltage and current are 11 kV and 3.788 A. Therefore, each transformer rating is 11/0.231 kV, 3.788/180.38 A, 41.67 kVA.

(*e*) For open delta, sum of the kVA ratings of the two transformers installed

$$= \frac{125}{0.866} = 144.34$$

∴ Rating of each transformer $= \dfrac{144.34}{2} = 72.17$ kVA.

Voltage rating of each transformer should be 11/0.4 kV.

Secondary current $= \dfrac{72.17}{0.4} = 180.43$ A

Primary current $= \dfrac{72.17}{11} = 6.56$ A

∴ Current rating of each transformer is 6.56/180.43 A.

Example 8.23. *Two 3-phase transformers Dd0 and Dy11 have their primaries energised from the same 3-phase source. One phase winding of the secondary delta has its mid-point grounded and the other secondary has its star point grounded as shown in Fig. 8.60 (a). If per phase secondary voltage of both the transformers is 400 V, then determine the voltage between the points (a) $a_2'b_2$ (b) c_2c_2' and (c) c_2b_2'.*

Solution. Since middle point of one phase winding and the star point are grounded as shown in Fig. 8.60 (*a*), the two grounded points overlap each other as illustrated in Fig. 8.60 (*b*).

(*a*) An examination of Fig. 8.60 (*b*) reveals that $a_2'a_2$ = 200 V and therefore

$$a_2'b_2 = a_2'a_2 + a_2b_2 = 200 + 400 = 600 \text{ V}.$$

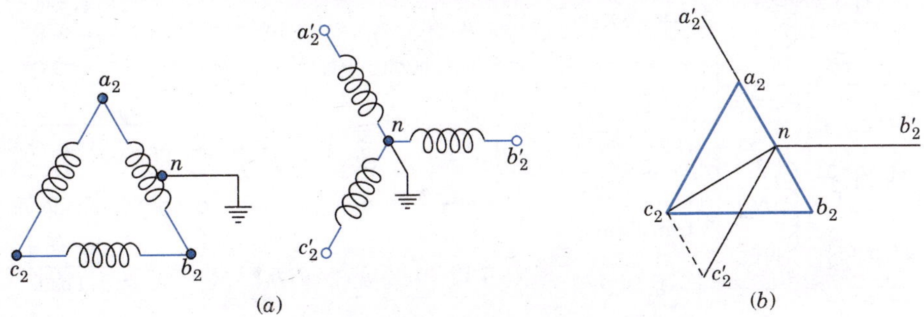

Fig. 8.60: Pertaining to Example 8.23.

(*b*) Fig. 8.60 (*b*) shows that $a_2n = c_2c_2'$ = 200 V.

(*c*) Fig. 8.60 (*b*) also reveals that $\angle c_2nb_2 = 90°$ and $\angle b_2nb_2' = 60°$.

$$\therefore \quad \angle c_2nb_2' = 150°$$

Now

$$c_2n = \sqrt{(c_2b_2)^2 - (b_2n)^2}$$

$$= \sqrt{(400)^2 - (200)^2} = 346.4 \text{ V}$$

$$\therefore \quad c_2b_2' = [(c_2n)^2 + (nb_2')^2 - 2 \times c_2n \times nb_2' \times \cos \angle c_2nb_2']^{1/2}$$

$$= \sqrt{(346.4)^2 + (400)^2 - 2 \times 346.4 \times 400 \cos 150°} = 721.10 \text{ V}.$$

8.9 THREE-PHASE TO TWO-PHASE CONVERSION (SCOTT CONNECTION)

At present three-phase energy systems are by far the most common, but for certain specialized applications two-phase supplies are essential. For example two-phase energy system is required to feed power to

(*i*) single-phase arc furnaces. (*ii*) low voltage single-phase rural supplies.
(*iii*) electrified tracks in electric traction. (*iv*) two-phase control motors.

Charles F. Scott converted two phases to three phases at Niagara Falls and the arrangement used by him is known as Scott-connection, in his honour. It may be argued at this juncture that single-phase supply can also be taken from a 3-phase system, by using any two lines or any line and the neutral. But with these arrangements, the 3-phase system becomes more unbalanced than with the use of Scott-connections.

It should be noted that two-phase system of voltages consist of two equal voltages displaced from each other by a time-phase angle of 90°.

The Scott-connection requires two single-phase transformers connected as shown in Fig. 8.61. In this figure, the transformer connected between the terminals *BC*, or B_1B_3, and provided with centre tap B_2 is called the *main transformer*. The second transformer between the terminals A_1A_3, is called the *teaser transformer*. Fig. 8.62 gives the schematic connection diagram for the Scott-connection. The three phase star-connected source *abc* is shown merely for convenience in analysis.

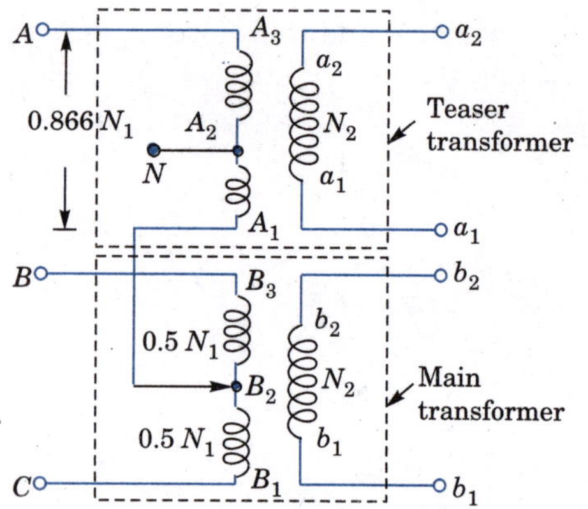

Fig. 8.61: Scott-connection of transformers.

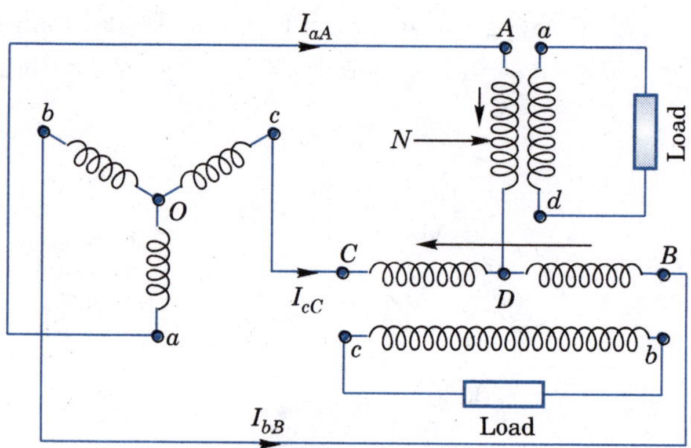

Fig. 8.62: Schematic connection diagram for Scott-connection.

Let the positive direction of primary voltage and current be taken arbitrarily along the arrows from *A* to *D* and from *B* to *C* as shown in Fig. 8.62. The supply voltage phasor diagram is shown in Fig. 8.63 (*a*), where V_{oa}, V_{ob}, V_{oc} are the phase voltages and V_{ab} (= $V_{ao} + V_{ob}$), V_{bc} (= $V_{bo} + V_{oc}$), V_{ca} (= $V_{co} + V_{oa}$), are the line voltages. Since the source terminals *a, b, c* are directly connected to transformer primary terminals *A, B, C*; voltages V_{AB}, V_{BC}, V_{CA} are equal to voltages V_{ab}, V_{bc}, V_{ca} respectively. Therefore, for transformer primary voltages, the phasor diagram is as shown in Fig. 8.63 (*b*).

Neglecting the transformer internal impedance drops, the voltage V_{ab} or V_{AB} must be equal to the voltages induced in *AD* and *DB*. Therefore, on traversing the circuit *aADBb*, we get

$$\overline{V}_{ab} = \overline{V}_{AB} = \overline{V}_{AD} + \overline{V}_{DB}$$

$$\therefore \quad \overline{V}_{AD} = \overline{V}_{AB} - \overline{V}_{DB}$$

Since $\overline{V}_{BD} = -\overline{V}_{DB}$, the above voltage equation can be written as

$$\overline{V}_{AD} = \overline{V}_{AB} + \overline{V}_{BD} \qquad \text{...(8.13)}$$

If $V_{AB} = V_{BC} = V_{CA} = V_L$ (line voltage), then with V_{BC} as reference phasor as shown in Fig. 8.63 (*b*), $\overline{V}_{BC} = V_L \angle 0°$, $\overline{V}_{BD} = \frac{1}{2}\overline{V}_{BC} = \frac{1}{2} V_L \angle 0°$; $\overline{V}_{AB} = V_L \angle 120°$ and $\overline{V}_{CA} = V_L \angle -120°$

Eq. (8.13) can now be re-written in terms of V_L as,

$$\overline{V}_{AD} = V_L \angle 120° + \tfrac{1}{2} V_L \angle 0°$$

But $\quad \angle 120° = \cos 120 + j \sin 120° = -0.5 + j0.866$

$$\therefore \quad \overline{V}_{AD} = V_L [-0.5 + j0.866 + 0.5]$$

$$= j\,[0.866\, V_L] = 0.866\, V_L \angle 90° \qquad \text{...(8.14)}$$

Hence V_{AD}, the voltage across the teaser, is 0.866 of that across the main and leads it by 90° as shown in Fig. 8.63 (*b*).

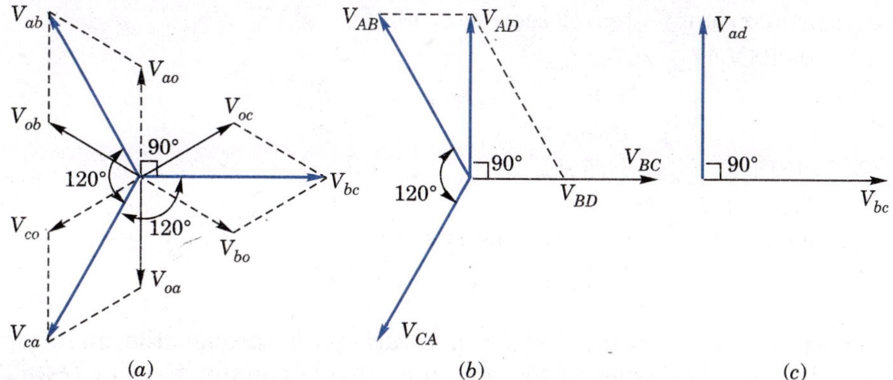

Fig. 8.63: (*a*) Supply voltage phasor diagram. Scott-connection phasor diagram for (*b*) the primary voltages and (*c*) the secondary voltages.

The voltages belonging to a phase winding, on the same core, are drawn parallel to each other in the phasor diagram. Therefore, the secondary voltages V_{ad}, V_{bc} as shown in Fig. 8.63 (*c*), are parallel to V_{AD}, V_{BC} respectively. Since the angle between voltages V_{ad} and V_{bc} is 90°, the voltages V_{ad}, V_{bc} form a 2-phase system of voltages. Thus a 3-phase system can be converted to a two-phase system. However, the converse is also true, *i.e.,* if two-phase voltages are applied to terminals *ad* and *bc* in Fig. 8.62 (*b*), the voltages at the terminals *A*, *B*, *C* would form a 3-phase system of voltages.

Since $V_{AD} = 0.866V_L$ and $V_{BC} = V_L$, the primaries of both the transformers would have equal voltage per turn only if the teaser primary tunrs are 0.866 times the primary turns of the main transformer. If both the transformers for Scott-connection are identical, then their primaries should have tappings both at the middle and at 0.866 of the windings. Note that the role of two identical transformers can be interchanged. If the transformers are not identical, then the main and teaser transformers must have a tapping respectively, at the middle and at 0.866 of their primary windings.

If voltage per turn $E_t = \sqrt{2}\,\pi f \phi_m$ is the same, then flux in the cores of both the main and teaser transformers are equal. This has the effect of giving equal core losses for both the transformers. Further, if the two secondaries have equal turns, then the secondary terminal voltages would be equal in magnitude but displaced from each other by 90° as shown in Fig. 8.63 (*c*).

The voltage between the lines and neutral point on the three-phase side is $V_L/\sqrt{3}$ = 0.578 V_L. Since the teaser voltage, equal to $0.866V_L$, is greater than $V_L/\sqrt{3}$, the neutral must be on the teaser primary. The neutral point is, therefore, $0.866V_L - 0.578V_L = 0.288V_L$ from *D*. In other words in Fig. 8.62 (*b*), $V_{AD} = 0.866V_L$, $V_{AN} = 0.578V_L$ and $V_{DN} = 0.288V_L$ and the neutral divides the teaser primary *AD* in the ratio of $V_{AN} : V_{DN} = 0.578 : 0.288 = 2 : 1$

$$\therefore \qquad \frac{\text{Number of turns in } AN}{\text{Number of turns in } DN} = 2.$$

Let N_1 be the number of turns in the main primary ($0.866N_1$ in the teaser primary) and N_2 in each of the two secondaries. If the exciting current is neglected, then the transformer action requires the balance between primary and secondary ampere-turns. For teaser transformer,

Teaser primary mmf = teaser secondary mmf

$$(0.866N_1)\, I_{AD} = N_2 \cdot I_{ad}$$

or
$$I_{AD} = \frac{1}{0.866} I_{ad} \frac{N_2}{N_1} = 1.155 I_{ad} \frac{N_2}{N_1} \qquad ...(8.15)$$

If $N_2/N_1 = 1$, then $I_{AD} = 1.155 I_{ad}$

For the main transformer,

Main primary mmf = main secondary mmf

$$I_{BC}N_1 = I_{bc}N_2 \quad \text{or} \quad I_{BC} = I_{bc} = N_2/N_1 \qquad ...(8.16)$$

If $N_2/N_1 = 1$, then $I_{BC} = I_{bc}$.

The teaser primary current I_{AD} has a return path through the main transformer primary. Since D is the mid-point of BC, I_{AD} must divide equally at point D and the total current in the main primary is the resultant of I_{BC} and $\frac{1}{2} I_{AD}$. The teaser currents $\frac{1}{2} I_{AD}$ in DB and $\frac{1}{2} I_{AD}$ in DC flow in opposite directions in the main primary, their magnetic effects, therefore, cancel each other and the mmf balance $I_{BC}N_1 = I_{bc}N_2$ remains uneffected.

The primary line currents I_{aA}, I_{bB}, I_{cC} can be obtained by applying Kirchhoff's current law at the points A, B and C in Fig. 8.62 (*b*).

At the point A, current entering is I_{aA} and current leaving is I_{AD}.

$$\therefore \quad \bar{I}_{aA} - \bar{I}_{AD} = 0 \quad \text{or} \quad \bar{I}_{aA} = \bar{I}_{AD} \qquad ...(8.17)$$

At the point B, the currents entering are I_{bB}, $\frac{1}{2}I_{AD}$ and the current leaving is I_{BC}.

$$\therefore \quad \bar{I}_{bB} + \frac{1}{2}\bar{I}_{AD} - \bar{I}_{BC} = 0 \quad \text{or} \quad \bar{I}_{bB} = \bar{I}_{BC} - \tfrac{1}{2}\bar{I}_{AD} \qquad ...(8.18)$$

Similarly, at the point C,
$$IcC = -\bar{I}_{BC} - \tfrac{1}{2}\bar{I}_{AD} \qquad ...(8.19)$$

(*a*) **Balanced load.** For a particular case of balanced load at unity pf, the secondary currents I_{ad} and I_{bc} can be expressed in terms of the current I_2. Here current I_2 is the magnitude of the secondary load current, *i.e.*, $I_{ad} = I_{bc} = I_2$. With I_{bc} as reference, $\bar{I}_{bc} = \bar{I}_2$ and $\bar{I}_{ad} = j\,\bar{I}_2$ as shown in Fig. 8.64 (*b*). For simplicity, unity turns ratio ($N_2/N_1 = 1$) is assumed.

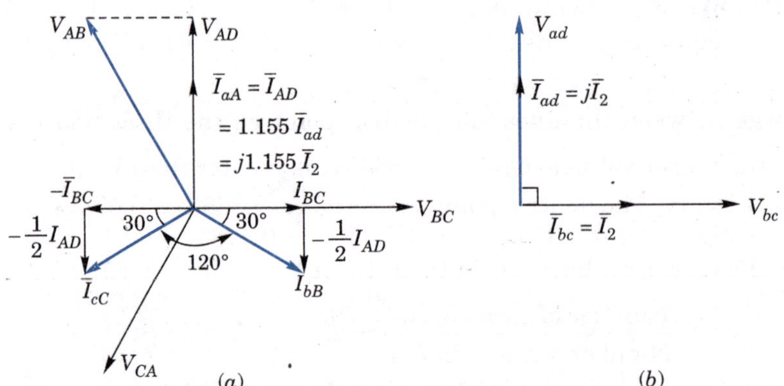

Fig. 8.64: Scott-connection phasor diagram for (*a*) primary side and (*b*) secondary side.

With the help of Eqs. (8.17) and (8.15)

$$\bar{I}_{aA} = \bar{I}_{AD} = 1.155\,\bar{I}_{ad} = 1.155\,(j\bar{I}_2) = 1.155 I_2 \angle 90°$$

Therefore, $I_{aA} = I_{AD}$ is in phase with V_{AD} as shown in Fig. 8.64 (*a*).

From Eqs. (8.18), (8.15) and (8.16),

$$\bar{I}_{bB} = \bar{I}_{BC} - \tfrac{1}{2}\bar{I}_{Ad} = \bar{I}_{bc} - \tfrac{1}{2}\,(1.155\,\bar{I}_{ad})$$

$$= \bar{I}_2 - \tfrac{1}{2}(1.155)\,(j\bar{I}_2) = 1.155\,(0.866 - j\,0.5)\,\bar{I}_2$$

Note that 1.155 × 0.866 = 1.

The expression for I_{bB} reveals that if I_{bB} is to be expressed as $I_2 \angle\theta$, then cosine and sine of θ must be positive and negative respectively and this can happen only in the fourth quadrant.

$$\therefore \qquad \bar{I}_2\,(0.866 - j0.5) = I_2 \angle -30°$$

Hence $\qquad \bar{I}_{bB} = 1.155\,I_2 \angle -30°$

In Fig. 8.64 (*a*), I_{bB} is drawn lagging behind the reference current I_{BC} by an angle of 30°.

From Eqs. (8.19), (8.15) and (8.16),

$$\bar{I}_{cC} = -\bar{I}_{BC} - \tfrac{1}{2}\bar{I}_{AD} = -\bar{I}_{bc} - \tfrac{1}{2}(1.155\,\bar{I}_{ad})$$

$$= -\bar{I}_2 - \tfrac{1}{2}(1.155)\,(j\bar{I}_2) = 1.155\,\bar{I}_2\,(-0.866 - j0.5)$$

$$= 1.155\,I_2 \angle 210° = 1.155\,I_2 \angle -150°$$

The line current I_{cC} has been drawn accordingly in Fig. 8.64 (*a*). An inspection of Fig. 8.64 reveals that for a balanced 2-phase load, the primary currents are also balanced — this is true whether load pf is unity or not.

(*b*) **Unbalanced load.** Suppose the secondary load is unbalanced. In Fig. 8.65 (*b*), I_{ad} and I_{bc} are assumed to lag behind their respective voltages by θ_1 and θ_2 respectively. The primary line currents are again obtained with the help of Eqs. (8.17), (8.18) and (8.19). The current $I_{aA} = I_{AD} = 1.155\,I_{ad}$ and is drawn parallel to I_{ad}. For I_{bB}, draw I_{BC} parallel and equal to I_{bc} (for unity turns ratio) and $-\tfrac{1}{2}I_{AD}$ parallel and opposite to I_{AD} as per Eq. (8.18). For I_{cC}, draw $-I_{BC}$ opposite to I_{BC} and $-\tfrac{1}{2}I_{AD}$ parallel and opposite to I_{AD}, as per Eq. (8.19). It is seen from the phasor diagram of Fig. 8.65 that for secondary unbalanced load, the primary currents are also unbalanced.

(*c*) **Utilization factor.** If V_2 and I_2 are the secondary voltage and current, then total available capacity at the output terminals = $2V_2I_2$ voltamperes.

For V_2, I_2 on the teaser secondary, the corresponding values on the teaser primary are $0.866V_2$ and $1.155I_2$, for $N_2/N_1 = 1$.

∴ VA rating of the teaser transformer primary = $(0.866V_2)\,(1.155I_2) = V_2I_2$.

∴ Rating of the teaser transformer = V_2I_2.

For V_2, I_2 on the main secondary, the corresponding values on the main primary are V_2 and $1.155I_2$, for $N_2/N_1 = 1$.

∴ VA rating of the main transformer primary = $(V_2)\,(1.155I_2) = 1.155V_2I_2$.

Note that for the main transformer, the secondary rating is V_2I_2, whereas the primary rating is $1.155V_2I_2$. The overall rating of the main transformer can, therefore, be taken as the mean of primary and secondary ratings.

∴ Main transformer rating = $\tfrac{1}{2}\,(V_2I_2 + 1.155V_2I_2) = 1.078V_2I_2$.

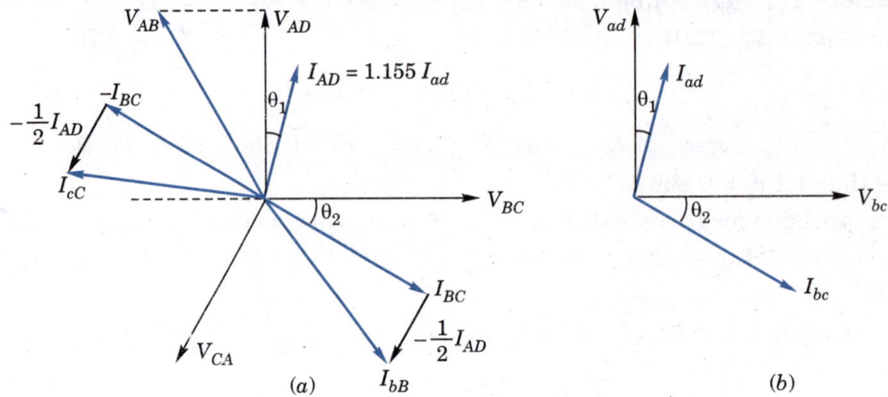

Fig. 8.65: Scott-connection phasor diagrams for an unbalanced secondary load.

The utilization factor has already been defined in Art. 8.6.

∴ Utilization factor for Scott-connection

$$= \frac{\text{Actual available kVA rating}}{\text{Sum of the kVA ratings of the transformers installed}}$$

$$= \frac{2V_2I_2}{V_2I_2 + 1.078V_2I_2} = 0.9625.$$

If the two transformers are identical, each being centre tapped and with a tap at 0.866, then available capacity in $VA = 2V_2I_2$.

VA rating of the teaser-transformer primary $= (V_2)\,(1.155I_2)$

∴ Mean rating of teaser transformer $= \frac{1}{2}\,(1 + 1.155)\, V_2I_2 = 1.078\, V_2I_2$

Similarly, mean rating of main transformer $= 1.078V_2I_2$

∴ Utilization factor for Scott-connection with identical transformers is given by

$$= \frac{2V_2I_2}{1.078V_2I_2 + 1.078V_2I_2} = 0.928$$

It should be noted that in the above analysis, no load transformer currents are neglected. Therefore, for rigorous analysis of Scott-connection scheme, the no-load or exciting currents must also be taken into account.

Example 8.24. *A 3-phase balanced voltage of 440 V is applied to two Scott-connected transformers. The main transformer has N_1 and N_2 turns in its primary and secondary windings respectively and turns ratio $\frac{N_2}{N_1} = \frac{1}{4}$.*

(a) Calculate

(i) the voltage across the teaser and the main transformer primaries,

(ii) the position of the neutral point,

and (iii) the secondary voltage of each phase.

(b) Out of the four terminals on the secondary side, any two are joined together. Determine the magnitude of the voltage across the remaining two terminals.

Solution. For this example, refer Fig. 8.62.

(*a*) (*i*) Voltage across the main transformer primary

$$= \text{line voltage } V_L = V_{BC} = 440 \text{ V}.$$

Voltage across the teaser transformer primary

$$= V_{AD} = 0.866\ V_L = 0.866 \times 440 = 381 \text{ V}.$$

(*ii*) The position of the neutral point on the teaser $= V_{DN} = \left(\frac{1}{3}\right)(V_{AD}) = \frac{381}{3} = 127$ V away from the mid-point D of the main transformer, or $V_{AN} = 381 - 127 = 254$ V away from the line of the teaser transformer.

(*iii*) For main transformer,

$$\frac{\text{Primary voltage, } V_1}{\text{Secondary voltage, } V_2} = \frac{N_1}{N_2} \quad \text{or} \quad V_2 = \left(\frac{440}{N_1}\right)N_2$$

Since the voltage per turn is equal for both teaser and main transformers, the voltage across each secondary is given by

$$440\left(\frac{N_2}{N_1}\right) = 440\left(\frac{1}{4}\right) = 110 \text{ V}$$

(*b*) With any two terminals joined together [say b_2a_1, b_2a_2, b_1a_1 or b_2a_2 in Fig. 8.61], the voltage across the remaining two terminals can be expressed in phasor form as $110 + j110$. The magnitude of this voltage is $\sqrt{(110)^2 + (110)^2} = 155.56$ V.

Example 8.25. *Resistive loads of 5 Ω and 10 Ω are connected respectively across the teaser and main transformer secondaries of a Scott-connected arrangement of transformers, fed from 3-phase, 230 V supply mains. If the main transformer primary to secondary turns ratio is 2, then determine the supply line currents. The magnetizing currents and the internal impedance drops are neglected.*

Solution. The magnitude of the secondary voltage of each phase is given by

$$V_{ad} = V_{bc} = 230\ \frac{\text{Secondary turns}}{\text{Primary turns}} = 230\left(\frac{1}{2}\right) = 115 \text{ V}$$

$\therefore$ Load current in the teaser-transformer secondary, $I_{ad} = \frac{115}{5} = 23$ A.

Load current in the main-transformer secondary, $I_{bc} = \frac{115}{10} = 11.5$ A

From Eq. (8.15), the teaser primary current is given by

$$I_{aA} = I_{AD} = 1.155 I_{ad}\frac{N_2}{N_1} = 1.155\ (23)\left(\frac{1}{2}\right) = 13.28 \text{ A}$$

From Eq. (8.16), the main-transformer primary current is given by

$$I_{BC} = I_{bc}\frac{N_2}{N_1} = 11.5 \times \frac{1}{2} = 5.75 \text{ A}.$$

By referring to Fig. 8.64, the phasor diagram for this example is drawn as shown in Fig. 8.66, from which currents I_{bB} and I_{cC} can be calculated. It may be seen from this phasor diagram that I_{BC} and $\frac{1}{2}I_{AD}$ are at right angles to each other.

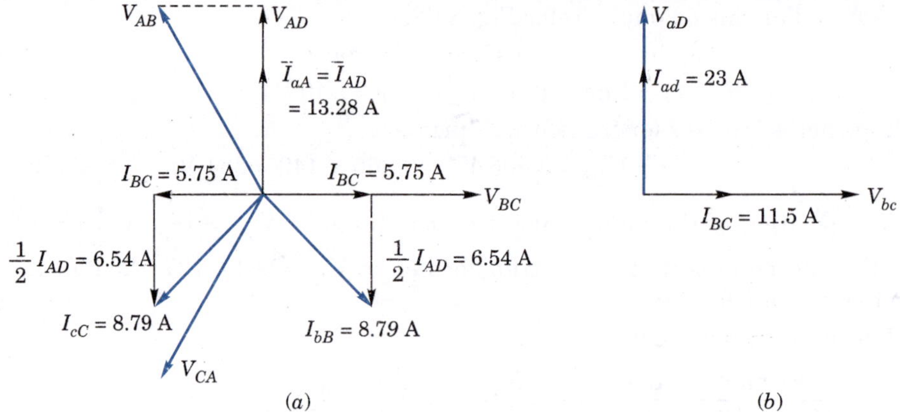

Fig. 8.66: Phasor diagram (not to scale) pertaining to Example 8.25.

$$\therefore \qquad I_{bB} = \sqrt{I_{BC}^2 + \left(\tfrac{1}{2} I_{AD}\right)^2} = \sqrt{(5.75)^2 + (6.64)^2} = 8.784 \text{ A}$$

and
$$I_{cC} = \sqrt{I_{BC}^2 + \left(\tfrac{1}{2} AD\right)^2} = 8.784 \text{ A}.$$

Thus the three line currents on the primary are 13.28 A, 8.784 A and 8.784 A.

Example 8.26. *Scott-connected transformers supply two single-phase loads at 100 V. The load across the teaser secondary is 300 kW at unity power factor and that across the main secondary is 200 kW at 0.8 power factor lagging. For a 3-phase input voltage of 11,000 V, calculate the primary line currents. The magnetizing currents and the leakage impedance drops are ignored.*

Solution. The current in the teaser secondary is $I_{ad} = \dfrac{300 \times 1000}{100 \times 1} = 3000$ A

The current in the main secondary is $I_{bc} = \dfrac{200 \times 1000}{100 \times 0.8} = 2500$ A.

Main transformer turns ratio from secondary to primary $= \dfrac{N_2}{N_1} = \dfrac{100}{11{,}000} = \dfrac{1}{110}$.

From Eq. (8.16), the main transformer primary current is

$$I_{BC} = I_{bc} \frac{N_2}{N_1} = 2500 \times \frac{1}{110} = 22.73 \text{ A}.$$

From Eq. (8.15), the line current is

$$I_{aA} = I_{AD} = 1.155\, I_{ad} \frac{N_2}{N_1} = 1.155\,(3000)\left(\frac{1}{110}\right) = 31.5 \text{ A}.$$

The phasor diagram for this example is illustrated in Fig. 8.67, where I_{AD} is parallel to I_{ad} and I_{BC} is parallel to I_{bc}. If this diagram is drawn to scale, the supply line currents can be determined graphically. The solution can also be carried out by using complex notation, or as given below.

For current I_{bB} :

H.C. (Horizontal component) of

$$I_{BC} = I_{BC} \cos 36.9° = (22.73)\,(0.8) = 18.2 \text{ A}$$

H.C. of $\frac{1}{2}\,I_{AD} = 0$

$\therefore$ Total H.C. = 18.2 A

V.C. (vertical component) of

$$I_{BC} = I_{BC} \sin 36.9° = (22.73)\,(0.6) = 13.64 \text{ A downward.}$$

V.C. of $\frac{1}{2}I_{AD}$ = 15.75 A downward.

$\therefore$ Total V.C. = 13.64 + 15.75 = 29.39 A

$$\therefore \quad I_{bB} = \sqrt{(\text{H.C.})^2 + (\text{V.C.})^2} = \sqrt{(18.2)^2 + (29.39)^2} = 34.57 \text{ A.}$$

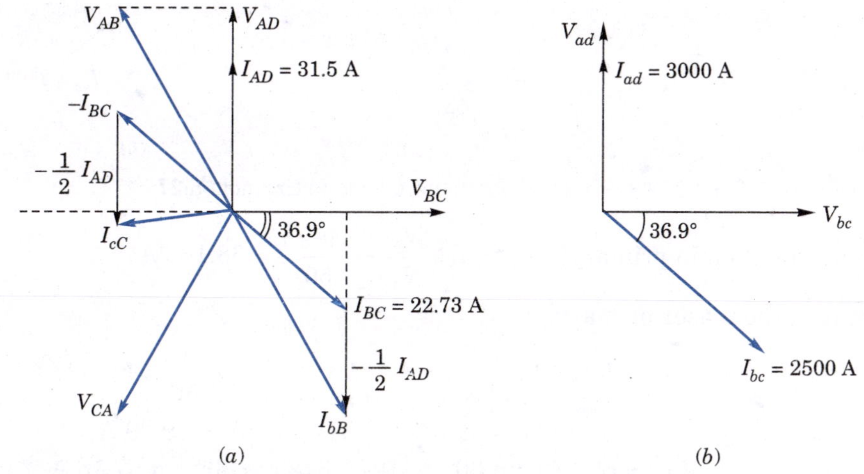

Fig. 8.67: Phasor diagram pertaining to Example 8.26.

For current I_{cC} ;

H.C. of I_{BC} = 18.2 A, H.C. of $\frac{1}{2}I_{AD} = 0$

Total H.C. = 18.2 A.

V.C. of I_{BC} = 13.64 A upward, V.C. of $\frac{1}{2}I_{AD}$ = 15.75 A downward.

$\therefore$ Total V.C. = 15.75 – 13.64 = 2.11 A

$$\therefore \quad I_{cC} = \sqrt{(\text{H.C.})^2 + (\text{V.C.})^2} = \sqrt{(18.2)^2 + (2.11)^2} = 18.32 \text{ A.}$$

Thus the three line currents are 31.5 A, 34.57 A and 18.32 A.

Example 8.27. *Two single-phase furnaces 1 and 2 are supplied at 220 V by means of two Scott-connected transformers with input voltage of 3-phase, 11 kV, 50 Hz. The voltage of furnace 1 is leading. Compute the currents on the 3-phase side if furnace 1 takes 500 kW at 0.866 p.f lagging and furnace 2 takes 600 kW at 0.8 p.f lagging.*

Solution. For main transformer, $\dfrac{N_1}{N_2} = \dfrac{11000}{220} = 50$

Current in main transformer secondary, $I_{bc} = \dfrac{600 \times 1000}{220 \times 0.8} = 3409.1$ A

Current in teaser transformer secondary, $I_{ad} = \dfrac{500 \times 1000}{220 \times 0.866} = 2624.4$ A

Furnace voltages V_{ad}, V_{bc} and currents I_{ad}, I_{bc} are drawn in the phasor diagram of Fig. 8.68.

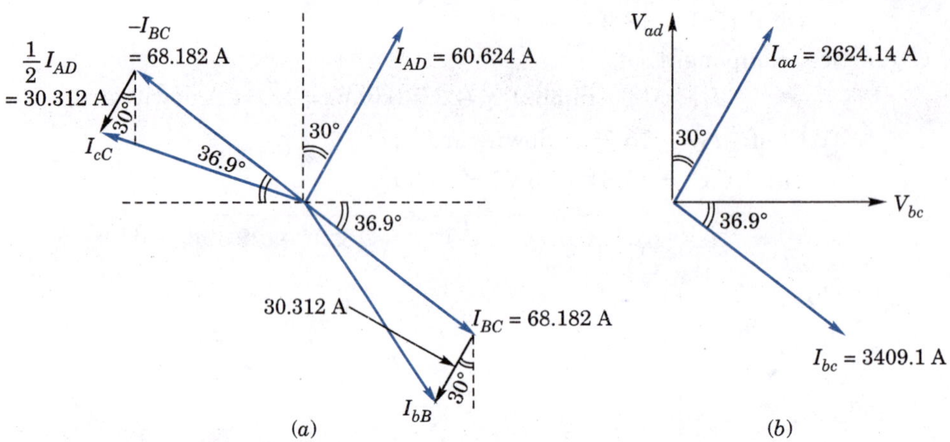

Fig. 8.68: Phasor diagram pertaining to Example 8.27.

Current in the main primary, $I_{BC} = I_{bc} \dfrac{N_2}{N_1} = \dfrac{3409.1}{50} = 68.182$ A

Current in the teaser primary,

$$I_{AD} = 1.155\, I_{ad} \cdot \frac{N_2}{N_1} = 1.155 \times 2624.4 \times \frac{1}{50} = 60.624 \text{ A}$$

For, $\quad I_{bB}$, H.C. = 68.182 cos 36.9° – 30.312 sin 30° = 39.39 A

V.C. = 68.182 sin 36.9° ↓ + 30.312 cos 30° ↓ = 67.16 A.

∴ Primary line current

$$I_{bB} = \sqrt{39.39^2 + 67.16^2} = 78.29 \text{ A}$$

for I_{cC}, H.C. = 68.182 cos 36.9° + 30.312 sin 30° = 69.70 A

V.C. = 68.182 sin 36.9° ↑ + 30.312 cos 30° ↓ = 14.66 A

∴ Primary line current, $I_{cC} = \sqrt{69.7^2 + 14.66^2} = 71.23$ A.

Primary line current, $I_{aA} = I_{AD} = 60.624$ A.

Example 8.28. *It is desired to transform 2400 V, 5000 kVA three-phase power to 2-phase power at 600 V by Scott-connected transformers. Determine the voltage and current ratings of both primary and secondary of each transformer. Neglect the transformer no-load currents.*

Solution. Voltage rating of main transformer is 2400/600 V.

$$\therefore \quad \frac{N_1}{N_2} = \frac{2400}{600} = 4.$$

Voltage rating of teaser transformer is 0.866 V_1/V_2 or 0.866 × 2400/600 or 2078.4/600 V.

For Scott-connected transformers,

$$\frac{\text{Actual available kVA rating}}{\text{Sum of the kVA ratings of the transformers installed}} = 0.9625.$$

$\therefore$ Sum of the kVA ratings of main and teaser transformers = $\dfrac{5000}{0.9625}$ = 5195 kVA.

Since the main and teaser transformer kVA ratings are in the ratio of 1.078 to 1, the teaser transformer kVA rating is given by, $\dfrac{5195}{2.078}$ = 2500 kVA.

$\therefore$ Main transformer rating = 5195 – 2500 = 2695 kVA.

For two-phase power, the secondary currents of both the transformers should be equal.

$\therefore$ Secondary current of main and teaser transformers = $\dfrac{2500}{0.6}$ = 4166.67 A.

Primary current of main and teaser transformers

$$= 1.155\,\frac{N_2}{N_1}\,I_2 = 1.155 \times \frac{1}{4} \times 4166.67 = 1203.13 \text{ A.}$$

$\therefore$ Current rating of both main and teaser transformer are 1203.13 A/4166.67 A.

8.10 THREE-PHASE TO SIX AND TWELVE PHASE CONVERSIONS

A rectifier equipment operates better if it is supplied from a larger number of phases. Transformers, for three to six phase conversion, are widely used for this purpose and many a time the conversion from 3 to 12 or even 24 phases is used for improving the performance of the rectifier equipment. For conversion from 3 to a larger number of phases, it is usually desirable to have the secondaries in sections. The object of this article is to discuss first 3 to 6 phase conversion and then 3 to 12 phase conversion.

It is usual to connect the primary in delta ; however, primary in star is permissible only if the secondary provides a closed path for the third harmonic magnetizing currents. If there is no closed path for third harmonic currents either in the primary or in the secondary, then the output voltage would contain objectionable harmonics.

8.10.1 Three to Six Phase Conversion

The methods of three to six phase conversion are known by the type of secondary connections employed and a few of them are (*a*) double-star (*b*) six-phase star (*c*) diametrical (*d*) mesh or ring and (*e*) double delta.

Each of these methods is now discussed in turn.

(*a*) **Double-star (or double-Y) connection.** Each transformer unit has its secondary winding in two equal sections. The primary must be connected in delta for this connection. The secondary half-sections, with appropriate markings, are joined together to form two reversed stars. Output terminals for one star are a_1 b_1 c_1 with a_2 b_2 c_2 joined together to give neutral n. The output terminals for second star are a_4 b_4 c_4 with a_3 b_3 c_3 joined together to form the second neutral n_1 as shown in Fig. 8.70. Terminals a_1 b_1 c_1 and a_4 b_4 c_4 are connected to 6-phase load

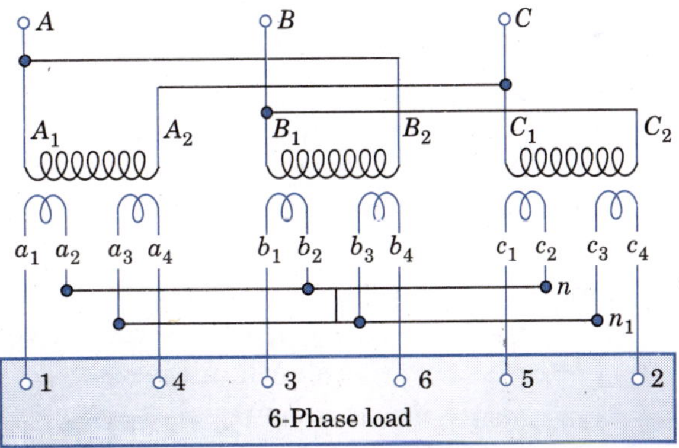

Fig. 8.69: Circuit diagram for double-star connection.

terminal 1, 3, 5, 4, 6, 2 respectively in Fig. 8.69. It may be seen from Fig. 8.70 (*a*) that two stars are reversed with respect to each other. If the two neutrals n and n_1 are joined together as shown in Fig. 8.70 (*b*), a true 6 phase star system is obtained and neutral is available. If n and n_1 are not joined, six phase load can even then be connected to a_1 a_4 b_1 b_4 c_1 c_4, but now the neutral would not be available.

If V_2 is the output line voltage, say across $a_1 c_4$ in Fig. 8.70 (*b*), then that secondary coil voltage ($a_1 a_2$, $b_1 b_2$ or $c_1 c_2$ etc) is also V_2.

How to know that transformer terminals a_1 b_1 c_1 and a_4 b_4 c_4 are to be connected respectively to load terminal 1, 3, 5, 4, 6, 2 ? For this, refer to Fig. 8.70 (*b*), where transformer terminal a_1 is first marked 1 and then the other transformer terminals are marked 2, 3, 4, 5, 6 clockwise. An inspection of this figure reveals that c_4 should be connected to 2, b_1 to 3 and so on.

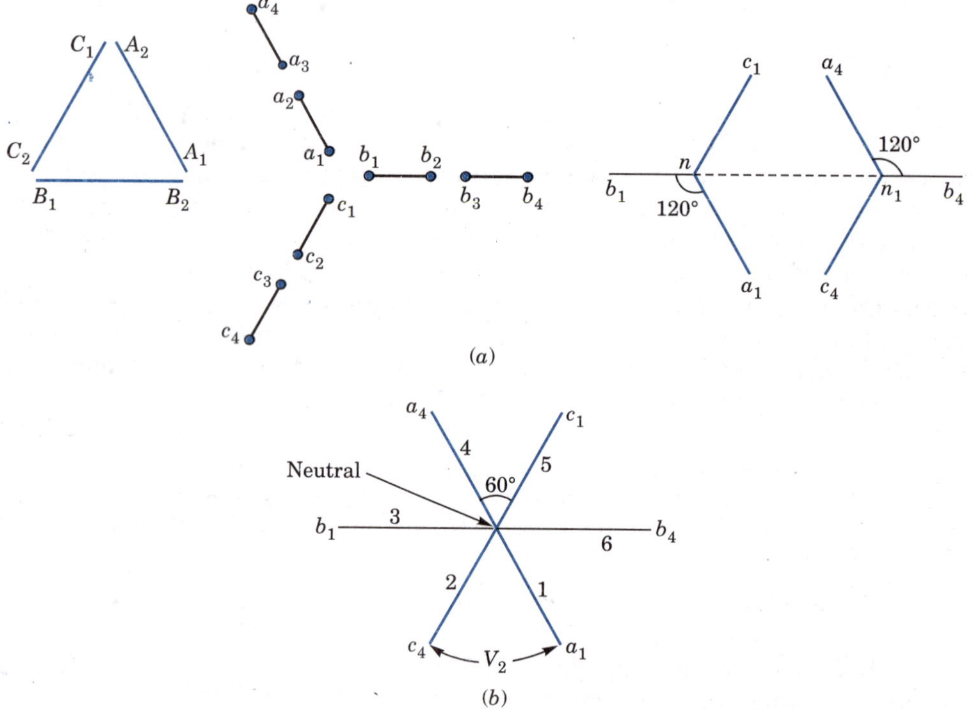

Fig. 8.70: Phasor diagrams for double-star connection.

(*b*) **Six-phase star connection.** The primary is delta connected and the mid-points a_2 b_2 c_2 of the three secondaries are joined together to form the neutral of the 6-phase star as shown in Fig. 8.71. It should be noted that this connection becomes identical with the double-star system provided the two neutrals n and n_1 are connected together in Fig. 8.70 (*a*). Six phase load terminals 1, 2, 3, 4, 5, 6 are connected to six transformer secondary terminals a_1 c_3 b_1 a_3 c_1 b_3 respectively as shown in Fig. 8.71 (*a*).

For an output voltage of V_2, say across a_1c_3 or c_3b_1, the coil voltage of a_1a_2, b_1b_2 or a_2a_3 etc. is also V_2.

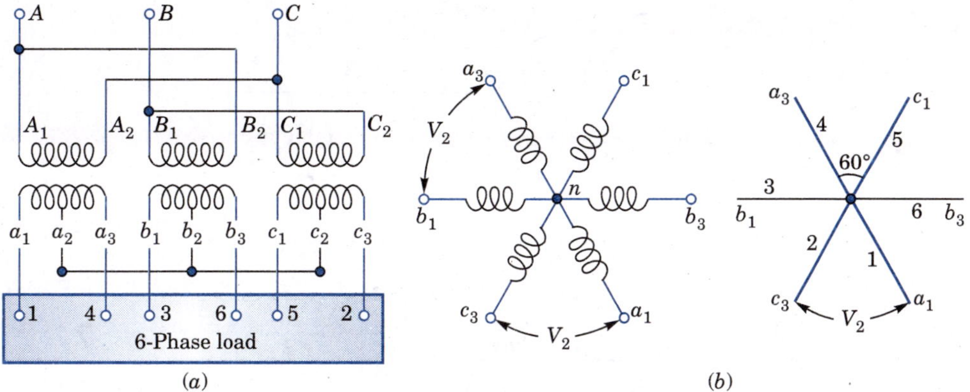

Fig. 8.71: Six phase star connection.

(*c*) **Diametrical or diametral connection.** If the midtaps of the secondary windings are not available, even then a six-phase load can be supplied from the three secondaries as shown in Fig. 8.72. However in order to fix the phase relations between the voltages, it is essential to connect the six-secondary terminals to the six-phase load. Transformer terminals marked a_1a_2 b_1b_2 c_1c_2 must be connected to load terminals 1 4 3 6 5 2 respectively. When neutral connection is not required, the diametral connection is most economical, because the secondary windings need not have mid-taps. Since the neutral is not available, this method can't be employed for rectifier circuits. If the output voltage is V_2, the coil voltage (a_1a_2 etc.) is $2V_2$.

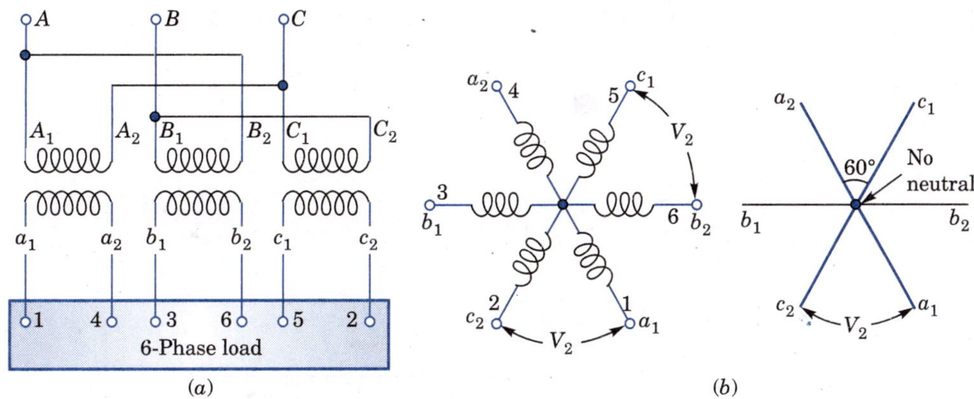

Fig. 8.72: Six-phase diametrical connection.

(*d*) **Six-phase mesh, or ring connection.** The primary is delta connected and the six half coils of the secondary windings are connected to the six-phase load as shown in Fig. 8.73 (*a*). The right side diagram of Fig. 8.73 (*b*) helps in making the various connections of the secondary half coils. Care should be taken to ensure that $a_1b_1c_1$ are 120° apart, with b_1 lagging a_1 as before. Further, the extreme ends of the same phase, *i.e.*, a_1a_4, b_1b_4, c_1c_4 should be diametrically opposite to each other in the right side diagram of Fig. 8.73 (*b*). The ring connection gives true six-phase supply, but the non-availability of the neutral makes it unsuitable for rectifier circuits.

In Fig. 8.73 (*a*), the terminals 1, 2, 3 of the six-phase load are only shown for the sake of clarity. The other load terminal connections can be made properly by referring to Fig. 8.73 (*b*). If V_2 is the output line voltage then the coil voltage a_1a_2, a_3a_4 etc. is also V_2.

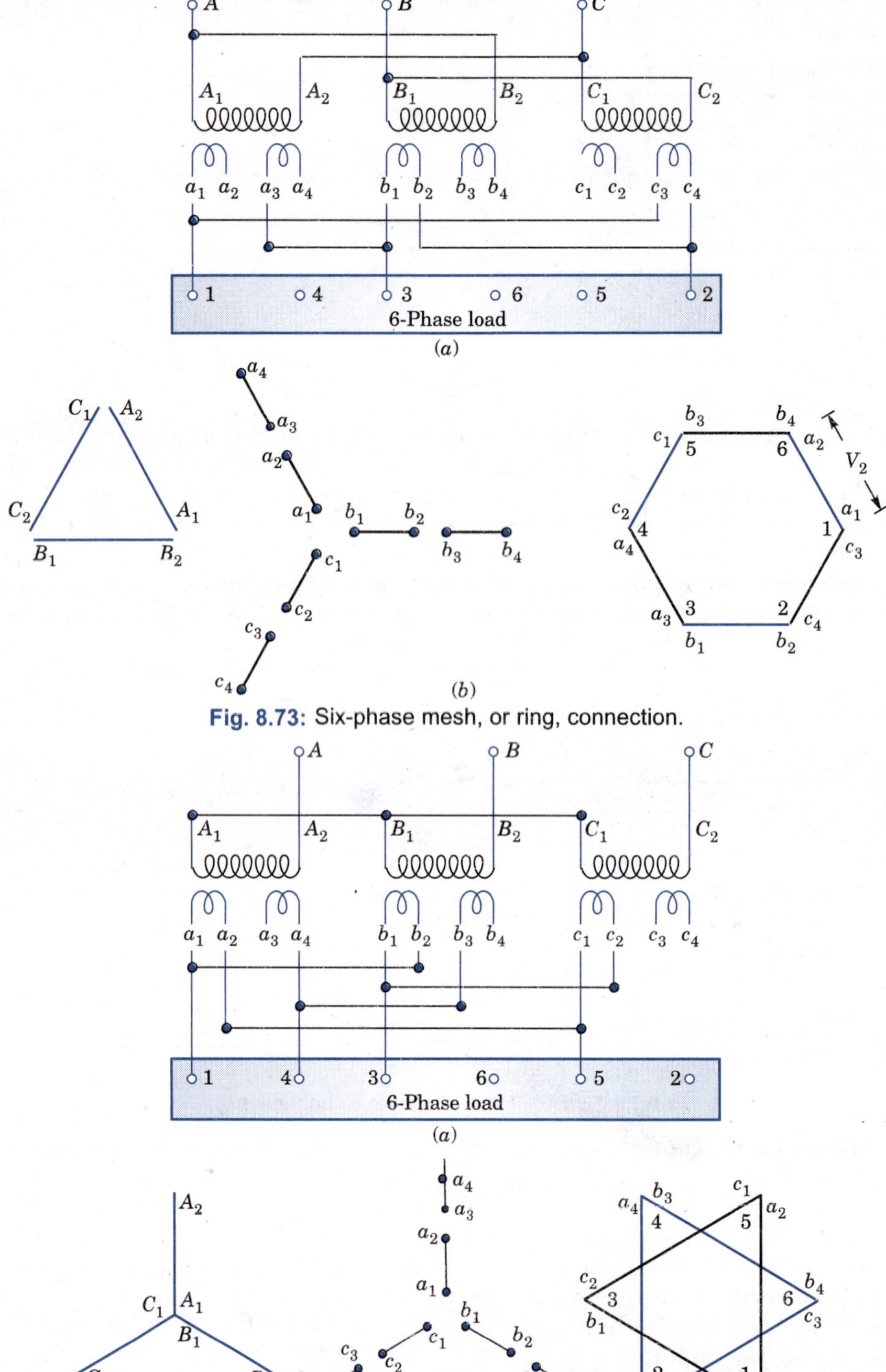

Fig. 8.73: Six-phase mesh, or ring, connection.

Fig. 8.74: Six-phase double-delta condition.

(*e*) **Double-delta connection.** The primary may be connected in star for this scheme of connections, because the two secondary deltas provide the required path for third harmonic magnetizing currents. The six half-sections of the secondary windings are connected so as to make two deltas. One delta is made by using the coils a_1a_2, b_1b_2, c_1c_2 and the second delta, by using the coils a_3a_4, b_3b_4, c_3c_4 in such a manner that the extreme ends of the secondary windings *i.e.*, a_1a_4, b_1b_4, c_1c_4 are diametrically opposite as shown in Fig. 8.74 (*b*). Note again that b_1 should lag a_1 by 120°. The two deltas are insulated from each other and get connected only through six-phase load. This scheme of connections is also unsuitable for rectifier equipments, because neutral is not available.

Let the line voltage for the double delta connection be V_2 as shown in Fig. 8.74 (*c*). In this fig., *OA* is the radius of the circle such that 2 (*OA*) is the diameter of the circle passing through points 1, 2, 3, 4, 5, 6 of Fig. 8.74 (*b*). In Fig. 8.74 (*c*), $OA = V_2$ = line voltage and $\angle OAB = 30°$.

$$\therefore \quad AB = OA \cos 30° = \sqrt{3}/2\, V_2$$

$$\therefore \quad \text{Coil voltage} = AB + BC = 2AB = \sqrt{3}\, V_2.$$

Thus the coil voltage a_1a_2 , a_3a_4 etc. is $\sqrt{3}\,V_2$ and the secondary winding phase voltage a_1a_4 etc. is $2\sqrt{3}\ V_2$ in double delta connection.

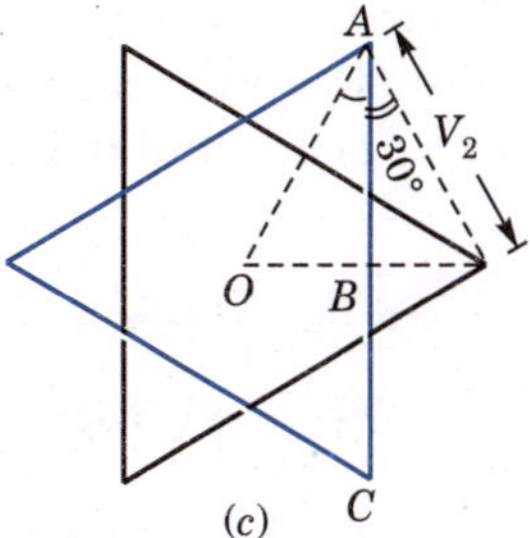

Fig. 8.74: (*c*) Pertaining to double-delta connection.

8.10.2 Three-phase to Twelve-phase Conversion

As stated earlier, the rectifier and inverter equipments have higher efficiency with large number of phases. In the case of a rectifier, the waveform of the output voltage is improved and the ripple voltage reduced, if the number of phases is increased. However, the increase in efficiency in going from 3 to 6 phases is more than the increase in efficiency in going from 6 to 12 phases. In addition, the twelve phase units are more complex and cost more than the 6-phase units. In view of this, the use of 12-phase equipment is recommended only in large installations.

In this section of the article, only one method of conversion from three to twelve phases is presented. The type of transformer secondary connections usually decide the name of the method employed.

(*a*) **Star-delta/double-star connection.** This method requires two, three-phase transformers with secondaries of each phase provided with a mid tap. The primary of one is connected in star and that of the other in delta.

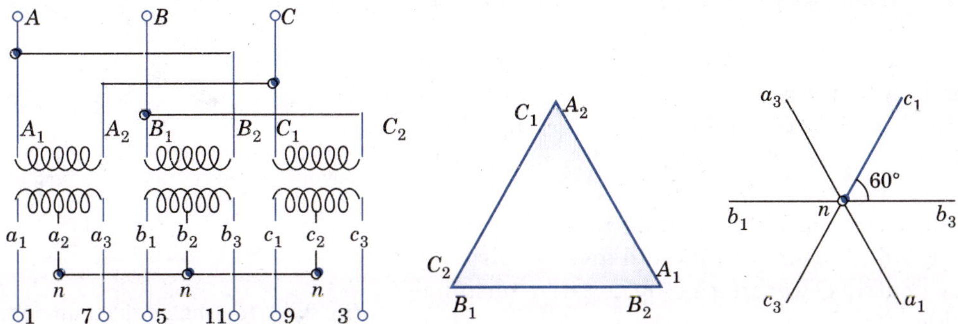

Fig. 8.75: (*a*) Pertaining to conversion from three to twelve phases.

In Fig. 8.75 (a), the primary is in delta and the mid-taps of the secondary windings are connected together to furnish double star, similar to Fig. 8.71. Note the position of $A_2B_2C_2$ in the phasor diagram of Fig. 8.75 (a).

In Fig. 8.75 (b), the primary is in star and the secondary is again in double star. The primary line voltages in Fig. 8.75 (a) and (b) must be in phase, since they are fed from the same voltage source. Hence the position of $A_2B_2C_2$ in phasor diagrams of Figs. 8.75 (a) and (b) should not alter. The secondary voltage phasor diagrams are illustrated in Figs. 8.75 (a) and (b). Note that a_1a_3, b_1b_3, c_1c_3 are parallel to A_1A_2, B_1B_2, C_1C_2 in Figs. 8.75 (a). In the other Fig. 8.75 (b); $a_1'a_3'$, $b_1'b_3'$, $c_1'c_3'$ are parallel to A_1A_2, B_1B_2, C_1C_2. If the two neutrals n and n' are connected, the secondary voltage phasor diagrams of Fig. 8.75 (a) and (b) get superimposed to result in the phasor diagram of Fig. 8.75 (c). The angle between adjacent phasors, say between oa_1, ob_3' is 30° and in this way, 12-phase system of voltages with neutral o is obtained.

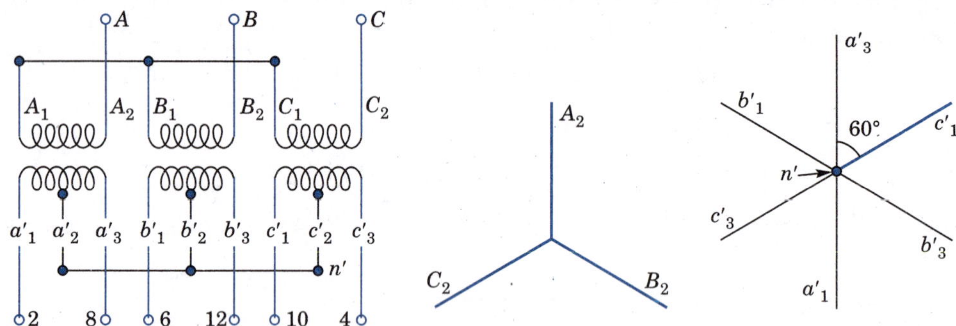

Fig. 8.75: (b) Pertaining to conversion from three to twelve phases.

Let V_2 be the line to line voltage on the 12-phase side, *i.e.*, V_2 is equal to the length of the phasor joining b_3c_1' or $c_1'c_1$ etc. Then in triangle ob_3c_1',

$$\frac{V_{ob3}}{\sin 75^\circ} = \frac{V_2}{\sin 30^\circ} \quad \text{or} \quad V_{ob3} = V_2 \frac{\sin 75^\circ}{\sin 30^\circ} = 1.932\ V_2$$

Line to neutral voltage on the secondary side is, $V_{ob3} = 1.932\ V_2$.

$\therefore$ The secondary with a mid-tap should be designed for a voltage of $2 \times 1.932\ V_2$ or $3.964\ V_2$ volts.

If V_1 is the primary line voltage, then phase windings of the star-primary should be designed for $V_1/3$ volts and that of the delta primary for V_1 volts.

The transformer, with its primary in star, must have a tertiary winding connected in delta, in order to allow the path for third harmonic magnetizing currents.

In Figs. 8.75 (a) and (b), the marking of the secondary terminals from 1 to 12 can be done by referring to Fig. 8.75 (c).

Since the neutral is available, this connection scheme is suitable for rectifier and inverter circuits, with the neutral O working as the negative terminal on dc side.

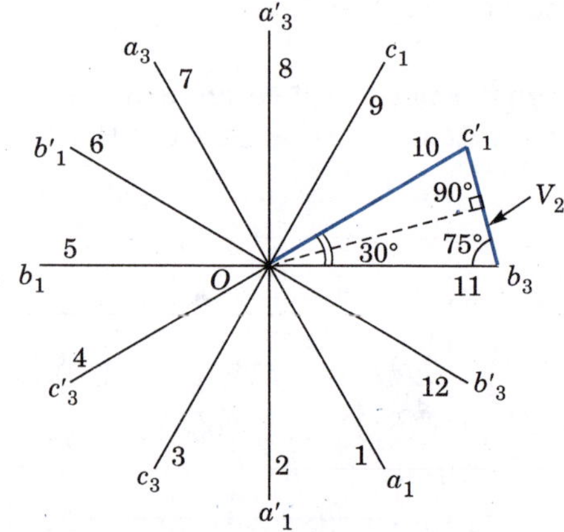

Fig. 8.75: (c) Phasor diagram pertaining to conversions from 3 to 12 phases.

8.11 THREE-WINDING TRANSFORMERS

A two-winding transformer has one primary winding and another secondary winding. A three-winding transformer has three windings on a common magnetic core; these windings are primary winding, secondary winding and a third winding. This third winding is usually called **tertiary winding**. Some of the applications of three-winding transformers are as follows :

1. The third winding is used to supply substation equipment (*e.g.*, pumps, fans etc.) at a voltage different from primary and secondary voltages.

2. The tertiary winding is used to supply power to phase-compensating devices such as static condensers or synchronous capacitors at a voltage different from those of primary and secondary voltages.

3. Tertiary winding can be used for measuring the voltage of high-voltage testing transformers.

4. For feeding two outgoing transmission lines at different voltages at a generating station.

5. A three-winding transformer, fed from one source, can deliver power to two loads independently and at different voltages. When used in this manner, a three-winding transformer is cheaper and more efficient than an equivalent two-winding transformers.

6. In star-star transformers, tertiary winding in delta (*i*) allows third harmonic current to flow and as a result, phase emfs are almost since waves (*ii*) allows sufficient flow of line to earth fault current for the operation of protective devices and (*iii*) limits voltage unbalance when main load is unsymmetrical.

A third winding is called **auxiliary winding** when used for supplying an additional load as in (1) above. It is also called **stabilizing winding** when used to limit the voltage unbalance as in (6) above.

8.11.1 Construction

A three-winding transformer has common magnetic core with primary, secondary and tertiary windings. Large transformers operate at different voltages, therefore, the three windings are termed as high voltage (H.V.), medium voltage (M.V.) and low voltage (L.V.) windings.

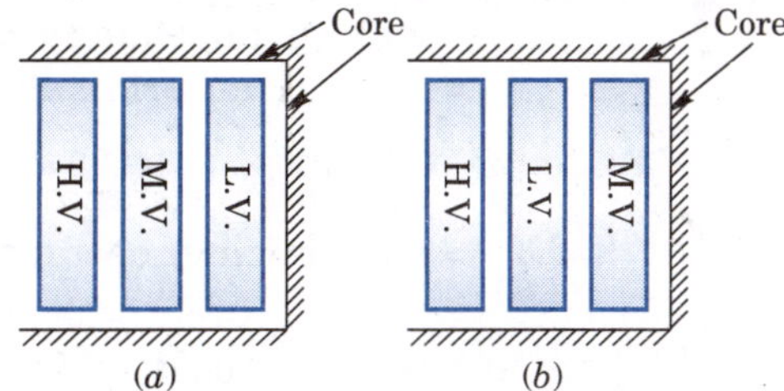

Fig. 8.76: Winding arrangement in a three-winding transformer.

There are two different arrangements of windings in a three-winding transformer as illustrated in Fig. 8.76. In Fig. 8.76 (*a*), L.V. winding is near the core and in Fig. 8.76 (*b*), M.V. winding is near the core. But H.V. winding in both cases is placed as the outermost winding from insulation considerations. The arrangement of these windings in the window determines their leakage impedences.

In two-winding transformer, kVA ratings of both H.V. and L.V. windings are equal. But in a three-winding transformer, kVA ratings of three windings are usually unequal. It is common to consider kVA rating of a three-winding transformer as equal to the largest kVA rating of any of its three windings.

8.11.2 Principle of Operation

The operating principle of a three-winding transformer is the same as for the two-winding transformer. The primary winding of a three-winding transformer is energized and exciting current, or no-load current, begins to flow. This exciting current provides for core loss and the magnetizing current. The flux produced by magnetizing current links all the three windings. Emfs are induced in primary, secondary and tertiary windings depending upon the number of turns in these windings.

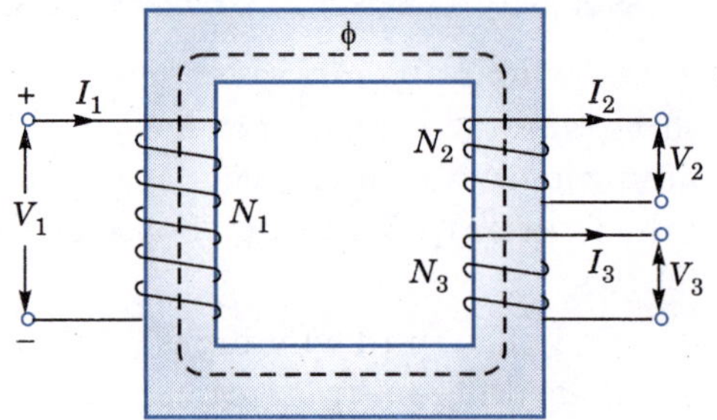

Fig. 8.77: Schematic diagram of a three-winding transformer

Fig. 8.77 shows a schematic diagram of a three-winding transformer. The subscripts 1, 2, 3 are used to denote primary, secondary and tertiary windings respectively. For an ideal three-winding transformer, emf per turn $= \dfrac{V_1}{N_1} = \dfrac{V_2}{N_2} = \dfrac{V_3}{N_3} = \sqrt{2}\, \pi\, f\, \phi_m$

For secondary and tertiary load current I_2 and I_3, the primary current I_1 can be obtained from the relation

$$\bar{I}_1 N_1 = \bar{I}_2 N_2 + \bar{I}_3 N_3$$

For a real transformer, $\bar{I}_1 N_1 = \bar{I}_0 N_1 + \bar{I}_2 N_2 + \bar{I}_3 N_3$, where I_0 is the no load current taken from the supply mains.

8.11.3 Equivalent Circuit

Equivalent circuit of a three-winding transformer can be represented by its single-phase star circuit as shown in Fig. 8.78. The terminals 1, 2, 3, indicate the primary (P), secondary (S) and tertiary (T) terminals respectively. In Fig. 8.78,

r_1, r_2, r_3 = resistances of P, S, T windings respectively
x_1, x_2, x_3 = leakage reactances of P, S, T windings respectively
z_1, z_2, z_3 = leakage impedances of P, S, T windings respectively
V_1, V_2, V_3 = voltages at terminals 1, 2, 3 respectively
I_1, I_2, I_3 = currents in P, S, T windings respectively
R_c = core-loss resistance
X_m = magnetizing reactance

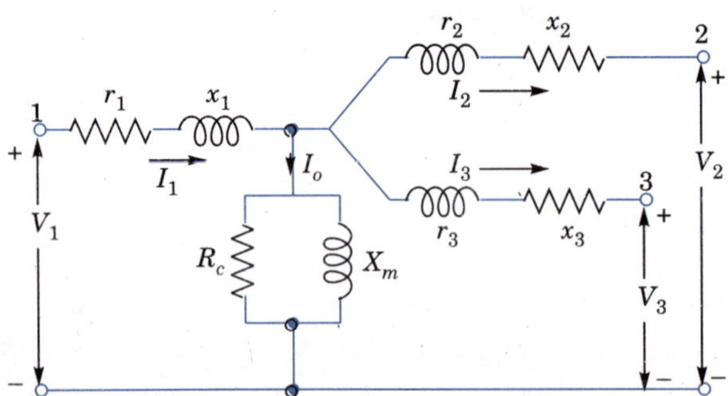

Fig. 8.78: Single-phase equivalent circuit of a three-winding transformer including exciting branch.

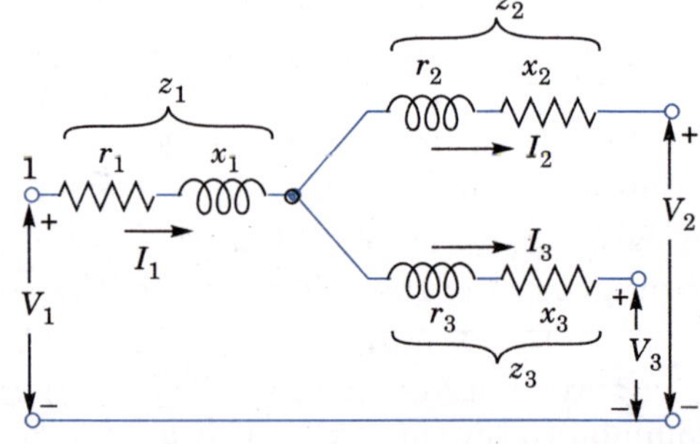

Fig. 8.79: Single-phase equivalent circuit of a three-winding transformer.

In practice, the magnetizing branch, consisting of R_C in parallel with X_m, is usually neglected. As a result, equivalent circuit of a three-winding transformer as shown in Fig. 8.79 is used for analysis purposes. In this equivalent circuit, leakage impedances z_1, z_2, z_3 are referred to one of the windings or are expressed in per unit using common kVA base.

8.11.4 Parameters of Three-winding Transformers

These parameters can be determined, as in two-winding transformers, by performing open-circuit and short circuit tests on three-winding transformers.

(*a*) **Short-circuit tests.** The equivalent leakage impedances z_1, z_2 and z_3 referred to a common base, can be determined by performing three-short-circuit tests as described below.

(*i*) Connect instruments in winding 1, short circuit winding 2 keeping winding 3 open as shown in Fig. 8.80 (*a*). Under these conditions, the equivalent circuit of Fig. 8.79 can be drawn as shown in Fig. 8.80 (*b*). If voltmeter, ammeter and wattmeter readings are respectively V_1, I_1 and P_1, then the magnitude of equivalent or short circuit impedance z_{12} of windings 1 and 2 is given by

$$z_{12} = \frac{V_1}{I_1} \qquad ...(8.20)$$

Equivalent resistance

$$r_{12} = \frac{P_1}{I_1^2} \qquad ...(8.21)$$

and equivalent leakage reactance $x_{12} = \sqrt{z_{12}^2 - r_{12}^2}$ ...(8.22)

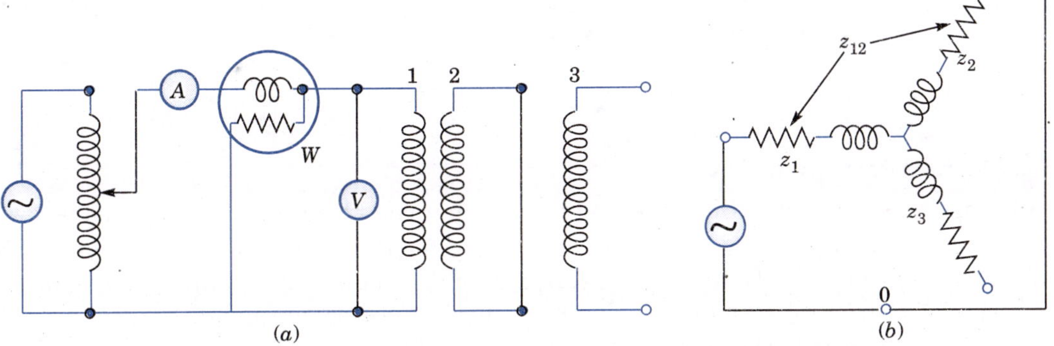

Fig. 8.80: Short-circuit test on a 3 winding transformer, (*a*) circuit diagram and (*b*) the corresponding equivalent circuit.

Note that subscripts 1, 2, associate with z, r and x indicate that windings 1 and 2 are in circuit. The order of subscripts has no significance. It means that if instruments are placed in winding 2 with winding 1 short circuited, the same value of equivalent in impedance would be obtained. In case the three-winding transformer is a polyphase one, then

$$z_{12} = \frac{\text{Per phase voltmeter reading}}{\text{Per phase ammeter reading}}.$$

Examination of the star equivalent-circuit of Fig. 8.80 (*b*) shows that z_{12} is a series combination of z_1 and z_2.

$$\therefore \quad z_{12} = r_{12} + jx_{12} = z_1 + z_2 \qquad ...(8.23)$$

(*ii*) Connect instruments in winding 1, short circuit winding 3 with winding 2 open. Then short-circuit impedance z_{13} of windings 1 and 3 is given by

$$z_{13} = r_{13} + jx_{13} = \frac{\text{Per phase voltmeter}}{\text{Per phase current}} = z_1 + z_3 \qquad ...(8.24)$$

(*iii*) Connect instruments in winding 2, short-circuit winding 3 and keep winding 1 open. These readings give

$$z_{23} = r_{23} + jx_{23} = \frac{\text{Per phase voltage}}{\text{Per phase current}} = z_2 + z_3 \qquad ...(8.25)$$

Simultaneous solution of Eqs. (8.23) to (8.25) gives

$$z_1 = r_1 + jx_1 = \tfrac{1}{2}\,(z_{12} + z_{13} - z_{23}) \qquad ...(8.26)$$

$$z_2 = r_2 + jx_2 = \tfrac{1}{2}\,(z_{12} + z_{23} - z_{13}) \qquad ...(8.27)$$

$$z_3 = r_3 + jx_3 = \tfrac{1}{2}\,(z_{13} + z_{23} - z_{12}) \qquad ...(8.28)$$

It may be seen from the above equations that the terms after the negative signs are z_{23} for z_1, z_{13} for z_2 and z_{12} for z_3.

The computed impedances z_{12} and z_{13} are referred to winding 1, because the instruments are connected in this winding. The impedance z_{23} is referred to winding 2, therefore, it must be referred to winding 1 $\left[= z_{23}(N_1/N_2)^2\right]$ and only then the Eqs. (8.26) to (8.28) employed for computing z_1, z_2 and z_3. Alternatively, z_{12}, z_{13} and z_{23} should be expressed in per unit and then Eqs. (8.26) to (8.28) used for determining z_1, z_2 and z_3.

(*b*) **Open circuit test.** This test can be performed, on any one of the three windings to determine core losses, magnetizing impedance and turns ratios. For example,

$$a_{12} = \frac{V_1}{V_2},\ a_{13} = \frac{V_1}{V_3} \quad \text{and} \quad a_{23} = \frac{V_2}{V_3} = \frac{V_2/V_1}{V_3/V_1} = \frac{a_{13}}{a_{12}}.$$

8.11.5 Voltage Regulation

The voltage regulation of a three-winding transformer can be obtained as outlined below:

(*i*) First determine the kVA in each winding for the load under consideration. Then obtain k for each winding. Here k is the ratio of the magnitude of the actual kVA loading of the winding to the base kVA employed in determining the network parameters.

(*ii*) Now calculate the p.u. leakage imedance drop (or voltage regulation) for each winding at its operating pf. For primary winding alone, the p.u. voltage regulation is

$$\varepsilon_1 = k_1\,(\varepsilon_{r1} \cos\theta_1 + \varepsilon_{x1} \sin\theta_1)$$

where, $k_1 = \dfrac{\text{primary kVA loading}}{\text{base kVA}}$

For secondary winding alone, $\varepsilon_2 = k_2\,(\varepsilon_{r2} \cos\theta_2 + \varepsilon_{x2} \sin\theta_2)$

where, $k_2 = \dfrac{\text{secondary kVA loading}}{\text{base kVA}}$

For tertiary winding alone, $\varepsilon_3 = k_3\,(\varepsilon_{r3} \cos\theta_2 + \varepsilon_{x3} \sin\theta_2)$

where, $k_3 = \dfrac{\text{tertiary kVA loading}}{\text{base kVA}}$

Here $\cos\theta_1$, $\cos\theta_2$, $\cos\theta_3$ are the operating power factors of windings 1, 2, 3 respectively.

ε_{r1}, ε_{r2}, ε_{r3} are the per unit resistance drops for windings 1, 2, 3 respectively.

ε_{x1}, ε_{x2}, ε_{x3} are the per unit leakage reactance drops for windings 1, 2, 3 respectively.

(iii) The voltage retulation for any pair of windings is obtained by the algebraic (not phasor) sum of the individual voltage regulations of this pair under consideration, if power flows from one to another. Otherwise a negative sign is used as detailed below.

For a three-winding transformer with primary energised from ac source and with both secondary and tertiary windings connected to loads, the voltage regulations are,

from primary to secondary, $\varepsilon_{12} = \varepsilon_1 + \varepsilon_2$ and

from primary to tertiary, $\varepsilon_{13} = \varepsilon_1 + \varepsilon_3$.

Since power flows from winding 1 to windings 2 and 3, ε_{12} and ε_{13} are obtained by adding individual regulations ε_1, ε_2, ε_3 accordingly.

The voltage regulation from secondary to tertiary, $\varepsilon_{23} = \varepsilon_2 - \varepsilon_3$

and from tertiary to secondary, $\varepsilon_{32} = \varepsilon_3 - \varepsilon_2$.

Since power does not flow from winding 2 to 3 or from 3 to 2, ε_{23} and ε_{32} are obtained by substracting ε_2, ε_3 accordingly.

Voltage regulation from secondary to primary, $\varepsilon_{21} = -(\varepsilon_1 + \varepsilon_2)$

and from tertiary to primary, $\varepsilon_{31} = -(\varepsilon_1 + \varepsilon_3)$.

Here negative sign is used before $(\varepsilon_1 + \varepsilon_2)$ because voltage regulation is determined from secondary to primary, whereas power flows from primary to secondary. Example 8.36 illustrates the determination of voltage regulation of a three-winding transformer.

Example 8.29. *A single-phase three-winding transformer gave the following data for three short-circuit tests :*

Secondary shorted ; primary excited : 120 V, 30 A, 750 W.

Tertiary shorted ; primary excited : 135 V, 30 A, 810 W

Tertiary shorted ; secondary excited : 30 V, 125 A, 815 W.

The ratings of the primary, secondary and tertiary windings are respectively 3300 V, 100 kVA ; 1000 V, 50 kVA and 400 V, 50 kVA.

Find the resistances and leakage reactances of the star equivalent circuit. Also calculate their values for each winding.

Solution. The resistances r_{12}, r_{13} and r_{23} can be determined, just like an ordinary two-winding transformer, from ammeter and wattmeter readings.

$$\therefore \quad r_{12} = \frac{750}{(30)^2} = 0.833\ \Omega, \qquad r_{13} = \frac{810}{(30)^2} = 0.90\ \Omega$$

and
$$r_{23} = \frac{815}{(125)^2} = 0.0522\ \Omega$$

Resistances r_{12} and r_{13} are referred to primary, since the instruments are connected in this winding. The resistance r_{23}, measured on the secondary side, must be referred to primary winding before r_1, r_2 and r_3 are computed.

$\therefore$ r_{23} when referred to primary winding

$$= (0.0522)\left(\frac{N_1}{N_2}\right)^2 = (0.0522)\left(\frac{3300}{1000}\right)^3 = 0.5685\ \Omega.$$

The equivalent circuit resistances r_1, r_2 and r_3 are

$$r_1 = \frac{1}{2}(r_{12} + r_{13} - r_{23}) = \frac{1}{2}(0.833 + 0.90 - 0.5685) = 0.5823\ \Omega$$

$$r_2 = \frac{1}{2}(r_{12} + r_{23} - r_{13}) = 0.251\ \Omega$$

and $$r_3 = \frac{1}{2}(r_{13} + r_{23} - r_{12}) = 0.318\ \Omega.$$

The short-circuit impedances are

$$z_{12} = \frac{120}{30} = 4\ \Omega, \qquad z_{13} = \frac{135}{30} = 4.5\ \Omega$$

and z_{23} when referred to primary winding $= \left(\frac{30}{125}\right)\left(\frac{3300}{1000}\right)^2 = 2.61\ \Omega$

From Eqs. (8.26) to (8.28), the leaking impedance referred to the primary side are,

$$z_1 = 2.945\ \Omega\ ;\ z_2 = 1.055\ \Omega \text{ and } z_3 = 1.555\ \Omega.$$

Primary winding leakage reactance is,

$$x_1 = \sqrt{z_1^2 - r_1^2} = \sqrt{(2.945)^2 - (0.5823)^2} = 2.885\ \Omega.$$

Similarly, $x_2 = 1.024\ \Omega$ and $x_3 = 1.520\ \Omega$.

Leakage impedance of primary winding, $z_1 = r_1 + jx_1 = 0.5823 + j2.885\ \Omega$

Leakage impedance of secondary winding

$$= (0.251 + j1.024)\left(\frac{1000}{3300}\right)^2 = 0.02305 + j0.094\ \Omega.$$

Leakage impedance of tertiary winding

$$= (0.318 + j1.52)\left(\frac{400}{3300}\right)^2 = 0.00467 + j0.0223\ \Omega.$$

Example 8.30. *A three-winding transformer in star-star-delta has the ratings of its primary, secondary and tertiary windings equal to 33 kV, 10 MVA ; 11 kV, 5 MVA and 3.3 kV, 5 MVA respectively. Three short-circuit tests on this transformer gave the following results:*

Secondary shorted, primary excited : 3200 V, 175 A, 120 kW.

Tertiary shorted, primary excited : 240 V, 15 A, 1.5 kW.

Tertiary shorted, secondary excited : 100 V, 50 A, 1.5 kW.

Compute the resistances and reactances in ohms of the star equivalent circuit of the three-winding transformer. Also determine z_1, z_2 and z_3 in per unit.

Solution. The instruments are connected in primary or secondary and since both of these are in star, the phase currents are equal to the line currents. Therefore, the resistances are :

$$r_{12} = \frac{120{,}000}{3\,(175)^2} = 1.305\ \Omega, \qquad r_{13} = \frac{1500}{3\,(15)^2} = 2.22\ \Omega$$

and $$r_{23} = \frac{1500}{3\,(50)^2} = 0.2\ \Omega.$$

For the equivalent circuit; r_{12}, r_{13} are already referred to primary and r_{23} with referred to primary is equal to $(0.2)\left(\frac{33}{11}\right)^2 = 1.8\ \Omega$.

$$\therefore \quad r_1 = \frac{1}{2}(r_{12} + r_{13} - r_{23}) = 0.862\ \Omega, \quad r_2 = \frac{1}{2}(r_{12} + r_{23} - r_{13}) = 0.442\ \Omega$$

and $$r_3 = \frac{1}{2}(r_{13} + r_{23} - r_{12}) = 1.357\ \Omega.$$

Primary is in star,

$$\therefore \quad z_{12} = \frac{\text{Per phase voltage}}{\text{Per phase current}} = \frac{2300}{\sqrt{3}\,(175)} = 10.56\ \Omega$$

Similarly, $$z_{13} = \frac{240}{\sqrt{3}\,(15)} = 9.24\ \Omega$$

Secondary is also in star, $\therefore$ z_{23} referred to primary

$$= \frac{100}{\sqrt{3}\,(50)} \cdot \left(\frac{33}{11}\right)^2 = 10.4\ \Omega.$$

With the help of Eqs. (8.26) to (8.28),

$$z_1 = 4.70\ \Omega\ ;\ z_2 = 5.86\ \Omega \text{ and } z_3 = 5.54\ \Omega.$$

$$\therefore \quad x_1 = \sqrt{(4.70)^2 - (0.862)^2} = 4.62\ \Omega$$

$$x_2 = \sqrt{(5.86)^2 - (0.442)^2} = 5.84\ \Omega$$

and $$x_3 = \sqrt{(4.54)^2 - (1.357)^2} = 4.34\ \Omega.$$

The leakage impedances z_1, z_2 and z_3 calculated above are in ohms and are referred to primary. In order to compute their per unit values, these should be divided by base impedance of the primary winding.

For primary ; per phase base voltage, $V_{b1} = \frac{33{,}000}{\sqrt{3}}$ V

and per phase base current, $$I_{b1} = \frac{10{,}000}{\sqrt{3}\,(33)}\ \text{A}$$

$\therefore$ Base impedance,

$$Z_{b1} = \frac{V_{b1}}{I_{b1}} = \left(\frac{33{,}000}{\sqrt{3}}\right)\left(\frac{\sqrt{3}\,(33)}{10{,}000}\right) = \frac{(33)^2}{10} = 108.9\ \Omega.$$

$$\therefore \quad z_1 \text{ in p.u.} = \frac{4.70}{108.90} = 0.0432, \quad z_2 \text{ in p.u.} = \frac{5.86}{108.90} = 0.0537$$

$$z_3 \text{ in p.u.} = \frac{4.55}{108.90} = 0.0417.$$

Example 8.31. *The primary, secondary and tertiary windings of a three-winding transformer are rated as 11 kV, 6 MVA, star/3.3 kV, 3 MVA, star/400 V, 3 MVA, delta respectively. Three short-circuit tests on this transformer gave the following results:*

secondary shorted ; primary excited : 500 V, 100 A,

tertiary shorted; primary excited : 600 V, 100 A,

and tertiary shorted ; secondary excited : 100 V, 200 A.

(a) Find the per unit leakage reactances of the star equivalent circuit. Neglect resistances.

(b) The primary is energised at rated voltage and the secondary is on open circuit. For a three-phase balanced short circuit at the tertiary terminals, calculate the short-circuit current and the secondary terminal voltage.

Solution. (*a*) From tests 1 and 2, the leakage reactances referred to primary are :

$$x_{12} = \frac{500}{\sqrt{3}\,(100)} = 2.885\ \Omega, \qquad x_{13} = \frac{600}{\sqrt{3}\,(100)} = 3.46\ \Omega$$

From test 3, the leakage reactance measured on the secondary side is

$$x_{23} = \frac{100}{\sqrt{3}\,(200)} = 0.2885\ \Omega$$

$$x_{23} \text{ when referred to primary} = (0.2885)\left(\frac{11}{3.3}\right)^2 = 3.20\ \Omega$$

$$\therefore \qquad x_1 = \tfrac{1}{2}\,(x_{12} + x_{13} - x_{23}) = 1.572\ \Omega$$

$$x_2 = \tfrac{1}{2}\,(x_{12} + x_{23} - x_{13}) = 1.312\ \Omega$$

and

$$x_3 = \tfrac{1}{2}\,(x_{13} + x_{23} - x_{12}) = 1.887\ \Omega.$$

For the primary, the base impedance is,

$$Z_{b1} = \frac{V_{b1}}{I_{b1}} = \frac{(11/\sqrt{3})}{\dfrac{6}{\sqrt{3} \times 11}} = \frac{(11)^2}{6} = 20.17\ \Omega$$

$$\therefore \qquad x_1 \text{ in p.u.} = \frac{1.572}{20.17} = 0.0779, \qquad x_2 \text{ in p.u.} = \frac{1.312}{20.12} = 0.0651$$

and

$$x_3 \text{ in p.u.} = \frac{1.887}{20.17} = 0.0936.$$

(*b*) For a short circuit at the tertiary terminals, $V_3 = 0$. From Fig. 8.81, the short circuit current I_{sc} in magnitude is

$$I_{sc} = \frac{V_1}{x_1 + x_3} = \frac{1.00}{0.1715} = 5.831 \text{ p.u.}$$

Fig. 8.81 reveals that the voltage across the secondary terminals is $I_{sc}x_3$.

$$\therefore \qquad V_2 = I_{sc}x_3 = (5.831)\,(0.0936) = 0.546 \text{ p.u.}$$

or

$$V_2 = (0.546)\,(3.3) = 1.802 \text{ kV.}$$

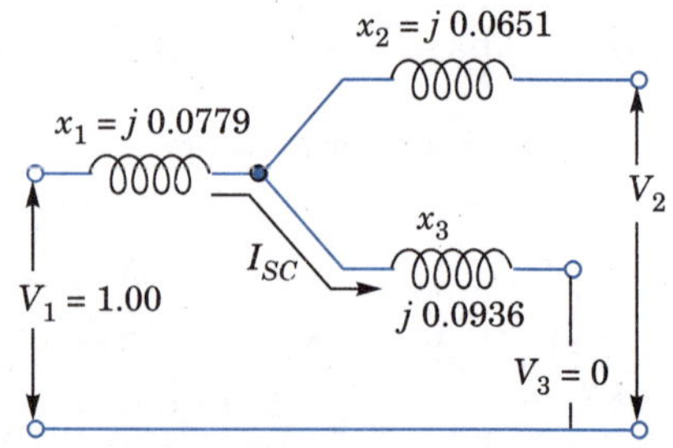

Fig. 8.81: Pertaining to Example 8.31.

Short-circuit current in primary winding

$$= I_{sc} \cdot I_{b1} = (5.831) \times \frac{6000}{\sqrt{3} \times 11} = 1836.34 \text{ A}$$

Short-circuit current in tertiary winding = $I_{sc} \cdot I_{b3}$

$$= (5.831) \times \frac{6000}{(0.40)\,(3)} = 29155 \text{ A.}$$

Note that for calculating base current I_{b3} for the tertiary winding, the base MVA of 6 should be used.

Example 8.32. *A three winding transformer is rated as follows:*

primary : star, 132 kV, 50 MVA
secondary : star, 33 kV, 25 MVA
tertiary : delta, 11 kV, 25 MVA

The per unit leakage reactances on 50 MVA base are ; x_{12} = 0.086, x_{13} = 0.062 and x_{23} = 0.090. Neglect resistances. (a) The primary is energised at a constant rated voltage. The secondary and tertiary windings, both supply rated currents at 0.8 p.f lag. Find the voltage of the secondary and tertiary terminals.

(b) In part (a), if tertiary load is disconnected, find the secondary terminal voltage.

(c) In part (a), if the tertiary is made to supply rated current at 0.6 p.f lead, compute the secondary terminal voltage.

Solution. The leakage reactances are referred to a common base of 50 MVA.

$$\therefore \quad x_1 = 1/2(0.086 + 0.062 - 0.090) = 0.029 \text{ p.u.}$$

$$x_2 = 1/2\,(0.086 + 0.090 - 0.062) = 0.057 \text{ p.u.}$$

and

$$x_3 = 1/2\,(0.062 + 0.090 - 0.086) = 0.033 \text{ p.u.}$$

(*a*) Both the secondary and tertiary windings operate at rated currents and at lagging power factor of 0.8. Assuming that secondary the tertiary terminal voltages are in phase, then with V_2 and V_3 as reference phasors,

secondary current $\quad \bar{I}_2 = 0.8 - j0.6$

and tertiary current $\quad \bar{I}_3 = 0.8 - j0.6$

The primary current $\quad \bar{I}_1 = \bar{I}_2 + \bar{I}_3 = 1.6 - j1.20.$

For the primary and secondary circuits, the voltage equation is

$$\bar{V}_1 = \bar{V}_2 + \bar{I}_2 \bar{z}_2 + \bar{I}_1 \bar{z}_1$$

$$= \bar{V}_2 + (0.8 - j0.6)\,(j0.057) + (1.6 - j1.2)\,(j0.029)$$

or

$$\bar{V}_1 = (\bar{V}_2 + 0.069) + j0.092$$

$$\therefore \quad V_1 = 1 = \sqrt{(V_2 + 0.069)^2 + (0.092)^2}$$

or

$$V_2 = \left[\sqrt{1 - (0.092)^2}\right] - 0.069 = 0.926 \text{ p.u.}$$

$\therefore$ Secondary terminal voltage = (0.926) (33) = 30.55 kV.

For primary and tertiary circuits, the voltage equation is

$$\bar{V}_1 = \bar{V}_3 + \bar{I}_3\bar{z}_3 + \bar{I}_1\bar{z}_1$$

$$= \bar{V}_3 + (0.8 - j0.6)\,(j0.033) + (1.6 - j1.2)\,(j0.029)$$

$$\bar{V}_1 = (\bar{V}_3 + 0.0546) + j0.0728$$

or $$1 = (V_3 + 0.0546)^2 + (0.0728)^2$$

or $$V_3 = \left[\sqrt{1-(0.0728)^2}\right] - 0.0546 = 0.9424 \text{ p.u.}$$

∴ Tertiary terminal voltage = 0.9424 × 11 = 10.37 kV.

(*b*) Here $I_3 = 0$, ∴ $\bar{I}_1 = \bar{I}_2 = 0.8 - j0.6$.

∴ $$\bar{V}_1 = \bar{V}_2 + \bar{I}_2(\bar{z}_1 + \bar{z}_2) = \bar{V}_2 + (0.8 - j0.6)\,(j0.086)$$

or $$V_2 = 0.9449 \text{ p.u.}$$

∴ Secondary terminal voltage = 0.9449 × 33 = 31.2 kV.

(*c*) The tertiary winding now supplies rated current at 0.6 p.f lead.

∴ $$\bar{I}_3 = 0.6 + j0.8,\ \bar{I}_2 = 0.8 - j0.6$$

and $$\bar{I}_1 = \bar{I}_2 + \bar{I}_3 = (0.8 - j0.6) + (0.6 + j0.8) = 1.4 + j0.2.$$

∴ $$\bar{V}_1 = \bar{V}_2 + \bar{I}_2\bar{z}_2 + \bar{I}_1\bar{z}_1$$

$$= \bar{V}_2 + (0.8 - j0.6)\,(j0.057) + (1.4 + j0.2)\,(j0.029)$$

$$= (\bar{V}_2 + 0.0284) + j0.0862. \quad \text{or} \quad V_2 = 0.9679 \text{ p.u.}$$

∴ Secondary terminal voltage = 0.9679 × 33 = 31.94 kV.

This example shows that the effect of connecting a leading pf load across the tertiary winding is to cause an increase in the secondary terminal voltage from 30.55 kV [part (*a*)] to 31.94 kV. This demonstrates the effects of connecting static capacitors or synchronous condensers across the tertiary winding for voltage regulation purposes.

Example 8.33. *A 3-winding, 132/33/11 kV, three-phase star-star-delta transformer, with negligible resistance, gave the following data for its reactances in per unit for a base of 50 MVA.*

H.V. to L.V. : 0.24
H.V. to M.V. : 0.19
M.V. to L.V. : 0.21

The l.v. winding supplies a balanced load current of 2400 A at power factor 0.8 lagging and the m.v. winding is connected to a star-connected load of 0 + j50 Ω per phase. For maintaining rated terminal voltage of 11 kV at its terminals, determine the voltage required at h.v. terminals.

Solution. It is given that $x_{13} = 0.24$, $x_{12} = 0.19$ and $x_{23} = 0.21$. From these, the per unit leakage reactances of the star-equivalent circuit are

$$x_1 = \tfrac{1}{2}\,(x_{12} + x_{13} - x_{23}) = \tfrac{1}{2}\,(0.19 + 0.24 - 0.21) = 0.11$$

Similarly, $x_2 = 0.08$ and $x_3 = 0.13$

Here base, MVA = 50.

For primary, base, kV = 132 ; base current $I_{1b} = \dfrac{50{,}000 \times \sqrt{3}}{3 \times 132}$ A

For secondary, base, kV = 33 ; base current $I_{2b} = \dfrac{50{,}000 \times \sqrt{3}}{3 \times 33}$ A

For tertiary, base, kV = 11 ; base current $I_{3b} = \dfrac{50{,}000}{3 \times 11}$ A

Per-phase load current in secondary $I_2 = \dfrac{33000}{\sqrt{3} \times 50}$ A

or
$$I_{2.pu} = \frac{I_2 \text{ in } A}{I_{2b} \text{ in } A} = \frac{33000}{\sqrt{3} \times 50} \times \frac{3 \times 33}{50{,}000\sqrt{3}}$$
$$= \left(\frac{33}{50}\right)^2 = 0.4356 \text{ at zero pf lagging}$$

Per-phase load current in tertiary,
$$I_{3\,.\,p.u.} = \frac{2400 \times 11 \times 3}{\sqrt{3} \times 50{,}000} = 0.9145 \text{ at pf 0.8 lagging.}$$

Per-phase primary current, $\bar{I}_1 = (\bar{I}_2 + \bar{I}_3)$ in per unit

or
$$\bar{I}_1 = -j0.4356 + j0.9145\,(0.8 - j0.6) = 0.7316 - j0.9843 \text{ p.u.}$$

The star equivalent circuit for this transformer gives the primary input voltage as
$$\bar{V}_1 = \bar{V}_3 + \bar{I}_3 z_3 + \bar{I}_1 z_1$$
$$= 1 + 0.9145\,(0.8 - j0.6)\,(j0.13) + (0.7316 - j0.9843)\,(j0.11)$$
$$= 1.17963 + j0.1756$$

or
$$V_1 = 1.9263 \text{ p.u.}$$

∴ Voltage required at h.v. terminals = 1.9263 × 132 = 157.427 kV.

Example 8.34. *A 3-phase bank, consisting of three single-phase three-winding transformers connected in star-delta-star, is used for stepping down the voltage of a 3-phase, 132-kV transmission line. Following is the data pertaining to one of the transformers :*

Ratings : Primary 1 : 15 MVA, 132 kV
Secondary 2 : 7.5 MVA, 33 kV
Tertiary 3 : 7.5 MVA, 11 kV

Short-circuit reactances on 7.5 MVA base :
$$x_{12} = 0.082,\ x_{23} = 0.064,\ x_{13} = 0.108$$

Transformer resistances are neglected. The delta-connected secondaries supply their rated current to a balanced load 0.8 pf lagging. The tertiaries deliver the rated current to a balanced load at unity p.f.

(a) Calculate the primary line voltage to maintain rated voltage at the secondary terminals.

(b) For the condition in part (a), find the line voltage at the tertiary terminals.

(c) If the primary voltage found in part (a) is held fixed, to what value will the tertiary voltage rise if the secondary load is reduced to zero?

Solution. The leakage reactances referred to common base of 7.5 MVA are

$$x_1 = \frac{1}{2}(0.082 + 0.108 - 0.064) = 0.063 \text{ p.u.}$$

$$x_2 = \frac{1}{2}(0.082 + 0.064 - 0.108) = 0.038 \text{ p.u.}$$

$$x_3 = \frac{1}{2}(0.064 + 0.108 - 0.082) = 0.09 \text{ p.u.}$$

(*a*) Secondary current $I_2 = 0.8 - j0.6$

Tertiary current $I_3 = 1.0 + j0.00$

The primary current $\bar{I}_1 = \bar{I}_2 + \bar{I}_3 = 1.8 - j0.6$ p.u.

For the primary and secondary circuits, the voltage equation is

$$\bar{V}_1 = \bar{V}_2 + \bar{I}_2\bar{z}_2 + \bar{I}_1\bar{z}_1$$

As the secondary voltage is equal to rated voltage, $V_2 = 1.0$

$$\therefore \quad \bar{V}_1 = 1 + (0.8 - j0.6)\,(j0.038) + (1.8 - j0.6)\,(j0.063)$$

$$= 1.0606 + j0.1438$$

$$\therefore \quad V_1 = 1.070304 \text{ p.u.} = 1.070304 \times 132 = 141.28 \text{ kV.}$$

(*b*) For the secondary and tertiary circuits, the voltage equation is

$$\bar{V}_3 = \bar{V}_2 + \bar{I}_2\bar{z}_2 - \bar{I}_3\bar{z}_3$$

$$= 1 + (0.8 - j0.6)\,(j0.038) - 1\,(j0.09) = 1.0228 - j0.0596$$

or $$V_3 = 1.02454 \text{ p.u.} = 11.27 \text{ kV.}$$

(*c*) With $I_2 = 0$, the voltage equation for primary and tertiary circuits is

$$\bar{V}_1 = \bar{V}_3 + \bar{I}_3\,(z_1 + z_3)$$

or $$1.0606 + j0.1438 = \bar{V}_3 + j0.153 \quad \text{or} \quad \bar{V}_3 = 1.0606 - j0.0092$$

$$\therefore \quad V_3 = 1.06064 = 11.667 \text{ kV}$$

With secondary load reduced to zero, the tertiary voltage rises from 11.27 kV to 11.667 kV.

Example 8.35. *A 11/3.3/0.4 kV, star/star/delta, three winding transformer has a magnetizing current of 3.0 amperes. At rated voltages, the secondary supplies a balanced load of 200 kVA at 0.8 pf lag and tertiary supplies a balanced load of 120 kW. The primary operates at a power factor of (a) 0.9 lagging and (b) 0.81 lagging.*

Find the primary and tertiary phase currents and also the power factor at which the tertiary operates. Neglect losses.

Solution. In a three-winding transformer, all the quantities should be referred to any one winding and here the quantities are referred to the primary winding.

Magnetizing current $\bar{I}_\phi = 0 - j3.0$ A

Secondary phase current $= \dfrac{200{,}000}{\sqrt{3}\,(3300)}$ A

$\therefore$ Secondary phase current referred to primary,

$$\bar{I}_2 = \frac{200{,}000}{\sqrt{3}\,(3300)} \cdot \frac{3300}{11{,}000} = \frac{200}{\sqrt{3}\,(11)} = 10.5 \text{ A}$$

In phasor form, $\bar{I}_2 = I_2 (\cos \theta_2 - j \sin \theta_2)$

$= 10.5\,(0.8 - j0.6) = (8.4 - j6.3)$ A.

Active component of tertiary phase current referred to primary

$$= I_3 \cos \theta_3 = \frac{120{,}000}{3 \times 400} \cdot \frac{400 \times \sqrt{3}}{11{,}000} = \frac{120}{\sqrt{3}\,(11)} = 6.3 \text{ A.}$$

Reactive component of tertiary current $= I_3 \sin \theta_3$.

Assuming lagging *pf* for the tertiary load,

$$\bar{I}_3 = I_3 (\cos \theta_3 - j \sin \theta_3) = 6.3 - jI_3 \sin \theta_3$$

Now total primary current,

$$\bar{I}_1 = \bar{I}_\phi + \bar{I}_2 + \bar{I}_3 = (0 - j3.0) + (8.4 - j6.3) + (6.3 - jI_3 \sin \theta_3)$$

$$= 14.7 - j(9.3 + I_3 \sin \theta_3).$$

(*a*) If θ_1 is the primary *pf* angle, then

$$\tan \theta_1 = \frac{9.3 + I_3 \sin \theta_3}{14.7} = \tan (\cos^{-1} 0.9) = 0.484,$$

or $9.3 + I_3 \sin \theta_3 = (14.7)\,(0.484) = 7.12$ or $I_3 \sin \theta_3 = -2.18$.

Since $I_3 \sin \theta_3$ has turned out to be negative, the tertiary is operating at a leading *pf*.
The magnitude of tertiary current is

$$\bar{I}_3 = \sqrt{(I_3 \cos \theta_3)^2 + (I_3 \sin \theta_3)^2}$$

$$= \sqrt{(6.3)^2 + (-2.18)^2} = 6.67 \text{ A.}$$

$\therefore$ Power factor at which the tertiary winding operates

$$= \frac{6.3}{6.67} = 0.945 \text{ leading.}$$

Primary current, $\bar{I}_1 = 14.7 - j(9.3 - 2.18) = 14.7 - j7.12$

$\therefore$ $I_1 = \sqrt{(14.7)^2 + (7.12)^2} = 16.33$ A.

Check: Power factor on the primary side $= \dfrac{14.7}{16.33} = 0.9$ lagging.

(*b*) Now, $\tan \theta_1 = \dfrac{9.3 + I_3 \sin \theta_3}{14.7} = \tan (\cos^{-1} 0.81) = 0.724.$

or $(9.3 + I_3 \sin \theta_3) = 10.64$ or $I_3 \sin \theta_3 = 1.34$.

Since $I_3 \sin \theta_3$ is positive, the tertiary is operating at a lagging power factor.

Now $\bar{I}_3 = \sqrt{(I_3 \cos \theta_3)^2 + (I_3 \sin \theta_3)^2} = \sqrt{(6.3)^2 + (1.34)^2} = 6.44$ A.

$\therefore$ Power factor on the tertiary side $= \dfrac{6.3}{6.43} = 0.980$ lagging.

Primary current $\bar{I}_1 = 14.7 - j\,(9.3 + 1.34) = 14.7 - j10.64$

or $\bar{I}_1 = \sqrt{(14.7)^2 + (10.64)^2} = 18.15$ A

Check: Power factor on the primary side $= \dfrac{14.7}{18.15} = 0.81$ lagging.

Example 8.36. *A 6600/3000/400 V, star/star/delta transformer has per unit resistance drops of 0.006, 0.007, 0.008 and per unit reactance drops of 0.03, 0.028, 0.034 for its primary, secondary and tertiary windings respectively on a 1500 kVA rated-voltage base. Its magnetizing current is 5 A. Find the voltage regulations for 3-phase balanced loads of 1500 kVA at pf 0.8 lagging on secondary and 600 kVA at pf 0.6 leading on tertiary.*

Solution. This example is solved in terms of 6600 V primary winding.

Magnetizing, $\text{kVA} = 0 - j\,\dfrac{\sqrt{3} \times 6600 \times 5}{1000} = 0 - j57.16$

Secondary load, $\text{kVA} = 1500\,(0.8 - j0.6) = 1200 - j900$

Tertiary load, $\text{kVA} = 600\,(0.6 + j0.8) = 360 + j480$

Total load on primary $= (0 - j57.16) + (1200 - j900) + (360 + j480)$

$= 1560 - j477.16 = 1631.34 \angle -17°$ kVA

The primary load is therefore, 1631.34 kVA at pf of cos 17° = 0.956 lagging.

For primary, $k_1 = \dfrac{1631.34}{1500} = 1.0876$

$\therefore$ Primary regulation component, $\varepsilon_1 = k_1\,(\varepsilon_{r1} \cos\theta_1 + \varepsilon_{x1} \sin\theta_1)$

$= 1.0876\,(0.006 \times 0.956 + 0.03 \times 0.2924) = 0.01578$

For secondary, $k_2 = \dfrac{1500}{1500} = 1.00$

$\therefore$ $\varepsilon_2 = k_2\,(\varepsilon_{r2} \cos\theta_2 + \varepsilon_{x2} \sin\theta_2)$

$= 1.00\,(0.007 \times 0.8 + 0.028 \times 0.6) = 0.0224$

For tertiary, $k_3 = \dfrac{600}{1500} = 0.4$

$\therefore$ $\varepsilon_3 = k_3\,(\varepsilon_{r3} \cos\theta_3 + \varepsilon_{x3} \sin\theta_3) = 0.4\,(0.008 \times 0.6 - 0.034 \times 0.8)$

$= -\,0.00896$

Primary to secondary voltage regulation,

$\varepsilon_{12} = \varepsilon_1 + \varepsilon_2 = 0.01578 + 0.0224 = 0.03818$ p.u. or $= 3.818\%$.

Primary to tertiary voltage regulation,

$\varepsilon_{13} = \varepsilon_1 + \varepsilon_3 = 0.01578 - 0.00896 = 0.00682$ p.u. or $= 0.682\%$.

Secondary to tertiary and tertiary to secondary voltage regulations are respectively,

$\varepsilon_{23} = \varepsilon_2 - \varepsilon_3 = 0.0224 + 0.00896 = 0.03136$ p.u. or 3.136%.

and $\varepsilon_{32} = -\,\varepsilon_{23} = -\,0.03136$ p.u. or $-\,3.136\%$.

8.12 THREE-PHASE AUTO-TRANSFORMERS

For the transformation of polyphase voltages, it is preferrable to use autotransformers instead of two-winding transformers in case the voltage ratio is not greater than 2. The advantages and disadvantages of polyphase auto-transformers are the same as discussed for single-phase auto-transformers.* In addition, three-phase autotransformers have the following disadvantages as compared to three-phase two-winding transformers :

(*i*) Since autotransformers have lower leakage impedances, these are subjected to severe mechanical stresses under short circuit conditions.

(*ii*) Connections on the primary and secondary sides in 3-phase autotransformers must be same, *i.e.*, only *Yy*, *Dd* are realisable.

The present day use of three-phase autotransformers are:

(*i*) for obtaining adjustable output voltages in testing circuits and laboratories,

(*ii*) for interconnecting two electrical systems of different voltages, *e.g.*, 220 kV and 400 kV systems and

(*iii*) as autotransformer starters for three-phase induction and synchronous motors.

The autotransformers in 3-phase circuits can be connected in many different ways**, but here only the most common type of connection schemes is discussed.

8.12.1 Star-connected Auto-transformers

A bank of three star-connected autotransformers shown in Fig. 8.82 behaves like a bank of three *Yy* connected two-winding transformers in many respects. For example, if autotransformer neutral is isolated, then line to neutral voltages contain large third-harmonic voltage components because of the suppression of third-harmonic exciting currents. This, however, does not occur in three-phase three-lagged core type autotransformers.

The behaviour of a bank of star-connected autotransformers is discussed below.

(*a*) When the autotransformer neutral is grounded but all other system neutrals are isolated, then, as usual, triple-frequency voltages induced in each transformer are present between line to ground but are absent from line to line. These triple frequency voltages cause the appearance of triple frequency exciting currents through line to ground capacitance *C* and through transformer windings. If line to ground current through *C* is taken as unity, the total return current from ground to star point *O* is 3 as shown in Fig. 8.83 (*a*). In case triple-frequency magnetizing reactances of transformer windings

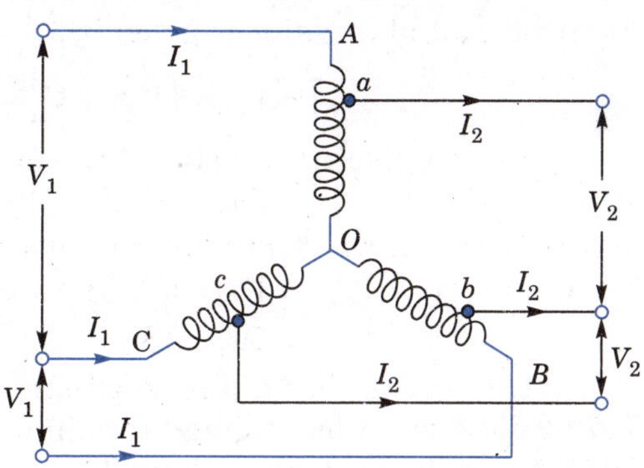

Fig. 8.82: Star-connected autotransformer.

become equal to the triple-frequency capacitive reactances $\left(\dfrac{1}{2\pi \cdot 3f \cdot C}\right)$ of the line wires to ground, then series resonance would take place. As a result of it, third-harmonic voltages from

* "Electrical Machinery" by the same author.

** "Transformer Engineering" by L.F. Blume.

line to neutral may become dangerously high which is undesirable. Therefore, if line to ground capacitance C is large*, then neutrals of autotransformer as well as the system network must be grounded so as to avoid the appearance of large triple-frequency voltages between line to neutral.

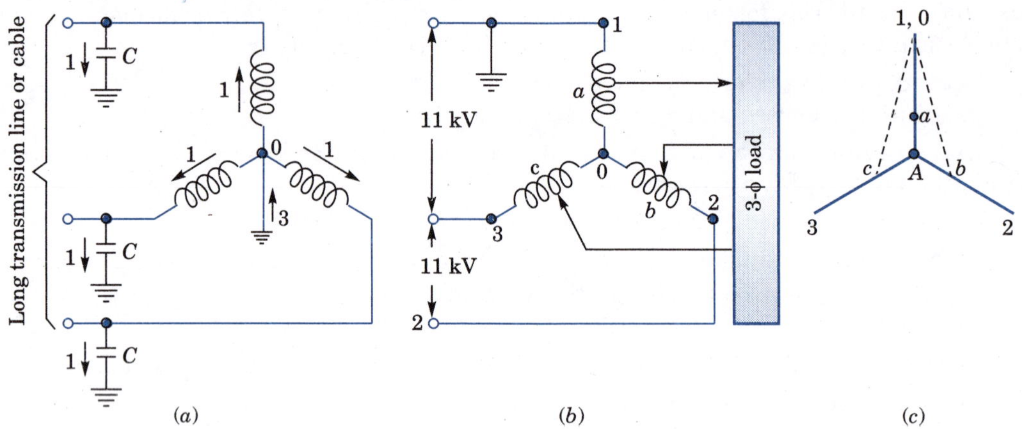

Fig. 8.83: (*a*) Paths of triple-frequency currents in *Yy* bank feeding a long transmission line or cable ; (*b*) A 3-phase auto-transformer subjected to line to ground fault ; and (*c*) phasor diagram for part (*b*).

(*b*) Consider a 3-phase system with auto-transformer neutral isolated and with all system neutrals ungounded, Fig. 8.84 (*b*). On such a system, a line to ground fault on h.v. side would cause the appearance of abnormally high voltages between the other two low-voltage terminals and the ground. In Fig. 8.83 (*b*), the line to ground fault is shown to occur on h.v. line 1. After the fault, the neutral 0 gets shifted to grounded line 1 and the voltage between l.v. terminal b and ground, or l.v. terminal c and ground, would rise to $V_{b1} = V_{c1}$ or $V_{bo} = V_{co}$, Fig. 8.83 (*c*) and its value is given by

$$V_{b1} = V_{c1} = [V_{A1}^2 + V_{Ab}^2 - 2V_{A1} \cdot V_{Ab} \cdot \cos 120°]^{1/2}$$

For example, assume that transformer windings are tapped at a, b, c such that $V_{oa} = 0.2\ V_{o1}$, $V_{ob} = 0.2\ V_{o2}$ etc in Fig. 8.83 (*b*). After the fault, the neutral gets shifted to faulted line 1 and voltage V_{b1}, V_{bo}, V_{c1} or V_{c0} is then given by

$$V_{b1} = V_{c1} = [(6351)^2 + (0.2 \times 6351)^2 - 2 \times 6351 \times (0.2 \times 6351) \cos 120°]^{1/2}$$
$$= 7072.2 \text{ V}.$$

This shows that a line to ground fault on h.v. side causes the appearance of voltage 7072.2 V between low-voltage terminal b, or c, and the ground. This voltage of magnitude 7072.2 V is much higher than 0.2 × 11000 = 2200 V. Thus, ungrounded star-connected autotransformers should not be used on ungrounded systems unless the voltage ratio is close to unity.

The problems associated with star-connected autotransformers can be overcome by the same methods as are adopted for a *Yy* bank and these are (*i*) by using delta-connected tertiary windings (*ii*) or by grounding the neutrals of both the autotransformer and the three-phase source.

* A long transmission line or cable has large line to ground capacitance.

As in single-phase autotransformers, the mmf of winding Aa is balanced by mmf of winding Oa in Fig. 8.82.

$$\therefore \quad \left.\begin{aligned} I_1 N_{Aa} &= I_{oa} N_{oa} \\ \text{and} \quad I_2 &= I_1 + I_{oa} \end{aligned}\right\} \qquad \text{...(8.29)}$$

The relations derived for single-phase autotransformers apply equally well to star-connected autotransformers on per phase basis.

Example 8.37. *A star-connected autotransformer has input to output voltage ratio of 2. A lamp load requiring 20 A is connected across terminals a, b and an inductive load requiring 30 A at 0.8 p.f lag is connected across terminals b, c ; refer to Fig. 8.82. Calculate the currents in each part of the three single-phase transformers.*

Solution. For this example, refer to Fig. 8.82.

Load across a, b :

For phase OA, $I_{Aa} + I_{oa} = I_2$, current leaving terminal a.

Since a is the mid-point, $I_{Aa} = I_{oa} = \frac{1}{2} I_2 = 10$ A at unity p.f.

Similarly, $I_{bo} = I_{bB} = \frac{1}{2} I_2 = 10$ A at unity p.f.

Load across b, c :

$$I_{bo} = I_{bB} = \frac{30}{2} = 15 \text{ A at 0.8 p.f lagging.}$$

and
$$I_{oc} = I_{Cc} = \frac{30}{2} = 15 \text{ A at 0.8 p.f lagging.}$$

Note that winding bo carries 10 A at unity pf and 15 A at 0.8 pf lagging. Same is true for winding bB.

Total current in winding bo or bB

$$I_{bc} = I_{bB} = \sqrt{(10 + 15 \times 0.8)^2 + (15 \times 0.6)^2} = 23.77 \text{ A.}$$

8.13 SEQUENCE IMPEDANCES OF TRANSFORMERS

In 3-phase systems, we come across positive-sequence, negative-sequence and zero-sequence voltages and currents and the associated sequence impedances. The object of this article is to discuss these sequence impedances of transformers.

The impedance of static apparatus, like transmission lines, cables and transformers, does not depend upon the phase sequence of the applied voltages. This is due to the fact that the operation of static apparatus is not effected whether they are fed with positive or negative sequence voltages. So the transformer impedances to positive-phase sequence and negative-phase sequence currents are the same. The impedance is that usually understood by the term as used in two-winding or three-winding transformers as shown in Fig. 8.84. The positive-phase sequence impedance of a two-winding transformer is equal to its leakage impedance z_{12}. It can be obtained by performing short-circuit test on a transformer and for a 2-winding transformer, positive sequence impedance = negative sequence impedance = transformer leakage impedance z_{12}. For a three-winding transformer, the positive and negative sequence impedances are equal to the leakage impedances between any pair of terminals of Fig. 8.84 (*b*).

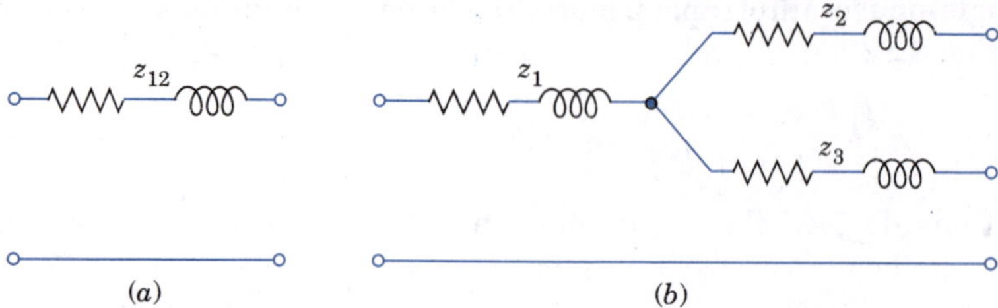

Fig. 8.84: Equivalent circuits for (*a*) two-winding and (*b*) three-winding transformers.

The positive and negative sequence components of voltages and currents in three-phases form balanced sets with phase order *abc* and *acb* as shown in Fig. 8.85 (*a*) and (*b*) respectively. Zero-phase sequence components of voltages and currents also form a symmetrical set as shown in Fig. 8.85 (*c*). Note that positive and negative sequence components are equal in magnitude but differ in phase by 120°; zero-phase sequence components are also equal in magnitude but are in phase with each other.

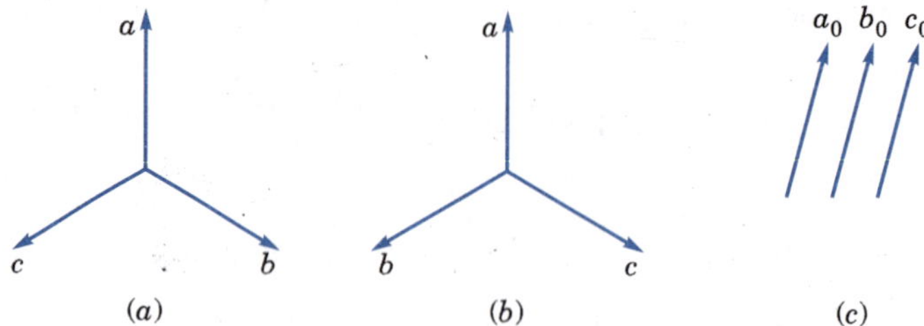

Fig. 8.85: Phasor diagrams for (*a*) positive-sequence (*b*) negative-sequence and (*c*) zero-sequence components.

In a three-phase system, zero-sequence components of current I_0 is defined as

$$I_0 = \frac{1}{3}(I_a + I_b + I_c)$$

or

$$\left.\begin{aligned} I_0 &= \frac{1}{3}(I_a + I_b + I_c) \\ I_0 &= \frac{1}{\sqrt{3}}(I_a + I_b + I_c) \end{aligned}\right\} \quad \text{...(8.30)}$$

Eq. (8.30) shows that if phasor sum of the three-phase currents is zero because of the circuit arrangement, then zero-sequence current is zero. This means that zero-sequence currents can't exist in star-connected rotating machines, transformers, transmission lines unless one or more neutral points are grounded or interconnected. In order to illustrate this, consider a single-phase line to ground fault on the primary of *Yd* transformer with primary neutral grounded as shown in Fig. 8.86. The fault current flows from ground to neutral, then current I_{NB} returns to fault. Mmf due to I_{NB} must be balanced by mmf due to secondary current I_{ba}. This current I_{ba} must flow in the other secondary phases *ac* and *cb* also. As a consequence of it, the primaries of phases *A* and *C* must carry oppositely directed currents as shown. Note that same current flows in the three secondaries, therefore the three primary currents are all equal and each has a magnitude equal to one third of the fault current. These primary and secondary currents, which are equal and in phase, are called zero-sequence currents in a three-phase system. In Fig. 8.86, if star point *N* were not grounded, then zero-sequence currents can't exist.

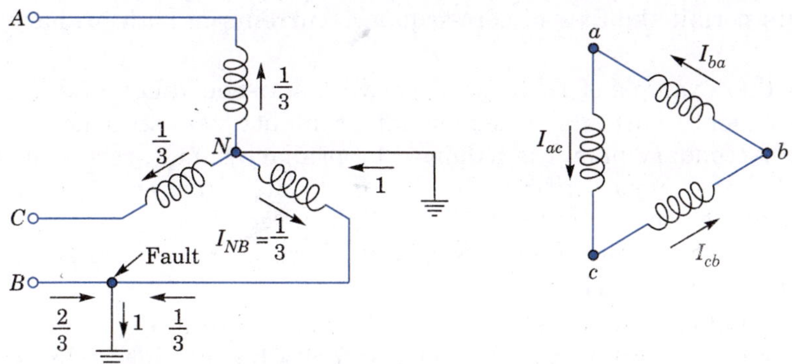

Fig. 8.86: Existence of zero-phase sequence currents for a line to ground fault on *Yd* transformer with primary neutral grounded.

In the delta-connected windings, the zero-sequence currents, which are equal and in phase with each other, simply circulate around the delta and not in the lines.

8.13.1 Zero-phase Sequence Equivalent Circuit

The zero-phase sequence equivalent circuits are required when 3-phase transformers; or 3-phase power networks, are operating under unbalanced or ground fault conditions.

The general principles pertaining to the existence of zero-sequence currents in 3-phase transformer windings are as follows :

(*i*) If the three-phase lines terminate in star-connected windings, with isolated neutral, then equivalent circuit is open circuited for zero-sequence currents. In case star-neutral is grounded or connected to source neutral, zero-sequence currents can exist.

(*ii*) If the three-phase lines terminate in delta-connected windings then equivalent circuit is open circuited for zero sequence currents, since there is no return path for these currents. Zero sequence currents can, however, flow in the delta-connected windings.

For drawing zero-sequence equivalent circuits, attention must be given to the winding connection (delta, star), earthing and also to the transformer construction in some cases. The general principles for drawing the zero sequence equivalent circuits for three-phase transformers are presented below.

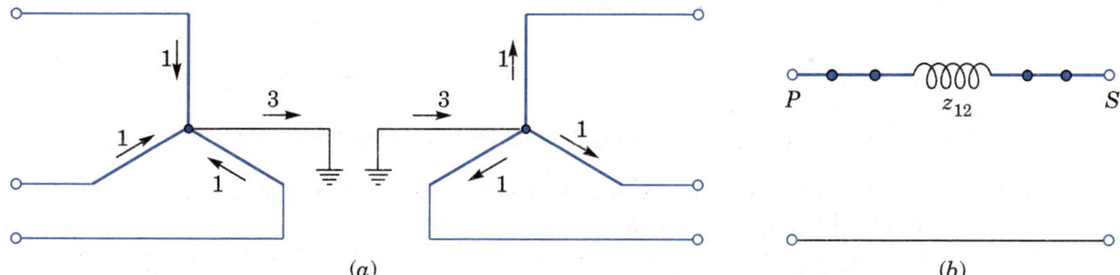

Fig. 8.87: Pertaining to z.s. equivalent circuits for 2-winding three-phase transformers.

(*a*) If external circuits on primary and secondary sides are so arranged that zero sequence current can flow freely in both primary and secondary windings, then secondary m.m.f. is balanced by primary m.m.f. (neglecting exciting currents). In such a case, the impedance to zero-sequence currents is equal to the leakage, or short circuit, impedance z_{12} per phase. For example, *Yy* transformer with both neutrals grounded, has zero-sequence equivalent circuit as shown in Fig. 8.87 (*b*), because zero-sequence currents can exist both in primary and secondary windings in Fig. 8.87 (*a*). Note that for Figs. 8.87 (*a*) and (*b*), the external circuits permit the flow of zero-sequence currents in both primary and secondary windings.

Take another example of *Yd* transformer with star-neutral grounded as shown in Fig. 8.87 (*c*). Zero-sequence currents in star-windings induce zero-sequence currents in delta windings. Since secondary m.m.f. is balanced by primary m.m.f., zero-sequence impedance offered is z_{12}. If zero sequence current can flow from external circuit to primary in star, the equivalent circuit is as shown in Fig. 8.87 (*d*). Since no zero-sequence current can flow from external circuit to the delta-connected windings, there is an open circuit to zero sequence currents on the secondary side.

Consider another example of *Dd* transformer as shown in Fig. 8.87 (*e*). Zero-sequence current can flow in both primary and secondary delta but not in the lines. Since primary m.m.f. balances secondary m.m.f., the impedance offerred to zero-sequence current is leakage impedance z_{12}. Zero-sequence currents can't flow from the external circuits to both the deltas, this is indicated by open circuits both on primary and secondary sides of the zero sequence equivalent circuits of Fig. 8.87 (*f*).

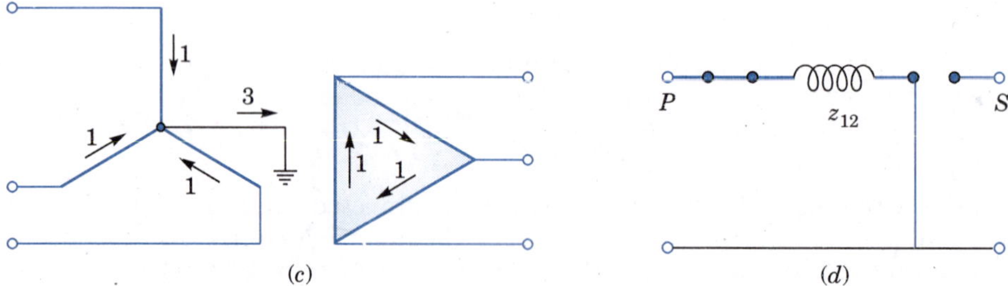

Fig. 8.87: Pertaining to z.s. equivalents circuits for 2-winding three-phase transformers.

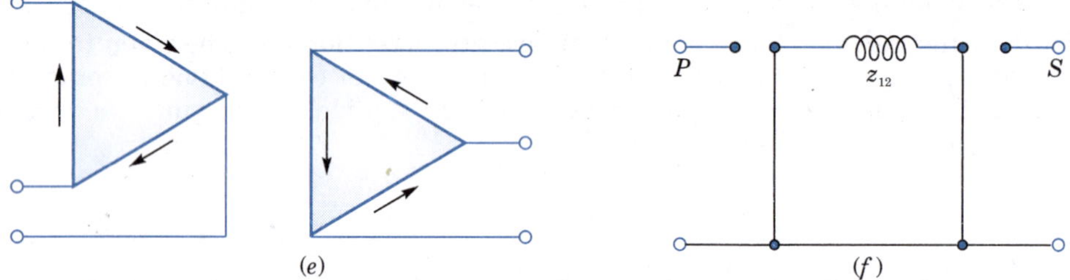

Fig. 8.87: Pertaining to z.s. equivalents circuits for 2-winding 3-phase transformers.

(*b*) If zero-sequence current can exist in one winding but not in the other, then m.m.f. of one side is not balanced by any other m.m.f. Consequently, the impedance to zero-sequence currents on the side where they can exist is the exciting (or open-circuit) impedance Z_ϕ of one phase. On the other side, the transformer acts as an open circuit for zero sequence currents. For *Yy* transformer with only primary neutral grounded as shown in Fig. 8.88 (*a*), the zero-sequence currents can exist only in primary and not in the secondary. Therefore, zero-sequence equivalent circuit for Fig. 8.88 (*a*) is as illustrated in Fig. 8.88 (*b*).

Consider another example of *Yd* transformer with isolated star neutral. The zero-sequence current can flow only in the secondary delta, but not in the external circuits. Therefore, zero-sequence currents can't exist both in primary and secondary external circuits and the equivalent circuit is as shown in Fig. 8.88 (*d*).

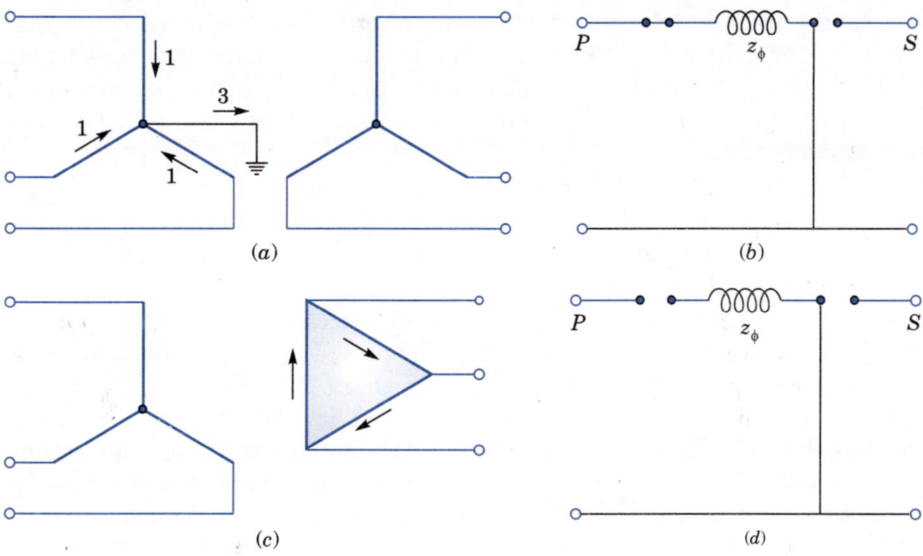

Fig. 8.88: Pertaining to z.s. equivalent circuits of 2-winding 3-phase transformer.

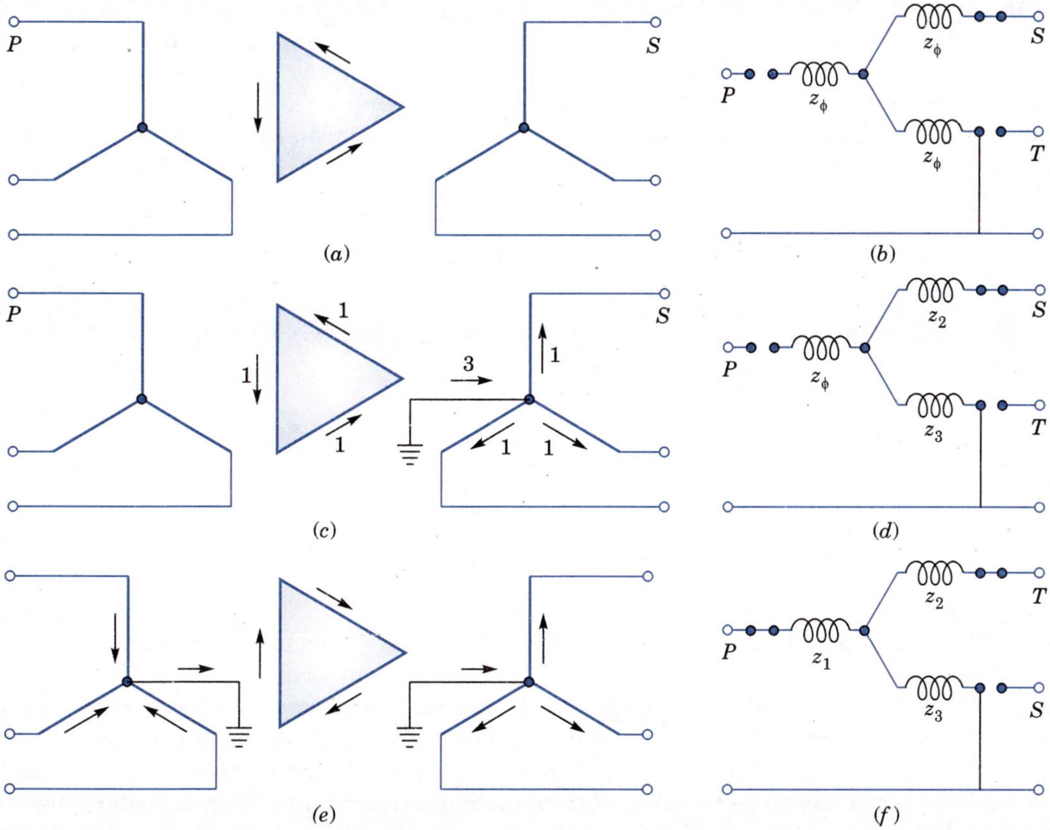

Fig. 8.89: Pertaining to zero-sequence equivalent circuits of 3-winding 3-phase transformers.

The general principles discussed above apply both to 3-phase transformer banks and to 3-phase transformers, the only difference is that the zero-sequence exciting impedance Z_ϕ is much smaller for a 3-phase core-type transformer than for a 3-phase transformer bank. The same general principles apply equally well to three-winding 3-phase transformers and some of these are discussed here.

Consider *Yyd* transformer with both neutrals isolated as shown in Fig. 8.89 (*a*). The zero-sequence currents can flow only in closed delta. No zero-sequence currents can flow from external circuits to primary and secondary in stars. Therefore, zero-sequence equivalent circuit is shown in Fig. 8.89 (*b*).

Take another example of *Yyd* transformer with secondary star grounded as shown in Fig. 8.89 (*c*). If external circuit on the secondary side provides path for zero-sequence currents, then zero sequence equivalent circuit, is as shown in Fig. 8.89 (*d*). Consider now *Yyd* transformer with both neutrals grounded as shown in Fig. 8.89 (*e*). Its zero-sequence equivalent is as shown in Fig. 8.89 (*f*) in case external circuits on primary and secondary sides provide path for zero-sequence currents. If primary source neutral is isolated in Fig. 8.89 (*e*), then equivalent circuit of Fig. 8.89 (*d*) is obtained. In case the external circuits on both primary and secondary sides do not provide path for zero-sequence currents in Fig. 8.89 (*e*), then equivalent circuit of Fig. 8.89 (*b*) is obtained.

For three-phase autotransformers, the same general principles apply. Here assume that the external circuits on both primary and secondary sides provide path for zero-sequence currents. Now consider a three-phase autotransformer with isolated neutral as shown in Fig. 8.90 (*a*). Since zero-sequence current can exist in winding *Aa* alone, the impedance offered is exciting impedance Z_ϕ in case of 3-phase bank or 3-phase shell type units and the equivalent circuit is as shown in Fig. 8.90 (*b*). In case transformer is 3-legged core type, the impedance offered is leakage impedance z_1 between legs and in Fig. 8.90 (*b*), Z_ϕ should be replaced by z_1.

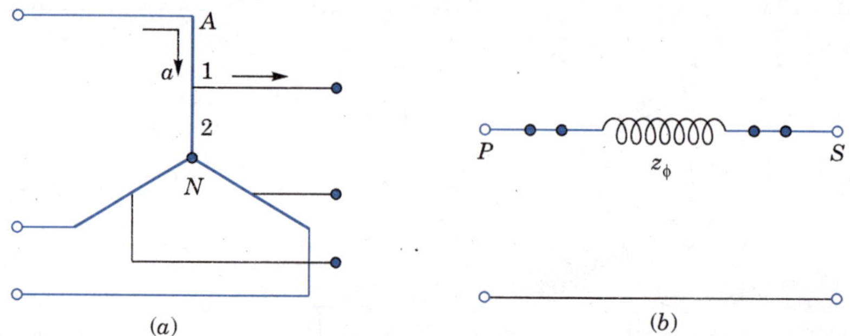

Fig. 8.90: Pertaining to z.s. equivalent circuits of 2-winding 3-phase autotransformers.

If autotransformer neutral is grounded as shown in Fig. 8.90 (*c*), zero-sequence currents can exist in both *Aa* and *Na* such that mmf balance exists. Therefore, the impedance offered is leakage impedance z_{12} and the equivalent circuit is as depicted in Fig. 8.90 (*d*). In Fig. 8.90 (*c*), note that the paths followed by zero-sequence currents are only shown. In case primary source neutral is isolated in Fig. 8.90 (*c*), then zero sequence current can flow only in winding 2, the zero-sequence equivalent circuit is, therefore, as shown in Fig. 8.90 (*b*) for transformers with separate magnetic circuits. For transformers with interlinked magnetic circuits, Z_ϕ should be replaced by z_2 (impedance between legs) in Fig. 8.90 (*b*).

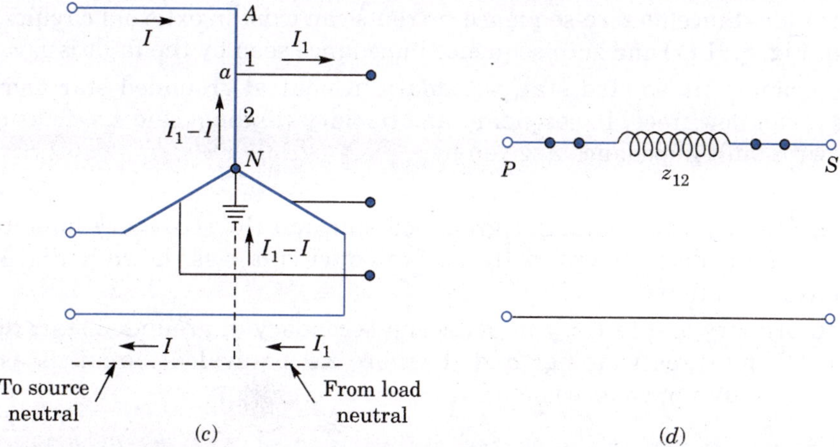

Fig. 8.90: Pertaining to z.s. equivalent circuits of 2-winding 3-phase autotransformers.

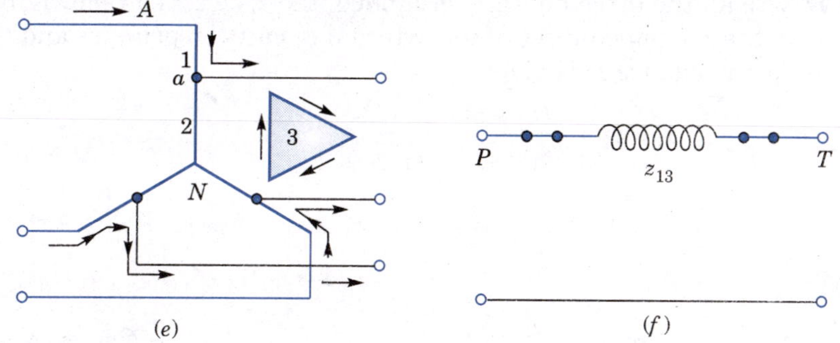

Fig. 8.90: Pertaining to z.s. equivalent circuits of 3-winding 3-phase autotransformers.

When autotransformer, with star neutral isolated, is provided with tertiary delta as shown in Fig. 8.90 (*e*), then mmf of winding *Aa* is balanced by tertiary winding mmf and zero-sequence equivalent circuit is as depicted in Fig. 8.90 (*f*). In this circuit, z_{13} is the leakage impedance between windings 1 and 3.

Zero-sequence equivalent circuit for 2-winding and 3-winding three-phase autotransformers and for three-phase autotransformers not discussed above can easily be drawn based on the basic general principles describes above. Zero-sequence equivalent circuit for a power system network can be drawn by combining the individual z.s.e.c. of the various parts of the system as illustrated in Example 8.39.

Example 8.38. *Draw the zero-sequence equivalent circuits for the following 3-winding transformers when any one phase of the secondary is grounded. Calculate the zero-sequence impedance as seen by the fault in each case. Assume that the external circuits on both primary and tertiary sides allow the existence of zero sequence currents.*

(*a*) *Ddd.*

(*b*) *Y/neutral grounded star/d.*

(*c*) *Neutral grounded star/d/neutral grounded star.*

(*d*) *D/neutral grounded star/d.*

(*e*) *Yyy with all the neutrals grounded.*

Solution. (*a*) Since no zero-sequence currents can exist in external circuits, the z.s.e.c. is as shown in Fig. 8.91 (*a*) and zero-sequence impedance seen by the fault is z_0 = infinity.

(*b*) For primary in isolated star, secondary in neutral grounded star and tertiary in delta, the z.s.c. can flow freely in secondary and tertiary windings and z.s.e.c. is as shown in Fig. 8.91 (*b*), with fault impedance z_0 given by,

$$z_0 = z_2 + z_3.$$

(*c*) With primary and tertiary in grounded star and the secondary in delta, the z.s.c. can't flow from fault to delta, therefore the equivalent circuit is as shown in Fig. 8.91 (*c*) with fault impedance z_0 = infinity.

(*d*) With primary and tertiary in delta and secondary in grounded star, the z.s.c. can flow freely in all the three windings and therefore z.s. equivalent circuit is as shown in Fig. 8.91 (*d*), with fault impedance given by,

$$z_0 = z_2 + \frac{z_1 \cdot z_3}{z_1 + z_3}$$

(*e*) For *Yyy* with all the three neutrals grounded, the z.s.e.c. is as shown in Fig. 8.91 (*e*) where z_1' and z_3' are the z.s. impedances of the external circuits on primary and tertiary sides respectively. The z.s. impedance z_0 is given by,

$$z_0 = z_2 + \frac{(z_1 + z_1')(z_3 + z_3')}{(z_1 + z_3) + (z_1' + z_3')}.$$

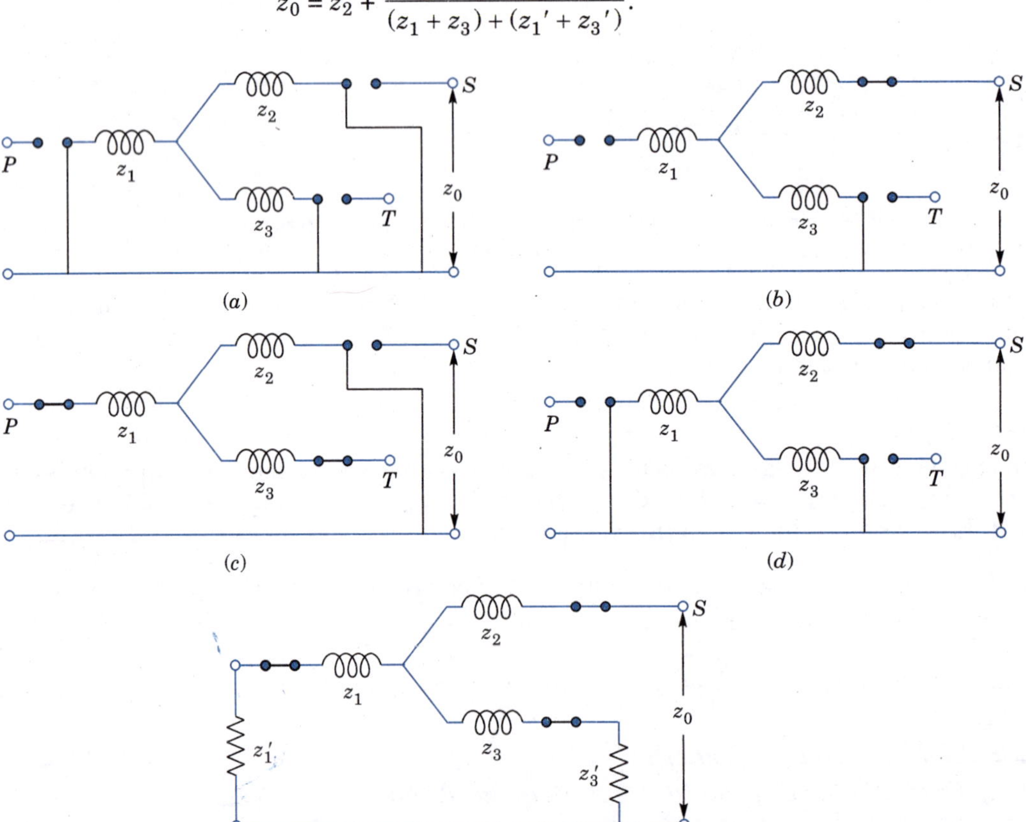

Fig. 8.91: Pertaining to Example 8.38.

Example 8.39. *In the power system network shown in Fig. 8.92 (a), a star-connected alternator grounded through Z_n feeds power to two a.c. motors. Draw the zero-sequence network of this system.*

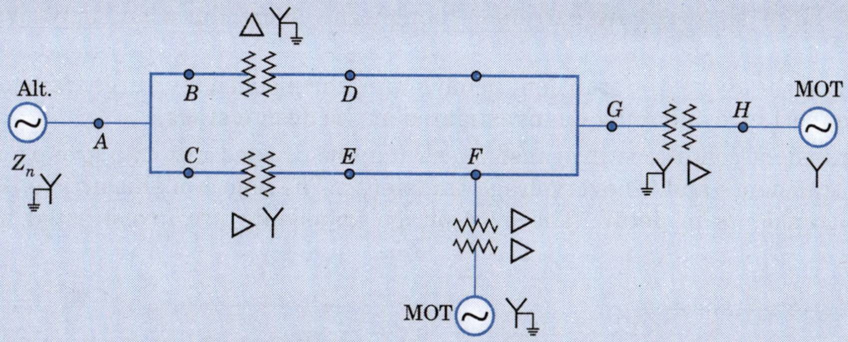

Fig. 8.92: (a) One line diagram of a power system network of Example 8.39.

Solution. The reference bus in Fig. 8.92 (b) represents common zero potential. Since four electrical machines are grounded, four terminals will be connected to the reference bus as shown. The neutral to ground connection carries the zero-sequence currents of all the three-phases. Therefore, an impedance between neutral and ground would cause three times the zero-sequence voltage drop as compared to the voltage drop across it when placed in each phase. As a consequence, an impedance of Z_n in the neutral to ground appears as $3Z_n$ in its zero-sequence equivalent circuit. The various other zero sequence impedances are, 1 for alternator, 2 for the transformer between *BD*, 3 for transformer between *CE*, 4 for line *DG*, 5 for line *EF*, 6 for line *FG* and so on.

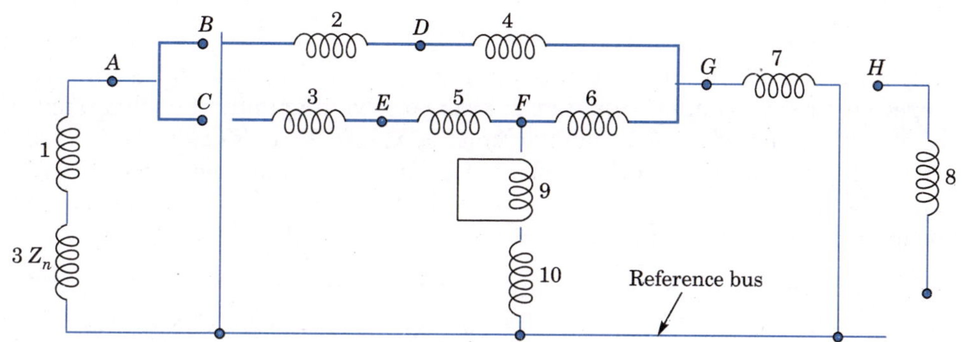

Fig. 8.92: (b) Zero-sequence network for Example 8.39.

8.14 TRANSFORMER TRANSIENTS

A transformer, under steady-state operating conditions, has a definite relation between its voltage, frequency, current etc. When any one or more of the quantities determining the transformer behaviour change, a transient condition appears between its initial steady state and final steady state. These transients, though of short duration, may produce detrimental effects in modern h.v. large power transformers. A few example of these detrimental effects are :

(*i*) the appearance of a surge voltage which may cause the breakdown of transformer insulation;

(*ii*) the occurrence of a short circuit giving rise to large currents in the windings which may be deformed due to severe mechanical stresses developed between them;

(*iii*) the large short-circuit currents, though the short duration, may overheat the transformers.

In view of the above, the transient behaviour of the modern h.v. large transformers is of paramount importance and must be investigated at the design stage.

The transient conditions in transformers may be divided into two groups, namely (*a*) overcurrent transients and (*b*) overvoltage transients. The object of this article is to discuss overcurrent transients in detail. The overvoltage transients are investigated in the next article.

8.14.1 Overcurrent Transients

These transient occur when an unloaded transformer is switched on to normal voltage on its primary side or when a short circuit occurs on its secondary side. The phenomenon pertaining to the switching on of an unloaded transformer is referred to as *switching-in phenomena* or *inrush phenomena* and is discussed below.

Switching-in (or inrush) phenomena. When the secondary side is open, the transformer takes only exciting (or no-load) current from the supply mains. Since the magnetizing component of current, 90° lagging the applied voltage V_1, is much larger than the core-loss component of current, the transformer at no-load behaves almost like a simple inductive reactor. As a result of it, the primary induced emf is equal and opposite to the applied voltage if small leakage impedance drop at no-load is neglected.

Here the inrush of magnetizing current is examined both qualitatively and analytically.

(*a*) **Qualitative approach.** The waveforms of the applied voltage v_1 and the core flux ϕ, under steady-state conditions, are illustrated in Fig. 8.93 (*a*). Note that at instant 1, v_1 is zero and ϕ is negative maximum and at instant 2, v_1 is positive maximum but flux ϕ is zero. For qualitative examination of inrush phenomena, *constant flux-linkage theorem* must be recalled. According to this theorem, the magnetic flux in an inductive circuit can't change suddenly, *i.e.*, the flux just after closing the switch (*i.e.*, at $t = 0+$) must remain equal to the flux just before closing the switch (*i.e.*, at $t = 0-$).

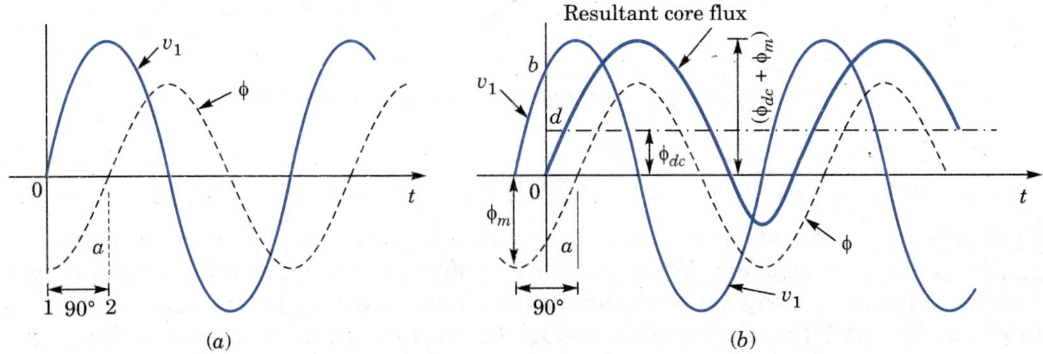

Fig. 8.93: (*a*) Applied voltage v_1 and flux ϕ waveforms for an ideal transformer (*b*) Effect of switching on an unloaded transformer when applied voltage is *ob*.

Consider an instant in between the two instants 1 and 2 as shown in Fig. 8.93 (*b*). Here switching voltage *ob* demands a steady-state flux *oa*. But the flux just before closing the switch, *i.e.*, at $t = 0 -$, is zero because v_1 is zero and it must remain zero at $t = 0 +$ as per constant flux-linkage theorem. Therefore, when the transformer is energised at the instant shown in Fig. 8.93 (*b*), a flux $\phi_{dc} = od = oa$ must be established in the transformer core so that resultant flux in the core at $t = 0 +$ remains zero. This flux ϕ_{dc} is called constant or d.c. flux and it remains constant in magnitude if primary-winding resistance r_1 is neglected. The d.c. flux adds to the steady-state alternating flux ϕ and the resultant core-flux wave becomes as shown by the thick curve in Fig. 8.93 (*b*). Note that maximum value of the core flux is $\phi_{dc} + \phi_m$.

Now consider instant 2, where the applied voltage v_1 is maximum positive and flux ϕ is zero. Here flux at both $t = 0 -$ and $t = 0 +$ is zero, therefore, $\phi_{dc} = 0$ and no transients take place. Core flux builds up as shown by curve ϕ in Fig. 8.94 (*a*). This shows that when a transformer is switched on at the instant its applied voltage is at peak value, then core flux ϕ attains its steady-state value immediately after the primary is energised and therefore no transients appear.

At the instant 1 of Fig. 8.93 (*a*), applied voltage v_1 is passing through zero and becoming positive whereas the flux is maximum negative. Suppose the transformer at no-load is switched on at instant 1. Here the flux at $t = 0 -$ (just before closing the switch) is zero and

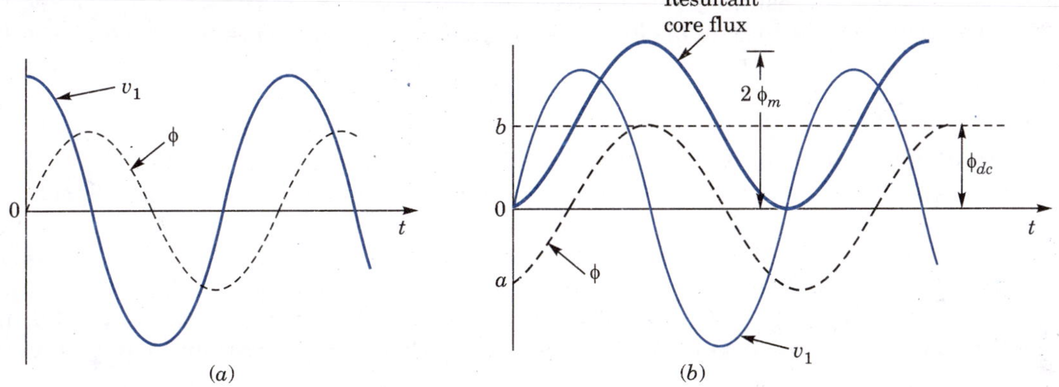

Fig. 8.94: Effect of switching on an unloaded transformer when (*a*) v_1 is maximum positive and ϕ is zero. (*b*) v_1 is zero and ϕ is maximum negative.

at $t = 0 +$ the flux is $oa = -\phi_m$ as shown in Fig. 8.94 (*b*). But as per constant flux-linkage theorem, the flux at $t = 0 +$ must remain zero. In view of this, a flux $\phi_{dc} = ob = oa = \phi_m$ must be set up in the core so that flux at $t = 0 +$ is zero. As before, constant flux ϕ_{dc} adds to the steady-state alternating flux ϕ and resultant core flux becomes as shown by thick curve in Fig. 8.94 (*b*). If time of closing the switch is considered at $t = 0$ in Fig. 8.94 (*b*), the general equation for the resultant corc flux is $\phi_{dc} - \phi_m \cos \omega t = \phi_m (1 - \cos \omega t)$. When $\omega t = 180°$, *i.e.* after half a cycle, the core flux becomes equal to twice the maximum flux — this is usually referred to as *doubling effect*. This doubling effect may saturate the core considerably. For normal flux, the flux density may be 1.6 Wb/m^2 and AT/cm, from a typical transformer *B-H* curve, are 40 ampere-turns per centimeter. For double the core flux, the flux density is 3.2 Wb/m^2 and AT/cm may become as high as 80 to 120 times their previous value. If normal magnetizing current is 5% of rated current, the doubling effect will raise the magnetizing current to about 4 to 6 $\left(\frac{80 \times 5}{100} \text{ to } \frac{120 \times 5}{100}\right)$ times its rated current. For such large magnetizing currents, the primary leakage impedance drop is quite large and induced emf is reduced considerably. This reduction in the induced emf restricts the core flux from attaining its double peak. This shows that doubling effect is not so dangerous as it appears. However, the effect of inrush magnetizing currents must be investigated at the design stage of large h.v. power transformers.

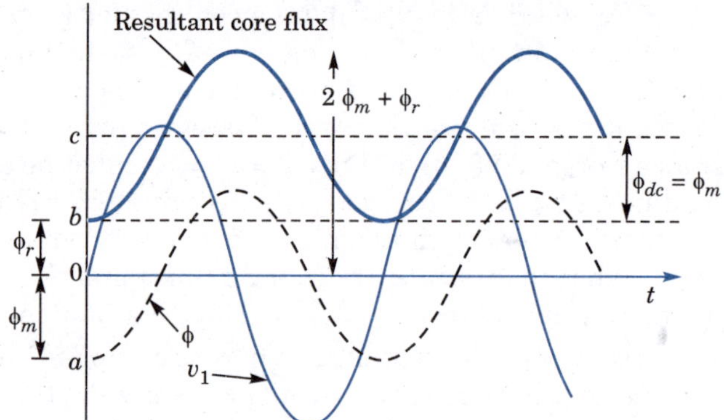

Fig. 8.95: Effect of switching on an unbalanced transformer when voltage is zero and residual magnetism ϕ_r is present.

Now suppose there is residual magnetism $\phi_r = ob$ present in the transformer core. If the primary is switched on at the instant voltage is passing through zero and becoming positive as shown in Fig. 8.95, then flux at $t = 0+$ must remain equal to ϕ_r (flux at $t = 0-$). This can happen only if there is established a constant flux $bc = \phi_{dc} = oa = \phi_m$. If primary resistance r_1 is neglected as before, then ϕ_r and ϕ_{dc} add to the steady-state alternating flux ϕ and the resultant core flux follows the thick curve as shown in Fig. 8.95. If time of closing the switch is considered at $t = 0$, then resultant core flux is given by $\phi_r + \phi_{dc} - \phi_m \cos \omega t = \phi_r + \phi_m (1 - \cos \omega t)$. After half a cycle from the instant of closing the switch, the core flux becomes equal to $\phi_r + 2\phi_m$ as shown. Actually, on account of the primary winding resistance r_1, both ϕ_{dc} and ϕ_r decay to zero with time and the core flux becomes a sine wave.

Hysteresis loops and waveforms of magnetizing currents for the cases illustrated in Figs. 8.94 (*a*), (*b*) and 8.95 are shown in Fig. 8.96 (*a*), (*b*) and (*c*) respectively. In Fig. 8.96 (*a*), hysteresis loop and magnetizing current i_ϕ are normal and symmetrical as per Fig. 8.94 (*a*). In Fig. 8.96 (*b*), core flux varies from zero to $2\phi_m$ as per Fig. 8.94 (*b*) and therefore hysteresis loop is reduced and i_ϕ is unidirectional in the beginning as shown. In Fig. 8.96 (*c*), core flux varies from $+\phi_r$ to $+(\phi_r + 2\phi_m)$ as per Fig. 8.95, core is supersaturated, hysteresis loop is negligibly small and i_ϕ is completely offset from zero in the beginning. In Fig. 8.96 (*b*) and (*c*), the waveforms of the magnetizing currents become symmetrical after some time on account of I^2R losses.

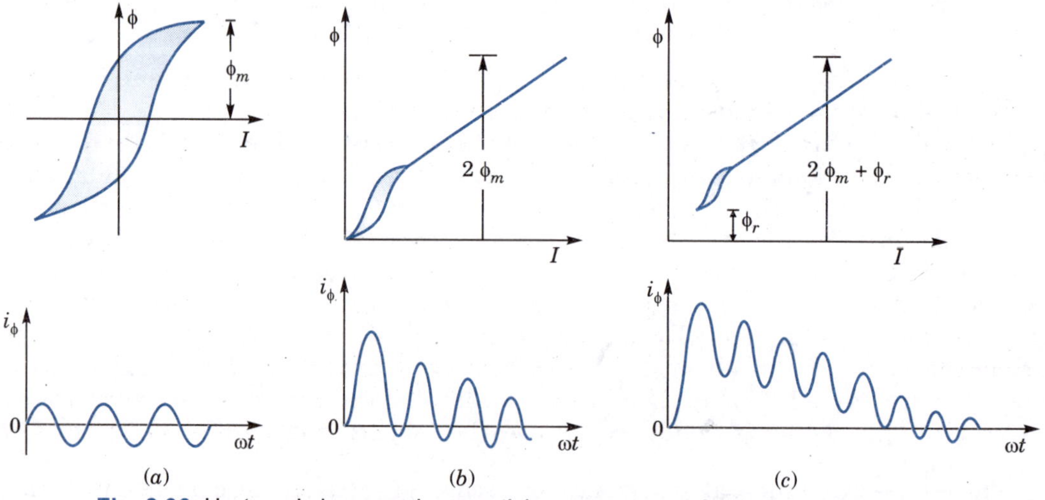

Fig. 8.96: Hysteresis loops and magnetizing current waveforms for a transformer.

Analytical approach. When voltage is switched on to the primary of an unloaded transformer, the e.m.f. equation for the primary circuit, as per Kirchhoff's voltage law, is given by

$$v_1 = V_{m1} \sin(\omega t + \theta_0)$$

$$= i_\phi r_1 + N_1 \frac{d\phi_t}{dt} \qquad \ldots(8.31)$$

where, v_1 = primary applied voltage at the instant of closing the switch,

ϕ_t = core flux at any time t,

i_ϕ = magnetizing current (core-loss component, being small, is neglected),

N_1 = primary turns,

V_{m1} = maximum value of the applied voltage wave,

and, θ_0 = the angle which the voltage wave makes with the time origin as shown in Fig. 8.97 (*a*).

Assuming that the core flux ϕ_t links all the primary turns, then primary winding inductance L_1 is given by

$$L_1 = \frac{N_1 \cdot \phi_t}{i_\phi}$$

The value of L_1 is not constant because of saturation in the transformer magnetization (*B-H*) curve, but here a linear relation between ϕ_t and i_ϕ is assumed.

$$\therefore \quad i_\phi = \frac{N_1 \cdot \phi_t}{L_1}$$

Substitution of this value of i_ϕ in Eq. (8.31) gives

$$\frac{N_1 \cdot \phi_t}{L_1} r_1 + N_1 \frac{d\phi_t}{dt} = V_{m1} \sin(\omega t + \theta_0)$$

or

$$\left(\frac{r_1}{L_1} + p\right) \phi_t = \frac{V_{m1}}{N_1} \sin(\omega t + \theta_0) \qquad \ldots(8.32)$$

Now solution of Eq. (8.32) is given by

$$\phi_t = \text{C.F.} + \text{P.I.}$$

C.F. The complementary function gives the transient part of the solution and is obtained from

$$\left(\frac{r_1}{L_1} + p\right) \phi_t = 0.$$

From this,

$$p = -\frac{r_1}{L_1}$$

$$\therefore \quad \text{C.F.} = Ce^{-\frac{r_1}{L_1}t}$$

where, C is a constant.

P.I. The particular integral gives the steady-state solution and is obtained by putting $p = j\omega$ in Eq. (8.32).

$$\therefore \quad \text{P.I.} = \frac{V_{m1}}{N_1\sqrt{\left(\frac{r_1}{L_1}\right)^2 + \omega^2}} \sin\left(\omega t + \theta_0 - \tan^{-1}\frac{\omega L_1}{r_1}\right)$$

If $r_1 = 0$, then $\quad \text{P.I.} = \dfrac{V_{m1}}{N_1\omega}\sin(\omega t + \theta_0 - \tan^{-1}\infty)$

$$= \phi_m \sin\left(\omega t + \theta_0 - \frac{\pi}{2}\right) = -\phi_m \cos(\omega t + \theta_0)$$

Therefore, the value of ϕ_t is given by

$$\phi_t = \textbf{C.F.} + \textbf{P.I.} = C \cdot e^{-\frac{r_1}{L_1}t} - \phi_m \cos(\omega t + \theta_0)$$

The value of constant C can be determined from the initial conditions. Now value of flux ϕ_t, at the instant of closing the switch, may be $\pm\,\phi_r$, where ϕ_r is the residual core flux.

$\therefore$ At time $t = 0$, $\phi_t = \pm\,\phi_r$

and $\quad \pm\,\phi_r = C - \phi_m \cos\phi_0 \quad$ or $\quad C = \pm\,\phi_r + \phi_m \cos\theta_0$

$$\therefore \quad \phi_t = (\phi_m \cos\phi_0 \pm \phi_r)\, e^{-\frac{r_1}{L_1}t_1} - \phi_m \cos(\omega t + \theta_0) \qquad \text{...(8.33)}$$

An examination of Eq. (8.33) shows that first terms in the bracket represents a constant d.c. flux $\phi_{dc} \pm \phi_r$, which has an exponential decay with time. Here $\phi_{dc} = \phi_m \cos\theta_0$. The second term consisting of $\cos(\omega t + \theta_0)$ represents the steady-state alternating flux of fundamental frequency ω.

Condition 1. If the primary is switched on when applied voltage is maximum, *i.e.*, when, $\theta_0 = \dfrac{\pi}{2}$ in Fig. 8.97 (*a*) and $\phi_r = 0$, then

$$v_1 = V_{m1}\sin\left(\omega t + \frac{\pi}{2}\right) = V_{m1}\cos\omega t.$$

and from Eq. (8.33), $\quad \phi_t = \left(\phi_m \cos\dfrac{\pi}{2}\right) e^{-\frac{r_1}{L_1}t} - \phi_m \cos\left(\omega t + \dfrac{\pi}{2}\right)$

$$= \phi_m \sin\omega t = \text{steady-state alternating flux.}$$

At time $t = 0$, $v_1 = V_{m1}$ and $\phi_t = 0$. This shows that flux corresponding to steady operation is established soon after the transformer is switched on at the instant of maximum applied voltage. This condition is, therefore, the most favourable for closing the transformer primary switch. This agrees with the results obtained qualitatively in Fig. 8.94 (*a*).

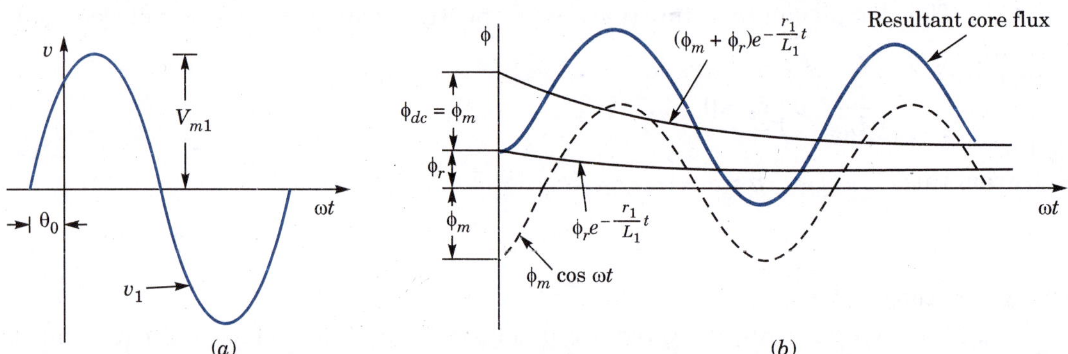

Fig. 8.97: Pertaining to inrush phenomena in transformers.

Condition 2. If the primary is switched on when applied voltage is passing through zero, *i.e.*, when $\theta_0 = 0$ and if ϕ_r is positive, then

$$v_1 = V_{m1}\sin\omega t$$

and from Eq. (8.33), $$\phi_t = (\phi_m + \phi_r)\, e^{-\frac{r_1}{L_1} t_1} - \phi_m \cos \omega t \quad ...(8.34)$$

After half a cycle, *i.e.* after $\omega t = \pi$ from the instant of closing the switch, Eq. (8.34) gives

$$\phi_t = (\phi_m + \phi_r)\, e^{-\frac{r_1}{L_1} \cdot \frac{\pi}{\omega}} - \phi_m \cos \pi$$

Usually $\omega L >> \pi r_1$, consequently $e^{-\frac{r_1 \pi}{\omega L_1}}$ $\left(\text{here } \omega t = \pi \text{ and } t = \frac{\pi}{\omega}\right)$ tends to $e^{-0} = 1$. Therefore, the resultant core flux after half a cycle of closing the switch is given by Eq. (8.34) as

$$\phi_{t \cdot m} = 2\phi_m + \phi_r \quad ...(8.35)$$

Eq. (8.35) agrees with the results obtained qualitatively. The plot of Eq. (8.34) is shown in Fig. 8.97 (*b*).

If primary resistance r_1 is neglected as in the qualitative examination, then Eq. (8.34) becomes

$$\phi_t = \phi_r + \phi_m (1 - \cos \omega t)$$

and after half a cycle, $\phi_{t \cdot m} = 2\phi_m + \phi_r$. This shows that switching on of the transformer primary at zero crossing of the applied voltage is the most unfavourable condition. For large value of core flux equal to $2\phi_m + \phi_r$, the transformer core is so much saturated that transformer behaves like an air-cored reactor because permeability then is almost equal to unity. The inrush of magnetizing current in a transformer settles down to steady-state magnetizing current in a time depending upon the transformer size. For large h.v. power transformers, the steady-state conditions may take 20 seconds or more from the instant of closing the primary switch.

The inrush of magnetizing current is not harmful to the transformer itself, but inadvertent operation of overload relays may trip the transformer out of circuit as soon as it is switched on to a.c. mains. Sometimes large inrush of magnetizing current causes an excessive momentary dip in the supply voltage and this may effect the operation of other electrical apparatus connected to it.

Estimation of inrush current. The peak value of the inrush magnetizing current in transformers can be estimated as follows.

Let A_i be the net iron (or core) area and A_t the mean area enclosed by a single turn of the primary winding. This means that $(A_t - A_i)$ is the area of the non-magnetic material enclosed by a turn. If B is the core flux density and H is the mmf per unit length of the air (or non-magnetic material), then maximum flux $2\phi_m + \phi_r$ enclosed by the primary winding is given by

$$2\phi_m + \phi_r = A_i B$$

i.e., flux carried by core + $(A_t - A_i)\,\mu_0 H$, *i.e.*, flux carried by the non-magnetic material.

or $$2\phi_m + \phi_r = A_t \mu_0 H + A_i (B - \mu_0 H) \quad ...(8.36)$$

The value of $(B - \mu_0 H)$, called the intrinsic flux density, is about 2.22 T for the usual type of transformer steels. In view of this, Eq. (8.36) becomes,

$$2\phi_m + \phi_r = A_t \mu_0 H + 2.22\, A_i \quad \text{or} \quad H = \frac{2\phi_m + \phi_r - 2.22 A_i}{\mu_0 A_t}$$

Now assuming that mmf per unit height of the primary winding is the same both for iron core and non-magnetic material around it, we get,

$$H = \frac{N_1 \cdot i_{\phi m}}{H_\omega} = \frac{2\phi_m + \phi_r - 2.22 A_i}{\mu_0 A_t}$$

Here $i_{\phi m}$ is the peak value of the inrush magnetizing current and H_ω is the primary winding height.

$$\therefore \qquad i_{\phi m} = \frac{H_\omega}{N_1}\left(\frac{2\phi_m + \phi_r - 2.22A_i}{\mu_0 A_t}\right)$$

If
$$B_m = \frac{\phi_m}{A_i} \text{ and } B_r = \frac{\phi_r}{A_i}$$

are the maximum and residual flux densities respectively, then

$$i_{\phi m} = \frac{H_\omega A_i}{N_1 A_t}\cdot\frac{1}{\mu_0}\,(2B_m + B_r - 2.22) \qquad ...(8.37)$$

The value of B_r is usually taken as $0.6B_m$. The actual value of the peak inrush magnetizing current may be less than that given by Eq. (8.37).

In transformers, l.v. winding is nearer to the core and area enclosed by its turn is small. But h.v. winding is outside the l.v. winding and area enclosed by its turn is comparatively large. Therefore, for a given transformer, the ratio A_i/A_t is large for l.v. winding and small for h.v. winding. This shows that inrush of magnetizing current, as given by Eq. (8.37) can be reduced if it is energised from its h.v. winding.

8.14.2 Inrush Current in 3-phase Transformers

When a three-phase transformer unit or a 3-phase transformer bank is switched on to three-phase supply mains, inrush of magnetizing current is bound to occur because of 120° phase displacement between the three voltages. If the condition is most favourable for one phase winding, then it would not be favourable for the other two phase windings. However, the magnitude of inrush current in 3-phase transformers is of lower intensity as compared to single-phase transformers. Inrush current in some of the three-phase transformer connections is discussed here in this part of the article.

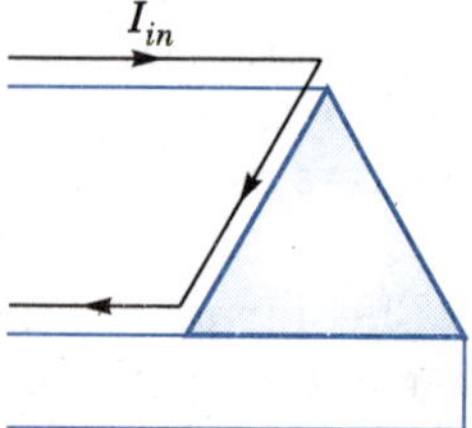

Fig. 8.98: Inrush line and phase currents are equal in delta.

(*a*) **Delta-connected primary.** With the primary winding in delta, each phase of the transformer gets connected to the source without effecting the other two phases. In view of this, inrush current phenomena for each phase winding takes place as in a single-phase transformer. But there is a difference in so far as the line currents are concerned. Under normal operation in delta, line current is $\sqrt{3}$ times the phase current. When a transformer in delta is switched on, inrush of magnetizing current takes place only in one phase pertaining to the saturated leg (others have negligible inrush current), consequently line and phase currents are equal under these conditions as shown in Fig. 8.98. Therefore, for a delta-connected primary,

$$\frac{\text{inrush line current in delta, } I_{in}}{\text{its rated line current } (= \sqrt{3}I_{ph})} = \frac{1}{\sqrt{3}}\,\frac{\text{inrush current in single-phase transformer}}{\text{its rated phase current, } I_{ph}}$$

This means that inrush line current in delta expressed in terms of its rated line current is $1/\sqrt{3}$ times (or 0.577 times) the inrush current in single-phase transformer expressed in terms of its rated phase current.

(*b*) **Three-phase transformer bank with star delta connections.** Let i_{1m} be the maximum inrush current for a single-phase transformer. Three such transformers are connected in star-delta as shown in Fig. 8.99. Assume that phase *A* has maximum inrush current i_a ($\therefore \quad v_a = 0$), then phases *B* and *C* would have almost negligible transients because voltage $v_b = v_c$ ($= 0.866\ V_{m1}$) are almost nearer to their maximum voltage V_{m1}. The return path for current i_a through phases *B* and *C* is indicated by currents i_b and i_c in Fig. 8.99.

Since cores of phases *B* and *C* have negligible transients, the magnetic effect of the return currents i_b and i_c must be neutralized by the current i_2 flowing in their closed secondaries as shown. This secondary current i_2 must have a return path through the secondary of phase *A*. Fig. 8.99 reveals that i_a and i_2 magnetize the core in the same direction. Since secondary is in delta, its primary neutral is stabilised. This means primary phase voltages remain balanced, equal to their values during single-phase operation. Therefore, the transient mmf $N_1\ (i_a + i_2)$ of phase *A* in Fig. 8.99 must be equal to the mmf $N_1 i_{1m}$ obtained during its single-phase inrush phenomena.

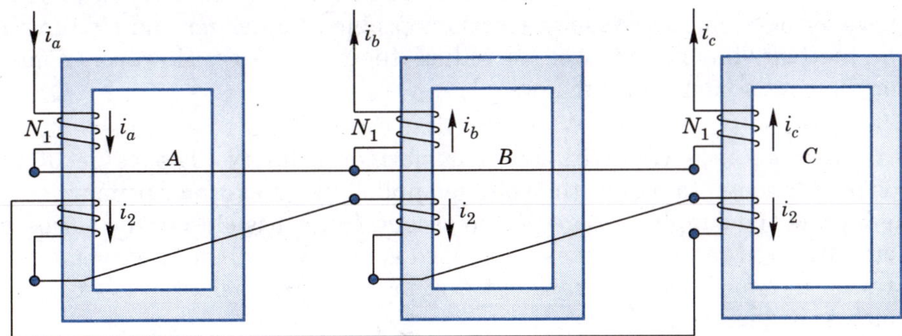

Fig. 8.99: Pertaining to inrush current in star-delta bank.

$$\therefore \qquad N_1\ (i_a + i_2) = N_1 i_{1m} \quad \text{or} \quad i_a + i_2 = i_{1m} \qquad \text{...(8.38)}$$

$$\left.\begin{aligned} &\text{For phase } B, && i_b - i_2 = 0 \\ &\text{and for phase } C, && i_c - i_2 = 0 \end{aligned}\right\} \qquad \text{...(8.39)}$$

The current i_a is returned through phases *B* and *C* as shown.

$$\therefore \qquad i_a = i_b + i_c$$

With the help of Eq. (8.39), $\quad i_a = 2i_2$

From Eq. (8.38), $\quad 2i_2 + i_2 = i_{1m}$

$$\therefore \qquad i_2 = \tfrac{1}{3} i_{1m} \quad \text{and} \quad i_a = \tfrac{2}{3} i_{1m} \qquad \text{...(8.40)}$$

Eq. (8.40) shows that the maximum inrush current for the case under consideration is 2/3 of that in a single-phase transformer.

(*c*) **Three-legged core-type star-connected transformer.** Consider again that phase *A* has maximum inrush current i_a. As before, i_b and i_c are the return currents for i_a. Let i_{1m} be the maximum inrush current when it operates as a single-phase transformer with windings *B* and *C* removed. Then, for legs *A* and *B*, mmfs produced by i_a and i_b help each other as shown in Fig. 8.100.

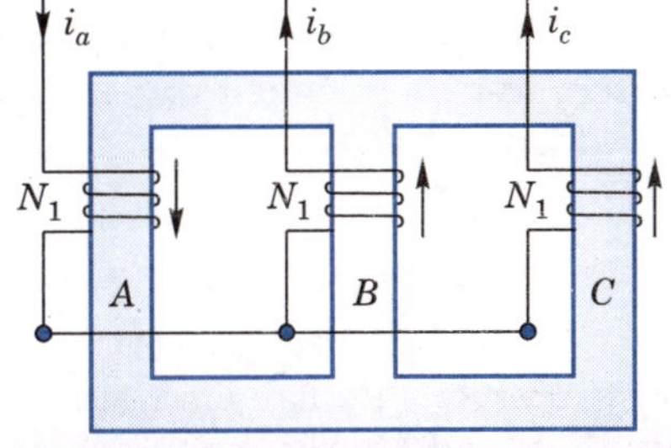

Fig. 8.100: Pertaining to inrush current in star-connected three-leg transformer.

$$\therefore \qquad N_1\ (i_a + i_b) = N_1 i_{1m}$$

For legs B and C, mmfs set up by i_b and i_c oppose each other.

$$\therefore \quad N_1(i_b - i_c) = 0$$

Since i_b and i_c are the return currents for i_a,

$$i_a = i_b + i_c$$

From above, $i_b = i_c$ and $i_a = 2i_b$.

But $i_a + i_b = i_{1m}$ or $3i_b = i_{1m}$

$$\therefore \quad i_b = i_c = \tfrac{1}{3} i_{1m} \quad \text{and} \quad i_a = \tfrac{2}{3} i_{1m} \qquad \ldots(8.41)$$

Eq. (8.41) shows that maximum inrush current in three-legged core-type star-connected transformer is two-thirds of that if it were operated on one leg as a single-phase transformer.

Reduction of high inrush currents. The inrush currents, associated with switching in of unloaded transformers, do not cause any serious problem under normal circumstances and therefore no methods have been used to reduce their intensity. However, some schemes proposed for their reduction are as follows.

(a) Use of a two-step switch. When the first contact of a two-step switch is closed, a resistance is inserted in series with the transformer primary. The value of this series resistance is large enough to reduce the voltage applied to transformer primary to a fraction, usually one-half, of the supply voltage. When second contact is closed, the series resistance gets short circuited and rated voltage is impressed across the transformer primary. Since the voltage is raised in two steps, the transient flux produced at each step is small and inrush current is almost negligible.

(b) Elimination of residual magnetism. In this method, a condenser is connected across the transformer primary. This condenser is suitably chosen so that it takes a charging current which is a good percentage of the transformer magnetizing current. When the transformer is switched off, damped oscillations occur between the transformer primary inductance and the condenser and in this manner, transformer gets demagnetized.

(c) Switching-in from h.v. side. If the transformer is switched-in on its h.v. side, the magnitude of inrush current can be reduced as per Eq. (8.37).

8.14.3 Primary Switching-in of Loaded Transformers

The power transformers may be switched-in with their secondaries disconnected from the loads, but distribution transformers are usually switched-in with their secondaries already connected to consumers terminals. The transients appearing with the switching-in of loaded transformers will not be examined in detail but here only an introduction would be given.

The transient currents produced in the primary and secondary windings, with the switching-in of a loaded transformer, are given by*

$$i_{1t} = \tfrac{1}{2}(\text{magnetizing current})\, e^{-\frac{r_1}{L_1}t} + Ie^{-\frac{r_1}{l_1}t}$$

and

$$i_{2t} = \tfrac{1}{2}\,(\text{magnetizing current})\, e^{-\frac{r_1}{L_1}t} + Ie^{-\frac{r_1}{L_1}t}$$

Here i_{1t} and $i_{2.t}$ are transient currents respectively in the primary and secondary windings and I is the mean of primary and secondary load currents I_1 and I_2.

* "Transient Performance of Electric Power Systems" by R. Rudenberg.

The transient load current decays with time constant l_1/r_1, which depends upon the leakage inductance l_1. The time constant L_1/r_1, with which magnetizing current decays, depends upon the self inductance L_1. Since l_1 is much less than L_1, the transient load currents vanish much more rapidly than the magnetizing currents. However, the time-constant l_1/r_1 is usually considerably larger than the time of half a cycle and this means that transient load current does not decay appreciably after half a cycle. Consequently, in the most unfavourable case ; load currents including the transient components, are almost doubled half a cycle after the instant of switching in of a loaded transformer.

The transformer inrush current with the unloaded transformer may attain 4 to 6 times their rated current after half a cycle from the instant of closing the switch, as explained earlier in this article. The total primary current, after half a cycle from the instant of switching-in the loaded transformer, is equal to 2 to 3 times the rated current contributed by inrush phenomena, plus (usually phasor sum) 2 times the load current contributed by the secondary load. Thus, peak value of total primary current after switching-in of a loaded transformer, may reach 4 to 5 times its rated current which is almost the same as obtained during the switching-in of an unloaded transformer. This shows that the magnitude of the total primary currents, obtained after the switching-in of an unloaded or loaded transformer, are almost the same.

8.15 OVERVOLTAGES (OR SURGES) IN TRANSFORMERS

If the voltage across transformer winding exceeds its rated voltage, then this voltage rise is called an overvoltage or a surge. Note, however, that the term is not applicable for long-time voltage rises, *e.g.*, the voltage rise caused by the runaway speed of an alternator is not termed as an overvoltage. The term overvoltage or surge refers to short-time voltage rises where the time interval between its origin and peak value is less than 100 μs.

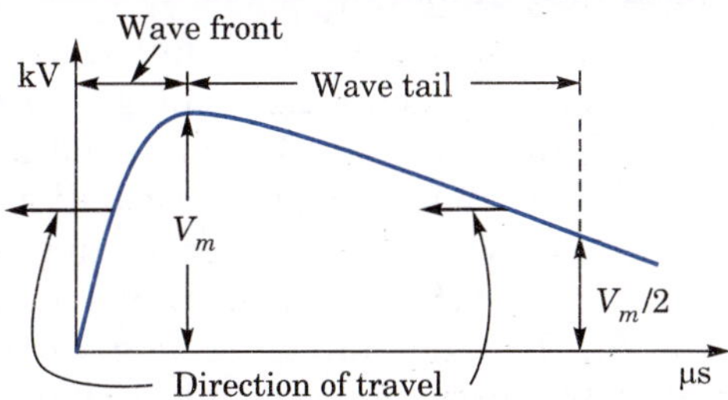

Fig. 8.101: A typical surge voltage waveform.

A transformer may be subjected to overvoltages produced in the transmission lines by switching, faults, lightning discharges etc. Fig. 8.101 shows a typical lightning and switching surge waveform.

8.15.1 Transformer Equivalent Circuit with Overvoltages

The surge or overvoltage phenomena in transformers occurs only in a few microseconds. In view of this, a surge voltage in transformers is equivalent to an overvoltage of very high frequency. Under steady-state conditions, the current passes through all the turns and only winding resistance and leakage reactance are encountered during its path. But when the transformer is subjected to overvoltages of very high frequency (kHz or MHz), the transformer equivalent circuit consits of a capacitance network as shown in Fig. 8.102 (*a*).

Here, K = Capacitance between turn to turn or coil to coil,

and, C = Capacitance of each hv coil (or turn) to tanks, core

and, l.v. winding, *i.e.*, to the earth.

Since the capacitance K are series connected, the total capacitance K_w along the winding length l is, $K_w = \frac{1}{n} . K$

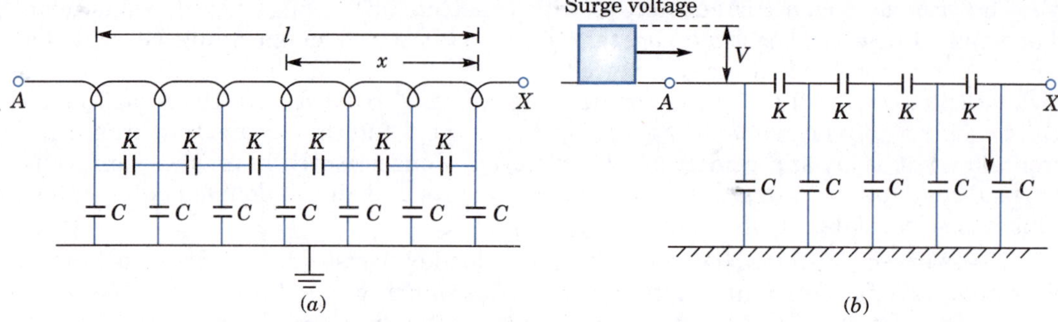

Fig. 8.102: (a) Transformer equivalent circuit for h.v. winding during surge phenomena (b) voltage surge on transformer h.v. winding.

Here n is the number of h.v. winding coils.

The capacitances C to earth are connected in parallel, therefore, the total winding capacitance C_g with respect to earth is $C_g = nC$

***(i)* Initial voltage distribution.** When surge voltage of rectangular wave impinges on the transformer terminals, the transformer inductances do not practically allow any current to flow through them. As a result, the transformer inductive network behaves as an open circuit. So the voltage distribution along the transformer winding is decided entirely by the capacitances K and C.

The transformer terminal A is subjected to step-function surge voltage of magnitude V as shown in Fig. 8.102 (*b*). For obtaining the mathematical analysis of the voltage distribution along the transformer winding, consider a winding element of length dx at a distance x from the neutral end X, Fig. 8.102 (*a*). Let the voltage of this winding element relative to the ground be v and its charge q as shown in Fig. 8.103. Since the shunt capacitance of a winding element relative to earth is proportional to its length, its shunt capacitance is $\frac{C_g}{l} \cdot dx$. The series capacitance is inversely proportional to its length, therefore the series capacitance of winding element dx is $\frac{K_\omega \cdot l}{dx}$.

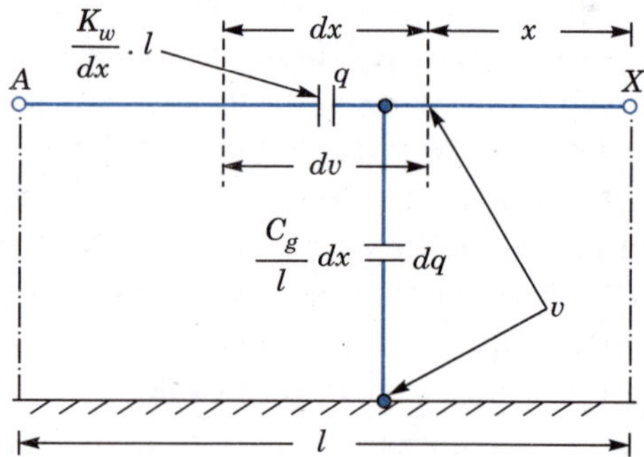

Fig. 8.103: Pertaining to the determination of initial voltage distribution.

Since the wave travels along from A to X, charge on capacitance $\frac{C_g}{l} \cdot dx$ must be less than that on capacitance $\frac{K_\omega \cdot l}{dx}$. Let the charge on $\frac{C_g}{l} \cdot dx$ be dq, less than q.

Now, $$\text{voltage} = \frac{\text{Charge}}{\text{Capacitance}}$$

For the capacitance $\frac{C_g}{l} \cdot dx$,

$$v = \frac{dq \cdot l}{C_g \cdot dx} \qquad \text{...(8.42)}$$

For the capacitance $\frac{K_\omega . l}{dx}$, $dv = \frac{q . dx}{l . K_\omega}$

or $$\frac{dv}{dx} = \frac{q}{l . K_\omega} \qquad ...(8.43)$$

Differentiating Eq. (8.43) with respect of x, we get

$$\frac{d^2v}{dx^2} = \frac{1}{l . K_\omega} \cdot \frac{dq}{dx}$$

From Eq. (8.42), $$\frac{d^2v}{dx^2} = \frac{1}{l . K_\omega} \cdot \frac{v . C_g}{l}$$

or $$\frac{d^2v}{dx^2} - \frac{C_g}{l^2 . K_\omega} v = 0 \qquad ...(8.44)$$

Put here $$\alpha = \sqrt{\frac{C_g}{K_\omega}} \qquad ...(8.45)$$

Eq. (8.44) now becomes $$\frac{d^2v}{dx^2} - \frac{\alpha^2}{l^2} . v = 0 \qquad ...(8.44)$$

or $$\left(D^2 - \left(\frac{\alpha}{l}\right)^2\right) v = 0, \quad \text{where,} \quad D = \pm \frac{\alpha}{l}$$

∴ Solution of Eq. (8.44) is, $v = A_1 . e^{\frac{\alpha}{l}x} + A_2 e^{-\frac{\alpha}{l}x}$ ...(8.46)

The constants of integration can be determined separately for grounded and isolated neutrals of the transformer end X, *i.e.* from the boundary conditions at the beginning and end of the transformer winding.

Solidly grounded neutral. When $x = 0$, the voltage v must be zero because end terminal X is grounded or earthed.

∴ For $x = 0$, $v = 0$ and from Eq. (8.46), $0 = A_1 + A_2$ or $A_1 = -A_2$

When $x = l$, the voltage at terminal A is V as shown in Fig. 8.102 (*b*).

∴ For $x = l$, $v = V$ and from Eq. (8.46),

$$V = A_1 e^{\alpha} + A_2 e^{-\alpha} = A_1 (e^{\alpha} - e^{-\alpha}) \qquad ...(8.47)$$

∴ $$A_1 = \frac{V}{e^{\alpha} - e^{-\alpha}} = -A_2$$

Thus the solution of Eq. (8.44) for the solidly grounded neutral is given by substituting the values of A_1 and A_2 in Eq. (8.46).

∴ $$v = \frac{V}{e^{\alpha} - e^{-\alpha}} [e^{\frac{\alpha}{l}x} - e^{-\frac{\alpha}{l}x}] = V \frac{\sinh \alpha \left(\frac{x}{l}\right)}{\sinh \alpha} \qquad ...(8.48)$$

Eq. (8.48) gives the magnitude of voltage at a point x in the winding. This equation shows that initial voltage distribution along the winding length, for a solidly grounded neutral depends upon $\alpha = \sqrt{C_g/K_\omega}$.

For $C_g = 0$, $\alpha = 0$ and $\dfrac{\sinh \alpha \left(\dfrac{x}{l}\right)}{\sinh \alpha} = \dfrac{0}{0}$ and it is indeterminate. Therefore, by applying L'Hospital's rule, we get

$$\left[\frac{dv}{d\alpha}\right]_{\alpha=0} = V \cdot \frac{x}{l} \cdot \frac{\cosh \alpha \left(\dfrac{x}{l}\right)}{\cosh \alpha}\Bigg|_{\alpha=0} = \frac{x}{l} \cdot V \qquad \text{...(8.49)}$$

Eq. (8.49) shows that for $\alpha = 0$, the initial voltage distribution at $t = 0$ is linear ($0.2V$ for $x = 0.2l$, $0.4V$ for $x = 0.4l$ etc.). However, in modern power transformers, α varies from 5 to 15 and therefore the initial voltage distribution along the transformer winding is considerably different from sloping straight line (when $\alpha = 0$). For different values of α and x, initial voltage distribution is plotted in Fig. 8.104 from Eq. (8.48).

The initial voltage gradient at the line end of the winding, where $x = l$, is given by

$$\frac{dv}{dx}\bigg|_{x=l} = V \cdot \frac{\alpha}{l} \cdot \frac{\cosh \alpha \left(\dfrac{x}{l}\right)}{\sinh \alpha}\Bigg|_{x=l} = \frac{\alpha}{l} \cdot V \coth \alpha$$

For $\alpha > 3$, $\coth \cong 1$.

$$\therefore \quad \frac{dv}{dx}\bigg|_{x=l} \cong \frac{\alpha}{l} \cdot V \qquad \text{...(8.50)}$$

The above equation for the voltage gradient at line end A is applicable for $\alpha > 3$.

For $\alpha = 0$, Eq. (8.49) shows that the initial voltage gradient at the line end A (where $x = l$) is V. Therefore, when α is more than 3,

$$\frac{dv}{dx}\bigg|_{x=l} = \alpha \quad \text{(initial voltage gradient at line end } A \text{ for } \alpha = 0)$$

or initial voltage gradient at line end $A = \alpha$ (initial voltage gradient corresponding to uniform gradient when $\alpha = 0$).

Thus, greater the value of α, greater is the voltage stress at the line end A. The voltage distribution along the line is shown in Fig. 8.104 for different values of α.

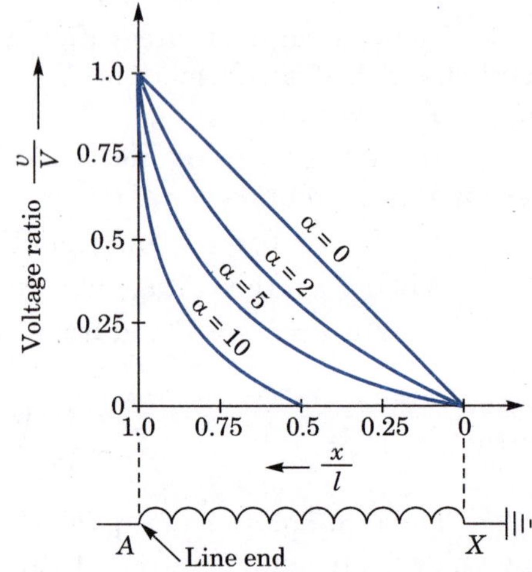

Fig. 8.104: Initial voltage distribution along transformer winding with grounded neutral and for different values of α.

Isolated neutral. In this case, when $x = 0$, $q = 0$, because no current can flow when neutral is isolated. Therefore, from Eq. (8.43),

$$\frac{dv}{dx}\bigg|_{x=0} = 0$$

In order to use the above condition, differentiate Eq. (8.46) with respect to x and put

$$\frac{dv}{dx} = 0 \text{ for } x = 0$$

$$\therefore \qquad \frac{dv}{dx} = 0 = A_1 . \frac{\alpha}{l} - A_2 . \frac{\alpha}{l} \quad \text{or} \quad A_1 = A_2$$

At the line end, $x = l$ and $v = V$. Using this condition, Eq. (8.46) gives

$$V = A_1 e^{\alpha} + A_2 e^{-\alpha} = A_1 (e^{\alpha} + e^{-\alpha}) \quad \text{or} \quad A_1 = A_2 = \frac{V}{e^{\alpha} + e^{-\alpha}}$$

Substitution of these values of A_1 and A_2 in Eq. (8.46) gives the solution of Eq. (8.44) as

$$v = \frac{V}{e^{\alpha} + e^{-\alpha}} \left[e^{\alpha . \frac{x}{l}} - e^{-\alpha . \frac{x}{l}} \right]$$

$$= V . \frac{\cosh \alpha . \left(\frac{x}{l}\right)}{\cosh \alpha} \qquad ...(8.51)$$

Eq. (8.51) gives the magnitude of voltage at a point x in the winding. This equation shows that initial voltage distribution along the winding length, for isolated neutral, depends upon α as before. In Eq. (8.51), for $\alpha = 0$, $v = V$ and therefore the initial voltage distribution along the winding is as shown in Fig. 8.105. This figure also shows the initial voltage distribution along the transformer winding for different values of α.

The initial voltage gradient at the line end of the winding, from Eq. (8.51), is

$$\left.\frac{dv}{dx}\right|_{x=l} = V . \frac{\alpha}{l} . \left.\frac{\sinh \alpha . \left(\frac{x}{l}\right)}{\cosh \alpha}\right|_{x=l}$$

$$= \frac{\alpha}{l} \cdot V \tanh \alpha$$

For $\alpha > 3$, tanh $\cong 1$

$$\therefore \qquad \left.\frac{dv}{dx}\right|_{x=l} = \frac{\alpha}{l} \cdot V \qquad ...(8.52)$$

Eq. (8.52) agrees with Eq. (8.50). This shows that the initial voltage gradient at the line end of the winding with isolated neutral is practically the same as in the case of grounded neutral for normal values of α.

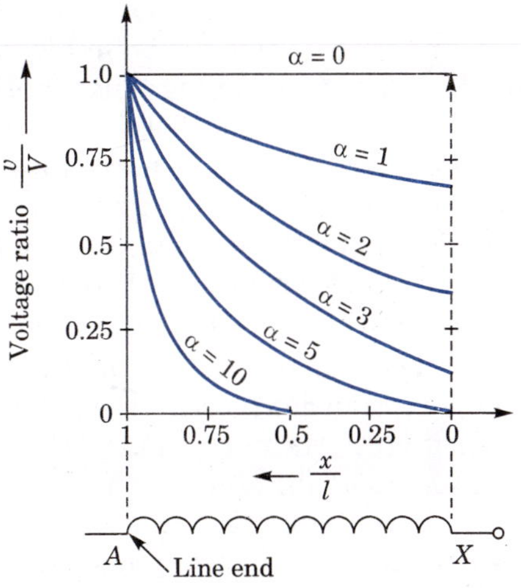

Fig. 8.105: Initial voltage distribution along transformer winding with isolated neutral and for different values of α.

Figs. 8.104 and 8.105 reveal that for $\alpha = 10$, first few turns near the line end A are subjected to severe voltage stress. The surge voltage itself may be several times the working voltage, the first few coils may, therefore, be subjected to an electric stress of about 200–300 times the normal stress for both grounded and isolated neutral type of transformers. This necessitates that steps must be taken to protect the winding insulation from breakdown, particularly the turns nearer the line end A.

***(ii)* Final voltage distribution.** The voltage distribution along the transformer winding, for different values of α, is depicted in Figs. 8.104 and 8.105 at the initial moment of transient process, *i.e.,* at $t = 0$. After a sufficiently long time, the voltage wave is uniformly distributed along the winding length. In the case of earthed neutral, the final voltage distribution, given by $x/l \cdot V$, is shown by sloping straight line PQ, marked $t = \infty$, in Fig. 8.106 (*a*).

For isolated neutral, the entire winding length attains same potential V as given by horizontal line $P'Q'$, marked $t = \infty$, in Fig. 8.106 (*b*). Note here that after the transients are over, the tail of the unit surge voltage is equal to sustained voltage V.

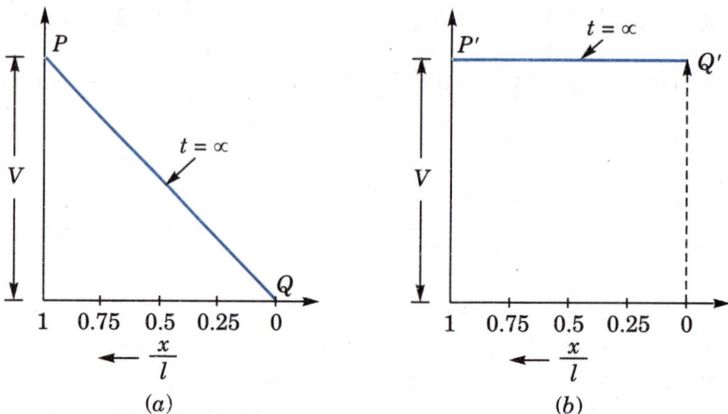

Fig. 8.106: Final voltage distribution for (*a*) earthed neutral and (*b*) isolated neutral.

***(iii)* Intermediate transients.** The initial voltage distribution along the transformer winding for $\alpha = 10$ is shown in Fig. 8.104 for earthed neutral and in Fig. 8.105 for an isolated neutral. The final voltage distribution for an earthed neutral is shown in Fig. 8.106 (*a*) by slopping straight line PQ. For an isolated neutral, the final voltage distribution along the transformer winding is horizontal line $P'Q'$ parallel to the abscissa, Fig. 8.106 (*b*). It is because no current can flow through the transformer winding with isolated neutral. A comparison between the initial and final voltage distributions along the transformer winding for $\alpha = 10$ shown in Figs. 8.104 to 8.106 reveals that initial and final voltage distributions along the transformer winding do not usually coincide.

The transition from the initial to final voltage distribution is always accompanied by complex transient oscillations because of the presence of transformer inductance and capacitance. These complex oscillations, during the transient process, put varying voltage stresses upon different parts of the winding length till finally oscilliations die out. At time $t = 0$, *i.e.*, initially, the largest voltage stress occurs at beginning of the winding terminal A for both earthed and isolated neutral types. Final voltage distributions, marked $t = \infty$, are shown in Fig. 8.106.

8.15.2 Transformer Protection against Surges

Surge voltage in transformers can cause large voltage gradients either between adjacent winding elements of a transformer or between transformer winding and earth. On account of any of these two causes, the transformer may be badly damaged and put out of service. So, the transformer protection against surges must be examined carefully. The transformer can be safeguarded against surges by two methods, namely,

(*a*) by external protection and (*b*) by internal protection

The external protection includes the methods leading to the reduction of surge-voltage amplitude reaching the transformer terminals and these are as follows :

(*i*) The route for the transmission and distribution lines should pass through areas which are immune to thunderstorms.

(*ii*) Overhead ground wires should be used.

(*iii*) There should be proper insulation co-ordination of the whole power system. This is done by proper choice of lightning arresters installed before the transformers at the substations.

Internal Protection:

The internal protection includes the methods adopted to increase the electric strength of the transformers. It has been stated before that the difference between initial and final voltage distributions is the major cause for the damage to a transformer winding. If, by using some special devices in the transformer, the initial and final voltage distributions are made to coincide, then the detrimental voltage gradients and oscillations would vanish. Transformers having such a protection, called *capacitive protection*, are referred to as surge-proof, or lightning proof, transformers.

Earlier, it was normal practice to reinforce the insulation of end turns in a transformer so that effect of surge voltages could be minimised. Now that the effect of surge voltage on transformer winding is understood, it is found that such a practice actually makes the matters worse. It is because reinforcement of end-turn insulation decreases the value of series capacitance K and increases the value of $\alpha = \sqrt{C_g/K_\omega}$, which has the effect of amplifying the voltage stress in the winding.

The basic concepts of capacitive protection are quite simple. If the transformer windings were so prepared that shunt capacitances C (and therefore C_g) are made negligibly small in comparison with series capacitances K (and therefore K_ω), then $\alpha = \sqrt{C_g/K_\omega}$, would be almost zero. Examination of Figs. 8.104 to 8.106 reveals that initial voltage distribution for $\alpha = 0$ in Figs. 8.104 and 8.105 is the same as the final voltage distribution marked $t = \infty$ in Fig. 8.106. This means that voltage distribution along the transformer winding length would become uniform soon after the surge appears in case $\alpha = 0$. In practice, however, earth capacitance C cannot be made negligibly small.

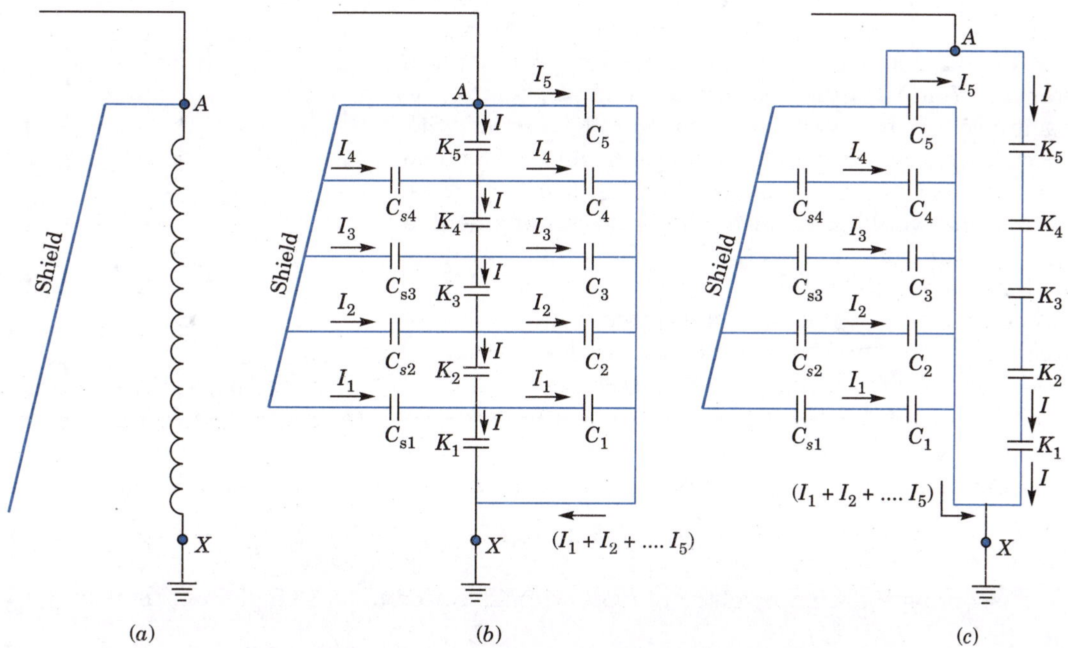

Fig. 8.107: Pertaining to the shield protection of H.V. winding against surges.

Note that the charging currents required by shunt capacitance C must flow through series capacitances K as shown in Fig. 8.102 (*b*). As a result, left capacitance K handles maximum charging current, whereas the right most K has minimum charging current through it. The main cause of the initial voltage distribution along the transformer winding being not uniform is that series capacitances K have to carry different charging currents as required by the shunt capacitances C. As a consequence of these unequal charging currents, voltage drops across capacitances K are unequal and voltage distribution along the transformer winding length is not uniform. In case series capacitances K are relieved of handling these charging currents, the transmitted process and voltage concentrations can be avoided. This can be achieved, to a greater extent, by providing screening capacitors C_{s1}, C_{s2} as depicted in Fig. 8.107 (*b*).

Fig. 8.107 (*a*) illustrate a transformer winding with earthed neutral and an insulated metal shield surrounding the winding connected to line end A. The shield is not made parallel to the axial length of the transformer winding in order that the different charging currents as required by earth capacitances C_1, C_2 ...... are delivered respectively by shield capacitances C_{s1}, C_{s2}, ... In this manner, the series capacitances K between coils are relieved of handling the charging currents needed for the earth capacitances C_1, C_2,... and the problem of voltage stresses is solved. For example, the current I_1 required for charging C_1 is delivered directly through shield capacitance C_{s1} as shown. Similarly I_2 required by C_2 passes through C_{s2}. This means that series capacitances K_2, K_3 etc are free of handling charging currents I_2, I_3 etc. Examination of Fig. 8.107 (*b*) leads to the modified equivalent circuit of Fig. 8.107 (*c*). Since same current flows through series capacitances K, a uniform voltage distribution is obtained initially and no voltage stresses occur in the transformer winding.

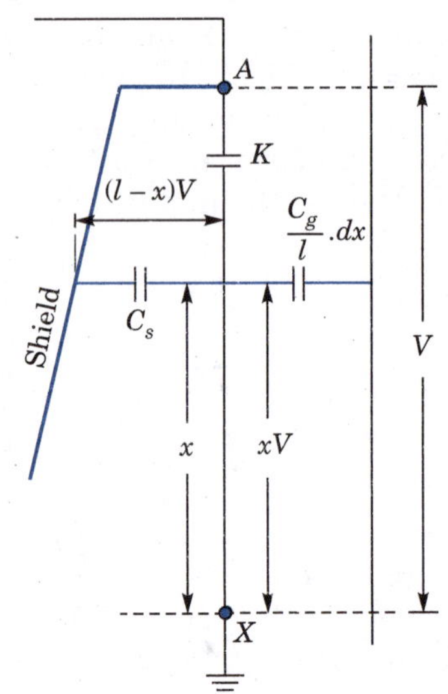

Fig. 8.108: Pertaining to the calculation of shield capacitance C_s.

The value of shield capacitance C_s for making the transformer surge proof can be determined by referring to Fig. 8.108. In this figure, consider a winding element at a distance x from the grounded neutral end. As before, the capacitance of this winding element is $C_g/l \cdot dx$ with respect to earth for winding length l and its shield capacitance (to be determined) is assumed to be C_s. Since no transients would occur after the provision of shield, a surge voltage of amplitude V would be uniformly distributed along the winding length l and its value is xV between the winding element and ground and $(l - x)\ V$ across this winding element and the shield screen, *i.e.*, across C_s as shown. In order that current through C_s is equal to the current through $C_g/l \cdot dx$, the charge across C_s and $C_g/l \cdot dx$ must be equal, *i.e.*,

Charge across $\quad C_s$ = charge across $C_g/l \cdot dx$

$$C_s\,(l - x)\,V = \left(\frac{C_g}{l}\,.\,dx\right)\cdot xV \quad \text{or} \quad C_s = \frac{C_g}{l}\cdot\frac{x\cdot dx}{l - x} \qquad \text{...(8.53)}$$

Assuming the winding element under consideration to be a single coil, then

$$\frac{C_g}{l}\cdot dx = \frac{C_g}{n} \qquad \text{...(8.54)}$$

Here C_g is the total ground capacitance of the winding and n is the number of winding coils.

Substitution of $C_g/l \cdot dx$ from Eq. (8.54) in Eq. (8.53) gives,

$$C_s = C_g \cdot \frac{x}{n\,(l - x)} \qquad \text{...(8.55)}$$

Eq. (8.55) gives the value of shielding capacitance C_s that must be available between winding and the shield in order to make the transformer surge proof. For the coils near the line terminal A, C_s must be more and therefore distance of the shield from winding is less. For coils away from terminal A, C_s decreases and likewise the distance between shield and winding becomes more as depicted in Figs. 8.107 (*a*) and 8.108. The beginning of winding (x = 1) requires C_s to be equal to infinity which is impossible to obtain physically. It is, however, possible to obtain a practically surge-proof transformer by suitably grading the shielding capacitance C_s.

Fig. 8.109 illustrates full capacitive protection of the h.v. winding of a transformer with disc coils. In this figure, 1 is a capacitive ring at the top of h.v. winding, 2 are shield turns and 3 is a shield. Note that the capacitance ring 1, shield turns 2 and the shield 3 are open circuited so as to avoid the formation of closed turns and these cover only a part (about two-third) of the h.v. winding circumference. The capacitive ring 1 consists of open-circuited copper band which is insulated properly. The copper band is connected to the line as shown. Shielding turns 2, made from the same material as used for the winding turns, are reliably insulated and placed in such a way as to ensure the required value of shielding capacitances. The shield 3 is inclined with respect to the winding appropriately so that shielding capacitances are suitably graded to avoid voltage concentrations.

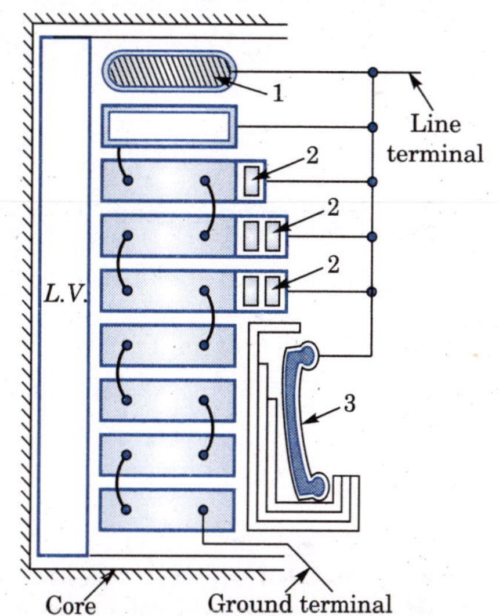

Fig. 8.109: Capacitive protection of h.v. winding by a graded shield.

The capacitive protection of the entire h.v. winding length complicates the transformer design and is expensive. Experience has shown that partial capacitive protection, consisting of capacitive ring 1 and shield turns 2 on both ends of h.v. winding provides sufficient protection against surge voltages. In addition, cost of the whole transformer is decreased considerably.

In addition to the capacitive protection of transformers, the use of interleaved coils also reduces the voltage concentrations and oscillations in transformers. Fig. 8.110 (*a*) illustrates two normal disc coils having 14 turns. If the order of turn-connection is altered to increase the voltage between turns, then the inter-turn series capacitance K_w becomes more and this reduces the factor $\alpha = \sqrt{C_g/K_w}$. Thus the windings of interleaved double-disc type coils as depicted in Fig. 8.110 (*b*) are better able to withstand surge voltages than the normal disc coils of Fig. 8.110 (*a*). Example 8.40 illustrates the effect of using interleaved coils for the reduction of surge-voltage effects.

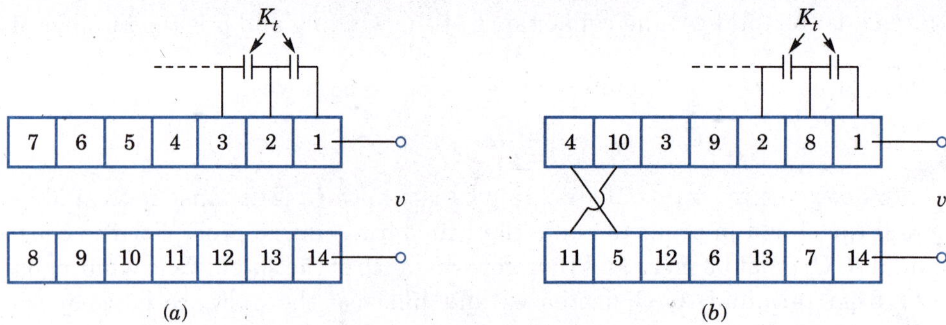

Fig. 8.110: (*a*) Two normal disc coils and (*b*) two interleaved coils.

Example 8.40. *Compare the effective series capacitance of the interleaved disc-coil pair in Fig. 8.110 (b) with that of normal pair of Fig. 8.110 (a).*

Solution. Let v = voltage per coil pair

n = number of turns = 14

and K_t = turn to turn capacitance or capacitance between adjacent turns as shown in Fig. 8.110.

Normal coil. Since there are 14 turns in series in this coil-pair, voltage between adjacent turns, *i.e.*, per turn, is given by $v_t = \dfrac{v}{14}$

The electric field energy W_t stored between adjacent turns is given by

$$W_t = 1/2 \text{ (capacitance between adjacent turns) (voltage between adjacent turns)}^2$$

$$= \frac{1}{2} K_t \cdot v_t^2 = \frac{1}{2} K_t \cdot \left(\frac{v}{14}\right)^2$$

Thus, total electric field energy W stored for the complete disc-pair, noting that there are 12 inter-turn gaps, is given by

$$W = \text{(energy stored in one gap) (number of gaps)}$$

$$= \left[\frac{1}{2} K_t \cdot \left(\frac{v}{14}\right)^2\right] \times 12 = \frac{1}{2} K_n \cdot v^2$$

Here K_n is the total effective series capacitance between turns 1 and 14 of the two normal disc coils of Fig. 8.110 (*a*).

$$\therefore \qquad K_n = \frac{12}{196} K_t$$

Interleaved coil. The arrangement of the coils is unchanged, therefore turn-to-turn capacitance remains K_t. But the effect of interleaving is to increase the voltage between adjacent (but not successive like 1, 2, 3 etc.) turns to $7v_t$ (1 to 8, 2 to 9, 3 to 10, ..., 7 to 14) and $6v_t$ (8 to 2, 9 to 3, ..., 13 to 7). Note that there are 6 adjacent turns where the voltage difference is $7v_t$ and another 6 adjacent turns across which the voltage is $6v_t$. Therefore, the total electric field energy stored is given by

$$\frac{1}{2} K_t\, [(7v_t)^2 \times 6 + (6v_t)^2 \times 6] = \frac{1}{2} K_t \times 6\left[\left(7 \cdot \frac{v}{14}\right)^2 + \left(6 \cdot \frac{v}{14}\right)^2\right] = \frac{1}{2} K_i \cdot v^2$$

Thus, the effective series capacitance K_i between turns 1 and 14 of the two interleaved coils of Fig. 8.110 (*b*) is given by

$$K_i = \frac{510}{196} K_t$$

Here series capacitance K_i for interleaved disc-coil pair is much more (510/12 ≑ 42.5 times) than series capacitance K_n for normal disc pair, so the value of $\alpha = \sqrt{C_g/K_\omega}$ is much smaller for interleaved coils. Consequently, the voltage stresses and oscillations with interleaved coils are considerably minimised.

8.16 MECHANICAL FORCES IN TRANSFORMERS

The currents in the primary and secondary windings of a transformer produce magnetic fluxes which oppose each other in the iron core. These fluxes are, however, cumulative in the space between two windings. This flux in between the two transformer windings, called leakage flux, gives rise to mechanical forces in a direction perpendicular to the directions of current and leakage flux, as per the so called left hand rule. The force per unit length between current carrying parallel conductors is given by

$$f = \frac{\mu_0 \cdot i_1 i_2}{4\pi d} \text{ newtons}$$

where d is the distance between two conductors carrying currents i_1 and i_2 respectively. Conductors are attracted to each other when currents in them have the same direction and they are repelled when the currents have opposite directions.

The mechanical forces on the transformer-winding conductors may be divided into two groups.

(*a*) **Internal forces.** These forces are produced due to interaction of currents in the same winding. For example, current in the primary (or secondary) turns are in the same direction, these primary turns therefore attract each other and internal forces are thus produced.

(*b*) **External force.** These forces are caused by interaction between currents in different windings, *e.g.* in primary and secondary windings.

The object of this article is to discuss these mechanical forces in transformers.

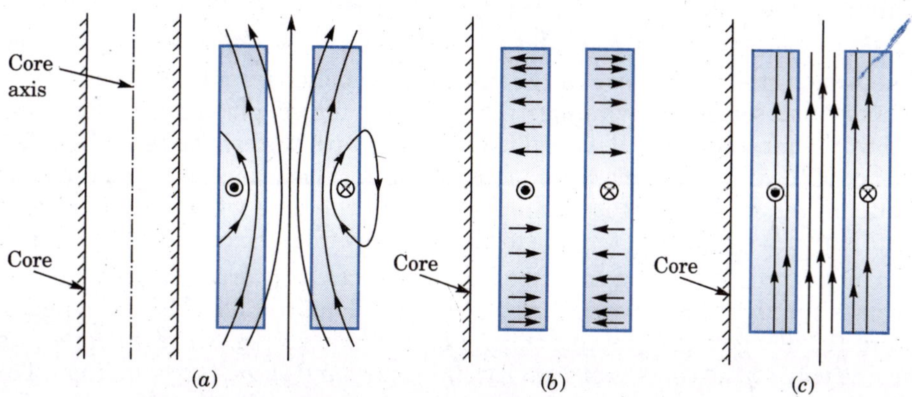

Fig. 8.111: (*a*) Leakage flux between two windings of a transformer (*b*) radial component of leakage flux and (*c*) axial component of leakage flux.

The leakage flux in radial space between the two windings, as shown in Fig. 8.111 (*a*), can be resolved into two components ; namely, radial component of leakage flux shown in Fig. 8.111 (*b*) and axial component of leakage flux shown in Fig. 8.111 (*c*). The interaction of radial component of leakage flux with current gives rise to internal forces and the interaction of axial component of leakage flux with current produces external forces and these are discussed below.

8.16.1 Internal Forces

Since currents in primary (or secondary) winding are in the same phase, separate conductors of a winding attract each other and as a result, there is an all round squeezing of the winding. The internal forces are directed parallel to the winding axis of primary and secondary windings and tend to compress each of the windings along its height as shown in Fig. 8.112 (*a*). The internal axial forces, given by the left hand rule, are the largest at the two end turns of the winding near the top and bottom, because there the radial component of leakage flux is maximum as is evident from Fig. 8.111 (*b*). The forces developed in the upper half of the winding *AB* are transmitted to turns placed at the middle *B* of the winding height.

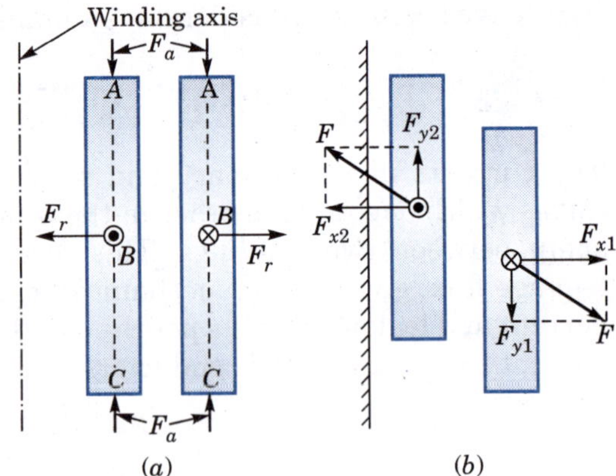

Fig. 8.112: Pertaining to mechanical forces in transformers.

Similarly, forces developed in the lower half *CB* are passed on to the turns placed at the middle *B*. In other words, the internal forces compress the primary and secondary windings from *A* to *B* and from *C* to *B*. It is because of this reason that the spacers of a coil placed at *B*, in the middle of winding height, are subjected to maximum mechanical stresses. These stresses have, however, been found unimportant even on short circuit for symmetrical arrangement of the two windings.

Since these forces act parallel to the axis of primary and secondary windings, these internal forces are also referred to as *axial compressive forces.*

8.16.2 External Forces

Currents in the primary and secondary windings of a transformer are almost in phase opposition to each other, therefore the windings are repelled from each other along the radius of the primary and secondary windings. These radial forces, given by the left hand rule, are developed by the interaction of the axial leakage flux with the coil currents, see Fig. 8.112 (*a*). The tendency of these radial forces is to increase the duct clearance between the two windings ; as a result the inner windings is compressed on to the core whereas the outer winding is subjected to outward radial force tending to burst it away from the core as shown in Fig. 8.113 (*a*).

It is, in general, possible to assume that the forces of interaction produced between two windings pass through the centres of gravity of their longitudinal (along the height) sections and are directed along the line joining them. For example, in Fig. 8.112 (*b*), force *F* is produced along the line joining the centres of gravity of primary and secondary windings. This *F* can be resolved into two components, one radial and the other axial. The radial-component forces F_{x1} and F_{x2} tend to burst out the outer winding and compress the inner winding respectively as shown in Fig. 8.112 (*b*). The axial-component forces F_{y1} and F_{y2} tend to increase the existing asymmetry.

In Figs. 8.112 and 8.113 are shown the mechanical forces in transformers with different winding arrangements. In Fig. 8.112 (*a*), internal force F_a squeezes spacers in the middle of the winding, but force F_a has no effect on the yokes. In Fig. 8.113 (*b*), external axial forces F_y tends to displace the two windings in axial direction and this force passes over to the yokes. The effect of force F_y in both the windings is $\frac{1}{2}F_y$ just above the middle and $\frac{1}{2}F_y$ just below the middle, so that total force is again F_y. Note for inner winding that the squeezing force is $\frac{1}{2}F_y - F_a$ (opposing each other) just above the middle of this winding and its value is $\frac{1}{2}F_y + F_a$ (aiding each other) just below the middle of this winding. Similar statements can be made for outer winding of Fig. 8.113 (*b*). For Fig. 8.113 (*c*), squeezing forces at the middle of inner and outer windings are $F_y + F_a$ and $F_y - F_a$ respectively but no force is passed over to the yokes. For Fig. 8.113 (*d*), external axial forces F_y cancel each other and no force is transmitted to the yokes. An examination of the various forces involved in Figs. 8.112 and 8.113 reveals that windings should be placed symmetrically with respect to each other so as to minimise the effect of external forces.

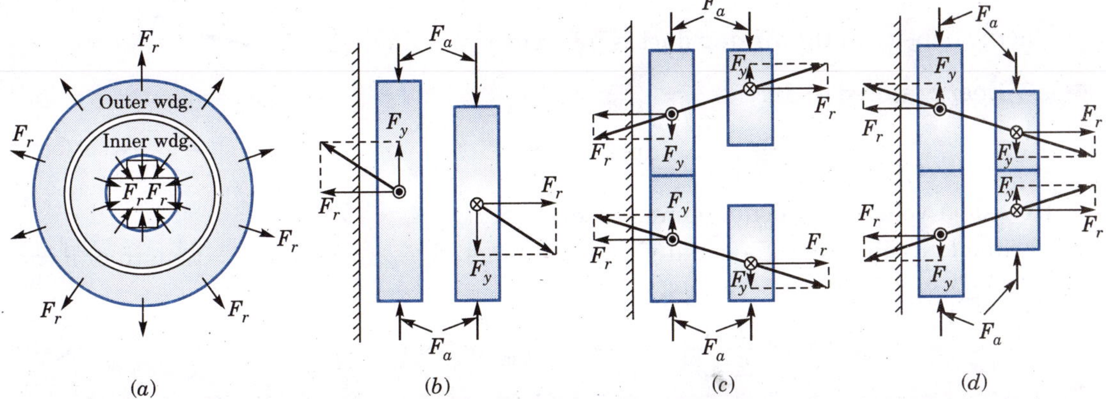

Fig. 8.113: (*a*) Cross-section of core and windings for showing the radial forces. Mechanical forces developed in transformer for (*b*) windings of unequal height, (*c*) windings tapped at the middle and (*d*) windings shortened symmetrically.

When the windings carry rated currents, the mechanical forces are not large. But under short circuit conditions, mechanical forces increase many times and can be dangerous for the transformers. In view of this, single-phase and three-phase transformers must be designed to withstand these large mechanical forces.

The methods of computing these mechanical forces are now presented in what follows.

8.16.3 Calculation of Mechanical Forces

Expressions for the external and internal forces are now derived from a consideration of the magnetic energy stored in the leakage flux.

(*a*) **External radial force.** First consider primary and secondary windings of equal height as shown in Fig. 8.114.

Let, N = numbers of turns in one winding,

i = instantaneous current in that winding.

and, H_w = winding height.

The m.m.f. variation along the radial width of the primary and secondary windings is as shown in the lower part of Fig. 8.114. Its magnitude in the air-gap duct of the two windings remains iN. Note that both primary and secondary m.m.f.s. are equal to iN and the transformer no-load current is neglected.

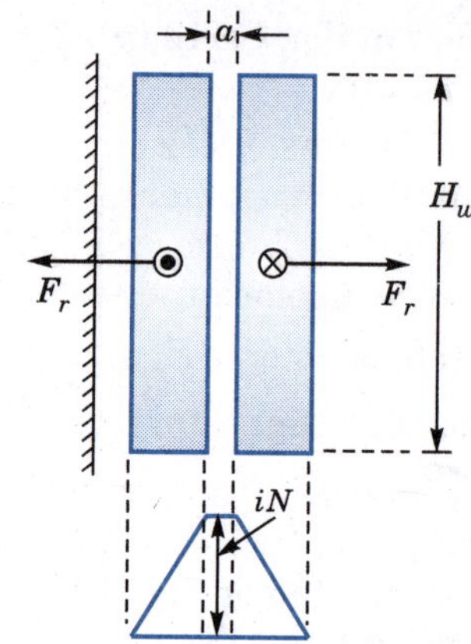

Fig. 8.114: M.m.f. variation over the radial width of primary and secondary windings.

Leakage flux in the duct

$$= \frac{\text{Duct m.m.f.}}{\text{Duct reluctance}} = \frac{(iN)\cdot \mu_0 \text{ (Area)}}{\text{Duct height } H_\omega \text{ along air gap}}$$

$$= \frac{iN \cdot \mu_0 \text{ (Area)}}{H_\omega}$$

Leakage flux density in duct, B_g

$$= \frac{\text{Leakage flux in duct}}{\text{Area}} = \frac{iN \cdot \mu_0 \text{ (Area)}}{H_\omega \text{ (Area)}}$$

or $$B_g = \mu_0 \frac{iN}{H_\omega} \text{ Wb/m}^2$$

Energy density in the air-gap duct is given by $\frac{1}{2}\frac{B_g^2}{\mu_0}$ Joules/m³.

∴ Energy stored in duct,

$$W_a = \frac{1}{2}\frac{B_g^2}{\mu_0} \text{ (duct volume)}$$

Here duct volume = (duct circumference) × a × H_ω.

The duct circumference is usually taken as equal to L_{mt}, where L_{mt} = Length of mean turn of primary and secondary windings

∴ $$W_a = \frac{1}{2}\frac{1}{\mu_0}\left(\frac{\mu_0 \cdot iN}{H_\omega}\right)^2 (L_{mt} \cdot a \cdot H_\omega)$$

$$= \frac{1}{2}\mu_0 \frac{(iN)^2}{H_\omega} \cdot L_{mt} \cdot a \qquad \text{...(8.56)}$$

Since the external radial forces F_r tend to vary the duct clearance "a" between the two windings, F_r can be obtained by differentiating W_a with respect to a.

∴ External radial force,

$$F_r = \frac{\partial W_a}{\partial a} = \frac{1}{2}\mu_0 (iN)^2 \cdot \left(\frac{L_{mt}}{H_\omega}\right) \text{ Newtons} \qquad \text{...(8.57)}$$

Positive sign before the force expression of Eq. (8.57) shows that F_r acts in such a direction as to increase the duct width a.

(*b*) **Internal axial forces.** Since F_a at the top and bottom of the winding are compressing it, the total axial force is $2F_a$. These forces tend to reduce the height of the windings. Therefore, internal axial force F_a can be calculated by taking the derivative of W_a with respect to H_ω and from Eq. (8.56), we get

$$2F_a = \frac{\partial W_a}{\partial H_\omega}$$

$$\therefore \qquad F_a = \frac{1}{4}\mu_0 (iN)^2 \cdot L_{mt}\, a\, (-H_\omega^2) = -\frac{1}{2}\left[\frac{1}{2}\mu_0 (iN)^2 \cdot \left(\frac{L_{mt}}{H_\omega}\right)\right]\left(\frac{a}{H_\omega}\right)$$

$$= -\frac{1}{2}\frac{a}{H_\omega} \cdot F_r \text{ Newtons} \qquad \text{...(8.58)}$$

The negative sign before the force expression of Eq. (8.58) indicates that the axial force acts in such a direction as to reduce the winding height H_ω.

Examination of Eqs. (8.57) and (8.58) reveals that both radial and axial forces are inversally proportional to winding height H_ω.

(*c*) **External axial forces due to asymmetry.** When inner and outer windings are not placed symmetrically with respect to the core as shown in Fig. 8.113 (*b*), external axial forces tending to increase the asymmetry are developed.

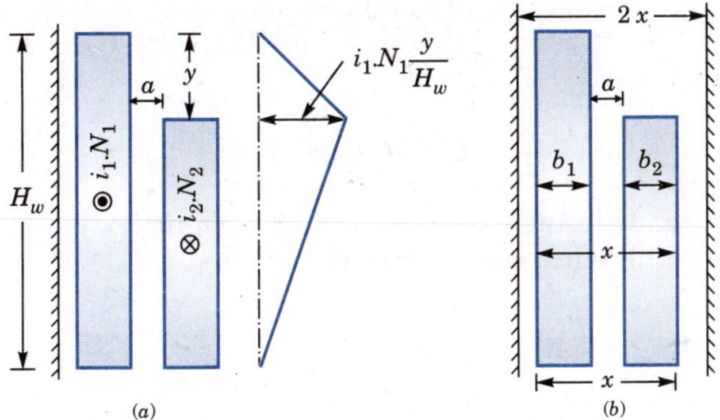

Fig. 8.115: (*a*) Out of balance cross ATs (*b*) Iron surfaces assumed at a distance of 2*x*.

Fig. 8.115 (*a*) shows two windings asymmetrically placed. In this fig.,

let, N_1 = number of turns in inner winding,

i_1 = current in the inner winding,

y = difference in height between l.v. and h.v. windings,

and H_ω = l.v. winding height.

Here (N_1/H_ω) are the l.v. turns per unit height. Since difference in the height of l.v. and h.v. windings is y, the out of balance mmf as shown in Fig. 8.115 (*a*) is given by

$$\left(\frac{i_1 N_1}{H_\omega}\right) y \text{ or } \frac{y}{H_\omega}(i_1 N_1)$$

For a transformer, $i_1 N_1 = i_2 N_2$, therefore a general expression for the out of balance mmf is $\frac{y}{H_\omega} \cdot (iN)$. This mmf gives rise to out of balance flux whose length is assumed to be $2x = 2(a + b_1 + b_2)$ as shown in Fig. 8.115 (*b*).

With this assumption, out of balance (or cross) flux

$$= \frac{\text{Out of balance mmf}}{\text{Reluctance}} = (\text{Out of balance mmf})\,\frac{\mu_0 . \text{Area}}{2x}$$

$$\text{Cross-flux density, } B_c = \frac{\text{Cross-flux}}{\text{Area}} = (\text{out of balance mmf})\,\frac{\mu_0}{2x}$$

or $$B_c = \frac{y}{H_\omega} \cdot iN \cdot \frac{\mu_0}{2x}$$

$$\text{Energy density of cross-flux} = \frac{1}{2}\frac{B_c^2}{\mu_0} = \frac{1}{2}\frac{y^2}{H_\omega^2} \cdot (iN)^2 \cdot \frac{\mu_0}{(2x)^2}$$

The above expression gives peak value of energy density. Since the energy density is not constant over the entire winding height H_ω, mean energy density should only be used for obtaining the energy stored in the cross-flux. The mean energy density is equal to half of the peak energy density, therefore the energy W_c stored in the cross-flux is given by

$$W_c = \text{(mean energy density) (volume)}$$

$$= \frac{1}{2} \text{(peak energy density) (volume)}$$

$$= \frac{1}{2} \cdot \left[\frac{1}{2} \cdot \frac{y^2}{H_\omega^2} \cdot \left(\frac{iN}{2x}\right)^2 \cdot \mu_0\right] [L_{mt} \cdot 2x \cdot H_\omega]$$

$$= \frac{1}{4} \cdot \frac{y^2}{H_\omega} (iN)^2 \cdot \frac{\mu_0}{2x} \cdot L_{mt}$$

Since axial force tends to increase the existing asymmetry y, the magnitude of axial force can be obtained by differentiating W_c with respect to y.

∴ External axial force,

$$F_b = \frac{\partial W_c}{\partial y} = \frac{1}{2}\frac{y}{H_\omega} (iN)^2 \cdot \frac{\mu_0}{2x} \cdot L_{mt}$$

$$= \frac{1}{2} \mu_0 \cdot \frac{y}{H_\omega} \cdot (iN)^2 \cdot \frac{L_{mt}}{2(a + b_1 + b_2)} \qquad ...(8.59)$$

Eq. (8.59) shows that greater the asymmetry y, greater is the external axial force tending to increase the asymmetry.

Let $$i = I_m \sin \omega t$$

Average value of i^2 or $I_m^2 \sin^2 \omega t$ is 1/2

From Eq. (8.57), maximum external radial force is

$$F_{r \cdot m} = \frac{1}{2} \mu_0 (I_m N)^2 \frac{L_{mt}}{H_\omega} \text{ Newtons}$$

$$F_{r \cdot av} = \frac{1}{2} \mu_0 (IN)^2 \frac{L_{mt}}{H_\omega} \text{ Newtons} \qquad ...(8.60\ a)$$

$$= \frac{1}{2} \mu_0 (IN)^2 \frac{L_{mt}}{H_\omega} \cdot \frac{1}{9.81} \cdot \frac{1}{1000} \text{ tons} \qquad ...(8.60\ b)$$

Here I is the rms value of current.

From Eq. (8.58), maximum internal axial force is

$$F_{a \cdot m} = -\frac{1}{2}\frac{a}{H_\omega} \cdot F_{r \cdot m}.$$

$$F_{a \cdot av} = -\frac{1}{2} \cdot \frac{a}{H_\omega} \cdot F_{r \cdot av} \text{ Newtons} \qquad ...(8.61)$$

From Eq. (8.59), maximum external axial force due to asymmetry is

$$F_{b \cdot m} = \frac{1}{2} \mu_0 \frac{y}{H_\omega} (I_m N)^2 \frac{L_{mt}}{2(a + b_1 + b_2)} \text{ Newtons}$$

$$F_{b \cdot av} = \frac{1}{2} \mu_0 \frac{y}{H_\omega} (IN)^2 \frac{L_{mt}}{2(a + b_1 + b_2)} \text{ Newtons} \quad ...(8.62)$$

As stated before, the various mechanical forces calculated above are small during normal operation of the transformer. However, under short circuit conditions, the mechanical forces attain dangerous values and the transformer may be damaged.

The transformer windings must be braced properly to withstand the various mechanical stresses. The tappings in the transformer should be so placed as to keep the unavoidable asymmetry in the windings as small as possible, so that axial forces due to asymmetry are limited. The mechanical arrangement of the windings in Fig. 8.113 (*c*) and (*d*) is superior over (*b*). In order to balance the external axial forces, *i.e.* F_{y1}, F_{y2}, the end supporters at the top and bottom of both the windings should have sufficient mechanical strength in addition to providing good insulation. The internal axial forces *i.e.*, F_a, are withstood by the winding itself. External radial forces, *i.e.*, F_r, are born by the formers, cores and packing pieces and supporters.

Under short-circuit conditions,

$$I_{sc} = \frac{V_r}{z_e \text{ in ohms}} = \frac{V_r \cdot I_r}{(I_r)\, z_e \text{ in ohms}}$$

$$= \frac{1}{z_e \text{ in per unit}} \cdot I_r \quad ...(8.63)$$

Here subscript r denotes rated value.

At the instant of short circuit, the current may become double of I_{sc} and in such a case, the short-circuit is given by

$$I_{sc} = \frac{2}{z_e \text{ in per unit}} \cdot I_r$$

But it is usual to take I_{sc} as 1.8 times $\dfrac{I_r}{z_e \text{ in per unit}}$.

Example 8.41. *A 500 kVA, 11000/400 V, delta/star transformer has the following data :*

Per phase turns, $N_1 = 1660$ *and* $N_2 = 36$.

$$L_{mt1} = 1.02 \text{ m},\ L_{mt2} = 0.84 \text{ m},\ H_\omega = 0.52 \text{ m}$$

$$a = 1.6 \text{ cm, per unit } z_e = 0.034.$$

(*a*) *The outer and inner windings of the transformer have equal heights. Find the magnitude of external radial and internal axial forces for a symmetrical short circuit across the secondary winding.*

(*b*) *If the h.v. winding is made 6% shorter than the l.v. winding at one end, then calculate the axial force due to asymmetry. Take radial thickness of each winding as 5.7 cm.*

Solution. (*a*) Primary rated phase current,

$$I_{r1} = \frac{500{,}000}{3 \times 11000} = 15.15 \text{ A.}$$

From Eq. 8.63, primary steady short-circuit current is

$$I_1 = \frac{1}{z_e \text{ in p.u.}} \times I_{r1} = \frac{1}{0.034} \times 15.15 = 445.6 \text{ A}$$

$$L_{mt} = \frac{1.02 + 0.84}{2} = 0.93 \text{ m.}$$

From Eq. [8.60 (*b*)], external radial force under steady-state conditions,

$$F_{r \cdot av} = \frac{1}{2} \times 4\pi \times 10^{-7} (445.6 \times 1660)^2 \frac{0.93}{0.52} \times \frac{1}{9.81} \times \frac{1}{1000} = 62.68 \text{ tons.}$$

At the time of short circuit, $F_{r \cdot av}$ may become double of 62.68 tons, but it is usual to take it as 1.8 times 62.68.

∴ External radial force at the moment of short circuit = 1.8 × 62.68 = 112.824 tons.

From Eq. (8.61), the magnitude of internal axial force is

$$F_{r \cdot av} = \frac{1}{2} \frac{a}{H_\omega} F_{r \cdot av} = \frac{1}{2} \frac{1.6}{52} \times 62.68 = 0.96 \text{ tons.}$$

Internal axial force at the moment of short circuit = 1.8 × 0.96 = 1.728 tons.

(*b*) Here $\frac{y}{H_\omega} = 0.06, \quad a + b_1 + b_2 = 1.6 + 2\,(5.7) = 13$ cm.

From Eq. (8.62), the axial force due to asymmetry is

$$F_{b \cdot av} = \frac{1}{2} \times 4\pi \times 10^{-7} \times 0.06 \times (445.6 \times 1660)^2 \times \frac{0.93}{2 \times 0.13} \times \frac{1}{9.81} \times \frac{1}{1000}$$

$$= 7.521 \text{ tons.}$$

Axial force due to asymmetry at the time of short circuit = 1.8 × 7.521 = 13.538 tons.

8.17 THE PER UNIT SYSTEM

For the analysis of electrical machines or electrical-machine systems, the calculations are often carried out in the per unit system. In this system, the relevant quantities such as voltage, current, kVA and impedance are expressed as decimal fractions of the appropriately chosen base values. For instance, if a voltage of 150 kV is chosen as base voltages then 90 kV becomes 0.6 per unit or 60% in terms of its base value of 150 kV. Out of the per unit and per cent methods, the per unit method is advantageous over the per cent method. It is because the product of two quantities in per unit gives the result in per unit itself whereas in per cent method, the product of two quantities in per cent must be divided by 100 to get the result in per cent.

For any system or device, the per unit quantity is defined by the following relation* :

$$\text{Per unit quantity} = \frac{\text{Actual value of the quantity in any unit}}{\text{Base value of that quantity in the same unit}} \qquad ...(8.64)$$

For any system, base values are selected arbitrarily. But it is common and preferable to choose the rated quantities of the device as its base values.

*The reader is advised to go through Art. 1.11 in the book "Electrical Machinery" by the same author.

The use of per unit system possesses the following two important advantages :

(*i*) Parameters of rotating electrical machines and transformers of widely different ratings lie within a narrow numerical range when expressed in per unit on the base of their nameplate ratings. This serves as a quick check on the correctness of their values. Further, a knowledge of the per unit parameters of electrical machines helps in the appraisal of their design and performance characteristics. This information further facilitates in the comparison of units of a given size made by the various manufacturers.

(*ii*) The second advantage is that the calculations in per unit quantities are easy, since during the transformer analysis, one need not bother whether the parameters are referred to h.v. or l.v. side. For complicated systems involving many transformers of different turns ratios, this advantage is more significant in that the possibility of serious mistakes is removed.

The per unit system is also useful in computer simulation of machine systems for their transient and dynamic analysis.

Base values of various quantities, once selected, must obey the normal electrical laws. For a single-phase system,

$$P_B, Q_B, (VA)_B = V_B I_B \qquad ...(8.65)$$

$$R_B, X_B, Z_B = \frac{V_B}{I_B} \qquad ...(8.66)$$

In Eqs. (8.65) and (8.66), V_B and I_B are the base values for voltage and current respectively. Further, *P, Q* and *VA* are the symbols for active power, reactive power and apparent power respectively. Subscript *B* indicates base value.

It is almost always a normal practice to choose first the values of base voltamperes $(VA)_B$ and base voltage V_B. Then values of I_B and other quantities in Eqs. (8.65) and (8.66) are automatically established. From above, it follows that

$$\text{base impedance, } Z_B = \frac{V_B}{I_B} = \frac{V_B^2}{(VA)_B} \qquad ...(8.67)$$

Expressing V_B in kV and $(VA)_B$ in kVA, Eq. (8.67) becomes

$$Z_B = \frac{[(kV)_B \times 1000]^2}{(kVA)_B \times 1000} = \frac{(kV)_B^2 \times 1000}{(kVA)_B}$$

$$= \frac{(kV)_B^2}{(MVA)_B} \qquad ...(8.68)$$

$$\therefore \qquad Z\text{ (p.u.)} = \frac{Z \text{ in ohms}}{Z_B} = \frac{(Z \text{ in ohms})\,(MVA)_B}{(kV)_B^2} \qquad ...(8.69)$$

Eq. (8.69) shows that per unit impedance is directly proportional to base MVA and inversely proportional to square of the base kV. Therefore, for changing the per-unit impedance on a given base to per-unit impedance on a new base, the following equation holds good.

$$Z\text{ (p.u.)}_{new} = Z\text{(p.u.)}_{old} \times \frac{(MVA)_{B.new}}{(MVA)_{B.old}} = \frac{(kV)_{B.old}^2}{(kV)_{B.new}^2} \qquad ...(8.70)$$

The per unit values of *R* and *X* can also be changed from a given base to a new base by using Eq. (8.70).

When several devices are interconnected, $(kVA)_B$ chosen arbitrarily must be the same for the overall system. Per unit values in one base can be changed to another base by the following relations.

$$(P,\ Q\ VA)\ (\text{p.u.})_{new} = (P,Q,VA)\ (\text{p.u.})_{old} \times \frac{(VA)_{B.old}}{(VA)_{B.new}} \quad ...(8.71)$$

$$V\ (\text{p.u.})_{new} = V\ (\text{p.u.})_{old} \times \frac{V_{B.old}}{V_{B.new}} \quad ...(8.72)$$

Base current, $I_B = \dfrac{(VA)_B}{V_B}$ A

per unit current, $$I\ (\text{p.u.}) = \frac{I \text{ in Amps.}}{I_B} = \frac{(I \text{ in } A) \cdot V_B}{(VA)_B} \quad ...(8.73)$$

As per Eq. (8.73),

$$I(\text{p.u.})_{new} = I(\text{p.u.})_{old} \times \frac{V_{B.new}}{V_{B.old}} \cdot \frac{(VA)_{B.old}}{(VA)_{B.new}} \quad ...(8.74)$$

When per unit is applied to 3-phase systems, the base values are chosen as under :

$$P_B,\ Q_B,\ (VA)_B = \text{3-phase VA} \quad ...(8.75)$$

$$(MVA)_B = \text{3-phase MVA} \quad ...(8.76)$$

$$(kV)_B = \text{line to line kV} \quad ...(8.77)$$

For star connected device, from Eq. (8.68),

base impedance, $$Z_B = \frac{(\text{Per phase base kV})^2}{\text{Per phase base MVA}} = \frac{[(kV)_B/\sqrt{3}]^2}{\frac{1}{3}(MVA)_B} = \frac{(kV)_B^2}{(MVA)_B}\ \Omega$$

and $$Z\ (\text{p.u.}) = \frac{(Z \text{ in ohms})\ (MVA)_B}{(kV)_B^2} \quad ...(8.78)$$

Eq. (8.78) for a 3-phase system is the same as Eq. (8.69) for a single-phase system.

For three impedances, each of Z ohms and connected in delta, we have,

$$Z_B\ (\text{delta}) = \frac{(\text{Per phase base } kV)^2}{\text{Per phase base } MVA} = \frac{(kV)_B^2}{\frac{1}{3}(MVA)_B} = \frac{3\,(kV)_B^2}{(MVA)_B}\ \Omega$$

$$\therefore \quad Z\ (\text{p.u.}) = \frac{Z \text{ in ohms}}{Z_B\ (\text{delta})} = \frac{(Z \text{ in } \Omega)\ (MVA)_B}{3\,(kV)_B^2} = \frac{\left(\frac{Z}{3} \text{ in } \Omega\right)(MVA)_B}{(kV)_B^2} \quad ...(8.79)$$

It is known for a three-phase device having three equal impedances in delta and each of Z ohms that $Z/3$ is its equilvalent star impedance. Therefore, as per Eq. (8.79), per unit impedance for delta or equivalent star is the same for a given 3-phase MVA base and line-to-line kV base.

8.18 TRANSFORMERS IN THREE-PHASE CIRCUITS

When three-phase transformers form a part of a three-phase balanced system, calculations are done by reducing the circuit to an equivalent single-phase circuit. Computations are carried out on a per-phase-star line-to-neutral basis, because then the transformer impedances can be added directly to the series-connected transmission-line impedances. In case transmission-line impedances are to be transferred from one to other side of the 3-phase transformer, use square of the *line-to-line* voltage ratio of the transformer. For star-delta or delta-star transformers, all quantities should be referred to star-connected side. For delta-delta transformers in series with transmission lines, the delta-connected impedances of the transformers should be replaced by equivalent star-connected impedances. It is already known that

$$Z_y = \frac{1}{3} Z_\Delta \qquad ...(8.80)$$

where, Z_Δ = per-phase impedance of balanced delta-connected circuit

and, Z_y = per-phase impedance of equivalent balanced star-connected circuit.

A few examples will illustrate how problems concerning the use of transformers in three-phase circuits can be handled.

Example 8.42. *Three identical single-phase transformers are connected with primaries in delta and secondaries in star. Each of the transformer is rated at 100 kVA, 6600/230 V and has an equivalent impedance referred to the h.v. side of (16 + j32) ohms. The primary side of the transformer is connected to a 3-phase supply through a feeder having resistance and leakage reactance of (2 + j4) ohms per phase.*

Calculate the line-to-line voltage at the sending end of the feeder when the transformer secondary is delivering rated load at 400 V (L-L) at 0.8 pf lagging.

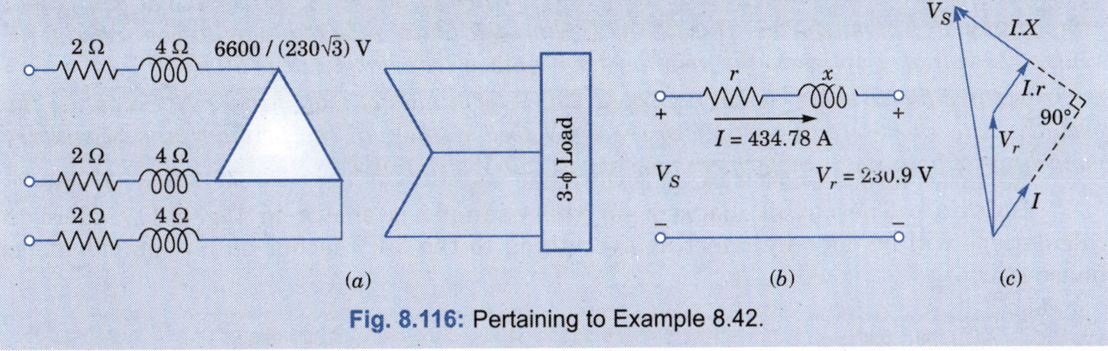

Fig. 8.116: Pertaining to Example 8.42.

Solution. Fig. 8.116 (*a*) shows the circuit diagram for this example. As stated before, the computations will be carried out on per phase basic referring all the quantities to l.v. star-connected side of the transformer bank.

H.V. feeder impedance referred to l.v. side is

$$Z_f = (2 + j4)\left[\frac{\text{line voltage on l.v. side}}{\text{line voltage on h.v. side}}\right]^2$$

$$= (2 + j4)\left[\frac{400}{6600}\right]^2 = 0.00735 + j0.0147\ \Omega \text{ per phase}$$

Transformer impedance referred to l.v. side is

$$Z_e = \left(\frac{230}{6600}\right)^2 (16 + j32) = 0.0194 + j0.0388\ \Omega \text{ per phase}$$

Total series impedance on the l.v. side, between source and load is

$$Z_f + Z_e = 0.02675 + j0.0535\ \Omega \text{ per phase}$$

Rated current on l.v. side $= \dfrac{100{,}000}{230} = 434.78$ A

Per-phase load voltage $= \dfrac{400}{\sqrt{3}} = 230.9$ V

The equivalent circuit for Fig. 8.116 (*a*) is as shown in Fig. 8.116 (*b*). For this equivalent circuit, the phaser diagram is drawn in Fig. 8.116 (*c*) which gives sending-end voltage per phase V_s on l.v. side as under:

$$V_s^2 = (230.9 \times 0.8 + 434.78 \times 0.02675)^2 + (230.9 \times 0.6 + 434.78 \times 0.0535)^2$$

$$V_s = 254.426 \text{ V}$$

$\therefore$ *L-L* voltage at the h.v. sending end

$$= 254.426 \times \frac{6600}{230} = 7300.92 \text{ V.}$$

Example 8.43. *Three identical single-phase transformers are connected delta-delta. Each of the transformer is rated at 100 kVA, 5000/250 V and has an equivalent impedance referred to h.v. side of (1 + j6) Ω. The primary side of this transformer A is fed from a second transformer B through a three-phase feeder of leakage impedance (0.4 + j1) ohms per phase. The transformer B is connected star-delta and is rated at 500 kVA, 50/5 kV. The equivalent impedance of the transformer B is (2 + j12) ohms per phase referred to delta-connected 5-kV side. The voltage applied to the primary terminals of transformer B is 50 kV.*

A three-phase short circuit occurs at 250-V terminals of transformer A. Calculate the steady-state short-circuit current in the 5 kV feeder lines, in the primary and secondary windings of both the transformers and at the 250-V terminals.

Solution. The circuit diagram for this example is shown in Fig. 8.117. Here the calculations will be done by referring everything to the 5-kV feeder on an equivalent per-phase-star.

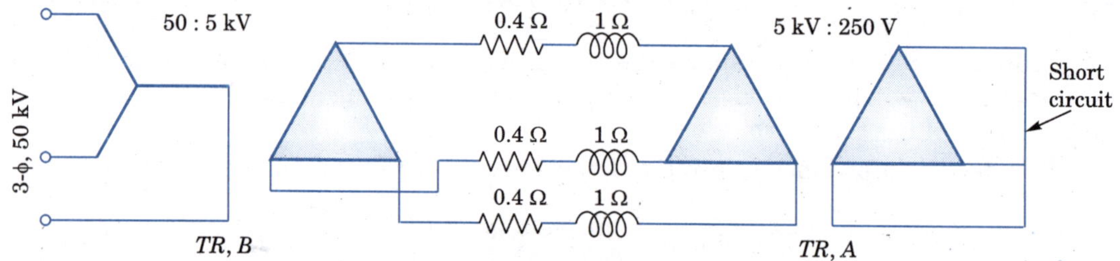

Fig. 8.117: Pertaining to Example 8.43.

For the feeder source voltage $= \dfrac{5000}{\sqrt{3}}$ V per phase

For transformer A, $z_{eg1} = \dfrac{1}{3}(1 + j6) = 0.33 + j2\ \Omega$

For transformer B, $z_{eg2} = \dfrac{1}{3}(2 + j12) = 0.67 + j4\ \Omega$

Feeder leakage impedance, $Z_f = 0.4 + j1\ \Omega$ per phase

Total impedance between source voltage and the fault

$$= z_{eg1} + z_{eg2} + Z_f = 1.4 + j7\ \Omega \quad \text{or} \quad 7.1386\ \Omega$$

Current in the 5-kV feeder $= \left(\dfrac{5000}{\sqrt{3}}\right) \times \dfrac{1}{7.1386} = 404.398$ A

Current in the 5-kV delta-connected windings of both the transformers

$$= \frac{404.398}{\sqrt{3}} = 233.486 \text{ A}$$

Current in the 250-V winding $= 233.486 \times 20 = 4669.72$ A

Current at the 250-V terminals = Short circuit line current

$$= \sqrt{3} \times 4669.72 = 8087.96 \text{ A}$$

Current in the 50-kV winding of star-delta transformer A

$$= \frac{233.486 \times \sqrt{3}}{10} = 40.44 \text{ A.}$$

Example 8.44. *Solve example 8.46 by using the per unit system.*

Solution. Choose a common three-phase base of 200 kVA (arbitrarily)

Line to line voltages are in the ratio of 50 kV : 5 kV : 250 V.

For transformer *A*, the base voltage and base kVA are taken equal to its individual ratings.

$$\therefore \qquad V_B = 5000 \text{ V}, (kVA)_B = 100 \text{ kVA}$$

Base impedance, $Z_{B1} = \dfrac{(kV)_B^2}{(MVA)_B} = \dfrac{5^2}{0.1} = 250\ \Omega$

Per unit impedance of transformer $A = \dfrac{1 + j6}{250}$

As individual transformer ratings are taken as base values, factor 1/3 does not appear here.

Total rating of transformer *A* is 300 kVA. Its per unit impedance on 200 kVA base is

$$z_{eg1} = \frac{1 + j6}{250} \times \frac{200}{300} = 0.00267 + j0.016 \text{ p.u.}$$

For transformer *B*, $V_B = 5$ kV, $(kVA)_B = 500$ kVA

Base impedance, $Z_{B2} = \dfrac{5 \times 5}{0.5} = 50\ \Omega$

Per unit impedance of transformer *B* on a base of 200 kVA is

$$z_{eg2} = \frac{1}{3}\left(\frac{2 + j12}{50}\right) \times \frac{200}{500} = 0.00533 + j0.032 \text{ p.u.}$$

For 5 kV feeder, $V_B = \dfrac{5000}{\sqrt{3}}$ V, $(kVA)_B = \dfrac{200}{3}$ kVA

$$I_B = \frac{200}{3} \times \frac{\sqrt{3}}{5.0} = \frac{40}{\sqrt{3}} = 23.095 \text{ A.} \quad Z_B = \frac{5000}{\sqrt{3}} \times \frac{\sqrt{3}}{40} = 125\ \Omega$$

Per unit impedance of feeder, $Z_f = \dfrac{0.4 + j1}{125} = 0.0032 + j0.008$

Total per unit impedance between source voltage and the fault

$$= z_{eg1} + z_{eg2} + Z_f = 0.0112 + j0.056$$

Source voltage $= 1.0$ p.u.

$$\text{Current in 5-kV feeder} = \frac{1.0}{\sqrt{0.0112^2 + 0.056^2}} = 17.51 \text{ p.u.} = 17.51 \times 23.095 = 404.393 \text{ A}$$

The result is consistent with the previous solution.

Example 8.45. *A 800 kVA, 11/0.4 kV, 3-phase delta-star transformer has ohmic loss of 3 kW on h.v. side and 2 kW on l.v. side under rated load. The total leakage reactance is 0.08 p.u. Calculate*

(*a*) *the ohmic values of the equivalent resistance and leakage reactance on both delta and star sides, and*

(*b*) *the per unit values of the resistance on both h.v. and l.v. sides.*

Solution. *H.V. side:*

Total ohmic loss $= 3 + 2 = 5$ kW.

$$\text{Full-load current} = \frac{800}{3 \times 11} \text{ A}$$

$$\text{Equivalent resistance in ohms,} \quad r_{e1} = \frac{5000 \times (33)^2}{(800)^2} = 8.508\ \Omega$$

For delta-connected impedances, it is known that

$$Z(\text{p.u.}) = \frac{\left(\frac{Z}{3} \text{ in ohms}\right)(MVA)_B}{(kV)_B^2}$$

$$\therefore \quad \text{Equivalent resistance in per unit} = \frac{8.508}{3} \times \frac{0.8}{(11)^2} = 0.01875 \text{ p.u.}$$

$$\text{Equivalent leakage reactance in ohms} = 3 \times \frac{(0.08)(11)^2}{0.8} = 36.3\ \Omega$$

L.V. side : Total ohmic loss $= 3 + 2 = 5$ kW

$$\text{Full-load current} = \frac{800 \times \sqrt{3}}{3 \times 0.4} = \frac{2000}{\sqrt{3}} \text{ A}$$

$$\text{Equivalent resistance in ohms,} \quad r_{e2} = \frac{5000 \times 3}{(2000)^2} = 0.00375\ \Omega.$$

For star-connected impedances, it is known that

$$Z(\text{p.u.}) = \frac{(Z \text{ in ohms})(MVA)_B}{(kV)_B^2}$$

$$\text{Equivalent resistance in per unit} = \frac{0.00375 \times 0.8}{(0.4)^2} = 0.01875$$

$$\text{Equivalent leakage reactance in ohms} = \frac{0.08 \times (11)^2}{0.8} = 12.1\ \Omega$$

It is seen that equivalent resistance in per unit is the same on both primary and secondary sides.

Example 8.46. *A Y-Δ connected bank of three identical 10 kVA, 2300/230 V single-phase transformers is used to step down the voltage. Per-phase impedance of the h.v. feeder is 0.4 + j 4Ω and that of the l.v. feeder is 0.004 + j 0.008 Ω. The load on l.v. side consists of a heater load of 2 kW per phase and a three-phase induction motor load of 15 kW at 0.8 pf lag at 230 V. Leakage impedance of each single-phase transformer, referred to l.v. side, is 0.1 + j0.2 Ω.*

Calculate the line current and line to line voltage at sending end of the h.v. feeder.

Solution. A single-line diagram for the three-phase system, given in this example, is shown in Fig. 8.118 (*a*). The calculations will be done on per-phase basis by referring all quantities to h.v. star-connected side of the transformer bank.

Heater load phase current, $I_H = \dfrac{2000}{2300} = 0.8696 \angle 0° \text{ A}$

Three-phase induction motor phase current,

$$I_M = \frac{15000}{3 \times 2300 \times 0.8} = 2.7174 \angle -36.87° \text{ A}$$

Total load current per phase,

$$I_L = I_H + I_M = 0.8697 \angle 0° + 2.7174 \angle -36.87°$$
$$= 0.8696 + j0 + 2.7174\,(0.8 - j0.6)$$
$$= 3.0435 - j1.6304 = 3.4527 \angle -28.178° \text{ A}$$

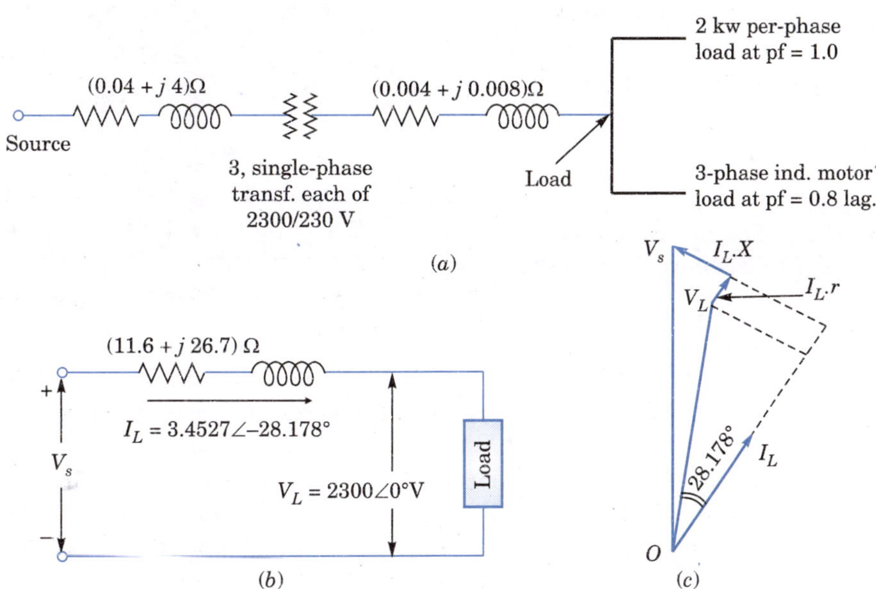

Fig. 8.118: (*a*) Single-line diagram (*b*) per-phase equivalent circuit referred to h.v. side and (*c*) phasor diagram, Example 8.46.

∴ Line current at sending end of h.v. feeder, because of star-connection, is **3.4527 A.**

L.V. feeder impedance referred to h.v. side,

$$Z_{f1} = (0.004 + j0.008)\left(\frac{2300 \times \sqrt{3}}{230}\right)^2 = 1.2 + j2.4 \ \Omega$$

Transformer leakage impedance referred to h.v. side,

$$Z_e = (0.1 + j0.2)\left(\frac{2300}{230}\right)^2 = 10 + j20\ \Omega$$

H.V. feeder impedance, $Z_{f2} = 0.4 + j4\ \Omega$

Total series impedance on h.v. side between source and load is

$$Z_{f1} + Z_e + Z_{f2} = 1.2 + j2.4 + 10 + j20 + 0.4 + j4 = 11.6 + j26.4\ \Omega$$

The per-phase equivalent circuit referred to h.v. side on per-phase *Y*-basis is shown in Fig. 8.118 (*b*), where V_s = per-phase sending end voltage of h.v. feeder, V_L = per-phase load voltage referred to h.v. side = 2300 $\angle 0°$ V and $I_L = 3.4527 \angle -28.178°$ A is the load currrent.

For the circuit of Fig. 8.118 (*b*), the phasor diagram, drawn in Fig. 8.118 (*c*) gives,

$$V_s^2 = [2300 \cos 28.178° + 3.4527 \times 11.6]^2 + [2300 \sin 28.178° + 3.4527 \times 26.4]^2$$
$$= [2067.47]^2 + [1177.24]^2$$

∴ Sending end voltage per phase, $V_s = \sqrt{2067.47^2 + 1177.24^2} = 2379.14$ V

Actual line to line voltage at the sending end of the h.v. feeder, because of star-connection is given by $2379.14 \times \sqrt{3} = 4120.67$ V.

Example 8.47. *Fig. 8.119 shows two single-phase transformers T_1 and T_2 of turns ratios 3 : 1 and 2 : 1 connected with their primaries in series across a 100-V, 50-Hz source. Assuming that the transformers are ideal, determine what the a.c. voltmeter V would read (i) when S_1 is closed (ii) when S_2 is closed (iii) when S_3 is closed. Take R = 100 ohms and the voltmeter to have infinite impedance. The dot points indicate ter-minals of the corresponding polarity on the primary and secondary sides.* [I.A.S., 1990]

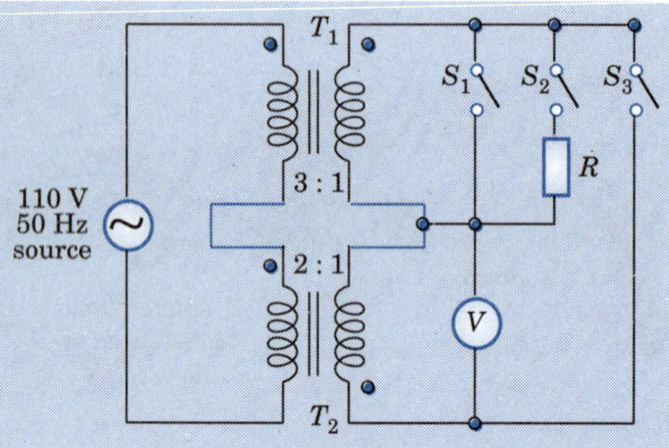

Fig. 8.119: Pertaining to Example 8.47.

Solution. (*a*) When switch S_1 is closed, secondary of transformer T_1 gets short circuited. As a result, its secondary voltage is zero, likewise primary voltage of T_1 is also zero. The entire source voltage of 100 V, therefore, appears across the primary of transformer T_2. Thus the voltage read by voltmeter V is 100/2 × 1 = 50 volts.

(*b*) When switch S_2 is closed, a current of 20/100 = 0.2 A begins to flow in the secondary of transformer T_1. As a result, its primary current is (0.02/3) = 0.067 A. Thus, for transformer 1, secondary mmf is balanced by its primary mmf. This current of 0.067 A must flow through the primary of T_2 as per the circuit requirement. Since the secondary of transformer T_2 is open-circuited, current of 0.067 A in its primary must be the magnetizing current.

∴ Voltage across primary of

$$T_2 = 0.067 \times \text{magnetizing impedance of } T_2$$

As the transformers are given to be ideal, the magnetizing impedance of transformer T_2 is large, the voltage across primary of T_2 is therefore greater than 40 V, *i.e.* that voltage of transformer 1 collapses. As a consequence, the voltage on the primary side of T_2 exceeds 40 V and voltmeter connected across secondary of T_2 must read much more than 20 V.

(c) When switch S_3 is closed, the two secondary windings get connected in parallel. Voltage across T_1 primary is 60 V and that across T_2 primary is 40 V. The voltmeter V, therefore, reads 20 Volts.

Example 8.48. *Two identical 200 V/200 V, 50 Hz single-phase transformer A and B have negligible power losses and negligible leakage fluxes. The magnetizing current taken by either transformer when fed from rated voltage is 0.1 A. If the windings of A and B are connected as shown in Fig. 8.120, estimate the currents drawn by P_A and S_A and the open-circuit voltage across $S_B \cdot P_A$ and S_A are the two windings of transformer A, while P_B and S_B are the two windings of transformer B.* [I.A.S., 1991]

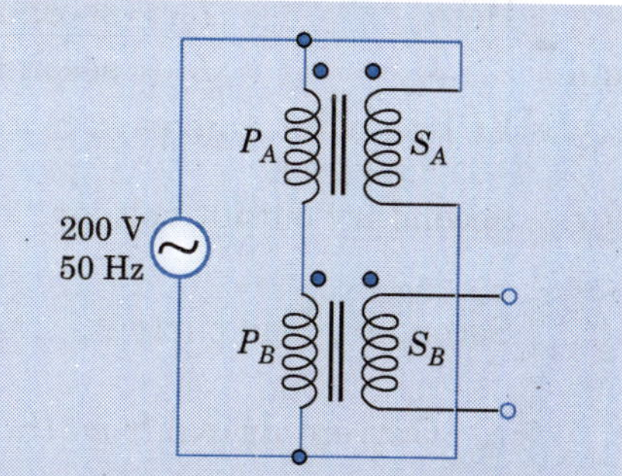

Fig. 8.120: Pertaining to Example 8.48.

Solution. The magnetizing current taken by transformer A or transformer B is 0.1 A. This means 0.1 A is sufficient to produce the required core flux in transformer A or transformer B. As per the given connection scheme, both the primary and secondary windings of transformer A combine together to produce the required core flux. Consequently, the current drawn by primary winding P_A is 0.05 A and that drawn by secondary winding S_A is also 0.05 A.

As P_B is in series with P_A, the current flowing in the primary winding P_B of transformer B is 0.05 A. A magnetizing current of 0.1 A gives an output voltage of 200 V across S_B. Likewise, a magnetizing current of 0.05 A in P_B would now give an open-circuit voltage of 100 V across winding S_B.

So the current drawn by windings P_A and S_A = 0.05 A each, and the open-circuit voltage across S_B = 100 V.

Example 8.49. *Fig. 8.121 (a) shows two single-phase transformers T_1 and T_2 of turns ratio 3 : 1 and 2 : 1 connected with their primaries in series across a 110 V, 50 Hz source. The dot-points indicate terminals of the corresponding polarity on the primary and secondary sides. Assume that the transformers are ideal and take R = 10 Ω. Determine the current drawn from the source.*

Solution. Let I_1 be the current in the two series-connected primaries. I_1 is also the source current as shown in Fig. 8.121 (b).

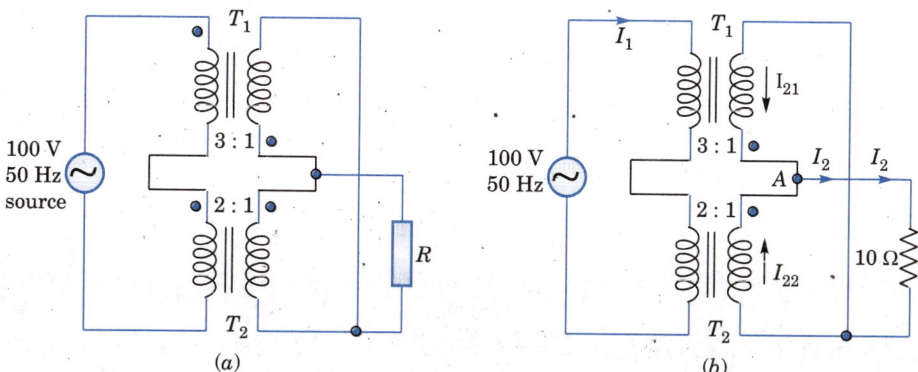

Fig. 8.121: Pertaining to Example 8.49.

For mmf balance, for transformer T_1, $I_1 \times 3 = I_{21} \times 1$

and for transformer T_2, $I_1 \times 2 = I_{22} \times 1$

This gives $I_{21} = 3I_1$ and $I_{22} = 2I_1$

Here I_{21} = secondary current of transformer T_1

and I_{22} = secondary current of transformer T_2

KCL at point A gives $I_2 = I_{21} + I_{22} = 3I_1 + 2I_1 = 5I_1$

Secondary output voltage, $V_2 = \frac{60}{3} = \frac{40}{2} = 20$ V

Secondary load current, $I_2 = \frac{V_2}{R} = \frac{20}{10} = 2 \text{ A} = 5I_1$

$\therefore$ Current drawn from the source, $I_1 = \frac{2}{5} = 0.4$ A.

Example 8.50. *Fig. 8.122 (a) shows two single-phase ideal transformers T_1 and T_2 of turns ratios 3 : 1 and 2 : 1 connected with their primaries in parallel across a 90-V, 50-Hz source. Their secondaries are connected in series as shown. The dot-points indicate terminals of the corresponding polarity on the primary and secondary sides. For R = 10 Ω, determine current taken from the source.*

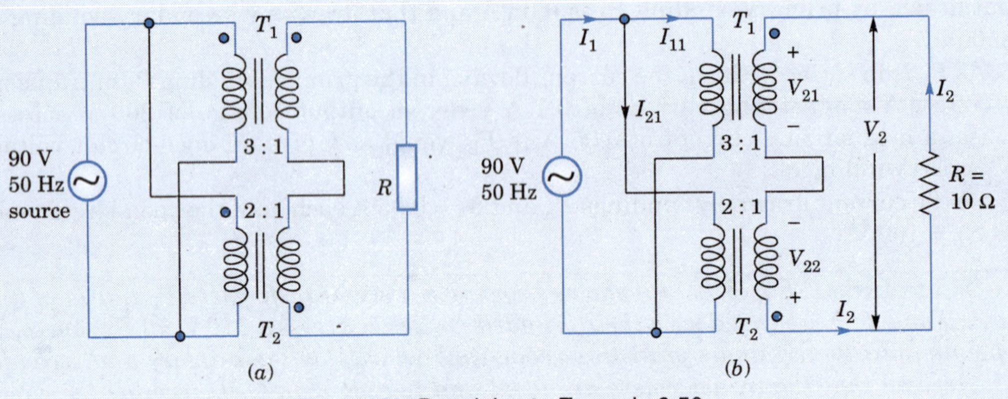

Fig. 8.122: Pertaining to Example 8.50.

Solution. For transformer T_1, secondary voltage is

$$\frac{V_{21}}{1} = \frac{90}{3} \quad \text{or} \quad V_{21} = 30 \text{ V}$$

For transformer T_2, secondary voltage is $\frac{V_{22}}{1} = \frac{90}{2}$ or $V_{22} = 45$ V

The two secondaries are connected in series with such polarity markings that voltages V_{21} and V_{22} oppose each other. Therefore, net output voltage, Fig. 8.122 (*b*), is given by

$$V_2 = V_{22} - V_{21} = 45 - 30 = 15 \text{ V}$$

Load current, $I_2 = \frac{V_2}{R} = \frac{15}{10} = 1.5$ A

For mmf balance, primary current of T_1 is $I_{11} = \frac{1.5}{3} = 0.5$ A.

and primary current of T_2 is $I_{21} = \frac{1.5}{2} = 0.75$ A.

$\therefore$ Source current $I_1 = I_{11} + I_{21} = 0.5 + 0.75 = 1.25$ A.

PROBLEMS

8.1. (*a*) What is the difference between a three-phase transformer bank and a 3-phase transformer unit ?

(*b*) Explain how the 3-phase core type transformer was evolved from three single-phase core type transformers having both their windings on one leg.

(*c*) In 3-phase shell type transformers, a considerable economy is achieved in the core material if the middle phase winding is wound in the reversed direction as compared with the outer two phase windings. Explain.

8.2. (*a*) The low voltage windings of a three-phase core type transformer have no electrical connection amongst them. If the middle l.v. winding is connected to single-phase of 300 V at rated frequency, then compute.

(*i*) the open circuit voltage across the l.v. windings on the outer two legs,

(*ii*) the open-circuit voltage across the l.v. winding in case the other l.v. winding is short circuited.

Assume that the magnetic flux is confined to the core and the winding resistances are negligible.

(*b*) In part (*a*), if single-phase supply of 300 V is given to the one l.v. winding on an outer leg, then calculate the open-circuit voltage across the other two l.v. windings. Assume that the ratio of window width to window height is half.

[**Hint :** (*a*) (*ii*): When one winding is short circuited, the voltage induced in it produces short circuit. The effect of this short circuit is to produce flux that opposes the inducing flux. As a result of it, most of the flux is forced to complete its path through the other core. Consequently, the voltage induced across the open-circuited winding is near to 300 V and the current in the short-circuited winding is very small.]

[**Ans.** (*a*) (*i*) 150 V (*ii*) 300 V (*b*) 200 V across middle winding and 100 V across outer winding]

8.3. (*a*) Describe the standard method of marking the terminals of 3-phase transformers.

(*b*) Explain the clock-method of angle designation for representing 3-phase transformers.

What points should be kept in mind for drawing the phasor diagrams of different groups of transformers ? Illustrate your answer with an example of star-delta transformer.

8.4. Describe in detail the four phasor groups pertaining to 3-phase transformers. Draw the phasor diagrams and connection schemes for each of these four groups.

8.5. (*a*) In *Yy0* transformer ; the polarities of phase winding *B* are reversed. Explain, with phasor diagram, its effect on the secondary output voltages.

(*b*) In a *Yy0*, 11000/433 V, 3-phase transformer, the polarities of phase-B winding get reversed. Find the magnitude of the output voltages with appropriate phasor diagrams.

[**Ans.** (*b*) V_{c2a2} = 433 V, $V_{a2b1} = V_{b1c2}$ = 250 V]

8.6. A *Yy0* transformer is fed from 3-phase supply leads marked A_2, B_2, C_2. If the primary leads are cyclically interchanged from

(*a*) A_2, B_2, C_2 to B_2, C_2, A_2 and (*b*) A_2, B_2, C_2 to C_2, A_2, B_2,

then investigate the effect of this changed phase sequence on the primary-line phasors and secondary-line phasors. Illustrate your answer with suitable connection and phasor diagrams. [**Ans.** Primary line phasors are uneffected. Secondary line phasors rotate through a time-phase of angle of (*a*) 120° anticlockwise (*b*) 120° clockwise].

8.7. (*a*) Explain the conditions that must be fulfilled for the successful parallel operation of 3-phase transformers.

(b) A 300 kVA, 3-phase transformer, having per phase leakage impedance of $0.016 + j0.07\ \Omega$, is connected in parallel with another transformer of the same voltage ratio having a rating of 500 kVA and per phase leakage impedance of $0.006 + j0.036\ \Omega$. Find the load shared by each transformer and their operating pfs for a total load of 800 kVA at 0.8 p.f. lagging.

[**Ans.** (b) 221.90 kW at p.f. 0.823 lagging and 417.67 kW at p.f. 0.7875 lagging].

8.8. (a) Discuss briefly the essential and desirable conditions to be fulfilled for operating two 3-phase transformers in parallel.

(b) Two delta-star 11000/433 V transformers are to be operated in parallel. Their primaries in delta are energised from the same voltage source of 11 kV. The secondary terminals are marked $a_2\ b_2\ c_2$ for one transformer and $a_2'\ b_2'\ c_2'$ for the second transformer.

With their neutrals joined together, the voltages are observed as follows:

$$a_2 - a_2' = 500 \text{ V},\ b_2 - b_2' = 433 \text{ V},\ c_2 - c_2' = 433 \text{ V}.$$

Describe with appropriate phasor diagrams, how the two secondaries can be connected in parallel. [**Ans.** (b) Reverse the polarities of phase A and then interchange b_2' and c_2' so that $a_2'\ b_2'\ c_2'$ overlap respectively $a_2 b_2 c_2$]

8.9. (a) Compare the behaviour of star/star transformer with star/zig-zag transformer.

(b) A star-star transformer is to be operated in parallel with delta-zigzag transformer. Calculate their h.v. to l.v. phase-turns ratio, in case primary and secondary voltages are respectively.

(i) 420 V and 140 V and (ii) 420 V and 1260 V.

[**Hint.** (b) (i) For zigzag, $140/\sqrt{3}$ V is the phase voltage, 140/3 V is the voltage rating of each half phase, ∴ 280/3 V is the phase voltage etc.] [**Ans.** (b) (i) 3, 4.5 (ii) 3, 2]

8.10. A three-phase step-down transformer is connected in star/delta and has a turn-ratio per phase of 30 to 1. Calculate the corresponding ratio of a second transformer connected delta/star to work on the same line voltages on each side. Explain in detail, with reference to phasor groups, whether these transformers would work in parallel.

[**Ans.** 90 to 1. These can work in parallel ; both may belong to the same phasor group 3 or 4 ; or to different phasor groups, see Example 8.1]

8.11. Two three-phase transformers operate in parallel between 33 and 11 kV busbars, the line voltages on the h.t. bus leading the corresponding voltages on the l.t. side by 30°. One transformer is delta/star connected and the other star/zigzag connected.

Draw a diagram showing the internal connections of all transformer windings and connections to the busbars, and show by means of phasor diagrams that these connections will not lead to any circulating currents. Calculate the voltage of each winding section of both the transformers. [I.E.S.]

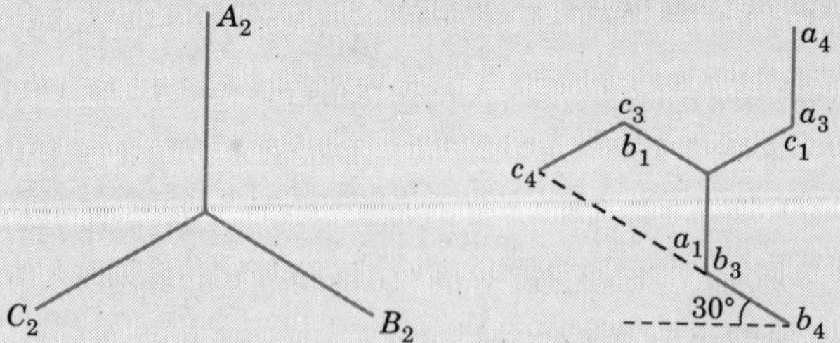

Fig. 8.123: Pertaining to the hint of problem 8.11.

[**Hint.** The delta/star transformer with line voltages on the h.t. bus is leading the corresponding voltages on the l.t. side by 30°, *Dy*1 as shown in Fig. 8.13. The corresponding star/zigzag transformer $Yz1$ phasor diagram is as shown in Fig. 8.129. The internal connections of transformer windings and connections to the bus-bars can be shown accordingly.] [**Ans.** Dy 1, 33 kV phase voltage/6.351 kV phase voltage. Yz1, 19.053 kV phase voltage/3.6667 kV for each half section.]

8.12. A 3-phase step-down transformer is connected to 6600 V mains and takes 10 A per line. Each secondary phase has two similar windings. Neglecting losses, calculate the secondary line voltage, line current and output for the connection : (*a*) delta/parallel star (*b*) delta/zig-zag. The ratio of primary turns per phase to each secondary winding per phase is 12.

[**Ans.** (*a*) 476.3 V, 138.57 A, 114.32 kVA (*b*) 825 V, 69.28 A, 99 kVA]

8.13. Two 11000/440 V, 3-phase, delta-star transformers have their ratings equal to 200 kVA and 300 kVA and their respective leakage impedances referred to secondary are $0.016 + j0.08\ \Omega$ per phase and $0.01 + j0.06\Omega$ per phase. For a total load of 500 kVA at a p.f. of 0.8 lagging, calculate (*a*) the output current of each transformer in terms of its rated current and (*b*) the output terminal voltage with primary voltage at 11 kV.

[**Hint.** First find the kVA shared by each transformer and their operating p.fs. Then,

$$\text{Voltage regulation} = \frac{I_2}{E_2}(r_{e2}\cos\theta_2 + x_{e2}\sin\theta_2)$$

$$= \frac{E_2 I_2}{(E_2)^2}[r_{e2}\cos\theta_2 + x_{e2}\sin\theta_2]$$

$$\text{or} \qquad \frac{E_2 - V_2}{E_2} = 1000 \times \frac{\text{kVA shared by transformer}}{(E_2)^2}[r_{e2}\cos\theta + x_{e2}\sin\theta_2]$$

[**Ans.** (*a*) 1.0674 I_{r1}, 0.955 I_{r2} (*b*) 410.967 V]

8.14. Two 11/3.3 kV, 3-phase, 500 kVA and 750 kVA transformers have their respective leakage impedances of $(1.2 + j4.6)\%$ and $(1.4 + j4.5)\%$.

(*a*) If no transformer is to be overloaded, calculate the maximum kVA load that can be supplied by these two transformers in parallel.

(*b*) If the total load on the transformers is 1200 kVA to 0.8 p.f. lagging, then calculate the load voltage with primary voltage at 11 kV.

[**Hint.** (*b*) Calculate the load shared by one transformer and then use the expression for transformer voltage regulation]. [**Ans.** (*a*) 1245.688 kVA (*b*) 3180.13 V]

8.15. (*a*) Explain how a three-phase transformer $Yd1$ of group number 3, can be successfully operated in parallel with another transformer Dy 11 of group number 4.

(*b*) Two transformers, $Yy0$, and $Dy1$ with same voltage and kVA ratings, are connected in parallel. Their primaries are energised from the same voltage source and the secondary neutrals are grounded. If their p.u. leakage impedances are 0.06, then determine the no-load circulating current in terms of rated current.

[**Hint.** (*b*) If ΔE is the resultant voltage in the local circuit, then circulating current

$$I_c = \frac{\Delta E}{z_{ea} + z_{eb}} = \frac{2E\sin\frac{\alpha}{2}}{z_{ea} + z_{eb}}$$

Since the transformers have same kVA and voltage ratings, their rated current I_r are equal.

$$\therefore \qquad \frac{I_c}{I_r} = \frac{2\sin\frac{\alpha}{2}}{\frac{I_r}{E}(z_{ea}) + \frac{I_r}{E}(z_{eb})} = \frac{2\sin\frac{\alpha}{2}}{z_{eapu} + z_{ebpu}} \text{ etc.]}$$

[**Ans.** (*b*) 4.314]

8.16. (*a*) State the conditions essential for the successful parallel operation of 3-phase power transformers.

(*b*) Two equal-ratio parallel-connected three-phase transformers deliver a total load of 1000 kVA at 11 kV, power factor 0.8 lagging. The equivalent impedances of the two transformers are $z_1 = 1 + j5\ \Omega$ and $z_2 = 1 + j3$ ohms. Calculate (*i*) current, (*ii*) phase displacement between V and I in each transformer secondary. Assume delta connection on the load side of the transformer.

[**Ans.** (*i*) 20.127 A (*Line*), 11.621 A (*phase*); 41.29° with phase current *I* lagging phase voltage V (*ii*) 32.463 A, 18.743 A, 34.16° with *I* lagging V.]

8.17. (*a*) Explain how the exciting (or no-load) current of a single-phase transformer contains harmonics even when the supply voltage is a sine wave.

(*b*) If transformer *B-H* curve is assumed without hysteresis, discuss how the results obtained in part (*a*) are effected.

8.18. (*a*) If the magnetizing current of a single-phase transformer is assumed a sine wave, then show that the flux wave must be flat-topped.

(*b*) The voltage applied to the primary of a single-phase transformer at no load is given by

$$v = 200 \cos \omega t + 80 \cos 3\omega t$$

If the primary has 300 turns, then calculate the maximum value of the flux in the core for a fundamental supply frequency of 50 Hz. [**Ans.** 1.839 m Wb]

8.19. (*a*) Show that the third harmonic voltages are in time phase, fifth harmonic voltages have a phase sequence opposite to the fundamental phase sequence and 7th harmonic voltages have the same phase sequence as that of the fundamental.

(*b*) The exciting current of a single-phase transformer, at rated voltage and frequency, is given by $i = 4 \sin \omega t + 1.2 \sin (3\omega t + \alpha_3) + 0.2 \sin (5\omega t + \alpha_5)$

If three such transformers are connected with their primary in delta and secondary in star, then calculate r.m.s. value of (*i*) primary line current and (*iii*) current in primary delta.

[**Hint.** (*b*) (*i*) Primary line current consists of fundamental and 5th harmonic currents. See Example 8-12] [**Ans.** (*b*) 4.9051 A, 2.9568 A]

8.20. (*a*) Compare the performance of two star-star transformers, one with separate magnetic circuits and the other with an interlinked magnetic circuit.

(*b*) A bank of three-single-phase transformers has its primary in star and secondary in delta. The primary is fed from 3-wire supply and the secondary per-phase voltage is 230 V. If the secondary delta is opened, a voltage of 380 V is measured across open delta. In case the neutrals of primary and source are connected together, the voltage across open-circuited delta reduces to zero. Explain how this happens.

8.21. Give the disadvantages of current and voltage harmonics in transformers. Explain how these harmonics can be eliminated.

8.22. (*a*) Explain the advantages of using a tertiary winding in a bank of star-star transformers.

(*b*) A 3-phase transformer is connected in star-star and the primary line to neutral voltage is given by $v = 200 \sin \omega t + 80 \sin (3\omega t + 100°)$.

If the phase turns ratio of primary to secondary is 1/3, then estimate the effective value of (*i*) the secondary line to line voltage ; (*ii*) the secondary line to neutral voltage.

In case this transformer is provided with third winding connected in delta, then determine the voltage across the open-delta of this winding. The phase turns ratio of secondary to tertiary is unity. [**Ans.** (*b*) 734.85 V, 456.95 V, 509.194 V]

8.23. The exciting current of a 231/462 V, 50 Hz transformer, when connected to rated sinusoidal voltage and frequency, is given by

$$i = 9 \sin \omega t + 3 \sin (3\omega t + \alpha_3) + 1 \sin (5\omega t + \alpha_5)$$

Three such transformers are connected in star/delta and at no load, their star is fed from 400 V, 50 Hz supply mains.

Calculate the effective value of current flowing in the primary coils and the secondary closed delta if

(*a*) the star neutral is not connected to supply neutral,

(*b*) the star neutral is connected to supply neutral.

[**Hint.** (*b*) Since the third harmonic current can flow both in the primary and secondary coils, the drop $I_3 z_3$ in the primary coil appears as $I_3 z_3 \times$ turns ratio in the secondary.

$$\therefore \text{ Third harmonic secondary phase voltage} = \frac{3}{\sqrt{2}} \cdot z_3 \cdot \frac{1}{2}$$

$$\therefore \quad \text{Current in secondary closed delta} = \frac{3}{\sqrt{2}} \cdot z_3 \times \frac{1}{2} \times \frac{1}{z_3} = 1.061 \text{ A}]$$

[**Ans.** (*a*) 6.403 A, 1.0608 A. (*b*) 6.7454 A, 1.061 A]

8.24. The primary windings of three identical single-phase transformers are joined in star and are connected to a 3-phase, 4-wire supply having voltages which are symmetrical and sinusoidal. The secondary windings are also joined in star and there is no external lead.

When the star points of the source and transformer primaries are connected, it is found that a current flows in the neutral conductor. Explain fully why this should occur and state what additional information would be needed in order to estimate the magnitude of the neutral current.

If now the secondary is connected in delta, will the neutral current decrease or increase? In case the star points of the source and transformer primaries are disconnected, will the secondary closed-delta current increase or decrease. Explain.

[**Ans.** Zero-sequence (or 3rd-harmonic) impedance of the closed circuit. Neutral current decreases. Secondary closed-delta current increases].

8.25. (*a*) What are the adverse effects of unbalanced currents in 3-phase transformers?

(*b*) Three identical 10 kVA transformers are connected to a balanced 3-phase supply. What is the greatest single phase load that can be supplied between any pair of lines on the secondary side without overheating any one of the transformers if they are connected in (*i*) *Yd*, (*ii*) *Dd* and (*iii*) *Dy*. [**Ans.** 15 kVA, 15 kVA, 17.32 kVA]

8.26. (*a*) Discuss the effect of connections used in three-phase transformer banks on the harmonic content of the magnetizing current.

(*b*) A single-phase load is connected across one pair of terminals of the secondaries of a transformer bank, the primaries of which are star-connected and secondaries delta-connected. Neglecting the no-load current, draw a phasor diagram, showing the distribution of currents in the primary and secondary windings.

8.27. (*a*) Why is the exciting current of a transformer non-sinusoidal although the applied voltage may be sinusoidal? Explain.

(*b*) Explain why it is not desirable to use star-star connection with a 3-phase shell-type transformer although it may be used with 3-legged core-type construction.

(*c*) The primary winding of a bank of three identical 10 kVA, 2400/240 V, single-phase transformers is supplied from another delta-star (neutral grounded) transformer. The line voltage is sinusoidal with effective value of 4160 V. The bank is connected *Yy* and a voltmeter connected between primary neutral and ground reads 1000 V. What are the line to neutral and line voltages across secondary of the bank? [**Ans.** (*c*) 260.17 V, 416 V]

8.28. (*a*) A bank of three transformers, connected in star-star, is fed from 3-phase 3-wire supply. If a single-phase load is applied between one line and neutral, then the voltage of loaded phase collapses, but this does not happen in a three-phase core type transformer. Explain.

(*b*) If *Yy* bank of three identical transformers is provided with third winding in delta ; explain how single-phase load, between one line and neutral, can be supplied without any collapse of-loaded-phase voltage.

8.29. Three identical single-phase transformers have their primary, secondary and tertiary windings connected in star, star and delta respectively. In each transformer, the secondary and tertiary turns are equal but the ratio of primary to secondary turns is 4. The primary is fed from 3-wire supply.

(*a*) For a single-phase load taking 60 A at 0.8 p.f. lag between one line and neutral, calculate the current in each winding of the transformer.

(*b*) In addition to the single-phase load of part (*a*), a balanced three-phase load taking a line current of 80 A at unity pf is supplied by transformer secondary. Calculate the current in each winding of the transformer.

[**Ans.** (*a*) I_1 = 10 A, I_2 = 60 A, I_3 = 20 A;
(*b*) I_{AN} = 28.64 A, I_{BN} = 20.024 A, I_{CN} = 24.677 A.
I_3 = 20 A; I_{na} = 132.97 A, I_{nb} = I_{nc} = 80 A]

8.30. A three-phase three-legged core type transformer connected in *Yy* can deliver single-phase line to neutral load without seriously unbalancing the phase voltages, but a 3-phase *Yy* transformer with independent magnetic circuits can't do so. Explain your answer with suitable diagram assuming the single-phase load to be inductive in nature.

8.31. (*a*) One supply line feeding the primaries of *Dy* transformer gets disconnected. For a phase turns ratio equal to unity, determine the line to line and line to neutral output voltages.

If one delta terminal disconnected from the supply mains is reconnected to any one of the remaining two supply lines, then investigate its effect on the line and line to neutral output voltages.

(*b*) One supply line feeding the primaries of 11/220 kV, *Yd* transformer gets disconnected. Obtain the magnitude of output voltages.

[**Ans.** (*b*) Single-phase output voltages are of magnitude 190.52 kV, 190.52 kV, 0]

8.32. (*a*) Discuss the adverse effects of unbalanced working of a three-phase transformer.

(*b*) A delta-star 11/0.4 kV bank of three identical single-phase transformers supplies a 3-phase balanced load of 500 kVA at 0.8 pf lag and a single-phase load of 100 kW at unity power factor between one line and neutral. Determine the magnitude of currents in each primary phase winding and in each supply line. Neglect internal voltage drop and their no-load currents. [**Ans.** Phase currents : 15.1547 A, 15.153 A, 23.077 A
Line currents : 35.291 A, 26.248 A, 30.96 A]

8.33. The transformer connections shown in Fig. 8.124 are connected to single-phase loads requiring VI voltamperes. For equal primary and secondary line voltages, determine the currents in the primary phase windings and the primary lines. The transformer exciting currents are neglected.

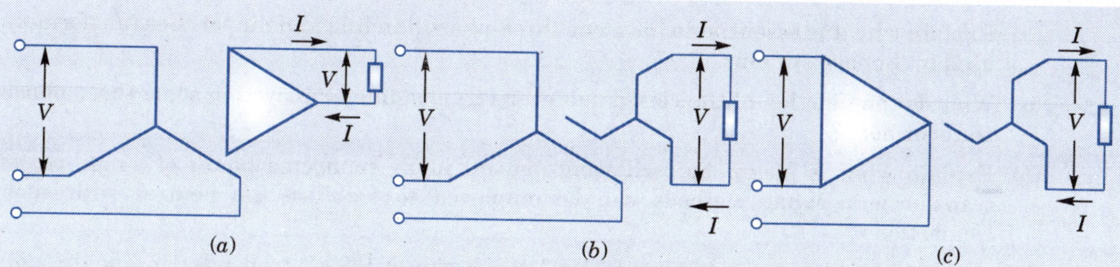

Fig. 8.124: Pertaining to Problem 8.33.

[**Ans.** (*a*) and (*b*) 1.1547*I*, 0.57735*I*, 0.57735*I*.

Same values are for lines (*c*) $\frac{2}{3}I, \frac{1}{3}I, \frac{1}{3}I$. (*I*, *I*, 0)]

8.34. (*a*) In open-delta transformers, show that the secondary line voltages form a balanced 3-phase system of voltages, in case the supply voltages are balanced.

(*b*) What is utilization factor? Find its value for open-delta connection.

8.35. (*a*) Show that the power delivered by open-delta transformers to a purely resistive load is equal to $\sqrt{3}\,EI$, where *E* and *I* are the line values.

(*b*) A load of 20 kW at 0.8 p.f. lagging is to be supplied at 230 V by transformers connected in open-delta from 11 kV line.

(*i*) Determine kVA rating of each of the two transformers and their turns ratio.

(*ii*) Determine the line currents on both h.v. and l.v. sides. At what p.f. is each transformer operating ? [**Ans.** (*b*) (*i*) 14.44 kVA, 47.826 (*ii*) 1.3122 A, 62.757 A, 0.993 lag, 0.392 lag]

8.36. Three identical single-phase transformers, connected in delta-delta, supply a balanced three-phase load. Each transformer carries rated current of 200 A at rated voltage.

(*i*) What is the current in each transformer secondary ?

(*ii*) One transformer develops fault and is removed. For the same temperature rise, determine the current in each transformer and the percentage reduction in kVA capacity of the open-delta. [**Ans.** (*i*) 200 A (*ii*) 115.473 A, 42.3%]

8.37. Two single-phase transformers, each rated for 200 kVA, 11/0.4 kV, 50 Hz, are connected in open-delta.

(*a*) Determine the load kVA that can be delivered by this connection scheme without overloading either transformer.

(*b*) This connection scheme supplies a three-phase balanced load of 200 kVA at 400 V, 0.866 power factor lag. Determine

(*i*) the transformer currents on the h.v. side and

(*ii*) power factors at which each transformer operates.

[**Ans.** (*a*) 346.4 kVA (*b*) 10.498 A, pfs are 1 and 0.5 lag]

8.38. Three 1910/230 V, single-phase transformers have no polarity marking on them. These three transformers are to be connected in (*a*) *Yd* (*b*) *Yy* (*c*) *Dy* (*d*) *Dd*, with their h.v. sides energised at suitable rated voltages. Explain how their secondaries can be connected with the help of a voltmeter only.

8.39. (*a*) Describe the merits and demerits of a bank of three single-phase transformers as compared to a 3-phase core type transformer.

(*b*) Explain why it is essential to have one three-phase winding in delta for the transformers used in 3-phase systems.

8.40. (*a*) What is the function of the closed delta tertiary winding employed in some three phase transformers ?

(*b*) Explain what is meant by oscillating neutral in *Yy* connected banks of single phase transformers. What methods can be employed to stabilise the neutral with such connections ?

8.41. A 3-phase, 11 kV alternator delivers 10 MVA to a 3-phase, 132 kV transmission line through three identical single-phase transformers. Determine the voltage, current and kVA ratings of each of the transformers if they are connected in (*a*) *Yy* (*b*) *Dd* (*c*) *Yd* (*d*) *Dy* (*e*) *V.v*.

[**Ans.** (*a*) 6.351/76.2125 kV, 524.88/43.74 A,
(*b*) 11/132 kV, 303.03/25.25 A
(*c*) 6.351/132 kV, 524.88/25.25 A
(*d*) 11/76.2125 kV, 303.03/43.74 A
Rating for parts (*a*) to (*d*) is 3.33 MVA
(*e*) 11/132 kV, 524.91/43.74 A ; 5.774 MVA]

8.42. (*a*) A 3-phase 11,000/400 V, *Yy*0 transformer has both its neutrals grounded as shown in Fig. 8.125. Find the voltage between terminals (*i*) *Nn* (*ii*) $A_2\,a_2$ (*iii*) $A_2\,b_2$.

(*b*) Repeat part (*a*), in case the three-phase transformer is *Yy*6.

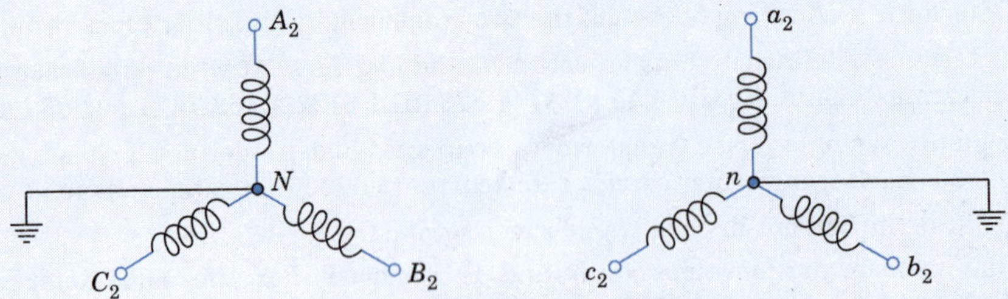

Fig. 8.125: Pertaining to Problem 8.42.

[**Ans.** (*a*) 0, 6120 V, 6469.6 V (*b*) 0, 6582 V, 6238.7 V]

8.43. (*a*) In Scott-connected transformers, show that if the load is balanced on the two-phase side, it is also balanced on the 3-phase side.

(*b*) A Scott-connected transformer is fed from 11 kV, 3-phase supply mains and delivers 2-phase power at 400 V. Each phase on the secondary side has 100 turns. Calculate the number of turns on the primary of both the transformers and the position of the neutral point.

[**Ans.** (*b*) 2750 turns, 2382 turns, 1588 turns from the line terminal of teaser primary]

8.44. (*a*) Explain with the help of connection and phasor diagrams, how Scott-connections are used to obtain two-phase supply from three-phase supply mains.

(*b*) Two Scott-connected transformers are used for transforming 6600 V, 3-phase to 400 V, 2-phase. The load on the main transformer secondary is 200 kVA at unity p.f. and the load on the other secondary is 300 kVA at unity p.f. Neglecting losses, compute currents in the transformer windings and in the primary supply lines.

[**Ans.** (*b*) 52.5 A, 40.09 A, 40.09 A]

8.45. (*a*) In Scott-connected transformers, explain whether the iron losses in the main and teaser transformers are equal or not.

(b) In Scott-connected transformers, teaser transformer supplies unity p.f. load of 500 kW at 200 V and the main transformer supplies 0.8 p.f. lagging load of 400 kW at 200 V. For a 3-phase input voltage of 6600 V, determine the primary line currents. Neglect magnetizing currents and the leakage impedance drops.

[**Ans.** (b) Teaser: 87.5 A ; Main: 107.85 A and 60.63 A]

8.46. (a) Two Scott-connected transformers are energised from 400 V, 3-phase source. For the main transformer, the primary to secondary turns ratio is 2. On the two-phase side, if any two terminals are joined together, then determine the voltage across the remaining two terminals.

(b) It is desired to transform 11 kV, 50 MVA three phase power to 2-phase power at 220 V by Scott-connected transformers. Determine the voltage and MVA ratings of both the transformers. [**Ans.** (a) 282.8 V (b) Teaser ; 9526/220 V, 25 MVA Main ; 11000/220 V, 26.95 MVA]

8.47. (a) Enumerate the advantages of six or twelve phase power over three-phase power.

(b) Describe at least three methods of conversion from 3 to 6 phases with suitable circuit and phasor diagrams.

8.48. Describe one method of conversion from three to twelve phases with suitable circuit and phasor diagrams.

8.49. The following is the data pertaining to a three winding transformer :

H.V. in star ; 10 MVA, 33 kV

M.V. in star ; 7.5 MVA, 11 kV

L.V. in delta ; 7.5 MVA, 3.3 kV.

The per unit leakage reactances are :

$$\left.\begin{aligned} x_{12} &= j0.092 \\ x_{13} &= j0.062 \end{aligned}\right\} \text{ – measured on H.V. side}$$

and $x_{23} = j0.069$] – measured on M.V. side.

For the *Y*-equivalent circuit, find the coil-leakage reactances in per unit and also in ohms.

[**Hint.** Choose a base of 10 MVA. Therefore, the proper base for per unit quantities on the primary side is 10 MVA, 33 kV ; on the secondary side is 10 MVA, 11 kV and on the tertiary side is 10 MVA, 3.3 kV. Since x_{23} is measured for a base of 7.5 MVA, 11 kV, its value on a base of 10 MVA, 11 kV is

$$0.069 \times \frac{10}{7.5} = 0.092 \text{ p.u.} \quad \text{Also} \quad x_{\text{p.u.}} = \frac{(x \text{ in ohms})(\text{MVA base})}{(\text{kV base})^2} \text{ etc.]}$$

[**Ans.** $x_1 = x_3 = 0.031$ p.u., $x_2 = 0.061$ p.u., $x_1 = x_3 = 3.376\ \Omega$, $x_2 = 6.643\ \Omega$]

8.50. (a) Describe the various applications of 3-phase, three-winding transformers.

(b) A three-phase, 50 MVA, 50 Hz, 66/33/3.3 kV, star/star/delta transformer gave the following test results :

Secondary short-circuited, primary excited : 4500 V, 250 A, 480 kW

Tertiary short-circuited, primary excited : 310 V, 17 A, 2.2 kW

Tertiary short-circuited, secondary excited : 160 V, 35 A, 2.2 kW.

Calculate the per phase resistance and leakage reactance of each winding.

In case the secondary and tertiary windings deliver load currents of 500 A at 0.8 p.f. lag and 500 A at unity p.f. respectively, then calculate the primary current and its p.f. Neglect the magnetizing current. [**Ans.** (b) $1.351 + j5.006\ \Omega$, $1.209 + j5.073$, $1.186 + j5.212\ \Omega$. 285.823 A at p.f. 0.8512 lagging]

8.51. (*a*) Give the equivalent circuit of a three-phase three-winding transformer. Explain how its parameters can be determined experimentally.

(*b*) A 3-phase 3-winding 132/11/33 kV transformer has the following measured leakage reactances to a base of 30 MVA:

Primary with secondary S.C. : 0.16 p.u.

Secondary with tertiary S.C. : 0.10 p.u.

Tertiary with primary S.C. : 0.12 p.u.

Calculate the primary terminal voltage in case a balanced load of 24 MVA at 0.8 p.f. lagging is taken from the l.v. terminals at 11 kV and the m.v. is permanently feeding a balanced star load of $j50\ \Omega$ per phase. **[Ans.** (*b*) 151.367 kV]

8.52. A single-phase 3-winding transformer has kVA ratings of 10000, 5000 and 5000 and their corresponding voltages are 132, 33 and 6.6 kV. Its open circuit test data are as follows :

132 kV, 1.3 A, 43.5 kW.

The leakage impedances of the three-windings are as under :

$z_1 = 8 + j77.6\ \Omega$, $z_2 = 0.52 + j4.1\ \Omega$, $z_3 = 0.018 + j0.144\ \Omega$.

Three such transformers are connected to form a 3-phase, 3-winding transformer. Winding 2 is connected in star to supply rated current at 0.8 p.f. lag and winding 3 in delta supplies rated current at 0.9 p.f. lag.

(*a*) For the primary in star, find line to line voltage to maintain rated line voltage at the winding 2 load terminals.

(*b*) Under the conditions of part (*a*), find the voltage across the tertiary load terminals. **[Ans.** (*a*) 143.293 kV (*b*) 6.6573 kV]

8.53. A 11000/3300/400 V, star/star/mesh transformer has per unit leakage impedance drops of $0.005 + j0.026$, $0.006 + j0.025$ and $0.008 + j0.033$ for its primary, secondary and tertiary windings respectively on a 1600 kVA rated-voltage base. Its magnetizing current is 3 A. Find the voltage regulations for 3-phase balanced loads of 1600 kVA at p.f. 0.8 lagging on secondary and 800 kVA at p.f. 0.7 leading on tertiary.

[Ans. $\varepsilon_{12} = 0.0328$, $\varepsilon_{13} = 0.00402$, $\varepsilon_{23} = 0.02878$]

8.54. Draw the zero-sequence circuits of the following 3-phase transformers when any one phase of the secondary is grounded and calculate the zero-sequence impedances.

(*a*) Neutral grounded star/ neutral grounded star/delta, with primary source neutral isolated.

(*b*) *Yy* with both neutrals and primary source neutral grounded.

(*c*) Neutral grounded star/ neutral grounded star/star, with primary source neutral grounded. **[Ans.** (*a*) $z_2 + z_3$ (*b*) $z_{12} + z_1'$ (*c*) $z_3 + (z_1 + z_1')$]

8.55. (*a*) Explain the basic principles of drawing the zero-sequence equivalent circuits for the following arrangements of transformers :

(*i*) Grounded star/Grounded star. (*ii*) Star/Grounded Star.

(*iii*) Delta/Delta/Grounded star.

(*b*) Explain why the impedance offered to the flow of zero-sequence currents in 3-phase transformers, is different from that offered to the flow of positive or negative sequence currents.

Draw the zero-sequence network and write down the zero-sequence impedance for each of the following cases. State the assumptions made.

(*i*) Star/delta/grounded star and (*ii*) Grounded star/delta/grounded star.

8.56. What is inrush phenomena in transformers ? Discuss qualitatively this phenomena if single-phase transformer is switched on at the instant applied voltage v is (*i*) maximum positive and (*ii*) zero with positive slope. Show that doubling effect is not so dangerous as it appears.

Discuss also the switching-in phenomena when residual magnetism is present in the transformer core.

8.57. Discuss switching in phenomena in single-phase transformers from a consideration of its voltage equation. Investigate the most favourable and unfavourable conditions for closing the transformer primary switch.

8.58. (*a*) What is the influence of connections in 3-phase transformers on the magnitude of the inrush current ? Discuss this with respect to the following :

Delta-connected primary, star-delta bank, star-connected 3-legged core-type transformer.

(*b*) Explain how the inrush magnetizing current in transformers can be estimated.

Suggest the methods employed to limit this inrush.

8.59. Explain clearly the inrush-current phenomena in transformers. Derive an approximate expression for the magnitude of core flux as a function of time, when an unloaded transformer is switched on to a voltage source. Sketch a typical oscillogram of this core flux and explain the nature of its shape.

8.60. (*a*) Show that the maximum inrush current in a star/delta bank of transformers is only two-third of that in a single-phase transformer.

(*b*) Give a brief account of the inrush phenomena in transformers with residual flux present.

8.61. (*a*) What is meant by overvoltages in transformers ? Give the various causes of transformer overvoltages.

(*b*) Draw and explain the transformer equivalent circuit for its h.v. winding during surge phenomena.

8.62. A step-function surge voltage of magnitude V strikes the transformer terminals. Discuss the following stages of surge phenomena in a transformer with solidly grounded neutral.

(*i*) Initial voltage distribution for different values of α.

(*ii*) Intermediate and final voltage distributions.

Show that the initial and final voltage distributions along transformer winding during surge phenomena do not coincide.

8.63. A rectangular travelling voltage wave with an infinitely long tail of magnitude V strikes h.v. transformer terminals. Discuss the following stages of surge phenomena in a transformer with an isolated neutral.

(*i*) Initial voltage distribution for different values of α.

(*ii*) Intermediate and final voltage distributions.

Show that the initial and final voltage distributions along the transformer winding during surge phenomena do not coincide.

8.64. Suggest the methods for safeguarding the transformers against surges.

Describe the basic concepts of capacitive protection in transformers.

Derive an expression for the shield capacitance that must be available between winding and the shield in order to make the transformer surge proof.

8.65. (*a*) Under what conditions, thc initial and final voltage distributions along the transformer winding during surge phenomena may coincide for grounded and isolated neutrals ? Is it possible to achieve it ? Discuss.

(*b*) Explain how the use of interleaved coils reduces the voltage concentrations and oscilliations in transformers.

(*c*) Compare the effective series capacitance of the interleaved disc-coil pair with that of a normal pair, with each layer having 6 turns. **[Ans.** (*c*) 31.6:1]

8.66. (*a*) Which flux is responsible for the existence of mechanical forces in transformers? Show the two components of this flux in relevant diagrams and enumerate the mechanical forces they gives rise to.

(*b*) Derive expressions for the mechanical forces developed in large transformers for (*i*) external radial forces and (*ii*) internal axial forces.

8.67. (*a*) Derive an expression for the mechanical axial forces developed due to asymmetrical arrangement of the windings.

(*b*) A 300 kVA, 6600/440 V, delta-star, 3-phase core type transformer has the following data :

$L_{mt1} = 0.96$ m, $L_{mt2} = 0.74$ m

Per-phase turns, $N_1 = 913, N_2 = 32, H_\omega = 0.47$ m

$a = 1.4$ cms, z_e in per unit = 0.035.

Radial thickness of h.v. winding = 5 cm

Radial thickness of l.v. winding = 6 cm.

For a symmetrical steady-state short circuit across the secondary winding, calculate the following :

(*i*) External radial and internal axial forces if the l.v. and h.v. windings are of equal height.

(*ii*) External axial forces if, at one end, the h.v. winding is made shorter than l.v. winding by 4 cms.

(*iii*) Various mechanical forces in parts (*i*) and (*ii*) at the time of short circuit.

[**Ans.** (*a*) 18.096 tons, 0.27 tons. (*b*) 2.9187 tons.
(*c*) 32.573 tons, 0.486 tons, 5.254 tons]

8.68. (*a*) What are the various mechanical forces acting on the windings of transformers with concentric coils ? What methods are employed to balance these forces and to limit their effects ?

(*b*) Derive expressions for the external radial and internal axial forces in transformers from a consideration of the magnetic energy stored in the leakage flux.

8.69. (*a*) What is per unit system ? Out of per unit and per cent methods, which one is preferable and why ?

Enumerate the advantages possessed by per unit system.

(*b*) In per unit system, which values are chosen first ? Derive the relation that gives Z (p.u.) in terms of MVA base etc.

(*c*) Define per unit impedance in terms of base MVA etc and obtain therefrom an expression for the new value of Z (p.u.) in terms of new MVA base etc.

8.70. (*a*) Define per-unit current. Express it in terms of new base VA etc.

(*b*) Describe the choice of base values for 3-phase systems.

(*c*) Show that Z (p.u.) in single-phase as well as three-phase star-connected systems has identical expressions.

(*d*) Find the per unit impedance of delta-connected impedances.

(*e*) When three-phase transformer forms a part of a three-phase system, discuss how the computations are carried out for star as well as delta connected transformers.

8.71. Repeat Example 8.42 in case secondary side of the transformer is connected to load through a three-phase feeder of impedance $(0.00735 + j0.0147)$ ohms per phase. [**Ans.** 7488.805 V]

8.72. A delta/star connected bank of three identical 100 kVA, 4000/200 V transformers is fed with power through a feeder whose impedance is $(0.2 + j0.6)$ Ω per phase. The voltage at the sending end of the feeder is held constant at 4 kV. A single-phase short-circuit test, when conducted with its l.v. winding short-circuited, gave the following data :

$$V_H = 40 \text{ V}, I_H = 25 \text{ A}, P = 320 \text{ W}$$

(*a*) Find the secondary line voltage in case the bank delivers rated current to a balanced three-phase unity pf load.

(*b*) If a solid three-phase short-circuit occurs at the secondary line terminals of the transformer, compute the currents in the transformer primary and secondary windings and in the feeder wires. [**Ans.** (*a*) 343.92 V (*b*) 22750.2 A, 22750.2 A, 1137.51 A]

8.73. (*a*) A 500 kVA, 6351/400 V, single-phase transformer has total leakage reactance of 0.12 per unit. Calculate the equivalent reactance in ohms referred to both l.v. and h.v. sides.

(*b*) if three transformers as described in (*a*) are connected in star-delta, compute

(*i*) the transformer-voltage and power ratings

(*ii*) per unit reactance of the transformer and

(*iii*) the equivalent reactance in ohms referred to l.v. and h.v. sides

[**Ans.** (*a*) 0.0384 Ω, 9.6804 Ω (*b*) (*i*) 11 kV/400 V, 1500 kVA (*ii*) 0.12 (*iii*) 0.1152 Ω, 29.04 Ω]

8.74. A single-phase ideal transformer has turns ratio from primary to secondary as '*a*'. Three such identical transformers, with input line voltage *V* and input line current *I*, are connected in (*a*) *Yy* (*b*) *Dd* (*c*) *Yd* (*d*) *Dy*.

For these connection schemes, calculate the values of currents and voltages for the transformer windings and for the output terminals.

[**Ans.** (*a*) $aI, aI; \dfrac{V}{a\sqrt{3}}, \dfrac{V}{a}$ (*b*) $\dfrac{aI}{\sqrt{3}}, aI; \dfrac{V}{a}, \dfrac{V}{a}$

(*c*) $aI, \sqrt{3}\,aI; \dfrac{V}{a\sqrt{3}}, \dfrac{V}{a\sqrt{3}}$ (*d*) $\dfrac{aI}{\sqrt{3}}, \dfrac{aI}{\sqrt{3}}; \dfrac{V}{a}, \dfrac{\sqrt{3}V}{a}$]

8.75. A 3-phase transformer, whose high-voltage side is delta-connected, is supplied at 11 kV. The star-connected secondary side has a terminal voltage of 415 V while delivering full load at 0.8 pf lagging. The equivalent resistance and reactance drops at full load are 1% and 5.5% respectively. Find the turns-ratio.

[**Ans.** Per-phase turns ratio from primary to secondary is 44.0264]

8.76. In Fig. 8.126, calculate

(*a*) the power delivered by each source

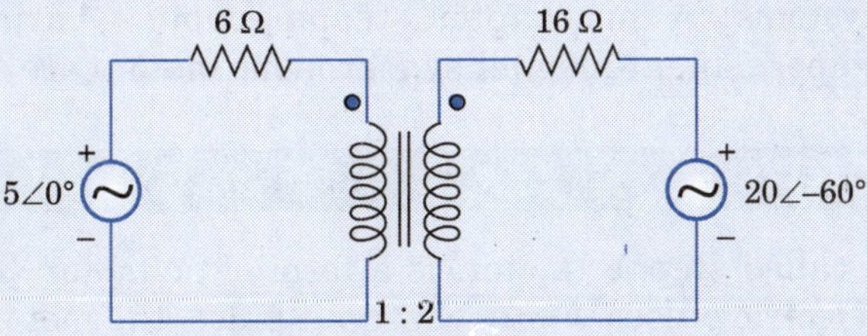

Fig. 8.126: Pertaining to Problem 8.76.

(*b*) the power dissipated in each resistor.

[**Hint.** Transfer 16 Ω and 20 ∠– 60° V to primary side and solve. Resultant voltage in the circuit = $5\sqrt{3}$ ∠90° V etc.] [**Ans.** (*a*) 7.5 watts by 20 ∠– 60° V source and zero watt by 5 ∠0° V source (*b*) 4.5 watts in 6 Ω and 3 watts in 16 Ω]

9 Special Machines

Common and conventional types of rotating electrical machines like dc, induction and synchronous machines have already been discussed in detail. Based on their operating principles, many new and unconventional types of machines have been developed. These machines having features different from conventional machines are described in this chapter. Out of the many types, special machines like stepping motors, variable reluctance motors etc. are only discussed in this chapter.

In some electric drives, an a.c. motor and its electronic controller are now designed together as one unit so that both are compatible with each other. This system approach of integrated design is becoming increasingly popular because

(*i*) of easy availability of electronic controllers at cheaper rates and

(*ii*) adjustable-speed drives so developed are more efficient and offer better performance characteristics.

An electronic controller consists of circuitry based on power electronics and microelectronics.

Examples of systems designed through integrated approach are variable-reluctance motor and brushless dc motor drives. In these motors, the stator phase winding is switched in synchronism with the rotor position which is monitored through a shaft position sensor. A variable-reluctance motor is also knows as *switched-reluctance motor*.

The stepping motors also offer brushless drive systems. These are extensively used in open-loop positioning systems. In this chapter, stepping motors, variable-reluctance motors, brushless dc motors and permanent-magnet synchronous motors are described.

9.1 STEPPING MOTORS

A stepping motor, also called stepper motor, is a form of ac motor. The input given to this motor is in the form of electric pulses. For every input pulse, the motor shaft turns through a specified number of degrees, called a *step*. The name stepping given to this motor is based on its working principle; one step rotation for one input pulse. Thus, a stepping motor is an ac motor whose shaft moves through one angular step for each input pulse. The range of step size may vary from 0.72° to 90°. Actually, a stepping motor can be regarded as a digital electromechanical device ; it translates the input digital information in the form of electric pulses into discrete steps of shaft rotation. In position control applications, if the number of input pulses sent to the motor is known, the actual position of the driven job can be obtained. Thus, a digital position-control system employing a stepping motor needs no rotor-position sensors and an expensive feedback loop.

A stepping motor differs from a conventional motor (CM) as under:

(*i*) Input to SM is in the form of electric pulses whereas input to a CM is invariably from a constant voltage source.

(*ii*) A CM has a free running shaft whereas shaft of SM moves through angular steps.

(*iii*) In control system applications, no feedback loop is required when SM is used but a feedback loop may be required when CM is used.

(*iv*) A SM is a digital electromechanical device whereas a CM is an analog electronomechanical device.

9.1.1 Principle of Operation

Stators of stepping motors have salient poles on which concentrated windings are wound. These windings may be appropriately connected so as to result in two, three or four phase windings, on the stator. The rotors of stepping motors carry no winding. The rotors are made from either permanent-magnet or ferromagnetic material.

A stepping motor is fed through an external drive circuit. The function of this drive circuit is to receive input voltage pulses and to deliver appropriate unidirectional current pulses to the stator windings of the stepping motor. These currents set up air-gap field which moves through one angular step for each input pulse. The rotor follows the axis of air-gap magnetic field on account of the development of reluctance torque and/or permanent-magnet torque. In this manner, for every input pulse the rotor moves through one step.

Some terms applicable to stepping motors are given below.

(*i*) Step angle. The angle through which the motor shaft rotates for each, input (or command) pulse is called step angle. This is expressed in degrees. For a step angle of 3.6°, the number of input pulses required for one revolution $\left(= \dfrac{360°}{\text{step angle}}\right)$ is 100.

The step angle α is given by, $$\alpha = \frac{N_s - N_r}{N_s \,.\, N_r} \times 360° \quad \text{...(9.1)}$$

where, N_s = number of stator poles

and, N_r = number of rotor teeth (or rotor poles)

The step angle α is also given by, $$\alpha = \frac{360°}{m \,.\, N_r} \quad \text{...(9.2)}$$

where, m = number of stator phases or stator stacks.

(*ii*) Resolution. Resolution of stepping motor is equal to the number of steps needed to complete one revolution of rotor.

$$\therefore \quad \text{Resolution} = \frac{360°}{\alpha} = \frac{\text{Number of steps for } n \text{ revolutions}}{\text{Rotor revolutions } n}$$

Greater the resolution, better is the accuracy of positioning of objects by the motor.

If f is the stepping frequency in pulses per second (pps), then for step angle α, the motor shaft speed n is given by,

$$n = \frac{\alpha \,.\, f}{360°} \text{ rps} \quad \text{...(9.3)}$$

***(iii)* Holding torque.** At standstill, the excited motor opposes the rotor rotation due to load torque. Holding torque is a term introduced to measure this opposing torque. Thus, *holding torque* is defined as the maximum load torque that can be applied to the shaft of an *excited motor* without causing continuous rotation.

***(iv)* Detent torque.** In case the motor is constructed with permanent magnets, then the stepping motor can develop torque to resist rotation even when motor is an unexcited. The term detent torque takes this into consideration. Thus, *detent torque* is defined as the maximum load torque that can be applied to the shaft of an *unexcited motor* without causing continuous rotation.

Stepping motors vary widely in their designs and configurations ; these can, however, be classified into three main types as under.

1. Variable reluctance stepping motors (VRSMs)
2. Permanent-magnet stepping motors (PMSMs)
3. Hybrid stepping motors (HSMs).

The three types derive their names from the type of rotor design and their basic principle of operation.

Stepping motors are usually designated as stator poles/rotor poles or teeth, for example, a 6/2 pole stepping motor means that this motor has 6 salient-poles on stator and 2 poles or teeth on rotor. The object of this article is to discuss the various types of stepping motors briefly.

9.1.2 Variable-Reluctance Stepping Motors

These motors consist of salient-pole stator with concentrated three or four phase windings and a salient-pole rotor. The rotor, made from ferromagnetic laminations, carries no winding. The stator-produced flux causes the rotor movement through a single step so that reluctance seen by the stator field is minimum and the stator-flux linkages are maximized for given stator currents.

VRSMs may be single-stack type or multi-stack type. These are now described here.

9.1.2.1 Single-stack VRSMs

A single-stack variable reluctance stepping motor is shown in Fig. 9.1. It has six salient poles with concentrated windings on stator. Rotor, made of ferromagnetic laminations has four teeth (or poles) with no rotor winding. The coils wound on radially opposite poles are connected in series (or parallel) so that stator has effectively three-phase winding. In Fig. 9.1, coils A and A' are in series. Similarly, coils BB' and CC' are in series.

The stator winding is excited from dc source through a suitable electronic switching device. With coils AA' excited, the rotor occupies the position shown in Fig. 9.1 (*a*) and $\theta = 0°$. When coils AA' are de-energized and coils BB' are excited, the rotor moves through a step angle of 30° counter-clockwise (CCW) as shown in Fig. 9.1 (*b*). Now, when current is withdrawn from coils BB' and coils CC' are excited, the rotor moves through a further step angle of 30° CCW so that $\theta = 60°$, Fig. 9.1 (*c*). In this manner, the rotor will complete one revolution in twelve $\left(\dfrac{360°}{\alpha = 30°}\right)$ steps.

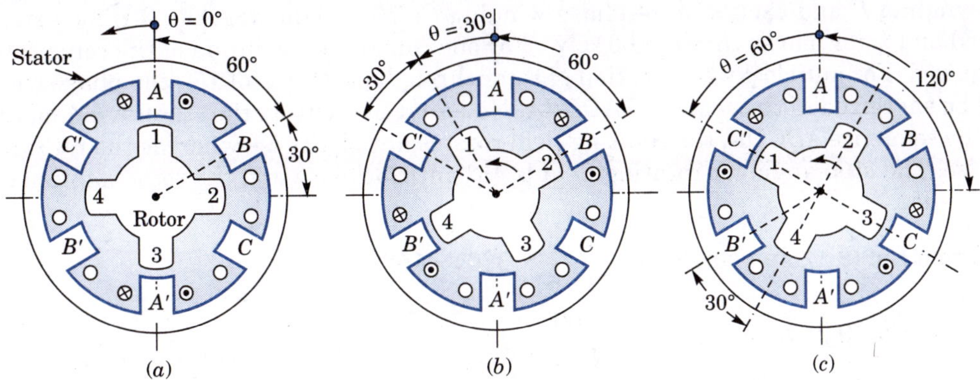

Fig. 9.1: Three-phase 6/4 pole single-stack variable reluctance stepping motor.

From Eq. (9.1), step angle, $\alpha = \dfrac{6-4}{6 \times 4} \times 360° = 30°$

Also from Eq. (9.2), step angle, $\alpha = \dfrac{360}{3 \times 4} = 30°$

In Fig. 9.1, with exciting sequence *ABCA*, rotor rotation is CCW. For clockwise (CW) rotation, the stator winding should be energized in the sequence *ACBA*. Further, note that by exciting the stator winding of Fig. 9.1 in the sequence ABCA, rotating field revolves *clockwise* whereas the rotor rotation is *anticlockwise or* CCW.

Lower values of step angle can be achieved by using a stepping motor with more number of poles on stator and teeth on rotor. Fig. 9.2 shows a 4-phase, 8/6-pole single-stack VRSM. The concentrated windings on diametrically opposite poles are connected in series (or parallel) so as to obtain an effective 4-phase winding on stator. For the sake of clarity, only phase *A* winding is shown in Fig. 9.2 (*a*).

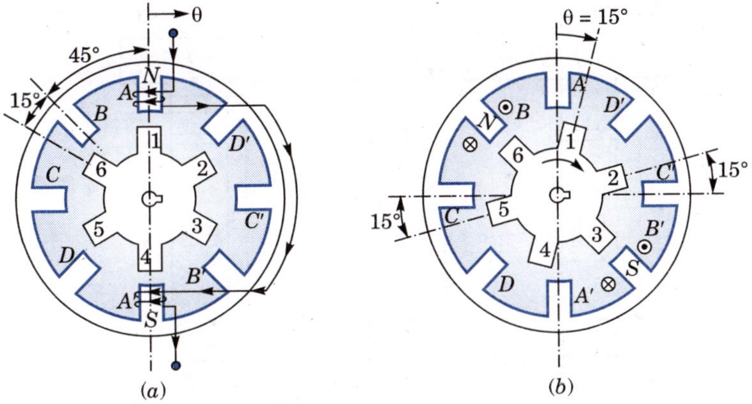

Fig. 9.2: Four-phase 8/ 6-pole VR stepping motor.

When phase *A* winding is excited, rotor teeth numbered 1 and 4 are aligned along the phase-*A* winding axis, rotor therefore occupies the position shown in Fig. 9.2 (*a*) and θ = 0°. When phase winding *A* is de-energized and phase winding *B* is excited, the poles numbered 3 and 6 get aligned along phase-*B* axis and the rotor moves through a step angle of 15° CW; this is shown in Fig. 9.2 (*b*). Further clockwise rotation of 15° is possible with de-energization of phase winding B and excitation of phase winding C. With sequence $ABCDA$, four steps are executed and rotor moves through 60° CW. For one complete revolution of the rotor, 24 steps are required. For anticlockwise rotation of rotor through each step of 15°, the phase windings should be energized in the sequence $ADCBA$. Note that by exciting the stator windings of Fig. 9.2 in the sequence $ABCDA$, the rotating field rotates anticlockwise whereas the rotor rotates clockwise. The step-angle for rotating field is 45° anticlockwise and the rotor rotation step is 15° clockwise.

From Eq. (9.1), step angle, $\alpha = \dfrac{8-6}{8 \times 6} \times 360° = 15°$

From Eq. (9.2), step angle, $\alpha = \dfrac{360}{4 \times 6} = 15°$

By choosing other pole numbers of stator poles and rotor teeth, any desired step angle can be achieved.

The relation between stator poles P_s, rotor teeth (or poles) P_r and the number of rotor phases m for a single-stack *VRSM* is generally given by

$$P_r = P_s \pm \frac{P_s}{m} \quad \text{...(9.4)}$$

If phase windings A and B in Fig. 9.1 are excited simultaneously, then rotor would move through a step angle of 15° CW. Now rotor poles numbered 1 and 3 would be alinged along the resultant field produced by stator phase winding A and B together. This technique of reducing the step angle is called *microstepping*.

Another technique of microstepping is to use multistack VRSMs. This type is now described below.

9.1.2.2 Multi-stack VRSMs

A three-stack VRSM is more common, it would therefore be described here.

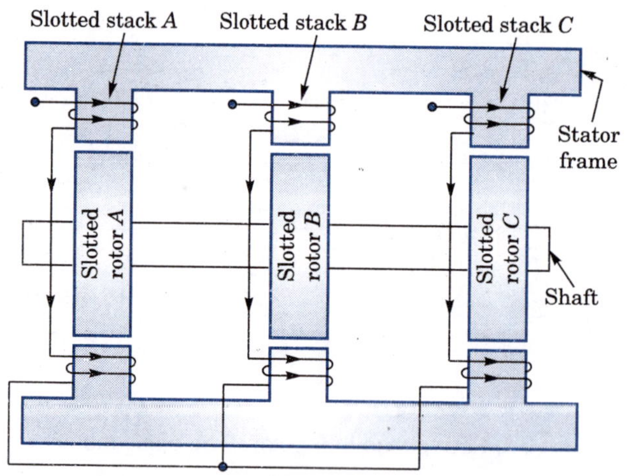

Fig. 9.3: Axial cross-section of a 3-stack variable reluctance stepping motor.

A three-stack VRSM has three separate magnetically isolated sections or stacks as shown in Fig. 9.3. The stator has common frame but the three stacks A, B, C are displaced axially (along the shaft axis) from each other as shown in Fig. 9.3. The stator poles (or teeth) of the three stacks have a progressive angular displacement of one-third (for a 3-stack motor) stator pole-pitch. For a 6-pole stator, the pole pitch is 360/6 = 60°, therefore stator teeth of the three stacks have angular displacement of 60/3 = 20° as shown in Fig. 9.4. In Fig. 9.4 (*a*) is shown stack *A* with stator poles 1, 2, 3, 4, ...; stack *B* is shown in Fig. 9.4 (*b*) with stator poles 1, 2, 3, 4..., having angular displacement of 20° CCW from stack *A*. Further, in Fig. 9.4 (*c*), the stack *C* shown with its stator poles 1, 2, 3, 4, ... has an angular displacement of 20° CCW from stack *B*. Note that the number of rotor teeth is equal to the number of stator poles. Also, stator stacks have an angular displacement from each other. But rotor teeth on the three stacks do not have any angular displacement from each other ; rotor teeth are aligned as shown in Fig. 9.4 (*a*), (*b*) and (*c*) (teeth 1 and 4 are along vertical axis).

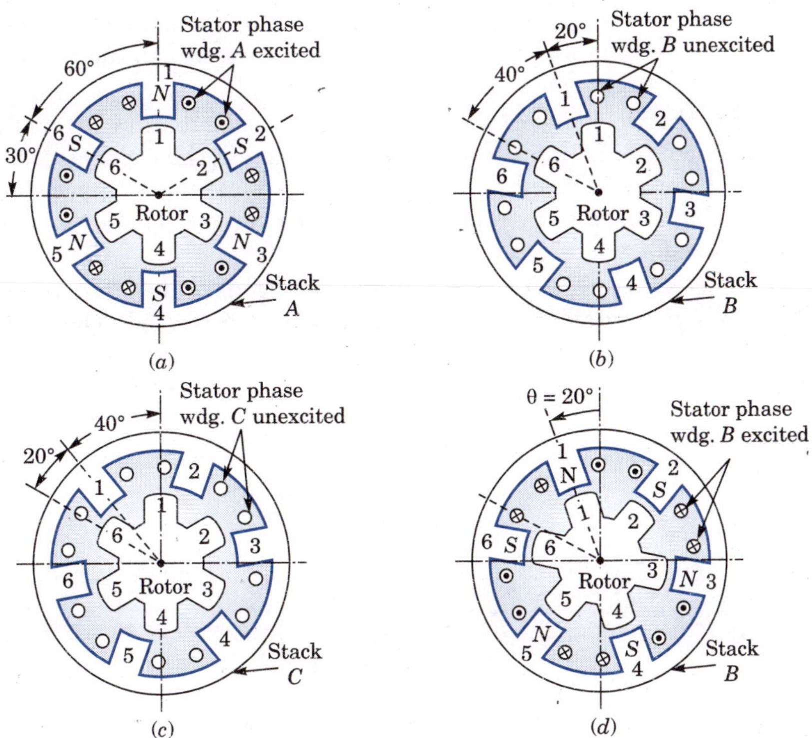

Fig. 9.4: Three-stack VRSM (*a*) stack *A* excited (*b*) stack *B* displaced from stack *A* by 20° CCW (*c*) stack *C* displaced from stack *A* by 40° CCW and (*d*) stack *B* energized and rotor moves 20° CCW.

When phase winding on stator stack *A* is excited by current i_a, alternate *N* and *S* poles are produced on stator, Fig. 9.4 (*a*). The rotor teeth align with stator poles so that reluctance seen by the flux of stator stack *A* is minimum, this is shown in Fig. 9.4 (*a*) where rotor teeth 1, 2, 3 ... align themselves with stator poles 1, 2, 3... respectively. When current i_a in stator winding of stack *A* is reduced to zero and stack *B* is energized, then rotor moves through a step of 20° CCW, so as to minimize the reluctance seen by the stack flux *B*, this is shown in Fig. 9.4 (*d*). If current i_b is reduced to zero and i_c is passed through winding of stack *C*, the rotor would rotate further by a step of 20° CCW with respect to stator stack *B*. Further, with $i_c = 0$ and re-establishment of i_a in phase winding of stack *A*, the rotor would again move by 20° CCW to execute one step to complete the rotation through one stator pole pitch of 60°. So, for CCW rotation, sequence of exciting the stator windings is *ABCABCA*. For CW rotation, sequence of exciting the stator windings is *ACBACBA*.

In Fig. 9.4, step angle, from Eq. (9.2), is

$$a = \frac{360°}{\text{Number of stacks} \times \text{Number of rotor poles}} = \frac{360}{3 \times 6} = 20°$$

For three-stack, 12/12 pole VRSM, the step angle would be $\alpha = \dfrac{360°}{3 \times 12} = 10°$.

9.1.3 Permanent-Magnet Stepping Motors

The stator of a permanent-magnet (PM) stepping motor consists of salient poles with concentrated windings, just like the stator of a VRSM. The rotor, as the name of this motor suggests, consists of permanent-magnet poles.

For illustrating the working principle of PMSM, an elementary form of 2-phase, 4/2-pole steping motor shown in Fig. 9.5 is considered. Here again the concentrated windings on diametrically opposite poles are connected in series so as to result in 2-phase winding on the stator. The rotor is magnetized to give two permanent magnets as shown. Working of this motor is described as under :

(*a*) In Fig. 9.5 (*a*), two coils *AA′* connected in series constitute phase *A* winding. When this winding is excited with current i_a as shown, the stator produced poles attract the rotor PM poles so that their magnetic axes coincide. Let the exciting of phase *A* winding in Fig. 9.5 (*a*) be denoted by + *A*.

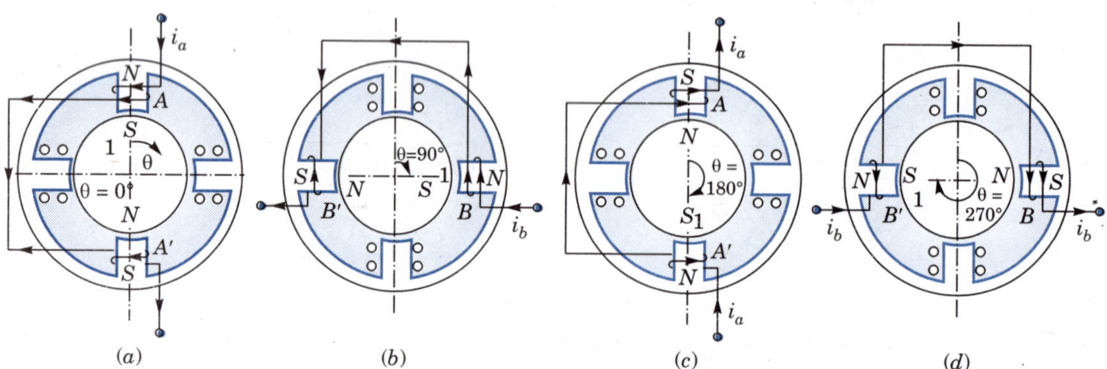

Fig. 9.5: Elementary form of 2-phase 4/2 pole permanent magnet stepping motor.

(*b*) In Fig. 9.5 (*b*), the current i_a in phase *A* winding is reduced to zero whereas phase *B* winding is energized with current i_b. Stator produced poles now attract the rotor causing a CW step rotation through θ = 90° as shown. Let the exciting of phase *B* winding in Fig. 9.5 (*b*) be designated + *B*.

(*c*) In Fig. 9.5 (*c*), the phase winding *A* is again excited but with current opposite to that in Fig. 9.5 (*a*). The rotor poles now move through a further step of 90° CW so that θ = 180°. This step of exciting the phase *A* winding must be designated – *A*.

(*d*) In Fig. 9.5 (*d*), the phase winding *B* is made to carry exciting current i_b opposite to that in Fig. 9.5 (*b*). The rotor again executes a further step of 90° CW so that θ = 270°. This method of exciting phase winding *B* must be designated – *B*.

For further 90°CW rotation so that $\theta = 360°$, phase winding B in Fig. 9.5 (d) is de-energized and phase winding A is energized as in Fig. 9.5 (a). This shows that four steps complete one revolution of the rotor movement.

It is seen from above that by the application of each current pulse to the stator winding in proper sequence, the rotor can be made to execute discrete angular steps of 90°. The sequence of exciting the stator phase windings is $+A$, $+B$, $-A$, $-B$, $+A$ ... for CW rotor movement. For CCW rotor rotation, the sequence of switching the phase winding must be reversed to $+A$, $-B$, $-A$, $+B$, $+A$, $-B$, ...

If both the phase windings are excited in the sequence $+A$ together with $+B$, then the resultant stator field is along the inter-polar axis, the rotor therefore moves a step of 45° CW as shown in Fig. 9.6. This shows that for obtaining an angular step of 45° CW, the switching sequence would be as under :

$$+A, (+A+B), +B, (+B-A), -A, (-A-B), -B, (-B+A), +A, ...$$

Here $(+A+B)$ means that phase windings A and B are excited together so as to produce stator poles as shown in Fig. 9.6. This method of reducing the step angle to half the normal step is called *half-step mode of excitation*. This, in general, is achieved by exciting, in appropriate sequence, one-phase winding, two-phase windings together, one phase winding etc as discussed above for Fig. 9.6. In Fig. 9.1 also, half-step is obtained by exciting the windings in sequence $+A$, $(+A+B)$, $+B$, $(+B+C)$, $+C$,... as stated before.

For a step angle of 45° in the basic PMSM of Fig. 9.6, the switching circuitry becomes more complex. In order that switching device is simple, a four-phase winding with 4/2-pole structure as shown in Fig. 9.7 (a) is used. Winding on each pole serves as one phase winding. This winding can be fed with voltages of single polarity as compared to that in Fig. 9.6 where voltages of two polarities are required. In Fig. 9.7, the four-phase winding has its four similar terminals connected together to form the neutral point N. Its other four terminals A, B, C, D are fed from four-phase supply in proper sequence. With winding A excited alone, the rotor occupies the position shown in Fig. 9.7 (a) where $\theta = 0°$. When both phase windings A and B are excited together, the rotor occupies a position of $\theta = 45°$, Fig. 9.7 (b).

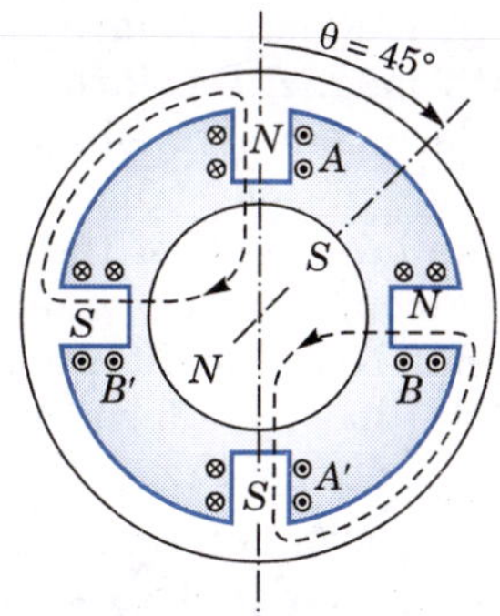

Fig. 9.6: Rotor rotation through 45° with both windings excited together in PMSM.

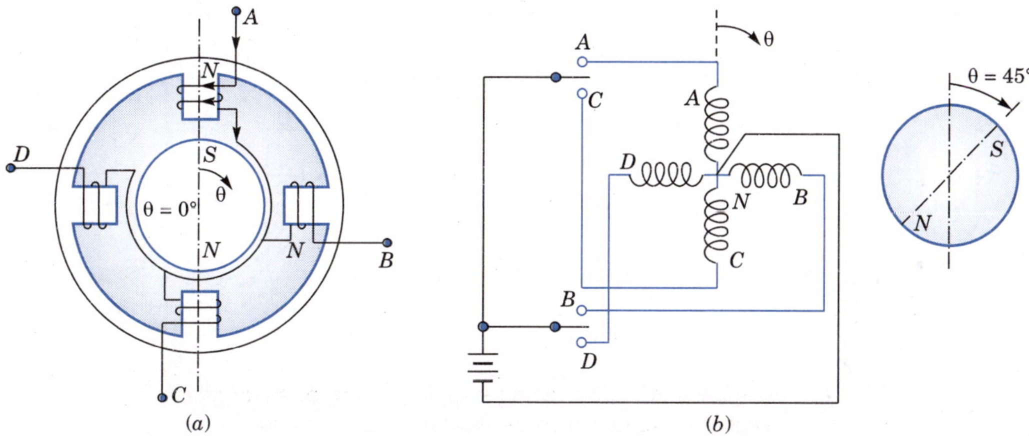

Fig. 9.7: Four phase 4/2-pole permanent magnet stepping motor.

The switching sequence for PMSM of Fig. 9.7 is simple. The rotor moves through steps of 45° CW and occupies position of $\theta = 0°, 45°, 90°, 135°, ...$ when windings are switched-on in the sequence *A, AB, B, BC, C, ...* For CCW movement of rotor, the switching sequence should be *A, AD, D, DC, D, CB, B, ...*

In PMSMs, even with zero exciting currents, some torque, called detent torque, is produced tending to align the permanent-magnet poles with the stator teeth ; this, however, is not the case in VRSMs. PMSMs have therefore, the advantage of developing detent torque to maintain position if the drive circuitry fails.

PMSMs have the disadvantage that smaller steps are not feasible because of the difficulties encountered in their construction.

9.1.4 Hybrid Stepping Motors

A hybrid stepping motor combines the features of both PM and VR stepping motors.

A schematic view of the rotor of a hybrid stepping motor (HSM) is shown in Fig. 9.8. It consist of an axial permanent magnet at the two ends of which are attached two identical ferromagnetic stacks as shown. These two stacks consists of equal number of teeth, in this figure there are three teeth on each stack. At one end, the stack attains north magnetic polarity and at the other end, stack gets south magnetic polarity. The two stacks have an angular displacement of one-half of the rotor tooth pitch. The stator has salient-pole structure which is continuous from one end to the other end of the stator structure. The stator poles carry concentrated windings like other types of stepping motors. Note the difference between three-stack VRSM and HSM; in the former the stator pole structure is discontinuous, Fig. 9.3, but in the later it is continuous.

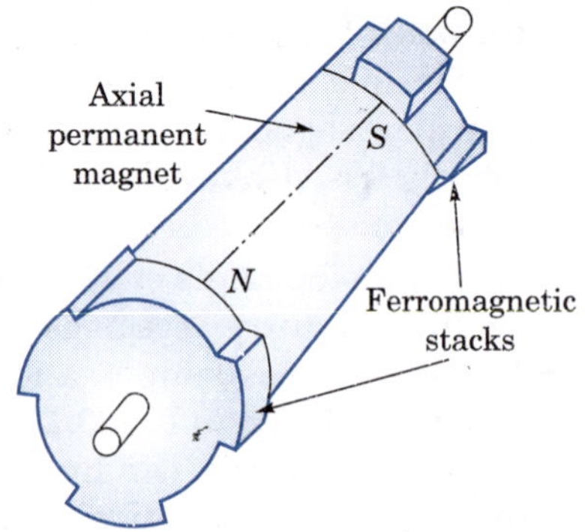

Fig. 9.8: Schematic view of rotor for hybrid stepping motor.

For understanding the working of HSM, refer to Fig. 9.9. In this fig., north poles at the front end of Fig. 9.8 are shown with full lines whereas the south poles at the far end are shown with dotted lines.

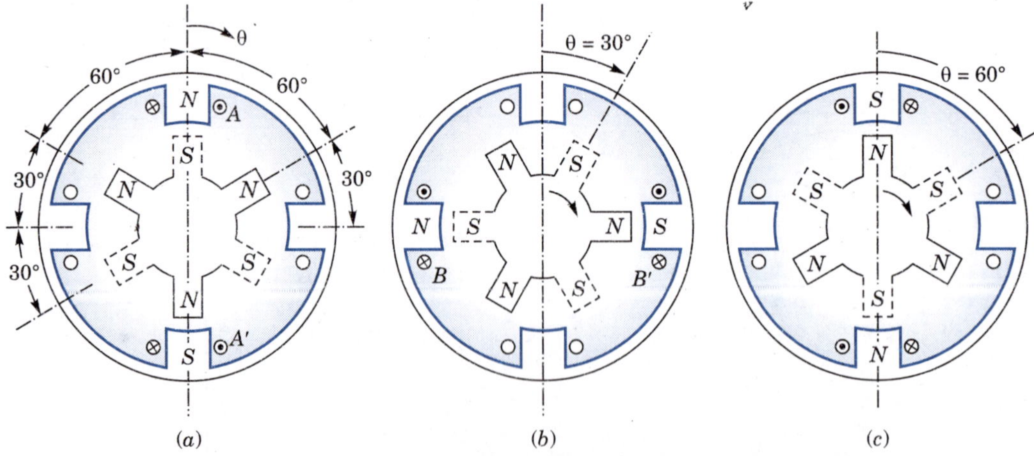

Fig. 9.9: Two-phase, 4/ 6-pole hybrid stepping motor (*a*) stator phase winding *A* excited (*b*) phase winding *B* excited and (*c*) phase winding *A* excited in the reversed direction.

When phase winding A is energized with current i_a, N pole at A and S pole at A' are created on the stator. Pole at A attracts S pole of far end and pole at A' attracts N pole of front end, this is shown in Fig. 9.9 (*a*). This equilibrium position of rotor structure results in maximizing the flux linkages with the phase winding A. For turning the rotor clockwise through a step, de-energize phase winding A and excite phase winding B so that N pole at B and S poles at B' are created on stator. Pole at B attracts S pole of rear end and pole at B' attracts N pole of front end, so a step angular rotation of 30° CW is achieved, Fig. 9.9 (*b*). In this equilibrium position, maximum flux linkages are now linked with phase winding B. If excitation is removed from phase winding B and reversed excitation is applied to phase winding A, pole on A attracts front N pole and pole at A' attracts rear S pole. This gives rise to a further step angle movement of 30° CW, Fig. 9.9 (*c*). In this manner, twelve steps will complete one revolution. Sequence of exciting the phase windings for clockwise rotation is $ABA'B'A$, and, therefore, for CCW rotation, the sequence will be $AB'A'BA$.

As in PMSMs, the rotor-poles in HSM also tend to align themselves with the stator teeth when stator exciting currents are absent.

The magnitude of step angle for a hybrid stepping motor is again given by Eq. (9.2). But now P must be equal to the total number of rotor poles on both the stacks.

From Eq. (9.2), step angle, $\alpha = \dfrac{360}{2 \times 6} = 30°$

If the motor excitation is removed in HSM, the rotor remains locked into the same position as before the removal of excitation. This is due to the production of detent torque by the permanent magnets of the rotor.

A HSM needs less excitation current to develop a given torque as compared to VRSM. Step angle in HSM can be reduced to very small steps by having more number of poles and teeth in its structure.

Example 9.1. *A stepping motor has a step angle 6°. Find (a) resolution (b) number of steps required for the shaft to complete 10 revolutions and (c) shaft-speed if the stepping frequency is 1800 pps.*

Solution. Here step angle, $\alpha = 6°$

(*a*) Resolution $= \dfrac{360°}{\alpha} = \dfrac{360°}{6} = 60$ steps/revolution.

(*b*) Number of steps for 10 revolutions

= Steps per revolution × Number of steps = 60 × 10 = 600 steps.

(*c*) Here pulses per second means steps per second.

For 60 steps per second, number of revolutions = 1 per sec

For 1800 steps per second, number of revolutions $= \dfrac{1}{60} \times 1800 = 30$ rps = 1800 r.p.m

$\therefore$ Shaft speed = 30 rps or 1800 r.p.m.

Example 9.2. *A 3-stack VRSM has 12 poles on each of the stator and rotor stacks. The motor is built such that rotor poles of each stack are aligned.*

(a) Calculate the angular displacement between the stator stacks and the step angle.

(b) Calculate the frequency of phase currents required to achieve a rotor speed of 1200 rpm.

Solution. (*a*) Stator pole pitch $= \dfrac{360°}{12} = 30°$

∴ Angular displacement between the stator stacks

$$= \frac{\text{Stator pole pitch}}{\text{Number of stator stacks}} = \frac{30}{3} = 10°$$

Now the step angle = angular displacement between stator-stacks = 10°

Also, from Eq. (9.2), $\alpha = \dfrac{360}{3 \times 12} = 10°$

(*b*) Here 1200 revolutions take = 60 sec.

∴ 1 revolution will take $= \dfrac{60}{1200} = \dfrac{1}{20}$ sec.

Now 30° (= 10 × 3) of revolution would require $= \dfrac{1}{20} \times \dfrac{30}{360} = \dfrac{1}{20} \times \dfrac{1}{12}$ sec $= T$

∴ Frequency of phase currents, $f = \dfrac{1}{T} = 20 \times 12 = 240$ pps or 240 Hz.

9.1.5 Characteristics of Stepping Motors

The two important characteristics of stepping motors are (*i*) torque-displacement characteristics and (*ii*) torque-stepping rate characteristics. These two characteristics are row described briefly.

9.1.5.1 Torque-displacement Characteristics

For a stepping motor, this characteristic gives the variation of electric torque developed as a function of the rotor position θ measured from its stable equilibrium position with one stator winding permanently excited.

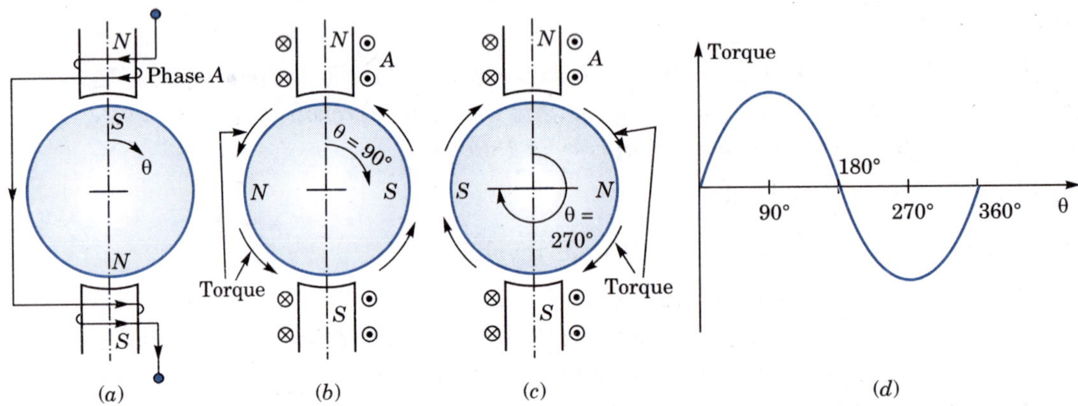

Fig. 9.10: Pertaining to PM stepping motor (*a*) no torque (*b*) CCW torque (*c*) CW torque (*d*) torque-displacement characteristic.

For a PM stepping motor in Fig. 9.10 (*a*), phase winding *A* alone is assumed to be permanently excited. In this fig., as the magnetic axes of stator and rotor poles are coincident θ = 0° and electromagnetic torque (proportional to stator mmf × rotor mmf × sin θ) is zero. When rotor is displaced so that θ increases from zero degree, torque increases. It becomes maximum when θ = 90° as shown in Fig. 9.10 (*b*). When θ increases beyond 90°, torque begins to decrease. Note that for 0 < θ < 180°, the torque is in CCW direction. When θ = 180°, torque is zero. For θ > 180°, torque increases but in the CW direction. When θ = 270°, the torque is maximum but negative, Fig. 9.10 (*c*). For 180° < θ < 360°, torque is in CW direction. The variation of electromagnetic torque with rotor position θ is illustrated in Fig. 9.10 (*d*).

For a VR stepping motor in Fig. 9.11 (*a*), only phase winding *A* is taken to be permanently excited. When long axis of rotor coincides with stator winding axis, θ = 0° and reluctance torque is zero. When rotor axis is taken away from position θ = 0°, the reluctance torque increases. This torque in CCW direction is maximum when rotor axis is 45° away, *i.e.*, when θ = 45°. Beyond θ = 45°, reluctance torque decreases. For 0° < θ < 90°, the torque is in CCW direction. When θ = 90° as shown in Fig. 9.11 (*b*), the reluctance torque is zero. When θ exceeds 90°, the torque also rises from zero in CW direction. At θ = 90°, the rotor can rotate either CW or CCW, therefore, the rotor orientation at θ = 90° is unstable. At θ = 135°, torque is again maximum but in CW direction. When θ = 180°, reluctance torque is again zero. For 90° < θ < 180°, reluctance torque is in CW direction. The variation of reluctance torque as a function of rotor position θ is shown in Fig. 9.11 (*c*).

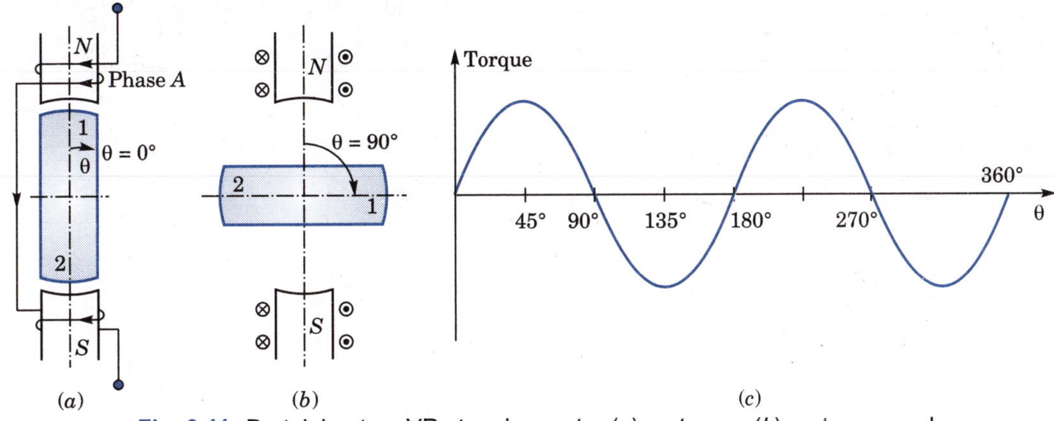

Fig. 9.11: Pertaining to a VR stepping motor (*a*) no torque (*b*) no torque and (*c*) torque-displacement characteristic.

As stated before, a hybrid stepping motor combines the characteristics of PM and VR stepping motors. Therefore, the resultant torque in a hybrid stepping motor is obtained by the addition of

(*i*) electromagnetic torque as in a PMSM

and (*ii*) reluctance torque as in a VRSM

This is illustrated in Fig. 9.12.

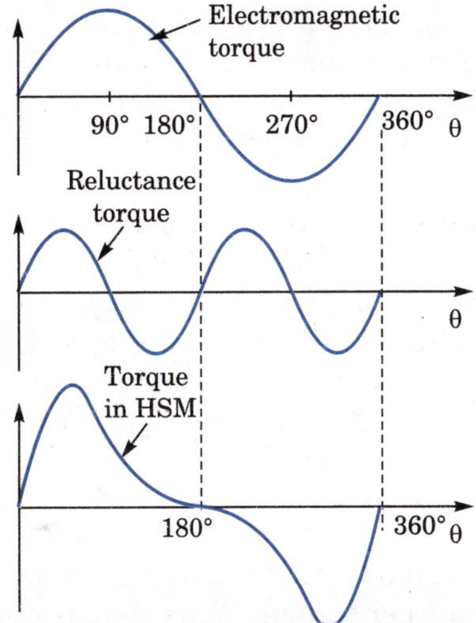

Fig. 9.12: Pertaining to torque in a hybrid stepping motor.

Example 9.3. *For each winding pattern in a stepping motor, the rotor of a PMSM has only one well-defined stable position whereas the rotor of a VRSM has two possible stable positions. Explain.*

Solution. In a stepping motor with PM rotor, when θ < 90° as in Fig. 9.13 (*a*), the electromagnetic torque is in CCW direction. As a result, the rotor also moves CCW to align the rotor magnetic axis with stator magnetic axis so that eventually θ = 0°. When θ > 90°, Fig. 9.13 (*b*), the torque is again in CCW direction, as a result rotor finally settles down at θ = 0°. Torque is also zero at θ = 180°, but this is an unstable position. A little angular disturbance away from θ = 180° position causes the permanent-magnet rotor to drift away from 180° position and it finally settles down at θ = 0° orientation. This shows that for one winding pattern, rotor of a PMSM has one stable and well-defined position at θ = 0° for 0° < θ < 360°.

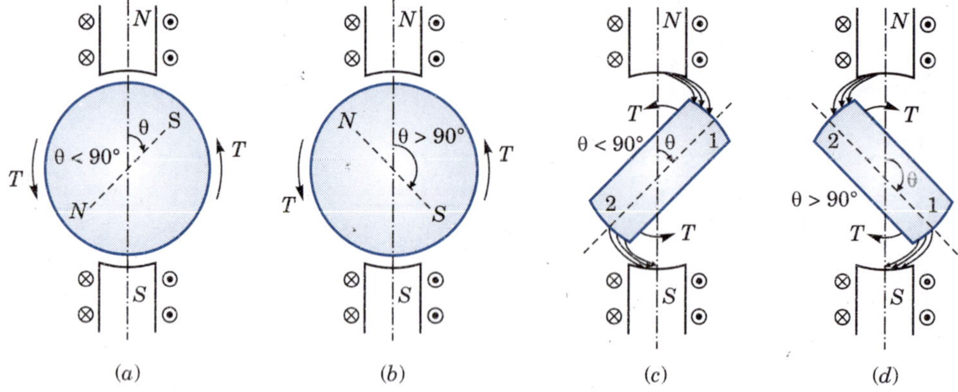

Fig. 9.13: Pertaining to Example 9.3.

In a VRSM with a ferromagnetic rotor, when θ < 90°, Fig. 9.13 (*c*), the reluctance torque is in CCW direction. As a result, the rotor moves CCW with rotor face marked 1 moving towards stator *N* pole and face 2 towards stator *S* pole. Finally, the long-rotor axis coincides with stator magnetic axis and reluctance torque reduces to zero when θ = 0°. In Fig. 9.13 (*d*), rotor face 1 is shown to occupy a position such that 90° < θ < 180°. Now rotor face 1 has *N* pole induced in it whereas rotor face 2 has *S* pole induced in it. As a result, reluctance torque is now CW with rotor face 1 moving towards stator *S* pole and rotor face 2 towards stator *N* pole. Finally, the rotor settles down at θ = 180°. Likewise, it can be shown that for rotor position in between θ > 180° and θ < 360°, the rotor will settle down eventually at θ = 180° or at θ = 360° (= 0°). Though reluctance torque is zero when θ = 90° or 270°, yet these are unstable positions. A little disturbance away from θ = 90° or 270° orientation will cause the rotor to move to positions of θ = 0° or θ = 180°. This shows that for one winding pattern on the stator, there are two possible stable positions for the ferromagnetic rotor, one at θ = 0° and the other at θ = 180° for 0° < θ < 360°.

9.1.5.2 Torque-pulse Rate Characteristics

This characteristic gives the variation of electric torque as a function of stepping rate in pulses per second. With increase in stepping rate, the rotor gets less time in driving the load from one position to the next, the driving torque is therefore reduced ; this is shown in Fig. 9.14.

A stepping motor is usually described by two characteristic curves 1 and 2, Fig. 9.14. Curve 1 gives the pull-in torque characteristic ; it shows the maximum stepping rate at which the motor can start, synchronize, stop or reverse as desired for different values of load torque. Curve 2 gives the pull-out torque characteristic, it shows the maximum stepping rate at which the motor can run for different values of load torque if already synchronized, but it cannot start, stop or reverse on command at this rate. For example, for load torque T_L, R_1 is the maximum stepping rate in pulses per second and at this rate, the motor can start and synchronize, stop or reverse as desired. Once started and synchronized to load torque T_L, pulsing rate can be increased beyond R_1 without losing synchronism up to the maximum pulse rate R_2. The stepping rate from R_1 to R_2 is called the slew rate for T_L. Between the curves 1 and 2, the torque-pulse rate characteristic gives the *slew range*. The characteristic between curve 1 and the zero-pulse-rate vertical line is called the start-range. The dotted portion of the curves 1 and 2 in Fig. 9.14 characterized by low-pulse rate is never used in practice. This is because of rotor oscillations caused by lack of damping at the low-pulse rate. So actually the start-range lies in between the dotted vertical line indicating the low-pulse rate and the pull-in torque curve 1.

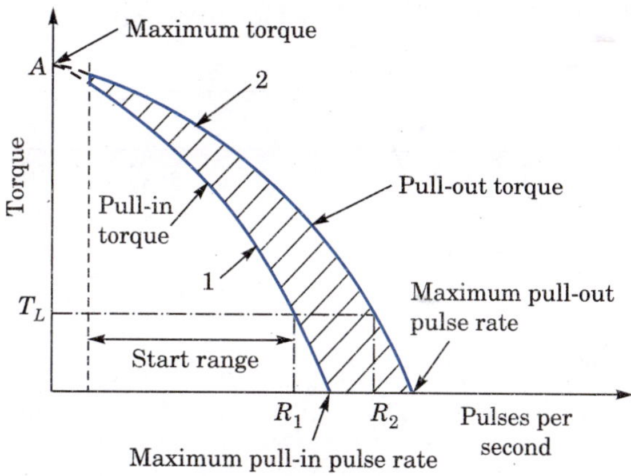

Fig. 9.14: Torque-pulse rate characteristics of a stepping motor.

The motor can start and synchronize with input pulses and can be stopped or reversed as desired in the start range. In the slew range, the motor cannot start, stop or reverse on command. For motor operation in the slew range, the motor has to be started in the start-range, then the pulse rate increased till it enters the slew range. In the slew range, the load follows the pulse rate up to pull-out torque curve 2. For pulse rate more than that given by pull-out torque, the load starts missing steps. In Fig. 9.14, the maximum torque point A gives the maximum holding torque of the excited motor to a steady load.

Example 9.4. *(a) For a permanent-magnet stepping motor, the 4-phase winding is arranged as shown in Fig. 9.15. The digital input to the motor is obtained from a 4-bit micro-processor. In binary language, '1' denotes ON and 'O' denotes OFF. Thus, 1000 means winding a is excited, 1010 means windings a and c are excited etc. Make a table of the 4-bit signals which correspond to the rotor angular positions clockwise at 0°, 45°, 90°, ..., 360°.*

(b) The motor of part (a) is made to rotate at a constant speed of 1500 rpm through the digital signal input to the four windings in proper sequence. Fing the time interval between the two digital signals applied to the motor.

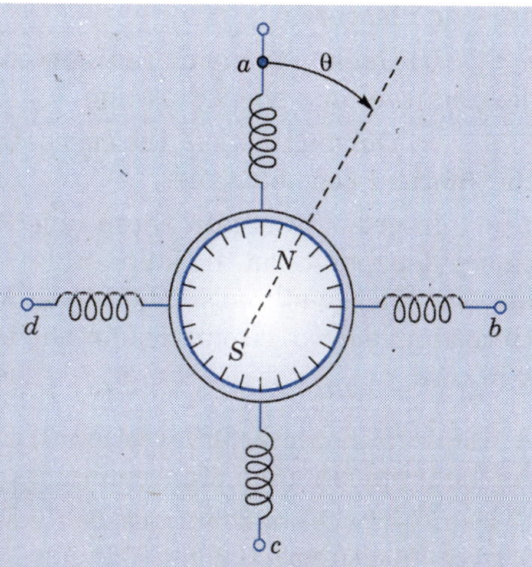

Fig. 9.15: Pertaining to Example 9.4.

Solution. (*a*) For clockwise rotation of the rotor, the table of the 4-bit signals is as under :

θ↓	*a*	*b*	*c*	*d*
0°	1	0	0	0
45°	1	1	0	0
90°	0	1	0	0
135°	0	1	1	0
180°	0	0	1	0
225°	0	0	1	1
270°	0	0	0	1
315°	1	0	0	1
360°	1	0	0	0

(*b*) For one revolution, 8 steps (each of 45°) are required. This means that time for one rotor revolution is also the time for 8 steps.

$$\therefore \quad \text{Time for one revolution} = \frac{60}{1500} \text{ sec}$$

$$\text{Time for 8 steps} = \frac{60}{1500} \text{ sec}$$

$$\text{Time for 1 step} = \frac{60}{1500} \times \frac{1}{8} \times 1000 = 5 \text{ m sec}$$

Thus the time interval between the digital signals should be 5 m sec.

9.1.6 Drive Circuits for Stepping Motors

The d.c. power supply to drive circuits should be as much free from harmonics as is possible. This is the reason single-phase rectifiers are not recommended. Three-phase rectifiers or batteries are, however, suitable as d.c. power sources for the drive circuits for stepping motors.

For optimum torque output from a stepping motor, the drive cicruits should possess the following features :

(*i*) During turn-on, the current in the phase winding should rise from zero to the desired level in a short duration.

(*ii*) During turn-off, the current in the phase winding should be forced to decay to zero in the shortest possible time.

In order to obtain these objectives, several drive circuits have been proposed. Their choice depends upon the step-angle, the power rating of the stepping motor and whether, or not, the energy-stored in the phase winding inductance is to be fed back to the d.c. supply. Here simple drive circuitries for the three types of stepping motors are described briefly.

9.1.6.1 Upipolar Drive Circuit for VRSM

A simple unipolar (or undirectional) drive circuit for a four-phase VRSM is shown in Fig. 9.16. As the torque in a reluctance motor is proportional to current squared, the direction of current in the phase windings for operating this motor is unimportant. The digital integrated circuit or a microprocessor generates the signals at the required instants to be applied to the transistors for turning them on. In this manner, the four-phase windings *A, B, C, D* are excited in appropriate sequence. The phase windings have large inductance, therefore, in series with each phase winding a *forcing resistance* R_f is inserted so as to reduce the circuit time constant. This arrangement, therefore, allows the rapid rise of current during turn-on, and and also a wider speed control is admissible. Forcing resistances however, reduce the circuit efficiency. A resistance R_d is also placed in series with freewheeling diode in order to dissipate the energy stored in the phase winding inductance.

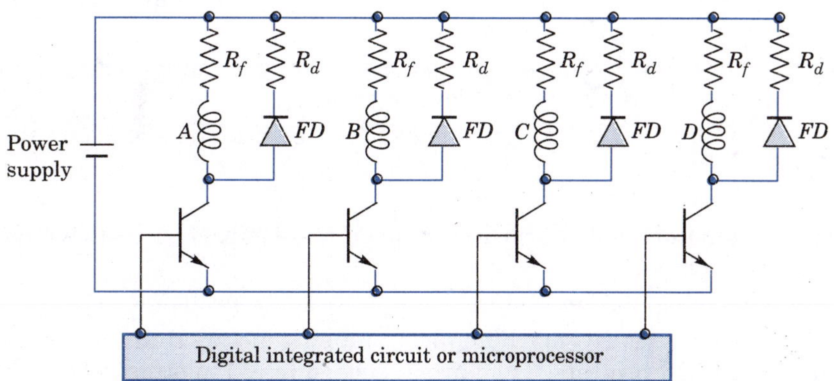

Fig. 9.16: Unipolar drive circuit for a four-phase VRSM.

For relatively high-power VRSM, the drive circuits are so designed that inductive energy stored in the magnetic circuit of the motor can be fed back to the d.c. supply.

9.1.6.2 Bipolar Drive Circuit for PM and HSM

In permanent-magnet and hybrid stepping motors, the torque is proportional to phase current. The direction of rotation in these motors is, therefore, dependent upon the direction of current in phase windings. For rotation in one direction, therefore, bipolar (or bidirectional) current in motor windings is essential. Thus, a bipolar drive circuit for each phase is required. A single-phase full-bridge d.c.-a.c. inverter as shown in Fig. 9.17 is commonly employed for PM and HSMs. Here T_1 to T_4 are four controllable switches. These switches may be transistors or thyristors depending upon the current to be handled by them. When these switches are closed, current flows in the direction of arrows associated with them. Single-chip drive modules are also available, at present, for use in the stepping motors.

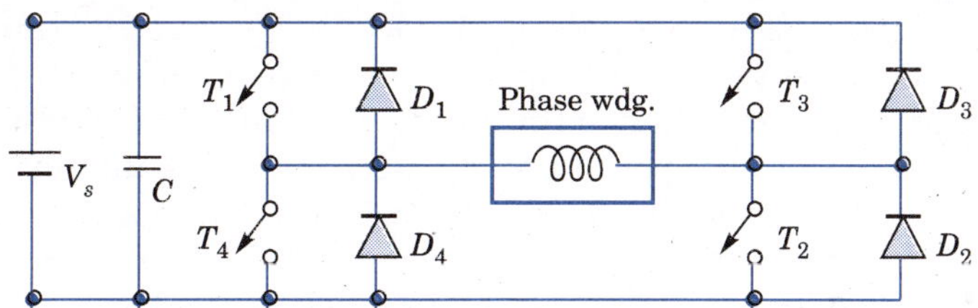

Fig. 9.17: Bipolar drive circuit for PM and HSMs.

9.1.7 Ratings and Applications

The power rating of stepping motors are usually low. The maximum power rating may be around 2.5 kW and the minimum power rating around a few microwatt. VR stepping motors (*i*) operate at small steps, 15° or less and (*ii*) can synchronize with signals upto 1200 pulses per second. PM stepping motors (*i*) operate at large steps, usually above 5° and up to a maximum 90° and (*ii*) are built to respond to maximum pulse rate of about 300 pulses per second. Hybrid stepping motors possess characteristics of both PM andVR stepping motors. A hybrid stepping motor

(*i*) can be designed to have small step-size (1.8°) with simple magnetic configuration as compared to PM stepping motor for which a complicated multipolar structure is required and (*ii*) requires less excitation as compared to VR motor for a given torque requirement, because some excitation is provided by the permanent magnets.

Stepping motors find wide use for tool positioning in numerically controlled (NC) machining systems. It is because of the following reasons :

(*i*) The output signal in NC systems is in the form of instructions on tape or punched paper. A stepping motor can directly work from such input signals without requiring analogue/digital (A/D) and D/A converters.

(*ii*) A stepping motor needs no position sensor and feedback circuits which, in machine tool drives, are quite complex.

(*iii*) Open-loop system design is simple and no stability problems arise.

In addition to its use in NC machine tools, stepping motors find wide use as paper-feed motors in typewriters and printers. They are also used in *X-Y* plotters, the textile industry, integrated-circuit fabrication, robotics, VCRs, video cameras, recorder pen-drives and disc drives in computer systems. In very small sizes, stepper motors are used as paper feeders in hand-held calculators. In the microwatt range, these are extensively employed in quartz-crystal wrist watches, time-pieces and clocks.

9.2 BRUSHLESS DC MOTORS

A brushless dc motor is a polyphase synchronous motor with a permanent-magnet rotor. This motor cannot operate without its electronic controller. Therefore, a brushless dc motor is a motor drive system that combines into one unit an ac motor, solid state inverter and a rotor position sensor. The solid state inverter uses transistors for low-power drives and thyristors for high-power drives. Rotor position sensor monitors the shaft position and sends the control signals for turning on the controlled switches of the inverter in an appropriate sequence. In this manner, inverter output excites the motor phase windings sequentially so as to produce the desired torque and speed.

A brushless d.c. motor is also viewed as 'inside-out' d.c. motor because its construction is opposite to that of a conventional d.c. motor. It has permanent-magnet field poles on the rotor and polyphase armature winding on the stator. The function of mechanical commutator in a conventional dc motor is now performed by electronic commutator in a brushless d.c. motor. This motor processes several advantages over conventional d.c. motor as outlined below :

(*i*) As no mechanical commutator and brushes are required, it has longer life.

(*ii*) Problems relating to radio frequency and electromagnetic interference are minimized.

(*iii*) It can run at speeds much higher than those obtained in a conventional d.c. motor.

(*iv*) Brushless dc motor is more efficient.

Types of brushless dc motor (BLDCMs) are as under:

(*i*) Trapezoidal BLDCMs, (*ii*) Sinusoidal BLDCMs.

In trapezoidal brushless dc motors, the air-gap flux density and generated emf waveforms are almost trapezoidal as in a conventional dc motor. Sometimes, trapezoidal brushless dc motor is just called "brushless dc motor". The trapezoidal BLDC motor is energized with quasi-square wave currents. The rotor position sensor is of the Hall-effect type.

In sinusoidal BLDC motor, the air-gap flux density and generated emf waveforms are sinusoidal as in a conventional synchronous motor. The sinusoidal BLDC motor is energized with sinusoidal currents. This BLDC motor requires more precise and expensive rotor-position sensor.

In BLDC motor, the torque-angle characteristic is trapezoidal whereas in sinusoidal type, the torque-angle characteristic is sinusoidal.

Basic operating principle. The basic operating principle of both types of BLDC motors is the same.

Fig. 9.18 shows an elementary form of brushless dc motor having three-phase stator winding and a permanent magnet rotor with two-poles. When phase winding A is energized with i_a ($i_b = i_c = 0$), stator S and N poles are created as shown in Fig. 9.18 (a). Stator S pole repels rotor S pole and attracts rotor N pole, thus producing clockwise torque.

When rotor has travelled to position shown in Fig. 9.18 (b), current i_a is reduced to zero and phase winding B is energized with current i_b. Here, again stator S pole, produced by winding B, repels rotor S pole and attracts rotor N pole, producing CW torque. Likewise, CW torque would be produced when rotor occupies appropriate position and phase winding C is excited. In this manner, sequence $ABCA$ of exciting the phase windings gives CW rotation. For CCW rotation, sequence of exciting phase windings should be $ACBA$.

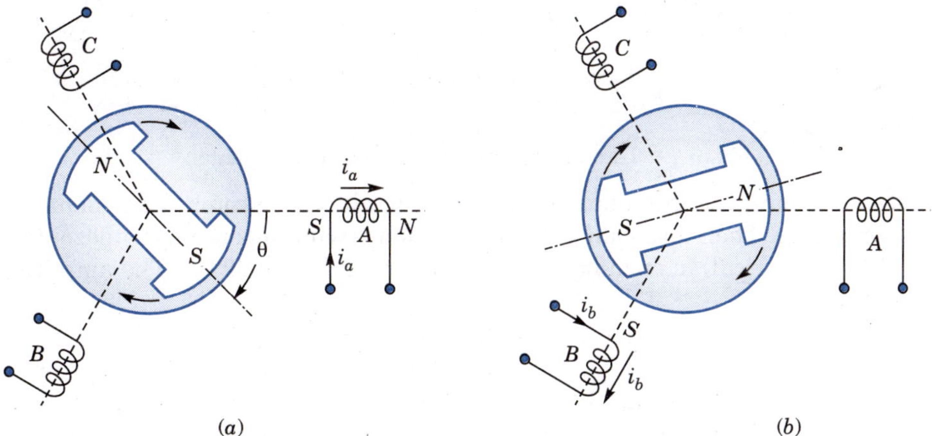

Fig. 9.18: An elementary form of three-phase brushless dc motor.

9.2.1 Trapezoidal Brushless DC Motors

These may be three-phase three pulse or three-phase six-pulse types. In both types, the stator three-phase winding has concentrated coils. The rotor, made from permanent magnets, is so shaped as to produce trapezoidal flux density waveform.

The two types of trapezoidal BLDC motors are now described.

9.2.1.1 Three-phase Three-pulse (or half-wave) Brushless dc Motor

Fig. 9.19 shows an elementary form of three-phase, three-pulse trapezoidal brushless dc motor along with its electronic controller. The stator has three-phase winding which is star-connected. The neutral, or star, point of the winding is connected to positive terminal of the dc supply. Full-bridge diode converts ac to dc and capacitor *C* serves as a filter circuit. The three transistors T_{R1}, T_{R2} and T_{R3} are turned on in an appropriate sequence so that unidirectional torque is developed. When T_{R1} is turned on, phase *A* winding is energized; when T_{R2} is on, phase *B* is energized and so on. When phase windings are energized in sequence *ABCA*, the rotor rotation is clockwise. With sequence *ACBA*, the rotor revolves anticlockwise.

The rotor-position sensor mounted on the motor shaft provides a position feedback. It monitors the shaft position and sends signals to the drive circuitry of the inverter circuit. In response to these signals, the inverter allows the flow of current to stator phase windings in a controlled sequence so that motor produces the desired torque and speed.

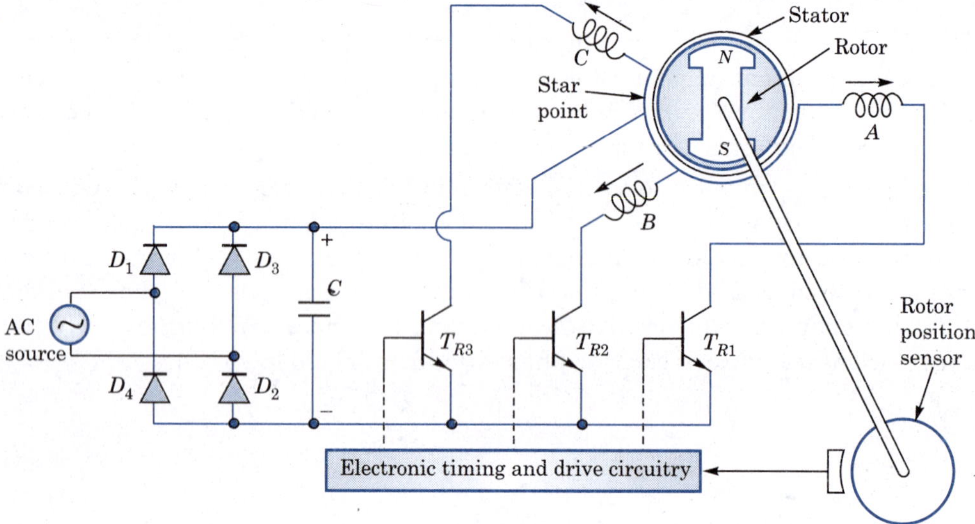

Fig. 9.19: Three-phase half-wave brushless dc motor.

As stated before, the flux density waveform produced by rotor permanent magnets is trapezoidal in nature. Therefore, emf generated in phase windings is also trapezoidal with flat portion for 120° (electrical) in each half cycle as shown in Fig. 9.20 (*a*). The amplitude of this generated emf is

$$E_a = \frac{\phi Z nP}{a} = \frac{\phi Z P}{2\pi a} . \omega_m = k\omega_m$$

where, k = motor voltage constant in V-s/rad.

Similar emf waveforms are generated in phases *b* and *c*, displaced from phase *a* emf, by 120° and 240° respectively.

The transistor T_{R1} is triggered at $\theta = 60°$ and is made to conduct a constant current I_a in phase winding *A* for 120° as shown in Fig. 9.20 (*b*). Developed torque T_{ea} is positive because both E_a and I_a are positive for period II ($\theta = 60°$ to $\theta = 180°$). Therefore, developed torque T_{ea} by phase winding *A* is given by

$$T_{ea} = \frac{E_a I_a}{\omega_m} = \frac{k\,\omega_m I_a}{\omega_m} = kI_a \quad ...(9.5)$$

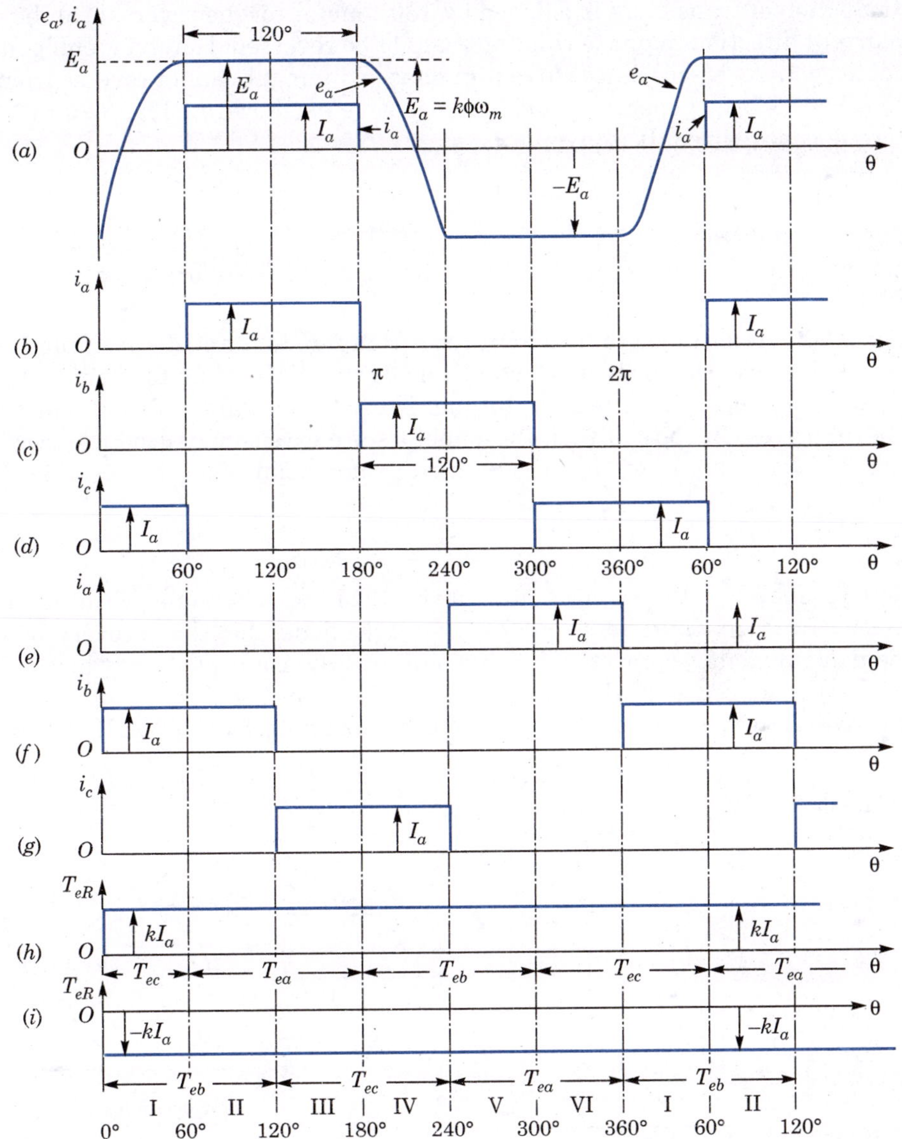

Fig. 9.20: Three-phase half-wave brushless dc motor, (*a*) trapezoidal emf wave generated in phase *A*; (*b*), (*c*), (*d*) phase currents for positive torque; (*e*), (*f*), (*g*) phase currents for negative torque; (*h*), (*i*) net positive and negative torque waveforms. Shaft angle θ is in electrical degrees.

The torque T_{ea} is developed by phase A for 120° only. Similarly, T_{R2}, T_{R3} are triggered to conduct from $\theta = 180°$ to 300° and $\theta = 300$ to 420° (= 60°) respectively. Since emfs E_b and E_c are positive (not shown) and current I_a is also positive, again positive torque is developed, where

$$T_{eb} = \frac{E_a \cdot I_a}{\omega_m} = \frac{k\omega_m I_a}{\omega_m} = kI_a = T_{ec}$$

This shows resultant torque T_{eR} is constant throughout and is given by $T_{eR} = T_{ea} = T_{eb} = T_{ec} = kI_a$. It is shown in Fig. 9.20 (*h*).

If conduction of transistors is delayed by 180°, motor torque reversal can be obtained. Note that current direction in phase windings cannot be reversed. However, emf generated in phase windings gets reversed. Since current in phase winding A cannot reverse from $\theta = 240°$ to 360°, Fig. 9.20 (*e*), but generated emf e_a is negative as shown in Fig. 9.20 (*a*), therefore negative torque is developed. It is given by

$$T_{ea} = -\frac{E_a I_a}{\omega_w} = -kI_a$$

Same is true for T_{eb} and T_{ec} and resultant torque T_{eR} is, therefore, negative as shown in Fig. 9.20 (*i*).

In Fig. 9.20, it is assumed that current rises from zero to I_a and decays from I_a to zero in zero time. This, however, is not true. Current takes some finite time to change. As a result, there would be some fluctuations in shaft torque. These torque ripples do not matter much in low power level drives. In spite of this, these motors are extensively used in record players, hard-disc drives for computers, low-cost instruments, small fans for cooling electronic equipment etc.

9.2.1.2 Three-phase Full-wave (or six-pulse) Brushless dc Motor

Fig. 9.21 shows a three-phase full-wave brushless dc motor with its electronic controller. There are six thyristors and six feedback diodes for the recovery of inductive energy. The neutral of star-connected stator winding is not connected anywhere. Thyristors are triggered in the sequence in which these are numbered in Fig. 9.21. Also, two of the three phases are active all the time as shown in Fig. 9.22. For example, for interval II ($\theta = 60°$ to 120°),

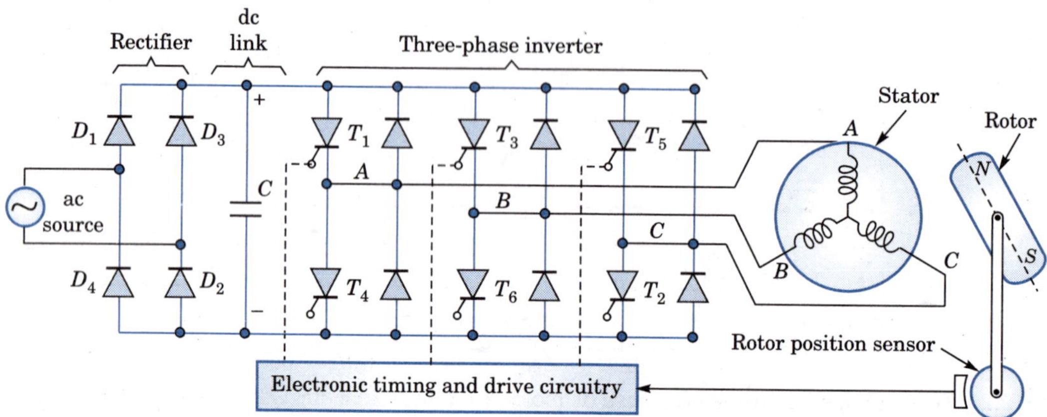

Fig. 9.21: Three-phase full-wave brushless dc motor.

SCRs 6 and 1 conduct and current flows from A to B; for interval III, SCRs 1, 2 conduct and current flows from A to C; for interval IV, SCRs 2, 3 conduct and current flows from B to C and so on. The magnitude of quasi-square current waveform is constant at I_a for 120° periods for all the three phases A, B, C as shown in Fig. 9.22 (*b*), (*c*), (*d*).

For interval II, torque T_{ea} is positive because both E_a and I_a are positive. For the same interval II, torque T_{eb} would also be positive, because both E_a and I_a are negative (E_a for phase b not shown). In this manner, torque waveforms for T_{ea}, T_{eb}, T_{ec} are drawn in Fig. 9.22 (*e*), (*f*), (*g*) respectively. Here the magnitude of torque $T_{ea} = T_{eb} = T_{ec} = T_e$ is given by

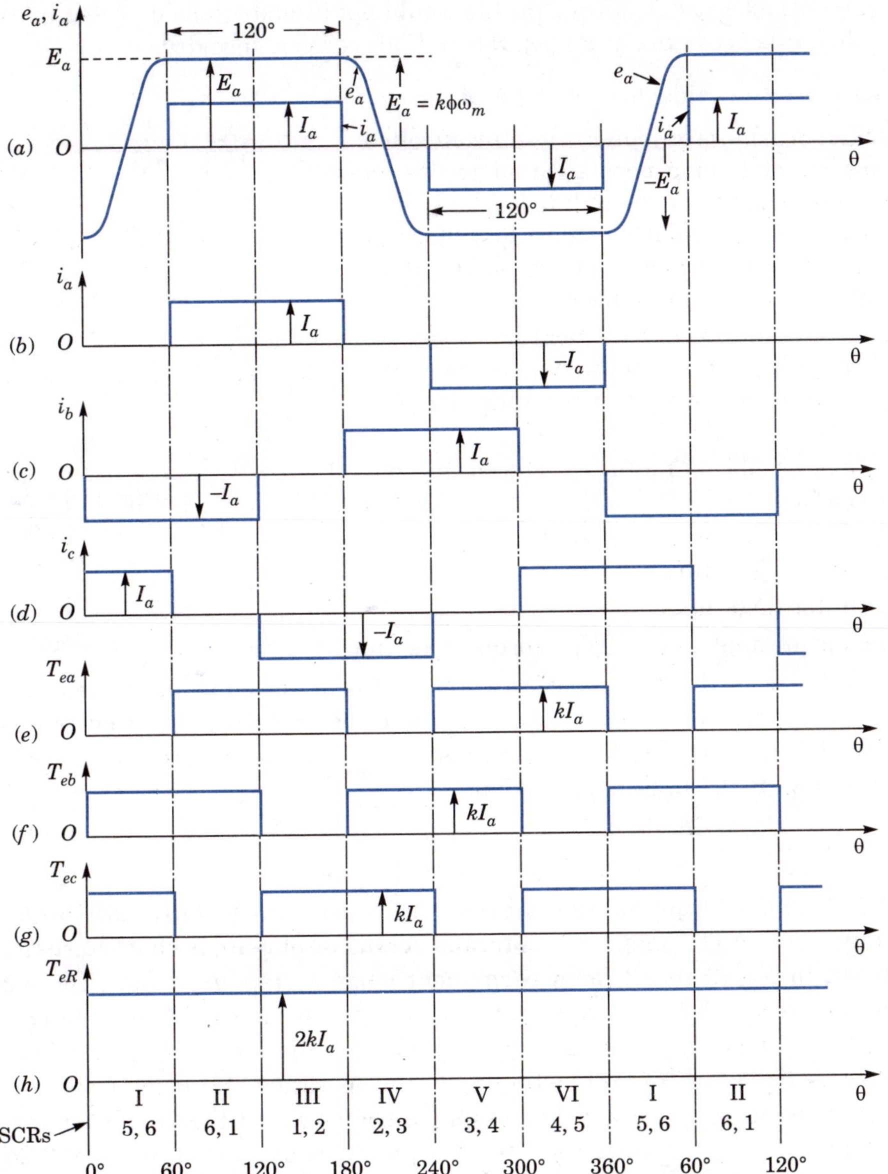

Fig. 9.22: Three-phase full-wave brushless dc motor. (*a*) trapezoidal emf wave generated in phase A; (*b*), (*c*), (*d*) phase currents for positive torque; (*e*), (*f*), (*g*) torque-angle characteristics; (*h*) net torque profile of constant amplitude. Angle θ in electrical degrees.

$$T_e = \frac{E_a I_a}{\omega_m} = \frac{k\,\omega_m\, I_a}{\omega_m} = k\, I_a$$

The net torque in period II is $T_{eR} = T_{ea} + T_{eb} = 2k\, I_a$. Same is true for other periods III, IV etc. The resultant torque $T_{eR} = 2kI_a$ is constand as shown in Fig. 9.22 (*h*).

As before, torque reversal can be obtained by shifting the triggering of thyristors by 180°. In VSI system, the inductive load would cause delay in the turn-on of current and turn-off of the current. As a result, torque profile would not be smooth as depicted in Fig. 9.22 (h). In spite of this, it is becoming quite popular in high performance drives.

9.2.2 Three-phase Sinusoidal Brushless DC Motor

The sinusoidal brushless dc motor is a self-controlled synchronous motor having permanent magnets on rotor and 3-phase distributed winding on the stator. As stated before, a sinusoidal brushless dc motor is a combination of synchronous motor, solid state inverter and a rotor position sensor.

Fig. 9.23 shows an elementary form of sinusoidal brushless dc motor having three-phase winding on stator and two-pole permanent magnet rotor.

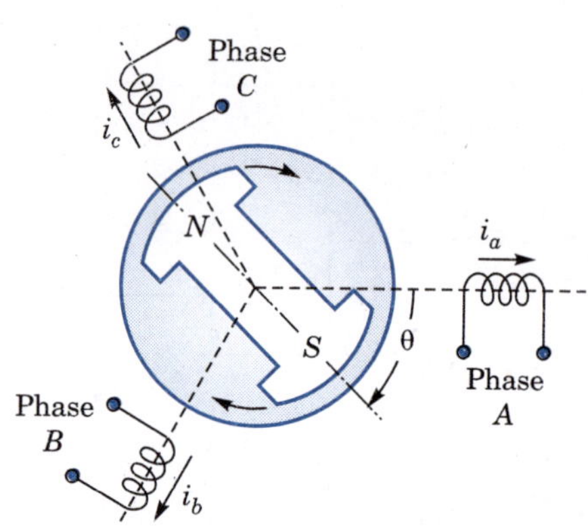

Fig. 9.23: An elementary form of three-phase sinusoidal brushless d.c. motor.

The magnitude of torque produced in this motor is given by

$$T_e = K_1 \cdot \phi_s \, \phi_r \sin \theta \quad \text{...(9.6)}$$

where, ϕ_s = stator field flux

ϕ_r = rotor field flux

θ = torque angle and K_1 = torque constant.

Strength of rotor-field flux ϕ_r is constant as it is produced by permanent magnets. The magnitude of stator field is proportional to stator current. As the stator current is constant, the stator field flux ϕ_s can also be treated constant. In view of this, the torque expression for phase A, from Eq. (9.6), can be expressed as

$$T_{ea} = KI_a \sin \theta \quad \text{...(9.7)}$$

where, I_a is the constant stator current in phase A.

As per Eq. (9.7), torque developed by phase A varies sinusoidally with torque angle θ as shown in Fig. 9.24 (a). The shape of this torque versus torque-angle characteristics is similar to that shown in Fig. 9.10 (d) for a permanent-magnet stepping motor. As axis of phase winding B is displaced by 120° from phase A axis, the torque T_{eb} developed by phase B is shifted by 120° from torque T_{ea} as shown in Fig. 9.24 (b). Similarly, torque developed by phase C is sketched as T_{ec} in Fig. 9.24 (c). Actually, for the operation of this motor as a brushless dc motor, phase winding A is energized through transistor T_{R1} of Fig. 9.18 from instant 1 (θ = 30°) to instant 1′ (θ = 150°) so that positive torque T_{ea} is developed, see Fig. 9.24 (d). From space instant 2 (θ = 150°) to instant 2′, phase winding B is energized through transistor T_{R2} for 120° so that positive torque T_{eb} is developed. From space position 3 (θ = 270°) to instant 3′, phase winding C is excited through transistor T_{R3} for 120° so that positive torque T_{ec} is produced. After this, phase winding A is again energized so as to result in continuous clockwise rotation of the brushless dc motor. It is seen that for a 3-phase three-pulse brushless dc motor, each winding conducts for 120-degree intervals in each cycle of 360°.

An examination of Figs. 9.23 and 9.24 shows that reversal of rotation is possible if the transistor conduction is delayed by 180° electrical ; from instant at 4 to 4′ for phase winding A, from instant 5 to 5′ for phase winding B etc. Reversal of the direction of rotation is also possible if the sequence of turning-on the stator winding is reversed.

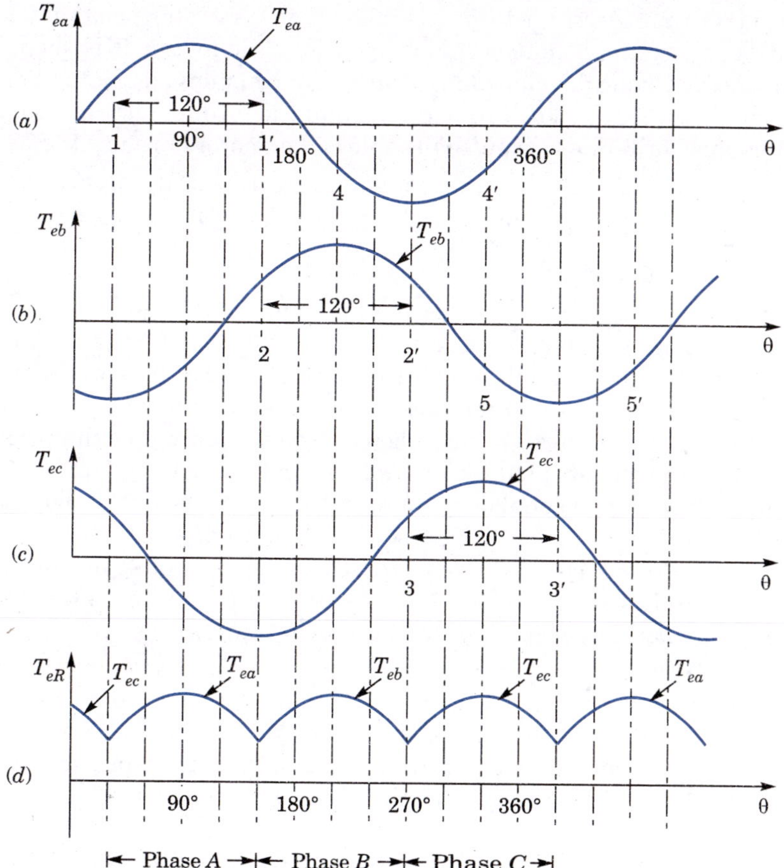

Fig. 9.24: Static torque-angle characteristics for a sinusoidal brushless d.c. motor.

In case phase windings carry instantaneous currents i_a, i_b and i_c; the instantaneous torque, from Eq. (9.7) and Fig. 9.24, can be expressed as

$$T_{ea} = Ki_a \sin \theta, \qquad T_{eb} = Ki_b \sin (\theta - 120°)$$

$$T_{ec} = Ki_c \sin (\theta - 240°)$$

If phase currents are assumed to vary sinusoidally with θ, then

$$i_a = I_m \sin \theta,\ i_b = I_m \sin (\theta - 120°) \text{ and } i_c = I_m \sin (\theta - 240°)$$

With these currents, the torque expressions for the three phases become,

$$T_{ea} = KI_m \sin^2 \theta,\ T_{eb} = KI_m \sin^2 (\theta - 120°)$$

and

$$T_{ec} = KI_m \sin^2 (\theta - 240°)$$

Resultant torque,

$$T_{eR} = T_{ea} + T_{eb} + T_{ec}$$

$$= KI_m [\sin^2 \theta + \sin^2 (\theta - 120°) + \sin^2 (\theta - 240°)]$$

$$= KI_m \left[\frac{1 - \cos 2\theta}{2} + \frac{1 - \cos 2(\theta - 120°)}{2} + \frac{1 - \cos 2(\theta - 240°)}{2}\right]$$

$$= \frac{3}{2} KI_m \qquad \text{...(9.8)}$$

Eq. (9.8) shows that the shaft torque is independent of rotor position θ and has linear relationship with current amplitude as in a conventional dc motor. It is seen from Fig. 9.24 that actually the motor torque developed in a sinusoidal brushless dc motor consists of torque pulsations. The ripple content in the torque profile and the torque fluctuations can be reduced if four-phase four-pulse or 3-phase 6-pulse brushless d.c. motors are used.

An examination of Fig. 9.24 shows that maximum torque is developed by phase winding *A* when rotor magnetic axis is at 90°, *i.e.* when $\theta = 90°$. Same is true for phase winding *B* and *C*.

9.2.3 Applications of BLDC Motors

As in a stepping motor, the frequency of exciting the phase windings determines the speed of brushless dc motors. The torque can be controlled by adjusting (*i*) the amplitude of phase-winding currents and (*ii*) the angle between the rotor-magnetic axis and the excited phase winding. Brushless dc motors are, therefore, able to display a wide variety of operating characteristics. As these characteristics can be controlled easily and the price of electronic controllers is falling sharply, brushless dc motors find increasing applications in drives previously dominated by conventional dc motors. Typical applications of these motors include turn-table drives for record players, hard-disc drives for computers, low-cost instruments, small fans for cooling electronics equipment etc. BLDC motors of somewhat higher ratings find applications in aircraft and satellite systems. In future, as the power ratings of these motors rise, these may perhaps be considered for use in traction systems.

A sinusoidal BLDC motor requires very expensive rotor position sensors. This adds significantly to the cost of this motor drive. However, a trapezoidal BLDC motor needs inexpensive sensors, this reduces its cost considerably. At the same time trapezoidal dc motor has sufficiently good performance characteristics. As a result, trapezoidal BLDC motor is more commonly used for a wide variety of applications as listed above.

9.3 VARIABLE-RELUCTANCE MOTORS

Variable-reluctance motor (VRM) is also known as *switched-reluctance motor* just to indicate that switching inverter is required to drive a VRM. Operating principle of this motor is similar to a single-stack variable-reluctance stepping motor studied earlier. However, design procedures and control strategies in VRM are different from those used in a stepping motor. For example, a VRM requires a rotor-position sensor whereas it is not needed in VR stepping motor. VRM is designed for continuous rotation whereas VRSM is designed to rotate in steps. VRM should not be confused with synchronous reluctance motor. A synchronous motor has cylindrical stator with distributed windings and salient-pole rotor with concentrated field winding. A VRM has salient poles on both stator and rotor. Also, VRM has concentrated windings on stator poles and no winding on the rotor teeth. A synchronous motor can run as a salient-pole synchronous motor with field winding energized and as a synchronous-reluctance motor with field winding de-energized.

VRMs are now finding increasing use in adjustable-speed drives because of the following features :

1. This motor is simple in construction with no winding on rotor and simple concentrated coils on stator.

2. It can run successfully at high speeds (about 2×10^5 rpm) because of no winding on rotor and rugged rotor construction.

3. Stator windings can be cooled easily and efficiently.

4. Because of effective stator cooling, the motor dimensions decrease for a given machine rating.

5. As VRM can be operated from unidirectional drive circuits, cost of mirco- and power-electronics is reduced.

6. VRM operates successfully, though at reduced output, even if one or more phases are out of circuit due to some fault.

7. As these motors can be manufactured with a large number of stator and rotor teeth, they give large torque per unit volume.

On account of the favourable features enumerated above, VRM drive is now emerging as an alternative for the general purpose adjustable speed drives. VRM drives can now compete with adjustable-speed d.c. and induction-motor drives.

9.3.1 Constructional Features

VRMs have either singly-salient construction as shown in Fig. 9.25 (*a*) or doubly-salient construction of Fig. 9.25 (*b*). In Fig. 9.25 (*a*), singly-salient VRM is shown to consist of a non-salient stator and a two-pole salient rotor. The rotor has no winding but the cylindrical stator has two-phase winding as shown. In an actual machine, the number of phase windings may be more than two. The inductance of each stator phase winding varies with rotor position ; it is maximum when axis of stator-phase winding coincides with the rotor axis. Doubly-salient VRM of Fig. 9.25 (*b*) consists of four salient poles on stator and the rotor has two salient poles

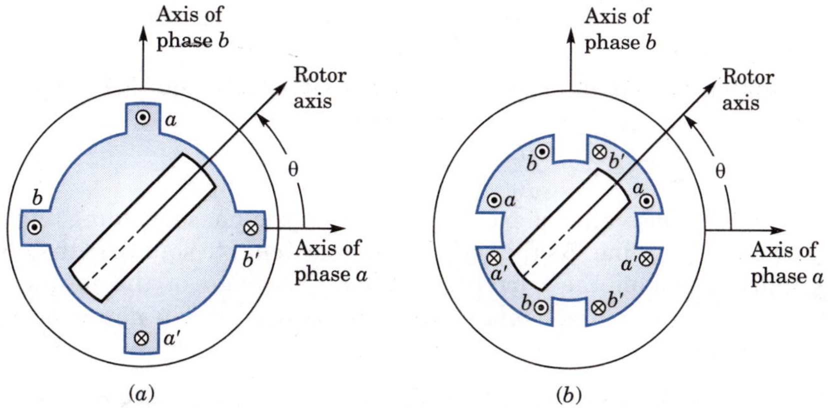

Fig. 9.25: Elementary two-phase VRMs (*a*) singly salient and (*b*) doubly salient.

with no winding. The concentrated windings on radially opposite poles are connected in either series or parallel to result in two-phase winding on stator. This shows that both VRMs of Fig. 9.25 have two-phase stator winding and a two-pole salient rotor.

For the same frame size, a doubly-salient VRM produces more torque as compared to singly-salient motor. Doubly-salient VRMs are, therefore, more common. Henceforth, in this article, doubly-salient VRMs will only be considered unless stated otherwise.

VRMs are usually made with unequal even number of poles on stator and rotor as in single-stack *VR* stepping motors. Stator and rotor magnetic circuits of these motors are laminated to reduce the core loss for achieving high efficiency of VRM drive.

9.3.2 Principle of Operation

As stated before, the working principle of VRM is the same as that of a single-stack VR stepping motor. Fig. 9.26 shows a three-phase 6/4 VRM. With phase winding *A* excited, the rotor orientation is as shown in Fig. 9.26 (*a*) and the flux linkages are maximized with *A*. When phase winding *A* is de-energized and phase winding *B* is excited, the rotor moves counterclockwise (CCW) so as to maximize the flux linkages with phase *B*, Fig. 9.26 (*b*). For further CCW rotation, phase winding *B* is de-energized and phase winding *C* is energized. The rotor rotates in CCW direction for excitation sequence in clockwise direction, *i.e.* *ABC* for the motor of Fig. 9.26. Actually, the phase currents to stator phases are switched on and off in synchronism with rotor position so that continuous rotor rotation is achieved and a steady average torque is developed. The synchronization of the switching of phase windings with the rotor position is essential for continuous rotor rotation. For this purpose, a shaft mounted sensor of the Hall-effect type or electro-optical type is a must. It may thus be concluded that VRM is basically a single-stack variable-reluctance stepping motor where the rotor position determines the turning-on and turning-off of appropriate phase windings.

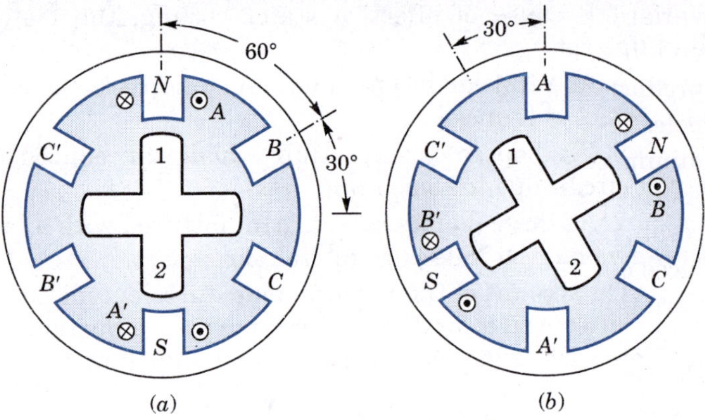

Fig. 9.26: Three-phase 6/4 VRM.

9.3.3 Torque Production

Under the assumption of magnetic linearity, the reluctance torque* developed in VRM is given by

$$T_e = \frac{1}{2} i^2 \frac{dL}{d\theta} \qquad ...(9.9)$$

where *i* is the instantaneous value of exciting current in the phase winding and *L* is the self-inductance of the phase winding. As the torque is proportional to square of the phase current, the torque is independent of the current direction. The sign of the torque is, however, dependent upon the variation of inductances with rotor position θ. The nature of the inductance

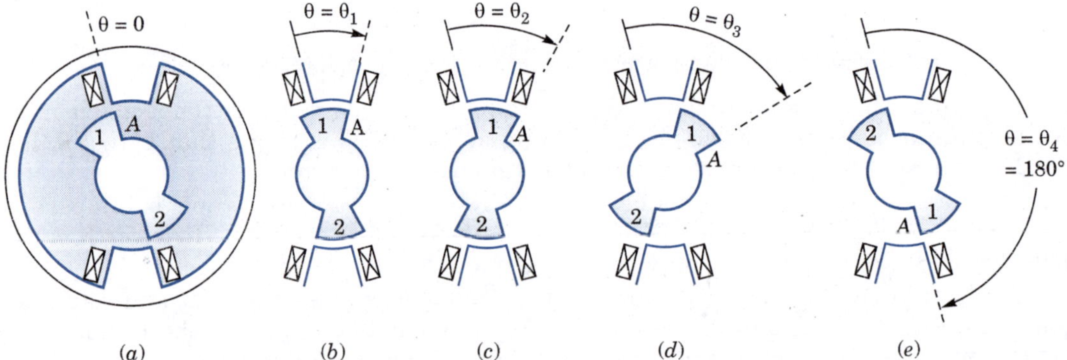

Fig. 9.27: A two-pole stator with two-pole rotor shown in different orientations for a VRM.

* Chapter 2 of the book "Electrical Machinery" by the same author.

variation with rotor angular position depends upon (*i*) the number of stator and rotor poles and (*ii*) the pole arcs of both stator and rotor poles. For understanding the concept of torque production, refer to Fig. 9.27 where an elementary doubly-salient VRM is shown with two poles on both stator and rotor. In Fig. 9.27 (*a*), angle θ is taken as zero and inductance is minimum L_{min}. In this figure, side A of rotor pole 1 is aligned along the left tip of stator pole. As the rotor is moved clockwise, stator and rotor poles begin to overlap each other and as a result, reluctance decreases and inductance increases linearly. When $\theta = \theta_1$, Fig. 9.27 (*b*), the pole faces overlap and reluctance is seen to be minimum and inductance is maximum L_{max}. The variation of inductance from L_{min} to L_{max} is taken linear. For rotor movement from θ_1 to θ_2, reluctance continues to be minimum and therefore inductance is maximum but constant for the overlap angle $(\theta_2 - \theta_1)$. As the rotor is moved beyond θ_2 of Fig. 9.27 (*c*), the overlapping of stator and rotor pole-faces begins to decrease and likewise the reluctance begins to rise and therefore inductance starts decreasing. When $\theta = \theta_3$, Fig. 9.27 (*d*), the inductance decreases to minimum value L_{min}; equal to the inductance already obtained for $\theta = 0°$ in Fig. 9.27 (*a*). For rotor movement from θ_3 to $\theta_4 = 180°$, the inductance remains constant at L_{min}. Beyond θ_4, the inductance begins to increase linearly as before ; this is shown in Fig. 9.28 (*a*). The variation of inductance in Fig. 9.28 (*a*) is ideal.

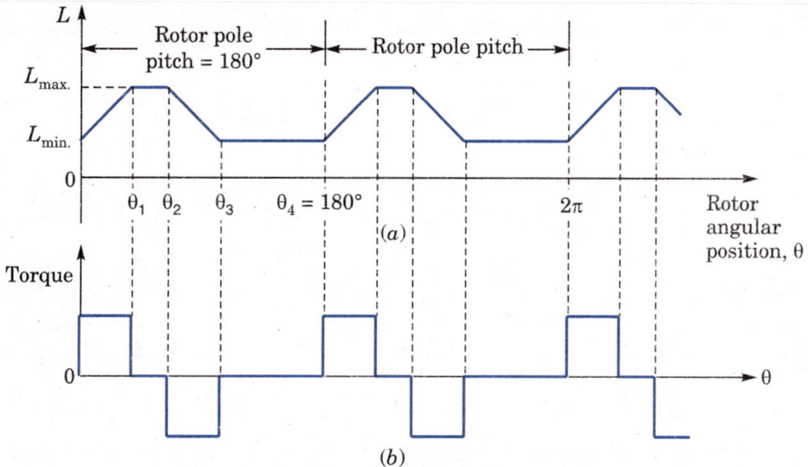

Fig. 9.28: (*a*) Inductance variation of stator phase winding with respect to θ and (*b*) torque-angle characteristics.

As per Eq. (9.9), the variation of relucance torque as a function of rotor angular position is as shown in Fig. 9.28 (*b*) for a constant stator current in the phase windings. It is seen from this figure that reluctance torque is positive when $dL/d\theta$ is positive and torque is negative for negative value of $dL/d\theta$. No reluctance torque is produced when L is constant.

An examination of Fig. 9.28 (*b*) reveals that average torque is zero for constant winding current. A positive value of average torque is produced when a phase winding is excited for the period $dL/d\theta$ is positive and not when $dL/d\theta$ is negative. This procedure is followed for all the stator windings in sequence so that a positive torque is developed and the rotor rotates. In order to determine the switching instants for different phase windings, a rotor-position sensor is essential.

In case all the phase windings are excited during the period $dL/d\theta$ is negative and not when $dL/d\theta$ is positive, an average negative torque results. Operation of motor for the condition of negative torque leads to regeneration process of VRM drive system. This shows that torque in VRM can be controlled merely by shifting the switching on and off instants of the phase windings during the cycle of inductance variation. As VRM drive is easily adaptable to four-quadrant operation, it is becoming a more popular drive motor.

9.3.4 General Considerations for VRMs

In this article, some operational characteristics of VRMs are examined. For this purpose, consider a 2-phase, 4/2 VRM as shown in Fig. 9.29 (*a*). In this fig., stator-pole angle β is assumed equal to rotor-pole angle $\alpha = 45°$. Angle θ is measured from the axis of phase A. When rotor pole axis and stator pole axis of phase A coicide, $\theta = 0°$, reluctance seen by stator pole flux is minimum and therefore flux linkages and inductance L_a of phase winding A is maximum, *i.e.* $L_a = L_m$.

In Fig. 9.29 (*b*), when $\theta = 45°$, lower tip of rotor pole 1 coicides with the upper tip of stator pole A. As a result, L_a has reduced from L_m at $\theta°$ to zero at $\theta = 45°$. This inductance, assumed linear, is shown in Fig. 9.30 (*a*).

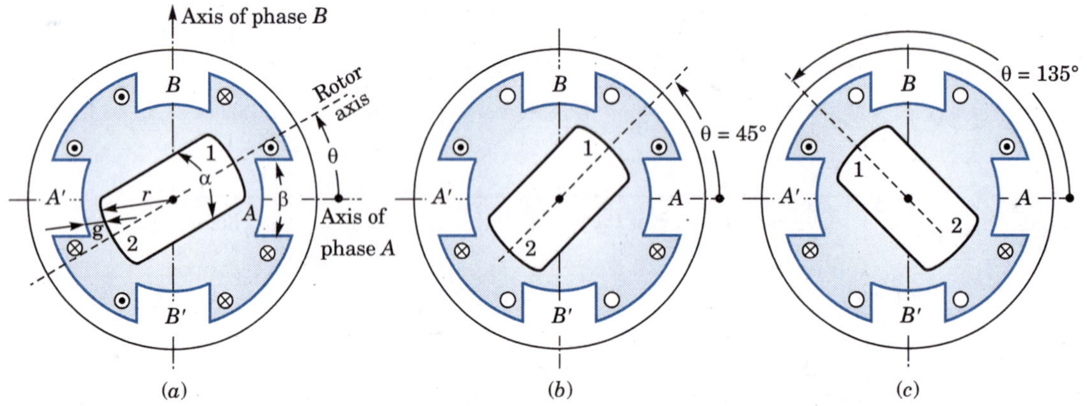

Fig. 9.29: (*a*) Two-phase 4/2 VRM (*b*) Rotor axis 45° away from stator phase A axis, $L_a = L_b = 0$ (*c*) $\theta = 135°$, $L_a = L_b = 0$.

In Fig. 9.29 (*c*), rotor-pole axis is 135° away from stator-pole A axis, *i.e.*, $\theta = 135°$. Here upper tip of rotor pole 2 is coinciding the lower tip of stator-pole A, therefore $L_a = 0$. As the rotor rotates clockwise L_a rises linearly and at $\theta = 180°$, $L_a = L_m$ as shown in Fig. 9.30 (*a*).

In Fig. 9.29 (*b*), when $\theta = 45°$, upper tip of rotor pole 1 coincides with the right tip of stator pole B. Therefore, inductance of phase B, *i.e.* $L_b = 0$. With CW rotor movement, L_b rises linearly and becomes maximum L_m when $\theta = 90°$ and zero when $\theta = 135°$ and so on. This is also shown in Fig. 9.30 (*a*).

The torque produced by phase A is given by $T_e = \dfrac{1}{2} i_a^2 \dfrac{dL_a}{d\theta}$

Assuming i_a = constant, the variation of torque T_{ea} with shaft angle θ is shown in Fig. 9.30 (*b*). Similarly, torque T_{eb} developed by phase B is shown in Fig. 9.30 (*c*). If both phase windings are excited together during the periods $dL/d\theta$ is positive, then the resultant positive torque wave shown in Fig. 9.30 (*d*) is obtained.

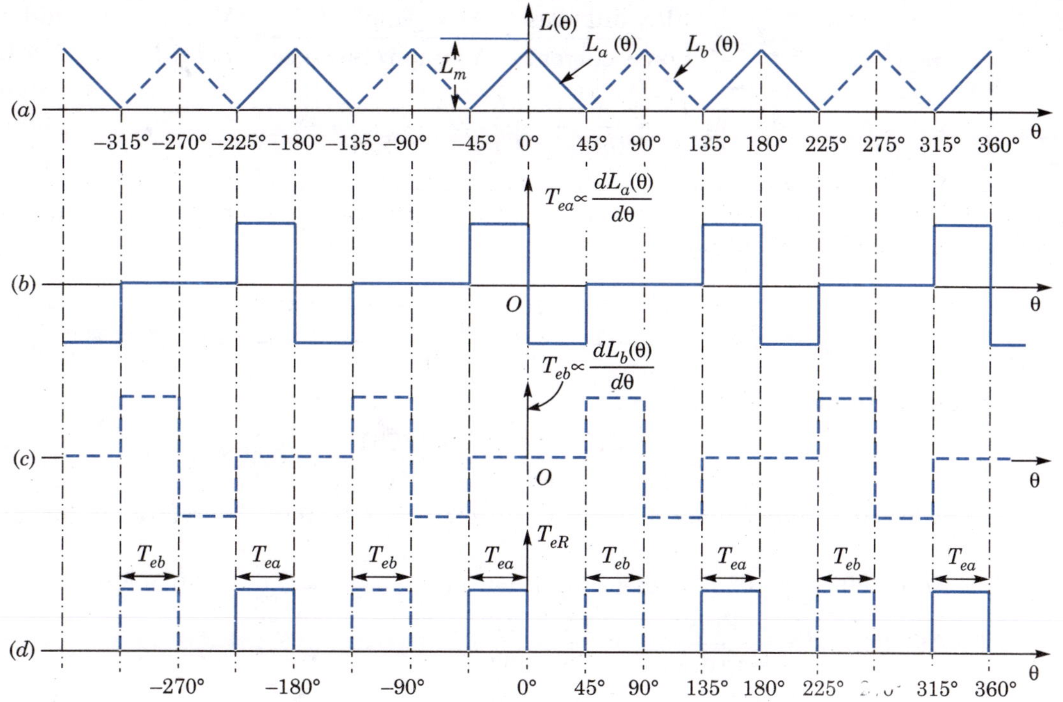

Fig. 9.30: (*a*) Ideal variation of inductances for phase *A* and *B* ; (*b*), (*c*) torque produced by the two phases and (*d*) net torque waveform.

From the waveform, of the resultant or net torque T_{eR}, the following observations can be made.

(*i*) There are zero torque positions which is an undesirable motor characteristic. For example, for rotor angles 0° < θ < 45°, 90° < θ < 135° etc., no positive torque is produced. At standstill, the rotor may get locked into these zero torque positions. Therefore, the rotor would have to be moved mechanically out of this zero torque region and only then the motor can be started.

(*ii*) In Fig. 9.30 (*d*), the time-average torque is positive. The motor would therefore rotate. Since the torque profile is not smooth, it would result in vibrations, noise and shaft fatigue which is undesirable.

The difficulties listed above can be overcome in 2-phase 4/2, VRM by constructing these motors with non-uniform air gap, but this will not be discussed here.

Example 9.5. *In two-phase 4/2 VRM shown in Fig. 9.29 (a), the dimensions are as follows :*

α = β = 45° ; rotor radius, r = 3 cm ; rotor-core length, l = 12 cm, gap length, g = 0.2 mm ; permeability of stator and rotor iron is infinity. Turns per pole = 60.

(a) Calculate the net torque developed when $i_a = i_b = 4$ *A and at angles of (i) 0° and (ii) 60°.*

(b) For rotor angle θ = 0°, phase A inductance is maximum. At this orientation, find the phase-A current so that an air-gap flux density of 1T is obtained under the pole face.

Solution. (*a*) When rotor-pole and stator-pole axes coincide, magnitude of inductance is L_m, where,

$$L_m = \frac{\text{Flux linkages}}{\text{Phase current}} = \frac{\text{mmf}}{\text{Air-gap reluctance}} \times \frac{N}{I}$$

$$= \frac{IN \cdot \mu_0 (r\alpha) l}{2g} \times \frac{N}{I} = \frac{N^2 \cdot \mu_0 (r\alpha) l}{2g}$$

Here $2g$ = total gap length, $(r\alpha)$ = air-gap pole face length and $(r\alpha) l$ = air-gap pole-face area. Here turns per phase = 60 + 60 = 120, because windings on opposite poles are connected in series to form 2-phase winding.

$$\therefore \quad L_m = \frac{120^2 \times 4\pi \times 10^{-7} \left(\frac{\pi}{4} \times 3 \times 10^{-2}\right) \times 0.12}{2 \times 2 \times 10^{-4}} = 0.12791 \text{ H}$$

Maximum torque, from Eq. (9.9), is

$$T_{em} = \frac{1}{2} i^2 \frac{L_m}{\alpha} = \frac{1}{2} \times 4^2 \times \frac{0.12791}{\pi/4} = 1.3029 \text{ Nm}.$$

(*i*) At $\theta = 0$, torque changes from $-T_{ea}$ to $+T_{ea}$, Fig. 9.30 (*b*), therefore net torque is zero.

(*ii*) At $\theta = 60°$, Fig. 9.30 (*b*) shows that net torque is $T_{eb} = T_{em}$ = 1.3029 Nm.

(*b*) Flux density, $B = \frac{\text{Flux, } \phi}{\text{Gap area, } A} = \frac{IN}{\text{Rel}} \times \frac{1}{A}$

$$= \frac{IN \cdot \mu_0 A}{2g} \times \frac{1}{A} = \mu_0 \frac{IN}{2g}$$

$$\therefore \quad \text{Phase-}A \text{ current, } I = \frac{2g \cdot B}{\mu_0 N} = \frac{2 \times 2 \times 10^{-4} \times 1}{4\pi \times 10^{-7} \times 120} = 2.6526 \text{ A}$$

Consider now a three-phase 6/4 VRM as shown in Fig. 9.31(*a*). In this figure, it is assumed that stator-pole angle = rotor-pole angle = 30°. Angle θ is measured from the axis of phase *A*. When angle $\theta = 0$ as shown in Fig. 9.31 (*a*), inductance L_a of phase *A* is maximum, *i.e.* $L_a = L_m$ at $\theta = 0$. Also, in Fig. 9.31 (*a*), upper tip of rotor pole 2 coincides with lower pole tip of phase *B*, so here $L_b = 0$. In addition, in this figure lower tip of rotor pole 2 is in line with upper pole tip of phase *C*, therefore $L_c = 0$. Thus at $\theta = 0°$ in Fig. 9.31 (*a*), $L_a = L_m$ and $L_b = L_c = 0$.

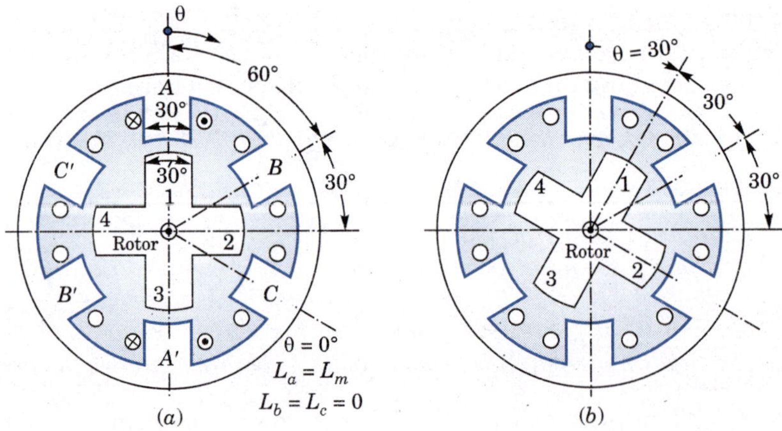

Fig. 9.31: A three-phase 6/4 VRM (*a*) $\theta = 0$, $L_a = L_m$ and $L_b = L_c = 0$ (*b*) $\theta = 30°$, $L_a = L_b = 0$ and $L_c = L_m$.

With clockwise rotor movement when $\theta = 30°$ as shown in Fig. 9.31 (*b*), left tip of rotor pole 1 coincides with right tip of stator pole *A*, therefore L_a reduces to zero. Also, here lower tip of rotor pole 1 begins to coicide stator pole *B*, therefore $L_b = 0$. At the same time, axis of rotor pole 2 coincides with the axis of stator pole *C*, therefore $L_c = L_m$. In this manner, inductance variations L_a, L_b and L_c for other values of rotor angle θ are plotted in Fig. 9.32 (*a*), (*b*) and (*c*) respectively.

Positive torque for phase *A* is developed when it is excited from $\theta = 60°$ to $90°$ etc. Similarly, positive torques T_{eb}, T_{ec} are developed when phase windings *B* and *C* are excited during the periods when $dL_b/d\theta$ and $dL_c/d\theta$ are positive. When phase windings *A*, *B*, *C* are excited only when $dL/d\theta$ is positive, then net positive torque waveform as shown in Fig. 9.32 (*d*) is obtained. Thus, a constant positive torque is developed when stator-pole angle = rotor-pole = 30°, $dL/d\theta$ is positive and stator phase windings are energized in the sequence *a*, *c*, *b*, *a*. If the phase windings are excited in the sequence *a*, *b*, *c*, *a* and $dL/d\theta$ is positive, then positive torque of constant magnitude, in the reversed direction, would be produced. For sequence *a*, *c*, *b*, *a*; the rotating field rotates anticlockwise but the rotor moves in clockwise direction in Fig. 9.31. For sequence *abca*, rotating field rotation is clockwise but rotor rotation is anticlockwise in Fig. 9.31. It is also observed from Fig. 9.32 that if the phase windings are energized in the sequence *acba* when $dL/d\theta$ is negative, a negative torque of constant magnitude would be produced.

It is seen from above that a positive torque of constant magnitude is produced when the phase windings are excited in a proper sequence when $dL/d\theta$ is positive. This smooth torque profile is obtained under the assumption that phase currents build up and fall instantaneously. In a practical VRM drive, build up and fall of phase currents get delayed because of winding inductances. As a result, torque profile is not so smooth as shown in Fig. 9.32 (*d*). In spite of this, VRMs in low power drives are becoming quite popular.

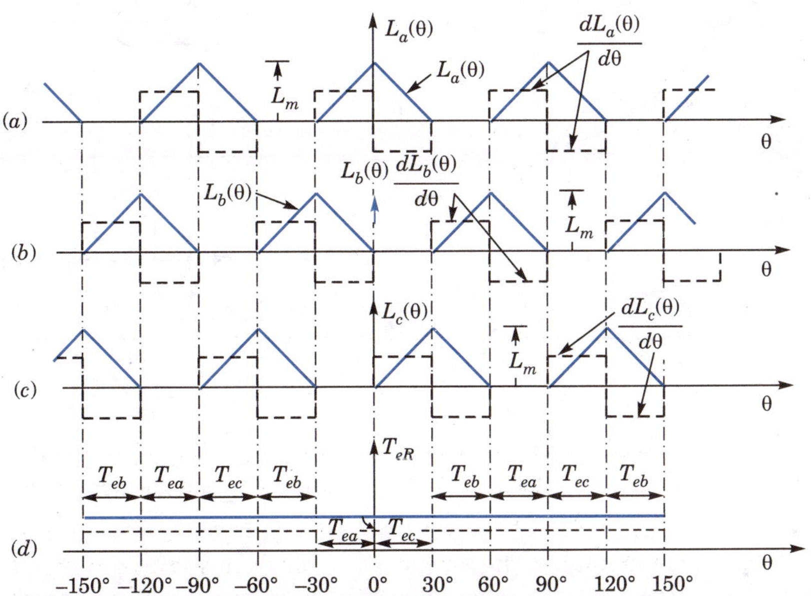

Fig. 9.32: Inductance variation L versus rotor angle θ for (*a*) phase A (*b*) phase B (*c*) phase C and (*d*) net torque versus θ.

9.3.5 Operating Modes of VRMs

A VRM can work in two distinctive operating modes; namely, single-pulse mode and pulse-width-modulation (PWM) mode. This classification is based on the nature of current waveforms in the phase windings of VRM.

Single-pulse mode. In single-pulse mode, also called *high-speed mode*, the current rise is within limits during the small time interval of excitation of each phase winding. This build-up of current is due to the winding inductance and motional counter emf generated in the stator winding. An ideal current waveform and variation of inductance with rotor angle θ is shown in Fig. 9.33 (*a*). In this figure, when inductance begins to rise, switch is closed and current at once reaches a constant value. When $L(\theta)$ stops rising, switch is opened and current decays to zero immediately. During the time current pulse is constant and positive, $L(\theta)$ is rising and therefore positive torque is produced. Actually, such ideal waveforms are non-existant.

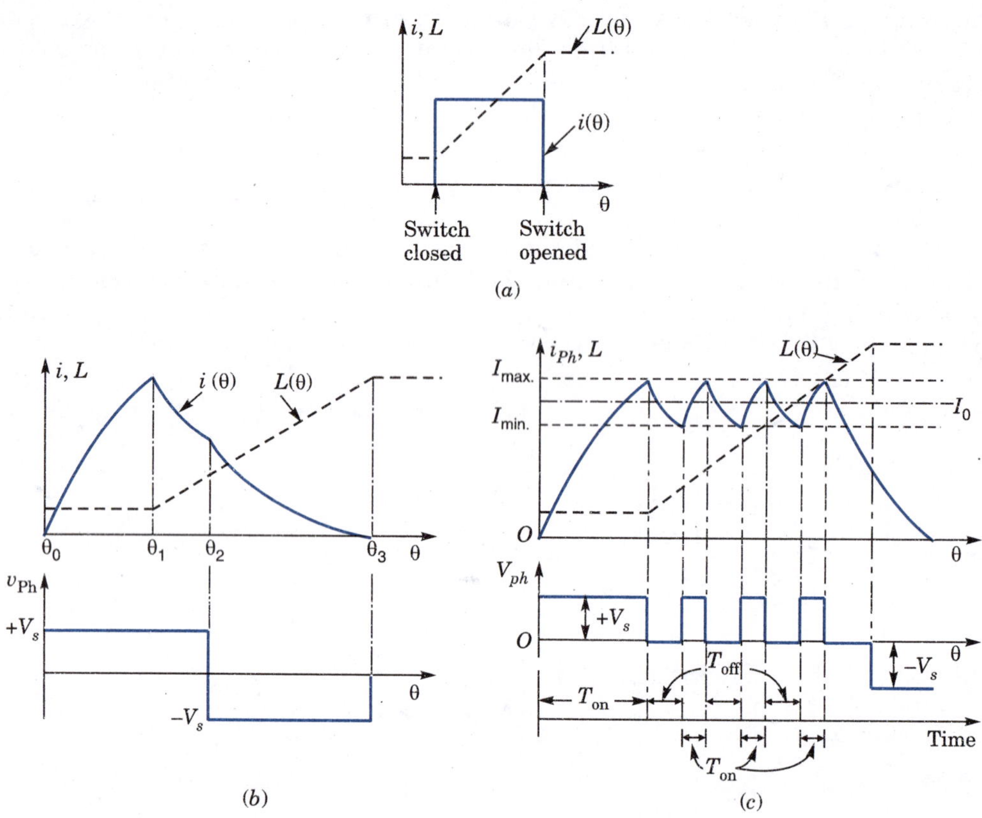

Fig. 9.33: Operation of VRM (*a*) ideal current waveform. Typical waveforms for phase current and phase voltage for (*b*) single-pulse mode and (*c*) chopping mode.

In practice, the instant of switching the phase windings with respect to rotor angle θ should be so adjusted as to maximize the torque available from VRM as in Fig. 9.33 (*b*). In this figure is shown that source voltage V_s should be applied to the winding somewhat in advance of the instant when inductance $L(\theta)$ begins to rise. Low inductance allows the current $i(\theta)$ to build up faster to a large value before torque producing region begins. After θ_1, current $i(\theta)$ begins to fall because of rising inductance $L(\theta)$ and the motional emf until switch is opened at

θ_2. At this rotor angle θ_2, negative voltage is applied to the phase winding. This causes rapid fall of current and finally $i(\theta)$ reduces to zero at extinction angle θ_3. Angle $(\theta_2 - \theta_0)$ is the transistor (or thyristor) conduction angle and $(\theta_3 - \theta_2)$ is the diode conduction angle of an inverter. Source delivers energy to motor during $(\theta_2 - \theta_0)$ and energy is fed back by the motor to source during $(\theta_3 - \theta_2)$. The angle $(\theta_3 - \theta_0)$, called conduction angle θ_c, is an important control parameter. The angle θ_0 is called the *switch-on angle* and θ_2 the *switch-off angle*. Angle $(\theta_1 - \theta_0)$ is called *angle of advance*.

The negative voltage to the phase winding at switch-off angle θ_2 should be applied much before the maximum value of inductance $L(\theta)$ is reached. This is done to ensure that current decays to zero and negative torque region is avoided. At high motor speeds, the angle of advance should be appreciably increased in order to allow the phase current to build-up rapidly to a significant value before the inductance begins to rise. For regeneration purposes, the current pulses and the falling inductance should occur simultaneously. In the regeneration mode, diode current exceeds the transistor (or thyristor) current and the net energy is returned to the d.c. source. It is thus seen that switch-on angle, angle of advance and switch-off angle of the devices are the controlling parameters of VRM drive.

PWM (or chopping) mode. In this mode, also called low-speed mode, each phase winding gets excited for a period which is sufficiently long. The current build up during this long period of time may be prohibitively high. In order to keep the current rise within acceptable ratings of the motor and the inverter components, a current-limiting device is incorporated before VRM as shown in Fig. 9.34. This is achieved by installing a current sensor in each phase so as to monitor current. This current sensor then controls alternately the on and off instants of power-converter components in order to hold the current between permissible upper and lower levels. The chopped phase current as a function of rotor position θ is shown in Fig. 9.33 (*c*). In this figure, I_{max} and I_{min} are the upper and lower prescribed levels of chopped phase current and I_0 is its mean value. When current reaches I_{max}, voltage V_s is switched off and when it decays to I_{min}, V_s is switched on as required. The inductance variation is also shown in this figure. If the upper and lower limits of each phase current are shifted up or down, then mean value of motor current would alter. This will result in torque control and hence speed adjustment as desired. Thus, an accurate monitoring of phase current is essential so as to obtain an adaptable VRM drive.

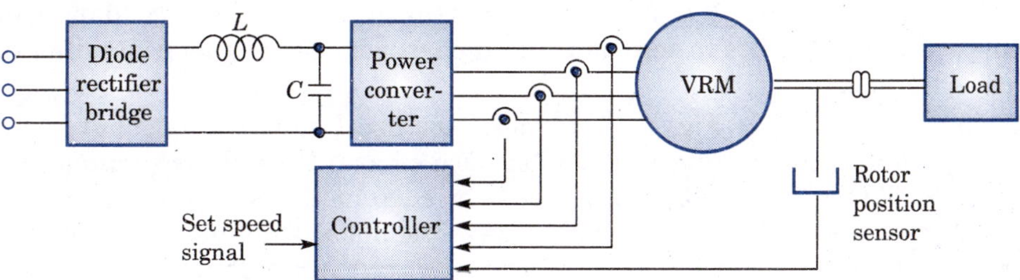

Fig. 9.34: Block diagram for 4-phase VRM drive system.

9.3.6 Inverter Drive Circuits for VRMs

As state before, phase windings of a VRM require unidirectional current pulse when rotor is appropriately positioned. The inverter should apply direct voltage to phase winding at such rotor orientation that phase current builds up rapidly. When it is required to turn off the phase winding, the inverter configuration should privide an alternative path for the rapid fall of phase current. In addition, during the decay of phase current through feedback diode (or diodes), much of the energy stored in the magnetic circuit of the motor should be returned to the source. This process, called regeneration, results in an inverter configuration which is more efficient than the one in which the magnetic stored energy is dissipated as heat. Most of these requirements are fulfilled by each of the inverter drive circuits shown in Fig. 9.35.

An examination of each of the three circuit configurations shows that phase winding is always in series with a power semiconductor device. As a result, there is no shoot-through fault current from the d.c. bus. Thus the drive circuit configuration shown in Fig. 9.35 are quite rugged and reliable. In these figures, the controlled switching device is either a thyristor, a GTO, power transistor, IGBT, MCT or MOSFET, but IGBT, MOSFET or MCT are better recommended for current chopping at reasonably high frequency during PWM mode. Inverter drive circuits in Figs. 9.35 (*a*) and (*b*) are shown for one phase winding and in Fig. 9.35 (*c*) for two phase windings so that these can be studied easily. These circuit configurations can, however, be extended for the excitation of more number of phase windings.

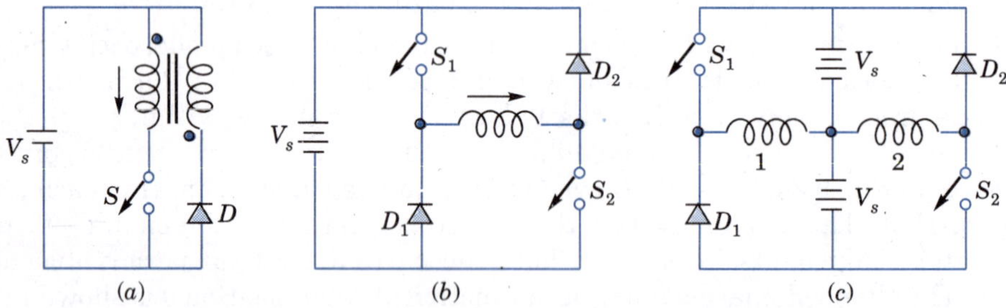

Fig. 9.35: Inverter drive circuit configurations for VRMs.

The inverter circuit of Fig. 9.35 (*a*) uses *bifilar* phase windings. A bifilar winding consists of two separate windings so arranged that these are closely coupled magnetically. These two windings can be regarded as the two windings of a transformer. When switch S is closed, the primary winding is energized with the current direction as shown and energy is delivered by source to phase winding. When switch S is opened, a decaying phase current in primary winding induces a voltage in the secondary winding in such a direction as to forward bias the diode D. The primary winding current transferred to the secondary winding by transformer action now decays to zero and stored energy in the magnetic circuit of the motor is returned to the source.

The inverter circuit of Fig. 9.35 (*b*) does not use bifilar winding but requires two switching devices and two feedback diodes in each phase. Both the switching devices are turned on and off together. When S_1, S_2 are on, current flows in the phase winding as indicated by arrow and energy flows from source to the phase winding. When switches S_1, S_2 are opened, current in the same direction begins to decay. As a result, a voltage appears across the phase winding which forward biases D_1 and D_2 and most of the inductive energy stored is returned to the d.c. source.

In the inverter circuit of Fig. 9.35 (*c*), two d.c. sources, each of voltage V_s, are required. Each phase needs one switch and one diode. With switch S_1 closed, phase winding 1 is excited from upper d.c. source. When switch S_1 is opened, the decaying phase current forward biases diode D_1. As a result, the decaying current now completes its path through lower d.c. source, diode D_1 and the phase winding 1. Inductive energy of phase 1 is, therefore, transferred to bottom d.c. source. It is thus seen that phase winding 1 is excited by upper d.c. source and regenerates into the bottom d.c. source. The circuit of Fig. 9.35 (*c*) is so arranged that phase 2 is connected opposite to phase 1. In other words, phase winding 2 is excited from bottom d.c. source and regenerates into the upper dc source. It shows that the circuit of Fig. 9.35 (*c*) allows the d.c. sources to discharge and charge equally and the amount of energy delivered by the two voltage sources is almost the same.

Example 9.6. *In a three-phase, 6/8 VRM, total time required to excite the three phases is 25 ms. Determine the rotor velocity in rad/sec and in rpm.*

Solution. In 6/8 VRM, step angle = $\dfrac{360}{3 \times 8} = 15°$

For three-phase excitation requiring 25 ms, rotor would execute three steps, *i.e.* rotor movement is $3 \times 15 = 45° = \dfrac{45}{360°} = \dfrac{1}{8}$ revolution in 25 ms.

In 25 ms, rotor rotation = $\dfrac{1}{8}$ rev.

In 1 sec, rotor rotation = $\dfrac{1}{8} \times \dfrac{1000}{25}$ rev = 5 rev.

In 1 minute, rotor rotation = 5 × 60 = 300 rev.

∴ Rotor speed, N_r = 300 rpm

Rotor angular velocity = $\dfrac{2\pi N_r}{60} = \dfrac{2\pi \times 300}{60}$ = 31.416 rad/sec

Rotor rotates in the direction of stator rotating magnetic field.

The analysis of VRM presented in this article assumes no magnetic saturation. Actually, VRMs are designed with short air-gap length so as to enhance the level of saturation in the pole faces. This is done to get more torque output from a VRM of given size.

9.3.7 VRM Applications

Switched-reluctance motors or VRMs possess several important features (listed earlier), which make them favourable for use in adjustable-speed drives. With the easy availability of low-cost power electronic circuitry and microprocesser-based systems, VRMs are now finding wide applications from fractional kW to several kW drives. Their applications include precision position control systems for robotics, low-power servomotors and high-power traction drives. Adjustable speed drive systems based on VRMs are becoming competitive with converter-fed dc drives and inverter-controlled induction-motor drives.

As rotor in a VRM carries no winding, VRMs with rotor speed more than 2×10^5 rpm have been built. VRMs with ratings upto about 25 kW are available at present.

9.4 PERMANENT MAGNET SYNCHRONOUS MOTORS

Permanent-magnet synchronous motors (PMSMs) have polyphase distributed winding on the stator and permanent magnets on the rotor. These motors may be fed from power supply, or from inverter or cycloconverter. When operated at a fixed frequency (50 Hz or some other constant frequency), synchronous motor behaves like a conventional synchronous motor with constant field excitation. Under these conditions, synchronous motor (*a*) runs at synchronous speed (*b*) power angle δ increases with load torque (*c*) may fall out of step if pull-out torque is exceeded and (*d*) has a tendency to hunt for sudden load changes. Under fixed frequency operation, the motor analysis can be done by the same techniques as already adopted for synchronous machines fitted with electromagnets. For PMSM, in phasor diagram of Fig. 4.12, excitation emf E_f is constant because it is generated by constant field flux produced by permanent magnets. The power developed by PMSM is given by Eq. (4.58). In PMSM, direct axis reactance is less than the quadrature-axis reactance ; as a result, reluctance power in Eq. (4.58) is negative. In salient-pole synchronous motors fitted with electromagnets, direct-axis reactance is more than the quadrature-axis reactance.

If PMSM is inverter fed in a closed loop, then the motor is called *self-controlled synchronous motor*. In the self-controlled mode, rotor-position sensor monitors the shaft position and sends the control signals for turning on the controlled switches of the inverter in a proper sequence. In this manner, speed and torque can be controlled. The behaviour of self-controlled SM is different from conventional SM; it now behaves like a conventional d.c. motor. The self-controlled SM (*a*) never pulls out of step because stator frequency is not fixed, it changes automatically with rotor speed (*b*) does not hunt under sudden load changes.

9.4.1 Constructional Features of PMSMs

The construction of PMSM is influenced by the duties to be performed by these motors.

9.4.1.1 Self-starting PMSMs

These motors have squirrel cage winding as in a three-phase cage induction motor. Fig. 9.36 shows a four-pole PMSM with cage winding. The permanent magnets are inserted below the bars as shown. When three-phase supply is given to PMSM, induction-motor torque is developed from standstill to near synchronous speed. Under favourable conditions, the rotor pulls into synchronism with stator rotating field and the motor now runs as a permanent-magnet synchronous motor at constant speed. A self-starting PMSM is also known as *line-start permanent-magnet synchronous motor*.

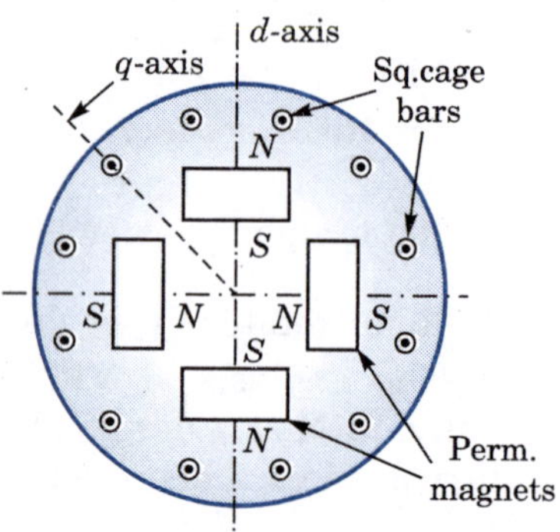

Fig. 9.36: Self-starting four-pole PM synchronous motor.

9.4.1.2 Self-controlled PMSMs

These types of synchronous motors may have surface mounted poles or poles placed in the rotor interior.

Fig. 9.37 (*a*) shows a surface mounted SM having four poles. These poles are glued to the outer periphery of rotor. This configuration is mechanically weak and therefore not suitable for high-speed applications. The variation between quadrature-axis (X_q) and direct-axis (X_d) reactances is not much. This fact affects the operating characteristics of PMSM considerably. Larger the variation between X_q and X_d, better is the SM performance.

Fig. 9.37 (*b*) shows surface inset PMSM having four poles. Here wide slots are cut in the rotor periphery and permanent magnets are inserted in these slots as shown. This arrangement is mechanically strong. The ratio X_q/X_d varies from 2 to 2.5.

Fig. 9.37 (c) shows the constructional features of interior PMSM. Here the permanent magnets are placed somewhere near the middle of rotor laminations.

In Fig. 9.37 (*d*), rare-earth magnetic material is laterally magnetized and is so placed that wedge-shaped poles retain the permanent magnets *N-S* in their position.

The interior PM structure of Fig. 9.37 (*c*) and (*d*) is more cumbersome but more robust mechanically, there are therefore suited for high-speed applications. In machines of Fig. 9.37 (*c*) and (*d*), the ratio between *q*-axis and *d*-axis reactances is around three.

Out of the four constructional forms shown in Fig. 9.37, the surface inset magnet configuration of Fig. 9.37 (*b*) is better because (*i*) its fabrication is easier (*ii*) it is mechanically strong and (*iii*) the ratio X_q/X_d is sufficiently large.

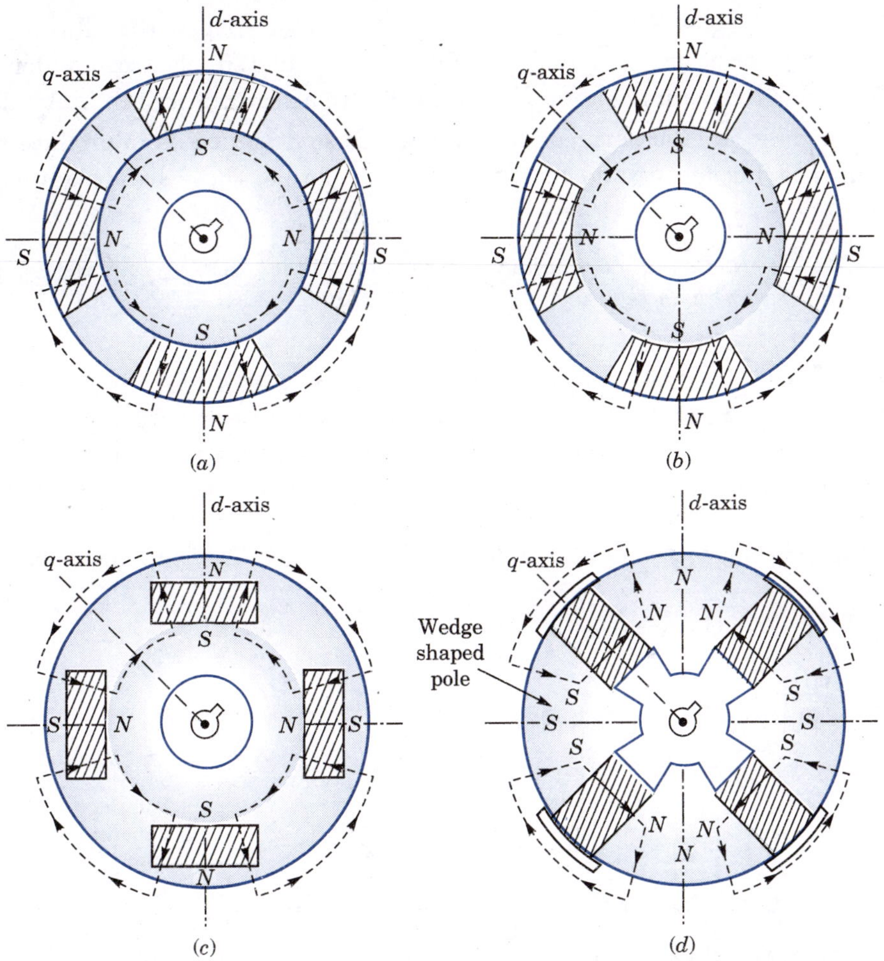

Fig. 9.37: Four-pole (*a*) surface mount PMSM (*b*) surface inset PMSM (*c*) interior PMSM and (*d*) interior PMSM with lateral magnetization.

In line-start PMSMs, cage windings play no role at synchronous speed. When rotor speed departs from synchronous speed due to sudden load change, slip-speed emfs are induced in cage winding. These slip emfs cause slip frequency currents to flow in cage winding in such a manner as to damp out rotor oscillations. There is thus an inherent feedback during rotor oscillations in self-starting PMSMs. But this is not so in self-controlled PMSMs. In these inverter controlled PMSMs, rotor oscillations can be controlled by an external feedback loop ; this renders the system more complex and less reliable than the self-starting, or line-start, PMSM drives.

9.4.2 PMSM Types

Self-controlled permanent-magnet synchronous motors can be broadly classified as under.

1. Trapezoidal type 2. Sinusoidal type

At present, trapezoidal type synchronous motor is known as permanent-magnet brushless dc motor and sinusoidal type as permanent-magnet synchronous motor.

In trapezoidal type, the permanent magnets are so shaped that flux density and generated emf waveforms are trapezoidal in nature for about 120° electrical under each pole. PM brushless dc motors with trapezoidal waveforms are already described in Art. 9.2.1.

In sinusoidal type, the permanent magnets are so designed as to produce sinusoidal waveforms for field flux density and generated emf waveforms. These are already described in Art. 9.2.2.

Example 9.7. *In permanet-magnent synchronous machines, direct-axis reactance X_d is less than quadrature-axis reactance X_q. Explain why?*

Solution. In synchronous machines, the rotor magnetic axis is called the direct-axis. Fig. 9.38 (*a*) shows the peak of armature mmf wave in line with *d*-axis. Neglecting two small air gaps, it is seen from this figure that reluctance offered to armature flux = reluctance offered by permanent magnets + reluctance offered by small iron in between two permanent magnets. Relative permeability of good quality permanent magnets is almost equal to that of air. Thus, the reluctance Rl_d seen by the armature *d*-axis flux in Fig. 9.38 (*a*) is primarily due to two permanent magnets only. Therefore, reluctance Rl_d is high. As a result, *d*-axis inductance $L_d = \frac{N^2}{Rl_d}$ has low value.

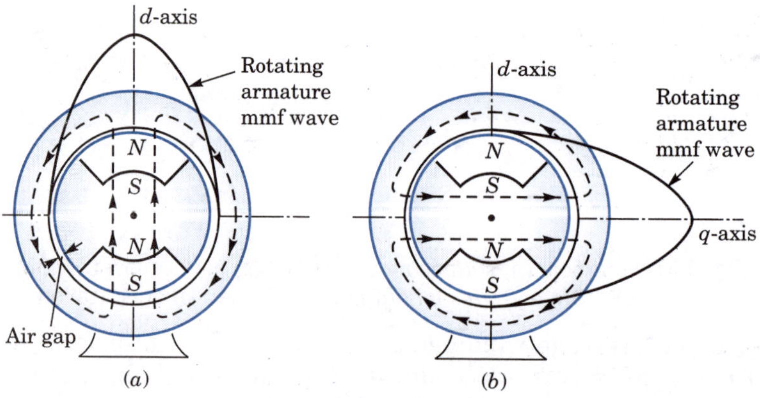

Fig. 9.38: Flux paths for (*a*) *d*-axis reactance and (*b*) *q*-axis reactance.

Fig. 9.38 (*b*) shows peak of armature mmf coinciding with the quadrature axis. Armature flux lines are also shown dotted. Here reluctance offered to armature flux = reluctance offered by iron $\left(=\dfrac{l}{\mu_a \cdot \mu_r A}\right)$ only and no permanent magnets. Since relative permeability μ_r of iron is very high (of the order of a few thousand), the reluctance Rl_q seen by q-axis flux is quite low. As a consequence,

$$L_q = \frac{N^2}{Rl_q} \text{ has high value.}$$

This shows that in PMSMs, $L_q > L_d$ or $X_q > X_d$.

9.4.3 Applications

Their applications are already described in Art. 9.2.3. In addition, these are now being used in air-conditioned equipment. In invertor air-conditioners, single-phase ac is first-converted to dc and then to 3-phase, 4-phase or 6-phase ac by inverter circuits. This ac supply is then fed to permanent-magnet brushless dc motor. Since PMBLDC motor has high efficiency (94 to 97%), an overall economical inverter ac system is obtained. These motors are also used in drones. Since PMBLDC motors possess high efficiency, long lifetime, low noise and good torque-speed characteristics, their use in electric vehicles, hybrid vehicles, elective bicycles, washing machines, CNC machine tools, blowers, robotics etc is also being explored.

PROBLEMS

9.1. (*a*) Why is the integrated design approach to drive systems becoming popular ?

(*b*) What is a stepping motor ?

(*c*) State the differences between a stepping motor and a conventional motor.

(*d*) Describe the operating principle of stepping motors.

9.2. (*a*) Define the following terms as applicable to stepping motors: step angle, resolution, holding torque, detent torque.

Is holding torque less or more than detent torque ? Explain.

(*b*) Describe the constructional features and working of a single-stack three-phase 6/8-pole variable reluctance stepping motor.

(*c*) For the motor of part (*b*), determine the excitation sequence of the three-phase winding for clockwise rotation of rotor through 90°.

(*d*) Repeat part (*c*) for half-step mode of operation through 45°.

[**Ans.** (*c*) *A*, *B*, *C*, *A*, *B*, *C*, ... (*d*) *A*, *AB*, *B*, *BC*, *C*, *CA*, ...]

9.3. (*a*) Describe, with appropriate sketches, a three-stack VRSM with eight poles on both stator and rotor.

(*b*) What is microstepping ?

(*c*) Find the step angle for a 3-stack VRSM with 16 poles on both stator and rotor.

9.4. (*a*) Describe, with appropriate sketches, a 2-phase 8/4-pole permanent magnet stepping motor.

(*b*) For the motor of part (*a*), determine the step-angle and the excitation sequence of the 2-phase windings for clockwise as well as counterclockwise rotation of the rotor.

[**Hint.** (*a*) For one phase excitation, poles numbered 1, 3, 5, 7 attain *N*, *S*, *N*, *S* magnetc polarity respectively etc.]

[**Ans.** (*b*) 45°; $+A$, $+B$, $-A$, $-B$, $+A$, $+B$ etc for CW.
$+A$, $-B$, $-A$, $+B$, $+A$, $-B$ etc for CCW]

9.5. A three-stack VRSM has 16 teeth on both stator and rotor. Find the angular displacement between stator stacks. For achieving rotation of the rotor at a speed of 810 rpm, find the frequency of the currents given to stator-phase windings. [**Ans.** 7.5°, 216 Hz]

9.6. Describe the constructional features and working of a two-phase 4/10 pole hybrid stepping motor with five teeth on each stack. Discuss its torque–displacement characteristics also.

9.7. A stepping motor has a step angle of 8°. Find (*a*) resolution (*b*) number of steps required for the shaft to complete 6 revolutions and (*c*) shaft speed in rpm if the stepping frequency is 1800 pps. [**Ans.** (*a*) 45 steps/revolution (*b*) 270 steps (*c*) 2400 rpm]

9.8. A three-stack VRSM has 16 poles on each of the stator and rotor stacks. The motor is built such that the stator poles of each stack are aligned.

(*a*) Calculate the angular displacement between the rotor stacks and the step angle.

(*b*) Determine the frequency of phase currents required to achieve a rotor speed of 900 rpm.

[**Ans.** (*a*) 7.5°, 7.5° (*b*) 240 pps]

9.9. (*a*) Discuss the torque-pulse rate characteristics of a stepping motor.

(*b*) Enumerate the features that the drive circuits for a stepping motor should possess for optimum torque output.

Describe the drive circuits used for VR, PM and hybrid stepping motors.

9.10. (*a*) Describe the slew range of stepping motors.

(*b*) Why are stepping motors more widely used in numerically controlled machines ?

Give other applications of stepping motors.

9.11. (*a*) What is a brushless dc motor ?

(*b*) What are the types of brushless dc motors ?

(*c*) Describe the difference between trapezoidal and sinusoidal BLDC motors.

(*d*) Give the basic operating principle of both types of BLDC motors.

9.12. Describe a 3-phase half wave brushless dc motor with appropriate diagrams. Discuss how torque is developed in this motor. In case constant phase currents are assumed to vary instantaneously; show, with the help of waveforms, that a constant resultant torque is produced.

How can the direction of rotation be reversed in this motor ?

9.13. Repeat Problem 9.12 for a 3-phase, full-wave brushless dc motor.

Show that resultant torque developed in three-phase full-wave BLDC motor is double of that developed in 3-phase half-wave BLDC motor.

9.14. Describe a three-phase, sinusoidal brushless dc motor. Discuss how torque is developed in this motor. In case phase currents are assumed to vary sinusoidally, show that output torque is independent of rotor-angular position.

9.15. (*a*) Give the applications of brushless d.c. motors.

(*b*) Enumerate the features which have made variable-reluctance-motor based adjustable drives more popular.

(*c*) Distinguish between single-stack variable-reluctance stepping motor and a variable-reluctance motor.

9.16. Describe the constructional features of VRM. Discuss how rotor rotates in a three-phase 6/4 VRM.

9.17. (*a*) In a VRM, the average output torque is zero in case phase winding current is constant. Discuss how it happens.

Is it possible to have average output torque non-zero ? Explain.

(*b*) Discuss the single-pulse mode of working of VRM.

9.18. (*a*) Discuss the principle of working of a VRM. Describe how motoring and regeneration is achieved in VRMs.

(*b*) Explain the working of VRM during PWM mode.

9.19. (*a*) Describe the inverter drive circuits used for switched reluctance motors.

(*b*) Give the applications of VRMs.

(*c*) A three-phase 6/8 VRM is running at a speed of 1000 rpm. Calculate the time between pulses required to excite the phase windings. [**Ans.** (*c*) 7.5 ms]

9.20. In a three-phase 6/4 VRM of Fig. 9.31, angle $\theta = 0$ when inductance of phase *A* is maximum. Plot and label the inductance variations of the three phases *A*, *B*, *C* if stator pole angle = rotor pole angle 40°. Plot the torque as a function of rotor position for the three phases.

Draw the net-torque T_{eR} waveform if each phase is excited with a constant current only at positions when $dL/d\theta$ is positive.

[**Ans.** (θ = 0° to 20°, $T_{eR} = T_{ec} = 1$); (θ = 20° to 30°, $T_{eR} = T_{eb} + T_{ec} = 2$); ($\theta$ = 30° to 50°, $T_{eR} = T_{eb} = 1$); (θ = 50° to 60°, $T_{eR} = T_{ea} + T_{eb} = 2$); etc.]

9.21. (*a*) Discuss the advantages of using hybrid stepping motor over PMSM and VRSM.

(*b*) Define the terms switch-on angle, switch-off angle and angle of advance for a variablereluctance motor during its single-pulse mode operation.

Explain how these angles control the working of VRM drive.

9.22. (*a*) Give the applications of VRMs.

(*b*) In a three-phase 6/4 VRM, the total time required for exciting the three-phase windings in proper sequence is 20 ms. Determine the rotor velocity in rad/sec and also in rpm.

[**Ans.** (*b*) 78.54 rad/sec, 750 rpm]

9.23. What is a permanent-magnet synchronous motor ?

Distinguish between the behaviour of a conventional synchronous motor and a self-controlled synchronous motor.

9.24. (*a*) Give the types of the PMSMs from the constructional viewpoint.

(*b*) Describe line-start PMSM with a relevant diagram.

(*c*) Give the applications of PMSMs.

9.25. Describe the various types of self-constrolled PMSMs with suitable diagrams for both surface mount and interior magnets. Out of the various configurations, which is the best type and why ?

APPENDIX

Objective Type Questions

In this appendix, multiple choice questions are given. The questions are so framed that four alternatives are provided, out of which one correct answer is to be tickmarked.

ELEMENTS OF GENERALIZED THEORY

1. Generalized theory of electrical machines is also called
   (*a*) unified theory of electrical machines (*b*) two-axis theory of electrical machines
   (*c*) primitive theory of electrical machines (*d*) either (*a*) or (*b*).
2. Generalized theory of electrical machines was developed by
   (*a*) W.J. Gibbs (*b*) A. Blondel
   (*c*) R.H. Park (*d*) Gabriel Kron.
3. All rotating electrical machines have
   (*a*) hetropolar system (*b*) homopolar system
   (*c*) either (*a*) or (*b*) (*d*) inductor system.
4. The axis of poles around which field winding is wound is called
   (*a*) *q*-axis (*b*) *d*-axis
   (*c*) interpolar axis (*d*) horizontal axis.
5. Generalized model of a dc compound machine with interpoles requires
   (*a*) 4 coils (*b*) 3 coils (*c*) 2 coils (*d*) 5 coils.
6. Generalized model of an amplidyne requires
   (*a*) 1 coil on stator (*S*) and 2 coils on rotor (*R*)
   (*b*) 1 coil on *S* and 3 coils on *R*
   (*c*) 2 coils on *S* and 1 coil on *R*
   (*d*) 2 coils on *S* and 2 coils on *R*.
7. Basic-two pole representation of a 3-phase synchronous machine with damper bars requires
   (*a*) 4 coils (*b*) 5 coils (*c*) 6 coils (*d*) 7 coils.
8. Idealized two-pole diagram of a 3-phase induction machine requires
   (*a*) 7 coils (*b*) 6 coils (*c*) 5 coils (*d*) 4 coils.
9. Speed voltage in a moving coil is maximum when its magnetic axis is
   (*a*) 270° away from other coil (*b*) 180° away from other coil
   (*c*) 90° away from other coil (*d*) 0° away from other coil.

10. Transformer voltage is maximum when the two coils are
(*a*) normal to each other (*b*) aligned along the same axis
(*c*) 60° away from each other (*d*) 270° away from each other.

11. Generalized model of rotating electrical machines is also called
(*a*) two-axis model (*b*) generalized machine diagram
(*c*) Kron's primitive machine diagram (*d*) all of these.

12. For speed voltage to be present in the coil of a generalized machine, it should be at the
(*a*) rotor (*b*) stator
(*c*) either (*a*) or (*b*) (*d*) both (*a*) and (*b*).

13. A torque can develop due to interaction between two coil currents if these are
(*a*) along the same axis (*b*) in quadrature
(*c*) 180° away from each other (*d*) 45° away from each other.

14. Power in terms of voltage and current phasors is given by
(*a*) Re $[\overline{V}\,\overline{I}^*]$ (*b*) Re $[\overline{V}^*\,\overline{I}]$
(*c*) Re $[\overline{V}\,\overline{I}]$ (*d*) either (*a*) or (*b*).

15. For power $P = \text{Re}\,[\overline{V}\,\overline{I}^*]$, the inductive load
(*a*) absorbs reactive power (*b*) delivers reactive power
(*c*) may be (*a*) or (*b*) (*d*) delivers capacitive power.

16. The main diagonal elements in the impedance matrix of a Kron's primitive machine contain
(*a*) only mutual inductances (*b*) resistances and mutual inductances
(*c*) only self-impedances (*d*) self and mutual impedances.

17. The two-axis model of a rotating electrical machine has two coils on d-axis as DS, DR and one coil on q-axis as QR. This model represents a .
(A) 3-phase synchronous machine without damper bars
(B) repulsion motor (C) amplidyne (D) 1-phase induction motor.
From above, the correct answer is
(*a*) A, D (*b*) A, B, D (*c*) A, B, C (*d*) B, C, D.

18. In two-axis model of a rotating electrical machine, voltage equation for the
(A) coil on stator has self and mutual impedance terms
(B) coil on rotor has self and mutual impedance terms
(C) coil on stator has self and mutual impedance and speed voltage terms
(D) coil on rotor has self and mutual impedance and speed voltage terms.
From above, the correct is
(*a*) A, D (*b*) B, C (*c*) A, C (*d*) B, D.

19. A single-phase load draws 12 kW at power factor 0.6 lagging. An ideal capacitor is connected across the load to improve the overall power factor to 0.8 lagging.
The reactive power delivered by ideal capacitor in kVAr is
(*a*) 9 (*b*) 6 (*c*) 9.6 (*d*) 7
[**Hint.** Use Eq. (1.38*a*)]

20. A single-phase load is supplied by a single-phase voltae source. If the current flowing from the load to the source is $10\angle -150°$ A and if the voltage at the load terminals is $100\angle 60°$, then the

(*a*) load absorbs real power and delivers reactive power

(*b*) load absorbs real power and absorbs reactive power

(*c*) load delivers real power and delivers reactive power

(*d*) load delivers real power and absorbs reactive power [*GATE, 2013*]

[**Hint.** Current from source to load = $-10\angle-150° = 10\angle30°$ A. Use Eq. (1.37)].

ANSWERS

1. (*b*)	**2.** (*d*)	**3.** (*c*)	**4.** (*b*)	**5.** (*a*)	**6.** (*d*)
7. (*c*)	**8.** (*b*)	**9.** (*c*)	**10.** (*b*)	**11.** (*d*)	**12.** (*a*)
13. (*b*)	**14.** (*d*)	**15.** (*a*)	**16.** (*c*)	**17.** (*b*)	**18.** (*a*)
19. (*d*)	**20.** (*b*)				

LINEAR TRANSFORMATIONS IN MACHINES

1. The electrical machines most closely resembling the Kron's primitive machine are
   (*a*) a.c. commutator machines (*b*) polyphase a.c. machines
   (*c*) single-phase machines (*d*) d.c. machines.
2. The term 'linear transformations in machines' means the transformation from
   (*a*) old to new set of variables (*b*) new to old set of variables
   (*c*) 3-phase to 2-phase variables (*d*) either (*a*) or (*b*).
3. The advantage of using transformations in electrical machines is to
   (*a*) obtain lesser number of equations (*b*) get a simpler solution
   (*c*) either (*a*) or (*b*) (*d*) both (*a*) or (*b*).
4. During transformations from old to new set of variables in electrical machines
   (*a*) their mmfs should be identical (*b*) their currents should be same
   (*c*) their emfs should be same (*d*) either (*a*) or (*b*).
5. For obtaining identical transformations for both voltages and currents during 3-phase to 2-phase transformation, change
   (*a*) the magnitude of 2-phase currents
   (*b*) the magnitude of 2-phase turns
   (*c*) both the magnitude of currents and number of turns
   (*d*) the conductor cross-section of 2-phase windings.
6. The transformation from rotating-reference frame to stationary-reference frame results in replacing the moving coils by
   (*a*) a, b, c coils (*b*) α, β coils (*c*) d, q coils (*d*) either (*b*) or (*c*).
7. If A is the transformation matrix, then for the power to be invariant in both the old and new set of variables,
   (A) $[A_t] = [A]$ (B) $[A_t] = [A^{-1}]$ (C) $[A^{-1}] = [A]$ (D) $[A_t]\ [A] = U$
   From above, the correct answer is
   (*a*) A, B (*b*) B, C (*c*) B, D (*d*) A, D.
8. During transformation, it is found that the coefficients of the transformation matrix are constant. This means that transformation has been done from
   (A) 3-phase winding to 2-phase winding, both on rotor
   (B) 3-phase winding to 2-phase winding, both on stator
   (C) 3-phase winding on rotor to d-q axes
   (D) 2-phase winding on stator to d-q axes.
   From above, the correct answer is
   (*a*) A, B, D (*b*) A, B, C (*c*) B, C, D (*d*) A, C, D.
9. If $[C]$ is the transformation or connection matrix from old to new set of variables, then the new impedance matrix is given by
   (A) $[C_t]\ [Z]\ [C]$ (B) $[C]\ [Z]\ [C_t]$ (C) $[C_t^*]\ [Z]\ [C]$ (D) $[C]\ [Z]\ [C_t^*]$
   From above, the correct answer is
   (*a*) A, B (*b*) B, C (*c*) C, D (*d*) A, C.
10. The torque produced in a 4-pole machine is 100 Nm. If this machine is re-wound with 6 poles, other things remaining unchanged, then the torque produced would be
    (*a*) 66.67 Nm (*b*) 100 Nm (*c*) 150 Nm (*d*) 133.33 Nm.

11. A 3-phase, 4-pole, 60 Hz, squirrel cage induction motor develops a torque of 360 Nm at rated phase voltage of 240 V. If 3-phase stator is re-wound with 2-phase stator winding for 6 poles and with the same number of turns per phase and the same conductor size, then rated phase voltage of the 2-phase induction motor would be

   (*a*) 160 V (*b*) 240 V (*c*) 300 V (*d*) 360 V.

12. For question No. 11, the 2-phase induction motor torque, if it is connected to rated 2-phase supply of 50 Hz system, would be

   (*a*) 192 Nm (*b*) 240 Nm (*c*) 288 Nm (*d*) 360 Nm.

13. For question No. 11, if the two-phase induction motor is energized from its rated 2-phase voltage at 60 Hz, then the torque would be

   (*a*) 192 Nm (*b*) 240 Nm (*c*) 288 Nm (*d*) 360 Nm.

14. A 3-phase, 8-pole, 50 Hz SCIM develops a torque of 200 Nm at rated phase voltage of 240 V. The 3-phase stator is rewound with 2-phase stator winding for 6 poles and with the same conductor size. If total number of stator turns in both 3-phase and 2-phase induction motors are the same, then rated phase voltage for 2-phase induction motor would be

   (*a*) 160 V (*b*) 240 V (*c*) 300 V (*d*) 360 V.

15. For question No. 14, the 2-phase induction motor torque, if it is energized from its rated 2-phase voltage at 50 Hz, would be

   (*a*) 125 Nm (*b*) 150 Nm (*c*) 175 Nm (*d*) 200 Nm.

16. For Question No. 14, if the 2-phase stator winding is energized from its rated 2-phase voltage of 60 Hz supply, then the torque would be

   (*a*) 125 Nm (*b*) 150 Nm (*c*) 175 Nm (*d*) 200 Nm.

ANSWERS

1. (*d*)	**2.** (*d*)	**3.** (*d*)	**4.** (*a*)	**5.** (*b*)	**6.** (*c*)
7. (*c*)	**8.** (*a*)	**9.** (*d*)	**10.** (*c*)	**11.** (*a*)	**12.** (*c*)
13. (*b*)	**14.** (*d*)	**15.** (*b*)	**16.** (*a*)		

D.C. MACHINES

1. A separately-excited d.c. generator is running at rated speed and at no load. If its field winding is suddenly connected to a d.c. source, then rise in armature generated voltage is governed by

(*a*) armature time constant (*b*) field time constant

(*c*) both armature and field time constants (*d*) mechanical time constant.

2. A separately-excited d.c. generator is running at rated speed with its field winding unexcited. Its armature is, however, connected to a load. If its field winding is suddenly connected to a d.c. source, then the build-up of armature current is governed by

(*a*) both armature and field time constants

(*b*) armature, field and mechanical time constants

(*c*) field and mechanical time constants

(*d*) armature and mechanical time constants.

3. If a separately-excited d.c. generator is operated with its brushes displaced from neutral axis, then its

(*a*) terminal voltage V_t decrease but armature current I_a increases

(*b*) V_t increases, I_a decreases

(*c*) both V_t and I_a increase

(*d*) both V_t and I_a decrease.

4. The supply both to field and armature circuits is disconnected simultaneously in a separately-excited d.c. motor and it comes to a standstill in 5 seconds. If armature circuit of this motor is disconnected from the supply with its field circuit remaining energized, the motor would come to rest in

(*a*) 5 sec (*b*) 7 sec (*c*) 4 sec (*d*) a very long time.

5. A separately-excited d.c. generator develops a no-load emf of 240 V at 1000 rpm. When run as a d.c. separately-excited motor with the same field current and 31.416 A as its armature current, the torque developed would be

(*a*) 60 Nm (*b*) 72 Nm (*c*) 90 Nm (*d*) 120 Nm.

6. A separately excited dc motor has an armature circuit resistance of 1Ω. When fed from 230 V dc supply, the motor draws an armature current of 21 A at 100 r.p.m. For an armature current of 15 A and for the same field current, the torque developed will be

(*a*) 31.92 Nm (*b*) 39.6 Nm (*c*) 31.513 Nm (*d*) 32.52 Nm.

7. A d.c. shunt generator is floating on the bus bar. It can be loaded by

(A) increasing its driving torque (B) decreasing its driving torque

(C) increasing its field current (D) decreasing its field current.

From above, the correct answer is

(*a*) B, C (*b*) B, D (*c*) A, D (*d*) A, C.

8. For successful parallel operation of d.c. shunt generators, the essential condition is that they should have

(*a*) same output voltage (*b*) same voltage regulation

(*c*) drooping $V_t - I_L$ characteristics (*d*) all of these.

9. For successful parallel operation of two d.c. compound generators,

(A) the equalizer resistance r_e should be very small as compared to series field resistance r_s

(B) r_e should be more than r_s

(C) r_s should be proportional to their ratings

(D) r_s should be inversely proportional to their ratings.

From above, the correct answer is

(*a*) A, C (*b*) A, D (*c*) B, C (*d*) B, D.

10. For successful parallel operation of d.c. generators, equalizer is required for

(*a*) series generators only (*b*) over-compounded generators only

(*c*) series and over compounded generators (*d*) series and undercompounded generators.

11. Plugging of d.c. motors is carried out by

(*a*) reversing both the field and armature polarities

(*b*) reversing only the field polarity

(*c*) reversing only the armature polarity

(*d*) disconnecting the armature from supply and connecting it across a resistance.

12. A 400 V, 50 A d.c. shunt motor has an armature resistance of 0.6 Ω. When running under rated conditions, the motor is braked by plugging. For limiting the initial armature current to 100 A, the external resistance in the armature circuit should be .... ohm.

13. In Question No. 12, if the motor is braked by dynamic braking, then the external resistance in the armature circuit at the moment of braking should be ..... ohm.

14. A 200 V d.c. shunt motor has torque constant of 4 Nm/A and armature circuit resistance of 0.4 Ω. For obtaining a regenerative braking torque of 200 Nm, the motor must be driven at a speed of .... rad/sec.

15. Two d.c. shunt generators, in parallel, share a load current of 125 A. Each generator has an armature resistance of 0.2 Ω and a field resistance of 120 Ω. The no-load generated emfs of these two machines are 245 V and 248 V. The current, in amperes, shared by generators 1 and 2 respectively are,

(*a*) 50, 75 (*b*) 75, 50 (*c*) 60, 65 (*d*) 65, 60.

16. Two compound generators are connected in parallel. If equalizer bar is not used

(*a*) one of the generators may stop (*b*) both generators may start hunting

(*c*) one of the generators may run as a motor

(*d*) both the generators may stop.

17. A d.c. shunt motor runs at 500 rpm at 220 V. A resistance of 4.5 ohm is added in series with the armature for speed control. The armature resistance is 0.5 ohms. The current to stall the motor will be

(*a*) 44 A (*b*) 50 A (*c*) 44.4 A (*d*) 60 A.

18. Consider the following statements regarding speed control of d.c. motors :

1. Ward-Leonard method is suitable for constant torque drives.
2. Field-control method facilitates speed control below base speed.
3. Armature-resistance-control method is more efficient when compared to Ward-Leonard method.
4. Field-control method is suitable for constant power drives.

From these statements, the correct are

(*a*) 1, 2 and 3 (*b*) 1, 3 and 4 (*c*) 2, 3 and 4 (*d*) 1 and 4.

19. Match List I with List II and select the correct answer using the codes given below the Lists :

LIST I	*LIST II*
A. Self-excitation of d.c. generators	1. Efficient and smooth speed control over a wide range
B. Speed control of a 3-phase induction motor by varying rotor resistance	2. Constant power applications
C. Speed control of a d.c. motor by field weakening	3. Associated with variation of load resistance, speed and field resistance
D. Variation of applied voltage to an induction motor with varying stator frequency.	4. Constant torque applications
	5. Dangerously high speeds at no-load.

Codes

(*a*) *A* *B* *C* *D*
3 4 5 1

(*b*) *A* *B* *C* *D*
3 4 2 1

(*c*) *A* *B* *C* *D*
3 2 4 5

(*d*) *A* *B* *C* *D*
4 3 2 5

20. Consider the following statements :

If the terminal voltage of a d.c. shunt motor is halved with the load torque varying as the square of speed, then

1. speed is halved
2. speed remains unaltered
3. armature current is doubled
4. armature current remains unaltered.

From these statements, the correct are

(*a*) 1 and 3 (*b*) 1 and 4 (*c*) 2 and 3 (*d*) 2 and 4.

21. For continuously running rolling mills with intermittent loading, the most suitable d.c. drive is a

(*a*) d.c. series motor (*b*) d.c. shunt motor

(*c*) d.c. differentialy compounded motor

(*d*) d.c. cumulatively compounded motor coupled to a heavy flywheel.

22. Neglecting all losses, the developed torque (*T*) of a d.c. separately-excited motor, operating under constant terminal voltage, is related to its output power (*P*) as under :

(*a*) $T \propto \sqrt{P}$ (*b*) $T \propto P$ (*c*) $T^2 \propto P^3$ (*d*) *T* independent of *P*.

23. Division of load between two dc shunt generators operating in parallel can be controlled more easily by

(*a*) adjustment of speeds (*b*) adjustment of field currents

(*c*) adjustment of armature circuit resistances

(*d*) using equalizer connections.

24. A pair of similar dc shunt generators operate in parallel and supply a common load. It is required to switch off machine number 1 and allow machine number 2 to supply the circuit load. The following operations are to be used to achieve this.

1. Switch off the main switch of machine 1.
2. Reduce the field current of machine 1.

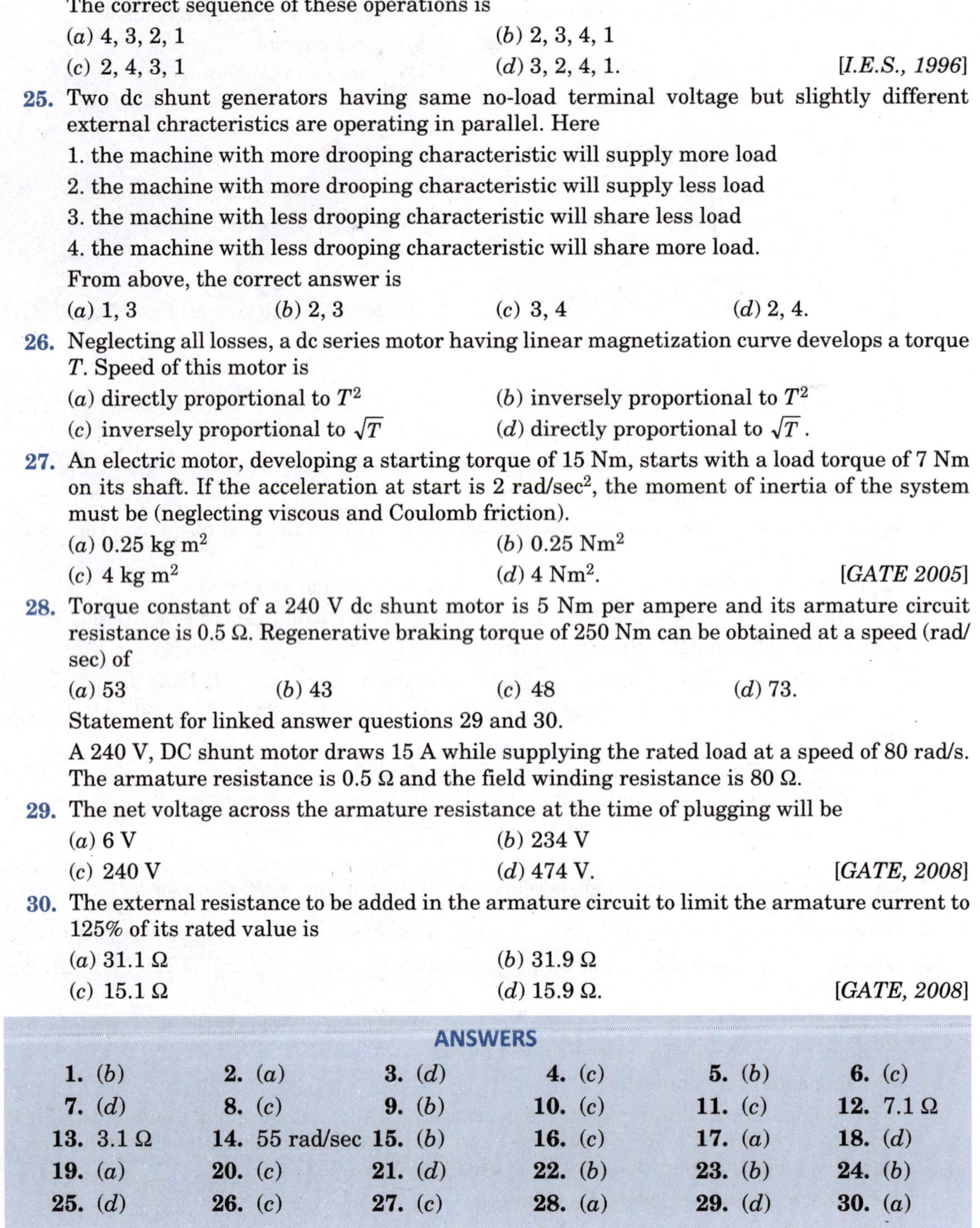

3. Increase the field curernt of machine 2.
4. Ensure that machine 1 just floats.

The correct sequence of these operations is

(*a*) 4, 3, 2, 1 (*b*) 2, 3, 4, 1
(*c*) 2, 4, 3, 1 (*d*) 3, 2, 4, 1. [*I.E.S., 1996*]

25. Two dc shunt generators having same no-load terminal voltage but slightly different external chracteristics are operating in parallel. Here

1. the machine with more drooping characteristic will supply more load
2. the machine with more drooping characteristic will supply less load
3. the machine with less drooping characteristic will share less load
4. the machine with less drooping characteristic will share more load.

From above, the correct answer is

(*a*) 1, 3 (*b*) 2, 3 (*c*) 3, 4 (*d*) 2, 4.

26. Neglecting all losses, a dc series motor having linear magnetization curve develops a torque *T*. Speed of this motor is

(*a*) directly proportional to T^2 (*b*) inversely proportional to T^2
(*c*) inversely proportional to $\sqrt{T}$ (*d*) directly proportional to $\sqrt{T}$.

27. An electric motor, developing a starting torque of 15 Nm, starts with a load torque of 7 Nm on its shaft. If the acceleration at start is 2 rad/sec^2, the moment of inertia of the system must be (neglecting viscous and Coulomb friction).

(*a*) 0.25 kg m^2 (*b*) 0.25 Nm^2
(*c*) 4 kg m^2 (*d*) 4 Nm^2. [*GATE 2005*]

28. Torque constant of a 240 V dc shunt motor is 5 Nm per ampere and its armature circuit resistance is 0.5 Ω. Regenerative braking torque of 250 Nm can be obtained at a speed (rad/sec) of

(*a*) 53 (*b*) 43 (*c*) 48 (*d*) 73.

Statement for linked answer questions 29 and 30.

A 240 V, DC shunt motor draws 15 A while supplying the rated load at a speed of 80 rad/s. The armature resistance is 0.5 Ω and the field winding resistance is 80 Ω.

29. The net voltage across the armature resistance at the time of plugging will be

(*a*) 6 V (*b*) 234 V
(*c*) 240 V (*d*) 474 V. [*GATE, 2008*]

30. The external resistance to be added in the armature circuit to limit the armature current to 125% of its rated value is

(*a*) 31.1 Ω (*b*) 31.9 Ω
(*c*) 15.1 Ω (*d*) 15.9 Ω. [*GATE, 2008*]

ANSWERS

1. (*b*)	**2.** (*a*)	**3.** (*d*)	**4.** (*c*)	**5.** (*b*)	**6.** (*c*)
7. (*d*)	**8.** (*c*)	**9.** (*b*)	**10.** (*c*)	**11.** (*c*)	**12.** 7.1 Ω
13. 3.1 Ω	**14.** 55 rad/sec	**15.** (*b*)	**16.** (*c*)	**17.** (*a*)	**18.** (*d*)
19. (*a*)	**20.** (*c*)	**21.** (*d*)	**22.** (*b*)	**23.** (*b*)	**24.** (*b*)
25. (*d*)	**26.** (*c*)	**27.** (*c*)	**28.** (*a*)	**29.** (*d*)	**30.** (*a*)

POLYPHASE SYNCHRONOUS MACHINES

1. If θ be the angle between phase-A axis and field-winding axis for a synchronous machine, the armature to field mutual inductance for phase B is

(A) $M_{afm} \cos \theta$ (B) $M_{afm} \cos (\theta - 120°)$

(C) $M_{afm} \cos (\theta + 120°)$ (D) $M_{afm} \cos (\theta - 240°)$.

From above, the correct answer is

(*a*) A, B (*b*) B, C (*c*) C, D (*d*) B, D.

2. If θ is the angle between phase-A axis and field-winding axis for a salient-pole machine, then armature self-inductance for phase B is

(*a*) $L_{ao} + L_{g2} \cos 2\theta$ (*b*) $L_{ao} + L_{g2} \cos (2\theta - 120°)$

(*c*) $L_{ao} + L_{g2} \cos (2\theta - 240°)$ (*d*) $-0.5\, L_{go} + L_{g2} \cos (2\theta - 240°)$.

3. If θ is the angle between phase-A axis and field-winding axis for a salient-pole machine, then armature mutual inductance between phases A and B is given by

(*a*) $-0.5\, L_{go} + L_{g2} \cos (2\theta - 120°)$ (*b*) $-0.5\, L_{go} + L_{g2} \cos 2\theta$

(*c*) $L_{ao} + L_{g2} \cos 2\theta$ (*d*) $-0.5\, L_{go} + L_{g2} \cos (2\theta - 240°)$.

4. If θ is the angle between phase-A and field-winding axes, then for phase A of a cylindrical-rotor synchronous machine

(A) armature to field mutual inductance is $M_{afm} \cos \theta$

(B) armature to field mutual inductance is M_{afm}

(C) armature self-inductance is $L_{ao} + L_{g2} \cos 2\theta$

(D) armature self-inductance is $l_a + L_{go}$

From above, the correct statement is

(*a*) A, C (*b*) B, C (*c*) B, D (*d*) A, D.

5. Self-inductance for phase-A of a 3-phase salient-pole machine is 18 + 4 cos 2θ mH and its leakage inductance is 2 mH. The ratio of X_d to X_q for this machine is

(*a*) $\frac{8}{5}$ (*b*) $\frac{9}{2}$ (*c*) $\frac{5}{3}$ (*d*) 4.

6. For Question 5 above, the ratio of X_{ad} to X_{aq} is

(*a*) $\frac{8}{5}$ (*b*) $\frac{9}{2}$ (*c*) $\frac{5}{3}$ (*d*) 4.

7. In the generalized model of a 3-phase synchronous machine, the open-circuit voltages are

(*a*) $v_{do} = 0, v_{qo} = 0$ (*b*) $v_{do} = M_d\, w\, I_f, v_{qo} = 0$

(*c*) $v_{do} = 0, v_q = M_d w I_f$ (*d*) $v_{do} = v_{qo} = M_d\, w\, I_f$.

8. A 4-pole, 3-phase, 50 Hz, star-connected uniform air-gap synchronous machine has mutual inductance between field and armature windings as 0.4 H (maximum). For a field current of 3 A, its excitation line voltage is

(*a*) π (110.23) V (*b*) π (73.48) V (*c*) π (63.643) V (*d*) π (90) V.

9. A salient-pole alternator has $X_d = 1.2$, $X_q = 1.0$, $r_a = 0$. If this alternator delivers rated kVA at unity pf and at rated voltage, its load angle is

(*a*) 60° (*b*) 90° (*c*) 45° (*d*) 30°.

10. For Question 9 above, the excitation voltage is

(*a*) 1.4142 (*b*) 1.5554 (*c*) 1.2726 (*d*) 1.6968.

11. A salient-pole alternator had $X_q = 0.7856$ pu and $r_a = 0$. If this generator delivers rated kVA at 0.8 pf lagging and at rated voltage, then its load angle is

(*a*) 60° (*b*) 36.9° (*c*) 23.1° (*d*) 25°.

12. SCR for a synchronous machine is the reciprocal of

(A) X_d in Ω (B) X_d in pu (C) X_s in Ω (D) X_s in pu.

From above, the correct answer is

(*a*) *A*, *C* (*b*) *B*, *D* (*c*) *A*, *D* (*d*) *B*, *C*.

13. Typical value of SCR for modern turboalternator is

(*a*) 1 (*b*) 1.2 (*c*) 0.5 (*d*) 1.5.

14. Typical values of SCR for hydrogenerators and synchronous condensers are respectively

(*a*) 1, 0.4 (*b*) 0.4, 1 (*c*) 1.5, 1 (*d*) 1, 0.8.

15. Per unit synchronous impedance of a synchronous machine is 1.20. Its SCR is

(*a*) 1.20 (*b*) 0.833 (*c*) 1.10 (*d*) 0.417.

16. A synchronous machine with large SCR has

(*a*) poor voltage regulation (*b*) poor stability

(*c*) low short-circuit current (*d*) more synchronizing power.

17. A synchronous machine with high value of SCR has

(*a*) bigger size (*b*) smaller size

(*c*) machine size independent of SCR (*d*) none of these.

18. In a 3-phase synchronous machine, if its air-gap length is increased, then for the same excitation voltage, its cost

(*a*) increases (*b*) decreases

(*c*) is unaffected by air-gap length (*d*) may increase or decrease.

19. A sudden 3-phase short circuit across an unloaded alternator was applied and armature current oscillograms were recorded. It was found that phase *A* current has no d.c. component. It means that at the instant of short circuit, axis of phase *A* was

(*a*) aligned along the field winding axis (FWA)

(*b*) displaced by 30° from FWA

(*c*) displaced by 90° from FWA

(*d*) displaced by 180° from FWA

20. During 3-phase short-circuit test on an unloaded alternator, the d.c. component may be zero in

(*a*) one phase only (*b*) any two phases

(*c*) all the three phases (*d*) none of the phases.

21. During 3-phase short-circuit test on an unloaded alternator, maximum value of d.c. component in the armature current is

(*a*) E_{fo}/X'_d (*b*) E_{fo}/X''_d (*c*) $\sqrt{2}\,E_{fo}/X'_d$ (*d*) $\sqrt{2}\,E_{fo}/X''_d$.

22. In case of 3-phase short circuit test, the maximum value of armature-phase current after one half cycle is

(*a*) $\sqrt{2}\,E_{fo}/X''_d$ (*b*) $2.\sqrt{2}\,E_{fo}/X'_d$ (*c*) $2\sqrt{2}\,E_{fo}/X''_d$ (*d*) $3\sqrt{2}\,E_{fo}/X''_d$.

23. In practice, maximum possible value of the sudden short-circuit armature current in a 3-phase alternator is taken as

(*a*) $2.\sqrt{2}\,E_{fo}/X''_d$ (*b*) $1.8\sqrt{2}\,E_{fo}/X''_d$ (*c*) $\sqrt{2}\,E_{fo}/X''_d$ (*d*) $3.\sqrt{2}\,E_{fo}/X''_d$.

24. In case prefault excitation voltage is 1.0 pu, then the minimum permissible value of X''_d for a salient-pole synchronous machine is

(*a*) 0.20 (*b*) 0.24 (*c*) 0.12 (*d*) 0.36.

25. A turbogenerator has no-load terminal voltage equal to 1.0 pu and X_d = 1.00 pu, X'_d = 0.20 p.u. When inductive load of X_L = 2.0 is suddenly applied, the load terminal voltage at $t = 0+$ is

(*a*) 0.91 (*b*) 0.667 (*c*) 1.00 (*d*) 0.8.

26. In Question 25 above, the steady-state terminal voltage across the load is

(*a*) 0.333 (*b*) 0.554 (*c*) 0.60 (*d*) 0.667.

27. A turbogenerator with X'_d = 0.2 pu is feeding a purely inductive load with X_L = 2 pu. The voltage across X_L is 1.00 pu. If now X_L is disconnected, the alternator terminal voltage at once

(*a*) reduces to 0.91 pu (*b*) rises to 1.1 pu
(*c*) rises to 1.2 pu (*d*) remains 1.0 pu.

28. The armature time constant T_a is applicable to

(A) d.c. component of armature current
(B) second harmonic component of armature current
(C) fundamental frequency component of armature current
(D) fundamental frequency component of field current

From above, the correct statement is

(*a*) A, B (*b*) A, B, C (*c*) A, B, D (*d*) B, C, D.

29. The various components of armature short-circuit current of a 3-phase alternator without amortisseurs are

(A) subtransient component (B) transient component
(C) second-harmonic component (D) d.c. component
(E) fundamental frequency component

From above, the correct statement is

(*a*) all the five (*b*) B, C, D (*c*) A, B, C, D (*d*) B, C, D, E.

30. In a salient-pole synchronous machine, the *d*-axis transient reactance X'_d is given by

(*a*) $\frac{1}{x_a} + \frac{1}{x_f} + \frac{1}{X_{md}}$ (*b*) $x_a + \frac{1}{x_f} + \frac{1}{X_{md}}$

(*c*) $x_a + \frac{x_f \,.\, X_{md}}{x_f + X_{md}}$ (*d*) $x_a + X_{md}$.

31. For a salient-pole synchronous machine

(*a*) $X_d = X_d' > X_d''$ (*b*) $X_q = X_q' > X_q''$
(*c*) $X_q' = X_q'' > X_d''$ (*d*) $X_d'' = X_q'' > X_2$.

32. In a synchronous machine, the effect of X_d'' and X_q'' is manifested only during

(*a*) steady state operation (*b*) transient operation
(*c*) subtransient operation (*d*) both (*a*) and (*c*).

33. In a 3-phase synchronous machine,

(*a*) $X_2 > x_0 > x_d''$ (*b*) $X_d'' > X_q'' > x_0$ (*c*) $X_q'' > X_2 > x_0$ (*d*) $X_q'' > X_2 < x_0$.

34. In a 3-phase synchronous machine,

(*a*) $T_{do}' > T_a > T_{do}''$ (*b*) $T_{do}' > T_{do}'' > T_a$ (*c*) $T_{do}' > T_a > T_d'$ (*d*) $T_d' > T_{do}' > T_d''$.

35. In a 3-phase synchronous machine, negative-sequence reactance is given by

(*a*) $(X_d'' - X_q'')/2$ (*b*) $(X_q'' - X_d'')/2$ (*c*) $(X_d'' + X_q'')/2$ (*d*) X_d''.

36. A salient-pole alternator develops a maximum power of 1.5 pu under steady state conditions. The amplitude of power developed under transient conditions and the corresponding load angle are, respectively

(*a*) 1.5 pu, $\delta = 90°$ (*b*) 2.0 pu, $\delta > 90°$ (*c*) 3.8, $\delta > 90°$ (*d*) 3.8, $\delta < 90°$.

37. A symmetrical 3-phase sudden short circuit was applied to an unloaded 3-phase alternator and current oscillograms were recorded. At the instant of short circuit, the peak value of alternating component of current was I_1, the d.c. component of current was I_d and the rms value of steady-state short circuit current was I_2. The excitation voltage before the short circuit was E_{fo}. The values of X_d and X_d'' are given by

(*a*) $X_d = \dfrac{\sqrt{2}\,.\,E_{fo}}{I_2},\; X_d'' = \dfrac{\sqrt{2}\,E_{fo}}{I_1 + I_d}$ (*b*) $X_d = \dfrac{E_{fo}}{I_2},\; X_d'' = \dfrac{\sqrt{2}\,E_{fo}}{I_1}$

(*c*) $X_d = \dfrac{E_{fo}}{I_1 + I_d},\; X_d'' = \dfrac{E_{fo}}{I_1 + I_d}$ (*d*) $X_d = \dfrac{2E_{fo}}{I_2 + I_d},\; X_d'' = \dfrac{2\sqrt{2}\,E_{fo}}{I_1 + I_d}$.

38. If x_a, x_f, x_{kd} and X_{md} are respectively the armature leakage reactance, field leakage reactance, *d*-axis damper winding leakage reactance and the *d*-axis mutual reactance, then X_d and X_d'' are expressed as

(*a*) $X_d = x_f + X_{md},\; X_d'' = x_a + x_f + x_{kd} + X_{md}$

(*b*) $X_d = x_a + X_{md},\; X_d'' = \dfrac{1}{\dfrac{1}{x_f} + \dfrac{1}{x_{kd}} + \dfrac{1}{X_{md}}}$

(*c*) $X_d = x_{kd} + X_{md},\; X_d'' = \dfrac{1}{x_a} + \dfrac{1}{\dfrac{1}{x_f} + \dfrac{1}{x_{kd}} + \dfrac{1}{X_{md}}}$

(*d*) $X_d = x_a + X_{md},\; X_d'' = x_a + \dfrac{1}{\dfrac{1}{x_f} + \dfrac{1}{x_{kd}} + \dfrac{1}{X_{md}}}$.

39. A synchronous generator has higher power handling capability when operating at

(*a*) a leading pf (*b*) a lagging pf

(*c*) it does not depend upon the pf of the generator

(*d*) it depends upon the load pf, as generator has no pf of its own.

40. In a synchronous machine connected to an infinite bus, if rotor speed departs from synchronous speed, then

(*a*) damping power comes into play (*b*) synchronizing power comes into play

(*c*) both (*a*) and (*b*) (*d*) none of these.

41. In a synchronous machine connected to an infinite bus, if rotor speed departs from synchronous speed, then the rotor oscillations can be investigated by including the

(A) damping power (B) synchronous power

(C) inertia power (D) shaft power.

From above, the correct answer is

(*a*) all of these (*b*) A, B, C (*c*) A, B, D (*d*) B, C, D.

42. In a synchronous machine connected to an infinite bus, if rotor speed N_r departs from synchronous speed N_s, then

(A) induction motor (IM) torque is developed if $N_r > N_s$

(B) IM torque is developed if $N_r < N_s$

(C) induction generator (IG) torque is developed if $N_r > N_s$

(D) IG torque is developed if $N_r < N_s$.

From these, the correct answer is

(*a*) A, C (*b*) A, D (*c*) B, C (*d*) B, D.

43. In a synchronous machine, synchronized with infinite bus, the resultant air-gap flux wave (AG) coincides with the field-pole (FP) axis at no load. As a generator, a sudden increment in the shaft power input would cause

(*a*) AG axis to go ahead of FP axis (*b*) AG axis to fall behind the FP axis

(*c*) AG axis to remain in line with FP axis; otherwise the synchronous machine will fall out of step

(*d*) none of these.

44. In a synchronous machine directly connected to a large power system network, the resultant air-gap flux wave (AG) coincides with the field-pole (FP) axis at no load. As a motor, a sudden increment of shaft load would cause

(*a*) AG axis to go ahead of FP axis (*b*) AG axis to fall behind FP axis

(*c*) AG axis to remain in line with FP axis, otherwise the synchronous machine will fall out of step

(*d*) none of these.

45. If J is the moment of inertia in kg.m^2, then inertia power P_j in watts per electrical rad/sec^2 is given by

(*a*) $\frac{8\pi f}{P^2} J$ (*b*) $\frac{4\pi f}{P^2} J$ (*c*) $\frac{8\pi f}{P} J$ (*d*) $\frac{P^2}{8\pi f} J$.

46. A 3-phase synchronous motor is running at synchronous speed N_s and is delivering power P_1 as shown in Fig. A-1. If shaft load is suddenly increased to P_2, then during the first forward swing of the rotor from A to C;

Fig. A-1

(A) from A to B rotor decelerates and at B, rotor speed $< N_s$

(B) from A to B rotor accelerates and at B, rotor speed $< N_s$

(C) from B to C rotor decelerates and at C, rotor speed $= N_s$

(D) from B to C rotor accelerates and at C, rotor speed $= N_s$.

From the above, the correct is

(*a*) A, C (*b*) A, D (*c*) B, C (*d*) B, D.

47. In Question 46, during the first backward swing of the rotor from C to A;

(A) from C to B rotor decelerates and at B, rotor speed $> N_s$

(B) from C to B rotor accelerates and at B, rotor speed $> N_s$

(C) from B to C rotor decelerates and at A, rotor speed $= N_s$

(D) from B to A rotor accelerates and at A, rotor speed $= N_s$.

From these the correct answer is

(*a*) A, C (*b*) A, D (*c*) B, C (*d*) B, D.

48. An alternator is running at synchronous speed N_s and is delivering power P_1 as shown in Fig. A-1. If steam input is suddenly increased to P_2, then during the first forward swing of the rotor from A to C;

(A) from A to B rotor decelerates and at B, rotor speed $< N_s$

(B) from A to B rotor accelerates and at B, rotor speed $> N_s$

(C) from B to C rotor decelerates and at C, rotor speed $= N_s$

(D) from B to C rotor accelerates and at C, rotor speed $= N_s$.

From above, the correct answer is

(*a*) A, C (*b*) A, D (*c*) B, C (*d*) B, D.

49. In Q. 48, during the first backward swing of the rotor from C to A;

(A) from C to B rotor decelerates and at B, rotor speed $< N_s$

(B) from C to B rotor accelerates and at B, rotor speed $< N_s$

(C) from B to A rotor decelerates and at A, rotor speed $= N_s$

(D) from B to A rotor accelerates and at A, rotor speed $= N_s$.

From above, the correct answer is

(*a*) A, C (*b*) A, D (*c*) B, C (*d*) B, D.

50. An alternator of frequency 50.2 Hz is to be synchronized with an infinite bus of frequency 50 Hz by means of three-dark-lamp method. The lamp-flicker per minute will be

(*a*) 6 (*b*) 25 (*c*) 30.6 (*d*) 12.

51. An alternator with frequency f_1 is to be synchronized with an infinite bus of frequency f. For proper synchronization,

(*a*) $f_1 = f$ (*b*) $f_1 < f$ (*c*) $f_1 > f$ (*d*) either (*b*) or (*c*).

52. A 3-phase alternator with line voltage V_L is to be synchronized with infinite bus. The maximum value of rms voltage across synchronizing switch would be

(*a*) $\sqrt{3}V_L$ (*b*) $2V_L$ (*c*) $2V_L/\sqrt{3}$ (*d*) $\sqrt{3}V_L/2$.

53. One alternator, with subtransient reactance of 0.25 pu, is to be synchronized with infinite bus by three-dark-lamp method. If the synchronizing switch is closed when the lamps are the brightest, then the synchronizing current would be

(*a*) 2 pu (*b*) 4 pu (*c*) 5 pu (*d*) 8 pu

54. An alternator of 300 kW is driven by a prime-mover of speed regulation 4% and another alternator of 400 kW by a prime-mover (PM) of speed regulation 5%. Governor settings of PMs are such that their no-load speed is the same. The total load the two alternators in parallel can take, without overloading any one of the two, is

(*a*) 600 kW (*b*) 620 kW (*c*) 650 kW (*d*) 720 kW.

55. In case of alternators, synchronous reactance is

(A) helpful for auto-synchronization of two alternators

(B) bad during the parallel operation of alternators

(C) helpful for the voltage regulation

(D) bad for the voltage regulation.

From above, the correct answer is

(*a*) A, C (*b*) A, D (*c*) B, C (*d*) B, D.

56. Two alternators running in parallel and supplying a fixed load operate with the same excitation voltages and the same armature currents. If steam input to alternator 1 is increased, then

(A) alternator 1 shares increased armature current I_a with improved pf

(B) alternator 1 shares increased I_a with worsened pf

(C) alternator 2 shares decreased I_a with improved pf

(D) alternator 2 shares decreased I_a with worsened pf.

From these, the correct answer is

(*a*) A, C (*b*) A, D (*c*) B, C (*d*) B, D.

57. Two alternators, with excitation voltages E_{f1} and E_{f2} are in parallel at no load. If E_{f1} is increased with no change in prime-mover input, then

(A) circulating current I_c is set up which magnetizes alternator 1

(B) I_c is setup which de-magnetizes alternator 1

(C) I_c is setup which magnetizes alternator 2

(D) I_c is setup but it produces no magnetizing effect.

From these, the correct answer is

(*a*) A, C (*b*) A, D (*c*) B, C (*d*) B, D.

58. Two alternators running in parallel have the same excitation voltages and armature currents and same pfs. If excitation of alternator 1 is increased, then for the same terminal voltage

(A) alternator 1 operates at a poor pf with increased armature current I_a

(B) alternator 1 operates at a better pf with increased I_a

(C) alternator 2 operates at a poor pf with decreased I_a

(D) alternator 2 operates at a better pf with decreased I_a.

From above, the correct answer is

(*a*) A, C (*b*) A, D (*c*) B, C (*d*) B, D.

59. The division of active power amongst alternators running in parallel depends upon

(*a*) speed-load characteristics of prime-movers

(*b*) volt-ampere characteristics of alternators

(*c*) excitation emfs of alternators

(*d*) all of these.

60. The division of reactive power amongst alternators running in parallel depends upon

(A) speed-load characteristics of prime-movers

(B) volt-ampere characteristics of alternators

(C) excitation voltages of alternators

From these, the correct answer is

(*a*) A, B (*b*) A, C (*c*) B, C (*d*) all of these.

61. An alternator is synchronized with infinite bus. Now if its field current is decreased, then its armature current

(*a*) increases with zero pf lagging (*b*) decreases with zero pf leading

(*c*) increases with zero pf leading (*d*) increases at any value of pf.

62. An alternator is synchronized with infinite bus. Now its field current is increased. With this, alternator armature current

(*a*) increases with zero pf lagging (*b*) increases with zero pf leading
(*c*) decreases with zero pf lagging (*d*) decreases with zero pf leading.

63. A 3-phase synchronous machine is synchronized with infinite bus. Now the prime-mover is disconnected from the synchronous machine. With this, the synchronous machine would
(*a*) work as a synchronous motor at a leading pf
(*b*) work as a synchronous motor at a lagging pf
(*c*) work as a 3-phase induction motor at a lagging pf
(*d*) stop.

64. A 3-phase synchronous machine is synchronized with an infinite bus. Now steam input to synchronous machine is increased. With this, synchronous machine starts working as
(*a*) alternator at a leading pf (*b*) alternator at a lagging pf
(*c*) synchronous motor at a leading pf (*d*) induction generator at a lagging pf.

65. A 3-phase alternator is supplying power to infinite bus at lagging pf. With constant steam input, alternator excitation is increased. With this,
(*a*) load angle δ decreases and pf increases (*b*) δ increases and pf decreases
(*c*) both δ and pf decrease (*d*) both δ and pf increase.

66. A synchronous machine has excitation voltage of $0.8 \angle 15°$ and the infinite bus voltage of 1.0 $\angle 0°$. The synchronous machine is working as
(*a*) an alternator and delivers reactive power at leading pf
(*b*) an alternator and absorbs reactive power at leading pf
(*c*) a synchronous motor and delivers reactive power at leading pf
(*d*) a synchronous motor and absorbs reactive power at lagging pf.

67. For a synchronous machine, the phasor diagram of Fig. A-2 (*a*) gets modified to that shown in Fig. A-2 (*b*). For this machine,

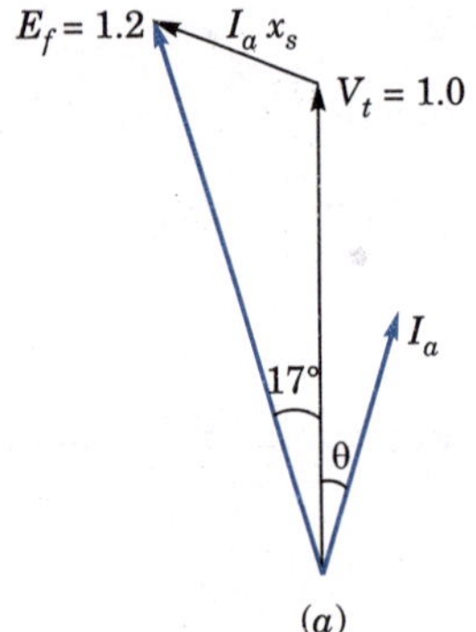

(*a*)

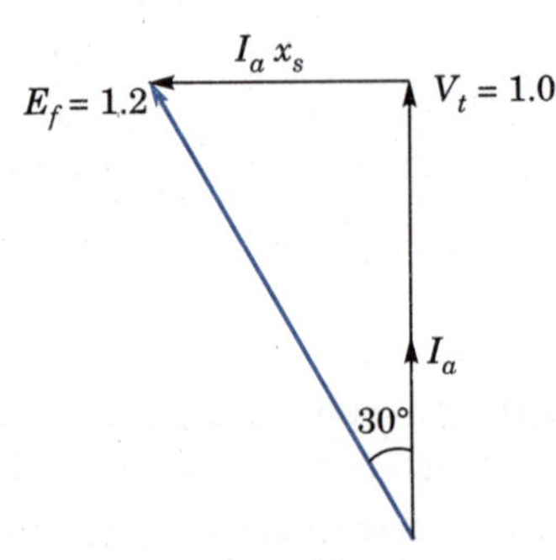

(*b*)

Fig. A-2

(*a*) field current has been increased (*b*) prime-mover input has been increased
(*c*) shaft load has been increased (*d*) prime-mover input has been reduced.

68. An alternator, driven by a d.c. shunt motor, is delivering power to an infinite bus. Now field current of d.c. motor is increased and as a consequence of it,
(*a*) speed ω_m decreases and alternator armature current I_a decreases
(*b*) ω_m increases and I_a decreases (*c*) ω_m remains constant and I_a increases
(*d*) ω_m remains constant and I_a decreases.

69. An alternator, driven by a d.c. shunt motor, is delivering 10 kW to an infinite bus. If field current of d.c. motor is increased, power flow from d.c. bus to a.c. bus would be

(*a*) > 10 kW (*b*) < 10 kW (*c*) 10 kW (*d*) reversed.

70. An alternator, driven by a d.c. shunt motor, is delivering 10 kW to an infinite bus. If the field current of dc motor is increased, power flow from d.c. bus to a.c. bus

(A) becomes more than 10 kW (B) becomes less than 10 kW

(C) remains 10 kW (D) may get reversed.

From above, the correct answer is

(*a*) A, B (*b*) B, D (*c*) A, D (*d*) C, D.

71. A 3-phase alternator is supplying active power to an infinite bus at a lagging pf. If its excitation is kept constant and steam input is increased, then

(*a*) load angle δ as well as armature current I_a increase but pf is worsened

(*b*) δ and I_a increase and pf is improved

(*c*) δ and I_a decrease and pf is improved

(*d*) δ increases, I_a decrease and pf is improved.

72. Two alternators of ratings 200 kVA and 300 kVA, working in parallel, are driven by prime-movers whose speed regulations are 3% and 5% respectively. The governor settings give the same no-load speed for the two prime-movers. A load of 190 kW will be shared by them, respectively, as

(*a*) 76 kW and 114 kW (*b*) 114 kW and 76 kW

(*c*) 100 kW and 90 kW (*d*) 90 kW and 100 kW.

73. A 3-phase synchronous generator is feeding rated power to an infinite bus. If its excitation fails, then it acts as a

(*a*) synchronous motor (*b*) synchronous generator

(*c*) reluctance generator (*d*) induction generator.

74. A 3-phase salient-pole alternator is delivering about 15% of its rated power to an infinite bus. If its excitation fails, then it acts as a

(*a*) synchronous motor (*b*) synchronous generator

(*c*) reluctance generator (*d*) induction generator.

75. Two alternators *A* and *B*, running in parallel, supply power to a resistive load. For the same terminal voltage and steam inputs, if excitation of alternator *A* is increased, then

(*a*) *A* will supply lagging kVAr

(*b*) *B* will supply leading kVAr

(*c*) As load is resistive, *A* cannot supply lagging kVAr

(*d*) As load is resistive, *B* cannot supply leading kVAr.

76. Two alternators *A* and *B*, running in parallel, supply power to a resistive load. For the same terminal voltage and steam inputs, if excitation of alternator *A* is increased, then

(A) *A* delivers reactive power at a leading pf

(B) *A* delivers reactive power at a lagging pf

(C) *B* absorbs reactive power at a leading pf

(D) *B* absorbs reactive power at a lagging pf

From these, the correct answer is

(*a*) B, D (*b*) A, C (*c*) B, C (*d*) A, D.

77. Two alternators A and B, running in parallel, share equal load for a total load power P. The load is resistive in nature. Driving torque of A is increased while that of B is adjusted so that load power P remains unchanged. With this, armature current I_a of alternator A and I_b of alternator B have the following relation :

(*a*) $I_a = I_b$ with I_a lagging I_b (*b*) $I_a = I_b$ with I_a leading I_b
(*c*) $I_a > I_b$ with I_a leading I_b (*d*) $I_a = I_b$ and both are in the same phase.

78. Two alternators A and B, running in parallel, supply power P to a resistive load. The two alternators share equal powers. For the same load power P, driving torque of alternator A is increased while that of B is suitably adjusted. With this,

(*a*) A supplies reactive power to load (*b*) B absorbs reactive power from load
(*c*) B delivers reactive power to A
(*d*) As load is resistive, no reactive power flow exists.

79. For Question 78,

(*a*) A delivers active and reactive powers to load
(*b*) A absorbs reactive power and delivers active power
(*c*) B absorbs both active and reactive powers
(*d*) As driving torques are only changed, there is no reactive power flow.

80. Prime-mover input to an alternator, delivering power to an infinite bus at a lagging pf, is gradually stopped and then prime-mover is disconnected from alternator. After this,

(*a*) it will stop (*b*) it will burn out
(*c*) it will act as a synchronous motor at a lagging pf
(*d*) it will act as a synchronous motor at a leading pf.

81. A 10 MVA, 11 kV, 3-phase star-connected alternator has $X_s = 1.1$ pu on machine rating. Its X_s in ohms is

(*a*) 26.61 Ω (*b*) 12 Ω (*c*) 6.655 Ω (*d*) 13.31 Ω.

82. For Question 81, if the alternator were delta connected, then X_s in ohms would be

(*a*) 26.61 Ω (*b*) 39.93 Ω (*c*) 13.31 Ω (*d*) 19.965 Ω.

83. A cylindrical-rotor alternator has a terminal voltage of 1 pu at a pf of 0.8 lagging. Its synchronous reactance is 1 pu on machine rating as the base. Its excitation voltage, with terminal voltage as the reference, is

(*a*) $1 + j0.8$ (*b*) $1.8 + j0.6$ (*c*) $1.6 + j0.8$ (*d*) $1.6 - j0.8$.

84. A uniform-air-gap synchronous motor is connected to an infinite bus of voltage $V_b = 1$ pu at pf 0.8 lagging. Its $X_s = 1$ pu on machine rating. Its excitation voltage, with V_b as reference, is

(*a*) $0.4 - j0.8$ (*b*) $1.6 + j0.8$ (*c*) $1.6 - j0.8$ (*d*) $0.4 + j0.8$

85. A 3-phase alternator is supplying power to an infinite bus at some pf. With constant steam input, its excitation is increased. With this, the following quantities would change :

(A) active power (B) reactive power (C) pf (D) armature current
(E) volt-amperes

From above, the correct answer is

(*a*) A, B, C, D (*b*) B, C, D, E (*c*) B, C, D (*d*) C, D, E, A.

86. Two alternators, working in parallel, supply power to a load. The excitation of one of them is increased. This will result in a change of their

(A) reactive powers (B) active powers
(C) terminal voltage (D) volt-amperes.

From above, the correct answer is

(*a*) A, B, C (*b*) A, C, D (*c*) B, C, D (*d*) A, D.

87. Two alternators supply power in parallel. Their kW and kVA sharing can be altered by changing respectively their

(*a*) driving torque and driving torque (*b*) excitation and driving torque
(*c*) driving torque and excitation (*d*) excitation and excitation.

88. Alternators 1 and 2 share inductive load equally. If excitation of alternator 1 is increased; then alternator 2 as compared to alternator 1 will deliver

(*a*) less current (*b*) more current (*c*) same current (*d*) zero current.

89. A cylindrical-rotor synchronous motor, connected to an infinite bus, is working with a load angle of 30°. If load on the synchronous motor is doubled, excitation remaining constant, then load angle would be

(*a*) 30° (*b*) 60° (*c*) 90° (*d*) 45°.

90. The maximum torque that a synchronous motor can deliver is proportional to

(*a*) $\frac{1}{V^2}$ (*b*) $\frac{1}{V}$ (*c*) V (*d*) V^2.

91. A 3-phase synchronous motor can be braked electrically by

(*a*) rheostatic braking (*b*) regenerative braking
(*c*) plugging (*d*) all of these.

92. When zero-sequence currents are flowing in the armature winding of a synchronous machine, the nature of air-gap field is

(*a*) rotating with constant amplitude (*b*) stationary but pulsating
(*c*) pulsating but rotating (*d*) stationary with constant amplitude.

93. When negative-sequence currents are flowing in the armature winding of a synchronous machine, the nature of air-gap field is

(*a*) rotating with constant amplitude against the direction of rotation
(*b*) rotating with varying amplitude against the direction of rotation
(*c*) rotating with constant amplitude in the direction of rotation
(*d*) stationary but pulsating.

94. Two similar synchronous generators are working in parallel to supply a common load demand with identical excitations and steam supplies to their prime-movers. Now, if the steam supply to the prime-mover of one of the generators is increased compared to the other, with field excitation kept unchanged, then

(*a*) its active power component will remain the same but the reactive power consumption will increase
(*b*) its active power will decrease while the reactive power will increase
(*c*) both active and reactive components of power will increase
(*d*) its active power contribution will increase but reactive power contribution of both will remain unchanged.

95. Two similar alternators running in parallel supply a common load demand with identical excitations and steam supplies to their prime-movers. Now, if the steam supply to the prime-mover of one of the alternators is increased compared to the other, with field excitation kept unchanged, then (*a*) its active power component will increase, reactive power component will decrease but operating frequency will remain unchanged

(*b*) its active power component, reactive power component and operating frequency, all will increase

(*c*) both its active power component and operating frequency will increase but its reactive power component will decrease

(*d*) both its active power component and operating frequency will increase but its reactive power component will remain unchanged.

96. Two similar alternators running in parallel supply a common load demand with identical excitations and steam supplies to their prime-movers. Now, if the excitation of one of the alternators is increased compared to the other, with its steam supply kept unchanged, then

(*a*) its active power component will remain unaltered, reactive power component will increase but the reactive power contributions of both will decrease

(*b*) both its active power and reactive power components will decrease but the reactive power contributions of both will increase

(*c*) its active power component as well as the reactive power contributions of both will remain unaltered but its reactive power component will decrease

(*d*) its active power component and the reactive power contributions of both will remain unaltered but its reactive power component will increase.

97. Consider the following statements :

1. A grid-connected induction generator always supplies leading reactive VARs to the bus
2. An overexcited synchronous motor draws current a lagging power factor
3. An under-excited synchronous generator connected to an infinite bus works at a leading power factor
4. The load angle of a synchronous machine is the angle between the excitation voltage and the gap voltage.

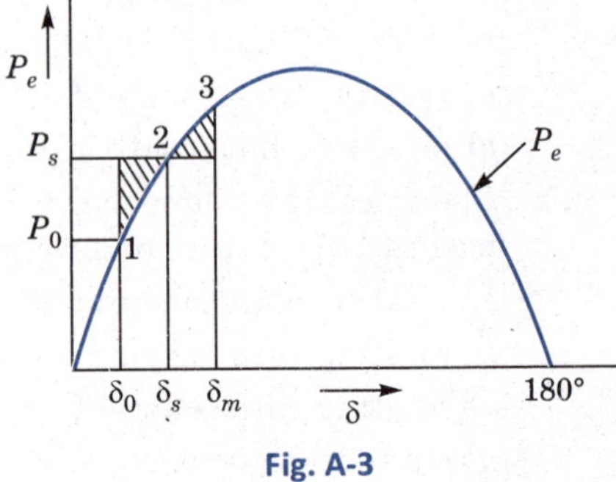

Fig. A-3

Of these statements, the correct are

(*a*) 1 and 2 (*b*) 2 and 3 (*c*) 1, 3 and 4 (*d*) 1, 2, 3 and 4.

98. Fig. A-3 shows electric power input P_e to a lose-less synchronous motor as a function of torque angle δ. The load is suddenly increased from P_o to P_s and the motor oscillates around δ_s between δ_0 and δ_m. List I given below shows the different positions in the oscillating cycle and List II gives the relationship between the motor kinetic energy *W* and the energy W_s at synchronous speed. Match List I with List II and select the correct answer using the codes given below the Lists.

List I (*Position in Oscillating Cycle*)	*List II* (*Relation between W and* W_s)
A. At point 1	1. $W = W_s$ and *W* is increasing
B. At point 2 while oscillating from 1 towards 3	2. $W > W_s$ and *W* is maximum
C. At point 3	3. $W < W_s$ and *W* is minimum
D. At point 2 while oscillating from 3 towards 1	4. $W = W_s$ and *W* is decreasing

Codes

	A	B	C	D			A	B	C	D
(*a*)	3	4	1	2		(*b*)	4	3	1	2
(*c*)	3	4	2	1		(*d*)	4	3	2	1

99. Fig. A-3 shows power-angle characteristic of a loss-less synchronous motor. The load is suddenly increased from P_o to P_s and the motor oscillates around δ_s between δ_o and δ_m. List I given below shows different positions in the oscillating cycle and List II gives the relationship between the motor speed ω_r and synchronous speed ω_s. Match List I with List II.

List I (*Position in Oscillating Cycle*)	*List II* (*Relation between ω_r and ω_s*)
A. $\delta_o < \delta < \delta_s$ while oscillating from 1 towards 2	1. $\omega_r > \omega_s$ and rotor accelerates
B. $\delta_s < \delta < \delta_m$ while oscillating from 2 towards 3	2. $\omega_r > \omega_s$ and rotor decelerates
C. $\delta_s < \delta < \delta_m$ while oscillating from 3 towards 2	3. $\omega_r < \omega_s$ and rotor decelerates
D. $\delta_o < \delta < \delta_s$ while oscillating from 2 towards 1	4. $\omega_r < \omega_s$ and rotor accelerates

(*a*) *A*–3, *B*–4, *C*–1, *D*–2 (*b*) *A*–2, *B*–3, *C*–4, *D*–1
(*c*) *A*–3, *B*–2, *C*–1, *D*–4 (*d*) *A*–1, *B*–3, *C*–2, *D*–4

100. A large synchronous generator is feeding power into an infinite bus at slightly lagging power factor. If a total loss of field occurs and the system can supply sufficient reactive power without a large terminal voltage drop, the unit will.

(*a*) continue to run as a synchronous generator and no tripping is necessary
(*b*) get short-circuited and it should be tripped instantaneously
(*c*) run as an induction generator and it should be tripped after a time delay
(*d*) run as a synchronous motor and it should be tripped after a time delay.

101. Two generators rated at 200 MW and 400 MW are operating in parallel. Their governor drop characteristics are respectively 4% and 5% from no-load to full-load. At no-load, the system frequency is 50 Hz. When supplying a load of 600 MW, the system frequency will be

(*a*) 50 Hz (*b*) 49 Hz (*c*) 51.3 Hz (*d*) 47.7 Hz.

102. Fig. A-3 shows power-angle characteristic of a loss-less synchronous generator connected to an infinite bus. The steam input to generator is suddenly increased from P_o to P_s and the rotor oscillates around δ_s between δ_o and δ_m. List I given below shows different positions in the oscillating cycle and List II gives the relationship between the rotor kinetic energy *W* and the energy W_s at synchronous speed. Match List I with List II.

List I	*List II*
(*A*) At point 1	1. $W = W_s$ and *W* is decreasing
(*B*) At point 2 while oscillating from 1 towards 3	2. $W = W_s$ and *W* is increasing
(*C*) At point 3	3. $W < W_s$ and *W* is minimum
(*D*) At point 2 while oscillating from 3 towards 1	4. $W > W_s$ and *W* is maximum

(*a*) *A*–2, *B*–4, *C*–1, *D*–3 (*b*) *A*–3, *B*–4, *C*–1, *D*–2
(*c*) *A*–2, *B*–4, *C*–1, *D*–3 (*d*) *A*–4, *B*–1, *C*–2, *D*–3

103. Fig. A-3 shows power-angle characteristic of a loss-less synchronous generator connected to infinite bus. The steam input to generator is suddenly increased from P_o to P_s and the rotor oscillates around δ_s between δ_o and δ_m. List I given below shows different positions in the oscillating cycle and List II gives relationship between the alternator speed ω_r and synchronous speed ω_s. Match List I with List II.

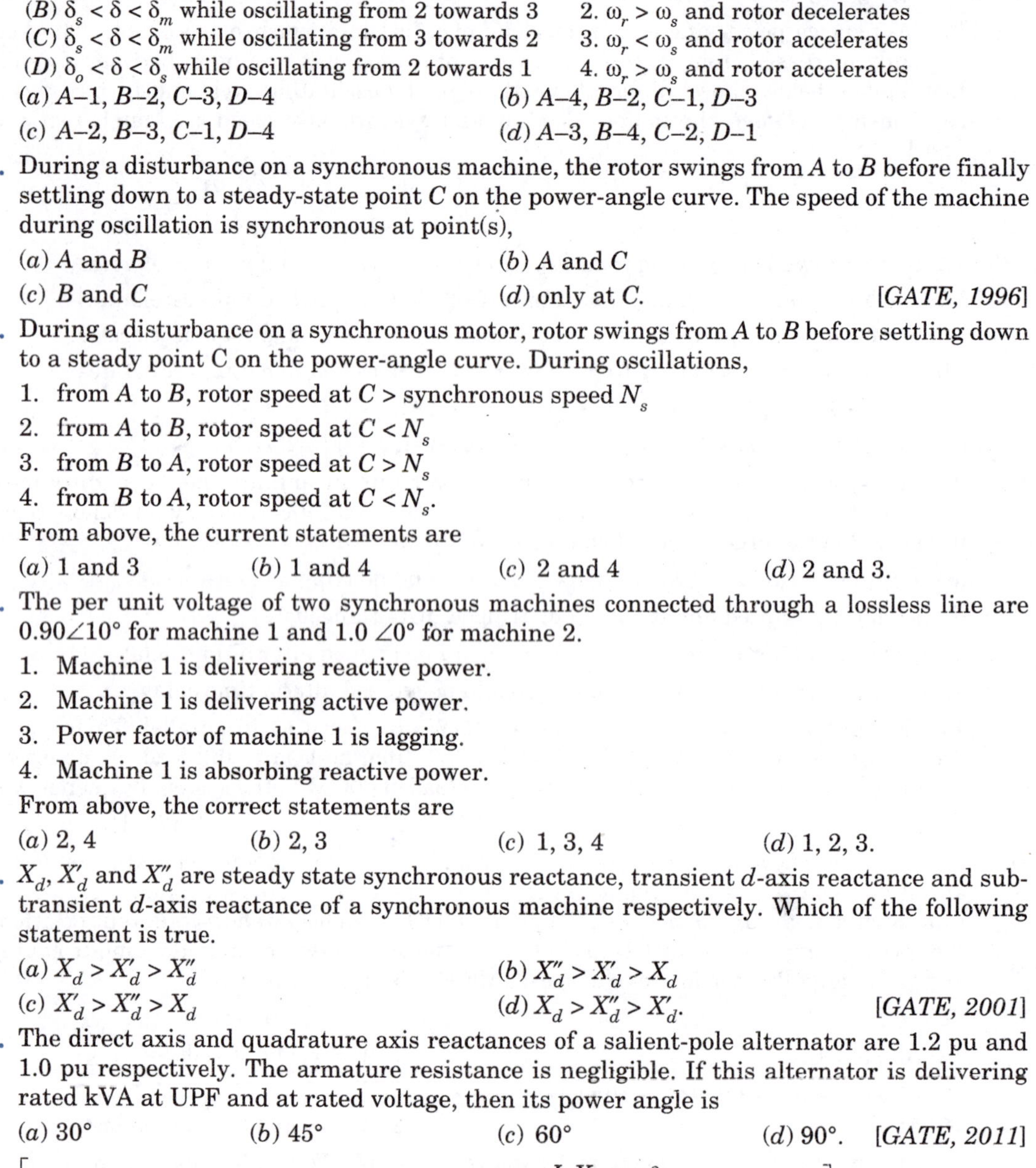

List I	*List II*
(*A*) $\delta_a < \delta < \delta_s$ while oscillating from 1 towards 2	1. $\omega_r < \omega_s$ and rotor decelerates
(*B*) $\delta_s < \delta < \delta_m$ while oscillating from 2 towards 3	2. $\omega_r > \omega_s$ and rotor decelerates
(*C*) $\delta_s < \delta < \delta_m$ while oscillating from 3 towards 2	3. $\omega_r < \omega_s$ and rotor accelerates
(*D*) $\delta_o < \delta < \delta_s$ while oscillating from 2 towards 1	4. $\omega_r > \omega_s$ and rotor accelerates

(*a*) *A*–1, *B*–2, *C*–3, *D*–4 (*b*) *A*–4, *B*–2, *C*–1, *D*–3
(*c*) *A*–2, *B*–3, *C*–1, *D*–4 (*d*) *A*–3, *B*–4, *C*–2, *D*–1

104. During a disturbance on a synchronous machine, the rotor swings from *A* to *B* before finally settling down to a steady-state point *C* on the power-angle curve. The speed of the machine during oscillation is synchronous at point(s),

(*a*) *A* and *B* (*b*) *A* and *C*
(*c*) *B* and *C* (*d*) only at *C*. [*GATE, 1996*]

105. During a disturbance on a synchronous motor, rotor swings from *A* to *B* before settling down to a steady point C on the power-angle curve. During oscillations,

1. from *A* to *B*, rotor speed at *C* > synchronous speed N_s
2. from *A* to *B*, rotor speed at $C < N_s$
3. from *B* to *A*, rotor speed at $C > N_s$
4. from *B* to *A*, rotor speed at $C < N_s$.

From above, the current statements are

(*a*) 1 and 3 (*b*) 1 and 4 (*c*) 2 and 4 (*d*) 2 and 3.

106. The per unit voltage of two synchronous machines connected through a lossless line are $0.90\angle 10°$ for machine 1 and $1.0\ \angle 0°$ for machine 2.

1. Machine 1 is delivering reactive power.
2. Machine 1 is delivering active power.
3. Power factor of machine 1 is lagging.
4. Machine 1 is absorbing reactive power.

From above, the correct statements are

(*a*) 2, 4 (*b*) 2, 3 (*c*) 1, 3, 4 (*d*) 1, 2, 3.

107. X_d, X'_d and X''_d are steady state synchronous reactance, transient *d*-axis reactance and sub-transient *d*-axis reactance of a synchronous machine respectively. Which of the following statement is true.

(*a*) $X_d > X'_d > X''_d$ (*b*) $X''_d > X'_d > X_d$
(*c*) $X'_d > X''_d > X_d$ (*d*) $X_d > X''_d > X'_d$. [*GATE, 2001*]

108. The direct axis and quadrature axis reactances of a salient-pole alternator are 1.2 pu and 1.0 pu respectively. The armature resistance is negligible. If this alternator is delivering rated kVA at UPF and at rated voltage, then its power angle is

(*a*) 30° (*b*) 45° (*c*) 60° (*d*) 90°. [*GATE, 2011*]

[**Hint.** From phasor diagram, derive $\tan\delta = \dfrac{I_a X_q \cos\theta}{V_t + I_q X_q \sin\theta}$ and use it.]

Statements for linked Answer Questions 109 and 110.

A synchronous motor is connnected to an infinite bus at 1 pu voltage and draws 0.6 pu current at unity power factor. Its synchronous reactance is 1.0 pu and resistance is negligible.

109. The excitation voltage (E_f) and load angle (δ) will respectively be

(*a*) 0.8 pu and 36.86° lag (*b*) 0.8 pu and 36.86° lead
(*c*) 1.17 pu and 30.96 lead (*d*) 1.17 pu and 30.96 lag. [*GATE, 2008*]

110. Keeping the excitation voltage same the load on the motor is increased such that the motor current increases by 20%. The operating power factor will become

(*a*) 0.995 lagging (*b*) 0.995 leading
(*c*) 0.791 lagging (*d*) 0.848 leading. [*GATE, 2008*]

111. A 3-phase, 400 V, 5 kW, star-connected synchronous motor having an internal reactance of 10 Ω is operating at 50% load, unity power factor. Now the excitation is increaed by 1%. What will be the new load in per cent, if the power factor is to be kept same? Neglect all losses and consider linear magnetic circuit.

(*a*) 67.9% (*b*) 56.9%
(*c*) 51% (*d*) 50%. [*GATE, 2006*]

112. In relation to the synchronous machines, which one of the following statement is false?

(*a*) In salient-pole machines, the direct-axis synchronous reactance is greater than the quadrature-axis synchronous reactance.
(*b*) The damper bars help the synchronous motor self start.
(*c*) Short circuit ratio is the ratio of the field current required to produce the rated voltage on open-circuit to the rated armature current.
(*d*) The V-curve of a synchronous motor represents the variation in the armature current with field excitation, at a given output power.

113. Two 3-phase, *Y*-connected alternators are to be paralleled to a set of common busbars. The armature has a per-phase synchronous reactance of 1.7 Ω and neligible armature resistance. The line voltage of the first machine is adjusted to 3300 V and that of the second machine is adjusted to 3200 V. The machine voltages are in phase at the instant they are paralleled. Under this condition the synchronizing current per phase will be

(*a*) 16.98 A (*b*) 29.41 A
(*c*) 33.96 A (*d*) 58.82 A. [*GATE, 2004*]

114. A three phase synchronous generator is to be connected to the infinite bus. The lamps are connected as shown in the fig. for the synchronization. The phase sequence of the bus voltage is *A*-*B*-*C* and that of incoming generator voltage is *A*′-*B*′-*C*′.

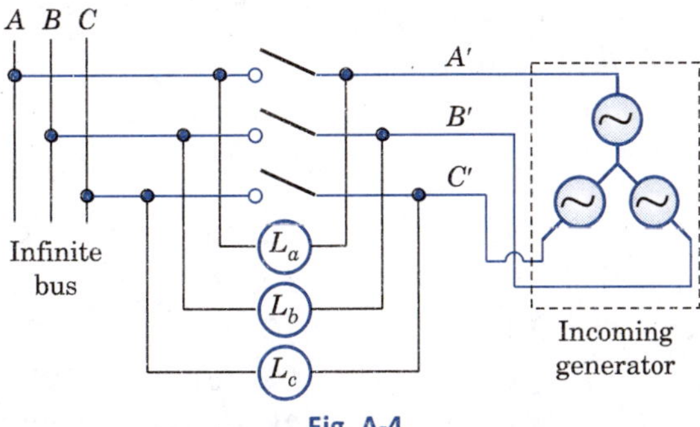

Fig. A-4

It was found that the lamps are becoming dark in the sequence L_a-L_b-L_c. It means that the phase sequence of the incoming generator is

(*a*) opposite to infinite bus and its frequency is more than infinite bus
(*b*) opposite to infinite bus and its frequency is less than infinite bus
(*c*) same as infinite bus and its frequency is more than infinite bus
(*d*) same as infinite bus and its frequency is less than infinite bus. [*GATE, 2014*]

115. A three phase synchronous generator is to be connected to the infinite bus. The lamps are connected as shown in the figure of Prob. 114 for the synchronization. The phas sequence of the bus voltage is *A*-*B*-*C* and that of the incoming geneator voltage is *A*′-*B*′-*C*′.

It was found that the lamps are becoming dark in the sequence L_a-L_c-L_b. It meas that the phase sequence of the incoming generator is

(*a*) opposite to infinite bus and its frequency is more than infinite bus
(*b*) opposite to infinite bus and its frequency is less than infinite bus
(*c*) same as infinite bus and its frequency is more than infinite bus
(*d*) same as infinite bus and its frequency is less than infinite bus.

116. A 3-phase synchronous generator is to be connectfed to an infinite bus. The lamps are connected as shown in the figure of Prob. 114 for the synchronization. The phaes sequence of the bus voltage is *A*-*B*-*C* and that of the incoming generator is *A*′-*B*′-*C*′. The frequency of inifnite bus is f_b and that of incoming generator is f_i.

If speed of the prime-mover driving the incoming generator is increased,

A. the lamp flickering decreases and $f_i > f_b$
B. the lamp flickering decreases and $f_i < f_b$
C. the lamp flickering increases and $f_i > f_b$
D. the lamp flickering increases and $f_i < f_b$

From above, the correct statements are

(*a*) A, C (*b*) A, D (*c*) B, C (*d*) B, D.

117. A 3-phsae synchronous generator is to be connected to an infinite bus. The lamps are connected as shown in the figure of Prob. 114 for the synchronization. The phase sequence of the bus voltage is *A*-*B*-*C* and that of the incoming generator is *A*′-*B*′-*C*′. The frequency of infinite bus is f_b and that of the incoming generator is f_i.

If speed of the prime mover driving the incoming generator is decreased,

A. the lamp flickering decreases and $f_i > f_b$
B. the lamp flickering decreases and $f_i < f_b$
C. the lamp flickering increases and $f_i > f_b$
D. the lamp flickering increases and $f_i < f_b$

From above, the correct statements are

(*a*) A, C (*b*) A, D (*c*) B, C (*d*) B, D.

ANSWERS

1. (*b*)	**2.** (*c*)	**3.** (*a*)	**4.** (*d*)	**5.** (*a*)	**6.** (*c*)
7. (*c*)	**8.** (*a*)	**9.** (*c*)	**10.** (*b*)	**11.** (*c*)	**12.** (*b*)
13. (*c*)	**14.** (*a*)	**15.** (*b*)	**16.** (*d*)	**17.** (*a*)	**18.** (*a*)
19. (*c*)	**20.** (*a*)	**21.** (*d*)	**22.** (*c*)	**23.** (*b*)	**24.** (*c*)
25. (*a*)	**26.** (*b*)	**27.** (*b*)	**28.** (*c*)	**29.** (*d*)	**30.** (*c*)
31. (*b*)	**32.** (*c*)	**33.** (*c*)	**34.** (*a*)	**35.** (*c*)	**36.** (*c*)
37. (*b*)	**38.** (*d*)	**39.** (*b*)	**40.** (*c*)	**41.** (*a*)	**42.** (*c*)

43. (*b*)	**44.** (*a*)	**45.** (*a*)	**46.** (*b*)	**47.** (*c*)	**48.** (*c*)
49. (*b*)	**50.** (*d*)	**51.** (*c*)	**52.** (*c*)	**53.** (*d*)	**54.** (*b*)
55. (*b*)	**56.** (*b*)	**57.** (*c*)	**58.** (*b*)	**59.** (*a*)	**60.** (*c*)
61. (*c*)	**62.** (*a*)	**63.** (*b*)	**64.** (*a*)	**65.** (*c*)	**66.** (*b*)
67. (*b*)	**68.** (*d*)	**69.** (*a*)	**70.** (*b*)	**71.** (*b*)	**72.** (*c*)
73. (*d*)	**74.** (*c*)	**75.** (*a*)	**76.** (*c*)	**77.** (*c*)	**78.** (*c*)
79. (*b*)	**80.** (*d*)	**81.** (*d*)	**82.** (*b*)	**83.** (*c*)	**84.** (*a*)
85. (*b*)	**86.** (*b*)	**87.** (*c*)	**88.** (*a*)	**89.** (*c*)	**90.** (*d*)
91. (*a*)	**92.** (*b*)	**93.** (*a*)	**94.** (*d*)	**95.** (*c*)	**96.** (*d*)
97. (*c*)	**98.** (*b*)	**99.** (*a*)	**100.** (*c*)	**101.** (*d*)	**102.** (*a*)
103. (*b*)	**104.** (*a*)	**105.** (*d*)	**106.** (*a*)	**107.** (*a*)	**108.** (*b*)
109. (*d*)	**110.** (*a*)	**111.** (*a*)	**112.** (*c*)	**113.** (*a*)	**114.** (*a*)
115. (*b*)	**116.** (*c*)	**117.** (*b*)			

POLYPHASE INDUCTION MACHINES

1. In a P-pole, f-Hz, 3-phase induction motor, synchronous angular velocity in mechanical and electrical radians per second is respectively given by

(a) $\frac{4\pi f}{P}, \frac{2\pi f}{P}$ (b) $\frac{2\pi f}{P}, \frac{4\pi f}{P}$ (c) $\frac{2\pi f}{P}, 4\pi f$ (d) $\frac{4\pi f}{P}, 2\pi f$.

2. Choose the correct statement/statements from the following in case both supply voltage V and supply frequency f are reduced so as to keep $\frac{V}{f}$ constant in a 3-phase induction motor.
   1. starting current I_{st} and starting torque $T_{e.st}$ increase
   2. I_{st} decreases but $T_{e.st}$ increases
   3. starting pf is improved but T_e decreases
   4. starting pf is improved but $T_{e.st}$ .increases

   From these, the correct statements are

   (a) 1, 3 (b) 1, 4 (c) 3, 4 (d) 2, 4

3. In a 3-phase induction motor, with negligible stator resistance, maximum torque is proportional to

(a) $\frac{V}{x_2}$ (b) $\frac{V^2}{\sqrt{x_2}}$ (c) $\frac{V^2}{x_2}$ (d) $\frac{\sqrt{V}}{x_2}$.

4. The rotor power output of a 3-phase induction motor is 15 kW and the correspoding slip is 4%. The rotor ohmic loss will be

(a) 600 W (b) 625 W
(c) 650 W (d) 700 W. [I.E.S., 1997]

5. In a 3-phase induction motor, if supply voltage and supply frequency are reduced by the same degree, then under maximum torque conditions :
(a) motor current decreases and pf is improved
(b) motor current increases and pf is improved
(c) motor current decreases and pf is worsened
(d) motor current increases and pf is worsened.

6. In a 3-phase induction motor, if supply voltage and supply frequency are reduced by the same ratio, then slip at which maximum torque occurs
(a) is more and maximum torque $T_{e.m}$ remains constant
(b) is more and $T_{e.m}$ decreases (c) is less and $T_{e.m}$ decreases
(d) is less and $T_{e.m}$ increases.

7. In a 3-phase induction motor with negligible stator resistance, if supply voltage and supply frequency are reduced by the same amount, then slip at which maximum torque occurs
(a) is more and maximum torque $T_{e.m}$ remains constant
(b) is more and $T_{e.m}$ decreases
(c) is less and $T_{e.m}$ decreases
(d) is less and $T_{e.m}$ increases.

8. In a 3-phase induction motor, maximum torque of 100 Nm occurs at a slip of 10%. The torque at a slip of 5% would be

(a) 50 Nm (b) 100 Nm (c) 80 Nm (d) 40 Nm.

9. If the supply voltage decreases by 4%, the torque in a 3-phase induction motor would decrease by

(*a*) 4% (*b*) 16% (*c*) 8% (*d*) 7.84%

10. A 3-phase induction motor runs at a slip of 3.2% at normal voltage. For the same load torque, if the supply voltage reduces to 80% of normal voltage, the motor would operate with a slip of

(*a*) 3.2% (*b*) 5% (*c*) 4% (*d*) 2.56%.

11. A 50-Hz, 3-phase induction motor with synchronous speed of 100 rad/sec develops a useful torque of 150 Nm when the rotor emf makes 120 complete cycles per minute. For this motor, the shaft power output is .... kW.

12. A 3-phase SCIM develops a torque of 100 Nm at 400 V, 50 Hz and at a slip of 0.03. The rotor circuit resistance is now increased to 4 times. For a supply voltage of 320 V, 50 Hz and for the same slip, the torque developed would be .... Nm.

13. A 6-pole, 3-phase induction motor develops the maximum torque at 1000 r.p.m when operated from a 60 Hz supply. Rotor resistance per phase is 1.2 Ω. Neglecting stator impedance, the speed at which it will develop maximum torque when operated from 50 Hz supply is

(*a*) 1000 r.p.m (*b*) 600 r.p.m

(*c*) 800 r.p.m (*d*) 200 r.p.m. [*GATE, 1990*]

14. In a 3-phase SCIM, stator voltage is reduced to half of its rated value. In terms of the rated values, the percentage reductions in stator current and developed torque are respectively given by

(*a*) 50, 75 (*b*) 75, 50 (*c*) 50, 25 (*d*) 50, 57.7.

15. In a 3-phase induction motor, a deep-bar rotor is used for obtaining

(*a*) more operating efficiency (*b*) more starting torque

(*c*) more pull-out torque (*d*) reduced rotor core loss.

16. In a polyphase SCIM, increased starting torque can be obtained by

1. increasing the frequency of operation 2. using deep-bar rotors

3. increasing the number of poles 4. using a double-cage rotor.

From these, the correct answer is

(*a*) 1, 2, 3 (*b*) 1, 3, 4 (*c*) 2, 3, 4 (*d*) 2, 4. [*GATE, 1991*]

17. In a polyphase IM using double-cage, the rotor current flows mainly through the

1. upper cage at starting 2. lower cage at starting

3. upper cage at normal speed 4. lower cage at normal speed.

From these, the correct answer is

(*a*) 1, 3 (*b*) 1, 4 (*c*) 2, 3 (*d*) 2, 4.

18. In a polyphase SCIM, increased starting torque can be obtained by

1. decreasing the supply frequency
2. decreasing the supply voltage only
3. decreasing both supply voltage and frequency by the same ratio
4. increasing the supply frequency only.

From these, the correct is

(*a*) 1, 3 (*b*) 1, 4 (*c*) 2, 3 (*d*) 2, 4.

19. In a double-cage IM, the inner-cage and outer-cage have respectively

(*a*) low r, high x and low r, high x (*b*) low r, low x and high r, low x

(*c*) low r, high x and high r, low x (*d*) high r, low x and low r, high x.

20. Total energy dissipated in the rotor circuit of a 3-phase SCIM, as slip changes from s_1 to s_2, is given by

(*a*) $3\, I_2^2\, r_2\, (s_1 - s_2)$ (*b*) $3\, I_2^2\, r_2\, (s_2 - s_1)$ (*c*) $\dfrac{Jw_s^2}{2}\,(s_1^2 - s_2^2)$ (*d*) $\dfrac{Jw_s^2}{2}\,(s_2^2 - s_1^2)$.

21. In a 3-phase SCIM, rotor energy losses during plugging from normal speed to rest and also from normal speed to backward normal speed are respectively

(*a*) $2Jw_s^2$, $3Jw_s^2$ (*b*) $\dfrac{3}{2}\,Jw_s^2$, $2Jw_s^2$ (*c*) $2Jw_s^2$, $\dfrac{3}{2}\,Jw_s^2$ (*d*) $3Jw_s^2$, $2Jw_s^2$.

22. Speed control of a 3-phase induction motor in the ratio other than 2 : 1 can be obtained by employing

(*a*) multiple stator winding (*b*) consequent-pole technique

(*c*) pole-amplitude modulation technique (*d*) any of the above.

23. Speed control in a 3-phase IM by pole-changing method is applicable to

(*a*) both squirrel-cage (SCIM) and slip-ring (SRIM) induction motors

(*b*) SRIM only (*c*) SCIM only (*d*) SRIM of small rating.

24. For the speed control of a polyphase SCIM by pole-changing method, the most expensive arrangement is

(*a*) constant-torque drive (*b*) constant-power drive

(*c*) variable-torque drive (*d*) variable-power drive.

25. A 3-phase SCIM can be connected to have either 4 or 8 poles. A fan operated by this motor takes 15 kW at lower speed. At higher operating speed, the fan would take... kW.

26. A 3-phase pole-changing IM has 72 slots with two independent double-layer windings. One winding has 3 coils/phase/pole and the other has 4 coils/phase/pole. The two respective operating speeds would be in the ratio of

(*a*) 3 : 4 (*b*) 4 : 3 (*c*) 1 : 2 (*d*) 2 : 1.

27. Supply frequency control for changing the speed in a 3-phase IM is generally carried out with (here V_1 and f_1 are supply voltage and supply frequency),

(*a*) $\dfrac{V_1}{f_1}$ constant as maximum torque $T_{e.m}$ remains always constant

(*b*) V_1, f_1 constant as $T_{e.m}$ remains constnat

(*c*) V_1 constant as $T_{e.m}$ remains constant

(*d*) $\dfrac{V_1}{f_1}$ constant as $T_{e.m}$ remains nearly constant.

28. For the speed control of a polyphase SCIM, if frequency of operation is decreased with

1. constant supply voltage V_1, starting torque $T_{e.st}$ decreases
2. constant supply voltage V_1, $T_{e.st}$ increases
3. $\dfrac{V_1}{f_1}$ constant, $T_{e.st}$ decreases
4. $\dfrac{V_1}{f_1}$ constant, $T_{e.st}$ increases.

From these, the correct answer is

(*a*) 1, 4 (*b*) 2, 4 (*c*) 1, 3 (*d*) 1, 2.

29. Line-voltage control for the speed regulation of a 3-phase SCIM is not so important because this method offers

(*a*) limited range of speed control (*b*) low operating efficiency

(*c*) low pull-out torque (*d*) all of these.

30. For a polyphase SRIM, when low speed is obtained by rotor-resistance control, then

(*a*) starting torque $T_{e.st}$ is low and efficiency η is low

(*b*) $T_{e.st}$ is more and η is low (*c*) both $T_{e.st}$ and η are high

(*d*) $T_{e.st}$ is low and η is more.

31. A 3-phase WRIM develops rated torque at s slip of 0.05 with slip rings short circuited. If the rotor circuit resistance is increased to four times by inserting external resistance in the rotor circuit, then at rated load torque, the slip would be

(*a*) 0.1 (*b*) 0.15 (*c*) 0.20 (*d*) 0.25.

32. In a 3-phase IM, speeds higher than synchronous speeds can be obtained by

(*a*) supply frequency control (*b*) supply voltage control

(*c*) rotor resistance control (*d*) rotor slip-power control.

33. In rotor-voltage-injection method of speed control for WRIM, if E_j = rotor voltage injected and I_2z_2 = rotor leakage impedance drop, then if

1. $E_j < I_2z_2$, rotor speed n_r < synchronous speed n_s
2. $E_j = I_2z_2$, $n_r = n_s$
3. $E_j > I_2z_2$, $n_r < n_s$
4. $E_j > I_2z_2$, $n_r > n_s$

From these, the correct answer is

(*a*) 2, 3, 4 (*b*) 1, 2, 3 (*c*) 1, 3 (*d*) 1, 2, 4.

34. In a 6-pole, 50 Hz, WRIM, the per-phase rotor emf at standstill is 30 V. For obtaining a rotor speed of 700 rpm at no-load, the voltage injected in the rotor circuit and its frequency are respectively

(*a*) 9 V, 15 Hz (*b*) – 9 V, 15 Hz (*c*) 21 V, 35 Hz (*d*) – 21 V, 35 Hz.

35. In a 4-pole, 50 Hz, WRIM, if voltage of 20 V is injected in phase with the standstill rotor emf of 50 V, then rotor speed at no-load would be

(*a*) 600 r.p.m (*b*) 900 r.p.m (*c*) 2100 r.p.m (*d*) 2400 r.p.m.

36. In slip-power recovery scheme for a 3-phase IM, if slip power is

1. returned to the supply, constant power drive (CPD) is obtained
2. added to main shaft, CPD is obtained
3. subtracted from the main shaft, constant torque drive (CTD) is obtained
4. obtained from the supply, CTD is obtained.

From above, the correct answer is

(*a*) 1, 3 (*b*) 2, 3 (*c*) 1, 4 (*d*) 2, 4.

37. The stator of a 3-phase, 4-pole slip-ring induction motor is fed from 50 Hz supply and its rotor from 30 Hz supply. Its rotor would run at (rpm),

(*a*) 900 or 600 (*b*) 600 or 1500 (*c*) 900 or 2400 (*d*) 600 or 2400.

38. In a slip-power recovery scheme for 3-phase SRIM, the load requires a constant power of 800 kW. For 6-pole, 50 Hz IM running at 700 rpm, the power handled by slip-power converter would be

(*a*) 240 kW at 50 Hz (*b*) 1040 kW at 15 Hz
(*c*) 240 kW at 15 Hz (*d*) 560 kW at 35 Hz.

39. The stator of a 4-pole, 3-phase, 50 Hz induction machine is supplied from 3-phase, 50 Hz supply and its rotor is driven at 750 rpm. The slip rings of the machine are open circuited. The frequency of the voltage across any two slip rings is

(*a*) 50 Hz or 25 Hz (*b*) 75 Hz or 50 Hz
(*c*) 100 Hz or 75 Hz (*d*) 25 Hz or 75 Hz. [*GATE, 1988*]

40. A prime-mover drives a 6-pole, 3-phase induction frequency converter. The converter is connected to 60 Hz, 3-phase supply on the primary. If the prime-mover speed is 3000 rpm, the frequencies of the possible outputs from the converter are

(*a*) 120 Hz, 60 Hz (*b*) 90 Hz, 210 Hz
(*c*) 176 Hz, 86 Hz (*d*) 180 Hz, 210 Hz. [*GATE, 1991*]

41. In a 3-phase SCIM, regenerative braking takes place when

1. number of stator poles is increased
2. number of stator poles is decreased
3. load is lifted up by crane
4. load is lowered by crane.

From above, the correct answer is

(*a*) 1, 3 (*b*) 2, 3 (*c*) 1, 4 (*d*) 2, 4

42. In a 3-phase induction motor, plugging requires that

(*a*) any two stator supply leads are short circuited
(*b*) any two stator supply leads are interchanged
(*c*) any two stator terminals are fed with d.c.
(*d*) d.c. is fed to two terminals obtained from 3-phase terminals.

43. D.C. dynamic braking in 3-phase IM is obtained by

(*a*) feeding d.c. to stator circuit
(*b*) feeding d.c. to rotor circuit
(*c*) interchanging any two stator supply terminals
(*d*) interchanging any two rotor terminals.

44. A 3-phase induction motor is connected to a 3-phase supply. One of the line fuses is blown out when the motor is running. Consequently,

1. the motor will come to standstill
2. the motor will continue to run at the same speed with line current unchanged
3. the motor will continue to run at a slightly reduced speed with an increased line current
4. the rotor currents will have both sf and $(2 - s) f$ component frequencies, where s is the slip and f is the supply frequency.

From these statements, the correct answer is

(*a*) 1, 3 (*b*) 2, 3 (*c*) 2, 4 (*d*) 3, 4. [*GATE, 1990*]

45. A single-phase induction motor is provided with a 3-phase slip-ring rotor connected to a starting resistance. This motor would

(*a*) not start (*b*) result in more starting torque
(*c*) produce no difference in the starting torque
(*d*) run at half the synchronous speed.

46. A 3-phase induction motor is to be connected to a 3-phase supply for the purpose of starting but in the supply line, one fuse is already blown out. Under these conditions, the motor would

(*a*) not start

(*b*) not start and there would be humming noise in the motor

(*c*) start and run at half the synchronous speed

(*d*) start and run at a speed slightly less than normal speed but would draw large current.

47. The rotor terminals of a 3-phase SRIM are open-circuited and stator is connected to balanced 3-phase supply. Under these conditions, the rotor will

(*a*) not start (*b*) run with more vibrations

(*c*) run at normal speed (*d*) run at a lower speed.

48. With rotor terminals of a 3-phase SRIM not short-circuited and with stator terminals connected to balanced 3-phase supply, the motor is seen to rotate at quite a low speed. The rotor rotation under these conditions is due to

(*a*) induction motor torque (*b*) hysteresis torque

(*c*) eddy-current torque (*d*) both hysteresis and eddy-current torques.

49. In a polyphase IM, the effect of skewing rotor slots is to

1. decrease both starting and maximum torques.
2. increase both starting and maximum torques.
3. decrease both rotor resistance and noise.
4. increase rotor resistance and decrease noise.

From above, the correct answer is

(*a*) 1, 3 (*b*) 2, 3 (*c*) 1, 4 (*d*) 2, 4.

50. The stator mmf wave in a 3-phase, 4-pole, 50 Hz IM is found to have fundamental, 5th and 7th harmonic component waves. The rotating fields due to by these harmonics rotate respectively at

(*a*) 1500 r.p.m, 300 r.p.m, 214.3 r.p.m (*b*) 1500 r.p.m, – 300 r.p.m, 214.3 r.p.m

(*c*) 1500 r.p.m, 300 r.p.m, – 214.3 r.p.m (*d*) 1500 r.p.m, – 300 r.p.m, – 214.3 r.p.m.

51. In a polyphase IM, the rotor slots are skewed by

1. one slot-pitch
2. two slot-pitches
3. one harmonic pole-pitch
4. two harmonic pole-pitches.

From above, the correct answer is

(*a*) 1, 4 (*b*) 1, 3 (*c*) 2, 4 (*d*) 2, 3.

52. In a 3-phase, 50 Hz IM running at 1440 rpm, the relative speed between 5th harmonic field and rotor is .... rpm and slip of rotor with respect to 5th harmonic field is ....

(*a*) 1440 rpm, 3.8 (*b*) 1740 rpm, 3.88 (*c*) 1740 rpm, 5.8 (*d*) 1440 rpm, 5.8.

53. In a 3-phase, 50 Hz IM running at 1440 rpm, the relative speed between 7th harmonic field and rotor is .... rpm and slip of rotor with respect to 7th harmonic field is ....

(*a*) 1654.3 rpm, 7.72 (*b*) 1225.7 rpm, – 5.72

(*c*) 1225.7 rpm, 5.72 (*d*) 1654.3 rpm, – 7.72.

54. A 3-phase, 50 Hz, 4-pole IM crawls at 740 rpm. This is due to

1. harmonic induction torque
2. harmonic synchronous torque
3. broken end-ring
4. unbalanced rotor phase.

From above, the correct answer is

(*a*) 1, 3 (*b*) 2, 3 (*c*) 2, 4 (*d*) 3, 4.

55. Crawling in a 3-phase IM may be due to

1. harmonic induction torque
2. harmonic synchronous torque
3. broken end-ring
4. broken rotor bar.

From above, the correct answer is

(*a*) 1, 2, 3 (*b*) 1, 3, 4 (*c*) 1, 2, 3, 4 (*d*) 2, 3, 4

56. A 3-phase IM crawls at one-seventh synchronous speed. This may be due to

(*a*) harmonic induction torque (*b*) harmonic synchronous torque
(*c*) both harmonic induction and synchronous torques
(*d*) broken-end-ring.

57. Cogging in a 3-phase IM occurs due to

(*a*) harmonic induction torque (*b*) harmonic synchronous torque
(*c*) both harmonic induction and synchronous torques
(*d*) broken end-ring.

58. In a 3-phase, 50 Hz, 4-pole, 30 cm diameter IM, the velocity of linear travelling field in m/sec is

(*a*) 23.56 (*b*) 47.12 (*c*) 11.78 (*d*) 35.34.

59. Slot harmonics in a 3-phase IM may be eliminated by

(*a*) skewing rotor slots (*b*) distribution of winding
(*c*) choosing suitable number of rotor slots (*d*) all of these.

60. Harmonic synchronous torque in a 3-phase IM

(*a*) can be avoided by a proper slot combination of stator and rotor slots
(*b*) may be avoided by a proper slot combination of stator and rotor slots
(*c*) can be avoided by skewing the rotor slots
(*d*) can be avoided by a proper choice of coil span.

61. In a cage rotor, standstill rotor leakage reactance is thrice the rotor resistance at 60 Hz. The frequency of supply at which maximum torque is obtained at starting is

(*a*) 60 Hz (*b*) 50 Hz (*c*) 20 Hz (*d*) 80 Hz.

62. A 3-phase, 4-pole SRIM may have the following types of windings for its rotor,

(*a*) 3-phase 6-pole (*b*) 2-phase 2-pole (*c*) 2-phase 4-pole (*d*) 3-phase 2-pole.

63. For a 3-phase SRIM, the slip for maximum torque

(*a*) may be between 1 and 2 (*b*) can never be more than 1
(*c*) cannot be more than 0.3 (*d*) none of these.

64. A squirrel cage IM having a rated slip of 4% on full-load has a starting torque same as the full-load torque. The starting current is

(*a*) equal to full-load current (*b*) twice full-load current
(*c*) four times full-load current (*d*) five times full-load current. [*GATE, 1991*]

65. Static Kramer drive for the speed control of a 3-phase slip-ring induction motor

1. requires 12 thyristors and a transformer
2. power can flow from rotor to bridge rectifier, inverter and to supply
3. power can flow from supply to bridge rectifier, inverter and to the rotor
4. offers constant torque drive
5. offers constant power drive.

From above, the correct answer is

(*a*) 1, 2, 5 (*b*) 1, 2, 4 (*c*) 2, 4 (*d*) 2, 5

66. A 3-phase induction motor has maximum torque of 200 Nm at a slip of 0.2 and at supply voltage of 400 V. For a supply voltage of 360 V,

(*a*) $s_{mT} < 0.2$ and $T_{e.m} = 180$ Nm (*b*) $s_{mT} = 0.2$ and $T_{e.m} = 180$ Nm

(*c*) $s_{mT} = 0.2$ and $T_{e.m} = 162$ Nm (*d*) $s_{mT} > 0.2$ and $T_{e.m} = 162$ Nm

67. Match the following :

Type of motor	*Characteristic / application*
A. 3-phase squirrel-cage IM	1. High-starting torque
B. 3-phase slip-ring IM	2. Wide speed control
C. 3-phase double-cage IM	3. Controllable starting torque
D. static Kramer drive	4. Low-starting torque

(*a*) *A*–4, *B*–3, *C*–1, *D*–2 (*b*) *A*–3, *B*–1, *C*–2, *D*–4

(*c*) *A*–2, *B*–1, *C*–3, *D*–4 (*d*) *A*–1, *B*–2, *C*–3, *D*–4

68. Match the following for a 3-phase induction motor.

Operation	*Rotor energy losses*
A. Rest to normal speed	1. $\frac{3}{2} Jw_s^2$
B. Normal speed to rest by plugging	2. $2\, Jw_s^2$
C. Reversal by plugging	3. $\frac{1}{8} Jw_s^2$
D. Half-normal to normal speed	4. $\frac{1}{2} Jw_s^2$

(*a*) *A*–4, *B*–2, *C*–3, *D*–1 (*b*) *A*–3, *B*–2, *C*–4, *D*–1

(*c*) *A*–1, *B*–2, *C*–3, *D*–4 (*d*) *A*–4, *B*–1, *C*–2, *D*–3

69. The torque-slip characteristic of a polyphase induction motor becomes almost linear at small values of slip, because in this range of slips

(*a*) the effective rotor-circuit resistance is very large compared to the rotor reactance

(*b*) the rotor resistance is equal to the stator resistance

(*c*) the rotor resistance is equal to the rotor reactance

(*d*) the rotor reactance is equal to the stator reactance.

70. Breakdown torque of a 3-phase induction motor of negligible stator impedance is

(*a*) directly proportional to rotor resistance

(*b*) inversely proportional to rotor resistance

(*c*) directly proportional to the reactance

(*d*) inversely proportional to the rotor leakage reactance.

71. While operating on variable frequency supplies, the a.c. motors require variable voltage as well in order to

(*a*) protect the insulation (*b*) aviod the effects of saturation

(*c*) improve the commutation capabilities of the inverter

(*d*) protect the thyristors from dv/dt.

72. The stator of a 2/4 pole changing cage motor is initially wound for 2-pole. The reconnection of the stator winding to 4-poles through a change-over switch, while the motor is running, would result in

(*a*) constant torque drive (*b*) constant power drive
(*c*) plugging to standstill
(*d*) regenerative braking to half the original speed. [*I.E.S., 1992*]

73. In figures given below, dotted curve gives torque-speed characteristic of a 3-phase induction motor under normal supply voltage V and frequency f. List I gives the variation of V and f while List II gives the torque-speed characteristics of this motor. Match List I with List II.

List I (*Variation of V and f*)

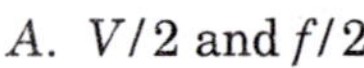
A. $V/2$ and $f/2$

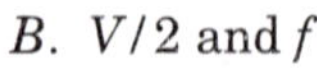
B. $V/2$ and f

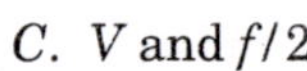
C. V and $f/2$

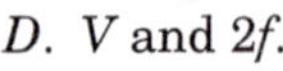
D. V and $2f$.

List II (*Torque-speed characteristics*)

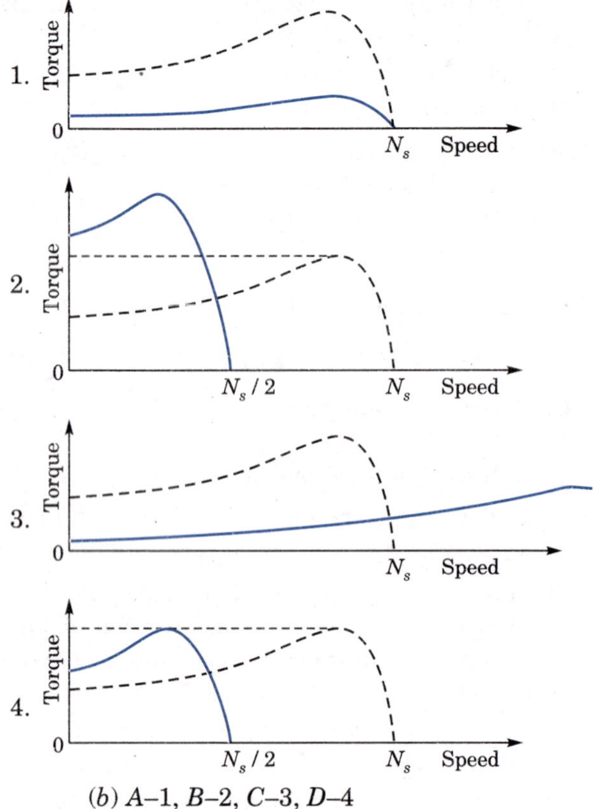

(*a*) A–4, B–1, C–2, D–3 (*b*) A–1, B–2, C–3, D–4
(*c*) A–3, B–2, C–1, D–4 (*d*) A–2, B–4, C–1, D–3

74. Match List I with List II

List I (*3-phase induction motor working under different operating conditions*)

List II (*Torque-speed characteristics of 3-phase induction motor*)

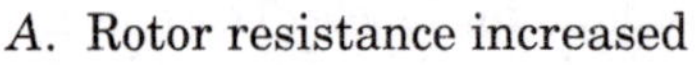
A. Rotor resistance increased

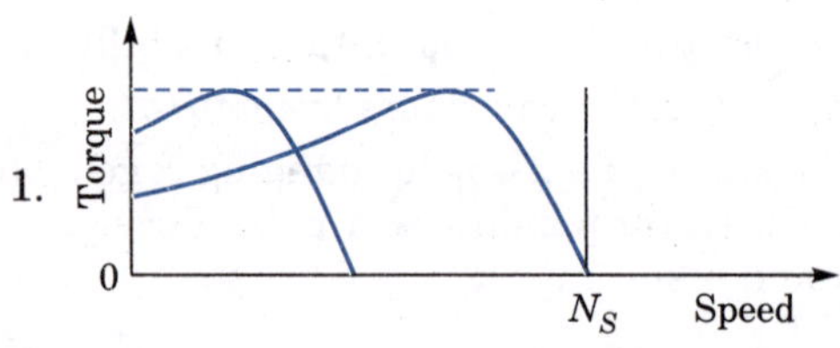

B. Emf injected in rotor circuit

2. 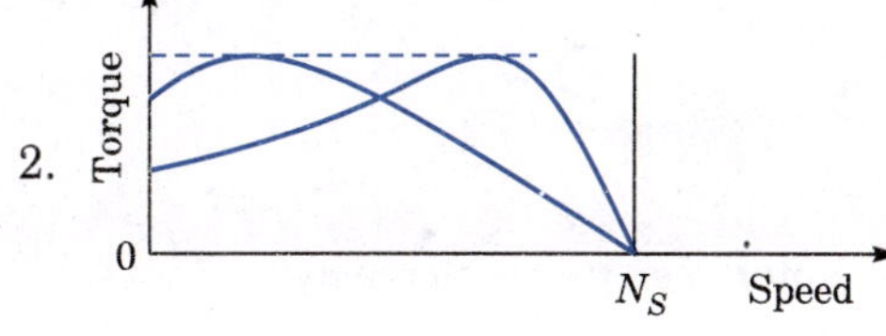

C. Constant gap flux

3. 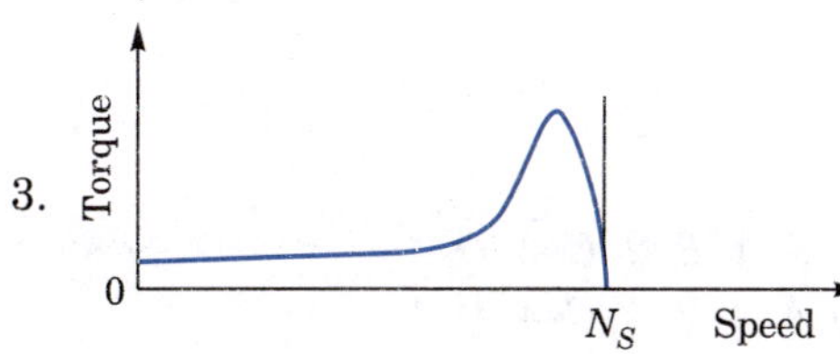

D. Constant stator current.

4. 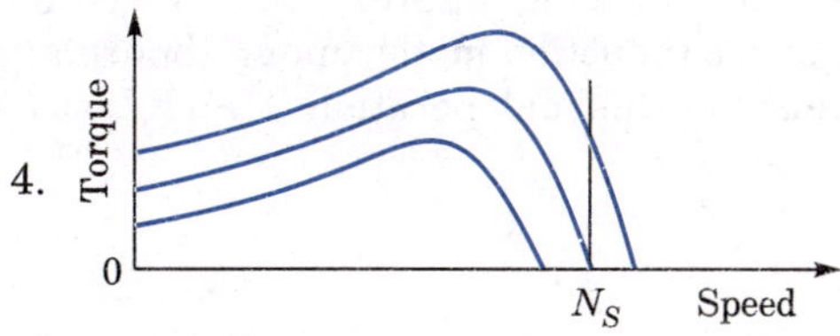

(*a*) *A*–1, *B*–2, *C*–3, *D*–4 (*b*) *A*–2, *B*–4, *C*–1, *D*–3
(*c*) *A*–3, *B*–4, *C*–2, *D*–1 (*d*) *A*–4, *B*–1, *C*–2, *D*–3

75. In figures given below, dotted curve gives torque-speed characteristic of a 3-phase induction motor under normal values of source voltage *V* and frequency *f*. List I gives different methods of speed control of a 3-phase induction motor and List II gives its torque-speed characteristics. Match List I with List II.

List I	*List II*
(Methods of speed control)	*(Torque / speed characteristics)*

A. Stator reactance increased

1. Torque, 0, N_S, Speed

B. Rotor reactance increased

2. Torque, 0, N_S, Speed

C. Pole changing with constant power

3. Torque, 0, N_S, Speed

D. Rotor resistance increased 4.

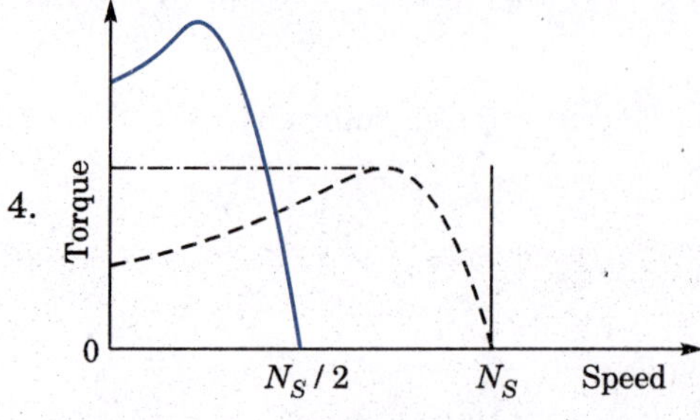

(*a*) *A*–1, *B*–2, *C*–3, *D*–4 (*b*) *A*–2, *B*–1, *C*–4, *D*–3
(*c*) *A*–3, *B*–2, *C*–4, *D*–1 (*d*) *A*–4, *B*–3, *C*–2, *D*–1

76. In the following figures, List II given below shows torque-speed characteristics of a 3-phase induction motor under abnormal operating conditions and List I gives the possible causes of this maloperation. Match List I with List II.

List I / *List II*

A. Motor with rotor bar broken 1.

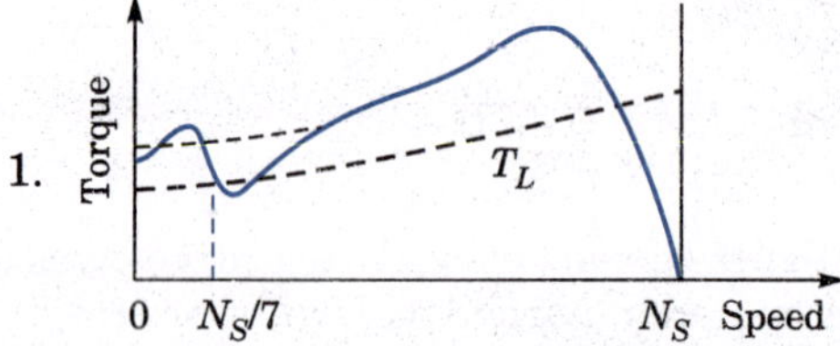

B. Harmonic synchronous torque 2.

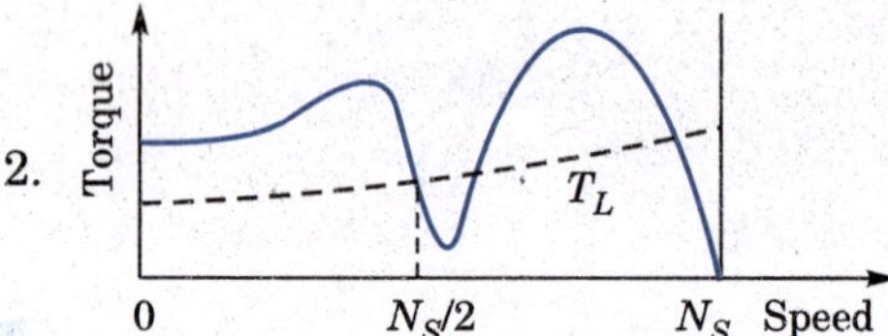

C. Harmonic induction torque 3.

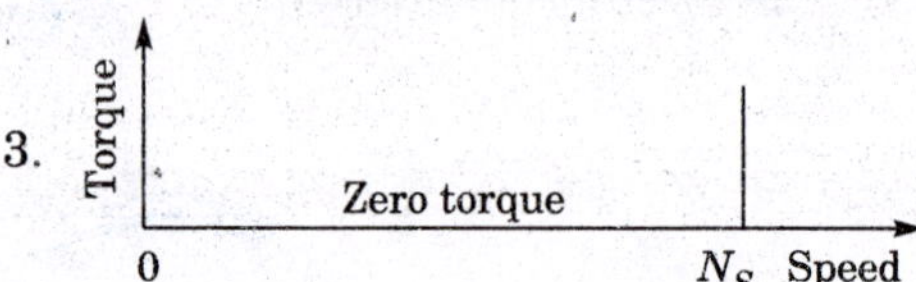

D. Motor with end-ring open-circuited 4.

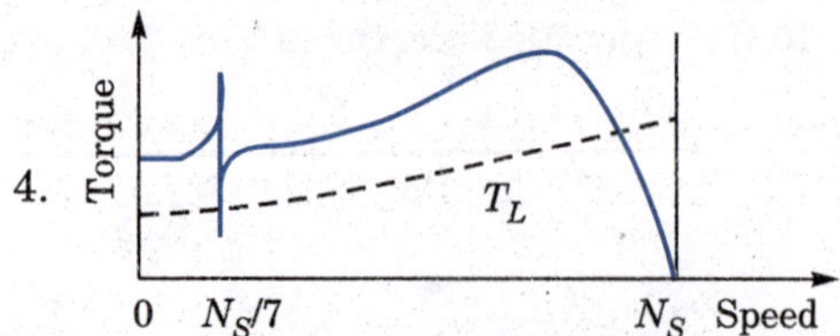

(*a*) *A*–4, *B*–2, *C*–3, *D*–1 (*b*) *A*–1, *B*–4, *C*–3, *D*–2
(*c*) *A*–3, *B*–1, *C*–4, *D*–2 (*d*) *A*–2, *B*–3, *C*–1, *D*–4

77. Match List I with List II

List I (*Type of 3-phase induction motor*)	*List II* (*Torque-speed characteristics*)
A. Deep-bar totor	1.
B. Single-cage rotor with copper bars	2.
C. Double-cage rotor	3.
D. Single-cage rotor with brass bars	4.

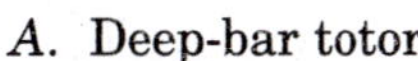

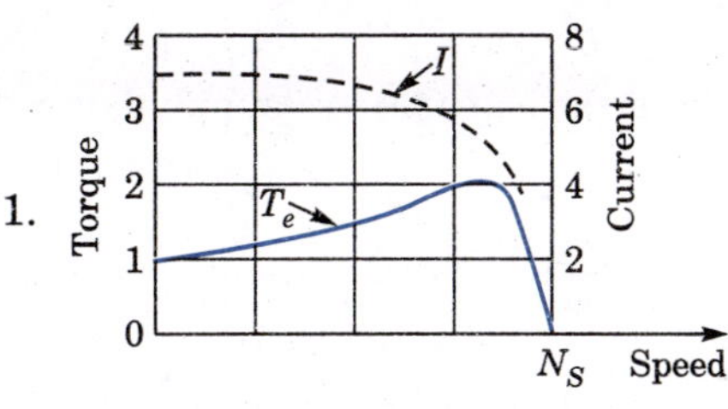

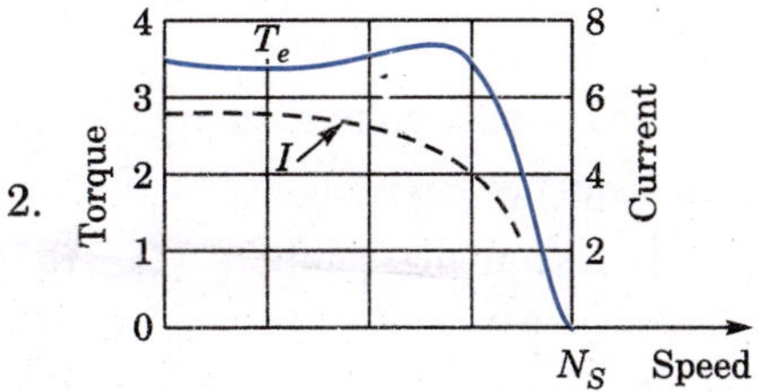

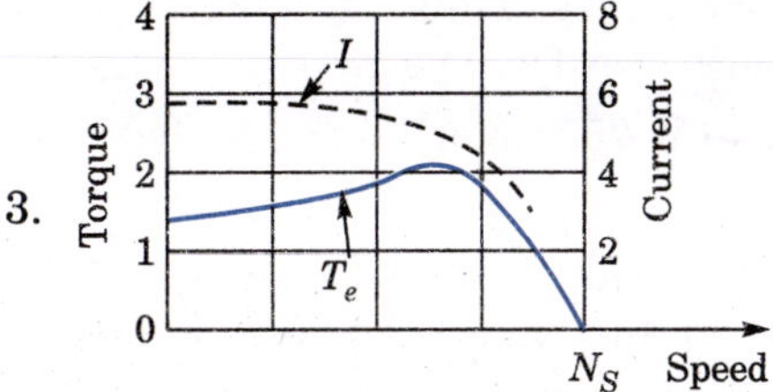

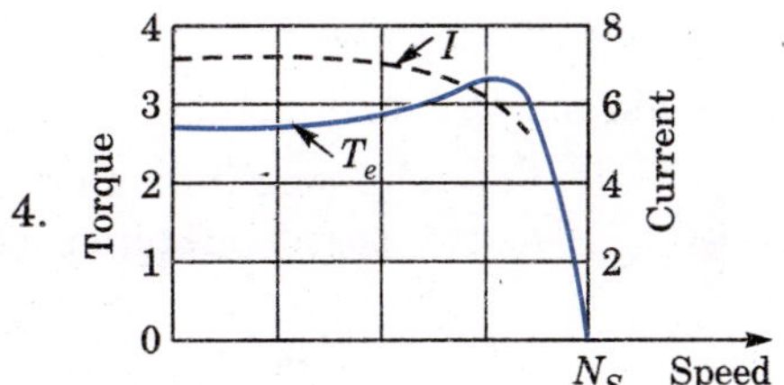

(*a*) *A*–4, *B*–1, *C*–2, *D*–3 (*b*) *A*–3, *B*–2, *C*–1, *D*–4
(*c*) *A*–2, *B*–3, *C*–4, *D*–1 (*d*) *A*–1, *B*–4, *C*–3, *D*–2

78. A 4-pole, 50 Hz, 3-phase slip-ring induction motor has standstill rotor emf of 40 V per phase. For obtaining a speed of 1800 rpm, the voltage to be injected into the rotor circuit and its frequency should be

(*a*) 32 V aiding original sE_2, 40 Hz (*b*) 8 V aiding original sE_2, 40 Hz
(*c*) 8 V aiding original sE_2, 10 Hz (*d*) 8 V opposing original sE_2, 10 Hz.

79. An induction motor is fed from a balanced 3-phase supply at rated voltage and frequency through a bank of three single-phase transformers connected in delta. One unit of the bank develops fault and is removed. Then

(*a*) single-phasing will occur and the machine fails to start

(*b*) single-phasing will not occur but the motor terminal voltage will become unbalanced and the machine can be loaded to the extent of 57.7% of its rating.

(*c*) the machine can be loaded to the extent of 57.7% of its rating with balanced supply at its terminals

(*d*) the machine can be loaded to the extent of $66\frac{2}{3}\%$ with balanced supply at its terminals.

[*GATE, 1995*]

80. An inverter capable of supplying a balanced three-phase variable voltage variable frequency output is feeding a three-phase induction motor rated for 50 Hz and 440 V. The stator winding resistances of the motor are negligibly small. During starting, the current inrush can be avoided without sacrificing the starting torque by suitably applying

(*a*) low voltage at rated frequency (*b*) low voltage keeping *V*/*f* ratio constant

(*c*) rated voltage at low frequency (*d*) rated voltage at rated frequency.

[*GATE, 1995*]

81. Unbalanced supply voltage given to a 3-phase, delta-connected induction motor will cause

(*a*) zero sequence currents (*b*) less heating of the rotor

(*c*) negative sequence component current (*d*) all of these. [*GATE, 1996*]

82. A 3-phase, 20 kW, 400 V, 1470 rpm, 50 Hz squirrel-cage induction motor develops a torque of 100 Nm at a speed of 1400 rpm. If the motor is connected to a 30 Hz supply, for keeping the same air-gap flux, the supply voltage should be .... V and for the same load torque, the new speed will be .... r.p.m.

(*a*) 240 V, 700 r.p.m (*b*) 240 V, 980 r.p.m (*c*) 300 V, 980 r.p.m (*d*) 240 V, 733.3 r.p.m.

[*GATE, 1997*]

83. In *V*/*f* speed control of a 3-phase induction motor having negligible stator resistance, with increase in supply frequency upto rated voltage, the maximum torque and the slip at maximum torque would respectively

(*a*) increase and decrease (*b*) remain constant and decrease

(*c*) remain constant and increase (*d*) decrease and decrease

84. Stator of a 3-phase slip-ring induction motor is fed from source V_1, f_1 and its rotor from source V_2, f_2. The two possible rotor speeds are

(*a*) $\frac{120 f_1}{P}\left(1-\frac{f_1}{f_2}\right), \frac{120 f_1}{P}\left(1+\frac{f_1}{f_2}\right)$ (*b*) $\frac{120 f_1}{P}\left(1+\frac{f_1}{f_2}\right), \frac{120 f_1}{P}\left(1+\frac{f_2}{f_1}\right)$

(*c*) $\frac{120 f_1}{P}\left(1-\frac{f_2}{f_1}\right), \frac{120 f_1}{P}\left(1+\frac{f_2}{f_1}\right)$ (*d*) $\frac{120 f_1}{P}\left(1-\frac{f_2}{f}\right), \frac{120 f_1}{P}\left(1+\frac{f_1}{f_2}\right)$.

85. A doubly fed 3-phase induction machine

1. can run as an induction generator at supersynchronous speed,
2. can run as an induction generator at subsynchronous speed,
3. cannot run as an induction generator at subsynchronous speed,
4. can run as an induction motor at super-synchronous speeds.

From above, the correct statements are

(*a*) 1, 3 (*b*) 2, 4 (*c*) 1, 2, 4 (*d*) 1, 3, 4.

86. A 3-phase squirrel-cage induction motor supplied from a balanced 3-phase source drives a mechanical load. The torque-speed characteristics of the motor (solid curve) and of the load (dotted curve) are shown. Of the two equilibrium points A and B, which of the following options correctly describes the stabilities of A and B?

(*a*) A is stable, B is unstable

(*b*) A is unstable, B is stable

(*c*) Both are stable.

(*d*) Both are unstable. [*GATE, 2009*]

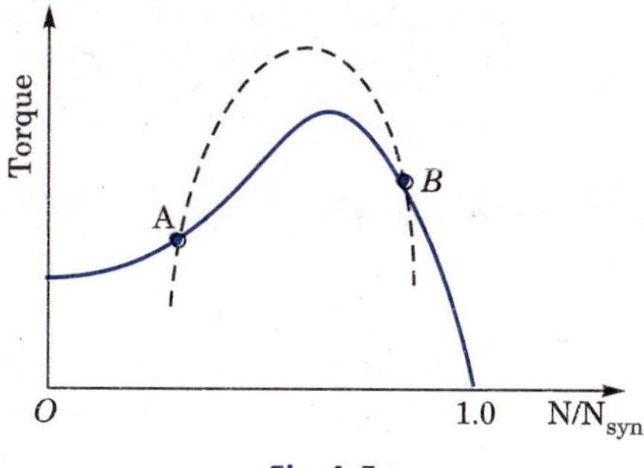

Fig. A-5

87. A 400 V, 50 Hz, 4-pole, 1400 rpm, star-connected squirrel-cage induction motor has the following parameters referred to the stator,

$$r_2 = 1.0\ \Omega,\ x_1 = x_2 = 1.5\ \Omega$$

Neglect stator resistance and core and rotational losses of the motor.

The motor is controlled from a 3-phase voltage source inverter with constant *V/f* control. The stator line-to-line voltage and frequency to obtain the maximum torque at starting will be

(*a*) 20.6 V, 2.7 Hz (*b*) 133.3 V, 16.7 Hz

(*c*) 266.6 V, 33.3 Hz (*d*) 323 V, 40.3 Hz. [*GATE, 2008*]

$$\left[\textbf{Hint. } s_{mT} = 1 = \frac{r_2}{x_1 + x_2}. \quad \therefore \quad 2\pi f_m (l_1 + l_2) = 1. \quad \text{Now } l_1 = \frac{1.5}{2\pi \times 50} = l_2 \text{ etc.}\right]$$

Common data for Questions 88 and 89.

A 3-phase, 440 V, 50 Hz, 4 pole, slip-ring induction motor is fed from the rotor side through an auto-transformer and the stator is connected to a variable resistance as shown in the figure here.

The motor is coupled to a 220 V, separately-excited DC generator feeding power to fixed resistance of 10 Ω. Two wattmeter method is used to measure the input power to induction motor. The variable resistance is adjusted such that the motor runs at 1410 r.p.m and the following readings were recorded: W_1 = 1800 W, W_2 = – 200 W.

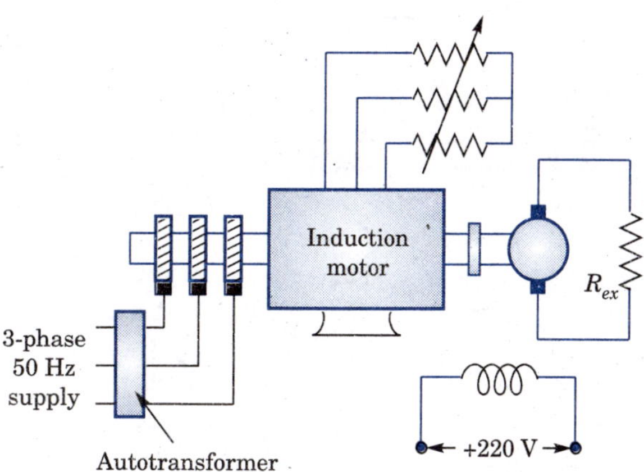

Fig. A-6

88. The speed of rotation of stator magnetic field with respect to rotor structure will be

(*b*) 90 rpm in the direction of rotation

(*b*) 90 rpm in the opposite direction of rotation

(*c*) 1500 rpm in the direction of rotation

(*d*) 1500 rpm in the opposite direction of rotation. [*GATE, 2008*]

89. Neglecting all losses of both the machines, the DC generator power output and the current through resistance (R_{ex}) will respectively be

(*a*) 96 W, 3.10 A (*b*) 120 W, 3.46 A (*c*) 1504 W, 12.26 A (*d*) 1880 W, 13.71 A.

[*GATE, 2008*]

90. The speed of a 4-pole induction motor is controlled by varying the supply frequency while maintaining the ratio of supply voltage to supply frequency (*V/f*) constant. At rated frequency of 50 Hz and rated voltage of 400 V, its speed is 1440 rpm. Find the speed at 30 Hz, if the load torque is constant.

(*a*) 882 rpm (*b*) 864 rpm (*c*) 840 rpm (*d*) 828 rpm.

[*GATE, 2006*]

91. Under no-load condition, if the applied voltage to an inductin motor is reduced from the rated voltage to half the rated value, then

(*a*) the speed decreases and the stator current increases

(*b*) both the speed and the stator current decrease

(*c*) the speed and the stator current remain practically constant

(*d*) there is negligible change in the speed but the stator current decreases. [*GATE, 2005*]

92. A 3-phase induction motor is driving a constant torque load at rated voltage and frequency. If both voltage and frequency are halved, following statements relate to the new condition. If stator resistance, leakage reactance and core loss are ignored.

P: The difference between synchronous speed and actual speed remains same

Q: The air-gap flux remains same

R: The stator current remains same

S: The pu slip remains same.

Among the above, the correct statements are

(*a*) All (*b*) *P*, *Q* and *R* (*c*) *Q*, *R* and *S* (*d*) *P* and *S*.

[*GATE, 2003*]

ANSWERS

1. (*d*)	**2.** (*d*)	**3.** (*c*)	**4.** (*b*)	**5.** (*a*)	**6.** (*b*)
7. (*a*)	**8.** (*c*)	**9.** (*d*)	**10.** (*b*)	**11.** 14.4 kW	
12. 16 Nm	**13.** (*c*)	**14.** (*a*)	**15.** (*b*)	**16.** (*c*)	**17.** (*b*)
18. (*a*)	**19.** (*c*)	**20.** (*c*)	**21.** (*b*)	**22.** (*c*)	**23.** (*c*)
24. (*b*)	**25.** 120 kW	**26.** (*a*)	**27.** (*d*)	**28.** (*b*)	**29.** (*d*)
30. (*b*)	**31.** (*c*)	**32.** (*d*)	**33.** (*b*)	**34.** (*a*)	**35.** (*c*)
36. (*d*)	**37.** (*d*)	**38.** (*c*)	**39.** (*d*)	**40.** (*b*)	**41.** (*c*)
42. (*b*)	**43.** (*a*)	**44.** (*d*)	**45.** (*b*)	**46.** (*b*)	**47.** (*d*)
48. (*d*)	**49.** (*c*)	**50.** (*b*)	**51.** (*a*)	**52.** (*c*)	**53.** (*b*)
54. (*d*)	**55.** (*c*)	**56.** (*c*)	**57.** (*b*)	**58.** (*a*)	**59.** (*a*)
60. (*a*)	**61.** (*c*)	**62.** (*c*)	**63.** (*a*)	**64.** (*d*)	**65.** (*c*)
66. (*c*)	**67.** (*a*)	**68.** (*d*)	**69.** (*a*)	**70.** (*d*)	**71.** (*b*)
72. (*d*)	**73.** (*a*)	**74.** (*b*)	**75.** (*c*)	**76.** (*d*)	**77.** (*a*)
78. (*c*)	**79.** (*c*)	**80.** (*b*)	**81.** (*c*)	**82.** (*d*)	**83.** (*b*)
84. (*c*)	**85.** (*c*)	**86.** (*a*)	**87.** (*b*)	**88.** (*b*)	**89.** (*c*)
90. (*c*)	**91.** (*b*)	**92.** (*b*)			

SINGLE PHASE MOTORS

1. In a single-phase induction motor, according to double-revolving field theory.
   (A) forward mmf F_f and backward mmf F_b are equal at standstill
   (B) F_f and F_b are equal at all rotor speeds
   (C) Forward flux ϕ_f and backward flux ϕ_b are equal at all rotor speeds
   (D) ϕ_f and ϕ_b are equal at standstill
   From above, the correct is
   (*a*) A, B, C (*b*) A, B, D (*c*) all the four (*d*) A, D.
2. A single-phase induction motor is labelled 1 and a 3-phase induction motor is labelled 2. When slip is zero
   (*a*) torque is zero in both motors 1 and 2
   (*b*) torque is non-zero but positive in both the motors
   (*c*) torque is non-zero negative in motor 1 and zero in motor 2
   (*d*) torque is non-zero negative in motor 1 and non-zero positive in motor 2.
3. A 3-phase induction motor is running from 3-phase source at a constant load. If fuse in one line is suddenly blown off, the motor
   (*a*) would stop
   (*b*) would continue running with line current $\sqrt{3}$ times the previous value
   (*c*) same as in (*b*) but with line current 3 times
   (*d*) same as in (*b*) but with line current 4 times.
4. A single-phase, 6-pole, 50 Hz induction motor has rotor resistance of $\sqrt{19}$ ohms and rotor self-reactance of 20 ohms. In addition to zero speed, the motor torque would be zero at a speed of
   (*a*) 1000 r.p.m (*b*) 995 r.p.m (*c*) 950 r.p.m (*d*) 900 r.p.m.
5. In various types of split-phase induction motors, the starting torques produced are in the following descending order :
   (*a*) capacitor-split, resistor-split, shaded pole
   (*b*) capacitor-split, shaded pole, resistor-split
   (*c*) resistor-split, capacitor-split, shaded pole
   (*d*) shaded pole, resistor-split, capacitor-split.
6. In a capacitor-split motor, if C_1 is the capacitance required for best starting torque and C_2 for best running performance, then
   (*a*) C_1 is much smaller than C_2 (*b*) C_1 is almost equal to C_2
   (*c*) C_1 is much larger than C_2 (*d*) C_1 and C_2 may have any values.
7. A single-phase, 50 Hz sub-synchronous motor has 2 stator poles and 10 rotor poles. It will run at a speed of
   (*a*) 3000 rpm (*b*) 600 rpm (*c*) 1800 rpm (*d*) 1000 rpm.
8. In a hysteresis motor, the rotor cylinder is made up of
   (*a*) magnetically soft chrome steel (*b*) magnetically hard cobalt steel
   (*c*) steel laminations (*d*) solid steel.
9. In capacitor start and run 1-phase induction motors, starting capacitor C_1 and permanent capacitor C_2 are as under :
   (*a*) C_1 – electrolytic type ; C_2 – mica type (*b*) C_1 – mica type ; C_2 – electrolytic type
   (*c*) C_1 – electrolytic type ; C_2 – paper type (*d*) C_1 – paper type ; C_2 – electrolytic type.

10. In a shaded-pole motor, if ϕ_1 is the flux in unshaded-pole and ϕ_2 in the shaded-pole, then the rotor

(*a*) runs from shaded to unshaded pole with ϕ_1 leading ϕ_2
(*b*) runs from shaded to unshaded pole with ϕ_2 leading ϕ_1
(*c*) runs from unshaded to shaded pole with ϕ_1 leading ϕ_2
(*d*) runs from unshaded to shaded pole with ϕ_2 leading ϕ_1.

11. Capacitor-start and run 1-phase induction motor is basically a

(*a*) 1-phase induction motor (*b*) 2-phase induction motor
(*c*) 3-phase induction motor (*d*) 1-phase reluctance motor.

12. The direction of rotation of a 1-phase induction motor can be reversed by

(*a*) reversing the leads of main winding (*b*) reversing the leads of auxiliary winding
(*c*) reversing the supply leads (*d*) either (*a*) or (*b*).

13. In a 1-phase split-phase induction motor, I_m and I_a are the currents in main and auxiliary windings respectively and β is the angle between them. The torque developed by this motor is proportional to

(*a*) $I_a I_m \sin \beta$ (*b*) $I_a I_m \cos \beta$ (*c*) $I_a I_m$ (*d*) $I_a I_m \sin \frac{\beta}{2}$.

14. In a single-phase induction motor, torque developed is proportional to

(*a*) supply voltage V_1 (*b*) V_1^2 (*c*) $\sqrt{V_1}$ (*d*) $V_1\sqrt{V_1}$.

15. A capacitor-star and run induction motor, as compared to capacitor-start induction motor, has

(*a*) more overload capacity (*b*) better pf and higher efficiency
(*c*) quieter operation (*d*) all of these.

16. In a capacitor-start 1-phase induction motor, the current in the auxiliary winding

(*a*) lags the current I_m in the main winding (*b*) is in phase with I_m
(*c*) leads I_m by 90° (*d*) leads I_m by about 80°.

17. Split-phase motors are designed to have

(A) low resistance and high leakage reactance for main winding
(B) low resistance and high leakage reactance for auxiliary winding
(C) high resistance and low leakage reactance for main winding
(D) high resistance and low leakage reactance for auxiliary winding.

From above, the correct is

(*a*) A, B (*b*) A, D (*c*) B, C (*d*) B, D.

18. When main winding of a 1-phase induction motor is connected to 200 V, 50 Hz source, it takes a current of 50 $\angle -60°$ A at standstill. Neglecting stator leakage impedance and magnetizing current, the rotor circuit parameters r_2 and x_2 in ohms are respectively.

(*a*) 2, 3.464 (*b*) 3.464, 2 (*c*) 4, 6.928 (*d*) 6.928, 4.

19. In a 1-phase induction motor, maximum starting torque may be obtained with auxiliary winding connected in series with

(*a*) resistor (*b*) capacitor (*c*) inductor (*d*) *R* and *L*.

20. The most suitable motor for a tape-recorder will be

(*a*) a.c. series motor (*b*) reluctance motor.
(*c*) hysteresis motor (*d*) 1-phase induction motor.

21. In 1-phase motors, almost constant torque during starting is produced by

(*a*) split-phase motor (*b*) reluctance motor

(*c*) shaded-pole motor (*d*) hysteresis motor.

22. A 1-phase motor which does not have any winding on its rotor is

(*a*) shaded-pole motor (*b*) hysteresis motor

(*c*) reluctance motor (*d*) repulsion motor.

23. The most suitable motor for a desk fan is

(*a*) shaded-pole motor (*b*) reluctance motor

(*c*) hysteresis motor (*d*) 1-phase split-phase motor.

24. A 2-phase a.c. servomotor, when energized from 2-phase, 120 V, 50 Hz supply gave the following data :

Slip	*0.4*	*1*	*1.6*
Torque, Nm	*6*	*10*	*14*

The motor is running with a slip of 0.4 with 120 V balanced two-phase voltages. If voltage of control phase is reduced to zero, the servomotor will develop a torque of

(*a*) 2 Nm (*b*) zero (*c*) – 1 Nm (*d*) – 2 Nm.

25. A 6-pole, 50 Hz single-phase induction motor runs at a speed of 900 rpm. The frequency/frequencies of current in the cage rotor will be

(*a*) 5 Hz (*b*) 5 Hz, 55 Hz (*c*) 5 Hz, 95 Hz (*d*) 55 Hz, 95 Hz.

26. List I contains the types of fractional kilowatt motors and List II their torque-speed characteristics. Match List I with List II.

List I (*Types of motor*)	*List II* (*Torque-speed characteristics*)
A. Hysteresis motor	1. 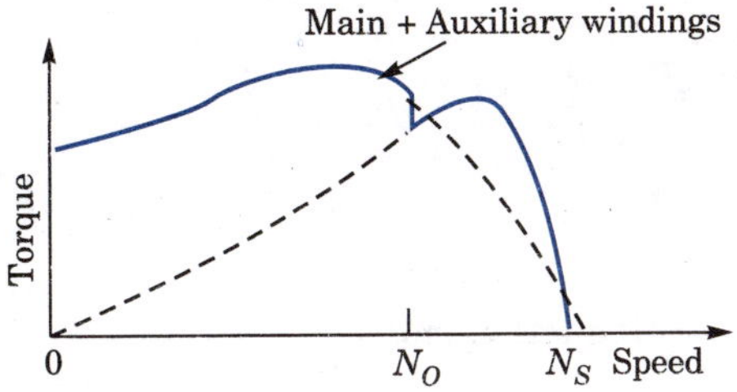
B. Capacitor-start split phase motor	2. 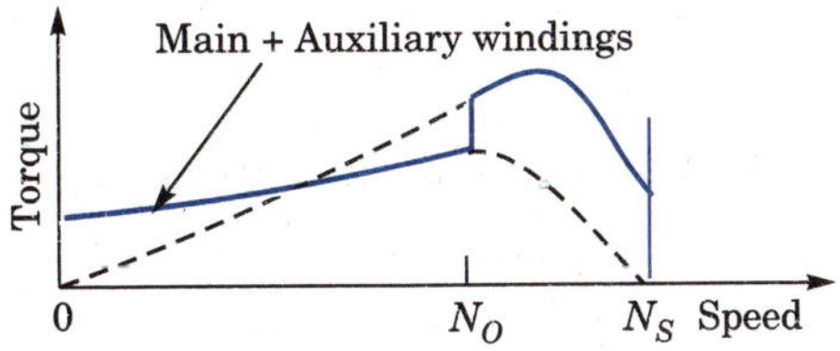
C. Reluctance motor	3. 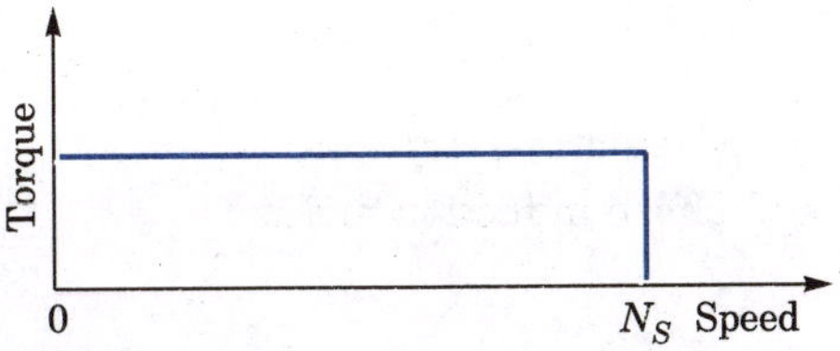

(*a*) *A*–3, *B*–1, *C*–2 (*b*) *A*–2, *B*–3, *C*–1
(*c*) *A*–1, *B*–2, *C*–3 (*d*) *A*–1, *B*–3, *C*–2

27. Which one of the following capacitor-start split-phase induction motors will have the largest value of capacitance ?

(*a*) 94 W, 3450 r.p.m (*b*) 187 W, 1725 r.p.m
(*c*) 373 W, 1140 r.p.m (*d*) 560 W, 1140 r.p.m.

28. While a 2-phase a.c. servomotor is in operation, if the voltage across the control field winding becomes zero, then the motor has a tendency to run as a single-phase induction motor. To prevent this,

(*a*) rotor having high mass moment of inertia is used for such a motor
(*b*) drag-cup type of light rotor with high rotor resistance is preferred
(*c*) a low rotor resistance is used
(*d*) the number of turns in the control field winding used is less than the main reference winding.

29. Match List I with List II

List I (Types of single-phase motors)	*List II (Types of appliances)*
A. Permanent magnet type	1. Rocket
B. Shaded pole	2. Refrigerator compressor
C. Universal	3. Sewing machine
D. Capacitor-start, capacitor-run induction motor	4. Photocopying machine

(*a*) *A*–2, *B*–3, *C*–4, *D*–1 (*b*) *A*–1, *B*–4, *C*–3, *D*–2
(*c*) *A*–3, *B*–4, *C*–1, *D*–2 (*d*) *A*–4, *B*–3, *C*–2, *D*–1

30. Match List I with List II

List I
(Types of single-phase motors)

A. Capacitor-run induction motor

B. Repulsion-induction motor

C. Capacitor-start split phase induction motor

List II
(Torque-speed characteristics)

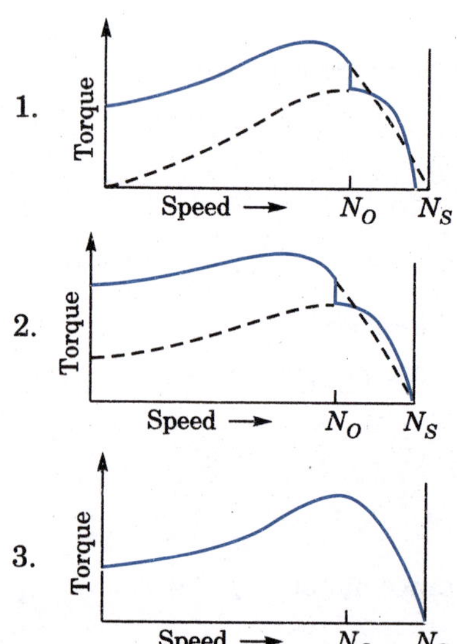

D. Capacitor-start and run Induction motor

4. 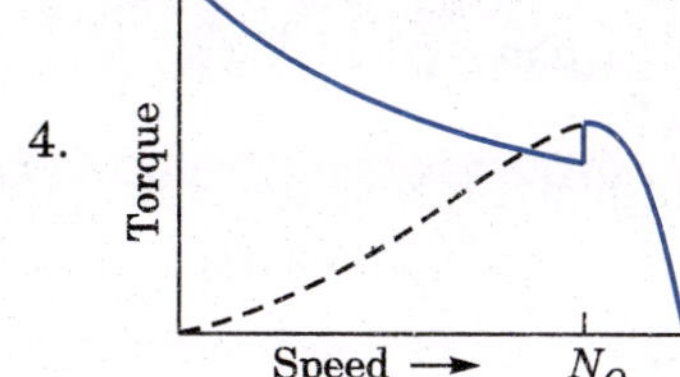

(*a*) *A*–3, *B*–4, *C*–1, *D*–2
(*b*) *A*–4, *B*–3, *C*–2, *D*–1
(*c*) *A*–2, *B*–1, *C*–4, *D*–3
(*d*) *A*–1, *B*–2, *C*–3, *D*–4

31. Match List I with List II

List I — *(Single-phase induction motors)*

List II — *(Torque-speed characteristics)*

A. Resistor split-phase motor

1. 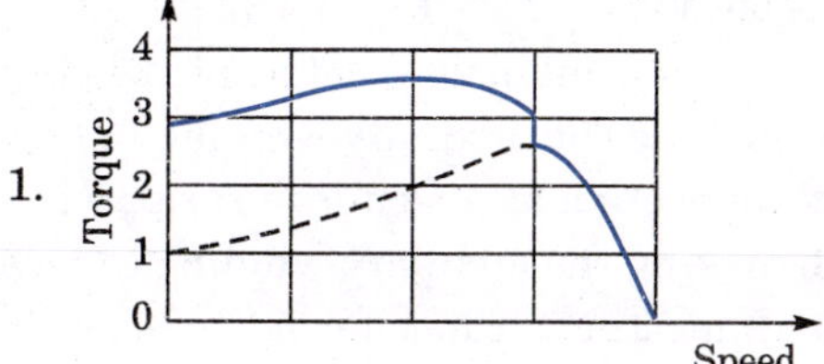

B. Capacitor-start motor

2. 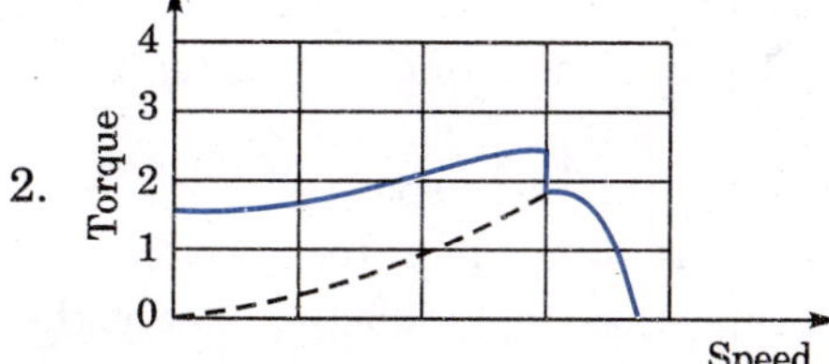

C. Capacitor-start and run motor

3. 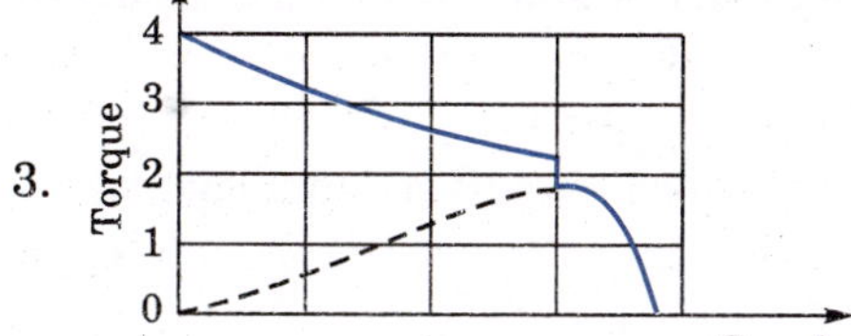

D. Repulsion-start motor

4. 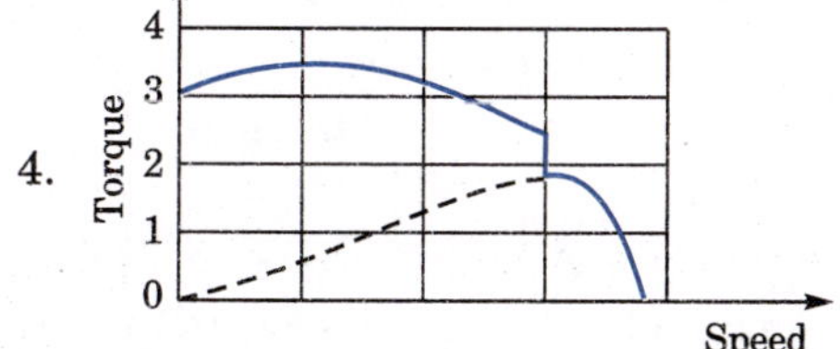

(*a*) *A*–4, *B*–3, *C*–2, *D*–1
(*b*) *A*–3, *B*–4, *C*–1, *D*–2
(*c*) *A*–1, *B*–3, *C*–2, *D*–4
(*d*) *A*–2, *B*–4, *C*–1, *D*–3

32. Which one of the following capacitor-start split-phase induction motor will have the largest value of capacitance ?

(*a*) 200 W, 705 r.p.m (*b*) 200 W, 940 r.p.m
(*c*) 200 W, 1410 r.p.m (*d*) 200 W, 2820 r.p.m.

33. In case of split-phase motor, the phase shift between currents in the two windings is around

(*a*) 30 degrees (*b*) 70 degrees (*c*) 90 degrees (*d*) 120 degrees.

[*GATE, 1996*]

34. No-load current of a 1-phase induction motor, as a percentage of its full-load current is about

(*a*) 5% (*b*) 20% (*c*) 40% (*d*) 80%.

35. Full-load operating power factor of a 1-phase induction motor is usually around

(*a*) 0.65 lag (*b*) 0.80 lag (*c*) 0.2 lead (*d*) unity.

36. A 100 W, 1-phase induction motor has full-load slip of 5%. Its friction and windage loss is 5 W and core loss is 18.5 W. The power input to rotor is equal to

(*a*) 130 W (*b*) 117.62 W (*c*) 123.5 W (*d*) 124.74 W.

37. In a 1-phase induction motor, phase-splitting is obtained by

1. making the auxiliary winding to have low reactance
2. connecting a capacitor in series with auxiliary winding
3. making the auxiliary winding to have high resistance
4. connecting a capacitor in series with main winding.

From above, the correct answer is

(*a*) 2 only (*b*) 2, 3, 4 (*c*) 1, 2, 3 (*d*) 1, 2, 3, 4.

38. In a 1-phase induction motor, centrifugal switch fitted on the rotor operates when rotor speed

(*a*) reaches its rated speed (*b*) exceeds synchronous speed
(*c*) exceeds 70% of its rated speed (*d*) exceeds 40% of its rated speed.

39. In a capacitor-start induction motor, the value of capacitor is determined by its

(*a*) voltage (*b*) frequency (*c*) power factor (*d*) starting torque.

40. In a capacitor-start single-phase induction motor, centrifugal switch fails to disconnect the capacitor as the motor accelerates. Under these conditions,

(*a*) the auxiliary winding will get damaged (*b*) the motor will stop
(*c*) the capacitor will get damaged (*d*) the main winding will get damaged

41. Consider the following statements regarding fractional kW shaded-pole motor.

1. Its direction of rotation is from unshaded to shaded portion of the poles.
2. Its direction of rotation is from shaded to unshaded portion of the poles.
3. It can remain stalled for short periods without any harm.
4. It has a very poor power factor.

From above, the correct statements are

(*a*) 1, 3, 4 (*b*) 2, 3, 4 (*c*) 2, 4 (*d*) 1, 3. [*I.E.S., 1997*]

42. In a split-phase motor (or resistor split-phase motor), ratio *X*/*R* of

(*a*) auxiliary winding is higher than that of main winding
(*b*) auxiliary winding is lower than that of main winding
(*c*) both windings are exactly equal
(*d*) both windings are nearly equal.

43. In a capacitor-start capacitor run induction motor,

(*a*) one capacitor is in circuit during starting and the other is in circuit during running

(*b*) both the capacitors are in circuit during starting and running

(*c*) both the capacitors are in circuit during starting and one capacitor during running

(*d*) one capacitor is in circuit during starting and both capacitors are in circuit during running.

44. A centrifugal switch is not required in

(*a*) split-phase motor (*b*) capacitor start motor

(*c*) capacitor start and capacitor run motor (*d*) permanent split capacitor motor.

45. In single-phase induction motors, the torque at synchronous speed is

1. zero in split-phase motors
2. zero in permanent-split capacitor motors
3. non-zero in capacitor-start and capacitor-run motors
4. non-zero in capacitor-start motors
5. zero in shaded-pole motors

From above, the correct statements are

(*a*) 2, 4, 5 (*b*) 1, 4, 5 (*c*) 1, 2, 3, 4 (*d*) 3, 4, 5.

46. In a two-phase servomotor, maximum torque is developed at

(*a*) synchronous speed

(*b*) at a speed somewhat less than synchronous speed

(*c*) at a slip of about – 0.5 (*d*) at a slip of about + 0.5.

47. Given that D = rotor diameter and L = rotor axial length, a high performance ac servometer is characterized by

(*a*) large D, large L (*b*) large D, small L

(*c*) small D, small L (*d*) small D, large L. [*I.E.S., 1993*]

48. In a 1-phase hysteresis motor,

(*a*) starting torque is produced by both eddy-current and hysteresis while running torque is produced by hysteresis

(*b*) starting as well as running torques are produced by eddy-curernt and hysteresis,

(*c*) starting torque is produced by only eddy-current while running torque is produced by only hysteresis

(*d*) starting as well as running torques both are produced by only hysteresis.

49. The mian reason for using a hysteresis motor for high quality tape-recorders and record-players is that

(*a*) its speed is constant (synchronous)

(*b*) it develops extremely steady torque

(*c*) it requires no centrifugal switch

(*d*) its operation is not affected by mechanical vibrations. [*I.E.S., 1995*]

50. A fluctuating voltage supply is deterimental to a referigerator motor but not to a ceiling fan, although both are 1-phase induction motors. It is because the referigerator motor

(*a*) is made more robust than the fan motor

(*b*) is subjected to short duty cycle but the fan motor is subjected to continuous duty

(*c*) is enclosed in a sealed unit while the fan motor is open to environment

(*d*) load is constant but the fan motor load is voltage dependent. [*I.E.S., 1993*]

51. Consider the following statements.

1. Reluctance-start 1-phase induction motor has non-salient pole rotor
2. 1-phase reluctance motor has salient-pole rotor
3. 1-phase reluctance motor has salient-pole stator
4. Reluctance-start 1-phase induction motor has non-uniform air gap
5. Single-phase reluctance motor working principle is similar to that of a shaded-pole motor.

From above, the correct statements are

(*a*) 1, 2, 4 (*b*) 1, 2, 4, 5 (*c*) 1, 2, 3, 5 (*d*) 1, 2, 3, 4.

52. A single-phase, 230 V, 50 Hz, 4-pole, capacitor-start induction motor has the following stand-still impedances

Main winding, $Z_m = 6.0 + j4.0\ \Omega$

Auxiliary winding, $Z_a = 8.0 + j6.0\ \Omega$

The value of the starting capacitor required to produce 90° phase difference between the currents in the main and auxiliary windings will be

(*a*) 176.84 μF (*b*) 167.24 μF (*c*) 265.26 μF (*d*) 280.86 μF

[**Hint.** Refer to Example 6.7] [*GATE, 2004*]

53. In a single-phase induction motor driving a fan load, the reason for having a high resistance rotor is to achieve

(*a*) low starting torque (*b*) quick acceleration

(*c*) high efficiency (*d*) reduced size [*GATE, 2005*]

54. A 220 V, 50 Hz, single-phase induction motor has the connection diagram and winding orientations shown in fig. here. MM' is the axis of the main stator winding (M_1M_2) and AA' is that of the auxiliary winding (A_1A_2). Directions of the winding axes indicate direction of flux when currents in the windings are in the directions shown. Parameters of each winding are indicated. When switsh S is closed, the motor

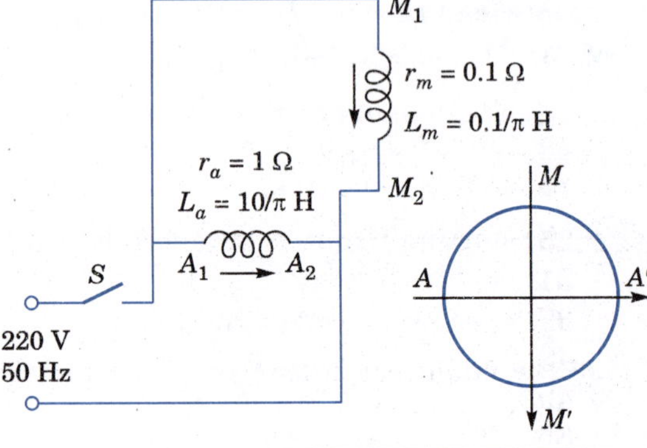

Fig. A-7

(*a*) rotates clockwise

(*b*) rotates anticlockwise

(*c*) does not rotate

(*d*) rotates momentarily and comes to a halt. [*GATE, 2009*]

[**Hint.** $\theta_m = \tan^{-1}\dfrac{10}{0.1} = 89.427°$, $\theta_a = \tan^{-1}\dfrac{1000}{1} = 89.943°$. Torque $\propto I_a I_m \sin(I_a, I_m)$ as $I_a I_m \sin(0.516°) \cong 0$]

55. A single-phase induction motor is provided with capacitor and centrifugal switch in series with auxiliary winding.

The switch is expected to operate at a speed of $0.7N_s$, but due to malfunctioning the switch fails to operate. The torque-speed characteristic of the motor is represented by

[*GATE, 2014*]

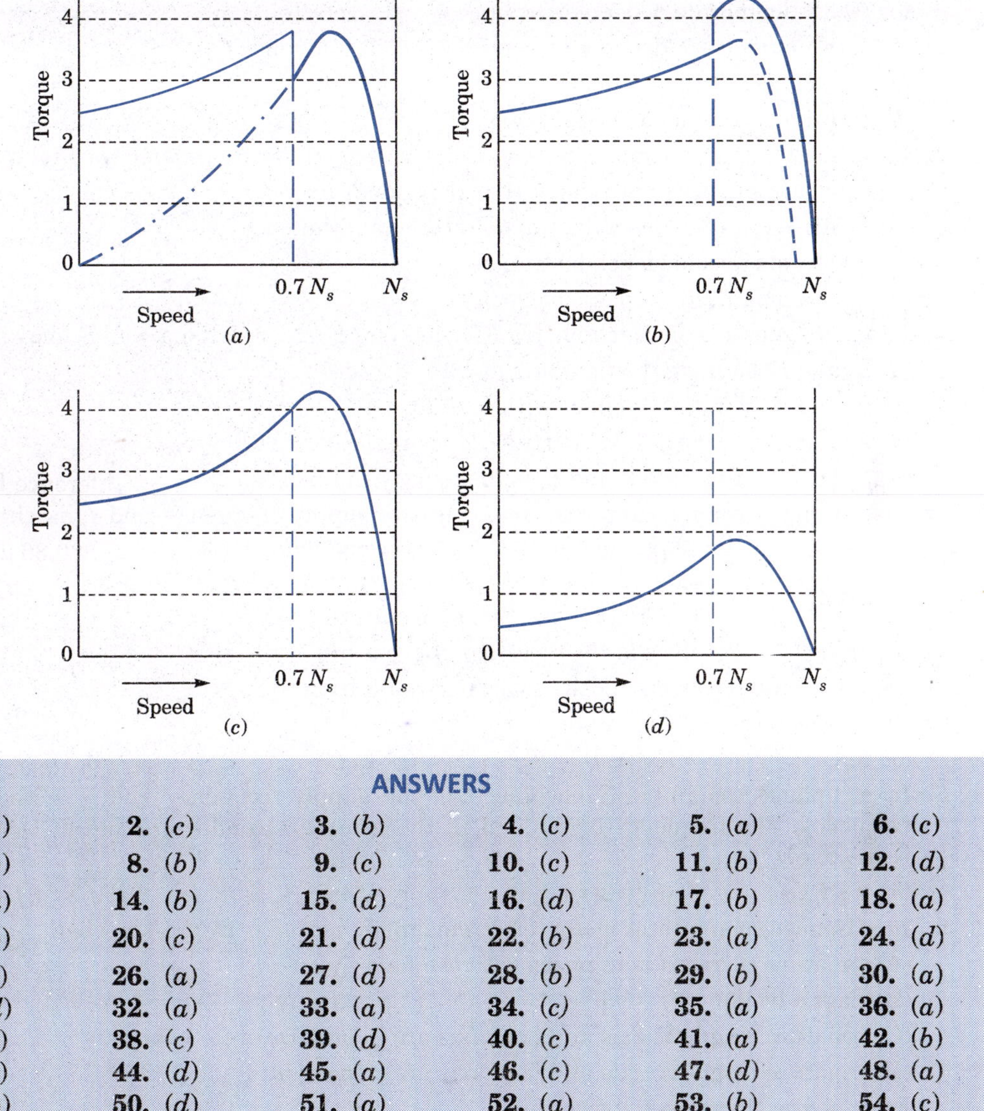

ANSWERS

1. (*b*)	**2.** (*c*)	**3.** (*b*)	**4.** (*c*)	**5.** (*a*)	**6.** (*c*)
7. (*b*)	**8.** (*b*)	**9.** (*c*)	**10.** (*c*)	**11.** (*b*)	**12.** (*d*)
13. (*a*)	**14.** (*b*)	**15.** (*d*)	**16.** (*d*)	**17.** (*b*)	**18.** (*a*)
19. (*b*)	**20.** (*c*)	**21.** (*d*)	**22.** (*b*)	**23.** (*a*)	**24.** (*d*)
25. (*c*)	**26.** (*a*)	**27.** (*d*)	**28.** (*b*)	**29.** (*b*)	**30.** (*a*)
31. (*d*)	**32.** (*a*)	**33.** (*a*)	**34.** (*c*)	**35.** (*a*)	**36.** (*a*)
37. (*c*)	**38.** (*c*)	**39.** (*d*)	**40.** (*c*)	**41.** (*a*)	**42.** (*b*)
43. (*c*)	**44.** (*d*)	**45.** (*a*)	**46.** (*c*)	**47.** (*d*)	**48.** (*a*)
49. (*b*)	**50.** (*d*)	**51.** (*a*)	**52.** (*a*)	**53.** (*b*)	**54.** (*c*)
55. (*c*)					

A.C. COMMUTATOR MACHINES

1. In an a.c. commutator motor, frequency of pulsating flux produced by field winding is f. The rotational emf across brushes has its frequency equal to

(*a*) f with magnitude dependent upon f

(*b*) f with magnitude dependent upon rotational frequency f_r

(*c*) f_r with magnitude dependent upon f_r

(*d*) f_r with magnitude dependent upon f.

2. In an a.c. commutator machine, the transformer emf has its frequency equal to

(*a*) supply frequency f with magnitude dependent upon f

(*b*) f with magnitude dependent upon rotational frequency f_r

(*c*) f_r with magnitude dependent upon f_r

(*d*) f_r with magnitude dependent upon f.

3. In an a.c. commutator machine, transformer emf E_t and rotational emf E_r may be as under:

(*a*) E_r and E_t both lag the field flux by 90°

(*b*) E_r and E_t both are in phase with field flux

(*c*) E_r is in phase with flux whereas E_t lags the flux by 90°

(*d*) E_r lags the flux by 90° and E_t is in phase with flux.

4. In a 3-phase commutator machine, f is the supply frequency and f_r is the rotational frequency. The frequency of emf in the armature conductors is

(A) $(f - f_r)$ if rotating field ϕ revolves opposite to armature rotation

(B) $(f - f_r)$ if ϕ revolves in the direction of armature rotation

(C) $(f + f_r)$ if ϕ revolves in the direction of armature rotation

(D) $(f + f_r)$ if ϕ revolves opposite to armature rotation.

From above, the correct answer is

(*a*) A, C (*b*) A, D (*c*) B, C (*d*) B, D.

5. In a 3-phase commutator machine, f is the supply frequency and f_r is the rotational frequency. The frequency of the emf in the armature conductors and at the brushes is respectively

(*a*) $(f \pm f_r), f$ (*b*) $(f \pm f_r), f_r$ (*c*) $(f + f_r), f_r$ (*d*) $(f - f_r), f$.

6. In a 1-phase commutator motor, electromagnetic torque is maximum when

(A) armature current i is in phase with the field flux ϕ

(B) i lags ϕ by 90°

(C) armature magnetic axis and field axis are in quadrature

(D) armature magnetic axis and field axis are coincident.

From above, the correct answer is

(*a*) A, C (*b*) A, D (*c*) B, C (*d*) B, D.

7. Operation of a dc shunt motor on ac supply is not successful due to

(*a*) low resistance of armature circuit (*b*) high resistance of field circuit

(*c*) high inductance of field circuit (*d*) reversal of polarity.

8. AC series motors are built with as few turns as possible to

(*a*) reduce flux (*b*) minimise eddy-current loss

(*c*) reduce reactance (*d*) increase speed

9. Consider the following statements regarding an ac series motor.

1. Its speed falls with increase in load.
2. Its power factor improves with increase in load.
3. Its torque-speed characteristic is similar to that of a dc shunt motor.
4. Its torque-speed characteristic is similar to that of a dc series motor.

From above, the correct statements are

(*a*) 1, 4 (*b*) 1, 2, 3 (*c*) 2, 3 (*d*) 1, 2, 4

10. Speed of an universal motor is

(*a*) not affected by supply frequency (*b*) proportional to supply frequency
(*c*) inversely proportional to supply frequency
(*d*) is affected by supply frequency

11. In a 1-phase series motor, as the load torque is increased,

(*a*) both power factor (pf) and speed (n) increase
(*b*) both pf and n decrease (*c*) pf improves but n decreases
(*d*) pf decreases but n increases.

12. The function of compensating winding in a 1-phase series motor is to

(*a*) reduce the reactance drop (*b*) improve the commutation
(*c*) reduce the reactance drop and degrade the commutation
(*d*) reduce the reactance drop and improve the commutation.

13. If a 1-phase series motor is operated at a frequency lower than its rated frequency, the motor would have

(*a*) improved commutation, low reactance drop and iron loss
(*b*) improved commutation only (*c*) low-reactance drop only
(*d*) low-reactance drop and iron loss.

14. If a single-phase series motor is operated at a frequency lower than its rated frequency, then

(*a*) both the speed and torque would decrease
(*b*) both the speed and torque would increase
(*c*) speed would decrease but torque would increase
(*d*) speed would increase but torque would decrease.

15. A universal motor

(A) can run satisfactorily both on a.c. and d.c. supplies
(B) has compensating winding
(C) has laminated stator and laminated rotor
(D) has unlaminated stator but laminated rotor

From these, the true is

(*a*) A, C (*b*) A, D (*c*) B, C (*d*) B, D.

16. Consider the following statements about a Schrage motor.

1. The magnitude of injected voltage into the secondary circuit depends on the angle between two brushes.
2. The phase angle between injected voltage and secondary voltage depends on the centre lines of rotor and secondary windings.
3. When the two brushes of each phase are on the same commutator segment, motor operates as an ordinary induction motor.

4. It offers constant power drive.

From above, the correct statements are

(*a*) 1, 2, 3, 4 (*b*) 1, 3, 4 (*c*) 1, 2, 4 (*d*) 1, 2, 3

17. Consider the following statements for a Schrage motor.

1. It does not require any special starting devices.
2. If the brushes are moved against the direction of rotation such that centre lines of rotor and stator windings do not coincide, the speed increases and pf is improved.
3. If the brushes are moved in the direction of rotation such that centre lines of rotor and stator windings do not coincide, the speed increases and pf is improved.
4. Rotor rotates in the direction of rotating field.

From above, the correct statements are

(*a*) 1, 3 (*b*) 2, 3 (*c*) 2, 3, 4 (*d*) 1, 3, 4

18. Consider the following statements regarding Schrage motor.

1. It is equivalent to an inverted polyphase induction motor.
2. Frequency of the emf at stationary brushes depends on the speed of rotating field in the air gap.
3. It is a constant torque drive motor.
4. Its operating power factor at low speed is high and at high speed is low.
5. The starting current can be kept low with brush-separation equal to pole pitch.

From above, the correct statements are

(*a*) 1, 3, 5 (*b*) 1, 2, 3, 5 (*c*) 1, 2, 3, 4, 5 (*d*) 1, 2, 4, 5

19. Consider the following statements about a Schrage motor.

1. Primary winding is located in lower part of rotor slots.
2. Primary winding is located in upper part of rotor slots.
3. Rotating field speed in air gap is slip speed.
4. It cannot operate at sychronous speed.

From above statements, the correct answer is

(*a*) 2, 3 (*b*) 1, 3 (*c*) 2, 3, 4 (*d*) 1, 3, 4

20. In a Schrage motor, k is the ratio of maximum value of injected emf to the rotor emf at standstill. The ratio of maximum no-load speed to synchronous speed is

(*a*) k (*b*) $1 - k$ (*c*) $1 + k$ (*d*) $\frac{1}{1-k}$.

21. In the Schrage motor, k is the ratio of maximum value of injected emf to the rotor emf at standstill. For a speed range of 5 : 1, the value of k is

(*a*) 1/2 (*b*) 2/3 (*c*) 3/2 (*d*) 1/3.

22. A Schrage motor is operating as a 3-phase induction motor. If the brush-shift is carried out against the direction of rotation, then

(*a*) speed rises and pf is worsened (*b*) speed decreases and pf is worsened
(*c*) speed rises and pf is improved (*d*) speed decreases and pf is improved.

23. A Schrage motor is running as a 3-phase induction motor. If brush shift is in the direction of rotor rotation, then

(*a*) speed rises and pf is worsened (*b*) speed decreases and pf is worsened
(*c*) speed rises and pf is improved (*d*) speed decreases and pf is improved.

24. A Schrage motor is a

(*a*) constant-power motor with shunt speed-torque characteristics

(*b*) constant-torque motor with shunt speed-torque characteristics

(*c*) constant-power motor with series speed-torque characteristics

(*d*) constant-torque motor with series speed-torque characteristics.

25. In a Schrage motor, power factor

(*a*) may become leading at sub-synchronous speed

(*b*) never becomes leading at super-synchronous speed

(*c*) may become leading at super-synchronous speed

(*d*) is always leading at super-synchronous speed.

26. In a Schrage motor, the speed regulation near synchronous speed n_s is

(A) more than its value near $\frac{3}{2} n_s$ (B) less than its value near $\frac{3}{2} n_s$

(C) more than its value near $\frac{n_s}{2}$ (D) less than its value near $\frac{n_s}{2}$.

From above, the correct is

(*a*) A, C (*b*) A, D (*c*) B, C (*d*) B, D.

27. For a 4-pole, 50 Hz Schrage motor, the ratio of maximum value of injected emf to the rotor emf at standstill is $\frac{2}{3}$. For a rotor speed of 1000 r.p.m, the brush separation in electrical degrees is

(*a*) 30° (*b*) 60° (*c*) 90° (*d*) 120°.

28. In a 4-pole, 50 Hz Schrage motor, the emf across the brushes, one pole-pitch apart, is 30 V. The secondary emf at standstill is 40 V. For this motor, no-load speed range is

(*a*) 7 : 1 (*b*) 5 : 1 (*c*) 9 : 1 (*d*) 3 : 1.

29. In a 4-pole, 50 Hz Schrage motor, rotor speed is 1800 r.p.m. Under this condition, air-gap flux speed with respect to stator and brush frequency are, respectively,

(*a*) 1500 rpm against the rotor rotation, 50 Hz

(*b*) 300 rpm against the rotor rotation, 10 Hz

(*c*) 300 rpm against the rotor rotation, 15 Hz

(*d*) 300 rpm in the direction of rotor rotation, 10 Hz.

30. In a 4-pole, 50 Hz Schrage motor, rotor runs at 1600 r.p.m clockwise. The speed of air-gap field and the brush frequency are, respectively.

(*a*) 1500 r.p.m anticlockwise, 50 Hz (*b*) 100 r.p.m clockwise, $53\frac{1}{3}$ Hz

(*c*) 100 r.p.m anticlockwise, $3\frac{1}{3}$ Hz (*d*) 100 r.p.m clockwise, $3\frac{1}{3}$ Hz.

31. In a 6-pole, 50 Hz Schrage motor, the rotor runs at 800 r.p.m clockwise. The speed of the air-gap field, with respect to stator and rotor, is respectively,

(*a*) 200 r.p.m anticlockwise, 1000 r.p.m anticlockwise

(*b*) 200 r.p.m clockwise, 1000 r.p.m anticlockwise

(*c*) 200 r.p.m clockwise, 1000 r.p.m clockwise

(*d*) 200 r.p.m anticlockwise, 1000 r.p.m clockwise.

32. In a 4-pole Schrage motor, rotor speed is 1500 r.p.m and air-gap field speed is 600 r.p.m, both speeds being in the same direction. The supply frequency and frequency of the emf at brushes are, respectively ,

(*a*) 30 Hz, 20 Hz (*b*) 70 Hz, 20 Hz (*c*) 30 Hz, 50 Hz (*d*) 20 Hz, 30 Hz.

33. The speed of a universal motor can be controlled by

(*a*) introducing a variable resistance in series with the motor

(*b*) tapping the field at various points

(*c*) centrifugal mechanism

(*d*) all of the above steps.

ANSWERS

1. (*b*)	**2.** (*a*)	**3.** (*c*)	**4.** (*d*)	**5.** (*a*)	**6.** (*a*)
7. (*c*)	**8.** (*c*)	**9.** (*a*)	**10.** (*d*)	**11.** (*b*)	**12.** (*d*)
13. (*a*)	**14.** (*b*)	**15.** (*a*)	**16.** (*d*)	**17.** (*a*)	**18.** (*b*)
19. (*b*)	**20.** (*c*)	**21.** (*b*)	**22.** (*d*)	**23.** (*c*)	**24.** (*b*)
25. (*c*)	**26.** (*d*)	**27.** (*b*)	**28.** (*a*)	**29.** (*d*)	**30.** (*d*)
31. (*a*)	**32.** (*a*)	**33.** (*d*).			

TRANSFORMERS

1. In a 3-phase core-type transformer, the exciting currents for
   (*a*) three primaries are equal (*b*) three primaries are unequal
   (*c*) outer two primaries are less than the middle primary
   (*d*) outer two primaries are more than the middle primary.
2. In a three-phase shell-type transformer, the direction of the winding on the central limb is reversed with respect to outer two limbs
   (*a*) to save the amount of core material (*b*) to save the amount of winding material
   (*c*) to reduce the third harmonics (*d*) to save both winding and core material.
3. The symbol *Yd*11 represents a 3-phase transformer with h.v. line phasor
   (*a*) leading the l.v. line phasor by 30° (*b*) leading the l.v. line phasor by 150°
   (*c*) lagging the l.v. line phasor by 30° (*d*) lagging the l.v. line phasor by 60°.
4. The secondary of a transformer in star has an output voltage of 400 V. If this secondary is reconnected in interstate, then the output voltage becomes
   (*a*) 346.4 V (*b*) 400 V (*c*) 460 V (*d*) 360 V.
5. The secondary of a transformer in interstar has an output voltage of 400 V. If this secondary is reconnected in star, then the output voltage becomes
   (*a*) 400 V (*b*) 461.87 V (*c*) 692.82 V (*d*) 450 V.
6. Tick the correct combination of phasor groups from the following:
   (*a*) *Yd*6, *Yy*1 (*b*) *Dd*6, *Yd*1 (*c*) *Yd*11, *Dy*6 (*d*) *Yy*11, *Dy*0.
7. A 3-phase transformer with h.v. in delta and l.v. in star can have the following symbol :
   (*a*) *Yd*1 or *Yd*11 (*b*) *Dy*1 or *Dy*11 (*c*) *Dy*0 or *Dy*6 (*d*) *Dy*1 only.
8. 3-phase transformer with h.v. in star and l.v. in delta can have the following symbol :
   (*a*) *Yd*1 or *Yd*11 (*b*) *Dy*1 or *Dy*11 (*c*) *Yd*0 or *Yd*6 (*d*) *Yd*1 only.
9. A delta-zigzag three-phase transformer can have the symbol:
   (*a*) *DzO* or *Dz*1 (*b*) *DzO* or *Dz*6 (*c*) *Dz*1 or *Dz*11 (*d*) *DzO* only.
10. A star-zigzag 3-phase transformer can have the symbol:
    (*a*) *YzO* or *Yz*1 (*b*) *Yz*1 or *Yz*11 (*c*) *YzO* or *Yz*11 (*d*) *Yz*1 only.
11. If the primary leads of a 3-phase transformer are interchanged cyclically once, the secondary line phasors get rotated through a time-phase angle of
    (*a*) 120° clockwise (*b*) 120° anticlockwise (*c*) 120° (*d*) 360°.
12. If the primary winding terminals of each of the three-phase are reversed, then the secondary line voltages are rotated through
    (*a*) 120° clockwise (*b*) 180° (*c*) 180° clockwise (*d*) 180° anticlockwise.
13. Consider the following statements :
    (A) *Dy*1 and *Yd*11 can operate in parallel (B) *Dy*11 and *Yd*1 can operate in parallel
    (C) *Dy*1 and *Yd*1 can operate in parallel (D) *Yd*1 and *Yz*1 can operate in parallel.
    From above, the correct statement is
    (*a*) C, D (*b*) A, B (*c*) A, C, D (*d*) All.
14. A 3-phase *Dy* transformer has input voltage of 1000 V and output voltage of 100 V. With primary and secondary windings reconnected respectively in star and zigzag and with the same input voltage, the output line voltage of *Yz* transformer would be
    (*a*) 50 V (*b*) 86.6 V (*c*) 100 V (*d*) 115 V.

15. A 3-phase *Yd* transformer has input voltage of 1000 *V* and output voltage of 100 V. With primary and secondary windings reconnected respectively in delta and zigzag and with the same input voltage, the output line voltage of *Dz* transformer would be

(*a*) 173.2 V (*b*) 100 V (*c*) 259.8 V (*d*) 150 V.

16. A 3-phase *Yd* transformer has secondary to primary per-phase turns ratio of *K*. If the ratio of primary to secondary line voltage is K_1 and the secondary line voltage leads the primary line voltage by an angle ϕ, then

(*a*) $K_1 = \frac{K}{\sqrt{3}}; \phi = 30°$ (*b*) $K_1 = \frac{\sqrt{3}}{K}; \phi = -30°$

(*c*) $K_1 = \frac{K}{\sqrt{3}}; \phi = -30°$ (*d*) $K_1 = \frac{\sqrt{3}}{K}; \phi = 30°$.

17. A 3-phase *Dy* transformer has secondary to primary turns ratio per phase of *K*. If the ratio of primary to secondary line voltage is K_1 and the secondary line voltage leads the primary line voltage by an angle ϕ, then.

(*a*) $K_1 = \frac{1}{K\sqrt{3}}$; $\phi = 30°$ (*b*) $K_1 = \frac{\sqrt{3}}{K}$; $\phi = 30°$

(*c*) $K_1 = \frac{\sqrt{3}}{K}$; $\phi = -30°$ (*d*) $K_1 = \frac{1}{K\sqrt{3}}$; $\phi = -30°$.

18. A 3-phase transformer has its primary connected in delta and secondary in star. Secondary to primary turns ratio per phase is *K*. If the ratio of secondary to primary line voltage is K_1, and the secondary voltage leads the primary voltage by an angle ϕ, then

(*a*) $K_1 = \sqrt{3}K$; $\phi = 30°$ (*b*) $K_1 = \frac{K}{\sqrt{3}}$; $\phi = -30°$

(*c*) $K_1 = \sqrt{3}K$; $\phi = -30°$ (*d*) $K_1 = \frac{K}{\sqrt{3}}$; $\phi = 30°$. [*GATE, 1988*]

19. A delta-star transformer 1 is operating in parallel with a star-delta transformer 2. If primary to secondary turns ratio per phase for transformer 1 is *K*, then for transformer 2, the primary to secondary turns ratio per phase would be

(*a*) *K* (*b*) 3*K* (*c*) $\frac{K}{3}$ (*d*) $\frac{K}{\sqrt{3}}$.

20. A star-delta transformer 1 is working in parallel with a delta-star transformer 2. If primary to secondary turns ratio per phase for transformer 1 is *K*, then for transformer 2, the primary to secondary turns ratio per phase is

(*a*) *K* (*b*) 3*K* (*c*) $\frac{K}{3}$ (*d*) $\frac{K}{\sqrt{3}}$.

21. Two transformers of different kVA ratings working in parallel share the load in proportion to their ratings when their

(A) per unit leakage impedances on the same kVA base are the same

(B) per unit leakage impedances on their respective ratings are equal

(C) ohmic values of the leakage impedances are inversely proportional to their ratings

(D) ohmic values of the magnetizing reactances are the same.

From above, the correct answer is

(*a*) A, C (*b*) A, B (*c*) B, C (*d*) A, D. [*GATE, 1992*]

22. The power associated with fundamental frequency applied voltage V_1 and third harmonic current I_1 is

(*a*) $V_1I_1 \cos \theta$ (*b*) zero (*c*) $\frac{1}{3} V_1I_1 \cos \theta$ (*d*) $\frac{1}{2} V_1I_1 \cos \theta$.

23. For a sinusoidal applied voltage in a single-phase transformer, the flux wave and the magnetizing-current are respectively

(*a*) sinusoidal, sinusoidal (*b*) peaky, flat-topped
(*c*) flat-topped, peaky (*d*) sinusoidal, peaky.

24. For a sinusoidal magnetizing current in a single-phase transformer, the waveforms of flux and induced emfs in both the windings are respectively

(*a*) peaky, sinusoidal (*b*) peaky, flat-topped
(*c*) flat-topped, peaky (*d*) sinusoidal, peaky.

25. In a transformer core, the third and fifth harmonic component of fluxes are 8% and 3% of the fundamental flux respectively. The third and fifth harmonic induced emfs, in terms of the fundamental induced emf, are respectively,

(*a*) 24%, 15% (*b*) 24%, 9% (*c*) 40%, 15% (*d*) 40%, 9%.

26. In a 3-phase transformer, phase sequence for the fundamental emf is *ABC*. Then phase sequences for the fifth and seventh harmonic emfs are respectively

(*a*) *ABC*, *ABC* (*b*) *ABC*, *ACB* (*c*) *ACB*, *ABC* (*d*) *ACB*, *ACB*.

27. Primary, or secondary, winding of a 3-phase transformer in delta helps to suppress

(*a*) third harmonic current (*b*) third harmonic voltage
(*c*) third harmonic flux (*d*) all of the above.

28. A single-phase transformer has fundamental, third harmonic and fifth harmonic voltages equal to 400 V, 200 V and 50 V respectively. Three such transformers are connected in star-delta. The voltage across the secondary open-circuited delta would be

(*a*) 1200 V (*b*) 600 V (*c*) 150 V (*d*) 650 V.

29. A single-phase transformer has fundamental, third harmonic and fifth harmonic voltages of 400 V, 200 V and 50 V respectively. Three such transformers are connected in star-delta. In addition, the transformer neutral is connected to source neutral. The voltage across the open-circuited secondary delta would be

(*a*) 600 V (*b*) 150 V (*c*) zero (*d*) 1200 V.

30. A delta-star transformer at no-load, has 1.5 A current circulating in the closed delta. If now the secondary is also connected in delta, the circulating current in the primary delta would

(*a*) reduce to 1.2 A (*b*) become more than 1.5 A
(*c*) become less than 1.5 A (*d*) become 0.75 A.

31. A delta-star transformer bank, at no-load, has 1.5 A current circulating in the closed delta. The three-phase transformer bank is assumed ideal with phase turns ratio as unity. If the secondary is now also reconnected in delta, the circulating current in the primary delta would

(*a*) reduce to 0.75 A (*b*) become more than 1.5 A
(*c*) become less than 1.5 A (*d*) reduce to 1.2 A.

32. A star-delta transformer can deliver 100 kVA load. If it is re-connected in delta-star, it can deliver a load of

(*a*) 173.2 kVA (*b*) 86.6 kVA (*c*) 300 kVA (*d*) 100 kVA.

33. Two 100 kVA single-phase transformers are connected in open delta. The maximum balanced 3-phase load that the combination can deliver without overloading either unit is

(*a*) 173.2 kVA (*b*) 200 kVA (*c*) 300 kVA (*d*) 115.5 kVA.

34. The utilization factor for transformers in open-delta is

(*a*) 0.75 (*b*) 0.667 (*c*) 0.866 (*d*) 0.5.

35. A single-phase transformer has primary to secondary turns ratio of 20. Three such transformers are used for three to six phase conversion by double-star method. If the output line voltage is 400 V, then the primary line voltage is

(*a*) 8 kV (*b*) 16 kV (*c*) 12 kV (*d*) 20 kV.

36. For three to six phase conversion by double-star connection, the output line voltage is V_2. The voltage rating of each secondary winding is

(*a*) V_2 (*b*) $\sqrt{3}\,V_2$ (*c*) $\frac{1}{2}\,V_2$ (*d*) $2\,V_2$.

37. For 3-to 6-phase conversion by diametral connection, the output line voltage is V_2. The voltage rating of each secondary winding is

(*a*) V_2 (*b*) $\sqrt{3}\,V_2$ (*c*) $\frac{1}{2}\,V_2$ (*d*) $2\,V_2$.

38. For three to six phase conversion by double-delta connection, the output line voltage is V_2. The voltage rating of each secondary winding is

(*a*) V_2 (*b*) $\sqrt{3}\,V_2$ (*c*) $\frac{1}{2}\,V_2$ (*d*) $2\,V_2$.

39. For three to twelve-phase conversion by star-delta/double-star connection, the output line voltage is V_2. The voltage rating of the secondary winding (with a mid tap) is

(*a*) $\frac{\sin 75°}{\sin 30°} \cdot V_2$ (*b*) $\frac{\sin 75°}{\sin 30°} \cdot 2V_2$ (*c*) $\frac{\sin 30°}{\sin 75°} \cdot 2V_2$ (*d*) $\frac{\sin 60°}{\sin 30°} \cdot 2V_2$.

40. A 3-phase transformer bank consists of three identical 2300/230 V, 15 kVA single-phase transformers connected in delta/delta. The bank supplies a 20 kVA unity pf 3-phase load. If one of the single-phase transformer develops a fault and is removed, the load carried by each of the two transformers, now operating in open-delta would be

(*a*) 10 kVA (*b*) 11.55 kVA (*c*) 17.31 kVA (*d*) 23.095 kVA.

[*GATE, 1997*]

41. Scott-connected transformers can convert

(*a*) 3 to 2 phases (*b*) 2 to 3 phases (*c*) both (*a*) and (*b*) (*d*) 2 to 4 phases.

42. In Scott-connected transformers, main transformer has unity turns ratio. For secondary balanced load current of 10 A, the primary current in amperes in the main and teaser transformers are respectively

(*a*) 10, 10, 10 (*b*) 11.55, 11.55, 11.55

(*c*) 10, 10, 11.55 (*d*) 11.55, 11.55, 10.

43. The function of using delta-connected tertiary winding in a star-star transformers is

(A) to permit the flow of sufficient fault current for the operation of protective devices

(B) to permit the single-phase loading

(C) to suppress harmonic voltages

(D) to provide low-reactance path for zero-sequence currents.

From above, the correct answer is

(*a*) A, B, C (*b*) A, B, D (*c*) B, C, D (*d*) all.

44. In order to reduce the effect of third harmonic flux and for minimum unbalance in the output voltages in star-star transformers, the three-phase transformer should be

(*a*) a three-legged core type (*b*) a five-legged core type

(*c*) a three-phase shell type (*d*) a bank of three 1-phase transformers.

45. A three-winding 132/66/11 kV transformer, as compared to two 132/66 kV and 132/11 kV two-winding transformers, is

(*a*) cheaper, less efficient and has good voltage regulation

(*b*) cheaper, more efficient and has good voltage regulation

(*c*) cheaper, more efficient and has poor voltage regulation

(*d*) costlier, more efficient and has poor voltage regulation.

46. In order to avoid the appearance of large third harmonic voltages between line to neutral of a star-connected auto-transformer (AT) bank, it is essential to

(*a*) ground AT neutral only (*b*) isolate AT neutral only

(*c*) ground neutral of both AT and source (*d*) ground source neutral only.

47. A voltage $v = 400 \sin 314.6t$ is applied to a single-phase transformer on no load. If the no-load current of the transformer is $2 \sin (314.6t - 85°)$, then magnetizing branch impedance will approximately be equal to

(*a*) $141 \angle 90°$ (*b*) $200 \angle -85°$ (*c*) $200 \angle 85°$ (*d*) $282 \angle -80°$.

[*GATE, 1997*]

48. Zero-sequence currents can flow from a line into a transformer bank if the windings are

(*a*) grounded star/delta (*b*) delta/star

(*c*) star/grounded star (*d*) delta/delta. [*I.E.S. 1992*]

49. Zero-sequence currents in a 3-phase system are

(*a*) equal and displaced from each other by 120°

(*b*) unequal and are in phase

(*c*) unequal and displaced from each other by 120°

(*d*) equal and are in phase.

50. For a 3-phase transformer, out of the positive, negative and zero sequence impedances, the minimum impedance is

(*a*) zero-sequence impedance (*b*) positive-sequence impedance

(*c*) negative-sequence impedance

(*d*) both positive and negative sequence impedances.

51. In a grounded-star/delta transformer, the zero-sequence current may flow from

(*a*) transformer secondary to load (*b*) source to transformer primary

(*c*) transformer primary to load (*d*) source to load.

52. If a transformer is switched on when the applied voltage is passing through zero and becoming positive, then inrush current is

(*a*) zero (*b*) minimum

(*c*) between minimum and maximum (*d*) maximum.

53. If a transformer is switched on when the applied voltage is maximum positive, then there occurs

(*a*) no current inrush (*b*) minimum current inrush

(*c*) average current inrush (*d*) maximum current inrush.

54. The inrush current of a transformer is at its worst, when switching on takes place at that point of the voltage wave when the corresponding steady-state current is

(*a*) the highest (*b*) the highest positive

(*c*) the highest negative (*d*) zero.

55. The inrush current in a transformer at no-load is maximum if the supply voltage is switched-on at

(*a*) peak voltage wave (*b*) zero voltage wave

(*c*) $\frac{V}{2}$ value (*d*) $\frac{\sqrt{3}\,V}{2}$ value.

56. The magnetizing-inrush-current in a transformer is rich in

(*a*) third harmonics (*b*) fifth harmonics

(*c*) seventh harmonics (*d*) second harmonics.

57. In transformers, the term overvoltage means the short-time voltage rise with a wavefront of

(*a*) 10 sec (*b*) 1 sec (*c*) 10 msec (*d*) 80μ sec.

58. Effect of surge voltage in a transformer can be minimized by

(*a*) increasing the winding capacitance

(*b*) decreasing the earth capacitance

(*c*) decreasing both the winding and earth capacitances

(*d*) increasing both the winding and earth capacitances.

59. Shield protection of h.v. winding against surge means

(*a*) reduction of winding capacitance (*b*) reduction of earth capacitance

(*c*) provision of screening capacitance (*d*) increasing of winding capacitance.

60. When a surge voltage strikes transformer terminals, voltage concentration can take place

(*a*) only at the line terminal (*b*) at any point of the winding length

(*c*) at farthest end from line terminal (*d*) at the middle of winding length.

61. Surge voltage effects on the transformers can be minimized by the use of

(A) surge absorbers (B) metal shields

(C) interleaved coils (D) reinforced insulation for end-turns.

From above, the correct answer is

(*a*) A, B, D (*b*) A, B, C (*c*) B, C, D (*d*) all.

62. The flux responsible for the development of mechanical forces in transformers is

(*a*) primary leakage flux (*b*) total flux

(*c*) mutual flux (*d*) leakage flux.

63. External radial forces in transformers are produced due to the interaction of

(*a*) currents in the primary and secondary windings

(*b*) current in the primary winding and leakage flux

(*c*) current in the secondary winding and leakage flux

(*d*) currents in both primary and secondary windings and the leakage flux.

64. The external and internal mechanical forces in transformers are

(*a*) directly proportional to winding height (H_w), and current squared

(*b*) inversely proportional to H_w, and current squared

(*c*) directly proportional to H_w, and inversely proportional to current squared

(*d*) inversely proportional to H_w and current.

65. When primary and secondary windings are not placed symmetrically with respect to the transformer core, the mechanical forces developed are

(*a*) external axial forces (*b*) external radial forces

(*c*) internal axial forces (*d*) internal axial forces.

66. A 500 MVA, 11 kV synchronous generator has 0.2 pu synchronous reactance. The per unit synchronous reactance on the base values of 100 MVA and 22 kV is

(*a*) 0.16 (*b*) 0.01 (*c*) 4.0 (*d*) 0.25.

[*GATE, 1991*]

67. In per unit system, the base values chosen first are

(*a*) voltampere, voltage (*b*) voltampere, current

(*c*) voltage, current (*d*) current, impedance.

68. Three single-phase transformers, each rated for 25 MVA, 38.1 kV/3.81 kV, are connected in *Yd*. The leakage reactance of each transformer on its own base is 0.1 p.u. The leakage reactance in p.u. on a base of 75 MVA, 66 kV is

(*a*) 0.1 p.u (*b*) 0.1732 p.u (*c*) 0.3 p.u (*d*) 0.033 p.u.

69. In which one of the following sets of 3-phase transformer connections will zero-sequence current be present in the transformer windings ?

(*a*) primary in star, neutral grounded; secondary in star, neutral not grounded

(*b*) primary in star, neutral grounded; secondary in delta

(*c*) primary in star, neutral not grounded ; secondary in star, neutral grounded

(*d*) primary in star, neutral not grounded; secondary in delta.

70. Short-circuit test is performed on a transformer with a certain impressed voltage at rated frequency. If the short-circuit test is now performed with the same magnitude of impressed voltage, but at a frequency higher than the rated frequency, then

(*a*) the magnitude of current and power factor will both increase

(*b*) the magnitude of current will decrease but the power factor will increase

(*c*) the magnitude of current will increase but the power factor will decrease

(*d*) the magnitude of current as well as the power factor will decrease.

71. Can a 50 Hz transformer be used for 25 Hz, if the input voltage is maintained constant at the rated value corresponding to 50 Hz?

(*a*) Yes. Since the voltage is constant, current levels will not change

(*b*) No. Flux will be doubled which will drive the core to excessive saturation

(*c*) No. Owing to decreased reactance of transformer, input current will be doubled at load

(*d*) Yes. At constant voltage, insulation will not be overstressed.

72. If the secondary winding of the ideal transformer shown in the circuit of Fig. A-8 has 40 turns, the number of turns in the primary winding for maximum power transfer to the 2 Ω resistor will be

(*a*) 20 (*b*) 40

(*c*) 80 (*d*) 160.

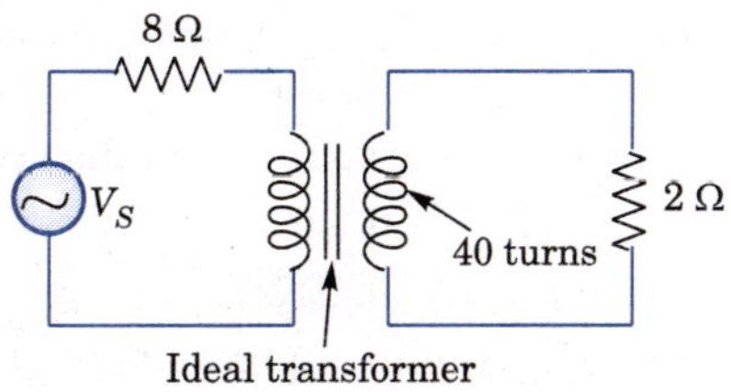

8 Ω
V_S
2 Ω
40 turns
Ideal transformer

Fig. A-8

73. Five-legged core-type transformer is preferred over three-legged core-type transformer because of

(*a*) reduced hysteresis loss (*b*) reduced eddy-current loss

(*c*) magnetic balance of the three phases (*d*) reduced ohmic loss

74. Which of the following connections of transformers will give the highest secondary voltage?

(*a*) Delta primary, delta secondary (*b*) Delta primary, star secondary

(*c*) star primary, star secondary (*d*) star primary, delta secondary. [*I.E.S., 1992*]

75. A 3-phase transformer has its primary in delta and secondary in star. Secondary to primary turn-ratio per phase is 5. For a primary voltage of 400, the secondary line voltage would be

(*a*) 2000 V (*b*) 80 V (*c*) 3464 V (*d*) $80 . \sqrt{3}$ V.

76. Which of the following connections of transformers will give the lowest secondary voltage ?

(*a*) Delta primary, delta secondary (*b*) Delta primary, star secondary

(*c*) star primary, star secondary (*d*) star primary, delta secondary.

77. A 3-phase *Yd* transformer has input line voltage of 1000 V and output line voltage of 100 V. If primary is reconnected in delta and secondary in star, for the same input voltage, the output line voltage will be

(*a*) 100 V (*b*) 173.2 V (*c*) 150 V (*d*) 300 V.

78. Three single-phase transformers, each of 100 kVA rating, are connected in a closed delta arrangement. If one of them is taken out, it would be possible to load the bank in such a manner that each one is loaded to the extent of

(*a*) 86.6 kVA (*b*) 66.67 kVA (*c*) 57.7 kVA (*d*) 33.33 kVA.

[*I.E.S., 1993*]

79. An 11 kV/400 V, 1000 kVA, *Yy* transformer is reconnected as delta-star with the h.v. side in delta. The rating for new connection will be

(*a*) $\frac{11}{\sqrt{3}}$ kV/400 V, 1000 kVA (*b*) 11 kV/400 V, 1732 kVA

(*c*) $11.\sqrt{3}$ kV/400 V, 1000 kVA (*d*) 11 kV/$400\sqrt{3}$ V, $\frac{1000}{\sqrt{3}}$ kVA

80. Supply to one terminal of delta-wye connected 3-phase core-type transformer, which is on no-load, fails. Assuming magnetic circuit symmetry, voltages on the secondary side will be

(*a*) 230, 230, 115 (*b*) 230, 115, 115 (*c*) 345, 115, 115 (*d*) 345, 0, 345.

[*GATE, 1995*]

81. Supply to one terminal of star-delta connected 3-phase core-type transformer, which is on no-load fails. Assuming magnetic circuit symmetry, voltages on the secondary side will be

(*a*) 230, 230, 230 (*b*) 230, 115, 115 (*c*) 230, 0, 230 (*d*) 345, 230, 345.

82. Three identical 10 kVA, 2400/240 V, single-phase transformers are connected in star-delta. Supply to one terminal of this three-phase transformer connection, which is at no-load, fails. Now voltages on the secondary side will be

(*a*) 207.8, 0, 207.8 (*b*) 120, 0, 120

(*c*) 311.7, 0, 311.7 (*d*) 207.8, 207.8, 207.8.

83. Two 3-limb, 3-phase delta-star connected transformers are supplied from the same source. One of the transformers is *Dy*1 and other is *Dy*11. The phase difference between the corresponding phase voltage of the secondaries would be

(*a*) 0° (*b*) 30° (*c*) 60° (*d*) 120°. [*I.E.S., 1997*]

84. Fig. A-9 shows a star-delta connected 3-phase transformer used to step down the voltage from 11000 V to 400 V line to line. It has two switches S_1 and S_2. Under normal conditions, S_1 is closed and S_2 is open. Under certain special conditions, S_1 is open and S_2 is closed. In such a case, the magnitude of voltage across the L.V. terminals would be

(*a*) 400, 0, 400
(*b*) 200, 0, 200
(*c*) 346.4, 346.4, 346.4
(*d*) 519.6, 519.6, 519.6.

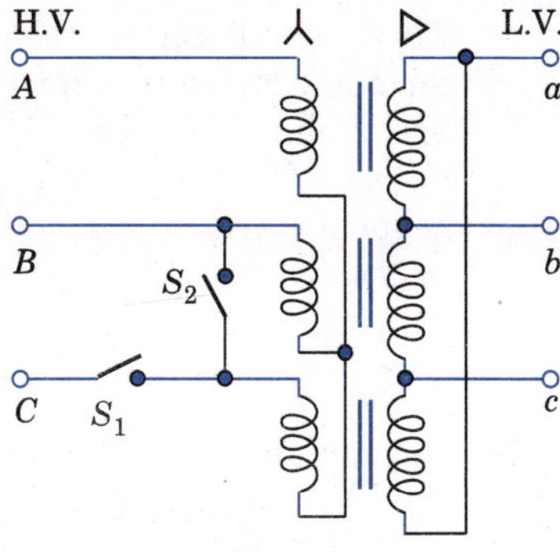

Fig. A-9

85. The windings of a Q kVA, V_1/V_2 volts, three-phase, delta-connected, core-type transformer are reconnected to work as a single-phase transformer. The maximum voltage and the power ratings of the new configuration are

(*a*) $3V_1/3V_2$, $3Q$ (*b*) V_1/V_2, $Q/3$ (*c*) $\sqrt{3}V_1/\sqrt{3}V_2$, $2Q$ (*d*) $2V_1/2V_2$, $2Q/3$.

[*GATE, 1999*]

86. The windings of a Q kVA, V_1/V_2 volt, three-phase, star-connected, core-type transformer are reconnected to work as a single-phase transformer. The maximum voltage and the power ratings of the new configuration are

(*a*) $\frac{V_1}{\sqrt{3}}\Big/\frac{V_2}{\sqrt{3}}, \sqrt{3}Q$ (*b*) $\sqrt{3}V_1/\sqrt{3}V_2, Q$ (*c*) $\frac{2V_1}{\sqrt{3}}\Big/\frac{2V_2}{\sqrt{3}}, \frac{2Q}{3}$ (*d*) $\frac{V_1}{\sqrt{3}}\Big/\frac{V_2}{\sqrt{3}}, \frac{Q}{3}$.

87. For the network shown in Fig. A-10, the zero-sequence reactances in p.u. are indicated. The zero-sequence driving point reactance of the node 3 is

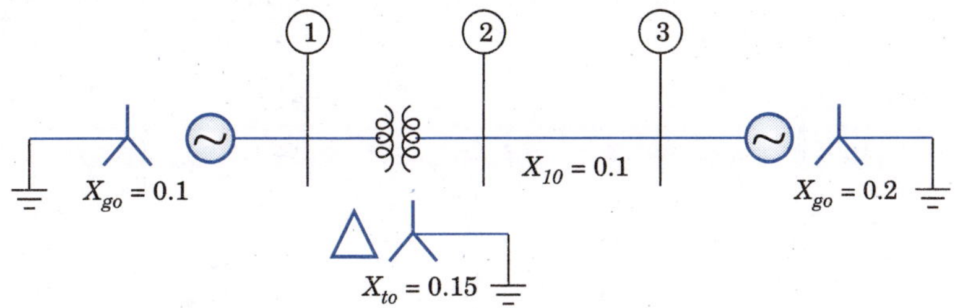

Fig. A-10

(*a*) 0.12 (*b*) 0.30 (*c*) 0.10 (*d*) 0.20. [*GATE, 1998*]

88. Three single-phase transformers are connected to form a 3-phase transformer bank. The transformers are connected as shown in Fig. A-11. The nomenclature of this connection scheme for phase sequence *ABC* is

(*a*) *Yd*0 (*b*) *Yd*6
(*c*) *Yd*11 (*d*) *Yd*1. [*I.E.S., 1996*]

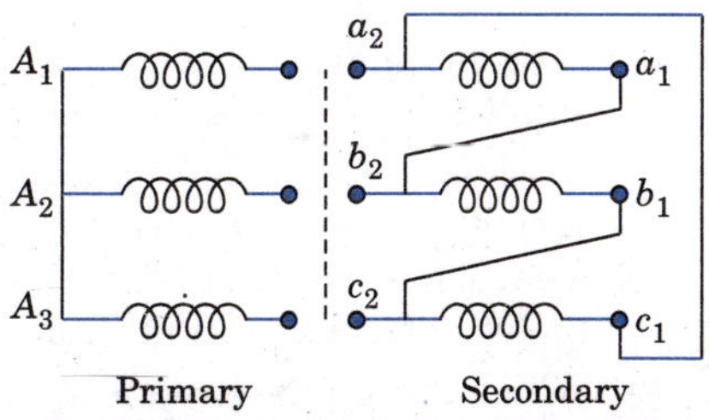

Fig. A-11

89. Three single-phase transformers are connected to form a 3-phase transformer bank. The transformers are connected as shown in Fig. A-12. The nomenclature of this connection scheme for phase sequence *ABC* is

(*a*) *Dy*0 (*b*) *Dy*1

(*c*) *Dy*6 (*d*) *Dy*11.

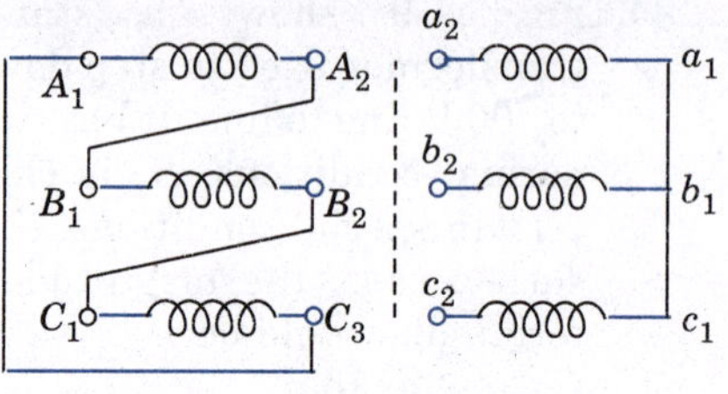

Fig. A-12

90. In example 8.17, if both switches S_1 and S_2 are open, then the magnitude of voltage across the LV terminals *a* and *c* would be

(*a*) 240 V (*b*) 0 V (*c*) 360 V (*d*) 480 V.

91. Fig. A-13 shows a star-delta connected 3-phase transformer used to step up the voltage from 415 to 9600 V line to line. It has two switches S_1 and S_2. Under normal conditions, S_1 is closed and S_2 is open. Under certain special conditions, S_1 is open and S_2 is closed. In such a case, the magnitude of voltage across the HV terminals *A* and *C* would be

(*a*) 8300 V (*b*) 9600 V

(*c*) 5542.7 V (*d*) 0 V.

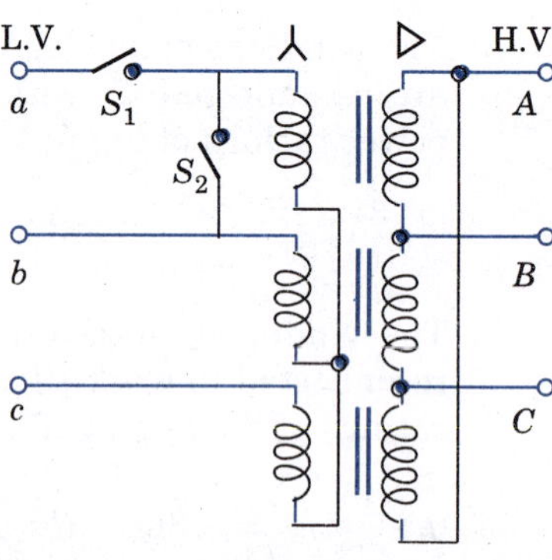

Fig. A-13

92. In Prob. 91 above, if both switches S_1 and S_2 are open, then the magnitude of voltage across the H.V. terminals *AB*, *BC*, *CA* would be

(*a*) 8300 V, 0 V, 8300 V (*b*) 0 V, 8300 V, 8300 V

(*c*) 8300 V, 8300 V, 0 V (*d*) 0 V, 0 V, 8300 V.

93. A single-phase air cored transformer, fed from a rated sinusoidal supply is operating at no load. The steady state magnetizing current drawn by the transformer from the supply will have the waveform

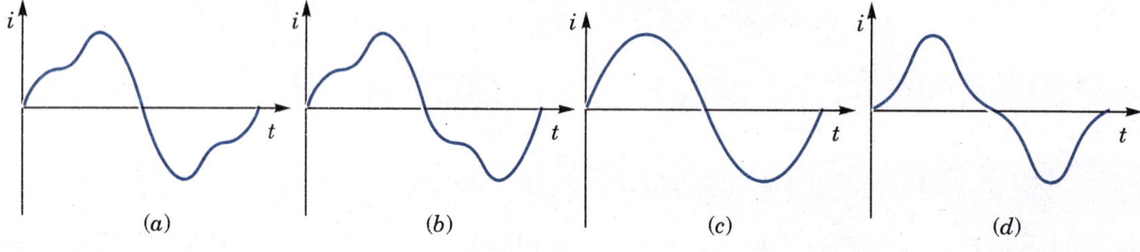

[*GATE, 2011*]

94. A single-phase iron-cored transformer, with no hysteresis loss, fed from a rated sinusoidal supply is operating at no load. The steady state magnetizing current drawn by the transformer from the supply will have the waveform shown in Prob. 93.

95. A single-phase iron-cored transformer, fed from a rated sinusoidal supply is operating at no load. The steady-state exciting current drawn by the transformer from the supply will have the waveform shown in Prob. 93.

96. Which three-phase connection can be used in a transformer to introduce a phase difference of 30° between its output and corresponding input line voltages ?

(*a*) Star-star (*b*) Star-Delta (*c*) Delta-Delta (*d*) Delta-Zigzag.

[*GATE, 2005*]

97. A balanced star-connected and purely resistive load is connected at the secondary of a star-delta transformer as shown in the figure. The line-to-line voltage rating of the transformer is 110/220 V. Neglecting the non-idealities of the transformer, the impedance Z of the equivalent star-connected load, referred to the primary side of the transformer is

(*a*) $(3 + j0)\ \Omega$ (*b*) $(0.866 - j0.5)\ \Omega$ (*c*) $(0.866 + j0.5)\ \Omega$ (*d*) $(1 + j0)\ \Omega$.

[*GATE, 2010*]

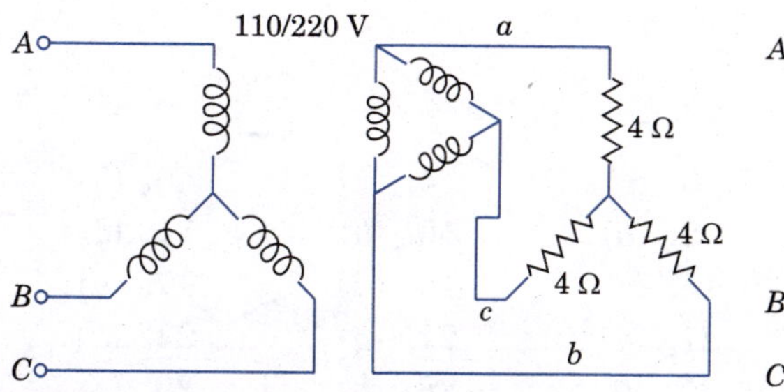

Common Data for Probs. 98 and 99

[*GATE, 2009*]

The star-delta transformer shown here is excited on the star side with a balanced 4-wire, 3-phase sinusoidal voltage supply of rated magnitude. The transformer is under no-load condition.

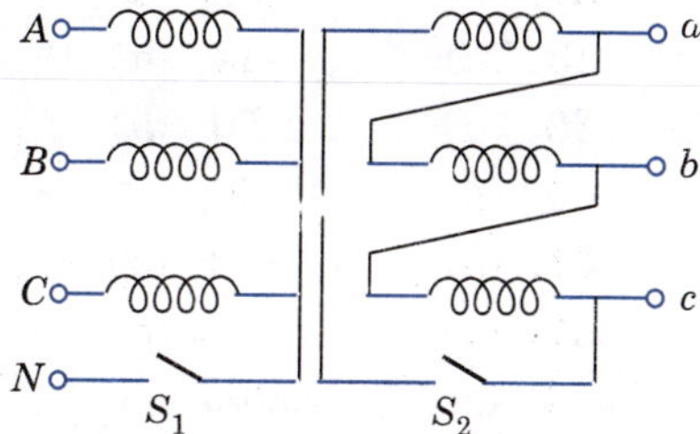

98. With both S_1 and S_2 opened, the core flux waveform will be

(*a*) a sinusoid at fundamental frequency
(*b*) flat-topped with third harmonic
(*c*) peaby with third harmonic
(*d*) none of the above.

99. With S_2 closed and S_1 opened, the current waveform in the delta winding will be

(*a*) a sinusoid at fundamental frequency (*b*) flat-topped with third harmonic
(*c*) only third harmonic (*d*) none of the above.

100. A 2-bus system and the corresponding zero sequence network are shown in the fig.

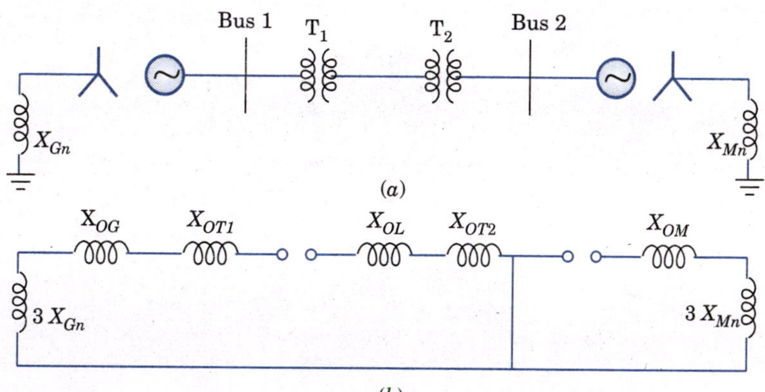

The transformers T_1 and T_2 are connecrted as

(*a*) ⅄ ⅄ and ⅄ ▷

(*b*) ⏚⅄ ⅄ and ⏚⅄ ▷

(*c*) ⏚⅄ ▷ and ▷ ⏚⅄

(*d*) ▷ ⏚⅄ and ⅄ ⏚⅄

[*GATE, 2014*]

ANSWERS

1. (*d*)	**2.** (*a*)	**3.** (*c*)	**4.** (*a*)	**5.** (*b*)	**6.** (*b*)
7. (*b*)	**8.** (*a*)	**9.** (*b*)	**10.** (*b*)	**11.** (*c*)	**12.** (*b*)
13. (*d*)	**14.** (*a*)	**15.** (*c*)	**16.** (*d*)	**17.** (*a*)	**18.** (*a*)
19. (*c*)	**20.** (*b*)	**21.** (*a*)	**22.** (*b*)	**23.** (*d*)	**24.** (*c*)
25. (*a*)	**26.** (*c*)	**27.** (*b*)	**28.** (*b*)	**29.** (*c*)	**30.** (*c*)
31. (*a*)	**32.** (*d*)	**33.** (*a*)	**34.** (*c*)	**35.** (*b*)	**36.** (*a*)
37. (*d*)	**38.** (*b*)	**39.** (*b*)	**40.** (*b*)	**41.** (*c*)	**42.** (*b*)
43. (*d*)	**44.** (*a*)	**45.** (*c*)	**46.** (*c*)	**47.** (*c*)	**48.** (*a*)
49. (*d*)	**50.** (*a*)	**51.** (*b*)	**52.** (*d*)	**53.** (*a*)	**54.** (*c*)
55. (*b*)	**56.** (*d*)	**57.** (*d*)	**58.** (*b*)	**59.** (*c*)	**60.** (*b*)
61. (*b*)	**62.** (*d*)	**63.** (*d*)	**64.** (*b*)	**65.** (*a*)	**66.** (*b*)
67. (*a*)	**68.** (*a*)	**69.** (*b*)	**70.** (*a*)	**71.** (*b*)	**72.** (*c*)
73. (*c*)	**74.** (*b*)	**75.** (*c*)	**76.** (*d*)	**77.** (*d*)	**78.** (*a*)
79. (*a*)	**80.** (*d*)	**81.** (*c*)	**82.** (*a*)	**83.** (*c*)	**84.** (*c*)
85. (*d*)	**86.** (*c*)	**87.** (*c*)	**88.** (*d*)	**89.** (*b*)	**90.** (*c*)
91. (*a*)	**92.** (*b*)	**93.** (*c*)	**94.** (*d*)	**95.** (*b*)	**96.** (*b*)
97. (*d*)	**98.** (*b*)	**99.** (*c*)	**100.** (*b*)		

SPECIAL MACHINES

1. The resolution, in steps per revolution, of a single-stack, four-phase, 8/6 pole VR stepping motor is

   (*a*) 12 (*b*) 24 (*c*) 36 (*d*) 48.

2. A stepping motor has a resolution of 200 steps/revolution. For obtaining a speed of 600 rpm, the pulse rate required, in pps, is

   (*a*) 500 (*b*) 1000 (*c*) 3000 (*d*) 2000.

3. The rotor of a stepping motor has

   (*a*) no brushes (*b*) no windings (*c*) no commutator (*d*) all of these.

4. A 1.8° step, 4-phase stepping motor has a total of 40 teeth on 8 poles of stator. The number of rotor teeth for this motor will be

   (*a*) 40 (*b*) 50 (*c*) 100 (*d*) 80. [*GATE, 2000*]

5. Which type of motor is most suitable for computer printer drive ?

   (*a*) Reluctance motor (*b*) Hysteresis motor

   (*c*) Shaded-pole motor (*d*) Stepper motor. [*GATE, 1996*]

6. A variable-reluctance stepping motor has four concentric coils on its four-pole stator. Rotor has five teeth. By successive switching of the individual stator coils to a dc source, the rotor moves by an angle of

   (*a*) 30° (*b*) 18° (*c*) 9° (*d*) 72°.

7. For a given stepping motor, the following torque has the highest numerical value.

   (*a*) Detent torque (*b*) Pull-in torque (*c*) Pull-out torque (*d*) Holding torque. [*GATE, 2004*]

8. In a stepping motor, holding torque is the

   (*a*) maximum load torque with phase winding unexcited

   (*b*) minimum load torque with phase winding unexcited

   (*c*) minimum load torque with phase winding excited

   (*d*) maximum load torque with phase winding excited.

9. In a stepping motor, the detent torque is the

   (*a*) maximum load torque with phase winding unexcited

   (*b*) minimum load torque with phase winding unexcited

   (*c*) minimum load torque with phase winding excited

   (*d*) maximum load torque with phase winding excited.

10. The following motor definitely has permanent magnet rotor.

    (*a*) DC commutator motor (*b*) Brushless dc motor

    (*c*) Stepper motor (*d*) Reluctance motor. [*GATE, 2004*]

11. For a 1.8°, 2-phase bipolar stepping motor, the stepping rate is 100 steps per second. The rotational speed of the motor in rpm is

    (*a*) 15 (*b*) 30 (*c*) 60 (*d*) 90. [*GATE, 2004*]

12. A three-phase three-stack, variable reluctance step motor has 20 poles on each rotor and stator stack. The step-angle of this step motor is

    (*a*) 3° (*b*) 6° (*c*) 9° (*d*) 18°. [*GATE, 2007*]

13. A three-stack, 12/12 pole VR stepping motor has the angular displacement between stator stacks is

    (*a*) 10° (*b*) 20° (*c*) 30° (*d*) 15°.

14. Which of the following excitation sequence for a 3-phase VRSM results in half-step mode ?
(*a*) *A*, *B*, *C*, *A*... (*b*) *A*, *C*, *B*, *A*... (*c*) *A*, *AB*, *B*, *BC*... (*d*) *AB*, *BC*, *CA*, *AB*...

15. In the slew range, a stepping motor
(*a*) can start, stop or reverse on command
(*b*) cannot start, stop or reverse on command
(*c*) cannot start but can stop or reverse on command
(*d*) cannot start and stop but can reverse on command.

16. In a 3-phase, 6/4 VRM, the frequency of exciting the phase windings, for a rotor speed of 600 rpm, is
(*a*) 40 Hz (*b*) 50 Hz (*c*) 60 Hz (*d*) 80 Hz.

17. A four-stack VRSM has 15 teeth on both stator and rotor. For achieving a rotor speed of 800 rpm, the frequency of currents given to stator phase winding is
(*a*) 100 Hz (*b*) 600 Hz (*c*) 200 Hz (*d*) 187.5 Hz.

18. In a 3-phase, 6/8 VRM, the total time required for exciting the three-phase windings is 30 ms. The rotor velocity in rpm is
(*a*) 250 (*b*) 333.33 (*c*) 500 (*d*) 111.11.

ANSWERS

1. (*b*)	**2.** (*d*)	**3.** (*d*)	**4.** (*b*)	**5.** (*d*)	**6.** (*b*)
7. (*d*)	**8.** (*d*)	**9.** (*a*)	**10.** (*b*)	**11.** (*b*)	**12.** (*b*)
13. (*a*)	**14.** (*c*)	**15.** (*b*)	**16.** (*a*)	**17.** (*c*)	**18.** (*a*)

APPENDIX

B

Typical Problems

In this appendix, some typical problems pertaining to electrical machines are solved.

B.1. *A separately-excited dc motor runs at 1000 rpm at no load when its armature terminals are connected to a 200 V dc source and the rated voltage is applied to field winding. The armature resistance of this motor is 1 Ω. The no-load armature current is negligible. With the motor developing its full load torque, the armature voltage is set so that the rotor speed is 500 rpm. When the load torque is reduced to 50% of the full-load value under the same armature voltage conditions, the speed rises to 520 rpm. Neglecting the rotational losses, the full-load armature current (in Amperes) is ....* [GATE 2015]

Solution. Here terminal or source voltage $V_t = 200$ V,

no-load speed, $N_0 = 1000$ rpm, $I_0 = 1$ A, $r_a = 0$

$\therefore \quad E_{a1} = V_t - I_0 r_a = 200 - 1 \times 0 = 200 \text{ V} \propto 1000 \times \phi$ ...(*i*)

At full load, speed = 500 rpm, $\therefore \; E_{a2} \propto 500 \times \phi$ ...(*ii*)

From Eqs. (*i*) and (*ii*), we get

$$\frac{E_{a2}}{200} = \frac{500 \times \phi}{1000 \times \phi}, \quad \therefore \; E_{a2} = \frac{500}{1000} \times 200 = 100 \text{ V}$$

Let the full-load current be I_{fl}, then

$$V_t = E_{a2} + I_{fl} \times r^a = 100 + I_{fl} \times 1 \qquad ...(iii)$$

With load torque reduced to half, new armature current = $\frac{I_{fl}}{2}$ at a speed of 520 rpm.

$$\therefore \quad \text{At speed 520 rpm,} \quad E_{a3} = \frac{520}{1000} \times 200 = 104 \text{ V}$$

$$\therefore \quad V_t = E_{a3} + \frac{I_{fl}}{2} \times 1 = 104 + \frac{I_{fl}}{2} \qquad ...(iv)$$

From Eqs. (*iii*) and (*iv*), $V_t = 100 + I_{fl} \times 1 = 104 + \frac{I_{fl}}{2}$

$$\therefore \quad \frac{I_{fl}}{2} = 104 - 100 = 4. \text{ This gives } I_{fl} = 4 \times 2 = \mathbf{8\ A.}$$

Common Data for Questions (B.2 and B.3)

A separately-excited dc motor runs at 1500 rpm under no-load with 200 V applied to the armature. The field voltage is maintained at its rated value. The speed of the motor, when it delivers a torque of 5 Nm, is 1400 rpm as shown in the figure B-1. The rotational losses and armature reaction are neglected.

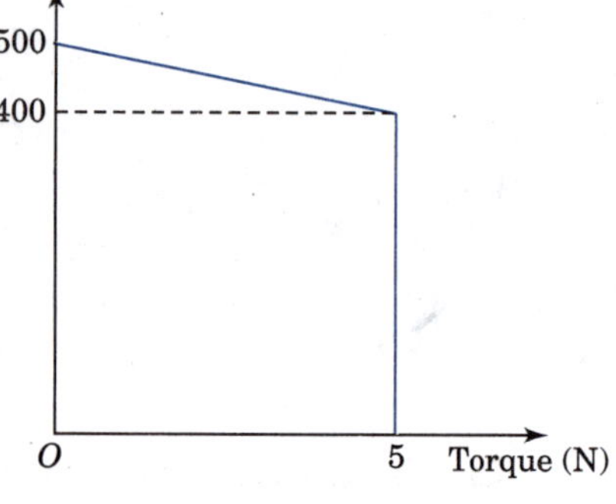

Fig. B-1

B.2. *The armature resistance of the motor is*

(*a*) 2 Ω (*b*) 3.4 Ω
(*c*) 4.4 Ω (*d*) 7.7 Ω

B.3. *For the motor to deliver a torque of 2.5 Nm at 1400 rpm, the armature voltage to be applied is*

(*a*) 125.5 V (*b*) 193.3 V (*c*) 200 V (*d*) 241.7 V

Solution. B.2. At no-load, speed, $N_0 = 1500$ rpm, $I_a = 0$, $V_t = 200$ V

$$\therefore \quad E_a = V_t - I_a r_a = 200 - 0 = 200 \text{ V} \propto 1500 \times \phi \quad \text{...}(i)$$

At 1400 rpm, torque = 5 Nm. $\therefore \; E_{a1} \propto 1400 \times \phi$ ...(*ii*)

From Eqs. (*i*) and (*ii*), we get, $\dfrac{E_{a1}}{200} = \dfrac{1400}{1500}$ or $E_{a1} = \dfrac{1400}{1500} \times 200 = 186.67$ V

With no rotational losses, $E_{a1} I_{a1} = T_e \cdot w_m = 5 \times \dfrac{2\pi \times 1400}{60}$

$\therefore$ Armature current, $I_{a1} = \dfrac{5 \times 2\pi \times 1400}{186.67 \times 60} = 3.927$ A

Now, $V_t = E_{a1} + I_{a1} \cdot r_a$ or $200 = 186.67 + 3.927 \times r_a$

$\therefore$ Armature circuit resistance, $r_a = \dfrac{200 - 186.67}{3.927} = 3.394\ \Omega \simeq 3.4\ \Omega$ $\therefore$ **Ans.** (*b*)

Solution. B.3. In a dc motor, torque $T_c \propto \phi I_a$

$$\therefore \quad 5 \propto \phi \times 3.927$$

For 2.5 Nm, $2.5 \propto \phi \times I_{a2}$

$\therefore$ New armature current, $I_{a2} = \dfrac{2.5}{5.0} \times 3.927 = 1.9635$ A

$\therefore$ Armature voltage to be applied at 2.5 Nm is

$$V_t = E_{a1} + I_{a2} \cdot r_a = 186.67 + 1.9635 \times 3.4$$
$$= 193.34 \text{ V} \simeq 193.3 \text{ V}. \quad \therefore \quad \textbf{Ans. } (b)$$

B.4. *A separately-excited dc generator has an armature resistance of 0.1 Ω and negligible armature inductance. At rated field current and rated rotor speed, its open circuit voltage is 200 V. When this generator is operated at half the rated speed, with half the rated field current, an uncharged 1000 μF capacitor is suddenly connected across the armature terminals. Assume that the speed remains unchanged during the transient. At what time (in microseconds) after the capacitor is connected with the voltage across it reach 25 V?*

(*a*) 62.25 (*b*) 69.3 (*c*) 73.25 (*d*) 77.3 [*GATE 2015*]

Solution. At rated field current I_f and rated speed N, the generated voltage is

$$V_g = 200 \propto NI_f \quad ...(i)$$

At half the rated field current $I_f/2$ and half the rated speed $N/2$; the generated voltage would be

$$V_s \propto \frac{N}{2} \cdot \frac{I_f}{2} \quad ...(ii)$$

From Eqs. (*i*) and (*ii*), we get

$$\frac{V_s}{200} = \frac{\frac{N}{2} \cdot \frac{I_f}{2}}{N\,I_f} = \frac{1}{4}; \quad \therefore V_s = \frac{200}{4} = 50 \text{ V}$$

In the circuit shown in Fig. B-2, R = armature circuit resistance, C = load capacitor and V_s = open-circuit voltage of separately excited generator at half the rated field current and half the rated speed = 50 V. For this circuit, KVL gives

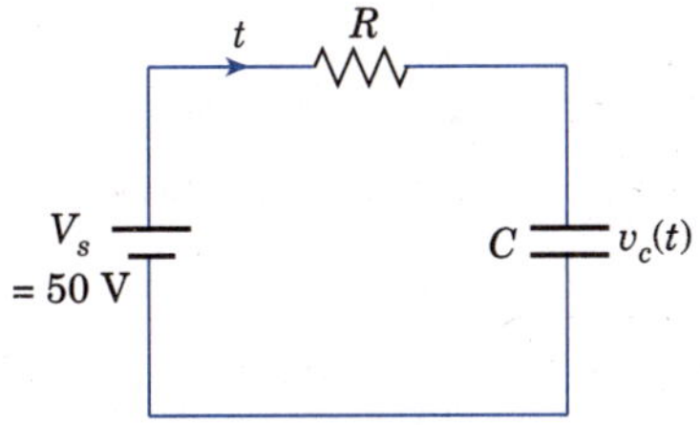

Fig. B-2

$$R \,.\, i + \frac{1}{C}\int i.dt = V_s$$

or
$$R \,.\, I(s) + \frac{1}{C}\left[\frac{I(s)}{s} + 0\right] = \frac{V_s}{s}$$

$\therefore$
$$I(s) = \frac{V_s}{s\left[R + \frac{1}{Cs}\right]} = \frac{V_s}{\left[\frac{1}{C} + R.s\right]} = \frac{V_s}{R}\frac{1}{\left[s + \frac{1}{RC}\right]}$$

$\therefore$
$$i(t) = \frac{V_s}{R}\, e^{-t/RC}$$

$\therefore$ Voltage across capacitor, $v_c(t) = \frac{1}{C}\int_0^t i.dt = \frac{1}{C}\int_0^t \frac{V_s}{R} e^{-t/RC} \,.\, dt$

$\therefore$
$$v_c\,(t) = \frac{V_s}{RC}\left[\frac{e^{-t/RC}}{-\frac{1}{RC}}\right]_0^t = -V_s\,[e^{-t/RC} - 1] = V_s\,[1 - e^{-t/RC}]$$

Here
$$RC = 0.1 \times 1000 \times 10^{-6} = 10^{-4} \text{ sec.}$$
$$V_s = 50 \text{ V}, v_c(t) = 25 \text{ V}$$

$\therefore$
$$25 = 50\left[1 - e^{-t/10^{-4}}\right] = 50\,[1 - e^{-1000\,t}]$$

or
$$e^{+10000t} = \frac{1}{1 - \frac{25}{50}} = \frac{1}{1 - \frac{1}{2}} = 2$$

or
$$1000t = \ln 2 = 0.69315$$

$\therefore$
$$t = \frac{0.69315}{10000} = 0.69315 \times 10^{-4} = 69.315 \times 10^{-6} \text{ sec}$$
$$= 69.315\ \mu \text{ sec} \quad \therefore \textbf{Ans. } (b)$$

B.5. *Two 550 kVA alternators operate in parallel to supply the following two loads:*

(*i*) *25 kw at 0.95 power factor lag* (*ii*) *100 kw at 0.8 power factor lead.*

One machine is supplying 200 kw at 0.95 pf lag. The power factor of the other machine must be

(*a*) *0.89 lead* (*b*) *0.95 lead* (*c*) *0.95 lag* (*d*) *0.89 lag*

[*GATE 1993*]

Solution. Load 1, L_1 = 250 kw at 0.95 pf lag

$= 250\ [0.95 - j\ 0.312] = [237.5 - j18]$ kVA

Load 2, L_2 = 100 kw at 0.8 pf lead

$= 100\ [0.8 + j0.6] = [80 + j60] = [317.5 - j18]$ kVA

Load shared by machine 1, M_1 = 200 kw at pf 0.9 lag

$= 200\ [0.9 - j0.436] = [180 - j87.2]$ kVA

Load on machine 1 + load on machine 2 = total load = $L_1 + L_2$

$\therefore$ Load on machine 2 = $[317.5 - j18] - [180 - j87.2]$

$= [137.5 + j69.2] = 153.931\ \underline{/+26.6715°}$

$\therefore$ Power factor of machine 2 = cos (+26.715) = 0.893 leading. $\therefore$ **Ans.** (*a*)

B.6. *The per unit voltage of two synchronous machines connected through a lossless line are 0.95 ∠10° and 1.0 ∠0°. Match the two sides in the following:*

List I	**List II**
(A) Real power of machine 1	(P) Positive real power
(B) Reactive power of machine 1	(Q) Positive reactive power
(C) Power factor of machine 1	(R) Negative real power
	(S) Negative reactive power
	(T) Leading power factor
	(U) Lagging power factor

Solution. Here machine 1 voltage 0.95 ∠10° leads the machine 2 voltage by an angle of 10°. The phasor diagram for these voltages is shown in Fig. 8-3. As machine 1 voltage V_1 is a head of machine 2 voltage V_2 by 10°, machine 1 is working as an alternator at a leading power factor cos θ_1 as shown in Fig. B-3. Therefore, $C \rightarrow T$.

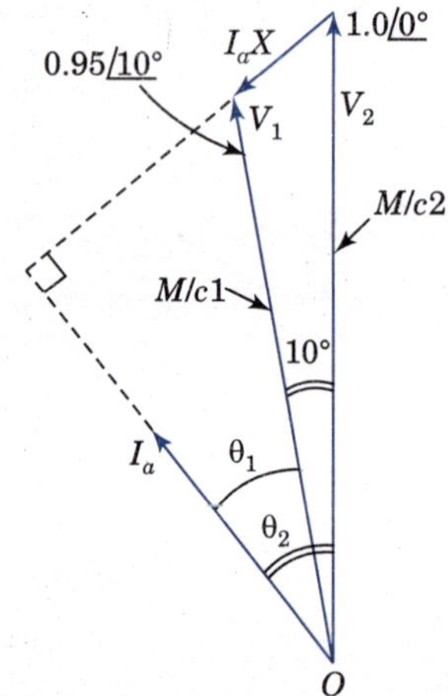

Fig. B-3

Machine 1 as an alternator delivers (treated positive) active power or real power. Therefore, for machine 1, real power is positive. Thus, $A \rightarrow P$.

Machine 1 works as an alternator at a leading power factor, therefore machine 1 absorbs the reactive power-treated negative (because active power going out of alternator is treated positive) the reactive power. Therefore, reactive power of machine 1 is negative. Thus, $B \rightarrow S$.

Machine 2 works as a synchronous motor at a leading power factor cos θ_2. Machine 2, therefore, absorbs active power but delivers reactive power.

$\therefore$ **Ans.** $A \rightarrow P$; $B \rightarrow S$; $C \rightarrow T$.

Statement for Linked Answers B.7 and B.8

A synchronous motor is connected to an infinite bus at 1.0 pu voltage and draws 0.6 pu current at unity power factors. Its synchronous reactance is 1.00 pu and resistance is negligible. *[GATE 2008]*

B.7. *The excitation voltage (E) and load angle δ will respectively be*

(*a*) *0.8 pu and 36.86 lag* (*b*) *0.8 pu and 39.86 lead*

(*c*) *1.17 pu and 30.96 lead* (*d*) *1.17 pu and 30.96 lag.*

B.8. *Keeping the excitation voltage same, the load on the motor is increased by 20%. The operating power factor will become*

(*a*) *0.995 lagging* (*b*) *0.995 leading* (*c*) *0.791 lagging* (*d*) *0.848 leading.*

Solution. B.7. The circuit and phasor diagrams pertaing to this problem are drawn in Fig. B.4. It is seen from the phasor diagram that

$$E = \sqrt{1^2 + 0.6^2} = 1.166 \simeq 1.17 \text{ pu}$$

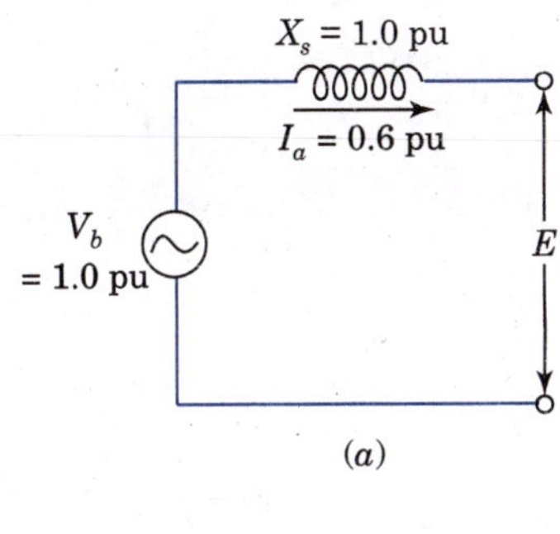

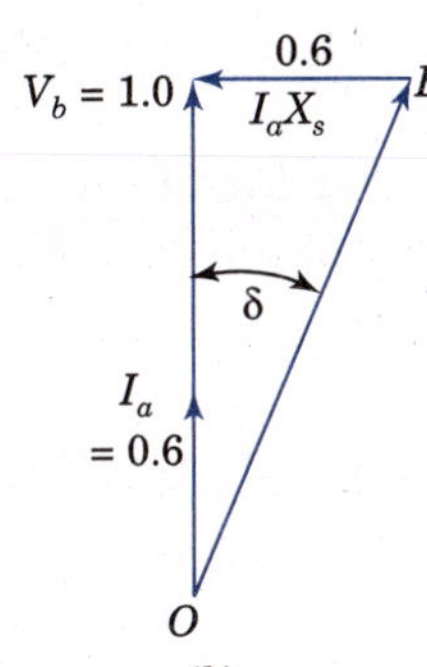

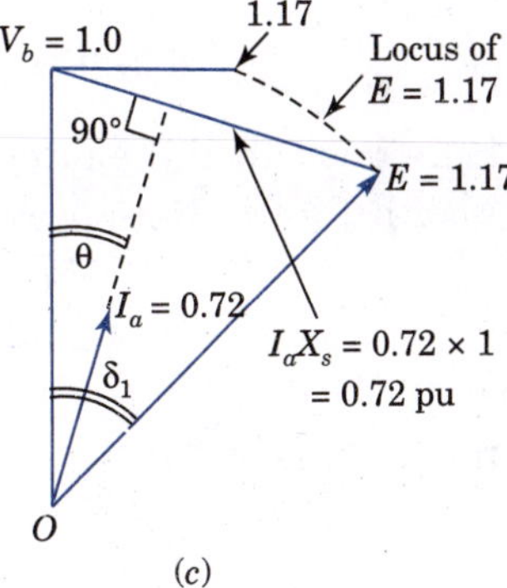

Fig. B-4

$$\text{Load angle } \delta = \tan^{-1}\frac{0.6}{1.0} = 30.96° \text{ lag.} \quad \therefore \quad \textbf{Ans. } (d)$$

Solution. B.8. For these operating conditions, the phasor diagram of Fig. B-4 (*b*) gets modified to that shown in Fig. B-4 (*c*), where excitation voltage remains constant at E = 1.17 pu but is shifted to a position with increased load angle δ_1, V_b = 1.0, $I_a X_s$ increases to (0.6 × 1.2) × 1 = 0.72 pu. From this figure,

$$E^2 + V_b^2 - 2EV_b \cos \delta_1 = (I_a X_s)^2$$

$$1.17^2 + 1^2 - 2 \times 1.17 \times 1 \times \cos \delta_1 = 0.72^2$$

$$\therefore \quad \delta_1 = \cos^{-1}\left[\frac{1.17^2 + 1^2 - 0.72^2}{2 \times 1.17}\right] = 37.74°$$

Now,

$$\text{power} = V_b I_a \cos \theta = \frac{E \cdot V_b}{X_s} \sin \delta_1$$

$$1 \times 0.72 \times \cos \theta = \frac{1.17 \times 1}{1.0} \sin 37.74°$$

$\therefore$ Operating power factor, $\cos\theta = \dfrac{1.17}{0.72}\sin 37.74° = 0.9946$

$\simeq 0.995$ lagging. $\therefore$ **Ans.** (*a*)

B.9. *A three-phase, 50 Hz salient-pole synchronous motor has per-phase direct-axis reactance (X_d) of 0.8 pu and a per-phase quadrature-axis reactance (X_q) of 0.6 pu. Resistance of the machine is negligible. It is drawing full load current at 0.8 pf (loading). When the terminal voltage is 1 pu, per-phase induced voltage, in pu, is ....* [*GATE 2016*]

Solution. Phasor diagram for a salient-pole synchronous motor working at a leading power factor cos θ, with zero armature resistance, is shown in Fig. B-5. From this figure, we get

$$\tan\psi = \frac{AC}{OA} = \frac{AB + BC}{OA}$$

$$= \frac{V_f \sin\theta + I_a X_q}{V_t \cos\theta}$$

$$\therefore \quad \psi = \tan^{-1}\left[\frac{1\times 0.6 + 1\times 0.8}{1\times 0.8}\right] = 56.31°$$

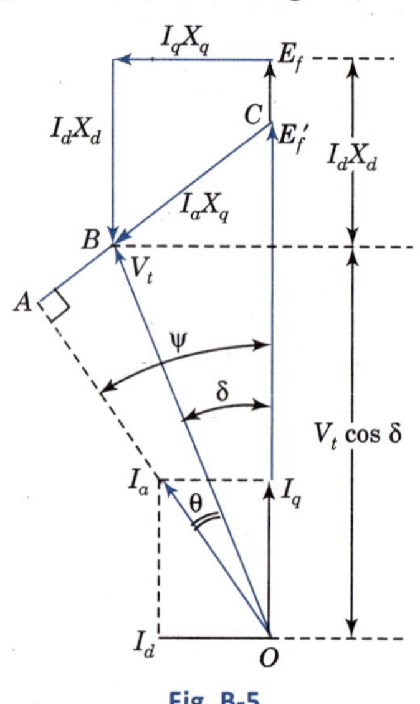

Fig. B-5

Here ψ is called the internal power-factor angle.

Also ψ = δ + θ. Here power-factor angle θ

$= \cos^{-1} 0.8 = 36.87°$.

$\therefore$ Load angle $\delta = 56.31 - 36.87° = 19.44°$

$\therefore$ $I_d = I_a \sin\psi = 1.\sin 56.31° = 0.832$ pu

It is seen from Fig. B.5 that per phase induced emf,

$$E_f = V_t \cos\delta + I_d X_d$$

$$= 1\,.\cos 19.44° + 0.832 \times 0.8$$

$$= 1.6085 \text{ pu.}$$

B.10. *A stand alone engine-driven synchronous generator is feeding a partly inductive load. A capacitor is now connected across the load to completely nullify the inductive current. For this operating condition,*

(*a*) *the field current and the fuel input have to be reduced*

(*b*) *the field current and the fuel input have to be increased*

(*c*) *the field current has to be increased and fuel input left unaltered.*

(*d*) *the field current has to be reduced and fuel input left unaltered.*

Solution. With inductive load, load current is I_{a1}, power factor is cos θ lagging and excitation emf $E_{f1} = V_t + j\,I_{a1}\,Xs$ as shown in Fig. B.6. With capacitor across the load, inductive current *ab* is nullified and now load current reduces to I_{a2} at unity power factor as shown in Fig. B.6. New value of excitation emf is $E_{f2} = V_t + jI_{a2}\,Xs$. Since $E_{f2} < E_{f1}$, field current must be reduced.

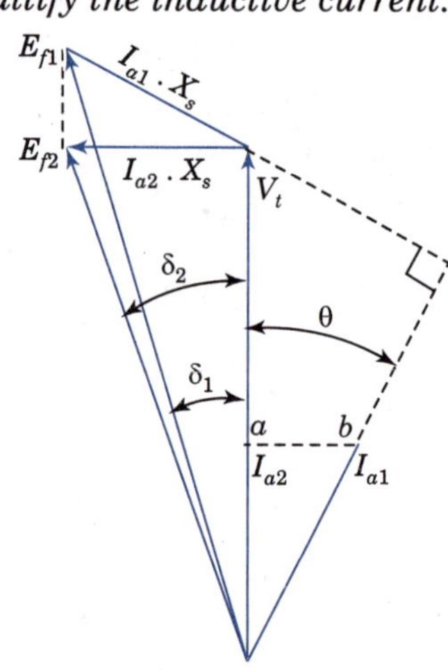

Fig. B-6

Further, power = $V_t I_{a1}$, $\cos\theta = V_t I_{a2}$ remains unchanged. Therefore fuel input must be left unaltered. $\therefore$ **Ans.** (d)

B.11. *A 3-phase induction motor is driving a constant load torque at rated voltage and frequency. If both voltage and frequency are halved, following statements relate to the new condition if stator resistance, leakage reactance and core loss are neglected.*

1. *The difference between synchronous speed and actual speed remains same.*
2. *The air-gap flux remains the same.*
3. *The stator current remain the same.*
4. *The per unit slip remain same.*

Among the above, the correct statements are

(*a*) *all* (*b*) *1, 2 and 3* (*c*) *2, 3, and 4* (*d*) *1 and 4.*

[*GATE 2003*]

Solution. With stator leakage impedance and core loss ignored, it is seen from Fig. 5.5 (a) that [V_1 replaced by V for convinience],

$$T_e = \frac{3}{w_s} \cdot I_2^2 \frac{r_2}{s} = \frac{3}{w_s} \frac{V^2}{\left(\frac{r_2}{s}\right)^2 + x_2^2} \cdot \frac{r_2}{s}$$

For small values of slips, $\frac{r_2}{s} >> x_2$.

$$\therefore \qquad T_e = \frac{3}{w_s} \cdot \frac{V^2}{\left(\frac{r_2}{s}\right)^2} \cdot \frac{r_2}{s} = \frac{3}{w_s} \cdot \frac{V^2}{r_2} \cdot s \qquad ...(5.32)$$

For rated voltage V_1 and rated frequency f_1, we have

$$V_1 = \sqrt{2}\pi\, f_1 \phi_1 N_1 \text{ kw}_1$$

or $$V_1 \propto f_1\, \phi_1 \qquad ...(i)$$

With voltage $\frac{V_1}{2}$ and frequency $\frac{f_1}{2}$, we have $\frac{V_1}{2} \propto \frac{f_1}{2} \cdot \phi_2$ ...(*ii*)

From eqs. (*i*) and (*ii*), $\frac{V_1}{V_1/2} = \frac{f_1 \cdot \phi_1}{f_1/2 \cdot \phi_2}$

or $$V_1 \cdot \frac{f_1}{2} \cdot \phi_2 = \frac{V_1}{2} \cdot f_1\, \phi_1 \text{ or } \phi_1 = \phi_2$$

Thus, air-gap flux remains the same. Therefore, **statement 2 is correct**.

At V_1, f_1; synchronous speed, $w_{s1} = \frac{4\pi f_1}{P}$

and at V_2, f_2; synchronous speed, $w_{s2} = \frac{4\pi f_2}{P} = \frac{4\pi \cdot \frac{f_1}{2}}{P} = \frac{4\pi f_1}{2P} = \frac{w_{s1}}{2}$

$$\therefore \qquad w_{s2} = \frac{1}{2}\, w_{s1}$$

At V_1, f_1; torque $T_{e1} = \dfrac{3}{w_{s1}} \cdot \dfrac{V_1^2}{r_2} s_1$

At V_2, f_2, torque $T_{e2} = \dfrac{3}{\omega_{s2}} \cdot \dfrac{[V_1/2]^2}{r_2} . s_2$

But $T_{e1} = T_{e2}$; $\therefore$ $\dfrac{3}{\omega_{s1}} \cdot \dfrac{V_1^2}{r_2} . s_1 = \dfrac{3}{\omega_{s2}} \cdot \dfrac{V_1^2}{4r_2} . s_2$

or $$\frac{s_1}{\omega_{s1}} = \frac{s_2}{4\omega_{s2}} = \frac{s_2}{4 \times \frac{1}{2}\omega_{s1}} = \frac{s_2}{2\omega_{s1}}$$

$\therefore$ $$\frac{s_2}{s_1} = \frac{2\omega_{s1}}{\omega_{s1}} = 2 \text{ or } s_2 = 2s_1$$

$\therefore$ Per unit slip does not remain the same. **Therefore, statement 4 is not correct.**

At V_1, f_1; slip speed = synchronous speed – actual rotor speed

$$= \omega_{s1} - \omega_{s1}(1 - s_1) = s_1 . \omega_{s1}$$

At V_2, f_2; slip speed $= \omega_{s2} - \omega_{r2}$

$$= \omega_{r2} - \omega_{r2}(1 - s_2) = s_2 . \omega_{s2}$$

$$= [2s_1] . \left[\frac{1}{2}\omega_{s1}\right] = s_1 . \omega_{r1}$$

Thus, the slip speed or the difference between synchronous speed and actual rotor speed remains the same. **Therefore, statement 1 is correct.**

Rotor current, $$I_2 = \frac{V}{\sqrt{\left(\frac{r_2}{s}\right)^2 + x_2^2}}$$

For small slips s, $\dfrac{r_2}{s} >> x_2$; $\therefore$ $I_2 = \dfrac{V.s}{r_2}$

At V_1, f_1; $$I_{21} = \frac{V_1}{r_2} . s_1$$

At V_2, f_2; $$I_{22} = \frac{V_1/2}{r_2} . s_2 = \frac{V_1}{2r_2} . 2s_1 = \frac{V_1}{r_2} . s_1 = I_{2s}$$

Thus, rotor current or stator current remains the same.

$\therefore$ **Statement 3 is correct.**

From above, statements 1, 2 and 3 are correct. $\therefore$ **Ans. (*b*)**

B.12. *The speed of a 4-pole, 3-phase induction motor is controlled by varying the supply frequency while maintaining the ratio of supply voltage to supply frequency (V/f) constant. At rated frequency of 50 Hz and rated voltage of 400 V, its speed is 1440 rpm. Find the speed at 30 Hz if load torque is constant.*

(*a*) *882 rpm* (*b*) *864 rpm* (*c*) *840 rpm* (*d*) *828 rpm*

[*GATE 2006*]

Solution. Here $\frac{V_1}{f_1} = \frac{V_2}{f_2}$ = constant. $\therefore \frac{400}{50} = \frac{V_2}{30}$

$$\therefore \quad V_2 = \frac{400}{50} \times 30 = 240 \text{ V, slip} = \frac{1500 - 1440}{1500} = 0.04$$

From Eq. (5.32), for small values of slips,

$$T_e = \frac{3}{\omega_s} \cdot \frac{V^2}{r_2} \cdot s \quad \text{...(5.32)}$$

For V_1, f_1; $$T_{e1} = \frac{3}{\omega_{s1}} \cdot \frac{V_1^2}{r_2} s_1$$

For V_2, f_2; $$T_{e2} = \frac{3}{\omega_{s2}} \cdot \frac{V_2^2}{r_2} s_2$$

For constant load torque, $T_{e1} = T_{e2}$

$$\therefore \quad \frac{3}{\omega_{s1}} \cdot \frac{V_1^2}{r_2} \cdot s_1 = \frac{3}{\omega_{s2}} \cdot \frac{V_2^2}{r_2} \cdot s_2.$$

$$\frac{3.P}{4\pi \times 50} \cdot \frac{400^2 \times 0.04}{r_2} = \frac{3P}{4\pi \times 30} \cdot \frac{240^2}{r_2} \cdot s_2$$

$$\therefore \quad s_2 = \left(\frac{400}{240}\right)^2 \times \frac{30}{50} \times 0.04 = 0.067$$

$$\therefore \quad \text{Speed at 30 Hz} = \frac{120 \times 30}{4} [1 - 0.067] = 839.7 \simeq 840 \text{ rpm.}$$ $\therefore$ **Ans.** (*c*)

B.13. *A 3-phase, 4-pole squirrel-cage induction motor has 36 stator and 28 rotor slots. The number of phases in the rotor is*

(*a*) 3 (*b*) 9 (*c*) 7 (*d*) 8 [*GATE 2000*]

[**Hint:** Number of phases in the rotor of squirrel-cage induction motor is equal to the number of rotor slots per pole]

Solution. Here, rotor slots per pole = $\frac{28}{4}$ = 7 = Number of phases in the rotor.

$\therefore$ **Ans.** (*c*)

B.14. *A three-phase slip-ring induction motor, provided with a commutator winding, is shown in Fig. B-7. The rotor rotates in clockwise direction when the rotor windings are closed.*

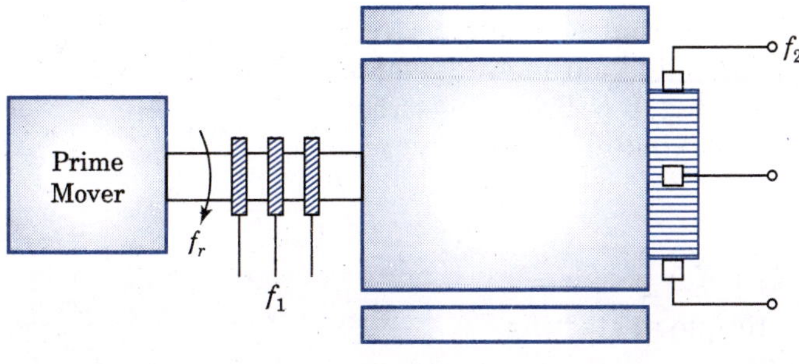

Fig. B-7

If the rotor winding is open circuited and the system is made to run at rotational speed f_r with the help of prime-mover in anticlockwise direction, then the frequency of voltage across slip rings is f_1 and frequency of voltage across commutator brushes is f_2. The values of f_1 and f_2 respectively are

(a) $f + f_r$ and f (b) $f - f_r$ and f (c) $f - f_r$ and f_2 (d) $f + f_r$ and $f - f_r$

[*GATE 2014*]

[**Hint:** Read Art. 5.10.1]

Solution. Frequency of voltage at commutator brushes depends upon the speed of air-gap flux with respect to brushes. Speed of air-gap flux or stator flux is $\frac{120f}{P} = N_s$ with respect to fixed brushes or stator. Therefore, speed of air-gap flux with respect to fixed brushes is N_s.

$\therefore$ Frequency of voltage across commutator brushes, $f_2 = \frac{120N_s}{P} = f.$

It is given that rotor rotates clockwise, therefore direction of rotation of stator flux must also be clockwise at $N_s = \frac{120f}{P}$ rpm. Rotor is rotated by prime-mover in anticlockwise direction at rotational speed N_r rpm where $\frac{120\,N_r}{P} = f_r$. Therefore speed of air-gap flux or stator flux with respect to rotor conductors is $(N_s + N_r)$ rpm.

$\therefore$ Frequency of emf at slip rings = f_1 = frequency of emf generated in the rotor conductors.

$$\therefore \qquad f_1 = \frac{P\,(\text{speed of air-gap flux with respect to rotor conductors})}{120}$$

$$= \frac{P\,(N_s + N_r)}{120} = \frac{P.N_s}{120} + \frac{P.N_r}{120} = f + f_r$$

$\therefore$ Values of f_1 and f_2 are respectively $f + f_r$ and f. $\therefore$ **Ans.** (*a*)

B.15. *A 400 V, 50 Hz, 4-pole, 1400 rpm star-connected squirrel cage induction motor has the following parameters refererred to the stator.*

$$R_r' = 1.0\ \Omega,\ X_s = X_r' = 1.5\ \Omega$$

Neglect stator resistance and core and rotational losses of the motor. The motor is controlled from a 3-phase voltage source inverter with constant V/f control. The stator line to line voltage (rms) and frequency to obtain the maximum torque at starting will be

(*a*) *20.6 V, 2.7 Hz* (*b*) *133.3 V, 16.7 Hz* (*c*) *266.6 V, 33.3 Hz* (*d*) *323.3 V, 40.3 Hz.*

[*GATE 2008*]

Solution. It is given that equivalent circuit parameters of a 3-phase induction motor, referred to stator, are as shown in Fig. B-8. From this circuit, the slip s_{mT} at which maximum torque occurs is given by

$$s_{mT} = \frac{R_r'}{X_s + X_r'}$$

For maximum torque at starting,

$$s_{mT} = 1.0$$

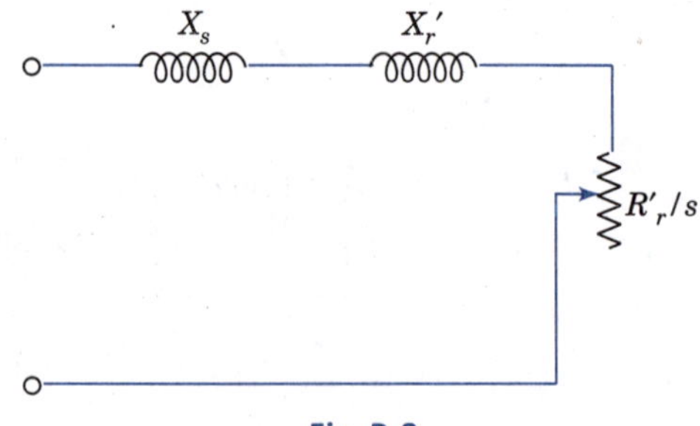

Fig. B-8

$$\therefore \qquad s_{mT} = 1.0 = \frac{R_r'}{X_{sm} + X_{rn}'} = \frac{1.0}{X_{sm} + X_{rn}'}$$

where X_{sm} and X_{rm}' are stator and rotor leakage reactances at frequency f_m at which maximum torque occurs at starting.

$$\therefore \qquad X_{sm} + X_{rm}' = 1.0 \ \Omega$$

$$\text{or} \qquad 2\pi f_m L_s + 2\pi f_m L_r' = 1.0$$

$$\text{or} \qquad f_m = \frac{1}{2\pi [L_s + L_r]}$$

$$\text{But} \qquad L_s = \frac{X_s}{2\pi f} = \frac{1.5}{2\pi \times 50} \text{ and } L_r = \frac{X_r'}{2\pi f} = \frac{1.5}{2\pi \times 50}$$

$$\therefore \qquad f_m = \frac{1}{25\left[\dfrac{1.5}{2\pi \times 50} + \dfrac{1.5}{2\pi \times 50}\right]} = \frac{50}{3} = 16.67 \text{ Hz}$$

For constant V/f, $\dfrac{V_1}{f_1} = \dfrac{V_2}{f_m}$ or $\dfrac{400}{50} = \dfrac{V_2}{16.67}$

$$\therefore \qquad V_2 = \frac{400}{50} \times \frac{50}{3} = \frac{400}{3} = 133.33 \text{ V}$$

∴ Answer is 133.3 V, 16.7 Hz. ∴ **Ans.** (*b*)

B.16. *In a constant V/f induction motor drive, the slip at maximum torque*

(*a*) *is directly proportional to the synchronous speed*

(*b*) *remains constant with respect to synchronous speed*

(*c*) *has the inverse relation with the synchronous speed*

(*d*) *has not relation with the synchronous speed.* [*GATE 2016*]

Solution. With stator leakage impedance ignored, the slip at maximum torque is given by

$$s_{mT} = \frac{r_2}{x_1 + x_2} = \frac{r_2}{2\pi f\,[l_1 + l_2]}$$

Now synchronous speed, $\omega_s = \dfrac{4\pi f}{P}$ or $2\pi f = \dfrac{P.\omega_s}{2}$

$$\therefore \qquad s_{mT} = \frac{2r_2}{P.\omega_s [l_1 + l_2]}$$

$$\therefore \qquad s_{mT} \propto \frac{1}{\omega_s} \text{ or } s_{mT} \propto \frac{1}{\text{synchronous speed}}. \qquad \therefore \textbf{ Ans. } (c)$$

B.17. *A cylindrical rotor synchronous generator with constant real power ouput and constant terminal voltage is supplying 100 A current to a 0.9 lagging power factor load. An ideal reactor is now connected in parallel with the load, as a result of which the total lagging reactive power requirement of the load is twice the previous value while the real power remains unchanged. The armature current is now .... A (rounded off to 2 decimal places.)*

[*GATE 2020*]

Solution. Fig. B-9 (*a*) shows a cylindrical rotor synchronous generator supplying constant real power $V_t \times 100 \times 0.9$ to a load. Here load voltage is V_t, load current is 100 A and load power factor is $\cos\theta = 0.9$ lag.

∴ Real constant power delivered to load, $P = V_t \times 100 \times 0.9$, W.

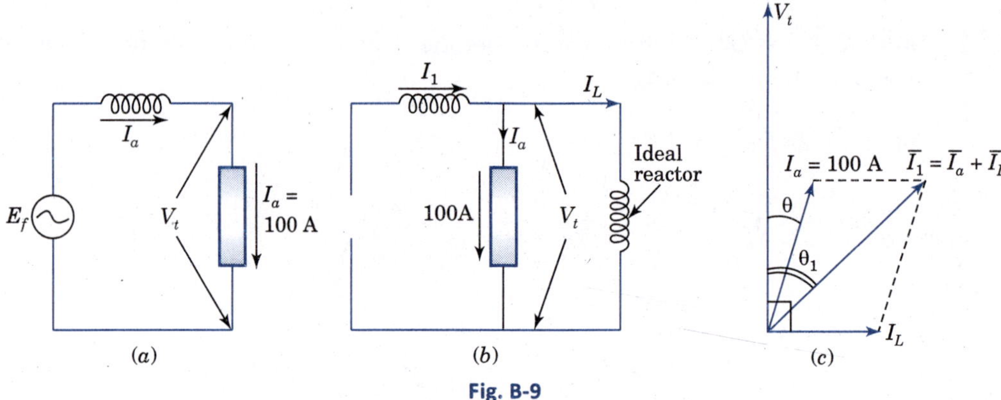

Fig. B-9

Reactive power requirement of the load

$$= V_t \times 100 \sin [\cos^{-1} 0.9]$$
$$= V_t \times 100 \times 0.436 \text{ VAr.}$$

When ideal reactor is connected in parallel with the load as shown in Fig. B.9 (*b*), the reactive current I_L lags V_t by 90° and total current taken from generator becomes $\bar{I}_1 = \bar{I}_a + \bar{I}_L$ as shown in Fig. B.9 (*c*). Here I_a = 100 A is shown lagging V_t by $\theta = \cos^{-1} 0.9$. Reactor current I_L lags V_t by 90°. New armature current is $\bar{I}_1 = \bar{I}_a + \bar{I}_L$ and it lags V_t by an angle θ_1.

From Fig. B.9 (*c*), total lagging reactive power is given by

$$V_t I_1 \sin \theta_1 = \text{twice the previous reactive power, } V_t \times 100 \times 0.436 \text{ VAr}$$

$$\therefore \quad V_t I_1 \sin \theta_1 = 2[V_t \times 100 \times 0.436]$$

$$\therefore \quad I_1 \sin \theta_1 = 200 \times 0.436 = 87.2 \text{ A} \qquad ...(i)$$

Fig. B.9 (*c*) also gives constant real power $= V_t I_a \cos \theta = V_t \times 100 \times 0.9 = V_t I_1 \cos \theta_1$

$$\therefore \quad I_1 \cos \theta_1 = 100 \times 0.9 = 90 \text{ A} \qquad ...(ii)$$

From Eqs. (*i*) and (*ii*), we get $I_1^2 = (I_1 \sin\theta_1)^2 + (I_1 \cos \theta_1)^2 = 87.2^2 + 90^2$

∴ New value of armature current, $I_2 = \sqrt{87.2^2 + 90^2} = 125.315$ A

B.18. *Windings 'A', 'B' and 'C' have 20 turns each and are wound on the same iron core as shown, along with winding 'X' which has 2 turns. The figure shows the sense (clockwise/anti-clockwise) of each of the windings only and does not reflect the exact number of turns. If windings 'A', 'B' and 'C' are supplied with balanced 3-phase voltages at 50 Hz and there is no core saturation, the no-load RMS voltage (in V, (rounded off to 2 decimal places) across winding 'X' is ....* [*GATE 2020*]

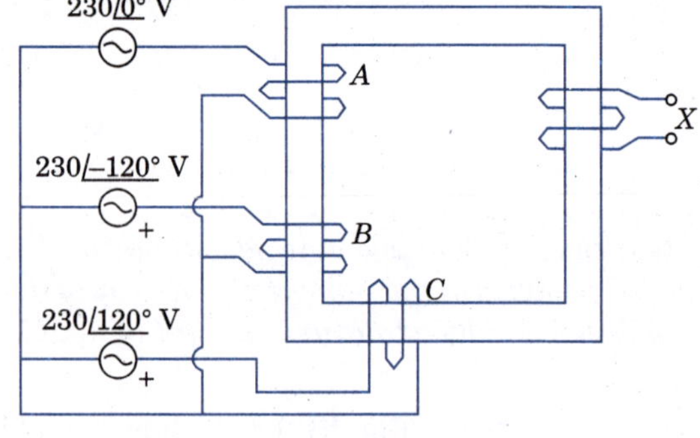

Fig. B-10

Solution. Voltage across winding *X* due to primary winding *A*

$$= \frac{230\angle 0°}{20} \times 2 = 23\angle 0° \text{ V}$$

Voltage across winding X due to primary winding B

$$= \frac{230\angle -120°}{20} \times 2 = 23\angle -120° \text{ V}$$

Voltage across winding X due to primary winding C

$$= \frac{230\angle 120°}{20} \times 2 = 23\angle 120° \text{ V}$$

In Fig. B-10, both windings B and C are wound in the same sense but opposite to the sense of winding A.

∴ Resultant voltage across X due to the combined action of all three windings A, B and C is given by

$$V_x = 23 \angle 0° - 23 \angle -120° - 23\angle 120°$$
$$= 23 \, [(\cos 0 + j \sin 0) - (\cos - 120° + j \sin - 120°) - (\cos 120° + j \sin 120°)]$$
$$= 23 \, [1 + j\, 0 + 0.5 + j0.866 + 0.5 - j\, 0.866]$$
$$= 23[1 + 1] = 46 \text{ V } \angle 0°$$

∴ Voltage across winding X is 46 V and is in phase with reference line voltage.

B.19. *In Fig. B-10, if all the three windings 'A', 'B' and 'C' are wound in the same sense, then calculate the resultant voltage across winding 'X'.*

Solution. With all the three windings 'A', 'B' and 'C' wound in the same sense, then resultant voltage across winding 'X' is given by

$$V_x = 23\angle 0° + 23\angle -120° + 23\angle 120°$$
$$= 23 \, [\cos 0 + j \sin 0 + \cos (-120) + j \sin (-120) + \cos (120 + j \sin 120°]$$
$$= 23 \, [1 + j\, 0 - 0.5 - j\, 0.866 - 0.5 + j\, 0.866]$$
$$= 23 \, [1 - 1] = 0 \text{ V}.$$

∴ Voltage across winding X is zero.

B.20. *In Fig. B-10, if both the windings A and B are wound in the same sense but winding C is wound in a sense opposite to both windings A and B, then calculate the resultant voltage across winding X.*

Solution. With winding C wound in a sense opposite to both the windings A and B, the resultant voltage across winding X is given by

$$V_x = 23\angle 0° + 23\angle -120° - 23\angle 120°$$
$$= 23 \, [\cos 0 + j \sin 0 + \cos (-120) + j \sin (-120) - (\cos 120 + j \sin 120)]$$
$$= 23 \, [1 + j\, 0 - 0.5 - j\, 0.866 + 0.5 - j\, 0.866]$$
$$= 23 \, [1 - j\, 1.732] = 23\sqrt{1^2 + 1.73^2} \;\underline{\big|-\tan^{-1} \frac{1.732}{1}}$$
$$= 23 \times 2\angle -60° = 46\angle -60° \text{ V}$$

∴ Voltage across winding X is V_x = 46 V and it lags the reference line voltage by 60°.

B.21. *Consider the table given:*

Constructional feature	Machine type	Mitigation
(P) Damper bars	(S) Induction motor	(X) Hunting
(Q) Skewed rotor slots	(T) Transformer	(Y) Magnetic locking
(R) Compensating winding	(U) Synchronous machine	(Z) Armature reaction
	(V) D.C. machine	

The correct combination that relates the constructional feature, machine type and mitigation is

(A) P-V-X, Q-U-Z, R-T-Y (B) P-U-X, Q-S-Y, R-V-Z

(C) P-T-Y, Q-V-Z, R-S-X (D) P-U-X, Q-V-Y, R-T-Z [*GATE 2021*]

Solution.

1. Damper bars (P) are used in a synchronous machine (U) to mitigate hunting (X); therefore correct combination is P-U-X.

2. Skewed rotor slots (Q) are used in an induction motor (S) to mitigate magnetic locking (Y), therefore correct combination is Q-S-Y.

3. Compensating winding (R) is used in a dc machine (V) to mitigate armature reaction (Z), therefore correct combination is R-V-Z.

Therefore, the correct combination that relates the construction features, machine type and mitigation is **B.** [P-U-X, Q-S-Y, R-V-Z].

B.22. *An alternator with internal voltage of 1 $\angle\delta_1$ pu and synchronous reactance of 0.4 pu is connected by a transmission line of reactance 0.1 pu to a synchronous motor having synchronous reactance 0.35 pu and internal voltage of 0.85 $\angle\delta_2$ pu. If the real power supplied by the alternator is 0.866 pu, then $(\delta_1 - \delta_2)$ is .... degree (Rounded off to two decimal places).* [*GATE 2021*]

Solution. Alternator voltage 1 $\angle\delta_1$ pu and synchronous motor voltage 0.85 $\angle\delta_2$ pu are shown in Fig. B-11. Alternator voltage leads the synchronous motor voltage by angle $(\delta_1 - \delta_2)$ as shown.

The power delivered by alternator to synchronous motor is given by

$$P = \frac{\text{alternator voltage } 1 \times \text{synch. motor voltage } 0.85}{\text{total reactance between alternator and synch. motor}} \times \sin(\text{angle between alternator voltage 1 and synch. motor voltage 0.85})$$

$$0.866 = \frac{1 \times 0.85}{0.4 + 0.1 + 0.35} \sin(\delta_1 - \delta_2)$$

$$= \frac{0.85}{0.85} \sin(\delta_1 - \delta_2) = \sin(\delta_1 - \delta_2)$$

$\therefore$ $(\delta_1 - \delta_2) = \sin^{-1}[0.866] = 60°$. **Ans.**

$1.0\angle\delta_1$, $0.85\angle\delta_2$, $\delta_1 - \delta_2$, δ_2, δ_1, O

Fig. B-11

B.23. *An 8-pole, 50 Hz, 3-phase, slip-ring induction motor has an effective rotor resistance of 0.08 Ω per phase. Its speed at maximum torque is 650 rpm. The additional resistance per phase that must be inserted in the rotor to achieve maximum torque at start is .... Ω (Rounded off to 2 decimal places). Neglect magnetizing current and leakage impedance. Consider equivalent circuit parameters referred to stator.* [GATE 2021]

Solution. Synchronous speed, $N_s = \dfrac{120 \times 50}{8} = 750$ rpm

Speed at maximum torque = 650 rpm

$\therefore$ Slip at maximum torque $= \dfrac{750 - 650}{750} = \dfrac{100}{750} = \dfrac{2}{15} = s_{mT}$

Effective rotor resistance per phase, $r_2 = 0.08\ \Omega$

Maximum torque occurs when $\dfrac{r_2}{x_2} = s_{mT}$. $\therefore \dfrac{0.08}{x_2} = \dfrac{2}{15}$

$\therefore$ Leakage reactance, $x_2 = \dfrac{0.08 \times 15}{2} = 0.6\ \Omega$

External resistance R that must be inserted in the rotor circuit to achieve maximum torque at start is given by

$$\frac{r_2 + R}{\text{slip at start}} = x_2, \text{ or } \frac{0.08 + R}{1} = 0.6\ \Omega$$

$\therefore$ External resistance $R = 0.6 - 0.08 = 0.52\ \Omega$. **Ans.**

B.24. *A three-phase balanced voltage is applied to the load shown. The phase-sequence is RYB. The ratio* $\left|\dfrac{I_B}{I_R}\right|$ *is ....* [GATE 2021]

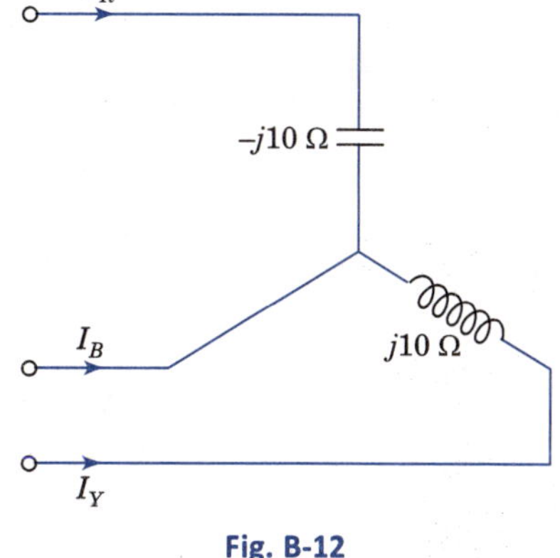

Fig. B-12

Solution. It is given that phase-sequence is RYB. Let V be the line voltage. Then, we can write

$$V_{RY} = V\angle 0°,\ V_{YB} = V\angle -120°$$

and $$V_{BR} = V\angle 120°$$

From Fig. B-12, we get

$$I_R = \frac{V_{RB}}{X_C} = \frac{-V_{BR}}{X_C} = \frac{-V\angle 120°}{10\angle -90°}$$
$$= -0.1\ V\ \angle 210°$$
$$= -0.1\ V\ [\cos 210° + j \sin 210°]$$
$$= -0.1\ V\ [-0.866 - j\ 0.5]$$
$$= V\ [0.0866 + j\ 0.05]$$

$$I_Y = \frac{V_{YB}}{X_L} = \frac{V\angle -120°}{10\angle 90°} = 0.1\ V\ \angle -210°$$
$$= 0.1\ V\ [\cos(-210) + j \sin(-210)] = 0.1\ V\ [-0.866 + j\ 0.5]$$
$$= V\ [-0.0866 + j\ 0.05]$$

Now $I_R + I_Y + I_B = 0$

$\therefore$

$$I_B = -[I_R + I_Y] = -V[0.0866 + j\,0.05 - 0.0866 + j\,0.05]$$
$$= -j\,0.1\text{ V} = 0.1\text{ V} \angle{-90°}$$

Also

$$I_R = V[0.0866 + j\,0.05] = V\sqrt{[0.0866^2 + 0.05^2} \Big| \tan^{-1}\frac{0.05}{0.0866}$$

$$= 0.1\text{ V} \angle 30°$$

$\therefore$

$$\left|\frac{I_B}{I_R}\right| = \left|\frac{0.1\text{ V} \angle{-90°}}{0.1\text{ V} \angle 30°}\right| = \frac{0.1\text{ V}}{0.1\text{ V}} = 1.$$ **Ans.**

APPENDIX

C

Some Useful Relations

(i) $\sin A + \sin\left(A - \frac{2\pi}{3}\right) + \sin\left(A - \frac{4\pi}{3}\right) = 0$

(ii) $\cos A + \cos\left(A - \frac{2\pi}{3}\right) + \cos\left(A - \frac{4\pi}{3}\right) = 0$

(iii) $\sin A \cos A + \sin\left(A - \frac{2\pi}{3}\right) . \cos\left(A - \frac{2\pi}{3}\right) + \sin\left(A - \frac{4\pi}{3}\right) \cos\left(A - \frac{4\pi}{3}\right) = 0$

(iv) $\sin^2 A + \sin^2\left(A - \frac{2\pi}{3}\right) + \sin^2\left(A - \frac{4\pi}{3}\right) = \frac{3}{2}$

(v) $\cos^2\left(A - \frac{2\pi}{3}\right) + \cos\left(A - \frac{4\pi}{3}\right) = \frac{3}{2}$

(vi) $\sin (A \pm B) = \sin A \cos B \pm \cos A \cos B$

(vii) $\cos (A \pm B) = \cos A \cos B \mp \sin A \sin B$

(viii) $\sin C + \sin D = 2 \sin \frac{C + D}{2} . \cos \frac{C - D}{2}$

(ix) $\sin C - \sin D = 2 \cos \frac{C + D}{2} . \sin \frac{C - D}{2}$

(x) $\cos C + \cos D = 2 \cos \frac{C + D}{2} \cos \frac{C - D}{2}$

(xi) $\cos C - \cos D = 2 \sin \frac{C + D}{2} \sin \frac{C - D}{2}$

(xii) $\sin 3A = 3 \sin A - 4 \sin^3 A$

(xiii) $\cos 3A = 4 \cos^3 A - 3 \cos A$

(xiv) $\int \sin nx . dx = -\frac{\cos nx}{n}$

(xv) $\int \cos nx . dx = \frac{\sin nx}{n}$

(xvi) In a triangle, $\angle A + \angle B + \angle C = 180°$ etc.

Index

A

B

C

D

E

F

G

H

I

Q

R

S

T

U

V

Z

References

1. R.H. Park, "Two-reaction Theory of Synchronous Machines—Generalized Method of Analysis—Part I," Trans. Vol. 48, July 1929, pp. 716-727.
2. W.J. Gibbs, "Electric Machine Analysis using Matrices," Pitman, 1962.
3. B. Adkins, "The General Theory of Electrical Machines," Chapman and Hall, London, 1964.
4. A.E. Fitzgerald, C. Kingsley and S.D. Umans, "Electric Machinery," Tata McGraw Hill, 2003.
5. J.M.D. Murphy and F.G. Turnbull, "Power Electronic Control of AC Motors," Pergamon Press, 1988.
6. P.C. Krause, O. Wasynczuk and S.D. Sudhoff, "Analysis of Electric Machinery and Drive Systems," John Wiley and Sons, 2002.